2/07

olivia RESORTS

For those of you who prefer to keep your feet on the ground, Olivia engages entire resorts for your pleasure. Make new friends, see the sights and enjoy a wide range of sports and activities. Our resort vacations are all-inclusive, so your tummy's as pampered as the rest of you. Indulge yourself at a relaxing resort surrounded by women.

olivia
FEEL FREE
800.631.6277 | www.olivia.com/resorts | info@olivia.com
CST#1009281-40

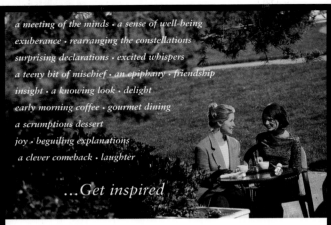

We all want the same thing.

KeyWest
the fabulous gay & lesbian destination

The Everglades · Miami

Key Largo

Islamorada

Key West · Big Pine Key
& The Lower Keys · Marathon

fla-keys.com/gaykeywest   1-888-327-9831

THE GREATEST
WOMEN'S WEEKEND
ON EARTH!

girlbar
Los Angeles

DINAH SHORE
WEEKEND 06
Palm Springs California
March 29 - April 2

For Hotel Bookings & Event Tickets
www.dinahshoreweekend.com
For VIP Weekend Packages
e-mail: dinahshorevip@aol.com

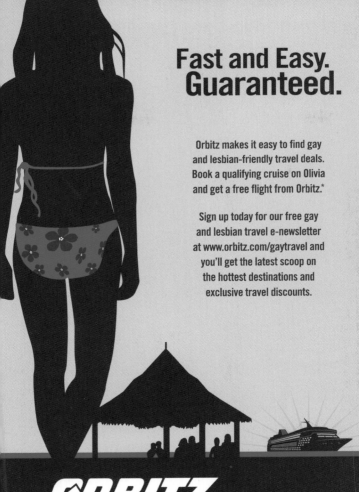

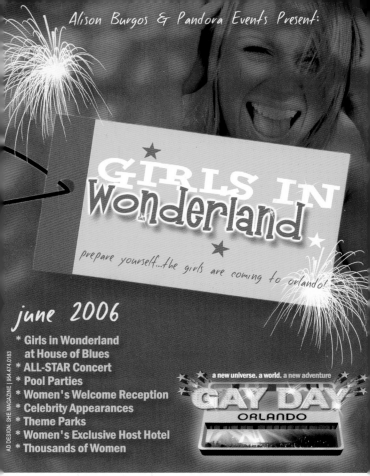

Alison Burgos & Pandora Events Present:

GIRLS IN wonderland

prepare yourself...the girls are coming to orlando!

june 2006

* Girls in Wonderland
  at House of Blues
* ALL-STAR Concert
* Pool Parties
* Women's Welcome Reception
* Celebrity Appearances
* Theme Parks
* Women's Exclusive Host Hotel
* Thousands of Women

AD DESIGN: SHE MAGAZINE | 954.474.0183

a new universe. a world. a new adventure

GAY DAY
ORLANDO

  DAMRON

BENEFITING THE NATIONAL
CENTER FOR LESBIAN RIGHTS

NCLR

FOR TICKET & HOTEL INFORMATION VISIT:
WWW.GIRLSINWONDERLAND.COM
OR CALL 954.288.8691

Like Nowhere Else

provincetown
BUSINESS GUILD

Find Out What's Happening
at our Event Schedule at Ptown.org

PROVINCETOWN

frameline30

San Francisco
International LGBT
Film Festival

June 15-25, 2006
www.frameline.org

GET OUT AND SEE A MOVIE

Subscribe Today!

Canadian Court Rules for Same-Sex Marriages •

The Incredible
Never-Shrinking

Lily Tomlin

LN
LESBIAN NEWS

Lucky in Love

Melissa Etheridge

Talks About Her Recent Wedding, Her New Book and Politics

The Lesbian News

The Longest-Running National Lesbian Publication

Subscriptions or Advertising

800. 458. 9888

E-mail: TheLN@sbcglobal.net ▪ P.O. Box 55 Torrance, CA 90507

Visit us at: www.LesbianNews.com

Curve

THE BEST-SELLING LESBIAN MAGAZINE

"[Curve is]. . . beautiful, sexy, and impossibly stylish. — New York Magazine

In 2006,
R Family Vacations
is headed west.

*from Seattle
through the
Gulf of Alaska
and back*

g.b.f magazine

connecting gay black females worldwide

models: Sphear and Naya'Hri
photo: Jen McClearly

www.gbfmag.com
since 1990

Women On A Roll,
the premier social lesbian organization invites you to...

climb aboard **Paradise**,
Carnival Cruise's 4-star luxury ship

And cruise on the largest-ever women's weekend party at sea!

September 15-18, 2006

Sail the beautiful Pacific Ocean from Long Beach, California to Ensenada, Mexico with 2000+ women!

Prices start as low as $499!
Information and reservations: 800-960-8842
www.womenonaroll.com, Women's Travel Page

All Women, All Weekend, Alright!

Save The Date!
WHITE PARTY WEEK
Thanksgiving Weekend
miami - miami beach - fort lauderdale

WHITE PARTY WEEK™

www.whiteparty.org

benefiting:

care | resource

Your One Source

www.CareResource.org

Care Resource would like to thank all the sponsors,
volunteers and everyone who attend
The White Party Week.
Without your support, this fundraiser
Would not be possible.

WE, THE PEOPLE, CREATE THIS MEMORIAL OF OUR OWN VOLITION TO HONOR THOSE LOST, CRAFTING THE PANELS IN OUR OWN WAY, BY OUR OWN DESIGN.

The AIDS Memorial Quilt

We continue to honor the dead
by fighting for the living.
—The NAMES Project Foundation

www.aidsquilt.org   101 Krog Street   Atlanta, Georgia 30307   404-688-5500

Haven't joined Damron OnLine yet?

Here's your chance to get a free trial membership.
Fill out the form below, and mail it back before December 31, 2006, when offer expires.

3-month membership offer is for brand-new members only. Current members will receive a 1-month extenstion to an existing account that is in good standing when they send back this form.

To help Damron better serve you, please tell us your:

Age: ❑ under 21 ❑ 21-25 ❑ 26-32
❑ 33-39 ❑ 40-49 ❑ 50-65 ❑ 66+

Personal Income: ❑ under $15K ❑ $15-25K ❑ $25-40K
❑ $40-65K ❑ $65-100K ❑ $100-200K ❑ $200K+

Where do you live? (City, State, Country)

Familiarity with the *Damron Women's Traveller*:
❑ This is the first copy I've seen ❑ I've used it before

Other Damron Publications You Have Used:
❑ *Damron City Guide* ❑ *Damron Accommodations*
❑ *Damron Amsterdam* ❑ *Damron Men's Travel Guide*
❑ *Damron OnLine* (http://www.damron.com)

Please Comment on the *Damron Women's Traveller* (compared to other travel guides). Any suggestions for improvements? What parts do you particularly like/use?

_____

_____

_____

New to Damron OnLine? Please complete for a free 3-month membership:
ALL FIELDS BELOW ARE REQUIRED ▶ PLEASE PRINT ▶ MEMBERSHIP INFO WILL BE EMAILED TO YOU

Name _____

Address _____

City/State/Zip _____

Email Address _____

Please Mail to: Damron 2006 OnLine Offer
PO Box 422458
San Francisco, CA 94142-2458

Traveller Codes

Most of the codes used in this book are self-explanatory. Here are the few, however, which aren't.

▲—This symbol marks an advertiser. Please look for their display ad near this listing, and be sure to tell them you saw their ad in the *Damron Women's Traveller*.

Popular—So we've heard from the business and/or a reader.

Mostly Women—80-90% lesbian crowd.

Mostly Gay Men—Women welcome.

Lesbians/Gay Men—60%(L)/40%(G) to a 40%(L)/60%(G) mix.

LGBT—Lesbian, Gay, Bisexual, and Transgendered.

Gay/Straight—A little bit of everything.

Gay-Friendly—LGBT folk are definitely welcome but are rarely the ones hosting the party.

Neighborhood Bar—Regulars and a local flavor, often has a pool table.

Dancing/DJ—Usually has a DJ at least Fri and Sat nights.

Transgender-Friendly—Transsexuals, cross-dressers, and other transgendered people welcome.

Live Shows—From an open mic to live music.

MultiRacial—A good mix of women of color and their friends.

Beer/Wine—Beer and/or wine. No hard liquor.

Smokefree—No smoking anywhere inside premises.

Private Club—Found mainly in the US South where it's the only way to keep a liquor license. Call the bar before you go out and tell them you're visiting. They will advise you of their policy regarding membership. Usually have set-ups so you can BYOB.

Wheelchair Access—Includes rest room.

the Damron Women's Traveller®

Publisher	Damron Company
President & Editor-in-Chief	Gina M. Gatta
Managing Editor	Ian Philips
Deputy Editor	Erika O'Connor
Assistant Editor	Maya Lara
Director of Art & Advertising	Kathleen Pratt
Cover Photo	Jack Slomovits
Cover Design	Rick Avila

Board of Directors

Mikal Shively, Gina M. Gatta,
Edward Gatta, Jr., Louise Mock

How to Contact Us

Mail: PO Box 422458, San Francisco, CA 94142-2458
Email: info@damron.com
Web: www.damron.com
Fax: 415/703-9049
Phone: 415/255-0404 & 800/462-6654

Table of Contents

United States

Table of Contents

ALABAMA

Statewide

PUBLICATIONS

Ambush Mag 504/522–8049 • LGBT newspaper for the Gulf South

Southern Voice 404/876–1819 • weekly LGBT newspaper for AL, FL (panhandle), GA, LA, MS, TN w/ resource listings

Birmingham

ACCOMMODATIONS

The Tutwiler Wyndham 2021 Park Pl N (at 21st St N) 205/322–2100 • gay-friendly • also restaurant & lounge • wheelchair access • $130+

BARS

Club 729 2830 7th Ave S (at 29th St) 205/324–0997 • 5pm-close • mostly women • dancing/DJ • live shows • karaoke • wheelchair access

NIGHTCLUBS

22nd Street Jazz Cafe 710 22nd St S (at 7th Ave S) 205/252–0407 • 4pm-close • gay-friendly • multiracial • live music • dancing/DJ • food served

The Quest Club 416 24th St S (at 5th Ave S) 205/251–4313 • 24hrs • mostly gay men • dancing/DJ • 19+ Wed-Sun • drag shows • private club • patio • wheelchair access • cover charge

RESTAURANTS

Anthony's 2131 7th Ave S (at 20th) 205/324–1215 • lunch & dinner, clsd Sun-Mon • lesbians/ gay men • cont'l/ Italian • some veggie • full bar • wheelchair access • gay-owned

Bottega Cafe & Restaurant 2240 Highland Ave (btwn 22nd & 23rd) 205/939–1000 • 5:30pm-10:30pm, clsd Sun • some veggie • full bar • wheelchair access

Highlands Bar & Grill 2011 11th Ave S (at 20th St) 205/939–1400 • 5:30pm-10pm, clsd Sun-Mon • wheelchair access

John's 112 21st St N (btwn 1st & 2nd Ave N) 205/322–6014 • lunch & dinner • seafood & steak • full bar • wheelchair access

Silvertron Cafe 3813 Clairmont Ave S (at 39th St S) 205/591–3707 • 11am-10pm, till 9pm Sun • also full bar • more gay Mon

Birmingham

LGBT PRIDE:
June. web: www.gaybham.com.

ANNUAL EVENTS:
April/May - Festival of the Arts.
June - City Stages 205/251–1272, web: www.citystages.org.
June - Shakespeare Renaissance Fair 334/271-5353 or 800/841-4273, web: www.asf.net.

CITY INFO:
800/458–8085 or 205/458-8000, web: www.birminghamal.org.

BEST VIEW:
Overlook Park.

WEATHER:
Hot and humid in the 80°s and 90°s during the summer, mild in the 50°s to low 40°s during the winter.

TRANSIT:
Americas United Cab Co 205/969-7177.
Birmingham Transit Authority 205/521-0101, web: www.bjcta.org.

ATTRACTIONS:
Alabama Jazz Hall of Fame 205/254-2731, web: www.jazzhall.com.
Birmingham Zoo & Botanical Gardens 205/879-0408, web: www.birminghamzoo.com.
Civil Rights Museum 205/328-9696, web: www.bcri.org.
Vulcan Statue at 20th St S & Valley Ave, atop Red Mountain.
Sloss Furnaces 205/324-1911, web: www.slossfurnaces.com.

ENTERTAINMENT & RECREATION

Magic City Diamonds 2117 University Blvd (at 22nd, at Baptist church) **205/591–4382, 205/592–4455** • 7pm-9pm Th only • alternative square dance club

Terrific New Theater 2821 2nd Ave S (in Dr Pepper Design Complex) **205/328–0868**

SPIRITUAL GROUPS

Covenant MCC 5117 1st Ave N (at 52nd St) **205/599–3363** • 11am & 7pm Sun

UCC- Pilgrim Congregational 3801 Montclair Rd **205/879–1624** • 11am Sun

EROTICA

Alabama Adult Books 801 3rd Ave N (at 8th) **205/322–7323** • 24hrs

Dothan

NIGHTCLUBS

The Bar 2563 Ross Clark Cr (at US 231 S) **334/712–6810** • 7pm-2am Th-Sat • lesbians/ gay men • dancing/DJ • multiracial • transgender-friendly • talent competition Th • drag shows • videos • wheelchair access

Geneva

ACCOMMODATIONS

Spring Creek Campground & Resort 163 Campground Rd (at Hwy 52 & Country Rd 4) **334/684–3891** • mostly gay men • cabins • also tent & RV sites • swimming • nudity ok • some theme wknds w/ DJ • gay-owned • $15-60

Huntsville

BARS

Club Ozz 1204 Posey (at Larkin) **256/534–5970** • 6pm-2am, from 4pm wknds • lesbians/ gay men • neighborhood bar • DJ Th-Sun • live shows • patio • wheelchair access

NIGHTCLUBS

Upscale 2021 Golf Rd **256/881–8820** • 8pm-close Fri-Sat • lesbians/ gay men • dancing/DJ • drag shows • 19+ • "Alabama's largest alternative entertainment complex" • also cafe • wheelchair access

SPIRITUAL GROUPS

MCC 3015 Sparkman Dr NW (at Pulaski Pike) **256/851–6914** • 11am & 6:30pm Sun

Mobile

see also Pensacola, Florida

INFO LINES & SERVICES

Bay Area Inclusion 100 S Florida St #C **251/450–1060** • LGBT community center

Pink Triangle AA Group at Cornerstone MCC **251/479–9994 (AA#), 251/476–4621 (CHURCH)** • 7pm Th & Sat

ACCOMMODATIONS

Berney/ Fly B&B 1118 Government St **251/405–0949** • gay-friendly • Victorian B&B • full brkfst • swimming • jacuzzi • $119-179

Riverhouse B&B 13285 Rebel Rd, Theodore **251/973–2233, 800/552–9791** • gay-friendly • B&B on Fowl River • full brkfst • hot tub • nonsmoking • gay-owned • $110-190

BARS

Gabriel's Downtown 55 S Joachim St (off Government) **251/432–4900** • 7:30pm-close, 4pm-close Sun • lesbians/ gay men • videos • karaoke • patio • private club

NIGHTCLUBS

B–Bob's Downtown 213 Conti St (at Joachim) **251/433–2262** • 5pm-close, from 3pm Sun • mostly men • dancing/DJ • also gift shop • wheelchair access

Troopers 215 Conti St (near Joachim) **251/433–7436** • 9pm-close Wed-Sat • lesbians/ gay men • dancing/DJ • drag shows Th • private club • patio • wheelchair access • open since 1976!

Visions 20 S Conception St (at Conti St) **251/432–9056** • 4pm-close, clsd Mon • mostly women • neighborhood bar • dancing/DJ • multiracial • transgender-friendly • videos • wheelchair access • lesbian-owned

RETAIL SHOPS

Over The Rainbow 18 S Conception (at Conti) **251/432–4291** • noon-midnight, from 4pm Sun, clsd Mon

SPIRITUAL GROUPS

Cornerstone MCC 2201 Government St (at Mohawk) **251/476–4621** • 11am & 7pm Sun

Montgomery

ACCOMMODATIONS

Rocky Mount B&B 2364 Rocky Mount Rd, Prattville **334/285-0490, 800/646-3831** • gay-friendly • Victorian house on 50 acres • full brkfst • nonsmoking • $110-150

NIGHTCLUBS

Oasis 6500 Lower Wetumpka Rd **334/264-4444** • 9pm-close Th-Sun • lesbians/ gay men • dancing/DJ • transgender-friendly • drag shows • gay-owned

SPIRITUAL GROUPS

New Hope MCC 566 Oliver Rd **334/213-0409** • 10:30am Sun

Tuscaloosa

BARS

Michael's 2201 6th St (at 22nd Ave) **205/758-9223** • 8pm-2am Th-Sat • lesbians/ gay men • dancing/DJ • drag shows

SPIRITUAL GROUPS

God's House 1053 MLK Dr, Northport **205/553-5244** • 11am Sun • wheelchair access

ALASKA

Anchorage

INFO LINES & SERVICES

AA Gay/ Lesbian 2110 E Northern Lights #103 (at Community Center) **907/344-2474, 907/344-2474** • 7pm Mon

Gay/ Lesbian Helpline **907/258-4777, 888/901-9876** • 6pm-11pm, ask about women's events: usually every Sat except summers when everyone's outdoors

Identity, Inc 2110 E Northern Lights Blvd #103 **907/929-4528** • LGBT • community center • newsletter

ACCOMMODATIONS

A Wildflower Inn B&B 1239 I St (at 13th) **907/274-1239, 877/693-1239** • gay/ straight • convenient, downtown location • close to hiking trails & scenic vistas • fun hosts • gay-owned • $69-129

Alaska Bear Company B&B 535 E 6th Ave (btwn Eagle & Fairbanks) **907/277-2327** • gay/ straight • in downtown Anchorage • gay-owned

Anchorage Jewel Lake B&B 8125 Jewel Lake Rd (at Rasberry) **907/245-7321** • gay/ straight • B&B • full brkfst • kids ok • nonsmoking • gay-owned • $100-250

City Garden B&B 1352 W 10th Ave (at N St) **907/276-2359** • gay-straight • beautiful views of Mt McKinley from bedrooms • 10-minute walk to downtown area • nonsmoking • gay-owned

Copper Whale Inn 440 L St **907/258-7999** • gay/ straight • located downtown • gay-owned • $69-185

Gallery B&B 1229 G St (at 12th) **907/274-2567** • gay/ straight • kids/ pets ok • wheelchair access • lesbian-owned • $35-85

Home Suite Home 1611 Cara Loop **907/345-2880, 888/345-2881** • seasonal • 1-bdrm suite • $115

"Off The Tracks" Women's Guesthouse 342 W 11th Ave **907/272-6537** • women only • • "a safe place for women" • kids welcome (boys under 12 only) • shared baths • $54-81

Susitna Sunsets B&B 9901 Conifer St **907/346-1067** • gay-friendly • B&B • overlooking Anchorage, Cook Inlet & Mt Susitna • full brkfst • nonsmoking • lesbian-owned • $75-159

BARS

Mad Myrna's 530 E 5th Ave (at Fairbanks) **907/276-9762** • 3pm-2:30am, till 3am wknds • lesbians/ gay men • neighborhood bar • dancing/DJ • karaoke • food served • drag shows

Raven 708 E 4th Ave **907/276-9672** • 1pm-2:30am, till 3am wknds • lesbians/ gay men • neighborhood bar • wheelchair access

RESTAURANTS

China Lights 12110 Business Blvd, Eagle River **907/694-8080** • 11:30am-10pm, till 10:30pm wknds

Garcia's 11901 Business Blvd #104 (next to Safeway), Eagle River **907/694-8600** • lunch & dinner, till midnight Fri-Sat • Mexican

O'Brady's Burgers & Brew 6901 E Tudor Rd (in Chugach Square) **907/338-1080** • 11am-midnight, noon-10pm Sun • gay-friendly • some veggie

Simon & Seafort's 420 L St (btwn 4th & 5th) **907/274-3502** • lunch weekdays, dinner nightly • seafood & prime rib • full bar

ENTERTAINMENT & RECREATION

Out North 3800 DeBarr Rd **907/279-3800** • community-based & visiting-artist exhibits, screenings & performances

BOOKSTORES

Title Wave Books 1360 W Northern Lights Blvd **907/278–9283** • largest independent bookstore in Alaska, new-and-used, LGBT section

RETAIL SHOPS

The Sports Shop 570 E Benson Blvd **907/272–7755** • 10am-7pm, till 6pm Sat, noon-5pm Sun • women's outdoor clothing • adventure gear & equipment

PUBLICATIONS

Anchorage Press **907/561–7737** • alternative paper • arts & entertainment listings

Klondyke Kontact **907/345–3818** • newsmagazine published every other month

SPIRITUAL GROUPS

Lamb of God MCC 2311 Pembroke (at Immanuel Presbyterian Church) **907/258–5266** • 2pm Sun

Unitarian Universalist Fellowship 3201 Turnagain St (at 32nd) **907/248–3737** • 9am & 10:45am Sun • wheelchair access

EROTICA

Le Shop 305 W Dimond Blvd (at C St) **907/522–1987** • 8am-2am

Swingers Adult Bookstore 710 W Northern Lights Blvd (at Arctic) **907/561–5039** • 8am-1:30am

Anchorage

LGBT PRIDE:
June. web:
www.anchoragepride.com.

ANNUAL EVENTS:
January - Anchorage Folk Festival 907/566-2334, web: www.anchoragefolkfestival.org.
March - Iditarod Sled Dog Race 907/376-5155, web: www.iditarod.com.
Int'l Ice Carving Competition 907/276-5015.
June - Midnight Sun Marathon 907/343-4474, web: www.mayorsmarathon.com.
August - Alaska State Fair 800/850–3247, web: www.alaskastatefair.org.
October - Quyana Alaska (native dance celebration) 907/274-3611, web: www.nativefederation.org.

CITY INFO:
907/276-4118 or 800/478-1255, web: www.anchorage.net.

BEST VIEW:
The 11-mile-long paved Tony Knowles Coastal Trail along Cook Inlet offers spectacular views of several mountains, including Denali (Mt McKinley).

WEATHER:
Anchorage's climate is milder than one might think, due to its coastal location. It is cold in the winter (but rarely below 0°F), and it does warm up considerably in June, July, and August. Winter sets in around October. Expect more rain in late summer/early fall.

TRANSIT:
Rideline (bus) 907/343-6543.

ATTRACTIONS:
Alaska Museum of Natural History, 907/247-2400, web: www.alaskamuseum.org.
Alaska Native Heritage Center 907/330-8000, web: www.alaskanative.net.
Alaska Wildlife Conservation Center (in Portage) 907/783-2025, web: www.alaskawildlife.org.
Portage Glacier.
Wolf Song of Alaska Museum 907/688-9653, web: www.wolf-songalaska.org.

Fairbanks

ACCOMMODATIONS

Billie's Backpackers Hostel 2895 Mack Rd
907/479-2034 • gay-friendly • hostel &
campsites • kids ok • food served • women-
owned • $25

SPIRITUAL GROUPS

Unitarian Universalist Fellowship 4448
Pikes Landing Rd (across from the Princess
Hotel) **907/451-8838** • 10:30am Sun, does
not meet in summer

Homer

ACCOMMODATIONS

Island Watch B&B 4241 Claudia St (at W
Hill Rd) **907/235-2265** • gay-friendly • also
cabins • full brkfst • kitchens • nonsmoking •
kids/pets ok • wheelchair access • women-
owned • $100-160/double

Skyline B&B 63540 Skyline Dr **907/235-3823**
• gay/straight • full brkfst • hot tub • kids ok •
lesbian-owned • $85-125

ENTERTAINMENT & RECREATION

Alaska Fantastic Fishing Charters
800/478-7777 • deluxe cabin cruiser for big-
game fishing (halibut) • $165 (per person)

Juneau

INFO LINES & SERVICES

**SEAGLA (Southeast Alaska Gay &
Lesbian Alliance)** • also publishes
newsletter • see www.seagla.org

ACCOMMODATIONS

**A Pearson's Pond Luxury Suites &
Adventure Spa** 4541 Sawa Circle
907/789-3772, 888/658-6328 • gay-friendly •
B&B resort & spa • hot tub • nonsmoking •
$109-299

Alaska Suites Juneau 2141-2145 Crowhill
Rd, Douglas **907/789-3772** • gay-friendly •
1-bdrm condos • waterview balconies • full
kitchen • kids ok • nonsmoking • 6-night
minimum • $99-169

The Silverbow 120 Second St
907/586-4146, 800/586-4146 • gay-friendly •
remodeled 1914 building • full brkfst • also
restaurant & bakery

RESTAURANTS

Inn at the Waterfront 455 S Franklin St
907/586-2050 • 5pm-10pm • American • full
bar

ENTERTAINMENT & RECREATION

Women Sail Alaska 245 Irwin St
888/272-4525 • gay-friendly • catered sailing
adventures for women • reserve months in
advance

Women's Prerogative KTOO 104.3 & 103.1
FM **907/586-1670** • 9pm Wed • women's
music

Ketchikan

ACCOMMODATIONS

Anchor Inn by the Sea 4672 S Tongass Hwy
907/247-7117, 800/928-3308 • gay-friendly •
nonsmoking • $85-135

ENTERTAINMENT & RECREATION

Southeast Sea Kayak 1007 Water St
907/225-1258, 800/287-1607 • trip planning •
tours • wilderness kayaking

Kodiak

SPIRITUAL GROUPS

**St James the Fisherman Episcopal
Church** 421 Thorsheim **907/486-5276** •
7:30am & 10am Sun

McCarthy

ACCOMMODATIONS

Ma Johnson's Hotel **907/554-4402** • gay-
friendly • full brkfst • kids ok • inside America's
largest nat'l park, Wrangell St Elias

Palmer

ACCOMMODATIONS

Alaska Garden Gate B&B 950 S Trunk Rd
907/746-2333 • gay/straight • B&B inn • full
brkfst • hot tub • kids/pets ok • lesbian-
owned • $79-119

Sitka

ACCOMMODATIONS

A Crescent Harbor Hideaway 709 Lincoln
St **907/747-4900** • gay-friendly • restored
historic waterfront home • nonsmoking • $90-
165

CAFES

Backdoor Cafe 104 Barracks (behind Old
Harbor Books on Lincoln St, no street sign)
907/747-8856 • 7am-5pm, 9am-3pm Sun •
pleasant & funky hangout

ENTERTAINMENT & RECREATION

Esther G Sea Taxi 215 Shotgun Alley
907/738-6481 • marine wildlife tours

ARIZONA

Apache Junction

ACCOMMODATIONS

Susa's Serendipity Ranch 4375 E Superstition Blvd **480/288-9333** • women only • guesthouses on 15-acre ranch • 2 RV hookups • great views! • hot tub • nonsmoking • pets ok • lesbian-owned • $45-75/ night, $1500/ month

ENTERTAINMENT & RECREATION

RVing Women Inc PO Box 1940 85217 **888/557-8464, 480/671-6226** • nonprofit RV club for women only

Bisbee

ACCOMMODATIONS

Casa de San Pedro B&B 8933 S Yell Ln (at Hwy 92 & Palominas Rd), Hereford **520/366-1300, 888/257-2050** • gay-friendly • full brkfst • pool • hot tub • nonsmoking • wheelchair access • gay-owned • $139-155+tax

Copper Queen Hotel 11 Howell Ave **520/432-2216** • gay-friendly • restored landmark hotel • kids ok • swimming • wheelchair access • $83-161

BARS

St Elmo's 36 Brewery Gulch Ave **520/432-5578** • 10am-1am • gay-friendly • live bands Fri-Sat

CAFES

Prickly Pear Cafe 105 Tombstone Cnyn **520/432-7337** • 11am-10pm, clsd Tue

Bullhead City

includes Laughlin, Nevada

BARS

The Lariat Saloon 1161 Hancock Rd (at 95) **928/758-8479** • 10am-1am • lesbians/ gay men • neighborhood bar • multiracial • DJ wknds • wheelchair access • woman-owned/ run

Flagstaff

ACCOMMODATIONS

Hotel Monte Vista 100 N San Francisco St (at Aspen) **928/779-6971, 800/545-3068** • gay-friendly • historic lodging circa 1927 • some shared baths • full bar • $55-160

Inn at 410 410 N Leroux St **520/774-0088, 800/774-2008** • gay-friendly • full brkfst • $150-210

Starlight Pines B&B 3380 E Lockett Rd (at Fanning) **928/527-1912, 800/752-1912** • gay friendly • full brkfst • nonsmoking • gay-owned

BARS

Charly's 23 N Leroux (at Aspen, at Weatherford Hotel) **928/779-1919** • 11am-1am • gay-friendly • food served • some veggie • live shows nightly • patio • wheelchair access

Monte Vista Lounge 100 N San Francisco St (at Hotel Monte Vista) **928/774-2403** • noon-1am, from 11am Fri-Sun • gay-friendly • live bands • karaoke

CAFES

Macy's European Coffee House 14 S Beaver St **928/774-2243** • food served • vegetarian/ vegan

RESTAURANTS

Cafe Olé 119 S San Francisco (at Butler) **928/774-8272** • lunch & dinner, clsd Sun • Mexican • plenty veggie • beer/ wine • wheelchair access

Gypsy's Hideaway 1926 N 4th St, Ste 8-B (off Rte 66) **928/526-4333** • 11am-1am, lunch & dinner • also cocktail bar • live shows • karaoke

Pasto 19 E Aspen (at San Francisco) **928/779-1937** • lunch & dinner • Italian • beer/ wine • wheelchair access

BOOKSTORES

Aradia Books 116 W Cottage (at Beaver) **928/779-3817** • 10:30am-5:30pm, clsd Sun • lesbian/ feminist • wheelchair access • women-owned • also mail order

RETAIL SHOPS

Crystal Magic 1 N San Francisco St **928/779-2528** • books & gifts

SPIRITUAL GROUPS

Episcopal Church of the Epiphany 423 N Beaver St **928/774-2911** • 5:30pm Sat, 8am, 9:15am & 10:45am Sun • does not meet in Aug • childcare provided at Sun services • wheelchair access

Golden Valley

EROTICA

Pleasure Palace Adult Bookstore 3583 US Hwy 68 #7 **928/565-5600**

Jerome

ACCOMMODATIONS

The Cottage Inn Jerome 928/634-0701 • gay/ straight • full brkfst • kids/ pets ok • gay-owned • $75 (B&B) – 95 (apt)

RESTAURANTS

Red Rooster Cafe 363 Main St 928/634-7087 • 11am-4pm, clsd Tue • some veggie • live music wknds • lesbian-owned

Kingman

ACCOMMODATIONS

Kings Inn Best Western 2930 E Andy Devine 928/753-6101, 800/750-6101 • gay-friendly • swimming • nonsmoking rooms available • food served • bakery on premises • kids/ pets ok • wheelchair access • $60-95

Lake Havasu City

INFO LINES & SERVICES

Lake Havasu City AA 928/453-0313 (24HR HOTLINE) • 7 groups

ACCOMMODATIONS

Nautical Inn 1000 McCulloch Blvd 928/855-2141, 800/892-2141 • gay-friendly • beachfront hotel • full restaurant & bar • private beach • swimming • $69-489

Lake Powell

ACCOMMODATIONS

Dreamkatchers of Lake Powell B&B 435/675-5828, 888/479-9419 • gay/ straight • 8-person spa on deck • full brkfst • $65-120

Mesa

EROTICA

Castle Megastore 8315 E Main St 480/986-6114 • 24hrs

Mohave Valley

EROTICA

Eros Adult Emporium 10185 Harbor Ave 928/768-6300

Phoenix

see also Scottsdale & Tempe

INFO LINES & SERVICES

1N10 602/264-5437 • 7pm Th • youth group • HIV peer education • call for location

AA Lambda Club 2622 N 16th St 602/264-1341 • noon, 6pm & 8pm, 10pm • call for more times & info

ACCOMMODATIONS

Cantera Fountains 2828 E Campbell Ave 928/300-3153, 888/661-6757 • gay-friendly • condo • fully equipped kitchen • nonsmoking • gay-owned • $35-65

Clarendon Hotel & Suites 401 W Clarendon Ave (at 3rd Ave) 602/252-7363 • gay/ straight • modern boutique hotel in midtown • swimming • wheelchair access • gay-owned • $89-149

Hotel San Carlos 202 N Central Ave 602/253-4121, 866/253-4121 • gay-friendly • boutique hotel • rooftop pool • restaurant • downtown • $79-289

Ivy Cottage Home Stay 2315 N 42nd St 602/955-5157 • gay-friendly • B&B in historic home • heated Roman pool • full brkfst • gay-owned • $85-95

Larry's B&B 502 W Claremont Ave (btwn Maryland & Bethany Home) 602/249-2974 • European-style B&B • lesbians/ gay men • full brkfst • swimming • hot tub • nudity • nonsmoking • wheelchair access • gay-owned • $50-70

Maricopa Manor B&B Inn 15 W Pasadena Ave 602/274-6302, 800/292-6403 • gay/ straight • in heart of N Central Phoenix • swimming • hot tub • wheelchair access • gay-owned • $99-199

Yum Yum Tree Guest House 90 W Virginia Ave #1 (at 3rd Ave) 602/265-2590, 877/986-8733 • gay/ straight • suites in historic neighborhood • courtyard • swimming • gay-owned • $89-139

BARS

Ain't Nobody's Bizness 3031 E Indian School #7 (at 32nd St) 602/224-9977 • 4pm-1am, till 2am Th-Sun • mostly women • dancing/DJ • multiracial • live music • karaoke • wheelchair access

Amsterdam 718 N Central Ave (btwn Roosevelt & Fillmore) 602/258-6122 • 4pm-2am • lesbians/ gay men • upscale bar • live music Sun-Mon

Apollo's 5749 N 7th St (S of Bethany Home) **602/277–9373** • 11am-1am, till 2am wknds • mostly gay men • neighborhood bar • karaoke

Cash Inn Country 2140 E McDowell Rd (at 22nd St) **602/244–9943** • 2pm-close, from noon wknds • mostly women • dancing/DJ • country/ western • wheelchair access

Friends 1028 E Indian School Rd (at 7th St) **602/277–7729** • 11am-1pm • mostly men • neighborhood bar • bears • videos • food served • gay-owned

Harley's 155/ Harley's II 155 W Camelback Rd (btwn 3rd & Central Aves) **602/274–8505** • noon-1am • mostly gay men • neighborhood bar • dancing/DJ • bears • leather • videos

Incognito Lounge 2424 E Thomas Rd (at 24th St) **602/955–9805** • 8pm-1am, till 3am Fri-Sat, clsd Mon-Wed • lesbians/ gay men • dancing/DJ • live shows • wheelchair access

Marlys' 15615 N Cave Creek Rd (btwn Greenway Pkwy & Greenway Rd) **602/867–2463** • 3pm-1am, till 2am Fri-Sat • lesbians/ gay men • neighborhood bar

Misty's 4301 N 7th Ave (at Indian School Rd) **602/265–3233** • 4pm-close, from 5pm wknds • mostly women • dancing/DJ • multiracial • karaoke • live shows • wheelchair access • women-owned

Nasty's Sports Bar 3108 E McDowell Rd (at 32nd St) **602/267–8707** • noon-2am, from 2pm Mon-Th • mostly women • karaoke

Oz 1805 W Bethany Home Rd **602/242–5114** • 1pm-2am • lesbians/ gay men • neighborhood bar

Plazma 1560 E Osborn Rd (at N 16th St) **602/266–0477** • 3pm-2am • lesbians/ gay men • neighborhood bar • live shows • videos

Phoenix

WHERE THE GIRLS ARE:
Everywhere. Phoenix doesn't have one section of town where lesbians hang out, but the area between 5th Ave & 32nd St, and Camelback & Thomas Streets does contain most of the women's bars.

LGBT PRIDE:
April. 602/279-1771, web: www.azpride.org.

ANNUAL EVENTS:
October - AIDS Walk 602/265–9255.
October - Rainbows Festival 602/770-8241, web: www.rainbowsfestival.com.

CITY INFO:
602/254-6500.
Arizona Office of Tourism 602/230-7733 or 800/842-8257, web: www.arizonaguide.com; www.azot.com.

BEST VIEW:
South Mountain Park at sunset, watching the city lights come on.

WEATHER:
Beautifully mild and comfortable (60°s-80°s) October through March or April. Hot (90°s-100°s) in summer. August brings the rainy season (severe monsoon storms) with flash flooding.

TRANSIT:
Yellow Cab 602/252-5252.
Super Shuttle 602/244-9000.
Phoenix Transit 602/253-5000.

ATTRACTIONS:
Castles & Coasters Park on Black Canyon Fwy & Peoria 602/997-7577, web: www.castlesncoasters.com.
Heard Museum 602/252-8840, web: www.heard.org.
Phoenix Zoo 602/273–1341, web: www.phoenixzoo.org.
Desert Botanical Garden in Papago Park 480/941–1225.
Golf Arizona 602/944–3035, web: www.azgolf.org.
Hiking trails in Papago Park, Squaw Peak & Camelback Mtns.

Reply **Forward**　　　　　　　　　　**Delete**

Date: Dec 17, 2005 11:51:33
From: Girl-on-the-Go
To: Editor@Damron.com
Subject: Phoenix

>Can't stand another cloudy day? Sick of spending your summers in a fog bank and your winters in a snowdrift? Try Phoenix, a sun worshiper's paradise. Here the winters are warm and the summers sizzle. And each day ends with a dramatic desert sunset.

>The people of Phoenix have perfected many ways to soak up the incredible sunshine. Some do it as they hike or ride horseback on the many trails along Squaw Peak (off Lincoln Drive) or Camelback Mountain. Some do it by the pool or on the golf course or tennis court. Some do it as they hover over the valley in a hot-air balloon.

>Some do it between galleries as they enjoy the popular Thursday night Art Walk along Main Street, Marshall Way, and 5th Avenue in Scottsdale. Others do it dashing from the car to the Scottsdale Galleria or Fashion Square. Still others get sun on the half-hour trip north to Rawhide (800/527-1880), Arizona's real live Old West town and Native American village, complete with gunfights and hayrides.*

>What do lesbians do in Phoenix? Pretty much the same things, but usually in couples. Whether traveling with your honey or on your own, you'll probably enjoy one of the many women's bars in town: **Ain't Nobody's Bizness (The Biz), Misty's, Cash Inn,** or **Nasty's Sports Bar.** You'll find the girls who want to have fun at **E-Lounge**, the women's dance club. Phoenix also has a large sober women's community and its own AA club house. And many lesbians just like to get away from it all on camping, fishing, or hiking trips. Call the **Lesbian Social Network** (480/946-5570) to find out what social events will be on while you're in town.

*Driving in the Arizona desert during the summer can be dangerous. Always carry a few gallons of water in your vehicle, and check all fluids in your car both before you leave and frequently during your trip.

Pookie's Cafe 4540 N 7th St (at Camelback) **602/277–2121** • 4pm-1am • lesbians/gay men • also restaurant • live shows • videos • wheelchair access

Roscoe's on 7th 4531 N 7th St (at Minnezona) **602/285–0833** • noon-1am, from 11am Sun • lesbians/ gay men • sports bar • food served

The Waterhole 8830 N 43rd Ave (at Dunlap) **623/937–3139** • 11am-1am • lesbians/gay men • neighborhood bar • food served • karaoke

Wild Card 801 N Arizona Ave, Chandler **480/857–3088** • lesbians/gay men • neighborhood bar • dancing/ DJ • karaoke • drag shows • videos

NIGHTCLUBS

E-Lounge 4343 N 7th Ave (btwn Camelback & Indian School Rd) **602/279–0388** • mostly women • dancing/DJ

Karamba 1724 E McDowell (at 16th St) **602/254–0231** • 4pm-close, clsd Mon-Wed • mostly men • dancing/DJ • Flava Th & Latin Night Sat • wheelchair access

RESTAURANTS

Alexi's 3550 N Central (in Valley Bank Bldg at Osborn) **602/279–0982** • lunch & dinner, dinner only Sat, clsd Sun • full bar • patio • wheelchair access

Hamburger Mary's 5111 N 7th St (N of Camelback) **602/240–6969** • 10am-2am • Sun brunch • also bar • karaoke • gay-owned

Katz's Deli 5144 N Central (at Camelback) **602/277–8814** • 6:30am-2:30pm, from 8am Sun • kosher-style deli

Los Dos Molinos 8646 S Central Ave **602/243–9113** • lunch & dinner, clsd Sun-Mon • robust homecooking

Persian Garden Cafe 1335 W Thomas Rd (at N 15th Ave) **602/263–1915** • 11am-9pm, till 10pm Fri-Sat, clsd Sun • plenty veggie

Pookie's Cafe 4540 N 7th St (at Camelback) **602/277–2121** • 11am-midnight, kitchen till 11pm, Sun brunch • lesbians/gay men • live shows • videos • also full bar • wheelchair access

Vincent Guerithault on Camelback 3930 E Camelback Rd #204 (at 40th St) **602/224–0225** • lunch Mon-Fri • dinner nightly • Southwestern • some veggie • wheelchair access

ENTERTAINMENT & RECREATION

Friends of Ellen Brunch 1949 E Camelback Rd (at Miracle Mile Deli behind Best Buy) **602/380–5848** • 11am 1st & 3rd Sun

Lesbian Social Network 480/946–5570 • 7:30pm-10pm Fri • popular informal social evenings of games, videos & discussions • smoke & alcohol-free • call for location

Phoenix Mercury 602/379–7878 • check out the Women's National Basketball Association while you're in Phoenix

BOOKSTORES

The Bookstore 4230 N 7th Ave **602/279–3910** • 9am-8pm, till 6pm Sat, till 5pm Sun • independent

RETAIL SHOPS

EXPOSED Studio & Gallery 3302 N 3rd St (at Osborn) **602/248–8030** • 1pm-5:30pm Mon-Fri • "new & established artists of all mediums" • wheelchair access • gay-owned

Root Seller Gallery 1605 N 7th Ave (at McDowell Rd) **602/712–9338** • 10am-7pm, 11am-5pm Sun • LGBT books & gifts

Unique on Central 4700 N Central Ave #105 (at Highland) **602/279–9691, 800/269–4840 (MAIL ORDER)** • 9am-9pm, noon-8pm Sun • cards & gifts • wheelchair access

PUBLICATIONS

Caliente flavAZ 320 E Willetta Ste 3 (at McDowell & 3rd St) **602/460–2346** • first gay English/Spanish magazine in AZ

Echo Magazine 602/266–0550, 888/324–6624 • bi-weekly LGBT newsmagazine

Ionaz 602/308–4662 • entertainment guide

Red Magazine 602/308–8310 • monthly gay nightlife & lifestyle magazine

Women's Community Connection 480/946–5570 • monthly newspaper w/ events listings, articles, personals & lesbian resources

SPIRITUAL GROUPS

Augustana Lutheran Church 2604 N 14th St (at Virginia) **602/265–8400** • 9am Sun

Casa de Cristo Evangelical Church 1029 E Turney (at Indian School) **602/265–2831** • 10am Sun, 6:30pm Wed

Community Church of Hope 4121 N 7th Ave (off 6th Dr) **602/234–2180** • 9am & 11am Sun • independent Christian church & counseling center

Gentle Shepherd MCC 2604 N 14th (at Augustana Lutheran) **602/864–6404** • 10:30am Sun

EROTICA

Adult Shoppe 111 S 24th St (at Jefferson) **602/306–1130** • 24hrs • also 5021 W Indian School Rd (at 51st Ave), 623/245–3008 & 2345 W Holly St, 602/253-7126

Castle Megastore 300 E Camelback (at Central) **602/266–3348** • 24hrs • also 5501 E Washington, 602/231–9837 • 8802 N Black Canyon Fwy, 602/995–1641 • 8315 E Apache Tr, 480/986–6114

International Bookstore 3640 E Thomas Rd (at 36th St) **602/955–2000**

Tuff Stuff 1716 E McDowell Rd (at 17th St) **602/254–9651, 877/875–4167** • 10am-6pm, till 4pm Sat, clsd Sun-Mon • custom leather shop

Prescott

INFO LINES & SERVICES

Prescott Pride Center 111 Josephine St **928/445–8800** • 1:30pm-5:30pm Tue, Th & Sat, call for calendar of events • wheelchair access

ACCOMMODATIONS

Briar Wreath Inn B&B 232 S Arizona Ave (at Gurley) **928/778–6048, 877/778–6048** • gay/ straight • Craftsman bungalow • full brkfst • hot tub • gay-owned • $110-165

Scottsdale

ACCOMMODATIONS

Inn at Eagle Mountain 9800 N Summer Hill Blvd, Fountain Hills **480/816–3000, 800/992–8083** • gay-friendly • on 18-hole championship golf course • 1/4 mile from Scottsdale • nonsmoking • $119-295

ResortQuest Arizona 14505 N Hayden, Suite 341 **480/515–2300, 888/868–4378** • rental homes, villas & condos • swimming • kids/ pets ok • nonsmoking • $85-500

BARS

BS West 7125 E 5th Ave (in pedestrian mall) **480/945–9028** • 1pm-1am • lesbians/ gay men • dancing/DJ • videos • karaoke • wheelchair access

RESTAURANTS

AZ-88 7553 E Scottsdale Mall **480/994–5576** • 11am-1am, food till midnight, from 5pm wknds • upscale American • some veggie

Ibiza Cafe 4400 N Scottsdale Rd (at the Canal) **480/421–2492** • 11am-11pm, clsd Sun-Mon • gay/straight • Mediterranean • tapas • full bar • patio

Malee's 7131 E Main **480/947–6042** • lunch & dinner, dinner only Sun • Thai • plenty veggie • full bar

Restaurant Hapa 6204 N Scottsdale **480/998–8220** • 5pm-10pm, clsd Sun • upscale • contemporary Asian • also lounge • wheelchair access • gay-owned

EROTICA

Zorba's Adult Book Shop 2924 N Scottsdale Rd (N of Thomas) **480/941–9891** • 24hrs • video rentals & arcade

Sedona

ACCOMMODATIONS

A Woman's Way PO Box 127, 86339 **928/282–7044** • women-only • "healing sanctuary"

A-Lodge at Sedona—A Luxury B&B Inn 125 Kallof Pl **928/204–1942, 800/619–4467** • gay/ straight • Mission-style B&B inn • Red Rock views • full gourmet brkfst • swimming • nonsmoking • wheelchair access • $160-325

Apple Orchard Inn 656 Jordan Rd **928/282–5328, 800/663–6968** • gay-friendly • full brkfst • hot tub • swimming • hiking • scenic views • nonsmoking • wheelchair access • $140-230

Iris Garden Inn 390 Jordan Rd **928/282–2552, 800/321–8988** • gay/ straight • motel • jacuzzi • nonsmoking • wheelchair access • gay-owned • $74-125

Southwest Inn at Sedona 3250 W Hwy 89–A **928/282–3344, 800/483–7422** • gay-friendly • swimming • spa • workout room • nonsmoking • $119-239

Two Angels Guesthouse 928/204–2083 • lesbians/ gay men • w/ Red Rock mtn views • nonsmoking • lesbian-owned • $105

RESTAURANTS

Judi's 40 Soldiers Pass Rd **928/282–4449** • lunch & dinner, dinner only Sun • some veggie • full bar

Piñon Bistro 1075 Hwy 260 (Rte 89A), Cottonwood **928/649–0234** • dinner Th-Sun only • upscale • wheelchair access • lesbian-owned

Tempe

RESTAURANTS

Restaurant Mexico 120 E University Dr **480/967-3280** • 11am-9pm, till 10pm Fri-Sat, clsd Sun

ENTERTAINMENT & RECREATION

Tuesday Night Lesbian Scrabble League 1032 S Terrace (at the Muse) **480/946-5570** • 6:30pm 2nd & 4th Tue

BOOKSTORES

Changing Hands 6428 S McClintock Dr **480/730-0205** • 10am-9pm, till 10pm Fri-Sat, from 9am wknds • new & used • LGBT section

EROTICA

Modern World 1812 E Apache (at McClintock Dr) **480/967-9052**

Tucson

INFO LINES & SERVICES

AA Gay/ Lesbian 3269 N Mountain Ave (at MCC) **520/624-4183** • 8pm Th

Wingspan, Southern Arizona's LGBT Community Center 300 E 6th St (at 5th Ave) **520/624-1779, 520/624-0348** • 10am-7pm Mon-Fri, till 5pm Sat • resources • youth support • library • film festival • call for more info

ACCOMMODATIONS

Adobe Desert Vacation Rentals **520/578-3998** • gay/ straight • custom adobe homes • outdoor hot tub • nonsmoking • kids/ pets ok • patio • $700-1,500/ week

Adobe Rose Inn B&B 940 N Olsen Ave (at E 2nd) **520/318-4644, 800/328-4122** • gay-friendly • full brkfst, always veggie option • swimming • hot tub • $65-185

Armory Park Guesthouse 219 S 5th Ave **520/206-9252** • gay-friendly • renovated 1896 residence w/ 2 detached guest units • gay-owned • $60-110

Catalina Park Inn 309 E 1st St **520/792-4541, 800/792-4885** • gay/ straight • full brkfst • nonsmoking • kids 10+ ok • gay-owned • $126-166

Clarion Hotel Randolph Park 102 N Alvernon Wy **520/795-0330, 800/252-7466** • gay-friendly • full brkfst • swimming • jacuzzi • kids/ pets ok • wheelchair access • $49-109

Coyote Moon Health Resort & Spa 7501 N Wade Rd **520/744-2355, 877/784-7430** • lesbians/ gay men • 30-acre resort • offers fitness, spa services, nutrition & holistic medicine • women-only & family-only weeks • swimming • sauna • wheelchair access • gay-owned • $97-234/ night

Desert Trails B&B 12851 E Speedway Blvd **520/885-7295, 877/758-3284** • gay-friendly • adobe hacienda on 3 acres bordering Saguaro Nat'l Park • far from the madding crowd • swimming • smoking outside only • $95-155

Hacienda del Sol Guest Ranch Resort 5601 N Hacienda del Sol Rd **520/299-1501, 800/728-6514** • gay-friendly • food served • swimming • wheelchair access • $89-485

Hotel Congress 311 E Congress **520/622-8848, 800/722-8848** • gay/ straight • historic hotel w/ vintage furnishings • $59-99 • also Cup Cafe • plenty veggie • also full bar & club

Milagras Guesthouse 11185 W Calle Pima **520/578-8577** • mostly women • natural adobe guesthouse • suites • garden courtyard • private patio • hot tub • nonsmoking • lesbian-owned • wheelchair access • $75-100 (cash or check only)

Montecito House **520/795-7592, 520/327-8586** • gay-friendly • nonsmoking • kids ok by arrangement • lesbian-owned • $45-55

Natural B&B **520/881-4582, 888/295-8500** • gay/ straight • full brkfst • nonsmoking • nontoxic/ allergenic • some shared baths • kids ok • massage available • gay-owned • $65-90

Royal Elizabeth B&B Inn 204 S Scott Ave (at Broadway) **520/670-9022, 877/670-9022** • gay/ straight • historic 1878 downtown mansion • full brkfst • swimming • hot tub • kids ok • nonsmoking • gay-owned • $102-215

BARS

Ain't Nobody's Bizness 2900 E Broadway #118 (at Tucson) **520/318-4838** • 2pm-1am • mostly women • dancing/DJ • wheelchair access

Congress Tap Room 311 E Congress (at Hotel Congress) **520/622-8848** • 10am-1am • gay-friendly • neighborhood bar • dance club from 9pm • alternative • live bands • theme nights

Howl At The Moon 915 W Prince Rd **520/293-7339** • 3pm-1am, 11am-2am wknds • gay/ straight • dancing/ DJ • country/ western • food served

Reply **Forward** **Delete**

Date: Dec 22, 2005 14:06:59
From: Girl-on-the-Go
To: Editor@Damron.com
Subject: Tucson

>Mention Tucson's torrid weather, and you're likely to hear, "Yeah, but it's dry heat!"

>Whether you believe that or know better, you can make the most of Tucson's sunshine. Leave your overcoat at home, pack your SPF 160 sun lotion and a good pair of shades, and prepare for a great time.

>You'll see the rainbow everywhere, but mainly around shops on 4th Avenue, the downtown Arts District, and residences in the Armory Park Historic neighborhood. (The annual homes tour might as well be called the "who's who of home-owning homos"!)

>Downtown is where you'll find such gay-friendly establishments as **Rainbow Planet Coffee House,** the **Grill on Congress** and **Hydra,** purveyor of fine BDSM gear. At night, grab a beer at the **Congress Tap Room** or **IBT's** or pay a visit to the women's bar, **Ain't Nobody's Bizness.**

>Just a few blocks northeast is 4th Avenue, where you'll find queer businesses standing strong between sports bars. In addition to gay-owned hair and skin care salons, real estate offices, restaurants, and retail stores, you'll find **Wingspan,** the LGBT community center, which hosts various women's groups and events, as well as **Antigone Books,** one of the best women's bookstores in the Southwest.

>LGBT spirituality and healing groups abound, as do Latina, discussion, writers, and readers groups. For films, try the Loft or Catalina Theater, or The Screening Room. Tucson also hosts three film festivals, including the Lesbian & Gay Film Festival in March. For general outdoor hilarity, Tucson's gay softball league can't be beat. The Desert Museum (520/883-2702) showcases 300 animal species and 1,200 different plants that call the Sonoran Desert home.

>When you're done with the entertainment, and the temperature at midnight has dropped its usual 30 or 40 degrees, settle in at one of the many gay-owned or gay-friendly B&Bs in town, such as **Milagras B&B** or the **Royal Elizabeth B&B Inn.**

IBT's (It's About Time) 616 N 4th Ave (at University) **520/882-3053** • noon-2am • lesbians/ gay men • dancing/DJ • live shows • wheelchair access

Woody's 3710 N Oracle (at Prince) **520/292-6702** • 10am-2am, from 11am wknds • mostly gay men • video/ sports bar • wheelchair access

The Yard Dog Saloon 2449 N Stone (N of Grant) **520/624-3858** • 6am-1am, from 10am Sun • mixed crowd • transgender-friendly • patio • wheelchair access

NIGHTCLUBS

Club Eon 520/620-6245 • 7pm-midnight 1st Sat only • dance party for queer youth 23 & younger

CAFES

The Cottage Bakery Cafe 800 N Kolb **520/722-1129** • 7am-9pm, till 11pm Fri-Sat, 8am-8pm Sun • lowfat • gourmet lunch menu

Rainbow Planet Coffee House 606 N 4th Ave (at 5th St) **520/620-1770** • 8am-10pm, till 6pm Sun-Mon, till midnight Fri-Sat, from 9am wknds • lesbians/ gay men • transgender-friendly • plenty veggie • live music Tue • lesbian-owned

RESTAURANTS

Blue Willow 2616 N Campbell (at Grant) **520/327-7577** • 7am-9pm, 8am-10pm Fri-Sat • brkfst served all day

Cafe Terra Cotta 3500 E. Sunrise **520/577-8100** • 11am-10pm, till 10:30pm wknds • full bar • wheelchair access

Colors Restaurant 5305 E Speedway **520/323-1840** • dinner nightly, Sun brunch, clsd Mon, also bar from 4pm • lesbians/ gay men • live entertainment

The Grill on Congress 100 E Congress (at Scott) **520/623-7621** • 24hrs • plenty veggie • full bar

November Bar & Grill 4001 N Romero Rd (at Roger) **520/407-9622** • 3pm-1am • full bar till late

BOOKSTORES

Antigone Books 411 N 4th Ave (at 7th St) **520/792-3715** • 10am-7pm, till 9pm Fri-Sat, noon-5pm Sun • LGBT/ feminist • gifts • wheelchair access

RETAIL SHOPS

Desert Pride 611 N 4th Ave **520/388-9829** • pride gifts • T-shirts • jewelry • videos • CDs • gay-owned

Tucson

LGBT PRIDE:
June.

ANNUAL EVENTS:
February - La Fiesta de los Vaqueros (rodeo & parade) 520/741-2233, web: www.tucsonrodeo.com.
March - Lesbian & Gay Film Festival 520/624-1779 (Wingspan #).
April - Int'l Mariachi Music Conference 520/838-3908, web: www.tucsonmariachi.org.

CITY INFO:
520/624-1817, web: www.visittucson.org.

BEST VIEW:
From a ski lift heading up to the top of Mount Lemmon.

WEATHER:
350 days of sunshine a year. Need we say more?

TRANSIT:
Arizona Shuttle 520/795-6771 or 800/888-2749, web: www.arizonashuttle.com.

ATTRACTIONS:
Arizona-Sonora Desert Museum 520/883-2702, web: www.desert-museum.org.
Arizona State Museum 520/621-6302, web: www.statemuseum.arizona.edu.
Biosphere 2 520/838-6200, web: www.bio2.edu.
Catalina State Park.
Colossal Cave.
Mission San Xavier del Bac, 520/294-6624.
Old Tucson.
Saguaro National Park.

PUBLICATIONS

The Observer 520/622–7176

SPIRITUAL GROUPS

Cornerstone Fellowship 2902 N Geronimo (at Laguna) **520/622–4626** • 10:30am Sun

Water of Life MCC 3269 N Mountain Ave (N of Fort Lowell) **520/292–9151** • 10:15am Sun

EROTICA

The Bookstore Southwest 5754 E Speedway Blvd **520/790–1500**

Caesar's Adult Shop 2540 N Oracle Rd (btwn Glen & Grant) **520/622–9479**

Hydra 145 E Congress (at 6th) **520/791–3711** • vinyl • leather • toys • shoes • lingerie

Wenden

RESTAURANTS

The Brooks Outback 35296 2nd St (at Hwy 60) **928/859–3176** • 11am-11pm • also full bar • wheelchair access • gay-owned

Yuma

EROTICA

Triple X Adult Super Store 3125 S Ave 3-E (32nd) **928/344–1799**

ARKANSAS

Statewide

PUBLICATIONS

Ozarks Star 918/835–7887 • 10am-4pm Mon-Fri, monthly LGBT news publication serving AR, KS, MO & OK

Eureka Springs

ACCOMMODATIONS

11 Singleton House B&B 11 Singleton **800/833–3394** • gay/ straight • 1890s Victorian • full brkfst • jacuzzi • nonsmoking • woman-owned • $75-145

1905 Basin Park Hotel 12 Spring St **479/253–7837, 877/643–4972** • gay/ straight • 1905 historic hotel • restaurant/ spa access • $89-199

Candlestick Cottage Inn 6 Douglas St (at N Main) **479/253–6813, 800/835–5184** • gay-friendly • private, romantic setting • full brkfst • swimming • lesbian-owned

Cliff Cottage Inn & Eureka Springs Cottages in historic downtown **479/253–7409, 800/799–7409** • gay/ straight • B&B inn in heart of downtown • full gourmet brkfst • hot tub & jacuzzis • nonsmoking • gay & straight-owned • $189-230

Comfort Inn of Eureka Springs Hwy 62 E (at Jct 23 S) **479/253–5241, 800/828–0109** • gay-friendly • 3-story Victorian hotel • swimming • wheelchair access • woman-owned/ run • $49-159

Enchanted Cottages 18 Nut St **479/253–6790, 800/862–2788** • gay-friendly • near downtown • hot tub • $79-149

Gardener's Cottage in Historic District **479/253–9111, 800/833–3394** • gay/ straight • cottage for 2 • jacuzzi • nonsmoking • woman-owned • $125-145

Heart of the Hills Inn 5 Summit (on Historic Loop) **479/253–7468, 800/253–7468** • gay/ straight • historic inn near downtown • full brkfst • private decks • gay-owned • $80-139

Home Suite Home 888/933–4050 • gay-friendly • vacation home in restored schoolhouse • jacuzzi • nonsmoking • gay-owned • $140-280

Log Cabin on Beaver Lake 585 Viewpoint Dr (off Mundell Rd) **479/253–7344** • gay/ straight • private lake access • jacuzzi • fireplace • nonsmoking • lesbian-owned • $125

Ozark Real Log Homes 170 W Van Buren (at Century 21 Woodland Real Estate) **479/253–7344 (CABIN ENQUIRIES), 479/253–7321 (LOG HOMES)** • precut, pretreated log home packages • custom or catalog packages • also 1 rental cabin ($125 for a couple) • lesbian-owned

Palace Hotel & Bath House 135 Spring St **479/253–7474** • gay-friendly • historic bath house open to all • $120-165

Pond Mountain Lodge & Resort **479/253–5877, 800/583–8043** • gay/ straight • mountaintop inn on 159 acres • cabins • swimming • nonsmoking • jacuzzi • wheelchair access • lesbian & straight-owned/ run • $79-165

Roadrunner Inn 3034 Mundell Rd **479/253–8281, 888/253–8166** • gay-friendly • views • reservations advised • $59-80

TradeWinds 141 W Van Buren (at 23 N) **479/253–9774, 800/242–1615** • gay/ straight • motel reminiscent of the motor inns of the '40s & '50s • jacuzzi • swimming • $49-150 • gay-owned

The Veranda Inn B&B 38 Prospect Ave (at Linwood) **479/253-7292, 888/295-2171** • gay-friendly • colonial revival mansion B&B in historic district • full brkfst • nonsmoking • gay-owned

Wildflower Cottages 22 Hale **479/253-9173, 866/847-9776** • gay/ straight • private cottages • hot tub • kids/ pets ok • $80-140

The Woods Resort 50 Wall St (off Hwy 62) **479/253-8281** • lesbians/ gay men • cottages • some treehouse cottages • treehouse hot tub • jacuzzis • kitchens • nonsmoking • gay-owned • $115-135

BARS

Chelsea's Corner Cafe 10 Mountain St (at Center St) **479/253-6723** • 11am-2am, till 10pm Sun • gay-friendly • dancing/DJ • patio • also restaurant • plenty veggie • women-owned

RESTAURANTS

Autumn Breeze Hwy 23 S **479/253-7734** • 5pm-9pm, clsd Sun • cont'l • opens in March • nonsmoking

Caribe 309 W Van Buren **479/253-8102** • 5pm-9pm, clsd Tue • gay-friendly • popular • Carribean • live music Fri-Sat • also bar

Cottage Inn 450 Hwy 62 W **479/253-5282** • opens in Feb • 5pm-9pm, clsd Mon-Wed • Mediterranean • full bar

Ermilio's 26 White St **479/253-8806** • 5pm-9pm • Italian • plenty veggie • full bar

Gaskins Cabin Steak House 2883 Hwy 23 N (Hwy 187) **479/253-5466** • 5pm-9pm Th-Sat • clsd winter • steak • seafood • some vegetarian • beer/ wine • reservations suggested

Sonny's Pizzeria 119 N Main St (at Mountain) **479/253-2329** • 11am-11pm wknds, weekday hours vary, clsd Mon & Tue • pizza & pasta • beer/ wine

ENTERTAINMENT & RECREATION

Diversity Pride **479/253-2555** • produces variety of LGBT events, concerts & dances, including events for Valentine's & during Fall & Spring Diversity Wknds

BOOKSTORES

Gazebo Books 86 Spring St **479/253-9556**

PUBLICATIONS

Ozarks Star **918/835-7887** • 10am-4pm Mon-Fri, monthly LGBT news publication serving AR, KS, MO & OK

SPIRITUAL GROUPS

MCC of the Living Spring 17 Elk St (at Unitarian church) **479/253-9337** • 7pm Sun

Fayetteville

INFO LINES & SERVICES

AA Gay/ Lesbian 902 W Maple (at Presbyterian church complex) **479/443-6366 (AA#)** • 7pm Mon

PRIDE ARKU-659 (in Arkansas Union, University of Arkansas) **479/575-3880** • official LGBT student association • call for office hours

NIGHTCLUBS

Five Squirrels 523 W Poplar **479/442-3052** • 9pm-2am Th-Sat • popular • gay/ straight • live music venue • dancing/DJ • check calendar for events

CAFES

The Common Grounds 412 W Dickson (at West) **479/442-3515** • 7am-2am, from 9am wknds • full bar • also restaurant • lots of veggie

BOOKSTORES

Hastings Bookstore 2999 N College Ave (Fiesta Square Shopping Center) **479/521-0244** • 9am-11pm, till midnight Fri-Sat

Passages 2332 N College Ave (near La Huerta) **479/442-5845** • 10am-6pm, till 8pm Fri, from noon Sun • New Age/ metaphysical • classes

EROTICA

Curry's Video Concepts 612 N College Ave **479/521-0009**

Fort Smith

BARS

Kinkead's 1004 1/2 Garrison Ave (at Towson) **479/783-9988** • 3pm-1am, till midnight Sat, clsd Sun • popular • lesbians/ gay men • dancing/DJ • multiracial • transgender-friendly • karaoke • drag shows • strippers • 18+

NIGHTCLUBS

Club 1022 1022 Dodson Ave (at N I St) **479/782-1845** • 9pm-5am, Fri-Sun, from 8pm Sun, clsd Mon-Th • lesbians/ gay men • dancing/ DJ • transgender-friendly • food served • karaoke • drag shows • strippers • private club • wheelchair access

Klub XLR8 917 N A St **918/774–3742** • 7pm-2am Fri-Sun • lesbians/ gay men • dancing/DJ • country/ western • bears • leather • live shows • karaoke • drag shows • videos • private club • wheelchair access

Helena

ACCOMMODATIONS

Foxglove B&B 229 Beech **870/338–9391, 800/863–1926** • gay-friendly • 100-year-old mansion • full brkfst • jacuzzi • nonsmoking • $89-119

Hot Springs

ACCOMMODATIONS

The Rose Cottage 218 Court St (at Exchange St) **501/623–6449** • gay-friendly • historic Victorian row house • kids/ pets ok • jacuzzi • $175

NIGHTCLUBS

Club One Eleven 111 Garden St (near Malvern Ave) **501/620–4111** • 8pm-2am, clsd Mon-Tue • gay-friendly • dancing/ DJ • live entertainment • karaoke • drag shows • private club • wheelchair access

Little Rock

ACCOMMODATIONS

Comfort Inn & Suites, Little Rock Airport 4301 E Roosevelt Rd (at Bankhead) **501/376–2466, 800/228–5150** • gay-friendly • wheelchair access • gay-owned

Legacy Hotel & Suites 625 W Capitol Ave (at Gaines) **501/374–0100** • nat'l historic property located in downtown area • gay-friendly • kids ok • brkfst included • wheelchair access

BARS

Backstreet 1021 Jessie Rd (btwn Cantrell & Riverfront) **501/664–2744** • 9pm-5am, clsd Tue-Th • lesbians/ gay men • dancing/DJ • drag shows • karaoke • male dancers • videos • 18+ Sun-Mon • private club • wheelchair access

The Factory 412 S Louisiana St (btwn 4th & Center) **501/372–3070** • 5pm-2am, 8pm-1am Sat, clsd Sun-Mon • gay/ straight • neighborhood bar • dancing/DJ • food served • live shows • karaoke • wheelchair access • gay-owned

Little Rock

WHERE THE GIRLS ARE:
Scattered. Popular hangouts are the Women's Project, local bookstores, and Vino's Pizza - women's coffeehouse.

LGBT PRIDE:
April.

ANNUAL EVENTS:
October - State Fair 501/372–8341, web: www.arkfairgrounds.com.

CITY INFO:
Arkansas Dept of Tourism 800/NATURAL, web: www.arkansas.com.
Little Rock Convention & Visitors Bureau 800/844-4781, web: www.littlerock.com.

BEST VIEW:
Quapaw Quarter (in the heart of the city).

WEATHER:
When it comes to natural precipitation, Arkansas is far from being a dry state. Be prepared for the occasional severe thunderstorm or ice storm. Summers are hot and humid (mid 90ºs). Winters can be cold (30ºs) with some snow and ice. Spring and fall are the best times to come and be awed by Mother Nature.

TRANSIT:
Black & White Cab 501/374-0333.
Central Arkansas Transit 501/375-1163.

ATTRACTIONS:
Check out Bill & Hillary's old digs at 18th & Center Sts.
Decorative Arts Museum 501/372-4000, web: www.arkarts.com.
Historical Quapaw Quarter.

Sidetracks 415 Main St, North Little Rock **501/244-0444** • 4pm-2am, till 1am Sat, clsd Sun-Mon • mostly gay men • neighborhood bar • also restaurant • country/ western • bears • leather • older crowd • wheelchair access

NIGHTCLUBS

Discovery: The Experience 1021 Jessie Rd (btwn Cantrell & Riverfront) **501/664-4784** • 9pm-5am Sat only • popular • gay/ straight • dancing/DJ • transgender-friendly • drag shows • live music • private club • wheelchair access

---

Reply	Forward		Delete

Date: Dec 21, 2005 12:16:35
From: Girl-on-the-Go
To: Editor@Damron.com
Subject: Little Rock

>If you want a city with a pace of life all its own, a city whose history reflects the dramatic changes within the South, and a city surrounded by natural beauty, you've made the right choice to visit Little Rock.

>Here you can enjoy relaxing summer days in the shade beside the slow-moving Arkansas River that winds through town. Or you can take off to the nearby lakes and national forests to camp, rock climb, or water-ski. Stay in town and you can spend your days exploring the state capital, touring the historic homes of the Quapaw Quarter district, or browsing in Little Rock's many shops. Rumor has it that Bill Clinton's boyhood home is owned by a friendly lesbian couple.

>At night, you can make an evening of it with dinner, a program at the Arkansas Arts Center, and a visit to the lesbian bar **UBU.** If you'd rather mix it up, mosey on over to the biggest LGBT bar in Little Rock, **Backstreet**

>Of course, if that isn't enough excitement, you can always head out for the northwest corner of the state. We've heard there are many lesbian landowners, living alone and in groups, throughout this region. And while you're out there, be sure to visit the funky Ozark Mountain resort town of Eureka Springs. There are loads of gay-friendly and women-owned B&Bs in this quaint, old-fashioned town, as well as a popular Passion Play. **Candlestick Cottage Inn B&B** and **Log Cabin on Beaver Lake** are lesbian-owned accommodations, and **Caribe** is a popular gay-friendly hangout.

UBU 824 W Capitol (at Izard) 501/375–8580
• 8pm-2am Fri, from 9pm Sat, clsd Sun-Th •
lesbians/ gay men • dancing/DJ • multiracial •
transgender-friendly • live shows • karaoke •
drag shows • private club • wheelchair access
• lesbian-owned

RESTAURANTS

Vino's Pizza 923 W 7th St (at Chester)
501/375–8466 • 11am-close • beer/ wine •
inquire about monthly women's coffeehouse

ENTERTAINMENT & RECREATION

The Weekend Theatre 1001 W 7th St (at
Chester) 501/374–3761 • beer & wine • plays
& musicals on wknds • gay-owned

BOOKSTORES

Women's Project 2224 Main St (at 23rd)
501/372–5113, 501/372–6853 (TDD) • 10am-
5pm Mon-Fri • feminist resource • call for info

RETAIL SHOPS

A Twisted Gift Shop 1007 W 7th St (at
Chester) 501/376–7723 • 11am-10pm, clsd
Tue • gift shop • also 7201 Asher Ave,
501/568–4262

Wild Card 400 N Bowman (at Maralynn)
501/223–9071 • 10am-8pm, noon-5pm Sun •
novelties & gifts

SPIRITUAL GROUPS

MCC Spirit of the Rock 2017 Chandler,
North Little Rock 501/753–7075 • 10:30am
Sun

Unitarian Universalist Church 1818
Reservoir Rd 501/225–1503 • 10:30am Sun •
wheelchair access

Mountain Home

ACCOMMODATIONS

Black Oak Resort 870/431–8363 • gay/
straight • quiet mtn resort bordering Bull
Shoals Lake • swimming • kids/ pets ok • $76-
155

CALIFORNIA

Statewide

PUBLICATIONS

The Lavender Lens 4094 Georgia St #2, San
Diego 92103 619/291–8223 • "California's bi-
weekly news & lifestyle magazine for lesbians
& friends"

▲ **Lesbian News (LN)** 800/995–8838,
800/458–9488 • nat'l w/ strong coverage of
southern CA • see ad front color section

Outword News Magazine 916/329–9280 •
statewide LGBT newspaper w/ N & S CA
editions

Amador City

ACCOMMODATIONS

Imperial Hotel 14202 Hwy 49 (at Water St)
209/267–9172 • gay-friendly • B&B • brick
Victorian hotel from Gold Rush era • full brkfst
• kids ok • gay-owned • $100-140

Anaheim

see Orange County

Arcata

BARS

The Alibi 744 9th St 707/822–3731 • 6pm-
9pm Th for "Family Night" • neighborhood bar
• also restaurant • live shows • young crowd

RESTAURANTS

Wildflower Bakery & Cafe 1604 G St
707/822–0360 • 8am-8pm, 9am-1pm Sun •
vegetarian

BOOKSTORES

Northtown Books 957 H St 707/822–2834 •
10am-7pm, till 9pm Fri, till 6pm Sat, noon-
5pm Sun • LGBT section • carries The L Word
paper

Arnold

ACCOMMODATIONS

Dorrington Inn at Big Trees 3450 Hwy 4
(at Boards Crossing), Dorrington
209/795–2164, 888/874–2164 • gay/ straight •
cottages & suites • 3 hours from San
Francisco, 18 miles from Bear Valley • gay-
owned • $59-199

Atascadero

EROTICA

Diamond Adult World 7253 El Camino Real
805/462–0404 • books • toys • videos

Auburn

CAFES

Wolf Mountain Coffee 13428 Lincoln Wy (at
Foresthill Rd/ I–80) 530/888–8195 • 5:30am-
6:30pm, from 7am Sun • relaxing woodsy
atmosphere • internet access • wheelchair
access • gay-owned

Bakersfield

ACCOMMODATIONS

Rio Bravo Resort, Hotel & Spa 11200 Lake Ming Rd **661/872–5000, 888/517–5500** • gay/ straight • swimming • wheelchair access • $80-128

NIGHTCLUBS

The Casablanca Club 1825 N St (at 19th St) **661/324–0661, 661/326–1872** • 8pm-2am, clsd Mon-Wed • mostly gay men • neighborhood bar • dancing/DJ • live entertainment • cabaret • drag shows • videos • gay-owned

EROTICA

Wildcat Books 2620 Chester Ave (at 21st) **661/324–4243**

Benicia

see Vallejo

Berkeley

see East Bay

Big Bear Lake

ACCOMMODATIONS

Alpine Retreats 433 Edgemoor (at Big Bear Blvd) **818/535–9272** • gay/ straight • indoor spas • fireplaces • private entrances • nonsmoking • kids ok • gay-owned • $135-225

Eagles' Nest B&B 41675 Big Bear Blvd **909/866–6465, 888/866–6465** • gay-friendly • 5 cottages • full brkfst • spa • $85-325

Grey Squirrel Resort **909/866–4335, 800/381–5569** • gay/ straight • 20 cabins & 30 private rental homes • swimming • lesbian-owned • $85-675

Hillcrest Lodge 40241 Big Bear Blvd **909/866–7330, 800/843–4449** • gay/ straight • motel • cabins • jacuzzi suites • kitchens • fireplaces • nonsmoking rooms available • kids ok • wheelchair access • $46-200

Knickerbocker Mansion Country Inn 869 Knickerbocker Rd **909/878–9190, 877/423–1180** • gay/ straight • log mansion on lake • full brkfst • jacuzzi • hiking • nonsmoking • wheelchair access • gay-owned • $110-250

Majestic Moose Lodge 39328 Big Bear Blvd (at Cienga) **909/866–2435, 877/585–5855** • gay-friendly • cabins • jacuzzi • swimming • kids/ pets ok • nonsmoking • $99-209

Rainbow View Lodge 2726 View Dr (at Hilltop), Running Springs **909/867–1810, 888/868–1810** • gay/ straight • kids ok • nonsmoking • women-owned • $69-149

Big Sur

ACCOMMODATIONS

Lucia Lodge 62400 Hwy 1 **831/667–2391, 866/424–4787** • gay-friendly • oceanview cabins (newly remodeled) • $175-250 • also restaurant • American/ seafood • Rockslide Lounge

Buena Park

BARS

Ozz Supper Club 6231 Manchester Blvd **714/522–1542** • 9pm-2am, from 6pm Fri-Sat, from 3pm Sun, clsd Mon & Wed • popular • lesbians/ gay men • more women Sun • dancing/DJ • live shows • cabaret • piano bar • 18+ • call for events • also restaurant • some veggie

Burney

ACCOMMODATIONS

Burney Mountain Guest Ranch 22800 Hat Creek, Powerhouse #2 (at Hwy 299), Cassel **530/335–4087** • gay-friendly • close to some of best fly-fishing in state • swimming • kids ok • wheelchair access • lesbian & gay-owned • $175-300/ night

Cambria

ACCOMMODATIONS

Blue Dolphin Inn 6470 Moonstone Beach Dr **805/927–3300, 800/222–9157** • gay-friendly • inn on Cambria's Moonstone Beach • wheelchair access • $89-319

The J Patrick House B&B 2990 Burton Dr (1/2 mile off Hwy 1) **805/927–3812, 800/341–5258** • gay-friendly • full brkfst • authentic log cabin • fireplaces • nonsmoking • $165-205

Leopold Cove 2183 Sherwood Dr **805/927–5396, 866/927–5396** • gay-friendly • vacation home on a bluff overlooking the Pacific Ocean • located in the Central Coast wine district • gay-owned • $200

Carmel

see also Monterey

ACCOMMODATIONS

Carmel River Inn Hwy 1 at Oliver Rd 831/624–1575, 800/966–6490 • gay-friendly • cottages & inn on 10 acres • kids/ pets ok • swimming • nonsmoking • $79-329

Chico

INFO LINES & SERVICES

Stonewall Alliance Center 341 Broadway #416 530/893–3336 • 1pm-5pm, till 7pm Tue-Fri • recorded info • meetings

Chula Vista

EROTICA

F St Bookstore 1141 3rd Ave (btwn Naples & Oxford) 619/585–3314 • 24hrs • wheelchair access

Clear Lake

ACCOMMODATIONS

Blue Fish Cove Resort 10573 E Hwy 20, Clearlake Oaks 707/998–1769 • gay-friendly • lakeside resort cottages • kitchens • kids ok • pets ok by arrangement • boat launch facilities & rentals • $60-120

Edgewater Resort 6420 Soda Bay Rd (at Hohape Rd), Kelseyville 707/279–0208, 800/396–6224 • "gay-owned, straight-friendly" • cabin • camping & RV hookups • lake access & pool • theme wknds • boat facilities • smoking outside • kids/ pets ok • lesbian-owned • $28-400

Gingerbread Cottages B&B 4057 E Hwy 20, Nice 707/274–0200, 888/880–5253 • gay/ straight • lakefront w/ private beach • antiques & art • hot tub • swimming • nonsmoking • $115-185

Lake Vacation Rentals 1855 S Main St, Lakeport 707/263–7188 • gay-friendly • rental homes on the lake • gay-owned • $185-500

Rocky Point Cottages 3884 Lakeshore Blvd (at Park Way Rd), Lakeport 707/263–5901 • gay-friendly • private 1920s-style lakefront resort on Clear Lake • cottages w/ private pier & decks • $135-350

Sea Breeze Resort 9595 Harbor Dr, Glenhaven 707/998–3327 • gay/ straight • cottages • swimming • nonsmoking • wheelchair access • gay-owned • $80-125 • 2-night minimum stay

RESTAURANTS

Kathy's Inn 14677 Lake Shore Dr, Clearlake 707/994–9933 • lunch Wed-Fri, open from 4pm wknds, clsd Mon-Tue • full bar • wheelchair access

Cloverdale

see also Healdsburg

ACCOMMODATIONS

Asti Ranch 25750 River Rd 707/894–5960 • women only • cottage near lake & river in Wine Country • tennis court • nonsmoking • wheelchair access • $500-750 weekly, $250-350 wknds

Vintage Towers B&B 302 N Main St (at 3rd) 707/894–4535, 888/886–9377 • gay-friendly • Queen Anne mansion • full brkfst • nonsmoking • $95-180

Columbia

ENTERTAINMENT & RECREATION

Zephyr Whitewater Expedition near Yosemite & Lake Tahoe 209/533–1401, 800/431–3636 • women-only, co-ed & charter rafting

Concord

INFO LINES & SERVICES

AA Gay/ Lesbian 2118 Willow Pass Rd 925/939–4155 (AA#) • 7:30pm Tue

Rainbow Community Center of Contra Costa County 3024 Willow Pass Rd #200 (btwn Mt Diablo & Grant) 925/692–0090 • 10am-5pm Mon-Fri • evening/ wknd support groups • library • social events • referral line

EROTICA

Lingerie Etc 2294 Monument Blvd (at Buskirk) 925/676–2962

Costa Mesa

see Orange County

Cupertino

BARS

Dar's Hideaway 10095 Saich Wy (at Stevens Creek Blvd) 408/255–7474 • 5pm-2am • lesbians/ gay men • neighborhood bar • DJ every other Sat • live shows

Dana Point

see Orange County

Davis

see also Sacramento

CAFES

Cafe Roma 231 E St (btwn 2nd & 3rd) 530/756-1615 • 6am-10pm, 6:30am-9pm wknds • popular • coffee & pastries • student hangout

East Bay

includes Berkeley & Oakland, see also Concord, Danville, Fremont, Lafayette, Hayward, Pleasant Hill, San Lorenzo, Walnut Creek

INFO LINES & SERVICES

La Peña 3105 Shattuck Ave, Berkeley 510/849-2568 • 10am-5pm Tue-Fri, box office open 1pm-6pm Wed-Sat • also cafe 5:30pm-9:30pm Wed-Sun • multicultural center • hosts meetings, events, performance art • multiracial clientele

Pacific Center 2712 Telegraph Ave (at Derby), Berkeley 510/548-8283 • 10am-10pm, noon-3pm & 7pm-10pm Sat, 6pm-9pm Sun

ACCOMMODATIONS

Bates House B&B 399 Bellevue Ave (at Van Buren), Oakland 510/893-3881, 866/344-5874 • gay/ straight • B&B-inn • nonsmoking • gay-owned • $95-175

East Bay

WHERE THE GIRLS ARE:
Though there's no lesbian ghetto, you'll find more of us in North Oakland (Rockridge) and North Berkeley, Lake Merritt, around Grand Lake & Piedmont, the Solano/Albany area, or at a cafe along 4th St in Berkeley.

ANNUAL EVENTS:
October - Community Celebration for the Days of the Dead 510/238-2200, web: www.muse-umca.org.

CITY INFO:
Oakland Convention & Visitors Bureau 510/839-9000, web: www.oaklandcvb.com.
Berkeley Visitor Info Center 800/847-4823, web: www.visit-berkeley.com.

ATTRACTIONS:
The Claremont Hotel & Restaurant, Berkeley 510/843-3000, web: www.claremontresort.com.
Emeryville Marina Public Market.
Jack London Square, Oakland.
Oakland Museum of California 510/238-2200, web: www.museumca.org.
The Paramount Theater, Oakland 510/465-6400, web: www.para-mounttheatre.com.
UC Berkeley.

BEST VIEW:
Claremont Hotel, Tilden Park, various locations in the Berkeley and Oakland Hills. Or from the top of Sather Tower on the UC Berkeley campus.

WEATHER:
While San Francisco is fogged in during the summers, the East Bay remains sunny and warm. Some areas even get hot (90°s-100°s). As for the winter, the temperature drops along with rain (upper 30°s-40°s in the winter). Spring is the time to come – the usually brown hills explode with the colors of green grass and wildflowers.

TRANSIT:
Yellow Cab (Berkeley) 510/527-8294.
Veteran's Cab (Oakland) 510/533-1900.
Bayporter Express 510/864-4000, web: www.bayporter.com.
AC Transit 510/817-1717, web: www.actransit.org.
BART (subway) 510/465-2278, web: www.bart.gov.
Ferry 510/749-5837, web: www.eastbayferry.com.

Reply Forward Delete

Date: Dec 22, 2005 14:06:59
From: Girl-on-the-Go
To: Editor@Damron.com
Subject: East Bay

>So what exactly is the East Bay? To most Northern Californians, it's simply the string of cities and counties across the Bay Bridge from San Francisco—with weather that's consistently sunnier and 10 to 20 degrees warmer than Fog City. For the *Damron Women's Traveller*, it is the more lesbian-friendly cities of Berkeley and Oakland.

>Berkeley—both the campus of the University of California and the city where it's located—was immortalized in the '60s as a hotbed of student/counterculture activism. Today, most of the people taking to the streets, especially Telegraph and College Avenues, are tourists or kids from the suburbs in search of consumer thrills such as a good book, exotic cuisine, and funky jewelry and crafts sold by street vendors.

>Locals and visitors alike will enjoy people-watching on Telegraph or University Avenue. Or you can just take to the hills—vast Tilden Park offers incredible views and trails to hike and bike.

>As for Oakland, Gertrude Stein once said, "There is no there there." Well, Gertrude, a lot has happened since you were in Oakland!

>Today Oakland is a city with an incredible diversity of races, cultures, and classes. The birthplace of the Black Panthers, this city has been especially influential in urban African American music, fashion, and politics. Lately Oakland has also become a vital artists' enclave, as Bay Area artists flee high rent in San Francisco for spacious lofts downtown or in West Oakland.

>And where are all the women? Well, many are in couples or covens or both, which can make them hard to find. But if you want to start a couple or a coven of your own, stop in at **White Horse** bar (in Oakland). Gastronomically inclined lesbians can often be found at popular weekend brunch spot **Mama's Royal Cafe** (also in Oakland), or at The Emeryville Marina Public Market (510/652-9300) in Emeryville.

Reply **Forward** **Delete**

>For more info on East Bay groups and events, cruise by the **Pacific Center** in Berkeley. The center hosts meetings for lesbian moms and kids, bisexuals, transgendered women, separatists, and more. Those interested in women's spirituality should drop by **Ancient Ways** (in Oakland), the pagan emporium extraordinaire.

>If you're the outdoors type, consider an adventure in Northern California with **Mariah Wilderness Expeditions** (510/233-2303). Or make a day of it at one of the nearby state parks: Point Reyes is a beautiful destination with a hostel, and Point Isabel is rumored to be a good meeting place for dykes with dogs.

>For plays, performances, and events, grab a copy of the **Bay Times** and check out the calendar section. Or pick up some entertainment of your own at the East Bay **Good Vibrations** (in Berkeley) a clean, women-friendly sex toy store.

>There are also lots of resources for women of color in the East Bay. Start with **La Peña Cultural Center** (in Berkeley), an active center with many events for Latina Americans and African Americans. There's also **What's Up!** an events hotline "for lesbian sistahs of African descent."

Washington Inn 495 10th St (at Broadway), Oakland **510/452-1776** • gay/ straight • historic boutique hotel • full brkfst • nonsmoking • wheelchair access • $89-178

Woodfin Suite Hotel 5800 Shellmound St (at Shellmound Wy), Emeryville **510/601-5880, 888/433-9042** • gay-friendly • full brkfst • pool • nonsmoking • $149-299

BARS

Bench & Bar 2111 Franklin St (at 21st St), Oakland **510/444-2266** • 3pm-2am • popular • mostly gay men • dancing/DJ • Latino/a clientele • Latin night Fri-Sat • drag shows • strippers • young crowd • wheelchair access

Cabel's Reef 2272 Telegraph Ave (at Grand), Oakland **510/451-3777** • 3pm-11pm, till 2am wknds • lesbians/ gay men • dancing/DJ • multiracial • karaoke • drag shows

White Horse 6551 Telegraph Ave (at 66th), Oakland **510/652-3820** • 1pm-2am, from 3pm Mon-Tue • popular wknds • lesbians/ gay men • dancing/DJ • wheelchair access

CAFES

Cafe Sorrento 2510 Channing (at Telegraph), Berkeley **510/548-8220** • 11am-9pm • Italian • vegetarian

Cafe Strada 2300 College Ave (at Bancroft), Berkeley **510/843-5282** • 6:30am-midnight • popular • students • great patio & white mochas • wheelchair access

Mimosa Cafe 462 Santa Clara (at Grand), Oakland **510/465-2948** • 11am-9pm, from 9am wknds, till 2pm Sun, clsd Mon • natural & healthy • plenty veggie • beer/ wine

Raw Energy 2050 Addison St (at Shattuck), Berkeley **510/665-9464** • 8am-7pm, clsd wknds • organic juice cafe • gay-owned

RESTAURANTS

Bette's To Go 1807 4th St (at Hearst), Berkeley **510/548-9494** • 6:30am-5pm, from 8am wknds • sandwiches • some veggie

Chez Panisse 1517 Shattuck Ave (at Cedar), Berkeley 510/548-5525 • clsd Sun • nouvelle Californian • beer/ wine • reservations required • also cafe

La Mediterranée 2936 College Ave (at Ashby), Berkeley 510/540-7773 • 10am-10pm, till 11pm wknds • beer/ wine

Mama's Royal Cafe 4012 Broadway (at 40th), Oakland 510/547-7600 • 7am-3pm, from 8am wknds • popular • mostly lesbians • come early for excellent wknd brunch • beer/ wine • wheelchair access

Sea Mi 856 San Pablo Rd, Albany 510/559-9191 • international fusion menu • some veggie • patio • also full bar • karaoke Th

ENTERTAINMENT & RECREATION

Scharffen Berger Chocolate Maker 914 Heinz Ave, Berkeley 510/981-4050 • a tasty chocolate factory tour • gay-owned

What's Up! Events Hotline for Sistahs 510/835-6126 • for lesbians of African descent

BOOKSTORES

Black Oak Books 1491 Shattuck Ave, Berkeley 510/486-0698 • 10am-10pm • independent • new & used • some LGBT titles • readings

Cody's 2454 Telegraph Ave (at Haste), Berkeley 510/845-7852 • 10am-10pm • general • LGBT section • frequent readings & lectures • wheelchair access

Diesel, A Bookstore 5433 College Avenue, Oakland 510/653-9965 • 10am-9pm, till 10pm Fri-Sat, till 6pm Sun • independent

RETAIL SHOPS

Ancient Ways 4075 Telegraph Ave (at 41st), Oakland 510/653-3244 • 11am-7pm • extensive occult supplies • classes • readings • runs several festivals annually • woman-owned/ run

▲ **See Jane Run Sports** 5817 College Ave, Oakland 510/428-2681 • 11am-7pm, 10am-6pm Sat, noon-5pm Sun • women's athletic apparel

PUBLICATIONS

San Francisco Bay Times 415/626-0260 • popular • a "must read" for Bay Area resources

SPIRITUAL GROUPS

Albany United Methodist Church 980 Stannage Ave (at Marin), Albany 510/526-7346 • 10am Sun

New Spirit Community Church 1798 Scenic Ave (Chapel of the Pacific School of Religion), Berkeley 510/704-7729 • 11am Sun & 7pm Wed

EROTICA

▲ **Good Vibrations** 2504 San Pablo (at Dwight Wy), Berkeley 510/841-8987 • 11am-7pm, till 8pm Fri-Sat • clean, well-lighted sex toy store • workshops & events • also mail order • wheelchair access • (see ad in front color section)

Hollywood Adult Books 5686 Telegraph Ave (at 57th), Oakland 510/654-1169

El Cajon

EROTICA

F St Bookstore 158 E Main (at Magnolia) 619/447-0381 • 24hrs • wheelchair access

Elk

RESTAURANTS

Queenie's Roadhouse Cafe 6061 S Hwy 1 707/877-3285 • 8am-3pm, clsd Tue-Wed • fabulous all-day brkfsts • some veggie • lesbian-owned

Encinitas

ACCOMMODATIONS

Ocean Inn 1444 N Hwy 101, Leucadia 760/436-1988, 800/546-1598 • gay-friendly • mission decor in quiet neighborhood setting • $69-189

Escondido

EROTICA

Romantix Video Specialties 2322 S Escondido Blvd 760/745-6697 • wheelchair access

Eureka

ACCOMMODATIONS

Abigail's Elegant Victorian Mansion Historic B&B Inn 1406 C St 707/444-3144 • gay-friendly • 1878 Nat'l Historic landmark • full brkfst • sauna • nonsmoking • $95-195

Carter House Victorians 301 L St 707/444-8062, 800/404-1390 • gay-friendly • enclave of 4 unique inns • full brkfst • nonsmoking • kids ok • restaurant • wine shop • wheelchair access • $155-497

Bars

Lost Coast Brewery Pub 617 4th St (btwn G & H Sts) **707/445–4480** • 11am–midnight • gay-friendly • food served • beer/ wine • wheelchair access • women-owned

The Shanty 213 3rd St (at C St) **707/444–2053** • noon–2am • lesbians/ gay men • neighborhood bar • lesbian-owned

Restaurants

Folie Deuce 1551 G St, Arcata **707/822–1042** • dinner only, Sun brunch, clsd Mon • bistro • beer/ wine • reservations recommended • wheelchair access

Bookstores

Booklegger 402 2nd St (at E St) **707/445–1344** • 10am–5:30pm, 11am–4pm Sun • mostly used • some lesbian titles • wheelchair access • women-owned

Publications

The "L" Word PO Box 272, Bayside 95524 • lesbian newsletter for Humboldt County • available at Booklegger & North Town Books in Arcata

Erotica

Good Relations 308 2nd St **707/441–9570** • lingerie • toys • books • videos • wheelchair access

Fairfield

see Vacaville

Ferndale

Accommodations

Collingwood Inn B&B 831 Main St (at Hwy 101) **707/786–9219, 800/469–1632** • gay-friendly • B&B • full brkfst • pets ok • nonsmoking • wheelchair access • gay-owned • $100-203

The Gingerbread Mansion Inn 400 Berding St **707/786–4000, 800/952–4136** • gay-friendly • a grand lady w/ beautifully restored interior • full brkfst • nonsmoking • kids ok • $150-400

Fontana

Erotica

Romantix 14589 Valley Blvd (at Cherry) **909/350–4717** • 24hrs

Fort Bragg

Accommodations

Aslan House 24600 N Hwy 1 **707/964–1952** • gay-friendly • beach house • partial ocean view • hot tub • kids 10+ ok • $160 + $12 extra person (4 max)

The Cleone Gardens Inn 24600 N Hwy 1 **707/964–2788, 800/400–2189 (CA ONLY)** • gay/ straight • nonsmoking • also cottages • country garden retreat on 9 1/2 acres • hot tub • $86-165 (2 persons)

Restaurants

Purple Rose Mill Creek Dr **707/964–6507** • 5pm-9pm, clsd Mon-Tue • Mexican

Entertainment & Recreation

Skunk Train California Western foot of Laurel St **800/777–5865** • scenic train trips

Bookstores

Windsong Books & Records 324 N Main (at Redwood Ave) **707/964–2050** • 10am-5:30pm, till 4pm Sun • mostly used • large selection of women's/ lesbian titles

Fountain Valley

see Orange County

Fremont

Info Lines & Services

The Edge 39160 State St **510/790–2887** • call for hours • drop-in center • community bulletin board • support groups & services • wheelchair access

Erotica

L'Amour Shoppe 40555 Grimmer Blvd (at Fremont) **510/659–8161**

Fresno

Info Lines & Services

Community Link **559/266–5465** • info • LGBT support • also publishes "Newslink"

Serenity Fellowship AA 942 N Van Ness Ave (btwn Olive & Belmont) **559/221–6907** • 7pm Mon • also 7pm Tue (lesbians/ gay men)

Bars

The Den 4538 E Belmont Ave (at Maple) **559/255–3213** • 4pm-2am • mostly men • country/ western • bears • leather • multiracial • videos • older crowd • beer/ wine • gay-owned

North Tower Circle 2777 N Maroa
559/229–4188 • 8pm-2am, from 5pm Th-Sun
• popular • lesbians/ gay men • patio

Red Lantern 4618 E Belmont Ave (at Maple)
559/251–5898 • 2pm-2am • mostly gay men •
neighborhood bar • country/ western •
multiracial • wheelchair access

NIGHTCLUBS

Deja Vu/ Starrz Lounge
708 N Blackstone (btwn Olive & Belmont, on
Bremer) 559/445–0878 • 9pm-2am • mostly
gay men • dancing/DJ • theme nights • videos
• gay-owned

CAFES

Caffe Fulton Coffee Company 1145 Fulton
Mall (at Fresno St) 559/485–3494 • 6am-5pm,
clsd wknds • food served

BOOKSTORES

Out of the Closet Book & Gift Emporium
35 E Olive Ave (W of Palm Ave) 559/233–5041
• 9am-7pm, 10am-2pm Sat-Sun, clsd Mon •
LGBT • events, poetry readings & book
discussions • wheelchair access • lesbian-
owned

RETAIL SHOPS

Only For You 3123 N Maroa Ave
559/225–3225 • LGBT • gay-owned

SPIRITUAL GROUPS

Wesley United Methodist Church 1343 E
Barstow Ave (at 4th) 559/224–1947 • 8:30am
& 11am Sun, summer hours vary • reconciling
congregation

EROTICA

G-Spot 1141 N Van Ness Ave (at Olive Ave)
559/264–6900 • 10am-midnight • largest
pride/ erotica store in Central Valley • gay-
owned

Suzie's Adult Superstores 1267 N
Blackstone 559/497–9613 • 24hrs

Wildcat Book Store 1535 Fresno St (at G
St) 559/237–4525 • video arcade • books •
adult novelties

Garden Grove

see Orange County

Geyserville

ENTERTAINMENT & RECREATION

Locals Tasting Room 21023 Geyserville Ave
(off Hwy 128) 707/857–4900 • 11am-6pm clsd
Tue-Wed • unique artisan wineries •
complimentary tastings • call for schedule •
wheelchair access

Grass Valley

see also Nevada City

BOOKSTORES

The Book Seller 107 Mill St 530/272–2131
• 9:30am-7pm, till 9pm Fri, till 5:30pm Sat •
independent

Gualala

ACCOMMODATIONS

Breakers Inn 39300 S Hwy 1 707/884–3200,
800/273–2537 • gay/ straight • oceanfront •
women-owned • $105-275

North Coast Country Inn 34591 S Hwy 1
707/884–4537, 800/959–4537 • gay-friendly •
B&B overlooking Mendocino coast • hot tub •
nonsmoking • $185-225

Half Moon Bay

ACCOMMODATIONS

Mill Rose Inn 615 Mill St 650/726–8750,
800/900–7673 • gay-friendly • classic
European elegance by the sea • full brkfst •
hot tub • nonsmoking • kids 10+ ok • $150-
360

RESTAURANTS

Moss Beach Distillery 140 Beach Wy (at
Ocean) 650/728–5595 • lunch & dinner, Sun
brunch • some veggie • patio

Pasta Moon 315 Main St (at Mill)
650/726–5125 • lunch & dinner • full bar •
wheelchair access

Hayward

INFO LINES & SERVICES

Lighthouse Community Center 1217 A St
(near 2nd St) 510/881–8167 • support groups
& social events

BARS

Rainbow Room 21859 Mission Blvd (at
Sunset) 510/582–8078 • noon-2am, from
10am wknds • lesbians/ gay men • dancing/DJ
• women-owned

Turf Club 22519 Main St (at A St)
510/881–9877 • noon-2am • lesbians/ gay
men • dancing/DJ • drag shows • patio

NIGHTCLUBS

Club Rumor 22554 Main St (btwn A & B Sts)
510/733–2334 • 11am-2am, from 10am wknds
• lesbians/ gay men • dancing/DJ • wheelchair
access

EROTICA

L'Amour Shoppe 22553 Main St (btwn A & B Sts) 510/886-7777

Healdsburg

see also Russian River

ACCOMMODATIONS

Camellia Inn 211 North St 707/433-8182, 800/727-8182 • gay-friendly • Italianate Victorian • nonsmoking • $119-239

Madrona Manor 707/433-4231, 800/258-4003 • gay-friendly • elegant Victorian country inn • full brkfst • swimming • nonsmoking • some rooms ok for kids • also restaurant • wheelchair access • $175-445

RESTAURANTS

Chateau Souverain 400 Souverain Rd, Geyserville 707/433-8281 • lunch daily, dinner Fri-Sun only, brunch Sun • fine dining

Hemet

NIGHTCLUBS

Club Don't You Know 133 N Harvard St (at Florida) 951/658-5939 • 3pm-1am, till 2am Fri-Sat • lesbians/gay men • dancing/DJ • transgender-friendly • karaoke • wheelchair access • gay-owned

SPIRITUAL GROUPS

House of Faith 1000 N State St, Ste 107-109 951/487-6290 • 10am Sun • group sing 6pm Sun • Bible study & potluck 5pm Wed • wheelchair access

Hermosa Beach

EROTICA

Tender Box 809 Pacific Coast Hwy (at 7th) 310/318-2882

Huntington Beach

see Orange County

Idyllwild

ACCOMMODATIONS

Quiet Creek Inn & Vacation Rentals 26345 Delano Dr (at Toll Gate Rd) 951/659-6110, 800/450-6110 • gay-friendly • vacation rentals • private spas • pets ok in certain cabins • nonsmoking • $90-500

The Rainbow Inn 951/659-0111 • gay/ straight • full brkfst • nonsmoking • patio • fireplaces • also conference center • gay-owned • $90-145+ tax

Strawberry Creek Inn B&B 26370 Hwy 243 (at S Cir Dr) 951/659-3202, 800/262-8969 • gay-friendly • relaxing getaway w/ sundeck, garden & hammocks • wheelchair access • gay-owned • $120-230

Imperial Beach

EROTICA

Romantix 1177 Palm Ave (at Florida) 619/575-5081 • 24hrs

Irvine

see Orange County

Jamestown

ACCOMMODATIONS

The Homestead at Table Mountain B&B 17307 Table Mountain Rd (at Chicken Ranch Rd) 209/984-3712 • gay-friendly • B&B • full brkfst • nonsmoking • lesbian-owned • $105-115

June Lake

ACCOMMODATIONS

June Lake Villager 2240 Hwy 158 (2.5 miles W of Hwy 395) 760/648-7712, 800/655-6545 • gay-friendly • jacuzzi • nonsmoking • kids/ pets ok • women-owned • $85-225

Kernville

ACCOMMODATIONS

River View Lodge 2 Sirretta 760/376-6019, 877/885-6333 • gay/ straight • riverfront resort • jacuzzi • kids/pets ok • nonsmoking • gay-owned • $79-129

Klamath

ACCOMMODATIONS

Rhodes' End B&B 115 Trobitz Rd 707/482-1654 • gay-friendly • full brkfst • hot tub • nonsmoking • $90-120

Laguna Beach

see Orange County

Lake Tahoe

see also Lake Tahoe, Nevada

ACCOMMODATIONS

Black Bear Inn 530/544-4411, 800/431-4411 • gay/ straight • full brkfst • hot tub • fireplaces • nonsmoking • gay-owned • $200-500

Grinnin' Bear Cabin 530/582–8703 • gay/ straight • 3-bdrm cabin on pine-treed lot • kids/ pets ok • nonsmoking • women-owned • $200+

Heavenly Lodge 930 Park Ave (at Manzanita Ave), South Lake Tahoe 530/544–2400, 800/884–4920 • gay/ straight • sauna • wheelchair access • gay-owned

Holly's Place 800/745–7041 • gay/ straight • cabins & cottages • fireplaces • kitchens • hot tubs • nonsmoking • kids/ pets ok • women-owned • $250-425

Silver Shadows Motel 1251 Emerald Bay Rd, South Lake Tahoe 530/541–3575 • gay-friendly • motel • swimming • kids/ pets ok • $55+

Tahoe Moon Properties 530/581–2771, 866/581–2771 • gay-friendly • $125-1,0005

Tahoe Retreat & Spa 2446 Lake Tahoe Blvd (at Sierra Blvd), South Lake Tahoe 530/544–6776, 888/824–6378 • gay/ straight • also day spa • kids/ pets ok • nonsmoking • $65-115

NIGHTCLUBS

Faces 270 Kingsbury Grade, Stateline, NV 775/588–2333 • 5pm-2am, 3pm-4am Fri-Sat • lesbians/ gay men • dancing/DJ

RESTAURANTS

Driftwood Cafe 4119 Laurel Ave (at Poplar) 530/544–6545 • 7am-2pm • homecooking • some veggie • wheelchair access

Passaretti's 1181 Emerald Bay Rd/ Hwy 50 530/541–3433 • 11am-9pm • Italian

Lancaster

NIGHTCLUBS

Back Door 1255 W Ave I (at 13th St W) 661/945–2566 • 6pm-2am • lesbians/ gay men • dancing/DJ • karaoke • occasional drag shows

Long Beach

INFO LINES & SERVICES

AA Gay/ Lesbian (Atlantic Alano Club) 1403 E 4th St 562/432–7476 • hours vary

The Gay & Lesbian Community Center of Greater Long Beach 2017 E 4th St (at Cherry) 562/434–4455 • 9am-10pm, till 6pm Sat, 5pm-9pm Sun • also newsletter

ACCOMMODATIONS

Beachrunners' Inn 231 Kennebec Ave (at Junipero & Broadway) 562/856–0202, 866/221–0001 • gay/ straight • B&B • near beach • hot tub • nonsmoking • $89-125

Turret House B&B 556 Chestnut Ave (at Sixth St) 562/624–1991, 888/488–7738 • gay/ straight • hot tub • gay-owned • $99-140

BARS

The Brit 1744 E Broadway (at Cherry) 562/432–9742 • 10am-2am • mostly gay men • neighborhood bar • patio

The Broadway 1100 E Broadway (at Cerritos) 562/432–3646 • 10am-2am • lesbians/ gay men • neighborhood bar • karaoke • wheelchair access

Club Broadway 3348 E Broadway (at Redondo) 562/438–7700 • 11am-2am • mostly women • neighborhood bar • videos • wheelchair access • women-owned

The Crest 5935 Cherry Ave (at South) 562/423–6650 • 2pm-2am • mostly gay men • leather

Pistons 2020 E Artesia (at Cherry) 562/422–1928 • 6pm-2am, till midnight Mon, till 3am Fri-Sat, from 3pm Sun • mostly gay men • bears • leather • patio

Que Será 1923 E 7th St (at Cherry) 562/599–6170 • 7pm-2am, from 5pm Fri, from 1pm Sun • gay/ straight • dancing/DJ • alternative • live music

Ripples 5101 E Ocean (at Granada) 562/433–0357 • noon-2am • popular • mostly gay men • dancing/DJ • multiracial clientele • food served • karaoke • videos • young crowd • patio • T-dance Sun • theme nights

Silver Fox 411 Redondo (at 4th) 562/439–6343 • 4pm-2am, from noon wknds • popular happy hour • mostly gay men • karaoke Wed & Sun • videos • wheelchair access

Sweetwater Saloon 1201 E Broadway (at Orange) 562/432–7044 • 10am-2am • popular days • mostly gay men • neighborhood bar • wheelchair access

NIGHTCLUBS

Club Flaunt 6400 E Pacific Hwy & 2nd (at Seaport Marina Hotel, at Fire Island bar) • 8pm-2am Fri only • mostly women • dancing/ DJ • live music

Executive Suite 3428 E Pacific Coast Hwy (at Redondo) 562/597–3884 • 8pm-close Th-Sat • popular • lesbians/ gay men • dancing/DJ • Latin night Th • women's night Sat • 2 levels

Venus Goddesses & Girls 3428 E Pacific Coast Hwy (at Redondo at Exec Suites) **562/597–3884, 526/591–2032** • every Fri • mostly women • dancing/DJ

CAFES

Cafe Haven 1708 E Broadway (at Gaviota) **562/437–3785** • 7am-11pm, till 2:30am Fri-Sat, till 11pm Sun

Hot Java 2101 E Broadway Ave **562/433–0688** • 6am-10pm, till midnight Fri-Sat • also soups, sandwiches, salads • Wi-Fi

RESTAURANTS

Choices 740 E Broadway (at Alamitos) **562/983–7001** • 11am-2am • lesbians/ gay men • full menu • full bar • dancing/DJ

Egg Heaven 4358 E 4th St **562/433–9277** • 7am-2pm, till 3pm wknds • some veggie

House of Madame JoJo 2941 E Broadway (btwn Temple & Redondo) **562/439–3672** • 4:30pm-close, from 5:30 wknds, clsd Mon • popular • lesbians/ gay men • cont'l • some veggie • beer/ wine, martinis • wheelchair access

Margarita Grille 70 Atlantic Ave (btwn 1st & Ocean) **562/437–4583** • brkfst, lunch & dinner • full bar • theme nights

Omelette Inn 108 W 3rd St (at Pine) **562/437–5625** • 7am-2:30pm

Original Park Pantry 2104 E Broadway (at Junipero) **562/434–0451** • lunch & dinner • int'l • some veggie • wheelchair access

RETAIL SHOPS

Hot Stuff 2121 E Broadway (at Junipero) **562/433–0692** • 11am-7pm, 10am-6pm wknds • cards • gifts • adult novelties • serving community since 1980 • lesbian-owned

Long Beach

WHERE THE GIRLS ARE:
Schmoozing with the boys on Broadway between Atlantic and Cherry Avenues, or elsewhere between Pacific Coast Hwy and the beach. Or at home snuggling.

LGBT PRIDE:
3rd wknd in May. 562/987-9191, web: www.longbeachpride.com.

ANNUAL EVENTS:
June - AIDS Walk, web: www.aidswalklb.org.
October - Out Loud art & film festival, web: www.centerlb.org

CITY INFO:
800/452–7829, web: www.visitlongbeach.com.

BEST VIEW:
On the deck of the Queen Mary, docked overlooking most of Long Beach. Or Signal Hill, off 405. Take the Cherry exit.

WEATHER:
Quite temperate: highs in the mid-80°s July through September, and cooling down at night. In the winter, January to March, highs are in the upper 60°s, and lows in the upper 40°s.

TRANSIT:
Long Beach Taxi Co-op 562/435-6111.
Long Beach Transit & Runabout (free downtown shuttle) 562/591-8753. web: www.lbtransit.com.

ATTRACTIONS:
Belmont Shores area on 2nd St, south of Pacific Coast Highway—lots of restaurants & shopping, only blocks from the beach.
Long Beach Downtown Marketplace, 10am-4pm Fri.
The Queen Mary 562/435-3511, web: www.queenmary.com.
"Planet Ocean" mural at 300 E Ocean Blvd.

Reply **Forward** **Delete**

Date: Dec 21, 2005 12:16:35
From: Girl-on-the-Go
To: Editor@Damron.com
Subject: Long Beach

>Though it's often overshadowed by its neighbor Los Angeles, Long Beach is a large harbor city with plenty of bars and shopping of its own...and, of course, lesbians.

>According to local rumor, Long Beach is second only to San Francisco in lesbian/gay population, at approximately 45,000—though many of these gay residents are "married," making Long Beach a bedroom community of professional couples.

>The city itself is melded from overlapping suburbs and industrial areas. The cleaner air, mild weather, and reasonable traffic make it an obvious choice for those looking for a livable refuge away from L.A. Of course the nightlife is milder as well, but nobody's complaining about the women's bar—**Club Broadway**, perfect for casual hanging out. Friday nights you can flaunt it at **Club Flaunt**. The **Executive Suite**'s dance floor welcomes women seven nights a week, and you'll find pussy galore at the monthly **PussyCat Lounge**. For breakfast & lunch after a night out, check out the lesbian-owned **Porch Café**. For other events, check with the **Lesbian/Gay Center**.

Soul Simple 2105 E Broadway Ave 562/434–9343 • soul-inspiring candles, oils, drums & more • also classes & workshops, including Reiki, chakra work & tea ceremonies • women-owned

Toto's Revenge 2947 E. Broadway (at Orizaba) 562/434–2777, 877/688–8686 • 10am-9pm • unique cards & gifts • dog-friendly • also mail order • gay-owned

PUBLICATIONS

▲ **Lesbian News (LN)** 800/995–8838, 800/458–9888 • nat'l w/ strong coverage of southern CA • see ad front color section

SPIRITUAL GROUPS

Christ Chapel 3935 E 10th St (at Termino) 562/438–5303 • 10am Sun • nondenominational • wheelchair access

First United Methodist Church 507 Pacific Ave (at 5th) 562/437–1289 • 10am Sun • wheelchair access

Open Door Ministries 4101 E Willow St (at The Grand, btwn Lakewood & Redondo) 562/925–3533 • 10am Sun

Refiner's Fire Fellowship 4140 Norse Wy 562/429–5111 • 10am Sun, Bible study 7pm Th

Trinity Lutheran Church 759 Linden Ave (btwn 7th & 8th) 562/437-4002 • 10:30am Sun • wheelchair access

EROTICA

The Crypt on Broadway 1712 E Broadway (btwn Cherry & Falcon) 562/983-6560 • 11am-10pm, till midnight Tue, Fri-Sat, from noon Sun • leather • toys

The Rubber Tree 5018 E 2nd St (at Granada) 562/434-0027 • 11am-9pm, till 10pm Fri-Sat, noon-7pm Sun • gifts for lovers • women-owned

LOS ANGELES

Los Angeles is divided into 7 geographical areas:

LA—Overview

INFO LINES & SERVICES

Alcoholics Together Center 1773 Griffith Park Blvd (at Hyperion) 323/663-8882, 323/936-4343 (AA#) • 12-step groups

LA Gay & Lesbian Center's Village 1125 N McCadden Pl (at Santa Monica) 323/860-7302 • cybercenter • cafe • theaters • library • classes • call for events & hours

Los Angeles Gay & Lesbian Center 1625 N Schrader Blvd 323/993-7400 • 9am-9pm, till 1pm Sat, clsd Sun • wide variety of services

ENTERTAINMENT & RECREATION

The Celebration Theatre 7051-B Santa Monica Blvd (at La Brea) 323/957-1884 • LGBT theater • call for more info

The Gay Mafia Comedy Company 323/634-2820 • lesbians/ gay men • improv/ sketch comedy • gay-owned

The Getty Center 1200 Getty Center Dr, Brentwood 310/440-7300 • clsd Mon • LA's shining city on a hill & world-class museum • of course, it's still in LA so you'll need to make reservations for parking (!)

Highways 1651 18th St (at the Arts Center), Santa Monica 310/315-1459 (RESERVATION LINE) • "full-service performance center"

Hollywood Walks 1850 Whitley Ave #620 90028 323/464-2440 • 2.5-hour walking tour • gay-owned

IMRU Gay Radio KPFK LA 90.7 FM 818/985-2711 • 7pm Mon

LA Sparks 877/447-7275 • check out the Women's National Basketball Association while you're in Los Angeles

Outfest 213/480-7088 • LGBT media arts foundation that sponsors the annual LGBT film festival each July • see listing in Film Festival Calendar in back Events section

Purple Circuit Hotline 818/953-5072 • LGBT theater listings

SoCalGirlGolf.com 714/420-5611 • women's golf organization • lesbian-owned

Sunwolf Farms 661/245-9653 • private ranch w/ customized day trips • lesbian-owned

Vox Femina 310/391-2402 • women's chorus

RETAIL SHOPS

Jewelry by Poncé 1417 S Coast Hwy, Laguna Beach 949/497-4154, 800/969-RING • 11am-7pm Wed-Sun, by appt Mon-Tue • LGBT commitment rings & other jewelry • see ad in back mail order section

PUBLICATIONS

Community Yellow Pages 323/848-3033, 800/745-5669 • annual survival guide to LGBT Southern CA & Bay Area

▲ **Flavor** 213/509-1536 • monthly coverage of LA & southern CA lesbian club scene

▲ **Lesbian News (LN)** 310/787-8658, 800/458-9888 • nat'l w/ strong coverage of southern CA • see ad front color section

Odyssey Magazine 323/874-8788 • dish on LA's club scene

Outword News Magazine 310/274-2146 • statewide LGBT newspaper w/ N & S CA editions

The Pink Pages 800/929-7465

The Women's Yellow Pages 818/995-6646

SPIRITUAL GROUPS

All Saints Episcopal Church 504 N Camden Dr, Beverly Hills 310/275-0123 • also LGBT social support group

Beth Chayim Chadashim (BCC) 6000 W Pico Blvd (at Crescent Hts) 323/931-7023 • 8pm Fri

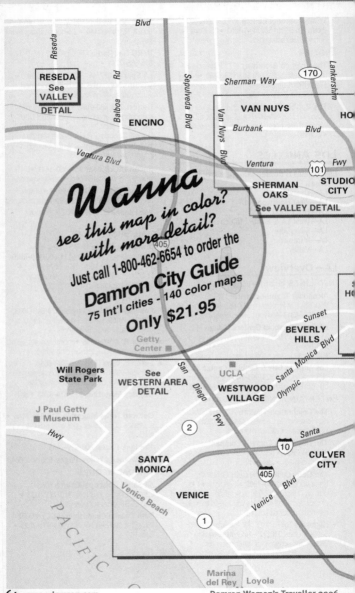

Wanna see this map in color? with more detail?

Just call 1-800-462-6654 to order the

Damron City Guide

75 Int'l cities - 140 color maps

Only $21.95

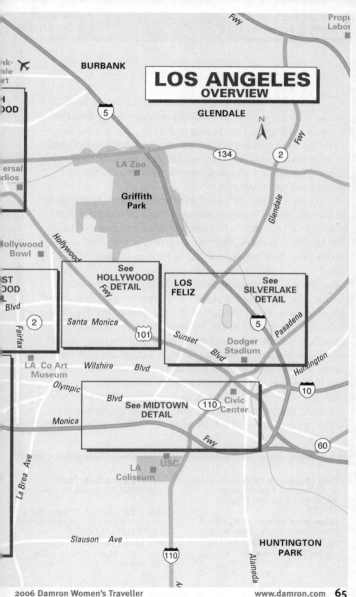

LOS ANGELES
OVERVIEW

BURBANK

GLENDALE

LA Zoo

Griffith
Park

Hollywood
Bowl

See
HOLLYWOOD
DETAIL

LOS
FELIZ

See
SILVERLAKE
DETAIL

Santa Monica

Sunset   Blvd

Dodger
Stadium

LA Co Art
Museum

Wilshire   Blvd

Olympic

Blvd

See MIDTOWN
DETAIL

Civic
Center

Monica

Fwy

La Brea Ave

LA
Coliseum

USC

Slauson   Ave

HUNTINGTON
PARK

Reply Forward Delete

```
Date: Dec 22, 2005 14:06:59
From: Girl-on-the-Go
To: Editor@Damron.com
Subject: Tucson
```

>There is no city that better embodies the extremes of American life than Los Angeles. Here fantasy and reality have become inseparable. The mere mention of the "City of Angels" conjures up images of palm-lined streets, sun-drenched beaches, and wealth beyond imagination, along with smog, overcrowded freeways, searing poverty, and urban violence.

>Most travelers come only for the fantasy. They want to star-gaze at Mann's Chinese Theatre in Hollywood; at movie and television studios (Fox, Universal) in Burbank; at famous restaurants (Spago, The Ivy, Chaya Brasserie, Morton's, etc.); and, of course, all along Rodeo Drive. (Our favorite star-gazing location is Canter's Deli after 2am.)

>But if you take a moment to focus your sights past the usual tourist traps, you'll see the unique—and often tense—diversity that L.A. offers as a city on the borders of Latin America, the Pacific Rim, Suburbia USA, and the rest of the world. You'll find museums, centers, and theaters celebrating the cultures of the many peoples who live in this valley. Cultural epicenters include Olvera Street, Korea Town, China Town, and the historically Jewish Fairfax District. Call the L.A. Visitor's Bureau for directions and advice.

>LA's art scene rivals New York's, so if you're an art lover be sure to check out the galleries and museums, as well as the performance art scene (check a recent *L.A. Weekly*).

Christ Chapel of the Valley 11050 Hartsook St (S of Magnolia), North Hollywood **818/985-8977** • 10am Sun • full gospel fellowship

Congregation Kol Ami 1200 N La Brea **323/606-0996** • 8pm Fri (6:45pm 1st Fri)

Dignity LA 126 S Ave 64 (S of York Ave), Highland Park **323/344-8064** • 5:30pm Sun

Holy Trinity Community Church **323/913-3870** • 4:30pm last Sat • call for info & location

MCC in the Valley 5730 Cahuenga Blvd (2 blocks N of Burbank Blvd), North Hollywood **818/762-1133** • 10:30am Sun

MCC LA 8714 Santa Monica Blvd (at Westbourne) **310/854-9110** • 9am, 11am, 1pm (en español) • wheelchair access

[Reply] [Forward]   [Delete]

>This is a car-driven city—remember the song, "Nobody Walks in LA."? Nobody takes the bus, either, if they can avoid it. So plan on spending a day just driving; don't miss Mulholland Drive at night.

>During the day, shop along trendy Melrose Avenue (that's right, Avenue not Place), or peruse women's sexuality boutique **Grand Opening!** in West Hollywood. Or check out Los Feliz (pronounced anglo-style: *Lahss Feel-iss*), the funky neighborhood to cruise between Silverlake and Hollywood. Los Feliz is home to many hip restaurants and shops.

>As for lesbian nightlife in L.A., there are several full-time women's bars (some of them in the Valley), and many women's nights. L.A. is where the one-nighter women's dance bar revolution began, so make sure to double-check the papers before you go out (**Flavor**, the more topical **Lesbian News**, or **Odyssey**). Thursday is the women-only party **Fuse** at Here Lounge. On Fridays, don't miss **Girl Bar** at Ultra Suede. The monthly party **Café con Leche** has been going strong for over 10 years!

St Andrew's Episcopal Church 1432 Engracia Ave (at Cabrillo), Torrance **310/328-3781** • 8am & 10am Sun

Unity Fellowship Church 5148 W Jefferson Blvd (at Sycamore) **323/938-8322, 323/936-4948** • 11:30am • uplifting service in the African American tradition • wheelchair access

West Hollywood Presbyterian Church 7350 Sunset Blvd (at Martel) **323/874-6646** • 11am Sun • wheelchair access

LA—West Hollywood

ACCOMMODATIONS

Élan Hotel Modern 8435 Beverly Blvd (at Croft) **323/658-6663, 888/611-0398** • gay/ straight • kids ok • wheelchair access • gay-owned • $135-215

The Grafton on Sunset 8462 W Sunset Blvd (at La Cienega) **323/654-4600, 800/821-3660** • gay/ straight • swimming • sundeck • panoramic views • located in heart of Sunset Strip • wheelchair access • $139-500

The Grove Guesthouse **323/876-7778, 888/524-7683** • lesbians/ gay men • 1-bdrm villa • hot tub • swimming • kitchens • pets ok by arrangement • gay-owned • $189+

Holloway Motel 8465 Santa Monica Blvd (at La Cienega) **323/654-2454, 888/654-6400** • gay/ straight • kitchens • nonsmoking • centrally located • $95-165

Hyatt West Hollywood 8401 Sunset Blvd (at Kings Rd) **323/656-1234, 800/233-1234** • gay/ straight • on the Sunset Strip • swimming • nonsmoking • wheelchair access • $99-299

Just Right Reservations **978/934-9931** • inns & B&Bs • also Palm Springs, Provincetown, MA & Boston, MA

Los Angeles

WHERE THE GIRLS ARE:

Hip dykes hang out in West Hollywood, with the boys along Santa Monica Blvd, or cruising funky Venice Beach and Santa Monica. The S&M ("Stand & Model") glamourdykes pose in chichi clubs and posh eateries in West L.A. and Beverly Hills. There's a scattered community of women in Silverlake. And more suburban lesbians frequent the gay bars in Studio City and North Hollywood. If you're used to makeup-free lesbians, you may be surprised that coiffed and lipsticked lesbian style is the norm in L.A.

LGBT PRIDE:

June. 323/969-8302. Christopher St West, web: www.lapride.org.

ANNUAL EVENTS:

June - AIDS LifeCycle 866/BIKE-4AIDS, web: www.aidslifecycle.org. AIDS benefit bike ride from San Francisco to LA.

July - Outfest 213/480-7088, web: www.outfest.org. Los Angeles' lesbian/ gay film & video festival.

August - Sunset Junction Fair 323/661-7771, web: www.sunsetjunction.org. Carnival, arts & information fair on Sunset Blvd in Silverlake to benefit Sunset Junction Youth Center.

October - Gay Days at Disneyland, web: www.gayday2.com.

October - AIDS Walk-a-thon 213/201-9255, web: www.aidswalk.net.

CITY INFO:

800/228-2452, web: www.lacvb.com.

West Hollywood Convention & Visitors Bureau, 800/368-6020, web: www.visitwesthollywood.com.

ATTRACTIONS:

3rd St outdoor mall in Santa Monica.

Chinatown, near downtown.

City Walk in Universal Studios.

The Getty Center 310/440-7300, web: www.getty.edu.

Mann's Chinese Theater on Hollywood Blvd 323/464-8111.

Melrose Ave, hip commercial district in West Hollywood.

Theme Parks: Disneyland, Knotts Berry Farm, or Magic Mountain.

Watts Towers, not far from LAX 323/860-9964, web: www.wattstower.net.

Westwood Village premiere movie theaters & restaurants.

Venice Beach.

BEST VIEW:

Drive up Mulholland Drive, in the hills between Hollywood and the Valley, for a panoramic view of the city, and the Hollywood sign.

WEATHER:

Summers are hot, dry, and smoggy with temperatures in the 80°s-90°s. LA's weather is at its finest — sunny, blue skies, and moderate temperatures (mid 70°s) — during the months of March, April, and May.

TRANSIT:

Yellow Cab 877/733-3305.

LA Express 800/427-7483.

Super Shuttle 310/782-6600.

Metro Transit Authority 213/626-4455.

▲ **Le Montrose Suite Hotel** 900 Hammond St (at Sunset) **310/855–1115, 800/776–0666** • popular • gay-friendly • hot tub • swimming • kitchens • fireplaces • nonsmoking • kids/pets ok • gym • also full restaurant • rooftop patio • wheelchair access • $195-595

▲ **Le Parc Suite Hotel** 733 N West Knoll Dr (at Melrose) **310/855–8888, 800/578–4837** • popular • gay-friendly • swimming • tennis courts • kids/pets ok • also restaurant • wheelchair access • $300-400 (corp rates from $170)

Mondrian 8440 Sunset Blvd **323/650–8999, 800/525–8029** • gay-friendly • home of trendy Sky Bar & Asia de Cuba • $185-425

Ramada Plaza Hotel—West Hollywood 8585 Santa Monica Blvd (at La Cienega) **310/652–6400, 800/845–8585** • gay-friendly • modern art deco hotel & suites • swimming • kids ok • wheelchair access • $109-275

Secret Garden B&B 8039 Selma Ave (at Laurel Canyon) **323/656–3888** • gay-friendly • unique B&B • wheelchair access • $95-165

Sunset Marquis Hotel & Villas 1200 Alta Loma Rd (1/2 block S of Sunset Blvd) **310/657–1333, 800/858–9758** • gay/straight • full brkfst • sauna • hot tub • swimming • kids ok • wheelchair access • $265-1500

Valadon Hotel 8822 Cynthia St (at Larrabee) **310/854–1114, 800/835–7997** • gay-friendly • all-suite hotel • hot tub • swimming • kids ok • wheelchair access • $118-265

Bars

Comedy Store 8433 Sunset Blvd (at La Cienega) **323/650–6268** • 8pm-2am • gay-friendly • stand-up club

Fuse 696 N Robertson Blvd (at Santa Monica, at Here Lounge) **310/360–8455** • Th only • mostly women • swank cocktail gathering • dancing/DJ

Here Lounge 696 N Robertson Blvd (at Santa Monica) **310/360–8455** • 4pm-2am • lesbians/gay men • more women Th • swanky & stylish • DJ nightly

Improvisation 8162 Melrose Ave (at Crescent Heights) **323/651–2583** • gay-friendly • stand-up comedy • also restaurant

The Normandie Room 8737 Santa Monica Blvd (at Hancock) **310/659–6204** • 5pm-2am • gay/straight • neighborhood bar • wheelchair access

The Palms on Las Olas 8572 Santa Monica Blvd (at La Cienega) **310/652–1595** • 5pm-2am, from 4pm wknds, after-hours Fri-Sat • popular • mostly women • multiracial • neighborhood bar • dancing/DJ • theme nights • BBQ Sun • karaoke • patio • wheelchair access

Tempest 7323 Santa Monica Blvd (E of Fuller Ave) **323/850–5115** • 8:30pm-close • popular • gay/straight • live shows • theme nights • also restaurant (dinner only) • Californian/Italian • some veggie • patio

Viper Room 8852 Sunset Blvd (btwn San Vicente & Larrabee) **310/358–1880** • 9pm-2am • gay-friendly • dancing/DJ • live shows • cover charge

Nightclubs

Beige 7213 Sunset Blvd (btwn Poinsettia & Formosa, at the Falcon) **323/850–5350** • Tue only • lesbians/gay men • popular • dancing/DJ • food served

Boytrade 5515 Wilshire Blvd (at El Rey Theatre) **323/936–6400** • 11pm last Fri only • mostly gay men • dancing/DJ • mostly African-American • male dancers

The Factory 652 N La Peer Dr (at Santa Monica) **310/659–4551** • 9pm-2am Fri-Sat • mostly gay men • dancing/DJ • videos

▲ **Girl Bar** 661 N Robertson Blvd (at Santa Monica, at Ultra Suede) **310/659–4551, 877/447–5252** • popular • 9pm-3am Fri only • women only • dancing/DJ • call hotline for events

Parlour Club 7702 Santa Monica Blvd (at Stanley) **323/650–7968** • lesbians/gay men • dancing/DJ • theme nights • live entertainment • drag shows

Rage 8911 Santa Monica Blvd (at San Vicente) **310/652–7055** • 11am-2am, lunch Tue-Sun, dinner nightly • popular • mostly gay men • dancing/DJ • live shows • videos • 18+ wknds • wheelchair access

Red Dragon 661 N Robertson Blvd (at Santa Monica, at Ultra Suede) • 2nd Sat • popular • mostly gay men • Asian-American clientele • 18+ • cover

Rush 8865 Santa Monica Blvd (at Fiesta Cantina) **310/652–8865** • 10pm-close Sun only • mostly gay men • dancing/DJ • 18+ • young crowd

Ultra Suede 661 N Robertson Blvd (at Santa Monica) **310/659–4551** • 9pm-2am Wed-Sun • gay/straight • mostly women Fri for Girlbar • dancing/DJ • alternative • live shows

It's last call then back to your suite.

Aren't you glad she chose Le Parc?

Le Parc. Good Times.

- 5 minutes to The Abbey, Fubar, Gold Coast, Mickey's, Normandie Room, Rage, Trunks and Ultra Suede.

- Convenient secluded location, twice-daily maid service, in-suite dining, two in-suite TV's, Direct TV, on-demand movies, VHS &DVD, data ports and internet access.

- Restaurant & lounge, rooftop tennis, heated rooftop pool & whirpool, full-service gym & spa, masseurs & trainers and business center.

CALL
- 800.5.SUITES
- 310.855.8888

CLICK
- reservations@leparcsuites.com
- leparcsuites.com

733 N. West Knoll Drive
West Hollywood, CA 90069

le parc
SUITE HOTEL

CAFES

Cabrini's Koffee Bar 5666 W 3rd St (at La Brea) 323/938-0259, 323/662-9923 • 10am-6pm • mostly women • live entertainment & music • multiracial clientele

Eat-Well 8252 Santa Monica Blvd (at La Jolla) 323/656-1383 • 7am-3pm & 5:30pm-10pm, 8am-3pm wknds • popular

Mani's Bakery 519 S Fairfax Ave (at Maryland Dr) 323/938-8800 • 6:30am-midnight • coffee & dessert bar • wheelchair access

Urth Caffe 8565 Melrose Ave 310/659-0628 • food served • patio

Who's On Third Cafe 8369 W 3rd St (at Orlando) 323/651-2928 • 7:30am-5pm, from 8am wknds

RESTAURANTS

The Abbey 692 N Robertson (at Santa Monica) 310/289-8410 • 8am-2am • lesbians/gay men • popular • American/cont'l • full bar • patio • wheelchair access

Alto Palato 755 N La Cienega Blvd (at Waring) 310/657-9271 • 6pm-10:30pm, clsd Mon • bargain pasta & comfortable chairs • full bar

AOC 8022 W Third St (at Crescent Heights Blvd) 323/653-6359 • dinner nightly • wine bar • eclectic • upscale

Benvenuto Cafe 8512 Santa Monica Blvd (at La Cienega) 310/659-8635 • lunch Tue-Fri, dinner nightly • Italian • full bar • wheelchair access

Bossa Nova 685 N Robertson Blvd (at Santa Monica) 310/657-5070 • 11am-11pm • Brazilian • beer/wine • patio • wheelchair access

Cafe La Boheme 8400 Santa Monica Blvd (btwn Benecia Ave & Fox Hills Dr) 323/848-2360 • 5:30pm-1am Fri-Sat, till midnight Sun-Th • American eclectic/California • full bar • patio w/fireplace • wheelchair access

Canter's Deli 419 N Fairfax (btwn Melrose & Beverly) 323/651-2030 • 24hrs • hip after-hours • Jewish/American • some veggie • wheelchair access

Gozar 8948 Santa Monica Blvd (at N Robertson) 310/657-4832 • dinner only • Latin fusion • wheelchair access

Hamburger Mary's Bar & Grill 8288 Santa Monica Blvd 323/654-3800 • 11am-1am • lesbians/gay men • Sun brunch • full bar • transgender-friendly • ladies night Wed • Latin Th • drag shows

Il Pastaio 400 N Canon Dr (at Brighton Wy), Beverly Hills 310/205-5444 • lunch & dinner, dinner only Sun • homemade pasta • full bar

Il Piccolino Trattoria 350 N Robertson Blvd (btwn Melrose & Beverly) 310/659-2220 • lunch & dinner, clsd Sun • full bar • patio • wheelchair access

Koo Koo Roo 8520 Santa Monica Blvd (at La Cienega Blvd) 310/657-3300 • 11am-11pm • lots of healthy chicken dishes • plenty veggie • beer/wine • wheelchair access

L'Orangerie 903 N La Cienega Blvd (btwn Melrose & Santa Monica) 310/652-9770 • dinner only, clsd Mon • haute French • patio • $28-38

Louise's Trattoria 7505 Melrose Ave (at Gardner) 323/651-3880 • 11am-11pm, till midnight Fri-Sat • Italian • great foccacia bread • beer/wine

Lucques 8474 Melrose Ave (at La Cienega) 323/655-6277 • lunch Tue-Sat, dinner nightly • French • full bar • patio • wheelchair access

Marco's Trattoria 8136 Santa Monica (at Crescent Hts) 323/650-2771 • 11am-10pm • wheelchair access

Marix Tex Mex 1108 N Flores (btwn La Cienega & Fairfax) 323/656-8800 • 11:30am-11pm • lesbians/gay men • some veggie • great margaritas • wheelchair access

Mark's Restaurant 861 N La Cienega Blvd (at Santa Monica) 310/652-5252 • 6pm-10pm, from 5pm Sun • full bar

Murakami 8730 Santa Monica Blvd #F (at San Vicente) 310/854-6212 • lunch & dinner, clsd Mon • Japanese • popular w/lesbians

O-Bar 8279 Santa Monica Blvd (at Sweetzer) 323/822-3300 • 6pm-2am • lesbians/gay men • full bar

Oasis 611 N La Brea (at Melrose) 323/939-8900 • 6pm-midnight, clsd Sun • Moroccan • patio

Real Food Daily 414 N La Cienega (btwn Beverly & Melrose) 310/289-9910 • 11:30am-11pm • organic vegetarian • beer/wine • wheelchair access

Sante Libre 345 N La Brea (btwn Melrose & Beverly) 323/857-0412 • 8am-10pm • pastas, salads & wraps • plenty veggie & vegan • cheap

Sapori Cucina 8945 Santa Monica Blvd (at Robertson) **310/275-9518** • Italian • some veggie • wheelchair access

Skewers 8939 Santa Monica Blvd (at Robertson) **310/271-0555** • 11am-10pm • Middle Eastern • grill, salads, dips • beer/ wine

Tango Grill 8807 Santa Monica Blvd (at San Vicente) **310/659-3663** • 11:30am-11:30pm • lesbians/ gay men • Argentinian • some veggie • beer/ wine • wheelchair access

Tommy Tang's 7313 Melrose Ave (at Poinsettia) **323/937-5733** • noon-10pm, till 11pm wknds • beer/ wine

Trocadero 8280 Sunset Blvd (at Sweetzer) **323/656-7161** • 6pm-2am • pastas & salads • full bar • patio • wheelchair access

Yukon Mining Co 7328 Santa Monica Blvd (at Fuller) **323/851-8833** • 24hrs • popular • champagne brunch Sun • beer/ wine • wheelchair access

BOOKSTORES

A Different Light 8853 Santa Monica Blvd (btwn San Vicente & Larrabee) **310/854-6601** • 10am-11pm • popular • LGBT • readings

Book Soup 8818 W Sunset Blvd (at Larrabee) **310/659-3110** • 9am-11pm • LGBT section

RETAIL SHOPS

Dorothy's Surrender 7985 Santa Monica Blvd #111 (at Laurel) **323/650-4111** • 10am-11:30pm • cards • magazines • gifts

Syren 7225 Beverly Blvd **323/936-6693, 800/667-9736** • clsd Sun-Mon • leather & latex

SPIRITUAL GROUPS

WeHo Church 8936 Santa Monica Blvd (at Robertson, in Hybrid Internet Cafe) **323/656-2400** • 11am Sun

GYMS & HEALTH CLUBS

Easton's Gym 8053 Beverly Blvd (at Crescent Hts) **323/651-3636** • gay-friendly

The Fitness Factory 650 N La Peer Dr (at Santa Monica) **310/358-1938** • 6am-9pm, till 8pm Fri, 7am-5pm Sat, 8am-1pm Sun

EROTICA

Circus of Books 8230 Santa Monica Blvd (at La Jolla) **323/656-6533** • 6am-2am

Drake's 8932 Santa Monica Blvd (at San Vicente) **310/289-8932** • 10am-2am • also 7566 Melrose Ave, 323/651-5600, 24hrs

Hustler Hollywood 8920 Sunset Blvd (at San Vicente) **310/860-9009** • chic erotic department store • also cafe

Pleasure Chest 7733 Santa Monica Blvd (at Genesee) **323/650-1022** • 10am-midnight, till 1am Fri-Sat

LA—Hollywood

ACCOMMODATIONS

Holiday Inn Hollywood 2005 N Highland (at Franklin) **323/876-8600** • gay-friendly • also restaurant & lounge • swimming • jacuzzi • wheelchair access • $109-149

Hollywood Metropolitan Hotel 5825 Sunset Blvd (btwn Bronson & Van Ness) **323/962-5800, 800/962-5800** • gay-friendly • kids ok • nonsmoking • wheelchair access • also restaurant • $79-145

Ramada Inn & Hollywood—Universal Studios 1160 N Vermont Ave (at Santa Monica) **323/660-1788, 800/800-9733** • gay-friendly • swimming • wheelchair access • $79-139

BARS

Faultline 4216 Melrose Ave (at Normandie) **323/660-0889** • 5pm-2am, from 2pm wknds, clsd Mon • popular • mostly gay men • dancing/ DJ • occasional women's events • leather • videos • patio

Spit 4216 Melrose Ave (at Faultine) **323/969-2530** • 9pm-3am 3rd Sat • popular • mostly gay men • DJ • leather • alternative • videos • cruisy

NIGHTCLUBS

The Circus/ Arena 6655 Santa Monica Blvd (at Seward) **323/462-1291** • 9pm-2am Tue & Fri-Sat, more gay Tue & Fri • popular • dancing/DJ

Miss Kitty's 6510 Santa Monica Blvd (at Wilcox, at Dragonfly) **323/466-6111** (CLUB) • 9pm Fri only • gay/ straight • dancing/ DJ • fetish/ goth/ rock 'n' roll • live shows

Revival 6801 Hollywood Blvd (at Highland, at Level 3) • 7pm-2am Sun only • mostly gay men • dancing/ DJ

TigerHeat 6655 Sunset Blvd (E of Highland, at Arena nightclub) **323/462-1291** • 10pm-2:30am Th only • mostly gay men • dancing/DJ • transgender-friendly • live shows • videos • 18+ • cover charge

Restaurants

Hollywood Canteen 1006 N Seward St (at Santa Monica) **323/465–0961** • 11:30am-midnight, till 1am Fri-Sat, dinner only Sat, clsd Sun • popular • classic • full bar

La Poubelle 5907 Franklin Ave (at Bronson) **323/465–0807** • 11:30am-1am • French/Italian • some veggie • wheelchair access

Lucy's Cafe El Adobe 5536 Melrose Ave (near Gower St) **323/462–9421** • lunch & dinner, clsd Sun • Mexican • patio

Musso & Frank Grill 6667 Hollywood Blvd (near Las Palmas) **323/467–7788** • 11am-11pm, clsd Sun-Mon • the grand-dame diner/steak house of Hollywood • great pancakes, potpie & martinis!

Off Vine 6263 Leland Wy (at Vine) **323/962–1900** • lunch & dinner, Sun brunch • beer/ wine

Prado 244 N Larchmont Blvd (at Beverly) **323/467–3871** • lunch & dinner, dinner only Sun • Caribbean • some veggie • wheelchair access

Quality 8030 W 3rd St (at Laurel) **323/658–5959** • 8am-3pm • homestyle brkfst • some veggie • wheelchair access

Rosco's House of Chicken & Waffles 1514 N Gower (at Sunset) **323/466–7453** • 8:30am-midnight

Entertainment & Recreation

The Erotic Museum 6741 Hollywood Blvd **323/463–7684** • noon-9pm, till midnight Fri-Sat • 18+

Bookstores

Skylight Books 1818 N Vermont Ave (at Melbourne Ave) **323/660–1175** • way cool independent in Los Feliz • great fiction & alt-lit sections

Retail Shops

Archaic Idiot/ Mondo Video-A-Go-Go 4328 Melrose (at Vermont) **323/953–8896** • noon-10pm • vintage clothes • cult & LGBT videos

Panpipes Magickal Marketplace 1641 N Cahuenga Blvd **323/462–7078** • 11am-7pm • "nation's oldest occult store" w/ custom spells & classes

Videoactive 2522 Hyperion Ave (at Griffith Park Blvd) **323/669–8544** • 10am-11pm, till midnight wknds • LGBT section • adult videos • wheelchair access

Y-Que Trading Post 1770 N Vermont Ave **323/664–0021** • noon-8pm • kitsch boutique that's home to the "Free Wynona" & "Free Martha" T-shirts

Gyms & Health Clubs

Gold's Gym 1016 N Cole Ave (near Santa Monica & Vine) **323/462–7012** • gay-friendly

Erotica

Romantix 6315–1/2 Hollywood Blvd (at Vine) **323/464–9435**

LA—West LA & Santa Monica

Accommodations

The Georgian Hotel 1415 Ocean Ave (btwn Santa Monica & Broadway), Santa Monica **310/395–9945, 800/538–8147** • gay-friendly • food served • wheelchair access • $195+

The Inn at Venice Beach 327 Washington Blvd (at Via Dolce), Marina Del Rey **310/821–2557, 800/828–0688** • gay-friendly • 43-room European-style inn • kids ok • wheelchair access • $99-159

The Linnington **310/441–9107** • lesbians/ gay men • B&B • jacuzzi • kids ok • lesbian-owned • $70-90

W Los Angeles 930 Hilgard Ave (at Le Conte) **310/208–8765, 800/421–2317** • gay-friendly • suites • also restaurant • gym • day spa • swimming • $219-379

Bars

Annex 835 S La Brea (at Arbor Vitae), Inglewood **310/671–7323** • 4pm-2am • mostly gay men • neighborhood bar • dancing/ DJ • African-American clientele • karaoke • wheelchair access

The Dolphin 1995 Artesia Blvd (at Aviation Blvd), Redondo Beach **310/318–3339** • 4pm-2am, from 2pm wknds • lesbians/ gay men • neighborhood bar • karaoke • patio • wheelchair access

Cafes

Anastasia's Asylum 1028 Wilshire Blvd (at 11th St), Santa Monica **310/394–7113** • 7am-2am • plenty veggie • live music evenings

Restaurants

12 Washington 12 Washington Blvd (at Pacific), Venice **310/822–5566** • dinner from 5pm, from 4pm Sun • cont'l

Baja Cantina 311 Washington Blvd (at Sanborn), Venice **310/821–2252** • lunch & dinner Mon-Fri, also brunch wknds

Border Grill 1445 4th St (at Broadway), Santa Monica **310/451–1655** • lunch & dinner

▲ **Cantalini's Salerno Beach Restaurant**
193 Culver Blvd (at Vista del Mar), Playa del
Rey 310/821-0018 • lunch 11:30am-3pm
Tue-Fri, dinner 4pm-10pm Tue-Sun, clsd Mon
• Italian • homemade pastas • beer/ wine •
live music Sun nights

Drago 2628 Wilshire Blvd (btwn 26th &
Princeton), Santa Monica 310/828-1585 •
lunch Mon-Fri, dinner nightly • Sicilian Italian
• wheelchair access

Golden Bull 170 W Channel Rd (at Pacific
Coast Hwy), Santa Monica 310/230-0402 •
dinner only, Sun brunch (summers) •
American • full bar

Joe's 1023 Abbot Kinney Blvd, Venice
310/399-5811 • lunch Tue-Fri, dinner nightly,
wknd brunch, clsd Mon • French/ Californian

Real Food Daily 514 Santa Monica Blvd
(btwn 5th & 6th), Santa Monica
310/451-7544 • 11:30am-10pm • organic
vegetarian • beer/ wine • wheelchair access •
$8-12

SPIRITUAL GROUPS

Lighthouse MCC of the South Bay 2235
Sepulveda (at the Center), Redondo Beach
310/535-7100 • 10:30am Sun

EROTICA

The Love Boutique 2924 Wilshire Blvd (W
of Bundy), Santa Monica 310/453-3459 •
toys • books

Pleasure Island 18426 Hawthorne Blvd,
Torrance 310/793-9477 • 11am-midnight, till
2am Fri-Sat

LA—Silverlake

ACCOMMODATIONS

Sanborn GuestHouse 1005 1/2 Sanborn
Ave (near Sunset) 323/666-3947 • gay/
straight • private unit w/ kitchen •
nonsmoking • gay-owned • $59-99

Silverview Guest Room 1707 Micheltorena
St #416 (at Effie St) 323/660-6109 • gay/
straight • hillside condo • nonsmoking •
wheelchair access • gay-owned • $69-89 (2-
night minimum)

BARS

Gauntlet II 4219 Santa Monica Blvd (at
Hoover) 323/669-9472 • 4pm-2am, from
2pm Sat • popular • mostly gay men •
women's night Wed • leather • wheelchair
access

NIGHTCLUBS

Cafe Con Leche 700 Almansor St (at Almansor Ct), Alhambra **626/282-0330 (CLUB INFO)** • 2nd Fri only • mostly women • dancing/ DJ • Latino/a

Dragstrip 66 1151 Glendale Blvd (off Park Ave, at Sunset Blvd, at the Echo) 213/413-8200 • 9pm-4am 2nd Sat • gay/ straight • popular • trashy pansexual rock 'n' roll club • dancing/ DJ • drag shows • cover charge

CAFES

The Coffee Table 2930 Rowena Ave **323/644-8111** • 7am-11pm, till midnight wknds • patio • fab mosaic magic

RESTAURANTS

Casita Del Campo 1920 Hyperion Ave **323/662-4255** • 11am-10pm, till 11:30pm Fri-Sat • popular • Mexican • patio • also The Plush Life cabaret Sat • call 323/969-2596 for details

Cha Cha Cha 656 N Virgil Ave (at Melrose) 323/664-7723 • 8am-10pm, till 11pm Fri-Sat • lesbians/ gay men • Caribbean • plenty veggie • wheelchair access

The Crest Restaurant 3725 Sunset Blvd (at Lucille) **323/660-3645** • 8am-10pm • diner/ Greek

Da Giannino 2630 Hyperion Ave (at Griffith Park Blvd) **323/664-7979** • dinner only, clsd Mon • beer/ wine • patio

Eat Well Coffeeshop 3916 Sunset Blvd (at Hyperion) 323/664-1624 • 8am-3pm • comfort food • some veggie

El Conquistador 3701 W Sunset Blvd (at Lucille) **323/666-5136** • lunch Tue-Sun, dinner nightly • Mexican • beer/ wine • patio

The Flying Leap Cafe 2538 Hyperion Ave (below The Other Side bar) • dinner Tue-Sun • cont'l • full bar • also Mary's Metro Station

Lunch to Latenite Kitchen 4348 Fountain Ave (at Sunset Blvd) **323/664-3663** • 5pm-1am, from noon wknds • neighborhood eatery • from veggie entrees to chicken & dumplings • gay-owned

Picholine 3360 W 1st St (at Beverly Blvd) **213/252-8722** • 10am-3pm, clsd wknds • French • gay-owned

Vida 1930 Hillhurst Ave (at Franklin, in Los Feliz) **323/662-1248** • 5pm-11pm, clsd Mon • hip w/ Asian accent • full bar

Zen Restaurant 2609 Hyperion Ave (at Griffith Park Blvd) **323/665-2929, 323/665-2930** • open late • Japanese • some veggie • full bar • live shows • karaoke

ENTERTAINMENT & RECREATION

Plush Life Cabaret 1920 Hyperion Ave (at Casita Del Campo) **323/969-2596** • Sat

BOOKSTORES

Serifos 3814 W Sunset Blvd **323/660-7467** • independent

GYMS & HEALTH CLUBS

Body Builders 2516 Hyperion Ave (at Tracy) **323/668-0802** • gay-friendly

EROTICA

Circus of Books 4001 Sunset Blvd (at Sanborn) **323/666-1304**

LA—Midtown

BARS

Cafe Club Fais Do-Do 5257 W Adams Blvd (btwn Fairfax & La Brea) **323/954-8080** • 7pm-11pm • gay-friendly • live music • also Cajun restaurant

Score 107 W 4th St (at Main) **213/625-7382** • 3pm-2am • lesbians/ gay men • neighborhood bar • dancing/DJ • mostly Latina/o • live shows

NIGHTCLUBS

Flamingos 825 James M Wood Blvd (at 9th & Figueroa, at Zita Bar) **626/282-0330 (CLUB INFO)**, **213/488-0400 (BAR#)** • 1st Sat only • mostly women • dancing/ DJ • Latino/a

Jewel's Catch One Disco 4067 W Pico Blvd (at Crenshaw) **323/734-8849** • 5pm-2am, clsd Mon-Tue • popular • lesbians/ gay men • dancing/DJ • alternative • mostly African-American • karaoke • more women Th & Sun • wheelchair access

RESTAURANTS

Cassell's 3266 W 6th St (at Vermont) **213/480-8668** • 10:30am-4pm, clsd Sun • great burgers

Du-Par's 6333 W 3rd St (at the Farmer's Market) **323/933-8446** • 6am-10pm • plush diner schmoozing

LA—Valley

includes San Fernando & San Gabriel Valleys

Bars

Club Fuel 11608 Ventura Blvd (at Laurel Canyon), Studio City **818/506-0404** • 3pm-2am • popular • mostly gay men • transgender-friendly • dancing/DJ • karaoke • theme nights • wheelchair access

The Lodge/ Club L 4923 Lankershim Blvd (at Vineland), North Hollywood **818/769-7722** • 2pm-2am, till 3am wknds • popular • mostly gay men • transgender-friendly • dancing/DJ • multiracial clientele • live shows • theme nights • wheelchair access

Moonshadow 10437 Burbank Blvd (at Cahuenga), North Hollywood **818/508-7008** • 1pm-2am • popular • lesbians/ gay men • neighborhood bar • dancing/DJ • karaoke • live shows • wheelchair access

Oxwood Inn 13713 Oxnard (at Woodman), Van Nuys **818/997-9666 (PAY PHONE)** • 3pm-2am, from 5pm Mon • mostly women • neighborhood bar • dancing/DJ • patio • one of the oldest lesbian bars in US • women-owned

Rawhide 10937 Burbank Blvd (near Vineland), North Hollywood **818/760-9798** • 7pm-midnight Wed, 8pm-2am Th-Sat, from 2pm Sun, clsd Mon-Tue • popular • mostly gay men • dancing/DJ • country/ western • Latin music wknds • wheelchair access

Silver Rail 11518 Burbank Blvd (btwn Colfax & Lankershim) **818/980-8310** • 4pm-2am, from noon wknds • lesbians/ gay men • neighborhood bar

Nightclubs

C Frenz 7026 Reseda Blvd (at Sherman Way), Reseda **818/996-2976** • 3pm-2am, after-hours Sat • popular • lesbians/ gay men • neighborhood bar • dancing/DJ • multiracial • karaoke • cabaret Tue • live shows • patio • wheelchair access • gay-owned

La Victoria 19655 Sherman Wy (at Corbin Ave), Reseda **818/998-8464** • 9pm-2am • gay/ straight • more gay Wed-Th • dancing/ DJ • mostly Latino/a clientele • dinner served 7:30pm-11pm • live shows

Cafes

Aroma 4360 Tujunga Ave, Studio City **818/508-6505** • 6am-11pm, 7am-10pm Sun

Coffee Junction 19221 Ventura Blvd (E of Tampa), Tarzana **818/342-3405** • 7am-5pm, from 8am Sat, from 9am Sun • live music Th-Sat • women-owned

RESTAURANTS

Du-Par's 12036 Ventura Blvd (at Laurel Canyon), Studio City **818/766-4437** • 6am-1am, till 3am Fri-Sat • plush diner schmoozing

Du-Par's 75 W Thousand Oaks Blvd, Thousand Oaks **805/373-8785** • 6am-10:30pm, till 11:30pm wknds • plush diner schmoozing

GYMS & HEALTH CLUBS

Gold's Gym 6233 N Laurel Canyon Blvd (at Oxnard), North Hollywood **818/506-4600**

EROTICA

Le Sex Shoppe 21625 Sherman Wy (at Nelson), Canoga Park **818/992-9801**

Le Sex Shoppe 4539 Van Nuys Blvd (at Ventura), Sherman Oaks **818/501-9609** • 24hrs

Le Sex Shoppe 4877 Lankershim Blvd (at Houston), North Hollywood **818/760-9529** • 24hrs

Romantix 12323 Ventura Blvd (at Laurel Canyon), Studio City **818/760-9352** • 24hrs

Manhattan Beach

see also LA—West LA & Santa Monica

ACCOMMODATIONS

▲ **Sea View Inn at the Beach** 3400 Highland Ave **310/545-1504** • gay-friendly • ocean views • pool • courtyard • nonsmoking rooms available • $105-345

RESTAURANTS

The Local Yolk 3414 Highland Ave (at Rosecranz) **310/546-4407** • 6:30am-2:30pm

Manteca

RETAIL SHOPS

Mystical Body 259 W Yosemite **209/825-1102** • noon-8pm, clsd Sun • body piercing

Marin County

includes Corte Madera, Mill Valley, San Rafael, Sausalito, Tiburon

INFO LINES & SERVICES

Spectrum Center for LGBT Concerns 1000 Sir Francis Drake Blvd #10, San Anselmo **415/457-1115** • 11am-5pm, 2pm-6pm Th, clsd Fri-Sun • referrals • social/ support groups • wheelchair access

ACCOMMODATIONS

▲ **Acqua Hotel** 555 Redwood Hwy, Mill Valley **415/380-0400, 888/662-9555** • gay-friendly • nonsmoking • kids ok • wheelchair access • $169-219

Beach House, Bolinas CA **415/927-2644** x2 • gay/ straight • cottage • kids ok • lesbian-owned • $200-260

Casa Madrona Hotel & Spa 801 Bridgeway, Sausalito **415/332-0502, 800/288-0502**

Marin Suites Hotel 45 Tamal Vista Blvd (at Lucky Dr), Corte Madera **415/924-3608, 800/362-3372** • gay-friendly • all-suite hotel w/ full kitchens • $99-199

Panama Hotel 4 Bayview St, San Rafael **415/457-3993, 800/899-3993** • gay-friendly cottage • some shared bath • nonsmoking • kids/ pets ok • restaurant • $75-160

Tiburon Lodge & Conference Center 1651 Tiburon Blvd, Tiburon **415/435-3133, 800/762-7770** • gay-friendly • hotel • swimming • $159-339

Waters Edge 25 Main St, Tiburon **415/789-5999, 877/789-5999** • gay/ straight • boutique hotel • kids ok • nonsmoking • wheelchair access • $175-425

RESTAURANTS

Guaymas 5 Main St (at ferry dock), Tiburon **415/435-6300** • gourmet Mexican • great views of the Bay

BOOKSTORES

The Depot Bookshop & Cafe 87 Throckmorton, Mill Valley **415/383-2665** • 7am-7pm, independent

RETAIL SHOPS

Cowgirl Creamery 80 4th St (at Tomales Bay Foods), Pt Reyes Station **415/663-9335** • 10am-6pm Wed-Sun • handmade cheeses • picnic lunches to go • women-owned

▲ **See Jane Run Sports** 15 E Blithedale, Mill Valley **415/384-0555** • 11am-7pm, 10am-6pm Sat, noon-5pm Sun • women's athletic apparel

SPIRITUAL GROUPS

Unitarian Universalist Congregation of Marin 240 Channing Wy, San Rafael **415/479-4131** • 11am Sun • call for directions

Marysville

INFO LINES & SERVICES

YSP 530/755-4847 • lesbians/ gay men • LGBT social group

Mendocino

ACCOMMODATIONS

Agate Cove Inn 11201 N Lansing 707/937-0551, 800/527-3111 • gay-friendly • full brkfst • fireplaces • nonsmoking • $139-309

Annie's Jug Handle Beach B&B 32980 Gibney Ln, Fort Bragg 707/964-1415, 800/964-9957 • gay/ straight • on Hwy 1 across from Pacific Ocean • full brkfst • $119-219

Bellflower Box 867 95460 707/937-0783 • lesbians only • secluded cabin w/ kitchen • hot tub • fireplaces • nonsmoking • kids/ pets ok (call first) • lesbian-owned • $65-85

Blair House & Cottage 45110 Little Lake St (at Ford St) 707/937-1800, 800/699-9269 • gay-friendly • nonsmoking • $100-210

Brewery Gulch Inn 9401 Coast Hwy 1 N 707/937-4752, 800/578-4454 • gay/ straight • oceanview B&B made of eco-salvaged redwood • full gourmet brkfst • jacuzzi • teens welcome • nonsmoking • $170-360

Glendeven Inn 8205 N Hwy 1, Little River 707/937-0083, 800/822-4536 • gay-friendly • charming farmhouse on the coast • also private rental home • full brkfst • nonsmoking • wheelchair access • $145-275

Inn at Schoolhouse Creek 7051 N Hwy 1, Little River 707/937-5525, 800/731-5525 • gay/ straight • B&B w/ cottages & suites • full brkfst • hot tub • fireplaces • nonsmoking • $149-350

John Dougherty House 571 Ukiah St (at Kasten St) 707/937-5266, 800/486-2104 • gay-friendly • jacuzzi • gay-owned • $140-250

MacCallum House Inn 45020 Albion St (at Lansing) 707/937-0289, 800/609-0492 • gay/ straight • nonsmoking • wheelchair access • kids ok • restaurant • full bar • $135-350

McElroy's Inn 998 Main St 800/1734780-7905 • gay-friendly • located in the village • nonsmoking • kids ok • $90-135

Mendocino Coastal Reservations 800/262-7801, 707/937-5033 • 9am-5pm • gay-friendly • call for available vacation rentals

Mendocino Hotel & Garden Suites 45080 Main St 707/937-0511, 800/548-0513 • gay-friendly • Victorian w/ garden cottages • nonsmoking • $95-295

Orr Hot Springs 13201 Orr Springs Rd, Ukiah **707/462-6277** • gay-friendly • mineral hot springs • swimming • hostel-style cabins, private cottages & campsites • clothing-optional • kids ok • guests must bring all own food • $40 (camping, 1 person) -$185 (cottage, 2 people)

Packard House 45170 Little Lake St (at Kasten St) **707/937-2677, 888/453-2677** • gay-friendly • full brkfst • jacuzzi • nonsmoking • gay-owned • $225

The Philo Pottery Inn 8550 Hwy 128, Philo **707/895-3069** • gay/ straight • historic country inn • full brkfst • nonsmoking • lesbian-owned • $110-165

Sallie & Eileen's Place **707/937-2028** • women only • cabins • hot tub • kitchens • fireplaces • kids/ pets ok • lesbian-owned • $80-100 • $15/ add'l person • 2-night minimum stay

Seagull Inn 44594 Albion St **707/937-5204, 888/937-5204** • gay-friendly • 9 units in the heart of historic Mendocino • nonsmoking • kids ok • wheelchair access • woman-owned/run • $55-165

Stanford Inn by the Sea—A Country Inn & Spa Coast Hwy 1 & Comptche-Ukiah Rd **707/937-5615, 800/331-8884** • gay-friendly • full brkfst • hot tub • swimming • organic vegetarian restaurant • nonsmoking • kids/pets ok • wheelchair access • $265-320

▲ **Stevenswood Spa Resort** 8211 N Hwy 1 **707/937-2810, 800/421-2810** • gay/ straight • wheelchair access • gay-owned • $149-325

RESTAURANTS

Cafe Beaujolais 961 Ukiah St **707/937-5614** • dinner from 5:45pm • reservations recommended • California country • some veggie • wheelchair access

Menlo Park

see Palo Alto

Mill Valley

see Marin County

Modesto

see also Stockton

BARS

Brave Bull 701 S 9th **209/529-6712** • 7pm-2am • lesbians/ gay men • dancing • levi/leather • live shows • karaoke • strippers

NIGHTCLUBS

The Mustang Club 413 N 7th St (at B St) **209/522-0393** • 6:30pm-2am, from 2pm wknds • ladies night Wed • open 35+ years! • lesbians/ gay men • dancing/DJ • live shows • karaoke Sun • women-owned

CAFES

Deva Cafe 1202 J St **209/572-3382** • 6am-3pm, till 9pm Tue-Th, till 10pm Fri-Sat • gay-friendly • food served • popular breakfast

Oasis Caffe 3025 McHenry Ave (at Rumble) **209/571-3337** • 8am-10pm, 10am-midnight Fri-Sat, clsd Sun • also Mediterranean food served

RESTAURANTS

Restaurant 1505 1505 J St **209/571-1505** • lunch Mon-Fri & dinner daily, also bar till 2am

RETAIL SHOPS

Mystical Body 121 Mchenry Ave **209/527-1163** • 10am-8pm, till 6pm Sun • body piercing

EROTICA

Liberty Adult Book Store 1030 Kansas Ave **209/524-7603**

Suzie's Adult Superstores 115 McHenry Ave (at Needham) **209/529-5546** • 24hrs

Monterey

ACCOMMODATIONS

Gosby House Inn 643 Lighthouse Ave (at 18th), Pacific Grove **831/375-1287, 800/527-8828** • gay-friendly • B&B • full brkfst • some shared baths • nonsmoking • kids ok • wheelchair access • $95-195

Monterey Fireside Lodge 1131 10th St **831/373-4172, 800/722-2624** • gay-friendly • hot tub • fireplaces • nonsmoking rooms available • kids ok • $59-399

The Monterey Hotel 406 Alvarado St **831/375-3184, 800/727-0960** • gay-friendly • turn-of-the-century boutique hotel • $89-259

BARS

Lighthouse Bar & Grill 281 Lighthouse Ave (at Dickman), New Monterey **831/373-4488** • 4pm-2am • lesbians/ gay men • ladies night Wed

NIGHTCLUBS

Franco's Bar/ Norma Jean's Cabaret 10639 Merritt, Castroville **831/633-2090, 831/758-9266** • 9pm-2am Sat only • lesbians/ gay men • dancing/DJ • Latino/a clientele • food served • live shows • drag shows

RESTAURANTS

Old Fisherman's Grotto 39 Fisherman's Wharf #1 **831/375-4604** • 11am-9pm

Tarpy's Roadhouse 2999 Hwy 68 (at Canyon Dr) **831/647-1444** • lunch & dinner

Mountain View

NIGHTCLUBS

King of Clubs Nightclub 893 Leong Dr (at Moffett Blvd) **650/968-6366** • 6pm-2am • lesbians/ gay men • neighborhood bar • dancing/DJ • theme nights • karaoke • multiracial • transgender-friendly

Myers Flat

ACCOMMODATIONS

Giant Redwoods RV & Camp **707/943-3198** • gay-friendly • campsites • RV • located off the Avenue of the Giants on the Eel River • shared baths • kids/ pets ok • $23(tent)-35

Napa Valley

ACCOMMODATIONS

Beazley House B&B Inn 1910 First St, Napa **707/257-1649, 800/559-1649** • gay-friendly • full brkfst • nonsmoking • wheelchair access • $205-299

The Chablis Inn 3360 Solano Ave (Redwood Rd at Hwy 29), Napa **707/257-1944, 800/443-3490** • gay-friendly • motel • hot tub • kids/ pets ok • nonsmoking • $125-265

Chateau de Vie 3250 Hwy 128, Calistoga **707/942-6446, 877/558-2513** • gay/ straight • full brkfst • pets ok • gay-owned • $209-329

The Ink House B&B 1575 St Helena Hwy, St Helena **707/963-3890** • gay-friendly • 1884 Italianate Victorian among the vineyards • full brkfst • nonsmoking • $122-230 + tax

La Belle Epoque B&B Inn 1386 Calistoga Ave, Napa **707/257-2161, 800/238-8070** • gay-friendly • B&B in Napa's historic Old Town • full brkfst • garden • in-room fireplaces • nonsmoking • $199-285

Meadowlark Country House 601 Petrified Forest Rd, Calistoga **707/942-5651, 800/942-5651** • gay-friendly • B&B • full brkfst • clothing-optional mineral pool, sauna & hot tub • gay-owned • $165-265 & $295-425 (pool house)

▲ **The Mount View Hotel** 1457 Lincoln Ave, Calistoga **707/942-6877, 800/816-6877** • swimming • jacuzzi • spa • also cottages • $159-329

Napa River Inn 500 Main St (at 5th), Napa **707/251-8500, 877/251-8500** • luxury boutique hotel with on-site spa • located in the historic Napa Mill • gay-friendly • 159-499

Oliver House B&B 2970 Silverado Trail N (at Deer Park), St Helena **707/963-4089, 800/682-7888** • gay-friendly • B&B • European-style chalet in heart of Wine Country • full brkfst • gay-owned • $165-295

Stone Oaks Vineyard Silverado Trail, Napa **707/226-2462** • gay/ straight • rental home • jacuzzi • swimming • kids ok • women-owned • $800-1,000/ night

White Sulphur Springs Resort & Spa 3100 White Sulphur Springs Rd, St Helena **707/963-8588, 800/593-8873 (IN CA & NV ONLY)** • gay-friendly • secluded Napa Valley retreat • swimming • natural sulphur pool • $95-210

NIGHTCLUBS

1351 Lounge 1351 Main St (btwn Adams & Hunt), St Helena **707/963-1969** • gay friendly • dancing/DJ • live shows

RESTAURANTS

Brannan's 1374 Lincoln Ave (at Washington), Calistoga **707/942-2233** • lunch & dinner, brunch wknds • new American/ Wine Country cuisine • full bar • gay-owned

Flat Iron Grill 1440 Lincoln Ave (at Washington), Calistoga **707/942-1220** • lunch & dinner • New York neighborhood-style restaurant, traditional American classics • gay-owned

Rainbow Room @ The Depot 806 Fourth St (at Soscol), Napa **707/252-4477** • 3pm-close, 4pm-9pm Sun, clsd Mon • gay/ straight • live music • wheelchair access • also Italian restaurant • gay-owned

Tra Vigne 1050 Charter Oak Ave (Hwy 29), St Helena **707/963-4444** • 11:30am-10pm • Northern Italian • also wine bar

Nevada City

ACCOMMODATIONS

The Flume's End 317 S Pine St **530/265-9665** • gay/ straight • full brkfst • women-owned • $125-189

CAFES

Java John's 306 Broad St **530/265-3653** • 6:30am-5pm • gay-owned

RESTAURANTS

Friar Tucks 111 N Pine St (at Commercial) **530/265-9093** • dinner from 5pm • popular • American/ fondue • full bar • wheelchair access

Newport Beach

see Orange County

Oakland

see East Bay

Oceanside

BARS

Greystokes 1903 S Coast Hwy (btwn Kelly & Vista Wy) 760/757-2955 • 2pm-2am, from noon wknds • lesbians/ gay men • also restaurant • patio

Orange County

includes Anaheim, Costa Mesa, Garden Grove, Huntington Beach, Laguna Beach, Irvine, Newport Beach, Santa Ana

INFO LINES & SERVICES

AA Gay/ Lesbian Laguna Beach 714/556-4555 (AA#)

The Gay & Lesbian Services Center of Orange County 12800 Garden Grove Blvd #F (btwn Harbor & Fairview), Garden Grove 714/534-0862 • 9am-9pm, 10am-2pm Sat, clsd Sun

ACCOMMODATIONS

By The Sea Inn 475 N Coast Hwy, Laguna Beach 949/497-6645, 800/297-0007 • gay-friendly • hot tub • swimming • kids ok • wheelchair access • $79-219

Casa Laguna B&B Inn 2510 S Coast Hwy, Laguna Beach 949/494-2996, 800/233-0449 • gay-friendly • inn & cottages overlooking the Pacific • swimming • kids/ pets ok • nonsmoking • gay-owned • $140-550

Holiday Inn Laguna Beach 696 S Coast Hwy, Laguna Beach 949/494-1001, 800/228-5691 • gay-friendly • swimming • kids ok • food served • wheelchair access • $99-299

Laguna Brisas Spa Hotel 1600 S Coast Hwy (at Bluebird), Laguna Beach 949/497-7272, 888/296-6834 • gay/ straight • resort hotel • free brkfst • swimming • in-room whirlpool spas • nonsmoking • wheelchair access • $99-350

Laguna Cliffs Marriott Resort & Spa 25135 Park Lantern, Dana Point 949/661-5000, 800/533-9748 • gay-friendly • swimming • wheelchair access • $129-438

Laguna Magical Cottages 217 & 223 Nyes Pl, Laguna Beach 949/494-4554 • gay/ straight • 2 rental cottages on Laguna Beach • kids/ pets ok • woman-owned/ run • $975-1,575/ week

BARS

Club Bounce 1460 S Coast Hwy, Laguna Beach 949/494-0056 • 2pm-2am • lesbians/ gay men • dancing/ DJ • karaoke • cabaret

Frat House 8112 Garden Grove Blvd (at Beach Blvd), Garden Grove 714/373-3728 • 3pm-2am • popular • lesbians/ gay men • dancing/DJ • multiracial • theme nights • drag shows • young crowd • wheelchair access

Tin Lizzie Saloon 752 St Clair (at Bristol), Costa Mesa 714/966-2029 • 11am-2am • mostly gay men • neighborhood bar • wheelchair access

Woody's at the Beach 1305 S Coast Hwy (at Cress), Laguna Beach 949/376-8809 • 4pm-2am • mostly gay men • also restaurant, 6pm-10pm • monthly T-dances in summer • patio

NIGHTCLUBS

Boom Boom Room 1401 S Coast Hwy (at The Coast Inn), Laguna Beach 949/933-9319 • 11:30am-2am, from 11am wknds • popular • mostly gay men • dancing/DJ • drag shows • videos

Bravo 1490 S Anaheim Blvd, Anaheim 714/533-2291 • lesbians/ gay men • Tue & Sat only • dancing/DJ • Latino/a • Pop Planet Tue w/ go-go boys, videos, 18+

El Calor 2916 W Lincoln Ave (at E Beach Blvd), Anaheim 714/527-8873 • 8pm-2am • lesbians/ gay men • dancing/ DJ • mostly Latino/a • Latin music

Lion's Den 719 W 19th St (at Pomona), Costa Mesa 949/645-3830 • 9pm-2am, clsd Mon-Tue • lesbians/ gay men • gay Th-Fri & Sun only • dancing/DJ • karaoke • drag shows Fri • Latino Fri • young crowd

CAFES

Fixx 2549 Eastbluff Dr, Newport Beach 949/644-9349 • 6am-10pm • food served • theme nights

The Koffee Klatch 1440 S Coast Hwy (btwn Mountain & Pacific Coast Hwy), Laguna Beach 949/376-6867 • 7am-11pm, till midnight Fri-Sat • brkfst & lunch • desserts

Zinc Cafe 350 Ocean Ave (at Broadway), Laguna Beach 949/494-6302 • 7am-4:30pm, till 5pm wknds • vegetarian • beer/ wine • patio • also market • wheelchair access

RESTAURANTS

Cafe Zoolu 860 Glenneyre, Laguna Beach **949/494-6825** • dinner only, clsd Mon • Californian • some veggie • wheelchair access

The Cottage 308 N Coast Hwy (at Aster), Laguna Beach **949/494-3023** • brkfst, lunch & dinner • homestyle cooking • some veggie

Dizz's As Is 2794 S Coast Hwy, Laguna Beach **949/494-5250** • open 5:30pm, seating at 6pm • cont'l • full bar • patio

Hamburger Mary's Bar & Grille OC 4221 Dolphin-Striker Wy, Newport Beach **949/756-8800, 888/834-MARY** • 11am-2am • lesbians/ gay men • dancing/ DJ

Madison Square & Garden Cafe 320 N Coast Hwy, Laguna Beach **949/494-0137** • 8am-3pm, clsd Tue

Sorrento Grille 370 Glenneyre St, Laguna Beach **949/494-8686** • dinner only • upscale American bistro & martini bar

ENTERTAINMENT & RECREATION

West St Beach Laguna Beach

RETAIL SHOPS

▲ **Jewelry by Poncé** 1417 S Coast Hwy, Laguna Beach **949/497-4154, 800/969-RING** • 11am-7pm Wed-Sun, by appt Mon-Tue • LGBT commitment rings & other jewelry • see ad in back mail order section

PUBLICATIONS

▲ **Lesbian News (LN)** **800/995-8838, 800/458-9888** • nat'l w/ strong coverage of southern CA • see ad front color section

Orange County/ Long Beach Blade **949/494-4898**

SPIRITUAL GROUPS

Christ Chapel MCC 720 N Spurgeon (at 8th & Main), Santa Ana **714/835-0722** • 10am Sun

Christ Chapel of Laguna 286 St Anne's Dr (at Glenneyre, at the Women's Club), Laguna Beach **949/376-2099** • 10am Sun

Unitarian Universalist Fellowship 429 Cypress Dr (S of Myrtle), Laguna Beach **949/497-4568** • 10:30am Sun

EROTICA

A-Z Bookstore 8192 Garden Grove Blvd (at Beach), Garden Grove **714/534-9349** • 24hrs wknds

Paradise Specialties 7344 Center (at Gothard), Huntington Beach **714/898-0400**

Romantix 12686 Garden Grove Blvd (at Harbor), Garden Grove **714/638-8595**

Video Horizons 31678 S Coast Hwy (at 3rd Ave), Laguna Beach **949/499-4519**

Pacific Grove

RESTAURANTS

Pasta Mia Trattoria/ The Pizza Grotto 481 Lighthouse Ave **831/375-7709, 831/375-9268** • 5pm-9pm • Italian • cocktails • beer/ wine

Palm Springs

INFO LINES & SERVICES

AA Gay/ Lesbian **760/324-4880 (AA#)**

Desert Pride Center 611 S Palm Canyon #201 (at The Sun Center) **760/327-2313** • noon-9pm, 9am-5pm wknds • programs & services • 12-step meetings

ACCOMMODATIONS

2022 Casa Diego Baristo 2022 E Baristo Rd (at Sunrise) **760/320-1124, 52-322/223-4676 (MEXICO #)** • lesbians/ gay men • 3-bdrm vacation rental • swimming • spa • gay-owned

Ballantines Hotel 1420 N Indian Canyon Dr **760/320-1178, 800/485-2808** • gay-friendly • '50s chic • swimming • $99-265

BauHouse in the Desert 2470 S Yosemite Dr (at Camino Real & Hwy 111) **760/320-6800** • gay/ straight • rental home • jacuzzi • pool • kids/ pets ok • wheelchair access • $425-700

Caliente Tropics Resort 411 E Palm Canyon Dr **760/327-1391, 866/468-9595** • gay/ straight • hot tub • swimming • nonsmoking resort • kids/ pets ok • food served • wheelchair access • gay-owned • $99-295

Calla Lily Inn 350 S Belardo Rd (at Baristo) **760/323-3654, 888/888-5787** • gay-friendly • swimming • "a tranquil oasis" • $99-350

▲ **Casitas Laquita** 450 E Palm Canyon Dr (near Camino Real) **760/416-9999, 877/203-3410** • lesbian resort • swimming • nonsmoking • small pets ok • wheelchair access • lesbian-owned • $135-350

Desert Palms Inn 67-580 E Palm Canyon Dr (at Gene Autry Tr), Cathedral City **760/324-3000, 800/801-8696** • mostly gay men • hot tub • swimming • courtyard • also restaurant • some veggie • full bar • wheelchair access • gay-owned • $69-159

Honeysuckle Inn Avenida Olancha (across from Queen of Hearts) **760/322-5793, 888/275-9903** • women only • swimming • full kitchens • small pets ok • lesbian-owned • $110-150

Reply Forward   Delete

Date: Dec 15, 2005 12:26:42
From: Girl-on-the-Go
To: Editor@Damron.com
Subject: Palm Springs

>Each and every spring, since 1972, the LPGA has converged upon the city of Palm Springs to present the premier event of its tournament schedule. Many women plan their vacations around the **Kraft Nabisco Golf Championship** (previously known as Dinah Shore!) and calendars are blocked out as soon as the tournament dates for the following year are released. Visitors pour into the valley to admire the beauty of springtime and to engage in the myriad events that occur between March and May.

>But did you know Palm Springs is open for business during the other nine months of the year as well? This has been a well-kept secret, but we are willing to divulge this information to expose the different faces and personalities of a truly year-round resort destination for women.

>Year-round businesses that welcome women are abundant. All you have to do is stroll along Arenas Road to find food, merchandise, and entertainment. Friendly faces welcome you at the door of **Ground Zero, Heaven, Spike's,** and **Toucan's Tiki Lounge**, and you can pick up sex supplies and pride items at **GayMart**; books, cards, and gifts at **Q Trading Company**; or just about all of the above can be found at **Mischief**. If you find yourself jonesing for a hoe-down on the right day of the month, you can check out **Boots in Squares** monthly lesbian and gay square dance.

>There is plenty of outdoor entertainment, as well. Take a day trip to the spectacular Joshua Tree National Park, or for a little danger and an amazing view, catch a ride on the Aerial Tram that goes from the desert floor to the top of Mount San Jacinto. When you come back to earth, it's time to lie back and treat yourself to some sun and outdoor fun.

>Of course, you're going to need a place to rest, rejuvenate, and recharge for the next day's activities. Two women-only establishments — **Casitas Laquita** and the **Queen of Hearts Resort** — provide travelers with comfortable and friendly accommodations. As you bask in the sun, soak up the warm desert air, and drift into a peaceful state of tranquillity, you'll ask yourself why you didn't visit paradise sooner.

La Casa Contenta 760/322–2500, 800/777–4606 • prestigious 5-bdrm estate property w/ lush gardens • lots of privacy • $375-550 (also weekly & monthly)

La Mancha Private Villas & Spas 444 Avenida Caballeros 760/323–1773, 866/673–7501 • gay-friendly • private 1, 2 & 3-bdrm villas • many w/ own pool & spa • also restaurant & bar • wheelchair access • $199-799

Mojave 73721 Shadow Mountain Dr, Palm Desert 760/346–6121, 866/846–8358 • gay-friendly • boutique hotel • swimming • hot tub • spa services • kids ok • wheelchair access • $69-169

Mountain View Villa on Farrell Dr 305/294–1525 (FL#) • vacation rental • jacuzzi • swimming • kids ok • nonsmoking • $139-225

Palm Springs Luxury Getaway 415/218–1920 • gay/ straight • vacation rental • pool • nonsmoking • pets ok w/ proprietor approval • gay-owned • $200+/night (2-night minimum)

▲ **Queen of Hearts Resort** 435 E Avenida Olancha 760/322–5793, 888/275–9903 • women only • swimming • full kitchens • lesbian-owned • $110-150

The Resort at Palm Springs 701 E Palm Canyon Dr 760/320–2700, 800/854–4345 • gay-friendly • swimming • hot tub • kids/ pets ok • also restaurant • wheelchair access • $79-129

Ruby Montana's Coral Sands Inn 210 W Stevens Rd (at N Palm Canyon) 760/325–4900, 866/820–8302 • gay/ straight • resort • swimming • kids/ pets ok • wheelchair access • lesbian & gay-owned • $107-120

Palm Springs

WHERE THE GIRLS ARE:
Vacationers will be staying on East Palm Canyon near Sunrise Way. Women do hang out at the boys' bars too. Try the bar at The Desert Palms Inn, or just about anywhere on Perez Rd.

LGBT PRIDE:
November, web: www.pspride.org.

ANNUAL EVENTS:
Spring - Kraft Nabisco Golf Tournament (aka "Dinah Shore") 760/324-4546, web: www.kncgolf.com. One of the biggest gatherings of lesbians on the continent.
White Party, web: www.jeffreysanker.com. Popular circuit party/fundraiser.
October - Out on Film 760/770-2042, lesbian/gay film & arts festival.

CITY INFO:
Palm Springs Visitors Bureau 760/778-8415 or 800/927-7256, web: www.palm-springs.org.

ATTRACTIONS:
Palm Springs Aerial Tramway to the top of Mt San Jacinto, on Tramway Rd, web: www.pstramway.com.

BEST VIEW:
Top of Mt San Jacinto. Driving through the surrounding desert, you can see great views of the mountains. Be careful in the summer—always carry water in your vehicle, and be sure to check all fluids in your car before you leave and frequently during your trip.

WEATHER:
Palm Springs is sunny and warm in the winter, with temperatures in the 70°s. Summers are scorching (100°+).

TRANSIT:
City Cab 760/416-2594.
Classic Cab 760/322-3111.
Desert Valley Shuttle 800/413-3999.
Sun Line Transit Agency 760/343-3451.

We're not just a place to stay...
We're an Experience!!

- PRIVATE GROUNDS WITH HEATED POOL
- FULL KITCHENS STOCKED WITH IN-ROOM COMPLIMENTARY CONTINENTAL BREAKFAST
- COZY FIREPLACE ROOMS
- RELAXING MASSAGE AVAILABLE AT YOUR REQUEST
- WIRELESS INTERNET
- PRIVATE ROMANCE SUITE WITH SPA AND TWO FIREPLACES

(760) 416.9999
Toll Free 877-203-3410

450 EAST PALM CANYON DRIVE
PALM SPRINGS, CA 92264

Casitas Laquita

e-mail: casitas@casitaslaquita.com   www.casitaslaquita.com

The Three Thirty Three B&B 333 E Ramon Rd 760/320–7744 (9AM-8PM PST) • gay/straight • intimate 3-bdrm B&B • hot tub • gay-owned • $85-150

Villa Mykonos 67–590 Jones Rd (at Cree), Cathedral City **800/471–4753** • lesbians/gay men • timeshare condos & rental units • swimming • $190-275 (rentals)/ $3,000-7,000 (condos)

Villa Royale 1620 Indian Trail 760/327–2314, 800/245–2314 • gay-friendly • "named one of the five best small inns in Southern California by Sunset Magazine" • $119-279

The Village Inn 855 N Indian Canyon Dr 760/320–8622, 866/320–8622 • gay/straight • hotel • hot tub • swimming • kids/pets ok • $59-189

BARS

Ground Zero 36–737 Cathedral Canyon Dr (at Commercial), Cathedral City **760/321–0031** • 2pm-2am • lesbians/gay men • neighborhood bar • karaoke • drag shows & cabaret wknds • patio

Hunter's Video Bar 302 E Arenas Rd (at Calle Encilia) **760/323–0700** • 10am-2am • popular • mostly gay men • dancing/DJ • video bar • go-go boys Fri

Spike's Wonder Bar & Grill 241 E Tahquitz Canyon Wy 760/322–5280 • 11am-11pm, clsd Mon • popular • lesbians/gay men • also restaurant • wknd brunch • patio

Toucan's Tiki Lounge 2100 N Palm Canyon Dr (at Via Escuela) 760/416–7584 • noon-2am • lesbians/gay men • dancing/DJ • cabaret Mon • drag shows Wed & Sun • male & female go-go dancers wknds

The Villa Palm Springs—Butterfield's 67–670 Carey Rd (at The Villa resort), Cathedral City 760/328–7211 • 11am-midnight • lesbians/gay men • poolside bar • patio • also cafe w/ lunch & dinner

NIGHTCLUBS

Heaven 611 S Palm Canyon Dr (in the Sun Center) 760/416–0950 • 7pm-1am Wed, 9pm-2am Th, 8pm-4am Fri-Sat, from 10pm Sun, clsd Mon-Tue • lesbians/gay men • dancing/DJ Fri-Sun • karaoke Wed • strippers Th • cabaret Fri-Sat • cover

CAFES

Palm Springs Koffi 515 N Palm Canyon Dr (at Alejo) 760/416–2244 • 6am-7pm

Queen of HEARTS RESORT

Toll Free 888-275-9903
www.queenofheartsps.com
Lesbian Owned & Operated

Full Kitchens and Outside BBQ
Poolside Misters & A/C in Rooms
Complimentary Continental Breakfast
2 Pools, Jacuzzi & Outdoor Fireplace
Ask about the Desert Hearts Inn - Pets Welcome

RESTAURANTS

Amici 71380 Hwy 111, Rancho Mirage 760/341–0738 • lunch & dinner, Sun brunch • Italian patio • full bar • $20-25 (dinner)

Atlas 210 S Palm Canyon Dr 760/325–8839 • 4pm-2am, clsd Mon-Tue • steak & seafood • dancing

Billy Reed's 1800 N Palm Canyon Dr (at Vista Chino) 760/325–1946 • 8am-9pm • some veggie • full bar • also bakery

Blame It on Midnight 777 E Tahquitz Canyon Wy 760/323–1200 • 5pm-10pm, till 11pm Fri-Sat, clsd Sun, clsd Mon in summer • also full bar • live shows • patio

Butterfield's Adobe 67–670 Carey Rd (at The Villa resort), Cathedral City 760/328–7211 • 11am-10pm • wknd champagne brunch by pool • full bar

Churchill's 665 S Palm Canyon Dr (at Sunny Dunes) 760/325–3716 • lunch & dinner • fish & chips, Southern comfort food, salads • gay-owned

Copley's 621 N Palm Canyon Dr 760/327–9555 • 5pm-10pm • "creative comtemporary American cuisine" • full bar • valet parking

Davey's Hideaway 292 E Palm Canyon Dr 760/320–4480 • from 5pm • steak, seafood & pasta "nightly piano entertainment" • patio • also full bar

El Gallito 68820 Grove St (at Palm Canyon), Cathedral City 760/328–7794 • 10am-9pm • homemade Mexican • beer/ wine

Hamburger Mary's 415 N Palm Canyon Dr 760/778–6279 • 11am-close • full bar

International Cafe 67-778 Hwy 111, Cathedral City 760/202–2390 • 7am-10pm, brkfst till 4pm • "best burgers in town"

Just Pizza 315 E Arenas 760/416–2818 • wknds till 2am, also delivers

Las Casuelas 368 N Palm Canyon Dr (btwn Amado & Alejo) 760/325–3213 • 11am-10pm • Mexican

Rainbow Cactus Restaurant & Bar 212 S Indian Canyon (at Arenas) 760/325–3868 • lunch & dinner, Sun brunch • Californian • piano bar

Red Tomato & House of Lamb 68–784 E Palm Canyon (btwn Date Palm & Cathedral Canyon), Cathedral City 760/328–7518 • 4pm-10pm • Italian • beer/ wine • wheelchair access

Shame on the Moon 69–950 Frank Sinatra Dr (at Hwy 111), Rancho Mirage 760/324–5515 • 5pm-10:30pm • cont'l • plenty veggie • full bar • patio • wheelchair access

Simba's 190 N Sunrise Wy 760/778–7630 • lunch & dinner • ribs • clsd summers

Spike's Baja Cantina 611 S Palm Canyon (in the Sun Center) 760/864–9775 • lunch & dinner, lunch only Mon, clsd Sun

Thai Kitchen II 787 N Palm Canyon Dr 760/323–4527 • lunch & dinner

Tootie's Texas Barbeque 68-703 Perez Rd, Cathedral City 760/202–6963

The Uptown Grill of Palm Springs 150 E Vista Chino (at Indian Canyon) 760/320–6116 • lunch & dinner • cont'l • full bar • piano lounge nightly • $12-20

Wang's in the Desert 424 S Indian Canyon Dr 760/325–9264 • from 5:30pm • Chinese

ENTERTAINMENT & RECREATION

Boots in Squares 68-727 E Palm Canyon (at Van Fleet, in Cathedral City Senior Center), Cathedral City 760/328–6303, 760/327–8684 • lesbian/ gay square dance club • monthly dances • classes Mon

Desert Dyners PO Box 5072, 92263-5072 760/202–6645 • lesbian social club • membership required • hosts mixers, dances, dinners & golf • singles & couples welcome

The Living Desert Zoo & Gardens Palm Desert 760/346–5694 • 9am-5pm (8am-1pm June-Aug) • "zoo & endangered species conservation center, botanical gardens, natural history museum, wilderness park, nature preserve, education center"

Ruddy's 1930s General Store Museum 221 S Palm Canyon Dr 760/327–2156 • 10am-4pm Th-Sun • "the most you can spend is 95¢"

BOOKSTORES

Peppertree Bookstore & Cafe 155 S Palm Canyon Dr 760/325–4821 • 10am-8pm, till 10pm Th-Sat • independent • some LGBT titles • readings

Q Trading Company 606 E Sunny Dunes Rd (at Indian Canyon) 760/416–7150, 800/756–2290 • 10am-6pm • LGBT • also cards, gifts, videos, etc

RETAIL SHOPS

GayMartUSA 305 E Arenas Rd (at Indian Canyon) 760/416–6436 • 10am-midnight

Mischief 210 E Arenas Rd (at Indian Canyon) **760/322-8555** • 11am-9pm, 10am-10pm Fri-Sat, 11am-7pm Sun • novelties, cards, pride items, gifts, toys, DVDs

PUBLICATIONS

The Bottom Line **760/323-0552** • the desert's LGBT bar guide & classifieds

Buzz **760/324-8299** • bi-weekly • news, entertainment & listings • covers San Diego & Palm Springs

Desert Daily Guide **760/320-3237** • LGBT weekly, travel, activity & lodging info for Palm Springs

Palm Springs Gay Yellow Pages **760/324-8299** • online directory of Palm Springs businesses

SPIRITUAL GROUPS

Bloom in the Desert Ministries 3601 E Mesquite Ave (in the Family YMCA of the Desert) **760/333-1221** • 9:30am • independent, interdenominational, progressive, inclusive, Christian, mainline-protestant worshipping congregation

Dignity Palm Springs 125 W El Alameda (St Paul in the Desert Episcopal Church) **760/321-9511, 866/321-9511** • mass 5:30pm Sun

Metropolitan Community Church of the Coachella Valley (MCCCV) 32150 Candlewood Dr, Ste 6, Cathedral City **760/328-3591** • 10am Sun

St Paul in the Desert 125 W El Alameda **760/320-7488** • 8am & 10:30am Sun, Holy Communion 6pm Wed • Episcopal • Integrity meets 6:30pm 4th Fri for potluck

Unity Church of Palm Springs 815 S Camino Real (at N Riverside Dr) **760/325-7377** • 11am Sun, 7:30pm Tue (silent prayer & meditation) • also bookstore & classes

GYMS & HEALTH CLUBS

Gold's Gym 4070 Airport Center Dr (at Ramon) **760/322-4653** • gay-friendly • 24hrs

Urban Yoga Center 750 N Palm Canyon Dr (at Healing Arts Community) **760/320-7702**

Palo Alto

ACCOMMODATIONS

Creekside Inn 3400 El Camino Real (at Page Mill Rd) **650/493-2411, 800/492-7335** • gay/straight • swimming • kids ok • nonsmoking • restaurant & lounge • wheelchair access • $179-259

▲ **Hotel Avante** 860 El Camino Real, Mountain View **650/940-1000, 800/538-1600** • gay/straight • swimming • jacuzzi • 120-279

BOOKSTORES

Books Inc 157 Stanford Shopping Center **650/321-0600** • 9:30am-9pm, 10am-8pm Sat, 11am-6pm Sun • general • LGBT section

SPIRITUAL GROUPS

First Presbyterian Church 1140 Cowper St (at Embarcadero) **650/325-5659** • 11am Sun • wheelchair access

Pasadena

BARS

Boulevard/ Club S Karaoke 3199 E Foothill Blvd (at Sierra Madre Villa) **626/356-9304** • 6pm-2am, from 3pm Fri-Sun • mostly gay men • neighborhood bar • karaoke

Encounters 203 N Sierra Madre Blvd (at Foothill) **626/792-3735** • 4pm-2am, from 3pm wknds • lesbians/ gay men • neighborhood bar • dancing/DJ • young crowd • patio

RESTAURANTS

Twin Palms 101 W Green St (at De Lacey Ave) **626/577-2567** • lunch & dinner • chic decor • reasonable prices • huge menu

SPIRITUAL GROUPS

First Congregational United Church of Christ 464 E Walnut (at Las Robles) **626/795-0696** • 10am Sun

EROTICA

Romantix 45 E Colorado (at Raymond) **626/683-9468** • 24hrs

Paso Robles

ENTERTAINMENT & RECREATION

Wine Attic 1305 Park St **805/227-4107** • 11am-7pm, till 4pm Sun, clsd Mon-Tue • tasting room & wine shop

Pescadero

ACCOMMODATIONS

Costanoa 2001 Rossi Rd **650/879-1100, 877/262-7848** • gay/ straight • also tent bungalows & cabins • 1 hour south of San Francisco • $40-350

Estancia del Mar **650/879-1500** • gay-friendly • cottage rentals w/ ocean views • nonsmoking • kids/ pets ok • wheelchair access • $150-225

Petaluma

ACCOMMODATIONS

Old Palms of Petaluma B&B 2 Liberty St (at 6th St) **707/658–2554** • gay-friendly • full brkfst • kids ok • wheelchair access • $125-200

RESTAURANTS

Brix 16 Kentucky St (in Lanmart Bldg) **707/766–8162** • dinner, clsd Sun • popular • also wine store

BOOKSTORES

Copperfield's Books 140 Kentucky St (btwn Western & Washington, downtown) **707/762–0563** • 9am-9pm, till 6pm Sun • new & used books • also great little cafe

Pismo Beach

ACCOMMODATIONS

The Palomar Inn 1601 Shell Beach Rd, Shell Beach **805/773–4204, 888/384–4004** • gay/ straight • $60-90

Placerville

ACCOMMODATIONS

Rancho Cicada Retreat 209/245–4841, **877/553–9481** • mostly gay men • secluded riverside retreat in the Sierra foothills w/ 2-person tents & cabin • swimming • nudity • gay-owned • $100-200 (lower during week)

Shafsky House B&B 2942 Coloma St (at Spring St/ Hwy 49) **530/642–2776** • gay-friendly • full brkfst • nonsmoking • kids ok • lesbian-owned • $115-145

Pleasant Hill

EROTICA

Lingerie Etc 2298 Monument Blvd (at Buskirk) **925/676–2962**

Pomona

BARS

Alibi East 225 S San Antonio Ave (at 2nd) **909/623–9422** • 10am-2am, till 4am Fri-Sat • mostly gay men • dancing/DJ

The Hookup 1047 E 2nd St (at Pico) **909/620–2844** • noon-2am, from 10am wknds • lesbians/ gay men • neighborhood bar • food served • karaoke • wheelchair access • gay-owned

NIGHTCLUBS

Robbie's 390 E 2nd St (at College Plaza) **909/620–4371** • 8pm-2am, clsd Mon-Th • lesbians/ gay men • dancing/DJ • Latino/a clientle • live shows • call for events

EROTICA

Mustang Books & Videos 961 N Central (at Foothill Blvd), Upland **909/981–0227** • 24hrs

Redding

NIGHTCLUBS

Club 501 1244 California St (at Center & Division, enter rear) **530/243–7869** • 6pm-2am, from noon Sun • lesbians/ gay men • dancing/DJ • young crowd

CAFES

Judy's Espresso 1100 Hartnell Ave (at Churncreek) **530/221–8081** • 6am-5pm, from 7am wknds, till 5pm Sat, till 1pm Sun • snow cones & coffee drinks • wheelchair access

Redondo Beach

see also Los Angeles—West LA & Santa Monica

ACCOMMODATIONS

Palos Verdes Inn 1700 S Pacific Coast Hwy **310/316–4211, 800/421–9241** • gay-friendly • jacuzzi • swimming • food served • kids ok • wheelchair access • $75-125

Redwood City

ENTERTAINMENT & RECREATION

Redwood Roller Rink 1303 Main St (at Beech St) **650/369–5558** • lesbians/ gay men • gay skate night Wed 8pm-10:30pm • multiracial • 18+

EROTICA

Secrets Adult Superstore 739 El Camino Real (at Brewster) **650/364–6913** • 24hrs

Riverside

see also San Bernardino

NIGHTCLUBS

Menagerie 3581 University Ave (at Orange) **951/788–8000** • 4pm-2am • lesbians/ gay men • dancing/DJ • karaoke • drag shows Th • wheelchair access

VIP Nightclub & Restaurant 3673 Merrill Ave (at Magnolia) **951/784–2370** • 5pm-2am, 3pm-2am Wed-Sun • lesbians/ gay men • dancing/DJ • karaoke • drag shows Fri • food served

EROTICA

Romantix 3945 Market St (at 9th) **951/788–5194** • 24hrs

Russian River

includes Cazadero, Forestville, Guerneville & Monte Rio

ACCOMMODATIONS

Applewood Inn 13555 Hwy 116 (at Mays Canyon), Guerneville **707/869–9093, 800/555–8509** • gay-friendly • full brkfst • swimming • nonsmoking • food served • wheelchair access • gay-owned • $185-345

Eagle's Peak 11644 Our Peak Rd (at McPeak Rd), Forestville **707/887–9218, 877/891–6466** • mostly gay men • vacation house w/ deck & spa on 26 acres • gay-owned • $195-225 (2-night mininum)

Far Reaches Highland Terrace (at Huckleberry St), Monte Rio **415/864–4554** • gay-friendly • cottage • kids/ pets ok • large deck • gay-owned • $150-250 (2-night minimum)

Fern Grove Cottages 16650 River Rd, Guerneville **707/869–8105** • gay-friendly • California craftsman cottages circa 1926 • swimming • kids/ pets ok • nonsmoking • $79-209

Fifes Guest Ranch & Roadhouse Restaurant 16467 River Rd (at Brookside Ln), Guerneville **707/869-0656, 800/734-3371** • gay/ straight • 49 cabins • 60 campsites • swimming • also restaurant • 3 full bars • gym • day spa • wheelchair access • gay-owned • $65-305

Grandma's House 20280 River Blvd, Monte Rio **707/865–1865** • lesbians/ gay men • B&B on the Russian River • private beach • hot tub • lesbian-owned • $100-175

HearthSide Cabin 2320 Cazadero Hwy, Cazadero **415/255–1099** • gay/ straight • 2-bdrm cabin (sleeps 6) • hot tub • private access to creek • wireless internet • gay-owned • $180-240

Highland Dell Resort 21050 River Blvd (at Bohemian Hwy), Monte Rio **707/865–2300** • gay-friendly • riverside hotel • full bar & restaurant

▲ **Highlands Resort** 14000 Woodland Dr, Guerneville **707/869-0333** • lesbians/ gay men • country retreat on 4 wooded acres • hot tub • swimming • clothing-optional pool • $45-145

Reply **Forward** **Delete**

Date: Dec 17, 2005 13:29:53
From: Girl-on-the-Go
To: Editor@Damron.com
Subject: Russian River

>The Russian River resort area is hidden away in the redwood forests of Northern California, an hour and a half north of the San Francisco Bay Area. The warm summer days and cool star-lit nights have made it a favorite secret getaway for many of San Francisco's lesbians and gays—especially when they can't stand another foggy, cold day in the City.

>Life at "The River," as it's fondly called, is laid back. You can take a canoe ride, hike under the redwoods, or just lie back on the riverbank and soak up the sun. There are plenty of good camping spots for those interested—you might want to try **The Willows** or **Fife's Guest Ranch**. If you're in the mood for other soothing and sensual delights, you're in luck. The River is in the heart of the famous California Wine Country. Plan a tour to the many wineries, and don't forget to designate a sober driver, so you can taste the world-class wines as you go. Or see some of the world's most beautiful coastline as you cruise along the Pacific Coast Highway—only fifteen minutes away!

>The River becomes a lesbian garden of earthly delights several times a year. **Women's Weekend** happens in June and late September, and women pack the tiny town as they enjoy the many entertainers, dances, and barbecues.

Huckleberry Springs Country Inn & Spa 8105 Old Beedle, Monte Rio **707/865–2683, 800/822–2683** • gay/ straight • private cottages • full brkfst • swimming • Japanese spa • massage therapy • no smoking anywhere on property • videos • women-owned • $160-175 (2-night minimum)

Inn at Occidental 3657 Church St, Occidental **707/874–1047, 800/522–6324** • gay-friendly • luxury Sonoma Wine Country inn • full brkfst • wheelchair access• $199-625

Inn at the Willows 15905 River Rd (at Hwy 116), Guerneville **707/869–2824 (8AM-8PM PST), 800/953–2828** • lesbians/ gay men • old-fashioned country lodge & campground • nonsmoking • gay-owned • $79-159 ($25+ camping)

Powder River Ranch 7390 Covey Rd (at River Rd), Forestville **707/887–7778** • gay/ straight • 1 studio cottage • jacuzzi • gay-owned • $95-125

Retreat Resort & Spa 14711 Armstrong Woods Rd, Guerneville **707/869–2706, 866/737–3529** • gay/ straight • newly renovated resort w/ full-service spa • kids/ pets ok • swimming • nonsmoking • jacuzzi • gay-owned • $150-325

Ridenhour Ranch House Inn & Cottages 12850 River Rd, Guerneville **707/887–1033, 888/877–4466** • gay-friendly • 1906 B&B • hot tub kids ok • nonsmoking • $125-185

Rio Villa Beach Resort 20292 Hwy 116 (at Bohemian Hwy), Monte Rio **707/865–1143** • gay-friendly • on the river • cabins • kids ok • nonsmoking • gay-owned • $79-199

River Village Resort & Spa 14880 River Rd, Guerneville **707/869–8139, 888/342–2624** • gay/ straight • cottages • swimming • hot tub • kids/ pets ok • nonsmoking • wheelchair access • $90-195

Russian River Getaways 14075 Mill St (at 4th St), Guerneville **707/869–4560, 800/433–6673** • lesbians/ gay men • vacation rental service • nightly & weekly rates • lesbian-owned

Russian River Reservations **707/869–0601, 800/403–1744** • reservation service for rental homes • gay-owned

Russian River Resort/ Triple R Resort 16390 4th St (at Mill), Guerneville **707/869–0691, 800/417–3767** • lesbians/ gay men • hot tub • swimming • nudity ok • also restaurant • some veggie • full bar • videos • wheelchair access • gay-owned • $55-180

Russian River View Retreat **707/869–3040** (8AM-8PM PST) • gay-friendly • vacation home • hot tub • kids/ pets ok • nonsmoking • deck • 2 bikes provided • private dock & boat • $400-600/ wknd, $850-1,350/ week

Santa Nella House 12130 Hwy 116, Guerneville **707/869–9488, 800/440–9031** • gay-friendly • B&B • $149-179

Russian River

WHERE THE GIRLS ARE:
Guerneville is a small town, so you won't miss the scantily clad, vacationing women walking toward the bars downtown or the beach.

ANNUAL EVENTS:
May & September - Women's Weekends 877/644-9001, web: www.russianriverwomensweek-ends.com.

July - Lazy Bear Weekend, thousands of bears take over the River, web: www.lazybearweek-end.com.

August - Sundance, web: www.guspresents.com. The circuit comes to the River.

September - Jazz Festival, web: www.jazzontheriver.com.

CITY INFO:
Russian River Chamber of Commerce & Visitors Center 877/644-9001, web: www.russianriver.com.

ATTRACTIONS:
Armstrong Redwood State Park.
Bodega Bay.
Mudbaths of Calistoga.
Wineries of Napa and Sonoma Counties.

BEST VIEW:
Anywhere in Armstrong Woods, the Napa Wine Country, and on the ride along the picture-postcard-perfect coast on Highway 1.

WEATHER:
Summer days are sunny and warm (80°s-90°s) but usually begin with a dense fog. Winter days have the same pattern but are a lot cooler and wetter. Winter nights can be very damp and chilly (low 40°s).

TRANSIT:
Bill's Taxi Service 707/869-2177. As far as public transit goes, this area is easiest to reach by car.

Tim & Tony's Treehouse 707/887–9531, 888/887–9531 • gay/ straight • studio cottage • swimming • hot tub • sauna • nudity ok • nonsmoking • gay-owned • $145+

Village Inn & Restaurant 20822 River Blvd, Monte Rio 707/865–2304, 800/303–2303 • gay/ straight • historic inn • nonsmoking • also restaurant & full bar • wheelchair access • gay-owned • $85-185

Wildwood Retreat Old Cazadero Rd (off River Rd), Guerneville 707/632–5321 • gay/ straight • facilities are for groups of 20 or more • swimming • nonsmoking • $110 + 15% (meals included)

BARS

Liquid Sky 16225 Main St (at Armstrong Woods Rd), Guerneville 707/869–9910 • 5pm-2am, 1pm-2am wknds • lesbians/ gay men • neighborhood bar • theme nights • DJ Th-Sun • wheelchair access

Mc T's Bullpen 16246 1st St (at Church), Guerneville 707/869–3377 • 8am-2am • gay/ straight • sports bar • patio • wheelchair access

The Pink Elephant 9895 Main St, Monte Rio 707/865–0500 • 11am-2am • gay-friendly • neighborhood bar • live music wknds

Rainbow Cattle Co 16220 Main St (at Armstrong Woods Rd), Guerneville 707/869–0206 • 6am-2am • gay/ straight • neighborhood bar

NIGHTCLUBS

Club Fab 16135 River Rd (at Armstrong Woods Rd, in the River Theater), Guerneville 707/869–5708 • 9pm-2am, till 4am Sat, 4pm-close Sun, clsd Mon-Wed • popular • mostly gay men • dancing/DJ • drag shows

CAFES

Coffee Bazaar 14045 Armstrong Woods Rd (at River Rd), Guerneville 707/869–9706 • 6am-8pm • cafe • soups • salads • sandwiches • wireless internet

RESTAURANTS

Applewood 13555 Hwy 116 (at Applewood Inn), Guerneville 707/869–9093, 800/555–8509 • gourmet meals in the heart of the redwoods • wheelchair access • gay-owned • $20+

Cape Fear Cafe 25191 Main St, Duncans Mills 707/865–9246 • 9am-9pm, clsd 3pm-5pm

Chez Marie 6675 Front St (Hwy 116), Forestville 707/887–7503 • dinner from 6pm, clsd Mon-Tue • lesbian-owned

Flavors Unlimited 16450 Main St/ River Rd, Guerneville 707/869–0425 • hours vary • custom-blended ice cream

Guerneville Grill 16390 4th St (at Triple R Resort), Guerneville 707/869–0691 • lesbians/ gay men • American • some BBQ • some veggie • full bar • patio • wheelchair access

Mom's Apple Pie 4550 Gravenstein Hwy N, Sebastopol 707/823–8330 • pie worth stopping for on your way to & from Russian River!

River Inn Restaurant 16141 Main St, Guerneville 707/869–0481 • seasonal hours • local favorite • wheelchair access

Underwood Bar & Bistro 9113 Graton Rd, Graton 707/823–7023 • lunch & dinner, clsd Mon

Willow Wood Market Cafe 9020 Graton Rd, Graton 707/823–0233 • 8am-9pm, from 9am Sat, brunch 9am-3pm Sun

BOOKSTORES

River Reader 16355 Main St (at Mill), Guerneville 707/869–2240 • 10am-6pm, till 5pm Sun (extended summer hours) • wheelchair access

RETAIL SHOPS

Guerneville 5&10 16252 Main St, Guerneville 707/869–3404 • 10am-6pm • old-fashioned five & dime • lesbian-owned

Touch of Greene 16377 B Main St, Guerneville 707/869–3180 • 10am-6pm, till 5pm Sun • bath & body shop • massage • lesbian-owned

Up the River 16212 Main St (at Armstrong Woods Rd), Guerneville 707/869–3167 • cards • gifts • T-shirts

PUBLICATIONS

We the People Santa Rosa 707/581–1809 • LGBT newspaper for Sonoma County

SPIRITUAL GROUPS

MCC of the Redwood Empire 16219 First Street (at The Redwood Lodge, Odd Fellows Hall), Guerneville 707/869–9882 • 10am Sun

Sacramento

INFO LINES & SERVICES

Gay AA 3460 2nd Ave 916/454–1100 • 8pm Mon & Wed, 6pm Tue [WO]

Lambda Community Center 1927 L St 916/442–0185 • noon-9pm, till 6pm Sun • youth groups • discussion groups • referrals • library

ACCOMMODATIONS

Governor's Inn 210 Richards Blvd (at I-5) 916/448-7224, 800/999-6689 • gay-friendly • pool • hot tub • internet • nonsmoking

Inn at Parkside 2116 6th St (at U St) 916/658-1818, 800/995-7275 • B&B inn • gay/ straight • full brkfst • jacuzzi • wheelchair access • gay-owned • $179-329

Verona Village River Resort 6985 Garden Hwy, Nicolaus 530/656-1321 • lesbians/ gay men • trailers for rent • full bar • restaurant • store • marina • RV space $18, tent space $12

BARS

The Depot 2001 K St 916/441-6823 • 4pm-2am, till 4am Fri-Sat, from 2pm wknds • popular • mostly gay men • neighborhood bar • transgender-friendly • live shows • strippers • videos • wheelchair access

NIGHTCLUBS

Club 21 1119 21st St (btwn K & L Sts) 916/443-1537 • 9pm-2am Wed-Sun • gay/straight • dancing/DJ • women's night Fri • multiracial clientele • also Isabella's Mexican/ Italian restaurant • men's night Wed & Sun • videos • lesbian-owned

Faces 2000 K St (at 20th St) 916/448-7798 • 4pm-2am • popular • lesbians/ gay men • dancing/DJ • country/ western Fri-Sat • transgender-friendly • strippers Th • karaoke • videos • patio • wheelchair access

RESTAURANTS

Hamburger Mary's 1630 J St (at 17th) 916/441-4340 • 11am-10pm • full bar • karaoke

Hukilau Island Grill 1501 16th St 916/444-5850 • lunch & dinner, brunch wknds • Hawaiian • full bar • wheelchair access

Jack's Urban Eats 1230 20th St (at Capitol Ave) 916/444-0307 • 11am-8pm, till 9pm Wed-Sat, from 5pm wknds • also at 2535 Fair Oaks Blvd, 916/481-5225

Paesano's Pizzeria 1806 Capitol Ave (at 18th) 916/447-8646 • 11:30am-9:30pm • funky artwork • patio

Rick's Dessert Diner 2322 K St (btwn 23rd & 24th) 916/444-0969 • 10am-11pm, till 1am wknds • coffee & dessert

Thai Palace 3262 J St (33rd St) 916/447-5353 • lunch & dinner, clsd Sun

Zocalo 1801 Capitol Ave (at 18th St) 916/441-0303 • 11am-10pm • Mexican • full bar

ENTERTAINMENT & RECREATION

Lambda Players 2791 24th St (near Broadway) 916/444-8229 • LGBT theater company

Lavender Library, Archives & Cultural Exchange of Sacramento 1414 21st St (btwn N & O Sts) 916/492-0558 • 7pm-9pm Th, 6pm-8pm Fri, noon-6pm wknds, clsd Mon-Wed

PUBLICATIONS

MGW (Mom Guess What) 916/441-6397 • bi-monthly glossy magazine • women-owned

Outword News Magazine 916/329-9280 • statewide LGBT newspaper w/ N & S CA editions

SPIRITUAL GROUPS

Integrity Northern California 916/446-2513, 916/394-1715 • LGBT Episcopalians • call for location

Lutheran Church of our Redeemer 4641 Marconi Ave (at Mission) 916/483-5691 • 10:15am Sun

EROTICA

G Spot 2009 K St (at 20th) 916/441-3200 • 10am-midnight, till 2am Fri-Sat • gay-owned

Goldie's I 201 N 12th St (at North B St) 916/447-5860 • 24hrs • also 2138 Del Paso Blvd, 916/922-0103

Goldie's Outlet 1800 Del Paso Blvd (at Oxford Blvd) 916/920-8659

Kiss-N-Tell 4201 Sunrise Blvd (at Fair Oaks) 916/966-5477

L'Amour Shoppe 2531 Broadway (at 26th) 916/736-3467 • 9am-1am

Suzie's Adult Superstores 4177 Florin Rd 916/429-8480 • 24hrs

Suzie's Adult Superstores 5138 Auburn Blvd 916/332-1051 • 24hrs

Salinas

SPIRITUAL GROUPS

St Paul's Episcopal Church 1071 Pajaro St (at San Miguel Ave) 831/424-7331 • 8am,10am, noon (Spanish) Sun

EROTICA

L'Amour Shoppe 325 E Alisal St 831/758-9600

San Bernardino

see also Riverside

INFO LINES & SERVICES

AA Gay/ Lesbian 909/825–4700 •
numerous meetings for Inland Empire

Gay/ Lesbian Community Center
909/882–4488 • 6:30pm-10pm • raps •
counseling • library

NIGHTCLUBS

The Lark 917 Inland Center Dr 909/884–8770
• noon-2am • lesbians/ gay men • DJ Fri-Sat
• live shows • karaoke Tue & Th • country/
western Fri • beer bust & CW dance lessons
Sun • huge patio • wheelchair access

ENTERTAINMENT & RECREATION

Camp Real Girls 818/985–8885 • women's
weekends in Southern California • see ad in
back tour section (Great Outdoor Adventures)

SPIRITUAL GROUPS

**First Congregational United Church of
Christ** 3041 N Sierra Wy 909/886–4911 •
10am Sun

Heartland Christian Fellowship UFMCC
2286 N Leroy St, Ste 1-2 951/318–1080 •
10:15am Sun

EROTICA

Bearfacts Book Store 1434 E Baseline
909/885–9176 • 24hrs

San Clemente

see Orange County

San Diego

INFO LINES & SERVICES

AA Gay/ Lesbian 1730 Monroe Ave (at The
Live and Let Live Alano Club) 619/298–8008
• 10:30am-10pm, from 8:30am wknds •
various LGBT meetings

San Diego LGBT Community Center
3909 Centre St (at University) 619/692–2077 •
9am-10pm, till 7pm Sat, clsd Sun

Women's Resource Center (WRC)
3909 Centre St (at University (in SD LGBT
Community Center)) 619/692–2077 • variety
of resources, health care referrals, social
services & community activities

ACCOMMODATIONS

Balboa Park Inn 3402 Park Blvd (at Upas)
619/298–0823, 800/938–8181 • gay-friendly •
charming guesthouse in the heart of San
Diego • theme rooms • $99-219

Beach Area B&B/ Elsbree House 5054
Narragansett Ave (at Sunset Cliffs Blvd)
619/226–4133, 800/607–4133 • gay-friendly •
near beach • nonsmoking • $95-135 (B&B) •
$1250-1600/ week (condo)

The Beach Place 2158 Sunset Cliffs Blvd (at
Muir) 619/225–0746 • lesbians/ gay men •
hot tub • nudity • kids ok • pets by
arrangement • 4 blocks from beach • gay-
owned • $59-69/ night • $350-400/ week

Best Western Blue Sea Lodge 707 Pacific
Beach Dr 858/488–4700, 800/258–3732 • gay-
friendly • beachfront hotel • swimming • hot
tub • kids ok • wheelchair access • $129-289

The Bristol Hotel 1055 First St
619/232–6141, 800/662–4477 • gay/ straight •
hotel • high-speed internet • kids/ pets ok •
restaurant • great collection of pop art •
wheelchair access • $119-239

Casa Granada 1720 Granada Ave (at Date
St) 619/501–5911, 866/524–2312 • gay/
straight • 3 separate units • near beach • kids
ok • nonsmoking • gay-owned • $99-199

Dimitri's Guesthouse 931 21st St (at
Broadway) 619/238–5547 • gay/ straight •
swimming • hot tub • nudity ok at pool •
nonsmoking • overlooks downtown •
wheelchair access • $110-125

Handlery Hotel & Resort 950 Hotel Circle
N 619/298–0511, 800/676–6567 • gay-friendly
• centrally located in Mission Valley •
swimming • hot tub • nonsmoking • kids ok •
wheelchair access • $89-169

Harbor House Resort 642 W Hawthorn
(btwn Columbia & State) 619/338–9966,
888/338–9966 • lesbians/ gay men • restored
1914 European-style resort • outdoor jacuzzis
• nonsmoking • also Moby Dick's bar • gay-
owned

Hillcrest Inn Hotel 3754 5th Ave (btwn
Robinson & Pennsylvania) 619/293–7078,
800/258–2280 • lesbians/ gay men • int'l hotel
in the heart of Hillcrest • hot tub • wheelchair
access • $69-149

Inn Suites Hotel 2223 El Cajon Blvd (btwn
Louisiana & Mississippi) 619/296–2101,
877/343–4648 • gay-friendly • swimming •
kids ok • also restaurant • wheelchair access •
$99-159

Keating House 2331 2nd Ave (at Juniper)
619/239–8585, 800/995–8644 • gay-friendly •
graceful Victorian on Bankers Hill • full brkfst •
nonsmoking • kids ok • straight & gay-owned
• $95-155

Park Manor Suites 525 Spruce St (btwn 5th & 6th) 619/291–0999, 800/874–2649 • gay-friendly • 1926 hotel • kids ok • $99-229

Villa Serena B&B 2164 Rosecrans St (btwn Udall & Voltaire) 619/224–1451, 866/559–2728 • gay-friendly • Italian villa in residential neighborhood • full brkfst • swimming • hot tub • nonsmoking • $110-380

W San Diego 421 W B St 619/231–8220, 877/WHOTELS (RESERVATIONS ONLY) • gay-friendly • restaurant • rooftop bar • swimming • wheelchair access • $249-379

BARS

The Brass Rail 3796 5th Ave (at Robinson) 619/298–2233 • 2pm-2am • lesbians/ gay men • dancing/DJ • Latin night Th & Sat • wheelchair access

Chee Chee Club 929 Broadway (at 9th Ave) 619/234–4404 • 6am-2am • mostly gay men • neighborhood bar • transgender-friendly • everyone welcome

The Flame 3780 Park Blvd (at University) 619/295–4163 • popular • mostly gay men Fri for Spin • mostly women Sat for Candy • dancing/DJ • patio

San Diego

WHERE THE GIRLS ARE:
Lesbians tend to live near Normal Heights, in the northwest part of the city. But for partying, women go to the bars near I-5, or to Hillcrest to hang out with the boys.

LGBT PRIDE:
July. 619/297-7683, web: www.sdpride.org.

CITY INFO:
San Diego Visitors Bureau 619/220-8601, web: www.sandiego.com.

ATTRACTIONS:
Fleet Space Center 619/238–1233, web: www.rhfleet.org.
Gaslamp Quarter, web: www.gaslamp.org.
Mingei Int'l Museum 619/239–0003, web: www.mingei.org.
The Old Globe Theatre 619/234–5623 (box office), web: www.oldglobe.org.
San Diego Museum of Art 619/232–7931, web: www.sdmart.org.
San Diego Wild Animal Park 760/747-8702, web: sandiego-zoo.org/wap/visitor_info.html.
San Diego Zoo 619/231-1515, web: www.sandiegozoo.org.
Sea World 800/257-4268, web: www.seaworld.com.

BEST VIEW:
Cabrillo National Monument on Point Loma or from a harbor cruise.

WEATHER:
San Diego is sunny and warm (upper 60°s-70°s) year-round, with higher humidity in the summer.

TRANSIT:
Yellow Cab 619/234-6161.
San Diego Cab 619/226-8294.
Silver Cab/Co-op 619/280-5555.
Cloud Nine Shuttle 800/974-8885.
San Diego Transit System 619/233-3004, 800/266-6883 (North County), web: www.sdcommute.com. San Diego Trolley (through downtown or to Tijuana).

Kickers 308 University Ave (at 3rd Ave) 619/491-0400 • 7pm-2am • popular • mostly gay men • dancing/DJ • theme nights • Latin Mon • karaoke Wed • country/ western Th-Sat • brunch Sun & T-dance from 5pm • wheelchair access

No 1 Fifth Ave (no sign) 3845 5th Ave (at University) 619/299-1911 • noon-2am • mostly gay men • neighborhood bar • videos nights • patio

Redwing Bar & Grill 4012 30th St (at Lincoln, North Park) 619/281-8700 • 10am-1am, till 2am Fri-Sat • mostly gay men • neighborhood bar • patio

Shooterz/ Club Odyssey 3815 30th St (at University) 619/574-0744 • 3pm-2am, till 4am Th-Sat • gay/ straight • sports bar • videos • dance club (from 9:30pm)

Reply **Forward** **Delete**

Date: Dec 9, 2005 13:01:44
From: Girl-on-the-Go
To: Editor@Damron.com
Subject: San Diego

>San Diego is a West Coast paradise. This city sprawls from the bays and beaches of the Pacific to the foothills of the desert mountains. The days are always warm, and the nights can be refreshingly cool.
>Stay at one of the city's lesbian-friendly inns, like women-owned **Dmitri's Guesthouse**. During the days, follow the tourist circuit which includes the world-famous San Diego Zoo and Sea World. Call the Visitor's Center for a brochure on all the sights.
>For a friendly neighborhood lesbian bar to take shelter in after a day of sightseeing, stop by lesbian-owned **Patti's Front Office**. Once the sun sets, you're ready to tour the lesbian circuit. Where to begin? Look for various ladies dance nights and various clubs like **The Flame** or **SRO Lounge** or check out **Six Degrees**, San Diego's only full-time women's bar. If you're a country/western gal, **Kickers** is a popular place to two-step with those boot-scooting boys.
>In mid-August, check out the Hillcrest Street Fair, popular with the many lesbian and gay residents of the happening Hillcrest district. (Be warned though: because of its location between super-freeways and construction, rush-hour traffic has been known to crawl through Hillcrest.)
>If you're feeling adventurous, cruise by the **Crypt** for some sex toys or a piercing or two. If you just want to network, stop in at the **Community Center** or pick up one of the LGBT papers at **Obelisk the Bookstore** for all the latest information about San Diego's lesbian community.

Six Degrees 3175 India St (enter on Spruce St) **619/296-6789** • 4pm-2am, from 2pm wknds • popular • mostly women • dancing/DJ • live shows • karaoke Wed & Sun • patio w/ smoking permitted • wheelchair access • women-owned/ run

SRO Lounge 1807 5th Ave (btwn Elm & Fir) **619/232-1886** • 10am-2am • mostly gay men • cocktail lounge • older, professional crowd • Ladies Night Out 1st, 3rd & 5th Sat • transgender-friendly

NIGHTCLUBS

Bacchus House 3054 University Ave (at 30th St) **619/299-2032** • 4pm-2am • mostly gay men • dancing/DJ • theme nights • Latin nights Wed & Sun • transgender-friendly • drag shows • strippers • videos • young crowd • wheelchair access • gay-owned

Club Montage 2028 Hancock St (at Washington Ave) **619/294-9590** • 9pm-2am Fri, till 4am Sat • popular • mostly gay men • dancing/DJ • live shows • videos • rooftop patio & sushi bar • wheelchair access • cover

CAFES

The Big Kitchen 3003 Grape St (at 30th) **619/234-5789** • 7am-2pm, 7:30am-3pm wknds • some veggie • wheelchair access • women-owned/ run • $5-10

Claire de Lune 2906 University Ave **619/688-9845** • 5am-midnight

David's Coffeehouse 3766 5th Ave (at Robinson) **619/296-4173** • 7am-11pm, till midnight wknds • lesbians/ gay men • coffeehouse for positive people & their friends • patio

Espresso Roma UCSD Price Center #76 (at Voight), La Jolla **858/450-2141** • 7am-midnight, hours vary wknds

Extraordinary Desserts 2929 5th Ave **619/294-2132** • 8:30am-11pm, till midnight Fri, 10am-midnight Sat, 10am-11pm Sun • the name says it all

Gelato Vero Caffee 3753 India St **619/295-9269** • 6am-midnight, 7am-1am wknds • great desserts (yes, the gelato is truly delicious) as well as coffee

Korova Coffee Bar 4496 Park Blvd (University Heights) **619/260-1917** • 6:30am-10pm, hours vary wknds

Urban Grind 3797 Park Blvd (at University) **619/299-4763** • 7am-midnight • popular • gay-owned

RESTAURANTS

The Abbey Café 127 E University Ave (in Hillcrest) **619/692-0311** • 5:30pm-10pm, 10am-8pm Sun • lesbians/ gay men • also coffee & tea house • specialty desserts • beer & wine • gay-owned

Adams Avenue Grill 2201 Adams Ave (at Mississippi) **619/298-8440** • lunch, dinner, brunch wknds • bistro • plenty veggie • beer/ wine • wheelchair access • gay-owned

Aqua Blu 734 5th Ave (near G St) **619/544-6456** • 11:30am-11pm,till midnight Fri-Sat • "fusion seafood" • upscale • wheelchair access

Bai Yook Thai 1260 University Ave **619/296-2700** • lunch & dinner, dinner only Sun

Baja Betty's 1421 University Ave (at Normal St) **619/269-8510** • 11am-midnight, till 1am Fri-Sat • lesbians/ gay men • Mexican • some veggie • also tequila bar • patio • wheelchair access • $5-10

Brian's American Eatery 1451 Washington St **619/296-8268** • 6am-10pm, 24hrs Fri-Sat • beer/ wine

Cafe Eleven 1440 University Ave (at Normal) **619/260-8023** • 5pm-close, opens 4pm Sun, clsd Mon • country French • some veggie • patio • wheelchair access • $15-20

California Cuisine 1027 University Ave (at 10th Ave) **619/543-0790** • lunch & dinner, clsd Mon • some veggie • also bar • wheelchair access • women-owned/ run • $17-21

Celadon 540 University Ave (at 6th) **619/297-8424** • lunch & dinner, upscale Thai

City Deli 535 University Ave (at 6th Ave) **619/295-2747** • 7am-midnight, till 2am wknds • NY deli • plenty veggie • full bar

The Cottage 7702 Fay (at Klein), La Jolla **858/454-8409** • 7:30am-3pm • fresh-baked items

Crest Cafe 425 Robinson (btwn 4th & 5th) **619/295-2510** • 7am-midnight • some veggie • wheelchair access • $5-10

Green Tomato 4090 Adams Ave **619/283-7546** • lunch Mon-Fri, dinner nightly, Sun brunch • gourmet meats, seafood & pastas • also full bar

Gulf Coast Grill 4130 Park Blvd **619/295-2244** • lunch & dinner, also Sun brkfst • New Orleans-inspired menu

Hamburger Mary's 308 University Ave (at 3rd) **619/491-0400** • 9am-2am (kitchen till 11pm) • some veggie • full bar • patio • wheelchair access • $5-10

Hash House A Go Go 3628 5th Ave **619/298-4646** • 7:30am-9pm, till 10pm Fri-Sat • great brkfst

Inn at the Park 525 Spruce St (btwn 5th & 6th, at Park Manor Suites) **619/296-0057** • popular • dinner nightly • piano bar

Jimmy Carter's Mexican Cafe 807 W Washington St (Mission Hills) **619/296-6952** • 11pm-9pm, till 10pm Fri, from 9am wknds for brunch

Kemo Sabe 3958 5th Ave **619/220-6802** • int'l • lesbian celeb chef Deborah Scott • reservations required

Liaison 2202 4th Ave (at Ivy) **619/234-5540** • dinner only, clsd Sun & Mon • French country • wheelchair access • $18-24 (prix fixe)

Lips 2770 5th Ave (at Nutmeg & Olive) **619/295-7900** • 5pm-close, Sun gospel brunch, clsd Mon • "the ultimate in drag dining" • Bitchy Bingo Wed • celeb impersonation Th • DJ wknds

The Lumberjack Grille 3949 Ohio St (North Park) **619/294-3804** • 7am-9pm • hearty food for your inner lumberjack • beer/wine

Martinis Above Fourth 3940 4th Ave, Ste 200 (btwn Washington & University) **619/400-4500** • 3pm-11pm, till midnight Fri-Sat, 11am-11pm Sun (brunch), clsd Mon • lesbians/gay men • also cabaret lounge • indoor & outdoor bar • gay-owned

The Mission 3795 Mission Blvd (at San Jose), Mission Beach **858/488-9060** • lesbians/gay men • brkfst & lunch • also 2801 University Ave in North Park, 619/220-8992

The Prado 1549 El Prado (in Balboa Park) **619/557-9441** • Latin/Italian fusion

Rice Jones 3687 5th Ave **619/291-1887** • from 11am • hip Vietnamese bistro • some veggie • full bar • patio

Roberto's 3202 Mission Blvd **858/488-1610** • the best rolled tacos & guacamole, multiple locations—imitators, even drive-thru versions—throughout San Diego

Rudford's 2900 El Cajon Blvd (at Kansas St) **619/282-8423** • 24hrs • popular homestyle cooking since 1949

South Park Bar & Grill 1946 Fern St (at Grape St) **619/696-0096** • dinner, clsd Mon • "California comfort food"

Taste of Szechuan 670 University Ave **619/298-1638** • 11am-midnight, till 1am Fri-Sat, noon-10pm Sun • Chinese

ENTERTAINMENT & RECREATION

Diversionary Theatre 4545 Park Blvd #101 (at Madison) **619/220-0097 (BOX OFFICE #), 619/220-6830** • LGBT theater

Sapphic Cinema 3909 Centre St (at University (in SD LGBT Community Center)) **619/692-2077** • 7pm Fri • monthly movie night "by, for & about Lesbian, Bisexual, Transgender & Feminist women"

BOOKSTORES

Groundworks Books UCSD Student Center 0323 (at Gilman Dr), La Jolla **858/452-9625** • 9am-7pm, till 6pm Tue, till 5pm Fri-Sat, clsd Sun • alternative • LGBT section • wheelchair access

▲ **Obelisk the Bookstore** 1029 University Ave (at 10th) **619/297-4171** • 10am-10pm, till 11pm Fri-Sat, 11am-10pm Sun • LGBT • wheelchair access

Traveler's Depot 1655 Garnet Ave (in Pacific Beach) **858/483-1421** • 10am-6pm, till 5pm Sat, from noon Sun • travel guides, maps, luggage & more

RETAIL SHOPS

Auntie Helen's 4028 30th St (at Lincoln) **619/584-8438** • 10am-4:30pm, clsd Sun-Mon • thrift shop benefits PWAs • wheelchair access

Babette Schwartz 421 University Ave (at 5th Ave) **619/220-7048** • 11am-9pm • campy novelties & gifts • gay-owned

Flesh Skin Grafix 1155 Palm Ave, Imperial Beach **619/424-8983** • tattoos • piercing

Jewelry by Poncé 1417 S Coast Hwy, Laguna Beach **949/497-4154, 800/969-RING** • 11am-7pm Wed-Sat, till 5pm Sun, clsd Mon-Tue • LGBT commitment rings & other jewelry • see ad in back mail order section

MacLeo Sexy Leather 3750 30th St (in North Park) **619/688-0504** • noon-8pm, by appt only Sun, clsd Mon • custom-made leather fashions

Mastodon 4638 Mission Blvd (at Emerald), Pacific Beach **858/272-1188** • body piercing

Rainbow Road 141 University Ave (at 3rd) **619/296-8222** • 10am-10pm • gay gifts

PUBLICATIONS

Buzz 3314 4th Ave **619/291-6690** • bi-weekly • news, entertainment & listings • covers San Diego & Palm Springs

▲ **Gay/ Lesbian Times** 1730 Monroe Ave, Ste A **619/299-6397, 800/438-8786** • LGBT newsmagazine

The Lavender Lens **619/291-8223** • "California's biweekly news & lifestyle magazine for lesbians & friends"

▲ **Lesbian News (LN)** **800/995-8838, 800/458-9888** • nat'l w/ strong coverage of southern CA • see ad front color section

Update **619/299-0500**

SPIRITUAL GROUPS

Dignity 4190 Front St (at First Unitarian Universalist Church in Hillcrest) **619/645-8240** • 6pm Sun, potlucks 3rd Sun after Mass

Evangelicals Concerned—San Diego PO Box 335656, 92163-3565 **619/281-6256** • worship group for lesbians & gays who are "reconciling our sexual orientation & our faith in Jesus Christ"

First Unitarian Universalist Church 4190 Front St (at Arbor) **619/298-9978** • 10am (July-Aug) • 9am & 11am (Sept-June)

MCC 3909 Centre St (in the SD LGBT Center) **619/521-2222** • 9am, 11am

New Creation United Church of Christ 4070 Jackdaw St (chapel of Mission Hills United Church of Christ) **619/293-0706** • 10am Sun

St Paul's Episcopal Cathedral 2728 Sixth Ave **619/298-7261** • Holy Eucharist 8am & 10:30am Sun

Temple Adat Shalom 15905 Pomerado Rd, Poway **858/451-1200** • Shabbat services Fri night & Saturday morning • Reform Jewish Congregation in North County Inland of San Diego

GYMS & HEALTH CLUBS

Evolution Fitness 526 Market St (at 6th Ave, near Horton Plaza) **619/231-9393** • 5am-10pm, till 8pm Fri, 8am-6pm wknds • gym & classes

Frog's Athletic Club 901 Hotel Circle S (at Washington), Mission Valley **619/291-3500**

PowerHouse Gym 734 University Ave #D (at 7th Ave) **619/296-7878** • 5am-11pm, till 10pm Fri, 8am-8pm wknds

EROTICA

The Crypt 3847 Park Blvd (at University) **619/692-9499** • 11am-11pm, till midnight Fri-Sat, till 9pm Sun

F St Bookstore 2004 University Ave (at Florida) **619/298-2644** • 24hrs

F St Bookstore 4650 Border Village (at San Ysidro Blvd), San Ysidro **619/690-2070** • 8am-midnight

F St Bookstore 751 4th Ave (at F St) **619/236-0841** • 24hrs

F St Bookstore 7865 Balboa Ave (btwn Mercury & Convoy Sts), Kearny Mesa **858/292-8083** • 24hrs

F St Bookstore 7998 Miramar Rd (at Dowdy) **858/549-8014** • 24hrs

The North Park Adult Video 4094 30th St (at Polk Ave) **619/284-4724** • 7am-2am, till 4am Fri-Sat

Ringold Alley 3408 30th St (at Upas St) **619/295-7464** • noon-10pm, till 2am Fri-Sat, till 5pm Sun • leather • fetish & accessories • gay-owned

Romantix Midnight Videos 1407 University Ave (at Richmond) **619/299-7186** • 24hrs, Hillcrest location

Romantix Midnight Videos 3606 Midway Dr (at Kemper) **619/222-9973** • 24hrs

Romantix Midnight Videos 4792 El Cajon Blvd (at 48th) **619/582-1997** • 24hrs

Romantix Midnight Videos 836 5th Ave (btwn E & F Sts) **619/237-9056** • 24hrs

Sensual Delights 1220 University Ave (at Vermont) **619/291-7400** • 11am-10pm, till 2am Fri-Sat, noon-8pm Sun • safer sex gifts for women & men • wheelchair access

SAN FRANCISCO

San Francisco is divided into 7 geographical areas:
SF—Overview
SF—Castro & Noe Valley
SF—South of Market
SF—Polk Street Area
SF—Downtown & North Beach
SF—Mission District
SF—Haight, Fillmore, Hayes Valley

SF—Overview

INFO LINES & SERVICES

AA Gay/ Lesbian 1821 Sacramento St **415/674-1821**

The Center for Sex & Culture 398 11th St (at Harrison) **415/255-1155** • very queer-friendly classes, workshops, gatherings, events, readings & more

GLBT Hotline of San Francisco **415/355-0999** • 5pm-9pm Mon-Fri • peer-counseling • info

LYRIC (Lavender Youth Recreation/ Information Center) 127 Collingwood (btwn 18th & 19th) **415/703-6150, 800/969-6884 (NATIONWIDE) & 246-7743 (CA ONLY)** • support & social groups • also Talkline 6:30pm-9:30pm Mon-Sat, peer-run support line for LGBT youth under 24, at 415/863-3636 (in SF) or 800/246-7743 (in CA) or 800/969-6884 (nationwide)

The San Francisco LGBT Community Center 1800 Market St (at Octavia) **415/865-5555** • noon-10pm, from 9am Sat, clsd Sun • includes cybercenter • meeting rooms • cafe • classes • child care & more

Women's Building 3543 18th St (btwn Valencia & Guerrero) **415/431-1180** • 9am-5pm Mon-Fri, till 6 Sat • space for many women's organizations • social/ support groups • housing & job listings • beautiful murals

ENTERTAINMENT & RECREATION

Beach Blanket Babylon 678 Green St (at Powell, in Club Fugazi) **415/421-4222** • the USA's longest running musical revue & wigs that must be seen to be believed • gay-friendly • very popular • also restaurant & full bar

Brava! 2781 24th St (btwn York & Hampshire) **415/641-7657, 415/647-2822** • culturally diverse performances by women • wheelchair access

Castro Theatre 429 Castro (at Market) **415/621-6120** • art house cinema • many LGBT & cult classics • live organ evenings

Cruisin' the Castro **415/255-1821** • 5-star walking lesbian/ gay history tour of the Castro

Femina Potens 465 S Van Ness (at 16th) **415/217-9340** • nonprofit art gallery & performance space promoting women & transfolk in the arts

▲ **Frameline** **415/703-8650** • LGBT media arts foundation • sponsors annual SF Int'l Lesbian/ Gay Film Festival in June • see Film Festival Calendar in back Events section

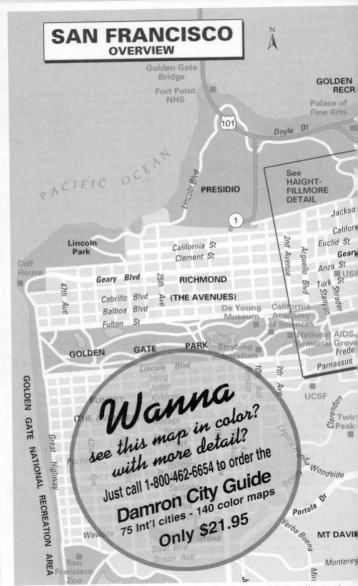

Reply **Forward** **Delete**

Date: Dec 15, 2005 12:26:42
From: Girl-on-the-Go
To: Editor@Damron.com
Subject: San Francisco

>San Francisco may be a top tourist destination because of its cable cars, beatniks, Victorians, and the Haight-Ashbury district, but we know what really makes it shine: its legendary lesbian, gay, bisexual, and transgender community. So unless standing in long lines for a little kitsch is your thing, skip Fisherman's Wharf and the cable cars, and head for San Francisco's queerest and quirkiest neighborhoods: the Mission, the Castro, Noe Valley, and South of Market (SoMa).

>Any lesbian walking along Valencia between Market Street and 24th Street can't miss all the hot women of all sizes and colors that live in this neighborhood. Valencia Street, the street that was put on the lesbian radar screen by Michelle Tea's amazing book *Valencia*, borders the upscale, predominantly gay Castro area, and the Mission, San Francisco's largest Latino neighborhood. This intersection of cultures results in a truly San Franciscan mix of punk dykes, dykes of color, lesbian-feminists, working-class straights, and funky artists. Many upscale eateries have sprung up, and more fancy cars line the streets, but the original flavor of this spicy neighborhood is still pungent.

>You'll get a taste of this yourself if you pick up a famous "San Francisco Mission-Style Burrito" (as they're advertised in New York these days) at one of the many cheap and delicious taquerias in the area. Walk it off afterward with a visit to the **Women's Building** on 18th Street. You can't miss the stunning murals. After that, rush over to 17th Street to the new (and larger) location of **Good Vibrations**, the fabulous women's sex toy store, before they close at 7pm.

>You might have heard the legends about the Mission's one-time women's bar, Amelia's. Sadly, it's long gone. Instead, head for its hip little sister, the **Lexington Club**, a popular dyke hangout. Another must for lesbians along Valencia Street is **Osento**, the women's bathhouse. Just off Valencia on 16th is the **Roxie**, a dyke-friendly repertory cinema.

Reply   Forward   Delete

>The Mission also hosts lots of fun queer performance at places like **Build** and **Brava!** and **Luna Sea**—check the biweekly **Bay Times** calendar. **Femina Potens** is the new kid on the block, offering women- and trans-oriented art and performance.

>You'll also find lots of lesbians in nearby Noe Valley, though this area tends to be a couples haven for professional women and lesbian moms. You'll enjoy an afternoon in one or all of the many quirky shops and cafes along upper 24th Street.

>If you cruise the Castro, you'll be surprised how many sisters—ranging from executives to queer chicks—you'll see walking the streets of what was the "Boys' Town" of the 1970s. Drop in at **A Different Light**, the LGBT bookstore, or **The Cafe** for a game of pool or girl-watching from the balcony. Thursday nights at **Mecca** you'll find lovely ladies three deep at the swank bar. The Castro also boasts three great 24-hour diners—**Bagdad Cafe**, **Sparky's**, and **Orphan Andy's**. For LGBT-themed films, don't miss an evening at the **Castro Theatre**.

>You still have energy? Wanna dance? SoMa (South of Market) is home to many of the city's dance clubs and live-music venues. Call the club hotlines to see if tonight's the night for one of the many monthly parties like **In Bed With Fairy Butch** or **Cream**. **The Stud** hosts several popular women's nights, and **Mango** is a seasonal hot spot for finding hot girls. Ladies of the Eighties will dig the vibe at the monthly **Respect** party.

>While you're south of Market, you might also want to check out the women's S/M scene in this kinky city: **Stormy Leather** and **Madame S** are two of our favorite women-oriented fetish stores. And if you're inspired to get that piercing you've been thinking about, visit one of the queer-friendly piercing parlors in town—we like **Body Manipulations**, right between the Mission and the Castro on 16th Street at Guerrero. When it comes to tattoos, there's only **Black & Blue**.

>Finally, if you're a fan of Diane Di Prima, Anne Waldman, the late Allen Ginsberg, or other beatniks, **City Lights Bookstore** in North Beach is a required pilgrimage. Afterward, have a drink or an espresso at beatnik hangout Café Vesuvius, just across Jack Kerouac Alley from City Lights.

>Sound like a lot? They don't call it Mecca for nothing.

San Francisco

WHERE THE GIRLS ARE:

Younger, radical dykes call the Mission or the lower Haight home, while upwardly mobile couples stake out Bernal Heights and Noe Valley. Hip, moneyed dykes live in the Castro. The East Bay is home to lots of lesbian feminists, older lesbians, and lesbian moms (see East Bay listings).

LGBT PRIDE:

June. 415/864-3733, web: www.sfpride.org.

ANNUAL EVENTS:

June - San Francisco Int'l Lesbian/Gay Film Festival 415/703-8650, web: www.frameline.org.

July - Up Your Alley Fair 415/861-3247, web: folsomstreetevents.org. Local SM/leather street fair held in Dore Alley, South-of-Market.

August-September - Festival of Babes, web: www.festivalofthe-babes.com. Annual women's soccer tournament.

September - Folsom Street Fair 415/861-3247, web: folsom-streetevents.org. Huge SM/leather street fair, topping a week of kinky events.

September-MadCat Women's Int'l Film Festival 415/436-9523, web: www.madcatfilmfestival.org.

October - Castro Street Fair 415/285-8546, web: www.castrostreetfair.org. Arts and community groups street fair.

CITY INFO:

San Francisco Convention & Visitors Bureau 415/391-2000, web: www.sfvisitor.org.

BEST VIEW:

After a great Italian meal in North Beach, go to the top floor of the North Beach parking garage on Vallejo near Stockton, next to the police station. If you're in the Castro or the Mission, head for Dolores Park, at Dolores and 20th St. Other good views: Golden Gate Bridge, Kirby Cove (a park area to the left, just past the Golden Gate Bridge in Marin), Coit Tower, Twin Peaks.

WEATHER:

A beautiful summer comes at the end of September and lasts through October. Much of the city is cold and fogged-in June through September, though the Castro and Mission are usually sunny. The cold in winter is damp, so bring lots of layers. When there isn't a drought, it also rains in the winter months of November through February.

TRANSIT:

Yellow Cab 415/626-2345.
Luxor Cab 415/282-4141.
Quake City Shuttle 415/255-4899.
Muni 415/673-6864, web: www.sfmuni.org.
Bay Area Rapid Transit (BART) 650/992-2278, subway, web: www.bart.gov.

ATTRACTIONS:

Alcatraz, web: www.nps.gov/alcatraz.
Asian Art Museum 415/ 581-3500, www.asianart.org.
Cablecars.
Chinatown.
Coit Tower, web: www.coittower.org.
Exploratorium 415/561-0360, web: www.exploratorium.edu.
Fisherman's Wharf.
Golden Gate Park.
Haight & Ashbury Sts.
Japantown.
North Beach.
Mission San Francisco de Assisi.
SF Museum of Modern Art 415/357-4000, web: www.sfmoma.org.
Twin Peaks.

Did you know there is a NATIONAL memorial dedicated to all lives touched by AIDS, and it is right here in San Francisco's Golden Gate Park? For more information go to www.AIDSmemorial.org, or call 415-750-8340.

A place for remembrance and renewal

NATIONAL
A I D S
MEMORIAL
GROVE

THE NATIONAL AIDS MEMORIAL GROVE ENSURES
THAT THE GLOBAL TRAGEDY OF AIDS WILL NEVER BE FORGOTTEN.

The Intersection for the Arts 446 Valencia St (btwn 16th & 15th Sts) **415/626-2787, 415/626-3311 (BOX OFFICE)** • San Francisco's oldest alternative arts space (since 1965!) w/ plays, art exhibitions, live jazz, literary series, performance art & much more

Jon Sims Center for the Arts 1519 Mission St (at 11th) **415/554-0402** • LGBT performing arts organization • check local listings for events

K'vetch 491 Potrero (at Mariposa, at Sadie's Flying Elephant) **415/551-7988** • 8pm 1st Sun, San Francisco's coolest queer open mic

Local Tastes of the City Tours **415/665-0480, 888/358-8687** • 3-hour walking tours of culture & cuisine of San Francisco's most colorful neighborhoods, including North Beach, Chinatown & the Haight-Ashbury • ends w/ optional dinner • "We eat our way through San Francisco"

The Marsh 1062 Valencia (at 22nd St) **415/641-0235** • queer-positive theater

Monday Night Gay Comedy 1800 Market St (at LGBT Community Center) **415/541-5610** • 7:30pm every other Mon • popular • lesbians/ gay men • call for info • cover charge (sliding scale)

▲ **National AIDS Memorial Grove** Golden Gate Park (on corner of Middle Drive East & Bowling Green Dr) **415/750-8340, 888/294-7683** • located in a lush, historic dell in Golden Gate Park • guided tours available 9:30am-12:30pm every Th • wheelchair access

San Francisco City Hikes 620 59th St, Oakland 94609 **510/601-9207** • 3-hour hiking tours of San Francisco for groups of 5+ • $20/ person • "the best way to see the city" • gay-friendly • wheelchair access • lesbian-owned

Theatre Rhinoceros 2926 16th St (at S Van Ness) **415/861-5079** • LGBT theater

Victorian Home Walks **415/252-9485** • custom-tailored walking tours w/ San Francisco resident • gay-owned

What's Up! Events Hotline for Sistahs **510/835-6126** • for lesbians of African descent

Yerba Buena Center for the Arts 701 Mission St (at 3rd St) **415/978-2787 (BOX OFFICE)**, **415/978-2700 (ADMINISTRATIVE)** • annual season includes wide variety of contemporary dance, theater & music, also film theater & gallery

PUBLICATIONS

BAR (Bay Area Reporter) **415/861-5019** • the weekly LGBT newspaper

Odyssey Magazine **323/874-8788** • all the dish on SF's club scene

Outword News Magazine **415/437-2886** • statewide LGBT newspaper w/ N & S CA editions

San Francisco Bay Times **415/626-0260** • popular • a "must read" for Bay Area resources

SPIRITUAL GROUPS

Bay Area Pagan Assemblies **408/559-4242** • open rituals • call for info

Dignity San Francisco 1329 7th Ave (at Presbyterian church, btwn Irving & Judah) **415/681-2491** • 5:30pm Sun • LGBT Roman Catholic services

Glide Memorial United Methodist Church 330 Ellis (at Taylor) **415/674-6000** • an only-in-San-Francisco Sunday worship service in truly diverse congregation

Hartford Street Zen Center 57 Hartford St (btwn 17th & 18th Sts) **415/863-2507** • daily sittings 6am & 6pm Mon-Fri, 9:10am Sat & by appt

Q-Spirit **415/281-9377** • queer spirituality events & discussions

Reclaiming PO Box 14404, 94114 • pagan infoline & network • classes • newsletter

SF—Castro & Noe Valley

ACCOMMODATIONS

24 Henry & Village House 24 Henry St & 4080 18th St (btwn Sanchez & Noe) **415/864-5686, 800/900-5686** • B&B • mostly gay men • some shared baths • nonsmoking • one-bdrm apt also available • gay-owned • $65-119

Albion House Inn 135 Gough St (at Fell) **415/621-0896, 800/625-2466 OR 800/ 400-8295** • gay-friendly • full brkfst • nonsmoking • kids ok • $89-165

Beck's Motor Lodge 2222 Market St (at Sanchez) **415/621-8212, 800/955-2325** • gay-friendly • in the heart of the Castro • kids/pets ok • wheelchair access • $95-114

▲ **Belvedere House** 598 Belvedere St (at 17th St) **415/731-6654, 877/226-3273** • popular • lesbians/ gay men • wall-to-wall books, art & style • just up the hill from the heart of the Castro • wireless internet • German spoken • nonsmoking • gay-owned • $95-135

Casa Buena Vista near Market & Castro **916/974-7409, 916/813-3119 (CELL)** • gay-friendly • rental apts • nonsmoking • kids ok • $205-250

Castro Suites 927 14th St (at Noe) 415/437–1783 • mostly gay men • furnished apts • nonsmoking • gay-owned • $200-220

Dolores Park Inn 3641 17th St (btwn Church & Dolores) 415/621–0482 • gay-friendly • Italianate Victorian mansion • hot tub • some shared baths • kitchens • fireplaces • nonsmoking • kids ok • $99-259

Edwardian San Francisco 1668 Market St (btwn Franklin & Gough) 415/864–1271, 888/864–8070 • gay-friendly • hot tub • jacuzzi • some shared baths • nonsmoking • $79-189

Friends 415/826–5972 • lesbians/ gay men • B&B in private home • gay-owned • $50-105

Inn on Castro 321 Castro St (btwn 16th & 17th) 415/861–0321 • lesbians/ gay men • B&B known for its hospitality & friendly atmosphere • full brkfst • nonsmoking • gay-owned • $85-250

Jersey Guest House 415/641–8882 • gay-straight • guest room in private home • overlooks garden • 1 block to shops & restaurants of 24th Street in Noe Valley • nonsmoking • lesbian-owned • $75-85

Le Grenier 347 Noe St (at 16th St) 415/864–4748 • lesbians/ gay men • suite • $65-90

Nancy's Bed 415/239–5692 • women only • cozy room in private lesbian home • kitchen • nonsmoking • kids ok • $25-35/ person

Noe's Nest B&B 3973 23rd St (at Noe) 415/821–0751 • gay-friendly • full brkfst • hot tub • fireplace • nonsmoking • kids ok • $99-195

Olive's Gate Guesthouse 415/821–6039 • gay/ straight • studio apt • full kitchen • private entrance & garden • nonsmoking • lesbian-owned • $115

▲ **The Parker Guest House** 520 Church St (at 17th) 415/621–3222, 888/520–7275 • popular • mostly gay men • guesthouse complex w/ gardens • steam spa • nonsmoking • gay-owned • $119-199

SF Noe Valley Tourist Apt 225 28th St (at Church) 415/695–9782, 415/312–0138 (CELL) • gay-friendly • cozy upstairs apt • kids ok • nonsmoking • gay-owned • $100 (per night, 2 persons, 3-day minimum) + $25 each additional adult

Terrace Place 415/241–0425 • mostly gay men • guest suite • gay-owned • $99-240

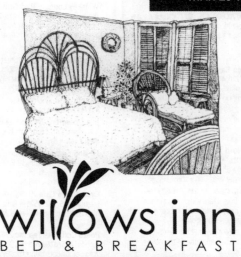

Travelodge Central 1707 Market St (at Valencia) 415/621–6775, 800/578–7878 • gay-friendly • nonsmoking rooms available • $99-179

▲ **The Willows Inn** 710 14th St (at Church) 415/431–4770, 800/431–0277 • lesbians/ gay men • "amenities, comfort, great location" • nonsmoking • lesbian & gay-owned • $105-165

BARS

The Bar on Castro 456 Castro St 415/626–7220, 415/626–1061 • 4pm-2am, from 1pm wknds • popular • mostly gay men • neighborhood bar • sidewalk patio

The Cafe 2367 Market St 415/861–3846 • 4pm-2am, from 1pm on wknds • popular • lesbians/ gay men • dancing/DJ • young crowd • deck overlooking Castro & Market

Cafe du Nord 2170 Market St (at Sanchez) 415/861–5016 • 6pm-2am, from 5pm Fri-Sat • gay-friendly • alternative • live music • theme nights • dinner Wed-Sun • some veggie

Daddy's 440 Castro St 415/621–8732 • noon-2am, from 11am wknds • popular • mostly gay men • neighborhood bar • leather • women genuinely welcome

Delicious 2369 Market St (at the Cafe) • 3pm-8pm 3rd Sat only, June-Oct • mostly women • T-dance

Harvey's 500 Castro St 415/431–4278 • 11am-1am, from 9am wknds • popular • lesbians/ gay men • neighborhood bar • also restaurant • wheelchair access

Ladies Night at Mecca 2029 Market St (at 14th) 415/621–7000 • popular • Th only • also swanky restaurant • live entertainment • valet parking • wheelchair access

Martuni's 4 Valencia St (at Market) 415/241–0205 • 4pm-2am • popular • gay/ straight • piano bar & lounge • great martinis

The Metro 3600 16th St (at Noe) 415/703–9751 • 11am-2am • mostly gay men • overlooks Market St

The Mint 1942 Market St (at Buchanan) 415/626–4726 • noon-2am • lesbians/ gay men • popular karaoke bar nights • videos • also restaurant • food served till 11pm (till midnight wknds)

The Mix 4086 18th St 415/431–8616 • 3pm-2am, from 8am wknds • mostly gay men • neighborhood bar • heated patio • wknd BBQ

Moby Dick's 4049 18th St • 2pm-2am, from noon wknds • mostly gay men • neighborhood bar • videos

Pilsner Inn 225 Church St (at Market) 415/621–7058 • 10am-2am • popular • mostly gay men • neighborhood bar • great patio

Whiskey Lounge/ Red Grill 4063 18th St (btwn Castro & Hartford) 415/255–2RED • 5pm-close • lesbians/ gay men • cozy bar upstairs, restaurant downstairs

CAFES

Cafe Flore 2298 Market St (at Noe) 415/621–8579 • 7am-10:30pm, till midnight wknds • popular • lesbians/ gay men • some veggie • full bar • great patio

Jumpin' Java 139 Noe St (at 14th St) 415/431–5282 • 6am-9pm, from 7am wknds

Just Desserts 248 Church St 415/626–5774 • 7am-8pm, 8am-11pm wknds • lesbians/ gay men • cafe • delicious cakes

Le Bon Gateau 476 Castro St 415/621–2767 • 7am-10pm, till midnight Fri-Sat (young crowd) • coffee, tea, très delicious desserts • live entertainment nights

Orbit Room Cafe 1900 Market St (at Laguna) 415/252–9525 • 8am-2am, till midnight Sun • great view of Market St • also bar

Peet's Coffee & Tea Inc 2257 Market St (at 16th St) 415/626–6416 • 6:30am-8pm, 7am-9pm Sat, till 8pm Sun • mostly gay men

Sweet Inspiration 2239 Market St 415/621–8664 • 7am-11:30pm, 8am-midnight wknds • popular wknd nights • food served • fabulous desserts

RESTAURANTS

2223 Market 2223 Market St 415/431–0692 • dinner, Sun brunch • popular • contemporary American • full bar • wheelchair access

Anchor Oyster Bar 579 Castro St (at 19th) 415/431–3990 • lunch & dinner • lesbians/ gay men • seafood • some veggie • beer/ wine • women-owned/ run

Bagdad Cafe 2295 Market St 415/621–4434 • 24hrs • lesbians/ gay men • diner • some veggie

Blue 2337 Market St (btwn Castro & Noe) 415/863–2583 • 11:30am-11pm, wknd brunch (hours vary) • popular • homecooking served w/ style • some veggie • beer/ wine

Chloe's 1399 Church St (at 26th St) 415/648–4116 • 8am-3pm • popular • come early for the excellent wknd brunch

Chow 215 Church St (at Market) **415/552–2469** • 11am-11pm, 10am-midnight wknds • popular • eclectic & affordable

Cove Cafe 434 Castro St **415/626–0462** • 8am-9pm • lesbians/ gay men • some veggie • wheelchair access

Eric's Chinese Restaurant 1500 Church St (at 27th St) **415/282–0919** • 11am-9pm • popular • some veggie

Home 2100 Market St (at Church) **415/503–0333** • dinner & Sun brunch • popular • American

It's Tops 1801 Market St (at Octavia) **415/431–6395** • 8am-3pm & 8pm-3am • classic diner • great hotcakes

Luna 558 Castro St (btwn 18th & 19th) **415/621–2566** • brkfst, lunch & dinner • popular • lesbians/ gay men • Californian • patio

M&L Market (May's) 691 14th St (at Market) **415/431–7044** • 11:30am-4pm, clsd wknds • great huge sandwiches

Ma Tante Sumi 4243 18th St (at Diamond) **415/552–6663** • 5:30pm-10pm • lesbians/ gay men • cont'l/ Japanese

Mecca 2029 Market St (at Dolores) **415/621–7000** • dinner from 5:30pm • popular • ladies night Th • American • swanky bar • DJ nightly • live entertainment • valet parking • wheelchair access

Michael's Octavia Lounge 1772 Market St (near Gough) **415/863–3516** • dinner only, wknd brunch, clsd Mon-Tue • live music • gay-owned

Miss Millie's 4123 24th St (at Castro) **415/285–5598** • dinner & very popular wknd brunch, worth the wait

Orphan Andy's 3991 17th St **415/864–9795** • 24hrs • diner • gay-owned

Pasta Pomodoro 2304 Market St **415/558–8123** • open till 11pm • popular • lesbians/ gay men • inexpensive Italian • also 24th & Noe location

Red Grill 4063 18th St (btwn Castro & Hartford) **415/255–2733** • steak & seafood • also Whiskey Lounge upstairs

The Sausage Factory 517 Castro St **415/626–1250** • 11:30am-12:30am • lesbians/ gay men • pizza & pasta • some veggie • beer/ wine

Sparky's 242 Church St (at Market) **415/626–8666** • 24hrs • diner • some veggie • popular late night

Swanky Steakhouse 2251 Market St **415/355–0986** • "ultracool Rat Pack styled supper club"

Tita's Hale 'aina 3870 17th St (btwn Sanchez & Noe) **415/626–2477** • dinner Tue-Sun, lunch wknds • popular • traditional Hawaiian • plenty veggie • wheelchair access • lesbian-owned

Welcome Home 464 Castro St **415/626–3600** • 8am-10pm • popular • lesbians/ gay men • homestyle • some veggie • beer/ wine

Zuni Cafe 1658 Market St (at Franklin) **415/552–2522** • lunch & dinner • clsd Mon • popular • upscale cont'l/ Mediterranean • full bar

ENTERTAINMENT & RECREATION

Castro Country Club 4058 18th St (at Castro) **415/552–6102** • noon-11pm, till 1am wknds • lesbians/ gay men • alcohol- & drug-free club

Pink Triangle Park near Market & Castro • "in remembrance of LGBT victims of the Nazi regime"

Three Dollar Bill Cafe 1800 Market St (at the SF LGBT Center) **415/503–1532** • 7am-10pm, 9am-10pm Sat, clsd Sun • cafe & so much more: hosts open mic, micro-cinema (film) night, games night

BOOKSTORES

A Different Light 489 Castro St **415/431–0891** • 10am-11pm • popular • LGBT • readings

Aardvark Books 227 Church St **415/552–6733** • 10:30am-10:30pm • mostly used • good LGBT section • say hello to Ace, the bookstore cat par excellence

Books, Inc 2275 Market St **415/864–6777** • 10am-11pm, till 10pm Sun • LGBT section • readings • wheelchair access

Get Lost 1825 Market St (at Guerrero) **415/437–0529** • 10am-7pm, till 6pm Sat, 11am-5pm Sun • travel books • LGBT section

RETAIL SHOPS

Best in Show 300 Sanchez St (at 16th St) **415/863–7387** • pet supplies

Cold Steel America 2377 Market St (at 17th St) **415/621–7233** • piercing & tattoo studio • also 1783 Haight St, 415/933–7233

Does Your Father Know? 548 Castro St **415/241–9865** • 9:30am-8pm, till 10pm Fri-Sat • LGBT gifts & videos

Does Your Mother Know? 4141 18th St (at Castro) 415/864-3160 • 9:30am-10pm, till 11pm Fri-Sat, till 9pm Sun • cards • T-shirts

Dragonfly Ink 3409 23rd St 415/550-1445 • tattoo studio • woman-owned/ run

Gotham Body Piercing 3991 17th St 415/701-1970 • noon-8pm, till 6pm Sun

Image Leather 2199 Market St (at Sanchez) 415/621-7551 • 9am-10pm, 11am-7pm Sun • custom leather clothing • accessories • toys

Just for Fun 3982 24th St (btwn Noe & Sanchez) 415/285-4068 • 9am-8pm, till 7pm Sat, 10am-6pm Sun • gift shop • wheelchair access

La Sirena Botanica 1509 Church St (at 27th St) 415/285-0612 • noon-6:30pm • Afro-Caribbean religious articles

National Product 1845 Market St (at Guerrero) 415/255-1920 • clsd Mon-Th • "art & unusual gifts" • all true & great cards, too

Rolo 2351 Market St 415/431-4545 • 11am-8pm, till 7pm Sun • designer labels • also 450 Castro location

▲ **See Jane Run Sports** 3910 24th St (at Noe) 415/401-8338 • 11am-7pm, 10am-6pm Sat, till 5pm Sun • women's athletic apparel

Under One Roof 549 Castro 415/503-2300 • 11am-8pm • 100% donated to AIDS relief • wheelchair access

SPIRITUAL GROUPS

Congregation Sha'ar Zahav 290 Dolores (at 16th) 415/861-6932 • call for services

MCC San Francisco 150 Eureka St (btwn 18th & 19th Sts) 415/863-4434 • worship 8:30am, 11am & 7pm Sun • Buddhist Q-Sangha 7pm Mon • home for queer spirituality

Most Holy Redeemer Church 100 Diamond St (at 18th St) 415/863-6259 • 8am daily, also 10am Sun, 5:30pm Mon-Fri, 5pm Sat (vigil mass) • mostly lesbian/gay Roman Catholic parish

GYMS & HEALTH CLUBS

Gold's Gym Castro 2301 Market St 415/626-4488 • popular • lesbians/ gay men • day passes available

EROTICA

The MMO (Mercury Mail Order) 4084 18th St 415/621-1188 • leather • toys

Romantasy Exquisite Corsetry 415/585-0760 • call for appt • corsets & fetish clothing • woman-owned/ run

Shoes and outfitting for adventure

See Jane Run
SPORTS
athletic gear for women

**The official sponsor
of the athlete in all of us**

yoga • running • cycling • swimming • hiking • triathlon • plus sizes

3910 24th St.
San Francisco, CA 94114
415-401-8338

5817 College Ave.
Oakland, CA 94618
510-428-2681

15 E Blithedale Ave.
Mill Valley, CA 94941
415-384-0555

www.SeeJaneRunSports.com

SF—South of Market

ACCOMMODATIONS

Argent Hotel 50 3rd St 415/974-6400, 877/222-6699 • gay-friendly • hip hotel w/ spectacular views • sauna • kids ok • nonsmoking • $179-249

European Guest House 761 Minna St 415/861-6634 • gay-friendly • hostel modeled on European guesthouse • shared baths • nonsmoking • $16-45

▲ **Hotel Vitale** 8 Mission St 415/278-3700, 888/890-8688 • gay-friendly • 4-star, full-service waterfront luxury hotel • rooftop spa • restaurant & bar • nonsmoking • wheelchair access • $199-399

Howard Johnson Express Inn 385 9th St (at Harrison) 415/431-5131, 800/446-4656 • gay/straight • motel • close to SOMA bars • limited parking • kids ok • wheelchair access • $69-139

The Mosser Hotel 54 4th St (btwn Market & Mission) 415/986-4400, 800/227-3804 • gay/straight • 1913 landmark hotel • some shared baths • nonsmoking • kids ok • also restaurant • SF cuisine • full bar • $69-229

Ramada Market St 1231 Market St (btwn 8th & 9th) 415/626-8000, 800/227-4747 • gay-friendly • wheelchair access

Renoir Hotel 45 McAllister (at Market St) 415/626-5200, 800/576-3388 • gay/straight • bar & restaurant • nonsmoking • wireless internet • wheelchair access • Damron discount • $89-350

W San Francisco 181 Third St 415/777-5300, 877/WHOTELS (RESERVATIONS ONLY) • gay-friendly • swimming • wheelchair access • $229-429

BARS

Cherry Bar & Lounge 917 Folsom St (at 5th St) 415/974-1585 • 4pm-2am • dancing/DJ • check calendar for theme nights

Cip Lounge 1225 Folsom St (at 8th) 415/863-1290 • from 5pm Tue-Sun, clsd Mon • gay/straight • lush lounge

The Eagle Tavern 398 12th St (at Harrison) 415/626-0880 • noon-2am • mostly gay men • popular • leather • occasional women's leather events • live music • patio

Gallery Lounge 510 Brannan (at 4th) 415/227-0449 • 4pm-close, from 7pm Sat • gay/straight • more gay Sun afternoon • patio • gay-owned

Hole in the Wall Saloon 289 8th St (at Folsom) 415/431-4695 • noon-2am • mostly gay men • neighborhood bar • leather

NIGHTCLUBS

1015 Folsom 1015 Folsom St (at 6th) 415/431-1200 • 10pm-close • gay/straight • popular • dancing/DJ • call for events • cover charge

Asia SF 201 9th St (at Howard) 415/255-2742 • 10pm-close Wed-Sat • popular • gay/straight • dancing/DJ • mostly Asian-American • theme nights • go-go boys • cover charge • also Cal-Asian restaurant w/ en-drag service 5pm-10pm

Chix 917 Folsom St (at The Cherry Bar) 415/974-1585 • 9pm-close Sat only • popular • mostly women • dancing/DJ • go-go dancers • cover

The Crib SF 715 Harrison St (at 3rd) • 9:30pm-2am Th only • lesbians/gay men • dancing/DJ • "hip-hop, pop, dance" • videos • younger crowd • 18+

Eight 1151 Folsom St (btwn 7th & 8th St) 415/431-1151 • 5pm-2am, from 8pm Sat • gay/straight • dancing/DJ

Endup 401 6th St (at Harrison) 415/357-0827 • clsd Tue • mostly gay men • dancing/DJ • multiracial • theme nights • popular Sun mornings

Hot Pants 1190 Folsom St (at Cat Club) • 9pm Fri only • lesbians/gay men • dancing/DJ • electro, hip hop, punk

Mezzanine 444 Jessie (at Mint) 415/625-8880 • 10pm-7am Fri-Sat • gay/straight • more gay Sat for Industry • dancing/DJ • multiracial clientele • transgender-friendly • theme nights • art shows • wheelchair access • cover charge

Miss Kitty's Scratching Post & Raucous Romp 917 Folsom St (at 5th St, at Cherry Bar) • 4th Sun • mostly women • gentlewoman's strip club • transgender-friendly • alternates between women-only & pansexual/queer • check local listings for details

Raw 401 6th St (at Harrison, at the Endup) 415/339-8310 • 10pm 3rd Sat only • mostly women • dancing/DJ • live entertainment • hip hop • multiracial crowd

The Stud 399 9th St (at Harrison) 415/252-7883 (INFO LINE), 415/863-6623 • 5pm-2am • popular • lesbians/gay men • dancing/DJ • theme nights • outrageous Trannyshack Tue

Sugar 399 9th St (at The Stud) 415/252–7883 (STUD #) • 9pm-4am Sat • popular • mostly gay men • dancing/DJ • great music & wall-to-wall alternababes • young crowd

Trannyshack 399 9th St (at The Stud) 415/863–6623 • 10pm-3am Tue, midnight show • popular • mostly gay men • dancing/DJ • weekly party for trannies & their friends & admirers • live shows • gay-owned

CAFES

Brain Wash 1122 Folsom St (at 7th St) 415/861–3663, 415/431–9274 • 7am-11pm • popular • cafe & laundromat • beer/ wine

Pick Me Up 298 9th St (at Folsom) 415/864–7425 • 6am-7pm, 8am-5pm wknds

RESTAURANTS

Ananda Fuara 1298 Market St (at 9th) 415/621–1994 • 8am-8pm, till 3pm Wed, clsd Sun • vegetarian

Bacar Restaurant & Wine Salon 448 Brannan St (btwn 3rd & 4th) 415/904–4100 • lunch Th-Fri, dinner nightly • some veggie • live shows • wheelchair access

Boulevard 1 Mission St (at Steuart) 415/543–6084 • lunch Mon-Fri & dinner daily • one of SF's finest

Butter 354 11th St (btwn Folsom & Harrison) 415/863–5964 • 5pm-2am, clsd Mon • "white trash bistro" • full bar • theme nights

Dogzilla Cafe 215 Fremont #2A (enter on Howard) 415/442–1889 • 10am-7pm • hot dog & sausage creations • soups & salads • beer/ wine • lesbian-owned

Don Ramon's Mexican Restaurant 225 11th St (btwn Howard & Folsom) 415/864–2700 • lunch Tue-Fri, dinner nightly, clsd Mon • some veggie • full bar

Fringale 570 4th St (btwn Bryant & Brannan) 415/543–0573 • lunch & dinner, clsd Sun • French bistro • wheelchair access

Hawthorne Lane 22 Hawthorne St (btwn 2nd & 3rd, off Howard) 415/777–9779 • dinner nightly, lunch Mon-Fri

Le Charm 315 5th St (at Folsom) 415/546–6128 • lunch & dinner, dinner only wknds

Lulu 816 Folsom St (at 4th St) 415/495–5775 • lunch & dinner • popular • upscale Mediterranean • some veggie • full bar • wheelchair access

Manora's Thai Cuisine 1600 Folsom (at 12th) 415/861–6224 • lunch & dinner Mon-Fri • some veggie

Rocco's Cafe 1131 Folsom St (at 7th) 415/554–0522 • brkfst & lunch daily, dinner Th-Fri only

The Slanted Door 1 Ferry Building #3 415/861–8032 • popular • Vietnamese • full bar • reservations recommended

Sneaky Tiki 1582 Folsom St (at 12th St) 415/701–8454 • restaurant & lounge • wheelchair access

Tu Lan 8 6th St (at Market) 415/626–0927 • lunch & dinner, clsd Sun • Vietnamese • some veggie • dicey neighborhood but delicious (& cheap) food

Woodward's Garden 1700 Mission St (at Duboce) 415/621–7122 • dinner seating at 6pm & 8pm, clsd Sun-Mon • wheelchair access

Yank Sing 101 Spear St (One Rincon Center, at Mission) 415/957–9300 • 11am-3pm Mon-Fri, 10am-4pm wknds • popular • dim-sum heaven! • also catering & delivery

RETAIL SHOPS

A Taste of Leather 1285 Folsom (btwn 9th & 10th) 415/252–9166 • noon-8pm

Dandelion 55 Potrero Ave (at Alameda St) 415/436–9500, 888/548–1968 • 10am-6pm, clsd Sun-Mon • gifts, books erotica & more • gay-owned

Leather Etc 1201 Folsom St (at 8th St) 415/864–7558 • 10:30am-7pm, 11am-6pm Sat, noon-5pm Sun

Madame S 321 7th St 415/863–9447 • women's fashion & equipment

Madame S Leather 321 7th St 415/863–9447 • noon-7pm, till 5pm Sun

Mr S Leather 385 8th St (at Harrison) 415/863–7764 • 11am-7pm • erotic goods • custom leather • latex

Stompers 323 10th St (at Folsom) 415/255–6422, 888/BOOTMAN • 11am-7pm, noon-6pm Sun • boots • cigars • gloves

Stormy Leather 1158 Howard St (btwn 7th & 8th) 415/626–1672 • noon-7pm • leather • latex • toys • magazines

GYMS & HEALTH CLUBS

Gold's Gym San Francisco 9th & Brannan 415/552–4653 • popular • day passes available

SEX CLUBS

Power Exchange Level 3 86 Otis St (btwn S Van Ness & Gough) 415/487–9944 • call for hours • playspace for female, transgendered, bi & straight couples

SF—Polk Street Area

ACCOMMODATIONS

Broadway Manor Inn 2201 Van Ness Ave (at Broadway) 415/776-7900, 800/727-6239 • gay-friendly • motel • close to Fisherman's Wharf • kids ok • lesbian, gay & straight-owned • $54-119

Hostelling International—San Francisco City Center 685 Ellis St (at Larkin) 415/474-5721, 800/909-4776 • gay-friendly • kids ok • nonsmoking • lesbian & gay & straight-owned/ run • $23-70

The Monarch Hotel 1015 Geary St (at Polk) 415/673-5232, 800/777-3210 • gay-friendly • kids ok • nonsmoking rooms available • up to $139

Nob Hill Motor Inn 1630 Pacific Ave (at Van Ness Ave) 415/775-8160, 800/343-6900 • gay-friendly • hotel • kids ok • nonsmoking • wheelchair access • $79-169

▲ **The Phoenix Hotel** 601 Eddy St (at Larkin) 415/776-1380, 800/248-9466 • gay-friendly • 1950s-style motor lodge • popular • fave of celebrity rockers • swimming • kids ok • $109-229

BARS

The Cinch 1723 Polk St (at Clay) 415/776-4162 • 6am-2am • mostly gay men • neighborhood bar • patio • lots of pool tables & no attitude • wheelchair access

Edinburgh Castle 950 Geary St (at Polk) 415/885-4074 • 5pm-2am • mostly straight but rockin' Scottish pub w/ single malts, beer, darts & authentic fish & chips • live bands

Gangway 841 Larkin St (btwn Geary & O'Farrell) 415/776-6828 • 8am-2am • mostly gay men • neighborhood bar

Kimo's 1351 Polk St (at Pine) 415/885-4535 • 8am-2am • mostly gay men • neighborhood bar • live bands upstairs

Lush Lounge 1092 Post (at Polk) 415/771-2022 • 4pm-2am • popular • gay/ straight • martini bar & piano lounge • wheelchair access

NIGHTCLUBS

Divas 1081 Post St (at Larkin) 415/474-DIVA • 6am-2am • mostly gay men • neighborhood bar • dancing/DJ • multiracial • transsexuals, transvestites & their admirers • live shows

Respect Broadway & Polk (at Harry Denton's Rouge) 415/647-8258 • 4pm till the last lady leaves, 2nd Sun only • "A Monthly Tea Dance For Women" • mostly lesbians • dancing/ DJ • multiracial • geared toward an older audience • $10 cover

CAFES

Quetzal 1234 Polk St (at Sutter) 415/673-4181 • 7am-9:30pm • popular • beer/ wine • live shows • videos • internet access

RESTAURANTS

Antica Trattoria 2400 Polk St (at Union) 415/928-5797 • dinner Tue-Sun • Italian

California Culinary Academy 625 Polk St (at Turk) 415/771-3500 • lunch & dinner Tue-Fri • popular • cooking school where future top chefs serve up what they've learned

El Super Burrito 1200 Polk St (at Sutter) 415/771-9700 • 9am-11pm

Grubstake II 1525 Pine St (at Polk) 415/673-8268 • 5pm-4am, from 10am wknds • lesbians/ gay men • diner • beer/ wine

Tai Chi 2031 Polk St (at Pacific) 415/441-6758 • lunch Mon-Fri, dinner nightly • popular • Chinese

BOOKSTORES

A Clean Well Lighted Place For Books 601 Van Ness Ave (at Turk) 415/441-6670 • 10am-11pm, till 9pm Sun • independent • LGBT section • many readings

EROTICA

▲ **Good Vibrations** 1620 Polk St (btwn Sacramento & Clay) 415/345-0400 • 11am-7pm, till 8pm Fri-Sat • clean, well-lighted sex toy store • also mail order

SF—Downtown & North Beach

ACCOMMODATIONS

Andrews Hotel 624 Post St (at Taylor) 415/563-6877, 800/926-3739 • gay-friendly • Victorian hotel • also restaurant • Italian • $99-175

Cartwright Hotel on Union Square 524 Sutter St (at Powell) 415/421-2865, 800/919-9779 • gay-friendly • B&B-inn on Union Square • afternoon tea • wine hour • $89-219

▲ **The Commodore Hotel** 825 Sutter St (at Jones) 415/923-6800, 800/338-6848 • gay/ straight • also popular Red Room lounge • kids ok • $109-169

Dakota Hotel 606 Post St (at Taylor) 415/931–7475 • gay-friendly • near Union Square • kids ok • $79-119

Executive Hotel Mark Twain 345 Taylor St (at Ellis) 415/673–2332, 888/388–3932 • gay-friendly • wheelchair access • $89-250

Galleria Park Hotel 191 Sutter St (at Kearny) 415/781–3060, 800/756–3036 • gay/ straight • boutique hotel • kids ok • wheelchair access • $99-199

Grand Hyatt San Francisco 345 Stockton St (at Sutter) 415/398–1234, 800/233–1234 • gay-friendly • restaurant & lounge • gym • $165-345

Halcyon Hotel 649 Jones St (at Post) 415/929–8033, 800/627–2396 • gay-friendly • kids ok • gay & straight-owned/ run • $79-129/ night • $510/ week

Handlery Union Square Hotel 351 Geary St 415/781–7800x145, 800/995–4874 • gay-friendly • steps from Union Square • swimming • wheelchair access • $194-294

Harbor Court Hotel 165 Steuart St (btwn Howard & Mission) 415/882–1300, 888/792–6283 • gay-friendly • in the heart of the Financial District • gym • pets ok • wheelchair access • $139-249

Hostelling International—San Francisco Downtown 312 Mason St (at O'Farrell) 415/788–5604, 800/909–4776 • gay/ straight • hostel • shared baths • kids ok • open kitchen • wheelchair access • internet access • $24-69

▲ **Hotel Bijou** 111 Mason St (at Eddy) 415/771–1200, 800/771–1022 • gay/ straight • nonsmoking • wheelchair access • kids ok • $119-149

Hotel Diva 440 Geary (at Mason) 415/885–0200, 800/553–1900 • gay-friendly • also gym • $139-249

Hotel Griffon 155 Steuart St (at Mission) 415/495–2100, 800/321–2201 • gay/ straight • also restaurant • bistro/ cont'l • wheelchair access • $139-435

Hotel Monaco 501 Geary St (at Taylor) 415/292–0100, 866/622–5284 • gay-friendly • nonsmoking rooms available • pets ok • full bar • $229-599

Hotel Nikko San Francisco 222 Mason St 415/394–1111, 800/645–5687 • gay/ straight • swimming • health club & spa • nonsmoking • also restaurant • wheelchair access • $200+

Hotel Palomar 12 4th St (at Market) 415/348–1111, 866/373–4941 • gay/ straight • boutique hotel • dogs ok • $199-959

▲ **The Hotel Rex** 562 Sutter St (at Powell) 415/433–4434, 800/433–4434 • gay-friendly • full bar • wheelchair access • $175-575

Hotel Triton 342 Grant Ave (at Bush) 415/394–0500, 800/433–6611 • gay/ straight • designer theme rooms • kids/ pets ok • wheelchair access • $149-299

Hotel Vintage Court 650 Bush St (at Powell) 415/392–4666, 800/654–1100 • gay-friendly • fireplaces • nonsmoking • also world-famous 5-star Masa's restaurant • French • $75 prix fixe • wheelchair access • $149-239

Hyatt Regency San Francisco 5 Embarcadero Center (at California) 415/788–1234, 800/233–1234 • gay-friendly • luxury waterfront hotel • $189-394

King George Hotel 334 Mason St (at Geary) 415/781–5050, 800/288–6005 • gay-friendly • also The Windsor Tearoom • kids ok • wheelchair access • $89-179

Luz Hotel 725 Geary Blvd (at Leavenworth) 415/928–1917 • jacuzzi • mostly men • gay-owned • $80-150

▲ **Maxwell Hotel** 386 Geary St (at Mason) 415/986–2000, 888/734–6299 • gay/ straight • newly restored 1908 art deco masterpiece • wheelchair access • $129-259

Nob Hill Hotel 835 Hyde St (btwn Bush & Sutter) 415/885–2987, 877/662–4455 • gay/ straight • European-style hotel • jacuzzi • nonsmoking • kids ok • also restaurant • wheelchair access • $50-245

▲ **Nob Hill Lambourne** 725 Pine St (at Powell) 415/433–2287, 800/274–8466 • gay-friendly • luxurious "business accommodation" • kitchens • kids ok • nonsmoking • $210-350

Pan Pacific San Francisco 500 Post St (at Mason) 415/771–8600, 800/538–4040 • gay-friendly, hotel, kids ok, nonsmoking, wheelchair access, $229-450

Savoy Hotel 580 Geary St (at Jones) 415/441–2700, 800/227–4223 • gay-friendly • also popular restaurant & bar • $109-209

The York Hotel 940 Sutter St (at Leavenworth) 415/885–6800, 800/808–9675 • gay/ straight • boutique hotel • nonsmoking • wheelchair access • also cabaret • $119+

BARS

Aunt Charlie's Lounge 133 Turk St (at Taylor) 415/441–2922 • noon-midnight, 10am-2am wknds • mostly gay men • neighborhood bar • drag shows wknds

The San Francisco Bay Area's Unique Collection of Boutique Hotels

Joie de Vivre Hospitality
800.738.7477
www.jdvhospitality.com

We guarantee the best available rates on our website.

Acqua Hotel • Mill Valley • 888.662.9555
Hotel Bijou • San Francisco - Union Square • 800.771.1022
Hotel Carlton • San Francisco - Lower Nob Hill • 800.922.7586
Commodore Hotel • San Francisco - Union Square • 800.338.6848
Hotel Del Sol • San Francisco - Marina District • 877.433.5765
Nob Hill Lambourne • San Francisco - Nob Hill • 800.274.8466
The Maxwell Hotel • San Francisco - Union Square • 888.734.6299

These hotels are distinctive Joie de Vivre properties and proud participants in the Experience Rewards Club.

Joie de Vivre
HOSPITALITY

Plush Room 940 Sutter St (at York Hotel) **415/885–2800, 800/808–9675** • gay/ straight • cabaret w/ world-class performers • wheelchair access

CAFES

Caffe Trieste 609 Vallejo St **415/392–6739** • popular • get a taste of the real North Beach (past & present)—a great cappuccino

RESTAURANTS

Cafe Claude 7 Claude Ln (near Bush & Kearny) **415/392–3505** • lunch Mon-Sat, dinner Tue-Sat, clsd Sun • live jazz wknds • as close to Paris as you can get in SF • beer/ wine

Dottie's True Blue Cafe 522 Jones St (at Geary) **415/885–2767** • 7:30am-3pm, clsd Tue • plenty veggie • great brkfst • gay-owned

Golden Era 572 O'Farrell St **415/673–3136** • 11am-9pm, clsd Tue • vegetarian/ vegan

Mario's Bohemian Cigar Store Cafe 566 Columbus Ave (at Union) **415/362–0536** • 10am-close • great foccacia sandwiches • some veggie • beer/ wine

Masa's 640 Bush St (at Hotel Vintage Court) **415/989–7154** • dinner Tue-Sat • world-famous 5-star French restaurant • wheelchair access

Max's on the Square 398 Geary St (at Mason) **415/646–8600** • lunch & dinner • popular • seafood • full bar

▲ **Millennium** 580 Geary St (at Jones, at the Savoy Hotel) **415/345–3900** • dinner only • Euro-Mediterranean • upscale vegetarian

Moose's 1652 Stockton (btwn Filbert & Union) **415/989–7800** • popular • upscale bistro menu

Original Joe's 144 Taylor (btwn Turk & Eddy) **415/775–4877** • lunch & dinner • Italian • since 1937 • also art deco cocktail lounge

BOOKSTORES

City Lights Bookstore 261 Columbus Ave, North Beach (at Pacific) **415/362–8193** • 10am-midnight • historic beatnik bookstore • many progressive titles • LGBT section • whole floor for poetry

Stacey's Bookstore 581 Market St **415/421–4687, 800/926–6511** • 8:30am-7pm, 11am-6pm Sat, clsd Sun • independent • LGBT section

SF—Mission District

ACCOMMODATIONS

Elements 2516 Mission St (at 21st St) **415/647–4100, 866/327–8407** • gay/ straight • hostel w/ private or shared rooms• brkfst included • also restaurant & cafe • $23-90

▲ **The Inn San Francisco** 943 S Van Ness Ave (btwn 20th & 21st) **415/641–0188, 800/359–0913** • gay-friendly • Victorian mansion • hot tub • some shared baths • kitchens • fireplaces • patio • nonsmoking • $95-265

BARS

Chaise Lounge 309 Cortland Ave, Bernal Heights (at Bocana) • 5pm-close • gay/ straight • neighborhood bar • lesbian-owned

El Rio 3158 Mission St (at Cesar Chavez) **415/282–3325** • 5pm-close Mon-Th, from 3pm wknds • gay/ straight • neighborhood bar • Latino/a clientele • live shows • patio

▲ **Lexington Club** 3464 19th St (btwn Mission & Valencia) **415/863–2052** • 5pm-2am, from 3pm Fri-Sun • popular • mostly women • neighborhood bar • hip young crowd • lesbian-owned

Phone Booth 1398 S Van Ness Ave (at 25th) **415/648–4683** • noon-2am, from 1pm wknds • lesbians/ gay men • neighborhood bar

Sadie's Flying Elephant 491 Potrero (at Mariposa) **415/551–7988** • 4pm-2am • popular • gay/straight • neighborhood bar • K'vetch queer open mic 8pm 1st Sun

Wild Side West 424 Cortland, Bernal Heights (at Bennington) **415/647–3099** • 1pm-2am • gay/ straight • neighborhood bar • patio • magic garden • wheelchair access

NIGHTCLUBS

2nd Saturdays: Rock Steady 3158 Mission (at El Rio) **415/339–8310** • 3pm-8pm 2nd Sat only • mostly women • dancing/ DJ • hip hop, dancehall • multiracial

Cream 550 Barneveld (at Space 550, 2 blocks off Bayview) **408/792–3466** • 2nd Sat • mostly women • dancing/ DJ • multiracial

Esta Noche 3079 16th St (at Mission) **415/861–5757** • 1pm-2am • mostly gay men • dancing/DJ • mostly Latino/a • transgender-friendly • live shows • salsa & disco in a classic Tijuana dive

In Bed With Fairy Butch 2565 Mission (at 22nd, at 12 Galaxies) **415/339–8000** • occasional parties • mostly women • strippers • cabaret • dancing/ DJ

The **Lexington Club**

Your friendly neighborhood dyke bar!

Mon - Thur 5 PM to 2 AM
Fri - Sun 3 PM to 2 AM

3464 19th Street
San Francisco
www.lexingtonclub.com

Mango 3158 Mission (at El Rio)
415/339–8310 • 3pm-8pm 4th Sat April-Nov • women only • dancing/DJ • multiracial • food served

Sundance Saloon 550 Barneveld (at Space 550, 2 blocks off Bayshore Blvd)
415/820–1403 • 5pm-10:30pm Sun, lessons at 5:30pm • mostly gay men • women welcome! • DJ from 7:30pm • country/western • gay-owned

Unleash 2522 Mission St (at 21st St, at Medjool) 415/550–9055 (RESTAURANT #) • 4pm-10pm 1st Sun only • mostly women • dancing/DJ • wheelchair access

CAFES

Cafe Commons 3161 Mission St (btwn Cesar Chavez & Valencia) 415/282–2928 • 7am-6:30pm, from 8am wknds • sandwiches • plenty veggie • patio • wheelchair access • women-owned/run

Dolores Park Cafe 501 Dolores St (at 18th St) 415/621–2936 • 7am-8pm • food served • outdoor seating overlooking Dolores Park • live music Fri till 9:30pm

Farleys 1315 18th St (at Texas St, Potrero Hill) 415/648–1545 • 6am-10pm, from 8am wknds • coffeehouse

Ritual 1026 Valencia St (at 21st St, next to Lost Weekend Video) 415/641–1024 • 7am-11pm, from 8am Sat, till 9pm Sun • coffee, pastries & Wi-Fi

Tartine Bakery 600 Guerrero St (at 18th St) 415/487–2600 • 8am-7pm, from 9am Sun, French bakery w/ a line out the door every day all day • wine & espresso bar • outside tables

RESTAURANTS

Charanga 2351 Mission St (at 20th St) 415/282–1813 • 5:30pm-close, clsd Sun-Mon • tapas • beer/wine/sangria • plenty veggie • wheelchair access • women-owned/run

Delfina 3621 18th St (at Dolores) 415/552–4055 • 5:30pm-10pm • popular • excellent Tuscan cuisine • full bar • reservations required

El Farolito 2777 Mission St (at 24th) 415/824–7877 • popular • 11am-8pm • delicious, cheap burritos & more

Firecracker 1007 Valencia St (at 21st) 415/642–3470 • popular • dinner only, clsd Sun • Chinese • some veggie

Herbivore 983 Valencia St (at 21st) 415/826–5657 • 9am-10pm, till 11pm wknds • moderately priced vegan food in upscale setting • beer/wine

Just For You 722 22nd St (at 3rd St) 415/647–3033 • 7:30am-3pm, 8am-3pm wknds • popular • lesbians/gay men • Southern brkfst • some veggie • women-owned/run

Klein's Delicatessen 501 Connecticut St (at 20th St, Potrero Hill) 415/821–9149 • 7am-7pm, 8am-5pm Sun • patio • sandwiches & salads • some veggie • beer/wine • women-owned/run

Medjool 2522 Mission St (at 21st St) 415/550–9055 • brkfst, lunch & dinner, also cafe, clsd Sun • tapas • plenty veggie • wheelchair access

Pancho Villa 3071 16th St (btwn Mission & Valencia) 415/864–8840 • 11am-midnight • popular • also El Toro at 18th & Valencia • some veggie • beer/wine • wheelchair access

Pauline's Pizza Pie 260 Valencia St (btwn 14th & Duboce) 415/552–2050 • 5pm-10pm, clsd Sun-Mon • popular • lesbians/gay men • gourmet pizza • beer/wine

Picaro 3120 16th St (at Valencia) 415/431–4089 • dinner only • Spanish tapas bar • beer/wine • wheelchair access

Pork Store Cafe 3122 16th St (at Valencia) 415/626–5523 • from 8am • popular • cool American/diner food • great brkfsts • also 1451 Haight St, 415/864-6981

Slow Club 2501 Mariposa (at Hampshire) 415/241–9390 • lunch Mon-Fri, dinner Mon-Sat, wknd brunch • full bar • wheelchair access

Spiazzino 995 Valencia St (at 21st) 415/643–8814 • 11am-11pm • Italian • some veggie • full bar

Ti-Couz 3108 16th St (at Valencia) 415/252–7373 • 11am-11pm, from 10am wknds • Breton dinner & dessert crepes • plenty veggie • beer/wine • wheelchair access

Yamo Thai Kitchen 3406 18th St (at Mission) 415/553–8911 • 11am-9:30pm, clsd Sun • small, no frills outfit w/ great cheap food • organic • veggie

ENTERTAINMENT & RECREATION

Brendita's Latin Tour 415/921–0625 • walking tours of the Mission District • call between 8am-10pm

Metronome Ballroom 1830 17th St (at De Haro) 415/252–9000 • gay/straight • dance lessons • salsa to swing • dance parties wknds • call for events • cover charge

Women's Building 3543 18th St (btwn Valencia & Guerrero) 415/431–1180 • check out some of the most beautiful murals in the Mission District

BOOKSTORES

Borderlands Books 866 Valencia St (at 19th) 415/824-8203, 888/893-4008 • noon-8pm • popular • new & used • "San Francisco's home for science fiction, fantasy & horror books"

Dog Eared Books 900 Valencia St (at 20th) 415/282-1901 • 10am-10pm, till 8pm Sun • new & used • good LGBT section • wheelchair access

Modern Times Bookstore 888 Valencia St 415/282-9246 • 10am-9pm, 11am-6pm Sun • progressive • LGBT section • readings • wheelchair access

RETAIL SHOPS

Black & Blue Tattoo 381 Guerrero (at 16th St) 415/626-0770 • noon-7pm • mostly women clientele • women-owned/ run

Body Manipulations 3234 16th St (btwn Guerrero & Dolores) 415/621-0408 • noon-7pm, from 2pm Mon-Th • piercing (walk-in basis) • jewelry

SPIRITUAL GROUPS

The Episcopal Church of St John the Evangelist 1661 15th St (btwn Mission & Valencia, enter on Julian Ave) 415/861-1436 • 11am Sun & 6pm Wed • Oasis congregation • wheelchair access

Freedom in Christ Evangelical Church 601 Dolores St (at 19th) 415/970-8149 • 6pm Sun

GYMS & HEALTH CLUBS

Osento 955 Valencia St 415/282-6333 • noon-midnight • women only • baths • hot tub • massage

EROTICA

▲ **Good Vibrations** 603 Valencia St (at 17th St) 415/522-5460, 800/289-8423 • 11am-7pm, till 8pm Th-Sat • popular • clean, well-lighted sex toy store • also mail order

SF—Haight, Fillmore, Hayes Valley

ACCOMMODATIONS

555 Haight Guesthouse 555 Haight St 415/551-2555, 800/785-5504 • gay/ straight • nonsmoking • $20-44

Alamo Square Inn 719 Scott St (at Fulton) 415/922-2055, 800/345-9888 • gay-friendly • 1895 Queen Anne & 1896 Tudor Revival Victorian mansions • full brkfst • nonsmoking • kids ok • $110+

▲ **The Archbishop's Mansion** 1000 Fulton St (at Steiner) 415/563-7872, 800/543-5820 • gay-friendly • nonsmoking • one of SF's grandest homes • gay-owned • $145-425

The Chateau Tivoli 1057 Steiner St (at Golden Gate) 415/776-5462, 800/228-1647 • gay-friendly • historic San Francisco B&B • nonsmoking • $99-265

Francisco Bay Inn 1501 Lombard St (at Franklin) 415/474-3030, 800/410-7007 • gay-friendly • motel • kids ok • nonsmoking • $74-169

Hayes Valley Inn 417 Gough St (at Hayes) 415/431-9131, 800/930-7999 • gay/ straight • European-style pension • close to opera & symphony • library w/ computer access • $49-99

Heritage Marina Hotel 2550 Van Ness Ave 415/776-7500, 866/714-6834 • gay-friendly • vintage '50s hotel remodeled in 2003, located in the Marina District • swimming • $89-169

Hostelling International—Fisherman's Wharf Fort Mason, Bldg 240 (at Franklin) 415/771-7277, 800/909-4776 • gay/ straight • hostel • shared baths • kids ok • cafe & kitchen • wheelchair access • $22-78

▲ **Hotel Del Sol** 3100 Webster St (at Greenwich) 415/921-5520, 877/433-5765 • popular • gay/ straight • swimming • nonsmoking • $129-269

Hotel Majestic 1500 Sutter St (at Gough) 415/441-1100, 800/869-8966 • gay-friendly • one of SF's earliest grand hotels • also restaurant • full bar • wheelchair access • $170-450

Inn 1890 1890 Page St (near Stanyan) 415/386-0486, 888/INN-1890 • gay/ straight • Victorian near Golden Gate Park • kitchens • fireplaces • kids/ pets ok • nonsmoking • apt available • gay-owned • $89-159

Inn at the Opera 333 Fulton St (at Franklin) 415/863-8400, 800/590-0157 • gay-friendly • nonsmoking • wheelchair access • $145-350

▲ **Jackson Court** 2198 Jackson St (at Buchanan) 415/929-7670 • gay-friendly • 19th-c brownstone mansion • nonsmoking • kids ok • $160-225

Metro Hotel 319 Divisadero St (at Haight) 415/861-5364 • gay-friendly • European-style pension • food served • $66-120

Queen Anne Hotel 1590 Sutter St (at Octavia) 415/441-2828, 800/227-3970 • gay-friendly • popular • 1890 landmark • wood-burning fireplaces • kids ok • wheelchair access • gay-owned • Damron discount • $139-350 (up to $40 lower Nov-April)

Radisson Miyako Hotel 1625 Post St (at Laguna) 415/922–3200, 800/333–3333 • gay-friendly • in the heart of Japantown • wheelchair access • $179-299

Scott St Properties 230 Scott St (at Haight) 415/552–8980, 800/484–6394 x 8466 • centrally located • wireless internet • nonsmoking • gay-owned $100-150

Shannon-Kavanaugh Guest House 722 Steiner St (at Hayes) 415/563–2727 • gay-friendly • 1-bdrm garden apt • kids/pets ok • nonsmoking • wheelchair access • gay-owned • $175-300

Southern Comforts 310/305–2984, 800/889–7359 • reservation service for several deluxe rental properties • gay-owned

Stanyan Park Hotel 750 Stanyan St (at Waller) 415/751–1000 • gay-friendly • restored Victorian hotel listed on the Nat'l Register of Historic Places • kids ok • wheelchair access • $130-325

BARS

An Bodhran 668 Haight St (btwn Pierce & Scott) 415/431–4724 • 4pm-2am, from 6pm Sat • gay-friendly • traditional Irish pub w/ live music Sun

Jade Bar 650 Gough St (at McAllister) 415/869–1900 • 5pm-2am, from 8pm Sun • gay-friendly • upscale cocktails & Asian-inspired "nibbles"

The Lion Pub 2062 Divisadero St (at Sacramento) 415/567–6565 • 4pm-2am• gay/straight • professional crowd

Marlena's 488 Hayes St (at Octavia) 415/864–6672 • 3pm-2am • mostly gay men • neighborhood bar • drag shows wknds • also piano bar • wheelchair access

Noc Noc 557 Haight St (at Fillmore) 415/861–5811 • 5pm-2am • gay-friendly • beer/wine

Traxx 1437 Haight St (at Masonic) 415/864–4213 • noon-2am • mostly gay men • neighborhood bar

NIGHTCLUBS

The Underground 424 Haight St (at Webster) 415/864–7386 • 5:30pm-2am • gay/straight • dancing/DJ • alternative • theme nights • call for events

CAFES

Fillmore Grind 711 Fillmore (at Hayes) 415/775–5680 • 6:30am-7pm

RESTAURANTS

Alamo Square Seafood 803 Fillmore (at Grove) 415/440–2828 • dinner only

Blue Muse 409 Gough St (at Fell) 415/626–7505 • 7am-9:30pm, Sun brunch • some veggie • full bar (open later) • wheelchair access

Cafe Delle Stelle 395 Hayes (at Gough) 415/252–1110 • lunch daily, dinner Sun only • popular • Italian • beer/wine

Cha Cha Cha 1801 Haight St (at Shrader) 415/386–7670 • open till 11pm • Cuban/Cajun • excellent sangria • worth the wait!

Citizen Cake 399 Grove St (at Gough) 415/861–2228 • 8am-10pm Tue-Fri, from 10am Sat, 10am-5pm Sun, clsd Mon • popular • lesbian chef

Eliza's 2877 California (at Broderick) 415/621–4819 • lunch & dinner • excellent Chinese food & stylish decor

Ella's 500 Presidio Ave (at California) 415/441–5669 • 7am-5pm weekdays • popular wknd brunch

Garibaldi's 347 Presidio Ave (at Sacramento) 415/563–8841 • open for lunch weekdays & dinner nightly • Mediterranean • full bar • wheelchair access • gay-owned

Greens Fort Mason, Bldg A (near Van Ness & Bay) 415/771–6222 • lunch Tue-Sat, dinner Mon-Sat, Sun brunch • gourmet vegetarian

Herbivore 531 Divisadero St 415/885–7133 • 9am-10pm, till 11pm wknds • moderately priced vegan food in upscale setting • beer/wine

Jardinière 300 Grove St (at Franklin) 415/861–5555 • 5pm-midnight, till 10:30pm Sun-Mon • popular • oh-so-chic Californian-French cuisine • full bar

Kan Zaman 1793 Haight (at Shrader) 415/751–9656 • 5pm-midnight, from 10:30am wknds • Mediterranean • some veggie • beer/wine • hookahs & tobacco available

Suppenküche 601 Hayes (at Laguna) 415/252–9289 • dinner, Sun brunch • German cuisine served at communal tables • gay-owned

Thep-Phanom 400 Waller St (at Fillmore) 415/431–2526 • 5:30pm-10:30pm • popular • excellent Thai food (worth the wait!) • beer/wine

ENTERTAINMENT & RECREATION

Kabuki Springs & Spa 1750 Geary Blvd (at Fillmore) 415/922–6000 • traditional Japanese bath w/ extensive menu of spa sevices

BOOKSTORES

The Booksmith 1644 Haight St
415/863-8688, 800/493-7323 (IN US) •
independent • readings

RETAIL SHOPS

Some 1391 Haight St (at Masonic)
415/552-1525 • 1pm-8pm • leather

SPIRITUAL GROUPS

St Agnes Church 1025 Masonic Ave
415/487-8560 • 8:30am, 10:30am & 6pm Sun
in 111-year-old Catholic parish • "inclusive,
diverse, Jesuit"

San Jose

INFO LINES & SERVICES

AA Gay/ Lesbian 274 E Hamilton Ave, Ste
D, Campbell 408/374-8511 • 24hr helpline

**Billy DeFrank Lesbian/ Gay Community
Center** 938 The Alameda 408/293-2429,
408/293-3040 • 3pm-9pm, from 10am Wed,
noon-6pm Sat, clsd Sun • wheelchair access

ACCOMMODATIONS

Hotel De Anza 233 W Santa Clara St
408/286-1000, 800/843-3700 • gay-friendly •
art deco gem • nonsmoking • Italian
restaurant • wheelchair access • $125-329

BARS

Mac's Club 39 Post (btwn 1st & Market)
408/288-8221 • noon-2am • mostly men •
neighborhood bar • dancing/DJ

Renegades 393 Stockton (at Julian)
408/275-9902 • noon-2am • mostly gay men
• neighborhood bar • leather • patio

NIGHTCLUBS

Splash 65 Post St (at 1st) 408/993-0861 •
4pm-close, noon-8pm Sun • mostly
gay men • dancing/ DJ • karaoke • videos •
theme nights • gay-owned

RESTAURANTS

Eulipia Restaurant & Bar 374 S 1st St (at
San Carlos) 408/280-6161 • dinner only, clsd
Mon • eclectic new American • full bar

ENTERTAINMENT & RECREATION

Tech Museum of Innovation 201 S Market
St (at Park Ave) 408/294-8324 • 10am-5pm,
open Fri & Sat nights, clsd Mon, open daily in
summer • IMAX Dome Theater • a must-see
for digital junkies

BOOKSTORES

Sisterspirit 938 The Alameda 408/293-9372
• 6:30pm-9pm, 5pm-8pm Wed, noon-6pm Sat,
1pm-4pm Sun • occasional coffeehouse •
women's open mic 2nd Sat

RETAIL SHOPS

Scott's Super Video 840 Willow St #700 (at
Bird) 408/298-7013 • 10am-11pm, till
midnight Fri-Sat • large gay/ lesbian video
selection

PUBLICATIONS

Out Now Newsmagazine 1020 The
Alameda 408/293-1598 • LGBT newspaper

SPIRITUAL GROUPS

Spirit Connection MCC 65 S 7th St (at
Santa Clara) 408/279-2711 • 10:30am Sun

EROTICA

Leather Masters 969 Park Ave
408/293-7660 • leather & fetish • clothes •
toys • publications

Pleasures from the Heart 1565 Winchester
Blvd, Campbell 408/871-1826 • woman-
owned

San Luis Obispo

INFO LINES & SERVICES

**Wayne McCaughan Community Pride
Center** 11573 Los Osos Valley Rd, Ste B
805/541-4252 • 2pm-6pm, clsd wknds

Women's Community Center 880 Industrial
Way 805/544-9313 • counseling • support •
referrals

ACCOMMODATIONS

The Madonna Inn 1000 Madonna Rd
805/543-3000, 800/543-9666 • gay-friendly •
theme rooms • $147-330

The Palomar Inn 1601 Shell Beach Rd,
Shell Beach 805/773-4204, 888/384-4004 •
gay/ straight • $60-100

CAFES

Linnaea's Cafe 1110 Garden (near Marsh)
805/541-5888 • 6:30pm-11pm, closes early
Sun • plenty veggie • live entertainment

Outspoken, A Beverage Bistro 1422
Monterey (at California) 805/545-7664 •
6:30am-5:30pm, 8am-2pm Sat, clsd Sun •
lesbian-owned

RESTAURANTS

Big Sky Cafe 1121 Broad St 805/545-5401 •
7am-10pm, 8am-9pm Sun

Bookstores

Coalesce Bookstore & Garden Wedding Chapel 845 Main St, Morro Bay **805/772-2880** • 10am-5:30pm, 11am-4pm Sun • LGBT section • women-owned/ run

Volumes of Pleasure 1016 Los Osos Valley Rd, Los Osos **805/528-5565** • 10am-6pm, noon-close Sun • general • LGBT section • wheelchair access • lesbian-owned

Retail Shops

Boxworks 778 Higuera St (in Network Downtown SLO) **805/545-9940** • 10am-5:30pm • unique cards & gifts • mention Damron & receive a 10% discount! • gay-owned

Publications

GALA News & Reviews **805/541-4252** • news & events for Central California coast

Spiritual Groups

Integrity **805/467-3042** • 5:30pm 3rd Sun • call for location

San Mateo

Spiritual Groups

Peninsula MCC 1150 W Hillsdale Blvd **650/515-0900** • noon Sun

San Rafael

see Marin County

Santa Ana

see Orange County

Santa Barbara

Info Lines & Services

Pacific Pride Foundation 126 E Haley St #A-11 **805/963-3636** • 9am-5pm Mon-Fri • social/educational & support services • youth groups • HIV/AIDS services • newsletter

Accommodations

Fess Parker's DoubleTree Resort 633 E Cabrillo Blvd (at Garden) **800/879-2929** • gay-friendly • swimming • $140-1,027

Inn of the Spanish Garden 915 Garden St (at Carrillo) **805/564-4700, 866/564-4700** • gay/ straight • swimming • nonsmoking • kids ok • wheelchair access • $235-465

Old Yacht Club Inn 431 Corona Del Mar Dr **805/962-1277, 800/676-1676** • gay-friendly • only B&B on beach • full brkfst • nonsmoking • $119-479

The Orchid Inn at Santa Barbara 420 W Montecito St **805/965-2333, 877/722-3657** • gay/ straight • 1900s Queen Anne Victorian • full brkfst • nonsmoking • wheelchair access • gay-owned • $175-275

Bars

Hades Bar & Nightclub 235 W Montecito St **805/962-2754** • 4pm-2am, clsd Mon • lesbians/ gay men • neighborhood bar • dancing/DJ • karaoke • shows

Cafes

Hot Spot Espresso Bar 505 State St **805/963-4233** • 24hrs

Restaurants

Sojourner Cafe 134 E Canon Perdido (at Santa Barbara) **805/965-7922** • 11am-11pm, till 10pm Sun • plenty veggie • beer/ wine • wheelchair access

Zelo 630 State St (at Ortega) **805/966-5792** • lunch & dinner, clsd Mon • full bar • also nightclub from 10pm nightly • popular • dancing/DJ • live jazz

Bookstores

Chaucer's Books 3321 State St (at Las Positas Rd) **805/682-6787** • 9am-9pm, till 10pm Fri-Sat, till 6pm Sun • general • LGBT section

Retail Shops

Boxworks 1221 State St, #11 (at Victoria, in Victoria Court Shops) **805/568-1115** • 10am-5:30pm • unique cards & gifts • mention Damron & receive a 10% discount! • gay-owned

Erotica

The Riviera Adult Superstore 4135 State St **805/967-8282** • 10am-midnight • pride items

Santa Clara

Nightclubs

Club Savoy 3546 Flora Vista **408/247-7109** • 5pm-2am • popular • mostly women • dancing/DJ • live shows • karaoke • wheelchair access • women-owned/ run

Tinker's Damn (TD's) 46 N Saratoga Ave (at Stevens Creek) **408/243-4595** • 3pm-2am, from 1pm wknds • mostly gay men • dancing/DJ

Erotica

Borderline 56 N Saratoga Ave (at Stevens Creek) **408/241-2177** • toys • videos

Santa Cruz

INFO LINES & SERVICES

AA Gay/ Lesbian 5732 Soquel Dr, Soquel 831/475–5782 (AA#)

The Diversity Center 177 Walnut Ave 831/425–5422 • open daily • call for events

ACCOMMODATIONS

Chateau Victorian B&B Inn 118 First St 831/458–9458 • gay/ straight • 1885 Victorian inn w/ warm friendly atmosphere • fireplaces • nonsmoking • woman-owned/ run • $130-160

Compassion Flower Inn 216 Laurel St 831/466–0420 • gay/ straight • medical marijuana–friendly • full brkfst • clothing-optional jacuzzi & spa • kids ok • wheelchair access • lesbian-owned • $125–175

The Grove: A Women's Country Retreat by the Sea 40 Lily Wy, La Selva Beach 831/724–3459 • women only • 2 cottages • kitchens • fireplaces • hot tub • on a mini-farm near the beach • $135-195

NIGHTCLUBS

Blue Lagoon 923 Pacific Ave 831/423–7117 • 3:30pm-2am • gay/ straight • dancing/DJ • alternative • transgender-friendly • videos • wheelchair access

Club Caution 516 Front St 831/425–2582 • lesbians/ gay men • dancing/DJ • also restaurant • game room • theme nights • karaoke • videos

Dakota 1209 Pacific Ave (at Soquel) 831/454–9030 • 4pm-2am, from 2pm wknd • lesbians/ gay men • dancing/DJ • women's night Wed • men's night Th • wheelchair access

RESTAURANTS

Costa Brava Taco Stand 505 Seabright Ave 831/423–8190 • 8am-11pm, till 10pm Sun-Mon • Mexican • some veggie

Crêpe Place 1134 Soquel Ave (at Seabright) 831/429–6994 • 11am-midnight, 10am-1am Fri-Sat • plenty veggie • full bar • garden patio • wheelchair access

Saturn Cafe 145 Laurel St (at Pacific) 831/429–8505 • 11:30am-3am, till 4:30am Fri-Sat • light fare • plenty veggie • lesbian-owned

BOOKSTORES

Bookshop Santa Cruz 1520 Pacific Ave 831/423–0900 • 9am-10pm • general • LGBT section • cafe • wheelchair access

PUBLICATIONS

Manifesto Monterey Bay 831/761–3176 • monthly

GYMS & HEALTH CLUBS

Kiva Retreat House Spa 702 Water St (at Ocean) 831/429–1142 • noon-11pm, till midnight Fri-Sat • women-only 9am-1:30pm Sun

Santa Maria

INFO LINES & SERVICES

Pacific Pride Gay/ Lesbian Resource Center 819 W Church St (at Depot) 805/349–9947 • 9am-5pm Mon-Fri

CAFES

Cafe Monet 1555 S Broadway (at Battles) 805/928–1912 • 6:30am-9pm, till 5pm Mon, till 3pm wknds

EROTICA

Diamond Adult World 938 W Main St (at Western) 805/922–2828 • large LGBT video section

Santa Rosa

INFO LINES & SERVICES

Santa Rosa AA 707/544–1300 (AA#)

ACCOMMODATIONS

Hyatt Vineyard Creek Hotel 170 Railroad St (at Third St) 707/636–7100 • gay-friendly • resort • swimming • kids/ pets ok • seafood restaurant • wheelchair access • $149-249

NIGHTCLUBS

The Other Side 720 Adams (at Michele's) 707/526–3416 • 9pm-2am, 2nd Sat only • mostly women • dancing/ DJ

CAFES

A' Roma Roasters 95 5th St (Railroad Square) 707/576–7765 • 6am-close, live music wknds • lesbians/ gay men • live music wknds • wheelchair access • lesbian-owned

RESTAURANTS

Syrah 205 5th St (at Davis) 707/568–4002 • 11:30am-2:30pm & 5:30pm-9pm, till 10pm Fri-Sat • clsd Sun-Mon • creative California/ French bistro fare • eclectic wine list • moderate prices

BOOKSTORES

Sawyer's News 733 4th St (btwn D & E Sts) 707/542–1311 • 7am-9pm, till 7pm Sun • general news & bookstand

Publications

We the People 707/581-1809 • Sonoma County's voice of the lesbian, gay, bisexual & transgendered community

Spiritual Groups

1st Congregational United Church of Christ 2000 Humboldt St (at Silva) 707/546-0998 • 10:30am Sun

New Hope MCC 855 7th St (at Masonic Hall) 707/526-4673 • 10am Sun

Erotica

Santa Rosa Adult Books 3301 Santa Rosa Ave (at Todd) 707/542-8248

Sausalito

see Marin County

Sebastopol

Accommodations

Cedars of Sonoma 10203 Barnett Valley Rd (at Burnside) 707/829-1000 • gay/ straight • cabin on 20 acres • kids/ pets ok • $185-225

The Ranch 6056 Ross Rranch Road (at Ross Station Rd) 707/696-1578 • men only • nudity • hot tub • gym • nonsmoking • gay-owned

Vine Hill Inn B&B 3949 Vine Hill Rd 707/823-8832 • gay-friendly • B&B in restored 1897 farmhouse • swimming • $150

Cafes

Coffee Catz 6761 Sebastopol Ave (at Hwy 116) 707/829-6600 • 7am-8pm, till 9pm Fri-Sat • live shows • wheelchair access

Restaurants

Mom's Apple Pie 4550 Gravenstein Hwy N 707/823-8330 • pie worth stopping for on your way to & from Russian River!

Retail Shops

Milk & Honey 123 N Main St 707/824-1155 • 10am-6pm, from 11am Mon, Wed & Sun • goddess- & woman-oriented crafts • books • jewelry

Erotica

The Sensuality Shoppe 2371-A Gravenstein Hwy S 707/829-3999 • open daily • toys • books • videos • jewelry • woman-owned/ run

Sequoia Nat'l Park

Accommodations

Organic Gardens B&B 44095 Dinely Dr, Three Rivers 559/561-4610 • gay-friendly • 5 miles from entrance to Sequoia Nat'l Park • hot tub • nonsmoking • lesbian-owned • $115-130

Sonoma

includes Cotati, Glen Ellen, Kenwood & Penngrove

Accommodations

A Wine Country Teahouse 9556 Frederica Ave, Kenwood 707/833-6998 • lesbians/ gay men • swimming • hot tub • gay-owned • $225-275

Gaige House Inn 13540 Arnold Dr, Glen Ellen 707/935-0237, 800/935-0237 • gay-friendly • swimming • full brkfst • in the Wine Country • $175-695

Glenelly Inn & Cottages 5131 Warm Springs Rd, Glen Ellen 707/996-6720 • gay-friendly • B&B in 1916 inn • full brkfst • $150-250

Magliulo's Rose Garden Inn 681 Broadway (at Andrieux) 707/996-1031 • one of Wine Country's most romantic Victorian B&Bs • gay-friendly • wheelchair access

Sonoma Chalet 18935 5th St W 707/938-3129, 800/938-3129 • gay-friendly • B&B inn & cottages • hot tub

Thistle Dew Inn 171 W Spain St (at First St W) 707/938-2909, 800/382-7895 • gay-friendly • located in Wine Country • whirlpool baths & fireplaces • free use of bikes • gay & straight-owned • $155-285

Trojan Horse Inn 19455 Sonoma Hwy (btwn W Spain & W Napa) 707/996-2430, 800/899-1925 • gay-friendly • turn-of-the-century inn • nonsmoking • full brkfst • $160-245

Warm Springs Getaway 415/841-0257 • gay-friendly (mostly women) • rental home • hot tub • nonsmoking • lesbian-owned • $295-450

Bars

Black Cat Bar & Cafe 10056 Main St, Penngrove 707/793-9480 • 4pm-2am, from 5pm Mon • mostly women • neighborhood bar • DJ Sat • also restaurant • live shows • lesbian-owned

RESTAURANTS

The General's Daughter 400 W Spain St 707/938-4004 • lunch & dinner, Sun brunch, clsd Mon • eclectic

BOOKSTORES

North Light Books 550 E Cotati Rd, Cotati 707/792-4300 • 9am-9pm, till 7pm Fri, 10am-8pm Sun • anti-establishment • strong LGBT emphasis • also coffeehouse • lesbian-owned

Springville

ACCOMMODATIONS

Great Energy 559/539-2382 • lesbians/gay men • retreat in foothills of Sierra Nevada mtns • swimming • hiking • kids ok • woman-owned/run • $85-125

Stockton

see also Modesto

NIGHTCLUBS

Paradise 10100 N Lower Sacramento Rd (near Grider) 209/477-4724 • 6pm-2am, from 3pm Sun • lesbians/gay men • dancing/DJ • live shows • videos • young crowd

EROTICA

Suzie's Adult Superstores 3126 E Hammer Ln 209/952-6900 • 24hrs

Sunnyvale

ACCOMMODATIONS

▲ **Wild Palms Hotel** 910 E Fremont Ave (at Wolfe Ave) 408/738-0500, 800/538-1600 • gay-friendly • swimming • hot tub • kids ok • wheelchair access • $89-225

Sutter Creek

ACCOMMODATIONS

The Foxes Inn of Sutter Creek 77 Main St (at Keys St) 209/267-5882, 800/987-3344 • gay-friendly • full brkfst • close to Shenandoah Valley wine region • gay-owned • $160-229

Tiburon

see Marin County

Torrance

INFO LINES & SERVICES

South Bay Center 2235 Sepulveda Blvd (btwn Crenshaw & Arlington) 310/328-6550 • support/education for Manhattan, Hermosa & Redondo Beaches, Torrance, Palos Verdes, El Segundo

Ukiah

BARS

Perkins St Lounge 228 E Perkins St 707/462-0327 • 3pm-2am • gay-friendly • dancing/DJ

Upland

EROTICA

Mustang Books 961 N Central (at Foothill) 909/981-0227 • 24hrs

The Toy Box 1999 W Arrow Rte (at Central) 909/920-1135 • 24hrs

Vacaville

INFO LINES & SERVICES

Solano Pride Center 1125 Missouri St #203-D, Fairfield 707/427-2356 • clsd Tue & Sun • call for meeting times

SPIRITUAL GROUPS

St Paul's United Methodist Church 101 West St (at Monte Vista) 707/448-5154 • 10:30am Sun

Vallejo

NIGHTCLUBS

Nobody's Place 437 Virginia St (at Sonoma Blvd) 707/645-7298 • noon-2am, from 4pm Mon-Wed • lesbians/gay men • dancing/DJ • patio • wheelchair access

Van Nuys

EROTICA

Diamond Adult World 6406 Van Nuys Blvd (at Victory) 818/997-3665 • 24hrs • books • toys • videos

Ventura

INFO LINES & SERVICES

AA Gay/Lesbian 805/389-1444 (AA#), 800/990-7750

Ventura County Rainbow Alliance 2021 Sperry Ave, Ste 3 805/339-6342 • 9am-9pm

ACCOMMODATIONS

La Mer B&B 411 Poli St (at Oak St) 805/643-3600 • gay-friendly • Victorian B&B "of the celebrities" • full brkfst • $95-235

BARS

Paddy McDermott's 2 W Main St (at Ventura) 805/652-1071 • 2pm-2am • lesbians/gay men • dancing/DJ • live shows • karaoke • beer busts

EROTICA
Three Star Books 359 E Main St
805/653-9068 • 23hrs

Victorville

BARS
West Side 15 16868 Stoddard Wells Rd (off I-15) **760/243-9600** • 3pm-2am, from 2pm Sun • lesbians/ gay men • neighborhood bar • ladies night Th

Walnut Creek

INFO LINES & SERVICES
AA Gay/ Lesbian 185 Mayhew Wy (at Buskirk) **925/939-4155** • call for times

NIGHTCLUBS
Club 1220 1220 Pine St (at Civic Dr) **925/938-4550** • 4pm-2am • lesbians/ gay men • dancing/DJ • country/ western • karaoke • wheelchair access

Whittier

INFO LINES & SERVICES
Together in Pride AA 11931 Washington Blvd (at the church) **562/696-6213** (CHURCH #) • 7:30pm Th

SPIRITUAL GROUPS
Good Samaritan MCC 11931 E Washington Blvd **562/696-6213** • 10am Sun

Willits

RESTAURANTS
Purple Thistle 50 S Main St **707/459-4750** • 4:30pm-8pm, till 9pm wknds • clsd Sun & Mon • Japanese

BOOKSTORES
Leaves of Grass 15 S Main St **707/459-3744** • 10am-5:30pm, noon-5pm Sun • alternative

Yosemite Nat'l Park

ACCOMMODATIONS
The Ahwahnee Hotel Yosemite Valley Floor **559/252-4848** • gay-friendly • swimming • also restaurant • $379-835

Apple Tree Inn 1110 Hwy 41, Fish Camp **559/683-5111, 888/683-5111** • gay-friendly • B&B-inn • 2 miles from park's south entrance • swimming • wheelchair access • $89-299

Highland House B&B 3125 Wild Dove Ln (at Jerseydale Rd), Mariposa **209/966-3737, 888/477-5089** • gay-friendly • B&B near Yosemite & Sierra Nat'l Forest • kids ok • $95-135

▲ **The Homestead** 41110 Rd 600, Ahwahnee **559/683-0495, 800/483-0495** • gay-friendly • cottages, suite & 2-bdrm house nestled under the oaks on 160 acres • close to restaurants, golf, hiking & biking • kitchens • fireplaces • nonsmoking • kids ok • $110-374

Narrow Gauge Inn 48571 Hwy 41, Fish Camp **559/683-7720** • gay-friendly • mtnside country inn • swimming • hot tub • 4 miles from Yosemite • kids/ pets ok • nonsmoking • $120-205

Yosemite Big Creek Inn B&B 1221 Hwy 41, Fish Camp **559/641-2828** • gay/ straight • B&B • full brkfst • closest B&B to Yosemite Nat'l Park's south entrance on Hwy 41 • hot tub • nonsmoking • women-owned/ run • $100-209

The Yosemite Bug Lodge & Hostel 6979 Hwy 140, Midpines **209/966-6666** • gay-friendly • hostel w/ dorms, cabins, private rooms & tents • some shared baths • kids ok • nonsmoking • wheelchair access • $18-120

Yosemite View Lodge 11136 Hwy 140, El Portal **209/379-2681, 888/742-4371** • gay-friendly • swimming

Yosemite's Apple Blossom Inn B&B 559/642-2001, 888/687-4281 • gay-friendly • B&B • 20 minutes from south entrance of Yosemite Nat'l Park • hot tub • kids/ pets ok • wheelchair access • $85-200

COLORADO

Statewide

PUBLICATIONS

Colorado Pride Guide 303/377-1826 • LGBT business & travel directory • visit www.GayColorado.com for free copy

▲ **Out Front Colorado** 303/778-7900 • statewide LGBT newspaper

Weird Sisters 970/482-4393 • statewide • calendar w/ political, social & arts coverage

Alamosa

ACCOMMODATIONS

Cottonwood Inn 123 San Juan Ave **719/589-3882, 800/955-2623** • gay-friendly • full brkfst • art gallery • near sand dunes • nonsmoking • $55-125

Aspen

INFO LINES & SERVICES

Aspen Gay/ Lesbian Community Hotline 970/925-9249, 970/925-4123 • recorded local info & events

ACCOMMODATIONS

Aspen Mountain Lodge 311 W Main St **970/925-7650, 800/362-7736** • gay-friendly • full brkfst • après-ski wine & cheese • kids/ pets ok • hot tub • swimming • nonsmoking • $89-359

Hotel Aspen 110 W Main St **970/925-3441, 800/527-7369** • gay-friendly • mountain brkfst • hot tub • swimming • nonsmoking • kids/ pets ok • $109-405

Hotel Lenado 200 S Aspen St **970/925-6246, 800/321-3457** • gay-friendly • full brkfst • hot tub • full bar • $125-525

Sardy House 128 E Main St **970/920-2525, 800/321-3457** • gay-friendly • hot tub • swimming • also restaurant • $115-1075

NIGHTCLUBS

Club Chelsea 415 Hyman Ave (at Galena) 970/920-0066 • 9pm-2am • gay-friendly • wheelchair access

RESTAURANTS

Jimmy's 205 S Mill St (at Hopkins) **970/925-6020** • 5:30pm-11:30pm • also bar

Syzygy 520 E Hyman, 2nd flr **970/925-3700** • seasonal • 6pm-10:30pm, bar till 2am • some veggie • live jazz • wheelchair access

BOOKSTORES

Explore Booksellers & Bistro 221 E Main (at Aspen) 970/925-5336, 800/562-7323 • 10am-9pm • also gourmet vegetarian restaurant • wheelchair access

Beaver Creek

ACCOMMODATIONS

Beaver Creek Lodge 26 Avondale Ln (at Village Rd) **970/845-9800, 800/583-9615** • gay-friendly • also restaurant w/ mtn views & fire pits • pool • wheelchair access

Boulder

ACCOMMODATIONS

The Briar Rose B&B 2151 Arapahoe Ave (at 22nd St) **303/442-3007, 888/786-8440** • gay-friendly • full brkfst • internet access • nonsmoking • $119-154

BARS

The FoundryBilliards Club 1109 Walnut
303/447–1803 • 11am-1:30am • also cafe
from 6am • gay-friendly • dancing/DJ • live
shows • wheelchair access

CAFES

Walnut Cafe 3073 Walnut (at 30th)
303/447–2315 • 7am-4pm • popular • plenty
veggie • patio • wheelchair access • women-
owned/ run

BOOKSTORES

Left Hand Books 1200 Pearl St, lower level
(E of Broadway) **303/443–8252** • 10am-9pm,
noon-6pm Sun • progressive literature

Word Is Out 2015 10th St (near Pearl)
303/449–1415 • 10am-7pm, noon-5pm Sun •
women's bookstore w/ LGBT sections •
wheelchair access

RETAIL SHOPS

Enchanted Ink 1200 Pearl St #35
303/440–6611 • tattoos, piercing, henna •
lesbian-owned

EROTICA

Pleasures 1720 15th St (at Grove)
303/442–9515 • 24hrs

Breckenridge

ACCOMMODATIONS

Allaire Timbers Inn 9511 Hwy 9, S Main St
970/453–7530, 800/624–4904 • gay-friendly •
full brkfst • hot tub • nonsmoking • wheelchair
access • $145-390

Valdoro Mountain Lodge 500 Village Rd
970/547–4089, 800/436–6780 • gay/ straight •
swimming • wheelchair access • condos w/
access to pool, massage facilities & outdoor
hot tub • $150-800

Colorado Springs

(includes Manitou Springs)

INFO LINES & SERVICES

**Pikes Peak Gay/ Lesbian Community
Center Helpline** 719/471–4429 • 2pm-6pm
Tue-Fri, noon-4pm Sat, clsd Sun-Mon • call for
events

ACCOMMODATIONS

**Authentic B&B Inns of the Pikes Peak
Region** 888/892–2237

Blue Skies Inn B&B 402 Manitou Ave (at
Mayfair), Manitou Springs **719/685–3899,
800/398–7949** • gay/ straight • Gothic Revival
built by artist/ innkeeper • full brkfst • gazebo
hot tub • kids ok • nonsmoking • $135-235

Old Town Guest House B&B 115 S 26th St
719/632–9194, 888/375–4210 • gay-friendly •
full brkfst • hot tub • nonsmoking • wheelchair
access • $99-237

Pikes Peak Paradise Woodland Park
719/687–6656, 800/728–8282 • gay-friendly •
mansion w/ view of Pikes Peak • full brkfst •
hot tub • fireplaces • nonsmoking • kids 12+
ok • $110-200

Quality Inn—Garden of the Gods
555 W Garden of the Gods **719/593–9119,
800/828–4347** • gay-friendly • seasonal pool •
mountain views • $50-110

Rockledge Country Inn 328 El Paso Blvd,
Manitou Springs **719/685–4515,
888/685–4515** • gay-friendly • Tudor country
home on historic estate • full brkfst • $125-325

Two Sisters Inn 10 Otoe Pl, Manitou
Springs **719/685–9684, 800/274–7466** • gay-
friendly • kids over 10 ok • full brkfst • women-
owned/ run • $69-125

RESTAURANTS

Dale Street Cafe 115 E Dale (at Nevada)
719/578–9898 • lunch & dinner, brunch wknds
• some veggie • full bar

SPIRITUAL GROUPS

Dignity Southern Colorado 21st & West
Colorado Ave **719/685–5343** • 7pm 1st Sat

Pikes Peak MCC 1102 S 21st St (at
Broadway) **719/634–3771** • 9am & 10:30am
Sun

EROTICA

First Amendment Adult Bookstore 220 E
Fillmore (at Nevada) 719/630–7676

Romantix 1613 La Shelle Wy (off B St)
719/538–9675

Denver

INFO LINES & SERVICES

AA Gay/ Lesbian 303/322–4440

**Lesbian/ Gay/ Bisexual Community
Services Center of Colorado** 1050
Broadway, 2nd flr **303/733–7743** • 10am-6pm
Mon-Fri • extensive resources & support
groups • wheelchair access

ACCOMMODATIONS

Capitol Hill Mansion B&B 1207
Pennsylvania (at 12th) **303/839–5221,
800/839–9329** • gay-friendly • B&B • full
brkfst • jacuzzi • kids ok • $95-175

Elyria's Western Guest House 1655 E 47th Ave (near I–70 & Brighton) **303/291-0915** • lesbians/gay men • Western ambiance in historic Denver neighborhood • shared baths • nonsmoking • gay-owned • $40-60

The Gregory Inn, LoDo 2500 Arapahoe St (at 25th St) **303/295-6570, 800/925-6570** • gay-friendly • full brkfst • jacuzzis • fireplaces • nonsmoking • straight & gay-owned • $119-259

Hotel Monaco 1717 Champa St (at 17th) **303/296-1717, 800/397-5380** • gay-friendly • gym • spa • nonsmoking • also Italian restaurant • pets ok • $125-915

Lumber Baron Inn 2555 W 37th Ave (at Bryant) **303/477-8205** • gay-friendly • Victorian mansion furnished w/ antiques • full brkfst • hot tub • $145-235

The Oxford Hotel 1600 17th St **303/628-5400, 800/228-5838** • gay-friendly • hotel • also 2 restaurants, art deco lounge • $169-369

Radisson Hotel Denver Stapleton Plaza 3333 Quebec St (at 35th) **303/321-3500, 800/333-3333** • gay-friendly • swimming • gym • also restaurant • wheelchair access • $75-139

Denver

WHERE THE GIRLS ARE:
Many lesbians reside in the Capitol Hill area, near the gay and mixed bars, but hang out in cafes and women's bars scattered around the city.

LGBT PRIDE:
June. 303/733-7743 x17, web: www.coloradoglbt.org.

ANNUAL EVENTS:
June/July- Pride Fest Denver, web: www.pridefestdenver.org.
July- 2nd weekend, Rocky Mountain Regional Rodeo (gay rodeo), web: cgra.net.
August- 3rd weekend, Cinema Q - Denver International LGBT film festival, web: www.cinemaq.org.
August - AIDS Walk, web: coloradoaidsproject.org
October- Great American Beer Festival, web: www.gabf.org.

CITY INFO:
303/892-1505,
web: www.denver.org.

ATTRACTIONS:
16th Street Mall.
Black American West Museum 303/292-2566.
Denver Art Museum 720/865-5000.
Six Flags Elitch Gardens 303/595-4386.
LoDo (Lower Downtown).
Molly Brown House 303/832-4092.

BEST VIEW:
Lookout Mountain (at night especially) or from the top of the Capitol rotunda.

WEATHER:
Summer temperatures average in the 90°s and winter ones in the 40°s. The sun shines an average of 300 days a year with humidity in the single digits.

TRANSIT:
Yellow Cab 303/777-7777.
Metro Taxi 303/333-3333.
Super Shuttle 303/370-1300.
RTD 303/628-9000 or 303/299-6000 (infoline).

Ramada Inn Denver Downtown 1150 E Colfax Ave (at Downing) **303/831-7700, 800/272-6232** • gay/ straight • hotel • swimming • hot tub • full brkfst • in the heart of Capitol Hill • wheelchair access • $55-99

BARS

The Atrium Bar & Grill 554 S Broadway **303/744-1923** • 7am-2am • mostly gay men • dancing/ DJ • food served • strippers Wed, Fri, Sat

BJ's Carousel 1380 S Broadway (at Arkansas) **303/777-9880** • noon-2am, from 10am wknds • popular • lesbians/ gay men • neighborhood bar • drag shows • also restaurant • karaoke Wed • transgender-friendly • wheelchair access • gay-owned

Broadways 1027 Broadway (at 11th Ave) **303/623-0700** • 3:30pm-2am, from 11am wknds • lesbians/ gay men • neighborhood bar

C's 7900 E Colfax Ave (at Trenton) **303/322-4436** • 5pm-midnight, till 2am Fri-Sat • mostly women • dancing/DJ

Cafe Cero 1446 S Broadway (btwn Arkansas & Florida) **303/282-1446** • 4pm-1:30am Tue-Sat • gay/ straight • neighborhood bar • food served 5pm-10:30pm

The Compound 145 Broadway (at 2nd Ave) **303/722-7977** • 7am-2am • mostly gay men • neighborhood bar • dancing/DJ • alternative

Coors Nightclub 3400 Navajo St (at 34th Ave) **303/433-5225** • 6pm-2am Th, from 3pm Fri-Sat, from 2pm Sun • lesbians/ gay men • dancing/ DJ • karaoke • ladies night Th

The Den 5110 W Colfax Ave (at Sheridan) **303/623-7998** • 1pm-2am, from 10am Sun • lesbians/ gay men • neighborhood bar • karaoke • wheelchair access

---

Date: Dec 18, 2005 14:11:59
From: Girl-on-the-Go
To: Editor@Damron.com
Subject: Denver

>Denver is a big city with a friendly small-town feel. To get the most out of your stay, start with a visit to the women's bookstore, **Sisters Books**, and pick up a copy of **Weird Sisters**, the local lesbian paper, or **Out Front Colorado**, the statewide LGBT paper. Next, drop by the **Lesbian/Gay/Bisexual Center** for the inside scoop on where to go and what to do in Denver.
>Look for local lesbians in Capitol Hill, soaking up sun in Cheesman Park, or sipping coffee at **Java Creek** or with the boys on 9th Avenue between Ogden and Marion.
At night, sample some live music at **Dazzle**, have a cocktail at the **Denver Detour**, or get down at **C's** dance bar.
>Be sure to take advantage of the Rocky Mountain snows with a ski trip to one of the many nearby resorts: Aspen, Telluride, or Rocky Mountain National Park.

Denver Detour 551 E Colfax Ave (at Pearl, use back entrance) **303/861–1497** • 11am-2am • popular • mostly women • neighborhood bar • live shows • lunch & dinner daily • some veggie • wheelchair access

Down Under Denver 266 S Downing, unit B (at Alameda, enter on alley) **303/777–4377** • 3pm-2am, from 11am wknds • lesbians/gay men • also restaurant • gay-owned

El Chapultepec 1962 Market St (at 20th) **303/295–9126** • 9am-2am • popular • gay-friendly • live jazz & blues • cover

Fox Hole 2936 Fox St (at 20th St) **303/298–7391** • 6pm-2am, from 3pm wknds • lesbians/gay men • outdoor dance Sun

JR's Bar 777 E 17th Ave **303/831–0459** • 3pm-2am • mostly gay men • videos • young crowd • gay-owned

R&R Denver 4958 E Colfax Ave (at Elm) **303/320–9337** • 3pm-2am, from 11am wknds • lesbians/gay men • neighborhood bar

Safari Bar 500 Denargo St (at 31st) **303/298–7959** • noon-2am • lesbians/gay men • more women Th-Fri • dancing/DJ • drag shows Sun

The Triangle 2036 Broadway (at 20th Ave) **303/293–9009** • 3pm-2am, from 1pm Sun • mostly gay men • leather

NIGHTCLUBS

The 2101 Denver 2101 Champa St (at 21st) **303/299–9283** • 9pm Wed for The Wave • lesbians/gay men • ladies' night Fri • dancing/DJ • wheelchair access

Club Evolution 821 22nd St (at Champa) **303/296–4604** • 2pm-2am, from 10am Sun • lesbians/gay men • dancing/DJ • 2 floors • upstairs lounge

Dream 3500 Walnut St (at 35th) **303/863–7326** • lesbians/gay men • dancing/DJ • theme nights • popular Sat

La Rumba 99 W 9th Ave (at Broadway) **303/572–8006** • gay-friendly• more gay for Lipgloss Fri • dancing/DJ

Rise 1909 Blake (at 19th) **303/383–1909** • 9pm-2am Wed, Fri-Sat • gay/straight • dancing/DJ • live shows • videos • theme nights

Serengeti 1037 Broadway **303/534–0222** • Inferno Fri • lesbians/gay men • dancing/DJ • live shows • theme nights

CAFES

Bump & Grind Cafe 439 E 17th Ave (at Pennsylvania) **303/861–4841** • 7am-2:30pm, wknd brunch 10am-2pm, clsd Mon

Common Grounds 3484 W 32nd Ave **303/458–5248** • also location at 1601 17th St, 303/ 296–9248

Diedrich Coffee 1201 E 9th Ave (at Downing) **303/837–1275** • 6am-11pm, from 7am wknds • popular

Java Creek 287 Columbine St (at 3rd Ave) **303/377–8902** • 7am-6pm, 8am-6pm Sat, 8:30am-3pm Sun • wheelchair access

Wired Coffee & Art 19 E Bayaud **303/733–3977** • 7am-5pm, till 10pm Fri-Sat • live entertainment • women-owned/run

RESTAURANTS

The Avenue Grill 630 E 17th Ave (at Washington) **303/861–2820** • 11:30am-11pm, till midnight Sat, 5pm-10pm Sun

Benny's Restaurant & Tequila Bar 301 E 7th Ave (at Grant St) **303/894–0788** • lunch & dinner weekdays, also brkfst wknds • Mexican • nonsmoking

Dazzle 930 Lincoln St (at 9th) **303/839–5100** • dinner from 4pm, from 5pm wknds • also lounge • live music

Dixon's Downtown Grill 1610 16th St (at Wazee) • 7am-10pm Sun-Mon, till 11pm Tue-Th, till midnight Fri, from 8am Sat • American

Goodfriends Restaurant 3100 E Colfax Ave (at St Paul) **303/331–1981** • lunch, brunch, dinner

Joseph's Southern Food, Carry Out & Drive In 2868 Fairfax St (at 29th) **303/333–5332** • 11am-9pm, clsd Mon • traditional Southern • also bakery, ice cream parlor, candy • gay-owned

Las Margaritas 1066 Olde S Gaylord St (btwn E Tennessee & E Mississippi, Washington Park) **303/777–0194** • 11am-10pm, bar till 2am • popular • Mexican • some veggie • wheelchair access

Manny's Underground/Wine Down 1836 Blake **303/308–0110** • 7am-3pm • clsd Sun

Painted Bench 400 E 20th Ave (at Logan) **303/863–7473** • lunch & dinner, dinner only Sat, clsd Sun • full bar

Paris on the Platte 1553 Platte St (at 15th) **303/455–2451** • 8am-1am, till 3am wknds • popular after-hours

Racine's 650 Sherman St (at 6th Ave)
303/595-0418 • brkfst, lunch, dinner & Sun
brunch • some veggie • full bar

Saverino 2191 Arapahoe (at 22nd St)
303/308-0764 • lunch weekdays, dinner
nightly, clsd Mon • Italian

Wazee Supper Club 1600 15th St (at
Wazee) 303/623-9518 • 11am-2am, noon-
midnight Sun • full bar

Zaidy's Deli 121 Adams (at First)
303/333-5336 • 6:30am-5pm, 7:30am-4pm
wknds

ENTERTAINMENT & RECREATION

Colorado OUT Spoken PBS KBDI, channel
12 303/861-0829 • 11pm Sun • LGBT news &
entertainment TV program

Denver Women's Chorus 303/274-4177

Mercury Cafe 2199 California St
303/294-9281 • 5:30pm-close, clsd Mon •
swing, tango, salsa dancing • live shows • also
restaurant • dinner only Tue-Sun, wknd brunch

BOOKSTORES

Isis Books & Gifts 5701 E Colfax Ave (at
Ivanhoe) 303/321-0867, 800/808-0867 •
10am-7pm, till 6pm Fri-Sat, noon-5pm Sun •
New Age • metaphysical • wheelchair access

Relatively Wilde 42 S Broadway (at
Ellsworth) 303/777-0766, 866/779-4533 •
11am-6pm Tue-Sat, noon-5pm Sun, clsd Mon
• LGBT books & videos • wheelchair access •
gay-owned

Sisters Books 2625 E 12th Ave (at Elizabeth)
303/399-2004 • 10am-6pm, noon-5pm Sun,
clsd Mon • feminist • gifts • toys • wheelchair
access • lesbian-owned

Tattered Cover Book Store 2955 E 1st Ave
(at Milwaukee) 303/322-7727, 800/833-9327
• 9am-11pm, 10am-6pm Sun • local
independent • also 1628 16th St • 4 flrs •
wheelchair access

RETAIL SHOPS

Arco Iris Design 82 S Broadway
303/765-5116 • pride jewelry & design

Bound By Design 1336 E Colfax (at
Humboldt) 303/830-7272, 303/832-TAT2 •
11am-11pm, noon-10pm Sun • piercing &
tattoos

Heaven Sent Me 116 S Broadway (btwn
Alameda & Virginia) 303/733-9000 • pride
items, clothing, gifts • wheelchair access

uBer 135 Broadway (at 2nd Ave)
303/777-1100 • 10am-9pm, till 6pm Mon •
fetish & pride gear

PUBLICATIONS

EXP Magazine 303/752-4300,
877/397-6244 • bi-weekly gay magazine

▲ **Out Front Colorado** 303/778-7900 •
statewide bi-weekly LGBT newspaper • since
1976

Pride Magazine 303/316-4688 • also
publishes Denver Pink Pages

SPIRITUAL GROUPS

Dignity Denver 1100 Fillmore (at Capitol
Hts Presb Church) 303/322-8485 • 5pm Sun,
social following service

MCC of the Rockies 980 Clarkson St (at
10th) 303/860-1819 • 8am, 9:30am & 11am
Sun • wheelchair access

St Paul's United Methodist Church 1615
Ogden (at E 16th Ave) 303/832-4929 •
10:30am Sun • reconciling congregation • also
Buddhist-Christian contemplative prayer •
5pm Sun

GYMS & HEALTH CLUBS

Broadway Bodyworks 160 S Broadway (at
Maple) 303/722-4342 • lesbians/ gay men •
wheelchair access

EROTICA

The Crypt 8 Broadway (at Ellsworth)
303/733-3112 • leather & more

Durango

ACCOMMODATIONS

Leland House B&B 721 E 2nd Ave
970/385-1920, 800/664-1920 • popular • gay-
friendly • rooms & suites w/ kitchens • full
brkfst • nonsmoking • wheelchair access •
$149-340

Rochester Hotel 726 E 2nd Ave
970/385-1920, 800/664-1920 • gay-friendly •
popular • newly renovated 1892 house
decorated in Old West motif • full brkfst •
nonsmoking • kids/ pets ok • wheelchair
access • $109-229

Estes Park

ACCOMMODATIONS

Stanley Hotel 333 Wonderview Ave
800/976-1377, 970/586-3371 • gay-friendly •
1909 lodge near Rocky Mtn Nat'l Park • the
inspiration for Stephen King's *The Shining* •
$180-300

Florissant

ENTERTAINMENT & RECREATION

McNamara Ranch 4620 County Rd 100 **719/748-3466** • horseback tours & more

Fort Collins

INFO LINES & SERVICES

The Lambda Community Center 149 W Oak, Ste 8 **970/221-3247**

ACCOMMODATIONS

Never Summer Nordic **970/482-9411** • gay/ straight • camping in yurts (portable Mongolian round houses) in Colorado Rockies • sleep 5-9 • kids/ pets ok • mtn-biking & skiing • $60-110

BARS

Choice City Shots 124 LaPorte Ave (at College) **970/221-4333** • 5-midnight, till 2am wknds • lesbians/ gay men • "womyn's night" Tue • neighborhood bar • dancing/DJ Fri-Sat • karaoke • live shows wknds • wheelchair access • lesbian/ gay-owned

NIGHTCLUBS

Club Static 1437 E Mulberry St (at Link Ln) **970/493-0251** • 9pm-2am, clsd Mon • popular • lesbians/ gay men • dancing/DJ • theme nights • videos • patio • wheelchair access

Grand Junction

BARS

Quincy's 609 Main St (btwn 7th & Main) **970/242-9633** • 7am-2am, gay after 8pm • gay-friendly • neighborhood bar • food served • theater crowd • wheelchair access

RESTAURANTS

Leon's Taqueria 505 30th Rd **970/242-1388** • lunch & dinner, brkfst wknds

Hotchkiss

ACCOMMODATIONS

Leroux Creek Inn & Vineyards 1220 3100 Rd **970/872-4746** • B&B • Southwestern-style adobe on 46 acres • $145-175

RESTAURANTS

North Fork Valley Restaurant & Thirsty Parrot Pub 140 W Bridge St **970/872-4215** • 11am-9pm, till 3pm Sun • American/ Mexican • bluegrass jam-session 3:30 pm Sun

Mancos

ACCOMMODATIONS

Old Mancos Inn 200 W Grand Ave **970/533-9019** • gay/ straight • some shared baths • gay-owned • $30-50

New Raymer

ACCOMMODATIONS

Colorado Cattle Company & Guest Ranch 70008 WCR 132 **970/437-5345** • gay-friendly • guests participate in cattle work & horseback riding in this Wild West adventure • pool • nonsmokng

Pueblo

BARS

Pirate's Cove 105 Central Plaza (off 1st & Union) **719/542-9624** • 2pm-2am, clsd Mon • lesbians/ gay men • neighborhood bar • wheelchair access

SPIRITUAL GROUPS

MCC Pueblo 1003 Liberty Ln (at Bonforte, at Christ Congregational) **719/543-6460** • 5pm Sun

Steamboat Springs

ACCOMMODATIONS

Elk River Estates **970/879-7556** • gay-friendly • suburban townhouse B&B • near hiking, skiing & natural hot springs • full brkfst • gay-owned • $35-40

Trinidad

ACCOMMODATIONS

Patmé Ranch PO Box 44, Aguilar 81020 **719/846-5724** • mostly women • B&B • camping • on 400 acres • full brkfst • hot tub • kids/ pets ok • nonsmoking • lesbian-owned • $60

Vail

ACCOMMODATIONS

Antlers at Vail 680 W Lionshead Pl **970/476-2471, 800/843-8245** • gay-friendly • apts • hot tub • swimming • fireplace • balcony • kids ok • pets ok w/ prior approval • $150-1,400

RESTAURANTS

Larkspur Restaurant & Market 458 Vail Valley Dr (in the Golden Peak Lodge) **970/479-8050** • lunch & dinner, seasonal hours • fine dining • also bar • patio • ski-in/ out • wheelchair access

Sweet Basil 193 E Gore Creek Dr 970/476-0125 • lunch & dinner • some veggie • full bar • wheelchair access

Winter Park

ACCOMMODATIONS

Bear Paw Inn 871 Bear Paw Dr 970/887-1351 • gay-friendly • massive log lodge on top of mtn w/ spectacular views of Rocky Mtn Nat'l Park • full brkfst • $170-215

Silverado II 490 Kings Crossing Rd 970/726-5753, 800/551-9943 • gay-friendly • condo ski resort • swimming • $81-560

CONNECTICUT

Statewide

PUBLICATIONS

▲ **Metroline** 860/233-8334 • regional newspaper & entertainment guide, covers CT, RI & MA

Bethel

RESTAURANTS

Bethel Pizza House 206 Greenwood Ave 203/748-1427 • 11am-11pm

Bridgeport

RESTAURANTS

Bloodroot Restaurant 85 Ferris St 203/576-9168 • lunch Tue & Th-Sat, dinner Tue-Sat, brunch only Sun, clsd Mon • feminist vegetarian • patio • wheelchair access • women-owned/ run

BOOKSTORES

Bloodroot 85 Ferris St 203/576-9168 • clsd Mon, call for hours • feminist • also vegetarian restaurant • wheelchair access

Danbury

ACCOMMODATIONS

Maron Hotel & Suites 42 Lake Ave Extension (off I-84) 203/791-2200, 866/811-2582 • gay-friendly • wheelchair access • kids/ pets ok • $89-189

BARS

Triangles Cafe 66 Sugar Hollow Rd, Rte 7 203/798-6996 • 5pm-1am, till 2am Fri-Sat • popular • lesbians/ gay men • dancing/DJ • live shows • patio • gay-owned

RESTAURANTS

Goulash Place 42 Highland Ave 203/744-1971 • lunch & dinner, clsd Mon • Hungarian • beer/ wine

Sesame Seed 68 W Wooster St 203/743-9850 • lunch & dinner, clsd Sun, Mediterranean/ Italian, funky decor, lots of veggie

Thang Long 56 Padanaram Rd (near North Street Shopping Center) 203/743-6049 • lunch & dinner, clsd Sun-Mon • Vietnamese • all-you-can-eat buffet wkdays

Enfield

EROTICA

Bookends 44 Enfield St/ Rte 5 860/745-3988

Groton

ACCOMMODATIONS

Flagship Inn & Suites 470 Gold Star Hwy (Rte 184, off I-95) 860/445-7458, 888/800-0770 • gay-friendly • gym passes • in-room movies • kids ok • wheelchair access • gay-owned • $50-165

Hartford

INFO LINES & SERVICES

Project 100/ The Community Center 1841 Broad St (at New Britain) 860/724-5542 • 10am-9pm • meetings & activities • wheelchair access

ACCOMMODATIONS

Butternut Farm 1654 Main St, Glastonbury 860/633-7197 • gay/ straight • 18th-c house furnished w/ antiques • full brkfst • $90-110

The Mansion Inn 139 Hartford Rd (at Main St), Manchester 860/646-0453 • gay-friendly • B&B • full brkfst • in-room fireplaces • $95-145

BARS

Chez Est 458 Wethersfield Ave (at Main St) 860/525-3243 • 3pm-1am, till 2am Fri-Sat • popular • lesbians/ gay men • karaoke • drag shows • monthly women's night

The Polo Club 678 Maple Ave (btwn Preston & Mapleton) 860/278-3333 • 8pm-1am, till 2am Fri-Sat • lesbians/ gay men • dancing/DJ • karaoke • drag shows

Women After Hours 860/930-844 • monthly dance/ social • call for schedule & location • cover

NIGHTCLUBS

Club Lucy 458 Wethersfield Ave (at Main St) **860/525-3243** • monthly women's party at Chez Est

Stage East 1022 Main St (at Bissell St), East Hartford **860/289-7400** • gay night Sun, call to verify

CAFES

Tisane Tea & Coffee Bar 537 Farmington Ave **860/523-5417** • 7am-1am, 8am-2am wknds

RESTAURANTS

Arugula 953 Farmington Ave, West Hartford **860/561-4888** • lunch & dinner, clsd Mon, Sun dinner only • Mediterranean • reservations recommended

Peppercorn's 357 Main St **860/547-1714** • lunch Mon-Fri, dinner Sat only • Northern Italian

Pond House Cafe 155 Asylum Ave **860/231-8823** • lunch Tue-Sat & dinner Wed-Sat, Sun brunch • bring your own bottle • patio

Trumbull Kitchen 150 Trumbull St (at Pearl St) **860/493-7417** • lunch & dinner Mon-Fri, dinner only wknds • global cuisine/ tapas

ENTERTAINMENT & RECREATION

Connecticut Sun 1 Mohegan Sun Blvd (Mohegan Sun Area), Uncasville **877/786-8499** • check out the Women's National Basketball Association while you're in Hartford

UConn Huskies 1266 Storrs Rd (Gampel Pavilion), Storrs **877/288-2666** • basketball • also plays at Hartford Civic Center, 860/ 727-8010

RETAIL SHOPS

▲ **MetroStore** 493 Farmington Ave (at Sisson Ave) **860/231-8845** • 8:30am-8pm, till 5:30pm Tue, Wed & Sat, clsd Sun • magazines • travel guides • DVD rentals • leather & more

PUBLICATIONS

▲ **Metroline** **860/233-8334** • regional newspaper & entertainment guide, covers CT, RI & MA

Hartford

LGBT PRIDE:
September. 860/524-8114, web: www.connecticutpride.com.

ANNUAL EVENTS:
June - Conneticut Gay & Lesbian Film Festival, web: ctglff.org

CITY INFO:
Greater Hartford Tourism District 800/793-4480, web: www.enjoy-hartford.com.

ATTRACTIONS:
Bushnell Park Carousel and Museum 860/585-5411.
Harriet Beecher Stowe House 860/522-9258.
Mark Twain House 860/247-0998.
Real Art Ways 860/232-1006.
Wadsworth Atheneum Museum of Art 860/278-2670.

WEATHER:
Summer highs are in the low 80°s. But that 50%+ humidity will make it feel like more. Humidity all year round. Summer drops into the low 20°s. January is the coldest and snowiest month. The full four seasons are in effect.

TRANSIT:
Yellow Cab 860/666-6666.
Airport Connection 860/529-7865 (downtown hotels only).
Connecticut Transit 860/525-9181, web: www.cttransit.com.

Spiritual Groups

MCC 1841 Broad St (at Hartford Community Center) **860/724-4605** • 10am Sun

Erotica

Very Intimate Pleasures 100 Brainard Ave (exit 27, off I-91) **860/246-1875**

Kent

Accommodations

Inn at Kent Falls 107 Kent Cornwall Rd **860/927-3197** • gay/ straight • wheelchair access • gay-owned • $155-325

Manchester

Cafes

Cafe on Main 985 Main St **860/647-7444** • 7am-2pm, till 1pm Sun, clsd Tue

Meriden

Erotica

The D/ S Toy Chest 975 Broad St (at rear) **203/639-0622** • 11am-9pm Mon-Th, till 10pm Fri-Sat, noon-5pm Sun • mostly women • huge fetish boutique!

Mystic

Accommodations

Mermaid Inn of Mystic 2 Broadway **860/536-6223, 877/692-2632** • lesbians/ gay men (straight-friendly) • B&B w/ village location & river views • full brkfst • lesbian-owned • $150-225

New Britain

Nightclubs

Club Shake 493 W Main St **860/223-1300** • lesbians/ gay men • Kitty Kat Club (mostly women) 3rd Fri • dancing/ DJ • drag shows

New Haven

Info Lines & Services

New Haven Gay/ Lesbian Community Center 50 Fitch St **203/387-2252** • events • meetings • resources • library • weekly movies • call for info

Accommodations

The Inn at Oyster Point 104 Howard Ave (at 6th St) **203/773-3334, 866/978-3778** • gay/ straight • jacuzzi • nonsmoking • gay-owned • $89-259

Bars

168 York St Cafe 168 York St **203/789-1915** • 3pm-1am, till 2am Fri-Sat • lesbians/ gay men • Sun brunch • patio • gay-owned

The Bar 254 Crown St **203/495-8924** • 4pm-1am • gay/ straight • more gay Tue • dancing/DJ • pizza • wheelchair access

Partners 365 Crown St (at Park St) **203/776-1014** • 5pm-1am, till 2am Fri-Sat • lesbians/ gay men • neighborhood bar • dancing/DJ • leather • occasional women's night

Nightclubs

Gotham Citi Cafe 130 Crown St (at Church) **203/498-2484** • 8pm-1am, till 5am Fri-Sat, clsd Sun-Tue • gay/ straight • dancing/DJ • gay night Sat • wheelchair access

Cafes

Chapel Sweet Shoppe 1042 Chapel St **203/624-2411** • 10am-8pm, noon-6pm Sun • full ice cream fountain • seasonal outside cafe

Restaurants

168 York St Cafe 168 York St **203/789-1915** • 3pm-1am, till 2am Fri-Sat • lesbians/ gay men • seasonal Sun brunch • some veggie • full bar • patio • gay-owned • $4-7

Beach Head Cafe 3 Cosey Beach Ave, East Haven **203/469-5450** • dinner only, clsd Mon • seafood • Italian • patio

Spiritual Groups

MCC 34 Harrison St **203/397-2312** • 9:15am Sun

Erotica

Very Intimate Pleasures 170 Boston Post Rd, Orange **203/799-7040**

New London

Bars

Club 251 9 Tilley St (at Bank) **860/443-8883** • 4pm-1am, 6pm-2am Fri-Sun • lesbians/ gay men • dancing/DJ • live shows • patio • wheelchair access

Bookstores

Greene's Books & Beans 140 Bank St **860/443-3312** • open 7 days • also cafe • wheelchair access

Norfolk

ACCOMMODATIONS

Manor House B&B 69 Maple Ave **860/542-5690** • gay-friendly • elegant & romantic 1898 Victorian Tudor estate • full brkfst • fireplaces • whirlpool • nonsmoking • $130-255

North Stonington Village

ACCOMMODATIONS

Antiques & Accommodations **800/554-7829** • gay-friendly • B&B • minutes from Mystic, CT • nonsmoking • $99-294

Norwalk

INFO LINES & SERVICES

Triangle Community Center 16 River St (Mechanic St entrance) **203/853-0600** • activities • newsletter • call for info

ACCOMMODATIONS

Silk Orchid **203/847-2561** • women only • 2 rooms • swimming • whirlpool • fireplace • lesbian-owned • $100-125

Norwich

BOOKSTORES

Magazines & More 77 Salem Tpke #105 **860/886-6247** • 10am-8pm, till 5pm Sat, clsd Sun • newsstand w/ 3,000 magazines & books

Preston

ACCOMMODATIONS

The Mandrake Inn 124 Rte 2A (at Rtes 2 & 12) **860/892-1485** • gay/ straight • B&B • full brkfst • hot tub • wheelchair access • $125-140 + tax

Ridgefield

RESTAURANTS

East Ridge Cafe 5 Grove St **203/894-1940** • 11am-2am • also mellow, upscale bar

Gail's Station House 378 Main St **203/438-9775** • brkfst & lunch, dinner Fri-Sat • great cheddar corn pancakes • beer/ wine

Stamford

NIGHTCLUBS

Club Mor 129 Atlantic St **203/357-7755** • gay Sun only • dancing/ DJ

Storrs

RESTAURANTS

Hideaway Roadhouse 12 Merrow Rd (at Rte 32) **860/487-6000** • 4pm-close, clsd Mon-Tue • gay-friendly • also bar • wheelchair access • gay-owned

Stratford

NIGHTCLUBS

Stephanie's Living Room **203/377-2119** • popular • women only • "quality social events for women" • dances • multiracial • all ages • wheelchair access • discounts for physically challenged

Washington Depot

RESTAURANTS

GW Tavern 20 Bee Brook Rd (Rte 47) **860/868-6633** • 5:30pm-10pm, till 11pm wknds

Waterbury

SPIRITUAL GROUPS

Integrity/ Waterbury Area 16 Church St (at St John's) **203/754-3116** • 5:30pm 2nd Sun

Westport

BARS

Cedar Brook Cafe 919 Post Rd E **203/221-7429** • 8pm-1am Mon, till 2am Fri-Sat, 6pm-11pm Sun, clsd Tue • lesbians/ gay men • dancing/DJ • karaoke • live shows • patio • wheelchair access

ENTERTAINMENT & RECREATION

Sherwood Island State Park Beach left to gay area

DELAWARE

Statewide

INFO LINES & SERVICES

Gay & Lesbian AA 302/856-6452

Rehoboth Beach

INFO LINES & SERVICES

Camp Rehoboth 39 Baltimore Ave 302/227-5620 • 9am-5:30pm Mon-Fri, 10am-4pm wknds • drop-in community center • support groups • magazine w/ extensive listings

ACCOMMODATIONS

An Inn by the Bay 205 Savannah Rd, Lewes 302/644-8878, 866/833-2565 • gay/ straight • nonsmoking • hot tub • gay-owned • $55-75

At Melissa's B&B 36 Delaware Ave (btwn 1st & 2nd) 302/227-7504, 800/396-8090 • gay/ straight • open year round • 1 block from beach • nonsmoking • women-owned/ run • $85-235

Cabana Gardens B&B 20 Lake Ave (at 3rd St) 302/227-5429 • lesbians/ gay men • lake & ocean views • deck • swimming • nonsmoking • gay-owned • $75-250

Canalside Inn Canal at 6th 302/226-2006, 866/412-2625 • gay/ straight • pool • hot tub • wheelchair access • gay-owned • $70-235

Chesapeake Landing B&B 101 Chesapeake St (at King Charles) 302/227-2973 • gay-friendly • full brkfst • swimming • nonsmoking • lakefront • near Poodle Beach • gay-owned • $125-275

Delaware Inn B&B 55 Delaware Ave 302/227-6031, 800/246-5244 • gay-friendly • country inn atmosphere • near beach • swimming • gay-owned • $80-210

The Homestead at Rehoboth B&B 35060 Warrington Rd 302/226-7625 • gay-friendly • small dogs ok • swimming • lesbian-owned • $80-170

Lazy L at Willow Creek 16061 Willow Creek Rd (at Hwy 1), Lewes 302/644-7220 • gay/ straight • full brkfst • pool • hot tub • very pet friendly • lesbian-owned • $75-165

The Lighthouse Inn B&B 20 Delaware Ave 302/226-0407 • seasonal • gay/ straight • B&B • also apt (weekly rental) • 1 block from beach • nonsmoking • kids/ pets ok • gay-owned • $135-195

Lord & Hamilton Seaside B&B Inn 20 Brooklyn Ave (at 1st) 302/227-6960, 877/227-6960 • lesbians/ gay men • Victorian home • 1/2 block to beach & boardwalk • lesbian & gay-owned • $95-225

The Pelican Loft 45 Baltimore Ave 302/226-5080, 800/550-9551 • mostly women • near beach & boardwalk • some shared baths • teens ok • nonsmoking • lesbian-owned • $75-165

Rehoboth Beach

ANNUAL EVENTS:
April - Cabaret Fest 302/227-2772, web: www.rehomain.com/Cabaret.
July - Fireworks 302/227-2772.
November - Rehoboth Beach Independent Film Festival 302/645-9095, web: www.rehobothfilm.com.

CITY INFO:
Rehoboth Beach-Dewey Beach Chamber of Commerce 302/227-2233 & 800/441-1329, web: www.beach-fun.com.

ATTRACTIONS:
Main Street 302/227-2772.
North Shores beach.

TRANSIT:
Seaport Taxi 302/645-6800.
Jolly Trolley 302/227-1197 (seasonal tour & shuttle), web: www.jollytrolley.com.

Rehoboth Guest House 40 Maryland Ave (btwn 1st & 2nd Sts) **302/227–4117, 800/564-0493** • lesbians/ gay men • Victorian beach house • deck • near boardwalk & beach • nonsmoking • gay-owned • $65-215

Sea Witch Manor Inn & Spa 71 Lake Ave (at Rehoboth Ave) **302/226–9482, 866/732-9482** • gay/ straight • B&B • full brkfst • hot tub • wheelchair access • gay-owned • $170-325

Silver Lake Guest House 133 Silver Lake Dr **302/226–2115, 800/842-2115** • lesbians/ gay men • near Poodle Beach • nonsmoking • lakefront • ocean views • gay-owned • $80-350

Summer Place Hotel 30 Olive Ave (at 1st) **302/226-0766, 800/815-3925** • gay/ straight • also apts • near beach • $39-175

BARS

The Blue Moon 35 Baltimore Ave (btwn 1st & 2nd) **302/227–6515** • 6pm-2am, clsd Jan • lesbians/ gay men • popular happy hour • also restaurant • Sun brunch • plenty veggie • $18-30

Dogfish Head Brewings & Eats 320 Rehoboth Ave **302/226–2739** • gay-friendly • micro-brewery • wood-grilled food • live music wknds

Double L Bar 622 Rehoboth Ave **302/227–0818** • 3pm-2am • open year round • mostly gay men • leather • bears • patio

Frogg Pond 3 S 1st St (near Rehoboth Ave) **302/227–2234** • 11am-1am • gay-friendly • popular w/ women in summer • neighborhood bar • food served • karaoke • popular happy hour

Partners Bistro & Piano Bar 404 Rehoboth Ave (at State St) **302/226–0207** • noon-1am, from 11am Sun • gay/ straight • also restaurant • piano bar • gay-owned

NIGHTCLUBS

Ladies 2000 856/869-0193 • seasonal parties, call hotline for details

CAFES

Java Beach 167 Rehoboth Ave **302/226–3377** • 7am-5pm, till 7pm wknds, open later in summer • cafe • patio

Lori's Café 39 Baltimore Ave (at 1st) **302/226–3066** • seasonal, call for hours • also sandwiches • woman-owned/ run

RESTAURANTS

Back Porch Cafe 59 Rehoboth Ave **302/227–3674** • lunch & dinner • Sun brunch • seasonal • some veggie • full bar • wheelchair access

CAMP REHOBOTH
CREATING COMMUNITY

FOR MORE INFORMATION ABOUT REHOBOTH BEACH VISIT US AT WWW.CAMPREHOBOTH.COM OR CALL 302-227-5620

Cafe Sole 44 Baltimore Ave **302/227-7107** • lunch & dinner, clsd Sun & Mon • casual

Cafe Zeus 37 Wilmington Ave **302/226-0400** • brunch, lunch, dinner • Mediterranean • $25 entrees • home of the Argos Bar • Sun T-dance • gay-owned

Celsius 50–C Wilmington Ave **302/227-5767** • dinner nightly, Sun brunch • French-Mediterranean • some veggie • wheelchair access • $15-25

Cloud Nine 234 Rehoboth Ave (at 2nd) **302/226-1999** • 4pm-2am • popular bar • fusion bistro • dancing/DJ wknds • summer T-dances • wheelchair access • $10-22

The Cultured Pearl 19-A Wilmington Ave (off 1st St) **302/227-8493** • dinner, lunch Th-Mon, clsd Mon-Wed off-season • pan-Asian • cocktail lounge • $15-29

Dish 26 Baltimore Ave **302/226-2112** • dinner nightly, clsd Wed & Th off-season • "a retro dining gallery"

Dos Locos 10 Wilmington Ave (btwn Baltimore & Rehoboth) **302/227-3353** • 5pm-10pm, till 11pm wknds, bar till 1am, seasonal variations • popular • Mexican • full bar

Eden 23 Baltimore Ave **302/227-3330** • dinner Wed-Sat • seasonal • "bold" American • wheelchair access

Espuma 28 Wilmington Ave **302/227-4199** • 6pm-10pm, clsd Mon • modern Mediterranean

Iguana Grill 52 Baltimore Ave **302/227-0948** • lunch & dinner (summers) • Southwestern • full bar • patio

La La Land 22 Wilmington Ave **302/227-3887** • 6pm-1am (seasonal) • seafood & more • full bar • patio • $19-28

Planet X Cafe 35 Wilmington Ave **302/226-1928** • lunch, dinner, Sun brunch • organic global cuisine • some veggie • friendly service • kitschy decor housed in converted Victorian

Purple Parrot Grill 134 Rehoboth Ave **302/226-1139** • lunch & dinner daily, brkfst wknds • karaoke & drag shows wknds • wheelchair access

Sydney's Side Street Restaurant & Blues Place 25 Christian St (at 2nd St) **302/227-1339** • dinner Wed-Sat (seasonal hours) • healthy entrees • full bar • live shows • patio • $12-20

Tijuana Taxi 207 Rehoboth Ave (at 2nd St) **302/227-1986** • dinner Wed-Sun, lunch wknds • full bar • wheelchair access • $6-13

Venus on the Halfshell 136 Dagsworth St, Dewey Beach **302/227-9292** • waterside Asian-inspired restaurant w/ fun Morocco-Meets-the-Far-East setting • also hosts Atmos dance party 10pm Sat • mostly gay men • dancing/DJ

ENTERTAINMENT & RECREATION

North Shores S end of Cape Henlopen State Park (at jetty S of watch tower) • popular women's beach • 20-minute walk from boardwalk • by car follow the shoreline road to State Park entrance

BOOKSTORES

Lambda Rising 39 Baltimore Ave (btwn 1st & 2nd) **302/227-6969** • 11am-8pm, till 10pm Fri-Sat, 10am-midnight summers • LGBT • wheelchair access

RETAIL SHOPS

Leather Central 4284A Hwy 1 (on the service road) **302/227-0700** • 10am-10pm, till 7pm Sun • leather uniforms, toys, accessories

PUBLICATIONS

EXP Magazine **302/227-5787, 877/397-6244** • bi-weekly gay magazine for Mid-Atlantic

▲ **Letters from Camp Rehoboth** **302/227-5620** • newsmagazine w/ events & entertainment listings

Visions Today **302/656-5876, 800/944-0100** • quarterly, covers Rehoboth, Philadelphia, New Hope, Wilmington & surrounding area

SPIRITUAL GROUPS

MCC of Rehoboth Beach 21 Midway Shopping Center/ Rte 1 (at Clubhouse at the Plantations) **302/645-4945** • 10am

GYMS & HEALTH CLUBS

Body Shop 401 N Boardwalk (at Virginia) **302/226-0920** • $12 day pass

Midway Fitness Midway Shopping Center #28B (on Rte 1, NW of John J Williams Hwy) **302/645-0407** • $11 day pass • racquetball

Wilmington

BARS

814 Club 814 Shipley St (btwn 8th & 9th) **302/657-5730** • 6pm-2am • lesbians/ gay men • dancing/DJ • transgender-friendly • also restaurant

NIGHTCLUBS

Baxter's 2006 Pennsylvania Ave
302/654–9858 • 4pm-2am • lesbians/ gay
men • dancing/ DJ • karaoke • country/
western • also restaurant

RESTAURANTS

Eclipse 1020 Union St 302/658–1588 • lunch
& dinner • upscale

Mrs Robino's 520 N Union (at Pennsylvania)
302/652–9223 • lunch & dinner • family-style
Italian • bar • wheelchair access

PUBLICATIONS

EXP Magazine 302/227–5787,
877/397–6244 • bi-weekly gay magazine for
Mid-Atlantic

Visions Today 302/656–1809, 800/944–0100
• quarterly, covers Rehoboth, Philadelphia,
New Hope, Wilmington & surrounding area

SPIRITUAL GROUPS

More Light 500 W 8th St (at West Presb
Church) 302/656–8326 • 11am Sun

DISTRICT OF COLUMBIA

Washington

INFO LINES & SERVICES

Gay/ Lesbian Hotline (at Whitman-Walker
Clinic) 202/833–3234 • 7pm-11pm •
resources • crisis counseling

Triangle Club 2030 P St NW 202/659–8641
• site for various 12-step groups • call for
times

▲ **Washington, DC Convention & Tourism**
1212 New York Ave NW #600
800/422–8644 • see ad in front color section

ACCOMMODATIONS

Bull Moose B&B on Capitol Hill 101 5th St
NE (at A St) 202/547–1050, 800/261–2768 •
gay/ straight • Victorian row house in historic
Capitol Hill district • nonsmoking • gay-owned
• $89-199

The Carlyle Suites Hotel 1731 New
Hampshire Ave NW (btwn R & S Sts)
202/234–3200, 866/468–3532 • gay/ straight •
art deco hotel • gym • also restaurant & bar •
popular gay Sun brunch • wheelchair access •
$89-209

Comfort Inn Downtown DC—Convention Center 1201 13th St NW **202/682-5300** • gay/ straight • near Dupont Circle • kids ok • $79-159

Creekside B&B 301/261-9438 • mostly women • private home on the shore of the Chesapeake • 40 minutes from DC • hot tub • swimming • nonsmoking • lesbian-owned • $85

DC GuestHouse 1337 10th St NW **202/332-2502** • gay/ straight • full brkfst • gay-owned • $170-250

The Embassy Inn 1627 16th St NW **202/234-7800, 800/423-9111** • gay-friendly • small hotel w/ B&B atmosphere • $79-149

Embassy Suites Alexandria 1900 Diagonal Rd, Alexandria, VA **703/684-5900, 800/362-2779** • gay/ straight • full brkfst • kids ok • swimming • $119-269

Embassy Suites Hotel at the Chevy Chase Pavilion 4300 Military Rd NW **202/362-9300, 800/362-2779** • gay-friendly • swimming • gym • wheelchair access • $149-289

Washington

WHERE THE GIRLS ARE:
Strolling around DuPont Circle or cruising a bar in the LGBT bar ghetto southeast of The Mall.

LGBT PRIDE:
May. Black Lesbian/ Gay Pride 202/737-5767, web: www.dcblackpride.org.
June. 202/986-1119, web: www.capitalpride.org.

ANNUAL EVENTS:
March - Women's History Month at various Smithsonian Museums 202/357-2700, web: www.smithsonianeducation.org.
October - Reel Affirmations Film Festival 202/986-1119, web: www.reelaffirmations.org.

CITY INFO:
DC Convention & Tourism Corporation. 202/789-7000, web: www.washington.org.

BEST VIEW:
From the top of the Washington Monument.

WEATHER:
Summers are hot (90°s) and MUGGY (the city was built on marshes). In the winter, temperatures drop to the 30°s and 40°s with rain and sometimes snow. Spring is the time of cherry blossoms.

TRANSIT:
Yellow Cab 202/544-1212.
Washington Flier 703/661-6655 (from Dulles or Ronald Reagan National).
Super Shuttle 800/258-3826.
Metro Transit Authority 202/637-7000, web: www.wmata.com.

ATTRACTIONS:
Ford's Theatre 202/347-4833, web: www.fordstheatre.org.
Jefferson Memorial.
JFK Center for the Performing Arts 800/444-1324, web: www.kennedy-center.org.
Lincoln Memorial.
National Gallery 202/737-4215, web: www.nga.gov.
National Museum of Women in the Arts 202/783-5000, web: www.nmwa.org.
National Zoo 202/673-4800, web: natzoo.si.edu.
Smithsonian 202/357-1300, web: www.smithsonianeducation.org.
Vietnam Veteran's Memorial.
United States Holocaust Memorial Museum 202/488-0400, web: www.ushmm.org.

Embassy Suites Tysons Corner 8517 Leesburg Pike, Vienna, VA **703/883-0707, 800/362-2779** • gay-friendly • full brkfst • kids ok • swimming • wheelchair access • $79-209

▲ **Embassy Suites Washington, DC** 1250 22nd St NW **202/857-3388, 800/362-2779** • gay-friendly • full brkfst • kids ok • swimming • $119-319

FourSeventeen—A Victorian Townhouse 417 A Street SE (at 5th St) **202/543-1481** • gay/ straight • B&B in private home • kids ok • gay-owned • $125-250

Hotel Helix 1430 Rhode Island Ave NW **202/462-9001, 800/706-1202** • gay-friendly • wheelchair access • $129-359

Hotel Madera 1310 New Hampshire Ave NW (at N) **202/296-7600, 800/430-1202** • gay-friendly • boutique hotel • kids/ pets ok • Firefly bistro adjacent • wheelchair access • $119-259

Hotel Monaco Washington DC 700 F St NW (at 7th) **202/628-7177, 800/649-1202** • gay-friendly • boutique hotel • kids/ pets ok • wheelchair access • $129-350

Hotel Rouge 1315 16th St NW (at Rhode Island) **202/232-8000, 800/368-5689** • gay-friendly • ultra-hip, high-tech luxury hotel • kids/ pets ok • also restaurant & bar • wheelchair access • $99-219

The Inn at Dupont Circle 1312 19th St NW (at N) **202/467-6777, 866/467-2100** • gay-friendly • 1885 Victorian town house formerly owned by astrolger Jeanne Dixon • woman-owned • $95-215

▲ **Kalorama Guest House at Kalorama Park** 1854 Mintwood Pl NW (at Columbia Rd) **202/667-6369** • gay/ straight • Victorian town house near Dupont Circle • $50-120

Kalorama Guest House at Woodley Park 2700 Cathedral Ave NW (off Connecticut Ave) **202/328-0860** • gay/ straight • near National Zoo & Washington Cathedral • nonsmoking • $45-100

Morrison-Clark Historic Inn & Restaurant Massachusetts Ave NW (at 11th St NW) **202/898-1200, 800/322-7898** • gay-friendly • hotel in 2 Victorian town houses • very popular restaurant • $155-325

Fashionable Inns In Fashionable Neighborhoods

o *Walk to Dupont Circle, fashionable clubs and restuarants, and the subway (Metro)*

o *Enjoy breakfast and evening aperitif*

THE KALORAMA GUEST HOUSES
Kalorama Park (202) 667-6369
Woodley Park (202) 328-0860

Reply **Forward** **Delete**

Date: Dec 1, 2005 12:26:42
From: Girl-on-the-Go
To: Editor@Damron.com
Subject: Washington, DC

>Even though Washington, DC, is known worldwide as a show-case of American culture and a command center of global politics, many people overlook this international "hot spot" when traveling in the United States. But DC is not all boring museums and stuffy bureaucrats.

>For instance, begin your stay in DC at one of the gay-friendly hotels or guesthouses in and around the city. **Creekside B&B** in Maryland has a strong lesbian following.

>Of course, you could tour the usual sites—starting with the heart of DC—the "Mall"—a two-mile-long grass strip bordered by many museums and monuments: the Smithsonian, the National Air and Space Museum, the National Gallery of Art, the Museum of Natural History, the Museum of American History, the Washington Monument, the Lincoln Memorial, and the Vietnam Veterans Memorial.

>For a truly interesting change of pace, check out these less touristy attractions: the outstanding National Museum of Women in the Arts, the hip shops and exotic eateries along Massachusetts Avenue, and of course, DuPont Circle, the pulsing heart of LGBT DC. The Circle is also home to the oldest modern art museum in the country, the Phillips Collection, as well as the LGBT bookstore **Lambda Rising,** and the kinky **Pleasure Place.**

>For nightlife, don't miss **Liquid Ladies** on Saturdays at **Apex. Phase One** is a more casual bar for lesbians, and there are several women's nights at the other mixed bars. Women of color get their groove on at monthly parties like **Merge** and **Sultry.** For the latest events for women in DC and its environs, pick up a copy of **Woman's Monthly** or **Women in the Life.**

One Washington Circle Hotel
One Washington Cir NW **202/872–1680, 800/424–9671** • gay-friendly • suites w/ kitchens • swimming • also restaurant & piano bar • kids ok • wheelchair access • $99-259

Radisson Barcelo Hotel Washington
2121 P St (at 21st St) **202/293–3100, 800/333–3333** • gay-friendly • in Dupont Circle • swimming • restaurant • wheelchair access • $99-285

The River Inn 924 25th St NW (at K St) **202/337–7600, 800/424–2741** • gay-friendly • suites w/ kitchen • gym • also Dish restaurant • wheelchair access • $69-265

Savoy Suites Hotel 2505 Wisconsin Ave NW (at Calvert, in Georgetown) **202/337–9700, 800/944–5377** • gay-friendly • also restaurant • Italian • wheelchair access • $99-209

Swann House Historic B&B 1808 New Hampshire Ave NW (at Swann St) **202/265–4414** • gay/ straight • 1883 Victorian mansion in Dupont Circle • swimming • roof deck • fireplaces • kids ok • $140-295

Topaz Hotel 1733 N St NW **202/393–3000, 800/424–2950** • gay-friendly • boutique hotel • kids/ pets ok • also restaurant & bar • wheelchair access • $109-249

Washington Plaza 10 Thomas Cir NW (at 14th & Massachusetts) **202/842–1300, 800/424–1140** • gay-friendly • full-service hotel • also restaurant • $109-249

Washington Terrace Hotel 1515 Rhode Island Ave NW, Washington DC **202/232–7000** • gay-friendly • $129-229

The Windsor Inn 1842 16th St NW **202/667–0300, 800/423–9111** • gay-friendly • small hotel w/ B&B atmosphere • $79-189

Bars

1409 Playbill Cafe 1409 14th St NW **202/265–3055** • 4pm-2am, till 3am Fri-Sat • lesbians/ gay men • food served • also theater

Apex 1415 22nd St NW (btwn O & P Sts) **202/296–0505** • 9pm-2am, till 3am Fri-Sat, clsd Sun-Mon & Wed • lesbians/ gay men • more women Sat for Liquid Ladies • dancing/DJ • videos • young crowd • wheelchair access • cover

Carlyle Cafe 1731 New Hampshire (at 18th & R Sts, in the Carlyle Suites) **202/234–3200** • 5pm-midnight, till 2am Fri-Sat • gay/ straight • art deco bar • dinner served • internet access • wheelchair access

Club Chaos 1603 17th St NW (at Q St) **202/232–4141** • 5pm-1am, till 2am Wed-Th, till 3am Fri-Sat, 11am-3pm Sun, clsd Mon • lesbians/ gay men • dancing/DJ • drag king/queen shows • women's night Wed • Latin Th • transgender-friendly • also restaurant • Sun brunch • some veggie • wheelchair access

DC Eagle 639 New York Ave NW (btwn 6th & 7th) **202/347–6025** • 4pm-2am, noon-3am wknds • popular • mostly gay men • leather • wheelchair access

DC Eagle Dyke Night 639 New York Ave NW (btwn 6th & 7th) • women's night 4th Wed only • mostly women • leather • wheelchair access

Ellington's on 8th 424-A 8th St SE **202/546–8308** • dinner, Sun brunch, clsd Mon-Tue • lesbians/ gay men • int'l cuisine • live jazz

The Fireplace 2161 P St NW (at 22nd St) **202/293–1293** • 1pm-2am, wknds till 3am • mostly gay men • neighborhood bar • multiracial • videos • wheelchair access

Halo 1435 P St NW **202/797–9730** • 5pm-close • lesbians/ gay men • neighborhood bar

JR's 1519 17th St NW (at Church) **202/328–0090** • 1pm-2am, till 3am Fri-Sat • popular • mostly gay men • neighborhood bar • videos • young crowd

Larry's Lounge 1840 18th St NW (at T St) **202/483–1483** • 4pm-1am, till 2am Fri-Sat • lesbians/ gay men • neighborhood bar • wheelchair access

Marx Cafe 3203 Mt Pleasant St NW **202/518–7600** • 4pm-2am, till 3am wknds, brunch wknds • gay/ straight • dancing/ DJ • food served • beer/ wine

Mr Henry's Capitol Hill 601 Pennsylvania Ave SE (at 6th St) **202/546–8412** • 11:30am-midnight, till 1am wknds • popular • gay-friendly • multiracial • live jazz • also restaurant

Phase One 525 8th St SE (btwn E & G Sts) **202/544–6831** • 7pm-2am, till 3am Fri-Sat (clsd Mon-Wed winter) • mostly women • neighborhood bar • dancing/DJ • multiracial • wheelchair access

Remington's 639 Pennsylvania Ave SE (btwn 6th & 7th) **202/543–3113** • 4pm-2am, till 3am Fri-Sat • popular • mostly gay men • dancing/DJ • 2 flrs • country/ western • dance lessons Sun-Mon & Wed • karaoke Wed • T-dance Sun • videos

Titan 1337 14th St NW (at Hamburger Mary's) **202/232–7010** • 5pm-midnight, till 2am Fri-Sat • dancing/DJ • food served • videos

Windows at Dupont Italian Kitchen 1637 R St NW (near 16th St NW) **202/234–5747** • 4pm-2am, wknd hours vary • gay-friendly • neighborhood bar • multiracial • food served

NIGHTCLUBS

Atlas/ Lizard Lounge 1223 Connecticut Ave NW (at 18th & N, at MCCXXIII) **202/331–4422** • 8pm Sun only • mostly gay men • call for info

Bachelors Mill 1104 8th St SE (downstairs at Back Door Pub) **202/544–1931** • 5pm-close • lesbians/ gay men • popular • dancing/DJ • 2 flrs • mostly African-American • live shows • wheelchair access

Cada Vez 1438 U St NW (at 15th) **202/667–0785** • gay/ straight • check local listings for gay events

Chief Ike's Mambo Room 1725 Columbia Rd NW (at Ontario) **202/332–2211** • 4pm-2am, till 3am Fri, 6pm-3am Sat, clsd Sun • gay-friendly • dancing/DJ • also restaurant • American • wheelchair access

The Edge 56 L St SE (at Half St) **202/488–1200** • from 10pm Mon, Wed, Fri-Sat only • lesbians/ gay men • ladies night Wed w/ female strippers • dancing/ DJ • multiracial • food served • videos • 18+ • wheelchair access • cover charge

Excursions 2321 18th St NW (at Kalorama, at The Blue Room) • lesbians/ gay men • dancing/ DJ • occasional parties (check local listings)

First Saturday 1438 U St NW (at 15th, at Cada Vez) **202/483–9819** • 1st Sat only • mostly women • dancing/ DJ • multiracial clientele

Liquid Ladies 1415 22nd St NW (btwn P & Q Sts, at Apex) **202/296–0505** • 9pm-2am Sat only • mostly women • dancing/DJ • videos • young crowd • wheelchair access • cover

Merge Happy Hour 1010 Vermont Ave NW (at Club Daedalus) **202/277–1583** • 6pm-1am 2nd Fri only • women only • dancing/ DJ • multiracial • dress code

Sultry Happy Hour 1800 M St NW (at Yuca Lounge) • 8pm-2am last Fri only • women only • dancing/ DJ • multiracial

Velvet 1015 Half St SE (corner of S Capitol & K St SE) **202/554–1500** • 10pm-6am Sat • popular • mostly gay men • dancing/DJ • food served • drag shows • videos • young crowd • cover charge

Wet 52 L St SE (at Half St) **202/488–1200** • 8pm-2am, till 3am Fri-Sat, clsd Sun, go-go boys • women go-go dancers from 4pm last Sat only

Ziegfeld's/ Secrets 1345 Half St SE (at O St) **202/554–5141** • 9pm-3am, till 2am Th & Sun, clsd Mon • lesbians/ gay men • dancing/DJ • alternative • multiracial • drag shows • wheelchair access

CAFES

Cosi 1647 20th St NW **202/332–6364** • 6:30am-midnight, till 2am Fri-Sat • full bar from 4pm • popular • make your own s'mores

Cyber STOP Café 1513 17th St NW (btwn P & O Sts NW) **202/234–2470** • 7am-midnight • popular • internet access • great people-watching

Jolt 'n' Bolt 1918 18th St NW (at Florida) **202/232–0077** • 8am-10pm, till midnight Fri-Sat • popular • patio

Soho Tea & Coffee 2150 P St NW **202/463–7646** • open 7am till late • cybercafe & more • food served • patio • wheelchair access

RESTAURANTS

18th & U Duplex Diner 2004 18th St NW (at Ave U) **202/265–7828** • 6pm-midnight • American comfort food • full bar

Annie's Paramount Steak House 1609 17th St NW (at Corcoran) **202/232–0395** • 11am-11pm, 24hrs Fri-Sat • popular • full bar

Armand's Chicago Pizza 4231 Wisconsin Ave NW (at Veazey) **202/686–9450** • 11:30am-10pm • full bar • also 226 Massachusetts Ave NE, Capitol Hill, 202/547-6600

Banana Cafe & Piano Bar 500 8th St SE (at E St) **202/543–5906** • lunch & dinner • Puerto Rican/ Cuban food • some veggie • famous margaritas • piano bar • gay-owned

Beacon Bar & Grill 1516 Rhode Island Ave NW (at 17th) **202/872–1126** • brkfst, lunch & dinner • popular Sun brunch • patio

Cafe Berlin 322 Massachusetts Ave NE (btwn 3rd & 4th) **202/543–7656** • lunch & dinner, dinner only Sun • German • some veggie • patio • wheelchair access

Cafe Japoné 2032 P St NW (at 21st)
202/223–1573 • 6pm-2am • mostly Asian-American • popular • Japanese food • full bar • live jazz Wed • karaoke

Cafe Luna 1633 P St NW (at 17th)
202/387–4005 • 8am-11pm, from 10am wknds, till 1:30am Fri-Sat • popular • lesbians/gay men • healthy • plenty veggie

Chartwell Grill 1914 Connecticut Ave (in The Churchill Hotel) 202/797–2000 • brkfst, lunch, dinner • cont'l • wheelchair access

Dupont Italian Kitchen & Bar 1637 17th St NW (at R St) 202/328–3222, 202/328–0100 • 11am-midnight, bar from 4pm • some veggie

Food For Thought 1811 14th St NW (at the Black Cat) 202/797–1095 • 8pm-1am, 7pm-2am Fri-Sat • gay-friendly • mostly vegan/veggie • nonsmoking • also live music • readings • indie/punk • young crowd

Guapo's 4515 Wisconsin Ave NW (at Albemarle) 202/686–3588 • lunch & dinner • Mexican • some veggie • full bar • wheelchair access

The Islander 1201 U St NW (at 12th)
202/234–4955 • lunch & dinner • Caribbean • some veggie • full bar • live music

Jaleo 480 7th St NW (at E St) 202/628–7949 • lunch & dinner • tapas • full bar • wheelchair access

La Frontera Cantina 1633 17th St NW (btwn R & Q Sts) 202/232–0437 • 11am-11pm, till 1am Fri-Sat • Tex-Mex

Lauriol Plaza 1835 18th St NW (at S St)
202/387–0035 • lunch & dinner • Latin American

Mercury Grill 1602 17th St NW
202/667–5937 • lunch Mon-Fri, dinner nightly • full bar • patio • gay-owned

Occidental Grill 1475 Pennsylvania Ave NW (btwn 14th & 15th) 202/783–1475 • lunch & dinner, upscale • political player hangout

Pepper's 1527 17th St NW (btwn P & Q Sts) 202/328–8193 • 11:30am-2am • popular • global American • Sun brunch • full bar • patio • great people-watching • wheelchair access

Perry's 1811 Columbia Rd NW (at 18th)
202/234–6218 • 5:30pm-10:30pm, till 11:30pm wknds, popular drag Sun brunch • contemporary American & sushi • full bar • roof deck

Rocklands 2418 Wisconsin Ave NW (at Calvert) 202/333–2558 • lunch & dinner • bbq & take-out

Sala Thai 2016 P St NW (at 21st)
202/872–1144 • lunch & dinner • some veggie

Skewers 1633 P St NW (at 17th)
202/387–7400 • 11:30am-11pm • popular • Middle-Eastern • full bar

Soul Vegetarian 2606 Georgia Ave NW
202/328–7685 • 11am-9pm, till 3pm Sun (brunch) • all-vegan menu

Tapatinis 711 8th St SE 202/546–8272 •
5pm-midnight, till 2am wknds • tapas & martinis

Trio 1537 17th St NW (at Q St NW)
202/232–6305 • 8am-midnight • American • some veggie • full bar • sidewalk cafe

Two Quail 320 Massachusetts Ave NE
202/543–8030 • lunch Mon-Fri, dinner nightly • popular • New American • some veggie • full bar • gay-owned

ENTERTAINMENT & RECREATION

Anecdotal History Tours 301/294–9514 •
gay-friendly • variety of guided tours

Bike the Sites 1100 Pennsylvania Ave NW (off 12th St) 202/842–2453 • 9am-6pm • tour the nation's capital on bike!

Hillwood Museum & Gardens
4155 Linnean Ave NW (at Tilden St NW)
202/686–5807, 877/445–5966 • 9am-5pm Tue-Sat • Fabergé, porcelain, furniture & more • reservations required

Lesbian & Gay Chorus of Washington, DC 202/546–1549

Phillips Collection 1600 21st St NW (at Q St) 202/387–0961 • clsd Mon • America's oldest museum of modern art • near Dupont Circle

Rainbow History Project 202/907–9007 •
self-guided walking tours of gay DC

Washington Mystics 202/661–5050 •
check out the Women's National Basketball Association while you're in DC

Women in the Life 1642 R St NW #220
202/483–9818, 202/483–9819 • party 1st Fri • sports teams • open mics • multiracial

BOOKSTORES

ADC Map & Travel Center 1636 I St NW (at 17th St) 202/628–2608, 800/544–2659 • 9am-6:30pm, till 5:30pm Fri, 11am-5pm Sat, clsd Sun • many maps & travel guides

G Books 1520 U St NW, BSMT (btwn 15th St & U St) 202/986–9697 • noon-10pm • new & used LGBT books & magazines • gay-owned

Kramer Books & Afterwords, a Cafe 1517 Connecticut Ave NW (at Q St) 202/387-1400 • 7:30am-1am, 24hrs wknds • general • also cafe • wheelchair access

Lambda Rising 1625 Connecticut Ave NW (btwn Q & R Sts) 202/462-6969 • 10am-10pm Sun-Th, till midnight Fri-Sat • LGBT • wheelchair access

RETAIL SHOPS

Leather Rack 1723 Connecticut Ave NW (btwn R & S Sts) 202/797-7401

Pulp 1803 14th St NW 202/462-7857 • 11am-7pm, noon-5pm Sun • cards • gifts • music

Universal Gear 1601 17th St NW (at Q St) 202/319-0136 • 11am-10pm Sun-Th, till midnight Fri-Sat • casual, club, athletic & designer clothing

PUBLICATIONS

EXP Magazine 302/227-5787, 877/397-6244 • bi-weekly gay magazine for Mid-Atlantic

MW (Metro Arts & Entertainment) 202/638-6830 • extensive club listings

Swirl Magazine 678/886-0711 (ATLANTA #) • magazine for "the African American lesbian, bisexual, bi-curious & 'straight but not narrow' community"

Washington Blade 202/797-7000 • huge LGBT newspaper • extensive resource listings

Woman's Monthly 202/965-5399 • articles • calendar of community/ arts events for greater DC/ Baltimore area

Women in the Life 202/483-9818 • quarterly

SPIRITUAL GROUPS

Bet Mishpachah 16th & Q Sts NW (at the DCJCC) 202/833-1638 • LGBT synagogue

Dignity Washington 1820 Connecticut Ave NW (at St Margaret's Church) 202/546-2235 • 6pm Sun

Faith Temple (Evangelical) 1313 New York Ave NW 202/232-4911 • 1pm Sun

Friends Meeting of Washington(Quaker) 2111 Florida Ave NW (enter on Decatur Pl) 202/483-3310 • 10:30am Sun, 7pm Wed • 10:30am Sun next door at 2121 Decatur Pl has special gay welcome

MCC Washington 474 Ridge St NW (btwn M & N Sts) 202/638-7373 • 9am & 11am Sun

GYMS & HEALTH CLUBS

Results—The Gym 1612 U St NW (at 17th St) **202/518-0001** • gay-friendly • also women-only fitness area • also cafe

Washington Sports Club 1835 Connecticut Ave NW (at Columbia & Florida) **202/332-0100**

EROTICA

▲ **Pleasure Place** 1063 Wisconsin Ave NW, Georgetown (btwn M & K Sts) **800/386-2386** • 10am-10pm, till midnight Wed-Sat, noon-7pm Sun • erotica • clubwear • leather • adult toys • DVDs • clothing & more • wheelchair access

▲ **Pleasure Place** 1710 Connecticut Ave NW (btwn Florida Ave & R St) **202/483-3297** • 10am-10pm, till midnight Wed-Sat, noon-7pm Sun • erotica • clubwear • leather • adult toys • DVDs • clothing & more

FLORIDA

Statewide

PUBLICATIONS

Ambush Mag 504/522-8049 • LGBT newspaper for the Gulf South

Clique Magazine 954/455-3394 • great glossy newsmagazine covering GA & FL's LGBT African American community • some nat'l club & event listings

HOTSPOTS! Magazine 954/928-1862 • South Florida's weekly bar guide

The Independent Gay News 954/563-0470 • LGBT newspaper for Southern FL

She Magazine, "The Source for Women" 954/474-0183 • "The hippest & hottest source for women of the rainbow community" • S Florida-based

Southern Voice 404/876-1819 • weekly LGBT newspaper for AL, FL (panhandle), GA, LA, MS, TN w/ resource listings

Alligator Point

ACCOMMODATIONS

Mermaid's Tale 866/794-9640 • mostly women • elegant & private waterfront vacation home on the Gulf of Mexico • lesbian-owned

Amelia Island

ACCOMMODATIONS

The Amelia Island Williams House B&B 103 S 9th St 904/277-2328, 800/414-9258 • gay-friendly • magnificent 1856 antebellum mansion • jacuzzi • fireplace • nonsmoking • wheelchair access • $219-279

Ash Street Inn 102 S 7th St (at Ash St) 904/277-6660, 800/277-6660 • gay/ straight • B&B • full brkfst • swimming • jacuzzi • kids ok/ small dogs ok • nonsmoking • wheelchair access • $129-299

Florida House Inn 20 S 3rd St 904/261-3300, 800/258-3301 • gay-friendly • B&B in Florida's oldest surviving hotel • kids/ pets ok • 2 restaurants & bar/ grille • $99-319

The Hoyt House 804 Atlantic Ave 904/277-4300, 800/432-2085 • gay-friendly • 1905 Queen Anne mansion • full brkfst • Wi-Fi • swimming • nonsmoking • wheelchair access • $139-209

RESTAURANTS

Beech Street Grill 801 Beech St (at 8th St), Fernandina Beach 904/277-3662 • 6pm-9pm • live music

Brett's Waterway Cafe 1 Front St 904/261-2660 • 11am-2:30am & 5:30pm-close • seafood • piano Th-Sat

Apalachicola

ACCOMMODATIONS

Coombs House Inn 80 6th St 850/653-9199, 888/244-8320 • gay-friendly • Victorian B&B • full brkfst • nonsmoking • wheelchair access • $89-225

Auburndale

BARS

Alternative Bar 404 Eaker St (at Hwy 92) 863/965-9018 • noon-2am, till Sun • gay/ straight • neighborhood bar • beer/ wine only • gay-owned

Boynton Beach

see also West Palm Beach

SPIRITUAL GROUPS

Church of Our Savior MCC 2011 S Federal Hwy 561/733-4000 • 10am Sun

Bradenton

see also Sarasota

INFO LINES & SERVICES

Gay AA 615 59th St W (Gratitude Room, in shopping center at corner of Manatee & 59th) **941/951–6810 (AA#)** • 1pm Sat

ACCOMMODATIONS

Summer House 111 & 113 36th St, Holmes Beach **941/778–2333, 800/431–0278** • gay-friendly • cottage-style inn, includes 4-bdrm cottage (sleeps 8-10) • swimming • nonsmoking • kids ok • $115-150 & $600-1,400/ weekly

NIGHTCLUBS

Club Heat 5520 14th St W (US-41) **941/727–2789** • from 9pm Wed only • popular • lesbians/ gay men • dancing/DJ • drag shows

EROTICA

14th Street Books 4949 14th St W **941/755–9076**

Cape Canaveral

ACCOMMODATIONS

Sand Pebbles Condominium 504 Filmore Dr, B-18 (at AIA/ Cocoa Beach) **321/436–3321** • women-only • furnished condo • swimming • kids ok • lesbian-owned • $800/ week

EROTICA

Fairvilla Megastore 500 Thurm Blvd **321/799–9961** • 9am-2am, from 10am Sun • clean, well-lighted adult store w/ emphasis on couples: "store for lovers"

Clearwater

see also Dunedin, New Port Richey, Port Richey & St Petersburg

ACCOMMODATIONS

Hampton Inn Clearwater/ St Petersburg Airport 3655 Hospitality Ln **727/577–9200** • gay-friendly • swimming • wheelchair access • off I-275 • $49-99

Holiday Inn Select 3535 Ulmerton Rd **727/577–9100** • gay-friendly • swimming • wheelchair access • close to airport & beach • $60-119

BARS

Pro Shop Pub 840 Cleveland St (at Prospect) **727/447–4259** • 1pm-2am • popular • mostly gay men • neighborhood bar • gay-owned

Z109 5858 Roosevelt Blvd/ State Rd 686 (at 58th) **727/538–0060** • 4pm-2am, from 1pm Sun, clsd Mon-Tue • lesbians/ gay men • neighborhood bar • karaoke Th • drag shows Fri-Sat • dancing/DJ Sun & BBQ • patio

RETAIL SHOPS

Skinz 2027 Gulf to Bay Blvd (aka State Rd 60) **727/441–8789** • 10am-6pm, noon-5pm Sun • men's & women's swimwear, gymwear & clubwear • also online store

SPIRITUAL GROUPS

Unitarian Universalist Church of Clearwater 2470 Nursery Rd **727/531–7704** • 10:30am Sun

Cocoa Beach

RESTAURANTS

Flaminias 3210 S Atlantic Ave **321/783–9908** • dinner only • Italian • beer/ wine

Lobster Shanty 2200 S Orlando Ave **321/783–1350** • 11:30am-9pm, till 10pm Fri-Sat • full bar • wheelchair access

Mango Tree 118 N Atlantic Ave **321/799–0513** • 6pm-10pm, clsd Mon • fine dining • wine list & single malt Scotch bar • wheelchair access

Daytona Beach

INFO LINES & SERVICES

Lambda Center 320 Harvey Ave (at Hollywood) **386/255–0280** • support groups • youth services • 12-step meetings • AA noon & 8pm daily • NA 6pm Sat

ACCOMMODATIONS

Acapulco Hotel & Resort 2505 S Atlantic Blvd (at Int'l Speedway Blvd) **386/761–2210, 800/245–3580** • gay-friendly • jacuzzi • right on beach • kids ok • restaurant • wheelchair access • $59-279

Atlantic Las Brisas Inn & Suites 700 N Atlantic Ave (Seabreeze) **386/255–3411, 866/255–3411** • gay/ straight • beachfront location • swimming • $54-199

Best Western Mayan Inn Beachfront 103 S Ocean Ave **386/252–2378, 800/443–5323** • gay-friendly • some rooms w/ ocean views • swimming • kids ok • wheelchair access • $79-215

Lilian Place B&B 111 Silver Beach Ave **386/323–9913, 877/893–7579** • gay/ straight • full brkfst • jacuzzi • wheelchair access • $135+

Mermaid Cottage 127 Arlington Wy, Ormond Beach **404/784–4447, 877/693–4068** • gay/ straight • 1938 Craftsman bungalow w/ fully equipped kitchen & courtyard • lesbian-owned • $1,195-3,195/ week

Miss Pat's Inn B&B 1209 S Peninsula Dr **386/248–8420, 866/464–7772** • gay-friendly • historic Victorian 1 block from ocean • full brkfst

The Villa B&B 801 N Peninsula Dr **386/248–2020, 888/248–7060** • gay-friendly • historic Spanish mansion • hot tub • swimming • nudity • nonsmoking • gay-owned • $85-250

BARS

The Groove Lounge 116-118 N Beach St **386/252–7600** • gay-friendly • dancing/DJ

Streamline Lounge 140 S Atlantic Ave (at Streamline Hotel) **386/258–6937** • 11am-3am (penthouse lounge) • gay-friendly • also NASCAR-themed lounge from 7pm • dancing/DJ • live entertainment • also game room w/ pool table

NIGHTCLUBS

Rumors Bar & Niteclub 1376 N Nova Rd (btwn 6th & 8th Sts, Holly Hill) **386/252–3776** • 2pm-2am • lesbians/ gay men • dancing/DJ • transgender-friendly • karaoke Th • drag shows Fri-Sat • videos • wheelchair access • gay-owned

CAFES

Connect Cafe 1500 Beville Rd #410 **386/238–3920** • 7am-6pm, till 10pm Fri, 9am-6pm Sat, clsd Sun • coffees & teas • pastries & soups/ sandwiches • internet • live entertainment Fri

RESTAURANTS

Anna's Trattoria 304 Seabreeze Blvd **386/239–9624** • dinner only, clsd Mon • Italian • beer/ wine

Barnacles Restaurant & Lounge 869 S Atlantic Ave, Ormond Beach **386/673–1070** • dinner nightly

Frappes North 123 W Granada St (at S Yonge St), Ormond Beach **386/615–4888** • lunch weekdays & dinner Mon-Sat, clsd Sun • "organically groovy" American • patio • full bar • reservations recommended

Sapporo 501 Seabreeze Ave **386/257–4477** • lunch Mon-Fri, dinner 7 days • Japanese steak house & sushi bar • full bar

PUBLICATIONS

Watermark 407/481–2243 (ORLANDO OFFICE) • bi-weekly LGBT newspaper for Central FL

SPIRITUAL GROUPS

Hope MCC 500 S Ridgewood Ave (at Loomis) **386/254–0993** • 11am Sun & 7pm Wed

Delray Beach

ACCOMMODATIONS

Crane's BeachHouse 82 Gleason St (at Atlantic Ave) **561/278–1700, 866/372–7263** • gay-friendly • hotel • swimming • kids/ pets ok • nonsmoking • $125-445

BARS

Lulu's Place 640 E Atlantic Ave Bay 6 (at E Federal Hwy) **561/278–4004** • 6am-2am • lesbians/ gay men • videos • wheelchair access

BOOKSTORES

Shining Through 426 E Atlantic Ave **561/276–8559** • metaphysical/ New Age • some LGBT titles • also incense, candles, crystals & gifts

Destin

ACCOMMODATIONS

Blue Skies Cottage 4442 Oceanview Dr (at Crystal Beach Dr) **251/608–7262, 888/299–6009** • gay-friendly • 2-bdrm rental home • pool • nonsmoking • kids ok • 6 person max • $95-1,325

Dunedin

see also St Petersburg

Fort Lauderdale

INFO LINES & SERVICES

Gay/ Lesbian Community Center of South Florida 1717 N Andrews Ave (btwn Sunrise & Oakland) **954/463–9005** • 10am-10pm, noon-5pm wknds • outreach • also Stonewall Library & Vida Latina • wheelchair access

Lambda South Inc 1231-A E Las Olas Blvd (alley access only) **954/761–9072** • meeting space for LGBT in recovery • wheelchair access

ACCOMMODATIONS

Alhambra Beach Resort 3021 Alhambra St **954/525–7601, 866/309–4014** • gay/ straight • motel • close to gay beach • swimming • gay-owned • $49-185

Comfort Suites Airport & Cruise Port 1800 S Federal Hwy (at 17th St) **954/767–8700, 800/760–0000** • gay/ straight • swimming • $69-209

Deauville Inn 2916 N Ocean Blvd (Oakland Park Blvd & A1A) 954/568-5000 • gay/ straight • in heart of Fort Lauderdale Beach • swimming • kids/ pets ok • wheelchair access • lesbian & straight-owned • $79-139

Doubletree Fort Lauderdale Oceanfront Hotel 440 Seabreeze Blvd 954/524-8733

Doubletree Guest Suites Fort Lauderdale Galleria 2670 E Sunrise Blvd 954/565-3800 • gay-friendly • bar & grille • patio w/ tiki bar • swimming • jacuzzi • health club

Embassy Suites Hotel 1100 SE 17th St 954/527-2700, 800/362-2779 • gay-friendly • full brkfst • hot tub • tropical outdoor pool • kids ok • wheelchair access • $229

Fort Lauderdale Vacation House 954/557-3312 • lesbians/ gay men • 3-bdrm house (sleeps 8) • gay nightlife & restaurants close by • swimming • gay-owned/ run • $200-310

Fort Lauderdale Vacation Rental 954/907-9069 • vacation rental • nonsmoking • gay-owned • $850-1,200/ week

Gigi's Resort by the Beach 3005 Alhambra St (at Birch) 954/463-4827, 800/910-2357 • gay-friendly • guesthouse on the beach • women-owned/ run • $61-192

Liberty Apartment & Garden Suites 1501 SW 2nd Ave (at Sheridan), Dania Beach 954/927-0090, 877/927-0090 • lesbians/ gay men • furnished apts • swimming • near beach • nonsmoking available • pets ok • wheelchair access • gay-owned • $350-995/ week

The Royal Palms Resort 2901 Terramar St (at Birch) 954/564-6444, 800/237-7256 • popular • mostly gay men • swimming • jacuzzi • nonsmoking • gay-owned • $169-339

Sheraton Yankee Trader Beach Hotel 321 N Fort Lauderdale Beach Blvd (A1A) 954/467-1111, 888/627-7109 • gay-friendly • beachfront hotel • sports deck & gym • 2 swimming pools • $169+

Fort Lauderdale

WHERE THE GIRLS ARE:
On the beach near the LGBT accommodations, just south of Birch State Recreation Area. Or at one of the cafes or bars in Wilton Manors or Oakland Park.

LGBT PRIDE:
March. 954/745-7070, web: www.pridesouthflorida.org.

ANNUAL EVENTS:
October-November - Int'l Film Fest, web www.fliff.com.
Fall - AIDS Run/Walk 954/463-9005.

CITY INFO:
Greater Fort Lauderdale Convention & Visitors Bureau 954/765-4466 or 800/227-8669 (code 187), web: www.sunny.org.

WEATHER:
The average year-round temperature in this sub-tropical climate is 75-90°.

TRANSIT:
Yellow Cab 954/565-5400.
Super Shuttle 954/764-1700.
Broward County Transit 954/357-8400.

ATTRACTIONS:
Broward Center for the Performing Arts 954/462-0222, web: www.browardcenter.org.
Butterfly World 954/977-4400, web: www.butterflyworld.com.
Everglades.
Flamingo Gardens 954/473-2955, web: www.flamingogardens.com.
Museum of Art 954/525-5500, web: www.moafl.org.
Museum of Discovery & Science 954/467-6637, web: www.mods.org.
Sawgrass Mills, world's largest outlet mall 954/846-2300, web: www.sawgrassmillsmall.com.

Soberano Resort La Casa Del Mar 3003 Granada St 954/467-2037, 866/467-2037 • gay-friendly • Mediterranean villa • swimming • nonsmoking • wheelchair access • gay-owned

Westin Fort Lauderdale 400 Corporate Dr (at Cypres Creek Rd) 954/772-1331, 800/937-8461 • gay-friendly • pool • hot tub • full brkfst • nonsmoking • $109-259

Windamar Beach Resort 543 Breakers Ave (near Bayshore) 954/561-0039, 866/554-6816 • mostly gay men • just steps from the ocean • swimming • gay-owned • $79-299

BARS

Beach Betty's 625 Dania Beach Blvd (at Federal Hwy), Dania 954/921-9893 • noon-2am, 1pm-2am Sun • mostly women • neighborhood bar • dancing/DJ • live music • gay-owned

Bill's Filling Station 1243 NE 11th Ave (at 13th St) 954/525-9403 • 2pm-2am, till 3am Fri-Sat, from noon Sat-Sun • neighborhood bar • patio • wheelchair access

Cathode Ray Club 1307 E Las Olas Blvd (at 13th Ave) 954/462-8611 • 2pm-2am, till 3am Fri-Sat • popular • mostly gay men • sports & piano bars • dancing/DJ • live shows • videos • also restaurant

Cloud 9 Lounge 7126 Stirling Rd, Davie 954/499-3525 • noon-4am, till 2am Sun • mostly women • live shows • drag shows • live bands

Flomingo's 3148 NE 12th Ave (NE corner Oakland & Dixie, Oakland Park) 954/563-8484 • mostly gay men • indoor & outdoor dining • happy hour daily

Georgie's Alibi 2266 Wilton Dr (at NE 4th Ave) 954/565-2526 • 11am-2am, till 3am Sat • popular • lesbians/ gay men • food served • videos • wireless internet • wheelchair access

Manhattan South 6890 Powerline Rd 954/971-1449 • from 2pm • lesbians/ gay men • dancing/DJ • country/western • dance lessons Tue & Sat • karaoke Th

Martini Cabaret 2500 Wilton Dr, Wilton Manors 954/565-1557 • 11am-2am • mostly women • lesbian-owned

Mona's 502 E Sunrise Blvd (at 6th Ave) 954/525-6662 • noon-2am, till 3am wknds • mostly gay men • neighborhood bar

New Moon 2448 Wilton Dr, Wilton Manors 954/563-7660 • 11am-close • mostly women • lounge • karaoke Th • dancing/DJ Fri • live music Sat

Ramrod 1508 NE 4th Ave (at 16th St) 954/763-8219 • 3pm-2am, till 3am wknds • popular • mostly gay men • dancing/DJ • leather/levi cruise bar • bbq Sun • patio • also LeatherWerks leather store

Smarty Pants 3038 N Federal Hwy (at Oakland Park Blvd) 954/561-1724 • 9am-2am, till 3am wknds • popular • mostly gay men • neighborhood bar • piano Th • karaoke Fri • wheelchair access

Torpedo 2829 W Broward Blvd (at 28th Ave) 954/587-2500 • open till 4am nightly • mostly men • dancing/ DJ • strippers

NIGHTCLUBS

Boom 2236 Wilton Dr, Wilton Manors 954/630-3556 • noon-2am, till 3am wknds • popular • mostly gay men • dancing/DJ • live shows • karaoke • drag shows • T-dance Sun • gay-owned

Circuit 2031 Wilton Dr, Wilton Manors • mostly gay men • dancing/DJ • Hi NRG club

Copa 2800 S Federal Hwy (N of airport) 954/463-1507, 954/463-1508 • 10pm-5am, till 6am wknds, clsd Mon & Tue • popular • mostly gay men • dancing/DJ • multiracial • live shows • food served • young crowd • inside & outside bars

Elements 3073 NE 6th Ave, Wilton Manors 954/567-2432 • 4pm-2am, from 1pm Sun, 1pm-3am Fri-Sat, lesbians/ gay men • more women Saturday for Ultra • dancing/ DJ

CAFES

Fantasia's of Boston 1826 E Sunrise Blvd (next to Gateway Theater) 954/522-4886 • noon-10pm

Java Boys 2230 Wilton Dr, Wilton Manors 954/564-8828 • 8am-midnight, coffee, tea & desserts

The Storks 2505 NE 15th Ave (at NE 26th St, Wilton Manors) 954/567-3220 • 6:30am-midnight, from 7am wknds • patio • also at 1109 E Las Olas Blvd, 954/522-4670 • wheelchair access

RESTAURANTS

Bite Me! 827 E Oakland Park Blvd 954/565-3225 • 11am-5pm, till 3pm Sat, clsd Sun • sandwiches, wraps & salads • gay-owned

Boulevard Cafe 1301 E Las Olas Blvd (at 13th) 954/467-3266 • lunch & dinner • dinner only Sat • Sun brunch w/ live jazz • popular • Italian • full bar

Canyon 1818 E Sunrise Blvd 954/765-1950 • dinner • Southwestern • full bar

| Reply | Forward | Delete |

Date: Dec 2, 2005 11:51:33
From: Girl-on-the-Go
To: Editor@Damron.com
Subject: Fort Lauderdale

>Fort Lauderdale, one of Florida's most popular cities and resort areas, has everything that makes the whole state a natural paradise—sunny skies, balmy nights, hot sands, and a clear blue sea.

>Honeycombed by the Intercoastal Waterway of rivers, bays, canals, and inlets, Fort Lauderdale is known as the American Venice. If you'd rather keep your feet on solid ground, you can tour Butterfly World or Flamingo Gardens, shop at Sawgrass Mills outlet mega-mall, or take in a jai alai game.

>For more breathtaking attractions, however, check out Fort Lauderdale's growing lesbian community. To get the full 411, pick up a copy of the local entertainment magazine named aptly **411** or a copy of **She** magazine, Florida's monthly lesbian magazine. Better still, make a call to the local lesbian social group Women in Network (954/564-4946), or pay a visit to the **Gay/Lesbian Community Center of South Florida**'s website (www.glccsf.org).

>Of course, you'll need a place to stay. You'll find a number of lesbian-friendly accommodations, including the world-class **Royal Palms Resort** and the lesbian- and straight-owned **Deauville Inn**.

>Now for the places to wine and dine and party. **Sublime** offers gourmet vegetarian and vegan meals while **Hamburger Mary's** serves up tasty diner fare with a side of screaming queens. Afterward, you can wind down (or up) with some coffee and dessert at **Fantasia's of Boston**. Then it's off to bed—or off to check out Fort Lauderdale's very-lesbian-friendly bars like **Cloud 9**, **Martini Cabaret**, **New Moon**, and **Beach Betty's** (in Dania) or nightclubs like the **Copa** and **Elements** where women mix it up with the gay boys. You can also head out to nearby Hollywood (Florida, that is) and pay a visit to **Ellen's**. For retro fun, take a trip on the wayback machine at Fort Lauderdale's Gay Skate Night on Tuesdays at the **Gold Coast Roller Rink**.

Chardee's 2209 Wilton Dr (at NE 6th Ave) 954/563-1800 • dinner from 6pm, also bar, open 4:30pm-2am • lesbians/ gay men • dancing • professional crowd • live shows • karaoke Sun • piano bar • wheelchair access • some veggie • $11-25

Colors 2736 N Federal Hwy (Rte 1) (at Wilton Manors) 954/566-2880 • dinner nightly & Sun brunch • bistro

Costello's 2345 Wilton Dr, Wilton Manors 954/563-7752 • dinner nightly • also Gin Mill martini bar next door

Dorothy's Deli 1015 NE 26th St (W of 5 Points), Wilton Manors 954/630-3354 • 7am-9pm, till 11pm Fri-Sat • deli-inspired restaurant • full bar • internet cafe

Galanga 2389 Wilton Dr, Wilton Manors 954/202-0000 • dinner nightly, lunch weekdays • Thai, also sushi

Grandma's French Cafe 3354 N Ocean Blvd (N of Oakland Park Blvd) 954/564-3671 • lunch & dinner, clsd Mon • also ice cream parlor

Hamburger Mary's 2449 Wilton Dr, Wilton Manors 954/567-1320 • 11:30am-11pm, till midnight Fri-Sat • popular • full bar till 1 hour after restaurant closes

Herban Kitchen 2823 E Oakland Park Blvd 954/566-1110 • dinner, clsd Sun-Mon • Italian/ Mediterranean • some veggie • beer/ wine

Hi-Life Cafe 3000 N Federal Hwy #12 (at Oakland Park Blvd, in the Plaza 3000) 954/563-1395 • dinner Tue-Sun • bistro • some veggie • $15-25

Kitchenetta 2850 N Federal Hwy 954/567-3333 • noon-10pm, till 11pm Fri-Sat, till 9pm Sun

Lester's Diner 250 State Rd 84 954/525-5641 • 24hrs • popular • more gay late nights • $9+

Simply Delish Cafe 2287 Wilton Dr, Wilton Manors 954/565-8646 • 8am-3pm daily, 5pm-9pm, clsd Mon & Sun nights • reservations recommended

Sublime 1431 N Federal Hwy 954/615-1431 • dinner nightly • vegan/ vegetarian

Tasty Thai 2254 Wilton Dr, Wilton Manors 954/396-3177 • lunch & dinner

Tequila Sunrise Mexican Cafe 4711 N Dixie Hwy 954/938-4473 • 11:30am-11pm, 1pm-10pm Sun, monster margaritas

Tropics Cabaret & Restaurant 2000 Wilton Dr (at 20th) 954/537-6000 • lunch & dinner • new American • also piano bar, till 3am Sat • lesbians/ gay men • live shows • wheelchair access

ENTERTAINMENT & RECREATION

Gallery at Beach Place 17 S Ft Lauderdale Beach Blvd 954/764-3460 • 11am-close • gay-friendly • plaza w/ bars/ shopping

Gold Coast Roller Rink 2604 S Federal Hwy 954/523-6783 • 8pm-midnight Tue • gay skate

BOOKSTORES

Pride Factory & CyberCafe 845 N Federal Hwy (at E Sunrise Blvd) 954/463-6600 • 10am-11pm, 11am-9pm Sun • books • clothing • pride gifts • coffee • also cybercafe

RETAIL SHOPS

Catalog X 850 NE 13th St 954/524-5050 • 10am-10pm, till 9pm Mon-Tue • toys • novelties

GayMartUSA 2240 Wilton Dr (at NE 6th Ave) 954/630-0360 • 11am-midnight • clothes & gifts

PUBLICATIONS

The 411 Magazine 954/567-1981 • weekly entertainment guide

Express South Florida 954/568-1880 • 9am-6pm Mon-Fri

The Independent Gay News 954/563-0470 • LGBT newspaper for Southern FL

TWN (The Weekly News) 305/757-6333 • LGBT newspaper for South Florida

SPIRITUAL GROUPS

Church of the Holy SpiritSong 555 W Cypress Creek Rd (at Sheraton Suites Cypress Creek) 954/418-8372 • 10am Sun

Congregation Etz Chaim 1881 NE 26th St, Ste 218 (btwn Federal Hwy & Dixie Hwy) 954/564-9232 • 8:30pm Fri • LGBT synagogue • social, educational & community services

Dignity Fort Lauderdale 1480 SW 9th Ave (at Sunshine Cathedral MCC) 954/463-4528 • 7:30pm Sun • Roman Catholic liturgy

First Congregational Church (UCC) 2501 NE 30th St 954/563-4271 • 10:30am Sun, "open & affirming"

Sunshine Cathedral MCC 1480 SW 9th Ave 954/462-2004, 877/750-6390 • 9am, 10:20am, 11:40am Sun, meditation 7pm Wed • wheelchair access

Unitarian Universalist Church of Fort Lauderdale 3970 NW 21st Ave, Oakland Park 954/484-6734 • 11am Sun

GYMS & HEALTH CLUBS

Better Bodies 1164 Oakland Blvd (at Dixie Hwy), Wilton Manors **954/561-7977** • also cafe & juice bar, gay-owned

Main Street Gym 2270 Wilton Dr, Wilton Manors **954/563-2655** • 5am-11pm, 8am-10pm wknds • also variety of classes

EROTICA

Fetish Factory 855 E Oakland Park Blvd **954/563-5777** • 11am-9pm, noon-6pm Sun • fetishwear • toys • books • magazine • videos

Strut Shoes 859 E Oakland Park Blvd **954/561-1001** • 11am-9pm, noon-6pm Sun • fetishwear • toys • books • magazine • videos

Tropixxx Video 1514 NE 4th Ave (at 16th St), Wilton Manors **954/522-5988** • 10am-1am, till 3am Fri-Sat, from noon Sun

Fort Myers

INFO LINES & SERVICES

Gay AA Lambda Drummers 3049 McGregor Blvd (at St John the Apostle MCC) **239/275-5111 (AA#)** • 8pm Tue & Sat in social hall

ACCOMMODATIONS

The Hibiscus House B&B 2135 McGregor Blvd **239/332-2651** • gay-friendly • nonsmoking • wheelchair access

Holiday Inn Gulfside 6890 Estero Blvd (at Bonita Beach Rd), Fort Myers Beach **239/463-5711, 800/690-9350** • gay-friendly • beachfront • swimming • kids ok • wheelchair access • $69-249

Lighthouse Resort Inn & Suites 1051 5th St, Fort Myers Beach **239/463-9392, 800/778-7748** • gay-friendly • resort across the street from Fort Myers Beach • swimming • Wi-Fi • kids ok • wheelchair access • $52-135

BARS

The Office Pub 3704 Cleveland Ave (at Grove) **239/936-3212** • noon-2am • mostly gay men • neighborhood bar • bears • leather nights Fri-Sat

Tubby's 4350 Fowler St (off Colonial Blvd) **239/274-5001** • 2pm-2am • mostly gay men • karaoke • live shows • gay-owned

NIGHTCLUBS

The Bottom Line (TBL) 3090 Evans Ave (at Hanson) **239/337-7292, 800/839-6823** • 2pm-2am • lesbians/ gay men • more women wknds • dancing/DJ • live shows • karaoke • videos • wheelchair access

RESTAURANTS

Jack Robert's Courtyard Cafe & Catering 1400 Colonial Blvd, unit 33 (in Royal Plum Square) **239/936-8118**

McGregor Food & Spirits Company 15675 McGregor Blvd, Ste 24 **239/437-3499** • 11am-2am • pub far • some outdoor dining • also full bar • gay-owned

Oasis 2260 Martin Luther King Blvd (at Hendry St) **239/334-1566** • brkfst & lunch only • beer/ wine • wheelchair access • women-owned/ run

SPIRITUAL GROUPS

St John the Apostle MCC 3049 McGregor Blvd **239/344-0012** • 10am & 7pm Sun, 6:30pm Wed • wheelchair access

Unitarian Universalist Church of Fort Myers 13411 Shire Ln **239/561-2700** • 10:30am Sun

Unity of Fort Myers 11120 Ranchette Rd **239/278-1511** • 8:30am, 10:15am & 11:45am Sun

Fort Pierce

ACCOMMODATIONS

Villa Nina Island Inn B&B 3851 N A1A **772/467-8969** • gay-friendly • B&B on 8-acre estate overlooking Indian River • swimming • nonsmoking • $125-215

Fort Walton Beach

see also Pensacola

Gainesville

INFO LINES & SERVICES

Free to Be AA 1624 NW 5th Ave (United Church of Gainesville) **352/372-8091 (AA#)** • 7:30pm Sun • LGBT AA group

Pride Community Center 1107 NW 6th St, Ste C **352/332-0700 (SWITCHBOARD #), 352/377-8915** • 3pm-7pm, noon-4pm Sat, clsd Sun • also switchboard

BARS

Spikes 4130 NW 6th St **352/376-3772** • 1pm-2am, till 11pm Sun • popular • lesbians/ gay men • neighborhood bar • wheelchair access

The University Club 18 E University Ave (enter rear) **352/378-6814** • 5pm-2am, till 11pm Sun • lesbians/gay men • 3 levels • young crowd • dancing/DJ • karaoke • live shows • patio • wheelchair access

RESTAURANTS

Emiliano's Cafe 7 SE 1st Ave **323/375-7381** • 11:30am-11pm, 11am-9:30pm Sun, clsd Mon • popular • Pan-Latin • also wine & tapas bar (11am-2am)

Natural Cafe 505 NW 13th St (at 5th Ave, in Books Inc) **352/384-0090, 352/374-4241** • vegetarian cafe

ENTERTAINMENT & RECREATION

Ponte Vedra LGBT Beach • Go N from Gainesville on Waldo Rd to N 301 then E on I-10. I-10 becomes 95. Go S on 95, then take a left. Go E onto Butler Blvd, which ends at A1A. Turn right onto A1A and then drive 5 to 7 minutes looking for Guana Boat Landing parking lot on the right. Park in a parking lot or get ticketed. Walk to beach.

BOOKSTORES

Goerings Book Store 3433 W University Ave **352/378-0363** • 10am-9:30pm, till 5pm Sun • independent • LGBT section

Wild Iris Books 802 W University Ave (at 8th St) **352/375-7477** • 11am-8pm, noon-6pm Sat, clsd Sun • feminist/LGBT • wheelchair access

PUBLICATIONS

Mama Raga • north-central FL newsletter • "primarily, but not solely, for lesbian women" • available at Wild Iris

SPIRITUAL GROUPS

Holy Trinity Episcopal 100 NE 1st St **352/372-4721** • 10:30am & 6pm Sun

Trinity MCC 11604 SW Archer Rd **352/495-3378** • 10:15am Sun • wheelchair access

Unitarian Universalist Fellowship 4225 NW 34th St **352/377-1669** • 11am Sun

High Springs

ACCOMMODATIONS

Grady House 420 NW 1st Ave **386/454-2206** • gay-friendly • B&B in historic 1917 Craftsman home • full brkfst • kids 8 yrs + ok • nonsmoking • $85-195

Holiday

BARS

Frank & Tony's Pub 2419 Grand Blvd (near Sunray Blvd) **727/942-9734** • 1pm-2am • lesbian/gay men • neighborhood bar • food served • karaoke Tue & Sun • beer & wine • patio • gay-owned

Hollywood

see also Miami

BARS

DinoPete's 4221 N State Rd 7 (at Stirling) **954/966-4441** • 4pm-close, clsd Sun • gay/straight • dancing/DJ • restaurant • live shows • karaoke Th

Ellen's 2217 N Federal Hwy **954/920-5479** • 3pm-2am • mostly women • neighborhood bar • beer/wine • karaoke Fri • open mic Sun • wheelchair access

Trixie's Show Bar 600 S Dixie Hwy (S of Hollywood Blvd) **954/923-9322** • 8pm-2am • mostly gay men • neighborhood bar • transgender-friendly (especially Th) • drag shows Th-Sat

RESTAURANTS

Sushi Blues Cafe 2009 Harrison St **954/929-9560** • lunch & dinner, dinner only Fri-Sat • sushi, seafood & sandwiches • live blues 9:30pm Fri-Sat • also full bar

EROTICA

Hollywood Book & Video 1235 S State Rd 7 (at Washington) **954/981-2164**

Islamorada

ACCOMMODATIONS

Casa Morada 136 Madeira Rd **305/664-0044, 888/881-3030** • gay-friendly • luxury all-suite hotel w/ private island • swimming • jacuzzi • kids/pets ok • women-owned • $199-389

Lookout Lodge Resort 87770 Overseas Hwy, mile marker 88 (at Plantation Blvd) **305/852-9915, 800/870-1772** • gay-friendly • waterfront resort • kids/pets ok • $79-325 (2-night minimum)

EROTICA

The Romance Store 82185 Overseas Hwy (Mile Marker 82) **305/664-8228, 800/326-8905** • 10am-6pm • lingerie • adult products • woman-owned

Jacksonville

Info Lines & Services

LGBT AA 1615 Hendricks Ave 904/399-8535 (AA#) • 6:30pm Mon • also 8pm Tue at 1140 McDuff Ave S

Women's Center of Jacksonville 5644 Colcord 904/722-3000

Accommodations

Hilton Garden Inn Jacksonville JTB/ Deerwood Park 9745 Gate Pkwy (at Southside Blvd) 904/997-6600, 877/782-9444 • gay-friendly • 15 minutes to beach • swimming • jacuzzi • kids ok

Spring Hill Suites Jacksonville 4385 Southside Blvd (at J Turner Butler Blvd) 904/997-6650, 888/287-9400 • gay-friendly • swimming • jacuzzi • kids ok • $89-114

Bars

616 616 Park St (at I-95) 904/358-6969 • 4pm-2am • lesbians/gay men • neighborhood bar • karaoke • patio

AJ's Bar & Grill 10244 Atlantic Blvd (in Regency Walk Shopping Center) 904/805-9060 • 4pm-2am • mostly women • dancing/DJ after 10pm (except Wed & Sat) • full menu • great venue for live music (wide array of bands Sat) • karaoke Wed • wheelchair access • women-owned/ run

Boot Rack Saloon 4751 Lenox Ave (at Cassat Ave) 904/384-7090 • 3pm-2am • mostly gay men • country/western • cruise bar • beer/wine • patio • wheelchair access

InCahoots 711 Edison Ave (btwn Riverside & Park) 904/353-6316 • 3pm-2am, from 8pm Sat, from 4pm Sun, clsd Mon-Tue • mostly gay men • 3 bars • dancing/DJ • alternative • multiracial • Latin night Fri • karaoke • drag shows • videos • wheelchair access

The Metro 2929 Plum St 904/388-8719 & 866/388-8719 (OUTSIDE JAX), 904/388-7192 (INFO LINE) • 4pm-2am, from 6pm Sat, till midnight Mon • popular • lesbians/gay men • 6 bars • dancing/DJ • drag shows • male strippers • videos • also piano bar • also The Loft • nonsmoking • 18+ • wheelchair access

The Norm 2952 Roosevelt Blvd (at College) 904/384-9929 • 4pm-close • mostly women but everyone welcome • dancing/DJ • live shows • wheelchair access

Park Place Lounge 931 King St (at Post) 904/389-6616 • noon-2am • lesbians/gay men • neighborhood bar • dancing/DJ • wheelchair access

Cafes

Fuel Coffeehouse 1037 Park St (at Post) 904/425-3835 • 10am-2am, noon-10pm Sun, till midnight Mon, 10am-midnight Tue • also sandwiches, soups & salads • beer • open mic & live music

Restaurants

Al's Pizza 1620 Margaret St, Ste 201 904/388-8384 • 11am-10pm, till 11pm Fri-Sat, noon-9pm • in Riverside/ Little 5 Points area

Biscotti's 3558 Saint Johns Ave 904/387-2060 • 10:30am-10pm, till midnight Fri, from 8am Sat, till 9pm Sun • popular • killer desserts • also cafe

Bistro Aix 1440 San Marco Blvd 904/398-1949 • 11am-10pm, till 11pm Fri, from 5pm Sat, till 9pm Sun • upscale French bistro fare • also pizza & salads • martini & wine list

Derby House 1068 Park St 904/356-0227 • brkfst & lunch • very popular wknds for brkfst

European Street Cafe 2753 Park St (at King) 904/384-9999 • 10am-10pm • popular • deli • salads • large beer selection • patio • gay-owned

Bookstores

Borders 8801 Southside Blvd, Ste 10 904/519-6500 • 9am-11pm, till 9pm Sun • LGBT section

Retail Shops

Rainbows & Stars 1046 Park St (in historic 5-Points) 904/356-7702 • 10am-8pm, 11am-6pm Sat, till 4pm Sun • pride giftstore • T-shirts • rainbow items • jewelry • also community bulletin board

Publications

Out in the City 904/389-8883 • monthly LGBT newspaper

Spiritual Groups

Christ Church of Peace 1240 S McDuff 904/387-2020 • 10:30am Sun

St Luke's MCC 1140 S McDuff Ave (at Remington) 904/389-7726 • 10:15am Sun & 7pm Wed

Unitarian Universalist Church of Jacksonville 7405 Arlington Expy 904/725-8133 • 11am Sun

Jacksonville Beach

ACCOMMODATIONS

Comfort Inn Oceanfront 1515 N 1st St
904/241–2311, 800/654–8776 • gay-friendly •
oceanfront • fitness center • restaurant •
swimming

BARS

Bo's Coral Reef 201 5th Ave N (at 2nd St)
904/246–9874 • 2pm-2am • lesbians/ gay
men • neighborhood bar • dancing/DJ • live
shows

Key West

INFO LINES & SERVICES

Gay/ Lesbian AA 305/296-8654 (HELPLINE #)

Gay/Lesbian Community Center 513
Truman Ave **305/292-3223** • many meetings
& groups • call for info

▲ **Key West Business Guild** 305/294–4603,
888/429–1893 • see ad in front color section

ACCOMMODATIONS

Alexander Palms Court 715 South St (at
Vernon) **305/296–6413, 800/858–1943** • gay-
friendly • swimming • hot tub • private patios
• gay-owned • $90-300

▲ **Alexander's Guest House** 1118 Fleming St
(at Frances) **305/294–9919, 800/654–9919** •
lesbians/ gay men • hot tub • swimming •
nudity • sundeck • wheelchair access • gay-
owned • $105-340

Ambrosia House Tropical Lodging
615 & 618-622 Fleming St (at Simonton)
305/296–9838, 800/535–9838 • gay-friendly •
swimming • hot tub • sea captain's house •
$120-499

Andrews Inn Zero Whalton Ln (at Duval)
305/294–7730, 888/263–7393 • gay-friendly •
swimming • kids ok • nonsmoking • $125-199

Key West

WHERE THE GIRLS ARE:
You can't miss 'em during
WomenFest in September, but
other times they're just off Duval
St., somewhere between Eaton
and South Streets. Or on the
beach. Or in the water.

LGBT PRIDE:
June. 305/292–3223, web:
www.pridefestkeywest.com.

ANNUAL EVENTS:
February - Kelly McGillis Classic
Women's & Girls' Flag Football
Tournament 888/464–9332, web:
www.iwffa.com.
September - WomenFest, web:
www.womenfest.net.
October - Fantasy Fest 305/296-
1817, web: www.fantasyfest.net.
Weeklong Halloween celebration
with parties, masquerade balls &
parades.

BEST VIEW:
Old Town Trolley Tour (1/2 hour),
web:
www.historictours.com/keywest.

WEATHER:
The average temperature year-
round is 78°, and the sun shines
nearly every day. Any time is the
right time for a visit.

TRANSIT:
Friendly Cab 305/292-0000.
Key West Shuttle 888/539–2628
Key West Transit Authority
305/293-6435.

ATTRACTIONS:
Audubon House and Gardens
305/294-4513.
Dolphin Research Center
305/289–1121, web:
www.dolphins.org.
Glass-bottom boats 305/293–0099.
Hemingway House, web:
www.hemingwayhome.com.
Sunset Celebration at Mallory
Square.
Red Barn Theatre 305/296-9911.
Southernmost Point USA.

Reply **Forward** **Delete**

Date: Dec 15, 2005 11:51:33
From: Girl-on-the-Go
To: Editor@Damron.com
Subject: Key West

>This tiny Caribbean island at the very tip of Florida, closer to Havana than to Miami, has had more crashing busts and facelifting booms than most Hollywood celebrities have had cosmetic surgeries. During its earliest boom days, it was home to pirates and those who salvaged the ships they and the reefs would wreck. Later came robber barons who made a killing in the cigar-rolling and sponge-harvesting businesses. With another boom came Harry Truman and his Little White House and Ernest Hemingway and his cats. And since the '80s, gays and lesbians have helped create the tropical boom town visited today by tourists from around the world.

>The famous Old Town area is dotted with Victorian homes and mansions. Many of them are now fully renovated as accommodations, such as the women-only guesthouse **Pearl's Rainbow**, which is also home to the popular lesbian bar and restaurant **Pearl's Patio**.

>As soon as you arrive, you realize Key West is a way of life, not just an exotic resort. Locals have perfected a laissez-faire attitude and you'll quickly fall into the relaxed rhythm. You'll be thoroughly entertained spending your days lounging poolside with warm tropical breezes in your hair and a cool drink in your hand.

>Or get out of that lounge chair and sail the emerald waters around Key West. This ocean is home to the hemisphere's largest living coral reef, accessible by snorkeling, which can be arranged for you by the **Mangrove Mistress** (in addition to commitment ceremonies) or by the lesbian-owned and lesbian-run **Venus Charters** (along with dolphin-watching and light-tackle fishing). For an inexpensive and fun way to get around the island, rent a bicycle or moped from one of the many bike rental shops.

>Don't miss **Womenfest** in September, the annual women's week in Key West—the ideal time and place to experience women entertainers, sailing, boating, snorkeling, a street fair, dances, and more. **Fantasy Fest** in October is seven days of Halloween in a tropical heaven: costumes, contests, parades, and parties galore.

>For information on other fun events, stop by Key West's LGBT bookstore and coffeehouse, **Flaming Maggie's**, and pick up a copy of local LGBT papers **Celebrate!** and **Southern Exposure**. Or call the **Gay/Lesbian Community Center**.

The Artist House 534 Eaton St (at Duval) **305/296-3977, 800/582-7882** • gay/ straight • Victorian guesthouse • swimming • jacuzzi • patio • nonsmoking • $129-299

Author's Key West 725 White St (entrance on Petronia) **305/294-7381, 800/898-6909** • gay-friendly • swimming • nonsmoking • $85-140

Avalon B&B 1317 Duval St (at United) **305/294-8233, 800/848-1317** • gay-friendly • restored Victorian • swimming • near beach • sundeck • $79-269

Beach Bungalow & Beach Guest Suite **305/294-1525** • gay/ straight • hot tub • vacation rental • nonsmoking • $119-169 (3-day minimum stay)

Big Ruby's Guesthouse 409 Appelrouth Ln (at Duval & Whitehead) **305/296-2323, 800/477-7829** • mostly gay men • full brkfst • swimming • nudity • evening wine • sundeck • wheelchair access • gay-owned • $102-499

Blue Parrot Inn 916 Elizabeth St (at Olivia) **305/296-0033, 800/231-2473** • gay-friendly • historic Bahamian home • swimming • nudity • sundeck • wheelchair access • gay-owned • $80-160

Casa de Luces 422 Amelia St (at Whitehead) **305/296-3993, 800/432-4849** • gay-friendly • early 1900s Conch house & condos • jacuzzi • wheelchair access • $99-269

Chelsea House 707 Truman Ave (at Elizabeth) **305/296-2211, 800/845-8859** • lesbians/ gay men • swimming • nudity • wheelchair access • gay-owned • $84-275

Cuban Club Suites 1102-1108 Duval St (at Virginia) **305/296-0465, 800/432-4849** • gay-friendly • award-winning historic hotel • suites w/ kitchens • kids/ dogs ok • $199-359

Cypress House 601 Caroline (at Simonton) **305/294-6969, 800/525-2488** • gay-friendly • guesthouse • swimming • sundeck • wheelchair access • $99-325

Duval House 815 Duval St (at Petronia) **305/292-9491, 800/223-8825** • gay-friendly • Victorians w/ gardens • swimming • sundeck • nonsmoking • gay-owned • $125-350

Eaton Lodge 511 Eaton St (at Duval) **305/292-2170, 800/294-2170** • gay-friendly • 1886 mansion & Conch house w/ gardens • hot tub • swimming • $105-315

Heartbreak Hotel 716 Duval St (near Petronia) **305/296-5558** • lesbians/ gay men • kitchens • lesbian & gay-owned • $43-199

Heron House 512 Simonton St (at Fleming) 305/294-9227, 800/294-1644 • gay-friendly • swimming • evening wine • wheelchair access • $119-369

Key Lodge Motel 1004 Duval St (at Truman) 305/296-9915, 800/845-8384 • gay-friendly • swimming • $115-259

Key West Harbor Inn B&B 219 Elizabeth St (at Greene) 305/296-2978, 800/608-6569 • lesbians/ gay men • swimming • hot tub • nonsmoking • wheelchair accessible • $115-400

Knowles House B&B 1004 Eaton St (at Grinnell) 305/296-8132, 800/352-4414 • gay/ straight • restored 1880s Conch house • swimming • nudity • nonsmoking • gay-owned • $89-199

La Te Da 1125 Duval St (at Catherine) 305/296-6706, 877/528-3320 • popular • lesbians/ gay men • full brkfst • tropical setting • nonsmoking • swimming • nudity • restaurant & 3 bars (piano bar & cabaret) • adults 21+ only • wheelchair access • gay-owned • $90-285

Lightbourn Inn 907 Truman Ave (at Packer) 305/296-5152, 800/352-6011 • gay-friendly • Conch mansion • swimming • sundeck • largest private teddy bear collection in Key West • nonsmoking • gay-owned • $98-298

Marquesa Hotel 600 Fleming St (at Simonton) 305/292-1919, 800/869-4631 • gay-friendly • swimming • also restaurant • full bar • wheelchair access • $175-430

Marrero's Guest Mansion 410 Fleming St (btwn Duval & Whitehead) 305/294-6977, 800/459-6212 • gay-friendly • 1890 Victorian mansion • swimming • hot tub • nonsmoking • $100-210

The Mermaid & the Alligator 729 Truman Ave (at Windsor Ln) 305/294-1894, 800/773-1894 • gay/ straight • full brkfst • swimming • nonsmoking • gay-owned • $168-248

Nassau House 1016 Fleming St (at Grinnell) 305/296-8513, 800/296-8513 • gay-friendly • swimming • nonsmoking • sundeck • hot tub • wheelchair access • gay-owned • $110-180

▲ **Pearl's Rainbow** 525 United St (at Duval) 305/292-1450, 800/749-6696 • popular • women only • hot tub • swimming • sundeck • nudity • nonsmoking • also bar & restaurant • wheelchair access • lesbian-owned • $99-329 • see color ad on inside front cover

Pier House Resort & Caribbean Spa 1 Duval St (at Front) 305/296-4600, 800/327-8340 • gay-friendly • private beach • hot tub • swimming • restaurants • live music • bars • spa • fitness center • kids ok • nonsmoking • wheelchair access • $200-1800

Pilot House Guest House 414 Simonton St (at Eaton) 305/293-6600, 800/648-3780 • gay/ straight • Victorian mansion in Old Town • hot tub • swimming • nudity • nonsmoking • wheelchair access • $100-300

Seascape Tropical Inn 420 Olivia St (at Duval) 305/296-7776, 800/765-6438 • gay-friendly • also cottages • swimming • hot tub • sundeck • nonsmoking • $99-189

Sheraton Suites Key West 2001 S Roosevelt Blvd 305/292-9800, 800/452-3224 • gay-friendly • swimming • hot tub • also restaurant • wheelchair access • $179-349

Simonton Court Historic Inn & Cottages 320 Simonton St (at Caroline) 305/294-6386, 800/944-2687 • gay-friendly • built in 1880s • hot tub • swimming • $150-540

Travelers Palm 915 Center St 305/294-9560, 800/294-9560 • gay-friendly • 3 locations in Old Town Key West • swimming • $98-308

Tropical Inn 812 Duval St (at Petronia) 305/294-9977, 888/611-6510 • gay-friendly • also cottage suites • hot tub • swimming • sundeck • $149-449

Bars

The 801 Bourbon Bar 801 Duval St (at Petronia) 305/294-4737 • 11am-4am • lesbians/ gay men • neighborhood bar • dancing/ DJ • popular drag shows • Sun bingo • also One Saloon • mostly gay men • leather

Bobby's Monkey Bar 900 Simonton St (at Olivia) 305/294-2655 • noon-4am • mostly gay men • neighborhood bar • wheelchair access

Bourbon Street Pub 724 Duval St (at Angela) 305/296-1992 • 11am-4am • mostly gay men • popular • strippers • videos • garden bar w/ pool & hot tub • wheelchair access

La Te Da 1125 Duval St (at Catherine) 305/296-6706 • popular • lesbians/ gay men • 3 bars (piano bar & cabaret) & restaurant • wheelchair access • gay-owned

▲ **Pearl's Patio** 525 United St (at Duval, at Pearl's Rainbow) 305/292-1450, 800/749-6696 • noon-8pm, later on wknds • women only • food served • special events

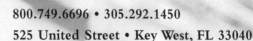

NIGHTCLUBS

Aqua 711 Duval St 305/294-0555 • 2pm-2am, till 4am Th-Sat, also Wet Bar, from 8pm Th-Sat • lesbians/ gay men • dancing/DJ • drag shows • karaoke • videos • garden w/ waterfall

The Blue Room 422 Appelrouth Ln (at Whitehead) 305/296-6667 • 9pm-4am, clsd Mon-Tue • gay-friendly • dancing/DJ • young crowd • patio

Virgilio's 524 Duval St (at Fleming in La Trattoria) 305/296-8118 • 7pm-4am • gay/ straight • live music • late-night DJ

CAFES

Croissants de France 816 Duval St (at Petronia) 305/294-2624 • 7:30am-6pm, restaurant open till 3pm, clsd Wed • French pastries • some veggie • beer/ wine • patio • $5-7

RESTAURANTS

Antonia's 615 Duval St (at Southard) 305/294-6565 • 6pm-11pm • popular • Italian • full bar • some veggie • $16-22

Bo's Fish Wagon 801 Caroline (at Williams) 305/294-9272 • lunch, dinner • popular • "seafood & eat it" • $4-12

Cafe Sole 1029 Southard St (at Frances) 305/294-0230 • lunch, dinner, Sun brunch • romantic • candlelit backyard

Camille's 1202 Simonton (at Catherine) 305/296-4811 • brkfst, lunch & dinner • bistro • hearty brkfst • $10-18

Half Shell Raw Bar 231 Margaret St 305/294-7496 • 11am-10pm • waterfront • full bar

Kelly's Caribbean Bar Grill & Brewery 301 Whitehead St (at Caroline) 305/293-8484 • lunch & dinner • full bar • owned by actress Kelly McGillis • $7-22

La Trattoria Venezia 524 Duval St (at Fleming) 305/296-1075 • 5:30pm-10:30pm • Italian • full bar • $10-22

Lobos 613 Duval St, #5 Key Lime Square (south of Southard St) 305/296-5303 • 11am-6pm, noon-5pm Sun • sandwiches • plenty veggie • beer/ wine • $4-7

Louie's Backyard 700 Waddell Ave (at Vernon) 305/294-1061 • lunch & dinner, bar 11:30am-2am • popular • fine cont'l dining • $22-30

Mangia Mangia 900 Southard St (at Margaret St) 305/294-2469 • dinner only • fresh pasta • beer/ wine • patio • $9-16

Mangoes 700 Duval St (at Angela) 305/292-4606 • 11:30am-1am • "Floribbean" cuisine • plenty veggie • full bar • patio • wheelchair access • $6-23

New York Pizza Cafe 1075 Duval St (Duval Square) 305/292-1991 • open till midnight • very reasonable prices

Ocean Grill Restaurant 1125 Duval St (at La Te Da accommodations) 305/296-6706 x39, 877/528-3320 • brkfst, lunch & dinner • popular • fusion • home of award-winning chef Alice Weingarten • piano bar • $7-28

Pisces 1007 Simonton St (at Truman) 305/294-7100 • 6pm-11pm • tropical French • full bar • $22-30

Rooftop Cafe 308 Front St (at Fitzpatrick) 305/294-2042 • brkfst, lunch & dinner • best Key Lime pie • some veggie • $15+

Salsa Loca 918 Duval St 305/292-1865 • clsd Mon, gay-friendly • tasty, inexpensive Mexican

Seven Fish 632 Olivia St (at Elizabeth) 305/296-2777 • 6pm-10pm, clsd Tue • popular • $12-15

Square One 1075 Duval St (at Truman) 305/296-4300 • 6pm-10pm • full bar • wheelchair access • $15-21

Upper Crust 611 Duval St 305/293-8890 • noon-11pm• excellent pizza

ENTERTAINMENT & RECREATION

Bahia Honda State Park & Beach 35 miles N of Key West • Viking Beach is best

BluQ Sailing 201 William St (at Caroline) 305/923-7245 • all-gay sails • mostly gay men • daily sailing, snorkeling, kayaking & sunset cruises • day trips include all gear & meals • gay-owned

Fort Zachary Taylor Beach • more gay to the right

Gay & Lesbian Trolley Tour 305/294-4603 • 11am Sat • check out all of the gay hotspots & historical points • look for rainbow-decorated trolley

The Key West Butterfly & Nature Conservatory 1316 Duval Street 305/296-2988, 800/839-4647 • gay-owned

Mangrove Mistress/ Intimate Island Ceremonies 305/745-8886 • gentle nature-exploring & snorkeling • also commitment ceremonies on land & sea • woman-owned/ run

Moped Hospital 601 Truman 866/296-1625 • forget the car—mopeds are a must for touring the island

The Rude Awakening Radio Extravaganza Ministry 92.7 FM WEOW 305/296-7511 • 6am-10am Mon-Fri • a morning zoo show w/a lesbian twist • music • comedy • contests • news

Sebago Gay Cruises 201 William St (at historic Key West Seaport) 305/292-4768, 305/294-5687 • lesbians/gay men • full cash bar on largest boat • cover

▲ **Venus Charters** Garrison Bight Marina slip #10 305/304-1181, 305/292-9403 • snorkeling • light-tackle fishing • dolphin-watching • personalized excursions • lesbian-owned

BOOKSTORES

Flaming Maggie's 830 Fleming St (at Margaret) 305/294-3931 • 10am-6pm • LGBT bookstore • also coffeehouse

Key West Island Books 513 Fleming St (at Duval) 305/294-2904 • 10am-9pm • new & used rare books • LGBT section

RETAIL SHOPS

Fast Buck Freddie's 500 Duval St (at Fleming) 305/294-2007 • 10am-6pm, till 8pm Th-Fri, till 10pm Sat, from 11am Sun • clothing • gifts • wheelchair access

In Touch 715 Duval St (at Angela) 305/292-7293 • 9am-11pm • gay gifts

PUBLICATIONS

Celebrate! 305/295-8292

Southern Exposure 305/294-6303

SPIRITUAL GROUPS

MCC Key West 1215 Petronia St (at White St) 305/294-8912 • 9:15am & 11am Sun • wheelchair access

St Paul's Episcopal Church 401 Duval (at Eden) 305/296-5142 • 7:30am, 9am & 11am Sun • Integrity meets 7:30pm 1st Wed • don't miss the stained glass window (!) • wheelchair access

Unitarian Universalist Fellowship of Key West 801 Georgia St 305/296-4369 • 11am Sun

GYMS & HEALTH CLUBS

Bodies on South 2740 N Roosevelt Blvd 305/292-2930

Club Body Tech 1075 Duval St (at Virginia) 305/292-9683 • lesbians/gay men • full gym • steam room • massage therapy available

EROTICA

Fairvilla Megastore 520 Front St 305/292-0448 • 9am-midnight • clean, well-lighted adult store w/emphasis on couples: "store for lovers"

Experience the sea in the company of women

VENUS CHARTERS

Snorkeling & Dolphin Watching
Light Tackle Fishing
Sunsets
Private Charters

Captain Karen Luknis
& Captain Debra Butler

305-292-9403
Cell: 305-304-1181
www.venuscharters.com

Lesbian Owned & Operated

P.O Box 4394 • Key West, FL 33041

Leather Master 418 Appelrouth Ln (btwn Duval & Whitehead) **305/292–5051, 800/565–9447** • 11am-11pm, noon-8pm Sun • custom leather, toys & more

Kissimmee

ACCOMMODATIONS

Ramada Plaza Gateway 7470 Hwy 192 W **407/396–4400, 800/327–9170** • gay-friendly • 1 mile from Walt Disney World • restaurant • wheelchair access

Lake Worth

see also West Palm Beach

BARS

DugRocks 6 S J St **561/493–1924** • 3pm-2am • mostly gay men • till midnight Sun

The Mad Hatter Bar & Grill 1532 N Dixie Hwy (16th Ave) **561/547–8860** • 11am-2am, noon-midnight Sun • lesbians/ gay men • neighborhood bar • food served

Lakeland

see also Tampa

ACCOMMODATIONS

Sunset Motel 2301 New Tampa Hwy **863/683–6464** • gay-friendly • motels, apts & private home on 3 acres • swimming • pets ok • wheelchair access • gay-owned • $55-100

BARS

Pulse 1030 E Main St **863/683–6021** • 4pm-2am, till midnight Sun • mostly gay men • dancing/DJ • drag shows Th-Sat • strippers Fri-Sat • wheelchair access

SPIRITUAL GROUPS

Rainbow Promise MCC 1145 US Hwy 92 E, Auburndale **863/802–6769** • 10:30am Sun

Madeira Beach

see St Petersburg

Marathon

ACCOMMODATIONS

Tropical Cottages 243 61st St Gulf **305/743–6048** • gay-friendly • outdoor hot tub • videos • pets ok • nonsmoking • gay-owned • $99-150+11.5%tax

Melbourne

ACCOMMODATIONS

Beach Bungalow 312 Wavecrest Ave, Indialantic by the Sea **321/984–1330** • gay-friendly • 3 2-bdrm beachfront villas (sleep 8) • private patios & spas • $115-160

Crane Creek Inn B&B 907 E Melbourne Ave **321/768–6416** • gay/ straight • full brkfst • swimming • hot tub • tropical waterfront setting • dogs ok • $139-199

BARS

Cold Keg 4060 W New Haven Ave (1/2 mile E of I-95) **321/724–1510** • 2pm-2am • popular • lesbians/ gay men • dancing/DJ • drag shows Fri-Sat • karaoke Wed • wheelchair access

SPIRITUAL GROUPS

East Coast MCC 2185 Meadowlane Ave (off US 192, in Unitarian Universalist Church) **321/759–5588** • 6pm 2nd & 4th Sat

MIAMI

Miami is divided into 3 geographical areas:
Miami—Overview
Miami—Greater Miami
Miami—Miami Beach/ South Beach

Miami—Overview

INFO LINES & SERVICES

Switchboard of Miami **305/358–4357** (HELPLINE #), **305/358–1640** (OFFICE #) • 24hrs • gay-friendly info & referrals for Dade County

ENTERTAINMENT & RECREATION

Sailboat Charters of Miami 3400 Pan American Dr (at S Bayshore Dr) **305/772–4221** • lesbians/ gay men • private sailing charters aboard all-teakwood 46-foot clipper to Bahamas & the Keys

PUBLICATIONS

TWN (The Weekly News) **305/757–6333** • LGBT newspaper for South Florida

Miami—Greater Miami

ACCOMMODATIONS

Miami River Inn 118 SW S River Dr **305/325–0045, 800/468–3589** • gay-friendly • B&B located in Miami's Little Havana district • swimming • jacuzzi • kids/ pets ok • wheelchair access • woman-owned/ run • $89-199

Bars

Uranus Bar 55 NE 24th St (at N Miami Ave) 305/573–1010 • 4pm-5am • mostly gay men • "video dance cruise bar"

Nightclubs

Azucar 2301 SW 32nd Ave (at Coral Wy) 305/441–6974 • 10pm-4am Fri, till 5am Sat, 8pm-3am Sun

Last Call Sundays 250 NE 183rd St, N Miami 305/405–1000 (CLUB#) • last Sun only • women only • dancing/ DJ • multiracial

Cafes

Gourmet Station 7601 Biscayne Blvd (at NE 71st St) 305/762–7229 • also catering • gay-owned

Restaurants

Magnum Lounge & Restaurant 709 NE 79th St 305/757–3368 • 6pm-midnight, bar open 5pm-2am, till 3am wknds, clsd Mon • popular • gay/ straight • neighborhood bar • cont'l • live shows • piano bar

Ortanique on the Mile 278 Miracle Mile (at Salzedo), Coral Gables 305/446–7710 • lunch Mon-Fri, dinner 7 days • popular • Caribbean • full bar • $11-19

Bookstores

Lambda Passages Bookstore 7545 Biscayne Blvd (at 76th) 305/754–6900 • 11am-9pm, noon-6pm Sun • LGBT/ feminist

Spiritual Groups

Coral Gables Congregational Church 3010 De Soto Blvd, Coral Gables 305/448–7421 • 11am Sun

Miami

Where the Girls Are:
In Miami proper, Coral Gables and the University district, as well as Biscayne Blvd. along the coast, are the lesbian hangouts of choice. You'll see women everywhere in South Beach, but especially along Ocean Dr., Washington, Collins and Lincoln Roads.

Annual Events:
March - Winter Party 305/572-1841, web: www.winterparty.com. AIDS benefit dance on the beach.
April/May - Gay & Lesbian Film Festival 305/534–9924, web: www.mglff.com.
November - White Party Vizcaya 305/576–1234, web: www.whiteparty.net. AIDS benefit.

City Info:
Greater Miami Convention & Visitors Bureau 305/539-3000. 701 Brickell Ave, web: www.miamiandbeaches.com.

Best View:
If you've got money to burn, a helicopter flight over Miami Beach is a great way to see the city. Otherwise, hit the beach.

Weather:
Warm all year. Temperatures stay in the 90ºs during the summer and drop into the mid-60ºs in the winter. Be prepared for sunshine!

Transit:
Yellow Cab 305/266–7799.
Metro Taxi 305/888-8888.
A Plus 305/219–8219.
Metro Bus 305/770-3131.

Attractions:
Art Deco Welcome Center 305/672-2014. web: mdpl.org.
Bayside Market Place 305/577-3344.
Miami Beach Botanical Garden 305/673-7256.
Miami Museum of Science & Planetarium 305/646-4200.
Museum of Contempory Art, N Miami 305/893-6211.
Parrot Jungle Island 305/258-6453.
Sanford L Ziff Jewish Museum of Florida 305/672-5044.

Reply **Forward** **Delete**

Date: Dec 18, 2005 11:51:33
From: Girl-on-the-Go
To: Editor@Damron.com
Subject: Miami Beach/ South Beach

>As a key center of business and politics in the Americas, Miami has an incredibly multicultural look and feel. You'll discover a diversity of people, from a growing population of transplanted seniors to large communities of Cubans, Latin Americans, and African Americans.

>Miami is also a tourist's winter wonderland of sun, sand, and sea. Make the most of it with trips to Seaquarium, Key Biscayne, or the nearby Everglades. Better still, hit the beach. South Beach, that is (SoBe, if you've gotta be hip at all costs).

>This section of Miami Beach has been given an incredible makeover by gays and lesbians, and has fast become one of the hottest spots on the East Coast. Much of the SoBe scene is gay boys, drag queens, and straight couples in little more than sunscreen and a thong, but svelte, hot-blooded, women-loving-women can be found. During the day, start your search and deepen your tan at the 12th Street gay beach. Or, go window-shopping along Lincoln Road.

>If you manage to look beyond the endless parade of bodies beautiful, you'll discover South Beach's historic Art Deco architecture. To make the most of the Art Deco District, take the $20 walking tour that leaves from the Art Deco Welcome Center at 1001 Ocean Drive.

>With all that walking, you're certain to build up quite an appetite. Try **Nexxt Cafe** or **Big Pink** or the 24-hour **Cafeteria** or the Italian restaurant **Tiramesu** for lunch or dinner, while **News Cafe** on Ocean Drive (open 24 hours) is always an option for late-night snacks.

>Unfortunately, there are no full-time women's bars in Miami or Miami Beach. But there are some women's nights like **Cherry Pie** and **Last Call Sundays**.

>There are also plenty of local lesbian promoters, so be sure to check out **She** magazine for roaming women's parties, or, if you have web access, be sure to visit www.pandoraevents.com. To learn about the rest of Miami's nightlife, pick up a copy of **TWN**, South Florida's LGBT newspaper, or the **Wire**, South Beach's gay tabloid.

>For a quieter evening with the girls back over in Miami, make reservations to dine at **Something Special**, a women-only restaurant in a private home. Afterward, curl up with a new book or magazine from **Lambda Passages**, Miami's LGBT bookstore.

St Stephen's Episcopal Church 2750 McFarlane Rd, Coconut Grove **305/448-2601** • 8am & 10am Sun

Temple Israel 137 NE 19th St **305/573-5900** • 6pm & 8pm Fri • also home to Ru'ach, "a havurah (fellowship) of lesbians and gay men who gather together throughout the year"

Unitarian Universalist Congregation of Miami 7701 SW 76th Ave **305/667-3697** • 11am Sun

Miami—Miami Beach/ South Beach

ACCOMMODATIONS

The AAA Shelborne Beach Resort—South Beach 1801 Collins Ave (at 18th) **305/531-1271, 800/327-8757** • gay-friendly • full brkfst • swimming • restaurant & bars • wheelchair access • $145-2,500

Abbey Hotel 300 21st St (btwn Washington & Collins) **305/531-0031, 888/612-2239** • gay/ straight • chic restored art deco • full brkfst • restaurant • gym • $89-225

Aqua Hotel & Lounge 1530 Collins Ave **305/538-4361** • gay/ straight • swimming • $95-395

The Bayliss 504 14th St **305/531-3488** • lesbians/ gay men • tropical art deco hotel • near beach • $60-80

Beachcomber Hotel 1340 Collins Ave (at 13th St) **305/531-3755, 888/305-4683** • gay-friendly • intimate art deco hotel • near beach • nonsmoking • $65-140

The Blue Moon Hotel 944 Collins Ave **305/673-2262, 800/724-1623** • gay-friendly • Mediterranean-style hotel • also bar • $89-400

Brigham Gardens 1401 Collins Ave (at 14th) **305/531-1331** • gay/ straight • art deco guesthouse • also apts w/ kitchens • kids/ pets ok • women-owned/ run • $70-145

The Cardozo Hotel 1300 Ocean Dr **305/535-6500, 800/782-6500** • gay-friendly • food served • Gloria Estefan's plush hotel • kids ok • wheelchair access • $150-450

The Century 140 Ocean Dr **305/674-8855, 888/982-3688** • gay-friendly • restored art deco • also Joia restaurant • celebrity hangout • $80-195

Chesterfield Hotel 855 Collins Ave **305/531-5831, 877/762-3477** • gay/ straight • $225-450

Circa 39 3900 Collins Ave (at 39th St) **305/538-4900, 877/824-7223** • gay-friendly, boutique hotel, swimming, also wine bar & lounge

The Colony Hotel 736 Ocean Dr (at 7th St) **305/673-0088, 800/226-5669** • gay-friendly • newly renovated art deco • bistro • oceanfront • wheelchair access • $129-256

Delano Hotel 1685 Collins Ave **305/672-2000, 800/555-5001** • gay-friendly • food served • great bar scene (see & be seen) • swimming • kids ok • wheelchair access • $350-950

Delores Guesthouse 1420 Collins Ave **305/673-0800** • gay/ straight • 1 block from beach • kids/ pets ok • $60-115

The European Guesthouse 721 Michigan Ave (btwn 7th & 8th) **305/673-6665** • lesbians/ gay men • B&B • full brkfst • hot tub • tropical garden w/ bar • gay-owned • $89-179

Florida Hotel Network 800/293-2419 • popular • gay-friendly • hotel reservations • vacation rentals

Florida Sunbreak 305/532-1516, 800/786-2732 • vacation rental condos, suite hotels & homes

Fountainbleu Hilton Resort & Spa 4441 Collins Ave **305/538-2000, 800/548-8886** • gay-friendly • restaurants • swimming • on beach • wheelchair access

Golden Tulip Casablanca Hotel 6345 Collins Ave (at 63rd St) **305/868-0010, 800/813-6676** • gay/ straight • swimming • studios & townhouses • $99-187

The Hotel 801 Collins Ave **305/531-2222, 877/843-4683** • gay-friendly • interior design by Todd Oldham • restaurant • also bar • swimming • $255-425

Hotel Astor 956 Washington Ave (at 10th St) **305/531-8081, 800/270-4981** • popular • gay-friendly • also Metro restaurant • wheelchair access • $125-900

Hotel Impala 1228 Collins Ave **305/673-2021, 800/646-7252** • gay/ straight • luxury hotel near beach • nonsmoking • wheelchair access • also award-winning Italian restaurant • $185-400

Hotel Lily Leon 835-841 Collins Ave (at 8th St) **305/673-3767** • gay-friendly • stylish decor • bar & restaurants • near ocean • kids/ pets ok • wheelchair access • $150-395

Hotel Nash 1120 Collins Ave **305/674-7800, 800/403-6274** • gay-friendly • sleek & modern new boutique hotel • spa • swimming • gardens • near gay beach • kids ok • nonsmoking • wheelchair access • $155-1400

Hotel Ocean 1230-38 Ocean Dr **305/672-2579, 800/783-1725** • popular • gay/ straight • great location • jacuzzi • pets ok • wheelchair access • $190-645

Hotel Shelley 844 Collins Ave **305/531–3341, 800/414–0612** • gay/ straight • 1930s art deco hotel • open bar eves • kids ok • wheelchair access • $89-249

The Indian Creek Hotel 2727 Indian Creek Dr **305/531-2727, 800/491-2772** • gay/ straight • food served • swimming • simple & away from the action • near ocean • kids ok • wheelchair access • $69-260

Island House Miami Beach 715 82nd St **305/864-2422, 800/382-2422** • all open-minded individuals welcome • nonsmoking • patio • $59-149

The Kent 1131 Collins Ave (at 11th St) **305/604-5068, 866/826-5368** • gay/ straight • on the beach • garden bar • wheelchair access • $79+

The Loft Hotel 952 Collins Ave **305/534-2244** • gay/ straight • upscale boutique hotel • 1 block to beach • kids/ small pets ok • $89-159

Marlin Hotel 1200 Collins Ave **305/604-3595** • gay/ straight • fabulous studios • full kitchens • stereo & WebTV • bar • wheelchair access • $175-1100

Miami Habitat 305/935-4641, **800/385-4644** • gay/ straight • furnished apts & hotel rooms in Art Deco District • also charter boats • $650-1,000/ week

The Nassau Suite Hotel 1414 Collins Ave **305/532-0043, 866/859-4177** • gay/ straight • renovated art deco • near beach • nonsmoking • $109-290

The National Hotel 1677 Collins Ave **305/532-2311, 800/327-8370** • gay/ straight • swimming • kids ok • restaurant & lounge • wheelchair access • $255-450

North Beach Guest House 7996 Crespi Blvd (at 80th) **305/807-7819** • gay/ straight • gay-owned • 3 blocks from beach & gay nudist areas • fully equipped kitchen • 3-night minimum stay • airport pickup

Ocean Surf Hotel 7436 Ocean Terrace (near 75th St & Collins Ave) **305/866-1648, 800/555-0411** • gay-friendly • beautiful restored art deco • in quiet North Beach • kids ok • wheelchair access • $80-150

The Park Central 640 Ocean Dr **305/538-1611, 800/727-5236** • gay-friendly • ocean views • food served • swimming • $115+

The Pelican 826 Ocean Dr (btwn 8th & 9th Sts) **305/673-3373, 800/773-5422** • popular • gay/ straight • designer theme rooms • restaurant w/ live DJ • on beach • $135-430

Penguin Hotel 1418 Ocean Dr **305/534-9334, 800/235-3296** • lesbians/ gay men • renovated art deco • full restaurant • kids ok • wheelchair access • $115-250

The Raleigh, Miami Beach 1775 Collins Ave (at Ocean Front) **305/534-6300, 800/848-1775** • gay-friendly • swimming • outdoor gym • restaurant & bars • kids/ pets ok • wheelchair access • $225-550

Royal South Beach 758 Washington Ave (at 8th St) **305/673-9009, 888/394-6835** • 1930s hotel restored to retro fabulousness by Jordan Mozer • $79-199

The Savoy Hotel 425 Ocean Dr (at 5th St) **305/532-0200, 800/237-2869** • gay/ straight • art-deco-meets-eclectic-boutique hotel • swimming • kids ok • nonsmoking • wheelchair access • $150-500

Something Special, A Lesbian Venture 10178 Collins Ave #106 **305/696-8826** • women only • 1-bdrm apt on beach • also camping & dining

South Seas 1751 Collins Ave **305/538-1411, 800/345-2678** • gay-friendly • clean & basic • beach access • swimming • $119-259

The Tides 1220 Ocean Dr **305/604-5070, 800/688-7678** • gay/ straight • food served • swimming • showcase Island Outpost hotel • $350-3500

The Tropics Hotel & Hostel 1550 Collins Ave (btwn 15th & 16th Sts) **305/531-0361** • gay/ straight • modern hotel rooms & hostel • swimming • near beach & attractions • $16-66

Villa Paradiso Guesthouse 1415 Collins Ave **305/532-0616** • gay-friendly • studios w/ full kitchens • courtyard • kids/ pets ok • $89-159

The Wave Hotel 350 Ocean Dr **305/673-0401, 800/501-0401** • gay-friendly • tropical style • newly renovated • bar • $129-500

The Winterhaven 1400 Ocean Dr **305/531-5571, 800/395-2322** • gay/ straight • ocean views • also bar • $109-339

BARS

Laundry Bar 721 N Lincoln Ln **305/531-7700** • noon-5am • lesbians/ gay men • neighborhood bar • live shows Mon, Wed & Fri • drag shows • video games • also laundromat

NIGHTCLUBS

Blue 222 Espanola Way (at Collins) **305/534-1009** • 10pm-5am • gay/ straight • dancing/ DJ • drag show Sun

Cherry Pie 6600 SW 57th Ave 305/495–6969, 954/288–8691 • 10 pm every Friday at Club Ozone

Crobar 1445 Washington Ave (at the Cameo Theater) 305/672–8084, 305/531–7736 • 10pm-5am • popular • gay-friendly • more gay Mon for Backdoor Bambi• dancing/DJ • wheelchair access

Mynt Ultra Lounge 1921 Collins Ave 786/276–6132 • 11pm-5am, clsd Sun-Tue • gay/ straight • dancing DJ

Pandora Events 305/975–6933 • monthly women's parties, locations rotate so check website: www.pandoraevents.com

Score 727 Lincoln Ave (at Meridian) 305/535–1111 • lounge opens 3pm, dance club 10pm-5am • popular • lesbians/ gay men • 4 bars • drag shows • karaoke • videos

Stallions 841 Washington Ave (btwn 8th & 9th) 305/673–0429 • 4am-close Fri-Sat • popular • mostly gay men • dancing • world-famous DJs • circuit crowd • wheelchair access

Twist 1057 Washington Ave (at 11th) 305/538–9478 • 1pm-5am • popular • mostly gay men • 7 bars • dancing/DJ • drag shows • live jazz • go-go boys • wheelchair access

CAFES

News Cafe 800 Ocean Dr 305/538–6397 • 24hrs • popular • healthy sandwiches • some veggie • also bookstore & bar

RESTAURANTS

11th Street Diner 11th & Washington 305/534–6373 • 24hrs • full bar

A Fish Called Avalon 700 Ocean Dr 305/532–1727, 800/933–3306 • 6pm-11pm • popular • some veggie • patio • full bar • wheelchair access

Balans 1022 Lincoln Rd (btwn Michigan & Lennox) 305/534–9191 • 8am-midnight, till 1am Fri-Sat • int'l • some veggie

Big Pink 157 Collins (at 2nd St) 305/532–4700 • 9am-1am, till 2am Fri-Sat • "real food for real people"

Cafeteria 546 Lincoln Rd (at Pennsylvania) 305/672–3663 • 24hrs

El Rancho Grande 1626 Pennsylvania Ave (S of Lincoln) 305/673–0480 • 10am-10pm • Mexican • 2nd location 72nd St (305/866–6516)

The Front Porch 1418 Ocean Dr (at Penguin Hotel) 305/531–8300 • 8am-10pm, till 10:30pm Fri-Sun • healthy homecooking • some veggie • full bar

Joe's Stone Crab 11 Washington Ave (near South Point Dr) 305/673–0365 • lunch & dinner, dinner only Sun-Mon • seasonal

Larios on the Beach 820 Ocean Dr 305/532–9577 • 11:30am-midnight • Cuban

Madame's Restaurant & Cabaret Lounge 239 Sunny Isles Blvd (at 163rd St & Collins Ave), Sunny Isles Beach 305/945–2040 • 6pm-midnight, till 1am Fri-Sat, clsd Tue-Wed • Southern comfort food • full bar • transgender-friendly • live shows • drag shows • cabaret • wheelchair access

Nemo 100 Collins Ave (at 1st St) 305/532–4550 • lunch & dinner, Sun brunch • Pacific Rim & South American cuisine • chic decor • $22

Nexxt Cafe 700 Lincoln Rd (at Euclid Ave) 305/532–6643 • 11:30am-11pm, till midnight Fri-Sat • popular

Pacific Time 915 Lincoln Rd (btwn Jefferson & Michigan) 305/534–5979 • lunch Mon-Fri, dinner nightly • pan-Pacific • some veggie

Palace 1200 Oean Drive (at 12th St) 305/531–7234 • also bar

Spiga 1228 Collins Ave (at 12th St) 305/534–0079 • dinner only • tasty homemade pastas

Sushi Rock Cafe 1351 Collins Ave (at 14th) 305/532–2133 • noon-midnight, 2pm-1am wknds • popular • full bar

Tiramesu 721 Lincoln Rd 305/532–4538 • lunch & dinner • Italian

Yuca 501 Lincoln Rd (at Drexel Ave) 305/532–9822 • noon-11:30pm • New Cuban cuisine • cocktails

ENTERTAINMENT & RECREATION

Beach Scooter Rentals 1435 Collins Ave 305/538–0977

Fritz's Skate & Bike 730 Lincoln Rd (at Euclid & Meridian) 305/532–1954 • rentals • in pedestrian mall

Lincoln Rd Lincoln Rd (btwn Bay Rd & Collins Aves) • pedestrian mall that embodies the rebirth of South Beach— fabulous restaurants, stores, galleries, museums, theaters, people at every step

BOOKSTORES

The 9th Chakra 530 Lincoln Rd (btwn Drexel & Pennsylvania) 305/538–0671, 866/538–0671 • New Age books • supplies • gifts

RETAIL SHOPS

Whittall & Shon 900 Washington Ave (at 9th) 305/538-2606 • 10am-9:30pm, till 10:30pm Fri-Sat • funky clothes & clubwear for boys

PUBLICATIONS

Wire 305/588-0000 • weekly gay tabloid

SPIRITUAL GROUPS

Circle of Light MCC 2100 Washington Ave (next to Convention Center) 305/535-2287 • 11am Sun

St John's on the Lake First Methodist Church 4760 Pine Tree Dr 305/531-7166 • 8am & 10am Sun

GYMS & HEALTH CLUBS

David Barton Gym 1685 Collins Ave (in the Delano Hotel) 305/674-5757 • gay-friendly

EROTICA

The Love Zone 19800 S Dixie Hwy 305/255-2190

The Love Zone 8831 SW 40th St 305/226-8332

Pleasure Emporium 1019 5th St 305/673-3311 • 24hrs

Pleasure Emporium 1671-A Alton Rd 305/538-6434

Mt Dora

ACCOMMODATIONS

The Dora Way B&B 1123 Dora Wy (at Old Rte 441) 352/735-5994 • gay-friendly • B&B furnished w/ antiques & 1950s collectibles • hot tub • $149

Naples

see also Fort Myers

INFO LINES & SERVICES

Lesbian/ Gay AA 2740 Bayshore Dr (at New Attitudes Club) 239/262-6535 (AA#) • 8pm Th

BARS

Snappers Nightclub 2634 Tamiami Trail E (at Bay Shore Dr) 239/775-4114 • 3pm-2am • lesbians/ gay men • neighborhood bar • dancing/ DJ • T-dance Sun • transgender-friendly • karaoke Mon & Wed • drag shows • wheelchair access

NIGHTCLUBS

Flash Up Club & Lounge 11901 US 41 N, North Naples 239/596-6449 • 5pm-2am, clsd Mon • lesbians/ gay men • dancing/DJ • Latin night Th • drag shows Th-Sun • drag kings Tue-Wed & Fri-Sun • wheelchair access

SPIRITUAL GROUPS

MCC Naples 6340 Tenth Ave SW (Unitarian Universalist Congregation bldg) 239/732-0092 • 5pm Sun

New Smyrna Beach

ACCOMMODATIONS

Night Swan B&B 512 S Riverside Dr 386/423-4940, 800/465-4261 • gay-friendly • B&B on Intracoastal Waterway • full brkfst • wheelchair access • $100-200

Ocala

BARS

441 North Lounge 4627 N US Hwy 441 352/629-8667 • 2pm-2am • mostly gay men • neighborhood bar • pizza served • karaoke Th • drag shows Sat • strippers Fri & Sun • 18+ • wheelchair access

NIGHTCLUBS

The Night Zone 9360 S Hwy 441 352/347-4877 • 2pm-2am, clsd Mon • lesbians/ gay men • 4 bars including techno bar (Fri), patio bar, CW bar (Wed) • karaoke Th • drag shows Fri-Sat • T-dance Sun • wheelchair access

BOOKSTORES

Barnes & Noble 3500 SW College Rd (at Hwy 200) 352/854-3999 • 8am-10pm, till 11pm wknds • LGBT section

SPIRITUAL GROUPS

Ocala MCC 4273 W Hwy 40 352/368-9929 • 11am & 7pm Sun, also 7pm Wed

EROTICA

Secrets of Ocala 815 N Magnolia Ave 352/622-3858

Orlando

INFO LINES & SERVICES

Gay, Lesbian & Bisexual Community Center of Central Florida 946 N Mills Ave 407/228-8272 • noon-9pm, till 4pm Fri-Sat, clsd Sun • full-service community center • helpline • extensive referrals

ACCOMMODATIONS

Clarion Hotel Universal 7299 Universal Blvd 407/351–5009, 800/445–7299 • gay-friendly • full-service hotel just outside Universal Studios • swimming • kids ok • wheelchair access • $69-119

Embassy Suites Orlando Downtown 191 E Pine St 407/841–1000, 800/362–2779 • gay-friendly • all-suite hotel • full brkfst • wheelchair access • $119-169

EO Inn & Spa 227 N Eola Dr (at Robinson) 407/481–8485, 888/481–8488 • gay/ straight • nonsmoking • sundeck • hot tub • cafe on-site • $129-219

Freedom Resort & Spa 8600 W Irlo Bronson Hwy, Kissimmee 407/396–7272, 800/327–9151 • exclusively lesbians/ gay men • membership-only resort • swimming • jacuzzi • bar & nightclub

Holiday Villas 2928 Vineland Rd (btwn SR 535 & 192), Kissimmee 407/397–0700, 800/344–3959 • gay-friendly • luxury villas just 5 miles from Walt Disney World • swimming • hot tub • $99-249

Mid-Century Modern Rental Home 407/758–1190 • gay-friendly • restored 1950s rental home • pool • outdoor hot tub • nonsmoking • near Disney

Oaktubb Inn 620 Tubb St, Oakland 407/654–4132, 888/625–8822 • lesbians/ gay men • B&B in 4-acre orange grove • 20 minutes N of Walt Disney World • swimming • nonsmoking • gay-owned • $70-110

Parliament House Motor Inn 410 N Orange Blossom Tr 407/425–7571 • lesbians/ gay men • swimming • restaurant • wheelchair access • $64-104+tax • also 6 bars • multiracial • live shows • dancing/DJ • young crowd • gay-owned

The Perri House Inn 10417 Vista Oaks Ct 407/876–4830, 800/780–4830 • gay-friendly • quiet oasis 3 miles from Disney • bird-watching • swimming • hot tub • kids ok • $99-143

Red Horse Inn 5825 International Dr 407/351–4100, 877/936–4100 • gay-friendly • hotel • swimming • nonsmoking • kids/ pets ok • wheelchair access • $59-179

Sandy Lake Towers 6137 Carrier Dr 407/996–6000, 877/996–6151 • gay-friendly • hotel, all 2-bdrm suites • swimming • wheelchair access • $69-89

Sheraton Studio City 5905 International Dr 407/351–2100, 800/327–1366 • gay-friendly • world-class amenities combined w/ elegance & sophisticated excitement of 1940s & 1950s Hollywood • swimming • nonsmoking • wheelchair access • $79-399

Sunny Orlando Resorts 866/337–5983 • gay/ straight • vacation rental • swimming • hot tub • kids ok • nonsmoking • $110-145

The Veranda B&B 115 N Summerlin Ave 407/849–0321, 800/420–6822 • gay-friendly • swimming • hot tub • nonsmoking • wheelchair access • $99-209

Westin Grand Bohemian 325 S Orange Ave 407/313–9000, 866/663–0024 • gay-friendly • luxury hotel in downtown Orlando • swimming • kids ok • wheelchair access • $129-209

The Winter Park Sweet Lodge 271 S Orlando Ave (at Fairbanks Ave), Winter Park 407/644–6099 • gay/ straight • motel • kids ok • gay-owned • $49-59

BARS

Copper Rocket 106 Lake Ave (at 17-92), Maitland 407/645–0069 • 2pm-2am • gay-friendly • also restaurant • microbrews • wheelchair access

Faces Club & Lounge 4910 Edgewater Dr 407/291–7571 • 4pm-2am • mostly women • popular • neighborhood bar • dancing/DJ wknds • live shows • karaoke • wheelchair access

Full Moon Saloon 500 N Orange Blossom Tr 407/648–8725 • noon-2am • popular Sun afternoon • mostly gay men • country/ western • bears • leather/ levi • patio • gay-owned

Hank's 5026 Edgewater Dr 407/291–2399 • noon-2am • mostly gay men • neighborhood bar • beer/ wine • patio • wheelchair access

Lava Lounge 1235 N Orange Ave, Ste 101 407/895–9790 • 5pm-2am, from 7pm Sat, clsd Sun-Mon • mostly gay men • upscale lounge • multiracial cliente • transgender-friendly • videos • patio • wheelchair accessible

Lee's Underground Tavern 431 E Central Blvd 407/841–1565 • gay/ straight

New Phoenix 7124 Aloma Ave (at Forsythe), Winter Park 407/678–9070 • noon-2am • lesbians/ gay men • neighborhood bar • dancing/ DJ • karaoke

The Peacock Room 1321 N Mills Ave (at Montana) 407/228–0048 • 4pm-2am, from 7pm Sat • gay-friendly • trendy lounge • live shows

Stable 410 N Orange Blossom Tr (at Parliament House) **407/425-7571** • 6pm-2am, from noon wknds • mostly gay men • country/ western • levi / leather • strippers • piano • also restaurant

Will's Pub 1850 N Mills Ave **407/898-5070** • 2pm-2am • gay-friendly • neighborhood bar • live shows • beer/ wine • wheelchair access • also Loch Haven Motor Inn, 407/896-3611

Wylde's 3557 S Orange Ave **407/852-0612** • 4pm-2am • mostly gay men • neighborhood bar

NIGHTCLUBS

The Club at Firestone 578 N Orange Ave **407/872-0066** • 10pm-3am Sat • popular • gay/ straight • more gay Sat • dancing/DJ • 18+ • live shows • videos • cover

Club Freedom 8600 W Irlo Bronson Hwy (at Freedom Resort & Spa), Kissimmee **407/396-7272, 800/327-9151** • 4pm-2am, clsd Mon-Wed • lesbians/ gay men • dancing/DJ • drag shows • wheelchair access

Club Quest 745 Bennett Rd **407/228-8226** • 10pm-3am Fri-Sat only • lesbians/ gay men • dancing/DJ • multiracial • drag shows • 18+

Parliament House Motor Inn 410 N Orange Blossom Tr **407/425-7571** • 10:30am-3am • lesbians/ gay men • 6 bars • dancing/DJ • multiracial • live shows • videos • also restaurant • wheelchair access • gay-owned

Southern Nights 375 S Bumby Ave **407/898-0424** • 4pm-3am, from 8pm Sat, from 9pm Sun • popular • lesbians/ gay men • Latin Mon • Lesbo-A-Go-Go Sat • dancing/DJ • multiracial • go-go dancers • drag shows • 18+ • wheelchair access

CAFES

The Coffee House of Thornton Park 712 E Washington St (at Summerlin) **407/426-8989** • 8am-4pm

White Wolf Cafe & Antique Shop 1829 N Orange Ave (at Princeton) **407/895-9911** • 11am-10pm, till 4pm Mon, till 11pm Fri-Sat, clsd Sun • salads • sandwiches • beer/ wine • wheelchair access

RESTAURANTS

Brian's 1409 N Orange Ave (at Virginia) **407/896-9912** • 6am-4pm • popular Sun

Dexter's of Thornton Park 808 E Washington St **407/648-0620** • lunch & dinner, brunch Sat-Sun • American • also wine bar • live bands • also trendy, 2nd location Winter Park, 407/629-1150

Harvey's Bistro 390 N Orange Ave (in Bank of America bldg) **407/246-6560** • lunch & dinner, clsd Sun • popular cocktail hour

Hemingway's at the Hyatt 1 Grand Cypress Blvd, Lake Buena Vista **407/239-1234** • dinner • popular • cont'l • $20-25

Orlando

WHERE THE GIRLS ARE:
Women who live here hang out at Faces bar. Tourists are—where else?—at the tourist attractions, including Disney World.

LGBT PRIDE:
June.

ANNUAL EVENTS:
May-June - Gay Days at Disney World, web: gaydays.com.

CITY INFO:
407/363-5872. 8723 International Dr, 8am-7pm, web: www.orlandoinfo.com.

WEATHER:
Mild winters, hot summers.

TRANSIT:
Yellow Cab 407/422-2222.
Atlas Motor Coaches 407/540-1006.
Lynx 407/841-5969.

ATTRACTIONS:
Sea World 800/327-2424, web: www.seaworld.com.
Universal Studios 407/363-8000, web: themeparks.universalstudios.com.
Walt Disney World 407/824-4321, web: www.disneyworld.com.
Wet & Wild Waterpark 407/351-3200.
Gatorland 407/855-5496.

Hue 629 E Central Blvd (at N Summerlin Ave) **407/849-1800** • lunch & dinner, wknd brunch • new American • full bar

The Rainbow Cafe at Parliament House **407/425-7571** • 7am-11pm, till 4am Fri-Sat, till 3am Sun • lesbians/ gay men

Taqueria Quetzalcoatl 480 N Orlando Ave #120 (at Gay Rd), Winter Park **407/691-0208** • 11am-8pm, till 11pm Fri-Sat, from noon Sun • some veggie • beer/ wine

---

Reply **Forward** **Delete**

Date: Dec 31, 2005 11:51:33
From: Girl-on-the-Go
To: Editor@Damron.com
Subject: Orlando

>For most vacationers, Orlando means one thing: Disney World. If you're a fan of the Mouse, show your appreciation during the first weekend of June at Disney's (unofficial) Gay Days. **Girls in Wonderland** is the popular women's party; check out **www.gaydays.com** or **www.girlsinwonderland.com** for details.

>Save some time for the enormous Epcot Center and MGM Studios, too. You'll need at least three days to traverse the 27,000 acres of this entertainment mecca. And if you still crave infotainment, visit Universal Studios, Wet 'n' Wild, Sea World, the Tupperware Museum (yes, Tupperware), Busch Gardens, or Cypress Gardens—a natural wonderland of lagoons, moss-draped trees, and exotic plants from around the world.

>Call the **Gay, Lesbian & Bisexual Community Center** to find out when the next Gay Day in the Busch (Gardens, that is) will be. If you like food on a stick, be sure to stop by the Central Florida Fair in February for Gay/Lesbian Day. After a long day of theme park-ing, settle in at one of the local lesbian-friendly accommoda-tions, like **Winter Park Sweet Lodge** or **Oaktubb Inn**, or stay at either of the two gay resort complexes, the **Parliament House** and **Freedom Resort and Spa**.

>**Faces** is the neighborhood lesbian bar, while **Southern Nights** and **The Club** (aka Firestone) are the places to dance, especially on Saturdays at Southern Nights when women show up in throngs.

>For more local info, stop by **Mojo**, the LGBT bookstore, or **Urban Think** bookstore or the Center, and pick up a copy of the LGBT paper **Watermark.** If you have internet access, also check out **www.gayorlando.com** for current events.

ENTERTAINMENT & RECREATION

The Enzian Theater 1300 S Orlando Ave (at Magnolia), Maitland **407/629-0054** • Central FL's only art house cinema • cafe • beer & wine

Gay Orlando Talk WPRK 91.5 FM **407/896-8431** • noon Fri • LGBT radio

Universal Studios Florida 1000 Universal Studios Plz **407/363-8000, 800/711-0080**

Walt Disney World Resort **407/824-4321** • don't even pretend you came to Orlando for any other reason

BOOKSTORES

Mojo 930 N Mills Ave (at E Marks St) **407/896-0204** • 1pm-7pm • LGBT

Urban Think Bookstore 625 E Central Blvd **407/650-8004** • 11am-9pm, till 6pm Sun-Mon • LGBT section • also bar

RETAIL SHOPS

Harmony Designs 496 N Orange Blossom Tr **407/481-9850** • 6:30pm-1am • pride store • wheelchair access • gay-owned

PUBLICATIONS

Watermark **407/481-2243** • bi-weekly LGBT newspaper for Central FL

SPIRITUAL GROUPS

Joy MCC 2351 S Ferncreek Ave **407/894-1081** • 8:30am, 10am, 11:30am & 7pm Sun • wheelchair access

EROTICA

Fairvilla Megastore 1740 N Orange Blossom Tr **407/425-5352** • 9am-2am, from 10am Sun • clean, well-lighted adult store w/ emphasis on couples: "store for lovers"

Palm Beach

ACCOMMODATIONS

Heart of Palm Beach 160 Royal Palm Wy **561/655-5600, 800/521-4278 (RESERVATIONS)** • gay-friendly • charming European-style hotel • swimming • kids/ pets ok • full-service salon & spa • also restaurant • full bar • $99-299

RESTAURANTS

Ta-boo 221 Worth Ave **561/835-3500** • 11:30am-10:30pm, till midnight Fri-Sat • cont'l • dancing/DJ Fri-Sat • piano nightly • wheelchair access

Panama City

ACCOMMODATIONS

Casa de Playa 20304 Front Beach Rd, Panama City Beach **850/236-8436** • lesbians/ gay men • guesthouse • steps from Gulf of Mexico • jacuzzi • heated pool • nonsmoking • patios • gay-owned • $150-175

Wisteria Inn 20404 Front Beach Rd, Panama City Beach **850/234-0557** • gay/ straight • tropical inn • hot tub • swimming • nonsmoking • $59-129

BARS

La Royale Lounge & Liquor Store 100 Harrison (at Beach Dr) **850/763-1755** • 3pm-3am • lesbians/ gay men • neighborhood bar • courtyard • wheelchair access

NIGHTCLUBS

Fiesta Room 110 Harrison Ave (at Beach Dr) **850/763-1755** • 8pm-3am Wed, till 4am Fri-Sat • popular • lesbians/ gay men • dancing/DJ • drag shows • wheelchair access

Panama City Beach

EROTICA

Condom Knowledge 7510-A Thomas Dr **850/230-3961** • 10am-10pm • "The Funniest, Sexiest Novelty Shop on the Beach" • also 13208 Front Beach Rd

Pensacola

INFO LINES & SERVICES

AA Gay/ Lesbian 461 Massachussetts (at W St, in MCC) **850/433-4191 (AA#)** • 7:30pm Mon & Fri

BARS

Jack & Ron's Piano & Video Bar 104 S Palafox Pl **850/434-0291** • 3pm-3am • gay-friendly • upscale lounge • piano Th • live jazz bands Fri-Sat • karaoke & videos Sun • pool table

Red Carpet 937 N New Warrington Rd **850/453-9918** • 5pm-3am • mostly women • dancing/DJ Sat • drag shows Fri • karaoke Wed • patio • "serving the gay community for 30 years!" • wheelchair access

Round-Up 706 E Gregory St (near 9th Ave) **850/433-8482** • 2pm-3am • popular • mostly gay men • neighborhood bar • bear- & leather/ levi-friendly • patio • wheelchair access

NIGHTCLUBS

Emerald City 406 E Wright St (at Alcaniz)
850/433–9491 • 3pm-3am (happy hour bar),
dance club from 9pm, clsd Tue • popular •
lesbians/ gay men • dancing/DJ • live shows •
18+ • patio • wheelchair access

CAFES

End of the Line Cafe 610 E Wright St
850/429–0336 • 11am-10pm, till 8pm Sun •
all-vegetarian cafe (vegan meals weekly) • fair
trade coffees • open mic, events, workshops •
live bands Fri-Sat • " as a 'safe space,' we have
no tolerance for sexism, racism, homophobia
or ageism"

RESTAURANTS

R Place Bistro 192 N Palafox St
850/437–5536 • lunch & dinner • soups,
salads, wraps & gourmet pizzas • beer & wine
• live music Fri-Sat

BOOKSTORES

Subterranean Books 9 E Gregory St
850/434–3456 • 10am-6pm, from 11am Sat,
clsd Sun • independent • new & used • from
punks to poets • includes women's & queer
studies sections

RETAIL SHOPS

Gulf Coast Pride 1615 E Scott St (in
schoolbus) **850/433–1443** • 8am-8pm • gifts
• toys • magazines • wheelchair access

SPIRITUAL GROUPS

Fire Dance Church of Wicca Milton
850/723–9877 (10AM-6PM EST) • celebrates
the holy days and festivals of the Wiccan
annual calendar • see www.fdcow.com for
dates

Holy Cross MCC 461 Massachusetts Ave (at
W St) **850/465–9900** • 9am & 11am Sun

**Unitarian Universalist Church of
Pensacola** 9888 Pensacola Blvd (N of 10
Mile Rd) **850/475–9077** • 10:30am Sun

Port Richey

see also St Petersburg

BARS

Waterside Landing 7737 Grand Blvd (2
blocks off US 19) **727/841–7900** • 6pm-2am,
from noon Wed-Fri • lesbians/ gay men •
more women Tue • dancing/DJ • karaoke Tue
& Sun • strippers Th-Fri • drag shows Sat •
wheelchair access

SPIRITUAL GROUPS

Spirit of Life MCC 4133 Thys Rd (off State
Rd 54), New Port Richey **727/849–6962** •
10:30am Sun • wheelchair access

Port St Lucie

NIGHTCLUBS

Rebar 8283 S Federal Hwy (at Fiesta Square)
772/340–7777 • 4pm-2am, 1pm-midnight
Sun • lesbians/ gay men • neighborhood bar •
dancing/DJ • videos • wheelchair access • gay-
owned

SPIRITUAL GROUPS

East Coast MCC 8438 US Hwy 1 (in Unity
Church, S of Rebar) **321/759–5588** • 5pm 1st
& 3rd Sun

Sarasota

INFO LINES & SERVICES

Gay AA 7225 N Lockwood Ridge Rd (in
Pierce Hall, Church of the Trinity MCC)
941/355–0847 (CHURCH #) • 7pm Sun

Gay Info Line **941/923–4636** • 24hrs •
recorded info

ACCOMMODATIONS

The Cypress 621 Gulfstream Ave S
941/955–4683 • gay-friendly • B&B inn •
overlooking Sarasota Bay • full gourmet brkfst
• nonsmoking • $150-240

Siesta Holidays 1017 Seaside Dr & 1011
Crescent St, Siesta Key **941/312–9882,
800/720–6885** • gay-friendly • pool •
nonsmoking • 2 locations • condos near
Crescent Beach • $475-1,425/ wk

BARS

Club Tri-Angles 1330 Martin Luther King Jr
Wy **941/953–5945** • 1pm-2am • popular •
mostly gay men • dancing/DJ • drag shows •
videos • patio • wheelchair access

PUBLICATIONS

Watermark **813/966–7295 (TAMPA OFFICE)** •
bi-weekly LGBT newspaper for Central FL

SPIRITUAL GROUPS

Church of the Trinity MCC 7225 N
Lockwood Ridge Rd **941/355–0847** • 9:15am
& 11am Sun • wheelchair access

Dignity 3975 Fruitville Rd (at Unitarian
Church) **941/359–9504 OR 359–3236,
941/371–4974 (CHURCH #)** • 5pm Sun

Temple Sinai 1802 Kenilworth St
941/924–1802 • 6pm Fri

Unitarian Universalist Church of Sarasota 3975 Fruitville Rd 941/371-4974 • 10:30am Sun

EROTICA

Tamiami Books 7338 S Tamiami Tr 941/923-7626 • 24hrs

Satellite Beach

EROTICA

Space Age Books & Temptations 63 Ocean Blvd 321/773-7660

South Beach

see Miami Beach/ South Beach

St Augustine

see also Jacksonville

INFO LINES & SERVICES

Lambda AA 1400 Old Dixie Hwy 904/399-8535 (AA#) • 7:30pm Th

ACCOMMODATIONS

Alexander Homestead 14 Sevilla St 904/826-4147, 888/292-4147 • gay-friendly • Victorian inn • full brkfst • $159-209

Casa Monica 95 Cordova St 904/827-1888, 800/648-1888 • gay-friendly • resort • restaurant & piano bar • fitness club • swimming • spa • oceanfront beach club • kids ok • wheelchair access • $99-1,000

Channel Marker 71 Barrier Island Inn & Restaurant 7601 A1A S (10 miles S of St Augustine) 904/461-4288, 866/461-4288 • gay-friendly • swimming jet spa

The Dolphin 617/216-8960 & 524-0224 (MA #s) • lesbians/ gay men • beach cottage 100 yds from ocean • lesbian community nearby • nonsmoking • lesbian-owned • $65-85/ night & $425-600/ week

Eve's Web Guest House & Retreat 904/823-9660 • mostly women • jacuzzi • nonsmoking • lesbian-owned • $110/ night, $600/ week

Our House B&B 7 Cincinnati Ave 904/824-9204 • gay/ straight • B&B in Victorian home in antiques district • full brkfst • gay-owned • $108-220

Saragossa Inn B&B 34 Saragossa St (at Sevilla) 904/808-7384, 877/808-7384 • gay/ straight • full brkfst • kids 12 years & up ok • gay-owned • $109-250

RESTAURANTS

La Parisienne 60 Hypolita St 904/829-0055 • lunch & dinner • French/ cont'l • wine list • reservations required

ENTERTAINMENT & RECREATION

Sheriff's Ghost Walk across from Old Water Wheel (St George St) 904/797-1950 • 8:30pm (clsd Tue) & midnight (Fri-Sat only) • 90-minute tours of St Augustine's most famous haunts

PUBLICATIONS

Out in the City 904/389-8883 • monthly LGBT newspaper

SPIRITUAL GROUPS

FirstCoast MCC 11 Old Mission Ave (in Limelight Theatre) 904/824-2802 • 10:30am Sun

St Petersburg

see also Tampa

INFO LINES & SERVICES

Gay Information Line (The Line) 727/586-4297 • touchtone 24hrs

ACCOMMODATIONS

Boca Ciega B&B 727/381-2755 • women-only • B&B in private home • swimming • lesbian-owned • $40-50

Changing Tides Cottages 225 Boca Ciega Dr, Madeira Beach 727/397-7706 • lesbians/ gay men • fully furnished rental cottages on harbor • women-owned/ run • $95-175

Dicken's House B&B 335 8th Ave NE 727/822-8622, 800/381-2022 • gay/ straight • swimming • newly restored 1900s home • near beach • full brkfst • jacuzzi • massage • gay-owned • $95-210

Inn at the Bay B&B 126 4th Ave NE (at 1st St) 727/822-1700, 888/873-2122 • gay-friendly • full brkfst • jacuzzi • nonsmoking • wheelchair access • $125-270

Mansion House 105 Fifth Ave NE 727/821-9391, 800/274-7520 • gay-friendly • B&B inn • full brkfst • swimming • jacuzzi • $99-220

Pass-A-Grille Beach Co-op 709 Gulf Wy, St Pete Beach 727/367-4726 • gay-friendly • swimming • kids ok • $60-95

Sea Oats by the Gulf 12625 Sunshine Ln, Treasure Island 727/367-7568, 866/715-9595 • gay-friendly • motel & apts • on the Gulf of Mexico • kids/ pets ok • wheelchair access • $250-795/ week

Reply **Forward** **Delete**

Date: Dec 8, 2005 11:51:33
From: Girl-on-the-Go
To: Editor@Damron.com
Subject: Tampa & St. Petersburg

>The Sunshine State has been a mix of cultures since the American Indians, Spanish, French and English clashed in the 16th century and onward. Today, it is even more diverse—and that is no less true of the hot spot of Florida's West Coast: the Tampa Bay Area. Whether it's the Greek sponge fisherman of Tarpon Springs or the Cuban cigar-rollers of Ybor City, a wide variety of peoples and cultures have left their mark on the architecture and food of Tampa and St. Petersburg.

>And Tampa Bay's lesbian communities are no exception, either. You'll find plenty of resources and activities here, and plenty of friendly women. When you arrive, call the **Women's Energy Bank (WEB)** 727/ 323-5706.

>Before you arrive, of course, you should reserve a place to stay. If you are interested in women-only accommodations, you have two choices: **Boca Ciega B&B** or **Changing Tides Cottages**, both of which are in St. Pete.

>Despite the popular postcard image of relaxed afternoons and sunset strolls on the gorgeous Gulf-side beaches, there is another side to Tampa and St. Pete: a great nightlife! There are two women's bars in the area: the long-time running lesbian bar **Sports Page** (in Largo) and the **Hideaway** (in St. Pete). If you prefer a more mixed venue, head over to **Peppers** (in St. Pete) or **The Chambers** (in Tampa) for drinks and dancing with the girls and boys.

>If partying is not your thang, don't fret! There are lots of other activities to keep you occupied while you're in town.... Pick up an espresso and stay for the open mic every Monday at queer-friendly **Sacred Grounds Coffeehouse** (in Tampa). For some good old-fashioned/retro fun, don your pink satin jacket and knee socks and strut your stuff on the waxed floor of the **United Skates of America** (Tampa), at Tuesday's LGBT skate night.

>Look for a copy of the latest edition of the **Gazette** and the **Watermark**—the local bi-weekly LGBT paper—for other ideas.

Suncoast Resort 3000 34th St S/ Hwy 19 S (at 32nd Ave S) 727/867–1111 • lesbians/ gay men • popular • dancing/DJ • live shows • swimming • 6 bars • 2 restaurants • gay shopping mall • wheelchair access • gay-owned • $49-89

Bars

The Back Room Bar @ Surf & Sand Bar 14601 Gulf Blvd, Madeira Beach 727/391–2680 • 1pm-2am • mostly gay men • neighborhood bar • karaoke • beach access • patio • wheelchair access

Grand Central Station 2612 Central Ave (at 26th) 727/327–8204 • 2pm-2am • mostly gay men • neighborhood bar • leather • male dancers • karaoke • patio • wheelchair access

The Hideaway 8302 4th St N (at 83rd) 727/570–9025 • 2pm-2am • mostly women • neighborhood bar • live shows • karaoke • wheelchair access

Oar House 4807 22nd Ave S 727/327–1691 • 2pm-2am, from 1pm Sun • lesbians/ gay men • neighborhood bar • karaoke

Peppers 4918 Gulfport Blvd S (at 49th), Gulfport 727/323-5724 • 2pm-2am • popular • lesbians/gay men • dancing/DJ • karaoke • wheelchair access

Sports Page Bar 13344 66th St N (at Ulmerton Rd), Largo 727/538-2430 • 4pm-2am, from 1pm Sun • mostly women • dancing/DJ • live bands • karaoke • wheelchair access

Suncoast Resort 3000 34th St S/ Hwy 19 S (at 32nd Ave S) 727/867–1111 • lesbians/ gay men • popular • dancing/DJ • drag shows • 6 bars (including piano & cabaret bars) • 2 restaurants • wheelchair access • gay-owned

VIP Lounge & Mexican Food Grill 10625 Gulf Blvd 727/360–5062 • 11am-2am • food served 11am-11pm • gay-friendly • wheelchair access

Nightclubs

Georgie's Alibi 3100 3rd Ave N (at 31st St N) 727/321–2112 • 11am-2am • lesbians/ gay men • 3 bars • neighborhood bar • dancing/DJ • food served • drag shows • videos • wireless internet • wheelchair access • patio • gay-owned

Z109 5858 Roosevelt Blvd (State Rd 686, at 58th), Clearwater 727/539–8903 • 4pm-2am, from 1pm Sun clsd Mon-Tue • lesbians/ gay men • live shows • karaoke • patio • wheelchair access

Restaurants

Suncoast Resort 3000 34th St S/ Hwy 19 S (at 32nd Ave S) 727/867–1111 • lesbians/ gay men • popular • Flamingo restaurant w/ indoor & patio dining • gay-owned

Entertainment & Recreation

Pontoon Pride Rides 813/728-3083 • Tampa Bay's only gay pontoon charter!

St Petersburg

LGBT Pride:
June. St Pete Pride, web: www.stpetepride.com.

Annual Events:
March - Tampa Bay Blues Festival 727/502–5000, web: www.tampabaybluesfest.com.

City Info:
Chamber of Commerce 727/821-4069, 8am-5pm Mon-Fri, web: www.stpete.com.

Best View:
Pass-A-Grille Beach in Tampa.

Weather:
Some say it's the Garden of Eden— winter temperatures occasionally dip into the 40°s, but for the rest of the year temperatures stay in the 70°-80°s.

Transit:
Yellow Cab 727/821-7777.

Attractions:
Great Explorations, interactive kids' museum, 727/821-8992, web: www.greatexplorations.org.
Salvador Dalí Museum 727/823-3767.
Florida International Museum 727/822-3693.

RETAIL SHOPS

The MC Film Festival Video & Music Store 3000 34th St S #2 (in Suncoast Resort) **727/866-0904** • noon-7pm • nonerotic LGBT videos • CDs & pride gifts • also at 1628 Central Ave • 727/894-6233

Tampa Bay Leather Company 3400 34th St S (in Suncoast Resort) **727/865-3010** • noon-midnight, till 2am Fri-Sat • leather • fetish

PUBLICATIONS

The Gazette **727/821-5009** • Tampa Bay's gay/ lesbian newsmagazine

Watermark **813/966-7295 (TAMPA OFFICE)** • bi-weekly LGBT newspaper for Central FL

SPIRITUAL GROUPS

Beth Rachamim Synagogue 719 Arlington Ave N (at Unitarian Universalist Church) **727/822-7503** • 8pm Fri

Bnai Emmunah 3374 Keystone Rd, Tarpon Springs **727/938-9000** • 8pm Fri

Christ The Cornerstone Church 5545 62nd Ave N, Pinellas Park **727/823-1806** • 10am & 6:30pm Sun

Holy Spirit Ecumenical Catholic Church 20162 US Hwy 19 N (at Druid Rd in Quality Inn), Clearwater **727/709-1542** • 10am Sun mass

King of Peace MCC 3150 5th Ave N **727/323-5857, 727/327-4567 (TTY/ TTD#)** • 10am Sun & 6:30pm Th • wheelchair access

Tallahassee

INFO LINES & SERVICES

The Family Tree 310 Blount St, Ste 204 **850/222-8555** • LGBT community center • call for hours

ACCOMMODATIONS

Twelve Oaks B&B 984 Boston Hwy/ County Rd 149 (at US Hwy 19), Monticello **850/997-0333** • gay/ straight • Victorian B&B plantation • full brkfst • 10-person hot tub • swimming • nudity permitted • gay-owned

BARS

Brothers 926 W Tharpe St (near Old Bainbridge) **850/386-2399** • 4pm-2am, from 9pm Sat, clsd Mon • lesbians/ gay men • dancing/DJ Wed-Sun • multiracial • drag shows Th & Sat • videos • 18+ • wheelchair access

NIGHTCLUBS

Club Jade 2122 W Pensacola St (at Ocala Dr) **850/574-1105** • 6pm-2am, clsd Mon • gay-friendly • dancing/DJ • T-dance Sun • live entertainment • drag shows

CAFES

Cool Grindz Coffee Shop 1700 N Monroe (at Tharpe) **850/561-3700** • gay-friendly • food served • nightly live, local talent on patio • beer/ wine

RESTAURANTS

The Village Inn 2690 N Monroe St (at Sharer Rd) **850/385-2903** • 6am-3am, 24hrs Fri-Sat, till midnight Sun • popular

SPIRITUAL GROUPS

Gentle Shepherd MCC 2810 N Meridian Rd (at Unitarian Universalist Church) **850/878-3001** • 7pm Sun

St Catherine of Sienna 1834 Mahan Dr (at United Church) **850/216-2348, 850/878-7385 (CHURCH #)** • 6pm Sun, "We are a Catholic community independent from Roman jurisdiction who seeks to serve all the people."

Tallahassee Friends Meeting Religious Society of Friends (Quakers) 2001 S Magnolia (1 mile S of Apalachee Pkwy) **850/878-3620** • 10:30am Sun

Unitarian Universalist Church of Tallahassee 2810 N Meridian Rd **850/385-5115** • 11am Sun

United Church (United Church of Christ) 1834 Mahan Dr **850/878-7385** • 10:30am Sun, "open & affirming"

Tampa

see also St Petersburg

INFO LINES & SERVICES

Gay Information Line (The Line) **727/586-4297** • touchtone service 24hrs

Gay/ Lesbian Community Center of Tampa 3708 W Swann Ave **813/875-8116** • call for hours

ACCOMMODATIONS

Gram's Place B&B GuestHouses/ Hostel & Music 3109 N Ola Ave **813/221-0596** • gay/ straight • nudity • hot tub • kids ok • BYOB • nonsmoking • $20-68 (hostel) & $65-95 (B&B)

Sawmill Camping Resort 21710 US Hwy 98, Dade City **352/583-0664** • popular • gay/ straight • theme wknds w/ entertainment • RV hookups • cabins • tent spots • dancing • karaoke • swimming • nudity • gay-owned • $10.25-89

BARS

2606 2606 Armenia Ave (at St Conrad) **813/875–6993** • 8pm-3am, from 6pm Sun • popular • mostly gay men • levi/ leather • strippers wknds • also leather shop from 9pm • wheelchair access • gay-owned

City Side 3703 Henderson Blvd (at Dale Mabry) **813/350–0600** • noon-3am • lesbians/gay men • neighborhood bar • karaoke • patio

Fling's 9002 N Florida Ave (at Busch) **813/935–9771** • 3pm-3am • mostly gay men • neighborhood bar • gay-owned

Metropolis 3447 W Kennedy Blvd (at Himes) **813/871–2410** • noon-3am, from 1pm Sun • lesbians/ gay men • neighborhood bar • dancing/DJ • strippers Fri-Sat • wheelchair access

Rainbow Room 421 S MacDill Ave (at Azeele St) **813/871–2265** • 3am-3pm, from 12:30pm wknds • mostly women • beer/wine

NIGHTCLUBS

The Chambers 1701 N Franklin St (at E Henderson Ave) **813/223–1300** • 5pm-3am, clsd Sun-Tue • lesbians/ gay men • dancing/DJ • 2 flrs • drag shows • 18+ • also restaurant

Flirt 1909 N 15th St (btwn 8th & 9th), Ybor City • Th & Sat • lesbians/ gay men • dancing/DJ • 2 flrs • drag shows • 18+

CAFES

Sacred Grounds Coffeehouse 4819 E Busch Blvd **813/983–0837** • 6pm-1am, till 2am Fri-Sat • all welcome but popular hangout for lesbians & gay men • live music • open mic Mon • bulk coffees & teas for sale • "Don't drink from the Mainstream!"

RESTAURANTS

Ho Ho Chinese 533 S Howard **813/254–9557** • 11am-10pm, dinner only wknds • full bar • wheelchair access • gay-owned

Taqueria Quetzalcoatl 402 S Howard Ave (at Azeele St) **813/259–9982** • 11am-10pm • Mexican • some veggie • beer/ wine

ENTERTAINMENT & RECREATION

United Skates of America 5121 N Armenia **813/876–5826, 813/876–6544** • LGBT skate 9pm-11:30pm every 3rd Tue

The Women's Show WMNF 88.5 FM **813/238–8001** • 10am-noon Sat

PUBLICATIONS

The Gazette **727/821–5009** • Tampa Bay's gay/ lesbian newsmagazine

Watermark **813/966–7295** • bi-weekly LGBT newspaper for Central FL

SPIRITUAL GROUPS

MCC of Tampa 408 E Cayuga St (at Central Ave) **813/239–1951** • 10:30am Sun (ASL interpreted) & 7pm Wed

---

Tampa

LGBT PRIDE:
June. Central Florida Black Pride 813/236–8809, web: www.florid-ablackpride.net.
June. St Pete Pride, web: www.stpetepride.com.

ANNUAL EVENTS:
October- Tampa International Gay & Lesbian Film Festival, web: www.pridefilmfest.com.

CITY INFO:
Greater Tampa Chamber of Commerce 813/228-7777, web: www.tampachamber.com.
Tampa/Hillsborough Convention & Visitors Bureau 813/223-1111. www.visittampa.com.

TRANSIT:
Yellow Cab 813/253-0121.
Super Shuttle 727/572-1111.
Hartline Transit (bus) 813/254-4278.

ATTRACTIONS:
Busch Gardens/Adventure Island 813/987-5082, web: www.4adventure.com.
Florida Aquarium 813/273-4000.
Harbour Island.
Museum of Science & Industry 813/987-6300.
Ybor Square.

Venice

ACCOMMODATIONS

Grandma Jean's B&B 720 Watersedge St, Englewood 305/394-7547 • gay-friendly • mostly women • B&B in private home • swimming • hot tub • nonsmoking • pets ok • woman-owned/ run • $55-65

SPIRITUAL GROUPS

Suncoast Cathedral MCC 3276 E Venice Ave (at Jackson St) 941/484-7068 • 9am & 11am Sun

Vero Beach

SPIRITUAL GROUPS

East Coast MCC 1590 27th Ave (off SR60, at Unitarian Universalist Fellowship) 321/759-5588 • 6pm 2nd & 4th Sun

West Palm Beach

INFO LINES & SERVICES

Compass LGBT Community Center 7600 S Dixie Hwy 561/533-9699 • 1pm-10pm, till 5pm Fri, 4pm-8pm Sat, clsd Sun • wheelchair access

The Whimsy 561/686-1354 • referrals, resources & academic archives • political clearinghouse • also feminist/ women's land camping, RV spaces (4), picnicking & guesthouse (feminist-friendly men welcome) • wheelchair access • sliding scale

ACCOMMODATIONS

Grandview Gardens B&B 1608 Lake Ave (at Palm) 561/833-9023 • gay-friendly • swimming • wheelchair • 1923 Spanish-Mediterranean home • gay-owned

Hibiscus House B&B 501 30th St 561/863-5633, 800/203-4927 • gay/ straight • full brkfst • swimming • jacuzzi • nonsmoking • gay-owned • $95-270

Scandia Lodge 625 S Federal Hwy (at 6th Ave), Lake Worth 561/586-3155 • gay/ straight • swimming • pets ok • gay-owned • $75-95

Tropical Gardens B&B 419 32nd St (Old Northwood Historic District) 561/848-4064, 800/736-4064 • gay-friendly • guesthouse • swimming • nonsmoking • $95-160

BARS

HG Rooster's 823 Belvedere Rd (btwn Parker & Lake) 561/832-9119 • 3pm-3am, till 4am Fri-Sat • popular • mostly gay men • neighborhood bar • strippers Sat • karaoke Wed & Sun • food served • wheelchair access

Kozlow's 6205 Georgia Ave (at Colonial) 561/533-5355 • 9am-3am, till 4am Fri-Sat, noon-3am Sun • popular • mostly gay men • neighborhood bar • dancing/DJ wknds • patio • wheelchair access

NIGHTCLUBS

Kashmir 1651 S Congress Ave 561/649-5557 • 5pm-close (Margarita Isles Lounge) 10pm-5am Wed-Sun (Kashmir) • mostly gay men • women-only party 8pm Mon in lounge • ladies night Wed • dancing/ DJ • live shows • 18+

Respectable Street 518 Clematis St 561/832-9999 • 9pm-3am, till 4am Fri-Sat, clsd Sun-Tue • gay-friendly • dancing/DJ • alternative • retro & new wave nights • live shows

RESTAURANTS

Palm Beach Fish Market & Bistro 3815 S Dixie Hwy 561/835-0300 • lunch & dinner, family-owned

Rhythm Cafe 3800-A S Dixie Hwy 561/833-3406 • 6pm-10pm, clsd Sun-Mon • some veggie • beer/ wine • $12-19

Thai Bay 1900 Okeechobee Blvd (in Palm Beach Market Pl) 561/640-0131 • lunch weekdays & dinner nightly

BOOKSTORES

Changing Times Bookstore 911 Village Blvd #806 (at Palm Beach Lakes) 561/640-0496 • 10am-7pm, till 5pm Sat, noon-5pm Sun • spiritual • LGBT section • community bulletin board • wheelchair access

RETAIL SHOPS

Eurotique 3109 45th St #300 561/684-2302, 800/486-9650 • 11am-7pm, noon-6pm Sat, clsd Sun • leather • books • videos

Studio 205 & Java Juice Bar 600 Lake Ave (at North L St), Lake Worth 561/533-5272 • 8am-9pm, till 5pm Sun • gay pride items • books & home accessories

SPIRITUAL GROUPS

MCC of the Palm Beaches 4857 Northlake Blvd, Palm Beach Gardens 561/775-5900 • 11am Sun

Wilton Manors

see Fort Lauderdale

Winter Haven

ACCOMMODATIONS

Ranch House Motor Inn 1911 Cypress Gardens Blvd 863/324-5994, 800/366-5996 • gay friendly • motel • swimming • restaurant • kids/ pets ok • wheelchair access • $47-82

GEORGIA

Statewide

PUBLICATIONS

Clique Magazine 954/455-3394 • great glossy newsmagazine covering GA & FL's LGBT African American community • some nat'l club & event listings

Southern Voice 404/876-1819 • weekly LGBT newspaper for AL, FL (panhandle), GA, LA, MS, TN w/ resource listings

Athens

BARS

Georgia Bar 159 W Clayton (at Lumpkin) 706/546-9884 • 3pm-2am, clsd Sun • gay-friendly • neighborhood bar • wheelchair access

The Globe 199 N Lumpkin (at Clayton) 706/353-4721 • 11am-2am, noon-midnight Sun • gay-friendly • 40 single-malt scotches

NIGHTCLUBS

Boneshakers 433 E Hancock Ave 706/543-1555 • 9pm-close, clsd Mon-Tue • lesbians/ gay men • dancing/DJ • live shows • 18+ • wheelchair access

Forty Watt Club 285 W Washington St (at Pulaski) 706/549-7871 • 9pm-2am • gay-friendly • alternative • live music • wheelchair access

CAFES

Espresso Royale Cafe 297 E Broad St (at Jackson) 706/613-7449 • 7am-midnight, from 8am wknds • best coffee in Athens • gallery • wheelchair access

RESTAURANTS

The Bluebird 493 E Clayton 706/549-3663 • 8am-3pm • popular brunch wknds • plenty veggie

The Grit 199 Prince Ave 706/543-6592 • 11am-9:30pm (clsd 3pm-5pm wknds) • ethnic vegetarian • great wknd brunch • wheelchair access

BOOKSTORES

Barnett's Newsstand 147 College Ave (at Clayton) 706/353-0530 • 7:30am-10pm, 8am-11pm Fri-Sat, 8am-10pm Sun

Atlanta

INFO LINES & SERVICES

Galano Club 585 Dutch Valley Rd (at Monroe) 404/881-9188 • LGBT recovery club • call for meeting times

ACCOMMODATIONS

Ansley Inn B&B 253 15th St 404/872-9000, 800/446-5416 • gay/ straight • full brkfst • nonsmoking • gay-owned • $120-250

The Georgian Terrace Hotel 659 Peachtree St 404/897-1991, 800/555-8000 • gay-friendly • "Atlanta's only historic luxury hotel" • hosted Gone with the Wind world-premier reception in 1939 • kids ok • $119-199

Hello B&B 1865 Windemere Dr 404/892-8111 • lesbians/ gay men • B&B in private home • hot tub • nonsmoking • gay-owned • $79-99

Hill Street Resort B& B 729 Hill St SE 404/627-4281, 404/627-6788 • gay/ straight • full brkfst • hot tub • gay-owned • $109-129

Hotel Indigo 683 Peachtree St NE 404/874-9200 • cozy, stylish no-frills hotel • workout room • wireless internet

Microtel Inn & Suites 1840 Corporate Blvd 404/325-4446 • gay-friendly • $55

Midtown Guest House 845 Penn Ave 404/931-8791 • gay/ straight • in the heart of midtown • $80-170 • gay-owned

Sheraton Atlanta Hotel 165 Courtland St (at International Blvd) 404/659-6500, 800/325-3535 • gay-friendly • swimming • 3 restaurants • also bar • wheelchair access • $169-349

W Atlanta 111 Perimeter Center W 770/396-6800, 877/WHOTELS (RESERVATIONS ONLY) • gay-friendly • swimming • nonsmoking • also restaurant • wheelchair access • $125-399

BARS

Atlanta Eagle 306 Ponce de Leon Ave NE (at Argonne) 404/873-2453 • 8pm-3am, till 4am Fri, 6pm-midnight Sun • popular • mostly gay men • dancing/DJ • bears • leather • also leather store • gay-owned/ run

Blake's (on the Park) 227 10th St (at Piedmont) 404/892-5786 • 3pm-3am, from 2pm wknds, till midnight Sun • lesbians/ gay men • neighborhood bar • upscale • drag shows • videos

Buddies 2345 Cheshire Bridge Rd (at La Vista) 404/634-5895 • 2:30pm-3am, till midnight Sun • mostly gay men • neighborhood bar • gospel drag show • gay-owned

Bulldogs 893 Peachtree St NE (btwn 7th & 8th) 404/872-3025 • 2pm-4am, till 3am Sat • popular • mostly gay men • neighborhood cruise bar • dancing/DJ • multiracial • videos

Burkhart's Pub 1492-F Piedmont Ave (at Monroe, in Ansley Mall) 404/872-4403 • 4pm-4am, 2pm-3am wknds • lesbians/ gay men • neighborhood bar • food served • karaoke • live shows • patio • wheelchair access

Eastside Lounge 485-A Flat Shoals Ave 404/522-7841 • 9pm-3am • gay/ straight • dancing/ DJ • multiracial • theme nights

Eddie's Attic 515-B N McDonough St (at Trinity Place), Decatur 404/377-4976 • 4pm-close • gay/ straight • occasional lesbian hangout • rooftop deck • live music 6 nights/ week • comedy 2nd & 4th Tue • also restaurant

Felix's on the Square 1510-G Piedmont Ave NE (Ansley Square) 404/249-7899 • 2pm-2:30am, from 12:30pm Sat, till midnight Sun • mostly gay men

Friends on Ponce 736 Ponce de Leon, NE (at Ponce de Leon Pl) 404/817-3820 • noon-2:30am, till 12:30am Sun • lesbians/ gay men • neighborhood bar • dancing/ DJ • rooftop patio

Halo Lounge 817 W Peachtree (6th St, btwn W Peachtree & Peachtree) 404/962-7333 • 4pm-3am, from 6pm Sat, clsd Sun • dinner • gay/ straight • DJ

Hoedowns 931 Monroe Dr #B (at Midtown Promenade) 404/876-0001 • 3pm-3am, till 2am Tue, 4pm-midnight Sun, clsd Mon • popular • mostly gay men • more women Th • dancing/DJ • country/ western • live shows • wheelchair access

Le Buzz 585 Franklin Rd A-10 (at S Marietta Pkwy, in Longhorn Plaza), Marietta 770/424-1337 • 5pm-3am, from 7pm Sat, clsd Sun • lesbians/ gay men • neighborhood bar • dancing/DJ • drag shows • karaoke • also restaurant • patio • wheelchair access

Mary's 1287 Glenwood Ave (at Flat Shoals) 404/624-4411 • 5pm-3am Fri-Sat, clsd Sun • lesbians/ gay men • friendly neighborhood cocktail bar • dancing/ DJ • karaoke • videos

My Sister's Room 222 E Howard Ave (at E Trinity Pl), Decatur 404/370-1990 • 8pm-2am, till 3am Fri-Sat, clsd Mon-Tue • popular • mostly women • DJ wknds • live music • karaoke • also restaurant • younger crowd • patio

Opus I 1086 Alco St NE (at Cheshire Bridge) 404/634-6478 • 9am-2:30am, 12:30pm-midnight Sun • mostly gay men • neighborhood bar • wheelchair access

Red Chair 550-C Amsterdam Ave (at Monroe) 404/870-0532 • 6:30pm-3am, 12:30pm-midnight Sun, clsd Mon • gay/ straight • videos • also restaurant • Sun brunch • nonsmoking • patio

Val's 3701 Lawrenceville Hwy, Tucker 770/938-0567 • 4pm-close • lesbians/ gay men • neighborhood bar • dancing/DJ • karaoke • food served

NIGHTCLUBS

The Armory 836 Juniper St NE (at 7th) 404/881-9280 • 7pm-3am, from 9pm Mon, clsd Sun • popular • lesbians/ gay men • 4 bars • dancing/DJ • multiracial • live shows • videos • young crowd • wheelchair access

Bazzaar 654 Peachtree St (at Ponce de Leon) 404/885-7505 • 5:30pm-midnight, till 3am Wed-Sat, clsd Mon-Tue • popular • gay/straight • dancing/DJ • full menu

Chaparral 2715 Burford Hwy 404/634-3737 • 10pm-4am Sun only • mostly gay men • dancing/ DJ

Girl 69 836 Juniper St NE (at 7th, at the Armory) 404/881-9280 • 10pm Fri only • women only • dancing/ DJ • mostly African-American

Jungle Club 2115 Faulkner Rd NE 404/844-8800 • 10pm-3am Fri-Sat only • lesbians/ gay men • dancing/ DJ • also Stars of the Century (drag shows) Mon 11pm • cover charge

Masquerade 695 North Ave NE 404/577-8178, 404/577-2002 • hours vary, clsd Mon • gay-friendly • dancing/DJ • live shows • call for events • food served • 18+ • private club • cover charge

MJQ Concourse 736 Ponce de Leon Ave (at Ponce de Leon Pl) 404/870-0575 • 11pm-4am Mon, Wed & Fri, till 3am Sat • gay-friendly • popular • dancing/DJ • alternative • live shows • young crowd

Phase One 4933 Memorial Dr, Decatur 678/296-0678 • mostly women 10pm Fri & Sun only • dancing/ DJ • mostly African-American • mostly men Th & Sat

The Tower II 735 Ralph McGill Blvd NE (at Freedom Pkwy) 404/523–1535 • lesbians/ gay men • dancing/ DJ • mostly women Sat & Tue • mostly men Fri for Manhunt • multiracial • younger crowd • wheelchair access

Traxx 800 Marietta St NW (at Club Library) 404/874–5400 • Tue & Fri only • mostly gay men • dancing/ DJ • mostly African-American clientele • live shows

Wet Bar 960 Spring St (at 10th) 404/745–9494 • 6pm-3am, from 8pm Sat • lesbians/ gay men • dancing/DJ • videos • patio

CAFES

Australian Bakery Cafe 463 Flat Shoals Rd (in East Atlanta Village) 404/653–0100 • 7:30am-7:30pm, till 9:30pm Fri-Sat, 9am-5pm Sun • authentic Australian bakery

Australian Bakery Cafe 48 S Park Square, Marietta 678/797–6222

Caribou Coffee 1551 Piedmont Ave NE (at Monroe) 404/733–5539 • 6:30am-11pm, 7am-midnight wknds

Intermezzo 1845 Peachtree Rd NE 404/355–0411 • 11am-3am, till 4am Fri-Sat • classy cafe • plenty veggie • full bar • great desserts

Urban Grounds 38 N Avondale Rd, Atltanta 404/499–2136

RESTAURANTS

Agnes & Muriel's 1514 Monroe Dr (near Piedmont) 404/885–1000 • 11am-11pm, till midnight Fri-Sat, from 10am wknds • popular • beer/ wine • patio

Apres Diem 931 Monroe Dr #C-103 404/872–3333 • lunch & dinner, brunch Sat-Sun • French bistro • live jazz Wed • full bar

Bacchanalia 1198 Howell Mill Rd NW 404/365–0410 • lunch Wed-Sat & dinner Mon-Sat• American

Bridgetown Grill 689 Peachtree St (across from Fox Theater) 404/873–5361 • 11am-10pm • popular • funky Caribbean • some veggie • wheelchair access

The Colonnade 1879 Cheshire Bridge Rd NE 404/874–5642 • lunch Wed-Sun, dinner nightly • traditional Southern

Cowtippers 1600 Piedmont Ave NE (at Monroe) 404/874–3469 • 11am-11pm, till midnight Fri-Sat • steak house • transgender-friendly • wheelchair access

Einstein's 1077 Juniper (at 12th) 404/876–7925 • 11am-midnight, till 1am Fri-Sat, wknd brunch • popular • some veggie • full bar • patio • wheelchair access • reservations accepted

The Flying Biscuit Cafe 1655 McLendon Ave (at Clifton) 404/687–8888 • 7am-10pm • popular • healthy brkfst all day • plenty veggie • beer/ wine • wheelchair access • also 1001 Piedmont Ave, 404/874-8887

Majestic Diner 1031 Ponce de Leon (at Clayton Terr) 404/875–0276 • 24hrs • popular diner right from the '50s w/ cantankerous waitresses included • at your own risk • some veggie • $3-8

Murphy's 997 Virginia Ave NE (at N Highland Ave) 404/872–0904 • 11am-10pm, till midnight Fri-Sat, from 8am wknds • popular • plenty veggie • wheelchair access

Patio Daddy-O 2714 E Point St (downtown East Point, off Langford Pkwy), East Point 404/767–6764 • 11am-4pm, till 9pm Th-Sat, clsd Sun-Mon • popular • BBQ • some veggie • take-out • screened-in porch • woman-owned/ run

R Thomas 1812 Peachtree Rd NE (btwn 26th & 27th) 404/872–2942 • 24hrs • popular • beer/ wine • healthy Californian/ juice bar • plenty veggie • wheelchair access • $5-10

Ria's Bluebird Cafe 421 Memorial Dr 404/521–3737 • 8am-3pm • very popular • gourmet brunch in quaint old diner in Grant Park • plenty veggie • woman-owned/ run

Swan Coach House 3130 Slaton Dr NW 404/261–0636 • lunch only Mon-Sat, clsd Sun • also gift shop & art gallery

Veni Vidi Vici 41 14th St 404/875–8424 • lunch Mon-Fri, dinner 5pm-11pm nightly • upscale Italian • some veggie • $14-25

Watershed 406 W Ponce de Leon, Decatur 404/378–4900 • 11am-10pm, Sun brunch • wine bar • also gift shop • owned by Emily Saliers of the Indigo Girls

ENTERTAINMENT & RECREATION

Atlanta Feminist Women's Chorus 770/438–5823

Lambda Radio Report WRFG 89.3 FM 404/523–8989 • 6pm Tue • LGBT radio program

Little 5 Points, Moreland & Euclid Ave S of Ponce de Leon Ave • hip & funky area w/ too many restaurants & shops to list

Martin Luther King, Jr Center for Non–Violent Social Change 449 Auburn Ave NE **404/524–1956** • 9am-5pm daily • includes King's birth home, the church where he preached in the '60s & his gravesite

Theatre OUTlanta 404/371-0212 • LGBT theater group • call for performance location

BOOKSTORES

Brushstrokes/ Capulets 1510–J Piedmont Ave NE (near Monroe) **404/876-6567** • 10am-10pm, till 11pm Fri-Sat • LGBT variety store • gay-owned

Atlanta

WHERE THE GIRLS ARE:

Many lesbians live in DeKalb county, in the northeast part of the city of Decatur. For fun, women head for Midtown or Buckhead if they're professionals, Virginia-Highlands if they're funky or 30ish, and Little Five Points if they're young and wild.

LGBT PRIDE:

June. 404/929-0071, web: atlantapride.org.

ANNUAL EVENTS:

May - Armory Sports Classic 404/881-9280 (Armory Bar). Softball & many other sports competitions.

June - Midtown Music Festival, web: www.musicmidtown.com.

November - Out on Film, lesbian/ gay film festival, web: www.outonfilm.com.

CITY INFO:

404/521-6600 or 800/285-2682, web: www.atlanta.com.

BEST VIEW:

70th floor of the Peachtree Plaza, in the 3-story revolving Sun Dial restaurant (404/589-7506). Also from the top of Stone Mountain (only 20 feet taller).

WEATHER:

Summers are warm and humid (upper 80°s to low 90°s) with occasional thunderstorms. Winters are icy with occasional snow. Temperatures can drop into the low 30°s. Spring and fall are temperate – spring brings blossoming dogwoods and magnolias, while fall festoons the trees with awesome fall colors.

TRANSIT:

Yellow Cab 404/521-0200.
Superior Shuttle 770/457-4794.
Marta 404/848-5000, web: www.itsmarta.com.

ATTRACTIONS:

Atlanta Botanical Garden 404/876-5859, web: www.atlantabotanicalgarden.org.

Centennial Olympic Park.

CNN Center 404/827-2300, web: www.cnn.com/StudioTour.

Coca-Cola Museum 770/578-4325 x1465, web: www.woccatlanta.com.

Margaret Mitchell House 404/249-7015, web: www.gwtw.org.

Martin Luther King Jr. Memorial Center 404/526-8900, web: www.thekingcenter.org.

Piedmont Park.

Underground Atlanta 404/523-2311, web: underground-atlanta.com.

Reply **Forward** **Delete**

Date: Nov 18, 2005 10:51:37
From: Girl-on-the-Go
To: Editor@Damron.com
Subject: Atlanta
_____

>If you watched the 1996 Olympic Games, you saw how proud the residents of Atlanta are of their city. Today's Southerners have worked hard to move beyond stereotypes of the Old South. Of course, Atlanta's large population of lesbians and gay men is an integral part of that work.

>Planning to go sight-see? Atlanta houses the Martin Luther King, Jr. Center and the Carter Presidential Center—both tributes to icons of peace and positive change. Be sure to also check out for the nationally known Black Arts Festival if you are visiting in July (404/730-7315).

>Lesbian culture in Atlanta is spread out between **Charis** women's bookstore in L'il Five Points (cruise their readings), the **Atlanta Gay/Lesbian Center** in posh Midtown, and in between, along Piedmont and Cheshire Bridge roads. Midway between the gay Ansley Square area (Piedmont at Monroe) and downtown, stop by **Outwrite,** Atlanta's LGBT bookstore and cafe. Pick up a copy of **Southern Voice,** the LGBT newspaper, to get the dish on the bar scene. For more shopping, **Brushstrokes** is Atlanta's LGBT goodies store.

>Unless you're a serious mall-crawler, skip the overly commercial (but much-hyped) Underground Atlanta, and head for Lenox Mall instead. And, just a couple miles south on Highland, you'll run smack into funky shopping, dining, and live music in the alternative capital of Atlanta: **L'il Five Points** (not to be confused with "Five Points" downtown).

>**Tower II** is the local neighborhood dyke bar, and the country/western flavored **Hoedowns** has a women's night on Thursdays as well. **Ria's Bluebird Cafe** and **Patio Daddy-O** are two great places to dine and dish. And don't miss nearby Decatur, home to two popular lesbian hangouts—**My Sister's Room** bar and restaurant and **Eddie's Attic,** featuring live music (and rumored to be a sometime hangout of the Indigo Girls). And speaking of the Indigo Girls, check out **Watershed** restaurant, owned by Emily Saliers!

>If you're looking for women's accommodations, head an hour north to one of the women's guesthouses in lush, wooded Dahlonega, such as **Above the Clouds** or **Swiftwaters.**

>If you're a fan of R.E.M. or the B-52s, head northeast on Highway 306 or 78 about an hour and a half to the university town of Athens, Georgia. (On weekends during football season, traffic is hellish.) Pick up a *Flagpole* magazine to find out what's going on, and stop by **Boneshakers,** Athens's LGBT dance bar.

Charis Books & More 1189 Euclid Ave NE (at Moreland) 404/524-0304 • 10:30am-6:30pm, till 8pm Wed, Fri-Sat, till 7:30pm Th, noon-6pm Sun • feminist • wheelchair access

▲ **Outwrite Bookstore & Coffeehouse** 991 Piedmont Ave (at 10th) 404/607-0082 • 10am-11pm • popular • LGBT • music • videos • gifts • cafe • wheelchair access

RETAIL SHOPS

Atlanta Leather Company 2111 Faulkner Rd NE (at Cheshire Bridge Rd) 404/320-8989 • 11am-8pm, 1pm-6pm Sun • leather • fetish

The Boy Next Door 1447 Piedmont Ave NE (btwn 14th & Monroe) 404/873-2664 • 10am-8pm, noon-6pm Sun • clothing

The Junkman's Daughter 464 Moreland Ave (at Euclid) 404/577-3188 • 11am-7pm, till 8pm Fri, till 9pm Sat, from noon Sun • hip stuff

Piercing Experience 1654 McLendon Ave NE (at Clifton) 404/378-9100, 800/646-0393 • noon-9pm, till 5pm Sun

PUBLICATIONS

David Atlanta 404/876-4076

Labrys Atlanta 404/888-3157

Out & About Newspaper 615/596-6210 (TN #) • LGBT newspaper for Nashville, Knoxville, Chattanooga & Atlanta area • monthly

Out & Active 404/873-6004 • free gay/lesbian resource & entertainment guide

Southern Voice 404/876-1819 • weekly LGBT newspaper for AL, FL (panhandle), GA, LA, MS, TN w/ resource listings

Swirl Magazine 678/886-0711 (ATLANTA #) • magazine for "the African American lesbian, bisexual, bi-curious & 'straight but not narrow' community"

SPIRITUAL GROUPS

All Saints MCC 2352 Bolton Rd 404/296-9822 • 10:45am Sun

Christ Covenant MCC 109 Hibernia Ave (off Adair), Decatur 404/373-2933 • 11am Sun

Congregation Bet Haverim 2676 Clairmont Rd NE, Decatur 404/315-6446 • 8pm Fri • LGBT synagogue

First MCC of Atlanta 1379 Tullie Rd NE (at I-85 & N Druid Hills Rd) 404/325-4143 • 11am Sun, 7:30pm Wed • wheelchair access

GYMS & HEALTH CLUBS

The Fitness Factory 500 N Amsterdam (in Amsterdam Outlets) 404/815-7900 • popular • gay-friendly • full gym

EROTICA

Aphrodite's Toy Box 3040 N Decatur Rd (at Ponce De Leon), Scottdale 404/292-9700 • noon-8pm, till 9pm Fri-Sat, till 6pm Sun • 18+ • erotic boutique for women & their partners & friends • transgender-friendly

Heaven 2628 Piedmont (at Sidney Marcus Blvd) 404/262-9113

Inserection 505 Peachtree St NE 404/888-0878 • call for other locations

The Poster Hut/ Scream Boutique 2175 Cheshire Bridge Rd 404/633-7491 • clothing • toys

Southern Nights Videos 2205 Cheshire Br Rd (at Lenox Rd) 404/728-0701 • 24hrs

Starship 2275 Cheshire Bridge Rd 404/320-9101 • leather • novelties • 7 locations in Atlanta

CRUISY AREAS

Publix on Ponce 1001 Ponce de Leon Ave • supermarket • dyke cruising territory

Augusta

see also Aiken, South Carolina

NIGHTCLUBS

The Coliseum 1632 Walton Wy 706/733-2603 • 8pm-3am, clsd Sun • lesbians/ gay men • dancing/DJ • live shows

Gravity 825 E Buena Vista Ave (at Carolina Springs), N Augusta, SC 803/279-9988 • 10pm-6am • mostly gay men • dancing/ DJ

RETAIL SHOPS

B&B Creations 103 Shartom Dr (at Washington) 706/650-8923 • 10am-close, clsd Sun-Mon • gay-owned

SPIRITUAL GROUPS

MCC Church of Our Redeemer 557 Greene St 706/722-6454 • 11am & 6pm Sun

Blue Ridge

RESTAURANTS

Great Eats Deli 611 E Main St (at Carter St) 706/632-3094 • 11am-4pm • soups • sandwiches • desserts • young crowd • bring your own bottle • patio • wheelchair access

BOOKSTORES

Mountain Scholar Bookshop 679-A E Main St (at Depot) 706/623-1993 • 10am-5pm, clsd Mon • gay-owned

Columbus

SPIRITUAL GROUPS

Forgiving Heart Community Church 1442 Double Churches Rd 706/681-5246

Dahlonega

ACCOMMODATIONS

Mountain Laurel Creek 202 Talmer Grizzle Rd (at Hwy 19 & McDonald Rd) 706/867-8134 • gay-friendly • B&B • full brkfst • jacuzzi • garden • creek • nonsmoking • gay-owned • $120-157

Swiftwaters Womanspace 706/864-3229, 888/808-5021 • women only • on scenic river • full brkfst • hot tub • seasonal • nonsmoking • deck • dogs ok • women-owned/ run • $69-95 (B&B)/ $40-50 (cabins)/ $10 (camping)

RESTAURANTS

Smith House 84 S Chestatee St 706/867-7000, 800/852-9577 • lunch Tue-Fri & dinner wknds only • clsd Mon • family-style Southern

Dalton

RESTAURANTS

Dalton Depot 110 Depot St 706/226-3160 • 11am-10pm, bar till 2am, clsd Sun

Decatur

see Atlanta

Dewy Rose

ACCOMMODATIONS

The River's Edge 2311 Pulliam Mill Rd 706/213-8081 • mostly gay men • cabins • camping • RV • live shows • swimming • nudity • nonsmoking • wheelchair access • $15-98

Jonesboro

ACCOMMODATIONS

Holiday Inn Atlanta South 6288 Old Dixie Hwy (at Tara Blvd) 770/968-4300 • gay/ straight • swimming • kids/ pets ok • wheelchair access

Lake Lanier

ENTERTAINMENT & RECREATION

Gay Cove between Athens Park Rd & Frank Boyd Rd • a rainbow rendezvous for the pleasure-boating crowd—look for the rainbow flag

Macon

ACCOMMODATIONS

Lumberjack's Camping Resort 50 Hwy 230 (at Hwy 41), Unadilla **478/783-2267** • mostly gay men • 200 campsites & 85 RV hookups • on 150 acres • swimming • jacuzzi • pets ok • gay-owned

NIGHTCLUBS

Club Synergy 425 Cherry St (at MLK, Jr Blvd) **478/755-9383** • 9pm-close, clsd Sun-Tue • lesbians/ gay men • 4 bars • dancing/DJ • live shows • karaoke • wheelchair access

Marietta

see Atlanta

Mountain City

ACCOMMODATIONS

The York House 416 York House Rd **706/746-2068, 800/231-9675** • gay-friendly • 1896 historic country inn • located between towns of Clayton & Dillard • full brkfst • nonsmoking • wheelchair access • $69-129

Savannah

INFO LINES & SERVICES

First City Network 307 E Harris St **912/236-2489** • complete info & events line • social group • also newsletter

ACCOMMODATIONS

912 Barnard Victorian B&B 912 Barnard St **912/234-9121** • lesbians/ gay men • fireplaces • period furnishings • nonsmoking • garden • sundeck • gay-owned • $120

Catherine Ward House Inn 118 E Waldburg St (at Abercorn) **912/234-8564, 800/327-4270** • gay/ straight • Victorian Italianate B&B • full brkfst • jacuzzi • gay-owned • $159-400

Park Avenue Manor 107–109 W Park Ave **912/233-0352** • lesbians/ gay men • 1889 Victorian B&B • full brkfst • nonsmoking • $95-150

Thunderbird Inn 611 W Oglethorpe Ave (at MLK Blvd) **912/232-2661, 866/324-2661** • gay-friendly • motel • kids ok • nonsmoking • gay-owned • $99-139

Typee Beach Condo 1217 Bay St Unit 105b (at Hwy 80 E), Tybee Island **404/320-3280** • pool • kids ok • nonsmoking • wheelchair access • gay-owned • $100-140

Under the Rainbow Inn 104-106 West 38th St **912/790-1005** • gay/ straight • kids ok • nonsmoking • gay-owned • $89-125

NIGHTCLUBS

Club One 1 Jefferson St (at Bay) **912/232-0200** • 5pm-3am, till 2am Sun • lesbians/ gay men • dancing/DJ • food served • live shows Th-Sun • cabaret • dancers • videos

CAFES

B Matthews Bakery–Eatery 325 E Bay St (at Habersham St) **912/233-1319** • 7am-8pm, from 8am wknds • gay-owned

RESTAURANTS

Clary's Cafe 404 Abercorn (at Jones) **912/233-0402** • 7am-4pm • country cookin'

Queeny's to Go-Go 1611 Habersham St (at 33rd) **912/443-0888** • gay-friendly • also bar • more gay Wed • wheelchair access • gay-owned

Sweet Leaf Smokery 606 Abercorn **912/447-5444** • lunch & dinner • eclectic cuisine • also Southern folk art gallery

Tango Restaurant & Tropical Bar 1106 Hwy 80, Tybee Island **912/786-8264** • dinner, Sun brunch, clsd Tue

ENTERTAINMENT & RECREATION

Savannah Walks, Inc **912/238-9255** • gay-friendly • walking tours of downtown Savannah

BOOKSTORES

Moon Dance 306 W St Julian St **912/236-9003** • 10am-6pm, till 8pm Fri-Sat, 11am-5pm Sun • metaphysical supplies • gifts

RETAIL SHOPS

Urban Cargo 135 Bull St **912/341-0061** • 10am-6pm, noon-5pm Sun • pride items • candles, gifts, etc • gay-owned

PUBLICATIONS

Network News PO Box 2442, 31402 **912/236-2489** • monthly newsletter for Savannah & surrounding regions

Valdosta

NIGHTCLUBS

The Voo Doo Lounge 206 E Hill Ave (at Ashley) **229/293-9166** • 9pm-2am Th-Sat only • gay/ straight • theme nights • dancing/ DJ • strippers • drag shows • karaoke • 18+

Washington

ACCOMMODATIONS

Holly Court Inn 301 S Alexander Ave (at Water St) **706/678-3982, 866/465-5928** • gay-friendly • historic home on 2 acres • 2 blocks from Washington's town square • 1 hour from Augusta & Athens • full brkfst • kids ok • $80-195

HAWAII

Please note that cities are grouped by islands:
Hawaii (Big Island)
Kauai
Maui
Molokai
Oahu (includes Honolulu)

STATEWIDE

Bed & Breakfast Honolulu (Statewide) 3242 Kaohinani Dr (at Pelekane), Oahu **808/595-7533, 800/288-4666** • clientele & ownership vary • represents 414 locations statewide • $55-250

Pacific Ocean Holidays Oahu **808/923-2400, 800/735-6600** • Hawaii vacation packages

HAWAII (BIG ISLAND)

Captain Cook

ACCOMMODATIONS

Affordable Hawaii at Pomaika'i (Lucky) Farm B&B 83-5465 Mamalahoa Hwy **808/328-2112, 800/325-6427** • gay/ straight • working, century-old Kona farm • full brkfst • nonsmoking • $60-75 + 11.25% tax

Areca Palms Estate B&B **808/323-2276, 800/545-4390** • gay-friendly • full brkfst • gardens • jacuzzi • nonsmoking • $95-130

Horizon Guest House **808/328-2540, 888/328-8301** • gay/ straight • full brkfst • swimming • nonsmoking • wheelchair access • gay-owned • $250

Kealakekua Bay B&B **808/328-8150, 800/328-8150** • gay/ straight • Mediterranean-style villa • nonsmoking • kids ok • also 2-bdrm guesthouse

Kona Hawaii B&B 84-4780 Mamalahoa Hwy **808/328-8955, 800/897-3188** • gay friendly • full brkfst • nudity • nonsmoking • kids ok • wheelchair access • $110-280

Rainbow Plantation B&B **808/323-2393, 800/494-2829** • gay-friendly • on coffee & macadamia nut plantation • kayak rentals • nonsmoking • $79-99 +11.25% tax

Hilo

ACCOMMODATIONS

Aloha Healing Women PO Box 1850,, Pahoa 96778 **888/967-8622** • women only • all-inclusive holistic healing retreats • full brkfst • swimming • accupuncture • guided tours • gourmet meals • women-owned/ run • $150-289

The Butterfly Inn for Women **808/966-7936, 800/546-2442** • women only • hot tub • kitchens • nonsmoking • women-owned/ run • $55-85

Hale Aulike—Hawaiian House of Kindness 39-3350 Hana Kalana Camp Rd (at Mamalahoa Hwy), Ookala **808/962-6253** • mostly women • B&B • ocean views • hostess can provide tours to volcano & local sites • lesbian-owned • $50

Mele Kohola 15-991 Paradise Dr (Paradise Ala Kai), Keaau **808/965-0400** • vacation rental • bay views • seasonal whale watching • $180-350

Oceanfront B&B 1923 Kalanianaole St (3 miles from intersection of Hwys 11 & 19) **808/934-9004, 800/363-9524** • gay-friendly • 2 units • ocean views • hot tub • kids/ pets ok • wheelchair access • $110-140

Our Place Papaikou's B&B 27-228 Old Mamalahoa Hwy, Papa'ikou **808/964-5250** • gay/ straight • 3-rm tropical healing retreat • 4 miles north of Hilo • organic meals available • lesbian-owned • $60-90

Seascape Gardens B & B 2107 A Kaiwiki Rd (at Wainaku) **808/961-3036** • women only • panoramic views • women-owned

CAFES

Kope-Kope 1261 Kilauea Ave #220 (in Hilo Shopping Center) **808/933-1221** • 6:30am-6pm, 7:30am-3pm wknds • espresso bar

RESTAURANTS

Cafe Pesto 308 Kamehameha Ave 808/969-6640 • lunch & dinner • Hawaiian/ Californian style bistro w/ pizzas, salads, pastas • on the waterfront • also at Kawaihae Shopping Center (808) 882-1071

ENTERTAINMENT & RECREATION

Richardson's Beach at end of Kalanianaole Ave (Keaukaha)

BOOKSTORES

Borders 301 Maka'ala St (at Kanoelehua Hwy) 808/933-1410 • 9am-9pm, till 10pm Fri-Sat • LGBT section

Honaunau-Kona

ACCOMMODATIONS

Dragonfly Ranch Healing Arts Center 1 1/2 miles down City of Refuge Rd 808/328-2159 • gay/ straight • near ancient sanctuary w/ friendly dolphins • hot tub • nonsmoking • $100-300

Kailua-Kona

ACCOMMODATIONS

1st Class B&B Kona Hawaii 77-6504 Kilohana St 808/329-8778, 888/769-1110 • gay-friendly • private luxury suites • ocean views • full gourmet brkfst • nonsmoking • $135-140 (3-night minimum)

▲ **Hale Kipa 'O Pele** 808/329-8676, 800/LAVAGLO • lesbians/ gay men • plantation-style B&B • also bungalow w/ kitchen • hot tub • gay-owned • $95-125

Hawaiian Oasis B&B 74-4958 Kiwi St 808/327-1701 • gay-friendly • B&B • swimming • hot tub • wheelchair access • $135-185

Leilani—The Kona Coast 77-6461 Leilani St (at Lako) 808/960-7040 • gay-friendly • vacation rental • kids/ pets ok • lesbian-owned • $65-475

Pu'ukala Lodge B&B 808/325-1729, 888/325-1729 • lesbians/ gay men • on the slopes of Mt Hualalai • full brkfst • nonsmoking • gay-owned • $85-165

Royal Kona Resort 75–5852 Ali'i Dr **808/329–3111, 800/222–5642** • gay-friendly • set atop dramatic lava outcroppings overlooking Kailua Bay • swimming • private beach • bar • live shows • wheelchair access • $105-250

BARS

Mask Bar & Grill 75–5660 Kopiko St (at Cathedral Plaza) **808/329–8558** • 10am-2am • popular • lesbians/ gay men • neighborhood bar • dancing/DJ • live shows • karaoke • only lesbian/gay bar on the island

RESTAURANTS

Cassandra's Greek Taverna 75-5719 Alii Dr **808/334–1066** • 11am-10pm, bar open later • karaoke Wed

Edward's at Kanaloa 78–261 Manukai St (at Kamehameha III) **808/322–1003** • 8am-3pm & 5pm-10pm • Mediterranean • full bar from 8am-9pm • gay-owned

Huggo's 75-5828 Kahakai Rd (on Kailua Bay) **808/329–1493** • lunch Mon-Fri, dinner nightly • seafood & steak • also bar • live entertainment • patio

Kamuela

ACCOMMODATIONS

Aaah, the Views! B&B Inn 66–1773 Alaneo (at Kawaihae Rd [Rte 19]) **808/885–3455, 866/885–3455** • gay/ straight • 15 minutes to world's best beaches • nonsmoking • wheelchair access • women-owned/ run • $65-145

Ho'onanea PO Box 6450, 96743 **808/882–1177** • vacation rental • hot tub • swimming • kids ok • nonsmoking • wheelchair access • lesbian-owned • $113-125

Na'alehu

ACCOMMODATIONS

Earthsong **808/929–8043** • mostly women • retreat center w/ cottages on 3 acres • Hawaiian massage • Goddess temple • substance-free • lesbian-owned • $35-45

Margo's Corner Wakea/Kaikane Loop (Discovery Harbor) **808/929–9614** • cottage & 4 campsites • full brkfst & dinner • kids ok • sauna • lesbian-owned • $35-125

Ninole

ACCOMMODATIONS

Pu'u Puanani Vacation Estate 32-949 Mamalahoa Hwy **808/963–6789** • gay/ straight • 2 units in 1 guesthouse on 11 acres • nonsmoking • hot tub • ocean views • wheelchair access • gay-owned • $700-1,000 (weekly)

Pahoa

ACCOMMODATIONS

Aloha Healing Retreats 14-4720 A Malulani Circle **808/965–1244, 888/967–8622** • women-only • holistic center for aloha & healing • ocean views • wheelchair access • $205-295

Hale 'Ae Kali Guesthouse 13-6768 Kapoho-Kalapana Beach Rd **808/936–856** • gay/ straight • kids ok • nonsmoking • lesbian-owned • $50-80

Hawaiian Dream Vacation **808/965–9523** • gay/ straight • cottage • swimming at beach • hot tub • nonsmoking • women-owned/ run • $85

Kalani Oceanside Retreat **808/965–7828, 800/800–6886** • gay/ straight • coastal retreat & spa • on 113 acres • swimming • nudity • nonsmoking • food served • wheelchair access • straight & gay-owned • $20-30 camping • $60-240

Pamalu—Hawaiian Country House **808/965–0830** • gay/ straight • country retreat on 5 secluded acres • swimming • near hiking • snorkeling • warm ponds • kids ok if family rents whole house • nonsmoking • gay-owned • $75-125

Paradise Cliffs **808/965–8640** • lesbians/ gay men • B&B • vacation rental • ocean views • kids ok • nonsmoking • gay & lesbian-owned • $90-100/ night, $660-730/ week

Rainbow Dreams Cottage 13–6412 Kalapana Beach Rd **415/824–7062** • gay/ straight • oceanfront cottage • kitchen • nonsmoking • kids ok • gay-owned • $600/ week, $1,750/ month

▲ **Rainbow's Inn & Adventures** **808/965–9011** • gay/ straight • B&B hideaway • swimming • hot tub • kids/ pets ok • nonsmoking • wheelchair access • offers activity desk to plan your Hawaii experience • see also Rainbow Adventures • lesbian-owned • $85-135/ night, weekly & monthly rates available

Rainbow's Inn & Adventures
A remote, quiet B&B Hideaway

Out & About's Editor's Choice Award 1998
Located on the Big Island of Hawaii

We are located in old style Pahoa Village just 20 miles south of Hilo, on 10 acres of tropical jungle…just minutes from the ocean surf, fabulous snorkeling, volcanically heated warm pond, steam vents, clothing optional black sand beach and with many fabulous restaurants.

On our 10 secluded acres of grounds we have a large salt water swimming pool, hot tub, large lanai for breakfast or lounging, Hawaiian library, DVD library.

We have 3 choices of suites available ranging from $95-$125/night, double occupancy or discounted weekly & monthly rates. Group rates also available. All suites have private bath/shower, kitchenettes, TV/DVD, living rooms/dining rooms.

The Ohana Suite is a studio with a queen size bed.

The Aloha Suite is a one bedroom with a queen size bed in the bedroom. There is a fold out queen-size futon in the living room.

The Bamboo Suite is a one bedroom with a king-size bed in the bedroom. There is a fold out queen-size futon in the living room.

Coming soon: $50/night off power junglos...stay tuned.

Lots of community events happen here, please inquire.

Also ask about vacation rental cottages in the area or alternative accommodations for women's transitional housing, work exchange for extended stays. We encourage all kinds of inquires about The Big Island & your desires.

"We're here for fun, let us help"

Also featuring a full service activities desk: * Cowgirl Kelly & her Happy Horses * helicopter tours * "work/fun" exchange program * Lesbian guided Rainbow Adventures lava tube hikes & secluded beaches   remote jungle adventures with Hawaiian ruins   snorkeling ponds with coral gardens trips to the volcano's active lava flow   commitment ceremonies

PO Box 983, Pahoa, HI 96778 • Phone: 808-965-9011
Email: alohafun911@aol.com

www.alohafun.com

BARS

Lava Zone 15-2929 Pahoa Village Rd
808/965-2222 • noon-11pm, till 2am Fri-Sat,
clsd Sun • lesbians/ gay men • neighborhood
bar • dancing/ DJ • karaoke • live shows • food
served

ENTERTAINMENT & RECREATION

Kehena Beach off Hwy 137 (trailhead at 19-
mile marker phone booth) • lava rock trail to
clothing-optional black sand beach

Rainbow Adventures 808/965-9011 •
custom-made remote land & sea excursions •
lesbian-owned

Volcano Village

ACCOMMODATIONS

The Chalet Kilauea Collection 998 Wright
Rd **808/967-7786, 800/937-7786** • gay-
friendly • full brkfst • hot tub • nonsmoking •
$49-399

Hale Ohia Cottages 808/967-7986,
800/455-3803 • gay/ straight • hot tub •
fireplaces • rainforest • gay-owned • $95-165

Kulana: The Affordable Artists Sanctuary
808/985-9055 • mostly women • artist retreat
• camping, cabins & guest rooms available •
no smoking, drugs or alcohol • kids/ pets ok •
women-owned/ run • $15 (campers) & $20-30
(cabin); $325/ month

KAUAI

INFO LINES & SERVICES

Lambda Aloha 808/823-6248 • recorded
info

Anahola

ACCOMMODATIONS

**Aliomanu Palms—A Beachfront Vacation
Rental** 4880 Aliomanu Rd (at Kuhio Hwy),
Anahola **808/822-1021** • gay/ straight • 3-
bdrm/3.5-bath rental • located on the beach •
gay-owned • $500/ night, $2,500/ week

Mahina Kai Ocean Villa 4933 Aliomanu Rd
808/822-9451, 800/337-1134 • popular • gay/
straight • Japanese style farmhouse B&B
overlooking Anahola Bay • swimming • hot
tub • nudity • nonsmoking • gay-owned •
$175-325

Hanalei

NIGHTCLUBS

Tahiti Nui 5-5134 Kuhio Hwy (near Hanalei
Center) **808/826-6277** • 11am-2am • gay-
friendly • live music most nights • also
restaurant from 7am-3pm, then 5pm-10pm •
Thai, Vietnamese & Chinese • luaus Wed •
karaoke • wheelchair access

Kapaa

ACCOMMODATIONS

17 Palms Kauai 808/822-5659,
888/725-6799 • gay/ straight • 2 secluded
cottages 200 steps from beach • kids ok •
nonsmoking • wheelchair access • gay-owned
• $110-165 (4-night minimum)

Kauai Kualapa Cottage 1471 Kualapa Pl
808/822-1626 • gay-friendly • private cottage
overlooking hidden valley • 10 minutes to
beaches • kitchen • $75-85

Kauai Waterfall B&B 5783 Haaheo St
808/823-9533, 800/996-9533 • lesbians/ gay
men • swimming • hot tub • overlooking
Wailua River State Park Waterfall •
nonsmoking • gay-owned • $90-100

**Mahina's Women's Guest House on
Kaua'i** 4433 Panihi Rd **808/823-9364** •
women-only beach house • shared bathrooms
• lesbian-owned • $65-110

Mohala Ke Ola B&B Retreat 5663 Ohelo
Rd (at Kuamoo Rd/ Hwy 580) **808/823-6398,
888/465-2824** • gay-friendly • swimming •
jacuzzi • nonsmoking • gay-owned • $100-125

Royal Drive Cottages 147 Royal Dr
415/788-7882 • gay/ straight • private garden
cottages w/ kitchenettes • near beach •
nonsmoking • wheelchair access • lesbian &
gay-owned • $85-140

RESTAURANTS

A Pacific Cafe 4-831 Kuhio Hwy #220
808/822-0013 • dinner only • gourmet •
reservations req'd

Bull Shed 796 Kuhio Hwy **808/822-3791** •
5:30pm-10pm • steak & seafood • full bar

Eggbert's 4-484 Kuhio Hwy (in Coconut
Plantation Marketplace) **808/822-3787** •
7am-3pm • popular • gay-owned

Mema 4-369 Kuhio Hwy (in shopping
center) **808/823-0899** • lunch Mon-Fri, dinner
nightly, Thai & Chinese

Kilauea

ACCOMMODATIONS

Kai Mana 808/828–1280, 800/837–1782 • gay-friendly • cottage at Shakti Gawain's paradise home • hot tub • kitchen • nonsmoking • $150-185

Kauai Vacation Hideaway 4180 N Waiakalua St 808/828–0228, 888/858–6562 • lesbians/ gay men • 2 private homes on upscale 3-acres • overlooking ocean • private path to secluded beach • jacuzzi • kids ok • nonsmoking • wheelchair access • $295-475

CAFES

Mango Mama's Fruitstand Cafe 4640 Hookui Rd (at Kuhio Hwy) 808/828–1020 • 7am-6pm • natural foods, fruit smoothies & more

Lihue

ACCOMMODATIONS

Radisson Kauai Beach Resort 4331 Kauai Beach Dr 808/245–1955, 800/333–3333 • gay-friendly • pool • jacuzzi • also restaurant/ bar

BOOKSTORES

Borders Bookstore & Cafe 4303 Nawiliwili Rd 808/246–0862 • 9am-10pm, till 11pm Fri-Sat, till 8pm Sun • large LGBT section

Poipu Beach

ACCOMMODATIONS

The Makahuena 1661 Pe'e Rd 808/742–2482, 800/367–5004 • gay/ straight • oceanside, resort condos • swimming • jacuzzi • nonsmoking rooms • kids ok • oceanside • $195-450

Poipu Plantation Resort 1792 Pe'e Rd, Poipu Beach 808/742–6757, 800/634–0263 • gay/ straight • rooms & cottages • full brkfst • hot tub • near beach • kids ok • gay-owned • $95-250

Princeville

ACCOMMODATIONS

Kauai Oceanfront Condo 5300 Ka Haku Rd (at Pali Ke Kua #220) 610/793–7539 • gay/ straight • nonsmoking • $1,350-1,500/week

Puunene

RESTAURANTS

Roy's Bar & Grill 2360 Kiahuna Plantation Dr 808/742–5000 • 5:30pm-9:30pm • Hawaiian fusion

Wailua

RESTAURANTS

Caffe Coco 4–369 Kuhio Hwy 808/822–7990 • lunch Tue-Fri, dinner nightly, clsd Mon • art gallery • live music nightly • patio

MAUI

Haiku

ACCOMMODATIONS

Halfway to Hana House 101 W Waipio Rd 808/572–1176 • gay/ straight • private guest studio w/ sunrise ocean view • nonsmoking • near waterfall & natural pool • woman-owned/ run • $85-105

Huelo Point Flower Farm 808/572–1850 • gay-friendly • vacation rentals • oceanfront estate & organic farm • swimming • 3 hot tubs • gay-owned • $170-450 + tax

Hana

ACCOMMODATIONS

Hale Ohia 49625 Hana Hwy (at mile marker 27) 808/248–7045 • gay/ straight • rental home • hot tub • $210-750

Hana Accommodations 808/248–7868, 800/228–4262 • gay/ straight • studios & tropical cottages • kids ok • gay-owned • $68-150

Hana Alii Holidays 808/248–7742, 800/548–0478 • reservations service

Heavenly Flora 70 Maia Rd (Ulaino Rd) 808/879–5445, 800/822–4409 • gay-friendly • private rental home • panoramic ocean views • swimming • nonsmoking • gay-owned • $120-195

Na Pualani 'Ohana 808/248–8935, 800/628–7092 • gay/ straight • studios & suites • ocean & mtn views • nonsmoking rooms available • kids/ pets ok • lanai • wheelchair access • gay-owned • $60-85

Huelo

ACCOMMODATIONS

Cliff's Edge 808/572–4530, 800/262–6284 • gay-friendly • rental homes, suites & cottages • $145-325

Huelo Point Lookout 808/573–0914 • gay-friendly • private cottages • full kitchens • swimming • hot tub • $175-550

Kaanapali

ACCOMMODATIONS

The Royal Lahaina Resort 2780 Kekaa Dr **808/661-3611, 800/447-6925** • gay-friendly • full-service resort • restaurants • swimming • wheelchair access • $149-790

Kapalua

RESTAURANTS

Vino 2000 Village Rd **808/661-8466** • lunch & dinner • Italian • good wine selection

Kihei

INFO LINES & SERVICES

AA Gay/ Lesbian Kalama Park South Pavilion **808/874-3589** • 7:30am Sun

ACCOMMODATIONS

Andrea's Maui Condos **800/289-1522, 877/445-5885** • gay/ straight • 1 & 2-bdrm beachfront condos • full brkfst • swimming • nonsmoking • wheelchair access • lesbian-owned

▲ **Anfora's Dreams** 323/467-2991, **800/788-5046** • gay/ straight • rental condo near ocean • hot tub • swimming • gay-owned • $89-135

Best Western Maui Oceanfront Inn 2980 S Kihei Rd **808/879-7744, 800/263-3387** • gay/ straight • hotel • kids ok • $99-234

Eva Villa 815 Kumulani Dr **808/874-6407, 800/884-1845** • gay-friendly • B&B • near Wailea beaches • hot tub • swimming • kids over 12yrs ok • wheelchair access • $135-155

Hale Kumulani (House at the Horizon) 808/891-0425 • gay-friendly • private cottage w/ gardens • near beaches • nonsmoking • $125 (waterfall suite) & $145 (garden cottage)

Jack & Tom's Maui Condos/ Maui Suncoast Realty 808/874-1048, 800/800-8608 • gay/ straight • fully equipped condos & apts • nonsmoking rooms available • gay-owned • $60-200

Ko'a Kai Rentals 1993 S Kihei Rd #401 **808/879-6058, 800/399-6058 x33** • gay/ straight • swimming • nonsmoking • gay-owned • $45 day/ $275 weekly

Koa Lagoon 800 S Kihei Rd **808/879–3002, 800/367–8030** • gay-friendly • oceanfront suites • swimming • wheelchair access • $110-170

Maui Sunseeker Resort 551 S Kihei Rd (at Wailana Place) **808/879–1261, 800/532–6432** • mostly men • ocean views • nonsmoking • gay-owned • $85-205

Two Mermaids on Maui B&B 2840 Umalu Pl **808/874–8687, 800/598–9550** • gay/straight • jacuzzi • swimming • near beach • nonsmoking • $115-140

NIGHTCLUBS

Ultra-Fabulous Tuesdays at Hapa's Brew Haus 41 E Lipoa St (in Lipoa Center) **808/879–9001** • 8pm-2am Tue only • lesbians/gay men • dancing/DJ

CAFES

Stella Blues 1215 S Kihei Rd **808/874–3779** • 7:30am-10pm

SPIRITUAL GROUPS

Dignity Maui **808/874–3950** • contact Ron

EROTICA

The Love Shack 1913 S Kihei Rd **808/875–0303** • intimate apparel • DVDs • gifts

Kula

ACCOMMODATIONS

The Upcountry B&B 4925 Lower Kula Rd (at Copp St), Kula **808/878–8083** • gay-friendly • jacuzzi • pets ok • $125

Lahaina

RESTAURANTS

Lahaina Coolers 180 Dickenson St **808/661–7082** • 8am-2am • international • patio • women-owned/run

RETAIL SHOPS

Skin Deep Tattoo 626 Front St (across from the Banyan Tree) **808/661–8531** • 10am-10pm, till 8pm Sun

Makawao

ACCOMMODATIONS

Hale Ho'okipa Inn B&B 32 Pakani Pl **808/572–6698, 877/572–6698** • gay-friendly • restored Hawaiian plantation home • also Kipa Cottage (1-bdrm + loft) • nonsmoking • wheelchair access • woman-owned • $95-165 + tax; cottage: $160/ night & $2,900/ month

I Ke Kala 3675 Brewer, Makawao **808/572–0664, 877/787–4440** • mostly women • also holistic healing & tour services • nonsmoking • wheelchair access • lesbian-owned • $70-80

RESTAURANTS

Casanova Restaurant & Deli 1188 Makawao Ave **808/572–0220** • lunch & dinner • Italian • full bar till 2am • gay-friendly • ladies night Wed • live music & shows Wed-Sat

Makena

ENTERTAINMENT & RECREATION

Little Beach at Makena • lesbians/gay men • Pilani Hwy south to Wailea • right at Wailea Ike Dr • left on Wailea Alanui Dr to public beach • then take trail up hill at end of beach

Pukalani

ACCOMMODATIONS

Heavenly Gate Vacation Rental 276 Hiwalani Loop (at Iolani St) **808/276–2917, 808/276–5783** • gay/ straight • bungalow home • tropical gardens • kids ok • nonsmoking • gay-owned • $100-200

Wailea

CAFES

Maui Rainbow Factory near Little Beach at Makena (1 mile S of Maui Prince Hotel) • shave ice • fresh fruit smoothies • vegetarian food • gay-owned

Wailuku

ACCOMMODATIONS

Maluhia Kai Guesthouse **808/283–8966** • women only • ocean view • hot tub • swimming • 2 campsites ($35/ night) • lesbian-owned • $95

SPIRITUAL GROUPS

Aloha MCC 2371 Vineyard St (at Iao Congregational Church) **808/283–8483** • noon Sun

EROTICA

Paradise Spice 1010 Lower Main #B **808/249–2449** • toys, magazines, DVDs

MOLOKAI

Kamalo

ACCOMMODATIONS

Wavecrest Oceanfront Condo
808/218–0408 • gay/ straight • 1-bdrm •
oceanfront • swimming • kids ok • lesbian-
owned • $75/ night, $473/ week

OAHU

INFO LINES & SERVICES

Lesbian Info Line 808/531–4140 •
recording of upcoming events

PUBLICATIONS

GayHawaii.com 808/923–2400 • travel,
entertainment and community information

Odyssey Magazine Hawaii 808/955–5959
• everything you need to know about gay
Hawaii

Aiea

EROTICA

C 'n' N Liquor Aiea Shopping Center
808/487–2944

Honolulu

INFO LINES & SERVICES

Gay/ Lesbian AA 277 Ohua (at Waikiki
Health Center) 808/946–1438 • 8pm daily

The Gay/ Lesbian Community Center
2424 S Beretania (btwn Isenberg & University)
808/951–7000 • 10am-7pm, clsd wknds •
lesbian support group 7:30pm Wed • also
library • church • home of Marriage Project
Hawaii

Leis of Hawaii 888/534–7644 •
personalized Hawaiian greeting service
complete w/ fresh flower leis

ACCOMMODATIONS

Aqua Palms at Waikiki 1850 Ala Moana
Blvd (at Kalia & Ena) 808/947–7256,
866/406–2782 • gay-friendly • swimming •
kids ok • nonsmoking • wheelchair access •
$116-375

Breakers Hotel 250 Beachwalk
808/923–3181, 800/426–0494 • gay-friendly •
swimming • also bar & grill • $96-171

The Cabana at Waikiki 2551 Cartwright Rd
(off Kapahulu Ave) 808/926–5555,
877/902–2121 • popular • mostly gay men •
1-bdrm suites w/ kitchens & lanais • hot tub •
gay-owned • $129-175

Nui Kai 719/783–2331 • lesbians/ gay men •
oceanfront/ Gold Coast condo • swimming •
nonsmoking • wheelchair access • gay-owned
• $250-300

Outrigger Hotels & Resorts 808/921–6600,
800/688–7444 • gay-friendly • many Waikiki
properties

Queen's Surf Vacation Rentals 134
Kapahulu (at Lemon Rd, in Waikiki Grand
Hotel) 808/923–1814, 888/336–4368 • gay/
straight • swimming • ocean views • kids ok •
nonsmoking • gay, lesbian & straight-owned/
run • $70-145

ResortQuest Coconut Plaza Hotel 450
Lewers St (at Ala Wai, Waikiki) 808/923–8828,
866/774–2924 • gay-friendly • boutique hotel
in the heart of Waikiki • near the Kuhio (gay)
District• swimming • kitchenettes • wheelchair
access

ResortQuest Waikiki Joy Hotel 320 Lewers
St (at Kalakaua Ave, Waikiki) 808/923–2300,
866/774–2924 • gay-friendly • boutique hotel
• swimming • jacuzzis • near beach • cafe •
also bar • karaoke • wheelchair access

Waikiki GLBT Vacation Rentals 2092
Kuhio Ave #1903 808/922–1659,
800/543–5663 • gay-friendly • reservation
service • ask for Walt Flood • nonsmoking •
$65-125

BARS

Angles 2256 Kuhio Ave, 2nd flr (at Seaside,
Waikiki) 808/926–9766, 808/923–1130
(INFOLINE) • 10am-2am • lesbians/ gay men •
neighborhood bar • dancing/DJ Wed-Sun • live
shows • videos • theme nights • free internet
access

Hula's Bar & Lei Stand 134 Kapahulu Ave
(2nd flr of Waikiki Grand Hotel) 808/923–0669
• 10am-2am • popular • lesbians/ gay men •
dancing/DJ • theme nights • transgender-
friendly • food served • live shows • videos •
young crowd • weekly catamaran cruise

In Between 2155 Lau'ula St (off Lewers,
across from Planet Hollywood, Waikiki)
808/926–7060 • 2pm-2am • mostly gay men•
neighborhood bar • karaoke

Nightclubs

Black Garter Cafe 1192 Alakea St (at Beretania, at Detox) **808/531–4140 x2** • 9pm-2am Fri • mostly women • dancing/DJ • wheelchair access

Fusion Waikiki 2260 Kuhio Ave, upstairs (at Seaside) **808/924–2422** • 9pm-4am, from 8pm Fri-Sat, from 10pm Sun • popular • mostly gay men • dancing/DJ • alternative • transgender-friendly • live shows • karaoke • videos

Cafes

Caffe Giovannini 1888 Kalakaua Ave (across from the Wave, Waikiki) **808/979–2299** • 8am-11:30pm, till 10pm wknds • great coffee • sandwiches & desserts • patio • gay-owned

Mocha Java Cafe 1200 Ala Moana Blvd (in Ward Center) **808/591–9023** • 7am-9pm, till 10pm Fri-Sat, till 6pm Sun • plenty veggie

Restaurants

Café Che Pasta 1001 Bishop St, Ste 108 (enter off Alakea St) **808/524–0004, 808/531–4140 (INFO LINE)** • lunch & dinner Mon-Fri, clsd wknds • full bar

Cafe Sistina 1314 S King St **808/596–0061** • lunch Mon-Fri, dinner nightly • northern Italian • some veggie • full bar • wheelchair access

Eggs 'n' Things 1911–B Kalakaua Ave **808/949–0820** • 11pm-2pm • diner • popular after-hours

Indigo 1121 Nu'uanu Ave **808/521–2900** • lunch Tue-Fri, dinner Tue-Sat • Eurasian • live music Tue

Keo's In Waikiki 2375 Kuhio Ave **808/951–9355** • 7am-2pm & 5pm-10:30pm • popular • reservations advised

La Cucaracha 102 Nahua (at Kuhio Ave) **808/922–2288** • 12pm-11pm • Mexican • full bar

Singha Thai 1910 Ala Moana Blvd **808/941–2898** • 4pm-11pm • live shows

Honolulu

WHERE THE GIRLS ARE:
Where else? On the beach. Or cruising Kuhio Ave.

LGBT PRIDE:
June, web:
www.thecenterhawaii.org.

ANNUAL EVENTS:
April - Merrie Monarch Festival, hula competition in Hilo, web: www.kalena.com/merriemonarch.
May - Gay & Lesbian Film Festival 808/381–1952, web: www.hglcf.org.
April-May - Golden Week, celebration of Japanese culture
September - Aloha Festival, web: alohafestivals.com.

CITY INFO:
808/923-1811, web:
www.gohawaii.com.

BEST VIEW:
Helicopter tour.

WEATHER:
Usually paradise perfect, but humid. It rarely gets hotter than the upper 80ºs.

TRANSIT:
Charley's 808/531–1333.
The Bus 808/848-5555, web:
www.thebus.org.

ATTRACTIONS:
Bishop Museum 808/847-3511, web: www.bishopmuseum.org.
Foster Botanical Gardens. web: www.hawaiimuseums.org/mc/isoahu_foster.htm.
Hanauma Bay.
Honolulu Academy of Arts 808/532-8700, web: www.honoluluacademy.org.
Polynesian Cultural Center 800/367-7060 or 808/293-3333, web: www.polynesia.com.
Waimea Falls Park.

Reply **Forward**   **Delete**

Date: Nov 15, 2005 11:11:59
From: Girl-on-the-Go
To: Editor@Damron.com
Subject: Honolulu

>The city of Honolulu suffers from a bad case of multiple identities. The high-rise tourist hotels of Waikiki, six miles away, overshadow the downtown area of Honolulu, the center of the state government that teems with a vibrant culture all its own. Chinatown, a designated National Historic Landmark, offers a living history of Asian immigration to Hawaii, with street vendors, grocers, herbalists, and acupuncture clinics. Authentic Chinese, Vietnamese, and Filipino restaurants cram the area north of downtown, off of North King Street.

>On the other side of downtown, on South King Street, sits 'Iolani Palace, the heart and soul of modern Hawaiian history. The graceful structure served as a prison for Queen Lili'uokalani, Hawaii's last reigning monarch, when she was placed under house arrest by armed US forces intent on her signing over the nation's sovereignty. Don't miss the Hawaii Maritime Center next door for a glance back at the history of the islands. If you're staying in Waikiki, you can catch a trolley downtown from any of the main streets, saving yourself a mountain of parking headaches.

>Waikiki sits on the southwest corner of Oahu and offers a mind-boggling number of hotels, restaurants, and shops that are just waiting to consume your tourist dollars. Campy though it is, enjoy the postcard pleasure of a mai tai on the veranda of the magnificently restored Sheraton Moana Surfrider while the sun sets over the Pacific. **Hula's,** a neighborhood bar with a homey feel, is the most welcoming of the local bars. On Friday's, head over to Detox for the weekly lesbian dance party **Black Garter Cafe**. If you want to shake it with the boys, you can dance the night away at **Fusion Waikiki**, or at **Angles**.

>**Odyssey Magazine** gives boys the dirt on the club scene. Occasionally, they have something for women. Also helpful for fun-finding is the monthly **DaKine**. You can pick either of these up, along with a good book to read on the beach, at the LGBT shop **Eighty Percent Straight.**

>If you'd like to see the Big Island from offshore, give lesbian-owned **Rainbow Sailing Charters** a call. They offer whale-watching cruises, snorkeling, and commitment ceremonies.

Tryst Restaurant & Lanai Bar 407 Seaside, 2nd flr (at Kuhio Ave) **808/921-2288** • 6pm-11pm, also Sun brunch 9am-1pm • East-West fusion • some veggie • live entertainment Fri • lanai • gay-owned

ENTERTAINMENT & RECREATION

Honolulu Gay/ Lesbian Cultural Foundation 1877 Kalakaua Ave **808/381-1952** • last wknd of May/ first of June is annual Honolulu Rainbow Film Festival • art exhibits • concerts • plays • call for events

LikeHike 808/455-8193 • gay hiking tours every other Sun • also gay kayaking trips • call for info & locations

Rainbow Sailing Charters 808/396-5995 • lesbians/ gay men • whale-watching • snorkeling • sunset cocktail cruises • commitment ceremonies • lesbian-owned

RETAIL SHOPS

Eighty Percent Straight 134 Kapahulu Ave (at Waikiki Grand Hotel) **808/956-1411** • 10am-10pm, till midnight Fri-Sat, noon-10pm Sun • LGBT clothing • books • videos • cards • toys

PUBLICATIONS

DaKine Magazine 808/923-7378 • LGBT newsmagazine for Oahu • club & nightlife listings • monthly

Odyssey Magazine Hawaii 808/955-5959 • everything you need to know about gay Hawaii

SPIRITUAL GROUPS

Dignity Honolulu 539 Kapahulu Ave (at St Mark's Church) **808/536-5536** • 7:30pm 2nd & last Sun

Interweave 808/623-4726 • Unitarian Universalists • call for meeting times

Unity Church of Hawaii 3608 Diamond Head Cir (at Montserrat) **808/735-4436** • 7:30am, 9am & 11am Sun • wheelchair access

EROTICA

Diamond Head Video 870 Kapahulu Ave (near Genki Sushi) **808/735-6066** • 24hrs

Velvet Video 2155 Lau'ula St, 2nd flr (above In Between, Waikiki) **808/924-0868** • videos for sale & rent • preview booths • toys

Windward Coast

ACCOMMODATIONS

Ali'i Bluffs Windward B&B 46-251 Ikiiki St, Kane'ohe **808/235-1124, 800/235-1151** • gay/ straight • swimming • nonsmoking • gay-owned • $65-80

IDAHO

Statewide

PUBLICATIONS

Diversity Newsmagazine 208/336-3870 #2 • statewide LGBT newspaper • monthly

Boise

INFO LINES & SERVICES

AA Gay/ Lesbian 23rd & Woodlawn (at First Congregational Church) **208/344-6611** • 8pm Sun, 7pm Tue

The Community Center 919-A N 27th St (at Jordan) **208/336-3870** • volunteer staff • 24hr info line

BARS

The Lucky Dog 1108 Front St (at 11th) **208/333-0074** • 5pm-close, 2pm-2am Sun • lesbians/ gay men • neighborhood bar • patio

NIGHTCLUBS

The Balcony Club 180 N 8th St #224 (at Idaho) **208/336-1313** • 2pm-2am • gay/ straight • popular • dancing/DJ • theme nights • wheelchair access • gay-owned

Emerald City Club 415 S 9th St (at Borah) **208/342-5446** • 10am-2am • lesbians/ gay men • dancing/DJ from 10pm • transgender-friendly • drag shows • wheelchair access

CAFES

Flying M Coffeehouse 500 W Idaho (at 5th St) **208/345-4320** • 6:30am-11pm, 7:30am-6pm Sun

RESTAURANTS

The Klatsch 409 S 8th (across from 8th St Marketplace) **208/345-0452** • brkfst, lunch & dinner, till 3pm Sun-Mon • organic & plenty veggie • live music evenings & wknds • beer/ wine

ENTERTAINMENT & RECREATION

The Flicks 646 Fulton St **208/342-4288** • opens 4pm, from noon wknds • 4 movie theaters • food served • beer/ wine • patio • wheelchair access

BOOKSTORES

Crone's Cupboard 712 N Orchard **208/333-0831** • 10am-7pm, 11am-5pm Sun • feminist/ lesbian books & art

RETAIL SHOPS

The Edge 1101 W Idaho St (at 11th) **208/344-5383** • 6:30am-10pm, 9am-7pm Sun • gifts • LGBT magazines • also cafe

SPIRITUAL GROUPS

Treasure Valley MCC 408 N Garden St (at Morris Hill) **208/342-6764** • 5:45pm Sun

EROTICA

Pleasure Boutique 5022 Fairview (at Orchard) **208/433-1161** • toys, videos

Coeur d'Alene

see also Spokane, Washington

ACCOMMODATIONS

The Clark House on Hayden Lake 5250 E Hayden Lake Rd, Hayden Lake **208/772-3470, 800/765-4593** • popular • gay-friendly • mansion on a wooded 12-acre estate • full brkfst • also fine dining • hot tub • nonsmoking • gay-owned • $125-275

BARS

Mik-N-Mak's 406 N 4th (at Wallace) **208/667-4858** • 4pm-2am, from noon wknds • gay/ straight • neighborhood bar • dancing/DJ • karaoke • live shows

Lava Hot Springs

see also Pocatello

ACCOMMODATIONS

Lava Hot Springs Inn **208/776-5830, 800/527-5830** • gay-friendly • full brkfst • mineral pools • kids/ pets ok • nonsmoking • wheelchair access • $69-195

BOOKSTORES

Aura Soma Lava 196 E Main St **208/776-5800, 800/757-1233** • open wknds, also open 10am-5pm weekdays during summer • metaphysical & LGBT books

Moscow

BOOKSTORES

Bookpeople 521 S Main (btwn 5th & 6th) **208/882-7957** • 9am-8pm • general

Pocatello

NIGHTCLUBS

Charleys 331 E Center **208/232-9606** • 5pm-2am, from 7pm Sun • lesbians/ gay men • dancing/DJ • live shows • wheelchair access

CAFES

Main St Coffee & News 234 N Main (btwn Lander & Clark) **208/234-9834** • 7am-5pm, till 4pm Sat, from 4pm Sun

EROTICA

The Silver Fox 143 S 2nd St (at Center) **208/234-2477**

ILLINOIS

Statewide

PUBLICATIONS

Prairie Flame 217/753-2887 • LGBT newspaper for downstate IL

Alton

see also St Louis, Missouri

NIGHTCLUBS

Bubby & Sissy's 602 Belle (at 6th) **618/465-4773** • 3pm-2am, till 3am Fri-Sat • lesbians/ gay men • dancing/DJ • drag shows • karaoke • wheelchair access

Arlington Heights

see Chicago

Aurora

see also Chicago

EROTICA

Denmark Book Store 1300 US Hwy 30 (2 miles S of Rte 34) **630/898-9838** • 24hrs

Belleville

SPIRITUAL GROUPS

Well of Living Water Ministries 403 N Illinois St **618/277-7497** • 10am Sun

Bloomington

INFO LINES & SERVICES

Connections Community Center 313 N Main St (at Monroe St) **309/827-2437** • 24hr recorded info, staffed 7pm-10pm Mon-Fri, youth group 7:30pm-10:30pm Fri, men's group 7:30pm-10:30pm Sat

BARS

Bistro 316 N Main St (at Jefferson) **309/829-2278** • 8pm-1am, till 2am Fri-Sat • lesbians/ gay men • dancing/DJ Wed-Sat • wheelchair access

SPIRITUAL GROUPS

Unitarian Universalist Church of Bloomington 1613 E Emerson **309/828-0235** • 9:30am & 11am Sun, 10:30am summers

Blue Island

NIGHTCLUBS

The Edge 13126 S Western (at Grove)
708/597-8379 • 8pm-2am, till 3am Fri-Sat,
from 4pm Sun, clsd Mon • lesbians/ gay men
• neighborhood bar • dancing/DJ •
transgender-friendly • cabaret • drag shows
• wheelchair access

Brookfield

SPIRITUAL GROUPS

Holy Covenant MCC 9145 Grant Ave
708/387-1611 • 9am & 11am Sun •
wheelchair access

Calumet City

see also Chicago & Hammond, Indiana

BARS

Dick's R U Crazee 48 154th Pl (at Forsythe)
708/862-4605 • 7pm-2am, from 9pm Mon, till
3am Wed, Fri-Sat • mostly gay men •
neighborhood bar

John L's Place 335 154th Pl **708/862-2386** •
7pm-close • lesbians/ gay men •
neighborhood bar • transgender-friendly •
wheelchair access

The Patch 201 155th St (at Wentworth)
708/891-9854 • 4pm-2am, from noon Th,
7pm-3am Sat, clsd Sun-Wed • mostly women
• neighborhood bar • dancing/DJ • live shows
• karaoke • women-owned/ run

NIGHTCLUBS

Pour House 103 155th Pl (at Forsythe)
708/891-3980 • 8pm-2am, till 3am Wed, Fri-
Sat, clsd Tue • gay/ straight • dancing/DJ

Carbondale

INFO LINES & SERVICES

AA Lesbian/ Gay 618/549-4633

NIGHTCLUBS

The Upside Downtown 213 E Main St
618/549-4270 • 9pm-2am, clsd Mon-Tue & Th
• gay-friendly • neighborhood bar • dancing/DJ
• live shows • videos • gay-owned

Champaign/Urbana

INFO LINES & SERVICES

AA Lesbian/ Gay 217/367-4413,
217/367-4349

NIGHTCLUBS

Chester Street 63 Chester St (at Water St),
Champaign **217/356-5607** • 5pm-2am •
lesbians/ gay men • dancing/DJ • drag show
Sun • gay-owned • wheelchair access

CAFES

Espresso Royale 602 E Daniel (at 6th St),
Champaign **217/328-1112** • 7am-11pm

RESTAURANTS

Boltini Lounge 211 N Neil, Champaign
217/378-8001 • dinner only • also full bar •
upscale

Fiesta Cafe 216 S 1st St (at White, near U of
IL campus), Champaign **217/352-5902** •
11am-1am • Mexican • gay-owned

BOOKSTORES

Jane Addams Book Shop 208 N Neil (at
University) **217/356-2555** • 10am-5pm from
1pm Sun • full-service antiquarian bookstore
w/ children's room • LGBT & women's sections

CHICAGO

**Chicago is divided into 5 geographical
areas:**
Chicago—Overview
Chicago—North Side
Chicago—Boystown/ Lakeview
Chicago—Near North
Chicago—South Side

Chicago—Overview

INFO LINES & SERVICES

AA Gay/ Lesbian Boystown Alano Club
909 W Belmont Ave, 2nd flr (btwn Clark &
Sheffield) **773/529-0321** • 5pm-11pm, from
8:30am wknds • wheelchair access

Horizons Community Services
961 W Montana (at Fullerton & Sheffield)
773/472-6469 • 9am-10pm, till 5pm Fri,
11am-3pm Sat, clsd Sun

ACCOMMODATIONS

Chicago Park Hotel 17040 S Halsted (off
I-80), Harvey **708/596-1500** • gay-friendly •
kids ok • swimming • 30 minutes from
Chicago • $33-50

Chicago Sisters' Place 1957 S Spaulding
Ave (at S 21st) **773/542-9126** • women-only •
furnished rooms in women's residence •
please call ahead • lesbian-owned • $45-55

NIGHTCLUBS

Chix Mix Productions • occasional parties
• mostly women • dancing/ DJ • call for info

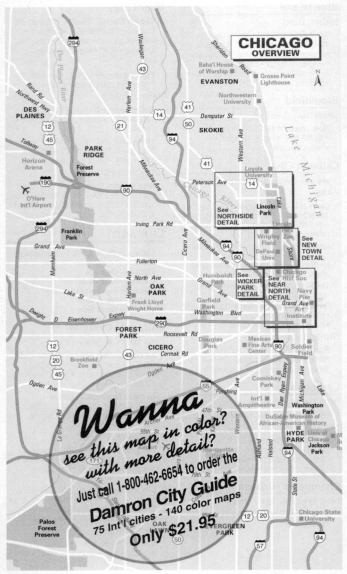

Hunters Night Club 1932 E Higgins (at Busse), Elk Grove Village **847/439-8840** • 4pm-4am • popular • mostly gay men • dancing/DJ • transgender-friendly • live entertainment • karaoke • videos • patio • wheelchair access

ENTERTAINMENT & RECREATION

Artemis Singers 773/764-4465 • lesbian feminist chorus

Bailiwick Arts Center 1229 W Belmont 773/883-1090 • many LGBT-themed productions w/ popular Pride Series & Lesbian Theater Initiative

Cafe Pride 716 W Addison (at Broadway, at Lakeview Presbyterian) **773/784-2635** • 8pm-midnight Fri • LGBT coffeehouse • for youth only

Chicago Neighborhood Tours 77 E Randolph St 312/742-1190 • gay-friendly • the best way to make the Windy City your kind of town

The Hancock Observatory 875 N Michigan Ave (in John Hancock Center) **888/875-8439** • renovated 94th-flr observatory w/ outside Skywalk

Leather Archives & Museum 6418 N Greenview 773/761-9200

The Neo-Futurarium 5153 N Ashland Ave 773/275-5255 • alternative theater group

Sears Tower Skydeck 233 S Wacker Dr (enter at Jackson Blvd) 312/875-9696 • see the city from one of the world's tallest buildings

PUBLICATIONS

The Alternative Phone Book 619 W Stratford Pl 773/472-6319 • directory of local businesses

Chicago Free Press 773/325-0005 • LGBT newspaper

Gay Chicago 773/327-7271 • weekly • extensive resource listings

Identity 773/871-7610 • monthly news & features for LGBTs of color

Pink Pages 773/769-6328 • LGBT business directory & lifestyle magazine

Swirl Magazine 678/886-0711 (ATLANTA #) • magazine for "the African American lesbian, bisexual, bi-curious & 'straight but not narrow' community"

Windy City Times 773/871-7610 • weekly LGBT newspaper & weekly calendar guide

SPIRITUAL GROUPS

Congregation Or Chadash 5959 N Sheridan 773/271-2148 • call for Shabbat services & monthly activities

Dignity Chicago 3344 N Broadway (at Broadway United Methodist Church, in Lakeview) **312/458-9438** • mass & social hour 5pm Sun

MCC Good Shepherd 7045 N Western Ave 773/262-0099, 773/275-7776 • 11am Sun

Chicago—North Side

BARS

Big Chicks 5024 N Sheridan (btwn Foster & Argyle) 773/728-5511 • 4pm-2am, from 3pm wknds • lesbians/ gay men • neighborhood bar • dancing/DJ • videos • patio • Sun BBQ • wheelchair access

Charmer's Lounge 1502 W Jarvis (at Greenview) 773/465-2811 • 6pm-2am, from 4pm wknds, till 3am Sat • lesbians/ gay men • neighborhood bar

Chicago Eagle 5015 N Clark St (at Argyle) 773/728-0050 • 8pm-4am, till 5am Sat • lesbians/gay men • leather • dress code Tue, Fri-Sat • wheelchair access

Clark's on Clark 5001 N Clark St (at Argyle) 773/728-2373 • 2am-4am, till 5am Sat • popular • mostly gay men • neighborhood bar

Crew 4804 N Broadway (at Lawrence) 773/784-2739 • 11:30am-2am • lesbians/ gay men • sports bar • food served

El Gato Negro 1461 W Irving Park 773/472-9353 • 4pm-close, from 7pm Mon-Wed • gay/ straight • dancing/DJ • transgender-friendly • mostly Latino-American • live shows

Lost & Found 3058 W Irving Park Rd (at Albany) 773/463-7599 • 7pm-2am, clsd Mon (also Tue summers) • mostly women • neighborhood bar

Madrigal's 5316 N Clark St (at Balmoral) 773/334-3033 • 5pm-2am, till 3am Sat • lesbians/gay men • Latino/a clientele • karaoke Mon • strippers Tue-Sun

Scot's 1829 W Montrose (at Damen) 773/528-3253 • 3pm-2am, from 11am wknds • lesbians/ gay men • neighborhood bar

Star Gaze 5419 N Clark (at Foster) 773/561-7363 • 5pm-2am, till 3am Sat, from noon Sun • mostly women • neighborhood bar • theme nights • food served • live shows

Reply **Forward** **Delete**

Date: Nov 18, 2005 11:16:32
From: Girl-on-the-Go
To: Editor@Damron.com
Subject: Chicago

>Not just another big Midwestern city, it is The City of the Midwest. Even those who've never been know about its winters, gangsters, pizza, music, museums, universities, and sports teams. But what makes Chicago our kind of town is its patchwork of diverse communities—especially African Americans, artists and performers, and of course, lesbians and gay men.

>If you remember the Chicago 7, you might want to stop by the Heartland Cafe (773/465-8005) in Rogers Park for a drink, some food, or a T-shirt from their radical variety store. Or check in with **Horizons Community Services** to find out about local LGBT political and social groups.

>The African American communities in Chicago are large and influential, making up about 40 percent of Chicago's population. In fact, Chicago was settled by an African French man, whose name graces the Du Sable Museum of African American History (773/947-0600). The South Side is the cultural center for Chicagoans of African descent and houses the South Side Community Art Center (773/373-1026) and the Olivet Baptist Church, a station on the Underground Railroad and the site of Mahalia Jackson's 1928 debut. We've heard the homecooking at Army & Lou's Restaurant (773/483-3100) will make you stand up and holler.

> Many of Chicago's other immigrant neighborhoods also house the museums, centers, and restaurants the city is famous for—call the Chicago Office of Tourism for details. If you love Indian food, don't miss the many delicious and cheap Indian buffets on Devon, just west of Sheridan.

>What else is there to do? For starters, take a cruise on Lake Michigan. You have your choice of wine-tasting cruises, narrated history cruises, and brunch, dinner, or cocktail cruises. On land, you'll find superb shopping, real Chicago-style deep dish pizza, and a great arts and theater scene. Don't miss the thriving blues and jazz clubs, like the Green Mill (773/878-5552), known for originating "poetry slams" and for its house big band. On a sunny day, head down to "the Rocks," the popular waterfront hang-out off Lakeshore Drive, at Belmont Harbor.

Reply Forward   Delete

>And you'll never have a dull moment in Chicago's women's scene. A lot of it happens in Chicago's North Side. Here, you'll find **Women & Children First** bookstore where you can check out the books while the women check out you. Be sure to pick up copies of **Pink Pages, Chicago Free Press,** and **Windy City Times** for the dish on what's hot. Grab a bite to eat at lesbian-owned **Tomboy,** then check out one of the North Side's two women's bars—**Lost & Found** and **Star Gaze**—or one of the mixed bars—our fave, **Big Chicks.** If you want something calmer and more sister-centered, then spend your Saturday at **Mountain Moving Coffeehouse,** a landmark in Chicago's womyn's scene.

>And while New Town may be known as "Boys' Town," sisters can be found getting down with their gay brothers at **Berlin** or the **Closet.** Or get the dish on current women's nightclub events by calling **Chix Mix Productions** (773/ 583-5049).

Touché 6412 N Clark St (at Devon) **773/465-7400** • 5pm-4am, from 3pm Sat, from noon Sun • popular • mostly gay men • leather

NIGHTCLUBS

Atmosphere 5355 N Clark (at W Balmoral Ave) **773/784-1100** • 3pm-2am, till 3am Sat • lesbians/ gay men • more women Fri • dancing/DJ • gay-owned

Chix Mix 5355 N Clark (at W Balmoral Ave) **773/784-1100 (CLUB #)** • Fri only • mostly women • dancing/DJ

RESTAURANTS

Chicago Diner 3411 N Halsted St **773/935-6696** • 11am-10pm, from 10am wknds • hip & vegetarian • beer/ wine

Deluxe Diner 6349 N Clark St (at Devon) **773/743-9900** • 24hrs

Fireside 5739 N Ravenswood (at Rosehill) **773/878-5942** • 11am-4am, from 10am Sun • Cajun & pizza • patio • full bar

South 5900 N Broadway **773/989-7666** • dinner nightly, Southern

Speakeasy Supper Club 1401 W Devon (at Glenwood) **773/378-0600** • dinner nightly • live music • full bar

Tendino's 5335 N Sheridan (at Broadway) **773/275-8100** • 11am-11pm, till midnight wknds • pizza • full bar • wheelchair access

Tomboy 5402 N Clark (at Balmoral) **773/907-0636** • 5pm-10pm, till 11pm wknds, clsd Sun • popular • full bar • wheelchair access • lesbian-owned

Topolobampo/ Frontera Grill 445 N Clark St **312/661-1434** • lunch & dinner, Sat brunch, clsd Sun • Mexican

Tweet 5020 N Sheridan Rd **773/728-5576** • dinner Tue-Sat, wknd brunch • cash only

Unique So Chique Tea & Chocolate Room 4600 N Magnolia, Ste C (entrance on Wilson, next to Starbucks) **773/561-0324** • lunch 11:30am-3pm, tea service 3pm-5pm, brunch 10am-2:30pm wknds, clsd Mon • also hosts special gay events like Gay-i-Tea

ENTERTAINMENT & RECREATION

Hollywood Beach at Hollywood & Sheridan Sts • popular • "the" gay beach

Mountain Moving Coffeehouse 1700 W Farragut (in basement of Summerdale church) **312/409-0276** • 7:30pm some Sats, check gay papers for dates • women & girls only • nonalcoholic beverages • live shows • collectively run

BOOKSTORES

KOPI: A Traveler's Cafe 5317 N Clark St (at Summerdale) 773/989–5674 • 8am-11pm, till midnight Fri, from 9am Sat, from 10am Sun • live shows • also boutique & gallery • mostly veggie • soup, sandwiches, pastries

Women & Children First 5233 N Clark St (at Foster) 773/769–9299, 888/923–7323 • 11am-7pm, till 9pm Wed-Fri, from 10am Sat, till 6pm Sun • wheelchair access • women-owned/ run

RETAIL SHOPS

Gay Mart 3457 N Halsted St (at Cornelius) 773/929–4272 • 11am-7pm, noon-8pm wknds

Mephisto Leathers 3922 N Broadway (at Irving Park) 773/549–0900, 800/910–0666 • noon-8pm, clsd Sun • also at 6410 N Clark, 773/262-9938 • gay-owned

Specialty Video Films 5307 N Clark St (at Foster) 773/878–3434 • 10am-10pm, till 11pm Fri-Sat • foreign, cult, art house, LGBT & erotic videos • gay-owned

Chicago

WHERE THE GIRLS ARE:
In the Belmont area—on Halsted or Clark streets—with the boys, or hanging out elsewhere in Boystown. Upwardly-mobile lesbians live in Lincoln Park or Wrigleyville, while their working-class sisters live in Andersonville (way north).

LGBT PRIDE:
June. 773/348-8243, web: www.chicagopridecalendar.org.

ANNUAL EVENTS:
February - Fireball circuit party 773/244-6000, web: www.thefireball.com.
March - Women's Film Festival 773/235-4301, web: www.widc.org.
May - International Mr. Leather 800/545-6753. Weekend of events and contest on Sunday, web: www.imrl.com.
Bear Pride 773/509-5135, web: www.GLBears.com.
May-June- Chicago Blues Festival 312/744-3370.
August - Northalsted Market Days 773/303-0167, web: www.northalsted.com/daze.htm.
November - Chicago Lesbian & Gay Film Festival 773/293-1447, web: www.reelingfilmfestival.org.

CITY INFO:
Chicago Office of Tourism 312/744-2400. web: www.chicago.il.org.

ATTRACTIONS:
900 North Michigan Shops.
The Art Institute of Chicago 312/443-3600, web: www.artic.edu.
Historic Water Tower.
Museum of Science and Industry 773/684-1414, web: www.msichicago.org.
Sears Tower Skydeck Observatory 312/875-9696, web: www.sears-tower.com.
Second City & the Improv Comedy Clubs.

BEST VIEW:
Skydeck of the 110-story Sears Tower, web: www.sears-tower.com.

WEATHER:
"The Windy City" earned its name. Winter temperatures have been known to be as low as -46°. Summers are humid, normally in the 80°s.

TRANSIT:
Yellow Cab 312/ 829-4222.
Continental Airport Express 888/284-3826.
Chicago Transit Authority 312/836-7000, web: www.transitchicago.com.
Metra Rail, web: www.metrarail.com.

Unique So Chique Boutique 4600 N Magnolia, Ste C (entrance on Wilson, next to Starbucks) 773/561-0324 • 11:30am-7:30pm, 10am-6pm Sat, till 5pm Sun, clsd Mon • clothing & accessories for men & women • gifts for kids & babies • also tea & chocolate room • serves lunch, brunch & tea

GYMS & HEALTH CLUBS

Cheetah Gym 5248 N Clark St (at Foster) 773/728-7777

EROTICA

Early to Bed 5232 N Sheridan Rd (at Foster) 773/271-1219, 866/585-2424 • clsd Mon • transgender-friendly • 18+ • lesbian-owned

Chicago—Boystown/ Lakeview

ACCOMMODATIONS

Best Western Hawthorne Terrace 3434 N Broadway (at Hawthorne Pl) 773/244-3434, 888/675-2378 • gay-friendly • located in the heart of Chicago's gay community • wheelchair access • $139+

City Suites Hotel 933 W Belmont Ave (btwn Clark & Sheffield) 773/404-3400, 800/248-9108 • gay-friendly • European style • nonsmoking rooms available • $139-189

Inn at Lincoln Park 601 W Diversey Pkwy (at N Clark St) 773/348-2810, 866/774-7275 • gay/ straight • vintage Victorian inn in Lincoln Park • straight & gay-owned • $85-225

Majestic Hotel 528 W Brompton Ave (at Addison) 773/404-3499, 800/727-5108 • gay-friendly • romantic 19th-c atmosphere • nonsmoking rooms available • $139-209

Villa Toscana B&B 3447 N Halsted St 773/404-2643, 800/404-2643 • lesbians/ gay men • 1890s coach house • nonsmoking • wheelchair access • gay-owned • $99-149

The Willows 555 W Surf St (at Broadway) 773/528-8400, 800/787-3108 • gay/ straight • 19th-c French flair • nonsmoking rooms available • $89-189

BARS

Annex 3 3160 N Clark St (at Belmont) 773/327-5969 • noon-2am, till 3am Sat • lesbians/ gay men • neighborhood bar • wheelchair access

Beat Kitchen 2100 W Belmont (btwn Hoyne & Damen) 773/281-4444 • 4pm-2am, from noon wknds • gay-friendly • live music • also grill • some veggie • wheelchair access

Berlin 954 W Belmont (at Sheffield) 773/348-4975 • 5pm-4am, from 8pm Sun-Mon • popular • lesbians/ gay men • dancing/DJ • women's night Wed • transgender-friendly • live shows • videos • wheelchair access

Blues 2519 N Halsted 773/528-1012, 773/549-9436 • 8pm-2am, till 3am Sat • gay-friendly • popular • classic Chicago blues spot • live shows

Bobby Love's 3729 N Halsted St (at Waveland) 773/525-1200 • 3pm-2am, from noon wknds, till 3am Fri-Sat • lesbians/ gay men • neighborhood bar • karaoke • wheelchair access

Buck's Saloon 3439 N Halsted St (btwn Cornelia & Newport) 773/525-1125 • noon-2am • mostly gay men • neighborhood bar • patio

Cell Block 3702 N Halsted (at Waveland) 773/665-8064 • 4pm-2am, from 2pm wknds • mostly gay men • dancing/DJ • leather • also Holding Cell from 10pm Th-Sat • strict leather/ latex/ uniform code • wheelchair access

Charlie's Chicago 3726 N Broadway (btwn Waveland & Grace) 773/871-8887 • 2pm-4am, till 5am Sat • mostly gay men • dancing/DJ • country/ western • club music after 1am

The Closet 3325 N Broadway St (at Buckingham) 773/477-8533 • 2pm-4am, till 5am Sat, from noon wknds • popular • lesbians/ gay men • neighborhood bar • videos

Cocktail 3359 Halsted St (at Roscoe) 773/477-1420 • 4pm-2am, from 2pm wknds, till 3am Sat • lesbians/ gay men • neighborhood bar • dancing/ DJ • videos • wheelchair access

Gentry on Halsted 3320 N Halsted (at Aldine) 773/348-1053 • 4pm-2am, till 3am Sat • mostly gay men • upscale piano bar

Little Jim's 3501 N Halsted St (at Cornelia) 773/871-6116 • noon-4am, till 5am Sat • popular • mostly gay men • neighborhood bar

The Lucky Horseshoe Lounge 3169 N Halsted St (at Briar) 773/404-3169 • 4pm-2am, from 2pm wknds • mostly gay men • neighborhood bar • dancers nightly • patio

The North End 3733 N Halsted St (at Grace) 773/477-7999 • 3pm-2am, till 3am Sat, from 1pm wknds • mostly gay men • neighborhood sports bar • wheelchair access

Roscoe's 3354–56 N Halsted St (at W Roscoe) 773/281–3355 • 2pm-2am, noon-3am Sat • popular • lesbians/gay men • neighborhood bar • dancing/DJ • live shows • videos • 6 bars • patio cafe in summer

Spin 800 W Belmont (enter on Halsted) 773/327–7711 • 4pm-2am, till 3am Sat, from noon wknds • lesbians/gay men • dancing/DJ • live shows • videos • theme nights • 3 bars • lounge

NIGHTCLUBS

Boom Boom Room 2200 N Ashland (at Green Dolphin Street bar) 773/395–0066 • 11pm-4am Mon only • popular • mostly gay men • dancing/DJ • live shows • cover charge

Circuit/ Rehab 3641 N Halsted St (at Addison) 773/325–2233 • 9pm-4am, till 5am Sat, clsd Mon-Tue • mostly gay men • more women Fri • dancing/DJ • multiracial clientele • karaoke • live shows • drag king show last Fri • theme nights • Latin T-dance Sun

Hydrate 3458 N Halsted St (at Cornelia) 773/975–9244 • 4pm-4am, 2pm-5am Sat, from 1pm Sun • popular • gay/ straight • dancing/DJ • live entertainment

Smart Bar 3730 N Clark St (downstairs at the Metro) 773/549–4140 • 10pm-4am, till 5am Sat • gay-friendly • dancing/DJ • popular • goth Tue • punk Wed • house/ techno Th-Sat

CAFES

Pick Me Up Cafe & All Nite Express Lounge 3408 N Clark 773/248–6613 • 3pm-3am, 24hrs Fri-Sat • brkfst all day

RESTAURANTS

Angelina Ristorante 3561 N Broadway (at Addison) 773/935–5933 • 5:30pm-11pm, Sun brunch • Italian • full bar • wheelchair access

Ann Sather's 929 W Belmont Ave (at Sheffield) 773/348–2378 • 7am-9pm, till 3pm Mon-Tue • popular • Swedish diner & Boystown fixture

Cornelia's 750 W Cornelia Ave (at Halsted) 773/248–8333 • dinner, clsd Mon • some veggie • upscale Italian • full bar • wheelchair access

Kit Kat Lounge & Supper Club 3700 N Halsted (at W Waveland Ave) 773/525–1111 • 5:30pm-1am Tue-Sun, brunch Sun (seasonal) • great martini menu • gay-owned

Kitsch'n On Roscoe 2005 W Roscoe (at Damen) 773/248–7372 • 9am-10pm, till 3pm Sun-Mon • brunch wknds • full bar

Mon Ami Gabi 2300 N Lincoln Park W 773/348–8886 • lunch & dinner • French bistro

The Pepper Lounge 3441 N Sheffield (btwn Newport & Clark) 773/665–7377 • 6pm-1:30am, till midnight Sun, clsd Mon • lesbians/gay men • supper club • gourmet Italian • plenty veggie • full bar

The Raw Bar & Grill 3720 N Clark St (at Waveland) 773/348–7291 • 3pm-2am, from noon Sun • seafood • lounge • live shows • wheelchair access

She She 4539 N Lincoln Ave (at Wilson) 773/293–3690 • dinner only, till 8pm Sun, clsd Mon, Sun brunch

X/O 3441 N Halsted 773/348–9696 • dinner nightly • full bar

BOOKSTORES

Unabridged Books 3251 N Broadway St (at Aldine) 773/883–9119 • 10am-10pm, till 8pm wknds • popular • large LGBT section

RETAIL SHOPS

Specialty Video Films 3221 N Broadway St (at Belmont) 773/248–3434 • 10am-10pm, till 11pm Fri-Sat • foreign, cult, art house, LGBT & erotic videos • gay-owned

Uncle Fun 1338 W Belmont (at Racine) 773/477–8223 • heaven for kitsch lovers

Universal Gear 3153 N Broadway (at Belmont) 773/296–1090 • 11am-10pm, till 11pm Fri-Sat • casual, club, athletic & designer clothing

GYMS & HEALTH CLUBS

Chicago Sweat Shop 3215 N Broadway (at Belmont) 773/871–2789 • gay-friendly

EROTICA

Batteries Not Included 3420 N Halsted (at Roscoe) 773/935–9900

The Pleasure Chest 3155 N Broadway (at Belmont Ave) 773/525–7152

Chicago—Near North

ACCOMMODATIONS

Allegro Chicago 171 W Randolph (at LaSalle) 312/236–0123, 800/643–1500 • gay-friendly • Kimpton hotel • upscale lounge & restaurant • live shows • kids/ pets ok • wheelchair access • $139-399

Best Western Inn of Chicago 162 E Ohio St (at Michigan Ave) 312/787–3100, 800/557–2378 • gay-friendly • food service • wheelchair access • $79-189

Comfort Inn & Suites Downtown 15 E Ohio St 312/894-0900, 888/775-4111 • gay-friendly • kids ok • wheelchair access • $149-279

Days Inn Gold Coast 1816 N Clark St (at Lincoln) 312/664-3040, 800/329-7466 • gay-friendly • also restaurant & lounge • wheelchair access • $129+

Flemish House of Chicago 68 E Cedar St (btwn Rush & Lake Shore Dr) 312/664-9981 • gay/ straight • B&B, studios & apts in greystone row house • gay-owned • $125-200

Gold Coast Guest House B&B 113 W Elm St (btwn Clark & LaSalle) 312/337-0361 • gay-friendly • 1873 townhouse • nonsmoking • garden • women-owned/ run • $119-189 • long-term rates available

The Hotel Burnham One W Washington St (at Dearborn) 312/782-1111, 877/294-9712 • gay-friendly • Chicago landmark • wheelchair access • $179+

Hotel Monaco 225 N Wabash (at S Water & Wacker Pl) 312/960-8500, 866/610-0081 • upscale • gay-friendly • gym • restaurant • $250+

Hyatt Regency Chicago 151 E Wacker Dr (at Michigan Ave) 312/565-1234, 800/233-1234 • gay-friendly • restaurant • cafe • bar

Millennium Knickerbocker Hotel 163 E Walton Pl (Michigan Ave) 312/751-8100, 800/621-8140 • gay-friendly • restaurant • martini bar • gym • right off Magnificent Mile • wheelchair access • $129-269

Old Town Chicago B&B Inn 312/440-9268 • gay/ straight • jacuzzi • roof deck • kids ok • gym • nonsmoking • $160-225

W Chicago—City Center 172 W Adams St 312/332-1200, 877/WHOTELS (RESERVATIONS ONLY) • gay-friendly • in the Loop • nonsmoking • also restaurant & bar • wheelchair access • $229-529

W Chicago—Lakeshore 644 N Lake Shore Dr 312/943-9200, 877/WHOTELS (RESERVATIONS ONLY) • gay-friendly • in the Loop • nonsmoking • also restaurant & bar • wheelchair access • $229-429

Bars

Artful Dodger 1734 W Wabansia (at Hermitage, in Wicker Park) 773/227-6859 • 5pm-2am, 8pm-3am Sat • gay-friendly • dancing/DJ

Club Foot 1824 W Augusta (in Wicker Park) 773/489-0379 • 8pm-2am, till 3am Sat • gay-friendly • neighborhood bar • dancing/ DJ • kitschy • alternative

Davenport's 1383 N Milwaukee (in Wicker Park) 773/278-1830 • gay/ straight • 7pm-midnight, till 2am Fri-Sat, clsd Tue • cabaret • piano bar

Gentry on State 440 N State (at Illinois) 312/664-1033 • 4pm-2am, till 3am Sat • popular • mostly gay men • live shows • professional crowd • videos

Nightclubs

Baton Show Lounge 436 N Clark St (btwn Illinois & Hubbard) 312/644-5269 • showtimes at 8:30pm, 10:30pm, 12:30am, clsd Mon-Tue • lesbians/ gay men • drag shows • reservations recommended • wheelchair access

The Crobar 1543 N Kingsbury (at Sheffield) 312/266-1900 • 10pm-4am, clsd Mon-Th • popular • gay-friendly • more gay Sun for Glee Club • dancing/DJ

The Rails 1675 N Elston Ave (at North Ave, at Prop House in Wicker Park) 708/802-1705, 312/486-2086 • 11pm-4am Fri only • mostly gay men • dancing/DJ • live shows • African-American & Latino clientele • cover charge

Second City 1616 N Wells St (at North) 312/337-3992, 877/778-4707 • gay-friendly • legendary comedy club • call for reservations

Cafes

Earwax Cafe 1564 N Milwaukee Ave (in Wicker Park) 773/772-4019 • 9am-11pm, till midnight Fri-Sat • plenty veggie

Restaurants

The Berghoff 17 W Adams St (at State) 312/427-3170 • 11am-9pm, till 10pm Sat, clsd Sun • German • great mashed potatoes

Blackbird 619 W Randolph (at Des Plaines) 312/715-0708 • lunch Mon-Fri, dinner nightly, clsd Sun

Fireplace Inn 1448 N Wells St (at North Ave) 312/664-5264 • dinner nightly, wknd brunch • bbq/ American • full bar

Iggy's 1840 W North Ave 312/829-4449 • dinner nightly from 7pm, till 4am Th-Sat, till 2am Sun • int'l • full bar • patio • live entertainment

Ina's 1235 W Randolph St 312/226-8227 • brkfst, lunch & dinner, full bar, free parking

Japonais 600 W Chicago Ave 312/822-9600 • lunch Mon-Fri, dinner nightly • Japanese

Kiki's Bistro 900 N Franklin St (at Locust) 312/335–5454 • lunch Mon-Fri, dinner nightly, clsd Sun • French • full bar

Manny's 1141 S Jefferson St (at Roosevelt) 312/939–2855 • 5am-4pm, clsd Sun • killer corned beef

Parthenon Restaurant 314 S Halsted St (near W Jackson) 312/726–2407 • 11am-close • full bar • Greek • "best gyros in Chicago"

Shaw's Crab House 21 E Hubbard (at State St) 312/527–2722 • lunch & dinner • full bar • wheelchair access

BOOKSTORES

After-Words New & Used Books 23 E Illinois 312/464–1110 • 10:30am-10pm, till 11pm Fri-Sat, noon-7pm Sun • internet access • cards • stationery • women-owned/ run

Quimby's Queer Store 1854 W North Ave (at Wolcott, in Wicker Park) 773/342–0910 • noon-10pm, till 6pm Sun • popular • alternative literature & comics • wheelchair access

GYMS & HEALTH CLUBS

Thousand Waves Spa 1212 W Belmont Ave (at Racine) 773/549–0700 • noon-9pm, 10am-7pm wknds, clsd Mon • women only • health spa only • women-owned/ run

Chicago—South Side

BARS

Club Escape 1530 E 75th St (at Stoney Island) 773/667–6454 • 4pm-2am, till 3am Sat • lesbians/ gay men • dancing/DJ • mostly African-American • food served • women's night Th

Inn Exile 5758 W 65th St (at Menard, near Midway Airport; 1 mile W of Midway hotel center at 65th & Cicero) 773/582–3510 • 8pm-2am, till 3am Sat • mostly gay men • dancing/DJ • videos • wheelchair access

Jeffery Pub 7041 S Jeffery (at 71st) 773/363–8555 • 5pm-4am, from noon Fri-Sun • popular • lesbians/ gay men • dancing/DJ • mostly African-American • live shows • wheelchair access

BOOKSTORES

57th St Books 1301 E 57th St, Hyde Park (at Kimbark St) 773/684–1300 • 10am-10pm, till 8pm Sun • LGBT section

Barbara's Bookstore 1218 S Halsted (at W Roosevelt) 312/413–2665 • 9am-10pm, 10am-9pm Sun • popular • women's/ LGBT section • wheelchair access • other locations: 700 E Grand Ave at Navy Pier, 312/222-0890 • Marshall Field's, 111 N State St, 312/781-3033 • Oak Park, 708/848-9140

EROTICA

Slightly Sinful 12300 S Cicero (at 123rd) 708/388–6902

Decatur

BARS

The Firehouse Bar 550 N Morgan (at Eldorado St) 217/428–7411 • 6pm-2am • lesbians/ gay men • dancing/DJ • live shows • karaoke • drag shows • videos • gay-owned/ operated

The Flashback Lounge 2239 E Wood St (at 22nd) 217/422–3530 • 9am-2am • lesbians/ gay men • neighborhood bar • dancing/DJ • karaoke

Du Quoin

ACCOMMODATIONS

The Pit 7403 Persimmon Rd 618/542–9470 • lesbians/ gay men • primitive camping • 18+ • nudity ok • swimming • gay-owned • free except $5 on holiday wknds

Elgin

see also Chicago

Elk Grove Village

see also Chicago

Forest Park

see also Chicago

NIGHTCLUBS

Hideaway 7301 W Roosevelt Rd (at Marengo) 708/771–4459 • 3pm-2am, till 3am Fri-Sat • mostly gay men • dancing/DJ • karaoke • drag shows • male dancers • videos

Nut Bush 7201 Franklin (at Harlem) 708/366–5117 • 3pm-2am, till 3am Fri-Sat, from 1pm wknds • mostly gay men • dancing/DJ • karaoke • drag shows • bingo • videos

Franklin Park

NIGHTCLUBS

Temptations 10235 W Grand Ave (at Mannheim) 847/455-0008 • 6pm-2am, till 3am Fri-Sat, clsd Sun-Mon • popular • lesbians/ gay men • dancing/DJ • transgender-friendly • live shows • drag shows • alternative • wheelchair access

Galesburg

ACCOMMODATIONS

The Fahnestock House 591 N Prairie St (at Losey) 309/344-0270 • gay/ straight • full brkfst • Queen Anne Victorian • gay-owned • $125

Granite City

see also St Louis, Missouri

Joliet

NIGHTCLUBS

Maneuvers & Co 118 E Jefferson (at Chicago) 815/727-7069 • 8pm-2am, till 3am Fri-Sat • lesbians/ gay men • dancing/DJ • transgender-friendly • drag shows • ladies night Sun • frequent events • patio

Long Grove

RETAIL SHOPS

The Long Grove Popcorn Shoppe 318 Old McHenry Rd 847/821-9101 • 10am-5pm, from 11am Sun • try the "Pride Pop" • also gourmet coffee & doggie treats • lesbian-owned

Oak Park

SPIRITUAL GROUPS

MCC of the Incarnation 542 S Scoville (at Adams) 708/383-3033 • 11am Sun

Ottawa

EROTICA

Brown Bag Video 3042 N Rte 71 (at I-80) 815/434-0820 • 24hrs

Peoria

BARS

Buddies 807 SW Adams (at Oak) 309/282-2125 • 4pm-1am, till 2am wknds • lesbians/ gay men • neighborhood bar

Sparky's Ringside Bar & Grille 1914 N Wisconsin Ave 309/682-0826 • 10am-1am • gay/ straight • neighborhood bar • karaoke

PUBLICATIONS

Prairie Flame 217/753-2887 • LGBT newspaper for downstate IL

EROTICA

Brown Bag Video 801 SW Adams (at Oak) 309/676-3003

Swingers World 335 SW Adams (at Harrison) 309/676-9275 • 24hrs

Quincy

NIGHTCLUBS

Irene's Cabaret 124 N 5th St (at Washington Park, enter rear) 217/222-6292 • 9pm-2:30am, from 7pm Fri-Sat, till 3:30am Sat, clsd Sun-Mon • lesbians/ gay men • dancing/DJ • multiracial • food served • karaoke • drag shows • wheelchair access • gay-owned

SPIRITUAL GROUPS

Church of the Holy Spirit 232 N 6th St (at Vermont) 217/224-2800 • 6pm Sun

Rock Island

see also Davenport, Iowa

BARS

Augie's 313 20th St (at 3rd) 309/788-7389 • 3pm-3am, from noon wknds • lesbians/ gay men • neighborhood bar

RETAIL SHOPS

Rainbow Gifts 311 17th St 309/786-0873, 877/606-4724 • noon-7pm, till 8pm wknds, till 6pm Sun • pride items • gay-owned

Rockford

BARS

Oh Zone 1014 Charles St (at E State) 815/964-9663 • 5pm-2am, noon-midnight Sun • lesbians/ gay men • dancing /DJ • live shows • karaoke Wed • shows

NIGHTCLUBS

The Office Niteclub 513 E State St (btwn 2nd & 3rd) 815/965-0344 • 5pm-2am, noon-midnight Sun • popular • lesbians/ gay men • dancing/DJ • live shows • drag shows • male & female strippers • videos

RESTAURANTS

Lucernes 845 N Church St (at Whitman)
815/968–2665 • 5pm-11pm, clsd Mon (also
Sun summers) • fondue • full bar • wheelchair
access

Maria's 828 Cunningham St (at Corbin)
815/968–6781 • 5pm-9pm, clsd Sun-Mon •
Italian • full bar

Springfield

INFO LINES & SERVICES

The Phoenix Center 118-122 E Laurel St
217/528–5253 • 9am-4pm, clsd wknds •
Phoenix Cafe group Th • youth group Fri

ACCOMMODATIONS

The Henry Mischler House 802 E Edwards
St (btwn 8th & 9th Sts) **217/525–2660** • gay-
friendly • full brkfst • nonsmoking • gay-
owned • $75-95

Quality Inn & Suites, State House 101 E
Adams (at First St) **217/528–5100** • gay-
friendly • hotel • full brkfst • kids/ pets ok •
wheelchair access • $89-159

BARS

Prisms 2143 N 11th St **217/525–6717** • 8pm-
1am, from 7pm wknds, clsd Mon • lesbians/
gay men • dancing/DJ • karaoke • drag shows
• strippers • food served • wheelchair access

The Station House 304–306 E Washington
(btwn 3rd & 4th Sts) **217/525–0438** • 10am-
1am, till 3am Fri-Sat, from noon Sun •
lesbians/ gay men • neighborhood bar •
dancing/DJ • wheelchair access

RESTAURANTS

Lil' Jimmy's Diner 1629 1/2 Peoria Rd (at
North Grand Ave) **217/753–1055** • 6am-8pm,
till 2pm Sun • brkfst, lunch & dinner • gay-
owned-run

BOOKSTORES

Sundance 1428 E Sangamon Ave (at Peoria
Rd) **217/788–5243** • 10am-6pm, clsd Sun •
New Age books & gifts • LGBT titles

PUBLICATIONS

Prairie Flame **217/753–2887** • LGBT
newspaper for downstate IL

SPIRITUAL GROUPS

Heartland Community MCC 501 W Monroe
(at Lewis) **217/523–4461** • 10:30am Sun

INDIANA

Bloomington

BARS

The Other Bar 414 S Walnut (btwn 2nd &
4th) **812/332–0033** • 5pm-2:30am, till
midnight Sun • lesbians/gay men •
neighborhood bar • patio • wheelchair access

Uncle Elizabeth's 502 N Morton (at 9th)
812/331–0060 • 4pm-3am, 5pm-midnight
Sun • lesbians/ gay men • neighborhood bar •
patio

CAFES

Soma Coffee House 322 E Kirkwood Ave
(below Laughing Planet) **812/331–2770** •
7am-11pm, from 8am Sun

RESTAURANTS

Laughing Planet Cafe 322 E Kirkwood Ave
(enter on Grant) **812/323–2233** • 11am-9pm •
outdoor seating

Village Deli 409 E Kirkwood **812/336–2303** •
7am-9pm, 8am-6pm wknds • lesbians/ gay
men • some veggie

RETAIL SHOPS

Athena Gallery 108 E Kirkwood Ave (at
Walnut) **812/339–0734** • 10:30am-7pm, till
8:30pm Fri, noon-5pm Sun • clothing, drums,
incense, gifts, etc • wheelchair access

SPIRITUAL GROUPS

Unity of Bloomington 1101 N Dunn (at
14th) **812/333–2484** • 9am & 11am Sun •
wheelchair access

Elkhart

see also South Bend

INFO LINES & SERVICES

Info Helpline 800/808–4357 • 24hrs

SPIRITUAL GROUPS

Unitarian Universalist Fellowship 1732
Garden St (at Cassopolis) **574/264–6525** •
10:30am Sun • wheelchair access

Evansville

NIGHTCLUBS

Slip-Er-N 2207 S Kentucky Ave (1/2 mile N of
I-164) **812/421–1092** • 4pm-3am, till 12:30am
Sun • lesbians/gay men • neighborhood bar •
dancing/DJ • food served • live shows •
karaoke Tue • drag shows • patio • also
leather/ pride shop upstairs

Someplace Else 930 Main St (at Sycamore) **812/424–3202** • 4pm-3am, 2pm-midnight Sun • lesbians/ gay men • dancing/DJ • drag shows • karaoke • patio

RESTAURANTS

Cafe Go Lightly 920 Main St **812/402–7378** • 10:30am-5pm

BOOKSTORES

Spiral Dance 1541 S Green River Rd (at Covert) **812/479–8979** • 11am-6pm • spiritual • wheelchair access

SPIRITUAL GROUPS

Unitarian Universalist Church 2910 E Morgan Ave • 10am Sun

Fort Wayne

INFO LINES & SERVICES

Gay/ Lesbian AA at Up the Stairs Community Center **260/424–1199 (HELPLINE #)** • 7:30pm Tue & Sat, 4pm Sun

Up the Stairs Community Center 514 E Washington Blvd **260/422–2450** • 7pm-10pm, till midnight Fri-Sat • youth group • library • space for various groups including lesbian/ gay helpline • also newspaper

BARS

Hide-n-Seeks Pub & Eatery 1008 N Wells St **260/423–2202** • 5pm-3:30am, till 1am Sun • mostly gay men • neighborhood bar • dancing/DJ • leather • karaoke • food served

Up the Street 2322 S Calhoun (at Creighton) **260/456–7166** • 7pm-3am Th-Sat • mostly women • dancing/DJ Fri-Sat • drag king shows • wheelchair access

NIGHTCLUBS

After Dark 1601 S Harrison St (at Grand St) **260/456–6235** • noon-3am, 6pm-1am Sun • mostly gay men • dancing/DJ • karaoke Mon • drag shows • go-go dancers • wheelchair access • gay-owned

RETAIL SHOPS

Boudoir Noir 512 W Superior St **260/420–0557** • 11am-10pm, till 11pm Fri-Sat, noon-6pm Sun • gifts • sex toys • leather

SPIRITUAL GROUPS

Open Door Chapel at Up the Stairs Community Center **260/424–1199 (HELPLINE #)** • 7pm Sun

Gary

see also Chicago, Illinois

Goshen

see also South Bend

CAFES

The Electric Brew 136 S Main St **574/533–5990** • 6:30am-10pm, till 11pm Fri-Sat, clsd Sun • "Goshen's original coffeehouse" • live music

Hammond

RESTAURANTS

Phil Smidt & Son 1205 N Calumet Ave (at Indianapolis Blvd) **219/659–0025** • lunch & dinner, dinner only Sun, clsd Mon • seafood • full bar

Indiana Dunes

ACCOMMODATIONS

The Gray Goose Inn B&B 350 Indian Boundary Rd (at I-95), Chesterton **219/926–5781, 800/521–5127** • gay/ straight • full brkfst • nonsmoking rooms available • $90-185

Indianapolis

INFO LINES & SERVICES

AA Gay/ Lesbian **317/632–7864, 317/416–5780 (EN ESPAÑOL)** • call for meeting times & locations

ACCOMMODATIONS

East Lake Retreat 335 W Lakeview Dr, Kinman **812/376–0784** • fully furnished 2-bdrm/2-bath rental home 30 minutes from Indianapolis • on wooded lot with waterfall, lake access, boating, firepit • lesbian-owned • $200-300/wknd & $500-700/wk

Renaissance Tower Historic Inn 230 E 9th St (btwn Delaware & Alabama) **317/261–1652, 800/676–7786** • gay-friendly • studio suites • full kitchens • downtown location • $95, $525/ week & $1,200/ month

Sycamore Knoll B&B 10777 Riverwood Ave, Noblesville **317/776–0570** • gay/ straight • fully restored 1886 estate near the White River • perennial gardens & apple orchard • quiet & casual • full brkfst • lesbian-owned • $95/ night

Yellow Rose Inn 1441 N Delaware St **317/636–7673** • gay/ straight • B&B in restored Victorian • rooftop hot tub

Bars

501 Eagle 501 N College (at Michigan St) 317/632–2100 • 5:30pm-3am, from 7:30pm Sat, clsd Sun • popular • mostly gay men • dancing/DJ • bears • leather

Downtown Olly's 822 N Illinois St (at St Clair) 317/636–5597 • 11am-1am • mostly gay men • neighborhood sports & video bar • popular Sun brunch • wheelchair access

Illusions 1446 E Washington (at Arsenal) 317/266–0535 • 7am-3am, noon-midnight Sun • gay/ straight • dancing/DJ • karaoke Th & Sat-Sun • drag shows Fri-Sat • wheelchair access

The Metro Restaurant & Nightclub 707 Massachusetts Ave (at College) 317/639-6022 • 11am-3am, from 4pm Sat, 11am-12:30am Sun • popular • lesbians/ gay men • neighborhood bar • piano bar • karaoke • patio • also restaurant • giftshop • wheelchair access

Varsity Lounge 1517 N Pennsylvania St (S of 16th) 317/635–9998 • 10am-3am, noon-midnight Sun • mostly gay men • neighborhood bar • food served (popular Sun buffet 5pm-9pm)

Nightclubs

Club Cabaret 151 W 14th St (at Capitol) 317/951–8569 • 8pm-3am Th only, call for show times (usually 11pm-1am) • lesbians/ gay men • dancing/DJ • drag shows • patio • wheelchair access

Talbott Street 2145 N Talbott St (at 22nd St) 317/931–1343 • 9pm-4am, till 1am Sun, clsd Mon-Th • popular • gay/ straight • dancing/DJ • theme nights • drag shows • lounge • gay-owned

The Ten 1218 N Pennsylvania St (at 12th, enter rear) 317/638–5802 • 6pm-3am, till midnight Sun • popular • lesbians/ gay men • dancing/DJ • live shows • drag shows • wheelchair access

The Unicorn Club 122 W 13th St (at Illinois) 317/262–9195 • 8pm-3am, 9pm-12:30am Sun • popular • mostly gay men • dancing/ DJ • male strippers • private club

Cafes

Vic's Coffeehouse 627 N East St (next door to Out Word Bound Books) 317/951–0335 • 7am-11pm • food served

Indianapolis

LGBT Pride:
June, web: www.indyprideinc.com.

Annual Events:
Memorial Day Weekend - Indy 500 auto race.

City Info:
Indianapolis Visitor's Bureau 317/639-4282, 800/958-INDY, web: www.indy.org.

Attractions:
Indianapolis Museum of Art 317/923-1331 & 317/920-2660 (24hr info line), web: www.ima-art.org.
Speedway 500 317/481-8500, web: www.indianapolismotorspeed-way.com.

Zoo 317/630-2001, web: www.indy-zoo.com.

Weather:
The spring weather is moderate (50°s-60°s) with occasional storms. The summers are typically midwestern: hot (mid-90°s) and humid. The autumns are mild and colorful in southeastern Indiana. As for winter, it's the wind chill that'll get to you.

Transit:
Yellow Cab 317/487-7777.
IndyGo 317/635-2100, web: www.indygo.net.

RESTAURANTS

Abbey Coffeehouse 825 N Pennsylvania St (btwn E St Claire & E 9th St) 317/269–8426 • 7am-midnight, 8am-1am wknds

Aesop's Tables 600 N Massachusetts Ave (at East) 317/631–0055 • lunch & dinner, clsd Sun • authentic Mediterranean • some veggie • beer/ wine • wheelchair access • $8-15

English Ivy's 944 S Alabama (at 10th) 317/822–5070 • lunch & dinner, till 3am Mon-Sat, 11am-midnight Sun • eclectic • also full bar

Mama Carolla's 1031 E 54th St 317/259–9412 • 5pm-close, clsd Sun-Mon • traditional Italian • wheelchair access

Mikado 148 S Illinois St 317/972–4180 • 11:30am-close • Japanese • wheelchair access

Naked Tchopstix 6253 N College Ave (in Broad Ripple) 317/252–5555 • lunch Mon-Fri, dinner Mon-Sat • popular • Korean, Japanese, Chinese cuisine • also sushi bar

ENTERTAINMENT & RECREATION

Indiana Fever Conseco Fieldhouse 317/917–2500 • check out the Women's National Basketball Association while you're in Indianapolis

Indianapolis Women's Chorus PO Box 2919, 46206-2919 317/931–9464

Key Cinemas 4044 S Keystone Ave (at S Carson Ave) 317/784–7454 • alternative cinema

Theatre on the Square 627 Massachusetts Ave 317/685–8687

BOOKSTORES

Borders 5612 Castleton Corner Ln (at 86th St) 317/849-8660 • 9am-10pm, 10am-8pm Sun • some LGBT titles

Out Word Bound 625 N East St (at Massachusetts Ave) 317/951–9100, 877/811–5471 • 11:30am-9pm, till 10pm Fri-Sat, from 10am Sat, noon-6pm Sun • LGBT books & gifts • special events including book group, live music concerts & Girl Friday Game Night every 4th Fri • gay & lesbian-owned

---

Reply | Forward | Delete

```
Date: Dec 20, 2005 11:26:57
From: Girl-on-the-Go
To: Editor@Damron.com
Subject: Indianapolis
```

>Indianapolis, the capital of the Hoosier state, may look like your typical Midwestern industrial city, but you'll find a few surprises under the surface.

>You probably won't find lesbians dancing in the streets (unless it's Pride Day), but they're there. Check out some of the fun boutiques and restaurants in the Broad Ripple district. Later, dance with the girls at **The Ten.** Or dance along with the boys at **Talbott St**. For the latest one-nighters and other events, check the latest issue of the **Word,** which you can pick up at the LGBT bookstore **Out Word Bound.**

>Ready for some hoops? You're sure to see some sporty girls in the stands at an **Indiana Fever** game, local representatives of the Women's National Basketball Association.

>If fast cars are more your style, be sure to be in Indianapolis for the Indy 500 on Memorial Day weekend.

PUBLICATIONS

EXP Magazine 317/267-0397, 877/397-6244 • gay magazine serving IN, OH & KY

Nuvo 317/254-2400 • Indy's alternative weekly

The Word 317/725-8840 • LGBT newspaper

SPIRITUAL GROUPS

All Saints Episcopal Church 16th & Central Ave 317/635-2538 • 10am Sun, 6pm Wed

Broadway United Methodist Church 609 E 29th St 317/924-4207 • 8:30am, 9:37am & 10:45am Sun, also service in Korean at 10:45 Sun

Jesus MCC 2950 E 55th Pl (at Keystone & 56th St) 317/722-0000 • 9am, 10:45am & 6pm Sun • wheelchair accesss

Unitarian Universalist Church of Indianapolis 615 W 43rd St 317/283-4760 • 10:30am Sun

EROTICA

Southern Nights Videos 3760 Commercial Dr (at 38th St) 317/329-5505 • 24hrs • videos • DVDs • toys, etc

Southside News 8063 Madison Ave 317/887-1020 • 6am-8pm, till 6pm Sun

Kokomo

BARS

Club Millennium 1400 W Markland Ave (at Park) 765/452-1611 • 6pm-close, 4pm-midnight Sun • lesbians/ gay men • dancing/DJ • karaoke • drag shows • food served

La Porte

RESTAURANTS

Holy Macaroni Cafe & Pizzeria 4318 W US Hwy 20 (E of I-94/Hwy 20/35 interchange) 219/871-1033 • 11am-9pm, till 10pm Fri-Sat, clsd Sun-Mon • outdoor dining • homemade deserts

Lafayette

INFO LINES & SERVICES

Pride Lafayette 658 Main St, Ste 218 • social/ support group w/ community center open 5:30pm-7:30pm Tue & 6pm-8pm Th

BARS

The Sportsman 644 Main St (at Columbia) 765/742-6321 • 4pm-close • lesbians/ gay men • neighborhood bar • dancing/DJ Fri-Sat

SPIRITUAL GROUPS

Unitarian Universalist Church 17 S 7th St 765/742-0460 • 10:30am Sun

EROTICA

Fantasy East 2311 Concord Rd (at Teal) 765/474-2417 • books & videos

Lake Station

NIGHTCLUBS

Encompass Nightclub & Lounge 2415 Rush St (at I-80/94 & Ripley St) 219/962-4640 • 7pm-3am, clsd Sun • popular • lesbians/ gay men • dancing/DJ • cabaret • food served • wheelchair access

Lowell

ACCOMMODATIONS

Inn Town B&B 1651 E Commercial Ave (Rte 2 or 181st) (at Burr St) 219/696-3338 • gay-friendly • full brkfst • kids/ pets ok • nonsmoking • women-owned/ run • $75-95

Merrillville

see also Gary & Hammond

Michigan City

ACCOMMODATIONS

Duneland Beach Inn & Restaurant 3311 Pottawattamie Trail (at Duneland Beach Dr) 219/874-7729, 800/423-7729 • gay-friendly • B&B/ restaurant/ bar • 1 block away from Lake Michigan & private beach • 60 miles outside of Chicago • jacuzzi suites available • 109-169

Tryon Farm Guest House 1400 Tryon Rd (at Hwy 212) 219/879-3618 • gay-friendly • full brkfst • hot tub • kids/ pets ok • nonsmoking • women-owned

Mishawaka

see also South Bend

Muncie

BARS

Mark III Tap Room 107 E Main St (at Walnut) **765/284-3840** • 2pm-2am, till 3am Wed & Fri-Sat • lesbians/ gay men • neighborhood bar • dancing/DJ • multiracial • transgender-friendly • food served • karaoke • drag shows • gay-owned

CAFES

The MT Cup 1606 W University Ave (at N Dill St) **765/287-1995** • 7:30am-11pm • sandwiches • baked goods

RETAIL SHOPS

Elements 1624 W University Ave **765/741-8840** • 11am-6pm, till 8pm Fri-Sat, 12:30pm-6pm Sun • gifts • pagan supplies • jewelry • books • includes LGBT items

Richmond

BARS

Tommy's 911 E Main St (at N 9th St) **765/939-8669** • noon-3:30am • gay/ straight • dancing/ DJ • karaoke • live shows • wheelchair access • also restaurant

South Bend

BARS

Jeannie's Tavern 621 S Bendix (at Ford St) **574/288-2962** • 11am-2am • gay-friendly • transgender-friendly • gay-owned

Vickies Inc 112 W Monroe (at S Michigan Ave) **574/232-4090** • 2pm-3am, from 3pm Mon, from noon Fri-Sat, 3pm-midnight Sun • gay/ straight • neighborhood bar • transgender-friendly • food served • karaoke Sat • football party every Sat in season • gay-owned

NIGHTCLUBS

Seahorse II Cabaret 1902 Western Ave (at Brookfield) **574/237-9139** • 7pm-3am • lesbians/ gay men • dancing/DJ • drag shows • wheelchair access

Terre Haute

NIGHTCLUBS

Truman's Nightclub & Lounge/ Little T's 100 N Center St, Mishawaka **574/259-2282, 574/259-7507** • 8pm-3am, from 10pm Fri-Sat • Little T's (sports bar, karaoke) open 6pm-2am Fri-Sat, till 12:30am Sun • popular • lesbians/ gay men • dancing/DJ • drag shows • also John's Grille • also gift shop • pride items • clothing

Zim Marss Nightclub & Restaurant 1500 Locust St (at 15th St) **812/232-3026** • 6pm-3am, clsd Sun-Mon • lesbians/ gay men • dancing/DJ • transgender-friendly • also restaurant • drag shows • strippers

Iowa

Statewide

PUBLICATIONS

Accessline 319/232-6805 • LGBT newspaper

Lavender Magazine 612/436-4660, 877/515-9969 • LGBT newsmagazine for MN, WI, IA, ND, SD

Ames

INFO LINES & SERVICES

LGBT Alliance—Iowa State University East Student Office Space (Memorial Union) 515/294-2104 • weekly meetings • also LGBT Student Services at 515/294-5670 (www.dso.iastate.edu/LGBTss)

RESTAURANTS

Boheme Bistro 2900 West St 515/296-4674 • 4:30pm-2am

Lucullan's 400 Main St (at Kellogg) 515/232-8484 • 11am-9pm, till 10pm Fri-Sat • Italian • some veggie • full bar

Burlington

ACCOMMODATIONS

Arrowhead Motel, Inc 2520 Mt Pleasant St 319/752-6353 • gay-friendly • kids/ pets ok • wheelchair access • gay-owned • $49-84

BARS

Steve's Place 852 Washington (at Central Ave) 319/752-9109 • 9am-2am, noon-6pm Sun • gay-friendly • neighborhood bar • restaurant • wheelchair access

Cedar Falls

see also Waterloo

Cedar Rapids

Info Lines & Services

Gay/ Lesbian Resource Center 305 2nd St SE #324 319/366-2055 • 7pm-9pm Mon (by appt) • 24hr recorded info • support groups • referrals • library

Nightclubs

Club Basix 3916 1st Ave NE (btwn 39th & 40th) 319/363-3194 • 5pm-2am, from noon wknds • lesbians/ gay men • transgender-friendly • dancing/DJ • karaoke Th • drag shows • gay/ lesbian-owned

Club Orbit 219 2nd St SE (at 2nd Ave) 319/362-6728 • 4pm-2am • mostly men • dancing/ DJ • live shows • drag shows • videos •

Dragon Nightclub 329 2nd Ave SE (2nd St) 319/286-9284 • 5pm-2am • gay/ straight • dancing/ DJ • transgender-friendly • live shows • karaoke • caberet • drag shows • strippers & go-go dancers • young crowd

Restaurants

The Happy Chef 1906 Blairs Ferry Rd NE 319/395-7793 • 24hrs • all-American • salad bar

Entertainment & Recreation

CSPS Arts Center 1103 3rd St SE 319/364-1580 • galleries • concerts • plays • many LGBT events

Spiritual Groups

Faith United Methodist Church 1000 30th St NE 319/363-8454 • 11am Sun

Council Bluffs

see also Omaha, Nebraska

Davenport

see also Rock Island, Illinois

Bars

811 Lockdown 811 W 2nd St (at Warren) 563/322-3292 • 4pm-2am, till 4am Fri-Sat • mostly gay men • also restaurant • gay-owned

Mary's on 2nd 832 W 2nd St 563/884-8014 • 4pm-2am, from 2pm Sun • lesbians/ gay men • neighborhood bar • dancing/DJ • occasional live shows • videos • patio • wheelchair access

Nightclubs

Club Fusion 813 W 2nd St (at Warren) 563/326-3452 • 4pm-2am, from noon Sun • lesbians/ gay men • dancing/DJ • drag shows • patio • deck • gay-owned

Liquid 822 W 2nd St (at Centennial Bridge) 563/324-9675 • 7pm-2am • mostly gay men • dancing/DJ • drag shows • male & female strippers • huge patio bar • volleyball • theme parties • wheelchair access • gay-owned

Spiritual Groups

MCC Quad Cities 3019 N Harrison 563/324-8281 • 11am Sun

Unitarian Universalist Church 3707 Eastern Ave 563/359-0816 • 11am Sun

Des Moines

Info Lines & Services

LGBT Community Center of Central Iowa 515/277-7884 • 24hr recorded info • library • youth groups • many other meetings • also publish newsletter

Accommodations

The Cottage B&B 1094 28th St (at Cottage Grove) 515/277-7559 • gay-friendly • 1929 Georgian • gay-owned • $89-99

Kingman House 2920 Kingman Blvd 515/279-7312, 515/996-2829 • lesbians/ gay men • turn-of-the-century B&B • full brkfst • wheelchair access • $50

The Renaissance Savery Hotel 401 Locust St (at 4th) 515/244-2151, 800/798-2151 • gay-friendly • historic luxury hotel & spa • swimming • kids ok • restaurant • wheelchair access • $99-695

Bars

The Blazing Saddle 416 E 5th St (btwn Grand & Locust) 515/246-1299 • 2pm-2am, from noon wknds • popular • mostly gay men • dancing/DJ • leather • drag shows • wheelchair access

Buddies Corral 418 E 5th St (btwn Grand & Locust) 515/244-7140 • noon-2am • gay-friendly • karaoke

Diesel 8980 Hickman (at 90th), Clive 515/331-2400 • 4pm-midnight, till 2am Fri-Sat, clsd Sun-Tue • lesbians/ gay men • neighorhood bar

Faces 416 E Walnut (at 4th St) 515/280-5463 • 9am-2am • lesbians/ gay men • dancing/DJ wknds • karaoke • drag shows • wheelchair access

NIGHTCLUBS

The Frathouse 508 Clifton Ave (Indianola Rd) (at 7th) **515/284-1074** • 8pm-2am, clsd Mon-Tue • lesbians/ gay men • drag shows

The Garden 112 SE 4th St **515/243-3965** • 8pm-2am, clsd Mon-Tue • lesbians/ gay men • dancing/DJ • live shows • karaoke • videos • patio • young crowd • wheelchair access

CAFES

The Breakroom Cyber Cafe 3015 Merle Hay Rd, Ste 4-B (at Urbandale) **515/279-6007** • 6:30am-6pm, 7am-4pm Sat, clsd Sun • internet

Java Joe's 214 4th St (at Court Ave) **515/288-5282** • 7am-11pm, till 12:30am Fri-Sat, from 9am Sun • live shows • community artist gallery next door

Zanzibar's Coffee Adventure 2723 Ingersoll (at 28th St) **515/244-7694** • 6:30am-9pm, till 11pm Fri-Sat, till 8am-6pm Sun

RESTAURANTS

Cafe di Scala 644 18th St (at Woodland) **515/554-6463** • lunch & dinner Fri-Sat only • Italian • beer/ wine • wheelchair access

Chicago Dog & Deli 523 Euclid (at 6th) **515/243-3085** • 10:30am-8pm, till 5pm Sat, clsd Sun • gay-owned

Paradise Pizza 2025 Grand, West Des Moines **515/222-9959** • 11am-9pm, till 10pm Fri-Sat, clsd Mon

BOOKSTORES

Borders 4100 University #115 (at 42nd, Water Tower mall), West Des Moines **515/223-1620** • 9am-10pm, till 11pm Fri-Sat, 11am-8pm Sun • LGBT section • also cafe • wheelchair access

PUBLICATIONS

LGBT Newsletter **515/277-7884** • monthly newsletter of the LGBT Community Center of Central Iowa

SPIRITUAL GROUPS

Church of the Holy Spirit MCC 2500 University **515/287-9787** • 10:30am Sun

EROTICA

Gallery Book Store 1000 Cherry (at 10th) **515/244-2916** • 24hrs

Dubuque

BARS

One Flight Up 44-48 Main St **563/582-8357** • 7pm-2am • lesbians/ gay men • dancing/DJ • restaurant • drag shows

Fort Dodge

EROTICA

Romantix Mini Cinema 15 N 5th St (on the square) **515/955-9756**

Grinnell

INFO LINES & SERVICES

Stonewall Resource Center Grinnell College 641/269-3327, 641/269-3761 • 4:30pm-11pm Mon-Th • library • also quarterly newsletter

Iowa City

INFO LINES & SERVICES

AA Gay/ Lesbian 130 N Madison (at Women's Resource Action Center) **319/335-1486** • 5pm Sun

Women's Resource & Action Center 130 N Madison (at Market) **319/335-1486** • 10am-5pm, till 7pm Tue & Th, clsd wknds • community center • support groups • counseling • wheelchair access

BARS

Deadwood 6 S Dubuque St **319/351-9417** • 9am-2am, from noon wknds • popular • mostly straight • neighborhood bar • college crowd

Studio 13 13 S Linn St (in the alley btwn Linn & Dubuque Sts) **319/338-7145** • 5pm-2am, clsd Mon-Tue • lesbians/ gay men • dancing/DJ • drag shows Fri & Sun • 19+ • gay-owned

BOOKSTORES

Prairie Lights Bookstore 15 S Dubuque St (at Washington) **319/337-2681, 800/295-BOOK** • 9am-10pm, till 6pm wknds • also cafe • wheelchair access

RETAIL SHOPS

New Pioneer Co-op & Bakehouse 22 S Van Buren **319/338-9441, 319/358-5513** • 7am-10pm • health food store & deli • also Coralville location at 1101 2nd St (at 12th Ave)

Vortex 211 E Washington **319/337-3434** • 10am-7pm, till 8pm Fri-Sat, noon-5pm Sun • unique gifts, some pride items

SPIRITUAL GROUPS

Faith United Church of Christ 1609 Deforest St (off Sycamore St, near Hwy 6) **319/338-5238** • 9:30am Sun • wheelchair access

Marshalltown

EROTICA

Adult Odyssey 907 Iowa Ave E **641/752-6550**
• videos • toys • leather

Newton

ACCOMMODATIONS

La Corsette Maison Inn 629 1st Ave E
641/792-6833 • gay-friendly • 3-course brkfst
• jacuzzi • 4-star restaurant • kids/ pets ok w/
pre-approval • nonsmoking • $85-225

Sioux City

BARS

3 Cheers 414 20th St **712/255-8005** • 8pm-
2am, clsd Mon-Tue • lesbians/ gay men •
neighborhood bar • dancing/DJ • live shows •
wheelchair access

Jones Street Station 412 Jones St
712/258-6922 • 5pm-2am, clsd Sun-Tue •
lesbians/ gay men • dancing/DJ • drag shows

Waterloo

INFO LINES & SERVICES

Access **319/232-6805** • weekly info &
support

NIGHTCLUBS

Kings & Queens Knight Club 304 W 4th St
(at Jefferson) **319/232-3001** • 6pm-2am • gay-
friendly • dancing/DJ • transgender-friendly •
drag shows • videos • young crowd •
wheelchair access

KANSAS

Statewide

PUBLICATIONS

▲ **The Liberty Press** **316/652-7737** •
statewide LGBT newspaper

Midwest Times **816/753-0900** • LGBT
magazine covering Missouri & Kansas

Emporia

BOOKSTORES

Town Crier 716 Commercial St
620/343-9649 • 9am-8pm, till 6pm Sat, 10am-
2pm Sun • some LGBT magazines • woman-
owned/ run

Junction City

NIGHTCLUBS

Xcalibur Club 384 Grant Ave **785/762-2050**
• 6pm-2am, from 2pm Fri-Sun, clsd Mon •
gay/ straight • dancing/DJ • live shows •
karaoke • gay-owned

RETAIL SHOPS

Phil's Leather 1706 N Washington St (at
Grant) **785/762-2242** • 1pm-6pm, call first

Kansas City

see also Kansas City, Missouri

Lawrence

BARS

Teller's Restaurant & Bar 746
Massachusetts St (at 8th) **785/843-4111** •
11am-10pm, till 11pm wknds • gay-friendly •
more gay Tue pm • also restaurant • southern
Italian/ pizza • some veggie • wheelchair
access

NIGHTCLUBS

Granada 1020 Massachusetts (at 11th)
785/842-1390 • hours vary, clsd Sun • gay/
straight • dancing/ DJ • live bands • wheelchair
access

Jazzhaus 926-1/2 Massachusetts St
785/749-3320, 785/749-1387 • 3pm-2am •
gay-friendly • live music

CAFES

Henry's 11 E 8th St (btwn Massachusetts St
& New Hampshire St) **785/331-3511** • 8am-
2am • espresso & sandwiches • plenty veggie
• also full bar upstairs

Java Break 17 E 7th St (btwn Massachusetts
& New Hampshire Sts) **785/749-5282** • 24hrs
• sandwiches • desserts • gay-owned

BOOKSTORES

The Dusty Bookshelf 708 Massachusetts St
785/749-4643 • 10am-8pm, till 10pm Fri-Sat,
noon-6pm Sun • used books, feminist & LGBT
section • gay-owned

RETAIL SHOPS

Naughty But Nice 1741 Massachusetts St
(btwn 17th & 18th) **785/832-1000** • 10am-
1am, till 3am Fri-Sat, noon-10pm Sun • pride
items • erotica

SPIRITUAL GROUPS

Ecumenical Christian Ministries at KU
1204 Oread 785/843–4933 • "Ecumenical Christian Ministries involves a diversity of people on the University of Kansas campus & in Lawrence."

Plymouth Congregational Church
925 Vermont St 785/843–3220 • 9:30am Sun (traditional worship) & 11:15am (contemporary worship) • "an open & affirming congregation"

Liberal

BOOKSTORES

Second Street Bookstore 11 W 2nd St 620/624–8105 • 9:30am-8pm, from 1pm Sun • large gay magazine selection

Manhattan

BOOKSTORES

The Dusty Bookshelf 700 N Manhattan 785/539–2839 • 10am-8pm, till 8pm Sat, 1pm-5pm Sun • used books • feminist & LGBT section • gay-owned

Overland Park

BARS

The Fox 7520 Shawnee Mission Pkwy (at Metcalf) 913/384–0369 • 2pm-2am • mostly gay men • neighborhood bar • transgender-friendly • videos

Strong City

BARS

Branding Iron Saloon 318 Cottonwood (at Hwy 50 & 177) 620/273–8388 • 3pm-1am • gay-friendly • neighborhood bar • live shows • wheelchair access • "true cowboy bar" • gay-owned

Topeka

INFO LINES & SERVICES

AA Gay/ Lesbian • 7:30pm Mon & 8pm Fri • call Marcus for location

BARS

Club Cosmos 1421 SW Lane St (at 15th) 785/290–2582 • 6pm-2am • lesbians/ gay men • neighborhood bar • dancing/ DJ • karaoke

BOOKSTORES

Barnes & Noble 6130 SW 17th St #101 785/273–9600 • 9am-11pm • LGBT section

RETAIL SHOPS

The Enchanted Willow Alchemy Shoppe
418 SW 6th Ave 785/235–3776 • 10am-6pm Sat-Mon, 4pm-6pm Tue-Fri (may vary) • pride items • pagan, occult & metaphysical supplies • herbs • aromatherapy • books • workshops • gay-owned

SPIRITUAL GROUPS

MCC Topeka 4425 SW 19th St 785/232–6196 • 10am Sun (9am summers)

MoonShadow Coven 785/224–3108 • eclectic Wicca/ pagan organization • call for info

Wichita

INFO LINES & SERVICES

One Day at a Time Gay AA 2821 S Hydraulic • 8pm Mon-Fri, 7pm Sat, 12:30pm Sun

ACCOMMODATIONS

Hawthorn Suites 2405 N Ridge Rd 316/729–5700 • gay-friendly • kids/ small pets ok • brkfst buffet • wheelchair access • $75-150

BARS

The Corner 3210 E Osie (at George Washington) 316/683–9781 • 3pm-2am • gay/ straight • neighborhood bar

J's Lounge 513 E Central (at Emporia) 316/262–1363 • 4pm-2am, till midnight Sun • lesbians/ gay men • cabaret • live shows • karaoke • patio • wheelchair access • "an upscale dive"

Kirby's Beer Store 3227 E 17th (at Holyoke) 316/685–7013 • 2pm-2am • gay-friendly • live bands • food served

The Other Side 447 N St Francis 316/262–7825 • 2pm-2am • lesbians/ gay men • neighborhood bar • leather

The Shatai 4000 S Broadway (at MacArthur) 316/522–2028 • 4pm-2am • mostly women • neighborhood bar • dancing/DJ • karaoke • live bands • food served • wheelchair access • women-owned/ run

Side Street 1106 S Pattie (near Lincoln & Hydraulic) 316/267–0324 • 2pm-2am • mostly gay men • dancing/DJ • country/ western • leather • wheelchair access

NIGHTCLUBS

Big Daddy's 458 N Waco (at Central) 316/262–8130 • 6pm-close, clsd Sun-Tue • mostly gay men • dancing/DJ • professional crowd • 18+ Fri & Sun • karaoke • live shows • also restaurant

Fantasy Complex 3201 S Hillside (at 31st) **316/682-5494** • 3pm-2am, clsd Mon • lesbians/ gay men • dancing/DJ • drag shows • also South Forty country/ western bar • wheelchair access

CAFES

Riverside Perk 1144 Bitting Ave (at 11th) **316/264-6464** • 7am-10pm, till midnight Fri-Sat, from 10am Sun • internet access • also Lava Lounge juice bar next door

RESTAURANTS

Moe's Sub Shop 2815 S Hydraulic (at Wassall) **316/524-5511** • 11am-8pm, clsd Sun

Old Mill Tasty Shop 604 E Douglas (at St Francis) **316/264-6500** • 11am-3pm, 8am-5pm Sat, clsd Sun • old-fashioned soda fountain • lunch menu • some veggie

Riverside Cafe 739 W 13th (at Bitting) **316/262-6703** • 6am-8pm, 8am-2pm Sun

The Upper Crust 7038 E Lincoln (at Governor) **316/683-8088** • lunch only, clsd wknds • homestyle • some veggie

Uptown Bistro 301 N Mead (at 2nd) **316/262-3232** • lunch & dinner daily, noon-8pm Sun

ENTERTAINMENT & RECREATION

Cabaret Oldtown Theatre 412 1/2 E Douglas (at Topeka) **316/265-4400** • edgy, kitschy productions

Mosley Street Melodrama 234 N Mosley St (btwn 1st & 2nd St) **316/263-0222** • melodrama, homestyle buffet & full bar!

Wichita Arts 334 N Mead **316/462-2787** • promotes visual & performing arts; ArtScene publication has extensive cultural calendar

RETAIL SHOPS

Holier Than Thou Body Piercing 1111 E Douglas Ave (at Washington) **316/266-4100** • 11am-8pm, noon-6pm Sun-Mon

PUBLICATIONS

▲ **The Liberty Press** **316/652-7737** • statewide LGBT newspaper

SPIRITUAL GROUPS

College Hill United Methodist Church 2930 E 1st St **316/683-4643** • 8:30am, 9:40am & 11am Sun

First Metropolitan Community Church 156 S Kansas Ave **316/267-1852** • 10:30am

First Unitarian Universalist Church 1501 Fairmount (near 13th St) **316/684-3481** • 11am Sun

Integrity/ South Central Kansas 3750 E Douglas (offices of St James Episcopal Church) **316/683-5686, x11** • worship 4pm 3rd Sun followed by discussion • LGBT Episcopalians & friends

Unity of Wichita 2160 N Oliver (at 21st) **316/682-7511** • 11am Sun

Wichita

LGBT PRIDE:
June.

ANNUAL EVENTS:
May- River Festival, web: www.wichitariverfestival.org.
October- Tallgrass Film Festival, web: www.tallgrassfilmfest.com. Gay-friendly independent film festival w/ some LGBT programming.

CITY INFO:
Kansas Travel & Tourism Dept 800/252-6727, web: www.travelks.com.

ATTRACTIONS:
Old Cowtown Museum 316/264-6398, web: www.old-cowtown.org.
Oldtown.
Pyradomes.
Wichita Art Museum 316/268-4921, web: www.wichitaartmuseum.org.

TRANSIT:
American Cab Co. 316/262-7511.
Metropolitan Transit Authority 316/265-7221.

EROTICA

Circle Cinema/ Video 2570 S Seneca St (at Crawford St) 316/264-2245 • 24hrs

Fetish Lingerie 2150 S Broadway (btwn E Clark & E Kinkaid Sts) 316/264-7800 • leather, toys, clubwear • all sizes available

Priscilla's 6143 W Kellogg (at Dugan) 316/942-1244

Wilson

EROTICA

After Dark Video 275 Hwy 232 785/658-3556 • 10am-midnight

KENTUCKY

Statewide

PUBLICATIONS

The Letter 502/636-0935 (NEWS), 502/772-7570 (ADVERTISING) • statewide LGBT newspaper

Covington

see also Cincinnati, Ohio

BARS

Rosie's Tavern 643 Bakewell St (at 7th St) 859/291-9707 • 3pm-2:30am • gay/ straight • neighborhood bar • lesbian-owned

Yadda Club 404 Pike St (at Main St) 859/491-5600 • 5pm-2:30am, from 7pm Sat, till 1am Sun, clsd Mon-Wed • lesbians/ gay men • neighborhood bar • dancing/ DJ • T-dance Sun • multiracial • live shows • karaoke • food served • patio • wheelchair access • lesbian-owned

Elizabethtown

SPIRITUAL GROUPS

Elizabethtown MCC 119 Brooks St (at Mulberry) 270/737-4404 • 11am Sun

Harned

ACCOMMODATIONS

Kentucky Holler House 270/547-4507 • rental cabin on 48 acres • gay/ straight • private decks • nonsmoking • also antique shop • $85

Lexington

INFO LINES & SERVICES

Gay/ Lesbian AA 472 Rose St (at St Augustine's Chapel) 859/276-2917 (AA#) • 8pm Mon & Wed • also 7:30pm Fri at 205 E Short St (church)

Pride Center of the Bluegrass 389 Waller Ave #100 859/253-3233 • 10am-3pm Mon-Sat

BARS

The Bar Complex 224 E Main St (at Esplanade) 859/255-1551 • 4pm-1am, till 2am Th-Fri, till 2:30am Sat, clsd Sun • popular • lesbians/ gay men • dancing/ DJ • drag shows • karaoke • live shows • wheelchair access

NIGHTCLUBS

Club 141 141 W Vine St (at Limestone) 859/233-4262 • 8:30pm-1am, till 3am wknds, clsd Sun-Mon • popular • lesbians/ gay men • dancing/ DJ • alternative • drag shows • wheelchair access

Club Liquid 2319 Woodhill Dr (at New Circle) 859/266-0911 • 4pm-1am, till 3am Th-Sat • lesbians/ gay men • dancing/ DJ • country/ western • bears • multiracial • transgender-friendly • drag shows • strippers • videos • gay-owned

RESTAURANTS

Alfalfa Restaurant 141 E Main St 859/253-0014 • lunch & dinner • healthy multi-ethnic • plenty veggie • folk music wknds

Natasha's Cafe & Boutique 112 Esplanade 859/259-2754, 888/901-8412 (SHOP #) • lunch & dinner, clsd Sun • eclectic • plenty veggie • Turkish coffee • internet access • also store

BOOKSTORES

Joseph-Beth 161 Lexington Green Circle 859/273-2911, 800/248-6849 • 9am-10pm, till 11pm Fri-Sat, 11am-9pm Sun • also cafe • wheelchair access

Sqecial Media 371 S Limestone St 859/255-4316 • 10am-8pm, noon-6pm • also pride items

PUBLICATIONS

GLSO (Gay/ Lesbian) News 859/253-3233 • local news & calendar

The Letter 502/636-0935 (NEWS), 502/772-7570 (ADVERTISING) • statewide LGBT newspaper

SPIRITUAL GROUPS

Pagan Forum 859/268-1640 • call for info on 10+ area pagan groups

Louisville

INFO LINES & SERVICES

LGBT Hotline 502/454-7613 • counseling 6pm-10pm • 24hr hotline • AA referrals

ACCOMMODATIONS

Bernheim Mansion B&B 1416 S 3rd St (at Hill) **502/638-1387, 800/303-0053** • gay/straight • Victorian mansion • full brkfst • hot tub • nonsmoking • gay-owned • $139-225

Columbine B&B 1707 S 3rd St (near Lee St) **502/635-5000, 800/635-5010** • gay-friendly • 1896 Greek Revivial mansion • full brkfst • nonsmoking • gay-owned • $95-155

Holiday Inn Southwest 4110 Dixie Hwy (at I-264) **502/448-2020** • gay-friendly • food served • swimming • lounge • wheelchair access

Inn at the Park 1332 S 4th St (at Park Ave) **502/637-6930** • gay-friendly • restored mansion • full brkfst • nonsmoking • $139-199

Louisville

WHERE THE GIRLS ARE:
On Main or Market Streets near 1st, and generally in the north-central part of town, just west of I-65.

LGBT PRIDE:
June.

ANNUAL EVENTS:
May - Kentucky Derby, web: www.kentuckyderby.com.
June-July - Kentucky Shakespeare Festival 502/637-4933, web: www.kyshakes.org.
October - World's Largest Halloween Party, Louisville Zoo, web: www.louisvillezoo.org.
October - St James Court Art Show 502/ 635-1842, web: www.stjamescourtartshow.com.

CITY INFO:
Louisville Visitor Center 800/792-5595.
Convention & Visitors Bureau, web: www.gotolouisville.com.

BEST VIEW:
Aboard the *Belle of Louisville* steamboat at Waterfront Park.

WEATHER:
Mild winters and long, hot summers!

TRANSIT:
Yellow Taxi 502/636-5511.
TARC Bus System 502/585-1234, web: www.ridetarc.org.
Toonerville II Trolley or Louisville Horse Trams 502/581-0100.

ATTRACTIONS:
Belle of Louisville steamboat 502/574-2992, 866/832-0011, web: www.belleoflouisville.org.
Churchill Downs 502/636-4400, web: www.churchilldowns.com.
Farmington Historic Home 502/452-9920.
Hadley Pottery 502/584-2171, web: www.hadleypottery.com.
Kentucky Derby 502/584-6383.
Louisville Slugger Tour 502/588-7228, web: www.sluggermuseum.org.
Locust Grove Historic Farm 502/897-4845, web: www.locustgrove.org.
St. James Court.
Waterfront Park, web: www.louisvillewaterfront.com.
West Main Street Historic District.

Reply Forward Delete

Date: Nov 14, 2005 12:22:05
From: Girl-on-the-Go
To: Editor@Damron.com
Subject: Louisville

>Beautiful Louisville sits on the banks of the Ohio River and is home to the world-famous Kentucky Derby. This spectacular race occurs during the first week of May at Churchill Downs.

>Louisville is also home to many whiskey distilleries, but if neither watching horses run in circles, nor swilling home-grown booze excites you, check out the Louisville Slugger Museum (502/588-7228). Then there's the *Belle of Louisville* (502/574-2992), one of the last authentic sternwheelers in the country as well as the oldest operating steamboat on the Mississippi River.

>Whatever you do, you're certain to enjoy this city's slower pace of life and Southern charm—Louisville is, after all, known as the "northern border for southern hospitality." The best way to get a feel for this Louisville is to walk among the elegant homes of St. James Court.

>Enjoy your morning brew at gay-owned **Day's Coffeehouse**, and before you leave, sample the whiskey and the hospitality at the popular **Connection Complex**, or drop in at the local watering-hole **Tink's Pub.** Enjoy a meal at lesbian-owned **Lynn's Paradise Cafe** or at gay-owned **Queenie's Pizza & Such,** and then get your groove on at the **Alternative,** Louisville's women's dance bar.

>Only a few hours to the east, make sure to rest a spell in the beautiful bluegrass country of Lexington, Kentucky. Then you can get up and dance at the **Bar Complex** or **Club Liquid.**

Mansion at River Walk 704 E Main St (at State St), New Albany, IN **812/941-8100** • gay-friendly • historic Italianate B&B • full brkfst • $95-145

Super 8 Scottsburg 1522 W McClain (off I-65), Scottsburg, IN **812/752-2122** • gay-friendly • pets ok • wheelchair access • $39-55

BARS

Magnolia Bar 1398 S 2nd St (at Magnolia) **502/637-9052** • noon-4am • gay-friendly • neighborhood bar • young crowd

Teddy Bears Bar & Grill 1148 Garvin Pl (at St Catherine) **502/589-2619** • 11am-4am, from 1pm Sun • mostly gay men • neighborhood bar • wheelchair access

Tink's Pub 2235 S Preston St **502/634-8180** • 2pm-close, from noon Sat, from 1pm Sun • lesbians/ gay men • neighborhood bar • live shows • karaoke

Tryangles 209 S Preston St (at Market) **502/583-6395** • 4pm-4am, from 1pm Sun • mostly gay men • strippers • wheelchair access

NIGHTCLUBS

The Alternative 1032 Story Ave (at Bickel Ave) **502/561-7613** • 6pm-midnight, 7pm-2am Fri-Sat • mostly women • dancing/ DJ • country/ western • live shows • 18+ • nonsmoking • wheelchair access • lesbian-owned

The Connection Complex 120 S Floyd St (at Market) **502/585-5752** • 5pm-4am • popular • lesbians/ gay men • dancing/DJ • piano bar & cabaret • videos • wheelchair access

Starbase Q 921 W Main St (at 9th St) • 4pm-close, from 8pm Sat, clsd Mon • mostly men • dancing/DJ • industrial video bar

CAFES

Days Coffeehouse 1420 Bardstown Rd (at Edenside) **502/456-1170** • 6:30am-10pm, till 11pm wknds • lesbian-owned

Sumshee's Family Room 204 S Preston **502/589-2018** • 7am-close • after-hours dancing/DJ Fri-Sat • also gallery • live shows • open mic

RESTAURANTS

Cafe Mimosa 1216 Bardstown Rd **502/458-2233** • lunch & dinner • Vietnamese, Chinese & sushi

El Mundo 2345 Frankfort Ave **502/899-9930** • 11:30am-9pm, full bar till 2am, clsd Sun • popular • Mexican

Greek Paradise 2113 Frankfort Ave **502/891-0003** • 11am-9pm, clsd Sun • lunch & dinner • outdoor seating • Greek dancing Fri-Sat

Gumby's Garden Room Cafe 911 S Brook St **502/625-1900** • 11am-2pm

Lynn's Paradise Cafe 984 Barret Ave (at Baxter) **502/583-3447** • 7am-10pm, till 2pm Mon • popular • lesbians/ gay men • colorful, funky decor • also bar • lesbian-owned

Porcini 2370 Frankfort Ave **502/894-8686** • dinner nightly, clsd Sun • Italian

Queenie's Pizza & Such 2622 S 4th St **502/636-3708** • 11am-10pm, till 11pm Fri-Sat, 4pm-8pm Sun, clsd Mon • gay-owned

Rudyard Kipling 422 W Oak St **502/636-1311** • lunch Mon-Fri, dinner from 5:30pm Wed-Sat • also English pub & theater • live music

Zen Garden 2240 Frankfort Ave **502/895-9114** • lunch & dinner • Asian • vegetarian

ENTERTAINMENT & RECREATION

Rainbow Cafe 2530 Frankfort Ave (at Open Door Community Fellowship) **502/893-6323** • 7pm-11pm 2nd & 3rd Sat only • women's music & coffeehouse

Voices of Kentuckiana **502/327-4099**

BOOKSTORES

Borders 3024 Bardstown Rd (in Gardiner Lane Shopping Center) **502/456-6660, 800/844-7323** • 9am-9pm, 10am-6pm Sun • also 4600 Shelbyville Rd, Shelbyville Plaza, 502/893-0133

Carmichael's 1295 Bardstown Rd (at Longest Ave) **502/456-6950** • 8am-10pm, till 11pm Fri-Sat, from 10am Sun • large LGBT section

PUBLICATIONS

EXP Magazine 317/267-0397 (INDY #), 877/397-6244 • gay magazine serving IN, OH & KY

Greater Cincinnati GLBT News PO Box 14971, Cincinnati, OH 45250-0971

The Letter 502/636-0935 (NEWS), 502/772-7570 (ADVERTISING) • statewide LGBT newspaper

SPIRITUAL GROUPS

B'nai Shalom 502/896-0475 • LGBT Jewish group

Central Presbyterian Church 502/587-6935 • 11am Sun • "More Light" congregation

MCC Louisville 1432 Highland Ave (at Rubel) 502/587-6225 • 10:30am • wheelchair access

Open Door Community Fellowship 2530 Frankfort Ave 502/893-6323 • 10:30am Sun

Midway

CAFES

Quirk Cafe & Coffee 104 E Main St E (inside Le Marché boutique mall) 859/846-4688 • 10am-5pm, clsd Mon • lesbian-owned

Morehead

ACCOMMODATIONS

Brownwood Bed & Breakfast & Cabins 46 Carey Cemetery Rd (at Cave Run Lake) 606/784-8799 • gay-friendly • special packages available • access to many outdoor activities • wheelchair access • gay-owned • $70 & up

Newport

see also Cincinnati, Ohio

BARS

The Crazy Fox Saloon 901 Washington Ave (at 9th) 859/261-2143 • 3pm-2:30am • gay/ straight • friendly neighborhood bar

Paducah

ACCOMMODATIONS

Mark Palmer Guest Retreat 524 Harrison St (at 6th St) 270/444-2056 • gay/straight • artist studio & guest suite in arts district • gay-owned

NIGHTCLUBS

DV8 2118 Bridge St (at Wayne Sullivan Dr) 270/575-1995 • 9pm-3am, clsd Sun-Mon • gay/ straight • neighborhood bar • dancing/DJ • live shows • wheelchair access

Somerset

INFO LINES & SERVICES

LGBT Info 606/678-5814 • call Linda for info

Versailles

ACCOMMODATIONS

Rose Hill Inn 233 Rose Hill 800/307-0460 • gay-friendly • 1823 Victorian mansion • full brkfst • near Lexington • women-owned/ run • $109-179

LOUISIANA

Statewide

PUBLICATIONS

Ambush Mag 504/522-8049 • LGBT newspaper for the Gulf South

Southern Voice 404/876-1819 • weekly LGBT newspaper for AL, FL (panhandle), GA, LA, MS, TN w/ resource listings

Alexandria

NIGHTCLUBS

Unique Bar & Lounge 3217 Industrial St 318/448-0555 • 9pm-3am, clsd Sun-Tue • popular • lesbians/ gay men • dancing/DJ • drag shows • transgender-friendly • drag shows • karaoke • patio • wheelchair access

Baton Rouge

INFO LINES & SERVICES

Freedom of Choice/ Gay AA 333 E Chimes St (at the Wesley Foundation) 225/924-0030 (AA#) • 8pm Th & 9pm Sat

The Lambda Group 225/907-3665 • info hotline

BARS

Doubleloons 7367 Exchange Pl 225/926-4744 • 7pm-close, 8pm-2am Fri-Sat, clsd Sun-Tue • gay/ straight • neighborhood bar

George's Place 860 St Louis 225/387-9798 • 3pm-2am, from 5pm Sat, clsd Sun • popular • lesbians/ gay men • neighborhood bar • karaoke Wed-Th • male strippers Tue & Fri-Sat • wheelchair access

Hound Dog 668 Main St (at 7th) 225/344-0807 • noon-2am, clsd Sun • lesbians/ gay men • neighborhood bar • shows monthly • also giftshop • wheelchair access

NIGHTCLUBS

L 174 South Blvd 225/389-1441 • 8pm-2am, clsd Sun-Tue • dancing/DJ • 18+

Splash 2183 Highland Rd 225/242-9491 • 9pm-2am, clsd Sun-Tue • lesbians/ gay men • dancing/DJ • drag shows • 18+ • wheelchair access

RESTAURANTS

Drusilla Seafood 3482 Drusilla Ln (at Jefferson Hwy) 225/923-0896 • 11am-10pm, till 9pm wknds

Ralph & Kacoo's 6110 Bluebonnet Blvd (off I-10 & Perkins) 225/766-2113 • 11am-9:30pm, till 10:30pm Fri-Sat • Cajun

BOOKSTORES

Hibiscus Bookstore 635 Main St (btwn 6th & 7th) 225/387-4264 • 11am-6pm, clsd Sun • LGBT

PUBLICATIONS

Ambush Mag 504/522-8049 • LGBT newspaper for the Gulf South

SPIRITUAL GROUPS

MCC of Baton Rouge 7747 Tom Dr (off Airline Hwy) 225/248-0404 • 11am Sun

Breaux Bridge

ACCOMMODATIONS

Maison des Amis 111 Washington St (at Bridge St) 337/507-3399 • gay-friendly • charming 1870 Creole/ Caribbean residence overlooking legendary Bayou Teche • one block from historic downtown • full brkfst • $100-200

Folsom

ACCOMMODATIONS

Woods Hole Inn 78253 Woods Hole Ln (at Thompson Rd) 985/796-9077 • gay-friendly • secluded getaway • 40 minutes from New Orleans • suites & cabin • fireplaces • nonsmoking • $85-138

Gretna

see New Orleans

Harvey

see New Orleans

Lafayette

INFO LINES & SERVICES

AA Gay/ Lesbian 115 Leonie St 337/991-0830 (AA) • call for time & locations

BARS

Back Side 209 Jefferson St (at Sound Factory) 337/269-0430 • 4pm-2am, noon-midnight Sun • lesbians/ gay men • neighborhood bar • male dancers Wed • gay-owned

Jules' Downtown 533 Jefferson St 337/264-8000 • 8pm-2am, clsd Sun-Mon • lesbians/ gay men • dancing/DJ • karaoke Th • strippers Wed & Sat • wheelchair access

NIGHTCLUBS

Sound Factory 209 Jefferson St (at Cypress) 337/269-6011 • 8pm-2am, till midnight Sun • mostly gay men • dancing/DJ • karaoke Tue • male dancers Wed • drag shows Sun • young crowd • gay-owned

Lake Charles

ACCOMMODATIONS

Aunt Ruby's 504 Pujo St (at Hodges) 337/430-0603 • gay/ straight • B&B • full brkfst • gay-owned • $85-120

NIGHTCLUBS

Crystal's 112 W Broad St 337/433-5457 • 8pm-2am, from 9pm Fri-Sat, till 4am Fri • lesbians/ gay men • dancing/DJ • country/ western • drag shows • wheelchair access

Illusion Nightclub 3905 Ryan St 337/562-8010 • 5pm-close, from 7pm Fri-Sat • gay/ straight • dancing/ DJ • transgender-friendly • live shows • videos • 18+ • young crowd • wheelchair access

CAFES

Creole Coffeehouse 311 Broad St (at Ryan) 337/433-0857 • 7am-4pm, till 1pm Sat, clsd Sun

RESTAURANTS

Pujo St Café 901 Ryan St (at Pujo) 337/439-2054 • 11am-9pm, till 10pm Fri-Sat • gay-owned • full bar

RETAIL SHOPS

Celtic Light 2024 Kirkman St (at 12th St) 337/497-0542 • 10am-7pm, 9am-5pm Sat, clsd Sun • gay-friendly • metaphysical bookstore • classes in Tarot & Wicca • gay pride items • gay-owned

Metairie

see New Orleans

Monroe

BARS

The Corner Bar 512 N 3rd St (at Pine) **318/329-0046** • 6:30pm-2am, clsd Sun, seasonal hours • lesbians/ gay men • neighborhood bar • multiracial • live shows • karaoke • drag shows • 18+ • gay-owned

Natchitoches

ACCOMMODATIONS

Chez des Amis B&B 910 Washington St (at Texas St) 318/352-2647 • gay/ straight • full brkfst • nonsmoking • gay-owned • $90-150

New Orleans

Please Note: Hurricane Katrina happened as this edition went to press. Please call ahead to make sure the listing has reopened. Here's to the new New Orleans—may it be bigger, better, and wilder than ever!

INFO LINES & SERVICES

AA Lambda Center 2106 Decatur (corner of Frenchmen) 504/779-1178 (GENERAL AA OFFICE #) • daily meetings

Lesbian/ Gay Community Center of New Orleans 2114 Decatur St (btwn Elysian Fields & Frenchmen) 504/945-1103 • 2pm-8pm, noon-6pm Fri-Sat, clsd Sun • call first • wheelchair access

ACCOMMODATIONS

1227 Easton House 1227 N Rendon St (btwn Esplanade & Grand Rte St John) 504/488-5543, 877/311-1023 • gay/ straight • B&B • full brkfst • near City Park • some shared baths • nonsmoking • gay-owned • $85-210

1850's Creole Cottage French Quarter 504/527-5360, 888/523-5235 • gay/ straight • 2 1-bdrm apts • kids ok • $95-330

1896 O'Malley House B&B 120 S Pierce St (at Canal St) 504/488-5896, 866/226-1896 • gay/ straight • B&B • jacuzzi • kids ok • gay-owned • $89-195

▲ **A Creole House** 1013 St Ann (btwn Burgundy & N Rampart) 504/524-8076, 888/251-0090 • gay/ straight • 1830s building furnished in period style • nonsmoking • kids ok • $49-225

Aaron Ingram Haus 1012 Elysian Fields Ave (btwn N Rampart & St Claude) 504/388-2224 • gay/ straight • guesthouse • apts • courtyard • gay-owned • $68-175

Alternative Accommodations/ French Quarter Accommodation Service 1001 Marigny St 504/949-5815, 800/209-9408 • 4 gay-friendly guesthouses

Andrew Jackson Hotel 919 Royal St (btwn St Philip & Dumaine) 504/561-5881, 800/654-0224 • gay-friendly • historic inn • tropical courtyard • $90-179

Antebellum Guest House 1333 Esplanade Ave (at Maris St) 504/943-1900 • gay/ straight • B&B • full brkfst • clothing-optional hot tub • private courtyard • nonsmoking • gay-owned • $100-175

Ashton's B&B 2023 Esplanade Ave (at Galvez) 504/942-7048, 800/725-4131 • gay-friendly • 1860s Greek revival mansion • quiet location • close by to French quarter • $120-180

Auld Sweet Olive B&B 2460 N Rampart (at Spain) 504/947-4332, 877/470-5323 • gay/ straight • kids 13+ ok • nonsmoking • $85-150

B&W Courtyards B&B 2425 Chartres St (btwn Mandeville & Spain) 504/945-9418, 800/585-5731 • gay-friendly • hot tub • gay-owned • $99+

Bed & Beverage Guest Apts 504/588-1483, 800/809-7815 • gay/ straight • furnished studios in the French Quarter • swimming • kids/ pets ok • wheelchair access • $75-265

Big Easy/ French Quarter Lodging 233 Cottonwood Dr, Gretna 504/433-2563, 800/368-4876 • gay/ straight • free reservation service • gay-owned

The Biscuit Palace 730 Dumaine (btwn Royal & Bourbon) 504/525-9949 • gay-friendly • 1820s Creole mansion • B&B & apts • in the French Quarter • kids ok • wheelchair access • $95-150

Block-Keller House 3620 Canal St (at Telemachus) 504/483-3033, 877/588-3033 • gay/ straight • B&B in restored Classical Revival villa • nonsmoking • kids ok • partial wheelchair access • gay-owned • $90-135

The Bohemian Armadillo 735 Touro St (at Dauphine) 504/947-8212, 866/947-8212 • gay/ straight • newly remodeled 1820s Creole cottage • hot tub • kids ok • nonsmoking • private courtyard • $89-200

Bon Maison Guest House 835 Bourbon St (btwn Lafitte's & Bourbon Pub) 504/561-8498 • popular • lesbians/ gay men • 1833 town house • nonsmoking • gay-owned • $95-175

Bourbon Orleans Hotel 717 Orleans (at Bourbon St) **504/523-2222** • popular • gay-friendly • swimming • also Palliard's restaurant & Snook's bar

Bourgoyne Guest House 839 Bourbon St (at Dumaine St) **504/524-3621, 504/525-3983** • popular • lesbians/ gay men • 1830s Creole mansion • courtyard • $93-190

The Burgundy B&B 2513 Burgundy St (at St Roch) **504/942-1463, 800/970-2153** • gay/ straight • close to French Quarter • clothing-optional hot tub • gay-owned

Bywater B&B 1026 Clouet St **504/944-8438** • gay-friendly • Victorian cottage • fireplace • nonsmoking • kids/ pets ok • lesbian & gay-owned • $75-125

Chartres Condo French Quarter **504/527-5360, 888/523-5235** • gay/ straight • jacuzzi • gay & straight-owned • $575-1,400/ night

The Chimes B&B Constantinople at Coliseum (in Garden District) **504/488-4640, 800/729-4640** • gay-friendly • 1876 home • nonsmoking • kids/ pets ok • $85-155

Creole Inn 2471 Dauphine St (at Spain) **504/948-3230** • B&B in private home • gay/ straight • nonsmoking • kids 12 years & up ok • garden • gay-owned • $78-173

The Degas House 2306 Esplanade Ave (at Tonti St) **504/821-5009, 800/755-6730** • gay-friendly • French Impressionist Degas' home (1872-1873) • full brkfst • jacuzzi • $99-250

Elysian Fields Inn 930 Elysian Fields Ave (at Burgundy) **504/948-9420, 866/948-9420** • gay/ straight • 1860s inn • full brkfst • jacuzzi tubs • nonsmoking • wheelchair access • gay-owned • $99-250

Elysian Guest House 1008 Elysian Fields Ave (at Rampart St) **504/940-0540** • lesbians/ gay men • 1880s Victorian "double" • large hot tub • kids/ small dogs ok • gay-owned • $80-200

Empress Hotel 1317 Ursulines Ave (btwn Treme & Marais) **504/529-4100, 888/524-9200** • gay-friendly • 2 blocks to French Quarter • kids/ pets ok •

Five Continents B&B 1731 Esplanade Ave (at Claiborne) **504/943-3536, 800/997-4652** • gay/ straight • B&B • full brkfst • kids/ pets ok • gay-owned • $100-300

| Reply | Forward | | Delete |

Date: Nov 21, 2005 11:23:19
From: Girl-on-the-Go
To: Editor@Damron.com
Subject: New Orleans

>If you haven't been to New Orleans for Mardi Gras, you've missed the party of the year. But there's still time to plan next year's visit to the French Quarter's blowout of a block party—complete with its elaborate balls, parades, and dancing in the streets. It all starts the day before Ash Wednesday (usually in February).

>Of course, there's more to "The Big Easy" than Mardi Gras, especially if you like life hot, humid, and spiced with steamy jazz and hot pepper. Park your bags in one of the MANY lesbian/gay inns in the area. Then venture into the French Quarter, where you'll find the infamous Bourbon Street with people strolling—or occasionally staggering—from jazz club to jazz club, bar to bar, restaurants to shops, twenty-four hours a day. Kitsch-lovers won't want to miss Pat O'Brien's, home of the Hurricane and the #1 bar in the country for alcohol volume sold—even if you don't drink, a campy photo in front of the fountain is a must. Jazz lovers, make a pilgrimage to Preservation Hall.

>Just across from Esplanade Avenue from the French Quarter is the less touristy but very hip Faubourg-Marigny neighborhood. This history-rich bohemian enclave has plenty to offer in the way of restaurants, cafes, but is also notable for its architecture and interesting, angular street layout.

>If you love to shop, check out the French Market, the Jackson Brewery, and Riverwalk. Antique hunting is best on Rue Royal or Decatur Street. And you can't leave New Orleans without a trip through the Garden District to see the incredible antebellum and revival homes—a trip best made on the St. Charles Trolley.

Reply **Forward**   **Delete**

>Gourmands must try real Cajun & Creole food in its natural environment—stop by **Commander's Palace** or **Sammy's Seafood** for a sampling. For melt-in-your-mouth, hot, sugar-powdered beignets, run, don't walk to **Café du Monde**.

>The morbidly inclined among us are bound to see shadows of vampires and other creatures of the night in this town of mysticism and the occult. With residents (past and present) like Anne Rice, Poppy Z. Brite, and Marie LaVeau stirring up the spirits, perhaps a protective amulet from Marie LaVeau's House of Voodoo (739 Bourbon St, 504/581-3751) would be a good idea. For a peek at traditional voodoo—the Afro-Caribbean religion, not the B-movie schlock—visit the Voodoo Museum (504/523-7685). Or sate that urge for blood with a body piercing at **Rings of Desire** or some fresh fetish wear from **Second Skin Leather.**

>So, pick a realm of the senses and go wild. You'll be happy to know that the women-loving-women of New Orleans know how to do wild very well. Get crazy with the boys (try the women-owned **Friendly Bar**) in the French Quarter—this Gay Central in New Orleans is also party central for everyone. And during **Southern Decadence,** the gay Mardi Gras on Labor Day weekend, the Quarter becomes a little queerer.

>To find out the current women's nights at the guys' bars, stop by the LGBT **Faubourg Marigny Art & Books** or **Alternatives** and pick up a copy of the Crescent City's LGBT newspaper, **Ambush.** Or drop by the **Lesbian/Gay Community Center** on Decatur.

French Quarter Corporate Apts
504/495-2387 • gay-straight • 1-bdrm apts & condos • gay-owned • $100-200

French Quarter Reservation Service
504/565-5344, 866/827-6652 • lesbians/gay men • kids ok • some w/ swimming • some w/ wheelchair access • gay-owned

French Quarter Suites Hotel 1119 N Rampart (at Ursulines) 504/524-7725, 800/457-2253 • gay-friendly • all-suite hotel • hot tub • swimming • kitchens • kids/pets ok • wheelchair access • $70+

▲ **The Frenchmen Hotel** 417 Frenchmen St (where Esplanade, Decatur & Frenchmen intersect) 504/948–2166, 800/831–1781 • popular • gay/straight • 1860s Creole town houses • spa • swimming • nonsmoking • kids ok • wheelchair access • $59-299

Garden District B&B 2418 Magazine St (at First St) 504/895–4302 • gay-friendly • 2 miles to French Quarter • kids ok • $80-150

The Gillham Pierce House B&B 1407 Esplanade Ave (at N Villere) 504/944–2115, 866/226–6392 • gay/straight • swimming • kids/pets ok • nonsmoking • gay-owned • $110-225

Glimmer Inn B&B 1631 7th St (at St Charles) 504/897–1895 • gay-friendly • 1891 Victorian & cottage • kids/pets ok • some shared baths • women-owned/run • $70-100

New Orleans

WHERE THE GIRLS ARE:
Wandering the Quarter, or in the small artsy area known as Mid-City, north of the Quarter up Esplanade St.

ANNUAL EVENTS:
February - Mardi Gras 504/566-5011. North America's rowdiest block party.

March - Gulf Coast Womyn's Sister Camp at Camp SisterSpirit (in Ovett, MS) 601/344-1411, web: www.campsisterspirit.com.

March - Tennesse Williams Festival, web: www.tennesseewilliams.net.

April - Gay Easter Parade, web: www.gayeasterparade.com.

April/May - New Orleans Jazz & Heritage Festival, web: www.nojazzfest.com.

May - Saints & Sinners, LGBT writers' festival, web: www.sasfest.org.

Labor Day - Southern Decadence 504/522-8047, web: www.southerndecadence.com. Gay mini-Mardi Gras.

CITY INFO:
504/566-5011 or 800/672-6124, web: www.neworleanscvb.com. Louisiana Office of Tourism 225/342-8100 or 800/334-8626, web: www.louisianatravel.com.

BEST VIEW:
Club 360 (504/522-9795) on the 33rd floor of the World Trade Center of New Orleans.

WEATHER:
Summer temperatures hover in the 90°s with subtropical humidity. Winters can be rainy and chilly. The average temperature in February (Mardi Gras month) is 58°, while the average precipitation is 5.23".

TRANSIT:
United Cab 504/522-9771.
Airport Shuttle 504/522-3500.
New Orleans Regional Transit Authority 504/827-7802, web: www.norta.com.

ATTRACTIONS:
Bourbon Street in the French Quarter.
Cabildo (to see the Louisiana Purchase) 504/568-6968.
Cafe du Monde for beignets 504/587-0835.
Garden District.
Haunted History Tour, 504/861-2727, web: www.hauntedhistory-tours.com.
Moon Walk.
New Orleans Museum of Art 504/488-2631, web: www.noma.org.
Pat O'Brien's for a hurricane 504/525-4823.
Preservation Hall 504/522-2841 or 888/946-5299, web: www.preservationhall.com.
Top of the Market.

The Green House Inn 1212 Magazine St (at Erato) 504/525–1333, 800/966–1303 • lesbians/ gay men • 1840s guesthouse • gym • hot tub • swimming • nonsmoking • pets ok • gay-owned • $69-199

HH Whitney House on the Historic Esplanade 1923 Esplanade Ave (btwn N Prieur and N Johnson) 504/948–9448, 877/944–9448 • gay/ straight • 1865 B&B • hot tub • some shared baths • kids ok • nonsmoking • gay-owned • $95-250

Hotel Monaco—New Orleans 333 St Charles Ave 504/561–0010, 866/561–0010 • gay-friendly • boutique hotel in former Masonic Temple • $99-329

Hotel Royal 1006 Royal St (at St Philip) 504/524–3900, 800/776–3901 • gay/ straight • historic 1830s Creole town house in the heart of the French Quarter • nonsmoking • wheelchair access • $95-350

Hotel St Pierre 911 Burgundy St 504/524–4401, 800/225–4040 • gay-friendly • European-style hotel • 2 blocks off Bourbon St • swimming • kids ok • $90-179

Inn The Quarter Reservation Service 888/523–5235 • gay-friendly • nonsmoking gay & straight-owned • $79-600

Kerlerec House 922-928 Kerlerec (at Dauphine St) 504/944–8544 • gay/ straight • 1 block from the French Quarter • gardens • kids/ pets ok, but call first • no unregistered overnight guests • gay-owned • $75-350

La Dauphine, Residence des Artistes 2316 Dauphine St (btwn Elysian Fields & Marigny) 504/948–2217 • gay/ straight • B&B • nonsmoking • gay-owned • $75-185 (3-night minimum)

La Maison Marigny B&B on Bourbon 1421 Bourbon St (at Esplanade) 504/948–3638, 800/570–2014 • gay-friendly • on the quiet end of Bourbon St • nonsmoking • gay-owned • $95-199

Lafitte Guest House 1003 Bourbon St (at St Philip) 504/581–2678, 800/331–7971 • popular • gay/ straight • elegant French manor house • nonsmoking • kids ok • full bar • gay-owned • $129-219

▲ **Lamothe House Hotel** 621 Esplanade Ave (btwn Royal & Chartres) 504/947–1161, 888/696–9575 • gay/ straight • Victorian guesthouse • courtyard • jacuzzi • swimming • kids ok • straight & gay-owned • $59-199

Lanata House 1220 Chartres St (at Gov Nicholls) 504/581–9060, 866/881–9060 • gay/ straight • furnished residential accommodations • swimming • gay-owned • $125-275

Le Papillon Guesthouse 2011 N Rampart St (at Touro St) 504/948–4993, 504/884–4008 (CELL) • gay/ straight • restored 1830s guesthouse • pets ok • gay-owned • $65-135

Lions Inn 2517 Chartres St (btwn Spain & Franklin) 504/945–2339, 800/485–6846 • gay/ straight • handsome 1850s home • swimming • hot tub • nudity ok • nonsmoking • semi-tropical patio • gay-owned • $50-165

Magnolia Mansion 2127 Prytania St (at Jackson) 504/412–9500, 888/222–9235 • gay/ straight • an enchanting antebellum mansion w/ uniquely themed guestrooms • located in historic garden district • $150-550

▲ **Marigny Guest House** 621 Esplanade (btwn Royal & Chartres) 504/944–9700 (LAMOTHE HOUSE #), 888/696–9575 • gay/ straight • Creole cottage annexed to Lamothe House • swimming at Lamothe • nonsmoking • $49-175

Mazant Guest House 906 Mazant (at Burgundy) 504/944–2662 • gay-friendly • 1870s Greek Revival • inexpensive

The McKendrick-Breaux House 1474 Magazine St (at Race St) 504/586–1700, 888/570–1700 • gay-friendly • 1860s restored Greek Revival • hot tub • kids ok • nonsmoking • $145-235

Mentone B&B 1437 Pauger St (at Kerlerec) 504/943–3019 • gay-friendly • suite in Victorian in the Faubourg Marigny district • nonsmoking • women-owned/ run • $125-175

New Orleans B&B/ French Quarter Accommodations 504/561–0447, 888/240–0070 • gay-friendly • reservation service • condos, apartments, & B&Bs available • pool • jacuzzi • nonsmoking • $100-500

New Orleans Guest House 1118 Ursulines Ave (at N Rampart) 504/566–1177, 800/562–1177 • gay-friendly • Creole cottage dated back to 1848 • courtyard • gay-owned • $79-99

Olde Town Inn 1001 Marigny St 504/949–5815, 800/209–9408 • gay/ straight • historic guesthouse • kids/ pets ok • lesbian & gay & straight-owned • wheelchair access • $49-129

Olde Victorian Inn & Spa—French Quarter 914 N Rampart St (at Dumaine St) **504/522–2446, 800/725–2446** • gay/ straight • B&B • full brkfst • swimming • nonsmoking • gay-owned • $99-250

The Park Plaza Hotel 1500 Canal St (at LaSalle St) **504/522–4500** • gay-friendly • 4 blocks from French Quarter • food served • swimming • $99-189

Parkview Marigny B&B 726 Frenchmen St (at Dauphine) **504/945–7875, 877/645–8617** • gay/ straight • 1870s Creole town house • nonsmoking • courtyard • gay-owned • $115-160

The Pontchartrain Hotel 2031 St Charles Ave (at Josephine St) **504/524–0581, 800/777–6193** • gay-friendly • landmark hotel in Garden District • jacuzzi • kids ok • $59-429

The Rathbone Mansions 1227 Esplanade Ave (at St Claude) **504/947–2100, 800/947–2101** • gay/ straight • 1850s Greek Revival mansion • also at 1244 Esplanade • swimming • gay-owned • $59-299

Rober House Condos **504/529–4663** • gay/ straight • condos around courtyard • swimming • nonsmoking room available • kids ok • wheelchair access • gay-owned • $89-135

Royal Barracks Guest House 717 Barracks St (at Bourbon) **504/529–7269, 888/255–7269** • gay-friendly • hot tub • nonsmoking • private patios • $89-149

Royal Street Courtyard 2438 Royal St (at Spain) **504/943–6818, 888/846–4004** • gay/ straight • suites in 1850s guesthouse • hot tub • pets ok • gay-owned • $55-164

Southern Comforts 310/305–2984, 800/889–7359 • reservation service for several deluxe rental properties • gay-owned

St Charles Guest House 1748 Prytania St (at Felicity) **504/523–6556** • gay-friendly • pensione-style guesthouse • some shared baths • swimming • patio • $55-125

▲ **St Peter House Hotel** 1005 St Peter St (at Burgundy) **504/524–9232, 888/604–6226** • gay/ straight • antique-furnished early-1800s building • historic location • $59-259

Sully Mansion 2631 Prytania St (at Fourth) **504/891–0457, 800/364–2414** • gay-friendly • 1890s mansion in heart of Garden District • nonsmoking • gay-owned • $99-250

Sun & Moon B&B 1037 N Rampart St (at Ursulines) **504/522–9716, 800/457–2253** • gay/ straight • Creole cottage • kids ok • women-owned/ run • $90-120

Sun Oak Museum & Guesthouse 2020 Burgundy St **504/945–0322** • gay/ straight • Greek Revival Creole cottage circa 1836 • gardens • gay-owned • $75-150

▲ **Ursuline Guest House** 708 Ursulines Ave (btwn Royal & Bourbon) **504/525–8509, 800/654–2351** • popular • gay/ straight • hot tub • evening socials • gay-owned • $85-125

Vieux Carré Rentals 841 Bourbon St **504/525–3983** • gay-friendly • 1 & 2-bdrm apts • nonsmoking • $100-200

W New Orleans 333 Poydras **504/525–9444, 877/WHOTELS (RESERVATIONS ONLY)** • gay-friendly • swimming • also popular bar & restaurant • wheelchair access • $239-479

W New Orleans—French Quarter 316 Chartres St **504/581–1200, 877/WHOTELS (RESERVATIONS ONLY)** • gay-friendly • swimming • also popular restaurant • wheelchair access • $289-489

Bars

Big Daddy's 2513 Royal St (at Franklin) **504/948–6288** • 24hrs • lesbians/ gay men • neighborhood bar • occasional shows • wheelchair access

Bourbon Pub & Parade 801 Bourbon St (at St Ann) **504/529–2107** • 24hrs • popular • lesbians/ gay men • dancing/DJ • theme nights • Sun T-dance • drag shows/ strippers • videos • 18+

Cafe Lafitte in Exile/ The Balcony Bar 901 Bourbon St (at Dumaine) **504/522–8397** • 24hrs • popular • mostly gay men • dancing/DJ • live shows • videos • Balcony Bar upstairs w/ cyberbar

Country Club 634 Louisa St (at Royal) **504/945–0742** • 11am-1am • popular • gay-friendly • food served • cabaret • swimming • volleyball • nude sunbathing • not your father's country club!

Cutter's 706 Franklin Ave (at Royal) **504/948–4200** • 11am-3am • lesbians/ gay men • neighborhood • wheelchair access

The Double Play 439 Dauphine St (at St Louis) **504/523–4517** • 24hrs • mostly gay men • neighborhood bar • transgender-friendly

The Four Seasons 3229 N Causeway Blvd (at 18th), Metairie **504/832–0659** • 3pm-4am • popular • mostly gay men • neighborhood bar • live music & shows in summer • karaoke • patio • also the Out Back Bar • gay-owned

The Friendly Bar 2301 Chartres St (at Marigny) **504/943–8929** • 11am-3am • popular • lesbians/ gay men • neighborhood bar • wheelchair access • women-owned

Golden Lantern 1239 Royal St (at Barracks) **504/529–2860** • 24hrs • mostly gay men • neighborhood bar • drag shows Sat • male dancers Sat-Sun

Good Friends Bar 740 Dauphine (at St Ann) **504/566–7191** • 24hrs • popular • mostly gay men • neighborhood bar • professional crowd • karaoke Tue • wheelchair access • also Queens Head Pub Th-Sun • piano sing-along Sun

Hi Ho Lounge 2239 St Claude Ave (at Marigny) **504/947–9344** • 8pm-close • gay-friendly • casual cocktail lounge • dancing/ DJ • alternative • Punk Rock Girl Nite Tue • live music some wknds • younger crowd • women-owned/ run

Le Roundup 819 St Louis St (at Dauphine) **504/561–8340** • 24hrs • mostly gay men • neighborhood bar • country/ western • transgender-friendly

Masquerades Lounge 3505 Division St, Metairie **504/888–4101** • noon-2am, till 3am Fri-Sat, from 5pm Sun • lesbians/ gay men • neighborhood bar • karaoke Sat • also Two Jokers Grill (504/454-5101), 11am-8pm, till midnight Fri-Sat

MRB 515 St Philip (at Decatur) **504/524–2558** • 24hrs • popular • lesbians/ gay men • neighborhood bar • patio

Napoleon's Itch Bourbon & St Ann (in Bourbon Orleans Hotel) **504/371–5450** • 3pm-close • gay/ straight • full-liquor wine & martini bar • smokefree

The New Bar 4929 Airline Dr, Metairie **504/780–1462** • 5pm-close, from 3pm Sun • lesbians/ gay men • dancing/ DJ • drag shows • karaoke Wed

Ninth Circle 700 N Rampart (at St Peter) **504/524–7654** • 24hrs • mostly gay men • neighborhood bar • transgender-friendly

Phoenix 941 Elysian Fields Ave (at N Rampart) **504/945–9264** • 24hrs • popular • mostly gay men • neighborhood bar • leather/ levi crowd • beer busts • also The Eagle upstairs • 9pm-5am • DJ • gay-owned

The Pub 2320 Belle Chasse Hwy, Gretna **504/362–4459** • 11am-close • lesbians/ gay men • neighborhood bar • live music/ bands • drag shows

Rawhide 2010 740 Burgundy (at St Ann) **504/525–8106** • 24hrs • popular • mostly gay men • neighborhood bar • dancing/ DJ • alternative, underground sound • karaoke • leather • videos

The Sanctuary 2301 N Causeway Blvd (at 34th), Metairie **504/834–7979** • 5:30pm-close, clsd Sun-Mon • lesbians/ gay men • neighborhood bar • dancing/DJ Sat • drag shows occasionally • wheelchair access

Voodoo at Congo Square 718 N Rampart (at Orleans) **504/527–0703** • 24hrs • mostly gay men • neighborhood bar

Wits Inn 141 N Carollton Ave (at Iberville) **504/486–1600** • 5pm-midnight Th only • ladies night drink specials • pool table

NIGHTCLUBS

735 Bourbon 735 Bourbon St (at Orleans) **504/581–6740** • noon-close, clsd Mon • gay/ straight • dancing/DJ • live shows

Oz 800 Bourbon St (at St Ann) **504/593–9491** • 24hrs • popular • mostly gay men • dancing/DJ • drag shows • live shows • videos • young crowd • wheelchair access

Starlight by the Park 834 N Rampart (at Dumaine) **504/561–8939** • noon-4am, 24hrs Fri-Sun • lesbians/ gay men • neighborhood bar • live shows • wheelchair access

CAFES

CC's Coffee House 941 Royal St **504/581–6996** • 6:30am-11pm, till midnight Fri-Sat, 7am-10pm Sun

Coffee, Friends and... 2401 Burgundy **504/948–7401** • lesbians/ gay men • food served

Croissants d'Or 617 Ursulines St **504/524–4663** • 7am-4:30pm, clsd Tue • delicious pastries

Royal Blend Coffee & Tea House 621 Royal St **504/523–2716** • 7am-8pm, till 11pm Fri-Sat, on a quiet, hidden courtyard, also serves salads & sandwiches

Z'otz 8210 Oak St **504/861–2224** • 24hrs • coffee shop & art space • live entertainment

RESTAURANTS

13 Monaghan's 517 Frenchmen St **504/942–1345** • 10am-3am • brkfst, lunch & dinner all the time • some veggie • full bar • wheelchair access

Bluebird Cafe 3625 Prytania St (btwn Foucher & Antonine) **504/895–7166** • 7am-10pm, from 8am wknds • popular • great brkfsts • cash only • $2-8

Bywater Bar-B-Que 3162 Dauphine St (at Louisa) **504/944-4445, 504/947-0000** • 7am-10pm, from 11am wknds • gay-owned

Cafe Sbisa 1011 Decatur St **504/522-5565** • dinner nightly & Sun Jazz Brunch • French Creole • patio • live jazz

Casamento's 4330 Magazine St (at Napoleon Ave) **504/895-9761** • lunch & dinner, clsd Mon (also clsd June-Aug) • best oyster loaf in city

Clover Grill 900 Bourbon St (at Dumaine) **504/598-1010** • 24hrs • popular • diner fare • $5-10

Commander's Palace 1403 Washington Ave (at Coliseum St, in Garden District) **504/899-8221** • lunch & dinner Mon-Fri • popular • upscale Creole & dress (no shorts) • jazz brunch wknds • reservations required

Daril's Diner & Shortstop 717 St Peter (at Royal & Bourbon) **504/524-3287** • 1950s-style diner • wheelchair access

Feelings Cafe 2600 Chartres St (at Franklin Ave) **504/945-2222** • dinner nightly, lunch Fri, Sun brunch • Creole • piano bar • courtyard

Fiorella's Cafe 45 French Market Pl (at Gov Nicholls & Ursulines) **504/528-9566** • 7am-2am, clsd Sun • homecooking

La Peniche 1940 Dauphine St (at Touro St) **504/943-1460** • 24hrs Fri-Mon, clsd Wed • Southern comfort foods • popular for brkfst • some veggie

Lafitte's Restaurant 2031 St Charles Ave (in Pontchartrain Hotel) **504/524-0581, 800/777-6193** • brkfst, lunch & dinner • Creole • the setting for part of Anne Rice's *The Witching Hour*

Mama Rosa 616 N Rampart (at Toulouse & St Louis) **504/523-5546** • 11am-10pm, till 11pm Fri-Sat • Italian • $6-11

Marigny Brasserie 640 Frenchmen St **504/945-4472** • lunch & dinner • French

Mona Lisa 1212 Royal St (at Barracks) **504/522-6746** • 11am-11pm, till midnight wknds • Italian • some veggie • beer/ wine • $10-15

Mona's 504 Frenchmen St **504/949-4115** • cheap Middle Eastern eats • some veggie

Moon Wok 800 Dauphine St **504/523-6910** • Chinese

Nola 534 St Louis St (btwn Chartres & Decatur) **504/522-6652** • lunch (except Sun) & dinner • fusion Creole from Emeril Lagasse • wheelchair access

Olivier's 204 Decatur St **504/525-7734** • lunch & dinner • Creole • wheelchair access • $10-15

Praline Connection 542 Frenchmen St (at Chartres) **504/943-3934** • 11am-10:30pm, till midnight Fri-Sat • soul food • also a location at 901 St Peters St, 504/523-3973 w/ a Sun gospel jazz brunch

Quarter Scene 900 Dumaine St (at Dauphine) **504/522-6533** • brkfst, lunch & dinner, dinner only Tue • Cajun/ Creole homecooking • some veggie

Quartermaster 1100 Bourbon St **504/529-1416** • 24hrs • "The Nellie Deli" • sandwiches & more

Sammy's Seafood 627 Bourbon St (across from Pat O' Brien's) **504/525-8442** • 11am-midnight • Cajun/ Creole • $9-28

Santa Fe 801 Frenchmen St (at Dauphine) **504/944-6854** • 5pm-10pm, till 11pm Fri-Sat, clsd Sun-Tue • Southwestern

The Upperline Restaurant 1413 Upperline **504/891-9822** • Creole • fine dining • full bar

Vera Cruz 7537 Maple (at Hillard) **504/866-1736** • 5pm-11pm, from 11am Th-Sat, clsd Sun • Mexican • wheelchair access

ENTERTAINMENT & RECREATION

Café du Monde 1039 Decatur St (Old Jackson Square) **504/587-0835, 800/772-2927** • till you've a had a beignet—fried dough, powdered w/ sugar, that melts in your mouth—you haven't been to New Orleans & this is "the" place to have them 24hrs a day

Gay Heritage Tour 909 Bourbon St **504/945-6789** • call for details • departs from Alternatives giftshop

Haunted History Tour 888/861-2727, 888/644-6787 • guided 2-1/2-hour tours of New Orleans' most famous haunts, including Anne Rice's home

Mardi Gras World 233 Newton St **504/361-7821, 800/362-8213** • tour this year-round Mardi Gras float workshop • take the free ferry from the base of Canal St • tour costs $14

Pat O'Brien's 718 St Peter St (btwn Bourbon & Royal) **504/525-4823, 800/597-4823** • gay-friendly • more than just a bar—come for the Hurricane, stay for the kitsch • also restaurant & cafe at 624 Bourbon

St Charles Streetcar Canal St (btwn Bourbon & Royal Sts) **504/827-7802 (RTA RIDELINE #)** • it's not named Desire, but you should still ride it, Blanche, if you want to see the Garden District

BOOKSTORES

Barnes & Noble 1601 Westbank Expwy, Harvey 504/263-1146 • 10am-10pm, till 11pm Fri-Sat, 11am-8pm Sun • wheelchair access

Beaucoup Books 3951 Magazine St (near Constantinople) 504/895-2663 • 9:30am-5:30pm, clsd Sun • independent • readings

FAB (Faubourg Marigny Art & Books) 600 Frenchmen St (at Chartres) 504/947-3700 • noon-7pm • LGBT

Garden District Bookshop 2727 Prytania St 504/895-2266 • 10am-6pm, 11am-5pm Sun • independent

RETAIL SHOPS

Alternatives 909 Bourbon St (at Dumaine) 504/524-5222 • 11am-7pm • LGBT cards • gifts

Eve's Market 4601 Freret (at Cadiz) 504/891-4015 • 9am-6:30pm, clsd Sun • natural foods store • women-owned/ run

Gargoyles 1201 Decatur St (at Gov Nicholls) 504/529-4384, 866/297-9207 (OUTSIDE LA) • 11am-6pm • leather/ fetish/ goth store

Hit Parade 741 Bourbon St 504/524-7700 • noon-midnight, 11am-2am Fri-Sat • popular • LGBT books • designer circuit clothing & more

Queen Fashions 3017 19th St, Metairie 504/524-4335 & 504/828-9888, 866/444-3357 • 9am-6pm, clsd Sun • sexy footwear (up to size 17), clothing & accessories

Rings of Desire 1128 Decatur St 504/524-6147 • noon-7pm, till 9pm Th-Sat, clsd Tue-Wed • piercing studio

Second Skin Leather 521 St Philip St (btwn Decatur & Chartres) 504/561-8167 • 10am-10pm

Something Different 5300 Tchoupitoulas (in Riverside Market) 504/891-9056 • 10am-9pm, till 7pm Sat, noon-6pm Sun • cards • novelties • gay-owned

PUBLICATIONS

Ambush Mag 504/522-8049 • LGBT newspaper for the Gulf South

Southern Voice 404/876-1819 • weekly LGBT newspaper for AL, FL (panhandle), GA, LA, MS, TN w/ resource listings

The Whiz 504/947-0816, 504/782-2056 • weekly gay guide to New Orleans

SPIRITUAL GROUPS

The Church of Christ the Liberator 1030 Marigny St 504/610-3971 • mass 11am Sun

First Unitarian Universalist Church 5212 S Claiborne Ave (at Jefferson Ave) 504/866-9010 • 10:30am Sun

EROTICA

Bourbon Strip Tease 205 Bourbon St 504/581-6633

Panda Bear 415 Bourbon St (at St Louis) 504/529-3593 • 9am-2am • leather • toys • wheelchair access

Paradise 41 W 24th St (at Crestview), Kenner 504/461-0000 • from 8am • wheelchair access

Shreveport

BARS

Korner Lounge II 800 Louisiana (near Cotton) 318/222-9796 • 5pm-midnight, till 2am Fri-Sat, from 7pm wknds • mostly gay men • neighborhood bar

NIGHTCLUBS

Central Station 1025 Marshall (btwn Fairfield & Creswell) 318/222-2216 • 3pm-6am • popular • lesbians/ gay men • dancing/DJ • country/ western • drag shows • transgender-friendly • live shows • wheelchair access

EROTICA

Fun Shop Too 9434 Mansfield Rd 318/688-2482 • clsd Sun

Slidell

see also New Orleans

BARS

Billy's 2600 Hwy 190 W 985/847-1921 • 5pm-midnight Th & Sun, till 2am Fri-Sat, clsd Mon-Wed • lesbians/ gay men • neighborhood bar

MAINE

Statewide

PUBLICATIONS

In Newsweekly 617/426-8246 • New England's largest LGBT newspaper

Aroostook County

ACCOMMODATIONS

Magic Pond Wildlife Sanctuary & Guest House Blaine 207/429-8787, 207/947-2240 • mostly women • artist-owned cottage • comfortable for women traveling alone • kitchen • nonsmoking • lesbian-owned • $595/ week

Augusta

includes Hallowell

ACCOMMODATIONS

Annabessacook Farm 192 Annabessacook Rd, Winthrop 207/377-3276 • popular • gay/ straight • restored 1810 farmhouse on 25 acres, 10 miles W of Augusta • lakefront • full brkfst • $65-300

Maple Hill Farm B&B Inn Hallowell 207/622-2708, 800/622-2708 • gay/ straight • Victorian farmhouse on 130 acres • full brkfst • whirlpools • clothing-optional swimming pond • nonsmoking • wheelchair access • gay-owned • $75-195

NIGHTCLUBS

PJ's (aka Papa Joe's) 80 Water St (btwn Laurel & Bridge) 207/623-4041 • 7pm-1am Th-Sat • popular • lesbians/ gay men • dancing/DJ • food served • piano bar • patio

RESTAURANTS

Slate's 167 Water St (Franklin), Hallowell 207/622-9575 • lunch & dinner, brunch only Sun • live shows Mon

SPIRITUAL GROUPS

Northern Lights MCC 1038 Riverside Dr (Rte 201) 207/621-2658 • 4pm Sun (6pm June-Aug)

Bangor

ACCOMMODATIONS

Maine Wilderness Lake Island 26 5th St 207/990-5839 • lesbians/ gay men • summer only • weekly rental cabins in the forest • $300+

BOOKSTORES

Pro Libris Bookshop 10 3rd St (at Union) 207/942-3019 • 10am-6pm, clsd Sun-Mon • new & used

Bar Harbor

ACCOMMODATIONS

Aysgarth Station 20 Roberts Ave 207/288-9655 • gay-friendly • 10-minute drive from Acadia • $70-130

Central House Inn 51 Clark Point Rd (at Rte 102), Southwest Harbor 207/244-0100, 877/205-0289 • gay/ straight • B&B inn • full brkfst • jacuzzi • kids ok • gay-owned $85-175

Manor House Inn 106 West St (near Bridge St) 207/288-3759, 800/437-0086 • open May-Nov • gay-friendly • 1880s Victorian mansion • full brkfst • jacuzzi • $75-250

RESTAURANTS

Mama DiMatteo's 34 Kennebec Pl (at Rodick St) 207/288-3666 • 5pm-9pm, open year-round • upscale casual dining • seafood, steak, pasta • full bar • gay-owned

Bath

ACCOMMODATIONS

The Galen C Moses House 1009 Washington St 207/442-8771, 888/442-8771 • gay/ straight • 1874 Victorian • full brkfst • nonsmoking • gay-owned • $99-259

The Inn at Bath 969 Washington St 207/443-4294, 800/423-0964 • gay/ straight • 1810 B&B • full brkfst • jacuzzi • nonsmoking • wheelchair access • $125-200

Belfast

ACCOMMODATIONS

ATBAY Coastal Rentals 207/338-1729 • mostly women • 2 apts for rental w/ lovely bay/ harbor views • proximity to good restaurants, kayaking & flea markets • gay-owned

Greenhope Farm 124 Underpass Rd (at Rte 1), Brooks 207/722-3999 • mostly women • coastal retreat on 25 private acres • camping • horseback-riding • nonsmoking • kids ok • lesbian-owned • $75-175

Belgrade Lakes

ACCOMMODATIONS

Yeaton Farm Inn 298 West Rd, Belgrade 207/495-7766 • gay-friendly • B&B in authentic 1826 stagecoach stop • full brkfst • nonsmoking • $135

Boothbay Harbor

ACCOMMODATIONS

Hodgdon Island Inn Barter's Island Rd (at Sawyer's Island Rd), Boothbay 207/633-7474, 800/314-5160 • gay/ straight • 1810 sea captain's home • full brkfst • swimming • nonsmoking • gay-owned • $125-175

Sur La Mer Inn 18 Eames Rd, PO Box 663, 04538 207/633-7400, 800/791-2026 • gay-friendly • luxury oceanfront B&B • nonsmoking • kids ok • gay-owned • $85-300

Brunswick

RESTAURANTS

Star Fish Grill 100 Pleasant St/ Rte 1 (at Mill St) 207/725-7828 • dinner only • clsd Mon • fresh seafood & natural meats • full bar • lesbian-owned

BOOKSTORES

Gulf of Maine Books 134 Maine St (at Pleasant) 207/729-5083 • 9:30am-5:30pm, clsd Sun • alternative

Camden

ACCOMMODATIONS

Norumbega 63 High St 207/236-4646 • gay-friendly • inn • circa 1886 • restaurant • $95-475

Cape Neddick

BOOKSTORES

Artistic Amazon Bookstore 182 Clay Hill Rd 877/422-0702 • women's • open by appointment only

Corea

ACCOMMODATIONS

The Black Duck Inn on Corea Harbor 207/963-2689 • gay/ straight • restored farmhouse • also cottages • full brkfst • nonsmoking • gay-owned • $120-180

Deer Isle

RESTAURANTS

Fisherman's Friend School St, Stonington 207/367-2442 • 11am-8pm • open April-Oct

Dexter

ACCOMMODATIONS

Brewster Inn 37 Zions Hill 207/924-3130 • gay-friendly • historic mansion • full brkfst • tennis • kids ok • wheelchair access • $79-119

Farmington

BOOKSTORES

Devany, Doak & Garrett Booksellers 193 Broadway 207/778-3454 • hours vary • LGBT section

Freeport

ACCOMMODATIONS

The Bagley House 1290 Royalsborough Rd, Durham 207/865-6566, 800/765-1772 • gay/ straight • full brkfst • nonsmoking • kids ok • conference room for 20 • lesbian-owned • $105-175

RESTAURANTS

Harraseeket Lunch & Lobster Co 162 Main St 207/865-9377, 800/342-6423 • lunch & dinner • open May-Oct

Greenville

ACCOMMODATIONS

Pleasant Street Inn at Moosehead Lake 26 Pleasant St 207/695-3400 • gay/ straight • B&B in 1889 home • full brkfst • nonsmoking • gay-owned • $110-260

Hancock

RESTAURANTS

Le Domaine Restaurant & Inn 207/422-3395, 800/554-8498 • 6pm-9pm, clsd Mon • open June-Oct

Kennebunkport

ACCOMMODATIONS

Arundel Meadows Inn 1024 Portland Rd (at Walker Ln), Arundel 207/985-3770 • gay-friendly • full brkfst • hot tub • swimming • nonsmoking • $115-150

The Colony Hotel 140 Ocean Ave (at Kings Hwy) 207/967-3331, 800/552-2363 • seasonal • gay-friendly • 1914 grand oceanfront property • private beach • swimming • nonsmoking • wheelchair access • lesbian-run • $129-435

White Barn Inn 37 Beach St 207/967-2321 • gay-friendly • swimming • restaurant • $320-785

RESTAURANTS

Bartley's Dockside by the bridge 207/967-5050 • lunch & dinner May-Dec, lunch only Jan-April • 11:30am-10pm • seafood • some veggie • full bar • wheelchair access

Kittery

see also Portsmouth, New Hampshire

Lewiston

ACCOMMODATIONS

Ware Street Inn B&B 52 Ware St (at College St) 207/783-8171, 877/783-8171 • gay-friendly • elegant 1940s colonial • full brkfst • nonsmoking • well-behaved kids ok • $70-175

BARS

The Sportsman's Club 2 Bates St (at Main) 207/784-2251 • 8pm-1am, clsd Mon-Tue • popular • lesbians/gay men • neighborhood bar • dancing/DJ • live shows • karaoke Th • drag shows • "oldest gay bah in Maine"

EROTICA

Paris Book Store 297 Lisbon St (at Chestnut) 207/783-6677

Naples

ACCOMMODATIONS

Lambs Mill Inn 207/693-6253 • gay/ straight • 1890s farmhouse on 20 acres • full brkfst • hot tub • swimming • lesbian-owned • $110-140

Newcastle

ACCOMMODATIONS

The Tipsy Butler B&B 11 High St 207/563-3394 • gay/ straight • on the Damariscotta River • full brkfst • nonsmoking • woman-owned • $90-150

Ogunquit

ACCOMMODATIONS

Abalonia 207/646-4804 • mostly gay men • B&B • renovated farmhouse • near beach & nightlife • nonsmoking • gay-owned • $49-169

Admiral's Inn Resort Hotel 87 Main St (at Agamenticus) 207/646-7093, 888/263-6318 • lesbians/gay men • swimming • hot tub • gay-owned • $69-169

Beauport Inn & Suites on Clay Hill 339 Agamenticus/ Clay Hill Rd 207/361-2400, 800/646-8681 • gay/ straight • English country manor on 11 acres • full brkfst • jacuzzi • nonsmoking • wheelchair access • $135-185

Beaver Dam Campground 551 School St, Rte 9, Berwick 207/698-2267 • gay-friendly • campground on beautiful 20-acre spring-fed pond • swimming • kids/pets ok • women-owned/ run • $25-38

Belm House Vacation Units 207/641-2637 • lesbians/gay men • private studio & 2-bdrm apt rentals • hot tub • dogs ok • gay-owned • $700-1,300/week

Black Boar Inn 277 Main St 207/646-2112 • lesbians/gay men • B&B built in 1674 • full gourmet brkfst • afternoon tea • kids ok • nonsmoking • also weekly cottages • gay-owned • $100-205

The Carriage Trade Inn 254 Shore Rd, PO Box 1793, 03907 207/646-0650, 866/500-0650 • lesbians/gay men • B&B • nonsmoking • also 1 suite for weekly rental • walking distance to Perkins Cove, beach & clubs • gay-owned • $85-250

Distant Sands B&B 207/646-8686 • gay/straight • 18th-c farmhouse • full brkfst • nonsmoking • overlooks Ogunquit River • also cottage • gay-owned • $95-195

▲ **The Heritage of Ogunquit** PO Box 1788, 03907 866/623-2647 • mostly lesbian clientele, gay men welcome • B&B/efficiency rentals • full baths • hot tub • deck • nonsmoking • kids ok • lesbian-owned • $80-145

The HideAway 65 Main St 207/646-3787, 617/524-0080 • guesthouse

The Inn at Tall Chimneys 108 Main St / US Rte 1 207/646-8974 • lesbians/gay men • open April-Nov • gay-owned/run • $50-95

Leisure Inn 73 School St 207/646-2737 • gay/straight • B&B & apts • seasonal • gay-owned • $99-229

MainEscape Rental House 66 Cottage St (at Shore Rd) 954/816-5286 • lesbians/gay men • located in village center • weekly rentals June-Aug • gay-owned

Meadowmere Resort 74 S Main St (at Rte 1) 207/646-9661, 800/633-8718 • gay-friendly • swimming • hot tub • kids ok • nonsmoking • wheelchair access • $45-339

Moon Over Maine B&B Berwick Rd 207/646-6666, 800/851-6837 • lesbians/gay men • hot tub • gay-owned • $69-129

Ogunquit Beach Inn & Vacation Apartments 67 School St 207/646-1112, 888/976-2463 • mostly men • guesthouse B&B • also cottage • 5 minutes to beach • some shared baths • gay-owned • $89-149

The Ogunquit Inn & Cottages 17 Glen Ave 207/646-2967, 866/999-3633 • clsd Jan-Feb • popular • lesbians/gay men • Victorian B&B • nonsmoking • also cottages • gay-owned • $49-189

OgunquitRentals.com 25 Mill St, N Reading, MA 01864 207/646-3840, 978/664-5813 • lesbians/gay men • weeekly rentals • seasonal (June-Sept) • near bars & beach • nonsmoking • pets/kids ok • gay-owned • $1,350-3,500/week

Old Village Inn 250 Main St 207/646-7088 • gay-friendly • 1880s B&B • ocean views • kids/pets ok • also restaurant • seafood • upscale • $60-125

Rockmere Lodge B&B 150 Stearns Rd 207/646-2985 • gay/straight • Maine shingle cottage • near beach • nonsmoking • gay-owned • $135-210

Two Village Square 14 Village Square Ln 207/646-5779, 412/431-1344 (WINTER #) • open May-Oct • mostly gay men • Victorian w/ ocean views • heated pool • nonsmoking • gay-owned • $110-169

Yellow Monkey Guest Houses/Hotel 280 Main St 207/646-9056 • gay/straight • seasonal • roofdeck • jacuzzi • fitness room • kids/pets ok • wheelchair access • gay-owned • $90-150

BARS

Admiral's Inn Bar 87 Main St (at Agamenticus) 207/646-7093, 888/263-6318 • 9am-1am • patio • BBQ

Front Porch Cafe Ogunquit Square 207/646-3976, 207/646-4005 • 4pm-1am, from 11:30am wknds (seasonal) • gay/straight • piano bar upstairs • full menu

Vine Cafe 478 Main St 207/646-0288, 877/646-0288 • 5pm-close • also restaurant • good wine selection

NIGHTCLUBS

Inside Out 237 Main St 207/646-6655 • open April-Jan, noon-close • popular • lesbians/gay men • dancing/DJ • tapas served • live shows Th-Mon • videos • also The Cafe & Martini Lounge • gay-owned

Maine Street 195 Main St/ US Rte 1 207/646-5101 • 6pm-1am, from 3pm Sat, from noon Sun • popular • lesbians/gay men • dancing/DJ • karaoke • cabaret • drag shows • videos • food served • gay-owned

CAFES

Bread & Roses 28 Main St 207/646-4227 • 7am-7pm, open later wknds, seasonal

Fancy That Cafe corner of Beach St & Rte 1 207/646-4118 • 6:30am-11pm • open April-Oct • pastries • sandwiches

Sister Mary Catherine's Internet Cafe, Inc 757A Post Rd (Rte 1) (at 9B & Rte 1), Wells **207/646-6611** • gay-friendly • hours vary by season • gay-owned

RESTAURANTS

Arrows Berrick Rd (18 miles W of Center) **207/361-1100** • open April-Dec, 6pm-9pm, clsd Mon-Tue • popular • eclectic country restaurant in 18th-c farmhouse • some veggie • herb, flower & vegetable gardens • reservations recommended

Clay Hill Farm 220 Clay Hill Rd, Cape Neddick (York) **207/361-2272** • dinner, clsd Mon-Tue • seafood • some veggie • also piano bar

Five-0 50 Shore Rd **207/646-6365** • popular • 5pm-1am, from 11am wknds • full bar

Grey Gull Inn 475 Webhannet Dr, Wells **207/646-7501** • dinner • New England fine dining • also oceanview rooms • $79-149

Joe Allen Restaurant 215 Main St (at Rte 1) **207/646-4477** • 5pm-11:30 pm • live shows • wheelchair access

Johnathan's 92 Bourne Ln **207/646-4777** • 5pm-8:30pm, till 10pm wknds • veggie/ seafood • full bar • wheelchair access

La Pizzeria 25 Main St (Rte 1) **207/646-1143** • lunch & dinner • open April-Dec • some veggie • beer/ wine • gay-owned

Poor Richard's Tavern 331 Shore Rd (at Pine Hill) **207/646-4722** • seasonal, 5:30pm-9:30pm, clsd Sun-Mon • New England fare • some veggie • full bar

Southside Pizza 185 Main St/ US Rte 1 **207/646-8800** • noon-10pm, wknds only • also wraps, smoothies, salads • gay-owned

PUBLICATIONS

In Newsweekly 617/426-8246 • New England's largest LGBT newspaper

Portland

ACCOMMODATIONS

Andrews-on-Auburn B&B 417 Auburn St **207/797-9157** • gay-friendly • 1780s farmhouse • full brkfst • jacuzzi • kitchen • nonsmoking • pets ok • patio • $89-190

Auberge by the Sea B&B 103 East Grand Ave, Old Orchard Beach **207/934-2355** • gay-friendly • private pathway to beach • nonsmoking • $79-159

Portland

LGBT PRIDE:
June. 207/773-4188, web: www.southernmainepride.org.

ANNUAL EVENTS:
August - Portland Chamber Music Festival 800/320-0257, web: www.pcmf.org.

CITY INFO:
207/772-5800, web: www.visitportland.com.

ATTRACTIONS:
Old Port.
Portland Head Light 207/799-2661, web: www.portlandheadlight.com.
Portland Museum of Art 207/775-6148, web: www.portlandmuseum.org.
Wadsworth-Longfellow House 207/774-1822.

WEATHER:
Portland has a mild marine climate. Winter temperatures are in the 20°s-40°s, and summers are breezy and mild, with temperatures in the 60°s-80°s.

TRANSIT:
Airport Limo/Taxi 800/517-9442.
Metro (bus) 207/774-0351, web: www.transportme.org.

The Danforth 163 Danforth St
207/879-8755, 800/991-6557 • gay-friendly •
1821 mansion • conference/ reception facilities
• nonsmoking • kids/ pets ok • also Rachel's
restaurant • woman-owned • $119-329

The Inn at St John 939 Congress St
207/773-6481, 800/636-9127 • gay/ straight •
unique historic inn • kids/ pets ok • wheelchair
access • gay-owned • $40-190

The Inn by the Sea 40 Bowery Beach Rd,
Cape Elizabeth 207/799-3134, 800/888-4287
• gay-friendly • condo-style suites w/ ocean
views • kids ok • nonsmoking • wheelchair
access • woman-owned • $179-679

The Percy Inn 15 Pine St (at Longfellow
Square) 207/871-7638, 888/417-3729 • gay-
friendly • B&B at Longfellow Square •
nonsmoking • $89-199

The Pomegranate Inn 49 Neal St
207/772-1006, 800/356-0408 • gay-friendly •
upscale B&B • full brkfst • private garden •
nonsmoking • $95-265

Sea View Motel 65 W Grand Ave (at Atlantic
Ave), Old Orchard Beach 207/934-4180,
800/541-8439 • gay/ straight • seasonal, April-
Oct • on the beach • swimming • patio • kids/
pets ok • gift shop • $50-260

West End Inn 146 Pine St 207/772-1377,
800/338-1377 • gay-friendly • 1870 town
house • full brkfst • nonsmoking • $99-209

Wild Iris Inn 273 State St 207/775-0224,
800/600-1557 • gay-friendly • B&B •
conveniently located in downtown Portland •
nonsmoking • kids 6+ ok • women-owned/
run • $85-125

BARS

Blackstones 6 Pine St (off Longfellow
Square) 207/775-2885 • 4pm-1am, from 3pm
Sun • mostly gay men • neighborhood bar •
leather/ fetish 3rd Sat • wheelchair access

Somewhere Else 117 Spring St (at High)
207/871-9169 • 4pm-1am • lesbians/ gay
men • neighborhood bar • dancing/ DJ •
multiracial clientele • karaoke • wheelchair
access

Una 505 Fore St 207/828-0300 • 4:30pm-
1am • gay/ straight • martini & wine bar • food
served

The Wine Bar 38 Wharf St 207/773-6667 •
5pm-close • gay/ straight • food served

NIGHTCLUBS

Styxx 3 Spring St 207/828-0822 • 7pm-1am
• popular • gay/ straight • dancing/DJ • live
shows • theme nights • karaoke • drag shows
• piano bar Tue • videos • gay-owned

CAFES

Coffee by Design 67 India St 207/879-2233
• 6:30am-6pm, 7am-5pm Sat, 8am-3pm Sun,
coffeeshop & micro-roastery • also 43
Washington Ave, 7am-6pm, clsd wknds • also
620 Congress St, 6:30am-9pm, till 7pm Sun

RESTAURANTS

Katahdin 106 High St (at Spring)
207/774-1740 • 5pm-10pm, till 11pm Fri-Sat,
clsd Sun-Mon • American menu • full bar

Siam Restaurant 339 Fore St (at Pearl)
207/773-8389 • lunch weekdays, dinner
nightly, clsd Mon • Thai • beer/ wine •
wheelchair access • gay-owned

Street & Co 33 Wharf St (btwn Dana &
Union) 207/775-0887 • 5:30pm-9:30pm, till
10pm Fri-Sat • popular • seafood • beer/ wine
• wheelchair access

UFFA 190 State St (at Congress)
207/775-3380 • dinner Wed-Sun, Sun brunch,
clsd Mon-Tue

Walter's Cafe 15 Exchange St 207/871-9258
• 11am-3pm & 5pm-9pm, dinner only Sun •
seafood/ pasta • some veggie

BOOKSTORES

Longfellow Books 1 Monument Square
207/772-4045 • 9am-6pm • LGBT section

RETAIL SHOPS

Communiques 3 Moulton St (at
Commercial) 207/773-5181 • 10am-5pm, till
9pm summers • cards • gifts • clothing

Condom Sense 424 Fore St (at Union)
207/871-0356 • hours vary • condoms, lube,
massage oils, novelties, etc

The Corner General Store 154 Middle St
207/253-5280 • 8am-1am • great wine
selection

Drop Me A Line 87 Market St (in Old Port)
207/773-5547 • 11am-6pm, till 5pm Sat,
noon-5pm Sun • card & gift shop • pride
items • gay-owned

SPIRITUAL GROUPS

Congregation Bet Ha'am 81 Westbrook St,
South Portland 207/879-0028 • 7:30pm Fri,
6:30pm 2nd Fri • gay-friendly synagogue

Richmond

ENTERTAINMENT & RECREATION

Kennebec Tidewater Charters 3 Swan
Island Landing 207/737-4695, 866/347-4874
• fly & spin fishing trips • April-Sept • women-
owned/ run • also bike & boat rentals & tours
(207/737-2112)

Rockland

ACCOMMODATIONS

Captain Lindsey House Inn 5 Lindsey St
207/596-7950, 800/523-2145 • gay-friendly •
19th-c Maine sea captain's home •
nonsmoking • wheelchair access • $85-195

The Old Granite Inn 546 Main St
207/594-9036, 800/386-9036 • gay-friendly •
stately 1880s stone guesthouse • full brkfst •
harbor views • wheelchair access • $85-170

Rockport

RESTAURANTS

Chez Michel Rte 1, Lincolnville Beach
207/789-5600 • dinner, Sun brunch, clsd Mon
• full bar • some veggie

Lobster Pound Rte 1, Lincolnville Beach
207/789-5550 • 11:30am-8pm • May-Oct •
full bar • patio

Searsport

ACCOMMODATIONS

Wildflower Inn 2 Black Rd S/ US Rte 1
207/548-2112, 888/546-2112 • gay/ straight •
close to hiking, kayaking, biking & antiquing •
lesbian-owned

Sebago Lake

RESTAURANTS

Sydney's Rte 302, Naples 207/693-3333 •
open April-Jan • 4pm-9pm, till 9:30pm Sat •
full bar

Tenants Harbor

ACCOMMODATIONS

Blueberry Cove Camp Harts Neck Road
207/372-6353, 617/876-2897 (OFF-SEASON) •
gay-friendly • cabins • private campsites •
near Penobscot Bay

Eastwind Inn 207/372-6366, 800/241-8439
• clsd Dec-April • gay-friendly • rooms & apts
• full brkfst • pets ok • $89-299 • also
restaurant • old-fashioned New England fare

White Mtns

ACCOMMODATIONS

Mountain Village Inn PO Box 216, 164
Main St, Kingfield 04947 866/577-0741 • gay-
friendly • upscale B&B on 17 acres in
renovated 1850 farmhouse • full brkfst • $104-
150

York Harbor

RESTAURANTS

York Harbor Inn Rte 1A 207/363-5119 •
lunch Mon-Sat, dinner nightly, Sun brunch •
also the Cellar Pub • also lodging

MARYLAND

Annapolis

INFO LINES & SERVICES

AA Gay/ Lesbian 199 Duke of Gloucester St
(at St Anne's Parish) 410/268-5441 • 8pm
Tue

ACCOMMODATIONS

Two-O-One B&B 201 Prince George St (at
Maryland Ave) 410/268-8053 • gay/ straight •
English country house • full brkfst •
nonsmoking • gay-owned

William Page Inn 8 Martin St
410/626-1506, 800/364-4160 • gay/ straight •
elegantly renovated 1908 home • full brkfst •
nonsmoking • teens ok • gay-owned • $125-
250

Baltimore

INFO LINES & SERVICES

AA Gay/ Lesbian 410/663-1922

Gay/ Lesbian Community Center 241 W
Chase St (at Read) 410/837-5445 • call for
hours • many groups & services

ACCOMMODATIONS

**Abacrombie Badger Fine Food &
Accommodations** 58 W Biddle St (at
Cathedral) 410/244-7227, 888/922-3437 •
gay/ straight • 1880s town house •
nonsmoking • also restaurant • $88-185

Biltmore Suites 205 W Madison St (at Park)
410/728-6550, 800/868-5064 • gay-friendly •
kids/ pets ok • $69-169

Clarion Hotel—Mt Vernon Square
612 Cathedral St (at W Monument)
410/727-7101, 800/292-5500 • gay-friendly •
restaurant • lounge • gym • jacuzzis • kids ok
• wheelchair access • $170-1550

Embassy Suites Hotel Baltimore at BWI
1300 Concourse Dr, Linthicum 410/850-0747,
800/362-2779 • gay-friendly • full brkfst • kids
ok • swimming • $139-219

Harbor Inn Pier 5 711 Eastern Ave (at
President) 410/539-2000 • gay/ straight • on
waterfront • full brkfst • restaurant •
wheelchair access • $219-1,495

Park Avenue B&B 2018 Park Avenue (at Reservoir St) 410/523-2625 • gay/ straight • nonsmoking • gay-owned • $135-145

Tremont Park Hotel 8 E Pleasant St 800/873-6668 • gay/ straight • 58-room hotel • swimming 1 blk away at Tremont Plaza • wheelchair access • $99-349

BARS

Baltimore Eagle 2022 N Charles St (enter on 21st) 443/524-3333 • 3pm-2am • popular • mostly gay men • also leather store • patio • wheelchair access

Club Bunns 608 W Lexington St (at Greene St) 410/234-2866 • 3pm-2am • lesbians/ gay men • dancing/DJ • multiracial • live shows • female strippers Sat

Club Phoenix 1101 Cathedral St (at Chase) 410/837-3906 • 4pm-2am, from noon wknds • lesbians/ gay men • women's night Th • dancing/DJ • drag shows • talent shows • karaoke • videos • food served • T-dance Sun

Coconuts Cafe 311 W Madison (at Eutaw) 410/383-6064 • 5pm-2am, clsd Mon • call for summer hours • popular • mostly women • dancing/DJ • food served • wheelchair access • lesbian-owned

Gallagher's 940 S Conkling St (at Dylan) 410/327-3966 • 10am-2am, from 11am wknds • mostly women • neighborhood bar • food served

The Gallery Bar & Studio Restaurant 1735 Maryland Ave (at Lafayette) 410/539-6965 • 2pm-1am • lesbians/ gay men • dinner Mon-Sat • wheelchair access

---

[**Reply**] [**Forward**]　　　　　　[**Delete**]

```
Date: Nov 12, 2005 19:28:01
From: Girl-on-the-Go
To: Editor@Damron.com
Subject: Baltimore
```

>Baltimore, one of the "hub" cities of the Chesapeake Bay, is a quaint, working-class city by the sea, with a friendly and diverse population. It's not far from Washington, DC, and, like the nation's capital, is packed with museums and history.

>To many, Baltimore is best known as the nation's capital of kitsch, home and movie-set for the fabulously filthy queer film-maker John Waters. You too can follow in the immortal foot-steps of Divine, the biggest drag queen movie star we know of. Baltimore is also the site of Edgar Allan Poe's home and grave.

>After visiting the Aquarium, dining on soft-shell crabs, and shopping, stop into **Lambda Rising**, Baltimore's LGBT bookstore, and pick up a copy of the **Woman's Monthly** or **Gay Life** to find out the latest goings on about town.

>At night, visit Baltimore's women's bar, **Coconuts**. Women of color and their friends should check out Saturdays at **Club Bunns**, and **Hippo** is always a popular spot to mix it up with the boys, especially on the first Sunday of each month.

Grand Central 1001 N Charles St (at Eager) 410/752-7133 • 4pm-close, from 3pm Sun • popular • lesbians/ gay men • 2 bars • dancing/ DJ • videos • karaoke • drag shows

Hippo 1 W Eager St (at Charles) 410/547-0069, 410/576-0018 • 4pm-2am • popular • lesbians/ gay men • more women 1st Sun for T-dance 6pm-11pm • dancing/DJ • transgender-friendly • karaoke • videos • piano bar • wheelchair access

NIGHTCLUBS

Orpheus 1001 E Pratt St (at Exeter) 410/276-5599 • gay-friendly • dancing/DJ • alternative • leather • goth Fri & 1st Th • fetish party Sat • disco Sun

The Paradox 1310 Russell St (at 13th) 410/837-9110 • 11pm-5am, midnight-6am Sat • popular • lesbians/ gay men • dancing/DJ • multiracial • food served • live shows • videos • 18+ Fri • wheelchair access

Sonar 407 E Saratoga St (at Holiday) 410/327-8333 • gay/ straight • more gay Fri & Sun • dancing/ DJ • live shows

Vibe 1722 N Charles St (at Lafayette) 410/727-7431 • after-hours Fri-Sat only • gay/ straight • dancing/DJ • 18+ • dress code

CAFES

Donna's Coffee Bar 2 W Madison (at Charles) 410/385-0180 • 7:30am-11pm, 8am-midnight wknds • beer/ wine

RESTAURANTS

23rd Degree 1225 Cathedral St (at Preston) 410/752-8144 • 5pm-11pm, till midnight Fri-Sat, Sun brunch 11am-3pm clsd Mon • tropical

Alonso's 415 W Cold Spring Lake (at Keswick Rd) 410/235-3433 • 11am-11pm, till midnight Fri-Sat • Italian • full bar • wheelchair access

---

Baltimore

WHERE THE GIRLS ARE:
The women's bars are in southeast Baltimore, near the intersection of Haven and Lombard. Of course, the boys' playground, downtown around Chase St. and Park Ave., is also a popular hangout.

LGBT PRIDE:
June. 410/837-5445 (GLCC #).

CITY INFO:
Baltimore Tourism Office 410/659-7300 or 800/543-1036, web: www.mdwelcome.org.

ATTRACTIONS:
Baltimore Museum of Art 410/396-7100, web: www.artbma.org.
Fort McHenry 410/962-4290.
Harborplace.
Lexington Market.
National Aquarium 410/576-3800, web: www.aqua.org.
Poe House & Museum 410/396-7932.
Walters Art Museum 410/547-9000, web: www.thewalters.org.

BEST VIEW:
Top of the World Trade Center at the Inner Harbor. 401 E Pratt, 410/837-8439.

WEATHER:
A temperate and, at times, temperamental climate. Spring brings great temperatures (50°-70°s) and unpredictable rains and heavy winds. In summer, the weather can be hot (90°s) and sticky. Fall cools off with an occasional "Indian Summer" in October. Winter brings cool days and colder nights, along with snow and ice.

TRANSIT:
Yellow Cab 410/685-1212.
Baltimore Airport Shuttle 410/821-5387 or 877/826-3678, web: www.baltimoreairportshuttle.com.
MTA Transit 410/539-5000, web: www.mtamaryland.com.

Cafe Hon 1002 W 36th St (at Roland)
410/243–1230 • 7am-9pm, till 10pm Fri-Sat,
from 9am wknds, till 8pm Sun • wheelchair
access

Loco Hombre 413 E Cold Spring Ln (at
Roland) **410/889–2233** • 11am-10pm, till
11pm Fri-Sat

Mount Vernon Stable & Saloon 909 N
Charles St (btwn Eager & Read)
410/685–7427 • 10:30am-midnight, till 1am
Fri-Sat • Sun brunch • some veggie • also bar

BOOKSTORES

Lambda Rising 241 W Chase St (at Read)
410/234–0069 • 10am-10pm • LGBT •
wheelchair access

PUBLICATIONS

EXP Magazine 302/227–5787,
877/397–6244 • bi-weekly gay magazine for
Mid-Atlantic

Gay Life 410/837–7748 • LGBT newspaper

Woman's Monthly 202/965–5399 • articles
• calendar of community/ arts events for
greater DC/ Baltimore area

SPIRITUAL GROUPS

Beit Tikvah 5802 Roland Ave (at Lake in
First Christian Church) **410/464–9402** •
welcoming Jewish Reconstructionist
congregation • call for services & times •
wheelchair access

Grace & St Peter's Episcopal Church
707 Park Ave (at Monument) **410/539–1395** •
10am Sun

MCC Baltimore 401 W Monument St
410/669–6222 • 9am & 11pm Sun, 7:30pm
Wed

St Mark's Lutheran Church 1900 St Paul St
(at 20th) **410/752–5804** • 11am Sun & 6:30pm
Th

Unity Fellowship Church 114 W Read St
410/244–0884 • 11am & 3:30pm Sun •
uplifting service in the African American
tradition

EROTICA

Chained Desires 136 W Read St
410/528–8441 • custom leather crafts &
apparel • adult toys

Boonsboro

NIGHTCLUBS

Deer Park Lodge 21614 National Pike
301/797–7672 • 7pm-2am, till midnight Sun,
clsd Mon-Wed • mostly gay men • dancing/DJ
• drag shows • gay-owned

Boyds

SPIRITUAL GROUPS

Open Door MCC 15817 Barnesville Rd
301/601–9112 • 10am Sun

Columbia

SPIRITUAL GROUPS

MCC New Covenant 14301 Laurel Bowie Rd
(at Oakland Presbyterian Church)
410/669–6222 • 6:30pm Sun

Cumberland

ACCOMMODATIONS

Red Lamp Post B&B 849 Braddock Rd
301/777–7476 • lesbians/ gay men • theme
rooms • some shared baths • full brkfst •
dinner available • hot tub • sundeck • gym •
nonsmoking • lesbian & gay-owned • $65-75

Rocky Gap Lodge & Golf Resort 16701
Lakeview Rd NE, Flintstone **301/784–8400,
800/724–0828** • gay-friendly • expansive
property w/ forests, lake & elegantly rustic
lodge • $110+

RESTAURANTS

Acropolis 47 E Main St, Frostburg
301/689–8277 • 4pm-10pm, clsd Sun-Mon •
Greek & American • full bar

Au Petit Paris 86 E Main St, Frostburg
301/689–8946, 800/207–0956 • 6pm-9:30pm,
clsd Sun-Mon • French • also lounge •
reservations suggested • wheelchair access

Havre de Grace

ACCOMMODATIONS

La Clé D'Or 226 N Union Ave (at
Chesapeake Bay) **410/939–6562,
888/484–4837** • gay/ straight • 1868 home of
the Johns Hopkins family • full brkfst • teens
ok (w/ prior approval) • gay-owned • $120-140

Princess Anne

ACCOMMODATIONS

The Alexander House Booklovers B&B
30535 Linden Ave (at corner of Beckford)
410/651–5195 • gay-friendly • literary-themed
B&B • full brkfst • nonsmoking • $70-140

Rock Hall

ACCOMMODATIONS

Tallulah's on Main 5750 Main St (at Sharp
St) **410/639–2596** • gay/ straight • small suite
hotel • kids ok • nonsmoking • wheelchair
access • gay-owned • $115-150

Rockville

RESTAURANTS

The Vegetable Garden 11618 Rockville Pk
301/468-9301 • lunch Mon-Fri, dinner nightly
• vegetarian/ vegan

Stevensville

RESTAURANTS

Love Point Cafe 401 Love Point Rd
410/604-0910 • 11am-10pm, lounge till 11pm

Towson

SPIRITUAL GROUPS

Towson Unitarian Universalist Church
1710 Dulaney Valley Rd, Lutherville
410/825-6045 • 9am & 11am Sun Sept-June,
10am Sun summers

Wheaton

BARS

De Lounge 11305 Georgia Ave 301/933-4176
• 4pm-close • lesbians/ gay men • dancing/ DJ
• live shows • ladies night Fri • also sports bar
• also restaurant

MASSACHUSETTS

Statewide

PUBLICATIONS

In Newsweekly 617/426-8246 • New
England's largest LGBT newspaper

Acton

RESTAURANTS

Acton Jazz Cafe 452 Great Rd/ Rte 2-A
978/263-6161 • 6pm-10pm, Sun jazz brunch
& lunch seasonal, clsd Mon • some veggie •
full bar • live shows • nonsmoking • cover
charge

Amherst

see also Northampton

ACCOMMODATIONS

Ivy House B&B 1 Sunset Ct 413/549-7554 •
gay/ straight • restored Colonial Cape • full
brkfst • nonsmoking • gay-owned • $60-90

BOOKSTORES

Food For Thought 106 N Pleasant St (at
Main) 413/253-5432 • 10am-6pm, till 7pm
Th-Fri, noon-5pm Sun • popular • progressive
bookstore • wheelchair access • collectively
run

Barre

ACCOMMODATIONS

Jenkins Inn & Restaurant 978/355-6444,
800/378-7373 • gay-friendly • full brkfst •
restaurant • full bar • nonsmoking • English
garden • gay-owned • $160-185

Winterwood 19 N Main St, Petersham
978/724-8885 • gay-friendly • Greek Revival
mansion • fireplaces • nonsmoking

RESTAURANTS

Barre Mill 90 Main St, South Barre
978/355-2987, 978/355-6417 • 5pm-9pm
Wed-Th, till 9:30pm Fri-Sat, noon-8pm Sun,
clsd Mon-Tue • Italian

Berkshires

ACCOMMODATIONS

The B&B at Howden Farm Rannapo Rd,
Sheffield 413/229-8481 • lesbians/ gay men •
250-acre working farm • near river • full brkfst •
nonsmoking • some shared baths • gay-
owned • $79-149

Broken Hill Manor 771 West Rd (at Rte 23),
Sheffield 413/528-6159, 877/535-6159 • gay-
friendly • B&B • full brkfst • hot tub • kids 12+
ok • wheelchair access • gay-owned • $125-
200

Cornell Inn 203 Main St, Lenox
413/637-0562, 800/637-0562 • gay-friendly •
located minutes from all cultural venues in the
Berkshires • same-sex wedding ceremonies
happily facilitated • full brkfst • jacuzzi •
wheelchair access • $80-350

River Bend Farm B&B 643 Simonds Rd,
Williamstown 413/458-3121 • gay-friendly •
restored 1770s home • shared baths •
seasonal • kids ok • $100

Walker House 64 Walker St, Lenox
413/637-1271, 800/235-3098 • gay/ straight •
1804 guesthouse • nonsmoking • kids 12+/
pets ok • wheelchair access • $80-220

Windflower Inn 684 S Egremont Rd, Great
Barrington 413/528-2720, 800/992-1993 •
gay-friendly • gracious country inn • full brkfst
• swimming • nonsmoking • kids ok • $100-
200

RESTAURANTS

Cafe Lucia 80 Church St, Lenox
413/637-2640 • dinner only, clsd Mon

Church Street Cafe 65 Church St, Lenox
413/637-2745 • lunch & dinner, clsd Sun-Mon
• some veggie

Gateways 51 Walker St, Lenox 413/637-2532
• dinner, clsd Sun-Mon • plenty veggie •
wheelchair access

Mezze Bistro & Bar 16 Water St,
Williamstown 413/458-0123 • 5pm-9pm
Sun-Mon, till 10pm Tue-Wed, till 11pm Th-Sat

ENTERTAINMENT & RECREATION

Tanglewood 197 Rte 183, Lenox
413/637-5376 • live music venue • summer
home of the Boston Symphony/ Pops

Williamstown Theatre Festival just E of
Rte 2 & Rte 7 junction, Williamstown
413/597-3400 • call for season calendar

Boston

INFO LINES & SERVICES

GLBT Helpline 617/267-9001 • 6pm-11pm,
5pm-10pm wknds

ACCOMMODATIONS

463 Beacon St Guest House 463 Beacon
St 617/536-1302 • gay-friendly • minutes
from Boston's heart • gay-owned • $69-149

82 Chandler B&B 82 Chandler St
617/482-0408, 888/482-0408 • gay/ straight •
historic town house in South End • great
views • nonsmoking • gay-owned • $85-160

Amsterdammertje 617/471-8454 •
lesbians/ gay men • Euro-American B&B • full
brkfst • nonsmoking • near Boston • gay-
owned • $75-110

Appleton Studio 30 Appleton St (at Berkely)
617/720-0522, 800/347-5088 • gay-friendly •
spacious studio apt • nonsmoking • also
weekly/ monthly rentals • gay-owned • $100-
160

Carolyn's B&B 102 Holworthy St (at Huron
Ave), Cambridge 617/864-7042 • gay-friendly
• near Harvard Square • nonsmoking •
women-owned/ run • $95-120

▲ **Chandler Inn** 26 Chandler St **617/482–3450, 800/842–3450** • gay-friendly • centrally located • $89-169

The Charles Street Inn 94 Charles St (at Mount Vernon, Beacon Hill) **617/314–8900, 877/772–8900** • gay/ straight • B&B • jacuzzi • kids/ pets ok • nonsmoking • lesbian-owned • $250-365

Clarendon Square Inn 198 W Brookline St (btwn Tremont & Columbus) **617/536–2229** • lesbians/ gay men • restored Victorian townhouse • hot tub • fireplaces • gay-owned • $119-289

The College Club 44 Commonwealth Ave (at Arlington St) **617/536–9510** • gay-friendly • B&B in Back Bay • some shared baths • kids ok • $75-160

Encore B&B 116 W Newton St (at Tremont) **617/247–3425** • gay-friendly • 19th-c town house in Boston's historic South End • nonsmoking • gay-owned • $130-190

Holiday Inn Select Boston Government Center 5 Blossom St (Cambridge St) **617/742–7630** • gay-friendly • swimming • wheelchair access • close to shops, restaurants & entertainment • full brkfst

Hotel 140 140 Clarendon St (at Stuart St) **617/585–5600** • gay/ straight • boutique hotel • near Copley Square • nonsmoking • women-owned/ run • $89-169

Just Right Reservations 978/934–9931 • gay/ straight • inns & B&Bs for Boston, Provincetown, West Hollywood, Santa Monica, Malibu & Palm Springs • gay-owned

Boston

Where the Girls Are:
Sipping coffee and reading somewhere in Cambridge or Harvard Square, strolling the South End near Columbus & Mass. Avenues, or hanging out in the Fenway or Jamaica Plain.

LGBT Pride:
June. 617/262-9405, web: www.bostonpride.org.

Annual Events:
May - Gay & Lesbian Film/Video Festival 617/369-3300 (Museum of Fine Arts #).

City Info:
Greater Boston Convention & Visitors Bureau 888/733-2678, web: www.bostonusa.com.

Weather:
Extreme—from freezing winters to boiling summers with a beautiful spring and fall.

Transit:
Boston Cab 617/536-5010.
Instyle Transportation limo service 617/ 641–2400 or 877/ 64–STYLE.
MBTA (the "T") 800/392-6100, web: www.mbta.com.

Attractions:
Beacon Hill.
Black Heritage Trail.
Boston Common.
Faneuil Hall.
Freedom Trail.
Harvard University.
Isabella Stewart Gardner Museum 617/566-1401, web: www.gardnermuseum.org.
Museum of Afro-American History 617/725-0022, web: www.afroammuseum.org.
Museum of Fine Arts 617/267-9300, web: www.mfa.org.
Museum of Science 617/723-2500.
New England Aquarium 617/973-5200, web: www.neaq.org.
Old North Church 617/523-6676, web: www.oldnorth.com.
Walden Pond.

Reply **Forward** **Delete**

Date: Nov 2, 2005 16:49:36
From: Girl-on-the-Go
To: Editor@Damron.com
Subject: Boston

>Home to 65 colleges and universities, Boston has been an intellectual center for the continent for over three centuries. Since that famed tea party, it's also been home to some of New England's most rebellious radicals. The result is a city whose character is both traditional and free-thinking, high-brow and free-wheeling*, stuffy and energetic.

Not only is this city complex, it's cluttered...with plenty of historic and mind-sparking sites to visit. Check out the high/low culture in Harvard Square and the shopping along Newbury Street in the Back Bay, as well as the touristy vendors in Faneuil Hall. Don't miss the North End's fabulous Italian food.

>Boston's women's community is, not surprisingly, strong and politically diverse. And it's decentralized: while you will find some women in the "gay ghetto" of the South End, local lesbians tend to gravitate toward Cambridge, Jamaica Plain, and Somerville. To find out what the latest hotspots are, pick up a copy of **Bay Windows** or **IN Newsweekly** at the well-stocked **Calamus Bookstore**. While you're there, check out the many national lesbian magazines published in Boston, such as feminist newsjournal **Sojourner**. Hungry? Grab a bite to eat at **City Girl Caffe** in Cambridge, or at one of the great restaurants on nearby Cambridge Street. If you're in Somerville, check out lesbian-owned **Diesel Cafe** where they have pool tables and are open late! Cute-as-a-bug **June Bug Cafe**, in Jamaica Plain, is another popular lesbian-owned hangout.

>Looking for something more exciting? On Thursday nights, dance with the girls at the funky **Midway Cafe** in Jamaica Plain. **Toast** (in Somerville) serves up good times for gals on Thursday and Friday, and **Tribe** is a popular new club night for the ladies.

* About driving in Boston: its drivers are notoriously the most freeform in the country. The streets of Boston can be confusing—often streets of the same name intersect, and six-way intersections are the rule.

Nine Zero Hotel 90 Tremont St (at Bosworth) 617/772–5800, 866/646–3937 • gay-friendly • luxury hotel • full brkfst • jacuzzi • kids/pets ok • $229-3,000

▲ **Oasis Guest House** 22 Edgerly Rd 617/267–2262, 800/230–0105 • popular • gay/straight • Back Bay location • some shared baths • nonsmoking • wheelchair access • gay-owned • $69-150

Rutland Square House B&B 56 Rutland Square 617/247–0018, 800/786–6567 • gay/straight • Victorian town house • nonsmoking • gay-owned • $85-150

Taylor House B&B 50 Burroughs St, Jamaica Plain 617/983–9334, 888/228–2956 • gay/straight • Italianate Victorian • nonsmoking • gay-owned • $110-190

Victorian B&B 617/536–3285 • women only • full brkfst • nonsmoking • kids ok • lesbian-owned • $75-95 (1-3 guests)

BARS

Boston Ramrod 1254 Boylston St (at Ipswich, 1 block from Fenway Park) 617/266–2986 • noon-2am • popular • mostly gay men • bears • leather • dress code Fri-Sat • dancing/DJ • videos • game room • wheelchair access

Chaps/ Club Rumor 100 Warrenton St (at Stuart) 617/422–0862, 617/695–9500 (INFO LINE) • 3pm-2am Wed Latino night, noon-2am Sun T-dance • popular • gay/ straight • dancing/DJ • videos

Club Cafe Lounge & Video Bar 209 Columbus (at Berkeley) 617/536–0966 • 11:30am-2am, from 2pm Sat • popular • lesbians/ gay men • 3 bars • upscale • karaoke • piano bar • live shows • videos • also restaurant • some veggie • wheelchair access

Dedo Lounge & Bistro 69 Church St (btwn Stuart & Arlington, in Theater District) 617/338–9999 • 5pm-1am, till 2am wknds • mostly gay men • neighborhood, bar • piano bar • also bistro

Dyke Night Productions • special events in various locations • mostly women • dancing/DJ • live shows • younger crowd • wheelchair access • check www.dykenight.com for info

Harp & Bard 1099 Dorchester Ave, Dorchester 617/265–2893 • 11pm-10pm, till 11pm Fri-Sat • gay-friendly • Irish pub & restaurant

Jacque's 79 Broadway (at Stuart) **617/426-8902** • 11am-midnight, from noon Sun • mostly gay men • popular • drag cabaret

Johnny D's Restaurant & Music Club 17 Holland St (in Davis Square), Somerville **617/776-2004** • 12:30pm-1am, from 9am wknds • Southern • plenty veggie • dancing • live music nightly

Machine 1256 Boylston St (below Boston Ramrod) **617/536-1950** • noon-2am, dancing Mon, Fri-Sat • popular • mostly gay men • more women days for pool • dancing/DJ • go-go boys • wheelchair access

Milky Way Lounge & Lanes 403 Centre St, Jamaica Plain **617/524-3740** • 6pm-1am • gay/ straight • food served • live music • poetry readings • karaoke • bowling

Ryles 212 Hampshire St (at Cambridge St, in Inman Square), Cambridge **617/876-9330** • gay/ straight • live shows • great wknd jazz brunch

Nightclubs

Avalon 15 Lansdowne St **617/262-2424** • 10pm-2am Th-Sun • popular • mostly gay men • dancing/DJ • more gay Sun • young crowd • $10 cover charge

Buzz 67 Stuart St **617/267-8969** • 10pm-2am Sat • popular • mostly gay men • dancing/DJ • cover charge

The Glamorous Life 30 Lansdowne St (at Embassy) **617/536-2100** • Th only • mostly men • dancing/DJ • hip hop

Manray/ Campus 21 Brookline St (off Mass Ave, in Central Square), Cambridge **617/864-0400** • 9pm-2am, clsd Sun-Tue • gay/ straight • more gay at Campus Th, goth Wed, fetish Fri • dancing/DJ • alternative • young crowd

The Middle East 472 Massachusetts Ave (in Central Square), Cambridge **617/497-0576** • 11am-1am, till 2am wknds • gay-friendly • alternative • live music • young crowd • also restaurant

Midway Cafe 3496 Washington St, Jamaica Plain **617/524-9038** • gay/ straight • more women Th • dancing/ DJ • theme nights • karaoke • live shows

Static 13 Lansdowne (at Axis) **617/262-2437** • 10pm-2am Mon • lesbians/ gay men • dancing/DJ • drag shows • 18+ • cover charge

Toast 70 Union Square, Somerville **617/623-9211** • 8pm-1am Th, 5:30pm-1am Fri • mostly women • dancing/ DJ

Tribe 533 Washington (at Club Felt) **617/350-5555** • 9pm-2am Th only • women only • dancing/ DJ

Cafes

1369 Cafe 757 Massachusetts Ave (in Central Square), Cambridge **617/576-4600** • 7am-11pm, from 8am wknds, till 10pm Sun • coffee & baked goods • also 1369 Cambridge St (Inman Square), 617/576-1369

Berkeley Perk 69 Berkeley St (at Chandler) **617/426-7375** • 6:30am-5pm, from 7am Sat, 8am-noon Sun • food served • gay-owned

Dartmouth 160 Commonwealth Ave **617/266-1122** • 4pm-1:30am, from 10am wknds • dinner • great desserts • beer/ wine • gay-owned

Diesel Cafe 257 Elm St (in Davis Square), Somerville **617/629-8717** • 7am-midnight, till 1am Fri-Sat, from 8am wknds • sandwiches • plenty veggie • pool tables • lesbian-owned

Fiore's Bakery 55 South St, Jamaica Plain **617/524-9200** • 7am-7pm, 8am-6pm wknds • bakery & organic coffees • gay-owned

Francesca's 564 Tremont St (at Clarendon) **617/482-9026** • 8am-11pm, till midnight Fri-Sat • popular • lesbians/ gay men • pastries • wheelchair access

JP Licks 352 Newbury St **617/236-1666** • "homemade ice cream cafe"—and yes, they serve coffee too

June Bug Cafe 403A Centre St, Jamaica Plain **617/522-2393** • 8am-11pm, from 9am Sat-Sun • Wi-Fi • also sandwiches • lesbian-owned

True Grounds 717 Broadway, Somerville **617/591-9559** • 7am-7pm

Restaurants

209 Boston 209 Columbus (at Berkeley, at Club Cafe) **617/536-0966** • dinner & wknd brunch • popular • some veggie • also 3 bars • videos • wheelchair access

Buddha's Delight 5 Beach St, 2nd flr **617/451-2395** • 11am-9:30pm • Chinese • vegetarian

Casa Romero 30 Gloucester St **617/536-4341** • 5pm-10pm, till 11pm wknds • Mexican

City Girl Cafe 204 Hampshire St (at Prospect), Cambridge **617/864-2809** • 11am-9pm, from 10am Sat, till 4pm Sun, clsd Mon • Italian • great sandwiches • plenty veggie • wknd brunch • lesbian-owned

Flux 1 Appleton St (at Tremont St) **617/695–3589** • 5:30pm-10pm, till 1pm Th-Sat • Sun brunch • popular • American comfort food • gay-owned

Icarus 3 Appleton St (off Tremont) **617/426–1790** • dinner only • New American

Laurel 142 Berkeley St (at Columbus) **617/424–6711** • lunch weekdays & dinner nightly, Sun brunch

Rabia's 73 Salem St (at Cross St) **617/227–6637** • lunch & dinner • fine Italian • some veggie • wheelchair access

Ristorante Lucia 415 Hanover St **617/367–2353** • lunch Th-Sun, dinner nightly • great North End pasta • some veggie

Trattoria Pulcinella 147 Huron Ave (at Concord), Cambridge **617/491–6336** • dinner 5pm-10pm • fine Italian

Entertainment & Recreation

Freedom Trail **617/357–8300** • start at the Visitor Information Center in Boston Common (at Tremont & West Sts), the most famous cow pasture & oldest public park in the US, then follow the red line to some of Boston's most famous sites

Isabella Stewart Gardner Museum 280 The Fenway **617/566–1401** • Venetian palazzo filled w/ Old Masters to Impressionists • gorgeous courtyard • clsd Mon

Jamaica Pond • great girl-watching

The Mapparium 175 Huntington Ave (in the Christian Science Center) **617/450–7000** • 10am-5pm, till 9pm Th-Fri, clsd Mon • the map's out of date, but where else can you walk through a 30-ft stained-glass globe

Museum of Afro-American History/ Black Heritage Trail 46 Joy St (at Smith Ct, on Beacon Hill) **617/725–0022** • 10am-4pm, clsd Sun • exhibits in the African Meeting House, the oldest standing African American church in the US

Theater Offensive **617/621–6090** • "New England's foremost presenter of LGBT theater" • Out on the Edge festival in Sept

Bookstores

Calamus Bookstore 92-B South St **617/338–1931, 888/800–7300** • 9am-7pm, noon-6pm • LGBT • also cards • music • jewelry • videos • magazines

Globe Corner Bookstore 28 Church St **617/497–6277** • travel books & maps

Trident Booksellers & Cafe 338 Newbury St (off Mass Ave) **617/267–8688** • 9am-midnight • good magazine browsing • food served • beer/ wine • wheelchair access

Unicorn Books 1210 Massachusetts Ave (at Appleton), Arlington Hts **781/646–3680** • 10am-7pm, till 6pm Sat, noon-5pm Sun • New Age & spiritual titles

Publications

Bay Windows **617/266–6670** • LGBT newspaper

In Newsweekly **617/426–8246** • New England's largest LGBT newspaper

Spiritual Groups

Am Tikva 50 Sewall Ave, Brookline **617/232–5543** • 8pm 1st & 3rd Fri • LGBT Jewish congregation for Greater Boston area

Dignity/ Boston 35 Bowdoin St (at St John the Evangelist Church, Beacon Hill) **617/421–1915** • 5:30pm Sun

MCC 131 Cambridge St (at Old West Church) **617/973–0404** • 6pm Sun

Gyms & Health Clubs

Columbus Athletic Club 209 Columbus **617/536–3006** • gay-friendly

Erotica

Eros Boutique 581–A Tremont St, 2nd flr **617/425–0345** • 10am-10pm • fetishwear • toys

Grand Opening! 318 Harvard St, 2nd flr (at Beacon, in Arcade Bldg), Brookline **617/731–2626** • 10am-7pm, till 9pm Th-Sat, from noon-6pm Sun • women's sex toy store • classes • readings

Hubba Hubba 534 Massachusetts Ave (at Brookline, in Central Square), Cambridge **617/492–9082** • fetish gear

Marquis de Sade 92 South St **617/426–2120** • 10am-11pm

Brookline

see Boston

Cambridge

see Boston

Cape Cod

see also Provincetown listings

INFO LINES & SERVICES

Gay/ Lesbian AA Cape Cod Hospital (at Whitcomb Pavilion), Hyannis **508/775-7060** • 6pm Sun

ACCOMMODATIONS

15 Park Square 15 Park Square (at Main St), Hyannis **508/771-4760** • gay-friendly • guesthouse • shared baths • nonsmoking • gay-owned • $50-100

Blue Heron B&B 464 Pleasant Lake Ave, Harwich **508/430-0219** • rental home on weekly basis • lesbians/ gay men • swimming • private beach • lesbian-owned • $1,900-2,800

The Capeside Cottage B&B 320 Woods Hole Rd, Woods Hole **508/548-6218, 800/320-2322** • gay-friendly • guesthouse & cottage • full brkfst • swimming • nonsmoking • $100-180

The Crow's Nest of West Dennis 230 Main St (at Station Ave), West Dennis **508/760-3335, 877/240-2769** • gay/ straight • B&B • pets ok • also restaurant • gay-owned • $125-165

Gull Cottage 10 Old Church St, Yarmouth Port **508/362-8747** • mostly gay men • near beach • shared baths • wheelchair access • $150/ week

Holbrook House 223 Main St (at Whit's Ln), Wellfleet **508/349-6706** • gay/ straight • restored 1820s capt's home • full brkfst • nonsmoking • $115-140/ night (rooms) $600-700/ week (apt)

Private Cape Cod Cottage 35 Rolling Ln (at Herring Brook Rd), Eastham **631/689-9456** • mostly women • 2-bdrm cottage • 2 miles to beach • 20 minutes to Provincetown • seasonal • nonsmoking • lesbian-owned • $800-1,050/ week

Woods Hole Passage 186 Woods Hole Rd, Falmouth **508/548-9575, 800/790-8976** • gay-friendly • full brkfst • near beaches • $100-195

NIGHTCLUBS

Club 477 477 Yarmouth Rd, Hyannis **508/775-9835, 800/393-6161** • 6pm-1am • lesbians/ gay men • Cape Cod's largest gay complex • dancing/DJ • wheelchair access

Cape Code

ACCOMMODATIONS

The Sleepy Rooster Guesthouse 125 Sea St (at South St) **508/771-5731** • gay-friendly • 1830s garden guesthouse • nonsmoking • gay-owned • $99-149

Chelsea

see Boston

Greenfield

ACCOMMODATIONS

Brandt House 29 Highland Ave **413/774-3329, 800/235-3329** • gay-friendly • full brkfst • kids ok • nonsmoking • woman-owned/ run • $110-325

The Charlemont Inn Rte 2, Mohawk Trail, Charlemont **413/339-5796** • gay-friendly • kids/ pets ok • $60-150 • also restaurant • some veggie • full bar • live music wknds • lesbian-owned

BOOKSTORES

World Eye Bookshop 156 Main St **413/772-2186** • 9am-6:30pm, till 6pm Fri-Sat, noon-5pm Sun • general • LGBT section • community bulletin board • women-owned/ run

Haverhill

BARS

Friend's Landing 85 Water St **978/374-9400** • 6pm-1am, till 2am wknds, clsd Mon • popular • lesbians/ gay men • dancing/DJ • 6 bars • 2 dance floors • cabaret • waterfront deck • wheelchair access

Indian Orchard

NIGHTCLUBS

Rainbow Connection 186 Main St **413/543-8400** • 7pm-2am Wed-Sun • mostly women • dancing/ DJ • transgender-friendly

Lenox

see Berkshires

Lincoln

ACCOMMODATIONS

Thoreau's Walden B&B 2 Concord Rd **781/259-1899** • gay/ straight • near historic Walden Pond • full brkfst • kids ok • nonsmoking • woman-owned • $75-100

Lowell

Bars

Downstairs Cafe 160 Merrimac St **978/937-3333** • 9pm-2am • lesbians/gay men • dancing/DJ • drag shows • live shows • videos

Lynn

Bars

Fran's Place 776 Washington (at Sagamore) **781/598-5618** • 2pm-2am • lesbians/gay men • dancing/DJ • theme nights • wheelchair access

The Pub at 47 Central 47 Central Ave **781/586-0551** • 2pm-2am • mostly gay men • neighborhood bar • dancing/DJ wknds • leather • karaoke • live shows Fri-Sat • gay-owned

Nightclubs

Club Central 649 Lynnway **781/599-6012** • 4pm-2am, clsd Mon-Tue • mostly gay men • dancing/DJ • live entertainment • karaoke • 18+ • patio • wheelchair access • gay-owned

Martha's Vineyard

Accommodations

Arbor Inn 222 Upper Main St, Edgartown **508/627-8137, 888/748-4383** • gay-friendly • B&B • some shared baths • $145-250

Four Gables 41 New York Ave, Oak Bluffs **508/696-8384** • gay/straight • turn-of-the-century inn • near beach • private sundecks • kids/pets ok • nonsmoking • $1,800-2,400/week

Martha's Vineyard Surfside 7 Oak Bluffs Ave, Oak Bluffs **508/693-2500, 800/537-3007** • gay-friendly • motel • some ocean views • wheelchair access • $70-305

The Shiverick Inn 5 Pease's Pt Wy, Edgartown (at Pent Ln) **508/627-3797, 800/723-4292** • gay/straight • restored 1840 mansion • antique-filled • nonsmoking • gay-owned • $130-385

Restaurants

The Black Dog Tavern Beach St Extension #21 **508/693-9020** • 7am-9pm, seasonal • wheelchair access

Le Grenier 96 Main St, Vineyard Haven **508/693-4906** • 5:30pm-close • French

Louis' Cafe 350 State Rd, Vineyard Haven **508/693-3255** • Italian • plenty veggie • gay-owned

Bookstores

Bunch of Grapes 44 Main St, Vineyard Haven **508/693-2291, 800/693-0221** • 9am-6pm, open later wknds • general • some LGBT titles & magazines

Nantucket

Accommodations

The Chestnut House 3 Chestnut St **508/228-0049** • gay-friendly • nonsmoking • kids ok • also cottage • $85-325

New Bedford

Bars

Le Place 20 Kenyon St **508/990-1248** • 2pm-2am • popular • lesbians/gay men • karaoke • dancing/DJ Fri-Sun • women-owned/run

Puzzles 428 N Front St (at Philips Ave) **508/997-0466** • 2:30pm-2am, from 4pm Sun-Wed • lesbians/gay men • dancing/DJ Fri-Sat • strippers Fri • karaoke Wed • wheelchair access

Newburyport

Restaurants

Glenn's Restaurant 44 Merrimac St **978/465-3811** • 5:30pm-9pm, from 4pm wknds, clsd Mon • full bar till midnight • live music • wheelchair access

Newton

see Boston

North Adams

Restaurants

Cafe Latino 1111 Mass MoCa Wy **413/662-2004** • 11am-11pm, clsd Tue • contemporary Latin American

Northampton

see also Amherst

Accommodations

Clarion Hotel & Conference Center 1 Atwood Dr **413/586-1211, 800/582-2929** • gay-friendly • swimming • tennis • kids ok • nonsmoking • also restaurant & bar • wheelchair access • $79-149

Clark Tavern Inn B&B 98 Bay Rd, Hadley **413/586-1900** • gay-friendly • 1740 colonial inn • swimming • nonsmoking • teens ok • $105-145

Corner Porches 82 Baptist Corner Rd, Ashfield **413/628–4592** • gay/ straight • 1880s farmhouse • 30 minutes from Northampton • shared bath • full brkfst • kids ok • nonsmoking • woman-owned/ run • $65-80

The Hotel Northampton 36 King St **413/584–3100, 800/547–3529** • gay-friendly • in the heart of downtown • gym • cafe & historic tavern • wheelchair access • $99-325

Reply **Forward** **Delete**

```
Date: Dec 10, 2005 09:45:12
From: Girl-on-the-Go
To: Editor@Damron.com
Subject: Northampton
```

>With all the hype from a while back about Northampton being the lesbian capital of the world, visitors are often surprised by the low-key atmosphere of this quaint and quiet New England town. It's the sort of place where the people are nice, the streets are safe, and most groups come in multiples of two.

>Sure, you'll be free to smooch with your honey just about every-where, but don't expect to see the throngs of Sapphic sisters you've heard about in the *National Enquirer* or on *20/20* milling around the streets. They're there all right, but they're probably home with the kids, cuddling with their other half, or studying for that big exam at one of the five colleges in the area.

>Still, there's plenty for a visiting lesbian to enjoy in Northampton. For lesbian-friendly accommodations, check out the **Tin Roof B&B** in Hadley. The **Green Street Cafe** and vegetarian, lesbian-owned **Bela** are popular with the local girls. At night, head to **Diva's** for dancing and drinks. For something different, make an appointment to view the **Sexual Minorities Archives,** or take a tour of Emily Dickinson's House in nearby Amherst.

>With two women's colleges, Smith and Mount Holyoke, progressive Hampshire College, Amherst College, and the University of Massachusetts all in the area, there's something fun to do every night of the week, from readings to performance art. Check out the website **LavenderLips.com** for a list of lesbian resources in Western Massachusetts. Also be sure to stop by **Pride & Joy** LGBT bookstore— and while you're there, pick up a copy of the Lesbian/Gay Business Guild's listing of "family" businesses in the area. If you're feeling frisky, squeeze into **Oh My**, the cozy local sex toy store.

The McKinley House 3 McKinley Ave (at Rte 10), Easthampton **413/695-6599** • lesbians/ gay men • full brkfst • some shared baths • 3 miles S of Northampton • nonsmoking • gay-owned • $95-155

Tin Roof B&B 413/586-8665 • mostly women • 1909 farmhouse w/ spectacular view of the Berkshires • shared baths • kids ok • lesbian-owned • $65-70

Bars

The Iron Horse 20 Center St 413/584-0610 • 7:30pm-close • gay-friendly • food served • live music • all ages • nonsmoking • some veggie

Nightclubs

Diva's 492 Pleasant St (at Conz St) **413/586-8161** • 9pm-2am, clsd Sun-Mon • lesbians/ gay men • dancing/DJ • live music • theme nights: Goth Tue (18+), drag & karaoke Wed (18+), '80s Th (18+), hip hop/ house Fri (18+) & Sat

Pearl Street 10 Pearl St **413/584-7771** • 7:30pm-1am • gay/ straight • dancing/DJ • live music • young crowd • women-owned/ run

Cafes

Haymarket Cafe 15 Amber Ln **413/586-9969** • 7am-10pm, till 11pm Fri-Sat • popular • also restaurant

Northampton

Where the Girls Are:
Just off Main St., browsing in the small shops, strolling down an avenue, or sipping a beverage at one of the cafes.

LGBT Pride:
May. 413/586-5602, web: www.northamptonpride.org.

Annual Events:
October - Paradise City Arts Festival 413/587-0772, web: www.paradise-city.com.

City Info:
413/584-1900, web: www.northamptonuncommon.com

Attractions:
Academy of Music 413/584-9032, web: www.academyofmusictheatre.com.
The Berkshires.
Emily Dickinson Homestead, Amherst 413/542-8161, web: www.emilydickinsonmuseum.org.
Historic Northampton 413/584-6011, web: www.historic-northampton.org.
Northampton Center for the Arts 413/584-7327, web: www.nohoarts.com.

Best View:
At the top of Skinner Mountain, up Route 47 by bus, car, or bike.

Weather:
Late summer/early fall is the best season, with warm, sunny days. Mid-summer gets to the low 90ºs, while winter brings snow from November to March, with temperatures in the 20ºs and 30ºs.

Transit:
Paradise Taxi 413/584-0055.
Peter Pan Shuttle 413/781-2900, 800/237-8747, web: www.peter-panbus.com.
Pioneer Valley Transit Authority (PVTA) 413/781-7882, web: www.pvta.com.

RESTAURANTS

Bela 68 Masonic St 413/586-8011 • noon-8:45pm, clsd Sun-Mon • vegetarian • wheelchair access • lesbian-owned

Green Street Cafe 64 Green St (at Main) 413/586-5650 • lunch & dinner • plenty veggie • beer/wine • gay-owned

Paul & Elizabeth's 150 Main St (in Thorne's Marketplace) 413/584-4832 • lunch & dinner • seafood • plenty veggie • beer/wine • wheelchair access

RETAIL SHOPS

Oh My 2-C Conz St (in Maplewood Shops) 413/584-9669 • 11am-6pm, till 8pm Fri-Sat, clsd Sun • cute & clean, well-lighted sex toy store

Pride & Joy 20 Crafts Ave 413/585-0683 • open 7 days • LGBT books & gifts • wheelchair access

PUBLICATIONS

In Newsweekly 617/426-8246 • New England's largest LGBT newspaper

▲ **Metroline** 860/233-8334 • regional newspaper & entertainment guide, covers CT, RI & MA

Plymouth

ACCOMMODATIONS

Symphony Hollow B&B 127 Brook St, Plympton 781/585-7823, 888/655-1200 • gay/straight • B&B • on 7 acres • full brkfst • gardens • fireplaces • gay-owned • $110-145

Provincetown

see also Cape Cod listings

INFO LINES & SERVICES

In Town Reservations, Real Estate & Travel 800/677-8696, 561/202-9889 • gay-owned

▲ **Provincetown Business Guild** 508/487-2313, 800/637-8696 • see ad in front color section

ACCOMMODATIONS

1807 House 54 Commercial St (btwn W Vine & Point St) 508/487-2173, 888/522-1807 • lesbians/gay men • apts & rooms in 1700s whaling capt's home • gay-owned • $70-225

Admiral's Landing Guest House 158 Bradford St (btwn Conwell & Pearl) 508/487-9665, 800/934-0925 • mostly gay men • 1840s Greek Revival home & studio efficiencies • nonsmoking • gay-owned • $55-140

Aerie House & Beach Club 184 Bradford St (at Miller Hill) 508/487-1197, 800/487-1197 • lesbians/gay men • intimate guesthouse on the tip of Cape Cod • hot tub • sundeck • gay-owned • $25-280

Anchor Inn Beach House 175 Commercial St **508/487-0432, 800/858-2657** • popular • gay/ straight • nonsmoking • central location • private beach • harbor view • wheelchair access • lesbian & straight-owned/ run • $115-375

Bayberry Accommodations 16 Winthrop St **508/487-4605, 800/422-4605** • lesbians/ gay men • award-winning home • hot tub • nonsmoking • gay-owned • $75-255

Bayshore 493 Commercial St (at Howland) **508/487-9133** • gay/ straight • apts • private beach • kitchens • pets ok • lesbian-owned • $105-230 ($1,200-2,300/ week in summer)

Beachfront Realty 139 Commercial St 508/487-1397 • vacation rentals

Beachpoint Condominiums 963 Commercial St **617/548-2300** • mostly women • 5 1-bdrm/ 1-bth condos • nonsmoking • $250-625/ week

Beaconlight Guest House 12 Winthrop St **508/487-9603, 800/696-9603** • popular • mostly gay men • award-winning • hot tub • fireplaces • sundecks • nonsmoking • parking • gay-owned • $70-290

Provincetown

WHERE THE GIRLS ARE:
In this small resort town, you can't miss 'em! At the beach, the girls gather on the left side at Herring Cove.

LGBT PRIDE:
August - Provincetown Carnival.

ANNUAL EVENTS:
May - Cabaretfest, web: www.cabaretfest.com.
June - Golden Threads. Gathering for lesbians over 50 & their admirers, at the Provincetown Inn. 781/229-9028, web: www.goldenthreadsptown.org.
August - Provincetown Carnival 800/637-8696.
October - Women's Week 800/637-8696. It's very popular, so make your reservations early!
October - Fantasia Fair - for trannies & their admirers.
December - Holly Folly, web: www.davidflower.com. Gay & Lesbian Holiday Festival.

CITY INFO:
Chamber of Commerce 508/487-3424, web: www.ptownchamber.com.

BEST VIEW:
People-watching from an outdoor cafe or on the beach.

ATTRACTIONS:
The beach.
Galleries.
Herring Cove Beach.
Pilgrim Monument.
Provincetown Museum 508/487-1310, web: www.pilgrim-monument.org.
Whale-watching.

WEATHER:
New England weather is unpredictable. Be prepared for rain, snow, or extreme heat! Otherwise, the weather during the season consists of warm days and cooler nights.

TRANSIT:
Cape Cab 508/487-2222.
Ferry: Bay State Cruise Company (from Commonwealth/World Trade Center Pier in Boston, during summer) 617/748-1428, web: www.baystatecruisecompany.com.

Reply **Forward** **Delete**

Date: Nov 4, 2005 12:09:11
From: Girl-on-the-Go
To: Editor@Damron.com
Subject: Provincetown

>Who would have thought that a little New England whaling village at the very tip of Cape Cod would be the country's largest gay and lesbian resort? But Provincetown is just that.

>The season in Provincetown runs according to a time-honored schedule of who does what, when, and where. According to one regular, the typical lesbian itinerary goes as follows:

>Arrival: Rent a bike and explore the town's LGBT shops and bookstores. (Nobody drives in Provincetown.) Pick up lunch at a deli on the way to Herring Cove. At the beach, head left to find the women.

>At the beach: Take off your top, if you like. Just keep an eye out for the cops, who'll give you a ticket if they catch you bare-breasted. If you simply MUST sunbathe in the nude, head over to **Spaghetti Strip**, the legal nude sand spit between Race Point Beach and Herring Cove. And a word to the wise: If you're heading toward the sand dunes for a tryst, don't forget your socks. The hot, white sand can burn your feet (Youch!).

>3pm: Bike back to your room for a shower, then head to the afternoon T-dance at **Boatslip Beach Resort** on Commercial Street. Drink and dance till dinnertime, then take a relaxing few hours for your meal.

>After dinner: Check out the bars; women have their choice between **Vixen, The Pied,** and **Chaser's**. If you're not into the bar scene or all the sun and surf has tired you out, you can always go shopping. Most stores stay open till 11pm during the summer. When the bars close, grab a slice of pizza and an espresso milkshake at **Spiritus**, and cruise the streets until they're empty—sometimes not till 4 or 5am.

>Before you leave, treat yourself to the excitement of a whale-watching cruise. There are several cruise lines, and **Portuguese Princess Whale Watch** is women-owned.

>But if you really want a whale of a good time, pencil in **Provincetown's Women's Week** in October. The **Women Innkeepers of Provincetown** will be sponsoring an opening party, a community dinner, a golf tournament and fun run, a prom, lots of entertainment...and more. Don't forget to call your favorite guesthouse early—really early—to make your reservations!

▲ **Benchmark Inn & Central** 6–8 Dyer St 508/487-7440, 888/487-7440 • lesbians/gay men • hot tub • sauna • fireplace • harbor views • swimming • in heart of Provincetown • nonsmoking • wheelchair access • gay-owned • $110-425

The Black Pearl Inn 11 & 18 Pearl St 508/487-0302, 800/761-1016 • lesbians/gay men • renovated 19th-c sea captain's home • hot tub • pets ok • "friends of Bill welcome"

▲ **Boatslip Resort** 161 Commercial St (at Atlantic) 508/487-1669, 800/451-7547 • popular • mostly gay men • resort • swimming • seasonal • also several bars • popular T-dance • gay-owned • $115-255

The Bradford Carver House 70 Bradford St 508/487-4966, 800/826-9083 • lesbians/gay men • restored mid-19th-c home • centrally located • nonsmoking • gay-owned • $49-199

Bradford House & Motel 41 Bradford St 508/487-0173 • gay-friendly • near town center • 1 block from the beach • wheelchair access • women-owned • $75-250

Brass Key Guesthouse 67 Bradford St (at Carver) 508/487-9005, 800/842-9858 • popular • lesbians/gay men • hot tub • swimming • nonsmoking • wheelchair access • gay-owned • $245-445

Burch House 116 Bradford St 508/487-9170 • gay/straight • studios • seasonal • some shared baths • kids/pets ok • $50-125

Cape Inn 508/487-1711, 800/422-4224 • gay/straight • swimming • nonsmoking • pets ok • also restaurant & lounge • wheelchair access • $69-179

Carpe Diem Guesthouse 12 Johnson St 508/487-4242, 800/487-0132 • lesbians/gay men • also cottage • full German brkfst • hot tub • nonsmoking • gay-owned • $70-335

The Carriage House Guesthouse 7 Central St 508/487-8855, 800/309-0248 • gay/straight • 1700s guesthouse w/ luxurious modern rooms • hot tub • courtyard • gay-owned • $100-295

Chicago House 6 Winslow St (at Bradford) 508/487-0537, 800/733-7869 • lesbians/ gay men • rooms & apts • hot tub • some shared baths • nonsmoking • gay-owned • $45-140

Christopher's by the Bay 8 Johnson St (at Bradford) 508/487-9263, 877/487-9263 • lesbians/ gay men • Victorian guesthouse • full brkfst • some shared baths • patio • nonsmoking • gay-owned • $65-175

The Clarendon House 118 Bradford St (btwn Ryder & Alden) 508/487-1645, 800/669-8229 • gay/ straight • also cottage • hot tub • roof deck • kids/ pets ok • nonsmoking • $75-185

The Commons Guest House & Bistro 386 Commercial St (at Pearl) 508/487-7800, 800/487-0784 • gay/ straight • deck w/ full bar • also restaurant • gay-owned • $129-199

Copper Fox 448 Commercial St 508/487-8583 • gay/straight • apts & suites • gay-owned

Crown & Anchor 247 Commercial St 508/487-1430 • lesbians/ gay men • swimming • nonsmoking • also bars • cabaret • gay-owned • $150-350

Crowne Pointe Historic Inn 82 Bradford St 508/487-6767, 877/276-9631 • lesbians/ gay men • 1800s mansion • full brkfst • hot tub • 2 large jacuzzis • nonsmoking • wheelchair access • gay-owned • $125-469

Designer's Dock 349 Commercial St 508/487-0385, 800/724-9888 • gay/ straight • weekly condos in town & on beach • June-Sept • kitchens • gay-owned • $800+ weekly (also 4-day wknd rates)

Dexter's Inn 6 Conwell St (at Railroad) 508/487-1911, 888/521-1999 • lesbians/ gay men • B&B • nonsmoking • sundeck • gay-owned • $75-150

The Dunes Motel & Apartments 508/487-1956, 800/475-1833 • lesbians/ gay men • rooms & apts • seasonal • decks • nonsmoking • $49-240

Dyer's Antique Barn Guest Suites 9 Winthrop St (at Commercial) 508/487-2061 • lesbians/ gay men • self-catering units • $2,500/ week

Esther's 186 Commercial St 508/487-7555, 888/873-5001 • gay/straight • restaurant & piano bar on premises

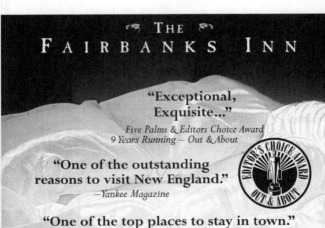

▲ **Fairbanks Inn** 90 Bradford St 508/487–0386, 800/324–7265 • popular • lesbians/gay men • kids ok • nonsmoking • Wi-Fi • lesbian-owned • $79-289

Four Gables 15 Race Rd 866/487–2427 • gay/straight • private cottages • kids/pets ok • gay-owned • $1,200-1,800/week in season

▲ **Gabriel's Apartments & Guest Rooms** 104 Bradford St 508/487–3232, 800/969–2643 • popular • mostly women • full brkfst • hot tub • nudity • nonsmoking • sundecks • lesbian & gay-owned • $95-350 • see ad on back cover

Gifford House Inn 9-11 Carver St 508/487–0688, 800/434–0130 • lesbians/gay men • seasonal • also several bars • also 11 Carver restaurant • dinner only • seafood • gay-owned • $60-220

Gracie House 152 Bradford St (at Conwell) 508/487–4808 • lesbians/gay men • historic, restored Queen Anne • seasonal • nonsmoking • lesbian-owned • $115-140

Grand View Inn 4 Conant St 508/487–9193, 888/268–9169 • lesbians/gay men • nonsmoking • kids/pets ok • decks • gay-owned • $45-155

▲ **Harbor Hill** 4 Harbor Hill Rd 508/487–0541 • gay-friendly • condo resort in West End • 500 yds from Nat'l Seashore • kids ok • gay-owned • $100-275

Harbor Hill at Provincetown 4 Harbor Hill Rd 508/487–0541 • mostly women • rental condos

Heritage House 7 Center St 508/487–3692 • lesbians/gay men • shared baths • lesbian-owned • $70-125

The Inn at Cook Street 7 Cook St 508/487–3894, 888/266–5655 • gay-friendly • intimate & quiet • nonsmoking • gay-owned • $85-180

Inn at the Moors 59 Provincelands Rd 508/487–1342, 800/842–6379 • gay-friendly • motel • across from Nat'l Seashore Province Lands • seasonal • nonsmoking • swimming • lesbian-owned • $60-130

John Randall House 140 Bradford St (at Standish) 508/487–3533, 800/573–6700 • lesbians/gay men • open year-round • kids ok • nonsmoking • gay-owned • $69-179

Labrador Landing 47 Commercial St 917/597–1500 • lesbians/gay men • luxury cottages on West End • kids/pets ok • gay-owned • $1,500-2,500/week

Land's End Inn 22 Commercial St **508/487-0706, 800/276-7088** • seasonal • gay/straight • nonsmoking • gay-owned • $135-495

Locust Court 32 Court St **860/896-1879** • gay/ straight • rental home • fireplace • kids ok • private yard & deck • $1,400-2,400/week, $750-1,200/ wknd

Lotus Guest House 296 Commercial St (at Standish) **508/487-4644, 888/508-4644** • lesbians/ gay men • seasonal • decks • garden • teens ok • lesbian & gay-owned • $90-275

Mayflower Apartments & Cottages 6 Bangs St (at Commercial St) **508/487-1916** • gay-friendly • kitchens • $140+

Moffett House 296-A Commercial St **508/487-6615, 800/990-8865** • lesbians/ gay men • leather/ levi-friendly • gay-owned • $60-150

Officers Quarters 164 Commercial St (btwn Winthrop & Central) **508/487-1850, 800/400-2278** • mostly men but all welcome • 19th-c sea captain's home • seasonal • sundeck • gay-owned • $100-250

The Oxford 8 Cottage St **508/487-9103, 888/456-9103** • lesbians/ gay men • recently renovated 1850 Revival • nonsmoking • parking • gay-owned • $90-290

Pilgrim House Inn 336 Commercial St **508/487-6424** • mostly women • seasonal • kids ok • also Vixen bar/ dance club • wheelchair access • $99-139

The Prince Albert Guest House 166 Commercial St **508/487-1850, 800/400-2278** • mostly gay men • Victorian • nonsmoking • gay-owned • $100-240

Provincetown Inn 1 Commercial St (at Rotary) **508/487-9500, 800/942-5388** • gay/ straight • swimming • private beach • poolside bar & grill • theater • wheelchair access • $59-369

Ravenwood Guest House 462 Commercial St (at Cook) **508/487-3203** • lesbians/ gay men • 1830 Greek Revival • also apts & cottage • nonsmoking • patio • private beach • wheelchair accessible cottage • lesbian-owned • $85-175

The Red Inn 15 Commercial St (at Point) **508/487-7334, 866/473-3466** • gay-friendly • boutique hotel on beach • nonsmoking • wheelchair access • gay-owned • $195-425

Revere Guesthouse 14 Court St (btwn Commercial & Bradford) **508/487-2292, 800/487-2292** • lesbians/ gay men • restored 1820s captain's home • also apt • nonsmoking • gay-owned • $90-275

Roomers 8 Carver St (at Commercial St) 508/487–3532 • seasonal • mostly gay men • Greek Revival guesthouse • gay-owned • $100-185

Rose Acre 5 Center St (at Commercial) 508/487–2347 • women only • also apts & cottage • nonsmoking • decks • gardens • parking • always open • women-owned/run • $125-200

Rose & Crown Guest House 158 Commercial St 508/487–3332 • gay/ straight • Victorian antiques • lavish gardens • some shared baths • lesbian-owned • $40-210 • also cottage • $160-230

Sandbars 570 Shore Rd, Beach Pt, North Truro 800/223–0088 x160 • gay/ straight • oceanfront rooms • kitchens • seasonal • private beach • woman-owned/run • $79-219

Sandpiper Beach House 165 Commercial St 508/487–1928, 800/354–8628 • gay/ straight • Victorian • sundeck • private beach • nonsmoking • gay-owned • $1,900-5,900/ week

Seasons, An Inn for All 160 Bradford St (at Pearl) 508/487–2283, 800/563–0113 • lesbians/ gay men • Victorian B&B • full brkfst • nonsmoking • gay-owned • $80-140

▲ **The Secret Garden Inn** 300–A Commercial St 508/487–9027, 866/786–9646 • lesbians/ gay men • central location • shared baths • kids ok • sundeck • garden • nonsmoking • $75-170

Shiremax Inn 5 Tremont St (btwn Franklin & School) 508/487–1233, 888/744–7362 • lesbians/ gay men • 1900s guesthouse • seasonal • pets ok • gay-owned • $70-115 & $750-900 (apt)

Snug Cottage 178 Bradford St 508/487–1616, 800/432–2334 • gay/ straight • boutique B&B • teens ok • nonsmoking • gay-owned • $90-235

Somerset House 378 Commercial St (at Pearl) 508/487–0383, 800/575–1850 • popular • lesbians/ gay men • Victorian mansion • nonsmoking • gay-owned • $75-280

The Stone Lion Inn 130 Commercial St, Wellfleet 508/349–9565 • gay-friendly • kids ok • full brkfst • 15 miles from P-Town • $120-170

Sunset Inn 142 Bradford St (at Center) 508/487–9810, 800/965–1801 • lesbians/ gay men • some shared baths • seasonal • clothing-optional sundeck • nonsmoking • gay-owned • $59-165

▲ **Surfside Hotel & Suites** 543 Commercial (at Kendall Ln) 508/487-1726, 800/421-1726 • gay/ straight • waterfront hotel • lots of amenities • private beach • swimming • kids/ pets ok • gay-owned • $139-329

The Tucker Inn 12 Center St 508/487-0381, 800/477-1867 • lesbians/ gay men • 1870s guesthouse • full brkfst • also cottage (rented weekly) • nonsmoking • gay-owned • $85-185

Victoria House 5 Standish St 508/487-4455, 877/867-8696 • lesbians/ gay men • gay-owned • $35-165

Watermark Inn 603 Commercial St 508/487-0165 • gay/ straight • suites w/ kitchens • beachside • kids ok • nonsmoking • $85-185/ night off-season & $1,200-2,500/ wk in-season

Watership Inn 7 Winthrop St 508/487-0094, 800/330-9413 • popular • mostly gay men • sundeck • gay-owned • $45-225

▲ **White Wind Inn** 174 Commercial St (at Winthrop) 508/487-1526, 888/449-9463 • lesbians/ gay men • 1800s Victorian • gay-owned • $95-265

Windamar House 568 Commercial St (at Conway) 508/487-0599 • lesbians/ gay men • 1840s sea captain's home • also apts • nonsmoking • lesbian-owned • $65-135

▲ **Women Innkeepers of Provincetown** PO Box 573, 02657 • women-owned accommodations in Provincetown

BARS

The Alibi 291 Commercial St (at Rider) 508/487-2890 • noon-1am • popular • gay/ straight • neighborhood bar • local favorite

▲ **The Boatslip Beach Resort** 161 Commercial St (at Central) 508/487-1669, 866/900-3892 • seasonal • popular • lesbians/ gay men • resort • T-dance 4pm daily during season • young crowd • special events • swimming • outdoor/ waterfront grill • some veggie

Chaser's 293 Commercial St (at Standish) 508/487-7200 • 6pm-1am, from 7pm winter • mostly women • neighborhood bar • dancing/DJ • live shows • karaoke

Governor Bradford 312 Commercial St (at Standish) 508/487-2781 • 11am-1am, from noon Sun • gay-friendly • "drag karaoke" in season • also restaurant in summer

PiedBar 193–A Commercial St (at Court St) 508/487–1527 • seasonal May-Oct, noon-1am • popular • lesbians/ gay men • dancing/DJ • all-women T-dance wknds

Vixen 336 Commercial St (at Pilgrim House Inn) 508/487–6424 • 4pm-1am, from 11am Fri-Sat, from noon Sun • mostly women • dancing/DJ • go go girls • live shows • videos

Wave Video Bar 247 Commercial St (in the Crown & Anchor) 508/487–1430 • 6pm-1am, from noon in season • lesbians/ gay men • neighborhood bar • karaoke Wed • more women Mon for G-Spot from 9pm in season • T-dance wknds from 6pm

NIGHTCLUBS

Atlantic House (The "A-House") 6 Masonic Pl 508/487–3169 • noon-1am • popular • mostly gay men • 3 bars • dancing/DJ • weekly theme parties • also The Little Bar from 11am • neighborhood bar • Macho Bar upstairs • leather

Club Purgatory 9-11 Carver St (at Bradford St, in the Gifford House) 508/487–8442 • 5pm-1am • lesbians/ gay men • dancing/DJ • levi/ leather • theme nights • popular leather night Sun

Paramount in the Crown & Anchor accommodations 508/487–1430 • 10:30pm-1am (seasonal) • popular • lesbians/ gay men • dancing/DJ • live shows • drag shows • cabaret • Power T 6pm-9pm Sun • cover Fri-Sat

CAFES

Cicchetti's Espresso Bar 353 Commercial St (at Angel's Landing) 508/487–0036 • from 7am • serves fair trade coffees (hot & frozen) & baked goods • women-owned

Joe's 148-A Commercial St (btwn Atlantic & Conant) 508/487–6656 • 7:30am-close • great coffee w/ a view

Post Office Cafe Cabaret 303 Commercial St (upstairs) 508/487–3892 • 8am-close, seasonal hours • lesbians/ gay men • some veggie

RESTAURANTS

Bayside Betsy's 177 Commercial St 508/487–6566 • brkfst, lunch & dinner on waterfront • clsd Tue-Wed, bar till 10pm • wheelchair access

Big Daddy's Burritos 205 Commercial St 508/487–4432 • 11am-9pm (May-Oct) • Tex-Mex, burritos, wraps • plenty veggie

Your room is ready . . .
year round

THE WOMEN INNKEEPERS OF PROVINCETOWN

Also join us for Women's Week every October

info@WomenInnKeepers.com
www.WomenInnKeepers.com

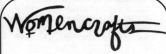

376 Commercial St.
Provincetown, MA 02657
508 487-2501

Here's a little bit about us.
Womencrafts is lesbian owned
and operated, and we are well into
our 3rd decade of celebrating women!

We represent over
50 women artists and artisans
from across the United States,
and offer a beautiful selection of
fine jewelry,
hand-thrown pottery,
porcelain,
sculpture,
photographs,
and
artwork.

In addition,
we carry over 700 lesbian and feminist
book titles, both fiction and non-fiction,
and a varied selection
of women's music and videos.

When you are visiting
Provincetown,
please stop in.

Or look for us at
www.womencrafts.com

Bubala's by the Bay 183–185 Commercial 508/487-0773 • 8am-11pm, bar till 1am • popular • seasonal • patio

Chester 404 Commercial St 508/487-8200 • dinner from 6pm • popular • seasonal hours, upscale

Ciro & Sal's 4 Kiley Ct (btwn Bangs St & Lovett's Ct) 508/487-6444 • dinner from 5:30pm, bar from 5pm • Northern Italian • reservations recommended

Clem & Ursie's 89 Shank Painter Rd 508/487-2333 • 11am-10pm • outdoor dining • cuisine theme nights • affordable • also fish market, deli & grocery • beer/ wine

Fanizzi's 539 Commercial St 508/487-1964 • seasonal • popular • lunch & dinner • some veggie • full bar • on the water • wheelchair access • $10-20

Front Street Restaurant 230 Commercial St 508/487-9715 • 6pm-10:30pm, bar till 1am • bistro beer/ wine • seasonal

Grand Central 5 Masonic Pl 508/487-7599 • seasonal • popular • dinner • full bar

L'Uva Restaurant 133 Bradford St 508/487-2010 • classic Mediterranean/ New American • outdoor garden & full bar

Lobster Pot harborside (at 321 Commercial St) 508/487-0842 • 11:30am-10pm (April-Nov) • seafood • some veggie • "a Provincetown tradition" • wheelchair access

Lorraine's 133 Commercial St 508/487-6074 • dinner • popular • lesbians/ gay men • Mexican• some veggie • full bar • woman-owned

Martin House 157 Commercial St (at Atlantic Street Landing) 508/487-1327 • 6pm-close, clsd Wed • outdoor dining • full bar • wheelchair access

The Mews Restaurant & Cafe 429 Commercial St (btwn Lovett's & Kiley) 508/487-1500 • dinner • Sun brunch • popular • cont'l • some veggie • Cafe Mews upstairs • live shows • wheelchair access • waterfront dining

Napi's Restaurant 7 Freeman St 508/487-1145, 800/571-6274 • dinner • lunch Oct-April • int'l/ seafood • plenty veggie • wheelchair access

Sal's Place 99 Commercial St 508/487-1279 • popular • seasonal • seafood/ Italian • publisher's choice: cheese & butter pasta • deck • on the water

Spiritus Pizza 190 Commercial St **508/487–2808** • noon-2am • popular • great espresso shakes & late-night hangout for a slice

Tofu A Go-Go! 336 Commercial St #6 (upstairs) **508/487–6237** • seasonal • lunch & dinner • vegetarian, vegan & macrobiotic • $7-12

ENTERTAINMENT & RECREATION

Art's Dune Tours 9 Washington Ave **508/487–1950, 800/894–1951** • day trips, sunset tours & charters through historic sand dunes & Nat'l Seashore Park • kids ok • gay-owned • $12-15

Portuguese Princess Whale Watch 70 Shank Painter Rd (at MacMillan Wharf) **800/442–3188** • day & evening cruises • women's event cruises • wheelchair access • women-owned/ run

Ptown Bikes 42 Bradford **508/487–8735** • 9am-7pm • rentals • gay-owned

Spaghetti Strip • nude beach • 1.5 miles south of Race Point Beach

BOOKSTORES

Now, Voyager Bookstore & Gallery 357 Commercial St **508/487–0848** • 10am-10pm (summers) • LGBT & general books • cards

Provincetown Bookshop 246 Commercial St **508/487–0964** • 11am-11pm (till 5pm off-season)

RETAIL SHOPS

Details in Whalers Wharf **508/487–4474** • 10am-11pm (in summer), call for off-season hours • LGBT gifts • T-shirts • books

Don't Panic 200 Commercial St **508/487–1280** • seasonal • 10am-10pm • LGBT gifts • T-shirts

MAP 141 Commercial St **508/487–4900** • swanky store • seasonal

Piercings by the Bearded Lady 336 Commercial St #4 **508/487–7979** • 1pm-7pm, clsd Sun • seasonal • lesbian-owned

Recovering Hearts 2–4 Standish St **508/487–4875** • 10am-11pm (in summer), call for off-season hours • recovery • LGBT & New Age books • wheelchair access

▲ **Womencrafts** 376 Commercial St **508/487–2501** • 10am-11pm (in summer), call for off-season hours • jewelry, pottery, books, music, gifts, etc

PUBLICATIONS

In Newsweekly 617/426–8246 • New England's largest LGBT newspaper

Provincetown Banner 508/487–7400 • newspaper

Provincetown Magazine 508/487–1000 • seasonal • Provincetown's oldest weekly magazine

GYMS & HEALTH CLUBS

Mussel Beach 35 Bradford St (btwn Montello & Conant) **508/487–0001** • 6am-9pm, till 8pm in winter • lesbians/ gay men

Provincetown Gym 82 Shank Painter Rd (at Winthrop) **508/487–2776** • 6am-8pm, 7am-7pm Sun, till 9pm in season • lesbians/ gay men • daily, weekly & monthly rates

EROTICA

MG Leather Inc 338 Commercial St (at Standish St) **508/487–4036** • 11am-6pm • leather • fetish • toys • gifts • gay-owned

Wild Hearts 244 Commercial St **508/487–8933** • 11am-11pm (in summer), noon-5pm (off-season) • toys for women

Quincy

see also Boston

NIGHTCLUBS

The Den 123 Sea St (at the Fox & Hound) **617/786–7469** • mostly gay men • cabaret • also restaurant

RETAIL SHOPS

Body Xtremes 417 Hancock St, North Quincy **617/471–5836** • body piercing & jewelry • also tattooing (617/984-0956)

Randolph

BARS

Randolph Country Club 44 Mazzeo Dr **781/961–2414** • 2pm-2am, from 10am summer • popular • lesbians/ gay men • dancing/DJ • food served • live shows • karaoke • male dancers • videos • volleyball court • swimming • wheelchair access

Rockport

ACCOMMODATIONS

Seven South Street Inn 7 South St **888/284–2730** • gay-friendly • swimming • nonsmoking • $69-159

Salem

NIGHTCLUBS

Roosevelvet 300 Derby St (at Roosevelt) **978/745–1133** • 7pm-1am Sun only • mostly gay men • dancing/ DJ

Salisbury

BARS

Hobo Cafe/ Lavender Lounge 5 Broadway **978/465–4626** • lesbians/ gay men • neighborhood bar • karaoke • gay-owned

Saugus

NIGHTCLUBS

Taboo 168 Broadway (Rte 1 N, Godfried's Plaza) **781/231–5111** • from 10pm • gay-friendly • dancing/DJ

Somerville

see Boston

Springfield

BARS

Pub/ Quarry 382 Dwight (at Taylor) **413/734–8123** • 2pm-2am, from noon wknds• mostly gay men • neighborhood bar • dancing/DJ wknds • live shows • leather

CAFES

Blue Moon Coffee Roasters 715 Sumner Ave (across from Bing Theater) **413/788–3965, 888/919–2627** • fresh-roasted coffee • also teas & baked goods • patio

Waltham

BOOKSTORES

Synchronicity Transgender Bookstore 13 Felton St (at Moody) **781/899–2212** • 10am-6pm, clsd wknds • over 100 TG titles

Watertown

see also Boston

Williamstown

see Berkshires

Worcester

INFO LINES & SERVICES

AA Gay/ Lesbian 1 Freeland St **508/752–9000** • 7pm Sat

BARS

MB Lounge 40 Grafton St (at Franklin) **508/799–4521** • 3pm-2am • lesbians/ gay men • neighborhood bar • wheelchair access

Water Street Mining Company 105 Water St **508/756–2227** • 7pm-2am Tue-Sun • lesbians/ gay men • neighborhood bar

NIGHTCLUBS

My Martini 1 Exchange Pl (at The Atrium) • 9pm-close • gay/ straight • more gay Wed

Rage 105 Water St **508/756–2227** • 10pm-2am Th-Sun • lesbians/ gay men • dancing/ DJ

CAFES

SPQR 82 Winter St **508/797–1011** • 4pm-midnight • gay night Sun

RESTAURANTS

86 Winter Street 86 Winter St **508/459–5400** • popular • from 4pm Wed-Sun, clsd Mon-Tue • upscale • full bar • gay-owned

ENTERTAINMENT & RECREATION

Face the Music WCUW 91.3 FM **508/753–2284** (REQUEST LINE) • 8pm Th • lesbian/ feminist music

RETAIL SHOPS

Glamour Boutique 850 Southbridge St, Auburn **508/721–7800** • noon-8pm, call for Sun hours • large-size dresses, wigs, etc

Vibes 116 Water St (at Harrison) **508/753–9969, 800/698–4237** • noon-9pm, till 3am Fri-Sat, clsd Mon • also cafe • gay-owned

SPIRITUAL GROUPS

North Star Cathedral of Hope 70 James St #146 **508/949–7939** • 9:45am Sun & 6:45pm Sun • wheelchair access

GYMS & HEALTH CLUBS

Midtown Athletic Club 22 Front St, 2nd flr (in Midtown Mall) **508/798–9703** • gay-friendly

MICHIGAN

Statewide

PUBLICATIONS

Between the Lines 248/615-7003, 888/615-7003 • LGBT weekly

Out Post 313/702-0272 • bi-weekly nightlife guide for SE Michigan

What Helen Heard PO Box 811, East Lansing 48826 517/371-5257 • what's happening for Michigan lesbians

Ann Arbor

INFO LINES & SERVICES

Lesbian/ Gay AA 734/482-5700

BARS

\aut\ Bar 315 Braun Ct (at Catherine) 734/994-3677 • 4pm-2am, from 10am Sun (brunch) • popular • lesbians/ gay men • 2 flrs • also restaurant • American/ Mexican • some veggie • patio • wheelchair access

NIGHTCLUBS

The Necto 516 E Liberty 734/994-5436 • 9pm-2am • gay/straight • dancing/DJ • videos • young crowd • 18+ • theme nights • gay night Fri

CAFES

Cafe Verde 216 N Fourth Ave 734/994-9174 • 7am-9:30pm, 9am-8pm Sun • fair trade & organic coffee & tea • also soups, sandwiches & salads • "Ann Arbor's only fair trade coffee bar"

RESTAURANTS

Dominick's 812 Monroe St (at Tappan Ave) 734/662-5414 • 10am-10pm , clsd Sun • Italian • full bar • wheelchair access

The Earle 121 W Washington (at Ashley) 734/994-0211 • 5:30pm-10pm, till 11:30 Fri-Sat, 5pm-9pm Sun • cont'l • some veggie • beer/ wine • wheelchair access

Seva 314 E Liberty 734/662-1111 • 11am-9pm, from 10am wknds • vegetarian • also cafe & wine bar

ENTERTAINMENT & RECREATION

The Ark 316 S Main St (btwn William & Liberty) 734/761-1818 • gay-friendly • concert house • women's music shows

BOOKSTORES

Common Language 317 Braun Ct 734/663-0036 • 11am-10pm, till midnight Fri-Sat, till 7pm Sun • LGBT • wheelchair access

Crazy Wisdom Books 114 S Main (btwn Huron & Washington) 734/665-2757 • 10am-10pm, till 11pm Wed-Sat • holistic & metaphysical

Nicola's Books 2513 Jackson Ave (at Maple, in Westgate) 734/662-4110 • 9am-9pm, till 6pm Sun

SPIRITUAL GROUPS

Northside Presbyterian Church 1679 Broadway St (at Baits Dr) 734/663-5503 • 11am Sun (10am June-Aug)

Tree of Life MCC 325 Braun Ct (near 4th Ave, across from \aut\ bar), Ypsilanti 734/449-4189 • 10:30am Sun

Zen Buddhist Temple 1214 Packard Rd 734/761-6520 • 9:30am & 4pm Sun

Battle Creek

NIGHTCLUBS

Partners 910 North Ave (at Morgan) 269/964-7276 • 6pm-2am, clsd Mon • lesbians/ gay men • dancing/DJ • karaoke • wheelchair access

SPIRITUAL GROUPS

Sign of the Covenant MCC 35 S Cass St (at Jackson) 269/965-8004 • 10:30am Sun

Bellaire

ACCOMMODATIONS

Applesauce Inn B&B 7296 S M-88 231/533-6448, 888/533-6448 • gay-friendly • B&B in 100-year-old farmhouse • dog-friendly • $75-105

Bellaire B&B 212 Park St (at Antrim) 231/533-6077, 800/545-0780 • gay/ straight • stately 1879 home • full brkfst • jacuzzi • nonsmoking • gay-owned • $95-225

Big Bay

ACCOMMODATIONS

Big Bay Depot Motel 906/345-9350 • gay-friendly • overlooking Lake Independence • kids/ pets ok • nonsmoking rooms available • lesbian-owned • $55

Cadillac

ACCOMMODATIONS

My Sister's Place 231/775-9730 • women's resort on lake • campsites, boats, bikes & other sports equipment available • kids welcome • women only • swimming • lesbian-owned • $20-135

Clarkston

SPIRITUAL GROUPS

Divine Peace MCC 5311 Sunnyside Dr 248/618-1186 • 10am Sun

Coldwater

EROTICA

The Lion's Den Adult Superstore 570 Jonesville Rd (exit 16, off I-69) 517/278-9577 • 24hrs

Copemish

ACCOMMODATIONS

Jeralan's Farm B&B 18361 Viaduct Rd 231/378-2926, 866/250-8444 • gay-friendly • B&B in 1872 farmhouse on 120 acres of woods & ponds • full brkfst • nonsmoking • $100-150

Detroit

INFO LINES & SERVICES

Affirmations Lesbian/ Gay Community Center 195 W 9 Mile Rd (at Woodward), Ferndale 248/398-7105 • 9am-9pm, till 11pm Fri-Sat, clsd Sun

Gay/ Lesbian AA 313/831-5550 (WAYNE COUNTY), 248/541-6565 (S OAKLAND COUNTY) • first number covers downtown Detroit, second covers N of 8 Mile Rd, including Royal Oak

Helpline 800/398-4297 • 4pm-9pm, till 11pm Fri-Sat • support & resources line

ACCOMMODATIONS

The Atheneum Suite Hotel 1000 Brush Ave (at Lafayette) 313/962-2323, 800/772-2323 • gay-friendly • luxury all-suite hotel • restaurant & lounge • gym • wheelchair access

Milner Hotel 1526 Centre St 313/963-3950, 877/645-6377 • gay-friendly • downtown

Shorecrest Motor Inn 1316 E Jefferson Ave 313/568-3000, 800/992-9616 • gay-friendly • downtown • restaurant • wheelchair access • $69-159

Woodbridge Star B&B 3985 Trumbull Ave 313/831-9668 • gay/ straight • inn in Victorian home • full brkfst • kids 12 years & up ok • gay-owned • $100-150

BARS

Club Gold Coast 2971 E 7 Mile Rd (at Conant) 313/366-6135 • 7pm-2am, open after hours till 5am Tue, Fri-Sat • popular • mostly gay men • dancing/DJ • male dancers nightly • wheelchair access

Diamond Jim's Saloon 19650 Warren (1 block E of Evergreen) 313/336-8680 • noon-2am, from 5pm wknds • mostly gay men • neighborhood bar • dancing/ DJ • country/ western nights • bears • leather • karaoke • multiracial clientele • dance lessons • also grill • gay-owned/ operated

Gigi's 16920 W Warren (at Clayburn, enter rear) 313/584-6525 • noon-2am, from 2pm wknds • mostly gay men • dancing/DJ • transgender-friendly • male dancers Mon & Fri • karaoke Sun • drag shows • talent contest • gay-owned

Pronto 608 S Washington (at 6th St), Royal Oak 248/544-7900 • 11am-2am Wed-Sat, till midnight Sun-Tue • popular • lesbians/ gay men • patio • also restaurant

Stingers Lounge 19404 Sherwood (at 7 Mile) 313/892-1765 • 6pm-5am, from 8pm wknds • lesbians/ gay men • neighborhood bar • drag shows • grill menu • gay-owned

Sugarbakers 3800 E 8 Mile Rd (at Ryan Ave) 313/892-5203 • 6pm-midnight, till 2am Fri-Sat, clsd Sun-Tue • mostly women • sports bar & grill

The Woodward Bar & Grill 6426 Woodward Ave (at Milwaukee, rear entrance) 313/872-0166 • 2pm-2am • mostly gay men • lounge • karaoke Mon & Wed

NIGHTCLUBS

Inuendo 744 E Savannah (at 6 1/2 Mile & I-75), Highland Park 313/891-5798 • 10pm-5am, till 2am Sun-Wed, clsd Mon • lesbians/ gay men • dancing/ DJ • karaoke • drag shows • strippers

Leland City Club 400 Bagley St (enter through unmarked door on First St side of Ramada Hotel building; club at top of stairwell) • 10pm-4:30am Fri-Sat • gay-friendly • dancing/DJ • goth/ alternative • 18+

Luna 1815 N Main St (at 12 Mile), Royal Oak 248/589-3344 • from 9pm, clsd Sun-Mon • gay-friendly • dancing/DJ • goth/ alternative • theme nights

Palladium 711 E McNichols Rd (btwn Woodward & I-75) **313/865–9700** • 10:30pm-4am Fri & Sat only • mostly women Fri • mostly men Sat • dancing/DJ • mostly African-American

Pandora's Box 6221 E Davison (at Mound) **313/892–8120** • 10pm-2am Wed & Fri-Sat, • popular • lesbians/ gay men • more women Sat • dancing/DJ • mostly African-American • karaoke • live shows • wheelchair access

Detroit

WHERE THE GIRLS ARE:
At the bars on 8-Mile Road between I-75 and Van Dyke Ave., with the boys in Highland Park or Dearborn, or shopping in Royal Oak.

LGBT PRIDE:
June. 313/537-3323 (Triangle Foundation #), web: www.pride-fest.net.

July. Hotter Than July, web: www.hotterthanjuly.com. "The Midwest's oldest black lesbian, gay, bi-affectionate and transgender pride celebration."

ANNUAL EVENTS:
January - Reel Pride Michigan Film Festival 313/537–3323 x103, web: www.reelpridemichigan.com.

End of April/early May - London Lesbian Film Festival 519/434-0246, web: www.www.llff.ca. Held in London, Ontario, Canada, but worth the trip. Women only.

August - Michigan Womyn's Music Festival 231/757-4766, web: www.michfest.com. One of the biggest annual gatherings of lesbians on the continent, in Walhalla.

CITY INFO:
313/202-1800 or 800/338-7648, web: www.visitdetroit.com.

BEST VIEW:
From the top of the 73-story Marriott Hotel at the Renaissance Center.

WEATHER:
Be prepared for hot, humid summers and cold, dry winters.

TRANSIT:
Checker Cab 313/963-7000, web: www.checkersedan.com.

Dynasty 800/445-5418, web: www.dynastyservices.com.

DOT bus service 313/933-1300 & 888/336-8287 (outside 313 area code), web: www.ci.detroit.mi.us/ddot.

Detroit People Mover 313/962-7245, web: www.thepeople-mover.com.

ATTRACTIONS:
Belle Isle Park 313/852-4075.

Detroit Institute of Arts 313/833-7900, web: www.dia.org.

Ford Detroit International Jazz Festival, web: www.detroitjazz-zfest.com.

Greektown.

Motown Historical Museum 313/875-2264, web: www.motownmuseum.com.

Museum of African American History 313/494-5800, web: www.maah-detroit.org.

North American Black Historical Museum in Windsor, Ontario, 800/713–6336, web: www.black-historicalmuseum.com.

Renaissance Center 313/259-5400, web: www.detroitrenaissance.com.

Reply **Forward** **Delete**

Date: Dec 11, 2005 10:14:22
From: Girl-on-the-Go
To: Editor@Damron.com
Subject: Detroit

>Known for its cars and stars, "Motown" is the home of General Motors and was the starting point for many living legends, including Aretha Franklin, Diana Ross & the Supremes, the Temptations, Stevie Wonder, Anita Baker, and Madonna.

>Detroit is also rich in African American culture. Be sure to check out the Museum of African American History, multi-cultural gallery Your Heritage House, the Motown Museum...and the lesbian/gay club **Pandora's Box.** And just across the river in Canada—via the underground Detroit/Windsor Tunnel—is the North American Black Historical Museum in Windsor, Ontario.

>You might want to start your stay with a visit to the **Affirmations Lesbian/Gay Community Center,** the LGBT bookstores **Chosen Books** and **Just 4 Us,** or **A Woman's Prerogative,** the women's bookstore. Later, check out **Sugarbakers,** a women's sports bar, or dance the night away at **Stiletto's** or the monthly **Palladium**.

>Downtown, discover the impressive Renaissance Center. This office and retail complex that dominates the city skyline houses shopping, restaurants, a 73-story hotel, even an indoor lake! Before moving on to explore the districts of Greektown, Bricktown, or Rivertown, take a spin around the Civic Center district on the Detroit People Mover, an elevated transit system that carries travelers in automated, weatherproof cars.

Q 141 W 9 Mile (at Woodward), Ferndale **248/582–7227** • 9pm-close Wed & Fri-Sat • popular • mostly gay men • dancing/ DJ • also cabaret Fri • 18+ Wed

The Rainbow Room 6640 E 8 Mile Rd (between Mound Rd & Van Dyke Ave) 313/891–1020 • 7pm-2am Wed-Sun • lesbians/ gay men • dancing/DJ • drag shows • karaoke • 18+

Score 23109 Harper (at E 9 Mile Rd), St Clair Shores **586/776–1320** • 8pm-close Wed-Sat • lesbians/gay men • more women Fri • dancing/ DJ • videos • karaoke Th • live bands Sat

Stiletto's 1641 Middlebelt Rd (between Michigan Ave & Cherry Hill Rd), Inkster **734/729–8980** • 8pm-2am Th-Sun • mostly women • dancing/DJ • live shows • karaoke

Temple 2906 Cass Ave (btwn Charlotte & Temple) 313/832–2822 • 11am-2am • mostly gay men • dancing/DJ • transgender-friendly • mostly African-American • popular wknds • wheelchair access

CAFES

Avalon International Breads 422 W Willis (at Cass) 313/832–0008 • 6am-6pm, clsd Sun-Mon • lesbian-owned

Cafe de Troit 1260 Liberty St 313/962–8050 • from 6:30am, from 10am wknds

Coffee Beanery Cafe 22871 S Woodward Ave, Ferndale 248/543–9434 • 7am-11pm

Trixie's Cafe 25925 Gratiot Ave, Roseville 586/776–9002 • 10am-1am, from 6pm Sun • live entertainment & open mics

RESTAURANTS

Cass Cafe 4620 Cass Ave (at Forest) 313/831–1400 • 11am-2am, 5pm-midnight Sun • plenty veggie • full bar

Como's 22812 Woodward (at 9 Mile), Ferndale 248/548–5005 • 11am-2am, till 3:30am Th-Sat • Italian • Sun brunch • full bar • patio • wheelchair access

La Dolce Vita 17546 Woodward Ave (at McNichols) 313/865–0331 • lunch & dinner, Sun brunch, clsd Mon • lesbians/ gay men • Italian • plenty veggie • full bar • patio • wheelchair access

Pronto 608 S Washington (at 6th St), Royal Oak 248/544–7900 • 11am-10pm, till midnight Fri, from 9am Sat, till 10pm Sun • popular • lesbians/gay men • patio • also video bar

Starving Artist 212 W 9 Mile (1/2 block W of Woodward), Ferndale 248/545–5650 • lunch & dinner, private parties Sun, clsd Mon • full bar • gay-owned

Sweet Lorraine's Cafe & Bar 29101 Greenfield Rd (at 12 Mile), Southfield 248/559–5985 • 11am-10pm, till midnight Fri-Sat • popular • modern American • some veggie • wheelchair access

Traffic Jam & Snug 511 W Canfield St (at SE corner of 2nd Ave) 313/831–9470 • 11am-10:30pm, till midnight Fri, from noon Sat, till 8pm Sun • eclectic • plenty veggie • also full bar, bakery, dairy & brewery

Vivio's 2460 Market St (btwn Gratiot & Russell) 313/393–1711 • lunch & dinner, clsd Sun • Italian • full bar

ENTERTAINMENT & RECREATION

Detroit Shock Palace of Auburn Hills, Auburn Hills • check out the Women's National Basketball Association while you're in Detroit

Pink Ice Productions 313/864–7743 • "promoting quality events for Women Loving Women" • visit web at www.pinkiceproductions.com

BOOKSTORES

A Woman's Prerogative Bookstore 175 W 9 Mile Rd (W of Woodward), Ferndale 248/545–5703 • 11am-8pm, till 9pm Th, till 7pm Sat, noon-4pm Sun • LGBT w/ strong emphasis on lesbian titles • wheelchair access

Chosen Books 120 W 4th St (btwn Main St & Woodward), Royal Oak 248/543–5758, 800/453–5758 • noon-10pm • LGBT • wheelchair access

Just 4 Us 211 W 9 Mile Rd (at Woodward), Ferndale 248/547–5878 • 1pm-8pm, 10am-6pm Sat, clsd Sun • also espresso bar • gay-owned

RETAIL SHOPS

Mia Mahalo 407 S Washington St, Royal Oak 248/546–1900 • 10am-6pm, till 7pm Fri, noon-5pm Sun • eco-friendly products for bed, bath, kitchen & baby

Royal Oak Tattoo 820 S Washington St, Royal Oak 248/398–0052 • noon-8pm, till 9pm Fri-Sat, clsd Sun • tattoo & piercing studio

PUBLICATIONS

Between the Lines 248/615–7003, 888/615–7003 • statewide LGBT weekly

Metra Magazine 248/543–3500 • covers IN, IL, MI, OH, PA, WI & Ontario, Canada

SPIRITUAL GROUPS

Birmingham Temple 28611 W 12 Mile Rd, Farmington Hills 248/477–1410 • Shabbat 8pm Fri • "a congregation for secular humanistic Judaism"

Congregation Shir Tikvah 3900 Northfield Pkwy, Troy 248/649–4418 • Shabbat 7:45pm Fri • Reform Judaism congregation

Dignity Detroit 8425 W McNichols Rd (in Sacred Heart Chapel, Marygrove College Campus) 313/278–4786 • 6pm Sun

First Unitarian Universalist Church 4605 Cass Ave 313/833–9107 • 11am Sun

MCC of Detroit 2441 Pinecrest (at Drayton Ave Presbyterian Church), Ferndale 248/399–7741 • 10am & 6pm Sun

Unity Fellowship Church 20846 Reimanville Ave, Ferndale 248/542–2301 • uplifting service in the African American tradition

Zion Lutheran Church 143 Albany (at Woodward), Ferndale 248/398–5510 • 10:30am Sun (9:30am summers) • wheelchair access

EROTICA

Noir Leather 124 W 4th St (at Center), Royal Oak 248/541–3979 • 11am-9pm, till 10pm Fri-Sat, noon-6pm Sun • leather • toys • fetishwear • wheelchair access

Flint

BARS

Club 501 2406 N Franklin St (at Davison) 810/234–9481 • 1pm-2am • popular • lesbians/ gay men • dancing/ DJ • multiracial

Pachyderm Pub G–1408 E Hemphill Rd (btwn I-475 & Saginaw St), Burton 810/744–4960 • 2pm-2am • lesbians/ gay men • neighborhood bar & restaurant • dancing/ DJ • professional crowd • multiracial clientele • transgender-friendly • outdoor courtyard • T-dance Sun • gay-owned

State Bar 2510 S Dort Hwy 810/767–7050 • 2pm-2am • popular • lesbians/ gay men • dancing/DJ • wheelchair access

The Zoo 4511 S Saginaw St (at Bristol Rd) 810/249–0267, 810/610–7195 • 2pm-close • lesbians/ gay men • dancing/DJ • food served • karaoke • theme nights • gay-owned

NIGHTCLUBS

Club Triangle 2101 S Dort (at Lippincott) 810/767–7550 • 7pm-2am, clsd Mon • popular • lesbians/ gay men • more women Wed • dancing/DJ • male dancers • 18+

CAFES

The Good Beans Cafe 328 N Grand Traverse (at 1st Ave) 810/237–4663 • 7:30am-4pm, till 9pm Th-Fri, open some wknds • espresso & pastries • live shows • gay-owned • wheelchair access

SPIRITUAL GROUPS

Redeemer MCC of Flint 1665 N Chevrolet Ave (at Welch) 810/238–6700 • 11am Sun • wheelchair access

Frankfort

ACCOMMODATIONS

Wayfarer Lodgings 1912 S Scenic Hwy (M-22) 231/352–9264, 800/735–8564 • gay-friendly • cottages • near Frankfort, Lake Michigan & Betsie River • kids/ pets ok • $42-80

Glen Arbor

ACCOMMODATIONS

Duneswood at Sleeping Bear Dunes Nat'l Lakeshore 231/334–3346 • women only • located in northern MI • nonsmoking • lesbian-owned • $50-95

Grand Rapids

BARS

The Apartment 33 Sheldon NE (at Library) 616/451–0815 • noon-2am, from 2pm Sun • mostly gay men • neighborhood bar • sandwiches served • wheelchair access

Diversions 10 Fountain St NW (at Division) 616/451–3800 • 8pm-2am • popular • lesbians/ gay men • dancing/DJ • karaoke • 18+ • videos • also cafe • wheelchair access

CAFES

Discussions 6 Jefferson SE (at Fulton) 616/456–5060 • 9am-1:30am, till 3am wknds, from 1pm-1am Sun • soup & sandwiches • gay-owned • wheelchair access

RESTAURANTS

Brandywine 1345 Lake Drive SE (in East town) 616/774-8641 • 7am-9pm, till 8pm Mon, 7:30am-9pm Sat, 8am-3pm Sun

Cherie Inn 969 Cherry St (at Lake Dr) 616/458-0588 • 7am-2pm, from 8am wknds, clsd Mon • some veggie • wheelchair access

Gaia Cafe 208 Diamond Ave SE (at Cherry St) 616/454-6233 • 8am-8pm, till 3pm wknds, clsd Mon • vegetarian

SPIRITUAL GROUPS

Reconciliation MCC 3864 Benjamin 616/364-7633 • 10am Sun

Honor

ACCOMMODATIONS

Labrys Wilderness Resort 231/882-5994 • women only • cabins in Sleeping Bear Dunes Nat'l Lakeshore • lesbian-owned • $50-80

Kalamazoo

INFO LINES & SERVICES

Kalamazoo Gay/ Lesbian Resource Center 629 Pioneer St 269/349-4234, 888/377-7271 • educational/ support groups • youth group • hotline

BARS

Tradewinds 562 Portage St (at Walnut) 269/383-1814 • 4pm-2am • lesbians/ gay men • neighborhood bar • dancing/DJ • theme nights

NIGHTCLUBS

The Zoo 906 Portage St (at Vine) 269/385-9191, 269/342-4229 • 4pm-2am • lesbians/ gay men • dancing/DJ • karaoke • 18+

SPIRITUAL GROUPS

Phoenix Community Church 394 S Drake (at Sky Ridge Church of the Brethren) 269/381-3222 • 6pm Sun • wheelchair access

EROTICA

Triangle World 551 Portage Rd (at Walnut) 269/373-4005 • LGBT books • leather • gifts • wheelchair access

Lansing

INFO LINES & SERVICES

LAHR LGBT Hotline 517/332-3200 • 7pm-10pm, 2pm-5pm Sun, clsd Sat

ACCOMMODATIONS

The Leaven Center Lyons 989/855-2606 • gay/ straight • some events women only • spiritual retreat center • nonsmoking • also guesthouse available for individual use

BARS

Club 505 505 E Shiawassee (at Cedar) 517/374-6312 • 6pm-2am, clsd Sun-Mon • mostly women • neighborhood bar • dancing/DJ

Esquire 1250 Turner (at Clinton) 517/487-5338 • 3pm-2am, from noon Wed & Sat • lesbians/ gay men • neighborhood bar

NIGHTCLUBS

Spiral 1247 Center St (at Clinton) 517/371-3221 • 8pm-2am, clsd Mon-Tue • mostly gay men • dancing/DJ • theme nights • videos • 18+

X-cel 224 S Washington Square (at Washtenaw St) 517/484-2399 • 9pm-2am • popular • mostly gay men • dancing/DJ • live shows • young crowd • cover charge

BOOKSTORES

Community News Center 418 Frandor Shopping Center 517/351-7562 • 9am-9pm, till 6pm Sun • wheelchair access

John David's Lightly Used Books 3308 S Cedar 517/410-0865 • noon-8pm, clsd Mon • used books • large LGBT section • gay-owned

RETAIL SHOPS

Splash of Color 515 E Grand River Ave, Ste F, East Lansing 517/333-0990 • open daily • tattoo & piercing studio

SPIRITUAL GROUPS

Dignity 1225 Ivanhoe Dr, East Lansing 517/351-7341 • call for info

Edgewood Church of Christ 469 N Hagadorn, East Lansing 517/332-8693

The Light House Chapel 1501 Windsor St (west of MLK) 517/394-2080, 517/694-7914 • 11am Sun • open & affirming

Unitarian Universalist Church of Greater Lansing 855 Grove St, East Lansing 517/351-4081 • 9:30am & 11:15am Sun • wheelchair access

Marquette

BOOKSTORES

Sweet Violets 413 N 3rd St (btwn Michigan & Arch) 906/228-3307 • 10am-5pm, clsd Sun • feminist

Muskegon

Nightclubs

Club Mo'z 80 E Seaway Dr (entrance on Norton Ave), Muskegon Heights 231/830-0190 • 3pm-2am • mostly gay men • dancing/DJ • multiracial clientele • young crowd • wheelchair access • gay-owned

R's 3236 Club 3236 Hoyt St, Muskegon Heights 231/733-4685 • 9pm-2am, clsd Sun-Th • lesbians/gay men • dancing/DJ • live entertainment • drag shows • wheelchair access • gay-owned • 18+

Owendale

Accommodations

Windover Resort 3596 Blakely Rd 989/375-2586 • women only • seasonal private resort • campsites & RV hookups • swimming • $25/year membership fee • $15-20 camping fee

Petoskey

Accommodations

Coach House Inn 1011 N US 31 (at Mitchell) 231/347-8281, 877/347-8088 • basic amenities • gay-owned • $39-105

Pontiac

Nightclubs

Club Flamingo 352 Oakland Ave (at Montcalm) 248/253-0430 • 4pm-2am, from 2pm Sat • lesbians/gay men • dancing/DJ • live shows • wheelchair access

Port Huron

Nightclubs

Seekers 3301 24th St (btwn Oak & Little) 810/985-9349 • 7pm-2am, from 4pm Fri-Sat, from 2pm Sun • lesbians/gay men • dancing/DJ • live shows

Rochester

Spiritual Groups

Paint Creek Unitarian Universalist Congregation 3rd St & Walnut Blvd (in American Legion Hall) 248/656-8219 • 10am Sun

Saginaw

Bars

The Heidelberg 411 S Franklin 989/771-9508 • 7pm-2am • lesbians/gay men • neighborhood bar • dancing/DJ

Saugatuck

Accommodations

The Belvedere Inn & Restaurant 3656 63rd St 269/857-5777 • gay-friendly • boutique inn in 1913 mansion • full gourmet brkfrst • nonsmoking • gay-owned • $180-295

The Bunkhouse B&B 6635 118th Ave, Fennville 269/543-4335, 877/226-7481 • lesbians/gay men • cabins • private baths • access to Campit Resort amenities (see listing below) • swimming • nonsmoking • lesbian & gay-owned • $60-125

Campit Outdoor Resort 6635 118th Ave, Fennville 269/543-4335, 877/226-7481 • lesbians/gay men • campsites • RV hookups • separate women's area • swimming • seasonal • pets ok • membership required • lesbian & gay-owned • $17-45

Deerpath Lodge 269/857-DEER, 888/DEERPATH • women only • studios on 40 waterfront acres • heated pool • hot tub • swimming • kayaks & canoes

Douglas House B&B 41 Spring St, Douglas 269/857-1119, 248/478-9392 • gay/straight • near gay beach • gay-owned • $125-145

▲ **The Dunes Resort** 333 Blue Star Hwy, Douglas 269/857-1401 • lesbians/gay men • motel & cottages • transgender-friendly • swimming • food served • women's wknds in April, June & Oct • dancing/DJ • live shows • pets ok • wheelchair access • gay-owned • $50-200

The Glenn Country Inn 1286 64th St (at 113th Ave), Fennville 269/227-3045, 888/237-3009 • gay/straight • "SW Michigan's #1 pet-friendly B&B" • gay-owned • $89-200

Hidden Garden Cottages & Suites 247 Bulter St 269/857-8109, 888/857-8109 • gay-friendly • cottages & suites • nonsmoking • $125-195

Hillby Thatch Cottages 71st St, Glenn 847/864-3553 • gay/straight • cottages • kitchens • fireplaces • kids ok • nonsmoking • woman-owned/run • $200-350/wknd package

Hooten Inn 6541 Blue Star Hwy (at Washinton) 269/857-1039 • gay/straight • boutique motel • pets ok w/ prior approval • $65-149

No matter where you live, Saugatuck is the great destination spot for GLBT travelers. With pristine beaches, miles of hiking trails, world-class galleries, exquisite dining, and amazing places to shop, we have everything you're looking for. No matter what you do, the Dunes Resort is the place to stay and party while visiting Saugatuck. We are one of the largest GLBT resorts in the country with 80 rooms, a pool and pool bar, and, of course, our famous disco/bar complex with plenty of room for you to see and be seen. Our in-house and guest DJs will keep you and your friends grooving all night long with their cutting edge dance mixes.

The Dunes Resort. *Plan on coming.*

The Hunter's Lodge 2790 Blue Star Hwy (at US 31), Douglas **269/857–5402** • gay/ straight • motel in rustic lodge • kids/ pets ok • $74-179

J Paules Fenn Inn 2254 S 58th St, Fennville **269/561–2836** • gay-friendly • B&B • full brkfst • pets ok • nonsmoking • $95-135

The Kingsley House B&B 626 West Main St, Fennville **269/561–6425, 866/561–6425** • gay-friendly • B&B in award-winning Victorian Queen Anne mansion • full brkfst • nonsmoking • gay-owned • $95-195

Kirby House 294 W Center (at Blue Star Hwy) **269/857–2904, 800/521–6473** • gay/ straight • Queen Anne Victorian • full brkfst • swimming • nonsmoking • gay-owned • $100-185

Lake Street Commons 790 Lake St **269/857–1680** • gay-friendly • suites w/ full kitchen & private decks • 8-person jacuzzi • 2–3-night minimum in season • gay-owned • $85-125

Lynn Dee Lea Boat & Breakfast, LLC 868 Holland St, Slip #1 **309/360–7498** • gay/ straight • B&B on houseboat • full brkfst • nonsmoking • $100-130

Maple Ridge Cottages 713-719 Maple **269/857–5211 (PINES #)** • gay/ straight • quaint 2-brdm & 1-bath cottages w/ private hot tubs • 3-night minimum or weekly rentals • nonsmoking • gay-owned • $150-275/ night & $950-1,150/ week

Moore's Creek Inn 820 Holland St (at Lucy) **269/857–5241** • gay-friendly • old-fashioned farmhouse • nonsmoking • $85-125

The Newnham SunCatcher Inn 131 Griffith (at Mason) **269/857–4249** • gay-friendly • full brkfst • hot tub • swimming • lesbian-owned • $75-130

The Park House Inn B&B 888 Holland St **269/857–4535, 866/321–4535** • gay-friendly • B&B in Saugatuck's oldest residence • full brkfst • nonsmoking • also cottages • $115-235

Saugatuck

ANNUAL EVENTS:
May - Tulip Time Festival, Holland 800/822–2770, web: www.tulip-time.org.
June - Waterfront Film Festival 269/857-8351, web: www.water-frontfilm.com.

CITY INFO:
Saugatuck-Douglas Convention & Visitors Bureau 269/857-1701, web: www.saugatuck.com. Holland Chamber of Commerce 616/392-2389, web: www.holland-chamber.org. City of the Village of Douglas, web: www.douglasmichi-gan.com.

TRANSIT:
Saugatuck Douglas Taxi Service 269/543-3355, web: www.saugatuckdouglas.com.
Interurban Transit Authority 269/857-1418.

ATTRACTIONS:
Galleries.
Historical Holland (home of the Wooden Shoe Factory).
Lakeshore Jazz Connection, web: www.lakeshorejazzconnection.org.
Saugatuck Dunes State Park.
Saugatuck-Douglas Historical Society Museum 269/857–7900.

The Pines Motor Lodge 56 Blue Star Hwy (at Center St), Douglas 269/857–5211 • gay/ straight • newly renovated boutique retro motel • nonsmoking • also retro gift gallery • gay-owned • $75-195

The Spruce Cutter's Cottage 6670 126th Ave (at Blue Star Hwy & M–89), Fennville 269/543–4285, 800/493–5888 • gay/ straight • full brkfst • gay-owned • $100-200

Timber Bluff 2731 Lakeshore Dr, Fennville 269/857–1370 • cottages on Lake Michigan • short drive to Saugatuck • kitchenettes • nonsmoking • kids ok • weekly & weekend rentals

Bars

▲ **Dunes Disco** 333 Blue Star Hwy (at the Dunes Resort) 269/857–1401 • 9am-2am • popular • lesbians/ gay men • 6 bars • dancing/DJ • transgender-friendly • live shows • cabaret • patio • gay-owned

Cafes

Uncommon Grounds 127 Hoffman (at Water) 269/857–3333 • 7:30am-9:30pm, open later on wknds • organic coffee & juice bar

The Yum Yum Gourmet Cafe & Gelateria 98 Center St, lower level (at Union St), Douglas 269/857–4567 • gay/ straight • also paninis, soup, salad • gay-owned

Restaurants

▲ **Blue Frog To Go** in the Dunes Resort 269/857–1401 x143 • 11am-7pm, till 9pm Fri-Sat (open May-Oct only) • lesbians/ gay men • take-out only

Blue Moon Bar & Grille 310 Blue Star Hwy (corner of Wiley Rd), Douglas 269/857–8686 • contemporary cuisine w/ int'l flair • full bar

Chaps Restaurant 8 Center St, Douglas 269/857–2699 • upscale American • Sun brunch • patio • fireplace • full bar

Pumpernickel's 202 Butler St (at Mason) 269/857–1196 • seasonal • brkfst, lunch & dinner • sandwiches & fresh breads • some veggie

Restaurant Toulouse 248 Culver St (at Griffith) 269/857–1561 • dinner only • country French • some veggie • full bar • reservations req'd • wheelchair access

Bookstores

Open Door Music & Books 403 Water St 269/857–4565, 888/613–8570 • New Age books, cards, gifts, CDs

Singapore Bank Bookstore 317 Butler St (upstairs) 269/857–3785 • general • new & used

Retail Shops

Amaru Leather 322 Griffith St 269/857–3745 • "original & custom creations in leather by two resident designers"

Circa Antiques, Arts & Accessories 98 Center St (at Union St), Douglas 269/857–7676 • antiques, art, furnishings & accessories from a range of periods • gay-owned

Glitter & Garden 98 Center St (at Union St), Douglas 269/857–7676 • garden & holiday shop, unique items & gifts • gay-owned

Groovy! Groovy! Retro Gift Gallery 56 Blue Star Hwy (at Center St), Douglas 269/857–2171 • seasonal hours • antiques, funky gifts & goods • gay-owned

Hoopdee Scootee 133 Mason (at Butler) 269/857–4141 • 10am-9pm, till 6pm Sun (till 5pm in winter) • clothing • gifts

Saugatuck Drug Store 201 Butler St 269/857–2300 • old-fashioned corner drug store including actual soda fountain!

Spiritual Groups

Douglas United Church of Christ 56 Wall St, Douglas 269/857–2085 • 10am Sun • "everyone welcome—no exceptions!"

Saugatuck United Methodist Church 250 Mason St 269/857–2295 • 9:30am Sun • 7pm Wed meditation

Gyms & Health Clubs

Pump House Gym 6492 Blue Star Hwy 269/857–7867

Sault Ste–Marie

Bookstores

Open Mind Books 223 Ashmun St (at Ridge, come through alley door) 906/635–9008, 877/635–9008 • 11am-5pm, clsd Sun-Wed, May-Dec • progressive

South Haven

Accommodations

Yelton Manor B&B 140 North Shore Dr (at Dyckman) 269/637–5220 • gay/ straight • full brkfst • jacuzzi • nonsmoking • wheelchair access • $100-295

St Clair

Accommodations

William Hopkins Manor 613 N Riverside Ave 810/329–0188 • gay-friendly • full brkfst • $80-100

St Ignace

ACCOMMODATIONS

Budget Host Inn & Suites 700 N State St **906/643–9666, 800/872–7057** • gay-friendly • swimming • facing harbor of Lake Huron & across from ferries to Mackinac Island • kids/ pets ok • wheelchair access • $58-157

Traverse City

ACCOMMODATIONS

Neahtawanta Inn 1308 Neahtawanta Rd **231/223–7315, 800/220–1415** • gay-friendly • swimming • sauna • nonsmoking • wheelchair access • $100-240

NIGHTCLUBS

Side Traxx Nite Club 520 Franklin **231/935–1666** • 5pm-2am • lesbians/ gay men • dancing/DJ • videos • wheelchair access • gay-owned

BOOKSTORES

The Bookie Joint 120 S Union St (btwn State & Front) **231/946–8862** • 10am-6pm, till 5pm Sat, 1pm-4pm Sun • pride gifts • used books

SPIRITUAL GROUPS

The Potter's House/ United Church of Christ 206 S Oak (at 5th) **231/649–9911** • 5:30 pm Sun

Union Pier

ACCOMMODATIONS

Blue Fish Guest House & Cottage 16070 Lake Shore Rd (at Union Pier Rd) **269/469–0468 x112** • gay/ straight • cottage & guesthouse available • some shared baths • nonsmoking • kids/ pets ok • gay-owned • $800-2,100/ week, nightly rates off season

Fire Fly Resort 15657 Lakeshore Rd **269/469–0245** • gay/ straight • 1 & 2-bdrm units • kitchens • nonsmoking • gay-owned • $80-150 • also weekly/ monthly rates

Ypsilanti

see also Ann Arbor

RETAIL SHOPS

Eklectic 105 W Michigan Ave **734/483–1030** • LGBT card & gift store • also handcrafted candles, incense & more

EROTICA

Magazine Rack 515 W Cross **734/482–6944**

Duluth

see also Superior, Wisconsin

INFO LINES & SERVICES

Aurora: A Northland Lesbian Center 32 E 1st St #104 (at 1st Ave) **218/722–4903** • drop-in center • social events • library • newsletter

CAFES

Jitters 102 W Superior St **218/720–6015** • 7am-7pm, till 5pm wknds

LakeView Coffee House 600 E Superior St (in Fitzgers Brewery Complex) **218/720–4464** • 7am-8pm, till 9pm Sat, 8pm-6am Sun • food served • beer/ wine

BOOKSTORES

At Sara's Table 1902 E 8th (at 19th) **218/723–8569** • 7am-8pm, clsd Tue in winter • also cafe • wheelchair access • women-owned/ run

Ely

ACCOMMODATIONS

Log Cabin Hideaways 1321 N Hwy 21 **218/365–6045** • gay-friendly • remote wilderness cabins • wood-fired sauna & hot tub • no running water/ electricity • nonsmoking • $395-1,200

Hastings

ACCOMMODATIONS

Thorwood & Rosewood Inns 315 Pine St (at 4th) **651/437–3297, 888/846–7966** • gay-friendly • circa 1880 mansion • full brkfst • nonsmoking • wheelchair access • $97-277

Hinckley

ACCOMMODATIONS

Dakota Lodge B&B 320/384–6052 • gay/ straight • full brkfst • hot tub • fireplaces • nonsmoking • wheelchair access • $109-145

Kenyon

ACCOMMODATIONS

Dancing Winds Farmstay Retreat 6863 County 12 Blvd **507/789–6606** • gay/ straight • B&B on working dairy farm • also tentsites • work exchange available • nonsmoking • lesbian-owned • $95-150

Mankato

CAFES

The Coffee Hag 329 N Riverfront
507/387–5533 • 7:30am-11pm, till midnight
Fri-Sat, from 8am Sat • veggie menu • live
shows • wheelchair access • women-owned/
run

Minneapolis/ St Paul

INFO LINES & SERVICES

AA Intergroup 7204 W 27th St, Ste 113, St
Louis Park 952/922–0880

OutFront Minnesota 310 38th St E #204,
Minneapolis 612/822–0127, 800/800–0350 •
info line w/ 24hr pre-recorded visitor info

ACCOMMODATIONS

Cover Park Manor 15330 58th St N (at
Peller), Stillwater 651/430–9292,
877/430–9292 • gay-friendly • full brkfst • in-
room jacuzzi & fireplace • nonsmoking • kids
ok • $119-195

Millennium Hotel Minneapolis 1313
Nicollet Mall (btwn W Grant & 13th St),
Minneapolis 612/332–6000, 800/522–8856 •
gay-friendly • food served • swimming •
wheelchair access • $139-289

Nan's B&B 2304 Fremont Ave S (at 22nd),
Minneapolis 612/377–5118 • gay-friendly •
1895 Victorian family home • full brkfst •
shared bath • nonsmoking • $60-70

Minneapolis/St Paul

LGBT PRIDE:
June. 952/852-6100, web:
www.tcpride.com.

ANNUAL EVENTS:
September - Gay Night at Knott's
Camp Snoopy in Mall of America.

CITY INFO:
888/676-6757, web:
www.minneapolis.org.

ATTRACTIONS:
American Swedish Institute.
Mall of America (the largest mall in
the US w/indoor theme park)
952/883-8800, web: www.mallo-
famerica.com.
Minneapolis American Indian Center
612/879–1700, web: www.maic-
net.org.
Minneapolis Institute of Arts
612/870-3131, web:
www.artsmia.org.
Museum of Questionable Medical
Devices at The Science Museum
of Minnesota 651/221-9444, web:
www.smm.org.
Walker Art Center/Minneapolis
Sculpture Garden 612/375-7622,
web: www.walkerart.org.
Frederick R Weisman Art Museum
612/625-9494.

BEST VIEW:
Observation deck of the 32nd story
of Foshay Tower, 821 Marquette
Ave (closed in winter).

WEATHER:
Winters are harsh. If driving, carry
extra blankets and supplies. The
average temperature is 19°, and it
can easily drop well below 0°,
and then there's the wind chill!
Summer temperatures are
usually in the upper-80°s to mid-
90°s and HUMID.

TRANSIT:
Yellow Cab (Minn) 612/824–4444.
Yellow Cab (St Paul) 651/222-4433.
Airport Express 612/827-7777.
MTC 612/373–3333, web:
www.metrotransit.org.

Reply **Forward** **Delete**

Date: Dec 17, 2005 12:01:07
From: Girl-on-the-Go
To: Editor@Damron.com
Subject: Minneapolis & St Paul

>If you're searching for a liberal oasis in the heartland of America, if you love Siberian winters, and if you crave a diverse, intensely political lesbian community, you'll fit right into the Twin Cities of Minneapolis and St. Paul.

>Located on the banks of the Mississippi River, these cities share the Minnesota Twins, 936 lakes, 513 parks, and a history of Native American and Northern European settlements. If you want more than glimpses into the various cultures of Minnesota, visit the Minneapolis American Indian Center or the American Swedish Institute.

>Of course, you'll probably have more fun checking out the lesbian cultural scene. The place to go to find out about the latest poetry reading, play, or concert is the **Amazon Bookstore** in Minneapolis. To find social groups for women of color, call **Outfront MN.**

>Or stop by the **Minnesota Women's Press** library in St. Paul. Then enjoy a meal in Minneapolis at the women-owned **Cafe Barbette.** For a night on the town, you won't find any full-time women's bars, but you can catch a drag show or hang out in the piano bar at the **Town House.** Also check out the **Gay 90s** complex, which has weekly drag king shows. **Diva Riot** produces monthly women's dance parties; check out divariot.com for current info. For a quieter atmosphere, head over to **Jetset** for cocktails.

>Whatever you do, don't stay indoors the whole time. In the summer, boating, fishing, sunbathing, water-skiing, walking, jogging, and bicycling are all popular. In winter, you can enjoy snowmobiling, ice hockey, cross-country skiing, or snuggling by a fire. For women's outdoor adventures, try **Adventures in Good Company** (877/439-4042).

Bars

19 Bar 19 W 15th St (at La Salle), Minneapolis **612/871-5553** • 3pm-2am • mostly gay men • neighborhood bar • wheelchair access

American Sports Cafe 2554 Como Ave, St Paul **651/646-1339** • 11pm-2am Wed • mostly women

Bev's Wine Bar 250 3rd Ave N (at Washington Ave), Minneapolis **612/337-0102** • 4:30pm-1am, from 6:30pm Sat, clsd Sun-Mon • gay-friendly • patio

Boom 401 E Hennepin Ave (at 4th), Minneapolis **612/378-3188** • 4pm-1am, till 2am Fri-Sat • mostly gay men • videos • also Oddfellows restaurant Wed-Sun • gay-owned

Brass Rail 422 Hennepin Ave (at 4th), Minneapolis **612/333-3016** • noon-2am • popular • mostly gay men • live shows • karaoke • drag shows • videos • wheelchair access

Bryant Lake Bowl 810 W Lake St (near Bryant), Minneapolis **612/825-3737** • 8am-2am • gay-friendly • alternative • also theater • restaurant ($5-9) • bowling alley • wheelchair access

The Independent 3001 Hennepin Ave (in Calhoun Square, upstairs), Minneapolis **612/378-1905** • gay/ straight • 11am-2am • Sun brunch • great martini selection

Jetset 115 N First St, Minneapolis **612/339-3933** • 5pm-close, from 6pm Sat, clsd Sun-Mon • lesbians/ gay men • upscale • nonsmoking

Over the Rainbow 719 N Dale St (at Minnehaha), St Paul **651/487-5070** • 11am-2am, from 2pm wknds • lesbians/ gay men • neighborhood bar • dancing/DJ • live shows • karaoke • male dancers • food served • gay-owned

Times Bar/ Jitters 201 E Hennepin Ave (at 2nd St NE), Minneapolis **612/617-8098** • 11am-1am, 10am-11pm Sun (jazz brunch) • gay-friendly • live music • cabaret • also cafe & restaurant

The Town House 1415 University Ave W (at Elbert), St Paul **651/646-7087** • 3pm-1am, from noon wknds • popular • lesbians/ gay men • dancing/DJ • karaoke • drag shows • theme nights • piano bar • open mic

Trikkx 490 N Robert St (at 9th St), St Paul **651/224-0703** • 5pm-2am • mostly gay men • dancing/DJ • karaoke • male dancers • videos • huge bear party 4th Fri • also restaurant • wheelchair access

Nightclubs

Diva Riot Minneapolis • monthly women's dance parties • check divariot.com for details

Euphoria 319 1st Ave N, Minneapolis **612/339-1968** • gay/ straight • theme nights

Gay 90s 408 Hennepin Ave (at 4th), Minneapolis **612/333-7755** • 8am-2am (dinner nightly) • popular • mostly gay men • 9-bar complex • dancing/DJ • multiracial clientele • karaoke • drag shows Wed-Sun • wheelchair access

Ground Zero/ The Front 15 NE 4th St (at Hennepin), Minneapolis **612/378-5115** • 10pm-2am, clsd Sun-Mon • popular • gay/ straight • more gay Th & Sat for Bondage-A-Go-Go • dancing/ DJ • alternative • live shows • wheelchair access • also The Front lounge from 9pm

Margarita Bella 1032 3rd Ave NE (at Central), Minneapolis **612/331-7955** • 9pm-2am • gay/ straight • more gay Th for drag shows • mostly Latino/a clientele • dancing/DJ • also restaurant 11am-9pm • nonsmoking • gay-owned

The Saloon 830 Hennepin Ave (at 9th), Minneapolis **612/332-0835** • 10pm-close • popular • lesbians/ gay men • dancing/DJ • food served after 5pm • karaoke • theme nights • young crowd • wheelchair access • gay-owned

Velvet Rope 2554 Como Ave (at Warehouse Nightclub), St Paul **651/645-4618** • 8:30pm-1am, 1st & 3rd Th of the month • mostly women • dancing/DJ • drag king shows • 18+ • wheelchair access

Cafes

Anodyne at 43rd 4301 Nicollet Ave (at 43rd), Minneapolis **612/824-4300** • 6:30am-10pm, till 11pm Fri, from 7am Sat, 8am-9pm Sun • wheelchair access

Cafe Barbette 1600 W Lake St (at Irving), Minneapolis **612/827-5710** • 8am-1am, till 2am Fri-Sat • lesbians/ gay men • French/ American • plenty veggie • beer/ wine • women-owned/ run

Cahoots 1562 Selby Ave (at Snelling), St Paul **651/644-6778** • 7am-10:30pm, from 7:30am Sun • coffee bar

Moose & Sadie's 212 3rd Ave N (at 2nd St), Minneapolis **612/371-0464** • 7am-11pm, from 8am Sat, 9am-10pm Sun

Uncommon Grounds 2809 Hennepin Ave (at 28th Ave), Minneapolis 612/872-4811 • 5pm-1am, from noon wknds • gay/ straight • outdoor seating

The Urban Bean 3255 Bryant Ave S (at 33rd), Minneapolis 612/824-6611 • 6:30am-11pm, from 7am wknds • patio

Vera's Cafe 2901 Lyndale Ave S (at 29th St W), Minneapolis 612/822-3871 • 7am-midnight • cozy coffeehouse w/ baked goods & light meals

Wilde Roast Cafe 518 Hennepin Ave E (at Central), Minneapolis 612/331-4544 • 7am-11pm, till 1am Fri-Sat • shares entrance w/ LGBT bookstore • beer/ wine • wheelchair access • gay-owned

RESTAURANTS

Al's Breakfast 413 14th Ave SE (at 4th), Minneapolis 612/331-9991 • 6am-1pm, from 9am Sun • popular • great hash

Birchwood Cafe 3311 E 25th St, Minneapolis 612/722-4474 • lunch & dinner • organic • plenty veggie

Bobino Cafe & Wine Bar 222 E Hennepin Ave, Minneapolis 612/623-3301 • lunch & dinner nightly • classic bistro • also martini bar

Cafe Brenda 300 1st Ave N (at 3rd), Minneapolis 612/342-9230 • lunch Mon-Fri, dinner Mon-Sat, clsd Sun • vegetarian & seafood • nonsmoking

Campiello 1320 W Lake St (at Hennepin), Minneapolis 612/825-2222 • dinner & Sun brunch • Italian

Chang O'Hara's 498 Selby Ave, St Paul 651/290-2338 • transgender-friendly • full bar • patio

D'Amico Cucina 100 N 6th St (btwn 1st & 2nd Aves), Minneapolis 612/338-2401 • dinner nightly • à la carte • full bar • live music Fri-Sat

Figlio 3001 Hennepin Ave S (in Calhoun Sq Mall), Minneapolis 612/822-1688 • lunch & dinner, bar till 2am

Goodfellows 40 S 7th (at Hennepin), Minneapolis 612/332-4800 • lunch weekdays & dinner Mon-Sat, clsd Sun • full bar • upscale American

Joe's Garage 1610 Harmon Pl, Minneapolis 612/904-1163 • cafe from 8am • lunch & dinner • full bar till 2am • rooftop seating

King & I Thai 1346 LaSalle Ave (at W Grant), Minneapolis 612/332-6928 • 4:30pm-10pm, till 11pm Fri-Sat, clsd Sun • full bar • plenty veggie • courtyard • free valet parking

Monte Carlo 219 3rd Ave N, Minneapolis 612/333-5900 • lunch & dinner, bar till 1am

Murray's 26 S 6th St (at Hennepin), Minneapolis 612/339-0909 • lunch Mon-Fri, dinner nightly • steak & seafood

Oddfellows 401 E Hennepin Ave (near 4th St), Minneapolis 612/378-3179 • 5pm-10pm, till 11pm Fri-Sat, clsd Mon-Tue • American

Palomino Euro Bistro 825 Hennepin Ave (at 9th St), Minneapolis 612/339-3800 • lunch Mon-Sat, dinner nightly • Italian/ Mediterranean

Rudolph's Bar-B-Que 1933 Lyndale (at Franklin), Minneapolis 612/871-8969 • 11pm-2am • full bar • wheelchair access

ENTERTAINMENT & RECREATION

Calhoun 32nd Beach E side of Lake Calhoun (33rd & Calhoun Blvd), Minneapolis

Fresh Fruit KFAI 90.3 FM, Minneapolis 612/341-0980 • 7pm-8pm Th • gay radio program • also a variety of LGBT programs 9pm-11pm Sun

Minnesota Lynx Target Center • check out the Women's National Basketball Association while you're in Minneapolis

Theatre de la Jeune Lune 105 N First St 612/333-6200 • 2005 Tony Award-winning regional theater

BOOKSTORES

Amazon Bookstore Co-operative 4755 Chicago Ave S, Minneapolis 612/821-9630 • 10am-8pm, till 6pm Sat, from 11am Sun • feminist bookstore since 1970 • also gifts, music & art • cafe • wheelchair access • women-owned/ run • no relation to Seattle's amazon.com

Magus Books, Ltd 1309 1/2 SE 4th St (at 13th/ 14th), Minneapolis 612/379-7669, 800/996-2387 • 10am-8pm, till 6pm wknds, from noon Sun • alternative spirituality books • also mail order

Query Booksellers 520 Hennepin Ave E (at Central), Minneapolis 612/331-7701 • noon-10pm, from 11am Sat, till 8pm Sun, clsd Mon • LGBT bookstore • wheelchair access • gay-owned

RETAIL SHOPS

The Rainbow Road 109 W Grant (at LaSalle), Minneapolis **612/872-8448** • 10am-10pm • LGBT retail & video • wheelchair access

Sister Fun 1604 W Lake St (at James), Minneapolis **612/672-0263** • noon-7pm, till 5pm Mon • kitschy stuff

PUBLICATIONS

Lavender Magazine 612/436-4660, 877/515-9969 • LGBT newsmagazine for MN, WI, IA, ND, SD

Minnesota Women's Press 771 Raymond Ave, St Paul 651/646-3968 • 8:30am-5pm Mon-Fri • bi-weekly newspaper • also library

SPIRITUAL GROUPS

All God's Children MCC 3100 Park Ave S (at 31st St), Minneapolis **612/824-2673** • 10am Sun & 7pm Wed • wheelchair access

Dignity Twin Cities 22 Orlin Ave (at Prospect Park United Methodist), Minneapolis **612/827-3103** • 7:30pm 2nd & 4th Fri

Lutherans Concerned 100 N Oxford (at Laurel), St Paul 651/222-1209, 651/224-3371 • call for info • wheelchair access

Shir Tikvah 5000 Girard Ave (at Minnehaha Pkwy), Minneapolis **612/822-1440** • 10:30am Sat, then 8pm every Fri • gay-friendly Jewish congregation • wheelchair access

GYMS & HEALTH CLUBS

The Firm 245 Aldrich Ave N Ste 220 (at Glenwood), Minneapolis **612/377-3003** • lesbians/ gay men • day passes

EROTICA

Fantasy Gifts 409 W Lake (at Lyndale), Minneapolis **612/824-2459** • 10am-10pm, noon-6pm Sun • adult gifts • wheelchair access • also located in St Paul 651/256-7484

SexWorld 241 2nd Ave N (at Washington), Minneapolis **612/672-0556** • 24hrs

The Smitten Kitten 2223 E 35th St, Minneapolis **612/721-6088, 888/751-0523** • 11am-9pm, till 10pm Fri-Sat, till 6pm Sun, clsd Mon • woman-centered sex toy store • transgender-friendly • lesbian-owned

Moorhead

see also Fargo, North Dakota

INFO LINES & SERVICES

Pride Collective & Community Center 116 12th St S (at Main Ave) 218/287-8034 • 3pm-5pm Tue & Sat • referrals • support • social groups

NIGHTCLUBS

The I-Beam 1021 Center Ave 218/233-7700 • 8pm-2am • lesbians/ gay men • dancing/DJ • videos • food served • wheelchair access

CAFES

Atomic Coffee 15 4th St S (at Main) 218/299-6161 • 7am-11pm, from 9am wknds, till 10pm Sun • also gallery • live shows • gay-owned

Rochester

INFO LINES & SERVICES

Gay/ Lesbian Community Service 507/281-3265 • 5:30pm-7:30pm Wed

SPIRITUAL GROUPS

Healing Spirit MCC 3703 Country Club Rd W 507/252-5016 • 5:30pm Sun • lesbians/ gay men • transgender-friendly • wheelchair access

Rushford

ACCOMMODATIONS

Windswept Inn 207 N Mill St 507/864-2545 • gay-friendly • gay-owned • $32-45

Two Harbors

ACCOMMODATIONS

Grand Superior Lodge 2826 Hwy 61 E (near Gooseberry Falls State Park) 218/834-3796, 800/627-9565 • gay/ straight • log cabins on Lake Superior • swimming • hot tub • nonsmoking available • kids ok • restaurant • wheelchair ramps available • $99-749

Wolverton

RESTAURANTS

District 31 Victoria's 101 First St 218/995-2000 • 5:30pm-9:30pm, clsd Sun • cont'l • beer/ wine • reservations required

MISSISSIPPI

Statewide

PUBLICATIONS

Ambush Mag 504/522-8049 • LGBT newspaper for the Gulf South

Southern Voice 404/876-1819 • weekly LGBT newspaper for AL, FL (panhandle), GA, LA, MS, TN w/ resource listings

Bay Saint Louis

ACCOMMODATIONS

Nella's RV Park 16145 Hwy 603 (near I-10), Kiln 228/586-0053 • gay/ straight • kids/ pets ok • friendly & clean w/ fishing dock • casino nearby • close to New Orleans • $20/ night

Biloxi

ACCOMMODATIONS

Lofty Oaks Inn 17288 Hwy 67 228/392-6722, 800/280-4361 • gay-friendly • full brkfst • hot tub • swimming • kids/ pets ok • woman-owned/ run • $79-125

BARS

Just Us Lounge 906 Division St (at Caillavet) 228/374-1007 • 24hrs • lesbians/ gay men • neighborhood bar • live shows • dancing/ DJ • drag shows • go-go boys • karaoke

NIGHTCLUBS

Werkz 153 Veterans Ave 228/388-0092 • 5pm-5am, from 3pm Th • lesbians/ gay men • dancing/DJ • live shows • karaoke • drag shows

Jackson

INFO LINES & SERVICES

Gay/ Lesbian Community Info Line 601/346-4379 • 24hrs • switchboard for many organizations, including youth group

Lambda AA 4866 N State St (at Unitarian Church) 601/856-5337 • 6:30pm Mon & Wed, 8pm Sat

BARS

Jack's Construction Site (JC's) 425 N Mart Plaza 601/362-3108 • 5pm-2am • mostly gay men • more women Wed & Fri • neighborhood bar • BYOB

NIGHTCLUBS

30601 200 N Mill St 601/353-0059 • 10pm-close Fri-Sat • lesbians/ gay men • dancing/DJ • mostly African-American • live shows • 18+ • beer/ wine • BYOB

Jack & Jill's 3911 Northview Dr (at Meadowbrook) 601/982-5225 • 9pm-close Fri-Sat • lesbians/ gay men • dancing/DJ • live shows • beer/ wine • BYOB • wheelchair access

Metro Entertainment Complex 4670 Hwy 80 W 601/922-8237 • Fri-Sat only • lesbians/ gay men • dancing/ DJ • drag shows • mostly African-American

SPIRITUAL GROUPS

MCC of Mississippi 1020-A N State St (at Fortification) 601/372-6644 • 11am Sun

Safe Harbor Family Church 2147 Henry Hill Dr #203 601/923-2728 • 6pm Sun • non-denominational • social events • support groups

Natchez

ACCOMMODATIONS

The Antebellum Music Room B&B at the Joseph Newman Stone House 804 Washington St 601/445-7466 • gay-friendly • antebellum Greek Revival on Nat'l Historic Register • gallery of rare antiques • full Southern brkfst • kids ok • gay-owned • $85-125

Mark Twain Guesthouse 25 Silver St 601/446-8023 • above Under the Hill Saloon • $35-150

BARS

Under the Hill Saloon 25 Silver St 601/446-8023 • 10am-close • gay-friendly • neighborhood bar • live music • also guestrooms

Ovett

ACCOMMODATIONS

Camp Sister Spirit 601/344-1411, 601/645-6479 • mostly women (some events women-only) • 120 acres of camping & RV sites • cabins • nonsmoking • clean & sober space • $15-30 (sliding scale includes kitchen use) • lesbian-owned

Tupelo

NIGHTCLUBS

Rumors 637 Hwy 145 (10 miles S of Tupelo), Shannon **662/767–9500, 662/213–4891** • 8pm-1am Th & Sat & 3rd Fri only • gay/ straight • dancing/DJ • live shows • wheelchair access

MISSOURI

Statewide

PUBLICATIONS

Ozarks Star 918/835–7887 • 10am-4pm Mon-Fri, monthly LGBT news publication serving AR, KS, MO & OK

Branson

see also Springfield & Eureka Springs, Arkansas

ACCOMMODATIONS

Branson Stagecoach RV Park 5751 State Hwy 165 417/335–8185, 800/446–7110 • gay-friendly • swimming • gay-owned • $24-149

Eden Roc Resort Motel 2652 State Hwy 176 (at Mineral Ct), Rockaway Beach 417/561–4163, 800/955–3459 • gay-friendly • swimming • all rooms have lake views • gay-owned • $45-80

Cape Girardeau

ACCOMMODATIONS

Rose Bed Inn 611 S Sprigg St 573/332–7673, 866/767–3233 • gay/ straight • B&B • full brkfst • hot tub • gourmet dining by reservation • nonsmoking • wheelchair access • gay-owned • $85-200

NIGHTCLUBS

Independence Place 5 S Henderson St (at Independence) 573/334–2939 • 7pm-1:30am, from 7pm Fri-Sat, clsd Sun • lesbians/ gay men • dancing/DJ • transgender-friendly • drag shows Sat

Columbia

BARS

SoCo Club 128 E Nifong Blvd #E (at Providence Rd) 573/499–9483 • 6:30pm-1:30am, clsd Sun • gay/ straight • dancing/DJ • alternative • food served • karaoke Tue • drag shows • patio • wheelchair access

NIGHTCLUBS

Club Phoenix 6870 E Mexico Gravel Rd (in Lake of the Woods area) 573/474–9060 • 9pm-1:30am Fri-Sat only • lesbians/ gay men • dancing/DJ • 18+ • lakeside patio

CAFES

Ernie's Cafe 1005 E Walnut (at 10th) 573/874–7804 • 6:30am-3pm

RagTag Cinemacafe 23 N 10th St 573/443–4359 • independent & alternative cinema • also theater, music & dance • food served • beer & wine

RESTAURANTS

Main Squeeze 28 S 9th St 573/817–5616 • 10am-8pm, till 3pm Sun • local organic ingredients

BOOKSTORES

The Peace Nook 804 C East Broadway (btwn 8th & 9th) 573/875–0539 • 10am-9pm, noon-6pm Sun • LGBT section • books • pride products • women's music

SPIRITUAL GROUPS

Christ the King Agape Church 515 Hickman Ave 573/443–5316 • 11am Sun

EROTICA

Eclectics 1122–A Wilkes Blvd 573/443–0873

Hermann

ACCOMMODATIONS

Healing Stone Retreat & Spa 800/486–5500 x238 • gay-friendly • full brkfst • nonsmoking • women-owned • $160-350

Jefferson City

ACCOMMODATIONS

Jefferson Inn B&B 801 W High St 573/635–7196 • gay-friendly • full brkfst • kids ok • $65-139

Joplin

PUBLICATIONS

Ozarks Star 918/835–7887 • 10am-4pm Mon-Fri, monthly LGBT news publication serving AR, KS, MO & OK

SPIRITUAL GROUPS

MCC Joplin- Spirit of Christ 2902 E 20th St (at Range Line Rd) 417/206–6179 • 6pm Sun • multiracial

United Church of Christ Family Fellowship 204 N Jackson Ave (at A & Jackson) 417/782–6647 • 10:30am Sun

Kansas City

INFO LINES & SERVICES

Gay/ Lesbian Community Center 207 Westport Rd #218 **816/931–4420** • 6pm-9pm Mon, Tue, Th-Fri • call for events

Live & Let Live AA 3535 Broadway, 4th Flr (at Knickerbocker Pl) **816/531–9668** • noon daily, 6pm Sun-Fri, 7pm Sat

ACCOMMODATIONS

40th St Inn 1007 E 40th St **816/561–7575** • gay/ straight • gay-owned • $75-90

Days Inn at Benjamin Ranch 6101 E 87th St (at I-435) **816/765–4331, 800/329–7466** • gay-friendly • swimming

Ken's Place 18 W 38th St (at Baltimore) **816/753–0533** • leabians/ gay men • some shared baths • nude sunbathing permitted • pets ok • near gay bars • gay-owned • $44-69

LaFontaine Inn 4320 Oak St **816/753–4434, 888/832–6000** • gay-friendly • full brkfst • hot tub • gay-owned • $139-184

The Porch Swing Inn 702 East St, Parkville **816/587–6282, 866/587–6282** • gay-friendly • B&B • full brkfst • hot tub • kids/ pets ok • lesbian-owned • $80-150

Quarterage Hotel 560 Westport Rd (at Mill St) **816/931–0001, 800/942–4233** • gay-friendly • in Westport district

Sleep Inn 7611 NW 97th Terrace (at Tiffany Springs Rd) **816/891–0111** • gay-friendly • hotel • swimming • kids/ pets ok • wheelchair access • $45-109

Southmoreland on the Plaza 116 E 46th St **816/531–7979** • gay-friendly • 1913 B&B • full brkfst • sundeck • nonsmoking • $125-235

Su Casa B&B 9004 E 92nd St **816/965–5647, 816/916–3444 (CELL)** • gay-friendly • Southwest-style home • full brkfst wknds • kids/ dogs/ horses ok • jacuzzi • swimming • nonsmoking • woman-owned/ run • $95-135

BARS

Back Door Bar 423 Southwest Blvd **816/472–0007** • mostly men • 9pm-close, from 6pm Sun, clsd Mon-Wed • bears • leather

Balanca's 1809 Grand Ave **816/474–6369** • 6pm-3am • gay/straight • multiracial • very diverse crowd • 2 flrs • dancing/DJ • live blues bands • food served

Bar Natasha 1911 Main St (at 20th) **816/472–5300** • gay/ straight • also tapas restaurant • open mic • cabaret • piano bar

---

Kansas City

LGBT PRIDE:
June. web: www.kansascity-gaypride.com.

CITY INFO:
Convention & Visitors Bureau 816/221-5242, web: www.visitkc.com.

TRANSIT:
Yellow Cab 816/471-5000.
KCI Shuttle 800/243-5000.
Metro 816/221-0660, web: www.cata.org.

ATTRACTIONS:
Black Archives of Mid-America 816/483-1300, web: www.blackarchives.org.
Historic 18th & Vine District (includes Kansas City Jazz Museum & the Negro Leagues Baseball Museum).
Nelson-Atkins Museum of Art 816/561-4000, web: www.nelson-atkins.org.
Thomas Hart Benton Home & Studio 816/931-5722, web: www.mostateparks.com/benton.htm.
Harry S Truman Nat'l Historical Site (in Independence, MO) 816/254-9929, web: www.nps.gov/hstr.

Club 1020 1020 McGee (at E 10th St) 816/842-4123 • 8am-1:30am, clsd Sun • popular • gay/ straight • neighborhood bar • dancing/ DJ • drag shows

DB Warehouse Complexx 1915 Main St (at 20th) 816/471-1575 • 11am-3am • popular • 5 bars • mostly gay men • dancing/DJ • food served • also leather shop • wheelchair access

Missie B's 805 W 39th St (at SW Trafficway) 816/561-0625 • noon-3am, clsd Sun • lesbians/ gay men • neighborhood bar • dancing/DJ • transgender-friendly • live shows • karaoke • drag shows

Sidekicks 3707 Main St (at 37th) 816/931-1430 • 2pm-3am, clsd Sun • lesbians/ gay men • dancing/DJ • country/ western • drag shows Fri • wheelchair access

Time Out 423 Southwest Blvd (at Broadway) 816/421-1288 • noon-3am, clsd Sun • lesbians/ gay men • transgender-friendly • neighborhood bar • dancing/DJ • karaoke • live shows • Latino night Sat • gay-owned

Tootsie's New Place 1822 Main (at 18th) 816/471-7704 • 11am-3am, from 5pm Sat-Sun, 11am-7pm Mon • popular • mostly women • dancing/DJ • wheelchair access • grill menu • some veggie

Wetherbee's 2510 NE Vivion Rd (at Antioch) 816/454-2455 • 6pm-3am • mostly women • dancing/DJ • food served • live shows • wheelchair access

NIGHTCLUBS

The Hurricane 4048 Broadway (at Westport Rd) 816/753-0884 • 2pm-3am, from 6pm wknds • gay-friendly • dancing/DJ • live bands • wheelchair access

NV 220 Admiral Blvd (at Grand Blvd) 816/421-6852 • 4:30pm-3am • mostly men • dancing/DJ • male dancers • videos • rooftop deck • wheelchair access

CAFES

Broadway Cafe 4106 Broadway Blvd (at Westport) 816/531-2432 • 7am-11pm, till midnight Fri-Sat, from 8am Sat-Sun • food served • no smoking

Planet Cafe 3535 Broadway Blvd (at 35th) 816/561-7287 • 7am-11pm, till midnight Fri, from 9am Sat, till 9pm Sun • popular • live shows • gay-owned

RESTAURANTS

Cafe Trio/ Starlet Lounge 3535 Broadway (at Knickerbocker Pl) 816/756-3227 • 4:30pm-11pm, clsd Sun • New American • piano • gay-owned

Classic Cup Cafe 301 W 47th St (at Central) 816/753-1840 • 7am-10pm • wheelchair access • great appetizers • Sun brunch

The Corner Restaurant 4059 Broadway (at Main) 816/931-6630 • 7am-7pm, till 3pm Sun • lots of veggie • wheelchair access

Sharp's 63rd St Grill 128 W 63rd St 816/333-4355 • 7am-10pm, from 8am wknds • beer/ wine • wheelchair access

Strouds 1014 E 85th St (btwn Troost & Holmes) 816/333-2132 • 4pm-10pm, from 11am Fri & Sun, till 11pm Fri-Sat • fried chicken

YJ's Snack Bar 128 W 18th St 816/472-5533 • eclectic menu • inexpensive

Zin 1900 Main St 816/527-0120 • dinner • contemporary

ENTERTAINMENT & RECREATION

Outspokin' • gay/lesbian bicycle club & other social events

Unicorn Theatre 3828 Main St (at 39th St) 816/531-7529 • contemporary American theater

RETAIL SHOPS

Out There 205 Westport Rd (btwn Main & Broadway) 816/753-4757 • 10am-7pm, till 6:30pm Sat, noon-5pm Sun • LGBT

PUBLICATIONS

EXP Magazine 314/367-0397, 877/397-6244 • bi-weekly gay magazine for MO, KS & IL

SPIRITUAL GROUPS

Abiding Peace Lutheran 5090 NE Chouteau Trafficway (1 block S of Vivion Rd) 816/452-1222 • 10am Sun • inclusive community of faith • wheelchair access

Broadway Church Broadway at 39th Terrace 816/561-3274 • 10am Sun

Spirit of Hope MCC 3801 Wyandotte (btwn Broadway & Main) 816/931-0750 • 10:15am Sun

EROTICA

Erotic City 8401 E Truman Rd (at I-435) 816/252-3370 • 24hrs • boutique • books • lounge

Hollywood at Home 9063 Metcalf (at 91st), Overland Park, KS 913/649-9666 • 10am-11pm

Lake Ozark

ACCOMMODATIONS

Paradise House 299 Flynn Rd (at Hwy 54) 573/365-4397, 573/280-7991 • gay/ straight • B&B in private home • hot tub • gay-owned • $80-90

Overland

EROTICA

TLC Priscilla's 10210 Page Ave (E of Ashby) 314/423-8422

Springfield

INFO LINES & SERVICES

AA Gay/ Lesbian 601 E Walnut St (at Christ Episcopal Church Annex) 417/823-7125 (AA #) • 6pm Sat

Gay & Lesbian Community Center of the Ozarks 518 E Commercial St 417/869-3978 • transgender support group 7pm Sun • youth group 4pm Tue • many other groups • newsletter • wheelchair access

BARS

The Edge 424 N Boonville 417/831-4700 • 4pm-1:30am, clsd Sun • lesbians/ gay men • dancing/DJ • karaoke • drag shows • wheelchair access • lesbian-owned

Martha's Vineyard 217-221 W Olive St 417/864-4572, 417/831-6144 • 4pm-1:30am, till midnight Sun, clsd Mon • lesbians/ gay men • neighborhood bar • dancing/DJ • drag shows • 18+ • also martini lounge • patio • wheelchair access • cover charge wknds

RoniSuz 821 W College St (at Grant) 417/864-0036 • 5pm-1:30am, from 7pm Sat, clsd Sun • gay/ straight • neighborhood bar • gay-owned

NIGHTCLUBS

Liquors & Kickers 1109 E Commercial (at National Ave) 417/873-2225 • lesbians/ gay men • dancing/DJ • country/ western • live shows

Rumors 1107 E Commercial (at National Ave) 417/873-2225 • 5pm-1:30am, clsd Sun • lesbians/ gay men • dancing/ DJ • transgender-friendly • drag shows • 18+ • gay-owned

BOOKSTORES

Renaissance Books & Gifts 1337 E Montclair 417/883-5161 • 10am-7pm, noon-5pm Sun • women's/ alternative • wheelchair access

EROTICA

TLC Priscilla's 1918 S Glenstone (at Sunshine) 417/881-8444

St Joseph

NIGHTCLUBS

Labels Nightclub 107 S 6th St (at Felix) 816/232-2269 • 7pm-1:30am, clsd Sun-Tue • gay/ straight • dancing/DJ • 2 floors • live shows • cabaret • drag shows • videos • wheelchair access

Shaft Nightclub 615 Felix (at 6th St) 816/248-0058 • lesbians/ gay men • dancing/ DJ • bears • transgender-friendly • videos • gay-owned

St Louis

INFO LINES & SERVICES

Gay/ Lesbian Hotline 314/367-0084 • 10am-6pm, clsd wknds

Steps Alano Club 1935-A Park Ave 314/436-1858 • LGBT 12-step meetings • call for schedule

ACCOMMODATIONS

A St Louis Guesthouse 1032-38 Allen Ave (at Menard) 314/773-1016 • mostly gay men • located in historic Soulard district • hot tub (nudity ok) • nonsmoking • gay-owned • $75-110

Brewers House B&B 1829 Lami St (at Lemp) 314/771-1542, 888/767-4665 • lesbians/ gay men • 1860s home • jacuzzi • pets ok • nonsmoking • gay-owned • $85

Lafayette Park B&B 1415 Missouri Ave (at Park) 314/771-9700, 866/338-1415 • gay/ straight • elegant B&B in historic neighborhood w/ decks & garden • full brkfst • gay-owned • $99-119

Napoleon's Retreat B&B 1815 Lafayette Ave (at Mississippi) 314/772-6979, 800/700-9980 • gay/ straight • restored 1880s town house • full brkfst • nonsmoking • gay-owned • $98-145

Park Avenue Mansion—A B&B Guesthouse 2007 Park Ave (at Mississippi) 314/588-9004, 866/588-9004 • gay/ straight • B&B inn • full brkfst • jacuzzi • $89-225

Bars

Absolutli Goosed Martini Bar, Etc 3196 S Grand (4 blocks S of Tower Grove Park) **314/772-0400** • 4pm-close, from 5pm Sat, from 2pm Sun, clsd Mon-Tue • lesbians/ gay men • neighborhood bar • also desserts • appetizers • patio • lesbian-owned

AMP (Alternative Music Pub) 4199 Manchester Ave (at Boyle) **314/652-5267** • 4pm-1am, from 6pm Sat, clsd Sun • lesbians/ gay men • neighborhood bar

Clementine's 2001 Menard (at Allen) **314/664-7869** • 10am-1:30am, 11am-midnight Sun • popular • mostly gay men • neighborhood bar • leather • food served • patio • wheelchair access

Club Escapades 133 W Main St, Belleville, IL **618/222-9597** • 6pm-2am • lesbians/ gay men • dancing/DJ • karaoke • live shows

Freddie's 4112 Manchester Ave **314/371-1333** • 3pm-1:30am, from noon Sun • lesbians/ gay men • neighborhood bar • video bar • karaoke Wed-Th

St Louis

Where the Girls Are:
Spread out, but somewhat concentrated in the Central West End near Forest Park. Younger, funkier crowds hang out in the Delmar Loop, west of the city limits, packed with ethnic restaurants.

LGBT Pride:
June. 314/772-8888, web: www.pridesaintlouis.com.

Annual Events:
June- Six Flags St Louis Gay Day 314/772-8888, web: www.pride-saintlouis.com.

City Info:
314/421-1023 or 800/ 888-3861, web: www.explorestlouis.com.

Best View:
Where else? Top of the Gateway Arch in the Observation Room, web: www.gatewayarch.com.

Weather:
100% midwestern. Cold winters— little snow and the temperatures can drop below 0°. Hot, muggy summers raise temperatures back up into the 100°s. Spring and fall bring out the best in Mother Nature.

Transit:
County Cab 314/993-8294, web: www.stlouiscountycab.com.
TransExpress 314/427-3311, web: www.transexpress-stl.com.
MetroBus 314/231-2345, web: www.metrostlouis.org.

Attractions:
Anheuser-Busch Brewery, web: www.budweisertours.com.
Argosy Casino 800/336-7568.
Cathedral Basilica of St Louis (world's largest collection of mosaic art), web: www.cathedral-stl.org.
Gateway Arch 877/982-1410, web: www.gatewayarch.com.
Grant's Farm 314/843-1700, web: www.grantsfarm.com.
Soulard, the "French Quarter of St Louis."
St Louis Art Museum 314/721-0072, web: www.slam.org.
Stone Hill Winery (in Hermann) 800/909-9463, web: www.stone-hillwinery.com.
The extremely quaint town of St Charles.

| Reply | Forward | | Delete |

Date: Dec 19, 2005 15:21:05
From: Girl-on-the-Go
To: Editor@Damron.com
Subject: St. Louis

>Most visitors come to St. Louis to see the famous Gateway Arch, the tallest monument in the U.S. at 630 feet, designed by renowned architect Eero Saarinen.

>After you've ridden the elevator in the Arch and seen the view, come down to earth and take a trip to historic Soulard, the "French Quarter of St. Louis." Established in 1779 by Madame and Monsieur Soulard as an open-air market, it's now the place for great food and jazz. And the Market still attracts crowds—LGBT and straight—on the weekends.

>Laclede's Landing is also a popular attraction. While you're down by the Gateway Arch, treat yourself to riverfront dining aboard any of the several riverboat restaurants on the Mississippi. Dining and shopping are most fun in the Central West End on Euclid Street between Delmar and Forest Park Boulevards, or in the University City Loop area near Washington University.

>Revive yourself with a cup of joe at **MokaBe's** café, then head upstairs to lesbian-friendly **Novak's Bar and Grill,** one of the many mixed bars in the city.

>For current women's events in the area, pick up a copy of **Vital Voice** or **EXP Magazine** at St Louis's coolest of the cool book-store, **Left Bank Books.**

Grey Fox Pub 3503 S Spring (at Potomac) **314/772–2150** • 2pm-1:30am, clsd Sun • lesbians/ gay men • neighborhood bar • drag shows • transgender-friendly • food served • patio

The Heights 2280 S Jefferson Ave (at Shenandoah) **314/772–9500** • 3pm-1:30am, 10am-midnight Sun • lesbians/ gay men • piano bar • food served

Korner's Bar 7101 S Broadway (at Blow St) **314/352–3088** • 5pm-1:30am, from 6pm Sat, clsd Sun-Tue • lesbians/ gay men • dancing/DJ • drag shows Wed, Fri-Sat

Loading Zone 16 S Euclid (at Forest Park Pkwy) **314/361–4119** • 4pm-1:30am, from 2pm Sun • popular • lesbians/ gay men • videos • wheelchair access • gay-owned

Novak's Bar & Grill 4121 Manchester
314/531–3699 • 4pm–1:30am, till midnight
Mon, till 3am Fri, noon–3am wknds • mostly
women • dancing/DJ • live shows • karaoke •
dancers Wed & Fri • patio • wheelchair access

Soulard Bastille 1027 Russell (at Menard)
314/664–4408 • 11am–1:30am • mostly gay
men • food served

NIGHTCLUBS

Attitudes 4100 Manchester 314/534–0044 •
7pm–3am, from 4pm Fri-Sat, clsd Sun-Mon •
popular • lesbians/ gay men • dancing/DJ

Bubby & Sissy's 602 Belle St (at 6th St),
Alton, IL 618/465–4773 • 5pm–2am, 3pm–
3am Fri-Sat, from noon Sun • lesbians/ gay
men • dancing/DJ • live shows • karaoke •
drag shows • videos • wheelchair access

The Complex Nightclub & Restaurant
3515 Chouteau (at Grand) 314/772–2645 •
9pm–3am, clsd Mon • popular • lesbians/ gay
men • 5 bars • dancing/DJ • drag shows •
videos • patio • food served • wheelchair
access

Faces Complex 132 Collinsville Ave (btwn
Missouri & Riverpark Dr), East St Louis, IL
618/271–7410 • 11pm–6am, from 10pm Wed
& Sun, clsd Mon-Tue • lesbians/ gay men •
dancing/DJ • live shows • food served • drag
shows • videos • 18+ Wed & Sun • 3 levels •
patio

Magnolia's 5 S Vandeventer (at Forest Park
Pkwy) 314/652–6500 • 6pm–3am • dinner
Wed-Sun • popular • mostly gay men •
dancing/DJ • country/ western • leather •
cabaret • karaoke • also • videos • wheelchair
access

The Spot 4146 Manchester 314/371–1330 •
mostly men • also restaurant • live shows

Velvet Lounge 1301 Washington Ave (at
13th Ave) 314/241–8178, 314/241–2997 •
9pm–3am Fri-Sat • gay/ straight • dancing/DJ •
lounge & house music

CAFES

Coffee Cartel 2 Maryland Plaza (at Euclid)
314/454–0000 • 24hrs • popular • internet
access

MokaBe's 3606 Arsenal (at S Grand)
314/865–2009 • 10am–1am • from 9am Sun •
popular • plenty veggie • occasional shows •
wheelchair access

Soulard Coffee Garden Cafe 910 Geyer St
314/241–1464 • brkfst, lunch, dinner

RESTAURANTS

Cafe Balaban 405 N Euclid Ave (at
McPherson) 314/361–8085 • popular • lunch,
dinner, Sun brunch • upscale dining room for
dinner only • some veggie • full bar •
wheelchair access

Chez Leon 4580 Laclede Ave (at Euclid)
314/361–1589 • 5:30pm–10pm, till 11pm Fri-
Sat, 5pm–9pm Sun, clsd Mon • French bistro •
full bar • gay-owned

Dressel's 419 N Euclid (at McPherson)
314/361–1060 • lunch & dinner • great Welsh
pub food • full bar • live shows

Duff's 392 N Euclid Ave (at McPherson)
314/361–0522 • lunch & dinner, clsd Mon,
brunch Sat-Sun • fine dining • some veggie •
full bar • wheelchair access

Majestic Bar & Restaurant 4900 Laclede
(at Euclid) 314/361–2011 • 6am–10pm •
Greek-American diner fare

Ted Drewes Frozen Custard
6726 Chippewa (at Jameson) 314/481–2652 •
11am–11pm • seasonal • a St Louis landmark
• also 4224 S Grand Blvd, 314/352-7376 •
wheelchair access

Tomatillo Mexican Grill 32 N Euclid Ave (at
W Pine Blvd) 314/367–7070 • 11am–8pm, till
7pm Sun • also 9641 Olive Blvd, 314/991-4995

Tony's 410 Market St (at Broadway)
314/231–7007 • dinner only, clsd Sun • Italian
fine dining • reservations advised

The Wildflower Restaurant 4590 Laclede
Ave 314/367–9888 • clsd Tue

Zinnia 7491 Big Bend Blvd (at Shrewsbury),
Webster Groves 314/962–0572 • lunch Tue-Fri
& dinner Tue-Sun, clsd Mon • California-style
bistro

ENTERTAINMENT & RECREATION

**Anheuser-Busch Brewery Tours/ Grant's
Farm** 12th & Lynch 314/577–2626,
314/843–1700 • all-American kitsch: see the
Clydesdales in their air-conditioned stables, or
visit the Busch family estate that was once the
home of Ulysses S Grant, www.grantsfarm.com

Int'l Bowling Museum & Hall of Fame
111 Stadium Plaza (across from Busch
Stadium) 314/231–6340 • 5,000 years of
bowling history (!) & 4 free frames

Living Out Loud KDHX 88.1FM
314/664–3688 • 7pm Wed • LGBT radio show

Opera Theatre of Saint Louis 539 Garden
Ave (at Edgar & Big Bend) 314/961–0171,
314/961–0644 • intimate theater w/ operas
sung in English • wheelchair access

Sistah Speak 6691 Delmar 314/719-2888 • 8pm 3rd Sun only • mostly women • multiracial • open mic & performance

BOOKSTORES

Left Bank Books 399 N Euclid Ave (at McPherson) 314/367-6731 • 10am-10pm, 11am-6pm Sun • popular • feminist & LGBT titles

RETAIL SHOPS

CheapTRX 3211 S Grand Blvd 314/664-4011 • alternative shopping • body piercing • tattoos

Heffalump's 387 N Euclid Ave (at McPherson) 314/361-0544 • 11am-8pm, till 6pm Mon, noon-5pm Sun • gifts

PUBLICATIONS

EXP Magazine 314/367-0397, 877/397-6244 • bi-weekly gay magazine for MO, KS, & IL

Vital Voice 314/865-3787 • bi-monthly news & feature publication

Women's Yellow Pages of Greater St Louis 314/997-6262

SPIRITUAL GROUPS

Dignity St Louis 600 N Euclid (at Trinity Church) 314/997-9897 • 7:30pm Sun

MCC of Greater St Louis 5000 Washington Pl (at Kings Hwy) 314/361-3221 • 9:30am & 11:30am Sun

The Reconstruction Minyan of St Louis 6267 Delmar Blvd 2-E, University City 314/721-1608 • "an inclusive, egalitarian & participatory community of Jews devoted to Torah, prayer & social justice"

St Louis Gay/ Lesbian Chavurah at Central Reform Congregation 5020 Waterman Ave (at Kings Hwy) 314/361-1564, 314/324-4936 • 7:30pm Fri, 10am Sat

Trinity Episcopal Church 600 N Euclid Ave (at Washington) 314/361-4655 • 8am & 10:30am Sun, 6pm Wed, 6:30am Th

EROTICA

Friends & Luvers 3550 Gravois (at Grand) 314/771-9405 • 10am-10pm, noon-7pm Sun • fetish clothes • toys • videos • dating service

Steelville

ACCOMMODATIONS

Country's Getaway 119 Big Bend Ln (near Hwy 8) 573/775-5534 • lesbians/ gay men • campground (open May 15-Oct 31) • 100 miles SW of St Louis • nudity ok • $10/ person (includes firewood)

MONTANA

Billings

NIGHTCLUBS

The Loft 2910 2nd Ave N (at 29th) 406/259-9074 • 4:30pm-2am • lesbians/ gay men • dancing/DJ • karaoke Wed • wheelchair access

RESTAURANTS

Eleven Cafe 2526 Montana Ave 406/238-0011 • lunch & dinner, clsd Sun

EROTICA

Big Sky Books 1203 1st Ave N (at 12th St) 406/259-0051

The Victorian 2019 Minnesota Ave (at 21st) 406/245-4293 • noon-midnight, clsd Sun-Mon • gay/ straight • videos • magazines • arcade • fireplace • fireplace & piano • also HIV testing 5pm-9pm Wed-Sat & monthly Hep B/C testing

Boulder

ACCOMMODATIONS

Boulder Hot Springs Inn & Retreat 406/225-4339 • gay-friendly • also B&B • massage • workshops • food served • swimming • nudity ok in hot springs • nonsmoking • kids ok • wheelchair access • $55-129

Bozeman

ACCOMMODATIONS

Gallatin Gateway Inn 76405 Gallatin Rd/ Hwy 191 406/763-4672, 800/676-3522 • gay-friendly • dinner nightly • hot tub • swimming • nonsmoking rooms available • kids ok • wheelchair access • $89-245

Lehrkind Mansion B&B 719 N Wallace Ave 406/585-6932, 800/992-6932 • gay/ straight • 1897 Queen Anne Victorian • full brkfst • hot tub • nonsmoking • gay-owned • $119-169

CAFES

The Leaf & Bean 35 W Main 406/587-1580 • 6am-10pm, from 7am Sun, till 11pm Fri-Sat • desserts • live shows • wheelchair access • women-owned/ run • also 1500 N 19th Ave, 406/587-2132

EROTICA

Ms Kitty's Adult Store 12 N Wilson 406/586-6989

Butte

ACCOMMODATIONS

Copper King Lodge & Convention Center
4655 Harrison Ave **406/494-6666,
800/332-8600** • gay/ straight • brkfst included
• kids ok • pets ok • swimming • hot tub •
sauna • located near I-15/ I-90 junction •
wheelchair access • $55-175

BARS

Snookums at the Skookum 3541 Harrison
Ave **406/533-0919** • 7pm-2am, clsd Mon-Tue
• lesbians/ gay men

RESTAURANTS

Matt's Place 2339 Placer (btwn Montana &
Rowe) **406/782-8049** • 11:30am-7pm, clsd
Sun-Mon • classic soda fountain diner

Pekin Noodle Parlor 117 S Main, 2nd flr
406/782-2217 • 5pm-11pm, till midnight Fri-
Sat, till 10:30pm Sun, clsd Tue • Chinese •
some veggie

Pork Chop John's 2400 Harrison Ave
406/782-1783, 800/782-0812 • 10:30am-
10:30pm, till 9:30 Sun • also 8 W Mercury,
406/782-0812

Uptown Cafe 47 E Broadway **406/723-4735**
• lunch weekdays & dinner nightly • bistro •
full bar • wheelchair access

Great Falls

RESTAURANTS

Black Diamond Bar & Supper Club
64 Castner, Belt **406/277-4118** • 5pm-10pm,
clsd Mon • steaks & seafood • 20 miles from
Great Falls

SPIRITUAL GROUPS

MCC Montana 1505 17th Ave SW
406/771-1070 • 10:30am Sun • call for social
activities

Hamilton

ACCOMMODATIONS

Happy Horse Ranch B&B 273 Fox Run
Trail (at Sheafman Creek Rd) **406/961-6893,
877/817-0422** • gay/ straight • located on 10
acres in spectacular Bitterroot Valley • farm-
fresh gourmet brkfst • $85-95

Helena

INFO LINES & SERVICES

PRIDE **406/442-9322, 800/610-9322 (IN MT)**
• info • newsletter • political advocacy &
education

Kalispell

INFO LINES & SERVICES

Flathead Valley Alliance **406/758-6707** •
LGBT referral service

ACCOMMODATIONS

Cottonwood Hill Farm Inn 2928 Whitefish
Stage Rd **406/756-6404, 800/458-0893** • gay/
straight • renovated farmhouse • full brkfst •
teens ok • nonsmoking • $65-135

Livingston

ACCOMMODATIONS

Yellowstone River Inn Cabins 4950 Hwy 89
S **406/222-2429, 888/669-6993** • gay/ straight
• cabins 40 ft from Yellowstone River • full
brkfst • nonsmoking • $110-135

Missoula

INFO LINES & SERVICES

Gay/ Lesbian AA 532 University Ave (at
Lifeboat) **406/543-0011** • 7pm Mon

**Western Montana Gay/ Lesbian
Community Center** 615 Oak St
406/543-2224 • LGBT resource center • call
for hours

ACCOMMODATIONS

Brooks St Motor Inn 3333 Brooks St (at
MacDonald) **406/549-5115, 800/538-3260** •
gay-friendly • motel • hot tub • nonsmoking
rooms available • kids/ pets ok • wheelchair
access • $37-125

Foxglove Cottage B&B 2331 Gilbert Ave
406/543-2927 • gay/ straight • 1800s
guesthouse • swimming • sun room • gardens
• some shared baths • nonsmoking • gay-
owned • $75-125

BARS

Amvets Club 525 Ryman (at Broadway)
406/543-9174 • noon-2am • gay/ straight •
dancing/DJ

The Oxford 337 N Higgins (at Pine)
406/549-0117 • popular • gay-friendly • 8am-
2am • 24hr cafe & casino

CAFES

The Catalyst 111 N Higgins **406/542-1337** •
7am-6pm

The Raven Cafe 130 E Broadway
406/829-8188 • 8am-10pm, till 5pm Sat, till
3pm Sun, clsd Mon • food served • live shows
• pool tables • internet access

RESTAURANTS

Montana Club/ Red Baron Casino 2620 Brooks **406/543-3200** • 6am-10pm, till 11pm Fri-Sat, casino open till 2am • full bar • wheelchair access

BOOKSTORES

Fact & Fiction 220 N Higgins **406/721-2881** • 9am-8pm, 10am-5pm Sat, noon-4pm Sun • many LGBT titles • wheelchair access

University Center Bookstore Campus Dr (at U of MT) **406/243-4921** • 8am-6pm, from 10am Sat, clsd Sun • gender studies section

SPIRITUAL GROUPS

University Congregation Christian Church 405 University Ave **406/543-6952** • 9am & 10:30am Sun, 10am Sun (summer)

Ovando

ACCOMMODATIONS

Lake Upsata Guest Ranch **406/793-5890, 800/594-7687** • gay-friendly • cabins • hot tub • seasonal • wildlife programs & outings • meals provided • kids ok • nonsmoking • $90-220 per person

Swan Valley

ACCOMMODATIONS

Holland Lake Lodge 1947 Holland Lake Rd (at Hwy 83) **406/754-2282, 877/925-6343** • gay-friendly • resort w/ lakefront cabins • full brkfst • hot tub • kids ok • restaurant & bar • wheelchair access • gay-owned • $95-115

NEBRASKA

Grand Island

ACCOMMODATIONS

Midtown Holiday Inn 2503 S Locust **308/384-1330** • gay-friendly • nonsmoking rooms available • kids/ pets ok • hot tub • swimming • also Images Pink Cadillac Lounge • wheelchair access • $59-75

Relax Inn 507 W 2nd St **308/384-1000** • gay-friendly • wheelchair access • $35-40

NIGHTCLUBS

Club Voodoo 3235 S Locust (at 34th) **308/381-8919** • 8pm-1am, clsd Sun-Th • gay-friendly • wheelchair access

RESTAURANTS

Nathan Detroit's 316 N Pine St **308/384-3655** • gay-friendly • wheelchair access

Tommy's 1325 S Locust **308/381-0440** • 24hrs

GYMS & HEALTH CLUBS

Health Plex Fitness Center 2909 Hwy 30 **308/384-1110** • gay-friendly

EROTICA

Exclusively Yours Shop 214 N Locust **308/381-6984** • adult toys • lingerie

Sweet Dreams Shop 217 W 3rd St **308/381-6349** • lingerie • adult toys

Kearney

RETAIL SHOPS

Hastings Entertainment 9 W 39th St **308/234-1130** • 10am-11pm • some LGBT books • also adult section

Lincoln

INFO LINES & SERVICES

Rainbow Group Gay/ Lesbian AA 2748 S St, 3rd flr (at 28th, at The Meeting Place) **402/438-5214** • 7:30pm Mon

BARS

Panic 200 S 18th St (at N St) **402/435-8764** • 4pm-1am, from 1pm wknds • lesbians/ gay men • live shows • karaoke • internet access • patio • wheelchair access • gay-owned

NIGHTCLUBS

The Q 226 S 9th St (btwn M & N Sts) **402/475-2269** • 8pm-1am, clsd Mon • lesbians/ gay men • dancing/DJ • live shows • karaoke • drag shows • also lounge • 19+ Tue

ENTERTAINMENT & RECREATION

Wimmin's Radio Show KZUM 89.3 FM **402/474-5086** • 11:30am Sun • also "TGI-Femmes" 10am-noon Fri

RETAIL SHOPS

Avant Card 1323 O St (btwn 13th & 14th) **402/476-1918** • hours vary • also Gateway Mall location (61st & O St), 402/476-1918

Omaha

INFO LINES & SERVICES

AA Gay/ Lesbian 851 N 74th (at Presbyterian Church) 402/556–1880 • 8:15pm Fri

Rainbow Outreach Center 1719 Leavenworth St 402/341–0330 • 7pm-9pm, 1pm-9pm Sat-Sun

ACCOMMODATIONS

Castle Unicorn 57034 Deacon Rd (at Hwy 34 & I-29), Pacific Jct, IA 712/527–5930 • gay/ straight • medieval style B&B • full brkfst • hot tub • sauna • patio • gay-owned • $169-189

The Cornerstone Mansion Inn 140 N 39th St (at Dodge) 402/558–7600, 888/883–7745 • gay-friendly • 1894 historic mansion • fireplaces • near downtown • food served • nonsmoking • commitment ceremonies • $85-125

BARS

Connections 1901 Leavenworth St (at 19th) 402/933–3033 • 4pm-1am,clsd Mon • lesbians/ gay men • dancing/DJ • live shows • karaoke • wheelchair access • lesbian-owned

DC's Saloon 610 S 14th St (at Jackson) 402/344–3103 • 2pm-1am • lesbians/gay men • neighborhood bar • dancing/DJ • country/ western • live shows • wheelchair access

Diamond Bar 712 S 16th St 402/342–9595 • 11am-2:30pm, then 9pm-close • mostly gay men • wheelchair access

Flixx 1019 S 10th St 402/408–1020 • 5pm-1am • mostly men • neighborhood bar • videos

Gilligan's Pub 1407 Harney St (at 14th St) 402/449–9147 • 4pm-1am, food served till 2:30am • lesbians/ gay men • neighborhood bar • karaoke • also restaurant • wheelchair access

NIGHTCLUBS

The Max 1417 Jackson (at 15th St) 402/346–4110 • 4pm-1am • popular • mostly gay men • 5 bars • dancing/DJ Wed-Sun • drag shows • strippers • videos • patio • wheelchair access • cover charge Fri-Sat

CAFES

Stage Right 401 S 16th (at Harney) 402/346–7675 • 7am-11pm, from 10am wknds, till 5pm Sun • live shows wknds

RESTAURANTS

Dixie Quick's 1915 Leavenworth St 402/346–3549 • dinner Wed-Fri, brunch Tue-Fri & Sun • Southern

French Cafe 1017 Howard St 402/341–3547 • lunch Tue-Fri, dinner nightly, wknd brunch, clsd Mon • full bar

ENTERTAINMENT & RECREATION

HGRA (Heartland Gay Rodeo Association) 402/203–4680

River City Mixed Chorus 402/341–7464 • LGBT chorus

BOOKSTORES

New Realities 1026 Howard St (in the Old Market) 402/342–1863 • 10am-10pm, till 11pm Fri-Sat, 11am-6pm Sun • progressive • wheelchair access

Next Millennium 2308 N 72nd St (N of Blondo St) 402/393–1121 • 11am-8pm Mon-Fri, till 5pm wknds, from noon Sun • metaphysical books & gifts • wheelchair access

The Reading Grounds 3928 Farnam St (at 40th) 402/502–2008 • 9am-9pm, till 11pm Fri-Sat, noon-6pm Sun, clsd Mon • LGBT • readings • also cafe w/ salads & sandwiches

RETAIL SHOPS

Villain's 3629 Q St 402/731–0202 • noon-8pm, till 5pm Sun • tattooing • piercing

SPIRITUAL GROUPS

MCC of Omaha 819 S 22nd St 402/345–2563 • 9am & 11am Sun • also support groups

Scottsbluff

RESTAURANTS

Pasta Villa 1455 10th St (at O St), Gering 308/436–5900 • 5pm-8pm, from 11am Sat, clsd Sun-Mon • lesbian-owned

NEVADA

Statewide

PUBLICATIONS

Nevada Pride Guide 702/882–7023 • LGBT business directory

Gerlach

ACCOMMODATIONS

▲ **F Ranch** 775/557–2804 • women only • B&B on remote NW Nevada working horse/cattle ranch • April-Sept • bird-watching • kids ok (no special acitivies for them) • nonsmoking • $2,500-3,500 (per couple per week)

Lake Tahoe

see also Lake Tahoe, California

ACCOMMODATIONS

The Mountain Retreat 275 Tramway Dr (at Boulder Ct), Stateline 530/582–5670 • lesbians/gay men • luxury town house • swimming • hot tub • sundeck • also skiing & hiking tours • gay-owned • $200-300

NIGHTCLUBS

Faces 270 Kingsbury Grade, Stateline 775/588–2333 • 5pm-close • lesbians/gay men • dancing/DJ

Las Vegas

INFO LINES & SERVICES

Alcoholics Together 2630 State St #233 702/737–0035 • noon & 8pm daily • call for directions

The Gay/ Lesbian Community Center of Southern Nevada 953 E Sahara Ave #B-25 702/733–9800 • 11am-7pm, 10am-3pm Sat, clsd Sun

ACCOMMODATIONS

LVR/ Chapman B&B 1800 Chapman Dr (at Oakey/ 15th St) 702/699–8977, 866/DOROTHY • gay/ straight • full brkfst • also bar • hot tub • sauna • swimming • gay-owned • $95-125

Viva Las Vegas Hotel 1205 Las Vegas Blvd 702/384–0771, 800/574–4450 • gay/ straight • campy themed rooms • nonsmoking • on-site disco • also commitment ceremonies • gay-owned • $59-225

BARS

8 1/2 Ultra Lounge & Dance Club 4633 Paradise Rd (at Naples) 702/791–0100 • lesbians/ gay men • neighborhood bar • videos • dancing/ DJ • wheelchair access

Backdoor Lounge 1415 E Charleston (near Maryland Pkwy) 702/385–2018 • 24hrs • mostly gay men • neighborhood bar • dancing/DJ • patio • Latino/a clientele Fri-Sat • wheelchair access

Backstreet 5012 S Arville Rd (at Tropicana) 702/876–1844 • popular • lesbians/ gay men • dancing/DJ Wed-Sun • country/ western • wheelchair access

Badlands Saloon 953 E Sahara #22 (in Commercial Center) 702/792–9262 • 24hrs • mostly gay men • neighborhood bar • dancing/DJ • country/ western • wheelchair access • gay-owned

The Buffalo 4640 Paradise Rd (at Naples) 702/733–8355 • 24hrs • popular • mostly gay men • leather • videos • wheelchair access

Flex 4371 W Charleston (at Arville) 702/385–3539 • 24hrs • lesbians/gay men • dancing/DJ • drag shows • go-go dancers

Freezone 610 E Naples 702/794–2300 • 24hrs • lesbians/gay men • women's night Tue • neighborhood bar • dancing/DJ • transgender-friendly • drag shows Fri-Sat • karaoke Sun • young crowd • also restaurant • gay-owned

Goodtimes 1775 E Tropicana Ave (at Spencer, in Liberace Plaza) 702/736–9494 • 24hrs • mostly gay men • more women Mon & Wed • neighborhood bar • dancing/DJ Mon & after-hours Sat • karaoke Wed • wheelchair access

The Las Vegas Eagle 3430 E Tropicana (at Pecos) 702/458–8662 • 24hrs • mostly gay men • leather • DJ Wed, Fri-Sat • also The Annex bar 8pm-4am Wed & Fri

Las Vegas Lounge 900 E Karen Ave (at Maryland Pkwy) 702/737–9350 • 24hrs • neighborhood bar • mostly transgender • drag shows

NIGHTCLUBS

Celebrity Vegas 201 N 3rd St (at Ogden St) 702/384–2582 • gay-friendly • dancing/DJ • transgender-friendly • also early sit-down show • karaoke • caberet • drag shows • erotic dancers • videos • young crowd • wheelchair access • gay-owned

F Ranch

Gerlach, NV
775.557.2804

LADIES!
DON'T BE LEFT OUT!

Beautiful, REMOTE, NW Nevada horse/cattle ranch
near the BLACK ROCK DESERT

We offer a Bed & Breakfast (3 meals day)
with relaxing solitude and bright heavens
in vast, awesome, spiritual high desert country.

Great food, immaculate quarters
Gracious, cheerful hostesses.

We are open April 1 through July 30
(weather permitting)

www.F-Ranch.com

The Gipsy 4605 S Paradise Rd (at Naples) **702/731–1919** • 9pm-close • popular • mostly gay men • dancing/DJ • Latin night Mon • live shows • go-go boys • videos • young crowd

House of Blues 3950 Las Vegas Blvd S (at Hacienda Ave, in Mandalay Bay) **702/632–7600** • gay-friendly • dancing/DJ • also restaurant • live shows • cover charge

Krave 3663 S Las Vegas Blvd (at Harmon, next to the Aladdin) **702/836–0830** • 9pm-close, clsd Mon-Th • popular • mostly gay men • dancing/DJ • live shows • also restaurant

RESTAURANTS

Cravings 3400 Las Vegas Blvd (at The Mirage) **800/627–6667** • buffet dining w/ imaginative layout • Sat-Sun brunch

Go Raw 2381 Windmill Ln **702/450–9007** • 10am-9pm, 11am-6pm Sun • organic vegan • also juice bar • also at 2910 Lake East Dr, 702/254-5382

Hamburger Mary's 4503 Paradise Rd **702/735–4400** • 10am-2am, from 10am wknds

Mama Jo's 3655 S Durango **702/869–8099** • lunch & dinner • Italian

Sushi Boy Desu 4632 S Maryland Pkwy #12 **702/736–8234** • 11am-10pm

Las Vegas

LGBT PRIDE:
May. 702/615-9429 (NVAPI Hotline), web: www.lasvegaspride.org.

ANNUAL EVENTS:
April - NGRA (Nevada Gay Rodeo Assn) Bighorn Rodeo 888/643-6472, web: www.ngra.com.

CITY INFO:
Convention & Visitors Authority 702/892-0711, web: www.vegas-freedom.com. Also www.lasvegas.com.

BEST VIEW:
Top of the Stratosphere. Or hurtling through the loops of the roller-coaster atop the New York New York Hotel. (Note: Do not ride immediately after the buffet.)

WEATHER:
It's in the desert. What do you think?

TRANSIT:
Western Cab 702/736-8000. Lucky Cab 702/477-7555. Various resorts have their own shuttle service. CAT (Citizens Area Transit) 702/228-7433, web: www.rtcsouthernnevada.com.

ATTRACTIONS:
Bellagio Art Gallery 702/693-7871, web: www.bellagio.com. Elvis-A-Rama 702/309-7200, web: www.elvisarama.com Guggenheim Hermitage Museum, 702/414-2440, web: guggenheimlasvegas.com. Hoover Dam & Museum, 702/294-1988, web: www.bcmha.org. Imperial Palace Auto Collection 702/794-3174, web: www.imperialpalace.com. King Tut Museum (at the Luxor) 702/262-4000. La Cage at the Riveria 702/794-9433. Las Vegas Art Museum 702/360-8000, web: www.lasvegasartmuseum.org. Liberace Museum 702/798-5595, web: www.liberace.org. Museum of Natural History 702/384-3466, web: www.lvnhm.org. StarTrek: The Experience (at the Hilton) 702/732-5111, web: www.startrekexp.com.

Entertainment & Recreation

Cupid's Wedding Chapel 827 Las Vegas Blvd S (1 block N of Charleston) 702/598-4444, 800/543-2933 • commitment ceremonies • "Have the Vegas wedding you've always dreamed of!"

The Forum Shops at Caesars 3570 Las Vegas Blvd S (in Caesars Palace) • you saw it in *Showgirls* & many other movies, now come shop for yourself

King Tutankhamun's Tomb & Museum 3900 Las Vegas Blvd S (in the Luxor Las Vegas) 702/262-4555 • exact replica of the tomb when Howard Carter opened it in 1922

La Cage 2901 Las Vegas Blvd (at the Riviera) 702/794-9433 • 7pm-9pm, clsd Tue • the biggest drag show in town: Frank Marino & friends impersonate the divas, from Joan Rivers to Tina Turner

Liberace Museum 1775 E Tropicana Ave 702/798-5595 • this is one queen's closet you have to look into—especially if you love your pianos, clothes & cars covered w/ diamonds • $12.50

O at the Bellagio 3600 Las Vegas Blvd S 888/488-7111 (RESERVATIONS ONLY), 702/693-7111 (GENERAL INFO) • Cirque du Soleil tops themselves w/ this showstopper in a specially constructed aquatic theater (it costs a pretty penny but is far more fun than losing your shirt in the casino)

Bookstores

Borders 2323 S Decatur (at Sahara) 702/258-0999 • 9am-11pm, till 9pm Sun • LGBT section • cafe • wheelchair access

Get Booked 4640 Paradise #15 (at Naples) 702/737-7780 • 10am-midnight, till 2am Fri-Sat • LGBT

Pride Factory Las Vegas 953 E Sahara, Ste E-1B (at Market St) 954/463-6600 • 10am-midnight • also internet cafe • also pride items, gifts & DVDs • open mic Mon • videos shown

Retail Shops

Glamour Boutique II 714 E Sahara Ave #250 702/697-1800, 866/692-1800 • clsd Sun, large-size dresses, wigs, etc

The Rack 953-35B E Sahara Ave, Ste 101 (in Commercial Center) 707/732-7225 • leather • fetish

Sin City 1013 E Charleston Blvd (at S 10th St) 702/387-6969 • 24hrs • piercing & tattoo studio

Publications

Las Vegas Night Beat 702/369-8441 • monthly news & entertainment paper

Out Las Vegas 702/650-0636 • monthly LGBT entertainment newspaper

Q Vegas Bugle 702/650-0636 • LGBT magazine

Spiritual Groups

Christ Church Episcopal 2000 S Maryland Pkwy (at E St Louis) 702/735-7655 • 8am, 10:30am & 6pm Sun

Dignity Las Vegas 2000 S Maryland Pkwy (at Holy Innocents American Catholic Church) 702/593-5395 • Catholic Mass 6:30pm Sat

MCC of Las Vegas 1140 Almond Tree Ln #302 (in the East Wing) 702/369-4380 • 10am Sun

Valley Outreach Synagogue 2020 W Horizon Ridge Rd (at Desert Willow Community Center), Henderson 702/436-4900 • 7:45pm 1st Fri

Gyms & Health Clubs

Hands On Therapeutic Massage 8335 S Las Vegas Blvd (at Cancun Resort) 702/458-8777 • licensed massage therapists visit home or hotel room • "open to all men & women" • mention ad for discount

The Las Vegas Athletic Club 5090 S Maryland Pkwy 702/798-5822 • gay-friendly • 5am-midnight, 7am-8pm wknds • day passes

Erotica

Bare Essentials Fantasy Fashions 4029 W Sahara Ave (near Valley View Blvd) 702/247-4711 • exotic/ intimate apparel • toys • gay-owned

Price Video 700 E Naples Dr #102 (at Swenson) 702/734-1342 • 10am-10pm

Rancho Adult Entertainment Center 4820 N Rancho #D (at Lone Mtn) 702/645-6104 • 24hrs

Video West 5785 W Tropicana (at Jones) 702/248-7055 • gay-owned • also 4637 S Paradise Rd, 702/735-1469

Laughlin

see Bullhead City, Arizona

Reno

INFO LINES & SERVICES

A Rainbow Place, Northern Nevada's GLBT Community Center 33 St Lawrence Ave (at Tahoe) **775/789-1780, 800/627-1168 (24HRS)** • resources • newsletter • also crisis line 800/627-1168

ACCOMMODATIONS

▲ **F Ranch** **775/557-2804** • women only • B&B on remote NW Nevada working horse/cattle ranch • April-Sept • bird-watching • kids ok (no special acitivies for them) • nonsmoking • $2,500-3,500 (per couple per week)

Holiday Inn & Diamonds Casino 1000 E 6th St (at Wells Ave) **775/786-5151** • gay-friendly • swimming • kids/pets ok • restaurant • wheelchair access • $59-139

BARS

1099 Club 1099 S Virginia St (at Vassar) **775/329-1099** • 24hrs, 10am-2am Tue-Th • popular • lesbians/gay men • neighborhood bar • live shows • videos • patio • wheelchair access

Five Star Saloon 132 West St (at 1st) **775/329-2878** • 24hrs • mostly gay men • neighborhood bar • dancing/DJ • wheelchair access

The New Quest 210 W Commercial Row (at West) **775/333-2808** • 24hrs • mostly gay men • dancing/DJ • transgender-friendly • Latin drag shows • young crowd • divey

The Patio 600 W 5th St (btwn Washington & Ralston) **775/323-6565** • 11am-2am • lesbians/gay men • neighborhood bar

NIGHTCLUBS

Revel Again 340 Kietzke Ln (btwn Glendale & Mill) **775/786-5455** • 2pm-close • popular • gay/straight • dancing/DJ • young crowd • patio

Tronix 303 Kietzke Ln (at E 2nd St) **775/333-9696** • 10am-3am • lesbians/gay men • neighborhood bar • dancing/DJ • multiracial clientele • trangender-friendly • karaoke • male dancers • videos • young crowd • wheelchair access • gay-owned

BOOKSTORES

Borders 4995 S Virginia St **775/448-9999** • 9am-10pm, till 11pm Fri-Sat, till 9pm Sun • LGBT section

Sundance Books 1155 W 4th St (at Keystone) **775/786-1188** • 9am-9pm, 10am-6pm wknds

PUBLICATIONS

The Outlands **775/324-7866** • calendar • resources • features • classifieds • listings

Sierra Voice **775/322-7866** • monthly • bar & resource listings • community events • arts & entertainment

SPIRITUAL GROUPS

MCC of the Sierras 3405 Gulling Rd (at Temple Sinai) **775/829-8602** • 5pm Sun

EROTICA

The Chocolate Walrus 160 E Grove **775/825-2267** • 10am-6pm, clsd Sun

Fantasy Faire 1298 S Virginia (at Arroyo) **775/323-6969** • adult novelties

G Spot 138 West St (btwn 1st & 2nd) **775/333-6969** • 11am-10pm, till 2am Fri-Sat, gay-owned

Suzie's 195 Kietzke Ln (at E 2nd St) **775/786-8557** • 24hrs

Tonopah

ACCOMMODATIONS

Best Western Hi-Desert Inn 320 N Main St (at Florence) **775/482-3511, 877/286-2208** • gay-friendly • swimming

Tonopah Station House Ramada 1137 S Main St **775/482-9777** • gay-friendly • casino/bar • pets ok • 24hr restaurant • nonsmoking • wheelchair access • $63

NEW HAMPSHIRE

Statewide

INFO LINES & SERVICES

Rainbow Resources of NH Inc **800/750-2524** • LGBT info for NH, VT, ME & MA

PUBLICATIONS

Equality Press 26 S Main St, PMB 145, Concord 03301 **603/738-3763** • non-profit LGBT newspaper of the granite state

In Newsweekly **617/426-8246** • New England's largest LGBT newspaper

Bristol

ACCOMMODATIONS

Cliff Lodge Lakeside Bistro & Cabins 77 Ravine Dr **603/744-8660** • cabins • restaurant • gay-owned • $60-95

Concord

SPIRITUAL GROUPS

South Congregational Church 27 Pleasant St 603/224–2521 • 8:15am & 10:30am

Dover

BARS

Dover Soul 364 Central Ave **603/834–6961** • gay/ straight • more gay Tue • live acoustic music Wed • also restaurant • live entertainment

CAFES

Cafe on the Corner 478 Central Ave 603/749–4711 • 6:30am-10pm • internet

Durham

ACCOMMODATIONS

Three Chimneys Inn 17 Newmarket Rd (Rte 108, off Rte 4) **603/868–7800, 888/399–9777** • gay-friendly • elegant 1649 house on Oyster River near Portsmouth • full brkfst • jacuzzi • nonsmoking • kids 6+ ok • wheelchair access • $139-209

Fitzwilliam

ACCOMMODATIONS

Hannah Davis House 603/585–3344 • gay/ straight • historic 1820 Federal bldg • full brkfst • kids ok • nonsmoking • $70-190

Keene

ACCOMMODATIONS

E. F. Lane Hotel 30 Main St **603/357–7070, 888/300–5056** • gay/ straight • rooms & suites • internet access • also restaurant • wheelchair access • $139-315

NIGHTCLUBS

The Back Door 30 Main St (at the E. F. Lane Hotel) **603/357–7070, 888/300–5056** • 9pm first Fri • lesbians/ gay men • dancing/DJ • food served

Lebanon

ENTERTAINMENT & RECREATION

Amelia's Underground Flying Society PO Box 746, 03766 • social group for lesbian & bisexual women in the Upper Valley region of VT & NH • also newsletter • calendar

Littleton

ACCOMMODATIONS

Comfort Inn & Suites 703 US Rte 5S (at I-91), St Johnsbury, VT **802/748–1500, 800/424–6423** • gay-friendly • hotel • swimming • hot tub • kids ok • wheelchair access • $99-359

Manchester

BARS

313 93 S Maple St **603/628–6813** • 6pm-1am, from 4pm Fri-Sat, from noon Sun • popular • lesbians/ gay men • dancing/DJ • food served • live entertainment • karaoke • drag shows • sports bar • piano bar Sun • videos • 18+ Tue, Th & Fri • "three clubs in one" • wheelchair access

The Breezeway 14 Pearl St **603/621–9111** • 4pm-1am • lesbians/ gay men • neighborhood bar • dancing/DJ • leather • gay-owned

Tudor of Manchester 361 Pine St (at Hanover) **603/626-4900** • 5pm-1am • mostly gay men • neighborhood bar • food served

Newfound Lake

ACCOMMODATIONS

The Inn on Newfound Lake 1030 Mayhew Tpke Rte 3–A, Bridgewater **603/744–9111, 800/745–7990** • gay/ straight • swimming • also restaurant • full bar • gay-owned • $105-345

Pelham

SPIRITUAL GROUPS

First Congregational Church 2 Main St **603/635–7025** • 8am & 10am Sun

Plymouth

ACCOMMODATIONS

Federal House Inn Historic B&B 27 Rte 25 (Rte 3 traffic circle) **603/536-4644, 866/536-4644** • gay/ straight • full brkfst • hot tub • gay-owned • $99-180

Portsmouth

CAFES

Breaking New Grounds 14 Market Square **603/436-9555** • coffee, tea, espresso shakes

EROTICA

Spaulding Book & Video 80 Spaulding Tpke **603/430-9760** • gay-owned

Surry

ACCOMMODATIONS

The Surry House 50 Village Rd (at Crain Rd) **603/352-2268** • gay/ straight • B&B in private home • full brkfst • swimming • kids/ pets ok • lesbian-owned • $75-100

White Mtns

ACCOMMODATIONS

Brookhill B&B PO Box 221, North Conway 03860 **603/356-3061, 888/356-3061** • gay/ straight • 2-bdrm suite • full brkfst • nonsmoking • $219-389

The Bungay Jar B&B 791 Easton Valley Rd, Franconia **603/823-7775, 800/421-0701** • gay-friendly • renovated post & beam barn • full brkfst • jacuzzi • nonsmoking • gay-owned • $140-245

Foxglove, A Country Inn **603/823-8840, 888/343-2220** • gay-friendly • 1898 country estate • full brkfst • nonsmoking • $110-175/ two people

▲ **Highlands Inn** Bethlehem **603/869-3978, 877/LES-B-INN (537-2466)** • a lesbian paradise • "one of 10 best gay/ lesbian guesthouses" (*Planet Out*) • full brkfst • outdoor & indoor spas • swimming pool • 100 mtn acres • special events • concerts • kids/ pets ok • ignore No Vacancy sign • lesbian-owned • $105-160 • see ad on page 1

The Horse & Hound Inn 205 Wells Rd, Franconia **603/823-5501, 800/450-5501** • clsd April & Nov • gay-friendly • 1830s farmhouse • full brkfst • kids/ pets ok • also restaurant • gay-owned • $90-150

Inn at Crystal Lake Rte 153 Eaton Center (at Rte 16), North Conway **603/447-2120, 800/343-7336** • gay/ straight • full brkfst • also restaurant • kids age 8+ ok • dogs ok • nonsmoking • gay-owned • $109-239

Mulburn Inn at Bethlehem 2370 Main St/ Rte 302, Bethlehem **603/869-3389, 800/457-9440** • gay/ straight • Victorian B&B • full brkfst • hot tub • nonsmoking • women-owned/ run • $85-175

The Notchland Inn Rte 302, Hart's Location **603/374-6131, 800/866-6131** • gay/ straight • 1860s granite mansion on 100 acres • full brkfst • other meals available • nonsmoking • gay-owned • $195-310

Riverbend Inn B&B 273 Chocorua Mtn Hwy (at Rte 113), Chocorua **603/323-7440, 800/628-6944** • gay/ straight • B&B • full brkfst • located on the Chocorua River • nonsmoking • gay-owned • $89-199

Top Notch Vacations Rte 302, Glen **603/383-4133, 800/762-6636** • gay-friendly • 1- to 6-bdrm condos, cottages & chalets • swimming • private wooded areas • mtn views • nonsmoking • $90-600

Wildcat Inn & Tavern Rte 16A, Jackson Village **603/383-4245, 800/228-4245** • gay-friendly • also cottage • full brkfst • 2 restaurants • $109-350

Will's Inn Rte 302, Glen **603/383-6757, 800/233-6780** • gay-friendly • traditional New England motor inn • 2-bdrm cottages available • swimming • nonsmoking • kids ok • $49-600

BARS

The Red Parka Steakhouse & Pub Rte 302, Glen **603/383-4344** • 3:30pm-close, from 3pm wknds • gay/ straight • open mic Mon • patio

The Up Country Restaurant & Tavern Rte 16, North Conway **603/356-3336** • more gay on wknds, dancing/DJ • live shows • karaoke • video

RESTAURANTS

Polly's Pancake Parlor Rte 117 (exit 38 off 93 N), Sugar Hill **603/823-5575** • 7am-2pm, till 3pm wknds, clsd winters

NEW JERSEY

Statewide

ENTERTAINMENT & RECREATION

Out & About **201/797-7827** • lesbian resources

PUBLICATIONS

PM Entertainment Magazine **516/845-0759** • events, listings, classifieds & more for Long Island, NJ & NYC

Asbury Park

ACCOMMODATIONS

Empress Hotel 101 Asbury Ave **732/774-0100** • gay-friendly • next to Paradise Club • lesbians/ gay men • dancing/DJ

BARS

Anybodys 108 St James Pl (at Cookman Ave) • 4pm-2am • mostly gay men • neighborhood bar • leather • multiracial clientele • transgender-friendly • live shows • 18+ • gay-owned

Georgie's 810 5th Ave (at Main) **732/988-1220** • 1pm-2am, from noon wknds • lesbians/ gay men • neighborhood bar • karaoke

NIGHTCLUBS

Paradise 101 Asbury Ave (at Ocean Ave) **732/988-6663** • 6pm-2am, from 4pm wknds, clsd Mon-Tue • lesbians/ gay men • dancing/DJ • 2 dance flrs • live shows • piano bar • tiki/ pool bar in summer

RESTAURANTS

Bistro Olé 230 Main St **732/897-0048** • lunch & dinner, dinner only Sun, clsd Mon • Spanish-Portuguese

Chat & Nibble 932 Asbury Ave **732/755-5100**

The Harrison Restaurant 800 5th Ave **732/774-2200** • 4pm-close, Sun brunch, clsd Tue

Moonstruck 517 Lake Ave (at Grand) **732/988-0123** • dinner only, clsd Mon-Tue • also bar • live music wknds

BOOKSTORES

Yellow Roof Bookstore 1019 Main St **732/774-8021**

SPIRITUAL GROUPS

Trinity Episcopal Church 503 Asbury Ave (at Grand Ave) **732/775-5084** • 8am & 10am Sun • call for Integrity meeting info

Atlantic City

ACCOMMODATIONS

Tropicana Casino & Resort Brighton & The Boardwalk **609/340-4000, 800/843-8767**

BARS

Brass Rail Bar & Grill 12 S Mt Vernon Ave (at Club Tru/ Studio Six Complex) **609/347-0808** • 24hrs • popular • gay/ straight • neighborhood bar • karaoke Mon & Th-Sat • live shows • food served • gay-owned

NIGHTCLUBS

Club Tru 9 S Martin Luther King, Jr Blvd (btwn Atlantic & Pacific Aves) **609/344-2222** • 10pm-2am • popular • gay/ straight • several bars • dancing/DJ

Studio Six Video Dance Club 18 S Mt Vernon Ave (near Kentucky) **609/348-3310** • 10pm-close • popular • lesbians/ gay men • 5 bars • dancing/DJ • live shows • videos

RESTAURANTS

Dock's Oyster House 2405 Atlantic Ave **609/345-0092** • 5pm-10pm, till 11pm Fri-Sat • wheelchair access

Mama Mott's 151 S New York Ave (at Pacific) **609/345-8218** • 4pm-10pm, clsd Mon • Italian & seafood • wheelchair access

White House Sub Shop 2301 Arctic Ave (at Mississippi) **609/345-1564** • 10am-10pm, till 11pm Fri-Sat, from 11am Sun

PUBLICATIONS

EXP Magazine 302/227-5787, 877/397-6244 • bi-weekly gay magazine for Mid-Atlantic

Boonton

NIGHTCLUBS

Connexions 202 Myrtle Ave (off Washington) **973/263-4000** • 4pm-2am • lesbians/ gay men • dancing/DJ • country/ western • food served • drag shows

Camden

see also Philadelphia, Pennsylvania

ENTERTAINMENT & RECREATION

The Walt Whitman House 328 Mickle Blvd (btwn S 3rd & S 4th Sts) **856/964-5383** • the last home of America's great & controversial poet

Cape May

ACCOMMODATIONS

Cottage Beside the Point **609/204-0549** • gay/ straight • studio • kids ok • nonsmoking • lesbian-owned • $115-135

Highland House 131 N Broadway (at York) **609/898-1198** • gay-friendly • B&B • kids/ pets ok • gazebo • nonsmoking • gay & straight-owned • $110-155

The Virginia Hotel 25 Jackson St (btwn Beach Dr & Carpenter's Ln) **609/884-5700, 800/732-4236** • gay-friendly • also The Ebbitt Room restaurant • seafood/ cont'l • $85-425

BARS

The King Edward Room 301 Howard St (at The Chalfonte Hotel) **609/884-8409** • 5pm-1am summer only • mostly gay men

Cherry Hill

see also Philadelphia, Pennsylvania

SPIRITUAL GROUPS

Unitarian Universalist Church 401 N Kings Hwy (btwn Chapel & Church) **856/667-3618** • 10:15am Sun

Edison

SPIRITUAL GROUPS

New Jersey's Lesbian & Gay Havurah
732/650-1010

Florence

EROTICA

Florence Book Store Rte 130 S (4 miles S
of Rte 206) 609/499-9853

Highlands

ACCOMMODATIONS

Sandy Hook Cottage B&B 36 Navesink Ave
(Rte 36) 732/708-1923 • gay/ straight • hot
tub • nonsmoking • gay-owned • $159-299

Hoboken

BARS

The Cage 32 Newark St 201/216-1766 •
5pm-2am, till 3am wknds • lesbians/ gay men
• neighborhood bar • dancing/ DJ • theme
nights

NIGHTCLUBS

Maxwell's 1039 Washington St
201/653-1703 • popular • gay-friendly •
alternative • live music venue • food served

Jamesburg

RESTAURANTS

Fiddleheads 27 E Railroad Ave
732/521-0878 • lunch & dinner, Sun brunch,
clsd Mon-Tue • upscale contemporary bistro •
feel free to bring your own wine

Jersey City

SPIRITUAL GROUPS

Christ United Methodist Church 2811
Kennedy Blvd 201/332-8996 • 10am Sun

Lambertville

see also New Hope, Pennsylvania

ACCOMMODATIONS

York Street House B&B 42 York St
609/397-3007, 888/398-3199 • gay-friendly •
full brkfst • nonsmoking • $105-225

Madison

BOOKSTORES

Pandora Book Peddlers 9 Waverly Pl (at
Main) 973/822-8388 • 10am-6pm, noon-5pm
Mon, till 8pm Th, clsd Sun • feminist
bookstore & book club

Maplewood

SPIRITUAL GROUPS

Dignity Metro New Jersey 550 Ridgewood
Rd (at St George's Episcopal Church)
973/857-4040 • 4pm 3rd Sun

Morristown

INFO LINES & SERVICES

GAAMC (Gay Activist Alliance in Morris
County) 21 Normandy Hts Rd (at Unitarian
Fellowship) 973/285-1595 • info line 7:30pm-
9pm, also recorded info • also women's
network

New Brunswick

INFO LINES & SERVICES

Pride Center of New Jersey 1048
Livingston Ave 732/846-2232 • info line •
meeting space for various groups • call for info

BARS

The Den 700 Hamilton St (at Douglas),
Somerset 732/545-7354 • 8pm-2am, from
9pm Sat, clsd Mon • popular • mostly gay
men • dancing/DJ Fri-Sat • country/ western •
multiracial • live shows • videos • also
restaurant • wheelchair access

RESTAURANTS

The Frog & the Peach 29 Dennis St (at
Hiram Square) 732/846-3216 • lunch Mon-
Fri, dinner nightly • full bar • wheelchair access

Stage Left 5 Livingston Ave (at George)
732/828-4444 • popular • lesbians/ gay men
• some veggie • full bar • patio • wheelchair
access • expensive

SPIRITUAL GROUPS

Emanuel Lutheran Church New &
Kirkpatrick 732/545-2673 • 9:30am Sun •
wheelchair access

Unity Fellowship Church 235-239 Jersey
Ave 732/393-0776 • 11am Sun • uplifting
service in the African American tradition

Newark

BARS

Murphy's Tavern 59 Edison Pl (btwn Broad & Mulberry) 973/622–9176 • 11:30am-2am • lesbians/ gay men • neighborhood bar • dancing/DJ Th-Sat • mostly African-American • also restaurant

SPIRITUAL GROUPS

Liberation in Truth Unity Fellowship Church 608 Broad St (in Trinity & St Phillip's Cathedral) 973/621–2100 • 3:30pm Sun • uplifting service in the African American tradition

North Brunswick

SPIRITUAL GROUPS

MCC Christ the Liberator 1048 Livingston Ave (at Clark, enter at the Loft), Piscataway 732/846–8227 • 10:45am Sun

Paterson

RESTAURANTS

E&V Restaurant 322 Chamberlain Ave 973/942–8080 • lunch Tue-Fri & dinner Tue-Sun • Italian

Plainfield

ACCOMMODATIONS

The Pillars of Plainfield B&B 922 Central Ave (at 9th St) 908/753–0922, 888/PILLARS (745–5277) • gay/ straight • Georgian/ Victorian mansion • full brkfst • nonsmoking • infants & kids over 12 ok • dogs ok (call first) • gay-owned • $114-255

Princeton

BOOKSTORES

Micawber Books 110-114 Nassau St 609/921–8454 • independent

Rahway

CAFES

Eat to the Beat Coffeehouse 44 Cherry St (at E Cherry) 732/381–0505 • 11am-9pm, till 10pm Fri-Sat, clsd Sun-Mon • plenty veggie • live shows

Red Bank

BOOKSTORES

Earth Spirit 25 Monmouth 732/842–3855 • 11am-7pm, till 8pm Fri, noon-5pm Sun • new age center & bookstore • LGBT sections

River Edge

NIGHTCLUBS

Feathers 77 Kinder Kamack Rd (at Grand) 201/342–6410 • 9pm-2am, till 3am Sat • popular • mostly gay men • dancing/DJ • karaoke • live shows • videos • young crowd • wheelchair access

Rosemont

RESTAURANTS

The Cafe 88 Kingwood-Stockton Rd 609/397–4097 • lunch Tue-Sun & dinner Wed-Sun • BYOB

Sayreville

NIGHTCLUBS

Colosseum 7090 Rte 9 N (at Rte 35 N) 732/316–0670 • 8pm-2am • lesbians/ gay men • dancing/DJ • live shows • drag

RESTAURANTS

Cagney's Pub & Restaurant 3276 Washington Rd 732/525–5586 • 3pm-2am • also bar • karaoke • dancing/ DJ

Sergeantsville

see New Hope, Pennsylvania

Stockton

ACCOMMODATIONS

Woolverton Inn 6 Woolverton Rd 609/397–0802, 888/264–6648 • gay-friendly • full brkfst • jacuzzi • wheelchair access • $130-425

Trenton

BARS

Buddies Pub 677 S Broad St (at Madison) 609/989–8566 • 5pm-1:30am, from 6pm Sat, clsd Sun-Mon • lesbians/ gay men • neighborhood bar • dancing/DJ • karaoke

The Mill Hill Saloon 300 S Broad (at Market) 609/394–7222 • 11:30am-2am, 5pm-2am Sat, clsd Sun, Brew Cellar from 10pm • gay-friendly • live bands from jazz to blues to rock to folk • also restaurant

CAFES

Cafe Ole 126 S Warren St 609/396–2233 • "alcohol-free, all-ages bistro w/ great food (some veggie dishes)" • hosts Trenton Q-Nite, queer coffeehouse, 6:30pm-9:30pm Fri

Westville

see also Philadelphia, Pennsylvania

NIGHTCLUBS

Bounce Night Club 1102 Rte 130 S (at I-295) **856/845-1010** • 9pm-2am Wed-Sat • mostly gay men • ladies nights • dancing/DJ • multracial clientele • transgender-friendly • food served • karaoke • drag shows • videos • 18+ • young crowd • wheelchair access

NEW MEXICO

Alamogordo

ACCOMMODATIONS

Best Western Desert Aire Motor Inn 1021 S White Sands Blvd **505/437-2110** • gay-friendly • swimming • wheelchair access • $68+

Albuquerque

includes Bernalillo, Corrales, Placitas & Rio Rancho

INFO LINES & SERVICES

AA Gay/ Lesbian 505/266-1900 (AA#) • call for times/ locations • nonsmoking meeting • wheelchair access

Common Bond Info Line 505/891-3647 • 24hrs • covers LGBT community

ACCOMMODATIONS

Brittania & W E Mauger Estate B&B 701 Roma Ave NW (at 7th) 505/242-8755, 800/719-9189 • gay-friendly • intimate 1897 Queen Anne residence • full brkfst • nonsmoking • $89-179

▲ **El Peñasco** 505/771-8909, 888/576-2726 • mostly women • private historic adobe guesthouse (sleeps 1-4) • stocked for brkfst • halfway between Albuquerque & Santa Fe • hot tub under the stars • kids ok • nonsmoking • lesbian-owned • $80-100

Golden Guesthouses 2645 Decker NW 505/344-9205, 888/513-GOLD • lesbians/ gay men • individual & shared units • nonsmoking • lesbian-owned • $90-140

Hacienda Antigua B&B 6708 Tierra Dr NW (close to corner of 2nd & Osuna) 505/345-5399, 800/201-2986 • gay/ straight • full brkfst • hot tub • swimming • nonsmoking • kids/ pets ok • $149-300

Nuevo Dia 11110 San Rafael Ave NE (at Browning) 505/856-7910 • gay-friendly • guesthouse • hot tub • kids/ pets ok • wheelchair access • $65-195

Reply Forward   Delete

Date: Nov 28, 2005 16:25:33
From: Girl-on-the-Go
To: Editor@Damron.com
Subject: Albuquerque

>We're going to let you in on a little secret: New Mexico is the overlooked gem of the Southwest. Arizona likes to take the lion's share of the credit for the Southwest style as it basks in its endless sun and endless supply of seniors and New Agers. Nevada cashes in on the image too, but goes for the glitz with its desert filled with more casinos that cacti. Colorado likes to brag about how it's God's little green heaven when not under several feet of fresh powder. Even Texas likes to horn in with its vibrant Tejano music and arts. But it's New Mexico, with its fermentation of 300 years of Native American, Spanish, and Anglo cultures, that is the true heart and soul of the Southwest.

>Sprawling in the shadow of Sandia Peak, New Mexico's largest city and cultural center is Albuquerque. The city's history can be glimpsed in its adobe constructions, cowboy decor, and proliferation of arts and crafts. And just outside of Albuquerque lies a more ancient piece of New Mexico's history: Petroglyph National Monument, covered with rock carvings created by the indigenous people of the area.

>During the day, stop in at New Mexico's largest independent bookstore **Page One** and pick up a copy of the LGBT bi-weekly newspaper **New Mexico Voice** for the scoop on the latest activities around town. Or, give the **Common Bond Info Line** a call. At night, visit Albuquerque's women's bar **Exhale** or **Foxes Lounge** for dancing and a drag show. Afterward, turn in for a good night's sleep at one of Albuquerque's lesbian-owned inns: **El Peñasco** or **Golden Guesthouses.**

>To see things from a new perspective, take to the air for a spectacular view with **Rainbow Ryders**. Albuquerque is a haven for those who enjoy the out-of-doors. Mountain bikers, especially, will love the scenery and endless terrain.

Wyndham Albuquerque Hotel 2910 Yale Blvd SE (at Gibson) 505/843-7000, 800/227-1117 • gay-friendly • 4-star hotel • swimming • also Rojo Bar & Grill • $179-209

Bars

Albuquerque Mining Co (AMC) 7209 Central Ave NE (at Louisiana) 505/255-4022 • 6pm-2am, till midnight Sun • popular • mostly gay men • dancing/DJ • live shows • wheelchair access • also Pit Bar • gay-owned

Albuquerque Social Club 4021 Central Ave NE (enter rear) 505/255-0887 • 3pm-midnight, till 2am Fri-Sat, noon-midnight Sun • popular • lesbians/gay men • dancing/DJ • private club

Exhale 6132 4th NW (near Osuna) 505/342-0049 • 6pm-close, from 4:30pm Sun, clsd Mon-Tue • mostly women • neighborhood bar • dancing/ DJ wknds • food served • karaoke • dance lessons

Foxes Lounge 8521 Central Ave NE (btwn Wisconsin & Wyoming) 505/255-3060 • 10am-2am, noon-midnight Sun • lesbians/ gay men • dancing/DJ • drag shows • wheelchair access

Sidewinders Ranch 8900 Central SE (at Wyoming) 505/275-1616 • noon-2am, till midnight Sun • mostly gay men • dancing/DJ • country/western • leather • wheelchair access

Nightclubs

Fire • monthly dance party • women only • check local listings for location

Pulse/ Blu 4100 Central Ave SE (at Montclaire, in Nob Hill) 505/255-3334 • 5pm-2am • popular • mostly gay men • Pulse Th-Sat only • dancing/DJ • cover charge

Restaurants

Artichoke Café 424 Central Ave 505/243-0200 • lunch Mon-Fri, dinner nightly • bistro • plenty veggie

---

Albuquerque

LGBT Pride:
June. 505/873-8084, web: www.abqpride.com.

Annual Events:
October - Albuquerque Int'l Balloon Fiesta 505/821-1000 or 888/422-7277, web: www.balloonfiesta.com.

City Info:
800/733-6396, web: www.abqcvb.org.

Best View:
Sandia Peak Tramway (505/856-7325) at sunset.

Weather:
Sunny and temperate. Warm days and cool nights in summer, with average temperatures from 65° to 95°. Winter is cooler, from 28° to 57°.

Attractions:
Albuquerque Museum 505/243-7255.
Indian Pueblo Cultural Center 505/843-7270 or 800/766-4405 (outside NM), web: www.indian-pueblo.org.
New Mexico Museum of Natural History & Science 505/841-2800, web: www.nmnaturalhistory.org.
Old Town.
Petroglyph National Monument 505/899-0205, web: www.nps.gov/petr/.
Rattlesnake Museum 505/242-6569, web: www.rattlesnakes.com.
Sandia Peak Tramway 505/856-7325, web: www.sandiapeak.com.
Wildlife West Nature Park & Chuckwagon 505/281-7655, web: www.wildlifewest.org

---

Chef du Jour 119 San Pasquale SW (at Central) **505/247-8998** • lunch only Mon-Fri • plenty veggie • wheelchair access

District Bar and Grill 115 4th St NW (downtown) **505/243-0003** • 11am-12am, till midnight Sun • New Mexican

Flying Star Cafe 3416 Central SE (2 blocks W of Carlisle) **505/255-6633** • 6am-11pm, till midnight wknds • plenty veggie • wheelchair access

Frontier 2400 Central SE (at Cornell) **505/266-0550** • 24hrs • good brkfst burritos

Graze 3128 Central SE **505/268-4729** • lunch & dinner, clsd Sun-Mon • also Gulp bar • patio

Martini Grille 4200 Central Ave NE **505/255-4111** • dinner nightly, bar from 4pm • swank

Romano's Macaroni Grill 2100 Louisiana NE (at Winrock Mall) **505/881-3400** • lunch & dinner • Italian

Sadie's Cocinita 6230 4th St NW (near Osuna) **505/345-5339** • 11am-10pm, till 9pm Sun • popular • New Mexican

ENTERTAINMENT & RECREATION

Rainbow Ryders 11520 San Bernadino NE **505/823-1111, 800/725-2477** • gay-friendly • scenic balloon rides

Women in Movement in New Mexico (WIMIN) **505/899-3627** • production company for the Southwest's premier women's music & art festival Wiminfest (Memorial Day wknd) • other events throughout year

BOOKSTORES

Bird Song 1708 Central SE **505/268-7204** • 11am-7pm • used • LGBT section

Page One 11018 Montgomery NE **505/294-2026, 800/521-4122** • 9am-10pm, till 8pm Sun

RETAIL SHOPS

Newsland 2122 Central Ave SE (at Yale) **505/242-0694** • some LGBT magazines

SPIRITUAL GROUPS

Dignity New Mexico 1815 Los Lomas (at University) **505/896-1095** • 7pm 1st Sun

Emmanuel MCC 341 Dallas NE (at Copper) **505/268-0599** • 10am Sun

First Unitarian Church 3701 Carlisle NE (at Comanche) **505/884-1801** • 9:30am & 11am Sun

MCC of Albuquerque 1103 Texas NE (near Lomas) **505/268-5252** • 10am Sun

GYMS & HEALTH CLUBS

Betty's Bath & Day Spa 1835 Candelaria NW **505/341-3456** • full-service spa w/ separate women-only hot tub

EROTICA

Castle Superstore 5110 Central Ave SE (at San Mateo) **505/262-2266**

Video Maxxx 810 Comanche NE (at I-25) **505/341-4000** • leather • novelties • books, etc

Chimayo

ACCOMMODATIONS

Casa Escondida B&B **505/351-4805, 800/643-7201** • gay-friendly • full brkfst • hot tub • nonsmoking • kids/pets ok • $89-149

Cloudcroft

ACCOMMODATIONS

Good Life Inn B&B & Wedding Chapel 164 Karr Canyon Rd (at Hwy 82) **505/682-5433, 866/543-3466** • gay-friendly • luxurious suites • full brkfst • hot tub • teens ok • lesbian-owned • $125-175

RETAIL SHOPS

Off The Beaten Path 100 Glorietta Ave (at 1st) **505/682-7284** • 9am-6pm • eclectic gifts • original artwork • wheelchair access • lesbian-owned

Farmington

ACCOMMODATIONS

Days Inn 1901 E Broadway **505/325-3700** • gay-friendly • kids/pets ok • wheelchair access • $39-99

Las Cruces

CAFES

Tommy's Cake Shop & Cafe 1609 El Paseo (at Montana) **505/526-6599** • 6:30am-6:30pm, 7am-5pm Sat, clsd Sun • patio

RETAIL SHOPS

Spirit Winds Gifts & Cafe 2260 S Locust St **505/521-0222** • 7:30am-8pm, till 6pm Sun • live music some wknds • patio

SPIRITUAL GROUPS

Holy Family Ecumenical Catholic Church 1809 El Paseo Rd (at Mesilla Valley Christian Church) **505/644-5025, 505/524-6807** • 10am Sun • inclusive Catholic community

Unitarian Universalist of Las Cruces 2000 S Solano (at corner of Wofford) 505/522–7281 • 9am & 10:30am Sun

Madrid

ACCOMMODATIONS

Madrid Lodging 14 Opera House Rd 505/471–3450 • gay-friendly • suite • full brkfst • hot tub • nonsmoking • kids/ pets ok • wheelchair access • $85-100

BARS

Mineshaft Tavern 2846 State Hwy 14 505/473–0743 • 11am-close • gay-friendly • live shows • hosts annual He/ She Bang in Sept • also restaurant • some veggie

CAFES

Java Junction 2855 State Hwy 14 505/438–2772 • 7:15am-6pm • also B&B

Ramah

ACCOMMODATIONS

Ancient Way Outpost 4018 Ice Caves Rd (at Hwy 53, mile marker 46), El Morro 506/783–4612 • cabins & RV park • also Ancient Ways Cafe • lesbian-owned

El Morro RV Park, Cabins & Cafe 4018 Hwy 53 505/783-4612 • gay/ straight • full brkfst • nonsmoking • lesbian-owned • $60-75

Ruidoso

RESTAURANTS

Mountain Annie's 2710 Sudderth (at Mechem) 505/257–7982 • 11am-9pm, clsd Tue-Wed (winter) • live shows • beer/ wine • patio • gazebos • nonsmoking • wheelchair access

Santa Fe

INFO LINES & SERVICES

AA Gay/ Lesbian 505/982–8932

ACCOMMODATIONS

Alexander's Inn 529 E Palace Ave (at Delgado) 505/986–1431, 888/321–5123 • gay/ straight • full brkfst • hot tub • kids/ pets ok • nonsmoking • gay-owned • $90-260

Bishop's Lodge Resort & Spa 1297 Bishops Lodge Rd 505/983–6377, 800/732–2240 • gay-friendly • on 450 acres 8 minutes from Plaza • kids/ pets ok • swimming • hot tub • wheelchair access • $149-389

Canyon Road Casitas 505/989–9930, 800/735-8453 • gay-friendly • 4 adobe casitas • kitchens • fireplaces • hot tub • patio • $100-275

El Farolito B&B 514 Galisteo St (at Paseo de Peralta) 505/988-1631, 888/634-8782 • gay/straight • adobe compound w/ romantic, private casitas • kids ok • nonsmoking • gay-owned • $150-225

Four Kachinas Inn 512 Webber St 505/988-1631, 888/634-8782 • gay/straight • courtyard • kids ok • nonsmoking • wheelchair access • gay-owned • $110-200

Hacienda Nicholas 320 E Marcy St 505/992-8385, 888/284-3170 • gay/straight • adobe home • full brkfst • kids/pets ok • nonsmoking • wheelchair access • gay-owned • $110-210

Heart Seed B&B Retreat & Spa 505/471-7026 • gay-friendly • located on Turquoise Trail (25 miles S of Santa Fe) • full brkfst • hot tub • nonsmoking • sundeck • also day spa • kids ok • lesbian-owned • $85-129

Hotel St Francis 210 Don Gaspar Ave 505/983-5700, 800/529-5700 • gay-friendly

Inn at Mountaintop 505/310-7958 • lesbians/gay men • private cottages • hot tub • secluded 10 acres • call for directions • gay-owned • $100-250

Inn of the Anasazi 113 Washington Ave 505/988-3030, 800/688-8100 • gay-friendly • luxury hotel 1/2 block from Plaza • kids ok • wheelchair access • $205-475

▲ **Inn of the Turquoise Bear B&B** 342 E Buena Vista St 505/983-0798, 800/396-4104 • lesbians/gay men • B&B in historic Witter Bynner estate • nonsmoking • gay-owned • $99-325

La Tienda Inn & Duran House 445-447 W San Francisco St 505/989-8259, 800/889-7611 • gay-friendly • adobe compound • kids ok • nonsmoking • wheelchair access • $100-190

Las Palomas 460 W San Francisco St 505/982-5560, 877/982-5560 • gay-friendly • luxury hotel 1/2 block from Plaza • kids ok • wheelchair access • $205-475

Leadfeather 3888 State Rd 14 (at Hwy 42) 505/438-3131 • lesbians/gay men • B&B on scenic Turquoise Trail • nonsmoking • kids/pets ok • gay-owned • $80-125

The Madeleine Inn 106 Faithway St 505/982–3465, 888/877–7622 • gay/ straight • Queen Anne Victorian • full brkfst • hot tub • kids ok • nonsmoking • gay-owned • $110-210

Marriott Residence Inn 1698 Galisteo St (at St Michaels) 505/988–7300, 800/331–3131 • gay-friendly • hot tub • swimming • nonsmoking • kids/ pets ok • wheelchair access • $89-219

Michael's Casa Quintana 114 Quintana St 505/984–1869, 888/443–2272 • gay/ straight • two 1,100-sq-ft adobe rental homes • kids/ pets ok • nonsmoking • wheelchair access • gay-owned • $75-195, $700-1,050/ week

Rainbow Vision Santa Fe 500 Rodeo Rd 505/474–9696 • LGBT retirement community set to open Jan 2006

Saltamontes Retreat—Grasshopper Hill Old Colonias Rd (at Llanitos Ln), East Pecos 505/757–2528, 877/PECOS2U • gay/ straight (mostly women) • 3 guestrooms in private home bordering Santa Fe Nat'l Forest • communal kitchen • hot tub • reservations required • nonsmoking • lesbian-owned • $60-85 (also weekly & monthly rates; 2-night minimum stay)

Tano Road Casita 15 Tano Pt Ln 505/989–7802, 505/989–7803 • gay/ straight • studio guesthouse • nonsmoking • $90

▲ **The Triangle Inn—Santa Fe** 14 Arroyo Cuyamungue (12 miles N of Santa Fe) 505/455–3375, 877/733–7689 • lesbians/ gay men • secluded rustic adobe compound • hot tub • nonsmoking casitas available • kids/ pets ok • wheelchair access • lesbian-owned • $70-160

Villas de Santa Fe 400 Griffin St 505/988–3000, 800/869–6790 • gay/ straight • villa-style suites • swimming • hot tub • kids ok • gym • courtyard • wheelchair access • $130-220

The Water Street Inn 427 W Water St 505/984–1193, 800/646–6752 • gay-friendly • historic adobe inn • jacuzzi • nonsmoking • kids/ pets ok • wheelchair access • $100-258

NIGHTCLUBS

Swig 135 W Palace Ave, 3rd flr (at Grant) 505/955–0400 • 5pm-2am, clsd Sun-Mon • gay/ straight • dancing/DJ • swank lounge • tapas served • gay-owned

CAFES

Longevity Cafe 112 W San Francisco St (Plaza Mercada) 505/986–0403 • 11am-midnight, till 7pm Sun • Zen-style tea house • food served • plenty veggie

RESTAURANTS

Anasazi Restaurant 113 Washington Ave (at The Inn of the Anasazi) 505/988–3236 • brkfst, lunch, dinner & Sun brunch • wheelchair access

Cafe Pasqual's 121 Don Gaspar (at Water St) 505/983–9340, 800/722–7672 • brkfst, lunch, dinner & Sun brunch • popular • Southwestern • some veggie • beer/ wine

The Compound Restaurant 653 Canyon Rd 505/982–4353 • lunch Mon-Fri, dinner nightly • upscale • Southwestern • nonsmoking • patio • reservations recommended

Cowgirl Hall of Fame 319 S Guadalupe (btwn Aztec & Guadalupe) 505/982–2565 • 11am-3am, from 8:30am wknds, till midnight Sun • Southwestern • plenty veggie

Dave's Not Here 1115 Hickox St (at Cortez) 505/983–7060 • 11am-9pm, clsd Sun • New Mexican • some veggie • beer/ wine • women-owned/ run

Geronimo's 724 Canyon Rd (at Camino del Monte Sol) 505/982–1500 • lunch Tue-Sun, dinner nightly • eclectic gourmet • full bar 11am-11pm

Kasasoba 544 Agua Fria 505/984–1969 • 6pm-10pm • popular • Japanese • patio

Paul's 72 Marcy St (at Lincoln & Washington) 505/982–8738 • lunch Mon-Fri, dinner nightly • modern int'l • some veggie • beer/ wine • wheelchair access

Santacafe 231 Washington Ave 505/984–1788 • lunch & dinner • New American • some veggie • full bar • wheelchair access

Vanessie of Santa Fe 434 W San Francisco (at Guadalupe) 505/982–9966 • 5:30pm-9pm (bar till midnight) • popular • lesbians/ gay men • steak house • piano bar

ENTERTAINMENT & RECREATION

One Railroad Circus 505/992–2588 • summer only • women's circus • check local listings for info

Ten Thousand Waves 3451 Hyde Park Rd (4 miles out of town) 505/992–5025 • Japanese health spa & lodging • sit under the stars & look out at the mtns • clothing-optional in all tubs • kids ok • call for more info

BOOKSTORES

Downtown Subscription 376 Garcia St (at Acequia Madre) 505/983–3085 • 7am-6pm • newsstand • coffee shop

RETAIL SHOPS

The Ark 133 Romero St (at Agua Fria)
505/988–3709 • 9:30m-7pm, 10am-6pm Sat,
11am-5pm Sun • spiritual

Silver City

ACCOMMODATIONS

West Street Inn 505/534–2302 •
guesthouse • kids/ pets ok (call for details) •
$85-105

CAFES

Shevek & Mi 602 N Bullard St (at 6th St)
505/534–9168 • wknd & holiday brunch •
Mediterranean cuisine • espresso • "the best
service in town" • beer/ wine • patio • gay-
owned

RESTAURANTS

Diane's Restaurant & Bakery 510 N
Bullard 505/538–1489 • lunch daily, dinner
Tue-Sat, wknd brunch • clsd Mon

RETAIL SHOPS

Many Moons 11786 US Hwy 180 E
505/534–2400 • 10am-6pm • Native
American arts & craft shop • gay-owned

Taos

ACCOMMODATIONS

Adobe & Stars B&B 584 State Hwy 150 (at
Valdez Rim Rd) 505/776–2776, 800/211–7076
• gay/ straight • luxurious pueblo • full brkfst •
near skiing & nat'l forest • fireplaces •
nonsmoking • patios • wheelchair access •
woman-owned/ run • $110-185

Brooks Street Inn 505/758–1489,
800/758–1489 • gay-friendly • B&B in adobe
home • full brkfst • nonsmoking • kids 10+ ok
• women-owned/ run • $99-149

Casa Europa Inn & Gallery 840 Upper
Ranchitos Rd (at Ranchitos Rd)
505/758–9798, 888/758–9798 • gay/ straight •
full brkfst • hot tub • sauna • nonsmoking •
$120-200

Casa Gallina 505/758–2306 • gay/ straight •
charming guesthouse in quiet, pastoral setting
• nonsmoking • wheelchair access • gay-
owned • $95-185

Dobson House 484 Tune Dr 505/776–5738 •
gay-friendly • luxury suites north of Taos • full
brkfst • nonsmoking • $110-130

Dreamcatcher B&B 416 La Lomita Rd (at
Valverde) 505/758–0613, 888/758–0613 • gay-
friendly • near Taos Plaza • full brkfst • hot tub
• nonsmoking • wheelchair access • $89-129

Orinda B&B 461 Valverde St (on Valverde
Park) 505/758–8581, 800/847–1837 • gay/
straight • full brkfst • nonsmoking • $80-145

San Geronimo Lodge 1101 Witt Rd (at Kit
Carson) 505/751–3776, 800/894–4119 •
popular • gay/ straight • full brkfst • swimming
• hot tub • massage available • kids/ pets ok •
nonsmoking • wheelchair access • $95-150

RESTAURANTS

Momentos de la Vida 474 State Hwy 150
505/776–3333 • New Mexican/gourmet
cuisine • organic produce • some veggie •
also full bar

NEW YORK

Adirondack Mtns

ACCOMMODATIONS

The Cornerstone Victorian 3921 Main St
(Rte 9), Warrensburg 518/623–3308 • gay-
friendly • close to skiing, hiking, Saratoga &
more • 5-course gourmet brkfst • beautiful
gardens & wraparound porch

Country Road Lodge B&B 115 Hickory Hill
Rd, Warrensburg 518/623–2207 • gay-friendly
• secluded riverside retreat at the end of a
country road • full brkfst • nonsmoking • $72-
109

The Doctor's Inn 282 Trudeau Rd, Saranac
Lake 518/891–3464, 888/518–3464 • gay-
friendly • full brkfst • some shared baths •
kids/ pets ok (call first) • nonsmoking • $75-
200

Falls Brook Yurts in Adirondacks John
Brannon Rd, Minerva 518/761–6187 • gay-
friendly • stay in a comfortable yurt w/ a sky
dome to view the stars • access to hiking,
fishing & boating

King Hendrick Motel 1602 State Rte 9,
Lake George 518/792–0418, 866/521–6883 •
gay-friendly • swimming • kids ok • cabins
available • wheelchair access • $70-120

The Merrill Magee House 3 Hudson St (off
Rte 9/ Main St), Warrensburg 518/623–2449,
888/664–4661 • gay-friendly • Victorian
country inn • full brkfst • 5 miles from Lake
George • wheelchair access • women-owned •
$115-145

Tea Island Motel 3020 Lake Shore Dr, Lake George 518/668-2776 • gay-friendly • motel • $80-135

Albany

see Capital District

Beacon

RESTAURANTS

Quinn's Restaurant 330 Main St 845/831-8065 • 5am-2pm • great bread

BOOKSTORES

World's End Books & Music 532 Main St 845/831-1760 • 11am-6pm, clsd Tue • used & rare books, CDs & more

RETAIL SHOPS

Kringle's Christmas House 475 Main St (at Tioronda Ave) 877/323-7660 • noon-5pm • gifts

Binghamton

INFO LINES & SERVICES

AA Gay/ Lesbian 438 Chenango St (at United Methodist Church) 607/722-5983 • 7pm Sat

BARA (Binghamton Area Rainbow Association) PO Box 3308, 13902 607/772-3216

ACCOMMODATIONS

Serenity Farms 607/656-4659 • gay/ straight • B&B • full brkfst • camping on 100 secluded acres • swimming • pets ok • gay-owned • $65-89

BARS

Merlin's 201 State St 607/722-1022 • 4pm-midnight, 7pm-3am Fri-Sat, clsd Mon-Tue • lesbians/ gay men • neighborhood bar • dancing/ DJ

Squiggy's 34 Chenango St (at Court) 607/722-2299 • 5pm-1am, 8pm-3am Fri-Sat, clsd Sun • lesbians/ gay men • neighborhood bar • dancing/DJ Fri-Sat

CAFES

Lost Dog Cafe 222 Water St 607/771-6063 • 11:30am-10pm, till 11pm Fri-Sat, clsd Sun • popular • some veggie • beer/wine • live shows • wheelchair access

RESTAURANTS

The Whole in the Wall 43 S Washington St 607/722-5138 • 11:30am-9pm, clsd Sun-Mon

SPIRITUAL GROUPS

Unitarian Universalist 183 Riverside 607/729-1641 • 9:15am & 11am Sun, 10am summer

Buffalo

BARS

Buddies 31 Johnson Park (at S Elmwood) 716/855-1313 • 1pm-4am, from noon wknds • lesbians/ gay men • dancing/DJ Th-Sat • live shows • wheelchair access • Rainbow Pride store inside

Cathode Ray 26 Allen St (at N Pearl) 716/884-3615 • 1pm-4am • mostly gay men • neighborhood bar • videos • wheelchair access

Friends 16 Allen St (at Main St) 716/883-7855 • 3pm-2am, noon-4am wknds • mostly men • multiracial • neighborhood bar • food served • patio • gay-owned

Fugazi 503 Franklin St (near Allen St) 716/881-3588 • 5pm-2am, from 8pm wknds • gay/ straight • intimate cocktail lounge • videos

Q 44 Allen St 716/332-2223 • 3pm-4am, from noon wknds • lesbians/ gay men • neighborhood bar

Roxy's Greenroom 884 Main St (at Carlton) 716/882-9293 • 6pm-close Wed-Sat • mostly women • dancing/ DJ • alternative • live shows • karaoke

The Underground 174 Delaware Ave (at Johnson) 716/853-0092 • noon-4am • mostly gay men • neighborhood bar • dancing/ DJ • karaoke

NIGHTCLUBS

Club Marcella 622 Main St 716/847-6850 • 9pm-4am, from 4pm Fri, clsd Mon,Tue & Th • lesbians/ gay men • dancing/DJ • drag shows • wheelchair access

CAFES

Cafe 59 59 Allen St (at Franklin) 716/883-1880 • 8am-9pm, 10am-5pm Sat, clsd Sun

RESTAURANTS

Solid Grounds 431 Elmwood Ave (at Bryant St) 716/882-5282 • 7:30am-3pm • home-made food • wheelchair access • lesbian-owned

BOOKSTORES

Talking Leaves 3158 Main St (btwn Winspear & Hertel Aves) 716/837-8554 • 10am-6pm, till 8pm Wed-Th, clsd Sun • also 951 Elmwood Ave, 716/884-9524

PUBLICATIONS

About Magazine 452 Franklin St (at Virginia St) 716/913-6406 • "the queer voice of western New York and southern Ontario"

Erie Gay News 814/456-9833 • covers news & events in the Erie, Cleveland, Pittsburgh, Buffalo & Chautauqua County, NY region

Outcome Buffalo 506 Linwood Ave Ste 6 716/883-2756 • monthly

SPIRITUAL GROUPS

Dignity 716/833-8995 • call for events

EROTICA

Adult Mart 3104 Delaware Ave (at Sheridan), Kenmore 716/877-5027 • 24hrs • women receive 20% off Wed

Capital District

includes Albany, Schenectady & Troy

INFO LINES & SERVICES

Gay AA at L/G Community Center, Albany 518/462-6138 • 7pm Sun

Lesbian/ Gay Community Center 332 Hudson Ave, Albany 518/462-6138 • 7pm-10pm • women's group 7pm Tue • also cafe

Women's Building 79 Central Ave, Albany 518/465-1597 • community center

ACCOMMODATIONS

Dreamer's B&B 48 Oneida St (at Cohoes Crescent Rd), Cohoes 518/233-7155 • gay/ straight • full brkfst • near Saratoga race track and gay shops • nonsmoking • lesbian-owned • $50-125

The Morgan State House 393 State St, Albany 518/427-6063, 888/427-6063 • gay-friendly • 1800s town house • nonsmoking • $160-260

BARS

Alibi's 1100 Madison Ave (at N Allen), Albany 518/489-0606 • 5pm-1am, till 4am Fri-Sat • gay/ straight • young crowd • casual retro lounge • also Peking restaurant • gay-owned

Big G's Restaurant & Nightclub 50 Oneida St (at Canvass), Cohoes 518/238-2133 • 5pm-close Th-Sat • mostly women • dancing/ DJ • food served • lesbian-owned

Blythewood 50 N Jay St (off Union), Schenectady 518/382-9755 • 8pm-4am, from 4pm Sun, clsd Mon • mostly gay men • neighborhood bar • wheelchair access

Cafe Hollywood 275 Lark St (at Hamilton), Albany 518/472-9043 • 3pm-4am • gay-friendly • neighborhood bar • young crowd • videos

Clinton Street Pub 159 Clinton St, Schenectady 518/377-8555 • 8am-2am, from noon Sun • lesbians/ gay men • neighborhood bar • dancing/ DJ • live shows • karaoke

Oh Bar 304 Lark St (at Madison), Albany 518/463-9004 • 2pm-4am • lesbians/ gay men • neighborhood bar • multiracial • karaoke • videos • wheelchair access

Waterworks Pub 76 Central Ave (btwn Lexington & Northern), Albany 518/465-9079 • 1pm-4am • popular • mostly gay men • neighborhood bar • dancing/DJ wknds • garden bar • food served • karaoke • wheelchair access

NIGHTCLUBS

Club Phoenix 348 Central Ave, Albany 518/462-4862 • 4pm-4am • lesbians/ gay men • dancing/DJ • transgender-friendly • karaoke • gay-owned

Fuze Box 12 Central Ave, Albany 518/432-4472 • 2pm-4am • gay/ straight • dancing/ DJ • live shows • swing dancing • karaoke • gay-owned

RESTAURANTS

Bomber's Burrito Bar 258 Lark St, Albany 518/463-9636 • 8am-11pm, till 9pm Sun • lots of veggie • gay-owned

Debbie's Kitchen 456 Madison Ave (btwn Lark St & Washington Park), Albany 518/463-3829 • lunch & dinner, clsd Sun • sandwiches • salads

El Loco Mexican Cafe 465 Madison Ave (btwn Lark & Willett), Albany 518/436-1855 • 11:30am-10pm, till 11pm Fri-Sat, clsd Mon • healthy Tex-Mex • some veggie • full bar

Magnolia's 462 Madison Ave, Albany 518/449-2492 • dinner, Sun brunch, bar till 2am Fri-Sat, clsd Mon • cont'l/ Indonesian • live music

ENTERTAINMENT & RECREATION

Face the Music WRPI 91.5 FM, Troy 518/276-6248 • 4pm-6pm Sun • feminist radio

Homo Radio WRPI 91.5 FM, Troy 518/276-6248 • noon-2pm Sun

Two Rivers 518/449-0758 • LGBT outdoor club

RETAIL SHOPS

Romeo's Gifts 299 Lark St (at Madison), Albany 518/434-4014 • noon-9pm, till 5pm Sun

PUBLICATIONS

Community 518/462-6138 x7 • monthly newsjournal

SPIRITUAL GROUPS

Congregation Berith Shalom 167 3rd St, Troy 518/272-8872 • 7:30 Fri

First United Presbyterian Church State & Willett Sts, Albany 518/449-7332 • 8:30am & 10:45am Sun • also 10am Sun in Troy • 1915 5th Ave • 518/272-2771

Grace & Holy Innocents Episcopal Church 498 Clinton Ave (at Robbins St), Albany 518/465-1112 • 9am Sun

Holy Trinity National Catholic Church 405 Washington Ave, Albany 518/434-8861 • 6pm Sun

MCC of Albany 275 State St (btwn Dove & Swan, at Emmanuel Baptist Church), Albany 518/785-7941 • 1pm Sun • wheelchair access

St Sebastian's Friary & Retreat Center 352 Glen Dr, Fultonville 518/853-1695 • retreats, Reiki healing & more

GYMS & HEALTH CLUBS

Fitness for Her 333 Delaware Ave, Delmar 518/478-0237 • 4am-9pm, 8:30am-4:30pm Sat, 9am-5pm Sun • women-only • child care available • wheelchair access • lesbian-owned

Catskill Mtns

INFO LINES & SERVICES

Wise Woman Center 845/246-8081 • women only • workshops • correspondence courses • newsletter

ACCOMMODATIONS

Bradstan Country Hotel 1561 Rte 17-B, White Lake 845/583-4114 • gay-friendly • also cottages • piano bar & cabaret • 6pm-1am Fri-Sat • $110-118

Carrier House B&B 64 Carrier St (at New St), Liberty 845/292-9742 • gay/ straight • walking distance to restaurants & hiking trails • gay-owned

Clark House 3292 Rte 23A, Palenville 518/678-5649, 877/689-5101 • gay/ straight • Victorian guesthouse • full brkfst • hot tub • nonsmoking • $105-205

ECCE B&B 19 Silverfish Rd, Barryville 845/557-8562, 888/557-8562 • gay/ straight • B&B 300 ft above Upper Delaware River • full brkfst • nonsmoking • gay-owned • $150-250

Full Moon Resort Valley View Rd (at County Rt 47), Oliverea 845/254-5117 • gay/ straight • hotel, campsites, cabins available • located on 100 acres • swimming • kids ok • nonsmoking • wknd weddings • $75-165

Inn at Stone Ridge Rte 209, Stone Ridge 845/687-0736 • gay-friendly • 1700s mansion • full brkfst • also fine dining • full bar • patio • $195-425

Kate's Lazy Meadow Motel 5191 Rte 28, Mt Tremper 845/688-7200 • gay-friendly • owned by Kate Pierson of the B-52s • $150+

Magical Land of Oz B&B 753 Shandelee Rd, Livingston Manor 845/439-3418 • gay/ straight • each room has Oz character theme • shared baths • hot tub • kids ok • gay-owned • $75-85

The Nightingale Inn 2372 State Rte 81, Earlton 518/634-7305 • gay/ straight • full brkfst • gay-owned • $85

Point Lookout Mountain Inn The Mohican Trail, Rte 23, East Windham 518/734-3381 • gay-friendly • near skiing • hot tub • nonsmoking • kids/ pets ok • also restaurant & cafe • wheelchair access • $80-165

River Run B&B 882 Main St, Fleischmanns 845/254-4884 • gay-friendly • Queen Anne Victorian • some shared baths • full brkfst • nonsmoking • $70-185

The Roxbury 2258 County Hwy 41 (at Bridge St), Roxbury 607/326-7200 • gay/ straight • hip country motel • kids ok • wheelchair access • gay-owned • $80-200

The Wild Rose Inn 66 Rock City Rd, Woodstock 845/679-8783 • gay-friendly • luxurious Victorian B&B • kids ok • nonsmoking • lesbian-owned • $150-250

The Woodstock Inn on the Millstream 48 Tannery Brook Rd, Woodstock 845/679-8211, 800/420-4707 • gay-friendly • swimming hole • wheelchair access • $109-219

RESTAURANTS

Catskill Rose 5355 Rte 212, Mt Tremper 845/688-7100 • 5pm-close Th-Sun • some veggie • full bar • patio

ENTERTAINMENT & RECREATION

Frog Hollow Farm Old Post Rd, Esopus 845/384-6424 • riding school

Healing Waters Farms State Rte 206 (1 mile W of Walton, at Lower Third Brook Rd) **607/865-4420** • seasonal • carriage museum • petting zoo • shops • gay-owned

BOOKSTORES

Golden Notebook 29 Tinker St, Woodstock **845/679-8000** • 10:30am-7pm, till 6pm Sun (till 9pm summers) • LGBT section • wheelchair access

Cherry Creek

ACCOMMODATIONS

The Cherry Creek Inn 1022 West Rd (at Center Rd) **716/296-5105** • gay/straight • B&B • full breakfast • in wine & Amish country • kids ok • gay-owned • $85-150

Cooperstown

see Sharon Springs

Corning

ACCOMMODATIONS

Hillcrest Manor B&B 227 Cedar St (at Fourth St) **607/936-4548** • gay-friendly • elegant 1890 neo-classic mansion in quiet neighborhood • gay-owned • $135-165

Rufus Tanner House B&B 60 Sagetown Rd, Pine City **607/732-0213** • gay/straight • full brkfst • hot tub • nonsmoking • wheelchair access • $77-135

Cortland

BOOKSTORES

Mandolin Winds Bookstore 33 Main St (at Central) **607/758-3165** • 10am-5pm, till 7pm Th, till 4pm Sat, clsd Sun • LGBT section

Croton-on-Hudson

ACCOMMODATIONS

Alexander Hamilton House 49 Van Wyck St **914/271-6737, 888/414-2539** • gay/straight • full brkfst • swimming • nonsmoking • kids ok • woman-owned/run • $120-300

Elmira

BARS

Chill 501 Erie St **607/732-1414** • 5pm-1am, till 3am Fri-Sat • lesbians/gay men • neighborhood bar • dancing/DJ • food served • drag shows • gay-owned

NIGHTCLUBS

ANGLES Ultimate Dance Club 511-513 Railroad Ave (btwn Clinton & 3rd) **607/737-7676** • 5pm-close, clsd Tue • popular • lesbians/gay men • dancing/DJ • live shows • game room • also restaurant • gay-owned

Endwell

SPIRITUAL GROUPS

Gay Catholic Mass 1501 Davis Ave (at Christ the King Church) **607/797-3642** • 5pm 1st Sun, also ask about LGBT service in Binghamton

Findley Lake

ACCOMMODATIONS

Blue Heron Inn 10412 Main St (at Shadyside Rd) **716/769-7852** • gay-friendly • B&B • full brkfst • kids ok • nonsmoking • $99-135

Fire Island

see also Long Island

INFO LINES & SERVICES

AA Gay/Lesbian **631/669-1124** • 7:30pm Th & 8pm Sat

ACCOMMODATIONS

A Summer Place Realty Bayview Walk (at Main Walk), Cherry Grove **631/597-6140** • rentals, private homes & apts • also sales • lesbian & gay-owned

Bob Howard Real Estate The Pines **631/597-9400, 212/819-9400** • great source for rentals

Dune Point Guesthouse **631/597-6261** • lesbians/gay men • hot tub • kids/pets ok • wheelchair access • lesbian & gay & straight-owned/run • $125+

GroveHotel Dock Walk, Cherry Grove **631/597-6600** • mostly gay men • swimming • nudity • nonsmoking room available • wheelchair access • gay-owned • $40-500

Hotel Ciel The Pines **631/597-6500** • mostly gay men • swimming • also restaurant • wheelchair access

Island Properties Real Estate 37 Fire Island Blvd, The Pines **631/597-6900** • weekly, monthly & seasonal rentals • lesbian & gay-owned

BARS

Blue Whale Fire Island Blvd, The Pines **631/597-6500** • seasonal • lesbians/ gay men • popular • dancing/DJ • popular Low Tea dance • also restaurant • wheelchair access

Cherry's 158 Bayview Walk, Cherry Grove **631/597-6820** • seasonal • noon-4am • popular • lesbians/ gay men • piano bar • live shows • drag shows • also restaurant • patio

Sip n' Twirl 36 Fire Island Blvd, The Pines **631/597-3196** • seasonal • noon-4am • mostly gay men • dancing/DJ • also piano bar

Sunsets on the Bay 83 Bayview Walk, Cherry Grove **631/597-9663** • noon-4am • lesbians/ gay men • dancing/ DJ

The Tides 177 Ocean Walk, Cherry Grove **631/597-3744** • mostly gay men • dancing/ DJ • shows • cabaret • strippers

NIGHTCLUBS

Ice Palace Bayview Walk, Cherry Grove **631/597-6600** • hours vary • popular • lesbians/ gay men • dancing/DJ • drag shows • wheelchair access

The Pavilion Fire Island Blvd, The Pines **631/597-6500** • seasonal • noon-8am • lesbians/ gay men • popular • dancing/DJ • popular High Tea dance • wheelchair access

RESTAURANTS

Cherry Grove Pizza Dock Walk (under the GroveHotel), Cherry Grove **631/597-6766** • 11am-11pm, till 1am Fri-Sat

Jumpin' Jack's Seafood Shack Ocean Walk, Cherry Grove **631/597-4174** • lunch & dinner • also piano bar

Marina Meat Market Harbor Park, The Pines **631/597-6588** • brkfst, lunch & dinner, all day take-out available

Sapin 36 Fire Island Blvd, The Pines **631/597-8888** • dinner only • upscale French

ENTERTAINMENT & RECREATION

Invasion of the Pines the Pines dock (July 4th wknd) • come & enjoy the annual fun as boatloads of drag queens from Cherry Grove arrive to terrorize the posh Pines

PUBLICATIONS

Island Scene 212/941-6701 • seasonal glossy mag w/ all you need to know about Fire Island

Geneva

ACCOMMODATIONS

Belhurst Rte 14 S (near Snell Rd) **315/781-0201** • gay-friendly • in historic castle overlooking Seneca Lake • fireplaces • also restaurant • $65-315

Glens Falls

ACCOMMODATIONS

Glens Falls Inn 25 Sherman Ave **518/743-9365, 800/208-9058** • gay-friendly • B&B in Victorian • full brkfst • woman-owned • $115-175

Hamptons

see Long Island—Suffolk/ Hamptons

Hudson Valley

Hudson Valley includes Catskill, Highland, Hudson, Hyde Park, Kingston, New Paltz, Poughkeepsie, Rhinebeck

ACCOMMODATIONS

The Country Squire B&B 251 Allen St (at 3rd), Hudson **518/822-9229** • kids ok • $125-195

Hudson City B&B 326 Allen St (at Rte 9-G/ 3rd St), Hudson **518/822-8044** • gay/ straight • 18th-c Victorian in antique district • hot tub • kids/small pets ok • gay-owned • $100-199

Inn at Applewood & The Would Restaurant 120 North Rd, Highland **845/691-2516** • gay/ straight • full brkfst • nonsmoking • also restaurant (wheelchair access) • lesbian-owned • $95

Lefevre House B&B 14 Southside Ave, New Paltz **845/255-4747** • gay/ straight • full brkfst • hot tub • kids ok • close to outdoor activities • gay-owned • $150-200

Roselawn 113 Roselawn, Highland **845/928-1440** • gay-friendly • 200-yr-old estate & mini-resort • full brkfst • swimming • hot tub • nonsmoking • $150-550 (rooms)/ $2,000-3,000 (estate)

St Charles Hotel 16–18 Park Pl, Hudson **518/822-9900** • gay-friendly • kids/ pets ok • also 2 restaurants

Van Schaack House 20 Broad St (at Albany Rd), Kinderhook **518/758-6118** • gay-friendly • B&B • full brkfst • nonsmoking • gay-owned • $120-185

BARS

Congress 411 Main St (off Academy), Poughkeepsie 845/486-9068 • 3pm-4am, from 7:30pm Sun • lesbians/ gay men • neighborhood bar • wheelchair access

Doolittle's Pub 49 S Partition St (at West Bridge), Saugerties 845/246-7682 • 4pm-midnight, till 2am Fri-Sat, clsd Sun • gay-friendly • neighborhood bar • alternative • country western • 18+ • live shows • food served • gay-owned

Griff's 47 Raymond Ave, Poughkeepsie 845/471-8913 • 7pm-2am, till 4am wknds • lesbians/ gay men • neighborhood bar • dancing/ DJ

NIGHTCLUBS

Prime Time Rte 9 W, Highland 845/691-8550 • 9:30pm-4am Th-Sat • mostly gay men • theme parties • dancing/DJ • male strippers • X-rated bingo • 18+

RESTAURANTS

Armadillo Bar & Grill 97 Abeel St, Kingston 845/339-1550 • lunch wknds, dinner Tue-Sat, clsd Mon • Southwestern • full bar • patio

Northern Spy Cafe Rte 213, High Falls 845/687-7298 • dinner nightly, Sun brunch • plenty veggie • full bar • wheelchair access

Ristorante Locust Tree 215 Hugenot St (behind conference center), New Paltz 845/255-7888 • lunch & dinner, clsd Tue • Euro-Italian • full bar • patio

Terrapin Rte 9, Rhinebeck 845/876-3330 • restaurant, bistro & bar

The Would Restaurant 120 North Rd (off Rte 9 W), Highland 845/691-9883 • dinner nightly • some veggie • full bar • patio • gay-owned • $16-22

PUBLICATIONS

▲ **InsideOUT** PO Box 908, New Paltz 12561 845/255-6500 • LGBT newsmagazine for Hudson Valley

Ithaca

INFO LINES & SERVICES

AA Gay/ Lesbian First Baptist Church (at Dewitt Park) 607/273-1541 • call for info

ACCOMMODATIONS

Frog Haven Women's B&B 578 W King Rd (off Rte 96B S) 607/272-3238 • women-only • in contemporary log-sided home • swimmable pond • kids ok • nonsmoking • lesbian-owned • $70-86

BARS

Common Ground 1230 Danby Rd/ Rte 96-B (at Comfort) 607/273-1505 • 4pm-1am, clsd Mon • popular • lesbians/ gay men • dancing/DJ • multiracial • live music Fri • also restaurant 5pm-8pm Wed-Sat & Sun brunch • some veggie • wheelchair access

Felicia's Atomic Lounge 508 W State St (Meadow St) 607/273-2219 • 4pm-1am • clsd Mon • gay-friendly • food served • live entertainment • piano bar • lesbian-owned

RESTAURANTS

ABC Cafe 308 Stewart Ave (at Buffalo) 607/277-4770 • brkfst, lunch & dinner, wknd brunch, clsd Mon • beer/ wine • vegetarian

ENTERTAINMENT & RECREATION

Out Loud Chorus 607/592-2003

BOOKSTORES

Colophon Books Inc 205 N Aurora St 607/277-5608 • 11am-8pm, till 7pm Tue, clsd Sun-Mon • independent alternative • LGBT section • wheelchair access

Jamestown

ACCOMMODATIONS

Fairmount Motel 138 W Fairmount (Rte 394) 716/763-9550 • gay-friendly • motel 10 minutes from Chautauqua Institution • kids ok • gay-owned • $40-70

BARS

Sneakers 100 Harrison (at Institute) 716/484-8816 • 2pm-2am, clsd Tue • lesbians/ gay men • dancing/DJ Fri-Sat • wheelchair access

ENTERTAINMENT & RECREATION

The Lucy-Desi Museum 212 Pine St 716/484-0800 • for those who love Lucy

LONG ISLAND

Long Island is divided into 2 geographical areas:
Long Island—Nassau County
Long Island—Suffolk County
see also Fire Island

Long Island — Nassau

INFO LINES & SERVICES

Gay/ Lesbian Switchboard of Long Island (GLSB of LI) 631/665-3700 • seasonal • 7pm-10pm weekdays only

Bars

Simple Pleasures 706 Main St, Farmingdale **516/249-6977** • 6pm-close • lesbians/gay men • neighborhood bar

Nightclubs

Deluxe 2686 Hempstead Tpke (at Club 2686), Levittown **516/520-1332** • 9pm-4am Wed only • lesbians/gay men • dancing/DJ

Luna Lounge 247 Jericho Tpke, New Hyde Park **516/488-1531** • open Wed-Sun • lesbians/gay men • more women Sat • dancing/DJ

Restaurants

RS Jones 153 Merrick Ave (off Sunrise), Merrick **516/378-7177** • dinner, clsd Mon • Tex-Mex • women-owned/run

Entertainment & Recreation

Pride for Youth Coffeehouse 2050 Bellmore Ave, Bellmore **516/679-9000** • 7:30pm-11:30pm Fri • ages 13-20 • live music

Publications

Outlook Long Island 631/968-7780 x1

PM Entertainment Magazine 516/845-0759 • events, listings, classifieds & more for Long Island, NJ & NYC

Spiritual Groups

Dignity Nassau at Church of the Advent, Westbury **516/781-6225** • 8pm 2nd Sat

Long Island—Suffolk/ Hamptons

Info Lines & Services

Gay/Lesbian Switchboard of Long Island (GLSB of LI) 631/665-3700 • 7pm-10pm weekdays only

LIGALY (Long Island Gay & Lesbian Youth) 34 Park Ave, Bay Shore **631/665-2300** • LGBT youth organization w/center • also Club LIGALY 9pm-1am Fri • substance-free youth nightclub

Accommodations

By the Sea 631/725-4952 • women only • swimming • nonsmoking • pets ok • $135-175

The Country Place 29 Hands Creek Rd, East Hampton **631/324-4125** • gay/straight • B&B on 3 acres w/pond • private entrances • nonsmoking • minutes to beach • $170-195

Cozy Cottages 395 Montauk Hwy, East Hampton **631/537-1160** • gay/straight • hot tub • pets ok • $89-350

East Hampton Village B&B 172 Newtown Ln (at McGuirk St), East Hampton **631/324-1858** • gay/straight • lovely turn-of-the-century home • nonsmoking

EconoLodge—Bay Shore 501 E Main St (at Saxon Ave), Bay Shore **631/666-6000, 800/553-2666** • gay/straight • comfortable budget motel • in-town, on Long Island's South Shore • close to beaches & ferries to Fire Island • $89-179

EconoLodge—MacArthur Airport 3055 Rte 454, Ronkonkoma **631/588-6800, 800/553-2666** • gay-friendly • budget motel • nonsmoking rooms available • wheelchair access • $86-175

EconoLodge—Smithtown/Hauppauge 755 Rte 347 (at Terry Rd), Smithtown **631/724-9000, 800/553-2666** • gay-friendly • centrally located • 12 miles from Fire Island • $88-114

Hampton Resorts & Hospitality 1655 Country Rd 39, Southampton **631/283-6100** • gay-friendly • boutique hotels • swimming • jacuzzi • kids/pets ok • wheelchair access • $120-550

Stirling House B&B 104 Bay Ave, Greenport **631/477-0654, 800/551-0654** • gay-friendly • full brkfst • jacuzzi • nonsmoking • gay-owned • $150-265

Sunset Beach 35 Shore Rd, Shelter Island **631/749-2001** • gay-friendly • seasonal • food served • $195-425

Bars

Club 608 608 Sunrise Hwy (at Belmont Ave), West Babylon **631/661-9580** • 8pm-4am • neighborhood bar • lesbians/gay men

One More Shot 841 N Broome Ave, Lindenhurst **631/226-6690** • 8pm-close, from 4pm Sun, clsd Mon • lesbians/gay men • neighborhood bar • dancing/DJ

Nightclubs

Bunkhouse 192 N Main St/Montauk Hwy (at Foster Ave), Sayville **631/567-2865** • 7pm-4am • popular • mostly gay men • dancing/DJ • karaoke • live shows • wheelchair access • gay-owned

Shi Bar 121 Woodfield Rd, West Hempstead **516/481-6438** • 8pm-4am, clsd Sun-Mon • popular • mostly women • dancing/DJ Fri • live shows Sat • wheelchair access

Restaurants

Babette's 66 Newtown Ln, East Hampton **631/329-5377** • brkfst, lunch & dinner • healthy • plenty veggie • woman-owned/run

ENTERTAINMENT & RECREATION

Fowler Beach Southampton

PUBLICATIONS

Outlook Long Island 631/968–7780 x1

PM Entertainment Magazine
516/845–0759 • events, listings, classifieds &
more for Long Island, NJ & NYC

SPIRITUAL GROUPS

Unitarian Universalist Fellowship
109 Browns Rd, Huntington 631/427–9547 •
10:30am

Montgomery

ACCOMMODATIONS

The Borland House B&B 130 Clinton St
845/457–1513 • gay-friendly • $85-185

Mt Morris

BARS

Fred's Tavern 36 Main St (at State)
585/658–3267 • noon-2am • gay/ straight •
neighborhood bar

NEW YORK CITY

New York City is divided into 8
geographical areas:
NYC—Overview
NYC—Soho, Greenwich & Chelsea
NYC—Midtown
NYC—Uptown
NYC—Brooklyn
NYC—Queens
NYC—Bronx
NYC—Staten Island

NYC—Overview

INFO LINES & SERVICES

AA Gay/ Lesbian Intergroup at Lesbian/
Gay Community Center 212/647–1680

Gay & Lesbian National Hotline
212/989–0099 • 4pm-8pm Mon-Fri, noon-
5pm Sat

Lesbian Herstory Archives 718/768–3953
• exists to gather & preserve records of lesbian
lives & activities • located in Park Slope,
Brooklyn • wheelchair access

LGBT Community Center 208 W 13th (at
7th Ave) 212/620–7310 • 9am-11pm •
popular • many group meetings & resources •
museum • wheelchair access

ACCOMMODATIONS

Manhattan Getaways 212/956–2010 • gay/
straight • B&B rooms & private apts
throughout Manhattan • kids over 10 years old
ok • woman-owned

NIGHTCLUBS

Kurfew • roving dance club for young
LGBTq's • 18+ • check listings

ENTERTAINMENT & RECREATION

**Before Stonewall: A Lesbian & Gay
History Tour** meet: Washington Square Arch
(at Big Onion Walking Tours) 212/439–1090 •
$10-15

Dyke TV 718/230–4770 • "only nat'l TV
show by & for lesbians" • also video
workshops

New York Liberty Madison Square Garden,
New York 212/465–6073 • check out the
Women's National Basketball Association
while you're in New York

Townhouse Tours 347/693–1484 • walking
tours of New York's gay history

PUBLICATIONS

Gay City News 646/452–2500 • LGBT
newspaper • weekly

GO NYC 888/466–9244 • "cultural road map
for the city girl" • listings, features,
entertainment, style, fitness & more

HX Magazine 212/352–3535 • complete
weekly guide to gay New York at night

New York Blade News 212/268–2701 •
weekly LGBT newspaper

Next 212/627–0165 • party paper

PM Entertainment Magazine
516/845–0759 • events, listings, classifieds &
more for Long Island, NJ & NYC

She's Out All Night E-zine 347/528–3663 •
online nightlife & event guide for lesbians
featuring an e-zine, video personal ads & chat
rooms

Swirl Magazine 678/886–0711 (ATLANTA #)
magazine for "the African American lesbian,
bisexual, bi-curious & 'straight but not narrow'
community"

Velvetpark Magazine 347/881–1025,
888/616–1989 • quarterly lesbian/ feminist
glossy w/ focus on the arts

SPIRITUAL GROUPS

**Buddhist Lesbians/ Gays: Diamond
Metta** at Lesbian/ Gay Community Center
212/803–5192 • 6pm 2nd Tue • silent
meditation • speaker

New York City

WHERE THE GIRLS ARE:
Upwardly mobile literary types hang in the West Village, hipster dykes cruise the East Village, upper-crusty lesbians have cocktails in Midtown, and working-class dykes live in Brooklyn.

LGBT PRIDE:
Last Sunday in June. 212/807-7433, web: www.hopinc.org.
Black Pride - June. 718/338-7557, web: www.blackpridenyc.com
Bronx Pride - June. bxpride@aol.com.
Brooklyn Pride - June. 718/670-3337.

ANNUAL EVENTS:
March - Saint-at-Large Black Party.
May - AIDS Walk 212/807-9255, web: www.aidswalk.net/newyork.
June - New York Int'l Gay/Lesbian Film Festival 212/571–2170, web: www.newfestival.org.
September - Wigstock. Outrageous wig/drag/performance festival in Tompkins Square Park in the East Village.
November - New York Lesbian/Gay Experimental Film/Video Fest 212/742–8880, web: www.mixnyc.org. Film, videos, installations & media performances.

CITY INFO:
212/397-8222.
nycvisit.com

BEST VIEW:
Coming over any of the bridges into New York or from the Empire State Building.

WEATHER:
A spectrum of extremes with pleasant moments thrown in. Spring and fall are the best times to visit.

TRANSIT:
Wave an arm on any streetcorner for a taxi.
Public transit MTA 718/330-1234, web: www.mta.nyc.ny.us.

ATTRACTIONS:
Broadway.
Carnegie Hall 212/903-9600, web: www.carnegiehall.org.
Central Park.
Ellis Island, web: www.ellisisland.org.
Empire State Building 212/736-3100, web: www.esbnyc.com.
Greenwich Village.
Guggenheim Museum 212/423-3500, web: www.guggenheim.org.
Lincoln Center 212/875-5456, web: www.lincolncenter.org.
Metropolitan Museum of Art 212/535-7710, web: www.metmuseum.org.
Museum of Modern Art 212/708-9400, web: www.moma.org.
Radio City Music Hall 212/247-4777, web: www.radiocity.com.
Rockefeller Center.
Statue of Liberty 866/782-8834.
Times Square.
United Nations 212/963-4475, web: www.un.org.
Wall Street.
World Trade Center Memorial.

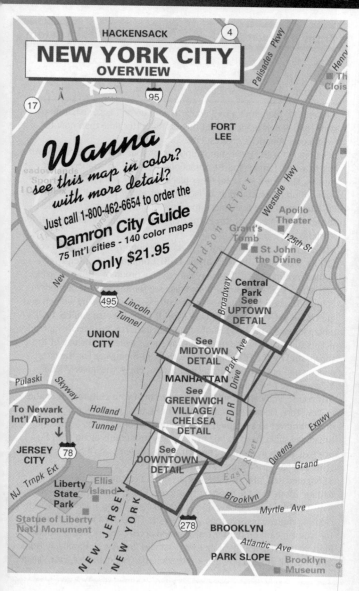

NEW YORK CITY
OVERVIEW

HACKENSACK

4

17

95

FORT LEE

Palisades Pkwy

Henry

The Clois

Hudson River

Westside Hwy

Apollo Theater

125th St

Grant's Tomb

St John the Divine

Wanna see this map in color? with more detail?

Just call 1-800-462-6654 to order the

Damron City Guide

75 Int'l cities - 140 color maps

Only $21.95

Meadowlands Sport 1

New

495

Lincoln Tunnel

Broadway

Central Park
See
UPTOWN
DETAIL

UNION CITY

See
MIDTOWN
DETAIL

Park Ave

Drive

Pulaski

Skyway

Holland Tunnel

MANHATTAN
See
GREENWICH
VILLAGE/
CHELSEA
DETAIL

FDR

Expwy

To Newark Int'l Airport
↓

JERSEY CITY

78

See
DOWNTOWN
DETAIL

Queens

Grand

NJ Trnpk Ext

Liberty State Park

Ellis Island

East River

Statue of Liberty Nat'l Monument

NEW JERSEY

NEW YORK

278

Brooklyn

Myrtle Ave

BROOKLYN

Atlantic Ave

PARK SLOPE

Brooklyn Museum

Reply **Forward** **Delete**

Date: Nov 7, 2005 12:26:42
From: Girl-on-the-Go
To: Editor@Damron.com
Subject: New York City

>After 9/11, there isn't a soul on earth who doesn't know what heroic stuff New York is made of. And there is no better time than now to (re)discover America's greatest city.

>Get ready for the most stimulating trip of your life! You've come to *the* city of world-famous tourist attractions: from the skyscrapers to the subway, New York is like no other place. Whether you pride yourself on your cultural sophistication, or lack thereof, you're going to find endless entertainment. There are plays, musicals, operas, museums and gallery shows, performance art, street theater, and street life...and that's just for starters.

>To get the most out of your visit, do your homework before you come. Call for a calendar of events at the **LGBT Community Center,** which houses meeting spaces for every conceivable group of LGBT+ people.

>New York's performance art is a must-see for any student of modern culture. The best bets for intelligent, cutting-edge shows by women and queers are **WOW (Women's One World) Cafe Theatre** and **PS 122,** where lesbian artist Holly Hughes got her start. For "two-fers"—half-price tickets to Broadway and off-Broadway shows available the day of the show—stop by the TKTS booth on 47th St. at Broadway. For the latest reviews and hot off-off-Broadway theaters, check the queer-friendly *Village Voice* newspaper.

>Of course, you can stimulate a lot more than your cultural sensibilities in New York. Gourmands cans experience oral orgasms ranging from a delicate quiver to a blinding throb every day. For instance, before that Broadway show, head to one of the many restaurants along 46th St. at 9th Ave. When in Brooklyn, brunch along 7th Ave.; you'll find plenty of LGBT company on a Sunday morning.

>Shopping, too, affords shivers of delight. Check out the fabulous vintage shops and the designer boutiques. Cruise Midtown on Madison Ave., E. 57th St., or 5th Ave. in the 50s, or tour Trump Tower and touch clothing more expensive than your last car. Other recommended districts for blowing cash on hipster fashions and accessories include St. Mark's Place in the Village (8th St. between 1st and 2nd Aves.); Broadway from 8th to Canal St.; and any major intersection in Soho and the East Village.

| Reply | Forward | | Delete |

>To titillate your mind, peruse the shelves at **Bluestockings** or **Oscar Wilde Memorial Bookshop**, or make an appointment to stop by the **Lesbian Herstory Archives** in Brooklyn. If you're in the mood for love, check out the wares at **Toys in Babeland**.

>You could spend days at the big art museums in Uptown near Central Park, but budget some time for the galleries in SoHo (south of Houston—pronounced How-ston, not like the city in Texas—between Broadway and 6th Ave.). Pick up a gallery map in the area.

>For musical entertainment, make your pilgrimage to the Kitchen, legendary site of experimental and freestyle jazz, or CBGB's, legendary home of noisy music (the Ramones started American punk here in 1974).

>Nightlife...we know you've been holding your breath! **Henrietta Hudson's** happens seven days a week, and **Girls Room** is a new alternative on the Lower East Side. **Shescape** & **LoverGirl NYC** produce women's club nights at various locations, so call for their latest events. You can get your groove on at one of the nightly events produced by Half N Half Productions (www.halfnhalfproductions.com), and no one should miss the Drag King scene in this gender-bending city. **Starlet** still shines Sunday nights at Starlight bar, and you can get your freak on with the boys and girls and everyone in between at Krash's mixed **Freaky Fridays** party.

>New York is home to plenty of one-nighters, so be sure to pick up a copy of **Go NYC** or **HX** or **Next** for up-to-the-minute club happenings. Also check out the online lesbian nightlife guide **www.shesoutallnight.com.**

>If this isn't enough excitement, experience the City in June when New York hosts numerous LGBT Pride–related cultural events, from their week-long Film Festival to the Pride March itself.

>One last bit of advice: there's more to New York City than Manhattan. Brooklyn has long been home to lesbians escaping the extortionist rents of Manhattan. To taste dyke life in this borough, stop by the **Metropolitan** or **Cattyshack**. If you'll be out on Long Island, stop by **Shi**.

Church of St Luke in the Fields (Episcopal) 487 Hudson St (at Christopher) 212/924-0562

Congregation Beth Simchat Torah 296 9th Ave (at 28th St) 212/929-9498 • 8:30pm Fri • LGBT synagogue • wheelchair access • also 57 Bethune St location • call for other meeting times

Dignity 218 W 11th St (at Waverly Pl, at St John's) 212/627-6488 • 7:30pm Sun

Integrity NYC 212/691-7181

MCC of New York 446 W 36th St (btwn 9th & 10th) 212/629-7440 • 10am & 7pm Sun

Society of Friends (Quakers) 120th St (at Riverside Church, btwn Riverside Dr & Claremont) 212/777-8866 • 11am Sun • also 15 Rutherford Pl

NYC—Soho, Greenwich & Chelsea

ACCOMMODATIONS

Abingdon Guesthouse 13 8th Ave (at W 12th St) 212/243-5384 • gay/ straight • quiet, mature clientele • nonsmoking • wheelchair access • $159-239

The Bank St B&B 92 Bank St (at Hudson) 212/645-4611 • mostly women • 1837 brownstone in West Village • roofdeck • lesbian-owned • $100-135

Chelsea Inn 46 W 17th St (btwn 5th & 6th Aves) 212/645-8989, 800/640-6469 • gay-friendly •European-style inn • $99-259

Chelsea Pines Inn 317 W 14th St (btwn 8th & 9th Aves) 212/929-1023, 888/546-2700 • mostly gay men • some shared baths • gay-owned • $109-169

The Chelsea Savoy Hotel 204 W 23rd St (at 7th Ave) 212/929-9353, 866/929-9353 • gay/ straight • wheelchair access • kids ok • $99-235

East Village B&B 244 E 7th St 212/260-1865 • mostly women • in the heart of the Village • nonsmoking • lesbian & gay & straight-owned • $75-100

Greenwich Village Home 877/878-2263 • lesbians/ gay men • B&B in private townhouse • kids ok • lesbian-owned • $165

Holiday Inn Downtown 138 Lafayette St (btwn Canal & Howard, in Chinatown) 212/966-8898 • gay-friendly • located at the crossroads of SoHo, Chinatown & Little Italy • convenient to subway, shopping & restaurants • $159-239

Hotel 17 225 E 17th St 212/475–2845 • gay-friendly • "East Village chic" budget hotel • shared baths • $100+

Hotel Washington Square 103 Waverly Pl (at MacDougal St) 212/777–9515, 800/222–0418 • gay-friendly • renovated 100-yr-old hotel • also North Square restaurant • $150+

Incentra Village House 32 8th Ave (at W 12th St) 212/206–0007 • lesbians/ gay men • nonsmoking • gay-owned • $119-259

Soho Grand Hotel 310 W Broadway (at Canal St) 212/965–3000, 800/965–3000 • gay-friendly • big, glossy, over-the-top hotel • wheelchair access • $374+

Southern Comforts 310/305–2984, 800/889–7359 • reservation service for several deluxe rental properties • gay-owned

Tribeca Grand 2 Avenue of the Americas 212/519–6500, 800/965–3000 • gay/ straight • $259+

W New York—Union Square 201 Park Ave S 212/253–9119, 877/WHOTELS (RESERVATIONS ONLY) • gay/ straight • also restaurant & bar • wheelchair access • $249-569

BARS

Barracuda 275 W 22nd St (at 8th Ave) 212/645–8613 • 4pm-4am • popular • mostly gay men • live DJs • drag shows

The Boiler Room 86 E 4th St (at 2nd Ave) 212/254–7536 • 4pm-4am • popular • mostly gay men • neighborhood bar

Boots & Saddle 76 Christopher St (at 7th Ave S) 212/929–9684 • noon-4am • mostly gay men • neighborhood bar

Clubhouse 700 E 9th St (at Ave C) 212/260–7970 • 6pm-4am • lesbians/ gay men • women's night Th • live DJs • lounge-y

Cubbyhole 281 W 12th St (at 4th St) 212/243–9041 • 4pm-4am, from 2pm wknds • lesbians/ gay men • neighborhood bar

The Dugout 185 Christopher St (at Weehawken St) 212/242–9113 • 4pm-2am, from 1pm Sun • mostly gay men • neighborhood bar • sports bar • wheelchair access

G Lounge 225 W 19th St (at 7th Ave) 212/929–1085 • 4pm-4am • popular • mostly gay men • lounge • live DJs • juice bar

Girls Room 210 Rivington (btwn Ridge & Pitt) 212/677–6149 • 7pm-close, clsd Sun-Mon • mostly women • theme nights

Gym Sportsbar 167 8th Ave (btwn 18th & 19th) • mostly gay men • neighborhood sports bar

Henrietta Hudson 438 Hudson (at Morton) 212/924–3347 • 4pm-4am, from 1pm wknds • mostly women • neighborhood bar • dancing/DJ • wheelchair access

The Hole 29 2nd Ave (at 2nd St) 212/473–9406 • 10pm-4am Th-Sat • lesbians/ gay men • dancing/ DJ

Luke & Leroy 21 7th Ave S (at Leroy) 212/929–8356 • gay/ straight • also restaurant

Marie's Crisis 59 Grove St (at 7th Ave) 212/243–9323 • 4pm-4am • lesbians/ gay men • piano bar from 9:30pm, from 5pm Fri-Sun

The Monster 80 Grove St (at W 4th St, Sheridan Square) 212/924–3558 • 4pm-4am, from 2pm wknds • popular • mostly gay men • dancing/DJ • piano bar & cabaret • Sabor Latino Mon • disco Tue • T-dance Sun • wheelchair access

Nowhere 322 E 14th St (btwn 1st & 2nd) 212/477–4744 • 3pm-4am • lesbians/ gay men • women's night Mon • neighborhood bar

Phoenix 447 E 13th (at Ave A) 212/477–9979 • 4pm-4am • lesbians/ gay men • neighborhood bar • patio

Rubyfruit Bar & Grill 531 Hudson St (at Charles St) 212/929–3343 • 3pm-2am, till 4am Fri-Sat • mostly women • full menu served 5pm-11pm, till midnight Fri-Sat, Sun brunch • live shows • bingo Tue

Sexy & Sophisticated 49 Grove St (btwn 7th Ave & Bleecker) 917/744–1270 • 7pm Fri only • mostly women

Starlight Bar & Lounge 167 Ave A (at 11th St) 212/475–2172 • 7pm-3am, till 4am Fri-Sun • lesbians/ gay men • more women Sun for Starlette • live DJs • live shows

Stonewall Inn 53 Christopher St (at 7th Ave) 212/463–0950 • 3pm-4am • mostly gay men • 4 bars • dancing/DJ • piano bar • martini bar

NIGHTCLUBS

Beige 40 E 4th St (at Bowery, at B-Bar) 212/475–2220 • 11pm Tue only • gay/ straight • swank lounge

Big Apple Ranch 39 W 19th St, 5th flr (btwn 5th & 6th, at Dance Manhattan) 212/358–5752 • 8pm-1am Sat only • lesbians/ gay men • dancing/DJ • country/ western • two-step lessons • beer only • cover charge

Caution Wednesdays 205 Chrystie St (at Stanton, at 6s & 8s) 212/477-6688 • 9pm Wed only • mostly women • dancing/ DJ

Detention 53 Christopher St (at 7th Ave, at Stonewall Inn) 212/463-0950 • Th only • mostly gay men • dancing/DJ • 18+

G's Spot/ Uninhibited Thursday's @ 2i's 248 W 14th St (btwn 7th & 8th Ave) 917/541-7176 • 8pm-3am Th only • mostly women • dancing/DJ • food served • multiracial

Heaven 579 6th Ave (off 16th St) 212/539-3982, 212/243-6100 • 5pm-4am Tue-Wed & Fri-Sun • mostly women Tue, Wed & Fri • dancing/DJ • multiracial • go-go girls • Latin night Wed • Fri Kaleidoscope (25+) • Gay College Party Sat (mostly gay men,18+) • lesbian-owned

Krash/ Freaky Friday 16 W 22nd St (btwn 5th & 6th, at Deep) 718/937-2400 • popular Fri party • lesbians/ gay men • dancing/ DJ • multiracial crowd

Noche Latina 579 6th Ave (off 16th St, at Heaven) 212/539-3982, 212/243-6100 • 5pm-4am Wed (18+ after 11pm) • mostly women • dancing/DJ • multiracial • go-go girls • "NYC's #1 Latina party" • lesbian-owned

Persuasion Mondays 68 W 3rd St (btwn Thompson & La Guardia, at Fuelray Lounge) 866/841-9139 x2307 • 8pm-2am Mon only • mostly women • dancing/ DJ • multiracial

Pyramid 101 Ave A (at 7th St) 212/473-7184 • lesbians/ gay men • 10pm-4am Fri for 1984 ('80s)

Roxy 515 W 18th St (at 10th Ave) 212/645-5156 • 11pm-5am Fri-Sat (rollerdisco from 8pm Wed) • popular • gay/ straight • gay Sat • dancing/DJ • alternative • live shows • cover charge

Sea Tea leaves from Pier 40 (at Christopher St) 212/675-4357 • 6pm-10pm Sun (June-Oct) • mostly gay men • dancing/DJ • professional • multiracial • buffet • live shows • gay-owned • cover

Shescape 212/686-5665 • women only • dance parties held at various locations throughout NYC area

Snapshot 9 Ave A (at Houston, at Boys Room) 212/358-1440 • Tue only • lesbians/ gay men • dancing/ DJ

CAFES

Big Cup 228 8th Ave (at 22nd St) 212/206-0059 • 7am-2am • popular • gay boy central

Brown Cup Cafe 334 8th Ave 212/675-7765 • 7am-8pm, from 8am Sat, clsd Sun

Caffe Raffaella 134 7th Ave S (at Charles St) 212/929-7247 • 11am-2am • armchair cafe

Factory Cafe 104 Christopher St 212/807-6900 • open till midnight

RESTAURANTS

7A 109 Ave A (at 7th St) 212/673-6583 • 24hrs • popular • American

Agave 140 Seventh Ave (btwn 10th St & Charles) 212/989-2100 • 11:30am-close • popular brunch • Southwestern

Angelica Kitchen 300 E. 12th St (at 1st Ave) 212/228-2909 • lunch & dinner • vegetarian/ vegan

Around the Clock 8 3rd Ave (at 9th St) 212/598-0402 • 8am-3am, 24hrs wknds

Benny's Burritos 93 Ave A (at 6th St) 212/254-2054 • 11:30am-midnight, bar till 2am • cheap & huge • also 113 Greenwich (at Jane) 212/727-0584

Better Burger 178 Eighth Ave (at 19th St) 212/989-6688 • 11am-midnight, till 1am Fri-Sun • burgers, hot dogs, salads & more • some plenty veggie

Blue Ribbon 97 Sullivan St (at Spring St) 212/274-0404 • 4pm-4am • chef hangout • wheelchair access

Bone Lick Park 75 Greenwich Ave (at 7th Ave) 212/647-9600 • 11:30am-11pm • gay-friendly • real pit BBQ • wheelchair access • gay-owned

Brunetta's 190 1st Ave (btwn 11th & 12th Sts) 212/228-4030 • popular • lesbians/ gay men • Italian • some veggie • patio

Chelsea Bistro & Bar 358 W 23rd St (at 9th Ave) 212/727-2026 • lunch & dinner • trendy French • full bar

The Chick Inn 420 Hudson St (at Leroy) 212/675-0810 • lunch & dinner • full bar • also juice bar • sidewalk cafe

Cola's 148 8th Ave (at 17th St) 212/633-8020 • lunch & dinner • popular • Italian • some veggie

Counter 105 1st Ave (at 7th St) 212/982-5870 • 5pm-midnight, from 11am wknds • vegan • '50s retro • organic beer/ wine • lesbian-owned

Cowgirl Hall of Fame 519 Hudson St (at W 10th) 212/633-1133 • lunch, dinner, wknd brunch

Deborah Stanton 43 Carmine St (near Beford St) 212/242-2606 • 11am-11pm, clsd Mon • lesbians/ gay men

East of Eighth 254 W 23rd St (at 8th) 212/352-0075 • lunch, dinner till midnight, till 2am wknds

Elmo 156 7th Ave (at 20th St) 212/337-8000 • lunch & dinner, also lounge

Empire Diner 210 10th Ave (at 22nd St) 212/243-2736 • 24hrs

Florent 69 Gansevoort St (at Washington) 212/989-5779 • 24hrs • popular • French diner

Food Bar 149 8th Ave (at 17th St) 212/243-2020 • 11am-midnight • Mediterranean

Garage 99 7th Ave S (at Grove St) 212/645-0600 • lunch Mon-Fri, dinner Th-Sun, brunch wknds • contemporary American • plenty veggie • live jazz

Gobo 401 Ave of the Americas 212/255-3242 • vegetarian/ vegan

Gonzo 140 W 13th St (btwn 6th & 7th Aves) 212/645-4606 • publisher's choice • 5:30pm-11pm • great Tuscan menu, over 60 wines by the glass • full bar

I Coppi 432 E 9th St (at 1st Ave) 212/254-2263 • 5pm-11pm, 11am-3pm Sat-Sun

Kate's Joint 58 Ave B (at 4th St) 212/777-7059 • from 11am (10am Sat-Sun) • supercool vegetarian

LaVagna 545 E 5th St (btwn Aves A & B) 212/979-1005 • dinner only • Italian • some veggie

Life Cafe 343 E 10th St (at Ave B) 212/477-8791 • 10am-1am, till 3am Fri-Sat • full bar • vegetarian • artist hangout

Lips 2 Bank St (at Greenwich) 212/675-7710 • 6pm-midnight, till 3am Sat, Disco Fever Brunch noon-6pm Sun • "the Hard Rock Cafe of drag" • Italian/ American served by queens

Lucky Cheng's 24 1st Ave (at 2nd St) 212/473-0516 • 5:30pm-midnight • popular • Asian/ fusion • full bar • drag shows • karaoke

Marco 142 W 10th St (at Greenwich Ave) 212/243-2222 • dinner Mon-Sat, Sun brunch • Italian • live jazz

Marion's Continental 354 Bowery St (btwn E 3rd & E 4th Sts) 212/475-7621 • 6pm-11pm, bar till 2am • also monthly Fashion Brunch

Med Cafe 99 2nd Ave (at 5th St) 212/477-8427 • 5pm-midnight • int'l tapas • full bar

Miracle Grill 112 1st Ave (at 6th St) 212/254-2353 • dinner, brunch • Southwestern • full bar • garden dining

O Mai 158 9th Ave (at 19th St) 212/633-0550 • dinner nightly • Vietnamese

The Pink Tea Cup 42 Grove St (btwn Bleecker & Bedford) 212/807-6755 • 8am-midnight, till 1am Fri-Sun, Southern homestyle

Sacred Chow 522 Hudson St (at W 10th St) 212/337-0863 • 7:30am-11pm • gourmet vegan • juice & smoothie bar • baked goods • wheelchair access

Sapa 43 W 24th St (btwn 6th Ave & Broadway) 212/929-1800 • lunch & dinner, Sun brunch • French/ Vietnamese

Sazerac House Bar & Grill 533 Hudson (at Charles) 212/989-0313 • lunch & dinner • Cajun • full bar

Stonewall Bistro 113 7th Ave S (at Christopher) 917/661-1335 • 5pm-11pm, Sun brunch from 11am • lesbians/ gay men • full bar • dancing/DJ • piano bar

Trattoria Pesce Pasta 262 Bleecker St (at 6th Ave) 212/645-2993 • noon-midnight

Tribeca Grill 375 Greenwich St (btwn N Moore & Franklin) 212/941-3900 • popular • chic neighborhood restaurant co-owned by Robert DeNiro • full bar • extensive wine list • reservations recommended

The Viceroy 160 8th Ave (at 18th St) 212/633-8484 • 11am-midnight • popular • fusion • full bar

Waikiki Wally's 101 E 2nd St (at 1st Ave) 212/673-8908 • 6pm-10pm, till 11pm Fri-Sat, tiki bar open later • new Polynesian • fun island atmosphere • live shows

ENTERTAINMENT & RECREATION

DrédKing Drag King/ Gender-Illusionist 212/946-4475 • one of the best known Drag Kings since 1995 • call for performance dates/ details

Leslie-Lohman Gay Art Foundation & Gallery 127-B Prince St, lower level 212/673-7007 • 1pm-6pm, clsd Sun-Mon

PS 122 150 1st Ave (at E 9th St) 212/477-5288, 212/477-5829 • it's rough, it's raw, it's real New York performance art

WOW Cafe Theatre 59 E 4th St, 4th flr (btwn 2nd Ave & Bowery) 212/777-4280 • open Th-Sat • women's theater

BOOKSTORES

Bluestockings Women's Bookstore 172 Allen St (btwn Stanton & Rivington) 212/777–6028 • 1pm-10pm • live music & performances • also cafe

Oscar Wilde Bookshop 15 Christopher St (at 7th Ave) 212/255–8097 • 11am-8pm, noon-7pm Sun • popular • LGBT

RETAIL SHOPS

DeMask 135 W 22nd St (btwn 6th & 7th Aves) 212/352–2850 • 11am-7pm • European fetish fashion

Flight 001 96 Greenwich Ave (btwn Jane & 12th) 212/691–1001 • 11am-8pm, noon-6pm Sun • travel gear

Rainbows & Triangles 192 8th Ave (at 19th St) 212/627–2166 • 11am-10pm, noon-9pm Sun • LGBT cards, books, gifts & more

Universal Gear 140 8th Ave (btwn 16th & 17th) 212/206–9119 • casual, club, athletic & designer clothing

Whittall & Shon 113 Christopher St 212/691–6964 • funky clothes & clubwear for boys

GYMS & HEALTH CLUBS

19th St Health & Fitness 22 W 19th St (btwn 5th & 6th) 212/414–5800 • lesbians/gay men • day passes available

David Barton Gym 215 W 23rd St (at 7th) 212/414–2022 • lesbians/gay men • day passes available

New York Sports Club 128 8th Ave (btwn 16th & 17th) 212/627–0065 • popular • mostly gay men • day passes available

SEX CLUBS

Submit 253 E Houston (btwn Aves A & B, at Studio 253) 718/789–4053 • monthly • women-only play party • call for location

EROTICA

Pleasure Chest 156 7th Ave S (at Charles) 212/242–2158

▲ **Toys in Babeland** 94 Rivington (btwn Orchard & Ludlow) 212/375–1701 • noon-10pm, till 8pm Sun

NYC—Downtown

ACCOMMODATIONS

Wall Street District Hotel 15 Gold St 212/232–7700, 212/232–7800 (RESERVATIONS) • gay/ straight • award-winning boutique hotel • NYC's most hi-tech hotel • San Marino Ristorante & Lounge • wheelchair access • $199-469

NIGHTCLUBS

Desilicious 95 Leonard (at Broadway) 212/713–5111 • monthly party • lesbians/ gay men • Bollywood, bhangra & house music • multiracial • call for dates

Ife's Monthly Dance Party 27 Park Pl (at Church, at Club Remix) 917/312–3090 (PROMOTER #) • 2nd Sat only • mostly women • dancing/ DJ • multiracial clientele

LipStik 27 Park Pl (at Church, at Club Remix) 212/942–8364, 212/267–5252 • 1st & 3rd Sat only • mostly women • dancing/ DJ • multiracial • Latin music

Remix After Hours 27 Park Pl (at Church, at Club Remix) 347/463–0125 • 11:30pm-6am Fri only • mostly women • dancing/ DJ • multiracial

RETAIL SHOPS

David Menkes Leather 114 Fifth Ave 212/989–3706 • custom-made leather & bondage wear

NYC—Midtown

ACCOMMODATIONS

Belvedere Hotel 319 W 48th St (at 8th Ave) 212/245–7000, 888/468–3558 • gay-friendly • hotel • wheelchair access • $160+

Buckingham Hotel 101 W 57th St (at 6th Ave) 212/246–1500, 888/511–1900 • gay-friendly • studios & 1-bdrm suites • $149+

Gershwin Hotel 7 E 27th St (at 5th Ave) 212/545–8000 • gay-friendly • artsy, seedy hotel w/ model's floor dorms & rooms • also bar & cafe • jazz room • art gallery • $99+

Habitat Hotel 130 E 57th St (at Lexington) 212/753–8841, 800/497–6028 • gay-friendly • upscale budget hotel • $75-270

Holiday Inn Martinique on Broadway 49 W 32nd St (btwn Broadway & 5th) 212/736–3800, 888/694–6543 • gay/ straight • also restaurant, cafe & cocktail lounge

The Hotel Metro 45 W 35th St (at 5th Ave) 212/947–2500, 800/356–3870 • gay-friendly • slick art deco hotel • 1 block from Empire State Bldg • $170-400

Hudson Hotel 356 W 58th St 512/554–6000 • magical hotel w/ trendy bar • $175+

Ivy Terrace 230 E 58th St 516/662–6862 • private studio rental • terrace • nonsmoking • women-owned/ run • $180-250

Lambda Mews 24 W 30th St (at 5th Ave & Broadway) 212/229–9339, 212/213–8798 • B&B in private home • lesbians/ gay men • views of Empire State Bldg • kids ok • gay-owned • $120-140

Park Central Hotel 870 7th Ave (at 56th St) 212/247–8000, 800/346–1359 • gay-friendly • also restaurant • wheelchair access • $169+

Travel Inn 515 W 42nd St (at 10th Ave) 212/695–7171, 800/869–4630 • gay-friendly • swimming • fitness center • $125-200

W New York 541 Lexington Ave 212/755–1200, 877/WHOTELS (RESERVATIONS ONLY) • gay/ straight • also restaurant & bar • wheelchair access • $249-569

W New York—The Court 130 E 39th St 212/685–1100, 877/WHOTELS (RESERVATIONS ONLY) • gay/ straight • also restaurant & bar • wheelchair access • $249-569

W New York—The Tuscany 120 E 39th St 212/686–1600, 877/WHOTELS (RESERVATIONS ONLY) • gay/ straight • also restaurant & bar at W The Court • wheelchair access • $249-569

W New York—Times Square 1567 Broadway 212/930–7400, 877/WHOTELS (RESERVATIONS ONLY) • gay/ straight • also restaurant & bar • wheelchair access • $299-569

BARS

Brite Bar 297 10th Ave (at 27th St) 212/279–9706 • 5:30pm-3am • gay/ straight • swank neighborhood bar

Cleo's Saloon 656 9th Ave (at 46th St) 212/307–1503 • 11am-4am, from noon Sun • mostly gay men • neighborhood bar

Danny's Skylight Room 346 W 46th St (at 9th Ave) 212/265–8133 • 4pm-midnight, brunch 11:30am-3pm Wed & wknds • gay-friendly • piano bar from 6pm • cabaret • Thai restaurant

Don't Tell Mama 343 W 46th St (at 9th Ave) 212/757–0788 • 4pm-4am • popular • gay-friendly • young crowd • piano bar & cabaret • cover + 2 drink minimum • call for shows

Dusk 147 W 24th St (btwn 6th & 7th) 212/924–4490 • 6pm-close, clsd Sun • gay/ straight

OW Bar 221 E 58th St (at 2nd Ave)
212/355-3395 • 4pm-4am, from 2pm Sun •
mostly gay men • live shows • drag/ strippers
• digital jukebox • videos • patio • gay-owned

Regents 317 E 53rd St (at 2nd Ave)
212/593-3091 • 4pm-4am, noon-midnight
Sun • mostly gay men • cabaret • piano bar

Therapy 348 W 52nd St (at 9th)
212/397-1700 • 5pm-4am, from noon Sun •
lesbians/ gay men • live shows • cabaret •
food served

The Web 40 E 58th St (at Madison)
212/308-1546 • 4pm-3am, till 4am Fri-Sat •
mostly gay men • dancing/DJ • Asian-
American clientele • go-go boys • theme
nights

NIGHTCLUBS

Escuelita 301 W 39th St (at 8th Ave)
212/631-0588 • 10pm-5am, 7pm-4am Sun,
clsd Mon-Wed • mostly gay men • more
women Fri for Freedom Fri • dancing/ DJ •
drag shows • Latino/a clientele • cover

Girlnation 12 W 45th St (btwn 5th & 6th Ave)
212/391-8053 • 10pm Sat only • mostly
women • popular lounge party • dancing/ DJ •
also restaurant

LoverGirl NYC 20 W 39th St, at Club Shelter
(btwn 5th & 6th Aves) 212/252-3397 • 10pm-
4am Sat • mostly women • dancing/DJ •
multiracial • live shows • cover charge

The Rambles 27th St (between 10th & 11th,
at Home) 212/352-3313 • 10pm Sun only •
mostly gay men • go-go boys

RESTAURANTS

44 & X Hell's Kitchen 626 10th Ave (at 44th
St) 212/977-1170 • 5:30pm-midnight, brunch
wknds • American comfort food • wheelchair
access • gay-owned

Beacon 25 W 56th St 212/332-0500 • lunch
& dinner, wknd brunch • open-fire cooking

Cafe Un Deux Trois 123 W 44th St (at
Broadway) 212/354-4148 • noon-midnight,
brunch wknds • popular • bistro • $12-26

Mangia e Bevi 800 9th Ave (at W 53rd St)
212/956-3976 • noon-midnight • Italian

Rice 'N' Beans 744 9th Ave (at 50th St)
212/265-4444 • 11am-10pm • Latin/ Brazilian
• plenty veggie • beer/ wine

Townhouse Restaurant 206 E 58th St (at
3rd Ave) 212/826-6241 • lunch & dinner, Sun
brunch (open late wknds) • popular • lesbians/
gay men • $10-23

ENTERTAINMENT & RECREATION

Sex and the City Tour 5th Ave, in front of
Pulitzer Fountain (at 58th St) 212/209-3370 •
3 hours • reservations a must!

BOOKSTORES

Coliseum Books 11 W 42nd St
212/803-5890 • 8am-8:30pm, from 11am Sat,
11am-7pm Sun • the daddy of all independent
bookstores in NYC is back & better than ever •
also cafe

EROTICA

Come Again 353 E 53rd St (at 2nd Ave)
212/308-9394 • clsd Sun • woman-owned
erotica store

Eve's Garden 119 W 57th St #1201 (btwn 6th
& 7th) 800/848-3837 • 11am-7pm, clsd Sun •
women's sexuality boutique

NYC—Uptown

ACCOMMODATIONS

The Carlyle 35 E 76th St (at Madison Ave)
212/744-1600, 888/767-3966 • gay-friendly •
full brkfst • $550-5,000

Country Inn the City W 77th St (at
Broadway) 212/580-4183 • gay-friendly •
studio apts in restored 1891 town house •
nonsmoking • $150-230

The Harlem Flophouse 212/662-0678 •
guesthouse • near Apollo Theatre • caters to
traveling artists • nonsmoking • kids ok • $75-
100

Hotel Newton 2528 Broadway
212/678-6500, 800/643-5553 • gay/ straight •
hotel on Upper West Side • nearest to
Columbia University • kids ok • $95-180

The Urban Jem Guest House 2005 Fifth
Ave (at 125th in Harlem) 212/831-6029,
888/264-8811 • gay-friendly • B&B •
renovated brownstone in heart of Harlem's
renaissance • some shared baths • kids ok •
$105-220

BARS

Brandy's Piano Bar 235 E 84th St (at 2nd
Ave) 212/650-1944 • 4pm-4am • mostly gay
men • piano bar

RESTAURANTS

Orbit East Harlem 2257 1st Ave E (at E
116th St) 212/348-7818 • dinner only •
creative cuisine • some veggie • full bar • live
jazz & blues • reservations recommended

NYC—Brooklyn

INFO LINES & SERVICES

Audre Lorde Project 85 S Oxford St
718/596–0342 • 10am-6pm, till 9pm Tue-Th,
11:30pm-7pm Sat, clsd Sun • LGBT center for
people of color • events • resources • HIV
services • library

BARS

The Abbey 536 Driggs Ave (btwn N 7th &
8th), Williamsburg **718/599–4400** • from 3pm
• gay/ straight • neighborhood bar •
dancing/DJ

Annie's 156 Montague St (at Henry)
718/596–0061 • gay/ straight • karaoke • also
restaurant • lunch & dinner

Bar 4 444 7th Ave (at 15th St, in Park Slope)
718/832–9800 • 11am-4am • gay/ straight •
neighborhood bar • DJ Fri-Sat • live music &
performances

Excelsior 390 5th Ave (btwn 6th & 7th)
718/832–1599 • 4pm-4am, from 2pm wknds •
lesbians/ gay men • patio

Ginger's Bar 363 5th Ave (btwn 5th & 6th
Sts, in Park Slope) **718/788–0924** • 5pm-4am,
from 2pm wknds • lesbians/ gay men • more
women Th • neighborhood bar • occasional
live shows

Kili 81 Hoyt St (at Boerum Hill)
718/855–5574 • 5pm-4am • popular • gay/
straight • neighborhood bar • live
entertainment • funky local bar • acoustic
music

Metropolitan 559 Lorimer St (at
Metropolitan), Williamsburg **718/599–4444** •
3pm-4am • lesbians/ gay men • comfy
neighborhood bar w/ 2 fireplaces • more
women Wed

R Bar 451 Meeker Ave (Graham Ave)
646/523–1813 • gay-friendly • more gay Tue •
neighborhood bar

NIGHTCLUBS

Cattyshack 249 4th Ave • mostly women •
dancing/ DJ • multiracial • hip hop/ R&B

Cirrah 249 4th Ave (at Cattyshack) • 10pm-
4am Fri only • women only • dancing/ DJ •
multiracial • hip hop/ R&B

RESTAURANTS

200 Fifth 200 5th Ave (btwn Union &
Sackett) **718/638–0023, 718/638–2925** • 4pm-
close, from 11am wknds • eclectic • full bar •
live shows

Aunt Suzie 247 5th Ave (at Garfield Pl)
718/788–2868 • dinner only • Italian

ChipShop/ The Curry Shop 383 5th Ave (at
6th St) 718/244–7746 • noon-10pm, till 11pm
Th-Sat, from 11am wknds • English/ Indian •
home of the famous fried Twinkie!

Faan 209 Smith St (at Baltic) **718/694–2277**
• lunch & dinner • pan-Asian • also bar
downstairs

Johnny Mack's 1114 8th Ave (btwn 11th &
12th) **718/832–7961** • 4pm-11pm, till 1am Fri-
Sat, Sun brunch

Red Hot 349 7th Ave (at 10th St, in Park
Slope) **718/369–0700** • delicious Chinese •
plenty veggie

Santa Fe Grill 62 7th Ave (at Lincoln)
718/636–0279 • 5pm-close, from 3pm wknds
• also bar

Superfine 126 Front St **718/243–9005** •
lunch Tue-Fri, dinner Tue-Sat, noon-5pm Sun,
clsd Mon • relaxed atmosphere • live shows •
lesbian-owned

ENTERTAINMENT & RECREATION

Rainbow Skate 200 Empire (at Bedford, at
Empire Skating Center) **718/462–1400** • every
other Th • lesbians/ gay men • roller skating
to hi-NRG music

SPIRITUAL GROUPS

All Souls Bethlehem Church 566 E 7th St
(near Cortelyou Rd) • 10:30am Sun

Brooklyn Heights Synagogue 131 Remsen
St (btwn Henry & Clinton) **718/522–2070** •
6:30pm Fri

First Unitarian Church of Brooklyn
48 Monroe Pl (btwn Pierpont & Clark)
718/624–5466 • 11am Sun

Park Slope United Methodist Church
6th Ave & 8th St **718/768–3093** • 11am Sun

GYMS & HEALTH CLUBS

The Training Academy 525 Waverly Ave
(btwn Fulton Ave & Atlantic Ave)
718/638–3888 • women-owned/ run

EROTICA

Pink Pussy Cat Boutique 355 5th Ave
718/369–0088

NYC—Queens

Bars

Albatross 36-19 24th Ave (at 37th), Astoria **718/204-9045** • 6pm-4am • gay/ straight • neighborhood bar • more gay wknds • gay-owned

Chueca 69-04 Woodside Ave (at 69th St), Woodside **718/424-1171** • 6pm-4am, clsd Mon-Tue • mostly women • mostly Latina • karaoke Th • lesbian-owned

Crescent Lounge 32-05 Crescent St (at Broadway), Astoria **718/728-9600** • 4pm-4am • gay/ straight • neighborhood bar • karaoke • live jazz • gay-owned

Nightclubs

Atlantis 2010 76–19 Roosevelt Ave (at 77th St), Jackson Hts **718/457-3939** • 10pm-4am Fri-Sun only • lesbians/ gay men • dancing/DJ • mostly Latina/o • drag shows

NYC—Bronx

Nightclubs

Girlz Night Out at Crimson Lounge 3031 Webster Ave (at E Mosholu Pkwy) **718/992-9073** • 10pm Fri only • mostly women • dancing/ DJ • multiracial

Liquid Fridays 1756 Tremont Ave (at Commonwealth, at Twins Lounge) **347/219-2882** • 1st Fri • lesbians/ gay men • dancing/ DJ • multiracial • transgender-friendly

The Warehouse 141 E 140th St (btwn Grand Concourse & Walton) **718/992-5974** • 11pm Sat only • lesbians/ gay men • dancing/DJ • mostly African-American • cover charge

Whateva Wednesdays 3031 Webster Ave (at E Mosholu Pkwy) **718/992-9073** • 6pm-midnight Wed only • mostly women • dancing/ DJ • multiracial

Niagara Falls

see also Buffalo, New York & Niagara Falls, Ontario, Canada

North Salem

Restaurants

Auberge Maxime Jct 116 & 121 (Ridgefield Rd) **914/669-5450** • dinner nightly • upscale French • terrace

Nyack

Nightclubs

Barz 327 Rte 9 W **845/353-4444** • 8pm-4am, from 3pm Sun • lesbians/ gay men • dancing/DJ • alternative • male dancers • karaoke

Restaurants

Sydney's Roadside Cafe 41 Rte 59 (at Rte 9W) **845/358-5475** • 7am-8:30pm, till 3pm Sun, clsd Tue • BYOB • gay-owned

Orange County

Info Lines & Services

Orange County Rainbow Alliance PO Box 304, Vails Gate 12584 **845/562-3086, 845/565-2189** • meets Fri in Newburgh

Restaurants

Gigi's Folderol 795 Rte 284, Westtown **845/726-3822** • 5pm-close, clsd Tue-Wed • French/farmhouse • some veggie • piano Fri-Sat • wheelchair access

Erotica

Exotic Gifts & Videos 658 Rte 211 E (exit 120, off Rte 17), Middletown **845/692-6664**

Orangeburg

Nightclubs

Club Blu 31 Blaisdell Rd **845/359-1948** • till 4am Fri-Sat • lesbians/ gay men • dancing/DJ • food served

Ossining

Spiritual Groups

Trinity Episcopal Church 7 S Highland/ Rte 9 **914/941-0806** • 7:30am & 10am Sun

Plattsburgh

Bars

Backstreet 30 Marion St (btwn Clinton & Court) **518/563-8211** • 5pm-2am, clsd Mon • lesbians/ gay men • dancing/DJ • special events • 18+ • live shows • transgender-friendly • wheelchair access • gay-owned

Port Chester

see also Greenwich & Stamford, CT

Bars

Sandy's Old Homestead 325 N Main St (at Wilkins) **914/939-0758** • 8am-4am • gay-friendly • karaoke • food • monthly women's parties w/ go-go girls • wheelchair access

Rochester

INFO LINES & SERVICES

AA Gay/ Lesbian 10 Manhattan Square Dr 585/232-6720 (AA#)

Gay Alliance of the Genesee Valley (GAGV) 179 Atlantic Ave (at Elton) 585/244-8640 • 10am-9pm, till 6pm Fri, clsd wknds • community center • also info line

BARS

Avenue Pub 522 Monroe Ave (at Goodman) 585/244-4960 • 4pm-2am • popular • mostly gay men • neighborhood bar • dancing/DJ • patio

Motor 113 State St (at Andrews) 585/262-2650 • 4pm-2am, from 2pm wknds • lesbians/ gay men • neighborhood bar • videos

Muther's 40 S Union St (at Gardiner Park) 585/325-6216 • 4pm-2am, till 3am Fri-Sun • popular • lesbians/ gay men • dancing/DJ • drag shows • gay-owned

Nasty D's 140 Alexander St (at Broadway) 585/256-1000 • 4pm-2am, 11am-2am Sun • mostly gay men • neighborhood bar • also restaurant • dancing/DJ • gay-owned

Tara Lounge 153 Liberty Pole Wy (at Andrews) 585/232-4719 • noon-2am • popular • lesbians/ gay men • neighborhood bar • piano bar Fri-Sat from 10am • older crowd

NIGHTCLUBS

Vertex 169 N Chestnut St 585/232-5498 • 10pm-3am Th-Sat • gay/ straight • dancing/DJ • goth club

CAFES

Little Theatre Cafe 240 East Ave 585/258-0412 • 5pm-10pm, till midnight Fri-Sat • popular • beer/ wine • soups • salads • live jazz • wheelchair access • art gallery

Patrick's Culinary Kreations 847 S Goodman St 585/271-0830 • 10am-10pm, till 3pm Sun • gay-owned

RESTAURANTS

Triphammer Grill 60 Browns Race (btwn Platt & Commercial), High Falls 585/262-2700 • lunch Mon-Fri, dinner nightly, clsd Sun • patio • full bar

RETAIL SHOPS

Outlandish 274 N Goodman St (in the Village Gate) 585/760-8383 • 11am-11pm, noon-5pm Sun • videos • pride items • books • toys • gay-owned

The Pride Connection 728 South Ave (1 block from Gregory) 585/242-7840 • noon-9pm, from 10am Sat, till 6pm Sun • LGBT gifts & books • also coffeehouse

PUBLICATIONS

Empty Closet 585/244-9030 • LGBT newspaper • resource listings

SPIRITUAL GROUPS

Dignity/ Integrity 17 S Fitzhugh St (at Broad, in Church of St Luke & St Simon Cyrene, look for pink steeple) 585/234-5092 • 5pm Sun

Open Arms MCC 175 Norris Dr (off Culver Rd, near Cobbs Hill Park) 585/271-8478 • 11am Sun • wheelchair access

Saratoga Springs

ACCOMMODATIONS

The Mansion Rte 29, Rock City Falls 518/885-1607, 888/996-9977 • gay/ straight • 1860 Victorian mansion • full brkfst • fireplaces • nonsmoking • wheelchair access • gay-owned • $95-335

Saratoga B&B/ Saratoga Motel 434 Church St 518/584-0920, 800/584-0920 • gay-friendly • B&B in 1850 farmhouse & motel • full brkfst • fireplaces • nonsmoking • gay-owned • $120-239

BARS

Desperate Annie's Caroline St (off Broadway) 518/587-2455 • gay-friendly • neighborhood bar

RESTAURANTS

Esperanto 6 1/2 Caroline St (off Broadway) 518/587-4236 • eclectic int'l • casual • inexpensive • popular w/ the college set

Little India 423 Broadway 518/583-4151 • lunch & dinner • tasty & authentic Indian food • lots of veggie • beer/ wine only

BOOKSTORES

Nahani 482 Broadway 518/587-4322 • 10am-6pm, noon-5pm Sun • wheelchair access

Schenectady

see Capital District

Seneca Falls

RETAIL SHOPS

WomanMade Products 91 Fall St
315/568-9364 • 10:30am-5:30pm, 11am-4pm
Sat, clsd Sun-Mon • lesbian & feminist T-shirts
• crafts

Sharon Springs

ACCOMMODATIONS

American Hotel Main St/ Rte 10
518/284-2105 • gay/ straight • 1847 Nat'l
Register hotel • also restaurant & bar • kids ok
• wheelchair access • gay-owned • $150

Brimstonia Cottage 173 Main St (on Rte 10)
518/284-2839 • gay-friendly • cottage suites
w/ kitchens • nonsmoking • $125+

Edgefield 153 Washington St 518/284-3339
• gay/ straight • full brkfst • nonsmoking •
well-appointed English Country house • gay-
owned • $125-185

New Yorker Guest House & Spa Center St
518/284-2126 • gay-friendly • seasonal • full
brkfst • kids ok • nonsmoking • $135-250

The TurnAround Spa 105 Washington St
518/284-9708, 212/628-9008 • lesbians/ gay
men • small hotel & health spa • full brkfst •
hot tub • food served • nonsmoking • kids ok
• clsd Nov-May • lesbian & gay-owned • $45-
75

RETAIL SHOPS

The Finishing Touch 165 Main St (Rte 10)
518/284-2884 • 11am-4pm Th-Sun only •
gallery & gift shop

Syracuse

INFO LINES & SERVICES

AA Gay/ Lesbian 315/463-5011 (AA#)

ACCOMMODATIONS

B&B Wellington 707 Danforth St (at Carbon)
315/474-3641, 800/724-5006 • gay-friendly •
kids ok • $95-150

BARS

Rain Lounge 218 N Franklin St (at Herald Pl)
315/474-3487 • 4pm-2am • mostly gay men •
neighborhood bar • professional • multiracial
• transgender-friendly • videos • gay-owned

Spirits 205 N West St (at W Genessee)
315/471-9279 • 3pm-2am, from noon wknds
• lesbians/ gay men • dancing/DJ wknds in
summer • neighborhood bar • live shows

NIGHTCLUBS

Trexx 319 N Clinton St (exit 18, off Rte 81)
315/474-6408 • 8pm-2am, till 4am Fri-Sat,
T-dance from 4pm Sun, clsd Mon-Tue • mostly
gay men • dancing/DJ • drag shows Sun •
videos • 18+ • wheelchair access

Troy

see Capital District

Utica

BARS

Chatterbox Lounge 239 Genesee St
315/266-0640 • 7pm-midnight, till 2am Fri-
Sat, clsd Sun-Mon • gay-friendly • live music

NIGHTCLUBS

That Place 216 Bleecker St (at Genessee)
315/724-1446 • 8pm-2am, from 4pm Fri, clsd
Sun-Mon • popular • mostly gay men •
dancing/DJ • leather • young crowd •
wheelchair access

Webster

RESTAURANTS

The Grill at Union Hill Country Store
1891 Ridge Rd 585/265-4443 • 6am-9pm,
from 7am Sun

White Plains

INFO LINES & SERVICES

Lesbian Line 914/949-3203 • 6pm-10pm
most nights, but hours vary

The Loft 180 E Post Rd (lower level)
914/948-2932, 914/948-4922 (HELPLINE) •
LGBT community center • call for hours • also
newsletter

Woodstock

see Catskill Mtns

NORTH CAROLINA

Statewide

PUBLICATIONS

▲ **The Front Page** 919/829–0181 • LGBT newspaper for the Carolinas

Arden

EROTICA

Southeastern Fantasy & Video 2317 Henderson Rd (Rte 25) (N of Buckshoals Rd) 828/684–2821 • toys

Asheville

includes Black Mountain

INFO LINES & SERVICES

Lambda AA Biltmore Village (at All Souls Episcopal Church) 828/254–8539 (AA#), 800/524–0465 • 7pm Mon

ACCOMMODATIONS

1889 WhiteGate Inn & Cottage 173 E Chestnut St 828/253–2553, 800/485–3045 • popular • gay/ straight • luxury, ull-service B&B • 3-course brkfst • gay-owned • $160-340

The 1900 Inn on Montford 296 Montford Ave 828/254–9569, 800/254–9569 • gay-friendly • popular • romantic luxury • English Arts & Crafts • full brkfst • $165-895

27 Blake Street 27 Blake St 828/252–7390 • women only • romantic room w/ private entrance in Victorian home • gardens • Southern hopsitality • nonsmoking • 2-night minimum wkdns/ holidays • woman-owned • reasonable rates

A Bird's Nest Bed & Kitchen 41 Oak Park Rd 828/251–2002, 828/713–0141 • lesbians/ gay men • comfortable, secluded & quiet B&K • in turn-of-the-century home • kids ok • nonsmoking • lesbian-owned • $135/ night & $850/ week

Abbington Green 46 Cumberland Circle (at Cumberland Ave) 828/251–2454, 800/251–2454 • gay-friendly • B&B in Montford historic district • gardens • $165-310

Acorn Cottage B&B 25 St Dunstans Cir 828/253–0609, 800/699–0609 • gay/ straight • 1925 granite home • full brkfst • nonsmoking • woman-owned/ run • $90-120

Asheville

ANNUAL EVENTS:
July - NC International Folk Festival (world cultural heritage celebration) 828/452-2997 or 877/365-5872, web: www.folkmoot.com.

CITY INFO:
828/258-6101, web: www.ashevillechamber.org.

ATTRACTIONS:
Biltmore Estate 800/624–1575, web: www.biltmore.com.
Blue Ridge Parkway.
North Carolina Arboretum 828/665-2492, web: www.ncarboretum.org.

WEATHER:
Gorgeous: temperate summers and mild winters, with a beautiful spring and fall.

TRANSIT:
New Bluebird Taxi 828/258-8331.
Sky Shuttle 828/253-0006.
Asheville Transit System 828/253–5691.

Asheville's Downtown Loft 55 1/2 Broadway St (at Walnut) **828/251–2002, 305/304-6151** • lesbian/ gay men • city loft space in the heart of downtown Asheville • "shabby chic decor" • accommodates up to 6 people • lesbian-owned • $120-175/ night & $750-1050/ week

Bat Cave Manor PO Box 271, Bat Cave 28710 **828/625-2104** • gay-straight • guesthouse on Rocky Broad River • full brkfst • kids ok • gay-owned • $75-85

Biltmore Village Inn 119 Dodge St (at Irwin) **828/274-8707, 866/274-8779** • gay-friendly • historic inn near Biltmore Estate • nonsmoking • gay-owned • $175-285

Bittersweet Cottage 458 Elk Mountain Scenic Hwy (at Beaverdam Rd) **828/712-2414** • gay/straight • "arts & crafts–style retreat" situated on Elk Mtn • convenient to downtown • all amenities included • gay-owned • $175-200

| **Reply** | **Forward** | | **Delete** |

```
Date: Nov 14, 2005 10:31:23
From: Ottersen@yahoo.com
To: Editor@Damron.com
Subject: Asheville
```

>Magical. This word tends to appear in any discussion of Asheville. Maybe it's the ancient blue mountains on every horizon, or the alchemy of mixing artists, New Agers, and an amazing lesbian population with mountain folk and Bible Belters, in one small Southern city. Whatever the reason, Asheville lives up to her magical reputation.

>Downtown you will find a lively, walkable city center brimming with galleries, eclectic shops, and coffeehouses. **Malaprop's Bookstore & Cafe** is a hub of womyn's community. Check out "Cafe of our Own," a women's poetry reading held every third Saturday. Malaprop's bulletin boards and free alternative newspapers are invaluable in finding things to see and do.

>While you're downtown, catch a film at the **Fine Arts Theater** or wander through the numerous art galleries. At night, sample cool jazz at **Tressa's**, or show off your sporting prowess in the game room of **Club Hairspray**. Weekends, dance late-nite at **Scandals**. You'll see lesbians everywhere—after all, Asheville is rumored to have one of the largest per capita populations of lesbians in the country as evidenced by the plethora of lesbian-owned B&B's. You can get a preview from Asheville's lesbian website: www.Sheville.org.

>Downtown is just a part of what this area has to offer. Check out New Morning Gallery and Blue goldsmiths, both in Biltmore Village. Hop on the Blue Ridge Parkway and you'll find mountains, overlooks, and waterfalls, with great hiking and whitewater to tantalize outdoor types. Explore it all!

Celie's Porch 828/281-4122 • women only • gracious older house north of downtown Asheville • nonsmoking • lesbian-owned • $60

Compassionate Expressions Mtn Inn 207 Robinson Cove Rd, Leicester **828/683-6633** • mostly women • cabins & rooms w/ a view of Blue Ridge Mtns • spa services • hot tub • on 40 acres • nonsmoking • wheelchair access • lesbian-owned • $60-120

The Hawk & Ivy B&B 133 N Fork Rd, Barnardsville **828/626-3486, 888/395-7254** • gay/ straight • full brkfst • nonsmoking • kids ok • swimming pond • wheelchair access • $100-140

Lofty Notions Campsite 411 Arrowood Rd (at Cove Rd), Rutherfordton **828/287-0069** • lesbians/ gay men • 1 campsite overlooking waterfall • SE of Asheville • swimming • kids ok • lesbian-owned • $200/week

Monthaven Guest Suite Apartments 21 Arborvale Rd #4 (at Montford Ave) **828/236-9089** • gay/ straight • located in historic neighborhood • nonsmoking • gay-owned • $90

Mountain Laurel B&B 139 Lee Dotson Rd, Fairview **828/628-9903, 828/712-6289** (CELL) • lesbians/ gay men • 25 miles from Asheville • full brkfst • nonsmoking • kids ok • lesbian-owned • $80-100

The Old Mill 100 Lake Lure Hwy (at 64 Junction), Bat Cave **828/625-4256** • gay-friendly • kids/ pets ok by arrangement • gay-owned • $50-90

▲ **Owl's Nest Inn & Engadine Cabins** 2630 Smokey Park Hwy (off I-40, at exit 37), Candler **828/665-8325, 800/665-8868** • gay/ straight • 1880s Victorian • full brkfst • fireplace • woman-owned • $135-225

The Tree House 395 Lakey Gap Acres, Black Mountain **828/669-3889** • mostly women • transgender-friendly • guesthouse • fireplace • 5 decks • sweat lodge • near Asheville • hiking trails • nonsmoking • lesbian/ trans-owned • $50-75

BARS

O'Henry's 237 Haywood St **828/254-1891** • 2pm-2am • lesbians/ gay men • neighborhood bar • drag shows • private club

Tressa's 28 Broadway **828/254-7072** • 4pm-2am, from 7pm Sat, clsd Sun • gay/ straight • jazz/ cigar bar • dancing/ DJ • live shows

Elegant 1885 Victorian inn nestled in the mountains just outside Asheville
- Full breakfast
- Private baths
- Fireplaces
- Whirlpool suite
- Evening wine and cheese
- Mountain views

OWL'S NEST INN AND ENGADINE CABINS
2630 Smokey Park Hwy, Candler, NC 28715
(828) 665-8325   800-665-8868
www.engadineinn.com

NIGHTCLUBS

Club Hairspray 38 N French Broad Ave (at Patton Ave) 828/258–2027 • 8pm-2am, clsd Sun • lesbians/ gay men • dancing/DJ • karaoke • cabaret • drag shows • game room • neighborhood bar

Scandals 11 Grove St (at Patton) 828/252–2838 • 10pm-3am, clsd Mon-Th • lesbians/ gay men • 3 bars • dancing/DJ • drag shows • videos • 18+ • private club • wheelchair access

CAFES

Beanstreets Coffee 3 Broadway (at College) 828/255–8180 • 7:30am-6pm, till midnight Th-Sat, 9am-10:30pm Sun • food served

Laurey's 67 Biltmore Ave 828/252–1500 • 10am-6pm, till 4pm Sat, clsd Sun • popular • bright cafe w/ delicious salads & cookies • also dinners to go • lesbian-owned • wheelchair access

RESTAURANTS

Laughing Seed Cafe 40 Wall St (at Haywood) 828/252–3445 • 11:30am-9pm, till 10pm Fri-Sat, Sun brunch from 10am, clsd Tue • vegetarian/ vegan • beer/ wine • patio • wheelchair access

Picnics Restaurant & Bake Shop 371 Merrimon Ave 828/258–2858 • 11:30am-7pm, clsd Sun-Mon • beer/ wine • wheelchair access • catering services available • gay-owned

Tupelo Honey Cafe 12 College St 828/255–4863 • 9am-3pm daily & 5:30pm-close Tue-Sun, clsd Mon • "Southern home cookin' w/ an uptown twist" • woman-owned/ run

ENTERTAINMENT & RECREATION

Fine Arts Theatre 36 Biltmore Ave 828/232–1536 • first-run art & independent films

BOOKSTORES

Downtown Books & News 67 N Lexington Ave (btwn Walnut & Hiawassee) 828/253–8654 • 8am-6pm, till 8pm Fri-Sat • used books & new magazines • LGBT section

Malaprop's Bookstore & Cafe 55 Haywood St (at Walnut) 828/254–6734, 800/441–9829 • 9am-9pm, till 10pm Fri-Sat, till 7pm Sun • readings • performances • women's poetry reading 8pm 3rd Sat

Reader's Corner 31 Montford Ave 828/285–8805 • 10am-7pm, till 8pm Fri-Sat, clsd Sun • used books

RETAIL SHOPS

Jewels That Dance: Jewelry Design 63 Haywood St 828/254–5088 • 10:30am-6pm, clsd Sun • gay-owned

PUBLICATIONS

Out in Asheville 828/687–7237 • LGBT newspaper

SPIRITUAL GROUPS

The Cathedral of All Souls 3 Angle St (Biltmore Village) 828/274–2681 • 8am, 9am & 11:15am Sun, noon & 5:45pm Wed • wheelchair access

MCC of Asheville 33 Grace Way (at Butler Ridge Rd), Arden 828/684–0838 • 10:30am Sun, 7pm Wed

St Joan of Arc Catholic Church 919 Haywood Rd (at Mitchell Ave) 828/252–3151 • 5pm Sat, 8:30am & 11:30am Sun, also Spanish Mass

Unitarian Universalist Church of Asheville 1 Edwin Pl (at Charlotte) 828/254–6001 • 10am Sun • wheelchair access

EROTICA

Bedtyme Stories 2334 Hendersonville Rd, Arden 828/684–8250

Atlantic Beach

ACCOMMODATIONS

Royal Pavilion Resort 125 Salter Path Rd 252/726–5188, 800/533–3700 • gay/ straight • oceanfront hotel • gym • swimming • kids ok • also restaurant & bar • wheelchair access • $65-350

Blowing Rock

ACCOMMODATIONS

Blowing Rock Cabins 229 Price St (Hwy 221 S) 828/295–4272 • gay-friendly • 1, 2 & 3-bdrm log cabins • full kitchens • kids ok • gay-owned • 119-189

Blowing Rock Victorian Inn 242 Ransom St (at US 321) 828/295–0034 • gay-friendly • B&B • full brkfst • jacuzzi • kids/ pets ok • gay-owned • $119-199

Stone Pillar B&B 144 Pine St 828/295–4141, 800/962–9955 • gay/ straight • historic 1920s house • full brkfst • wheelchair access • gay-owned • $90-150

Burnside

ACCOMMODATIONS

Riverside Treehouse 8035 State Hwy 80 S (above Sally's Kitchen) **828/675-1881** • gay-friendly • 2-bdrm apt overlooking river • women-owned/ run • $60/ night, $395/ week

RESTAURANTS

Sally's Kitchen 8035 State Hwy 80 S **828/675-1881** • 11am-8pm, from noon wknds • "If it's not good, we don't serve it" • women-owned/ run

Cashiers

ACCOMMODATIONS

Jane's Aerie Cottage **828/743-9002** • mostly women • cottage in great mtn location • $100/ night, $500/ week

Chapel Hill

see Raleigh/Durham/Chapel Hill

Charlotte

INFO LINES & SERVICES

Acceptance Group Gay/ Lesbian AA 1200 E Blvd (at First Christian Church) **704/332-4387 (AA#), 877/233-6853** • 8pm Fri

Gay/ Lesbian Switchboard **704/535-6277** • 6:30pm-9:30pm Sun-Th

The Lesbian/ Gay Community Center 1401-B Central Ave (at Clement Ave) **704/333-0141** • 4pm-8pm, till 7pm Fri, 10am-4pm Sat, clsd Sun

ACCOMMODATIONS

Doubletree Guest Suites Charlotte/ South Park **704/364-2400, 800/222-8733** • gay-friendly • pool

The Morehead Inn 1122 E Morehead St **704/376-3357, 888/667-3432** • gay-friendly • antique-filled suites in historic neighborhood • full brkfst • kids ok • wheelchair access • $120-190

Morgan Suites Hotel 315 E Woodlawn Rd **704/522-0852** • gay/ straight • fitness center • sundeck

Vanlandingham Estate 2010 The Plaza **704/334-8909, 888/524-2020** • gay-friendly • bungalow-style estate • full brkfst • nonsmoking • wheelchair access • gay-owned • $120-190

BARS

Central Station 2131 Central Ave (at The Plaza) **704/377-0906** • 5pm-2am • lesbians/ gay men • neighborhood bar • multiracial • private club

DAKS Tavern 1704 Shamrock Dr **704/347-6826** • 8pm-2am, clsd Sun • lesbians/ gay men • neighborhood bar • live music • patio

---

Charlotte

LGBT PRIDE:
May. 888/626-2329, web: www.charlottepride.com.

CITY INFO:
Convention & Visitors Bureau 704/334-2282 or 800/722-1994, web: charlottecvb.org.

TRANSIT:
Yellow Cab 704/332-6161.
Various hotels have their own shuttles.
Charlotte Transit 704/336-7433.

ATTRACTIONS:
Blumenthal Performing Arts Center 704/372-1000, web: www.blumenthalcenter.org
Daniel Stowe Botanical Gardens 704/825-4490, web: www.dsbg.org
Discovery Place 704/372-6261, web: www.discoveryplace.org.
Lowes Motor Speedway web: lowesmotorspeedway.com
Mint Museum of Art 704/337-2000, web: www.mintmuseum.org.
Paramount's Carowinds Amusement Park 704/588-2600, web: www.carowinds.com

---

Hartigan's Irish Pub 601 S Cedar St 704/347–1841 • 11am-10pm, till 2am wknds, from 5pm Sun • gay/ straight • neighborhood bar • dancing/ DJ Fri-Sat • country-western • live shows • food served • popular lesbian hangout • gay-owned

Liaisons 316 Rensselaer Ave (at South Blvd) 704/376–1617 • 5pm-1am • popular • lesbians/ gay men • neighborhood bar • live shows • also restaurant Wed-Sun • videos • 2 flrs • private club • women-owned/ run

Morehead Street Tavern 300 E Morehead St (btwn South Blvd & S Tryon) 704/334–2655 • 11:30am-2am, from 3:30pm Sun • gay-friendly • neighborhood bar • dancing/DJ Sat • live music • karaoke • food served

The Woodshed 4000 S I-85 Service Rd (at Little Rock) 704/394–1712 • 5pm-2am, from 3pm Sun • men only • neighborhood bar • leather • private club • food served • wheelchair access

NIGHTCLUBS

Club Myxx 3110 S Tryon St 704/525–5001 • 10:30pm-close Sat only • lesbians/ gay men • dancing/DJ • mostly African-American • live shows • private club

Scorpio's 2301 Freedom Dr 704/373–9124 • 9pm-3am Wed & Sun • lesbians/ gay men • dancing/DJ • multiracial • videos • 18+ • private club • also Diva's show bar • wheelchair access

Tremont Music Hall 400 W Tremont Ave 704/343–9494 • gay-friendly • live music venue

Velocity 935 S Summit Ave (at Morehead St) 704/333–0060 • 10pm-close Fri-Sat only • popular • mostly gay men • dancing/DJ • cabaret • private club • wheelchair access

CAFES

Caribou Coffee 1531 East Blvd (near Scott) 704/334–3570 • 6am-11pm, from 7am Sat-Sun, till midnight Fri-Sat • popular gay hangout Wed nights

Smelly Cat Coffee 514 E 36th St 704/374–9656 • 7am-9pm, till midnight Fri-Sat, 9am-5pm Sun • gay-friendly • food served

Tic Toc Coffeeshop 512 N Tryon St (btwn 8th & 9th) 704/375–5750 • 7am-3pm, clsd wknds • plenty veggie

RESTAURANTS

300 East 300 East Blvd (at Cleveland) 704/332–6507 • 11am-10pm, from 10am Sun, till 11pm Fri-Sat • eclectic fusion • some veggie • full bar • wheelchair access

Alexander Michael's 401 W 9th St (at Pine) 704/332–6789 • lunch & dinner, clsd Sun • pub fare • full bar • wheelchair access

Cosmos Cafe 300 N College (at 6th) 704/372–3553 • 11am-2am, from 5pm Sat, clsd Sun • gay-friendly • new world cuisine • some veggie • also martini lounge

Lupie's Cafe 2718 Monroe Rd (near 5th St) 704/374–1232 • 11am-10pm, from noon Sat, clsd Sun • homestyle cookin' • some veggie

The Pewter Rose Bistro 1820 S Blvd (near E Blvd) 704/332–8149 • lunch, dinner, brunch Sat-Sun • int'l/ american • live entertainment • outdoor dining • also nightclub

ENTERTAINMENT & RECREATION

Charlotte Sting Charlotte Coliseum 877/962–2849 • check out the Women's National Basketball Association while you're in Charlotte

BOOKSTORES

Paper Skyscraper 330 East Blvd (at Euclid Ave) 704/333–7130 • 10am-7pm, till 6pm Sat, from noon Sun • books • funky gifts • wheelchair access

Rainbow Path Metaphysical Bookstore 1412-F E Blvd (near Scott Ave) 704/332–3404, 800/294–8896 • gifts • books • music • health products

White Rabbit Books & Things 1401 Central Ave 704/377–4067 • 10am-9pm, noon-8pm Sun • LGBT • books • magazines • T-shirts • gifts

RETAIL SHOPS

Charlotte Leather Company 4544-H South Blvd (in Charlotte Eagle) 704/527–1126 • 8pm-2am Wed-Sat • leather • fetish

Naughty Naughteaze 4037 E Independence Blvd #611 704/531–9988 • apparel for strippers & cross-dressers

PUBLICATIONS

▲ **The Front Page** 919/829–0181 • LGBT newspaper for the Carolinas

Q Notes 704/531–9988 • bi-weekly LGBT newspaper for the Carolinas

SPIRITUAL GROUPS

MCC Charlotte 1825 Eastway Dr (btwn Windham Pl & Shamrock Dr) 704/563–5810 • 10:45am & 7pm Sun, 7pm Wed

Unitarian Universalist of Charlotte 234 N Sharon Amity Rd (at Hardwick) 704/366–8623 • 9am & 11:15am Sun (in summer 10:30 am only)

Erotica

Carolina Video Source 8829 E Harris Blvd (at Albemarle Rd) **704/566-9993**

Duck

Accommodations

Advice 5¢, a B&B 111 Scarborough Ln **252/255-1050, 800/238-4235** • gay-friendly • welcoming seaside cottage in village of Duck on North Carolina's outer banks • women-owned/ run • $135-245

Durham

see Raleigh/Durham/Chapel Hill

Fayetteville

Bars

Shady Lady Lounge 2906 Fort Bragg Rd **901/484-2054** • 6pm-2am, from 4pm Fri • gay/ straight • neighborhood bar

Nightclubs

Alias 984 Old McPherson Church Rd (at Raeford Rd) **910/484-7994** • 9pm-2:30am Fri-Sat, also Th in summers • lesbians/ gay men • dancing/DJ • multiracial • trangender-friendly • go-go dancers • videos • 18+ • gay-owned

Club Spektrum 107 Swain St (at Bragg Blvd) **910/868-4279** • 8pm-3am, clsd Mon • lesbians/ gay men • dancing/DJ • multiracial • live shows • drag shows • male dancers 3rd Fri • patio

Erotica

Fort Video & News 4431 Bragg Blvd (near 401 overpass) **910/868-9905**

Priscilla's 3800 Sycamore Dairy Rd (at Bragg Blvd) **910/860-1776**

Franklin

Accommodations

Phoenix Nest 850/421-1984 • lesbians/ gay men • mtn cabin • sleeps 4 • seasonal • kids ok • nonsmoking • wheelchair access • lesbian-owned • $85 or $385/wk

Rainbow Acres (Honey's) 850/997-8847 • gay/ straight • mostly women • rental home • nonsmoking • fireplace • some shared baths • great views • women-owned/ run • $750/ week

Greensboro

Info Lines & Services

Principles AA 5603 Hilltop Rd (at Unitarian Church) **336/854-4278 (AA#)** • 8pm Mon

Accommodations

Biltmore Greensboro Hotel 111 W Washington (at Elm St) **336/272-3474, 800/332-0303** • gay/ straight • fully restored historic hotel • kids/ pets ok • gay-owned • $69-139

O. Henry Hotel 624 Green Valley Rd (at Benjamin Pkwy) **336/854-2000, 800/965-9200** • gay-friendly • pool • full brkfst • $219-500

Bars

Time Out Saloon 330 Bellemeade St **336/272-8108** • 7pm-2:30, clsd Sun-Mon • mostly women • neighborhood bar • dancing/DJ • karaoke Th & Sat • private club • lesbian-owned

Nightclubs

360 360 Federal Pl (at Spring Garden) **336/275-1834** • 9pm-2:30am • gay-friendly • dancing/ DJ • country/ western • drag shows • strippers • karaoke • transgender-friendly

Warehouse 29 1011 Arnold St **336/333-9333** • 9:30pm-2:30am Wed, Fri-Sun, T-dance Sun (summer), add'l summer hours • mostly gay men • dancing/DJ • T-dance Sun (summer) • drag shows Sun • videos • patio bar • volleyball court (games Sun) • private club

Spiritual Groups

Unitarian Universalist Church of Greensboro 5603 Hilltop Rd (btwn Bridford Pkwy & Guilford) **336/856-0330** • 9:30am & 11am Sun

Erotica

Xanadu 1205 E Bessemer **336/373-9849**

Greenville

Nightclubs

Barcode 2217 S Memorial Dr **252/353-2623** • 9pm-close • lesbians/ gay men • dancing/DJ • transgender-friendly • karaoke • drag shows • private club • wheelchair access • gay-owned

The Great American Mining Co. of New Guinea, Inc 1008 B Dickinson Ave **252/758-5883** • 2am-7am • lesbians/ gay men • dancing/DJ • Latino/a clientele • drag shows •strippers • videos • private club • gay-owned

Spiritual Groups

Unitarian Universalist Congregation 131 Oakmont Dr (at Charles Blvd) **252/355-6658** • 10:30am Sun

EROTICA

Late Show Video 1101 Charles Blvd (at 10th St) 252/758–5883 • noon-midnight • adult DVDs • toys • gay-owned

Hickory

NIGHTCLUBS

Club Cabaret 101 N Center St (at 1st Ave) 828/322–8103 • 10pm-2am, 8pm-midnight Sun, clsd Mon-Wed • lesbians/ gay men • dancing/DJ • live shows • private club • wheelchair access

CAFES

Taste Full Beans 16 2nd St NW 828/325–0108 • 7am-6pm, wknd hours vary • gay-owned • art exhibits • gay-owned

SPIRITUAL GROUPS

Christ's Church of the Foothills 109 11th Ave NW (at Unitarian Church) 828/261–0403 • 11am Sun

Hot Springs

ACCOMMODATIONS

The Duckett House Inn 828/622–7621 • gay/ straight • Victorian farmhouse • full brkfst • shared baths • nonsmoking • creek swimming • also vegetarian restaurant (reservations required) • gay-owned • $95-120

Jacksonville

CAFES

Corner Cafe Coffeehouse 715 Gum Branch Rd (at Hwy 17) 910/938–2535 • 6pm-midnight or later • gay/ straight • internet access • full bar • patio

EROTICA

Priscilla's 113–A Western Blvd 910/355–0765

Lexington

SPIRITUAL GROUPS

Holy Rainbow Church 721 S Main St 336/798–3567 • 11am & 6:30pm Sun, 7pm Fri

Mt Mitchell

ACCOMMODATIONS

Serendipity Cabin 2160 S Toe River Rd, Burnsville 954/448–8371 • gay/ straight • kids/ pets ok • nonsmoking • $90-125

New Bern

ACCOMMODATIONS

Harmony House Inn 215 Pollock St 252/636–3810, 800/636–3113 • gay-friendly • 1850 Greek Revival • full brkfst • kids ok • nonsmoking • $99-160

Raleigh/Durham/Chapel Hill

INFO LINES & SERVICES

Common Solutions Gay/ Lesbian AA 505 Alexander Ave (at Episcopal Student Cntr), Durham 919/286–9499 (AA#) • 6:30pm Mon

Gay/ Lesbian Helpline of Wake County 919/821–0055 • 6:30pm-9:30pm Sun-Th

ACCOMMODATIONS

Fickle Creek Farm 919/304–6287 • gay/ straight • passive solar B&B • full brkfst • jacuzzi • some shared baths • kids ok • gay-owned • $75-85

Joan's Place 919/942–5621 • gay/ straight • 2 guest rooms w/ shared bath • nonsmoking • infants/ pets ok • lesbian-owned • $65-75

Morehead Manor B&B 914 Vickers Ave (at Morehead), Durham 919/687–4366, 888/437–6333 • gay/ straight • splendid colonial home • full brkfst • teens ok • nonsmoking • woman-owned/ run • $135-450

The Oakwood Inn B&B 411 N Bloodworth St (at Oakwood), Raleigh 919/832–9712, 800/267–9712 • gay-friendly • Victorian in the heart of Raleigh • full brkfst • kids ok • $125-175

NIGHTCLUBS

Boxer's Ringside 308 W Main St (at Market St), Durham 919/682–2100 • gay/ straight • dancing/DJ • private club

The Capital Corral (CC) 313 W Hargett St (at Harrington), Raleigh 919/755–9599 • 8pm-close, from 6pm Sun • mostly gay men • dancing/DJ • more multiracial Th • live shows • 18+ • also piano bar • private club • wheelchair access

Cat's Cradle 300 E Main St, Carrboro 919/967–9053 • gay-friendly • live music venue

Club Black Tie 3201 New Bern Ave (at Milburnie), Raleigh 919/255–1314 • 5pm-3am, from 8pm wknds • gay/ straight • dancing/DJ • theme nights • live shows • patio • gay-owned

Legends 330 W Hargett St, Raleigh
919/831–8888 • 9pm-close • theme nights •
deck • lesbians/ gay men • dancing/ DJ •
strippers • drag shows • young crowd • private
club • wheelchair access

The Office 310 S West St, Raleigh
919/828–9994 • Fri-Sun only • gay friendly •
dancing/DJ • preppy dance club • 3 rooms •
martini lounge • young crowd • private club

Visions 711 Rigsbee Ave, Durham
919/688–3002 • 9pm-close Fri-Sat only •
mostly women • dancing/DJ • deck •
nonsmoking Oldies night 2nd Fri (18+) • drag
king shows 3rd Fri • private club • wheelchair
access

CAFES

Caribou Coffee 110 West Franklin St (at N
Columbia St), Chapel Hill **919/933–5404** •
6:30am-11pm, till midnight Fri-Sat

Reverie: A Coffee Den 2522 Hillsborough
St (at Pogue), Raleigh **919/839–2233**

RESTAURANTS

Crazie Mae's 100 Westgreen Dr
919/933–0623 • 11am-10pm, till 8pm Sun •
diner fare, vegan options

Crooks Corner 610 Franklin St (at Merritt
Mill Rd), Chapel Hill **919/929–7643** • dinner
nightly • Southern • some veggie • full bar •
patio • wheelchair access

Elmo's Diner 776 9th St (in the Carr Mill
Mall), Durham **919/416–3823** • 6:30am-10pm,
till 11pm Fri-Sat • some veggie

Irregardless Cafe 901 W Morgan St (at
Hillsborough), Raleigh **919/833–8898** • lunch
Tue-Fri, dinner Tue-Sat, Sun brunch • plenty
veggie • live music • dancing Sat

Magnolia Grill 1002 9th St (at Knox),
Durham **919/286–3609** • 6pm-9:30pm, clsd
Sun-Mon • upscale Southern • full bar •
wheelchair access

Spotted Dog 111 E Main St, Carrboro
919/933–1117 • 11:30am-midnight, clsd Mon
• beer/ wine • some veggie

Raleigh/Durham/Chapel Hill

LGBT PRIDE:
October, Durham. web:
www.ncpride.org.

ANNUAL EVENTS:
August - North Carolina Gay and
Lesbian Film Festival, web:
www.carolinatheatre.org/ncglff.

CITY INFO:
919/834-5900 or 800/849-8499,
web: www.visitraleigh.com.
Chapel Hill/Orange County Visitors
Bureau, web: www.chocvb.org.

TRANSIT:
Regional Transit Information
919/549-9999, web: www.gotri-
angle.org.

ATTRACTIONS:
African-American Dance Ensemble,
Durham 919/560-2729.
African-American Cultural Complex,
Raleigh 919/250–9336, web:
www.aaccmuseum.bizland.com.
City Market, Raleigh.
Duke University, Durham.
Exploris (interactive global learning
center), Raleigh 919/834-4040,
web: www.exploris.org.
Morehead Planetarium & Science
Center 919/549-6863, web:
www.moreheadplanetarium.org.
NC Museum of Art, Raleigh
919/839-6262, web: www.ncart-
museum.org.
NC Museum of Life & Science,
Durham 919/220-5429, web:
www.ncmls.org.
Oakwood Historic District, Raleigh.
University of North Carolina, Chapel
Hill.
W. Franklin St. in Chapel Hill, south
of UNC and into Carrboro—
charming and hip shopping area.

Vertigo Diner 426 S McDowell St (at Cabarrus), Raleigh 919/832–4477 • 11am–11pm, till 2am Fri-Sat, from 5pm Sat, clsd Sun • retro chic

Weathervane Cafe Eastgate Shopping Center, Chapel Hill 919/929–9466 • 7am-9pm, till 10pm Fri-Sat, 10:30am-6pm Sun • plenty veggie • full bar • great brunch • patio • wheelchair access • live jazz

BOOKSTORES

Internationalist Books & Community Center 405 W Franklin St (at Columbia), Chapel Hill 919/942–1740 • 11am-8pm, till 6pm Sun • progressive/ alternative • cooperatively run • nonprofit • literature readings & events

Quail Ridge Books 3522 Wade Ave (at Ridgewood Center), Raleigh 919/828–1588, 800/672–6789 • 9am-9pm • LGBT section

Reader's Corner 3201 Hillsborough St (at Rosemary), Raleigh 919/828–7024 • 10am-8pm, till 6pm wknds, from noon Sun • used books

Regulator Bookshop 720 9th St (btwn Hillsborough & Perry), Durham 919/286–2700 • 9am-9pm, till 6pm Sun • also cafe

White Rabbit Raleigh 309 W Martin St (btwn Dawson & Harrington), Raleigh 919/856–1429 • 11am-9pm, 1pm-7pm Sun • LGBT • music • movies • cards • gifts • wheelchair access

PUBLICATIONS

▲ **The Front Page** 919/829–0181 • LGBT newspaper for the Carolinas

SPIRITUAL GROUPS

Community Church (Unitarian Universalist) 106 Purefoy Rd (at Mason Farm Rd), Chapel Hill 919/942–2050 • 9:30am & 11:15am Sun, 10:30am summer

Imani MCC of Durham 304 E Trinity Ave (at Calvary United Methodist Church), Durham 919/403–6881, 877/404–0922 • 2:45pm Sun

St John's MCC 805 Glenwood Ave, Raleigh 919/834–2611 • 11am & 7pm Sun

Unitarian Universalist Fellowship 3313 Wade Ave (at Dixie Tr), Raleigh 919/781–7635 • 10:30am

EROTICA

Castle Video & News 1210 Capitol Blvd, Raleigh 919/836–9189 • 24hrs

Spruce Pine

ACCOMMODATIONS

The Lemon Tree Inn 872 Greenwood Rd 828/765–6161 • gay/ straight • gay-owned • $35-50

Shepherd's Ridge 828/765–7809 • open March-Nov • mostly women • cottage in the woods • sleeps 2-4 • nonsmoking • $70/ night, $350/ week • woman-owned/ run

Statesville

ACCOMMODATIONS

Madelyn's in the Grove 1836 W Memorial Hwy, Union Grove 704/539–4151, 800/948–4473 • gay/ straight • B&B • full brkfst • "murder mystery" wknds • nonsmoking • $85-175

Wilkesboro

ACCOMMODATIONS

The Old Traphill Mill Inn & Resort 452 Traphill Mill Rd, Traphill 336/957–3713 • gay-friendly • rustic mountain retreat • different types of lodging available • reservations • clothing optional • swimming • nudity permitted • gay-owned • required • $15-100

Wilmington

ACCOMMODATIONS

Best Western Coastline Inn 503 Nutt St 910/763–2800, 800/617–7732 • gay/ straight • kids ok • internet access • nonsmoking • wheelchair access • gay-owned • $69-169

Blue Heaven B&B 517 Orange St 910/772–9929 • gay-friendly • 1800s historic home • full brkfst • nonsmoking • pets ok • $90-130

Hidden Treasure Beach 113 S 4th Ave (at K Ave), Kure Beach 910/458–3216 • gay/ straight • 3 private units w/ kitchens • swimming • nonsmoking • $75-115

Rosehill Inn B&B 114 S 3rd St (at Dock St) 910/815–0250, 800/815–0250 • gay-friendly • full brkfst • jacuzzi • nonsmoking • $99-199

The Taylor House Inn 14 N 7th St 910/763–7581, 800/382–9982 • gay/ straight • romantic 1905 house • full brkfst • nonsmoking • kids ok • $110-225

NIGHTCLUBS

Ibiza 118 Market St (rear) **910/251–1301** • 8pm-3am, clsd Mon-Wed • mostly gay men • dancing/DJ • more women Th for Girls Night Ou • karaoke • drag shows • young crowd • private club • wheelchair access • gay-owned

RESTAURANTS

Caffé Phoenix 9 S Front St **910/343–1395** • lunch & dinner • gay-owned

The Forks 3151 S 17th St (at Louise Wells Cameron Museum) **910/395–5999** • 11:30am-3pm, jazz brunch Sun, clsd Mon • upscale Southern • beer/ wine • gay-owned

BOOKSTORES

Bristol Books 1908 Eastwood Rd, Ste 116 (in Lumina Station) **910/256–4490** • 10am-7pm, from 9am-6pm Sun • also cafe

SPIRITUAL GROUPS

St Jude's MCC 507 Castle St (at 5th) **910/762–5833** • 9:30am, 11am & 7pm Sun

Unity Christ Church 717 Orchard Ave **910/763–5155** • 8:30am & 11am Sun

Wilson

SPIRITUAL GROUPS

GLAD (Gay & Lesbian Affirming Disciples) Alliance 252/291–7370

Winston-Salem

INFO LINES & SERVICES

Gay/ Lesbian Hotline 336/855–8558, 336/748–0031 • 7pm-10pm

NIGHTCLUBS

Club Odyssey 4019–A Country Club Rd 336/774–1077, 336/774–7071 • 9pm-2:30am, clsd Mon • popular • lesbians/ gay men • dancing/DJ • drag shows Fri • 18+ • cover charge

SPIRITUAL GROUPS

Holy Trinity Church 2873 Robinhood Rd 336/725–5355 • 10:30am

MCC of Winston-Salem 2315 Huff St 336/784–8009 • 11am & 6pm Sun

NORTH DAKOTA

Statewide

PUBLICATIONS

Lavender Magazine 612/436–4660, 877/515–9969 • LGBT newsmagazine for MN, WI, IA, ND, SD

Fargo

INFO LINES & SERVICES

Pride Collective & Community Center 116 12th St S (at Main Ave) **218/287–8034** • 3pm-5pm Tue & Sat, 8:30pm-10pm Th • referrals • support • social groups

NIGHTCLUBS

I-Beam 1021 Center Ave (at 11th), Moorhead, MN **218/233–7700** • 8pm-2am, clsd Sun • lesbians/ gay men • dancing/DJ • karaoke

RESTAURANTS

Fargo's Fryn' Pan 301 E Main St (at 4th) **701/293–9952** • 24hrs • popular • wheelchair access

RETAIL SHOPS

One World Imports 618 Main Ave (at Broadway) **701/297–8882** • 10am-7pm, till 6pm Sat, noon-4pm (clsd summer) Sun• gay-owned

Zandbroz Variety 420 Broadway **701/239–4729** • 9am-9pm, noon-5pm Sun • books & gifts

SPIRITUAL GROUPS

St Mark's Lutheran 670 4th Ave N **701/235–5591** • 10am Sun

EROTICA

ABC Fargo Romantix 417 N Pacific Ave **701/232–9768** • 24hrs

Grand Forks

EROTICA

Plain Brown Wrapper Romantix 102 S 3rd St (at Kittson) **701/772–9021** • 24hrs

Minot

EROTICA

Risque's 1514 S Broadway **701/838–2837**

Ohio

Statewide

Publications

Gay People's Chronicle 216/631-8646, 800/426-5947 • Ohio's largest weekly LGBT newspaper w/ extensive listings

OUTlines Magazine 216/433-1280 • free bi-weekly club magazine covering Akron, Canton Cleveland, Columbus, Dayton, Sandusky, Toledo & more

Outlook News 614/268-8525, 866/452-6397 • statewide LGBT newsweekly • good resource pages

Akron

Info Lines & Services

AA Intergroup 330/253-8181 (AA#)

Akron Pride Center 71 N Adams St (off E Market St) 330/253-2220 • call for meeting schedule

Bars

Adams Street Bar 77 N Adams St 330/434-9794 • 4:30pm-2:30am, from 9pm Sun • popular • mostly gay men • piano bar Wed • dancing/DJ Fri-Sat • drag shows • strippers

Cocktails 1009 S Main St 330/376-2625 • 4pm-2:30am, clsd Sun • mostly gay men • videos • drag shows • Daddy's leather bar upstairs wknds

Lydia's 1348 S Arlington St (in Arlington Plaza) 330/773-3001 • 6pm-2:30am, from 8pm Tue-Th • gay/ straight • neighborhood bar • blues • live shows wknds • karaoke

The Roseto Club 627 S Arlington St 330/724-4228 • 6pm-2:30am, till 1am Mon-Tue • mostly women • dancing/DJ • karaoke Wed • wheelchair access

Tear-Ez 360 S Main (near Exchange St) 330/376-0011 • 11am-2:30am, from noon Sun • lesbians/ gay men • neighborhood bar • drag shows Th & Sun • wheelchair access

Nightclubs

Interbelt 70 N Howard St (near Perkins & Main) 330/253-5700 • 10pm-2:30am, from 9pm Fri-Sat • lesbians/ gay men • dancing/DJ • live shows • videos • patio

Metro 820 W Market St (btwn Portage Pass & Rhodes Ave) 330/252-9000 • 4pm-2:30am, from 8pm Sun • mostly gay men • dancing/DJ • drag shows • strippers • videos • wheelchair access • gay-owned

Cafes

Angel Falls Coffee Company 792 W Market St (btwn S Highland & Grand) 330/376-5282 • lunch & desserts • patio • wheelchair access • gay-owned

Restaurants

Aladdin's Eatery 782 W Market St 330/535-0110 • 11am-10pm • Middle Eastern

Bricco 1 W Exchange St (at S Main St) 330/475-1600 • 11am-midnight, till 1am Fri-Sat • Italian • also bar • gay-owned

Bruegger's Bagels 1821 Merriman Rd 330/867-8394 • 6am-4pm

Two Amigos Mexican Grill 804 W Market St 330/762-8226 • 11:30am-9pm, till 10pm Fri-Sat, from 3pm Sun, clsd Mon

Spiritual Groups

Cascade Community Church 1196 Inman St 330/773-5298 • 11am Sun

Emmanuel Fellowship Church 60 N Arlington St (N of Market) 330/376-8725 • 11am Sun

Athens

Accommodations

Rose Cottage Inn B&B 10764 Hooper Ridge Rd, Glouster 740/448-7673, 866/225-9621 • gay/ straight • historic 1880s country inn • full brkfst • $80-100

SuBAMUH (Susan B Anthony Memorial UnRest Home) Women's Land Trust PO Box 5853, 45701 740/448-7242 • women only • cabins & camping • summer workshops • swimming • hot tub • nonsmoking • lesbian-owned • $7 (tent) – $12 (cabin) sliding scale

Brunswick

see also Akron & Cleveland

Restaurants

Pizza Marcello 67-A Pearl Rd (near Boston Rd) 330/225-1211 • 11am-10pm, till midnight Fri-Sat, from 1pm wknds • Italian

Canton

Nightclubs

540 Eagle 540 Walnut Ave NE (at 6th) 330/456-8622 • 9pm-2:30am, 10pm-close Sun • mostly gay men • neighborhood bar • leather

Exile 2360 Mahoning Rd 330/452-8098 • 5pm-2:30am • lesbians/ gay men • neighborhood bar • dancing/ DJ

Studio 704 704 4th St SW **330/453–1220** • 9pm-2:30am, clsd Sun-Tue • lesbians/ gay men • dancing/DJ • drag shows • male strippers Th-Sat

EROTICA

Tower Bookstore 219 12th St NE (near Walnut) **330/455-1254**

Cincinnati

INFO LINES & SERVICES

AA Gay/ Lesbian 320 Resor Ave (in St John's Unitarian Church), Clifton **513/351-0422 (AA#)** • call for locations of wknd meetings

Gay/ Lesbian Community Center of Greater Cincinnati 4119 Hamilton Ave (near Blue Rock) **513/591-0200** • 6pm-9pm, till 11pm Fri, noon-4pm Sat, clsd Sun

ACCOMMODATIONS

Cincinnatian Hotel 601 Vine St (at 6th St) **513/381-3000, 800/942-9000** • gay-friendly • restaurant & lounge • kids ok • $158-1,500

Clarion Cinncinnati 5901 Pfeiffer Rd (at I-71) **513/793-4500** • gay-friendly • pool • kids ok • wheelchair access • $59-109

First Farm Inn 2510 Stevens Rd, Idlewild, KY **859/586-0199, 800/277-9527** • gay-friendly • 1800s farmhouse B&B • 20 minutes from Cincinnati • full brkfst • horseback riding • massage • nonsmoking • wheelchair access • $99-154

Millennium Hotel Cincinnati 141 W Sixth St **513/352-2100, 800/876-2100** • gay-friendly • centrally located hotel w/in walking distance to gay bars & clubs & all of the city's major attractions • city's only outdoor rooftop pool & sundeck (seasonal) • 24hr business & fitness cetner • wheelchair access • $89-179

The Vernon Manor Hotel 400 Oak St **513/281-3300, 800/543-3999** • gay-friendly • restaurant • pub • gym • $109-129

Weller Haus B&B 319 Poplar St, Newport, KY **859/431-6829, 800/431-4287** • gay-friendly • B&B in 2 side-by-side historic homes

BARS

Bullfishes 4023 Hamilton Ave (at Blue Rock) **513/541-9220** • 7pm-2:30am, clsd Sun-Mon • mostly women • neighborhood bar • dancing/DJ • live shows • karaoke

Golden Lion 340 Ludlow (at Telford), Clifton **513/281-4179** • 11am-2:30am, from 1pm Sun • mostly gay men • neighborhood bar • dancing/ DJ • karaoke • live shows • dive bar

---

Cincinnati

LGBT PRIDE:
June. 513/681-4627, web: www.cincypride.com.

CITY INFO:
513/621-2142 or 800/246-2987, web: www.cincyusa.com.

BEST VIEW:
Mt Adams & Eden Park.

TRANSIT:
Yellow Cab 513/241-2100.
Queen City Metro 513/621-4455, web: www.sorta.com.

ATTRACTIONS:
The Beach waterpark (in Mason) 513/398-7946, web: www.thebeachwaterpark.com.
Carew Tower 513/241-3888.
Cincinnati Art Museum 513/721-2787, web: www.cincinnatiartmuseum.org.
Fountain Square.
Krohn Conservatory 513/421-4086.
Museum Center at Union Terminal 513/287-7000, web: www.cincymuseum.org.
Paramount King's Island (24 miles N of Cincinnati) 513/754-5700, web: www.pki.com.

Junkers Tavern 4156 Langland (at Pullan) 513/541–5470 • 7:30am-1am • gay-friendly • neighborhood bar

"Little Bit" Bar 2401 Vine St (at Hollister, Clifton Heights) 513/721–8484 • 5pm-2am, from 7pm Sat, from 3pm Sun • lesbians/ gay men • neighborhood bar • dancing/DJ • karaoke Wed-Th & Sun • drag shows • wheelchair access

Milton's 301 Milton St (at Sycamore) 513/784–9938 • 4pm-2:30am, from 7pm wknds • gay-friendly • neighborhood bar

The Serpent 4042 Hamilton Ave (at Blue Rock) 513/681–6969 • 7pm-2:30am, from 9pm Fri-Sat, clsd Mon, dress code Fri-Sat • mostly gay men • leather

Shooters 927 Race St (at Court) 513/381–9900 • 4pm-2:30am • mostly gay men • dancing/DJ • country/ western • more women Th • karaoke Wed

Simon Says 428 Walnut St (at 5th) 513/381–7577 • 11am-2:30am, from 1pm Sun • popular • mostly gay men • professional • neighborhood bar • wheelchair access

Spurs 1121 Race St (N of Central Pkwy) 513/621–2668 • 4pm-2:30am • popular • mostly gay men • leather • patio • wheelchair access

The Subway 609 Walnut St (at 6th) 513/421–1294 • 5:30am-2:30am, from noon Sun • mostly gay men • neighborhood bar • dancing/DJ • live shows • food served

Nightclubs

The Dock 603 W Pete Rose Wy (near Central) 513/241–5623 • 5pm-2:30am, till 4am wknds (from 8pm winter) • popular • lesbians/ gay men • dancing/DJ • live shows • 19+ • volleyball court • wheelchair access

Jacobs' on the Avenue 4029 Hamilton Ave (at Blue Rock) 513/591–2100 • 6pm-2:30am, from 4pm Fri-Sun, clsd Mon • mostly gay men • dancing/DJ • live shows • karaoke • videos • wheelchair access • gay-owned

Cafes

Kaldi's Cafe & Books 1204 Main St (at 12th) 513/241–3070 • 9am-7pm,10am-4pm Sun brunch • plenty veggie • full bar • live shows • wheelchair access

Zen & Now Book Cafe 4453 Bridgetown Rd 513/598–8999 • 7am-11pm, from 9am Sat, clsd Sun • coffeehouse & New Age bookstore

Restaurants

Boca 3200 Madison Rd, Oakley 513/542–2022 • dinner Tue-Sat, popular Sun brunch • nouvelle int'l • full bar • patio • wheelchair access

Hamburger Mary's 911 Vine St (at 9th St) 513/381–6279 • 11am-10pm, till midnight Fri-Sat, bar open till 2:30am • also nightclub • dancing/ DJ Wed, Fri-Sat • karaoke • drag shows • wheelchair access

Entertainment & Recreation

Alternating Currents WAIF 88.3 FM 513/749–1444 (during show) • 3pm Sat • LGBT public affairs radio program • also "Everywoman" 1pm Sat

Ensemble Theatre of Cincinnati 1127 Vine St 513/421–3555

Know Theatre 1425 Sycamore St 513/300–5669 • contemporary LGBT theater

Retail Shops

Elyse's Passion 1569 Chase Ave (at Hamilton) 513/541–0800 • noon-8pm, clsd Sun • spiritual/ erotic books, videos & more

Pink Pyramid 907 Race St (btwn 9th & Court) 513/621–7465 • noon-9pm, till 11pm Fri-Sat, 1pm-8pm Sun • pride items • also leather

Publications

EXP Magazine 317/267–0397 (Indy #), 877/397–6244 • gay magazine serving IN, OH & KY

Greater Cincinnati GLBT News

Spiritual Groups

Dignity 3960 Winding Wy (near Xavier Univ, at Friends Mtg House) 513/557–2111 • 7:30pm 1st & 3rd Sat

EarthSpirit 320 Resor Ave (at St John's Unitarian Universalist Church) 513/961–1938 (St John's #) • group for "earth-centered" spirituality

New Spirit MCC 4033 Hamilton Ave (at Belmont, in Grace Episcopal Church) 513/661–6464 • 10:30am & 7pm Sun

St John's Unitarian Universalist Church 320 Resor Ave 513/961–1938 • 10:30am

Cleveland

INFO LINES & SERVICES

AA Gay/ Lesbian 7801 Detroit Ave (at St Augustine Manor) **216/241–7387** • call for meeting times

Cleveland Lesbian/ Gay Community Center 6600 Detroit Ave **216/651–5428, 888/429–8761** • noon-10pm, 10am-6pm Sat, clsd Sun • wheelchair access

ACCOMMODATIONS

Clifford House 1810 W 28th St (at Jay) **216/589–0121** • gay/ straight • 1868 historic brick home • near downtown • fireplaces • nonsmoking • gay-owned • $85-165

Edgewater Estates 9803 Lake Ave **216/961–1764** • gay/ straight • English Tudor on Lake Erie • full brkfst • pets ok • patio • women-owned/ run • $80-150

Glendennis B&B 2808 Bridge Ave (at 28th St) **216/589–0663** • gay/ straight • 3-room suite • full brkfst • $100

Radisson Hotel Cleveland—Gateway 651 Huron Rd **216/377–9000, 800/333–3333** • gay-friendly • kids ok • wheelchair access • $79-129 + tax

Stone Gables B&B 3806 Franklin Blvd (at W 38th) **216/961–4654, 877/215–4326** • gay/ straight • full brkfst • jacuzzi • kids/ pets ok • wheelchair access • gay-owned • $100-150

| **Reply** | **Forward** | | **Delete** |

```
Date: Dec 17, 2005 14:21:22
From: Girl-on-the-Go
To: Editor@Damron.com
Subject: Cleveland
```

>Cleveland has made quite a comeback, since the recession and several economic facelifts in the '90s. Actually, only some districts, like the Flats, have had a beauty makeover. Other districts never lost their funky charm in this city that's home both to the Rock 'N' Roll Hall of Fame and the Cleveland Symphony Orchestra.

>Speaking of funky, flash back to the '60s with a trip down Coventry Road. University Circle is rumored to be another hang-out of the avant-garde, as is Murray Hill, known for its many galleries. While you're at it, make time for some serious art appreciation in the galleries of the world-famous Cleveland Museum of Art.

>To touch base with the lesbian community, pick up a copy of the **Gay People's Chronicle** or **Outlines** and find out more about the ever-changing bar/coffeehouse scene. For a whole-some meal, try the women-run **Inn on Coventry.** After dinner, check out bars **Paradise Inn** or the **Five Cent Decision** (known to locals as the **Nickel**).

BARS

A Man's World 2909 Detroit Ave (at 29th St) 216/574–2203 • 7am-2:30am, from noon Sun-Mon • mostly men • more women Sun eve for line dancing • dancing/DJ wknds • patio

Deco 11213 Detroit Ave (at 112th St) 216/221–8576 • 3pm-2:30am, from 4pm Sun • lesbians/gay men • neighborhood bar • dancing/DJ • karaoke • drag shows

The Hawk 11217 Detroit Ave (at 112th St) 216/521–5443 • 11am-2:30am, from 1pm Sun • lesbians/gay men • neighborhood bar • wheelchair access

Longevity 2032 W 25th St (at Lorain & 24th) 216/781–9191 • 10am-2:30am, from 11am Sat, from noon Sun • mostly gay men • neighborhood bar • strippers • wheelchair access

Muggs 3194 W 25th St (near Clark) 216/398–7012 • 11am-2:30am, from 10am Sat, clsd Sun • lesbians/gay men • neighborhood bar • dancing/DJ Fri-Sat • karaoke

The Nickel/Five Cent Decision 4365 State Rd (Rte 94, at Montclair) 216/661–1314 • 6pm-2am • mostly women • neighborhood bar • DJ • country/western • karaoke • live shows

Paradise Inn 4488 State Rd (Rte 94, at Rte 480) 216/741–9819 • 11am-2:30am • mostly women • neighborhood bar

Rec Room 15320 Brookpark Rd (at Smith Rd) 216/570–6580 • 6:30pm-2:30am, from 5pm Sun • mostly women

Twist 11633 Clifton (at 117th St) 216/221–2333 • 9am-2:30am, from 1pm Sun • popular • lesbians/gay men • neighborhood bar • dancing/DJ • professional crowd

Union Station Video Café 2814 Detroit Ave (at W 28th) 216/357–2997 • 5pm-2:30am, also Sun brunch • popular • lesbians/gay men, more women Sat night • dancing/DJ • drag shows • videos • full restaurant

NIGHTCLUBS

Best of Both Worlds 1059 Old River Rd (at Heaven and Earth) 216/443–4710 • 10pm-3:30am Sun • lesbians/gay men

---

Cleveland

WHERE THE GIRLS ARE:
Dancing downtown near Public Square, hanging out on State Rd below the intersection of Pearl and Broadview/Memphis.

LGBT PRIDE:
June. 216/371-0214, web: www.clevelandpride.org.

CITY INFO:
216/621-4110 or 800/321–1004, web: www.travelcleveland.com.

TRANSIT:
Yellow Cab 216/623-1500.
AmeriCab 216/881-1111.
Regional Transit Authority (RTA) 216/621-9500, web: www.gcrta.org.
Lolly the Trolley 216/771-4484, web: www.lollytrolley.com.

ATTRACTIONS:
Cleveland Metroparks Zoo 216/661-6500, web: www.clemetzoo.com.
Cleveland Museum of Art 216/421-7340, web: www.clemusart.com.
Coventry Road district.
Cuyahoga Valley National Recreation Area 216/524–1497.
The Flats.
Rock and Roll Hall of Fame 216/781-7625, web: www.rockhall.com.

Club 727 727 Bolivar Rd (at E 8th Pl) **216/861-5787** • 10pm-3:30am Sat • lesbians/gay men

CAFES

Johnny Mango 3120 Bridge Ave (btwn Fulton & W 32nd) **216/575-1919** • 11am-10pm, from 9am Fri-Sun, till 11pm Fri-Sat • healthy world food • juice bar • also full bar • wheelchair access

RESTAURANTS

Cafe Tandoor 2096 S Taylor Rd (at Cedar), Cleveland Hts **216/371-8500, 216/371-8569** • lunch & dinner, 3pm-9pm Sun • Indian • plenty veggie

Club Isabella 2025 University Hospital Rd (at Cornell) **216/229-1177** • lunch Mon-Fri & dinner nightly, clsd Sun • eclectic int'l • full bar • live jazz

Hecks 2927 Bridge Ave (at W 30th) **216/861-5464** • lunch & dinner • popular • gourmet burgers • wheelchair access

The Inn on Coventry 2785 Euclid Heights Blvd (at Coventry), Cleveland Hts **216/371-1811** • 7am-9pm, from 8:30am Sat-Sun, from 8am Mon, till 3pm Sun-Mon, Sun brunch • homestyle • popular Bloody Marys • some veggie • full bar • wheelchair access • women-owned/ run

My Friend's Deli & Restaurant 11616 Detroit Ave **216/221-2575** • 24hrs

ENTERTAINMENT & RECREATION

Rock & Roll Hall of Fame 1 Key Plaza (at E 9th & Lake) **216/781-ROCK** • even if you don't like rock, be sure to stop by & check out IM Pei's architectural gift to Cleveland

BOOKSTORES

Bookstore on W 25th St 1921 W 25th St (at Lorain) **216/566-8897** • 11am-5pm, 10am-6pm Sat, clsd Sun • LGBT section

Borders Bookshop & Espresso Bar 2101 Richmond Rd (at Cedar, in LaPlace Mall), Beachwood **216/292-2660** • 9am-11pm, till 9pm Sun

RETAIL SHOPS

Big Fun 1827 Coventry Rd **216/371-4386** • noon-6pm, 11am-10pm Fri-Sat, variety store

City Dweller 12005 Detroit Ave, Lakewood **216/226-7106** • 10am-9pm, noon-6pm Sun • cards, gifts & home decorations • gay-owned

The Clifton Web 11512 Clifton Blvd (at W 115th) **216/961-1120** • 11am-7pm, from 10am Sat, till 5pm Sun • cards & gifts

Diverse Universe 12011 Detroit Ave (at Hopkins), Lakewood **216/221-4297** • 10am-9pm, 11am-6pm Sun • LGBT • books • videos • music • clothing • pride gifts • wheelchair access • gay-owned

Shoptalk Lingerie 13351 Madison Ave, Lakewood **216/228-5557** • noon-8pm, till 5pm Sun, 10am-10pm Th-Sat • "your romance headquarters" • clothing, videos, toys

PUBLICATIONS

Erie Gay News **814/456-9833** • covers news & events in the Erie, Cleveland, Pittsburgh, Buffalo & Chautauqua County, NY region

Gay People's Chronicle **216/631-8646, 800/426-5947** • Ohio's largest weekly LGBT newspaper w/ extensive listings

OUTlines Magazine **216/433-1280** • free bi-weekly club magazine covering Akron, Canton Cleveland, Columbus, Dayton, Sandusky, Toledo & more

SPIRITUAL GROUPS

Chevrei Tikva 23737 Fairmont Blvd (at Anshe Chesed Temple), Beachwood **216/464-1330** • 8:15pm 1st & 3rd Fri • LGBT group

Liberation UCC 13714 Madison Ave, Lakewood **216/521-5556** • 10:30am Sun

Trinity Cathedral 2230 Euclid Ave **216/771-3630** • 8am, 9am & 11:15am Sun • Episcopal

EROTICA

Laws Leather Shop 11112 Clifton Blvd **216/961-0544** • 1pm-9pm, clsd Sun-Tue

Columbus

INFO LINES & SERVICES

AA Gay/ Lesbian **614/253-8501, 800/870-3795** (IN OH)

Stonewall Columbus Community Center/ Hotline 1160 N High St (at E 4th Ave) **614/299-7764** • 10am-6pm, till 5pm Fri, clsd wknds • wheelchair access

ACCOMMODATIONS

Courtyard by Marriott 35 W Spring St (at Front St) **614/228-3200, 800/321-2211** • gay-friendly • wknd discounts • wheelchair access • $89-170

BARS

Blazer's Pub 1205 N High St (at 5th) **614/299-1800** • 4pm-close • lesbians/ gay men • neighborhood bar • karaoke

Blondie's 2507 Summit St (at Hudson St) **614/267–3480** • 3pm-2:30am • lesbians/gay men • food served • karaoke • drag shows • strippers • gay-owned

Club Diversity 863 S High St **614/224–4050** • 4pm-midnight, till 2:30am wknds, opens 6:30pm Sat, clsd Sun • lesbians/gay men • live shows nightly • piano bar

Columbus Eagle Bar 232 N 3rd St (at Hickory) **614/228–2804** • 8pm-2:30am • popular • mostly gay men • young crowd • dancing/DJ • drag shows • strippers • wheelchair access • 18+

Downtown Connection 1126 N High St (at 4th Ave) **614/299–4880** • 5pm-2am, from 3pm wknds • mostly gay men • sports bar

The Far Side 1662 W Mound St (at Reed) **614/276–5817** • 5pm-1am, till 2:30am Fri-Sat, from 6pm Sat • mostly women • older crowd • neighborhood bar • food served • live bands wknds • karaoke • lesbian-owned

Havana Video Lounge 862 N High (at 1st Ave) **614/421–9697** • 5pm-2am • popular • lesbians/gay men • neighborhood bar • dancing/DJ • drag shows • martini & cigar lounge • videos • male strippers • food served

Slammer's/ Club 202 202 E Long St (at 5th St) **614/469–7526** • 11am-12:30am, 5pm-2:30am wknds • mostly women • dancing/DJ • open mic Tue • wheelchair access

Somewhere Else 1312 S High St (at Moler) **614/443–4300** • 1pm-2:30am • lesbians/gay men • live shows • karaoke • drag shows • strippers

The South Bend Tavern 126 E Moler St (at 4th St) **614/444–3386** • noon-2:30am • lesbians/gay men • neighborhood bar • drag shows Sat • wheelchair access

Summit Station 2210 Summit St (btwn Alden & Oakland) **614/261–9634** • 4pm-2:30am • mostly women • neighborhood bar • karaoke • live shows

Union Station Video Cafe 630 N High St (at Goodale) **614/228–3740** • 11am-2am • popular • lesbians/gay men • video bar • also restaurant • plenty veggie • internet access • wheelchair access

The Vine Cocktails & Café 73 E Gay St (at 3rd St) **614/221–8463** • 5pm-1am, Sun brunch from 11am • lesbians/gay men • martinis • also restaurant • karaoke • videos • wheelchair access

Columbus

WHERE THE GIRLS ARE:
Downtown with the boys, north near the University area, or somewhere in-between.

LGBT PRIDE:
June. 614/299-7764 (Stonewall #).

ANNUAL EVENTS:
June - Pagan Spirit Gathering in Athens campground, 1.5 hours south of Columbus 608/924-2216 (Wisconsin office), web: circle-sanctuary.org/psg/site.
September - Ohio Lesbian Festival, web: www.ohiolba.org.

CITY INFO:
614/221-2489, web: www.ohio-tourism.com.

WEATHER:
Truly midwestern. Winters are cold, summers are hot.

TRANSIT:
Yellow Cab 614/444-4444.
Northway Taxicab 614/299-1191.
Acme Taxi 614/299–9990.
Central Ohio Transit Authority (COTA) 614/228-1776, web: www.cota.com.

ATTRACTIONS:
Brewery District.
Columbus Jazz Orchestra 614/294–5200, web: www.columbusjazzorchestra.com.
Columbus Museum of Modern Art 614/221-6801, web: www.columbusmuseum.org.
Columbus Zoo 614/645-3550, web: www.colszoo.org.
German Village district.
The Short North neighborhood (popular "Gallery Hop" 1st Sat).
Wexner Center for the Arts 614/292-3535, web: www.wexarts.org.

Woofs Columbus 1409 S High St (at Jenkins) **614/443–4224** • 10am-2:30am, clsd Sun • mostly gay men • dancing/DJ • country/western • bears • leather • neighborhood bar • karaoke • strippers

Axis 775 N High St (at Hubbard) **614/291–4008** • 10pm-2:30am Fri-Sat only • popular • mostly gay men • dancing/DJ • go go boys • cabaret • 18+ • wheelchair access • gay-owned

La Barca Nightclub 1120 N High St (at 4th St) **614/291–6113, 614/351–4969** • 2pm-2am • lesbians/ gay men • Latino night Fri-Sat • drag shows

---

| Reply | Forward | | Delete |

```
Date: Fri, Dec 17, 2005 14:21:22
From: Girl-on-the-Go
To: Editor@Damron.com
Subject: Columbus
```

>The center of lesbian life in Columbus is Clintonville (affectionately known as "Clitville"), just north of the OSU campus. While you're in the neighborhood, stop by the popular dyke hangout **Summit Station**. Don't leave before picking up a copy of one of the several newspapers and magazines that cover Columbus and central Ohio, including the locally based national publication **Lesbian Health News**, which has been covering all aspects of lesbian health since 1993.

>Besides Clintonville, there is the Short North—the stretch of High Street just north of downtown. This funky, artsy neighborhood hosts a Gallery Hop the first Saturday of every month. After the shops start closing around 10pm (or later), check out **Blazer's Pub**. If you need to refuel, try the **Coffee Table**; we hear it's as popular with local dykes as with the cruisin' gay boys.

>Sports dykes, check out Berliner Park, any season, to watch women's softball, volleyball, or basketball leagues. Even the non-athletic head to the **Far Side** or **Slammers** afterward to celebrate the thrill of victory.

>The best time of all to be in Columbus is during the Gay Pride March that always falls the same weekend in June as ComFest. This is the community festival at Goodale Park in Victorian Village, which hosts a wide variety of merchants, food, information, and music.

Millenium 747 Chambers Rd (off King Ave) 614/291–7867 • after-hours Fri-Sat only (2:30am-5am), mostly gay men, dancing/DJ

Tradewinds II 117 E Chestnut (at 3rd St) 614/461–4110 • 4pm-2:30am, clsd Mon • mostly gay men • 3 bars • dancing/DJ • leather • videos • also restaurant • wheelchair access

Wall Street 144 N Wall St (at Long) 614/464–2800 • 8pm-2:30am, from 9pm Wed & Sun, clsd Mon-Tue • popular • lesbians/ gay men • TGIF party 1st Fri • dancing/DJ • country/ western Th • special events Sun • young crowd • wheelchair access

CAFES

The Coffee Table 731 N High St (at Buttles) 614/297–1177 • 7am-10pm, 8am-midnight Fri-Sat, 8am-11pm Sun • lesbians/ gay men

Cup-O-Joe Cafe 627 3rd St (at Sycamore) 614/221–1563 • 7am-10:30pm, till 11pm Fri-Sat, till 10pm Sun • food served

The Waiting Room Cafe & Deli 874 N High St 614/297–8844 • 7am-midnight, from 10am wknds • also art space • internet access

RESTAURANTS

Chinese Village 2124 N High St (at Lane St) 614/297–7979 • 11am-9:30pm, till 11pm wknds

L'Antibes 772 N High St #106 (at Warren) 614/291–1666 • dinner from 5pm, clsd Sun-Mon • French • full bar • wheelchair access • gay-owned

Lemon Grass 641 N High (at Russell) 614/224–1414 • lunch weekdays & dinner nightly • popular • Asian cuisine • reservations advised

BOOKSTORES

An Open Book 685 N High St (at Lincoln) 614/221–6339 • noon-10pm• LGBT • also pride items, music, videos & gifts • wheelchair access

The Book Loft of German Village 631 S 3rd St (at Sycamore) 614/464–1774 • 10am-11pm, till midnight Fri-Sat • LGBT section

RETAIL SHOPS

Columbus Leather Company 642 N High St, Ste B (in Short North) • leather • fetish

Hausfrau Haven 769 S 3rd St (at Columbus) 614/443–3680 • 10am-7pm, noon-5pm Sun • greeting cards • wine • gifts

Piercology 872 N High St (S of 1st, 2nd flr) 614/297–4743 • 1pm-9pm, till 7pm Sun • body-piercing studio • gay-owned

Torso 772 N High St (at Warren) 614/421–7663 • 11am-9pm, till 10pm Fri-Sat, noon-5pm Sun, clsd Mon • clothing • also above the Eagle 614/228-3250

PUBLICATIONS

EXP Magazine 317/267–0397 (INDY #), 877/397–6244 • gay magazine serving IN, OH & KY

OUTlines Magazine 216/433–1280 • free bi-weekly club magazine covering Akron, Canton Cleveland, Columbus, Dayton, Sandusky, Toledo & more

Outlook News 614/268-8525, 866/452-6397 • statewide LGBT newsweekly • good resource pages

Spotlight Magazine 614/805–5664 • bi-weekly LGBT paper for Central Ohio

The Stonewall Journal 614/299–7764 • quarterly paper

SPIRITUAL GROUPS

Dignity USA- Columbus 444 E Broad St (at First Congregational Church UCC, side entrance) 614/447–6546 • Roman Catholic Mass 5pm 2nd & 4th Sun

Lutherans Concerned 1555 S James Rd 614/447–7018 • 1:30pm 1st Sun

New Creation MCC 787 E Broad St (at St Paul's Episcopal Church) 614/224–0314 • 10:30am Sun, 7:30pm Wed

St Paul's Episcopal Church 787 E Broad St (at I-71 intersection) 614/221–1703 • 5pm Sun • wheelchair access

EROTICA

The Garden 1174 N High St (btwn 4th & 5th Ave) 614/294–2869 • 11am-3am, noon-midnight Sun • adult toys

Dayton

INFO LINES & SERVICES

AA Gay/ Lesbian 20 W 1st St (off Main, at Christ Episcopal Church) 937/222–2211 • 8pm Sat

Dayton Lesbian/ Gay Center 937/274–1776

BARS

Argos Bar 301 Mabel Ave (btwn Linden & 5th) 937/252–2976 • 5pm-2am Sat (call first) • uniform dress code • men only • neighborhood bar • leather • gay-owned

City Cafe 121 N Ludlow St (in Talbot Tower Bldg) 937/223–1417 • 5pm-2:30am • mostly gay men • DJ Fri-Sat • karaoke Wed & Sun • wheelchair access

Lady Hawk Social Club 2600 Valley St
937/233-5879 • 7pm-2:30am • mostly
women • free buffet Fri • karaoke

Right Corner 105 E 3rd St (at Jefferson)
937/228-1285 • noon-2:30am, from 1pm Sun
• mostly gay men • neighborhood bar •
wheelchair access • gay-owned

Stage Door 44 N Jefferson (at 2nd)
937/223-7418 • noon-2:30am, from 2pm Wed
& wknds • mostly gay men • leather •
wheelchair access

NIGHTCLUBS

Celebrity 850 N Main St (off I-75)
937/461-2582 • 9:30pm-2:30am, till 4am Fri-
Sat, clsd Sun-Tue • popular • mostly gay men
• dancing/DJ • karaoke • strippers • drag
shows • 18+ • wheelchair access

Masque 34 N Jefferson St (btwn 2nd & 3rd)
937/228-2582 • 7pm-2:30am, till 5am wknds
• popular • mostly men • dancing/DJ • drag
shows • strippers • 18+

Up On Main 1919 N Main St **937/278-3650**
• 8pm-close, clsd Mon-Tue • mostly lesbians •
neighborhood bar • dancing/DJ • live shows •
karaoke • wheelchair access • lesbian-owned

RESTAURANTS

Cold Beer & Cheeseburgers 33 S Jefferson
St (at 4th St) **937/222-2337** • 11am-close,
clsd Sun • grill • full bar • wheelchair access

The Spaghetti Warehouse 36 W 5th St (at
Ludlow) **937/461-3913** • 11am-10pm, till
11pm Fri-Sat, from noon wknds • more gay
Tue w/ Friends of the Italian Opera

BOOKSTORES

Books & Co 350 E Stroop Rd (at Farhills)
937/298-6540 • 9am-11pm, till 8pm Sun

RETAIL SHOPS

Q Gift Shop 1904 N Main St (at Ridge Ave)
937/274-4400 • noon-7pm • LGBT gifts

PUBLICATIONS

Gay Dayton **937/623-1590** • monthly LGBT
publication

SPIRITUAL GROUPS

Community Gospel Church 546 Xenia Ave
(at Steele Ave) **937/252-8855** • 10am Sun,
6:30pm Wed • wheelchair access

Eternal Joy MCC 2382 Kennedy Ave (at
Highridge) **937/254-2087** • 10:30am Sun

Kent

BARS

The Zephyr Cafe 106 W Main St
330/678-4848 • 5pm-close • gay-friendly •
live shows • wheelchair access

Lima

NIGHTCLUBS

Somewhere in Time 804 W North St
419/227-7288 • 6pm-2:30am, from 8pm
wknds • lesbians/ gay men • dancing/DJ • drag
shows • male & female strippers

Logan

ACCOMMODATIONS

**Glenlaurel—A Scottish Country Inn &
Cottages** 14940 Mt Olive Rd (off State Rte I-
80), Rockbridge **740/385-4070, 800/809-7378**
• gay/ straight • on 133 acres • full brkfst &
dinner • hot tub • nonsmoking • wheelchair
access • straight & gay-owned • $119-319

Lorain

BARS

Tim's Place 2223 Broadway (btwn 22nd &
23rd) **440/246-9002** • 8pm-2:30am • lesbians/
gay men • neighborhood bar • dancing/DJ •
drag shows • patio • wheelchair access

Marietta

ACCOMMODATIONS

Fourth St B&B 627 4th St **614/638-1187** •
gay/ straight • nonsmoking • gay-owned •
$69-99

Marietta 428 6th St **513/602-3178** • mostly
men • 3 rm suite w/ spacious workout rm •
nonsmoking • gay-owned • $75-100

Monroe

BARS

Old Street Saloon 13 Old St **513/539-9183**
• 8pm-2am Th-Sat, till 1am Wed, clsd Sun-Tue
• lesbians/ gay men • neighborhood bar •
dancing/ DJ • drag shows • karaoke

Oberlin

RETAIL SHOPS

Stitch by Stitch 31 S Main St **440/774-4544,
866/729-7248** • noon-6pm, till 5pm Sat, clsd
Sun • many LGBT items

Pickerington

CAFES

Planet Coffee & Tea Coffee Company
1252 Hill Rd N **614/861-2040** • 5:30am-
10pm, till 11pm Fri-Sat, wknd hours vary

Sandusky

NIGHTCLUBS

Crowbar 206 W Market St (at Jackson St)
419/239-6851 • 4pm-2:30am • lesbians/ gay
men • dancing/DJ • karaoke • drag shows •
strippers • 18+ • gay-owned

Xcentricities 306 W Water St **419/624-8118**
• 8pm-2:30am • lesbians/ gay men •
dancing/DJ • drag shows • male & female
strippers • patio

Springfield

NIGHTCLUBS

Chances 1912-14 Edwards Ave (at N
Belmont Ave) **937/324-0383** • 8:30pm-
2:30am, clsd Tue • gay-friendly • dancing/DJ •
live shows • karaoke • patio

Steubenville

NIGHTCLUBS

Club Maxx 122 N 6th St (at Market)
740/284-1291 • 8pm-close, clsd Sun-Tue •
lesbians/ gay men • dancing/DJ • karaoke • live
shows • videos

Toledo

INFO LINES & SERVICES

AA Gay/ Lesbian 2272 Collingwood Blvd (at
St Mark's Episcopal Church) **419/380-9862** •
8pm Wed

ACCOMMODATIONS

Hotel Seagate 141 N Summit St (at
Jefferson) **419/242-8885, 866/744-5711** •
located in Toledo's business district • kids/
pets ok • gay-friendly • wheelchair access

BARS

Hooterville Station 119 N Erie St (btwn Jeff
& Monroe) **419/241-9050** • 5:30am-2:30am •
lesbians/ gay men • dancing/DJ • karaoke •
patio

Rip Cord 115 N Erie (btwn Jefferson &
Monroe) **419/243-3412** • 1pm-2:30am •
mostly gay men • neighborhood bar • Sun
brunch • karaoke • drag shows • strippers •
also Rip Room Fri (military theme) • food
served

NIGHTCLUBS

Bretz 2012 Adams St **419/243-1900** • 4pm-
2:30am, till 4:30am Fri-Sat, clsd Mon-Tue •
lesbians/ gay men • dancing/DJ • karaoke •
drag shows • strippers • videos • 18+ •
wheelchair access

Caesar's Show Bar 725 Jefferson
419/241-5140 • 8pm-2:30am Fri-Sun only •
lesbians/ gay men • dancing/DJ • live shows •
wheelchair access

BOOKSTORES

Borders 5001 Monroe St (in Franklin Park
Mall) **419/537-9259** • 9am-11pm, till 9pm
Sun

People Called Women 3153 W Central Ave
(in Cricket West Center) **419/535-6455** •
11am-7pm, clsd Sun, clsd Mon • multicultural
• feminist

SPIRITUAL GROUPS

A New Life MCC 1 Trinity Plaza
419/244-2124 • 10am Sun

Warren

BARS

The Queen of Hearts 132-136 Pine St
(btwn Market & Franklin) **330/395-1100** •
4pm-2:30am • lesbians/ gay men •
neighborhood bar • dancing/DJ • live shows •
karaoke Wed • patio

NIGHTCLUBS

The Alley 441 E Market St (enter rear)
330/394-9483 • 4pm-2:30am, from 2pm Fri-
Sun • lesbians/ gay men • dancing/DJ • live
shows • wheelchair access

Yellow Springs

RESTAURANTS

Winds Cafe & Bakery 215 Xenia Ave
937/767-1144 • lunch & dinner, Sun brunch,
clsd Mon • plenty veggie • full bar •
wheelchair access • women-owned/ run

Youngstown

INFO LINES & SERVICES

The Pride Center of Greater Youngstown
264 Madison Ave (btwn Elm & 5th)
330/747-7433

BARS

The Mixx 21 W Hylda Ave (off Market)
330/782-6991 • 4pm-2:30am • lesbians/ gay
men • neighborhood bar • dancing/DJ Th-Sun
• karaoke Wed • drag shows Sun • wheelchair
access

OKLAHOMA

Statewide

PUBLICATIONS

Gayly Oklahoman 405/528-0800 • LGBT newspaper

Ozarks Star 918/835-7887 • 10am-4pm Mon-Fri, monthly LGBT news publication serving AR, KS, MO & OK

Enid

EROTICA

Priscilla's 4810-A W Garriott (at Garland) 580/233-5511 • toys • lingerie • books • videos

Grand Lake

ACCOMMODATIONS

Southern Oaks Resort & Spa 2 miles S of Hwy 28/82 Junction, Langley 918/782-9346 • gay-friendly • 19 cabins on 30 acres • pool • hot tub • hiking • gay-owned

RESTAURANTS

The Artichoke Restaurant & Bar Langley 918/782-9855 • 5pm-10pm, clsd Sun-Mon

Frosty's & Edna's Café Langley 918/782-9123

Lighthouse Supper Club Ketchum 918/782-3316

Lawton

BARS

Triangles 29 D Ave (at 1st) 580/351-0620 • 8pm-2am, clsd Mon-Tue • lesbians/gay men • neighborhood bar • dancing/DJ • drag shows • karaoke

BOOKSTORES

Ingrid's Books 1124 NW Cache Rd 580/353-1488 • 10am-10pm, clsd Sun • new & used books • magazines • also adult novelties

Lexington

ACCOMMODATIONS

Blue Sky Ranch 14001 Banner 405/872-2583 • mostly women • cabin • camping • 2 RV hookups ($25) • swimming • pets ok • wheelchair access • lesbian-owned • $100-125

Norman

see also Oklahoma City

INFO LINES & SERVICES

OU GLBT & Friends 405/325-4452

BOOKSTORES

Borders Books 300 Norman Center 405/573-4907 • 9am-11pm, 10am-10pm Sun • LGBT section

Oklahoma City

INFO LINES & SERVICES

AA Live & Let Live 405/524-1100

The Center 2135 NW 39th St 405/524-6000 • 5pm-9pm, clsd wknds • wheelchair access

Herland Sister Resources 2312 NW 39th St 405/521-9696 • 1pm-5pm wknds • women's resource center w/ books, crafts & lending library • also sponsors monthly events • wheelchair access

ACCOMMODATIONS

America's Crossroads B&B 405/495-1111 • reservation service for private homes • gay-owned • $35-55

▲ **Habana Inn** 2200 NW 39th Expwy (at Youngs) 405/528-2221, 800/988-2221 (RESERVATIONS ONLY) • popular • lesbians/gay men • resort • swimming • nonsmoking • also 3 clubs • piano bar • restaurant • gift shop • wheelchair access • $40-108

The Hollywood Hotel & Suites 3535 NW 39th St (at Portland) 405/947-2351 • mostly gay men • swimming • also restaurant & bar • pets ok • $30-91

BARS

Alibi's 1200 N Pennsylvania (at NW 11th) 405/605-3795 • 3pm-2am • gay/straight • neighborhood bar • transgender-friendly • karaoke • gay-owned

Excuses 2024 NW 11th (at Pennsylvania) 405/525-3734 • 3pm-2am, from 5pm Sat • mostly women • neighborhood bar • dancing/DJ • beer bar • wheelchair access

▲ **The Finishline** at Habana Inn 405/525-2900 • noon-2am • lesbians/gay men • neighborhood bar • dancing/DJ • country/western • lessons 7pm Tue • poolside bar • wheelchair access

Hi-Lo Club 1221 NW 50th St (btwn Western & Classen) 405/843-1722 • noon-2am • lesbians/gay men • neighborhood bar • live bands weekly • drag shows

▲ **The Ledo** at Habana Inn 405/525–0730 •
9pm-close • lesbians/ gay men • cabaret &
lounge • piano bar • food served • karaoke Th-
Fri • drag shows Sat • wheelchair access

Partners 2805 NW 36th St (at May Ave)
405/942–2199 • 6pm-close, from 7pm Fri-Sat,
clsd Mon-Tue • popular • mostly women •
neighborhood bar • patio • dancing/DJ •
karaoke • live shows • wheelchair access

Rockies 3201 N May Ave (at 30th)
405/947–9361 • noon-2am, till midnight
Mon-Tue • lesbians/ gay men • neighborhood
bar • beer only • patio • gay-owned

Sisters 2120 NW 39th St 405/521–9533 •
5pm-close, from 7pm Sat, clsd Mon-Tue •
mostly women • dancing/DJ • karaoke • live
shows Sun • gay-owned

Tramps 2201 NW 39th St (at Barnes)
405/521–9888 • noon-2am, from 10am wknds
• popular • mostly gay men • dancing/DJ •
drag shows • wheelchair access

NIGHTCLUBS

Angles 2117 NW 39th St (at Pennsylvania)
405/524–3431 • 9pm-2am Fri-Sun • popular •
lesbians/ gay men • dancing/DJ • live shows •
wheelchair access

Club Rox 3535 NW 39th Expressway (at
Hollywood Hotel & Suites) 405/947–2351 •
lesbians/ gay men • dancing/DJ • gay-owned

▲ **The Copa** at Habana Inn 405/525–0730 •
9pm-2am, clsd Mon • lesbians/ gay men •
dancing/DJ • theme nights • drag shows •
male dancers Fri-Sat • wheelchair access

Wreck Room 2127 NW 39th St (at
Pennsylvania) 405/525–7610 • 10pm-close
Th-Sun • popular • lesbians/ gay men •
dancing/DJ • live shows • drag shows • young
crowd • 18+ after 1am

CAFES

The Red Cup 3132 N Classen Blvd
405/525–3430 • coffeehouse • nonsmoking •
also sandwiches • free Wi-Fi

Oklahoma City

LGBT PRIDE:
June. 405/524-2131, web:
www.okcpride.com.

ANNUAL EVENTS:
May - Herland Spring Retreat
405/521-9696. Music, workshops, web: www.herlandsis-
ters.org.
May - Paseo Arts Festival 405/525-
2688, web: www.thepaseo.com.
September - Herland Fall Retreat.

CITY INFO:
405/297-8912, web:
www.okccvb.org.

TRANSIT:
Yellow Cab 405/232-6161.
Airport Express 405/681-3311.
Metro Transit 405/235-7433, web:
www.gometro.org.

ATTRACTIONS:
Bricktown, web: www.brick-
townokc.com.
Historic Paseo Arts District, web:
www.thepaseo.com.
Myriad Gardens' Crystal Bridge
405/297-3995, web: www.myri-
adgardens.com.
National Cowboy and Western
Heritage Museum 405/478-2250,
web: www.nationalcowboymu-
seum.org.
National Softball Hall of Fame
405/424-5266, web: www.soft-
ball.org.
Oklahoma City National Memorial
405/235-3313, web: www.okla-
homacitynationalmemorial.org.
Omniplex 405/602-6664, web:
www.omniplex.org.
Sylvan Goldman monument (inven-
tor of the shopping cart).
Will Rogers Park.

RESTAURANTS

Bricktown Brewery Restaurant 1 N Oklahoma (at Sheridan) **405/232–2739** • 11am-10pm, till midnight wknds, noon-8pm Sun • live bands wknds • full bar

▲ **Gusher's** at Habana Inn **405/525–0730** • 11am-10:30pm, from 9am wknds, till 3:30am Fri-Sat for after-hours brkfst • wheelchair access

Terra Luna Grille 7408 N Western (at 73rd) **405/879–0009** • lunch & dinner, clsd Sun-Mon

Topanga Restaurant 3535 NW 39th Expressway (at Hollywood Hotel & Suites) **405/947–2351** • 11am-close • lesbians/ gay men • Southwestern • full bar • gay-owned

ENTERTAINMENT & RECREATION

Carpenter Square Theater 400 W Sheridan, Oklahoma Ctiy **405/232–6500** • occasional gay-themed material

BOOKSTORES

Full Circle Bookstore 50 Penn Pl (in NE corner of 1st level) **405/842–2900, 800/683–7323** • 10am-9pm, till 10pm Fri-Sat, noon-5pm Sun • independent • readings • also cafe & coffee bar

RETAIL SHOPS

23rd St Body Piercing 411 NW 23rd St (btwn Hudson & Walker) **405/524–6824**

A Piece to Remember 2131 NW 39th St (at Pennsylvania) **405/528–2223** • 6pm-2:30am, clsd Mon • pride items, fetish gear & gay community info

Ziggyz 4005 N Pennsylvania (at I-240) **405/521–9999** • novelty gifts • smokeshop • also 924 SW 59th, 405/632-0810

PUBLICATIONS

Gayly Oklahoman **405/528–0800** • LGBT newspaper

The Herland Voice **405/521–9696** • newsletter

SPIRITUAL GROUPS

Cathedral of Hope OKC 600 NW 13th St (at First Unitarian Church) **405/232–4673** • 9am & 11am Sun

Epworth United Methodist Church 1901 N Douglas Ave **405/525–2346** • 10:45am Sun

Friends Meeting (Quakers) 2712 NW 23rd (at St Andrews) **405/632–7574** • 7pm Sundays

Open Arms UCC 3131 N Pennsylvania **405/525–9555** • 10:45am Sun

EROTICA

Christie's Toy Box 3126 N May Ave (at 30th) **405/946–4438** • also 1039 S Meridian, 405/948-3333

▲ **Jungle Red** at Habana Inn **405/524–5733** • 1pm-close • novelties • leather • gifts • wheelchair access

Priscilla's 615 E Memorial **405/755–8600**

Tulsa

INFO LINES & SERVICES

Gay/ Lesbian AA 4936 E 49th St **918/627–2224**

The Tulsa LGBT Community Center 5545 E 41st St (in Highland Plaza) **918/743–4297** • touchtone info • center open 6pm-9pm, from 3pm Fri-Sat, clsd Sun-Mon • wheelchair access

ACCOMMODATIONS

Holiday Inn Select 5000 East Skelly Dr (at I-44 & Yale Ave) **918/622–7000, 800/836–9635** • gay-friendly • swimming • kids/ pets ok • $57-109

BARS

Bamboo Lounge 7204 E Pine **918/836–8700** • noon-2am • oldest gay bar in OK • mostly gay men • neighborhood bar • dancing/DJ • live shows • patio • wheelchair access

Detour 7944 E 21st St (at Memorial) **918/270–2428** • 5pm-2am, from 7pm Sat, from 3pm Sun • mostly women • neighborhood bar

New Age Renegade/ The Rainbow Room 1649 S Main St (at 17th) **918/585–3405** • 4pm-2am • popular • lesbians/ gay men • neighborhood bar • live shows • karaoke • patio

TNT's 2114 S Memorial **918/660–0856** • noon-2am, clsd Sun-Tue • popular • mostly women • neighborhood bar • dancing/DJ • karaoke

White Lion Pub 6927 S Canton Ave (off 71st) **918/491–6533** • 4pm-9:30pm, clsd Sun-Mon • gay-friendly • food served

The Yellow Brick Road 2630 E 15th (at Harvard) **918/293–0304** • 3pm-2am • lesbians/ gay men • neighborhood bar • wheelchair access

NIGHTCLUBS

Club Majestic 124 N Boston **918/584–9494** • 9pm-2am Th-Sun • lesbians/ gay men • dancing/ DJ • drag shows

Club Maverick 822 S Sheridan (at 9th) **918/835-3301** • 6pm-2am • lesbians/ gay men • dancing/ DJ • country/ western • karaoke

RESTAURANTS

St Michael's Alley 3324 E 31st (in Ranch Acres) **918/745-9998** • lunch & dinner, clsd Sun

Wild Fork 1820 Utica Square **918/742-0712** • 7am-10pm, clsd Sun • full bar • wheelchair access • women-owned/ run

ENTERTAINMENT & RECREATION

Gilcrease Museum 1400 N Gilcrease Museum Rd **918/596-2700** • one of the best collections of Native American & cowboy art in the US

Nightingale Theater 1416 E 4th St **918/583-8487** • savvy, unconventional productions by the Midwestern Theater Troupe

Philbrook Museum of Art 2727 S Rockford Rd (1 block E of Peoria, at end of 27th St) **918/748-5309, 800/324-7941** • clsd Mon • Italian villa built in the '20s oil boom complete w/ kitschy lighted dance flr, now a museum • the gardens are a must in spring & summer

RETAIL SHOPS

Body Piercing by Nicole 3314 Peoria **918/712-1122** • noon-9pm, till 6pm Sun

The Pride Store 5445 E 1st St (in LGBT Community Center) **918/743-4297** • 6pm-9pm, from 3pm Sat, clsd Sun • LGBT cards • gifts • shirts • some books • wheelchair access

SPIRITUAL GROUPS

MCC United of Tulsa 1623 N Maplewood **918/838-1715** • 11am Sun

OREGON

Statewide

PUBLICATIONS

Just Out 503/236-1252 • LGBT newspaper w/ extensive resource directory

Ashland

INFO LINES & SERVICES

The Abdill-Ellis Lambda Community Center 208 Oak St, Ste 112 **541/488-6990** • 3pm-6pm, noon-3pm Sat, clsd Sun-Mon • meetings • events • library

Gay/ Lesbian AA 175 N Main St upstairs (at Methodist Church) 541/732-1850 • 6:30pm Mon

Womansource Rising 541/862-2240 • lesbian/ feminist group • sponsors cultural activities like 1st Fri Dance & annual Fall Gathering (wheelchair access) • also publishes Community News

ACCOMMODATIONS

The Arden Forest Inn 261 W Hersey St **541/488-1496, 800/460-3912** • gay/ straight • full brkfst • nonsmoking • swimming • kids 10+ ok • wheelchair access • gay-owned • $110-200

Blue Moon B&B 312 Helman St (at Hersey) **541/482-9228, 800/460-5453** • gay-friendly • full brkfst • kids ok • nonsmoking • gay-owned • $85-195

Country Willows Inn 1313 Clay St **541/488-1590, 800/945-5697** • gay-friendly • full brkfst • swimming • jacuzzi • nonsmoking • teens ok • wheelchair access • gay-owned • $115-245

Dandelion Garden Cottage 541/488-4463 • women only • peaceful retreat • nonsmoking • lesbian-owned • $55

Lithia Springs Inn 2165 W Jackson Rd **541/482-7128, 800/482-7128** • gay/ straight • full brkfst • natural hot-springs-fed whirlpools in rooms • nonsmoking • teens ok • $129-250

Neil Creek House B&B 341 Mowetza Dr **541/482-6443, 800/460-7860** • gay-friendly • full brkfst • swimming • nonsmoking • teens ok • $90-200

Romeo Inn B&B 295 Idaho St **541/488-0884, 800/915-8899** • gay-friendly • full brkfst • jacuzzi • swimming • nonsmoking • $80-200

CAFES

Ashland Bakery/ Cafe 38 E Main **541/482-2117** • 8am-8pm, till 3pm Mon-Tue • plenty veggie • wheelchair access

RESTAURANTS

The Black Sheep 51 N Main St (on the Plaza) **541/482-6414** • 11:30am-1am • eclectic pub fare • woman-owned

Geppetto's 345 E Main **541/482-1138** • 8am-midnight • Italian • full bar • wheelchair access

Greenleaf Restaurant 49 N Main St (on The Plaza) **541/482-2808** • 8am-8pm • Mediterranean/ Italian • creekside dining • beer/ wine • lots of veggie

BOOKSTORES

Bloomsbury Books 290 E Main St (btwn 1st & 2nd) 541/488-0029 • 8am-10pm, from 9am Sat, 10am-9pm Sun

RETAIL SHOPS

Travel Essentials 252 E Main St 541/482-7383, 800/521-6722 • 10am-5:30pm, 11am-4pm Sun • luggage • books • accessories

Astoria

ACCOMMODATIONS

Rosebriar Hotel 636 14th St 503/325-7427, 800/487-0224 • gay-friendly • upscale classic hotel in former convent • full brkfst • kids ok • wheelchair access • $69-275 incl tax

Beaverton

RESTAURANTS

Swagat Indian Cuisine 4325 SW 109th Ave 503/626-3000 • lunch & dinner • beer/ wine

Bend

NIGHTCLUBS

The Grove 1033 NW Bond St (Newport Ave) 541/318-5875 • 6pm-close, clsd Sun-Mon • popular • queer night Tue • veggie food served • nonsmoking

CAFES

Royal Blend 1075 NW Newport 541/383-0873 • 6:30am-6pm • also 3 other locations

RESTAURANTS

Blacksmith Restaurant 211 NW Greenwood Ave 541/318-0588 • 5:30pm-close • new American • upscale

Corvallis

BOOKSTORES

Book Bin 215 SW 4th St 541/752-0040 • 7am-9pm, till 10pm Fri-Sat, 9am-7pm Sun

Grass Roots Bookstore 227 SW 2nd St (btwn Jefferson & Madison) 541/754-7668 • 9am-7pm, till 9pm Fri, till 5:30pm Sat, 11am-5pm Sun • music section • espresso bar • wheelchair access

Eugene

INFO LINES & SERVICES

Gay/ Lesbian AA 1414 Kincaid (at Koinonia Center) 541/342-4113 • 7pm Wed, 8pm Fri

LGBTQ Alliance 541/346-3360 • 9am-5pm • various drop-in groups • wheelchair access

BARS

Neighbors Bourbon Street Bar 1417 Villard 541/338-0334 • 4pm-close, from 7pm Sun • lesbians/ gay men • women's night Th • dancing/DJ Sat

Sam's Place Tavern 825 Wilson St (at 11th St W) 541/484-4455 • 11am-2:30am, from 9am wknds, till midnight Sun • gay-friendly • neighborhood bar • dancing/DJ • also restaurant • drag shows • lesbian-owned

RESTAURANTS

Glenwood Restaurant 1340 Alder St (at 13th St) 541/687-0355 • 7am-10pm

Keystone Cafe 395 W 5th (at Lawrence) 541/342-2075 • 7am-3pm, till 2pm Tue-Th • popular brkfst • plenty veggie

ENTERTAINMENT & RECREATION

Soromundi 541/342-1490 • lesbian chorus of Eugene

BOOKSTORES

Mother Kali's Books 1849 Willamette (at 18th St) 541/343-4864 • 10am-7pm • LGBT, feminist, multiracial, kids, new & used • events & resources • women's community calendar • wheelchair access

RETAIL SHOPS

High Priestess Piercing 675 Lincoln St (at 7th St) 541/342-6585 • noon-8pm, 11am-10pm Wed-Sat • piercing studio

Ruby Chasm 152 W 5th Ave #4 (btwn Olive & Charnelton) 541/344-4074 • 10am-6pm, noon-5pm Sun • goddess gifts • books • wheelchair access

EROTICA

Exclusively Adult 1166 South A St (at 10th St), Springfield 541/726-6969 • 24hrs

Grants Pass

ACCOMMODATIONS

WomanShare 541/862-2807 • women only • country retreat center • cabins • shared kitchen • bathhouse • hot tub • special events • girls/ pets ok • nonsmoking • lesbian-owned • $15-35 (sliding scale)

CAFES

Sunshine Natural Foods Cafe 128 SW H St (btwn 5th & 6th Sts) 541/474-5044 • 9am-6pm, till 5pm Sat, clsd Sun • vegetarian • also market

SPIRITUAL GROUPS

Unitarian Universalist Fellowship
229 SW G St (at 4th St, in the art museum)
541/476–5600 • 10:30am Sun Sept–June

Jacksonville

ACCOMMODATIONS

The Touvelle House 455 N Oregon St (at
E St) **541/899–8938, 800/846–8422** • gay-
friendly • 1916 Craftsman on 1 1/2 acres • full
brkfst • swimming • $145-185

Lincoln City

RESTAURANTS

Dory Cove Restaurant 5819 Logan Rd (at
59th St) **541/994–5180** • 11:30am-8pm, till
9pm Fri-Sat, from noon Sun • steak & seafood
• beer/ wine

Ki West Restaurant 2945 NW Jetty Ave
541/994–3877 • 8am-9pm, till 10pm wknds

McMinnville

ACCOMMODATIONS

Middle Creek Run 25400 Harmony Rd,
Sheridan **503/843–7606** • gay/ straight •
Victorian B&B • full brkfst • swimming • some
shared baths • nonsmoking • gay-owned •
$100-115

Medford

ACCOMMODATIONS

The Bybee House B&B 4491 Jackson Hwy,
Central Point **541/773–3026** • gay-friendly •
nonsmoking • $125

NIGHTCLUBS

Ground Zero 123 S Front St **541/779–4827** •
9pm-2am, from 8pm Fri, clsd Sun-Tue • gay-
friendly • dancing/DJ • more gay Th at
Alternative Night • comedy Fri

RESTAURANTS

Cadillac Cafe 207 W 8th St (at Holly)
541/857–9411 • 10:30am-2pm Mon-Fri

Mac's Rock & Rod Diner 2382 Jacksonville
Hwy **541/608–7625** • 9am-9pm, 8am-10pm,
8am-3pm Sun

SPIRITUAL GROUPS

Medford First Christian Church 1900
Crater Lake Ave (at Brookhurst) **541/772–8030**
• 10:30am Sun

EROTICA

Castle Megastore 1113 Progress Dr (at
Bittle) **541/608–9540**

Newport

ACCOMMODATIONS

The Beach House B&B 107 SW Coast St
541/265–9141 • gay/ straight • full brkfst •
ocean view • jacuzzi • nonsmoking • kids ok •
wheelchair access • lesbian-owned • $110-125

Cliff House B&B **541/563–2506** • gay-
friendly • oceanfront • full brkfst • hot tub •
nonsmoking • $110-225

RESTAURANTS

Mo's Annex 657 SW Bay Blvd **541/265–7512**
• 11am-10pm • great chowder • live music

Portland

see also Vancouver, Washington

INFO LINES & SERVICES

Lesbian Community Project **503/227–0605**
• an organization for women who love women,
offers social, educational & political events

Live & Let Live Club 1210 SE 7th
503/238–6091 • 12-step meetings • call for
schedule

**Sexual Minority Youth Recreation Center
(SMYRC)** 2100 SE Belmont **503/872–9664** •
4pm-9pm Wed, till midnight Fri-Sat • drop-in
center for LGBTQ youth

ACCOMMODATIONS

The Clyde Hotel 1022 SW Stark St (at 10th)
503/224–8000 • gay/ straight • some shared
baths • kids ok • nonsmoking • $70-189

Fifth Avenue Suites Hotel 506 SW
Washington (at 5th Ave) **503/222–0001,
866/861–9514** • gay-friendly • restaurant •
gym • pets ok • $79+

The Grand Ronde Place 250 NE
Tomahawk Island Dr, Slip A-15 (I-5, at north
exit 308) **503/808–9048, 866/330–7245** • gay/
straight • B&B on 34-ft yacht • also private
charter cruises • gay-owned • $139-169 +
12.5% tax

Hotel Vintage Plaza 422 SW Broadway
503/228–1212, 800/263–2305 • popular • gay-
friendly • upscale hotel • restaurant & lounge
• wheelchair access • $109-399

Jupiter Hotel 800 E Burnside **503/230–9200,
877/800–0004** • popular • gay-friendly •
boutique hotel • restaurant & lounge (7am-
4am daily) • wheelchair access • $89-139

MacMaster House 1041 SW Vista Ave (at
Park Pl) **503/223–7362, 800/774–9523** • gay-
friendly • historic mansion near the Rose
Gardens • nonsmoking • $85-155

The Mark Spencer Hotel 409 SW Eleventh Ave (near Stark) **503/224–3293, 800/548–3934** • gay-friendly • kids/pets ok • $89-169

Sullivan's Gulch B&B 1744 NE Clackamas St (at 17th) **503/331–1104** • lesbians/gay men • full brkfst • hot tub • nonsmoking • $95-125

BARS

Boxxes 1035 SW Stark (at SW 11th Ave) **503/226–4171** • noon-2:30am • popular • mostly gay men • karaoke • videos • wheelchair access • also Brig • lesbians/gay men • dancing/DJ • also Red Cap Garage

Brazen Bean 2075 NW Glisan St (at 21st Ave) **503/294–0636** • 5pm-close, from 6pm Sat, clsd Sun • gay/straight • swank cigar & martini bar • food served • live shows • wheelchair access

Candlelight Bar & Cafe 2032 SW 5th (at Lincoln) **503/222–3378** • 10am-2:30am • gay-friendly • live blues • food served

CC Slaughter's 219 NW Davis (at 3rd) **503/248–9135** • 3pm-2:30am • popular • mostly gay men • dancing/DJ • country/western Wed • karaoke Tue • videos • also martini lounge • wheelchair access

Chopsticks Express 2651 E Burnside St (at SE 26th) **503/234–6171** • 8pm-close • gay/straight • karaoke venue • young crowd • food served • wheelchair access

Crush 1412 SE Morrison (at SE 14th) **503/235–8150** • 5pm-close • gay/straight • wine & martini bar

Portland

WHERE THE GIRLS ARE:
Try along SE Hawthorne & Belmont streets where some of the women's businesses are, or the NW section, 21st & 23rd Aves, for the more upscale lesbians.

LGBT PRIDE:
June. 503/295-9788, web: www.pridenw.org.

ANNUAL EVENTS:
October - Portland LGBT Film Festival 866/206–2315, web: www.sensoryperceptions.org.

CITY INFO:
877/678-5263, web: www.pova.com.
Oregon Tourism Commission 800/547-7842.

ATTRACTIONS:
Microbreweries.
Mount Hood Festival of Jazz, web: www.mthoodjazz.com.
Old Town.
Pioneer Courthouse Square, web: www.pioneercourthousesquare.org
Rose Festival, web: www.rosefestival.org.
Washington Park.

BEST VIEW:
International Rose Test Gardens at Washington Park.

WEATHER:
The wet and sometimes chilly winter rains give Portland its lush landscape that bursts into beautiful colors in the spring and fall. Summer brings sunnier days. (Temperatures can be in the 50°s one day and the 90°s the next.)

TRANSIT:
Radio Cab 503/227-1212.
Raz 503/684-3322.
Tri-Met System 503/238-7433, web: www.tri-met.org.

Darcelle XV 208 NW 3rd Ave (at NW Davis St) **503/222-5338** • 8:30pm-2:30am, from 10:30pm Fri-Sat, clsd Sun-Tue • gay/ straight • dancing/ DJ • cabaret • strippers • drag shows • food served • wheelchair access

Dirty Duck Tavern 439 NW 3rd (at Glisan) **503/224-8446** • 3pm-1am, till 2am Fri-Sat, from noon wknds • mostly gay men • neighborhood bar • leather • older crowd • beer/ wine • wheelchair access

---

[**Reply**] [**Forward**]   [**Delete**]

```
Date: Mon, Dec 13, 2005 09:45:12
From: Girl-on-the-Go
To: Editor@Damron.com
Subject: Portland
```

>Sprawling along the Columbia River at the foot of Mount Hood, you'll find this city that's home to rainy days, roses, and an active women's community. If you're searching for the proof that Portland is a lesbian-friendly city, look no further than the Portland Building. Atop the roof you'll find a statue of Portlandia, a city landmark and an amazon icon.

>Nearby you can explore the Mount St. Helens National Volcanic Monument or the 5,000 acres of Macleay Park. And if you love jazz, head for the hills: the Mount Hood Festival of Jazz brings the best of the jazz world to town every August.

>Lesbian life here focuses on the outdoors and cocooning at home with small groups of friends. To get in touch, pick up a recent copy of the statewide newspaper **Just Out,** or contact **Sisterspirit,** a women's spirituality resource.

>The **Egyptian Club** is the heart of women's nightlife in Portland. For a nourishing meal, visit **Old Wives Tales,** or head to lesbian-owned **Dingo's Mexican Grill,** which hosts the popu-lar "Girls Night Out" on Thursdays. Or savor the java and art at the smokefree **Cup & Saucer Cafe.** On weekends, you can enjoy live music at lesbian-owned cafes such as **Touchstone Coffee House** or **Haven Coffee.**

>Culturally minded visitors won't want to miss **In Other Words,** the only women's bookstore in town. They carry music along with a large selection of women's literature. **Powell's** is a new/used bookstore that's both legendary and huge, and we've heard that its LGBT section is a good meeting place on weekend nights—there's even a little cafe. **It's My Pleasure** serves up erotica for women.

Doug Fir 830 E Burnside (at NE 9th) **503/231-9663** • gay-friendly • popular • more women for monthly Snatch party • hipster log cabin lounge • also restaurant • live bands

Eagle PDX 1300 W Burnside (at 13th Ave) **503/241-0105** • 4pm-2am • mostly gay men • leather • videos • wheelchair access

The Egyptian Club 3701 SE Division (at SE 37th Ave) **503/236-8689** • 1pm-2:30am, from 4pm wknds • popular • mostly women • dancing/DJ • karaoke • strippers • food served • wheelchair access • lesbian-owned

Fox & Hound 217 NW 2nd Ave (btwn Everett & Davis) **503/243-5530** • 7am-2am • popular • mostly gay men • also restaurant • brunch Sun • karaoke • wheelchair access

Hobo's 120 NW 3rd Ave (btwn Davis & Couch) **503/224-3285** • 4pm-2am • gay/ straight • piano bar • also restaurant • some veggie • wheelchair access

Porky's 835 N Lombard (at Albina) **503/283-9734** • 2pm-2:30am, from 4pm Sun, gay/ straight • more gay Th for Booty • rockin' dive bar • transgender-friendly • food served • live bands • wheelchair access

Shanghai Steakery 16 NW Broadway **503/228-9325** • 7am-2am • gay/ straight • transgender-friendly • wheelchair access

Silverado 1217 SW Stark St (btwn SW 11th & 12th Aves) **503/224-4493** • 9am-2:30am • popular • mostly gay men • dancing/DJ • strippers • karaoke Mon • food served • wheelchair access

Starky's 2913 SE Stark St (at SE 29th Ave) **503/230-7980** • 11am-2am • popular • lesbians/ gay men • neighborhood bar • also restaurant • Sun brunch • some veggie • patio • wheelchair access

NIGHTCLUBS

Embers 110 NW Broadway (at NW Couch St) **503/222-3082** • 11am-2:30am, from 2pm wknds • popular • mostly gay men • dancing/DJ • drag shows • also restaurant • wheelchair access

Holocene 1001 SE Morrison (at E 10th) **503/239-7639** • gay/ straight • popular dance club • many LGBT theme nights • check local listings

Tarts 1001 SE Morrison (at SE 10th Ave, at Holocene) **503/239-7639** • 8pm-2:30am 2nd Sun • mostly women • dancing/ DJ • multiracial • food served

Women's After Hours Party 535 NW 16th Ave (at Hoyt, at Vitis Enoteca) **503/241-0355** • 10pm 1st & 3rd Sat only • mostly women • also Italian restaurant • lesbian-owned

CAFES

Blend 2327 E Burnside **503/234-8610** • 7am-6pm, from 8am Sun

Bread & Ink Cafe 3610 SE Hawthorne Blvd (at 36th) **503/239-4756** • 8am-9pm, till 10pm Fri-Sat, packed for Yiddish Brunch on Sun • popular • beer/ wine • wheelchair access

Cup & Saucer Cafe 3566 SE Hawthorne Blvd (btwn 34th & 36th) **503/236-6001** • 7am-9pm • popular w/ lesbians • full menu • some veggie • nonsmoking

Garbero's 414 SW 13th Ave (at Burnside) **503/225-4400** • 8am-8pm, till late Th-Sat, from 10am wknds • food served • live jazz Th • queer literature 1st Wed • internet access

Haven Coffee 3551 SE Division St **503/236-6890** • 7:30am-9pm, till 10pm wknds • mostly women • live shows • wheelchair access • lesbian-owned

Jackman Joe 1111 NW 16th Ave (at Marshall) **503/222-0121** • 7am-5pm, till 9pm Th-Fri, 8am-1pm Sat, clsd Sun • dog-friendly

Marco's Cafe & Espresso Bar 7910 SW 35th (at Multnomah Blvd), Multnomah **503/245-0199** • 7am-9:30pm, from 8am wknds, till 2pm Sun • food served • plenty veggie

The Pied Cow 3244 SE Belmont (at 33rd Ave) **503/230-4866** • 4pm-midnight, till 1am Fri-Sat, from 10am wknds • funky Victorian • great desserts • patio • wheelchair access

Three Friends Coffeehouse 201 SE 12th Ave (at Ash) **503/236-6411** • 7am-10pm, till midnight Fri-Sat, from 9am wknds

Touchstone Coffee House 7631 NE Glisan St **503/262-7613** • 6:30am-9pm, 8am-5pm Sun • tarot Tue • astrology Wed • live music Fri-Sat • also cards/ gifts & community resource room • lesbian-owned

RESTAURANTS

The Adobe Rose 1634 SE Bybee Blvd (at Milwaukee) **503/235-9114** • 11:30am-2pm, also 5pm-9pm Fri-Sat, clsd Sun-Mon • New Mexican • some veggie • beer/ wine

Assaggio 7742 SE 13th (at Lambert) **503/232-6151** • 5pm-9pm, clsd Sun • Italian • plenty veggie • wine bar

Aura Restaurant & Lounge 1022 W Burnside St (btwn SW 10th & 11th) 503/597-2872 • dinner, clsd Sun-Mon • also bar • wheelchair access

Bastas Trattoria 410 NW 21st (at Flanders) 503/274-1572 • dinner nightly • northern Italian • some veggie • full bar till 1am

Bernie's 2904 NE Alberta St 503/282-9864 • 4pm-10pm, clsd Sun • Southern bistro • patio

Bijou Cafe 132 SW 3rd Ave (at Pine St) 503/222-3187 • 7am-2pm, from 8am wknds • popular • plenty veggie • "farm-fresh brkfst" • wheelchair access

Blue Hour 250 NW 13th Ave (at NW Everett St) 503/226-3394 • 5pm-10pm, till 10:30pm Fri-Sat, bar open till midnight, clsd Sun-Mon • extensive wine list • upscale • wheelchair access

Brasserie Montmartre 626 SW Park (at Alder) 503/224-5552 • 11am-1am, till 3am Fri-Sat, brunch wknds • bistro • live jazz • full bar

Delta 4607 SE Woodstock (at 46th) 503/771-3101 • 5pm-10pm, bar open till 2am • Southern • plenty veggie • wheelchair access

Dingo's Mexican Grill 4612 SE Hawthorne Blvd (at SE 39th) 503/233-3996 • 11:30am-10pm, till midnight Th-Sat • popular Girls Night Out Th • lesbian-owned

Dot's Cafe 2521 SE Clinton (at 26th) 503/235-0203 • noon-2am • popular • full bar • eclectic American • plenty veggie • wheelchair access

Equinox 830 N Shaver St 503/460-3333 • dinner Wed-Sun, wknd brunch, clsd Mon-Tue • int'l • patio

Esparza's Tex-Mex Cafe 2725 SE Ankeny St (at 28th) 503/234-7909 • 11:30am-10pm, clsd Sun • popular • funky

Fish Grotto 1035 SW Stark (at SW 11th Ave, at Boxxes) 503/226-4171 • 5pm-close, clsd Mon • popular • some veggie • full bar • live shows • wheelchair access

Mayas Taqueria 1000 SW Morrison 503/226-1946 • 11am-9pm

Montage 301 SE Morrison 503/234-1324 • lunch & dinner till 2am, till 4am Fri-Sat • popular • Louisiana-style cookin' • full bar • wheelchair access

Nicholas' 318 SE Grand 503/235-5123 • 10am-9pm, from noon Sun • Middle Eastern

Old Wives Tales 1300 E Burnside St (at 13th) 503/238-0470 • 8am-9pm, till 10pm Fri-Sat • multi-ethnic vegetarian • beer/ wine • popular • wheelchair access

The Original Pancake House 8600 SW 24th Ave 503/246-9007 • brkfst & lunch, clsd Mon-Tue • crowded on wknds

Paradox Palace Cafe 3439 SE Belmont 503/232-7508 • brkfst & lunch daily, dinner Th-Sun • popular • vegetarian diner • killer Reuben

Pizzacato 505 NW 23rd (at Glisan) 503/242-0023 • 11:30am-10pm, till 11pm Fri-Sat, noon-9pm Sun • popular • plenty veggie • beer/ wine • many locations

The Roxy 1121 SW Stark St 503/223-9160 • 24hrs, clsd Mon • popular • lesbians/ gay men • retro American diner • wheelchair access

Saucebox 214 SW Broadway (at Stark) 503/241-3393 • 5pm-close, clsd Sun-Mon • lesbians/ gay men • pan-Asian • plenty veggie • full bar • DJ • wheelchair access • gay-owned

Vista Spring Cafe 2440 SW Vista (at Spring) 503/222-2811 • 11am-10pm, from noon wknds, till 9pm Sun • pasta & pizza • beer/ wine • wheelchair access

Vitis Enoteca 535 NW 16th Ave (at Hoyt) 503/241-0355 • lunch Tue-Fri, dinner Tue-Sat, clsd Sun-Mon • Italian tapas & wine bar • also Women's After Hours Party 10pm 1st & 3rd Sat • lesbian-owned

Wildwood 1221 NW 21st Ave (at Overton) 503/248-9663 • lunch & dinner Mon-Sat • full bar • upscale

ENTERTAINMENT & RECREATION

Sauvie's Island Beach 25 miles NW (off US 30) • follow Reeder Rd to the Collins beach area, park at the farthest end of the road, then follow path to beach

BOOKSTORES

Countermedia 927 SW Oak (btwn 9th & 10th) 503/226-8141 • 11am-7pm, noon-6pm Sun • alternative comics • vintage gay books/ periodicals

In Other Words 3734 SE Hawthorne Blvd (at 37th) 503/232-6003 • 10am-9pm, 11am-6pm Sun • women's books • music • resource center • wheelchair access

Laughing Horse Bookstore 3652 SE Division (at 37th) 503/236-2893 • 11am-7pm, clsd Sun • alternative/ progressive • wheelchair access

Looking Glass Bookstore 318 SW Taylor (btwn 3rd & 4th) **503/227-4760** • 9am-6pm, from 10am Sat, clsd Sun • general • some LGBT titles

Powell's Books 1005 W Burnside St (at 10th) **503/228-4651, 866/201-7601** • 9am-11pm • popular • largest new & used bookstore in the world • cafe • readings • wheelchair access

Reading Frenzy 921 SW Oak St (at 9th) **503/274-1449** • 11am-7pm, noon-6pm Sun • zines • comics • LGBT selection • wheelchair access

Twenty-Third Ave Books 1015 NW 23rd Ave (at Lovejoy) **503/224-5097** • 9:30am-9pm, from 10am Sat, 11am-7pm Sun • general • LGBT section • wheelchair access

RETAIL SHOPS

Hip Chicks do Wine 4510 SE 23rd Ave (SE Holgate & 26th) **503/753-6374** • 11am-6pm

It's My Pleasure 3106 NE 64th Ave (at Sandy Blvd) **503/280-8080** • noon-7pm • books • erotica • toys • gifts • workshops

The Jellybean 721 SW 10th Ave (at Morrison) **503/222-5888** • 10am-6pm, noon-5pm Sun • cards • T-shirts • gifts • wheelchair access

Presents of Mind 3633 SE Hawthorne (at 37th Ave) **503/230-7740** • 10am-7pm • jewelry • cards • unique toys • wheelchair access

PUBLICATIONS

Just Out **503/236-1252** • LGBT newspaper w/ extensive resource directory

Magazine 99 **206/529-4257, 877/408-7289** • quarterly arts, entertainment & lifestyle magazine for Pacific NW

Odyssey Magazine Northwest **206/621-8950** • dish on Pacific Northwest's club scene

SPIRITUAL GROUPS

Congregation Neveh Shalom 2900 SW Peaceful Ln (at Beaverton/ Hillsdale Hwy) **503/246-8831** • 8:15pm Fri & 9am Sat • conservative synagogue w/ LGBT outreach • call for directions

MCC Portland 2400 NE Broadway (at 24th Ave) **503/281-8868** • 9am & 11am Sun • wheelchair access

Sisterspirit 3430 SE Belmont #102 **503/736-3297** • celebration of women sharing spirituality • also 12-step pagan group • wheelchair access

St Stephen's Episcopal Church 1432 SW 13th Ave (at Clay) **503/223-6424** • 7:45am & 9:30am Sun

GYMS & HEALTH CLUBS

Inner City Hot Tubs 2927 NE Everett St (btwn 29th & 30th) **503/238-1065** • 10am-11pm, from 1pm Sun • gay-friendly • wellness center • reservations required

Princeton Athletic Club 614 SW 11th Ave (at Alder) **503/222-2639**

EROTICA

Fantasy for Adults 3137 NE Sandy Blvd (near NE 39th) **503/239-6969** • 24hrs

Spartacus Leathers 302 SW 12th Ave (at Burnside) **503/224-2604**

Roseburg

INFO LINES & SERVICES

Gay/ Lesbian Switchboard **541/672-4126** • 24hrs • support & referrals

Salem

RESTAURANTS

Off Center Cafe 1741 Center St NE (at 17th) **503/363-9245** • brkfst & lunch Tue-Fri, brunch wknds, clsd Mon • some veggie • wheelchair access

BOOKSTORES

Borders 2235 Lancaster Dr NE **503/375-9588** • 9am-10pm, 10am-9pm Sun • LGBT section

Jackson's Books 320 Liberty St SE (Pringle Park Plaza) **503/399-8694** • LGBT section

SPIRITUAL GROUPS

Sweet Spirit MCC 4774 Lilac Ln NE (at American Legion Hall) **503/315-7923** • 11am Sun

Unitarian Universalist Congregation of Salem 5090 Center St NE **503/364-0932** • 10:30am & 11:45am Sun

Sunriver

ACCOMMODATIONS

DiamondStone Guest Lodge & Gallery 16693 Sprague Loop, La Pine **541/536-6263, 866/626-9887** • gay-friendly • Western hotel-style B&B • full brkfst • hot tub • kids ok • pets ok (extra fee) • nonsmoking • $80-135

Yachats

ACCOMMODATIONS

Ocean Odyssey 541/547–3637,
800/800–1915 • gay-friendly • coastal
vacation rental homes in Yachats & Waldport •
kids ok • nonsmoking • women-owned/ run •
$75-425

The Oregon House 94288 Hwy 101
541/547–3329 • gay-friendly • ocean views •
patio • massage • nonsmoking • kids ok •
wheelchair access • $85-165

See Vue Motel 95590 Hwy 101
541/547–3227 • gay/ straight • kids/ pets ok •
nonsmoking • wheelchair access • lesbian-
owned • $65-90

Shamrock Lodgettes 105 Hwy 101 S (at
Yachats Ocean Rd) 541/547–3312,
800/845–5028 • gay-friendly • 5-acre resort •
hot tub • kids/ pets ok • wheelchair access •
gay-owned • $59-200

PENNSYLVANIA

Adamstown

ACCOMMODATIONS

The Barnyard Inn & Carriage House 2145
Old Lancaster Pike, Reinholds 717/484–1111,
888/738–6624 • gay/ straight • full brkfst •
150-year-old restored German school house •
petting zoo • nonsmoking • kids ok/ pets ok •
$85-165 (double occupancy)

Allentown

see also Bethlehem

BARS

Candida's 247 N 12th St (at Chew)
610/434–3071 • 2pm-2am • lesbians/ gay
men • neighborhood bar • food served

Stonewall, Moose Lounge Bar & Grille
28–30 N 10th St (at Hamilton) 610/432–0706
• 7pm-2am, clsd Mon • popular • lesbians/
gay men • dancing/DJ • food served • live
shows • karaoke • drag shows • male dancers
• videos • 18+ Th

SPIRITUAL GROUPS

MCC of the Lehigh Valley 1901 S 12th St,
#208 (in Merchants Square Mall)
610/709–8800 • 10:30am & 6pm Sun

EROTICA

Adult World 80 S West End Blvd/ Rte 309,
Quakerstown 215/538–1522 • 24hrs

Altoona

NIGHTCLUBS

Escapade 2523 Union Ave, Rte 36
814/946–8195 • 8pm-2am, clsd Sun •
lesbians/ gay men • dancing/DJ • karaoke •
gay-owned

Rumors 1413 11th Ave (enter rear)
814/941–0803 • 9pm-2am, clsd Sun •
lesbians/ gay men • dancing/DJ • karaoke •
patio • gay-owned

RESTAURANTS

Michael's Cafe 1413 11th Ave 814/941–0803
• 11am-9pm, till 2pm Mon, clsd Sun • upscale
full bar • gay-owned

Bethlehem

NIGHTCLUBS

Diamonz 1913 W Broad St (at Pennsylvania
Ave) 610/865–1028 • 4pm-2am, from 3pm
wknds • mostly women • dancing/DJ • live
shows • karaoke • also restaurant • some
veggie • wheelchair access

Bridgeport

NIGHTCLUBS

The Lark 302 DeKalb St/ Rte 202 N
610/275–8136 • 8pm-2am, clsd Sun • mostly
gay men • dancing/DJ • karaoke • drag shows

Bristol

EROTICA

Bristol News World 576 Bristol Pike/ Rte 13
N 215/785–4770

Erie

ACCOMMODATIONS

The Boothby Inn 311 W 6th St
814/456–1888, 866/266–8429 • gay-friendly •
$120-160

NIGHTCLUBS

Trance Dance Club 1607 Raspberry St
814/456–3027 • 8pm-2am, clsd Sun • gay/
straight • dancing/ DJ

The Zone 133 W 18th St (at Peach)
814/452–0125 • 8pm-2am • lesbians/ gay
men • dancing/DJ • food served

CAFES

Aroma's Coffeehouse 2164 W 8th St
814/456–5282 • 7am-9pm, from 8am wknds,
till 4pm Sun • light fare • nonsmoking

RESTAURANTS

Matthew's Trattoria 153 E 13th St (at Lovell Place) 814/459-6458 • dinner, clsd Sun-Mon • martini lounge • live music • courtyard

Papermoon 1325 State St (at 14th) 814/455-7766 • 4:30pm-9pm, till 10pm Th-Sat, jazz brunch Sun • seafood/ int'l • piano • reservations reccommended

Pie in the Sky Cafe 463 W 8th St (at Walnut) 814/459-8638 • 7:30-2pm Tue-Fri, dinner from 5:30pm Fri-Sat, clsd Sun-Mon • BYOB • reservations recommended • wheelchair access

Radicchio Deli 16501 State St (at E 10th St) 814/454-3616 • 8am-3pm, till 9pm Fri, 11am-9pm Sat • gay-owned

PUBLICATIONS

Erie Gay News 814/456-9833 • covers news & events in the Erie, Cleveland, Pittsburgh, Buffalo & Chautauqua County (NY) region

Gay People's Chronicle 216/631-8646, 800/426-5947 • Ohio's largest weekly LGBT newspaper w/ extensive listings

SPIRITUAL GROUPS

Temple Anshe Hesed 930 Liberty St 814/454-2426 • 7:30pm Fri

Unitarian Universalist Congregation of Erie 7180 New Perry Hwy 814/864-9300 • 10:30am Sun

Gettysburg

ACCOMMODATIONS

Battlefield B&B Inn 2264 Emmitsburg Rd (at Ridge Rd) 717/334-8804, 888/766-3897 • B&B • full brkfst • Civil War home on 30 acres of Gettysburg Battlefield • daily history demonstrations • kids ok • lesbian-owned • $160-250

Sheppard Mansion B&B 117 Frederick St (at High St), Hanover 717/633-8075, 877/762-6746 • gay/ straight • B&B • full brkfst • kids 12 years & up ok • nonsmoking • $140-250

Glen Mills

ACCOMMODATIONS

Sweetwater Farm B&B 50 Sweetwater Rd 610/459-4711, 800/793-3892 • gay-friendly • B&B • swimming • full brkst • $125-275

Greensburg

NIGHTCLUBS

Long Bada Lounge 108 W Pittsburgh St (at Pennsylvania Ave) 724/837-6614 • 9pm-2am, clsd Sun • popular • lesbians/ gay men • dancing/DJ • karaoke • drag shows • patio • wheelchair access

Harrisburg

INFO LINES & SERVICES

Gay/ Lesbian Switchboard 1300A N 3rd St 717/234-0328 • 6:30pm-9pm Mon-Fri (volunteers permitting)

BARS

704 Strawberry 704 N 3rd St 717/234-4228 • 2pm-2am • popular • mostly gay men • neighborhood bar • karaoke • videos • older crowd • wheelchair access

The Brownstone Lounge 412 Forster St (btwn 3rd & 6th) 717/234-7009 • 11am-2am, from 5pm Sat, from 3pm Sun • lesbians/ gay men • neighborhood bar • karaoke • also restaurant • wheelchair access

Neptune's Lounge 268 North St (at 3rd) 717/233-0581 • 4pm-2am, from 2pm Sun • popular • lesbians/ gay men • neighborhood bar • dancing/ DJ • young crowd • also restaurant

The Pink Lizard 891 Eisenhower Blvd (near exit 19) 717/939-1123 • 7pm-2am, till midnight Th, clsd Sun-Wed • lesbians/ gay men • transgender-friendly • dancing/DJ • food served • live shows • drag shows • videos • women-owned/ run • popular

NIGHTCLUBS

Stallions 706 N 3rd St (enter rear) 717/232-3060 • 7pm-2am, clsd Sun • popular • mostly gay men • dancing/DJ • live shows • karaoke Wed • drag shows • strippers • videos • also Shimmer 10pm-2am Fri-Sat (mostly gay men • dancing/DJ • 16+) • wheelchair access

BOOKSTORES

Forever Books 41 N Front St, Steelton 717/939-5507 • 6pm-8pm, noon-8pm Sat, clsd Sun • LGBT • multiracial clientele • open-mic poetry • bi-weekly LGBT movie night • weekly game night • lesbian-owned

PUBLICATIONS

Lavender Letter 717/232-8382 • newsletter & monthly calendar of events for womyn in south-central PA

SPIRITUAL GROUPS

MCC of the Spirit 2973 Jefferson St (near Uptown Shopping Plaza) 717/236-7387 • 9am, 10:30am & 7pm Sun

Irwin

NIGHTCLUBS

The Link 91 Wendel Rd, Herminie 724/446-7717 • 6pm-2am, clsd Sun • lesbians/ gay men • dancing/ DJ • live shows • drag shows • male dancers • food served

Johnstown

NIGHTCLUBS

Lucille's 520 Washington St (near Central Park) 814/539-4448 • 6pm-2am, clsd Sun-Mon • lesbians/ gay men • dancing/DJ • drag shows • strippers • karaoke

Kutztown

ACCOMMODATIONS

Grim's Manor B&B 10 Kern Rd 610/683-7089 • lesbians/ gay men • 200-yr-old stone farmhouse on 5 acres • full brkfst • nonsmoking • gay-owned • $75-80

Lancaster

ACCOMMODATIONS

Cameron Estate Inn 1855 Mansion Ln (at Donegal Springs Rd), Mount Joy 717/492-0111, 888/422-6376 • gay/ straight • B&B inn • full brkfst • located on 15 acres of lawn & woods • jacuzzi • nonsmoking • restaurant • wheelchair access • gay-owned • $119-289

Candlelight Inn B&B 2574 Lincoln Hwy E (at Rte 896/ Hartman Bridge Rd), Ronks 717/299-6005, 800/772-2635 • gay-friendly • full brkfst • jacuzzi • in the heart of PA's Dutch/ Amish countryside • $85-169

The Noble House B&B 113 W Market St, Marietta 717/426-4389, 888/271-6426 • gay/ straight • full brkfst • nonsmoking • $115-225

BARS

Tally Ho 201 W Orange (at Water) 717/299-0661 • 8pm-2am • popular • lesbians/ gay men • dancing/DJ • karaoke • drag shows • young crowd

NIGHTCLUBS

Sundown Lounge 429 N Mulberry St (at James) 717/392-2737 • 6pm-2am, from 3pm Fri-Sat, clsd Sun • mostly women • neighborhood bar • dancing/DJ

RESTAURANTS

The Loft above Tally Ho bar 717/299-0661 • lunch Mon-Fri, dinner Mon-Sat • contemporary American / French

BOOKSTORES

Borders 940 Plaza Blvd (at Harrisburg Pike) 717/293-8022 • 9am-11pm, 11am-9pm Sun • LGBT section

SPIRITUAL GROUPS

MCC Vision of Hope 130 E Main St, Mountville 717/285-9070 • 10:30am & 6pm Sun

Lebanon

SPIRITUAL GROUPS

St Macrina's ONA UCC Church Lebanon Optimists Bldg, at 14th & Washington St 717/272-7844 • 10am Sun

Lehighton

ACCOMMODATIONS

The Woods Campground 845 Vaughn Acres Ln 610/377-9577 • lesbians/ gay men • tent/ RV spots • also cabins • swimming • 18+

Meadville

SPIRITUAL GROUPS

Be Ye Kind to One Another 346 Chestnut St (at S Main St, at Unitarian Universalist Church) • 7pm 2nd & 4th Tue • Christian group for LGBT people • email before attending: rseddig@allegheny.edu

Monroeville

EROTICA

Monroeville News - Adult Mart 2735 Stroschein Rd (off Rte 22) 412/372-5477 • 24hrs

Montgomeryville

EROTICA

Adult World Book Store Rtes 202 & 309 215/362-9560 • 24hrs

New Hope

see also Lambertville & Sergeantsville, New Jersey

ACCOMMODATIONS

Ash Mill Farm B&B 5358 York Rd (at Rte 202), Holicong 215/794-5373 • gay-friendly • full brkfst

Best Western New Hope Inn 6426 Lower York Rd/ Rte 202 215/862–5221, 800/467–3202 • gay-friendly • swimming • also restaurant & lounge • kids/pets ok • wheelchair access • $89-169

Cordials B&B of New Hope 143 Old York Rd (at Sugan Rd) 215/862–3919, 877/219–1009 • lesbians/gay men • hot tub • nonsmoking • wheelchair access • gay-owned • $85-145

Fox & Hound B&B 246 West Bridge St 215/862–5082, 800/862–5082 • gay-friendly • 1850s stone manor • full brkfst • nonsmoking • $90-200

The Lexington House 6171 Upper York Rd 215/794–0811 • gay/straight • 1749 country home • swimming • nonsmoking • gay-owned • $120-200

The Mansion Inn 9 S Main (at Bridge St) 215/862–1231 • lesbians/gay men • B&B inn • full brkfst • jacuzzi • swimming • nonsmoking • gay-owned • $155-295

The New Hope Motel 400 W Bridge St/ Rte 179 215/862–2800 • gay/straight • patios • lounge • swimming • $69-149

Silver Maple Organic Farm & B&B 483 Sergeantsville Rd (Rte 523), Sergeantsville, NJ 908/237–2192 • gay/straight • 200-year-old farmhouse • full brkfst • hot tub • swimming • nonsmoking • kids/pets ok • wheelchair access • gay-owned • $99-159

The Victorian Peacock B&B 309 E Dark Hollow Rd, Pipersville 215/766–1356 • gay/straight • swimming • spa • nonsmoking • women-owned/run • $100-190

The Wishing Well Guesthouse 144 Old York Rd 215/862–8819 • gay/straight • B&B • nonsmoking • kids ok • gay-owned • $85-150

York Street House B&B 42 York St, Lambertville, NJ 609/397–3007, 888/398–3199 • gay-friendly • 1909 Manor house • nonsmoking • $105-225

BARS

The Raven Bar & Restaurant 385 West Bridge St 215/862–2081 • 11am-2am • mostly gay men • also motel • swimming • drag shows • male dancers • gay-owned • $85-169

RESTAURANTS

Eagle Diner 463 Old York Rd/ Rte 202 215/862–5575 • 24hrs • full bar • wheelchair access

Havana 105 S Main St 215/862–9897 • noon-midnight, from 11am wknds, bar till 2am • some veggie • live shows • karaoke

Karla's 5 W Mechanic St (at Main) 215/862–2612 • noon-11pm, till midnight Fri-Sat, from 10am Sun • New American • some veggie • full bar

Mother's 34 N Main St 215/862–5857 • 11am-9pm, till 10pm Fri-Sat • some veggie

Odette's 274 South River Rd 215/862–2432 • lunch & dinner, Sun brunch, clsd Tue • piano bar & cabaret till 1am • cont'l • some veggie • wheelchair access

The Raven 385 West Bridge St 215/862–2081 • 11am-2pm & 6pm-10pm • popular • gay/straight • fine-dining cont'l • also motel • swimming • gay-owned

Wildflowers 8 W Mechanic St 215/862–2241 • seasonal, noon-9:30pm, till 10:30pm Fri-Sat • some veggie • full bar • outdoor dining

RETAIL SHOPS

Bucks County Video & CD Exchange 415–C York Rd (at Rte 202) 215/862–0919 • 10am-10pm • general video store w/ art house, gay-themed & adult videos • gay-owned

PUBLICATIONS

EXP Magazine 302/227–5787, 877/397–6244 • bi-weekly gay magazine for Mid-Atlantic

Visions Today 302/656–5876, 800/241–5803 • quarterly, covers Rehoboth, Philadelphia, New Hope, Wilmington & surrounding area

EROTICA

Grownups 2 E Mechanic St (at Main) 215/862–9304 • toys etc • gay-owned

Le Chateau Exotique 27 W Mechanic St 215/862–3810 • fetishwear

New Milford

ACCOMMODATIONS

Oneida Camp & Lodge 570/465–7011 • mostly gay men • oldest gay-owned/operated campground dedicated to the gay community • 12 RV hookups • also 1 guest cottage available • swimming • nudity • seasonal

Oil City

EROTICA

Movie Stop 2 E First St 814/677–7368 • 11am-10pm, till 11pm Fri-Sat • LGBT section

Philadelphia

Info Lines & Services

AA Gay/ Lesbian 215/923-7900, 877/934-2522

Colours, Inc 1201 Chestnut St, 15th flr 215/496-0330 • serving the LGBTQ Community of Color • special emphasis on health

William Way LGBT Community Center 1315 Spruce St (at Juniper) 215/732-2220 • 11:30am-10pm, till 7pm Sat, from 10:30am Sun

Accommodations

▲ **Alexander Inn** Spruce (at 12th St) 215/923-3535, 877/253-9466 • gay/ straight • restored hotel • gym • gay-owned • $99-149

Antique Row B&B 341 S 12th St (at Pine) 215/592-7802 • gay-friendly • 1820s town house in heart of gay community • full brkfst • $65-110

Doubletree Hotel 237 S Broad St (at Locust) 215/893-1600, 800/222-8733 (Reservations) • gay-friendly

Embassy Suites Center City 1776 Ben Franklin Pkwy (at 18th) 215/561-1776, 800/362-2779 • gay-friendly • $129-209

Gaskill House B&B 312 Gaskill St (btwn Lombard & South St) 215/413-0669 • gay/ straight • on Society Hill • full brkfst • nonsmoking • gay-owned • $120-200

Glen Isle Farm 30 miles out of town, in Downingtown 610/269-9100 • gay/ straight • full brkfst • nonsmoking • older kids ok (call first) • gay-owned • $60-75

Hampton Inn Center City Philadelphia 1301 Race St (13th St) 267/765-1110, 800/426-7866 • gay/ straight • hotel • brkfst included • swimming • jacuzzi • wheelchair access • $79-209

Holiday Inn Historic Disctrict 400 Arch St (at Market) 215/923-8660, 800/843-2355 • gay-friendly • swimming • kids/ pets ok • $99-199

Latham Hotel 135 S 17th St (at Walnut) 215/563-7474, 800/528-4261 • gay-friendly

Philadelphia Marriott 1201 Market St (btwn 12th & 13th) 215/625-2900, 800/228-9290 • gay-friendly • swimming • 2 restaurants • near the gay area in Philly • wheelchair access

Rittenhouse Hotel 210 W Rittenhouse Square (at 19th) 215/546-9000, 800/635-1042 • gay-friendly • food served • $210+

Rodeway Inn 1208 Walnut St (btwn 12th & 13th) 215/546-7000, 800/887-1776 • lesbians/gay men • kids ok • nonsmoking • $99-149

Shippen Way Inn 416-18 Bainbridge St (4th & 5th Sts) 215/627-7266, 800/245-4873 • gay-friendly • 18th-c B&B • includes brkfst & afternoon tea

BARS

Bump 1234 Locust St (at 13th) 215/732-1800 • 5pm-2am • lesbians/gay men • also restaurant • Sun brunch • drag shows • "Austin-Powers chic"

Hamburger Mary's/Dragonfly 1716 Chestnut St 215/568-6969 • 11am-2am, also restaurant till 11pm • lesbians/gay men • Fabric 2nd Sat • food served

Key West 207-209 S Juniper (btwn Walnut & Locust) 215/545-1578 • noon-2am, from 2pm Sun • lesbians/gay men • neighborhood bar • 4 bars • dancing/DJ • lunch served daily • live shows • piano bar • sports bar • Elevate 4th Sat (mostly women) • wheelchair access

The Khyber 56 S 2nd St (btwn Market & Chestnut) 215/238-5888 • noon-2am, from 4pm Sat • gay-friendly • live bands • wheelchair access

---

Philadelphia

WHERE THE GIRLS ARE:
Partying downtown near 12th St., south of Market.

LGBT PRIDE:
June. 215/875-9288, web: www.phillypride.org.

ANNUAL EVENTS:
April/May - Equality Forum 215/732-3378, web: www.pride-fest.org. Weekend of LGBT film, performances, literature, sports, seminars, parties & more.
June - Gay & Lesbian Theatre Festival 215/922-1122, web: www.philagaylesbiantheatre-fest.org.
June - Womongathering 856/694-2037, web: www.womongather-ing.com. Women's spirituality fest.
July - Philadelphia International Gay & Lesbian Film Festival 267/765-9700 ext. 4, web: www.phillyfests.org

CITY INFO:
Philadelphia Convention & Visitors Bureau 215/636-3300, web: www.pcvb.org.

BEST VIEW:
Top of Center Square, 16th & Market.

WEATHER:
Winter temperatures hover in the 20°s. Summers are humid with temperatures in the 80°s and 90°s.

TRANSIT:
Quaker City Cab 215/728-8000.
Transit Authority (SEPTA) 215/

ATTRACTIONS:
Academy of Natural Sciences 215/299-1000, web: www.acnatsci.org.
African American Museum 215/574-0380, web: www.aampmuseum.org.
Betsy Ross House 215/686-1252, web: betsyrosshouse.org.
Independence Hall 215/965-2305, web: www.nps.gov/inde.
Liberty Bell Pavilion.
National Museum Of American Jewish History 215/923-3811, web: www.nmajh.org.
Philadelphia Museum of Art 215/763-8100, web: www.phila-museum.org.
Reading Terminal Market, web: www.readingterminalmarket.org.
Rodin Museum 215/763-8100, web: www.rodinmuseum.org.

North Third 3rd & Brown 215/413–3666 • 4pm-2am, Sun brunch • gay/ straight • Rock 'N' Roll Queer Bar 2nd Wed • also restaurant

Tavern on Camac 243 S Camac St (at Spruce) 215/545–0900 • noon-2am • lesbians/ gay men • dancing/DJ wknds • piano bar • food served

Tyz 1418 Rodman St (near 15th & Richmond) 215/546–4195 • 11pm-3am • mostly gay men • dancing/DJ wknds

Venture Inn 255 S Camac St (at Spruce) 215/545–8731 • 11am-2am • lesbians/ gay men • neighborhood bar • food served

The Westbury 261 S 13th (at Spruce) 215/546–5170 • 11am-2am, dinner till 10pm, till 11pm wknds • lesbians/ gay men • neighborhood bar • wheelchair access

Woody's 202 S 13th St (at Walnut) 215/545–1893 • 11am-2am • popular • mostly gay men • dancing/DJ • country/ western • dance lessons • videos • full restaurant • karaoke Mon • Latin Th • strippers • young crowd • 18+ Wed • wheelchair access

NIGHTCLUBS

Bike Stop 204-206 S Quince St (btwn 11th & 12th, Walnut & Locust) 215/627–1662 • 4pm-2am, from 2pm wknds • popular • mostly gay men • 4 flrs • dancing/DJ • leather (very leather-women-friendly) • live bands Sun • also The Gear Box custom leather shop

Club Libations 231 S Broad St (at Race St) • Fri-Sat • mostly women • dancing/DJ • multiracial • private club

Elevate 207–209 S Juniper (btwn Walnut & Locust) 215/545–1578 • 4th Sat • mostly women • dancing/DJ

Fluid 613 S 4th St (at Kater) 215/629–3686 • 10pm-2am • gay-friendly • more gay wknds • dancing/DJ • drag shows • theme nights • cover charge

Girl 200 S 12th St (at Sal's Restaurant) 215/574–2110 • 3rd Sat • mostly women • dancing/DJ

L'Hexagone 1718 Sansom St 215/569–4869 • 5pm-close, clsd Mon • more gay Sun • gay/ straight • dancing/ DJ

| Reply | Forward | | Delete |

Date: Nov 9, 2005 11:23:46
From: Girl-on-the-Go
To: Editor@Damron.com
Subject: Philadelphia

>Though it's packed with sites of rich historical value, don't miss out on Philadelphia's multicultural present. To get a feel for this city, browse the Reading Terminal Market, a quaint old farmer's market preserved within the new Convention Center. Here, smalltime grocers and farmers of many cultures sell their fresh food.

>A vital element in many of these cultures is the growing lesbian community. To connect with the scene, call the **William Way LGBT Community Center**, or check out **Sisters**, a women's dance bar that also serves dinner Wednesday-Sunday.

>And don't even think of leaving town before you visit **Giovanni's Room**, Philadelphia's legendary LGBT bookstore. Here you can pick up the latest lesbian bestseller, the love of your life, or a copy of the **Philadelphia Gay News**.

Lounge 125 125 S 2nd St (at Chestnut) 215/351–9026 • midnight-3:20am, from 11pm Wed-Sat • gay/ straight • dancing/DJ • live shows • food served

Palmer Social Club 601 Spring Garden St (at 6th) 215/925–5000 • 11pm-3am Fri-Sat only • gay-friendly • dancing/DJ • 3 flrs • private club

Pousse Cafe 1734 Snyder Ave (at R Club) 215/849–7444 • 9pm-1am • monthly women's strip night

Pure 1221 St James St (off 13th & Locust) 215/735–5772 • 9pm-3:30am Wed-Sun, from 1am Mon-Tue • mostly gay men • dancing/DJ • piano bar • karaoke • cabaret • private club

Pure Party Girl 1221 St James St (at Pure) 856/869–0193, 215/735–5772 • 9pm-close • mostly women • dancing/DJ • karaoke

Shampoo 417 N 8th St (at Willow) 215/922–7500 • 9pm-2am, clsd Mon-Tue • gay/ straight • more gay Fri • dancing/DJ • alternative

▲ **Sisters** 1320 Chancellor St (at Juniper) 215/735–0735 • 5pm-2am • mostly women • dancing/DJ • live shows • karaoke • also restaurant • dinner Wed-Sat, Sun brunch • wheelchair access

Cafes

10th Street Pour House 262 S 10th St (at Spruce) 215/922–5626 • 7:30am-3pm, popular brunch spot wknds • wheelchair access

Millennium Coffee 212 S 12th St (btwn Locust & Walnut) 215/731–9798 • 6am-11pm, till midnight Fri-Sat

Stellar Coffee 1101 Spruce St (at 11th) 215/625–7923 • 7am-6:30pm

Restaurants

Abbraccio 3601 Locust Walk (at 36th) 215/727–8247 • lunch Sun-Fri & dinner, bar till 1am • wheelchair access

The Adobe Cafe 4550 Mitchell St (at Greenleaf), Roxborough 215/483–3947 • lunch Th-Sun & dinner nightly • plenty veggie • live shows

Astral Plane 1708 Lombard St (btwn 17th & 18th) 215/546–6230 • dinner nightly • Sun brunch • some veggie • full bar till 2am

Blue in Green 719 Sansom St 215/923–6883 • lunch daily, dinner Fri-Sat • comfort food • full bar

The Continental 138 Market St (at 2nd) 215/923–6069 • 11:30am-2am, from 10:30am wknds • also bar until 2am • eclectic • some veggie

Cresheim Cottage Cafe 7402 Germantown Ave (at Gowen Ave) 215/248–4365 • lunch & dinner, Sun brunch • eclectic menu • some veggie • full bar • transgender-friendly • available for commitment ceremonies • wheelchair access

Figs 2501 Meredith St 215/978–8440 • dinner nightly • wknd brunch • clsd Mon • eclectic Mediterranean • BYOB • wheelchair access

The Happy Rooster 118 S 16th St (at Sansom St) 215/963–9311 • lunch & dinner, clsd Sun • cont'l • upscale • karaoke • full bar till 2am

Harmony Vegetarian 135 N 9th St (at Cherry) 215/627–4520 • 11am-11pm

The Inn Philadelphia 251 S Camac St (btwn Locust & Spruce) 215/732–2339 • 5:30pm-10:30pm, 5pm-9pm Sun, Sun brunch, clsd Mon • some veggie • full bar • piano bar • live shows • no smoking

Judy's Cafe 627 S 3rd St (at Bainbridge) 215/928–1968 • 5:30pm-10pm, till 11pm Fri-Sat, Sun brunch • full bar • women-owned/ run

L2 2201 South St (at 22nd) 215/732–7878 • dinner nightly, clsd Mon • also bar • live jazz

Liberties 705 N 2nd St (at Fairmount) 215/238–0660 • lunch & dinner • full bar till 2am

My Thai 2200 South St (at 22nd) 215/985–1878 • 5pm-10pm, till 11pm Fri-Sat • full bar

The Plough & the Stars 123 Chestnut St (at 2nd) 215/733–0300 • 11:30am-2am, popular brunch from 10:30am Sun • Irish pub fare • full bar • live music Sun

▲ **Sisters** 1320 Chancellor St (at Juniper) 215/735–0735 • dinner 5pm-10pm Wed-Sat, Sun brunch • mostly women

Striped Bass 1500 Walnut St (at 15th) 215/732–4444 • dinner nightly, brunch 11:30am-2:30pm Sun • upscale • seasonal

Sushi Bar 1431 Spruce St (across from The Kimmel Center) 215/732–5585 • 11:30am-10pm, clsd Sun

Swanky Bubbles 10 S Front St (at Market) 215/928–1200 • 5pm-1am • also bar till 2am • Asian-fusion

Valanni 1229 Spruce St 215/790-9494 • dinner nightly, Sun brunch • Mediterranean/ Latin • full bar

El Vez 121-127 S 13th St (at Sansom) 215/928-9800 • lunch Mon-Sat, brunch Sun, dinner nightly • Latin American/ Mexican • bar open till 2am

White Dog Cafe 3420 Sansom St (at Walnut) 215/386-9224 • lunch & dinner, brunch Sun • full bar • eclectic American • cool Mon reading & Sun film series

Zócalo 3600 Lancaster Ave (in University City) 215/895-0139 • lunch Mon-Fri, dinner nightly, clsd Sun • Mexican/ New Southwestern

ENTERTAINMENT & RECREATION

Amazon Country WXPN-FM 88.5 215/898-6677 • 11pm Sun • lesbian radio

Q Zine WXPN-FM 88.5 215/898-6677 • 11:30pm • LGBT radio

The Walt Whitman House 328 Mickle Blvd (btwn S 3rd & S 4th Sts), Camden, NJ 856/964-5383 • the last home of America's great & controversial poet, just across the Delaware River

BOOKSTORES

Giovanni's Room 345 S 12th St (at Pine) 215/923-2960 • 11:30am-7pm, till 10pm Fri-Sat, from 10am Sat, from 1pm Sun • popular • legendary LGBT bookstore

Robin's Bookstore 108 S 13th St 215/735-9600 • 10am-8pm, from noon Sun • oldest independent bookstore in Philly

RETAIL SHOPS

Amoeba Art Shop 7174 Germantown Ave (at W Mt Airy Ave) 215/242-4568 • 10am-7pm, clsd Sun • gay-owned

Infinite Body Piercing 626 S 4th St (at South) 215/923-7335 • noon-10pm, till midnight Fri-Sat, till 8pm Sun

PUBLICATIONS

EXP Magazine 302/227-5787, 877/397-6244 • bi-weekly gay magazine for Mid-Atlantic

PGN (Philadelphia Gay News) 215/625-8501 • LGBT newspaper w/ extensive listings

Visions Today 302/656-5876, 800/241-5803 • quarterly, covers Rehoboth, Philadelphia, New Hope, Wilmington & surrounding area

Women's Yellow Pages of Greater Philadelphia 610/446-4747

SPIRITUAL GROUPS

Beth Ahavah 8 Letitia St (btwn Market & Chestnut) 215/923-2003 • 8pm Fri

Christ Episcopal Church 2nd St above Market (at Church) 215/922-1695 • 9am & 11am Sun, also daily tours of church built in 1727

Dignity 330 S 13th St (btwn Spruce & Pine) 215/546-2093 • 7pm Sun

Integrity 1904 Walnut St (at the Church of the Holy Trinity) 215/382-0794 • 7pm 1st Wed • pastoral counseling available

MCC 1315 Spruce St (at William Way GLBT Center) 215/735-6223 • 11am Sun

Old First Reformed Church (United Church of Christ) 4th & Race Sts 215/922-4566 • 11am Sun (10am summer)

GYMS & HEALTH CLUBS

12th St Gym 204 S 12th St (btwn Locust & Walnut) 215/985-4092 • 5:30am-11pm, till 10pm Fri, 8am-8pm Sat, 8am-7pm Sun • gay-friendly • day passes

EROTICA

Condom Kingdom 437 South St (at 5th) 215/829-1668 • safer sex materials • toys

Passional 704 S 5th St (at Bainbridge) 215/829-4986, 877/2-CORSET • noon-10pm • corsets • fetish wear • toys • woman owned

The Pleasure Chest 2039 Walnut (btwn 20th & 21st) 215/561-7480 • 11am-7pm, clsd Sun-Mon

Scorpio Adult Boutique & Video 205 S Juniper St (btwn Walnut & Locust) 215/545-2181

Touch of Class 3342 Kensington Ave 215/739-3348 • open daily • gay videos & toys

Phoenixville

NIGHTCLUBS

Frank Jeffrey's 231 Bridge St (above Lojo's) 610/935-7154 • 7pm-2am, clsd Mon-Wed, also clsd Th & Sun in summer • lesbians/ gay men • also restaurant

Pittsburgh

INFO LINES & SERVICES

AA Gay/ Lesbian 239 4th Ave 412/471-7472 • call for times & location

Gay/ Lesbian Community Center 5808 Forward Ave (at Murray, 2nd flr) 412/422-0114 • 6:30pm-9:30pm, 3pm-6pm Sat, clsd Sun

ACCOMMODATIONS

Camp Davis 311 Red Brush Rd, Boyers **724/637–2402** • 2nd wknd April thru 2nd wknd in Oct • cabins, trailer, & campsites • lesbians/ gay men • adults 21+ only • dance 9pm-2am Sat • 1 hour from Pittsburgh • $17 (tent sites); $25 (cabins); $30 (trailer); rates per person

The Inn on the Mexican War Streets 604 W North Ave **412/231–6544** • lesbians/ gay men • located on the historic & gay-friendly North Side • nonsmoking • also restaurant • gay-owned • $99-169

The Priory 614 Pressley St (near Cedar Ave) **412/231–3338** • gay-friendly • 24-room Victorian • fitness center • kids ok • $134-195

BARS

Blue Moon Bar & Lounge 5115 Butler St, Lawrenceville **412/781–1119** • noon-2am, 4pm-midnight Mon-Tue, clsd Sun • mostly men • neighborhood bar • transgender-friendly • go-go dancers

Brewery Tavern 3315 Liberty Ave (at Herron Ave) **412/681–7991** • 10am-2am, from 11am Sun • gay-friendly

Images 965 Liberty Ave (at 10th St) **412/391–9990** • 2pm-2am, from 6pm Sat, clsd Sun • mostly gay men • karaoke • videos

Jaxx Nightclub 2424 Wylie Ave **412/475–4694** • lesbians/ gay men • dancing/DJ • African-American clientele

Liberty Avenue Saloon 941 Liberty Ave (at Smithfield) **412/338–1533** • 2pm-2am, from 5pm Sat, from 1pm Sun • lesbians/ gay men • neighborhood bar • also restaurant

New York, New York 5801 Ellsworth Ave (at Maryland) **412/661–5600** • 4pm-2am • popular • lesbians/ gay men • also restaurant • some veggie • piano sing-along Sat • wheelchair access

Pittsburgh Eagle 1740 Eckert St (near Beaver) **412/766–7222** • 9pm-2am, clsd Sun-Tue • popular • mostly gay men • dancing/DJ • leather • wheelchair access

Pittsburgh

LGBT PRIDE:
June. 412/422-0114 (GLCC #), web: glccpgh,org.
August. Pittsburgh Unity Black Pride 412/657-0142.

ANNUAL EVENTS:
June - Three Rivers Arts Festival 412/281–8723, web: www.arts-festival.net.

CITY INFO:
412/281-7711 or 800/359-0758, web: www.visitpittsburgh.com.

TRANSIT:
Yellow Cab 412/665-8100.
Airlines Transportation Co. 412/321–4990.
Port Authority Transit (PAT) 412/442-2000, web: www.portau-thority.org.

ATTRACTIONS:
Andy Warhol Museum 412/237-8300, web: www.warhol.org.
Carnegie Museums of Pittsburgh 412/622-3131, web: www.carnegiemuseums.org.
Fallingwater (in Mill Run) 724/329-8501, web: www.paconserve.org.
Frick Art & Historical Center 412/371-0600, web: www.frickart.org.
Golden Triangle District.
Shopping & dining in the Strip District.
National Aviary 412/323-7235, web: www.aviary.org.
Phipps Conservatory 412/622-6914, web: www.phipps.conservatory.org.
Rachel Carson Homestead (in Springdale) 724/274-5459, web: rachelcarsonhomestead.org.
Station Square.

Ray's Marlin Beach Bar & Grill 5121 Butler St, Lawrenceville 412/781-6771 • 11:30am-2am, from 1pm Sun • gay/ straight • multiracial • neighborhood bar • also Caribbean restaurant on upper level

Real Luck Cafe 1519 Penn Ave (at 16th) 412/566-8988 • 4pm-2am • lesbians/ gay men • neighborhood bar • go-go dancers • food served • some veggie • wheelchair access

Sidekicks 931 Liberty Ave (at Smithfield) 412/642-4435 • 5pm-midnight, clsd Sun • lesbians/ gay men • wheelchair access

True Love & Bartini 900 Western Ave (at Galveston Ave) 412/321-8783 • 5pm-2am, from 6pm Sat, from 3pm Sun, clsd Mon • gay/ straight • DJ Sat • food served till 9pm • live shows

Zebra Lounge 910 Constitution Blvd (at 9th), New Kensington 724/339-0298 • 4pm-2am, clsd Sun • lesbians/ gay men • dancing/DJ

NIGHTCLUBS

Angel's 2604 Josephine St 412/488-2700 • lesbians/ gay men • dancing/DJ

Club Hot 941 Liberty Ave (at Smithfield St, 2nd flr) 412/391-0804 • 11pm-3:30am • popular • lesbians/ gay men • dancing/DJ

Donny's Place 1226 Herron Ave (at Liberty) 412/682-9869 • 4pm-2am • popular • lesbians/ gay men • mostly women upstairs Fri-Sat • Leather Central mostly men downstairs Fri-Sat • food served

Pegasus 818 Liberty Ave (at 9th) 412/281-2131 • 9pm-2am, clsd Mon, Wed, Sun • popular • lesbians/ gay men • dancing/ DJ • young crowd

CAFES

Tuscany Cafe 1501 E Carson St (at 15th) 412/488-4475 • 8am-2am • full bar

ENTERTAINMENT & RECREATION

Andy Warhol Museum 117 Sandusky St (at General Robinson) 412/237-8300 • 10am-5pm, till 10pm Fri, clsd Mon • is it soup or is it art?—see for yourself

BOOKSTORES

Jay's Bookstall 3604 5th Ave (at Meyran) 412/683-2644 • 10am-5:45pm, till 4pm Sat, clsd Sun

RETAIL SHOPS

A Pleasant Present 2301 Murray Ave (at Nicholson) 412/421-7104 • 10am-8pm, till 6pm Fri-Sat, clsd Sun • wheelchair access

Slacker 1321 E Carson St (btwn 13th & 14th) 412/381-3911 • 11am-9pm, till 11pm Fri-Sat, noon-6pm Sun • magazines • clothing • leather • piercing • wheelchair access

PUBLICATIONS

Erie Gay News 814/456-9833 • covers news & events in the Erie, Cleveland, Pittsburgh, Buffalo & Chautauqua County, NY region

EXP Magazine 302/227-5787, 877/397-6244 • bi-weekly gay magazine for Mid-Atlantic

Out 412/243-3350 • LGBT newspaper

SPIRITUAL GROUPS

First Unitarian Church 605 Moorewood Ave (at Ellsworth) 412/621-8008 • 9:30am & 11am Sun, 10am summers

MCC of Pittsburgh 4836 Ellsworth Ave (at Devonshire, at Friends Mtg House) 412/683-2994 • 7pm Sun

Poconos

ACCOMMODATIONS

The Arrowheart Inn 3021 Valley View Dr (at Fox Gap Rd), Bangor 610/588-0241 • gay/ straight • B&B • full brkfst • hot tub • near skiing, hiking, biking, river • nonsmoking • kids ok • 1 1/2 hours from NYC • gay-owned • $85-125

▲ **Blueberry Ridge** 570/629-5036 • women only • full brkfst • hot tub • nonsmoking • holiday packages • lesbian-owned • $65-100

▲ **Frog Hollow** 570/595-2814 • lesbians/ gay men • secluded 1920s cottage • deck • fireplace • kids/ pets ok • lesbian-owned • $100-150

Home in the Mountain 1 Monomonock Rd, Mountainhome 570/595-9540 • lesbians/ gay men • B&B-inn in heart of Poconos • full brkfst • swimming • lesbian-owned • $75-115

Rainbow Mountain Resort 570/223-8484 • lesbians/ gay men • transgender-friendly • resort w/ suites • cabins (seasonal) • swimming • gay-owned • $46-248 • also restaurant & full bar • dancing/DJ Fri-Sat • piano bar • karaoke

▲ **Stoney Ridge** 570/629-5036 • lesbians/ gay men • secluded log home • kitchen • kids/ pets ok • lesbian-owned • $250 (for 2) – 350 (for 4) / wknds; $550 (2) – 750 (4)/ week

Quakertown

RESTAURANTS

The Brick Tavern Inn 2460 Old Bethlehem Pike (at Brick Tavern Rd) 215/529–6488 • lunch Tue-Sat & dinner nightly, full bar open later

Reading

BARS

The Peanut Bar & Restaurant 332 Penn St 610/376–8500, 800/515–8500 • 11am-11pm, till midnight Fri-Sat, clsd Sun • a Reading landmark!

RESTAURANTS

Judy's...on Cherry 332 Cherry St 610/374–8511 • lunch Tue-Fri, dinner Tue-Sat, clsd Sun-Mon • Mediterranean

The Ugly Oyster 21 S 5th St (at Cherry) 610/373–6791 • 11:30am-10pm, from noon Sat, clsd Sun • traditional Irish pub (bar open till 2am)

GYMS & HEALTH CLUBS

Gold's Gym 1119 Bern Rd, Wyomissing 610/372–9131 • gay-friendly

YMCA of Reading 631 Washington St 610/378–4700

Scranton

BARS

Twelve Penny Saloon 3501 Birney Ave, Moosic 570/941–0444 • 6pm-2am, clsd Sun • mostly men • neighborhood bar • gay-owned

State College

INFO LINES & SERVICES

Women's Resource Center 140 W Nittany Ave (at Frasier) 877/234–5050 (24HR HOTLINE), 814/234–5050 • 9am-7pm, clsd wknds

BARS

Chumley's 108 W College 814/238–4446 • 5pm-2am, from 6pm Sun • popular • lesbians/gay men • neighborhood bar • wheelchair access

NIGHTCLUBS

Players 112 W College Ave 814/234–1031 • 9pm-2am, clsd Mon & Wed • gay/ straight • "Alternative" night Sun • dancing/DJ • videos • young crowd

Uniontown

NIGHTCLUBS

Illusions 231 Pittsburgh St/ Rte 51 (at Fulton) 724/430–1477 • 5pm-close, clsd Sun • mostly men • neighborhood bar • dancing/ DJ • transgender-friendly • food • karaoke • drag shows • served • gay-owned

Wilkes-Barre

INFO LINES & SERVICES

AA Gay/ Lesbian 570/654–0488 • call for info

NIGHTCLUBS

Sneaker's Cafe 465 Main St, Kingston 570/283–9680 • 8pm-2am, clsd wknds • mostly women • dancing/DJ • food served • karaoke

Twist 1170 Hwy 315 (in Fox Ridge Plaza) 570/825–7300 • 8pm-2am, from 6pm Sun • popular • mostly gay men • dancing/DJ • patio • also restaurant • wheelchair access

Williamsport

BARS

Peachie's 144 E 4th St 570/326–3611 • 3pm-2am, from 7pm Sat, clsd Sun • lesbians/ gay men • dancing/DJ wknds • food served • wheelchair access

York

INFO LINES & SERVICES

York Area Gay Info 648 W College Ave 717/846–2560 • York area gay info

NIGHTCLUBS

Altland's Ranch 8505 Orchard Rd, Spring Grove 717/225–4479 • 8pm-2am Fri-Sat only • lesbians/ gay men • dancing/DJ • karaoke

The Velvet Rope 36 W 11th Ave 717/812–1474 • 7pm-2am Tue-Sun • lesbians/gay men • dancing/ DJ • retro night 1st & 3rd Fri • transgender-friendly • food served • drag shows • wheel chair access

EROTICA

Cupid's Connection Adult Boutique 244 N George St (at North) 717/846–5029

RHODE ISLAND

Statewide

PUBLICATIONS

In Newsweekly 617/426-8246 • New England's largest LGBT newspaper

Options 401/781-1193 • extensive resource listings

East Greenwich

RETAIL SHOPS

Scrumptions Bakery 5600 Post Rd 401/884-0844 • 9am-5pm, 10am-6pm Sat, clsd Mon

Newport

INFO LINES & SERVICES

Sobriety First 135 Pelham St (at Channing Memorial Church) 401/438-8860 • 8pm Fri

ACCOMMODATIONS

Brinley Victorian Inn 23 Brinley St 401/849-7645, 800/999-8523 • gay-friendly • nonsmoking • $89-229

Captain James Preston House 378 Spring St (at Pope) 401/847-7077, 866/238-3952 • gay-friendly • elegant Victorian B&B • nonsmoking • $130-230

Francis Malbone House Inn 392 Thames St (at Memorial Blvd) 401/846-0392, 800/846-0392 • gay-friendly • nonsmoking • wheelchair access

Hydrangea House Inn 16 Bellevue Ave 401/846-4435, 800/945-4667 • popular • gay/ straight • full brkfst • near beach • nonsmoking • gay-owned • $225-425

Inn Bliss B&B 10 Bliss Rd (at Broadway) 401/845-2547 • gay/ straight • gay-owned • 1888 Victorian B&B • close walk to beaches & downtown area • $47-175

The Melville House Inn 39 Clarke St 401/847-0640, 800/711-7184 • popular • gay-friendly • full brkfst • nonsmoking • $110-189

The Spring Seasons Inn 86 Spring St (btwn Mary St & Touro) 401/849-0004 • gay-friendly • B&B • full brkfst• jacuzzi baths • $1125-275

BARS

Castaways 28 Prospect Hill St 401/849-9928 • 6pm-1am, from 4pm wknds • lesbians/ gay men • neighborhood bar

RESTAURANTS

Restaurant Bouchard 505 Thames St 401/846-0123 • dinner, clsd Tue

Whitehorse Tavern 26 Marlborough (at Farewell) 401/849-3600 • lunch Wed-Sun, dinner nightly • upscale dining • no smoking

Pawtucket

INFO LINES & SERVICES

Gay & Lesbian AA 71 Park Place (at Congregational church) 401/438-8860 • 7:30pm Tue

Providence

INFO LINES & SERVICES

GLBT Helpline of Rhode Island 401/751-3322 • 7pm-10pm Mon, Wed & Fri

ACCOMMODATIONS

Courtyard by Marriott 32 Exchange Terr 401/272-1191, 888/887-7955 • gay-friendly

BARS

Alleycat 17 Snow St (at Washington) 401/273-0951 • 3pm-1am, till 2am Fri-Sat • lesbians/ gay men • neighborhood bar • videos • gay-owned

Deville's 150 Point St 401/751-7166 • 7pm-1am, till 2am Fri-Sat, from 4pm Sun, clsd Mon • popular • mostly women • neighborhood bar • dancing/DJ Th-Sat • wheelchair access

European Tavern 828 Charles St (at Raphael) 401/831-3327 • 3pm-midnight, clsd Sun • lesbians/ gay men • neighborhood bar

The Providence Eagle 200 Union St (at Weybosset) 401/421-1447 • 3pm-1am, from noon wknds, till 2am Fri-Sat • mostly gay men • leather • wheelchair access

Union 200 Union St (next to the Providence Eagle) 401/831-5366 • 5pm-1am, from 8pm Wed, till 2am Fri-Sat, clsd Mon-Tue • lesbians/ gay men • karaoke Th-Fri • piano bar Wed & Sun • DJ Sat

Wheels 125 Washington (at Mathewson) 401/272-6950 • noon-1am, till 2am Fri-Sat • lesbians/ gay men • dancing/DJ wknds • karaoke • videos • wheelchair access

NIGHTCLUBS

Bar One 1 Throop Alley (off S Main St) 401/621-7112 • 9pm-close, clsd Sun-Mon • gay/ straight • dancing/DJ • 18+ • call for events

Club Energy 69 Union St • mostly gay men • dancing/ DJ • theme nights

Fuel @ Diesel 79 Washington St **401/751–2700** • 9pm–1am Sun only • lesbians/ gay men • dancing/DJ • go-go boys • huge space • 18+ • cover

Mirabar 35 Richmond St (at Weybosset) **401/331–6761** • 3pm–1am, till 2am Fri-Sat • mostly gay men • dancing/DJ • karaoke Mon • live shows • male dancers • wheelchair access

Splash at Pulse 86 Crary St (at Plain) **401/272–2133** • Sat only • mostly women • dancing/DJ • 18+

Therapy/ INSANE 7 Dike St (at Troy) **401/490–7202** • 9pm–2am Tue-Th, till 4am Fri-Sat, clsd Sun-Mon • gay/ straight • also gallery & cafe from 10am • young crowd • wheelchair access

CAFES

Coffee Exchange 207 Wickenden St **401/273–1198** • 6:30am-11pm • deck

Nicks on Broadway 259 Broadway **401/421–0286** • brkfst & lunch, clsd Mon-Tue

Reflections Cafe 8 Governor St (at Wickenden) **401/273–7278** • 7am-11pm, from 8am wknds • food served • fresh baked goods & specialty coffees • also sidewalk seating

White Electric 150 Broadway **401/453–3007** • 7am-5:30pm, from 9am wknds

RESTAURANTS

Al Forno 577 S Main St **401/273–9760** • dinner only, clsd Sun-Mon • popular • Little Rhody's best dining experience • patio

Angelo Bianco 178 Atwells Ave **401/383–8199** • lunch & dinner • Italian • also lounge

Camille's 71 Bradford St (at Atwell's Ave) **401/751–4812** • lunch & dinner • full bar

Downcity 151 Weybosset St **401/331–9217** • lunch weekdays & dinner Tue-Sun • wknd brunch • full bar • wheelchair access

Julian's 318 Broadway (at Vinton) **401/861–1770** • 9am-1am • gourmet • plenty veggie

Lot 401 44 Hospital St **401/490–3980** • lunch Tue-Fri, dinner nightly, clsd Sun-Mon

Rue de l'Espoir 99 Hope St (at John) **401/751–8890** • brkfst, lunch & dinner, clsd Mon • full bar • women-owned/ run • American Bistro • wheelchair access

Viola's 58 DePasquale Plaza (on Federal Hill) **401/861–5766** • dinner nightly, clsd Mon-Tue, open for lunch in summer • patio

ENTERTAINMENT & RECREATION

Perishable Theatre 95 Empire St **401/331–2695** • plays • also late-night comedy

WaterFire Waterplace Park • May-Oct only • bonfire installations along the Providence River at sunset • check local listings for dates

BOOKSTORES

Books on the Square 471 Angell St (at Wayland) **401/331–9097** • 9am-9pm, noon-6pm Sun • some LGBT

Providence

LGBT PRIDE:
June. 401/467-2130, web: www.prideri.com.

ANNUAL EVENTS:
Oct - International Women's Playwriting Festival 401/621–6123, web: www.aboutwpf.com.

CITY INFO:
401/274-1636 or 800/233-1636, web: www.goprovidence.com.

ATTRACTIONS:
Newport.
RISD Museum 401/454-6500, web: www.risd.edu.
Waterfire 401/272-3111, web: www.waterfire.com.

TRANSIT:
Yellow Cab 401/941-1122.
RIPTA Bus Service 401/781-9400, web: www.ripta.com.

Oakwells 100 Gaspee St (inside Amtrack Station) 401/373–5190 • 6am-7pm • LGBT section

PUBLICATIONS

In Newsweekly 617/426–8246 • New England's largest LGBT newspaper

▲ **Metroline** 860/233–8334 • regional newspaper & entertainment guide, covers CT, RI & MA

Options 401/781–1193 • extensive resource listings

SPIRITUAL GROUPS

Bell Street Chapel (Unitarian) 5 Bell St 401/273–5678 • 10am Sun

St Peter's & Andrew's Episcopal Church 25 Pomona Ave 401/272–9649 • 8am & 10am Sun (9am summers)

SEX CLUBS

Black Key Club 401/274–3700 • call for hours • members-only playspace for lesbian, gay, bi, transgendered & straight couples & singles • nonsmoking

EROTICA

Miko 653 N Main St (at Doyle) 401/421–6646, 800/421–6646 • women-oriented • fetishwear • sex toys • classes

Smithfield

BARS

The Loft 325 Farnum Pike 401/231–3320 • 2pm-1am, from 1pm wknds, from 4pm Mon-Tue • lesbians/ gay men • dancing/DJ • strippers • swimming • wheelchair access • gay-owned

Westerly

ACCOMMODATIONS

The Villa 190 Shore Rd 401/596–1054, 800/722–9240 • gay-friendly • near beach • hot tub • swimming • nonsmoking • $105-295

RESTAURANTS

Mary's Rte 1 & Post Rd (off I-A) 401/322–0444 • lunch & dinner • Italian

SOUTH CAROLINA

Statewide

PUBLICATIONS

▲ **The Front Page** 919/829–0181 • LGBT newspaper for the Carolinas

Aiken

see also Augusta, Georgia

NIGHTCLUBS

Marlboro Station 141 Marlboro St 803/644–6485 • 10pm-close Fri-Sun • lesbians/ gay men • dancing/DJ • live shows

Beaufort

RESTAURANTS

Old House Restaurant 7868 Low Country Dr, Ridgeland 843/258–4444 • 5pm-9pm, till 10pm Fri-Sat, clsd Sun • BYOB • wheelchair access • gay-owned

Charleston

INFO LINES & SERVICES

Acceptance Group (Gay AA) 67 Anson St (btwn Society & George, at St Stephen's Episcopal) 843/723–9633 (AA#) • 7pm Mon, 8pm Tue & 6:30pm Sat

ACCOMMODATIONS

1854 B&B 34 Montagu St 843/723–4789 • lesbians/ gay men • private home in historic district • kids/ small pets ok • gay-owned • $115-125

A B&B @ 4 Unity Alley 4 Unity Alley 843/577–6660 • gay/ straight • full brkfst • nonsmoking • parking inside • $125-245

Alice's Carriage House B&B 22 New St (at Tradd St) 843/973–3458 • gay-friendly • swimming • hot tub • nonsmoking • $165-195

Blue Heron Inn 122 E Arctic Ave (corner of E Artic Ave, E Ashley Ave & 2nd St), Folly Beach 843/588–3343 • gay-friendly • 1-bdrm villas w/ ocean view • kids ok • nonsmoking • $500-900/ week

Folly Flamingo 116 E Ashley Ave (at Center St), Folly Beach 843/588–3351 • gay-friendly

The Gateway House Inn 20 Burns Ln (at King & Calhoun St) 843/722–3969, 800/706–1802 • gay-friendly • B&B • nonsmoking • pets ok • $139-199

Phoebe Pember House 26 Society St (at East Bay) 843/722-4186 • gay-friendly • an oasis in the heart of historic Charleston • yoga studio on property offers classes • $125-225

BARS

Patrick's Pub 1377 Ashley River Rd/ Hwy 61 843/571-3435 • 6pm-2am • lesbians/ gay men • neighborhood bar • transgender-friendly • DJ Fri-Sat • karaoke Th • live shows & music • wheelchair access

NIGHTCLUBS

Club Pantheon 28 Ann St (at King) 843/577-2582 • 10pm-2am Fri-Sun only • mostly gay men • more women Th • dancing • multiracial • live shows • drag shows •18+ • karaoke • gay-owned

Deja Vu II 4628 Spruill Ave 843/554-5959 • 8pm-3am Fri-Sat, from 5pm Th, clsd Sun-Wed • mostly women • dancing/DJ • live shows • karaoke • food served • private club • wheelchair access • lesbian-owned

CAFES

Bear E Patch 1980 Ashley River Rd 843/766-6490 • 7am-9pm, 8am-8pm Sat, clsd Sun • patio • wheelchair access

RESTAURANTS

Blossom Cafe 171 E Bay St 843/722-9200 • 11:30am-11pm, till midnight wknds • Sun brunch • healthy • courtyard • wheelchair access

Cafe Cafe 177 Meeting St (near Hasell) 843/723-3622 • 7am-close, soups, sandwiches & desserts

Cafe Suzanne 4 Center St 843/588-2101 • lunch Tue-Sat, dinner nightly, Sun brunch, clsd Mon • live jazz

Fig 232 Meeting St (near Hasell) 843/805-5900 • 6pm-11pm, till 1am Fri-Sat • some veggie • serves locally grown food

Joe Pasta 428 King St (at John) 843/965-5252 • 11:30am-10pm, till midnight Fri-Sat • also full bar

Magnolias 185 E Bay St #200 843/577-7771 • lunch & dinner, Southern

Melvin's Legendary Bar-B-Que 538 Folly Rd 843/762-0511 • "the #1 cheeseburger in America"

St Johns Island Cafe 3140 Maybank Hwy, St Johns Island 843/559-9090 • 7am-9pm, till 10pm Fri-Sat, Sun brunch • popular • Southern homecooking • beer/ wine

Sweetwater Cafe 137 Market St (at King St) 843/723-7121 • 7am-3pm, till 4pm Fri-Sat • popular

Vickery's of Beaufain Street 15 Beaufain St (at St Philip) 843/577-5300 • 11:30am-2am • popular • Cuban influence • some veggie • full bar

ENTERTAINMENT & RECREATION

Historic Charleston Foundation 108 Meeting St 843/723-1623 • call for info on city walking tours

Spoleto Festival USA 843/722-2764 • 2-week avant-garde performing art festival in late May–early June

PUBLICATIONS

▲ **The Front Page** 919/829-0181 • LGBT newspaper for the Carolinas

Q Notes 704/531-9988 • bi-weekly LGBT newspaper for the Carolinas

SPIRITUAL GROUPS

MCC Charleston 7860 Dorchester Rd, North Charleston 843/760-6114 • 11am Sun • wheelchair access

Columbia

INFO LINES & SERVICES

AA Gay/ Lesbian 5220 Clemson (in the house behind St Martin's Church) 803/254-5301(AA#) • 8pm Fri

South Carolina Pride Center 1108 Woodrow St 803/771-7713 • 24hr message, live 2pm-10pm Sat

BARS

Capital Club 1002 Gervais St 803/256-6464 • 5pm-2am • mostly gay men • neighborhood bar • professional crowd • private club • wheelchair access

NIGHTCLUBS

PTS 1109 1109 Assembly St (at Gervais St) 803/253-8900 • 5pm-3am, till 2am wknds • lesbians/ gay men • dancing/ DJ • live shows • multiracial clientele • transgender-friendly • private club • gay-owned

RESTAURANTS

Alley Cafe 911 Lady St 803/255-0257 • dinner Wed-Sat • mostly women • dancing/DJ • full bar • live music • karaoke

SPIRITUAL GROUPS

MCC Columbia 1111 Belleview (at Main St) 803/256-2154 • 11am Sun

Greenville

ACCOMMODATIONS

Walnut Lane Inn 110 Ridge Rd (at Groce Rd), Lyman 864/949–7230, 800/949–4686 • gay-friendly • B&B • full brkfst • kids ok • gay-owned • $90-115

NIGHTCLUBS

The Castle 8-B Legrand Blvd 864/235–9949 • 9:30pm-4am, till 3am Sun, clsd Mon-Th • popular • lesbians/ gay men • dancing/DJ • drag shows • videos • young crowd • private club • wheelchair access

BOOKSTORES

Out of Bounds 21 S Pleasanturb Dr 864/239–0106 • 11am-7pm, from noon Sat, clsd Sun • cards • gifts • magazines

SPIRITUAL GROUPS

MCC 2180 E Poinsett St Ext Hwy 290, Duncan 864/787–3734 • 11am Sun

Myrtle Beach

ACCOMMODATIONS

The Myrtle Beach Resort 518/330–1163 • gay/ straight • oceanview condo in 33-acre family-friendly resort • kids ok • nonsmoking • lesbian-owned • $500-1,200

BARS

Time Out 520 8th Ave N (at Oak) 843/448–1180 • 5pm-close, till 2am Sat • popular • mostly gay men • neighborhood bar • dancing/DJ • karaoke • live shows • patio bar • private club • wheelchair access

NIGHTCLUBS

Rainbow House 815 N Kings Hwy 843/626–7298 • 3pm-5am, till 2am wknds • lesbians/ gay men • dancing/DJ • karaoke • patio • wheelchair access

RESTAURANTS

Cedar Hill Landing Seafood & Oyster Roast 5225 Hwy 17 (Business), Murrells Inlet 843/651–8706 • 11am-close • live shows • wheelchair access • full bar

Rock Hill

BARS

Hideaway 405 Baskins Rd 803/328–6630 • 9pm-close Th-Sat • lesbians/ gay men • neighborhood bar • drag shows • karaoke • private club

Statewide

PUBLICATIONS

Lavender Magazine 612/436–4660, 877/515–9969 • LGBT newsmagazine for MN, WI, IA, ND, SD

Aberdeen

BARS

Baby Boomers 208 S Main St 605/226–2140 • 3pm-2am, from noon Sat, clsd Sun • gay-friendly • more gay late

Batesland

ACCOMMODATIONS

Wakpamni B&B (on the Pine Ridge Indian Reservation) 605/288–1800 • gay-friendly • unique rooms & tipis • full brkfst • dinner available • hot tub • gift shop • on Indian reservation • nonsmoking • $60-100

Hot Springs

ENTERTAINMENT & RECREATION

Springs Bath House 146 N Garden St 605/745–4424, 888/817–1972 • 10am-9pm (seasonal) • gay-friendly • 1880s bathhouse w/ hot mineral-water soaking pools (indoor & outdoor) • massage center • day-spa services

Rapid City

INFO LINES & SERVICES

Unified Live & Let Live AA 522 7th St #218 605/381–1325 • 8pm Fri

NIGHTCLUBS

TW's 702 Box Elder Rd W (I-90 E, exit 63), Box Elder 605/923–2153 • 8pm-2am, clsd Sun-Mon • lesbians/ gay men • dancing/ DJ • karaoke • live shows • country/ western • leather • volleyball • BBQ pit • also camping & RV • gay-owned

EROTICA

Monument Bookstore 912 Main St 605/394–9877

Salem

ACCOMMODATIONS

Camp America 25495 US 81 605/425–9085 • gay-friendly • 35 miles west of Sioux Falls • camping • RV hookups • kids/ pets ok • nonsmoking • lesbian-owned • $14-24

Sioux Falls

INFO LINES & SERVICES

The Center 3504 S Minnesota #108 (enter on 43rd) **605/331–1153** • support groups • counseling • library & more

Rainbow Wildbunch AA 400 N Western **605/332–4017** • 7pm Wed & Sat

NIGHTCLUBS

Touchez 323 S Phillips Ave (enter rear) **605/335–9874** • 8pm-2am, from 5pm Fri • popular • lesbians/ gay men • dancing/DJ • food served • karaoke • drag shows • also Downstairs Bar from 10pm Sat

EROTICA

Romantix 311 N Dakota Ave (btwn 6th & 7th) **605/332–9316** • 24hrs

Spearfish

CAFES

The Bay Leaf Cafe 126 1/2 W Hudson St **605/642–5462** • lunch & dinner • plenty veggie • espresso bar

TENNESSEE

Statewide

PUBLICATIONS

Southern Voice **404/876–1819** • weekly LGBT newspaper for AL, FL (panhandle), GA, LA, MS, TN w/ resource listings

Chattanooga

BARS

Chuck's II 27–1/2 W Main (at Market) **423/265–5405** • 6pm-1am, till 3am Fri-Sat • lesbians/ gay men • neighborhood bar • dancing/DJ • karaoke • patio

NIGHTCLUBS

Alan Gold's 1100 McCallie Ave (at Central) **423/629–8080** • 4:30pm-3am • popular • lesbians/ gay men • dancing/DJ • drag shows Tue-Sun • food served • young crowd • wheelchair access

Images 6005 Lee Hwy **423/855–8210** • 5pm-3am • lesbians/ gay men • dancing/DJ • drag shows • also restaurant • wheelchair access

PUBLICATIONS

Out & About Newspaper **615/596–6210** • LGBT newspaper for Nashville, Knoxville, Chattanooga & Atlanta area • monthly

SPIRITUAL GROUPS

MCC of Chattanooga 1601 Foust St **423/629–2737** • 11am & 6pm Sun

Clarksville

SPIRITUAL GROUPS

Christian Community Church Commerce & 10th St (at L&N Train Station) **931/906–8525** • 4pm Sun

Gatlinburg

ACCOMMODATIONS

Big Creek Stables & Big Creek Outpost 5019 Rag Mtn Rd, Hartford **423/487–5742, 423/487–3490** • gay/ straight • cabins • camping • horseback-riding • kids ok • wheelchair access • gay-owned • $75-150

Christopher Place, An Intimate Resort 1500 Pinnacles Wy, Newport **423/623–6555, 800/595–9441** • gay/ straight • full brkfst • swimming • nonsmoking • wheelchair access • $150-300

Stonecreek Cabins **865/429–0400** • lesbians/ gay men • 23-acre paradise in Smoky Mtns • hot tub • nonsmoking • lesbian-owned • $160-185

Johnson City

ACCOMMODATIONS

Iron Mountain Inn B&B & Creekside Chalet 138 Moreland Dr, Butler **423/768–2446, 888/781–2399** • gay-friendly • mtn-top B&B or private chalet • full brkfst • kids/ pets ok • nonsmoking • also lakeside luxury cottage • wheelchair access • woman-owned/ run • $160-350

Safehaven Farm 336 Stanley Hollow Rd, Roan Mountain **423/725–4262** • gay-friendly • cabins • creekside privacy • fireplace & wraparound porch • kids/ pets ok • $90/ night, $450/ week

NIGHTCLUBS

Fuzzy Holes 1410 E Main St (at S Broadway St) **423/929–9800** • 7pm-1:30am, till 3am Fri-Sat, clsd Sun-Mon • transgender-friendly • sex-positive strip club • food served • 18+ • wheelchair access • lesbian-owned

New Beginnings 2910 N Bristol Hwy **423/282–4446** • 9pm-3am, from 8pm Fri-Sat, clsd Mon • popular • mostly gay men • dancing/DJ • drag shows • also restaurant • wheelchair access

RETAIL SHOPS

Spikes Gift Shop 2910 N Bristol Hwy (inside New Beginnings) **423/282-4446** • 10pm-3am Fri-Sat only • pride gifts

Jonesborough

RESTAURANTS

Dogwood Lane Cafe 109 Courthouse Square **423/913-1629** • brkfst & lunch Tue-Sun, dinner served Fri-Sat, clsd Mon • Southern

Knoxville

INFO LINES & SERVICES

AA Gay/ Lesbian 865/522-9667 (AA#)

Gay/ Lesbian Helpline 865/531-2539 (MCC#) • 7pm-11pm

Lesbian Social Group 865/531-7788 • meet 8pm Wed • call for info

NIGHTCLUBS

Carousel II 1501 White Ave (on U Tenn campus, behind the law library) **865/522-6966** • 9pm-3am • popular • lesbians/ gay men • dancing/DJ • drag shows • also restaurant till 4am

Club XYZ 1215 N Central **865/637-4999** • 9pm-2am, from 6pm Fri, clsd Mon-Tue & Th • lesbians/ gay men • dancing/ DJ

Electric Ballroom 1213 Western Ave **865/525-6724** • 9pm-3am, from 6pm Fri-Sat, clsd Mon-Wed • mostly gay men • dancing/DJ • karaoke • drag shows • food served • 18+ • wheelchair access

The New Rainbow Club West 7211 Kingston Pike **865/588-8030** • 5pm-3am • lesbians/ gay men • dancing/DJ • food served • karaoke • drag shows • wheelchair access

PUBLICATIONS

Out & About Newspaper 615/596-6210 • LGBT newspaper for Nashville, Knoxville, Chattanooga & Atlanta area • monthly

SPIRITUAL GROUPS

MCC Knoxville 7820 Redeemer Ln (off Nubbins Ridge, look for unmarked driveway to church) **865/531-2539** • 11am & 6pm Sun

Madison

SPIRITUAL GROUPS

Covenant of the Cross 916 W Old Hickory Blvd **615/612-5040** • 11am & 6pm Sun

Memphis

INFO LINES & SERVICES

AA Intergroup 5119 Summer Ave #315 **901/454-1414** • call for times & locations

Memphis Gay/ Lesbian Community Center 892 S Cooper **901/278-6422, 901/278-4297 (HOTLINE)** • groups, 24hr recorded info

ACCOMMODATIONS

French Quarter Suites 2144 Madison **901/728-4000, 800/843-0353** • gay-friendly • also Bourbon St Cafe • $89-119

Shellcrest Guesthouse 671 Jefferson Ave (at N Orleans St) **901/277-0223** • gay/ straight • suites in downtown Victorian • swimming • gay-owned • $170-250 (3-night minimum)

Talbot Heirs Guesthouse 99 S 2nd St (btwn Union & Peabody Pl) **901/527-9772, 800/955-3956** • gay-friendly • suites w/ kitchens • funky decor • nonsmoking • kids ok • $150+

BARS

Crossroads 111 N Claybrook (at Jefferson) **901/276-1882** • noon-3am • lesbians/ gay men • neighborhood bar • drag shows Fri-Sat • beer & set-ups only • karaoke Th

The Jungle 1474 Madison (at McNeil) **901/278-0521** • 3pm-3am • mostly gay men • neighborhood bar • leather • food served • beer & set-ups only

Lorenz 1528 Madison Ave (at Avalon) **901/274-8272** • 24hrs • lesbians/ gay men • dancing/DJ • country/ western • live shows • patio

Madison Flame 1588 Madison (at Avalon) **901/278-9839** • 7pm-3am Wed-Sun • mostly women • neighborhood bar • dancing/DJ

The Metro 1349 Autumn St (at Cleveland) **901/274-8010** • 6pm-3am • lesbians/ gay men • dancing/DJ • karaoke • food served • patio • wheelchair access

One More 2117 Peabody Ave (at Cooper) **901/278-6673** • 11am-3am, from noon Sun • gay-friendly • neighborhood bar • multiracial • food served • patio

NIGHTCLUBS

Allusions 3204 N Thomas (in Northgate Shopping Center) **901/357-8383** • from 10pm Fri-Sat only • lesbians/ gay men • ladies night Fri • multiracial • dancing/DJ • drag shows • BYOB

Reply **Forward**   **Delete**

Date: Dec 13, 2005 15:38:12
From: Girl-on-the-Go
To: Editor@Damron.com
Subject: Memphis

>Many people around the world know Memphis as the city of two musical phenomena—the blues and the King. The blues were born when W.C. Handy immortalized "Beale Street," and, as for the King, Elvis lived and died here. From everywhere on earth, people come to visit his home and pay their respects at Graceland (800/238-2000).

>There are a number of mixed bars and clubs, like the popular **Backstreet** and **Madison Flame**, which are often patronized by women. For a complete rundown of local groups and events, check out the latest edition of **Family & Friends**.

Memphis

WHERE THE GIRLS ARE:
On Madison Ave., of course, just east of US-240.

CITY INFO:
901/543-5300, web: www.memphistravel.com.

ATTRACTIONS:
Beale Street.
Graceland 800/238-2000, web: www.elvis.com/graceland.
Mud Island 800/507–6507, web: www.mudisland.com.
Nat'l Civil Rights Museum 901/521–9699, web: www.civil-rightsmuseum.org.
Overton Square.
Sun Studio 901/521–0664, web: www.sunstudio.com.

BEST VIEW:
A cruise on any of the boats that ply the river.

WEATHER:
Suth'n. H-O-T and humid in the summer, cold (30°s-40°s) in the winter, and a relatively nice (but still humid) spring and fall.

TRANSIT:
Yellow Cab 901/577–7700.
MATA 901/274-6282, web: www.matatransit.com.

Backstreet 2018 Court Ave (at Morrison) **901/276–5522** • 8pm-3am Fri-Sun only • lesbians/ gay men • dancing/DJ • karaoke • wheelchair access • beer & set-ups only

CAFES

Buns on the Run 2150 Elzey Ave (at Cooper) **901/278-2867** • 7am-2pm, till1:30pm Sat, clsd Sun

Java Cabana 2170 Young Ave (at Cooper) **901/272–7210** • 11am-10pm, till midnight wknds, from noon Sun • poetry readings & live shows • also art gallery

Otherlands Coffee Bar 641 S Cooper (at Central) **901/278-4994** • 7am-8pm • plenty veggie • also gift shop • live music

P&H Cafe 1532 Madison (at Adeline) **901/726-0906** • 11am-3am, from 5pm Sat, clsd Sun • beer/ wine • food served • live shows • wheelchair access

RESTAURANTS

Automatic Slim's Tonga Club 83 S 2nd St (at Union) **901/525–7948** • lunch & dinner Mon-Fri, dinner till 11pm Fri-Sat, clsd Sun • Caribbean & Southwestern • plenty veggie • full bar • wheelchair access

Cafe Society 212 N Evergreen Ave (btwn McLean & Belvedere) **901/722–2177** • lunch & dinner, till 10pm Fri-Sat • full bar • wheelchair access

Dish 948 S Cooper (at Young) **901/276-0002** • dinner till 10pm Fri-Sat • tapas

Leonard's Pit Barbeque 5465 Fox Plaza Dr **901/360-1963** • 11am-9pm • Elvis ordered the pork sandwich at the original Leonard's (now closed), but the food is just as good here!

Saigon Le 51 N Cleveland **901/276–5326** • 11am-9pm, clsd Sun • Chinese/ Vietnamese/ Thai

ENTERTAINMENT & RECREATION

Center for Southern Folklore 119 S Main St (at Peabody Pl) **901/525-3655** • 11am-7pm, till 11pm Th-Sat • live music • gallery • cybercafe • food served

Graceland 3734 Elvis Presley Blvd **901/332-3322, 800/238-2000** • no visit to Memphis would be complete w/out a trip to see The King

Memphis Rock 'N Roll Tours **901/359-3102** • historical tour of Memphis music scene

BOOKSTORES

Davis-Kidd Booksellers 387 Perkins Rd Ext (at Poplar & Walnut Grove) **901/683-9801** • 9am-10pm, 10am-8pm Sun • general • some LGBT titles • also cafe

RETAIL SHOPS

Inz & Outz 553 S Cooper **901/728-6535** • 10am-6pm, from 1pm Sun • pride items • books • gifts • wheelchair access

PUBLICATIONS

Family & Friends **901/682-2669** • LGBT newsmagazine

SPIRITUAL GROUPS

First Congregational Church 1000 S Cooper (at Young) **901/278-6786** • 10:30am Sun, 6pm Wed

Holy Trinity Community Church 685 S Highland (at Spottswood Ave) **901/320-9376** • 8:15am &11:45am Sun

Integrity 102 N Second St (at Calvary Episcopal Church) **901/525-6602** • 6:30pm 3rd Tue

EROTICA

Cherokee Books 2947 Lamar **901/744-7494**

Nashville

INFO LINES & SERVICES

AA Gay/ Lesbian 1808 Woodmont (at Unitarian church) **615/831-1050** • 8pm Mon & 7:30pm Th

ACCOMMODATIONS

Savage House 167 8th Ave N (btwn Church & Commerce) **615/254-1278** • gay/ straight • 1840s Victorian townhouse • full brkfst • also Gas Lite Lounge • gay-owned • $95-125

Top O' Woodland 1603 Woodland St **615/228-3868, 888/228-3868** • gay-friendly • full brkfst • woman-owned/ run • $110-160

BARS

Blu 1713 Church St (at 17th & 18th) **615/329-3838** • 6:30pm-3am, clsd Tue • lesbians/ gay men • dancing/DJ • live shows • theme nights • patio

The Cabaret: Episode 2 833 Murfreesboro Rd **615/367-1995** • 8pm-3am, clsd Mon-Tue • lesbians/ gay men • dancing/ DJ • karaoke • drag shows • cabaret

DeVil's 339 Wilhagen Rd (at Murfeesboro) **615/366-6696** • 4pm-3am, till 1am Sun • mostly men • dancing/ DJ • transgender-friendly • karaoke • drag shows

The Gas Lite Lounge 167–1/2 8th Ave N (btwn Church & Commerce) **615/254–1278** • 4:30pm-3am • mostly gay men • also restaurant

TC's Triangle 1401 4th Ave S (btwn Lafayette & Chestnut) **615/242–8131** • noon-3am • lesbians/ gay men • neighborhood bar • food served • wheelchair access

Tribe/ Red 1517 Church St (at 15th Ave S) **615/329–2912** • 4pm-midnight, till 2am wknds • lesbians/gay men • live entertainent • videos • upscale • full restaurant • wheelchair access • gay-owned

NIGHTCLUBS

The Chute Complex 2535 Franklin Pike (at Wedgewood) **615/297–4571** • 5pm-3am • 6 bars • popular • mostly gay men • dancing/DJ • country/ western • leather • karaoke • drag shows • also Silver Stirrup restaurant/piano bar • wheelchair access

Excess/ Orbit 909 Church St (at 9th) **615/255–4331** • 2am-6am Wed, Fri-Sat only • lesbians/gay men • dancing/DJ • 18+ • alcohol-free • juice bar

---

[**Reply**] [**Forward**]   [**Delete**]

Date: Mon, Dec 20, 2005 11:25:39
From: Girl-on-the-Go
To: Editor@Damron.com
Subject: Nashville

>There's only one "Country Music Capital of the World," and that's Nashville. And there's no better place on earth to enjoy country and western music than at the Grand Ole Opry (615/889-6611). Be sure to plan ahead and get a performance schedule.

>Many of the greats of country music have homes in Nashville, and there are plenty of bus tours to show you exactly where your favorite stars live. The Country Music Hall of Fame and Museum (615/416-2001) is also a favorite stop for diehard fans.

>If listening to all that great music has you twitching in your seat, maybe it's time to get up and dance. For a change of pace, try **Lipstick Lounge**, which has a jazz lounge and a mostly lesbian crowd, or check out one of the several mixed bars, such as **TC's Triangle** or **Tribe**, which has a full restaurant. Keep your star-gazing eyes open while you're cloggin' away on the floor; you never know who you might see! For more sedate activities, check out the latest issue of **Xenogeny** and **Out & About Nashville**, which you can pick up at **Outloud Books**.

>If you're driving east, you'll pass through Knoxville—a small city with a quaint old town section and the main University of Tennessee. Call the **Gay/ Lesbian Helpline** about local events.

Kiss After Hours 508 Lea Ave (at 6th) **270/469-0171** • midnight-7am Fri-Sat night only • gay/straight • dancing/DJ

Lipstick Lounge 1400 Woodland St (at 14th) **615/226-6343** • 6pm-3am, from 4pm Tue-Fri • mostly women • jazz lounge • also smoking lounge

Play Dance Bar 1519 Church St **615/322-9627** • 9pm-3am Wed-Sun • mostly gay men • dancing/DJ • multiracial • transgender-friendly • karaoke • drag shows • wheelchair access

CAFES

Bongo Java 2007 Belmont Blvd **615/385-5282** • coffeehouse • deck • also serves brkfst, lunch & dinner

Fido 1812 21st Ave S **615/777-3436** • 7am-11pm, from 8am wknds • also full menu

RESTAURANTS

Calypso Cafe 2305 Elliston Pl **615/321-3878** • 11am-9pm • Caribbean

International Market 2010 Belmont Blvd (at International) **615/297-4453** • lunch & dinner • Thai/Chinese • plenty veggie

The Mad Platter 1239 6th Ave N (at Monroe) **615/242-2563** • lunch Tue-Fri, dinner nightly by reservation only, clsd Mon • Californian • some veggie • wheelchair access

Mirror 2317 12th Ave S (at Linden) **615/383-8330** • dinner only, clsd Sun • also bar

Rumours Wine & Art Bar 304 12th Ave S **615/292-9400** • 5pm-midnight, clsd Sun-Mon

Towne House Tea Room 165 8th Ave N (btwn Church & Commerce) **615/254-1277** • brkfst & lunch Mon-Fri, clsd wknds • buffet

ENTERTAINMENT & RECREATION

Tennessee Repertory Theater 505 Deaderick St **615/782-4000**

BOOKSTORES

Davis-Kidd Booksellers 4007 Hillsboro Rd (at Abbot-Martin) **615/385-2645** • 9am-10pm, till 11pm Fri-Sat, 10am-7pm Sun • LGBT section

Outloud Books & Gifts 1703 Church St (btwn 17th & 18th Ave) **615/340-0034** • 10am-10pm, till 11pm Fri-Sat • LGBT • also cafe • gay-owned

Nashville

WHERE THE GIRLS ARE:
Just north of I-65/40 along 2nd Ave. S. or Hermitage Ave.

LGBT PRIDE:
June 615/650-6736, web: www.nashvillepride.org.

CITY INFO:
800/657-6910, web: www.nashvillecvb.com.

BEST VIEW:
Try a walking tour of the city.

WEATHER:
See Memphis.

TRANSIT:
Yellow Cab 615/256-0101.
Gray Line Airport Shuttle 615/275-1180.
MTA 615/862-5969, web: www.nashvillemta.org.

ATTRACTIONS:
Country Music Hall of Fame 615/416-2001, web: www.countrymusichalloffame.com.
Grand Ole Opry & Opryland USA 615/871-OPRY, web: www.opry.com.
Jack Daniel's Distillery 615/279-4100, web: www.jackdaniels.com.
The Parthenon 615/862-8431, web: www.parthenon.org.
Ryman Auditorium 615/889-3060, web: www.ryman.com.
Tennessee Antebellum Trail 800/381-1865, web: www.antebellumtrail.com.

PUBLICATIONS

Church Street Freedom Press
615/582–5963 • weekly news, arts & events • weekly

Out & About Newspaper 615/596–6210 • LGBT newspaper for Nashville, Knoxville, Chattanooga & Atlanta area • monthly

Xenogeny/ Southern X-posure
615/831–1806 • LGBT newspaper & bar guide

SPIRITUAL GROUPS

Christ Community Church of Metropolitan Nashville 4425 Ashland City Hwy (at Briley Pkwy) 615/259–9636 • 10am Sun

First Unitarian Universalist Church 1808 Woodmont Blvd 615/383–5760 • 8:50am & 10:50am Sun

Stonewall Mission Church 419 Woodland St (at St Ann's Episcopal Church, Howe Hall) 615/269–3480 • 6pm Sun

EROTICA

Southern Vibe 700 Division (at 8th Ave S) 615/256–5775

Pigeon Forge

ENTERTAINMENT & RECREATION

Dollywood 1020 Dollywood Ln
865/428–9488 • Dolly Parton's "wholesome Smoky Mountain theme park" • 35 miles SE of Knoxville

TEXAS

Statewide

PUBLICATIONS

Ambush Mag 504/522–8049 • LGBT newspaper for the Gulf South

Shout Magazine 512/320–8678 • 1st & 3rd Th, LGBT entertainment & events magazine for central Texas

TXT Newsmagazine 214/754–8710, 877/903–8407 • LGBT weekly newsmagazine w/ lifestyle & entertainment section

Abilene

SPIRITUAL GROUPS

Exodus MCC 1933 S 27th 915/692–9830 • 11am

Amarillo

BARS

212 Club 212 W 6th St (at Taylor)
806/372–7997 • 2pm-2am • lesbians/ gay men • neighborhood bar • dancing/DJ • drag shows • wheelchair access

Sassy's 309 W 6th St 806/374–3029 • 5pm-2am, from 3pm Fri-Sun • lesbians/ gay men • dancing/ DJ • karaoke • drag shows

T Time 521 E 10th St 806/371–3535 • 2pm-midnight, till 1am Sat • lesbians/ gay men • neighborhood bar • karaoke Th • lesbian-owned

Whiskers 1219 W 10th Ave 806/371–8482 • 4pm-2am • lesbians/ gay men • neighborhood bar

RESTAURANTS

Lena's 2710 W 10th Ave (at Georgia)
806/372–5444 • lunch Mon-Fri & dinner wknds • some veggie • beer/ wine • wheelchair access

SPIRITUAL GROUPS

Amarillo Unitarian Universalist Fellowship 4901 Cornell (at 49th)
806/355–9351 • 11am Sun

MCC of Amarillo 2123 S Polk St (at 22nd St) 806/372–4557 • 10:30am Sun

Soul Journers Church 2650 Dumas Dr #138 806/355–4566 • 11am Sun

EROTICA

Fantasy Gifts & Video 440 N Lakeside 806/372–6500

Studio One 9000 Triangle Dr 806/372–0648 • 24hrs

Arlington

see also Fort Worth

INFO LINES & SERVICES

Tarrant County Lesbian/ Gay Alliance 817/877–5544 • info line • meetings

NIGHTCLUBS

The 1851 Club 1851 W Division (at Fielder) 817/801–9303 • 3pm-2am • lesbians/ gay men • dancing/DJ • drag shows • karaoke • videos • wheelchair access

SPIRITUAL GROUPS

Trinity MCC 1846 W Division St, Ste 305 817/265–5454 • 11am Sun • call for other events

Austin

INFO LINES & SERVICES

Lambda AA (Live & Let Live) 2700 W Anderson Ln #412 (in the Village Shopping Center) **512/444-0071** • 6:30pm Mon-Fri & 11am Sun

ACCOMMODATIONS

1888 Miller Crockett House 112 Academy Dr (at Congress Ave) **512/441-1600, 888/441-1641** • gay-friendly • New Orleans–style estate • full brkfst • kids/ pets ok • wheelchair access • woman-owned • $109-169

A Summit House B&B 1204 Summit St (at Lupine) **512/445-5304** • lesbians/ gay men • reservations required • full brkfst • swimming pool 1 block from house • nonsmoking • gay-owned • $69

Austin Folk House 506 W 22nd St **512/472-6700, 866/472-6700** • gay/ straight • B&B in restored 1880 house • kids/ pets ok • nonsmoking • wheelchair access • $95-145

Carrington's Bluff 1900 David St (at W 22nd St) **512/479-0638, 888/290-6090** • gay-friendly • full brkfst • kids/ pets ok • nonsmoking • wheelchair access • $89-149

Days Inn North 820 E Anderson Ln (Hwy 183) **512/835-4311, 866/835-4311** • gay-friendly • swimming • kids/ pets ok • wheelchair access • $49-55

Driskill Hotel 604 Brazos St (at 6th) **512/474-5911, 800/252-9367** • gay-friendly • food served • wheelchair access • $175-400 (even if you don't stay in this landmark hotel, be sure to check out the lobby)

Austin

WHERE THE GIRLS ARE:
Downtown along Red River St., or 4th/5th St. near Lavaca, or at the music clubs and cafes downtown and around the University.

LGBT PRIDE:
June. www.austinprideparade.org.

ANNUAL EVENTS
March - South by Southwest Music Festival, web: www.sxsw.com.
May & Labor Day - Splash Days. Weekend of parties in clothing-optional Hippie Hollow, web: www.splashday.com.
August/September - Austin G/L Int'l Film Festival 512/302-9889, web: www.agliff.org.

CITY INFO:
Austin Convention & Visitors Bureau 800/926-2282, web: www.austintexas.org.
Greater Austin Chamber of Commerce 512/478-9383.

BEST VIEW:
Texas State Capitol.

WEATHER:
Summers are real scorchers (high 90°s—low 100°s) and last forever. Spring, fall, and winter are welcome reliefs.

TRANSIT:
Yellow Cab 512/452-9999.
Various hotels have their own shuttles.
Capital Metro 512/474-1200, web: www.capmetro.org.

ATTRACTIONS:
Aqua Festival.
Elisabet Ney Museum 512/458-2255, web: www.ci.austin.tx.us/elisabetney/.
George Washington Carver Museum 512/974-4926, web: www.ci.austin.tx.us/carver/.
Hamilton Pool, web: www.texasoutside.com/hamiltonpool.htm.
Laguna Gloria Art Museum 512/458–8191.
McKinney Falls State Park.
Mount Bonnell.
Museo del Barrio de Austin.
Zilker Park/Barton Springs.

Reply **Forward** **Delete**

Date: Nov 18, 2005 10:41:26
From: Girl-on-the-Go
To: Editor@Damron.com
Subject: Austin

>Austin is a cultural oasis in the fiery heart of Texas. A refreshing bastion of left-wing, non-confrontational radicalism, and the home of the South By Southwest (SXSW) music festival, this most collegiate of cities seems to belong anywhere but the Lone Star State. But it does. In fact, Austin is actually the state capital and the seat of the Texas legislature.

>When harried urbanites in Dallas and Houston want a quick getaway, many head to the natural beauty of the Texas Hill Country. Just outside of the capital city, local boys and girls entertain themselves in the naturally cool (68° year-round) waters of Barton Springs. And Hippie Hollow, site of the LGBT First and Last Splash Festivals, has long been a favorite of the clothing-optional crowd.

>In town, entertainment centers around the Mardi Gras atmosphere of 6th Street downtown, where live and recorded music offerings run the gamut from hardcore punk to tear-jerkin' country & western. Most of the bars are mixed, female and male, straight and gay. Check out **'Bout Time** for their drag shows and volleyball court and **Rainbow Cattle Company** for some Texas 2-steppin'.

>The popular bookstore, **Book Woman,** is a great resource for connecting with like-minded women of every hue. The store regularly schedules seminars, book signings, and discussion groups; check in here for details on all the women's events around town. Austin Women's Rugby Club matches are also popular, as are spring and summer softball and volleyball leagues. Try Fans of Women's Sports for the latest schedules and contacts.

>Austin's LGBT newsweekly, the **TXT Newsmagazine,** is the best source for checking out all the current goings-on.

Hotel San Jose 1316 S Congress Ave 512/444-7322, 800/574-8897 • gay/ straight • small boutique hotel • swimming • nonsmoking • kids/ pets ok • wheelchair access • $85-290

Omni Hotel 700 San Jacinto (at 7th) 512/476-3700, 800/843-6664 • gay-friendly • rooftop pool • health club • wheelchair access

Park Lane Guest House 221 Park Ln (at Drake) 512/447-7460, 800/492-8827 • gay/ straight • full brkfst • swimming • also cottage • wheelchair access • lesbian-owned • $89-149

riverbarnsuites 30 minutes from Austin airport, Kingsbury 512/488-2175 • women-only • river resort w/ lots of outdoor activities • swimming • lesbian-owned • $125

Star of Texas Inn 611 W 22nd St (at Rio Grande) 512/499-8070, 877/499-8070 • gay-friendly • neo-classical Victorian • full brkfst • nonsmoking • kids/ pets ok • $95-155

BARS

'Bout Time 9601 N IH-35 N (at Rundberg) 512/832-5339 • 2pm-2am • popular • lesbians/ gay men • neighborhood bar • transgender-friendly • drag shows • karaoke • volleyball court • wheelchair access

Casino El Camino 516 E 6th St (at Red River) 512/469-9330 • 4pm-2am • gay-friendly • neighborhood bar • psychedelic punk jazz lounge • great burgers • wheelchair access

Rainbow Cattle Company 305 W 5th St (btwn Guadalupe & Lavaca) 512/472-5288 • 3pm-2am, from 8pm Sun, clsd Mon • lesbians/ gay men • dancing/DJ • country/ western • karaoke • classes Sun

NIGHTCLUBS

1920's Club 918 Congress Ave (btwn 9th & 10th) 512/479-7979 • 5pm-midnight, from 6pm wknds, till 2am Fri-Sat • lesbians/gay men • jazz club • food served • piano

Club Skirt PO Box 10314, 78766 • women only • dancing/ DJ • monthly dance parties • check local listings for dates & location • www.austinclubskirt.org

Dick's Silver Spur Saloon 113 San Jacinto Blvd (btwn 1st & 2nd) 512/457-8010 • noon-2am • mostly gay men • dancing/DJ • country/ western • Latin night Fri-Sat • male dancers Fri-Sat • patio

Fabric 101 W 5th St (at Congress Ave) 512/322-9333 • lesbians/gay men • dancing/DJ

Rain 217B W 4th St (at Colorado St) 512/494-1150 • 3pm-2am • mostly men • upscale gay lounge

Sidekicks Austin/ Xtreme 110 E Riverside Dr (at Congress Ave) 512/804-2797 • 4pm-2am, from 2pm wknds • lesbians/gay men • dancing/ DJ • live shows • karaoke

CAFES

Joe's Bakery & Coffeeshop 2305 E 7th St 512/472-0017 • 7am-3pm, clsd Mon • Tex-Mex

Little City Espresso Bar & Cafe 916 Congress Ave (at E 11th St) 512/476-2489 • 8am-midnight, from 9am wknds, till 10pm Sun • popular gay hangout

RESTAURANTS

Castle Hill Cafe 1101 W 5th St (at Baylor) 512/476-0728 • lunch weekdays & dinner nightly, clsd Sun • romantic • some veggie • wheelchair access

Chuy's 1728 Barton Springs Rd 512/474-4452 • 11am-10:30pm, till 11pm Fri-Sat • Tex-Mex

Eastside Cafe 2113 Manor Rd (at Coleto, by bright yellow gas station) 512/476-5858 • 11:30am-9:30pm, till 10pm Fri-Sat, from 10am wknds, wknd brunch • some veggie • beer/ wine • wheelchair access

El Sol y La Luna 1224 S Congress Ave (at Academy) 512/444-7770 • 7am-10pm, till 3pm Sun-Wed • great brkfst • live music Fri-Sat • wheelchair access • lesbian-owned

Fonda San Miguel 2330 W North Loop (at Hancock Rd) 512/459-4121 • dinner only, popular Sun brunch • Mexican • full bar • gay-owned • $15-28

Jo's Coffee Shop 1300 S Congress Ave 512/444-3800 • 7am-9pm, till 10pm Sat • "best lazy day outdoor dining scene" • wheelchair access • lesbian-owned

Katz's 618 W 6th St (at Rio Grande) 512/472-2037 • 24hrs • NY-style deli • full bar • wheelchair access

Mother's Cafe & Garden 4215 Duval St (at 43rd) 512/451-3994 • lunch, dinner, wknd brunch • vegetarian • popular

Romeo's 1500 Barton Springs Rd (near Lamar) 512/476-1090 • 11am-10pm, till 11pm Fri-Sat • Italian • some veggie • beer/ wine • wheelchair access

Starlite 624 W 34th St (at Guadalupe) 512/374-9012 • 6pm-11pm, Sun brunch till 3pm, clsd Mon-Tue • located in a hip, refurbished vintage 1930s home • gay-owned

Threadgill's 6416 N Lamar (at Koenig) 512/451–5440 • 11am-10pm, till 9pm Sun • great chicken-fried steak

West Lynn Cafe 1110 W Lynn (at W 12th St) 512/482–0950 • lunch & dinner, clsd Mon, wknd brunch • vegetarian • beer/ wine

ENTERTAINMENT & RECREATION

Barton Springs Barton Springs Rd • natural swimming hole

Bat Colony Congress Ave Bridge (at Barton Springs Dr) • everything's bigger in Texas— including the colony of bats that flies out from under this bridge every evening March-Oct

Historic Austin Tours 209 E 6th St (in the Visitor Information Center) 512/478–0098, 866/468–8784 • free guided & self-guided tours of the Capitol, Congress Ave & 6th St, Texas State Cemetery, Hyde Park

Zachary Scott Theatre Center 1510 Toomey Rd 512/476–0541 • diverse theater

BOOKSTORES

Book Woman 918 W 12th St (at Lamar) 512/472–2785 • 10am-9pm, noon-6pm Sun • cards • jewelry • music • videos • posters • T-shirts • wheelchair access • women-owned/ run

Bookpeople 603 N Lamar Blvd (at 6th) 512/472–5050, 800/853–9757 • 9am-11pm, clsd Thanksgiving Day • independent • readings

Lobo 3204–A Guadalupe (btwn 32nd & 33rd) 512/454–5406 • 10am-10pm, till 11pm Fri-Sat, from noon Sun • LGBT • wheelchair access

Resistencia Bookstore 1801-A S 1st St (at W Annie) 512/416–8885 • emphasis on Chicana/o, Latina/o & Native American titles • also some LGBT of color titles • readings

RETAIL SHOPS

Celebration! 108 W 43rd (at Speedway) 512/453–6207 • 10am-6pm, noon-5pm • eclectic gift shop • women-owned/ run

Tapelenders 1114 W 5th St, #201 512/472–0844 • 10am-10pm, till midnight Fri-Sat, from noon Sun • LGBT videos • novelties • gay-owned

PUBLICATIONS

Ambush Mag 504/522–8049 • LGBT newspaper for the Gulf South

Shout Magazine 512/320–8678 • 1st & 3rd Th • LGBT entertainment & events magazine for central Texas

TXT Newsmagazine 512/485–3126 • LGBT weekly newsmagazine w/ lifestyle & entertainment section

SPIRITUAL GROUPS

First Unitarian Universalist Church 4700 Grover Ave (at 49th) 512/452–6168 • 10am & 11:30 am Sun • wheelchair access

MCC Austin 8601 S First St (at Slaughter Ln) 512/291–8601 • 9am, 11am & 7pm Sun

GYMS & HEALTH CLUBS

Hyde Park Gym 4125 Guadalupe (at 42nd St) 512/459–9174 • gay-friendly • day passes $8

EROTICA

Forbidden Fruit 512 Neches (btwn 5th & 6th) 512/478–8358

Beaumont

INFO LINES & SERVICES

Lambda AA 1385 Calder Ave 409/866–6165 • 8pm Wed & Sat

BARS

Hooligan's 6025 Martin Luther King 409/832–0808 • mostly women • dancing/DJ • live music • karaoke

NIGHTCLUBS

Copa 304 Orleans St (at Liberty) 409/832–4206 • 9pm-2am, till 3am Fri-Sat • popular • lesbians/ gay men • dancing/DJ • talent night Wed • drag shows • wheelchair access

RESTAURANTS

Carlo's 2570 Calder (btwn 9th & 10th) 409/833–0108 • 11am-10pm, till 2am Fri-Sat • Italian/ Greek • live shows • full bar

SPIRITUAL GROUPS

Spindletop Unitarian Church 1575 Spindletop Rd (off Martin Luther King Pkwy) 409/833–6883 • 10:30am Sun

Bryan

BARS

Revolution Cafe & Bar 211 B S Main St (btwn 26th & 27th) 979/823–4044 • 3pm-2am, clsd Mon • gay-friendly • neighborhood bar • food served • live jazz/ funk/ reggae nightly

NIGHTCLUBS

Halo Video Bar 121 N Main St (at William J Bryan Pkwy) 979/823–6174 • 9:30pm-2am Th-Sat • gay-friendly • dancing/ DJ • drag shows • videos • 2 levels • wheelchair access

Buffalo

ACCOMMODATIONS

Buffalo RV Park 9928 US Hwy 79E, Oakwood 903/322-3854 • gay-friendly • swimming • kids/pets ok • wheelchair access • $16-23

Corpus Christi

INFO LINES & SERVICES

Clean & Serene AA 1315 Craig (at MCC Corpus Christi) 361/882-8255 • 8pm Fri

ACCOMMODATIONS

Anthony's By The Sea 732 S Pearl St, Rockport 361/729-6100, 800/460-2557 • gay/ straight • quiet retreat 4 blocks from water • full brkfst • swimming • hot tub • wheelchair access • lesbian-owned • $95-115

Christy Estates Suites 3942 Holly Rd (at Weber) 361/854-1091, 800/678-4836 • gay-friendly • hot tubs & spas • swimming • nonsmoking rooms available • wheelchair access • $69-169

BARS

Get Happy 526 S Staples (at Park St) 361/881-8910 • noon-2am • lesbians/gay men • neighborhood bar • dancing/DJ • food served • karaoke Th • gay-owned

The Hidden Door 802 S Staples St (at Coleman) 361/882-5002 • 3pm-2am, from noon wknds • lesbians/gay men • neighborhood bar • dancing/DJ • patio • wheelchair access

The Rose 213 S Staples 361/881-8181 • 6pm-2am, from 3pm Sun • mostly women • neighborhood bar

NIGHTCLUBS

Sixx 1212 Leopard St 361/888-7499 • 9pm-2am Wed & Sun, till 4am Fri-Sat • mostly men • drag shows • strippers • 18+

SPIRITUAL GROUPS

MCC of Corpus Christi 1315 Craig St (at 11th St, near Morgan & Staples) 361/882-8255 • 11am Sun • wheelchair access

Crockett

ACCOMMODATIONS

Warfield House B&B 712 Houston Ave (in Town Square) 936/544-4037 • gay/straight • turn-of-the-century B&B • gay-owned • $79-109

Dallas

see also Fort Worth

INFO LINES & SERVICES

John Thomas Gay/Lesbian Community Center 2701 Reagan St (at Brown) 214/528-9254, 214/528-0022 • 9am-9pm, 10am-6pm Sat, noon-5pm Sun • wheelchair access

Lambda AA 2438 Butler #106 214/267-0222

ACCOMMODATIONS

Amelia's Place 1108 S Akard St #13 214/421-7427 • gay-friendly • full brkfst • $95-115

Holiday Inn Select Dallas Central 10650 N Central Expwy (at Meadow) 214/373-6000, 888/477-STAY • gay/straight • swimming • $65-149

Melrose Hotel 3015 Oak Lawn Ave (at Cedar Springs) 214/521-5151, 800/635-7673 • gay-friendly • nonsmoking rooms available • also piano bar & lounge • also 4 1/2-star restaurant • wheelchair access • $149-335

BARS

Buddies II 4025 Maple Ave (at Throckmorton) 214/526-0887 • 11am-2am, from noon Sun, clsd Mon • mostly women • dancing/DJ • country/western wknds • karaoke • volleyball court • swimming

The Hidden Door 5025 Bowser Ave (at Mahanna) 214/526-0620 • 7am-2am, from noon Sun • mostly gay men • neighborhood bar • leather

Hideaway Club 4144 Buena Vista (at Fitzhugh) 214/559-2966 • 8am-2am, from noon Sun • lesbians/gay men • upscale crowd • piano bar • patio • cabaret • older crowd • wheelchair access

JR's Bar & Grill 3923 Cedar Springs Rd (at Throckmorton) 214/528-1004 • 11am-2am, from noon Sun, from 1pm Mon • upscale • popular • lesbians/gay men • grill till 4pm • live shows Sun • videos • young crowd • wheelchair access

Mickey's 3851 Cedar Springs Rd 214/219-6425 • 2pm-2am • mostly men • karaoke • videos

Side 2 Bar 2615 Oak Lawn Ave, Ste 101 (btwn Fairmount & Brown) 214/528-2026 • 8am-2am, from noon Sun • lesbians/gay men • neighborhood bar • live shows • karaoke • wheelchair access

Reply **Forward** **Delete**

Date: Nov 11, 2005 12:26:42
From: Girl-on-the-Go
To: Editor@Damron.com
Subject: Dallas

>Despite Dallas' conservative reputation as the buckle of the Bible Belt, this city has mellowed a great deal since the economic melt-down of the late 1980s. Two openly gay men have been elected to the City Council and sexual orientation is included in the city's anti-discrimination policy.

>Dallas is a relatively young city, but wealthy residents have created a legacy of art museums, historical sites, and entertain-ment districts that will keep you busy. The Arts District in down-town is home to the Dallas Museum of Art (DMA) and a fabulous collection of modern masters, pre-Columbian artifacts, and the Reeves Collection of Impressionist art and decorative pieces. The 6th Floor Museum, on the site where Oswald allegedly perched while assassinating JFK, is a fascinating exploration of the facts and conspiracy theories. Old City Park recreates a pioneer village with original dwellings, period reenactments, and exhibits. The West End, home of Planet Hollywood, the West End Marketplace, and the Dallas World Aquarium, offers a concentration of shops, restaurants, and diversions in one spot.

>East of downtown is Deep Ellum, one of Dallas' earliest African American communities ("ellum" is the way early residents pronounced Elm). Today it's live music central, featuring a variety of clubs offering a host of local and national bands, seven nights a week. Just about anything goes here, as long as it's left of center. Every segment of the population is represented in an ever-growing collection of offbeat bars, restaurants, shops, and tattoo parlors.

>Further east is Fair Park, site of the State Fair of Texas every fall. Any time of the year you can enjoy a wonderful day here touring the African American Museum, the Science Place and its IMAX theater, and the Dallas Aquarium and Horticulture Center. The surrounding neighborhood is the current habitué of choice for artists, with studios, showrooms, and gathering places along State and Parry Streets. Also on Parry St is the must-see Women's Museum.

Reply Forward   Delete

>The lesbian and gay community of Dallas is thriving, concentrated in Oak Lawn, just north of downtown. Most of the businesses along the Cedar Springs Strip (Cedar Springs Road between Douglas and Oak Lawn Avenue) are gay-owned, and all are LGBT-friendly. Same-sex couples populate the sidewalks and restaurant tables day and night. Parking can be next to impossible on weekend nights, though, and take care if you decide to park on darkened side streets.

>The local women's community is less visible than the gay men's, but you will find two full-time women's bars—**Buddies II** and **Sue Ellen's**—and several active women's organizations. Want just the facts, ma'am? Then call the **John Thomas Gay/Lesbian Community Center**. Dallas' churches and sports groups are also popular meeting places for singles. Lesbian couples are concentrated in the suburb of Oak Cliff or in Casa Linda, near White Rock Lake.

Sue Ellen's 3903 Cedar Springs Rd (at Reagan) **214/559-0707** • 5pm-2am, from noon-close wknds • popular • mostly women • dancing/DJ • live shows/ bands • Sun BBQ (summers) • patio • wheelchair access

Woody's 4011 Cedar Springs Rd (btwn Douglas & Throckmorton) **214/520-6629** • 2pm-2am • lesbians/ gay men • live shows • sports bar • videos • nonsmoking upstairs • wheelchair access

NIGHTCLUBS

The Brick 4117 Maple Ave (at Throckmorton) **214/521-2024** • 9pm-4am Fri-Sun • lesbians/ gay men • dancing/DJ • multiracial clientele

Havana 4006 Cedar Springs Rd (at Throckmorton) **214/526-9494** • bar & grill 5pm-10pm, lounge 10pm-2am, clsd Mon • gay/ straight • dancing/ DJ

Joe's Dallas 4125 Maple Ave (at Throckmorton) **214/219-5637** • noon-2am • mostly gay men • more women Wed & Fri • neighborhood bar • dancing/DJ • karaoke • food seved • female dancers Fri • patio • cover charge • wheelchair access

Kaliente 4350 Maple Ave (at Hondo) **214/520-6676** • 9pm-2am, clsd Mon-Tue • mostly gay men • mostly Latino • drag shows

One 3025 Main (in Deep Ellum) **214/741-1111** • 10pm-4am Fri-Sat, till 2am Tue • gay/ straight • more gay Fri • dancing/DJ • alternative house • 18+ • cover

Round-Up Saloon 3912 Cedar Springs Rd (at Throckmorton) **214/522-9611** • 3pm-2am, from noon wknds • popular • mostly gay men • dancing/DJ • country/ western • karaoke Sun-Th • dance lessons • 6 bars • wheelchair access

Station 4 3911 Cedar Springs Rd (at Throckmorton) **214/526-7171** • 9pm-4am Wed-Sun• popular • lesbians/ gay men • dancing/DJ • drag shows • videos • also Rose Room cabaret • 18+

CAFES

Cosmic Cafe 2912 Oak Lawn Ave **214/521-6157** • 11am-11pm, noon-10pm Sun • vegetarian food served • also yoga & meditation • live events

Dream Cafe 2800 Routh St (in the Quadrangle) **214/954-0486** • 7am-9pm, till 10pm Fri-Sat, brkfst served till 5pm • plenty veggie • beer/wine • wheelchair access

Restaurants

Ali Baba Cafe 1905 Greenville Ave (near Ross) 214/823–8235 • lunch & dinner, clsd Sun-Mon • Middle Eastern

Black-Eyed Pea 3857 Cedar Springs Rd (at Reagan) 214/521–4580 • 11am-10pm • Southern homecookin' • some veggie • wheelchair access

Blue Mesa Grill 5100 Beltline Rd (at Tollway), Addison 972/934-0165 • 11am-10pm, 10am-9pm Sun, till 10:30pm Fri-Sat • great fajitas • full bar

Bread Winners 3301 McKinney 214/754-4940 • brkfst & lunch daily, dinner Tue-Sun, Sun brunch • gay/ straight • int'l • some veggie • full bar

The Bronx Restaurant & Bar 3835 Cedar Springs Rd (at Oak Lawn) 214/521–5821 • lunch & dinner, Sun brunch, clsd Mon • some veggie • wheelchair access • gay-owned

Cremona Bistro & Cafe 3136 Routh St (at Cedar Springs) 214/871–1115 • lunch weekdays & dinner nightly • Italian • full bar

Fitness Essentials 4108 Oak Lawn (near Avondale) 214/528–5535 • 9am-7pm, till 6pm Sat, 1-6pm Sun • organic • plenty veggie • wheelchair access • gay-owned

Hunky's 4000 Cedar Springs Rd (at Throckmorton) 214/522-1212 • noon-10pm, till 11pm Fri-Sat, from 10am Sun • popular • beer/ wine • patio • wheelchair access • gay-owned

Monica Aca y Alla 2914 Main St (at Malcolm X) 214/748–7140 • lunch Mon-Fri, brunch wknds, dinner Tue-Sun • popular • trendy • contemporary Mex • full bar • live music wknds • Latin jazz/ salsa • transgender-friendly • wheelchair access

Sushi on McKinney 4500 McKinney Ave (at Armstrong) 214/521-0969 • lunch weekdays & dinner nightly • full bar • wheelchair access

Thai Soon 101 S Coit, Ste 401 (at Beltline) 972/234-6111 • lunch & dinner

Vitto 316 W 7th St (at Bishop) 214/946–1212 • lunch & dinner • Italian • beer/ wine • wheelchair access • gay-owned

Dallas

WHERE THE GIRLS ARE:
Oak Lawn in central Dallas is the gay and lesbian stomping grounds, mostly on Cedar Springs Ave.

LGBT PRIDE:
September. www.dallastavernguild.org.

CITY INFO:
214/571–1000, web: www.dallascvb.com.

BEST VIEW:
Hyatt Regency Tower.

WEATHER:
Can be unpredictable. Hot summers (90°s — 100°s) with possible severe rain storms. Winter temperatures hover in the 20°s through 40°s range.

TRANSIT:
Yellow Cab 214/426-6262.
Dallas Area Rapid Transit (DART) 214/979-1111, web: www.dart.org.

ATTRACTIONS:
Dallas Arboretum & Botanical Garden 214/327-8263, web dallasarboretum.org.
Dallas Museum of Art 214/922-1200, web: www.dm-art.org.
Dallas Theatre Center/ Frank Lloyd Wright 214/522–8499, web: www.dallastheatercenter.org.
Deep Ellum district.
Texas State Fair & State Fair Park 214/565-9931, web: www.bigtex.com.
The Women's Museum 214/915–0860, web: www.thewomensmuseum.org.

Ziziki's 4514 Travis St, #122 (in Travis Walk) 214/521–2233 • 11am-10pm, till 11pm Fri-Sat, Sun brunch • Greek • full bar • wheelchair access

ENTERTAINMENT & RECREATION

Conspiracy Museum 110 S Market (in the Katy Bldg) 214/741–3040 • 10am-6pm • dedicated to infamous US assassinations since 1835 & their cover-ups

Lambda Weekly KNON 89.3 FM 972/263–5305 • 1pm Sun • LGBT radio show for northern TX

The Women's Chorus of Dallas (TWCD) 3630 Harry Hines Blvd (at Sammons Center for the Arts) 214/520–7828 • several subscription concerts throughout year & "beaucoup CDs"

The Women's Museum 3800 Parry Ave 214/915–0860, 888/337–1167 • noon-5pm, clsd Mon

BOOKSTORES

Crossroads Market Bookstore/ Cafe 3930 Cedar Springs Rd (at Throckmorton) 214/521–8919 • 7am-10pm, till 11pm Fri-Sat • LGBT • wheelchair access

RETAIL SHOPS

An Occasional Piece 3922 Cedar Springs Rd (at Throckmorton) 214/520–0868 • gifts • cards • collectibles

Leather Masters 2525 Wycliff Ave #124 (w/ Leather by Boots) 214/528–3865 • noon-8pm, clsd Sun-Mon • custom leather & more

Obscurities 4000-B Cedar Springs 214/559–3706 • noon-10pm, till midnight Fri-Sat, from 2pm Sun • tattoo & piercing

Off the Street 4001–B Cedar Springs (at Throckmorton) 214/521–9051 • 10am-9pm, noon-6pm Sun • LGBT gifts

Tapelenders 3926 Cedar Springs Rd (at Throckmorton) 214/528–6344 • 9am-midnight • LGBT gifts • video rental • gay-owned

PUBLICATIONS

Dallas Voice 214/754–8710 • LGBT newspaper w/ extensive resource listings

TXT Newsmagazine 214/754–8710 • LGBT weekly newspaper w/ arts calendar & statewide resource list

SPIRITUAL GROUPS

Cathedral of Hope 5910 Cedar Springs Rd (at Inwood) 214/351–1901, 800/501–4673 • 9am & 11am Sun • wheelchair access

Dignity Dallas 4523 Cedar Springs Rd (at Bethany Presbyterian Church) 214/521–5342 x1732 • 6pm Sun • wheelchair access

First Unitarian Church of Dallas 4015 Normandy (at Preston) 214/528–3990 • 9am & 11:15am Sun (10am Sun summers)

St Thomas the Apostle Episcopal Church 6525 Inwood Rd (at Mockingbird Ln) 214/352–0410 • 8am, 10am & 5:30pm Sun

White Rock Community Church 9353 Garland Rd 214/320–0043 • 10:45am Sun

EROTICA

Alternatives 1720 W Mockingbird Ln (at Hawes) 214/630–7071 • 24hrs

Leather Masters/ Leather by Boots—Dallas 2525 Wycliff #124 (at Maple) 214/528–3865 • noon-8pm, clsd Sun-Mon

Shades of Grey Leather 3930-A Cedar Springs Rd (at Throckmorton) 214/521–4739 • 11am-8pm, till 10 pm Fri-Sat, noon-6pm Sun • wheelchair access

Denison

BARS

Good Time Lounge 2520 Hwy 91 N 903/463–6086 • 7pm-2am, clsd Mon • lesbians/ gay men • karaoke Th & Sun • drag shows

Denton

NIGHTCLUBS

Mable Peabody's Beauty Parlor & Chainsaw Repair 1215 E University Dr 940/566–9910 • 9pm-2am, clsd Mon • lesbians/ gay men • dancing/DJ • live shows • drag shows • wheelchair access • lesbian-owned

CAFES

Cupboard Natural Foods 200 W Congress St (at Elm) 940/387–5386 • 8am-9pm, 11am-6pm Sun • health food store & cafe

SPIRITUAL GROUPS

Harvest MCC 525 S Loop 288, Ste E 940/320–6150 • 11am Sun

El Paso

see also Ciudad Juárez, Mexico

INFO LINES & SERVICES

El Paso GLBT Community Center 216 S Ochoa 206/600–4297 • 24hr hotline • events • counseling • pride store • also cafe (10am-6pm, till 3am Fri-Sat)

Lambda Line 206/350-4283 • crisis help & info

BARS

Briar Patch 508 N Stanton (at Missouri) 915/577-9555 • noon-2am • lesbians/ gay men • neighborhood bar • karaoke • patio

Chiquita's Bar 310 Missouri (at Stanton) 915/351-0095 • 2pm-2am • lesbians/ gay men • neighborhood bar • mostly Latina/o clientele • wheelchair access

The Whatever Lounge 701 E Paisano St (at Ochoa) 915/533-0215 • 2pm-2am • lesbians/ gay men • dancing/DJ • karaoke • mostly Latino/a • wheelchair access

NIGHTCLUBS

The New Old Plantation 301 S Ochoa St (at Paisano) 915/533-6055 • 9pm-2am, till 4am Fri-Sat, clsd Mon-Wed • popular • lesbians/ gay men • dancing/DJ • drag shows Sun • videos • wheelchair access • also Generation Q II pride store upstairs

San Antonio Mining Co 800 E San Antonio Ave (at Ochoa) 915/533-9516 • 3pm-2am • popular • lesbians/ gay men • dancing/DJ • drag shows Wed • videos • patio • wheelchair access

The Zone 209 S El Paso 915/542-3800 • 9pm-2am, till 4am Fri-Sat, clsd Mon-Wed • dancing/DJ • live music • drag shows • go-go dancers • 18+

CAFES

De Ambiente Cafe 216 S Ochoa (at GLBT Community Center) 206/350-4283 • 3pm-6pm, 8pm-3am Fri-Sat, till 10pm Sun

RESTAURANTS

The Little Diner 7209 7th St, Canutillo 915/877-2176 • 11am-8pm, clsd Wed • true Texas fare

SPIRITUAL GROUPS

MCC of El Paso 900 Chelsea 915/591-4155 • 10:30am Sun

Fort Worth

see also Dallas

INFO LINES & SERVICES

Tarrant County Lesbian/ Gay Alliance 817/877-5544 • info line • newsletter

ACCOMMODATIONS

Best Western InnSuites Hotel 2000 Beach St 817/534-4801, 800/989-3556 • gay-friendly • all-suite hotel • nonsmoking • kids/ pets ok • wheelchair access • $55-99

BARS

Best Friends Club 2620 E Lancaster Ave 817/534-2280 • 3pm-2am • lesbians/ gay men • neighborhood bar • dancing/DJ wknds • karaoke & CW dance lessons Wed

Crossroads 515 S Jennings Ave (at Pennsylvania) 817/332-0071 • 11am-2am, from noon Sun • mostly gay men • neighborhood bar

NIGHTCLUBS

Changes 2637 E Lancaster 817/413-2332 • mostly men • dancing/DJ • video bar • dancers

Hot Shots 651 S Jennings Ave (at Pennsylvania) 817/820-0079 • 1pm-2:30am • mostly gay men • dancing/DJ • theme nights • wheelchair access

CAFES

Paris Coffee Shop 704 W Magnolia (at Hemphill) 817/335-2041 • 6am-2:30pm, till 11am Sat, clsd Sun

RESTAURANTS

Coffee House Gallery 609 S Jennings (at Pennsylvania) 817/335-4646 • mostly men • live shows • beer/ wine • also cafe • internet access • wheelchair access • gay-owned

SPIRITUAL GROUPS

Agape MCC 4615 E California Pkwy (take the Anglin exit off I-20) 817/535-5002 • 10:30am Sun • wheelchair access

First Jefferson Unitarian Universalist 1959 Sandy Ln (at Meadowbrook Dr) 817/451-1505 • 11am Sun • wheelchair access

Fredericksburg

ACCOMMODATIONS

Town Creek B&B 304 N Edison (at W Travis) 830/997-6848 • gay/ straight • full brkfst • $125-190

Galveston

ACCOMMODATIONS

Cottage by the Gulf 810 Ave L (at Seawall & 8th) 409/770-9332 • gay-friendly • 6 private rental homes • patio • pets ok • wheelchair access • gay-owned • $90-500

Oasis Beach Cottage 713/256-3000 • gay-friendly • on the Gulf of Mexico • kids ok • nonsmoking • gay-owned • $125-175 & $750-950/ week

Paradise Guesthouse & Resort 2317 Ave P
409/762–6677, 877/919–6677 • lesbians/ gay
men • swimming • hot tub • 1 block from
beach • Bloody Marys w/ brkfst • nonsmoking
• wheelchair access • gay-owned • $50-250

BARS

3rd Coast Beach Bar 3102 Seawall (at 31st
& Seawall) **409/765–6911** • noon-2am •
mostly men • karaoke • male dancers • deck

Robert's Lafitte 2501 Q Ave (at 25th St)
409/765–9092 • 7am-2am, from 10am Sun •
mostly gay men • drag shows wknds • patio •
wheelchair access

Undercurrent 2409 Market St (btwn 24th &
25th) **409/750–8571** • 4pm-2am, from 2pm
summers • lesbians/ gay men • dancing/DJ •
caberet • male dancers Fri-Sun • T-dance Sun
• gay-owned

NIGHTCLUBS

Garza's Kon Tiki 315 23rd St (at Market)
409/765–5805 • noon-2am • lesbians/ gay
men • neighborhood bar • dancing/DJ •
multiracial • transgender-friendly • live shows
• karaoke Wed • drag shows Th-Sun • gay-
owned

CAFES

Mod Coffee & Tea House 2126 Postoffice
(at 22nd) **409/765–5659** • 7am-10pm, from
8am wknds • gay-friendly • baked goods,
veggie wraps & salads • also art gallery

RESTAURANTS

Mosquito Cafe 628 14th St (at Winnie)
409/763–1010 • 7am-2pm, till 9pm Th-Sat,
8am-3pm Sun • some veggie

Groesbeck

ACCOMMODATIONS

Rainbow Ranch Campground 1662 LCR
800 **254/729–5847, 888/875–7596** • lesbians/
gay men • open all year • on Lake Limestone
• swimming • campsites & RV hookups •
lesbian-owned • $10+/ person, $28/ RV site

Gun Barrel City

BARS

Friends 410 S Gun Barrel/ Hwy 198
903/887–2061 • 4pm-midnight, from 3pm
wknds, till 1am Sat • lesbians/ gay men •
neighborhood bar • food served • karaoke
Wed • patio • wheelchair access

Houston

INFO LINES & SERVICES

Gay/ Lesbian Switchboard Houston
713/529–3211 • 24hrs

Houston LGBT Center 3400 Montrose, Ste
207 **713/524–3818** • noon-9pm

Lambda AA Center 1201 W Clay (btwn
Montrose & Waugh) **713/528–9772** •
wheelchair access

ACCOMMODATIONS

The Lovett Inn 501 Lovett Blvd, Montrose
(at Whitney) **713/522–5224, 800/779–5224** •
popular • gay/ straight • historic home of
former Houston mayor & Federal Court judge
• hot tub • swimming • nonsmoking • gay-
owned • $95-150

Patrician B&B Inn 1200 Southmore Blvd (at
San Jacinto) **713/523–1114, 800/553–5797** •
gay-friendly • 1919 three-story mansion • full
brkfst • $95-150

BARS

Chances 1100 Westheimer (at Waugh)
713/523–7217 • 2pm-2am • mostly women •
dancing/DJ • live shows • wheelchair access

Cousins 817 Fairview (at Converse)
713/528–9204 • 11am-2am, from noon Sun •
lesbians/ gay men • neighborhood bar • drag
shows

Decades 1205 Richmond (btwn Mandel &
Montrose) **713/521–2224** • 11am-2am, from
noon Sun • lesbians/ gay men • neighborhood
bar • women-owned/ run

Guava Lamp 570 Waugh **713/524–3359** •
4pm-2am • lesbians/ gay men • swanky
lounge w/ martinis & more • karaoke Wed &
Sun • cabaret Th • drag shows Sat •
wheelchair access

JR's 808 Pacific (at Grant) **713/521–2519** •
noon-2am • popular • mostly gay men • more
women Sun • karaoke • drag shows • videos •
patio • wheelchair access

Keys West 817 W Dallas (btwn Arthur &
Crosby) **713/571–7870** • 3pm-2am • lesbians/
gay men • neighborhood bar • piano • large
2-level deck

Mary's 1022 Westheimer (at Waugh)
713/527–9669 • 7am-2am, from 10am Sun •
popular • lesbians/ gay men • neighborhood
bar • leather • live shows • also patio bar •
wheelchair access

Meteor 2306 Genesee (at Fairview)
713/521–0123 • 4pm-2am, from 6pm Fri •
mostly gay men • cocktail lounge •
professional crowd • videos • gay-owned

Michael's Outpost 1419 Richmond (at Mandell) **713/520-8446** • 11am-2am, from noon Sun • mostly gay men • neighborhood bar • country/western • live entertainment • drag shows • older crowd

The New Barn 1100 Westheimer (at Waugh) **713/523-7217** • 8pm-2am, clsd Sun-Wed • mostly women • dancing/DJ • country/western

Rainbow Room 527 Barren Springs Dr (at Ella Blvd) **281/872-0215** • noon-2am • lesbians/gay men • dancing/DJ wknds • live shows

NIGHTCLUBS

Amazonia Discoteque 11449 I-49 N (at Aldine Bender) **281/260-9885** • Axis Tue only • mostly men • dancing/DJ • Latino clientele • Drag shows • male revue • also women's night second Th

Club Rainbow 1417-B Westheimer **713/522-5166** • 9pm-2am, clsd Mon-Wed • mostly women • dancing/DJ • live shows

G Spot 1100 Westheimer (at Montrose) **713/522-4065** • 8pm-2am Th-Sat • mostly women • dancing/DJ • wheelchair access

---

| Reply | Forward | | Delete |

Date: Nov 9, 2005 12:45:11
From: Girl-on-the-Go
To: Editor@Damron.com
Subject: Houston

>With mild winters and blazing summers, Houston is the hottest lesbian spot in the Southwest. From the Astrodome to San Jacinto, Houston welcomes sports fans, historians, and shoppers. This thriving urban center even has bars bigger than your home-town where you can dance the night away.

>First things first, get yourself copies of the **Houston Voice** and **OutSmart**. You can find them at **Houston's LGBT Center.** Stay and enjoy their hip coffee bar and periodicals.

>Later, grab a bite. Good eats and beautiful women can be found all over the cruisy Montrose (where lesbians are said to shop and party) and Heights neighborhoods. Try the elegant **Baba Yega's** or saddle up to a plate of Southern comfort food at the **Black-Eyed Pea**. Relax after your meal with a cup of coffee at—where else—**Java Java**. While you're in the neighbor-hood, take some time to admire the mansions of the Montrose and the elegant Victorian homes of the Heights. Then head over to Houston's hotspot for women, **Club Rainbow**, featuring two levels of dancing and go-go girls!

>After you've seen and done all that Houston has to offer, collapse in your jacuzzi suite at the historic **Lovett Inn.**

Inergy 5750 Chimney Rock (at Glenmont) 713/666–7310 • 9pm-3am, clsd Tue • popular • lesbians/ gay men • dancing/DJ • mostly Latina/o • karaoke • drag shows • videos • also Mango Lounge Fri-Sat (mostly women, dancing/DJ)

Numbers 300 Westheimer (at Taft) 713/526-6551 • gay-friendly • dancing/DJ • 80's Fri • also live music venue • young crowd

Ranch Hill Saloon 24704 I-45 (Glen Loch Dr), Ste 103, Spring • lesbians/ gay men • neighborhood bar • dancing/DJ • country/ western • professional crowd • live music wknds • karaoke Th • lesbian-owned

Rich's 2401 San Jacinto (at McIlhenny) 713/759–9606 • 9pm-5am, clsd Sun-Wed • popular • mostly gay men • dancing/DJ • alternative • 18+ Th-Fri • live shows • drag shows • videos

CAFES

Diedrich Coffee 4005 Montrose (btwn Richmond & W Alabama) 713/526–1319 • 5:30am-11pm, till midnight Fri-Sat, 7am-10pm Sun

Empire Cafe 1732 Westheimer Rd 713/528–5282 • 7:30am-10pm, till 11pm Fri-Sat

Houston

WHERE THE GIRLS ARE:
Strolling the Montrose district near the intersection of Montrose and Westheimer or out on Buffalo Speedway at the Plaza.

LGBT PRIDE:
June. 713/529-6979, web: www.pridehouston.org.

ANNUAL EVENTS:
Juneteenth Freedom Festival 713/529-4195.
Sept - Gay & Lesbian Film Festival, web: www.hglff.org.

CITY INFO:
713/227-3100, web: www.visithoustontexas.com.

BEST VIEW:
Spindletop, the revolving restaurant on top of the Hyatt Regency 713/654-1234.

WEATHER:
Humid all year round—you're not that far from the Gulf. Mild winters, although there are a few days when the temperatures drop into the 30ºs. Winter also brings occasional rainy days. Summers are very hot.

TRANSIT:
Yellow Cab 713/236-1111.
Metropolitan Transit Authority 713/635-4000, web: www.ridemetro.org.

ATTRACTIONS:
Contemporary Arts Museum 713/284-8250, web: www.camh.org.
The Galleria.
Menil Museum 713/525-9400, web: www.menil.org.
Museum of Fine Arts 713/639-7300, web: www.mfah.org.
Rothko Chapel 713/524-9839, web: www.rothkochapel.org.
San Jacinto Monument.
Six Flags Astroworld/ Waterworld, 713/799-1234.

Restaurants

Baba Yega's 2607 Grant (at Pacific) 713/522-0042 • 11am-10pm, till 11pm Fri-Sat, from 10:30am Sun • popular • plenty veggie • full bar • patio • wheelchair access

Barnaby's Cafe 604 Fairview (btwn Stanford & Hopkins St) 713/522-0106 • 11am-10pm, till 11pm Fri-Sat • popular • beer/ wine • wheelchair access • also 1701 S Shepard, 713/520-5131

Black-Eyed Pea 2048 W Gray (at Shepherd) 713/523-0200 • 10:30am-10pm, till 11pm Fri-Sat • popular • Southern • wheelchair access

Brasil 2604 Dunlavy (at Westheimer) 713/528-1993 • 8:30am-midnight, drinks served until 2am • bistro • plenty veggie • beer/ wine

Cafe Annie 1728 Post Oak Blvd (at San Felipe) 713/840-1111 • lunch Tue-Fri, dinner Mon-Sat, clsd Sun • fine dining

Captain Benny's Half Shell 8506 S Main 713/666-5469 • lunch & dinner • beer/ wine

Chapultepec 813 Richmond (btwn Montrose & Main) 713/522-2365 • 24hrs • Mexican • some veggie • beer/ wine

Hollywood Diner 2409 Grant (at Fairview St) 713/523-8855 • 10am-close

House of Pies 3112 Kirby (at Richmond/ Alabama) 713/528-3816 • 24hrs • popular • wheelchair access

Java Java Cafe 911 W 11th (at Shepherd) 713/880-5282 • 7:30am-3pm, from 8:30am wknds • popular

Magnolia Bar & Grill 6000 Richmond Ave (at Fountainview Dr) 713/781-6207 • Cajun • full bar • wheelchair access

Ming's Cafe 2703 Montrose (at Westheimer) 713/529-7888 • 11am-10pm • Chinese

Mo Mong 1201 Westheimer #B (at Montrose) 713/524-5664 • 11am-11pm, till midnight Fri-Sat, till 10pm Sun • Vietnamese • full bar

Ninfa's 2704 Navigation 713/228-1175 • 11am-10pm • popular • Mexican • some veggie • full bar

Ninos 2817 W Dallas (btwn Montrose & Waugh Dr) 713/522-5120 • lunch Mon-Fri, dinner Mon-Sat, clsd Sun • Italian • some veggie • full bar

Spanish Flower 4701 N Main (at Airline) 713/869-1706 • 24hrs, till 10pm Tue • Mexican • beer/ wine

Entertainment & Recreation

After Hours KPFT 90.1 FM (also 89.5 Galveston) 713/526-4000, 713/526-5738 (request line) • midnight-4am Sat • LGBT radio • also Queer Voices 8pm Mon

Houston Comets 1510 Polk St (at Toyota Center) 877/266-3879 • check out the Women's National Basketball Association while you're in Houston

Retail Shops

Hollywood Super Center 807 Fairview St (at Crocker St) 713/527-8510 • 10am-2am, till 3am Fri-Sat • gifts • T-shirts • novelties

Lucia's Garden 2216 Portsmouth (at Greenbriar) 713/523-6494 • 10am-6pm, till 7pm Tue & Th, clsd Sun • spiritual herb center

Publications

Houston Voice 713/529-8490 • LGBT newspaper

OutSmart 713/520-7237 • free monthly LGBT newsmagazine

Red Magazine 602/308-8310 • monthly gay nightlife & lifestyle magazine

Swirl Magazine 678/886-0711 (Atlanta #) • magazine for "the African American lesbian, bisexual, bi-curious & 'straight but not narrow' community"

TXT Newsmagazine 713/529-0322 • LGBT weekly newsmagazine w/ lifestyle & entertainment section

Spiritual Groups

Dignity Houston 2515 Waugh Dr (at Grace Lutheran) 713/880-2872 • 7:30pm Sat

Maranatha Fellowship House of Glory 3333 Fannin #106 713/528-6756 • 10am Sun

Mishpachat Alizim 602 Fairview (at Baby Barnaby's) 866/841-9139 x1834 • 8pm 2nd Fri • Jewish worship & social/ support group

Resurrection MCC 2025 W 11th St 713/861-9149 • 9am & 11am Sun, Spanish service 7pm Sat

Gyms & Health Clubs

Fitness Exchange 4040 Milam 713/524-9932 • 5am-10pm, 8am-8pm wknds • gay-friendly

Houston Gym 1501 Durham Rd (at Washington & Shepherd) 713/880-9191 • 5am-10pm, 8am-6pm wknds • gay-owned

YMCA Downtown 1600 Louisiana St (btwn Pease & Bell) 713/659-8501 • gay-friendly • swimming

Erotica

BJ's 24 Hour News 6314 Gulf Fwy
713/649–9241 • 24hrs

Diners News 240 Westheimer (at Mason)
713/522–9679 • 24hrs

Eros 1207 1207 Spencer Hwy (at Allen
Genoa) 713/944–6010 • 10am-midnight •
gay-owned

Leather Forever 604 Westheimer (at
Stanford) 713/526–6940 • 11am-7pm, noon-
6pm Sun

Q Video 1415 California St 713/522–4485 •
11am-midnight

Longview

Bars

Decisions 2103 E Marshall (2 blocks E of
Eastman Rd) 903/757–4884 • 5pm-2am •
lesbians/gay men • 2 bars • dancing/DJ Fri-
Sun • country/western • drag shows Fri & Sun
• wheelchair access

Spiritual Groups

MCC Longview (Church With A Vision)
420 E Cotton St 903/753–1501 • 11am Sun •
wheelchair access

Lubbock

Info Lines & Services

AA Lambda 4501 University Ave (at MCC)
806/792–5562 • 8pm Fri

Nightclubs

Club Luxor 2211 4th St (at V) 806/744–3744
• 9pm-2am Th-Sun • gay/straight • dancing/DJ
• drag shows Sun

Heaven Nightclub 1928 Buddy Holly Ave (at
I-27) 806/762–4466 • gay-friendly • dancing/DJ
• multiracial • drag shows • 18+ • young
crowd

Spiritual Groups

MCC 4501 University Ave (at 45th)
806/792–5562 • 11am & 6pm Sun •
wheelchair access

McAllen

see Rio Grande Valley

Mission

Accommodations

Seldon Left Ranch 3000 Bentsen Palm Dr
(I-83) 956/585–1215 • gay-friendly • RV
hookups, furnished apts & park models •
outdoor hot tub • located 10 miles outside
Mexico & 1 hour from beach • wheelchair
access • gay-owned • $10-30/night &
$165-500/month

Mt Vernon

Accommodations

The Veranda 3264 County Rd SE 4115
903/588–2402 • lesbians/gay men • B&B on
68 private acres • lake • jacuzzi • swimming •
nonsmoking • gourmet restaurant Fri-Sat •
$85-150

Odessa/Midland

Spiritual Groups

God's Rainbow Promises Fellowship
501 N Loraine (at Tennessee), Midland
432/570–5624 • 11am & 6:30pm Sun

Erotica

B&L Adult Bookstore 5890 W University
Blvd (at Mercury) 432/381–6855

Plano

Restaurants

Roy's Hawaiian Seafood 2840 Dallas Pkwy
(btwn Park & Parker) 972/473–6263 • 5:30pm-
9pm, till 10pm Wed-Th, till 11pm Fri-Sat •
Hawaiian fusion • wheelchair access

Entertainment & Recreation

Collin County Area Gay Outings
469/855–6575 • lesbians/gay men • social
events Tue & some Fri & Sun

Port Aransas

Accommodations

The Belles by the Sea 361/749–6138 •
gay/straight • Euro-style inn on dunes of
Mustang Island & Port Aransas • swimming •
hot tub • kids/pets ok • nonsmoking • $89-
145

Rio Grande Valley

includes McAllen

Bars

PBD's 2908 Ware Rd (at Daffodil), McAllen
956/682–8019 • 8pm-2am, clsd Mon • mostly
gay men • dancing/DJ Th-Sat • drag shows •
male strippers Fri-Sat • wheelchair access

Trade Bar 2010 Nolana (at Bicentennial), McAllen 956/630-6304 • 9pm-2am • lesbians/ gay men • dancing/DJ • strippers • 18+ • young crowd • gay-owned

San Antonio

INFO LINES & SERVICES

Diversity Center 611 E Myrtle 210/223-6106, 866/452-2724 • noon-8pm, 10am-10pm Sat, clsd Sun-Mon • GLBTQI community center • counseling • social activities • wheelchair access

Lambda AA 923 E Mistletoe (at Hwy 281) • 8:15pm Sat-Th

LISA Line (Lesbian Information San Antonio) 210/828-5472

ACCOMMODATIONS

Adams House B&B 231 Adams St (at S Alamo) 210/224-4791, 800/666-4810 • gay/ straight • full brkfst • nonsmoking • also carriage house • $99-169

Alamo Lodge 1126 E Elmira (at Wilmington) 210/222-9463 • gay-friendly • kids/ pets ok • $34-69

Arbor House Suites B&B 109 Arciniega (btwn S Alamo & S St Mary's) 210/472-2005, 888/272-6700 • gay/ straight • kids/ pets ok • hot tub • nonsmoking • wheelchair access • gay-owned • $125-150

Desert Hearts Cowgirl Club Bandera 830/796-7001 • women only • 1-room cabin on 30-acre ranch • swimming • horseback riding • nonsmoking • lesbian-owned • $75

The Garden Cottage 210/828-7815 • gay-friendly • private cottage • swimming • nonsmoking • woman-owned/ run • $200/week (call for monthly rates)

The Painted Lady Inn on Broadway 620 Broadway (at 6th) 210/220-1092 • popular • lesbians/ gay men • full brkfst • private art deco suites • kids/ pets ok • rooftop deck & spa • wireless internet • lesbian & gay-owned • $109-229

Shady Lady Lakeshore Lodge 110 Lakeshore Dr N (at Whartons Dock Rd), Bandera 830/796-7001 • lesbians/ gay men • guesthouse • located on Lake Medina • lesbian-owned • $175 (2-night minimum)

BARS

2015 Place 2015 San Pedro (at Woodlawn) 210/733-3365 • 4pm-2am • mostly gay men • neighborhood bar • patio

San Antonio

WHERE THE GIRLS ARE:
Coupled up in the suburbs or carousing downtown.

LGBT PRIDE:
June. web: www.pridesanantoniotexas.org.

ANNUAL EVENTS:
Late April - Fiesta San Antonio 877/723-4378, web: www.fiesta-sa.org.

CITY INFO:
800/447-3372, web: www.sanantoniocvb.com.

BEST VIEW:
High in the Sky Lounge in the Tower of the Americas, or from the deck of The Painted Lady Inn on Broadway.

WEATHER:
60°s-90°s in the summer, 40°s-60°s in the winter.

TRANSIT:
Yellow-Checker 210/222-2222.
Via Info 210/362-2020, web: www.viainfo.net.

ATTRACTIONS:
The Alamo 210/225-1391, web: www.thealamo.org.
Hemisfair Park.
El Mercado.
Plaza de Armas.
River Walk.
San Antonio Museum of Art 210/978-8100, web: www.sa-museum.org.
McNay Art Museum 210/824-5368, web: www.mcnayart.org.

Reply **Forward** **Delete**

Date:Nov 12, 2005 09:22:21
From: Girl-on-the-Go
To: Editor@Damron.com
Subject: San Antonio

>Although its moment of glory was more than 150 years ago, the Alamo has become a mythological symbol that still greatly influences San Antonians of today. Here at this mission, a handful of Texans—including Davy Crockett and Jim Bowie—kept a Mexican army of thousands at bay for almost two weeks.

>San Antonians are fiercely proud of this heritage, and maintain a rough-n-ready attitude to prove it. This is just as true of the dykes in San Antonio as anyone else. You'll find most of them at **Petticoat Junction** or **Bermuda Triangle**, the local women's bars.

>Though there's no gay ghetto in this spread-out city, there are some lesbian-friendly businesses clustered along various streets, including the 5000 blocks of S. Flores and McCullough, the 1400–1900 blocks of N. Main, and scattered along Broadway and San Pedro. But get the real 411 by calling **LISA**, the **Lesbian Information Line**, at 210/828-5472.

>For more traditional sight-seeing, there's always the Alamo or the River Walk. The architecture in old San Antonio is quaint and beautiful—stop by the **Bonham Exchange** for an eyeful and stay for a twirl or two around their dance floor. Better yet, try out the view from the deck of **The Painted Lady Inn on Broadway** bed-and-breakfast.

The Annex 330 San Pedro Ave (at Euclid) **210/223–6957** • 2pm-2am • mostly gay men • neighborhood bar • patio • wheelchair access

Bermuda Triangle 119 El Mio (at San Pedro) **210/342–2276** • 7pm-2am, clsd Mon • mostly women • neighborhood bar • dancing/DJ wknds • live shows • karaoke Wed • wheelchair access

Cobalt Club 2022 McCullough (at Ashby) **210/734–2244** • 7am-2am, from noon Sun • lesbians/ gay men • neighborhood bar • live shows • wheelchair access

Electric Company 820 San Pedro Ave (at W Laurel) **210/212–6635** • 9pm-3am Wed-Sun • lesbians/ gay men • dancing/ DJ • live shows • 18+

Petticoat Junction 1818 N Main (at Dewey) 210/732-0333 • 8pm-2am Wed-Sun • mostly women • dancing/DJ • country/ western • also martini bar • wheelchair access

Silver Dollar Saloon 1418 N Main Ave (at Laurel) 210/227-2623 • 2pm-2am • lesbians/ gay men • dancing/DJ • country/ western • live shows • theme nights • patio bar • wheelchair access

Tagz 5307 McCullough (near Basse) 210/828-4222 • noon-2am • lesbians/ gay men • neighborhood bar • patio • wheelchair access

NIGHTCLUBS

The Bonham Exchange 411 Bonham St (at 3rd/ Houston) 210/271-3811 • 4pm-2am, from 8pm wknds, till 4am Fri-Sat • popular • in 111-year-old mansion • lesbians/ gay men • dancing/DJ • videos • 18+ • gay-owned

The Boss 1006 VFW Blvd 210/534-6600 • gay-friendly • 8pm-2am, clsd Sun-Tue • open mic Th •

The Saint 1430 N Main (at Evergreen) 210/225-7330 • 4pm-3am • lesbians/ gay men • dancing/DJ • alternative • drag shows • 18+

CAFES

Candlelight Coffeehouse & Wine Bar 3011 N St Mary's (at Rte 281) 210/738-0099 • 4pm-midnight, clsd Mon-Tue

RESTAURANTS

Chacho's 7870 Callaghan Rd (at I-10) 210/366-2023 • 24hrs • Mexican • live bands • karaoke

Giovanni's Pizza & Italian Restaurant 913 S Brazos (at Guadalupe) 210/212-6626 • 10am-6pm, till 9pm Th-Fri, 5pm-close Sat, clsd Sun • some veggie

Lulu's Bakery & Cafe 918 N Main (at W Elmira) 210/222-9422 • 24hrs, clsd 7pm Fri-7pm Sat • Tex-Mex • wheelchair access

Madhatter's Tea 320 Beauregard 210/212-4832 • 7am-9pm, till 6pm Sun, Sun brunch • BYOB • patio • wheelchair access

El Mirador 722 S St Mary's St (at Durango St) 210/225-9444 • 6:30am-9pm, till 3pm Mon, till 10pm Fri-Sat, 9am-2pm Sun • Tex-Mex • plenty veggie • beer/ wine • patio • wheelchair access

ENTERTAINMENT & RECREATION

San Antonio Silver Stars SBC Center 210/444-5050 • check out the Women's National Basketball Association while you're in San Antonio

RETAIL SHOPS

Backbone Body Mods 4741 Fredericksburg Rd (off Loop 10) 210/349-6637 • 2pm-9pm, till 11pm Fri-Sat, clsd Sun • tattoo • no piercing Mon

On Main 2514 N Main (btwn Woodlawn & Mistletoe) 210/737-2323 • 10am-6pm, till 5pm Sat, clsd Sun • gifts • cards • T-shirts

ZEBRAZ.com 1608 N Main Ave (at E Park Ave) 210/472-2800, 800/788-4729 • 10am-10pm • LGBT dept store • also online version

PUBLICATIONS

Shout Magazine 512/320-8678 • 1st & 3rd Th • LGBT entertainment & events magazine for Central Texas

WomanSpace 210/828-5472 • monthly newsletter

SPIRITUAL GROUPS

MCC of San Antonio 611 E Myrtle (btwn McCullough & N St Mary's) 210/472-3597 • 10:30am Sun

River City Living MCC 202 Holland Ave (near McCullough & Hildebrand) 210/822-1121 • 11am Sun

EROTICA

Apollo News 2376 Austin Hwy (at Walzem) 210/653-3538 • 24hrs

Shelbyville

ACCOMMODATIONS

English Bay Marina 186 D English Ln 936/368-2554 • gay/ straight • motel, cabins & RV hookups • in remote area overlooking Toledo Bend Lake • kids/ pets ok • wheelchair access • lesbian-owned • $35-50

South Padre Island

ACCOMMODATIONS

New Upper Deck Hotel & Bar 120 E Atol St (at Padre Blvd) 956/761-5953 • mostly gay men • swimming • nudity at hot tub • bar open from 2pm, from 5pm off-season (Oct-April) • pets ok • wheelchair access • gay-owned • $19.95-195

Spring Branch

ACCOMMODATIONS

Mermaid's Cove 3660 Tanglewood Trail (at Eagle Rock Rd) 830/885-4297 • gay-straight • rustic campground w/ cabins • nonsmoking • lesbian-owned • $45-65 (cabins)/ $18-26 (RV)

Tyler

NIGHTCLUBS

Outlaws Hwy 110 (4 miles S of Loop 323) **903/509–2248** • 8:15pm Th College Night, 9pm Sat Alternative Night • dancing/DJ • 18+

SPIRITUAL GROUPS

St Gabriel's Community Church 13904 Country Rd 193 **903/581–6923** • 10:30am Sun, 6:30pm Wed • newsletter • wheelchair access

Waco

INFO LINES & SERVICES

Eddie & Velma Dwyer Community Center 507 Jefferson (at N 5th St) • gay & lesbian center, 2nd & 4th Fri social & movie night

Gay/ Lesbian Alliance of Central Texas 254/715–6501 • info • newsletter • events

NIGHTCLUBS

Club Trix 110 S 6th St 254/714–0767 • 8pm-2am Wed-Sun • lesbians/ gay men • dancing/DJ • drag shows 2nd & 4th Sun • videos

SPIRITUAL GROUPS

Central Texas MCC From the Heart 1601 Clay Ave (at 16th) **254/752–5331** • 11am Sun

Unitarian Universalist Fellowship of Waco 4209 N 27th St (at 19th) **254/754–0599** • 10:45am Sun • also Waldo's Coffeehouse • live shows • nonsmoking • 7:30 pm 1st Fri

Unity Church of Greater Waco 400 S 1st, Hewitt **254/666–9102** • 11am Sun

Wichita Falls

BARS

Odds 1205 Lamar (at 12th) **940/322–2996** • 3pm-2am • lesbians/ gay men • more women Th • neighborhood bar • dancing/ DJ • karaoke Th • drag shows • 18+ • beer/ wine

Wimberley

ACCOMMODATIONS

Bella Vista 2121 Hilltop **512/847–6425** • lesbians/ gay men • swimming • nonsmoking • gay-owned • $95-125

UTAH

Bryce Canyon

ACCOMMODATIONS

The Red Brick Inn of Panguitch B&B 161 N 100 West (at 200 North), Panguitch **435/676–2141, 866/733–2745** • gay-friendly • full brkfst • kids/ pets ok • $79-189

Escalante

ACCOMMODATIONS

Rainbow Country B&B 435/826–4567, 800/252–8824 • gay-friendly • full brkfst • hot tub • nonsmoking • kids/ pets ok • $55-85

Holladay

RESTAURANTS

Loco Lizard Cantina 6550 Big Cottonwood Canyon Rd (at 6500 S & 3000 E) 801/453–9400 • 11am-10pm, till 11pm Fri-Sat, brunch wknds • Mexican • full bar • trangender-friendly • wheelchair access

Logan

INFO LINES & SERVICES

Utah State University Pride Alliance Taggart Student Center, Rm 335 **435/797–5694** • Mon 7:30pm Sept-May • open to students & community • also Gay & Lesbian Student Resource Center (in Military Science Bldg. #122), 435/797–4297

Moab

ACCOMMODATIONS

Los Vados Canyon House 801/971–5304 • gay/ straight • retreat house in a red rock canyon • swimming • kids 10 & over ok • nonsmoking • gay-owned • $275

Mayor's House B&B 505 East Rose Tree Ln (at 400 E) **435/259–6015, 888/791–2345** • gay-friendly • full brkfst • swimming • hot tub • kids ok • nonsmoking • gay-owned • $90-200

Mt Peale Resort Inn/ Spa/ Cabins 1415 East Hwy 46, mile mark 14.1 (at mile mark 14.1), Old La Sal **435/686–2284, 888/687–3253** • gay/ straight • popular • B&B & cabins • full brkfst • hot tub • hiking • nonsmoking • kids ok • lesbian-owned • $85-199

Red Cliffs Lodge Hwy 128, mile post 14 **435/259–2002, 866/812–2002** • gay-friendly • resort • on Colorado River • swimming • hot tub • kids ok • nonsmoking • $99-269

Monument Valley

ACCOMMODATIONS

Pioneer House Inn 435/672-2446, **888/637-2582** • gay-friendly • full brkfst • also guided tours • $60-70

Ogden

BARS

Brass Rail 103 27th St (at Wall) **801/399-1543** • 6pm-2am • popular • lesbians/gay men • women's night Fri • dancing/DJ Th-Sat • drag shows • appetizers served • private club

SPIRITUAL GROUPS

Glory to God MCC 375 Harrison Blvd **801/394-0204** • 9am, 11am & 6pm Sun

Unitarian Universalist Church of Ogden 2261 Adams Ave (at YCC) **801/394-3338** • 10:30am Sun

Park City

ACCOMMODATIONS

Resort Property Management 800/243-2932

Salt Lake City

INFO LINES & SERVICES

Gay & Lesbian Community Center of Utah 355 N 300 W, 1st flr **801/539-8800, 888/874-2743** • info • resource center • meetings • coffee shop • programs • much more

ACCOMMODATIONS

Anton Boxrud B&B 57 S 600 E (at S Temple) **801/363-8035, 800/524-5511** • gay-friendly • full brkfst • hot tub • some shared baths • kids ok • $69-140

Hotel Monaco Salt Lake City 15 W 200 S **801/595-0000, 877/294-9710** • gay-friendly • restaurant & bar • gym • kids/pets ok • wheelchair access • $129-199

Parrish Place 720 E Ashton Ave **801/832-0970, 888/832-0869** • gay/straight • Victorian mansion • hot tub • nonsmoking • gay-owned • $79-109

Peery Hotel 110 W 300 S **801/521-4300, 800/331-0073** • popular • gay-friendly • full brkfst • kids ok • also 2 restaurants • full bar • wheelchair access • $129+

Salt Lake City

LGBT PRIDE:
June. 801/539-8800, web: www.utahpride.org.

ANNUAL EVENTS:
Jan-Feb - Gay/Lesbian Ski Week 877/429-6368, web: www.gayskiing.org.

CITY INFO:
801/521-2822, web: www.visitsaltlake.com.

WEATHER:
Home of "The Greatest Snow on Earth," the Wasatch Mtns get an average of 535 inches of powder, while the valley averages 59 inches. Spring is mild with an average of 62°, while summer temps average 88°, topping out at an average of 92° in July.

TRANSIT:
Yellow Cab 801/521-2100.
Utah Transit Authority (UTA) 801/743-3882, web: www.utabus.com.

ATTRACTIONS:
Family History Library, one of the largest genealogical research databases in the country 801/240-4085.
Great Salt Lake.
Mormon Tabernacle Choir 801/240-4150, web: www.mormontabernaclechoir.org.
Temple Square.
Skiing!
Trolley Square.

Saltair B&B/ Alpine Cottages 164 S 900 E 801/533–8184, 800/733–8184 • popular • gay-friendly • full brkfst • hot tub • also cottages from 1870s • nonsmoking • $55-185

Bars

MoDiggity's 3424 S State St 801/832–9000 • 4pm-midnight, till 2am Fri-Sat, from 2pm Sun, 11am-11pm Sun • live DJs wknds • mostly women • dancing/ DJ • videos • private club

Paper Moon 3737 S State St 801/713–0678 • 3pm-1am • mostly women • dancing/DJ • karaoke • country/ western Th • live music • private club • food served • wheelchair access

Radio City 147 S State St (btwn 1st & 2nd) 801/532–9327 • 10am-1am • mostly gay men • beer only • wheelchair access

Todd's Bar & Grill 1051 S 300 W (at 900 S) 801/328–8650 • 10am-1am • gay-friendly • more gay Wed • dancing/DJ • food served • live shows • karaoke • videos • private club • gay-owned

The Trapp 102 S 600 W 801/531–8727 • 11am-2am • lesbians/ gay men • dancing/DJ • country/ western • food Sun • private club • wheelchair access

Nightclubs

Club Manhattan 5 E 400 S (at Main) 801/364–7651 • 11am-close • lunch & dinner • live music • dancing/ DJ • wheelchair access

Club Sound 579 W 200 S (at 600 W) 801/328–0255 • Fri-Sat only • mostly gay men • dancing/ DJ • live bands rest of the week

Heads Up 163 W Pierpont Ave 801/359–2161 • 8pm-2am • mostly gay men • neighborhood bar • dancing/ DJ • karaoke • private club

The Trapp Door 615 W 100 S 801/533–0173 • 9pm-2am • mostly gay men • dancing/ DJ • multiracial • transgender-friendly • drag shows • private club • wheelchair access

Cafes

Coffee Garden 898 E 900 S 801/355–3425 • 6am-11pm, till midnight wknds • light fare • wheelchair access

Cup of Joe 353 W 200 S (btwn 300 & 400 W) 801/363–8322 • 7am-midnight, 9am-8pm Sun • internet access • gallery • live shows

Restaurants

Baci Trattoria 134 W Pierpont Ave 801/328–1333 • lunch weekdays & dinner Mon-Sat, clsd Sun • festive Italian • full bar • wheelchair access

Lambs Restaurant 169 S Main St 801/364–7166 • 7am-9pm, from 8am Sat, clsd Sun • wheelchair access • live shows • "oldest restaurant in Utah"

Market St Grill 48 W Market St 801/322–4668 • lunch Mon-Sat & dinner nightly, Sun brunch • seafood & steak • full bar • wheelchair access

The Metropolitan 173 W Broadway 801/364–3472 • dinner only Mon-Sat • upscale New American

Panini 299 S Main St 801/535–4300 • lunch & dinner • Italian

Rio Grande Cafe 270 S Rio Grande 801/364–3302 • lunch Mon-Sat & dinner nightly • popular • Mexican • some veggie • full bar • wheelchair access

Sage's Cafe 473 E 300 S 801/322–3790 • lunch & dinner, brkfst wknds, clsd Mon-Tue • vegan/ vegetarian

Entertainment & Recreation

Lambda Hiking Club 700 E 200 S (S of Chevron station) 801/532–8447 • activities 10am every 1st & 3rd Sat

Bookstores

Golden Braid Books 151 S 500 E 801/322–1162, 801/322–0404 (cafe) • 10am-9pm, till 6pm Sun • also Oasis Cafe, 7am-9pm, 8am-10pm wknds • gay/ straight

Retail Shops

Cahoots 878 E 900 S (at 900 E) 801/538–0606 • 10am-9pm • unique gift shop • wheelchair access • gay-owned

Gypsy Moon Emporium 1011 E 900 S 801/521–9100 • hours vary • New Age, goddess-oriented gifts

Publications

The Pillar of the Gay/Lesbian Community 801/265–0066 • LGBT newspaper

Salt Lake Metro 801/323–9500 • bi-weekly LGBT newspaper

Spiritual Groups

Restoration Church (Mormon) 2900 S State #205 801/359–1151 • 1pm Sun • call for midweek schedule

Sacred Light of Christ MCC 823 S 600 E 801/595–0052 • 11am Sun

South Valley Unitarian Universalist Society 6876 S Highland Dr 801/944–9723 • 10:30am Sun

EROTICA

All For Love 3072 S Main St (at 33rd St S)
801/487–8358 • clsd Sun • lingerie & S/M boutique • transgender-friendly • wheelchair access

Blue Boutique 2106 S 1100 E (at 2100 S)
801/485–2072 • also piercing

Mischievous 559 S 300 W (at 6th St S)
801/530–3100 • clsd Sun

Torrey

ACCOMMODATIONS

Capitol Reef Inn & Cafe 360 W Main St
435/425–3271 • gay-friendly • seasonal • hot tub • gift shop • $44-57 • also restaurant • plenty veggie • beer/ wine

SkyRidge Inn B&B 435/425–3222 • gay-friendly • full brkfst • hot tubs • near Capitol Reef Nat'l Park • nonsmoking • $107-188

Torrey Inn 600 E Hwy 24 (near Hwy 12)
435/425–3688 • gay-friendly • nonsmoking • wheelchair access • full brkfst • pool • near Capitol Reef Park • gay-owned

Zion Nat'l Park

ACCOMMODATIONS

Red Rock Inn 998 Zion Park Blvd, Springdale **435/772–3139** • gay/ straight • cottages w/ canyon views • full brkfst • hot tub • 1 mile to Zion Nat'l Park • nonsmoking • wheelchair access • lesbian-owned • $85-225

VERMONT

Statewide

INFO LINES & SERVICES

▲ **Vermont Gay Tourism Association** PO Box 164, Waterbury 05676 • Vermont's official organization to promote gay & lesbian travel throughout the state

ENTERTAINMENT & RECREATION

The Vermont Rainbow Connection
802/849–2739 x3 • TV show by & for VT's LGBT community • call for channels & show times

PUBLICATIONS

In Newsweekly 617/426–8246 • New England's largest LGBT newspaper

Out in the Mountains (OITM) PO Box 1122, Burlington 05402 **802/861-6486** • monthly newspaper covering Vermont & beyond

Andover

ACCOMMODATIONS

The Inn At HighView 753 E Hill Rd **802/875-2724** • gay/ straight • full brkfst • swimming • hot tub • spa services on site • nonsmoking • $135-265

Arlington

ACCOMMODATIONS

Arlington Inn Rte 7-A **802/375-6532, 800/443-9442** • country inn • internet • $95-315 • also restaurant • dinner from 5:30pm, clsd Sun-Mon • cont'l

Berkshire

ACCOMMODATIONS

Hummingbird Haven 956 Richford Rd, Richford **802/848-7037** • lesbians/ gay men • guest suite in the Green Mtns • nonsmoking • $90

Brattleboro

ACCOMMODATIONS

The Maples of Poocham Poocham Rd (at Paine Rd), Westmoreland, NH **603/399-8457, 800/659-6810** • B&B • near hiking & ski trails • shared baths • nonsmoking • children 10 years & up ok • dogs ok • nonsmoking • gay-owned • $50-75

BARS

Rainbow Lounge 940 Rte 5 (btwn exits 3 & 4, off I-91), Dummerston **802/254-9830** • 8pm-2am, clsd Sun-Tue • lesbians/ gay men • dancing/DJ • drag shows • wheelchair access

RESTAURANTS

Peter Haven's 32 Elliott St (at Main) **802/257-3333** • 6pm-10pm, clsd Sun-Mon • cont'l • gay-owned

BOOKSTORES

Everyone's Books 23 Elliott St **802/254-8160** • 9:30am-6pm, till 8pm Fri, till 7pm Sat, 11am-5pm Sun • wheelchair access

Bridgewater Corners

RESTAURANTS

Blanche & Bill's Pancake House US Rte 4 **802/422-3816** • 7am-2pm Wed-Sun • great flapjacks & maple syrup

Brookfield

RESTAURANTS

Ariel's Restaurant & Pond Village Pub Rte 65 (at Stone Rd) **802/276-3939** • dinner, clsd Sun-Tue • eclectic • overlooking Sunset Lake

Burlington

INFO LINES & SERVICES

R.U.1.2? Community Center 34 Elmwood Ave (across from Burlington post office) **802/860-RU12 (7812)** • social events • support group • coffeehouse nights

ACCOMMODATIONS

The Black Bear Inn 4010 Bolton Access Rd, Bolton Valley **802/434-2126, 800/395-6335** • gay/ straight • full brkfst • hot tub • swimming • nonsmoking • wheelchair access • gay-owned • $53-185

Hartwell House B&B 170 Ferguson Ave **802/658-9242, 888/658-9242** • gay-friendly • swimming • shared bath • woman-owned/ run • $55-70 + tax

The Inn at Essex 70 Essex Way, Essex **802/878-1100, 800/727-4295** • gay-friendly • VT's culinary resort featuring the acclaimed New England Culinary Institute • swimming • kids/pets ok • wheelchair access • $159-499

Wyndham Burlington 60 Battery St **802/658-6500** • gay-friendly • swimming • kids ok • wheelchair access • $159-289

BARS

135 Pearl 135 Pearl St **802/863-2343** • 7:30pm-2am, clsd Sun-Mon • gay/ straight • dancing/DJ • nonsmoking dance flr Fri-Sat • karaoke • cabaret • monthly women's dance

CAFES

Muddy Waters 184 Main St **802/658-0466** • coffeehouse • also teas, beer • try the white hot chocolate

Radio Bean Coffeehouse 8 N Winooski Ave **802/660-9346** • cool bohemian coffeehouse • live bands & open mic nights

RESTAURANTS

Daily Planet 15 Center St (at College) **802/862-9647** • 4pm-close, also bar till 2am • plenty veggie

Loretta's 44 Park St (near 5 Corners), Essex Junction 802/879-7777 • lunch weekdays, dinner nightly, clsd Sun-Mon • Italian • plenty veggie • lesbian-owned

Parima Thai 185 Pearl St 802/864-7917 • lunch & dinner • courtyard garden

Shanty on the Shore 181 Battery St 802/864-0238 • 11am-10pm • seafood • views of Lake Champlain

Silver Palace 1216 Williston Rd 802/864-0125 • 11:30am-9pm, till 10pm wknds • Chinese • some veggie • full bar

RETAIL SHOPS

Peace & Justice Store 21 Church St (at Pearl) 802/863-8326 • 10am-6pm, till 8pm Fri-Sat, noon-5pm Sun • pride store • books

SPIRITUAL GROUPS

First Unitarian Universalist Society 152 Pearl St (at top of Church St) 802/862-5630 • 11am, 10am (summer) • Interweave (LGBT group) • 12:30pm 2nd Sun (except July-Aug) • also civil unions

Chester

ACCOMMODATIONS

Chester House Inn 266 Main St 802/875-2205, 888/875-2205 • gay/ straight • full brkfst • nonsmoking • kids ok • wheelchair access • gay-owned • $95-189 • also restaurant • beer/ wine

Craftsbury Common

ACCOMMODATIONS

Greenhopefarm on Wylie Hill 2478 Wylie Hill Rd (at VT Rte 14) 802/586-7577 • mostly women • kids/pets ok • lesbian-owned

East Burke

RESTAURANTS

Inn at Mountain View Farm Darling Hill Rd 802/626-9924, 800/572-4509 • dinner nightly, clsd Tue • farm-fresh, organic cuisine • also inn

Greensboro

ACCOMMODATIONS

Highland Lodge 1608 Craftsbury Rd 802/533-2647 • gay-friendly • open May-Oct & Dec-March • 50km groomed x-country skiing • private beach & boats • includes brkfst & dinner • nonsmoking • wheelchair access • $125-310

Jay Peak

ACCOMMODATIONS

Grey Gables Mansion 122 River St, Richford 802/848-3625, 800/299-2117 • gay-friendly • circa 1888 B&B inn • full brkfst • kids ok • nonsmoking • available for civil unions & receptions • $89-139

Killington

ACCOMMODATIONS

Cortina Inn & Resort Rte 4 802/773-3333, 800/451-6108 • gay-friendly • hot tub • also tavern • kids/ pets ok • food served • wheelchair access • $99-239

Salt Ash Inn 4758 Rte 100A (at Rte 100), Plymouth 802/672-3748, 800/725-8274 • gay/ straight • 1830s country inn • full brkfst • hot tub • swimming • food served • pub • near skiing • kids/ small pets ok • gay-owned • $95-275

Ludlow

ACCOMMODATIONS

Cavendish Inn 1589 Main St (off Rte 131), Cavendish 802/226-7080 • gay-friendly • food served • at the historic Glimmerstone Mansion • wheelchair access • $48-260

Happy Trails Motel 321 Rte 103 S 802/228-8888 • gay-friendly • rooms, suites & cottage • seasonal hot tub • near skiing • $65-425

Lyndonville

RESTAURANTS

Miss Lyndonville Diner Rte 5 802/626-9890 • 6am-8pm, till 9pm Fri-Sat, from 7am Sun

Manchester

ACCOMMODATIONS

Hill Farm Inn 458 Hill Farm Rd (at Historic Rte 7A), Arlington 802/375-269, 800/882-2545 • gay-friendly • full brkfst • $80-195

CAFES

Little Rooster Cafe Rte 7-A, Manchester Center 802/362-3496 • 7am-2:30pm, clsd Wed (winters)

RESTAURANTS

Bistro Henry 1942 Rte 11/30 (.5 mile E Rte 7) 802/362-4982 • dinner only, clsd Mon • Mediterranean • also bar • reservations advised • seasonal

The Black Swan Rte 7-A S **802/362–3807 •** dinner from 5:30pm, clsd Wed • cont'l/ game • wheelchair access

Chanticleer Rte 7-A N, Manchester Center **802/362–1616 •** call for hours • seasonal

BOOKSTORES

Northshire Bookstore 4869 Main St, Manchester Center **802/362–2200 •** 10am-9pm, till 7pm Sun-Mon

Marlboro

ACCOMMODATIONS

Colonel Williams Inn Rte 9 (at Staver Rd) **802/257–1093 •** gay/ straight • full brkfst • hot tub • kids/ pets ok • nonsmoking • also restaurant • wheelchair access • $100-250

RESTAURANTS

Skyline Restaurant Rte 9, Hogback Mountain **802/464–5535 •** 7am-3pm, clsd Tue-Wed • wheelchair access

Montgomery Center

ACCOMMODATIONS

Phineas Swann B&B 802/326–4306 • gay/ straight • Gingerbread Victorian • full brkfst • nonsmoking • gay-owned • $109-165

CAFES

Trout River Traders 91 Main St (at Rte 242) **802/326–3085 •** 9am-5pm • gay-friendly • food served • also gift shop • gay-owned

Montpelier

ACCOMMODATIONS

Marshfield Inn & Motel 5630 US Rte 2, Marshfield **802/426–3383 •** gay-friendly • motel w/ great views of Green Mtns & Winooski River • full brkfst • lesbian-owned • $60-95

RESTAURANTS

Julio's 54 State **802/229–9348 •** 11:30am-10pm, till midnight wknds • Mexican

Sarducci's 3 Main St **802/223–0229 •** 11:30am-9:30pm, till 10pm wknds, from 4:30pm Sun • Italian • some veggie • full bar • wheelchair access

Wayside Restaurant Rte 302 **802/223–6611 •** 6:30am-9:30pm • wheelchair access

RETAIL SHOPS

Phoenix Rising 34 State St **802/229–0522 •** 10am-5:30pm, till 6pm Fri, 11am-5pm Sat, 12pm-4pm Sun • metaphysical • jewelry • gifts • pride items • music • gay-friendly

Rutland

ACCOMMODATIONS

The Inn of the Six Mountains 2617 Killington Rd, Killington **802/422–4302, 800/228–4676 •** gay-friendly • hotel • swimming • jacuzzi • kids ok • wheelchair access • $99-249

Lilac Inn 53 Park St, Brandon **802/247–5463, 800/221–0720 •** full brkfst • teens ok • wheelchair access • $145-295

Maplewood Inn 1108 S Main St (Rte 22-A), Fair Haven **802/265–8039, 800/253–7729 •** gay/ straight • romantic, historic-register 1843 Greek Revival • full brkfst • beautiful antiques • centrally located • nonsmoking • $110-250

NIGHTCLUBS

Shooka Dookas 13 Evelyn St (at West St) **802/773–6969 •** 6pm-2am, clsd Sun-Mon • lesbians/ gay men • dancing/DJ • karaoke • drag shows • gay-owned

Saxtons River

ACCOMMODATIONS

The Inn at Saxtons River 27 Main St (at Academy Ave) **802/869–2110 •** gay-friendly • historic Victorian inn w/ charming pub & restaurant • located in quaint New England village • $110-150

St Albans

RESTAURANTS

Jeff's Maine Seafood 65 N Main St **802/524–6135 •** lunch daily, dinner Tue-Sat

St Johnsbury

INFO LINES & SERVICES

Umbrella Women's Center 970 Memorial Dr **802/748–8645, 802/748–8141 •** 8am-4:30pm Mon-Fri • lesbian support & resources

ACCOMMODATIONS

▲ **Highlands Inn** Bethlehem, NH **603/869–3978, 877/LES–B–INN** (537-2466) • a lesbian paradise • "one of 10 best gay/ lesbian guesthouses" (*Planet Out*) • 19 antique-filled rooms • full brkfst • outdoor & indoor spas • swimming pool • 100 mtn acres • special events • concerts • VT civil union honeymoons • kids/ pets ok • ignore No Vacancy sign • lesbian-owned • $105-155 • see ad on page 1

Tallulahs B&B 745 Center St (at Broad), Lyndonville 802/626-4695 • gay/ straight • historic Dutch colonial • also large guesthouse • wheelchair access • $95-250

Stowe

ACCOMMODATIONS

Arbor Inn 3214 Mountain Rd 802/253-4772, 800/543-1293 • gay/ straight • full brkfst • hot tub • swimming • nonsmoking • $79-265

Fitch Hill Inn 802/888-3834, 800/639-2903 • gay/ straight • full brkfst • hot tub • older kids ok • $85-205

Gardner's Eden 150 Upper Sky Acres Dr 802/253-8464 • gay-friendly • luxury apt rental • hot tub • nonsmoking • $150-200 & $800-1,000/ week

The Green Mountain Inn 18 Main St 802/253-7301, 800/253-7302 • gay-friendly • restored 1833 private residence in the heart of Stowe Village • heated pool • 2 restaurants • $119-649

Honeywood Inn 4583 Mountain Rd 802/253-4846, 800/821-7891 • gay/ straight • full brkfst • jacuzzi • swimming • kids 11 years & up ok • nonsmoking • $89-269

Northern Lights Lodge 4441 Mountain Rd 802/253-8541, 800/448-4554 • gay-friendly • full brkfst • hot tub • swimming • sauna • kids/ pets ok • gay-owned • $58-148

The Old Stagecoach Inn 18 N Main St (at Stowe St), Waterbury 802/244-5056, 800/262-2206 • gay-friendly • historic village inn • full brkfst • kids/ pets ok • also full bar • nonsmoking • $65-180

▲ **Timberholm Inn** 452 Cottage Club Rd 802/253-7603, 800/753-7603 • gay/ straight • B&B • full brkfst • hot tub • nonsmoking • gay-owned • $89-179

Winding Brook, A Classic Mountain Lodge 199 Edson Hill Rd 802/253-7354, 800/426-6697 • gay/ straight • rustic mtn retreat • nonsmoking • full brkfst • kids ok • gay-owned • $85-195 + 12% service charge

Stratton Mountain

ACCOMMODATIONS

Stratton Mountain Inn 61 Middle Ridge Rd
802/297–2500, 877/887–3767 • gay-friendly •
resort • swimming • hot tub • also restaurant
& tavern

Townshend

ACCOMMODATIONS

Townshend State Park 2755 State Forest
Rd **802/365–7500** • gay-friendly •
campground • great hiking • open Memorial
Day wknd to Labor Day wknd

Waterbury

ACCOMMODATIONS

Grünberg Haus B&B & Cabins 94 Pine St,
Rte 100 S **802/244–7726, 800/800–7760** • gay/
straight • Austrian chalet & cabins • full brkfst
• fireplace • nonsmoking • $70-185

Moose Meadow Lodge 607 Crossett Hill
802/244–5378 • gay/ straight • log home on
86-acre wooded estate • full brkfst • hot tub •
gay-owned • $129-169

West Dover

ACCOMMODATIONS

Deerhill Inn **802/464–3100, 800/993–3379** •
gay/ straight • inn • teenagers ok •
nonsmoking • also restaurant • $135-285

Red Oak Inn 45 Rte 100 (at Rte 9)
802/464–8817 • gay-friendly • swimming •
also tavern & gameroom • gay-owned • $69-
189

Wilmington

ACCOMMODATIONS

Averill Stand B&B 236 Rte 9 East (at Rte
100) **802/464–9951** • lesbians/ gay men •
1787 farmhouse • near Mt Snow • some
shared baths • gay-owned • $59-99

Windham

ACCOMMODATIONS

A Stone Wall Inn RFD 133 **802/875–4238** •
gay-straight • B&B inn • hot tub •
nonsmoking • gay-owned • $110-140

Woodstock

ACCOMMODATIONS

The Ardmore Inn 23 Pleasant St
802/457–3887, 800/497–9652 • gay-friendly •
1880s Greek revival • full brkfst • jacuzzi •
nonsmoking • $135-195

Cabin in the Woods 1944 Chateauguay Rd,
Bridgewater Corners **802/672–5141** (NO CALLS
AFTER 9PM EST) • gay-friendly • secluded rustic
cabin • hot tub • swimming hole • fireplace •
smoking outdoors only • seasonal May-Oct •
pets ok • transgender-owned/ run • $225

Deer Brook Inn 535 Woodstock Rd
802/672–3713 • gay-friendly • B&B • full
brkfst • kids ok • gay-owned • $105-165

Village Inn of Woodstock 41 Pleasant St
802/457–1255, 800/722–4571 • gay-friendly •
restored Victorian Inn • full brkfst • internet
access • nonsmoking • $100-240

VIRGINIA

Alexandria

see also **Washington, District of
Columbia**

SPIRITUAL GROUPS

Church of the Resurrection (Episcopal)
2280 N Beauregard St **703/998–0888** • 8am &
10am Sun

Mt Vernon Unitarian Church 1909
Windmill Ln (off Fort Hunt Rd) **703/765–5950**
• 9:30am & 11:15am Sun (10am summer)

Arlington

see also **Washington, District of
Columbia**

INFO LINES & SERVICES

Arlington Gay/ Lesbian Alliance •
monthly meetings • outreach events • check
website for schedule: www.agla.org

BARS

Freddie's Beach Bar & Restaurant 555 S
23rd St **703/685–0555** • 3pm-2am, wknd
brunch • lesbians/ gay men • karaoke • drag
show • patio • live bands • food served

CAFES

Java Shack 2507 N Franklin Rd (at Wilson
Blvd & N Barton) **703/527–9556** • 7am-8pm •
lesbians/ gay men

PUBLICATIONS

Woman's Monthly 202/965–5399 • articles
• calendar of community/ arts events for
greater DC/ Baltimore area

SPIRITUAL GROUPS

Clarendon Presbyterian Church 1305 N
Jackson St (at 13th St) 703/527–9513 • 10am
Sun

Ashland

CAFES

Coffee Talk Cafe 9563 Kings Charter Dr
804/550–0887 • 7am-close, clsd Sun-Mon •
pasta • live music

Cape Charles

see also Norfolk & Virginia Beach

ACCOMMODATIONS

Cape Charles House B&B 645 Tazewell Ave
(at Fig) 757/331–4920 • gay-friendly • 1912
colonial revival home filled w/ antiques •
nonsmoking • $100-160

Sea Gate B&B 9 Tazewell Ave 757/331–2206
• gay-friendly • full brkfst • afternoon tea •
near beach on quiet, tree-lined street • gay-
owned • $95-110

Sterling House B&B 9 Randolph Ave (at
Bay Ave) 757/331–2483 • gay/ straight • 1913
beach bungalow • full brkfst • hot tub • teens
ok • gay-owned • $110-135

Charlottesville

ACCOMMODATIONS

CampOut 804/301–3553 • women only •
100-acre rustic campground w/ 50 campsites •
nonsmoking • wheelchair access • women-
owned/ run • $20 membership fee

Fiddlestick Lane 1889 Fiddlestick Ln (at 5th
St) 434/296–6545 • gay/ straight • B&B in
private home • full brkfst • kids over 9 years ok
• gay-owned • $125-210

The Inn at Court Square 410 E Jefferson St
434/295–2800, 866/466–2877 • gay-friendly •
restored house w/ period antiques • jacuzzi •
lunch served Mon-Fri • kids ok • nonsmoking
• women-owned/ run • $129-269

Mark Addy Inn 56 Rodes Farm Dr,
Nellysford 434/361–1101, 800/278–2154 •
gay/ straight • full brkfst • dinner available •
swimming • tennis • hot tub • nonsmoking •
wheelchair access • gay-owned • $100-195

The Summer Kitchen B&B 6482 Dick
Woods Rd 540/456–7009 • gay/ straight •
cottage • full brkfst • hot tub • sauna •
nonsmoking • lesbian-owned • $125-135

NIGHTCLUBS

Club 216 218 W Water St (enter on South St)
434/296–8783 • 10pm-5am Fri-Sat, some Sun
events popular • lesbians/ gay men •
dancing/DJ • live shows • private club •
wheelchair access

RESTAURANTS

Escafe in West End downtown mall (next to
the Omni Hotel) 434/295–8668 • 5:30pm-
11pm Tue-Sat, 4:30pm-9:30pm Sun, clsd Mon
• Asian/ American fusion • full bar • live
music • gay-owned

ENTERTAINMENT & RECREATION

The Eclectic Woman WTJU 91.1 FM
434/924–3418 • 7pm Th • women's music
show

BOOKSTORES

Quest Bookshop 619 W Main St
434/295–3377 • LGBT section

EROTICA

Hole in the Wall 30 S Main St, Harrisonburg
540/433–3366 • sex toys & videos

Sneak Reviews Video 2244 Ivy Rd
434/979–4420

Chincoteague Island

ACCOMMODATIONS

1848 Island Manor House 4160 Main St
(at Smith St) 757/336–5436, 800/852–1505 •
gay/ straight • B&B • full brkfst • nonsmoking
• gay-owned • $95-175

Christiansburg

ACCOMMODATIONS

River's Edge 6208 Little Camp Rd, Riner
540/381–4147, 888/786–9418 • gay-friendly •
full brkfst • dinner served • nonsmoking •
$150-165

Fairfax

SPIRITUAL GROUPS

MCC of Northern VA 10383 Democracy Ln
703/691–0930 • 11am Sun

Fredericksburg

RESTAURANTS

Merriman's Restaurant & Bar 715 Caroline St (btwn Charlotte & Hanover) **540/371–7723** • lunch & dinner, wknd brunch, lounge till 2am • popular • lesbians/ gay men • fresh natural homemade cuisine • plenty veggie • full bar • dancing/DJ • wheelchair access

Hampton

see also Newport News

CAFES

The Coffee Connection 768 Settlers Landing Rd **757/722–6300** • 7am-6pm, from 8am wknds, till 3pm Sun • food served

Harrisonburg

CAFES

Artful Dodger Coffeehouse 47 W Court Square **540/432–1179** • 8am-2am, noon-midnight Sun • wheelchair access

Luray

see Shenandoah Valley

Lynchburg

INFO LINES & SERVICES

Gay/ Lesbian Helpline 434/847–5242 • live 7pm-10pm Mon, Wed & Fri • info for central & SW VA

Mechanicsville

RETAIL SHOPS

Amore 7067 Mechanicsville Tpke (in Brandy Hill Pl) **804/730–1712** • exotic lingerie for men & women

Newport News

see also Norfolk & Virginia Beach

BARS

Corner Pocket 3516 Washington Ave (at 36th) **757/247–6366** • 5pm-2am • lesbians/ gay men • neighborhood bar • shows • food served till midnight • wheelchair access

EROTICA

Mr D's Leather & Novelties 9902–A Warwick Blvd (at Randolph Rd) **757/599–4070**

Norfolk

see also Virginia Beach

INFO LINES & SERVICES

Saturday Night Live Gay/ Lesbian AA 1301 Colley Ave (at First Lutheran Church) **757/625–1953 (CHURCH #)** • 8pm Sat

ACCOMMODATIONS

Tazewell Hotel & Suites 245 Granby St (at Tazewell St) **757/623–6200** • gay-friendly • full brkfst • kids ok • wheelchair access • $120-200

BARS

The Garage 731 Granby St (at Brambleton) **757/623–0303** • 8am-2am, from noon wknds • popular • mostly gay men • neighborhood bar • food served • wheelchair access

Hershee Bar 6117 Sewells Pt Rd (at Norview) **757/853–9842** • 4pm-2am, 1pm-2am Sun • mostly women • dancing/DJ • live shows • food served • some veggie • Sun buffet • wheelchair access • woman-owned/ run

Nutty Buddy's 143 E Little Creek Rd **757/588–6474** • 4pm-2am Wed-Sun • mostly gay men • more women Wed • dancing/DJ • multiracial • drag shows • also restaurant • some veggie • wheelchair access

The Wave 4107 Colley Ave (at 41st St) **757/440–5911** • 4pm-2am, from 5pm Sat, clsd Sun • lesbians/ gay men • dancing/DJ • live shows • also restaurant • dinner only • wheelchair access

CAFES

Oasis Cafe 142 W York St #101A (in York Center bldg) **757/627–6161** • 7:30am-4pm Mon-Fri • gay-owned

RESTAURANTS

Charlie's Cafe 1800 Granby St (at 18th) **757/625–0824** • 7am-2pm, till 3pm wknds • some veggie • beer/ wine

Uncle Louie's 132 E Little Creek Rd (at Granby) **757/480–1225** • 8am-11pm, till midnight Fri-Sat, till 10pm Sun • Jewish fine dining • also bar & deli • karaoke • wheelchair access

BOOKSTORES

Lambda Rising 322 W 21st St (at Llewellyn) **757/626–0969** • 10am-9pm • LGBT • wheelchair access

Norfolk

LGBT Pride:
www.hamptonroadspride.com.

Attractions:
Busch Gardens (in Williamsburg)
800/343-7946, web:
www.buschgardens.com.
The Chrysler Museum of Art
757/664-6200, web:
www.chrysler.org.
Douglas Macarthur Memorial
757/441-2965, web:
www.macarthurmemorial.org.
The Ghent historic district.
Hermitage Foundation Museum
757/423-2052, web:
www.hermitagefoundation.org.
Historic Williamsburg.
Norfolk Naval Base 757/322-2330,
web: www.navstanorva.navy.mil.
St Paul's Episcopal Church
757/627-4353, web:
www.saintpaulsnorfolk.org.
Waterside Festival Marketplace,
web:
www.watersidemarketplace.com.

City Info:
800/368-3097, web:
www.norfolkcvb.com.

Transit:
Checker Cab 757/855-3333, web:
www.norfolkcheckertaxi.com.
Norfolk Airport Shuttle 757/857-
3991, web:
www.norfolkairportexpress.com.
Hampton Roads Transit
757/222-6100, web:
www.hrtransit.org.

Retail Shops

Kindred Spirit 7510-C Granby St (at Wards Corner) **757/480-0424** • gifts • books • massage • readings & more

Spiritual Groups

New Life MCC 2605 Cunningham Dr **757/896-1213** • 6pm Sun

Erotica

Leather & Lace 149 E Little Creek Rd (at Granby) **757/583-4334**

Petersburg

Accommodations

Walker House B&B 3280 S Crater Rd (at Wagner) **804/861-5822** • gay-friendly • antebellum farmhouse • full brkfst • nonsmoking • kids ok • gay-owned • $98-120

Portsmouth

Cafes

The Lofty Bean 359 Broad St **757/399-3838** • 9am-close, clsd Sun-Mon • also art gallery • food served • live shows

Richmond

Info Lines & Services

AA Gay/ Lesbian 1205 W Franklin (at St James Episcopal Church) **804/355-1212**

Bars

Babes of Carytown 3166 W Cary St (at Auburn) **804/355-9330** • 11am-midnight, till 2am Th-Sat, 9am-3pm Sun, clsd Mon • mostly women • dancing/DJ • country/ western • karaoke • live music • food served • homecooking • some veggie • wheelchair access • women-owned/ run

Barcode 6 E Grace St (btwn 1st & Foushee Sts) **804/648-2040** • 11am-2am, from 3pm wknds • mostly gay men • neighborhood bar • karaoke • videos • food served • some veggie • wheelchair access

Godfrey's 308 E Grace St (btwn 3rd & 4th) **804/648-3957** • lunch Tue-Fri, dinner Wed-Sun, drag brunch Sun • lesbians/ gay men • also restaurant • dancing/DJ • karaoke • drag shows

Z2 2729 W Broad St **804/249-9930** • 4pm-close • neighborhood bar • cabaret • drag shows

NIGHTCLUBS

Club Colours 536 N Harrison St (at Broad) **804/353-9776** • 9pm-3am Wed & Sat • lesbians/gay men • more women until 11:30pm • dancing/DJ • multiracial • food served • live shows • wheelchair access

Fieldens 2033 W Broad St **804/359-1963** • midnight-close, clsd Mon-Wed • popular • mostly gay men • dancing/DJ • live shows • BYOB • private club (not a sex club) • wheelchair access

RESTAURANTS

Galaxy Diner 3109 W Cary St **804/213-0510** • all-day brkfst • some veggie • full bar

The Village 410 N Harrison **804/353-8204** • 8:30am-11:30pm, bar till 2am • American • plenty veggie

ENTERTAINMENT & RECREATION

Richmond Triangle Players 2033 W Broad St (at Fieldens Cabaret Theater) **804/346-8113** • alternative theater group

BOOKSTORES

Carytown Books 2930 W Cary St (at Sheppard) **804/359-4831** • 10am-7pm, till 5pm Sun • LGBT section • wheelchair access

Phoenix Rising 19 N Belmont Ave **804/355-7939, 800/719-1690** • 11am-7pm, clsd Tue • LGBT • wheelchair access

RETAIL SHOPS

Amore 173 Wadsworth Dr (in Midlothian Shopping Center), Midlothian **804/272-5666** • exotic lingerie for men & women

SPIRITUAL GROUPS

Gentle Shepherd 3700 Elwood Ave (at Cameron) **804/355-1377** • 11am Sun

MCC Richmond 2501 Park Ave (at Davis) **804/353-9477** • 10:45am Sun

New Beginnings Christian Church 4500 Kensington Ave (at Commonwealth Ave) **804/231-0321** • 6pm Sun

Roanoke

BARS

Backstreet Cafe 356 Salem Ave (off Jefferson) **540/345-1542** • 7pm-2am, till midnight Sun • lesbians/ gay men • neighborhood bar • food served

Cuba Pete's 120 Church Ave SW (at First St SW, inside Macado's) **540/342-7231** • 11am-2am • gay-friendly • more gay wknds • also Macado's restaurant • karaoke • wheelchair access

NIGHTCLUBS

The Park 615 Salem Ave **540/342-0946** • 9pm-close Fri-Sun • popular • lesbians/gay men • dancing/DJ • drag shows Sun • videos • young crowd • wheelchair access

PUBLICATIONS

Blue Ridge Lambda Press **540/345-2243** • covers western VA

SPIRITUAL GROUPS

MCC of the Blue Ridge 806 Jamison Ave SE **540/344-4444** • 10am Sun

Unitarian Universalist Church 2015 Grandin Rd SW **540/342-8888** • 11am Sun (10am summers)

Shenandoah Valley

INFO LINES & SERVICES

SVGLA (Shenandoah Valley Gay/ Lesbian Assoc) **540/574-4636** • 24hr touchtone info • weekly meetings • also dances & potlucks

ACCOMMODATIONS

Frog Hollow B&B 492 Greenhouse Rd (at Rte 11), Lexington **540/463-5444** • gay/ straight • full brkfst • hot tub • also cottage • gay-owned • $115-155

MayneviewB&B 439 Mechanic St **540/743-7921** • gay-friendly • full brkfst • Victorian w/ mountain views • near Luray Caverns, wineries & hiking • nonsmoking • $110-150

The Olde Staunton Inn 260 N Lewis St, Staunton **540/886-0193, 866/653-3786** • gay/ straight • B&B • hot tub • nonsmoking • $49-120

Piney Hill B&B 1048 Piney Hill Rd (at Mill Creek Crossroads), Luray 540/778–5261, 800/644–5261 • gay/ straight • 1750s farmhouse in Shenandoah Valley • full brkfst • hot tub • gay-owned • $109-179

Twelfth Night Inn 402 E Beverley St (at Coalter), Staunton 540/885–1733 • gay-friendly • B&B • full brkfst • kids/ pets ok • nonsmoking • $89-129

White Fence B&B 275 Chapel Rd, Stanley 540/778–4680, 800/211–9885 • gay-friendly • 1890 Victorian w/ cottages • full brkfst • jacuzzi • nonsmoking • kids ok • $129-189

Urbanna

ACCOMMODATIONS

Inn at Urbanna Creek 804/758–4661 • gay-friendly • full brkfst • jacuzzi • nonsmoking

Virginia Beach

see also Norfolk

BARS

In Between 5266 Princess Anne Rd (btwn Witchduck & Newton Rds) 757/490–9498 • 4pm-2am, from 5pm Sat • lesbians/ gay men • drag shows • male dancers • also restaurant • Sun brunch • gay-owned

Klub Ambush 475 S Lynnhaven Rd (at Lynnhaven Pkwy) 757/498–4301 • 5pm-2am • lesbians/ gay men • neighborhood bar • dancing/DJ • food served • shows • karaoke • gay-owned

Rainbow Cactus 3472 Holland Rd (at Diana Lee) 757/368–0441 • 7pm-2am, clsd Mon-Tue • mostly gay men • dancing/DJ • country/ western • drag shows • food served • wheelchair access

PUBLICATIONS

Lambda Directory 757/486–3546

SPIRITUAL GROUPS

The Christian Church Uniting 6049 Indian River Rd 757/420–1422 • 11am Sun

EROTICA

Nancy's Nook 1301 Oceana Blvd 757/428–1498 • also lingerie • toys

Williamsburg

ACCOMMODATIONS

Lavender Sea B&B 507 Capitol Landing Rd (at Washington St) 757/345–0198 • mostly women • 1938 home & haven for arts • kids ok • nonsmoking • lesbian-owned • $75-95

Windsor

ACCOMMODATIONS

Blackwater Campground 7651 Whispering Pines Trail 757/357–7211 • gay-friendly • RV hook-ups & primitive camping • swimming • pagan, medieval & gay events on wknds • kids/ pets ok • $25 (full hookup) & $22 (water & electric) & $5 per night (primitive camping)

WASHINGTON

Bellevue

see also Seattle

SPIRITUAL GROUPS

East Shore Unitarian Church 12700 SE 32nd St (1 1/2 blocks from Richards Rd) 425/747–3780 • 9am & 11am Sun (10am summers) • wheelchair access

Bellingham

BARS

Rumours 1119 Railroad Ave (at Chestnut) 360/671–1849 • 4pm-2am • lesbians/ gay men • dancing/DJ • multiracial • also restaurant • wheelchair access

CAFES

Tony's Coffee 1101 Harris Ave (at 11th), Fairhaven 360/738–4710 • 7am-8pm, till 10pm wknds • plenty veggie • patio • wheelchair access

RESTAURANTS

Skylark's Hidden Cafe 1308–B 11th St (at McKenzie) 360/715–3642 • 7am-9pm, till 10pm Fri-Sat • brkfst, lunch & dinner • great soups • beer/ wine • outdoor seating

BOOKSTORES

Village Books 1210 11th St (at Harris) 360/671–2626 • 9am-10pm, 10am-8pm Sun • new & used

RETAIL SHOPS

Kalamalka Studio 2518 Meridian 360/733–3832 • 11am-7pm, clsd Sun-Mon • tattoos • piercings

EROTICA

Great Northern Bookstore 1308 Railroad Ave (at Holly) 360/733–1650

Bremerton

INFO LINES & SERVICES

AA Gay/ Lesbian 700 Callahan Dr (at St
Paul's Episcopal) 360/475–0775 • 7:30pm Tue

OutKitsap 360/373-6150 • community
center • events • education

BARS

Brewski's 2810 Kitsap Wy (enter off Wycuff
St) 360/479–9100 • 11am-2am • gay-friendly
• neighborhood bar • food served •
wheelchair access

Chelan

ACCOMMODATIONS

Mary Kay's Romantic Whaley Mansion
415 S 3rd St 509/682–5735, 800/729–2408 •
gay-friendly • full brkfst • nonsmoking •
woman-owned • $85-135

Coupeville

ACCOMMODATIONS

Morris Farmhouse B&B 105 W Morris Rd
360/678–0939, 866/440–1555 • gay-friendly •
restored 1908 farmhouse on 10 acres •
lesbian-owned • $75-185

Everett

INFO LINES & SERVICES

AA Gay/ Lesbian 2624 Rockefeller
425/252–2525 • 7pm Sun

NIGHTCLUBS

Everett Underground 1212 California St (at
Grand Ave) 425/339–0807 • 4pm-2am •
lesbians/ gay men • dancing/DJ • multiracial •
karaoke Wed • drag shows Th • food served •
wheelchair access

Glacier

ACCOMMODATIONS

Mt Baker B&B 9447 Mt Baker Hwy
360/599–2299 • gay/ straight • modern chalet
• full brkfst • hot tub • kids ok • some shared
baths • $80-100

Hoquiam

ACCOMMODATIONS

Rivendell Ranch 100 Hensel Rd (at Hwy
101) 360/987–0088 • gay/ straight •
campground & working ranch on Olympic
Peninsula • kids ok • $10 • gay-owned

Kent

BARS

The Trax Terminal 226 1st Ave S (btwn
Titus & Gowe) 253/854–8729 • 11am-2am,
from 3pm wknds, till 4am Fri-Sat • lesbians/
gay men • dancing/DJ wknds • karaoke • also
Cha Cha Palace Showroom & Iron Horse
Saloon (country/ western) wknds

BOOKSTORES

New Woman Books 213 W Meeker (at 3rd
Ave W) 253/854–4311 • 10am-5:30pm, clsd
Sun-Mon • also Wild Woman Gallery

EROTICA

The Voyeur 604 Central Ave S 253/850–8428
• videos • toys • clothing

La Conner

ACCOMMODATIONS

The White Swan Guesthouse 15872 Moore
Rd, Mt Vernon 360/445–6805 • gay/ straight •
farmhouse B&B • also cottage • nonsmoking
• kids ok • $75-160

The Wild Iris 121 Maple Ave 360/466–1400
• gay-friendly • inn • nonsmoking • full brkfst
• restaurant w/ dinner wknds only • teens ok •
wheelchair access • $109-189

Long Beach Peninsula

ACCOMMODATIONS

Anthony's Home Court 1310 Pacific Hwy N,
Long Beach 360/642–2802, 888/787–2754 •
gay/ straight • cabins & RV hookups • gay-
owned • $70-110

**The Historic Sou'wester Lodge, Cabins &
RV Park** Beach Access Rd/ 38th Pl, Seaview
360/642–2542 • gay-friendly • inexpensive
suites • cabins w/ kitchens • vintage trailers •
RV hookups • pets ok • nonsmoking • $49-149

Senator TC Bloomer's Mansion 1004 41st
Pl (at Oceanfront), Seaview 360/642–3471 •
gay-friendly • rental home • hot tub • kids ok •
lesbian & gay-owned • $400

Shakti Cove Cottages 360/665–4000 •
lesbians/ gay men • cabins on the peninsula •
pets ok • nonsmoking • lesbian-owned • $70-
85

Lynnwood

RETAIL SHOPS

Lynnwood Tattoo 15315 Hwy 99, #7 (at
153rd) 425/742–8467 • noon-10pm, till
midnight Fri-Sat

Mt Vernon

RESTAURANTS

Deli Next Door 210 S 1st St (at Memorial Hwy) **360/336-3886** • 8am-9pm, 9pm-8pm Sun • healthy American • plenty veggie • wheelchair access

BOOKSTORES

Scott's Bookstore 121 Freeway Dr **360/336-6181** • 9am-8pm, till 5pm Sun, till 6pm Mon

Olympia

INFO LINES & SERVICES

Free at Last AA 11th & Washington (at United Church) **360/352-7344** • 7pm Mon

BARS

Hannah's 123 5th Ave W (at Columbia) **360/357-9890** • 11am-2am, from 10am Fri-Sat, till midnight Sun-Mon • gay/straight • neighborhood bar • food served

CAFES

Darby's Cafe 211 SE 5th Ave (at Washington) **360/357-6229** • 7am-3pm, 8am-2pm wknds, clsd Mon-Tue • gay/straight • gay-owned

Otto's 111 Washington St NE **360/352-8640** • 7am-6pm • espresso & fresh bagels

RESTAURANTS

Saigon Rendez-Vous 117 5th Ave SW (btwn Columbia & Capitol Wy) **360/352-1989** • lunch & dinner • Vietnamese • plenty veggie

Urban Onion 116 Legion Wy SE (at Capitol) **360/943-9242** • 7am-9pm, till 10pm wknds • plenty veggie • wheelchair access

RETAIL SHOPS

Dumpster Values 117 Washington St NE **360/705-3772** • 11am-7pm, noon-5pm Sun • new & used clothing • zines • records • toys • women-owned/run

EROTICA

Desire Video 3200 Pacific Ave SE (off I-5, at exit 107) **360/352-0820** • 24hrs • videos • toys • 100-channel video arcade • extensive LGBT section

Pasco

NIGHTCLUBS

Out & About Restaurant & Lounge 327 W Lewis **509/543-3796, 877/388-3796** • 6pm-2am, clsd Mon • lesbians/gay men • dancing/DJ wknds • karaoke • drag shows • cabaret • all ages Fri & Sun • also restaurant • wheelchair access

Port Townsend

ACCOMMODATIONS

Aunt Jenny's Guest House 504 Root St **360/385-2899** • gay/straight • quiet cottage • kids ok • nonsmoking • wheelchair access • woman-owned/run • $65-125/night & $300-600/week

The James House 1238 Washington St **800/385-1238, 360/385-1238** • gay-friendly • Victorian B&B • full brkfst • nonsmoking • gardens • $110-195

Ravenscroft Inn 533 Quincy St (at Clay St) **360/385-2784, 800/782-2691** • gay-friendly • seaport inn w/ views of Puget Sound • gourmet brkfst • hot tub • nonsmoking • $94-199

Quinault

ACCOMMODATIONS

Lake Quinault Lodge South Shore Rd (off US 101) **360/288-2900** • gay-friendly • $80-183

San Juan Islands

ACCOMMODATIONS

Blue Rose B&B 1811 9th St, Anacortes **360/293-5175, 877/293-3285** • gay-friendly • private home • full brkfst • near waterfront • $105-115

Lopez Farm Cottages & Tent Camping 555 Fisherman Bay Rd, Lopez Island **360/468-3555, 800/440-3556** • gay/straight • on 30-acre farm • hot tub • nonsmoking • also camping • $33 (camping) – 175 (cottages)

Spring Bay Inn on Orcas Island **360/376-5531** • gay/straight • full brkfst • hot tub • kayak tour included in price • nonsmoking • $220-260

The Whidbey Inn 106 1st St, Langley **360/221-7115, 888/313-2070** • gay/straight • full brkfst • located on bluff over Saratoga Passage Waterway & Mtns • nonsmoking • $95-175

ENTERTAINMENT & RECREATION

Western Prince Whale & Wildlife Tours
2 Spring St (at Front), Friday Harbor
360/378-5315, 800/757-6722 • whale-watching & wildlife tours April-Oct

Seattle

INFO LINES & SERVICES

Capitol Hill Alano 1222 E Pine St, 2nd flr (at 13th) **206/860-9560 (CLUB), 206/587-2838 (AA#)** • 12-step meetings daily

Lesbian Resource Center 2214 S Jackson St (at 23rd St) **206/322-DYKE (3953)** • drop-in noon-7pm Tue-Fri, & till 5pm Sat

Seattle LGBT Community Center 1115 E Pike St (btwn 11th & 12th Aves) **206/323-5428**

ACCOMMODATIONS

Ace Hotel 2423 1st Ave (at Wall St)
206/448-4721 • gay/ straight • modern & stylish • some shared baths • kids/ pets ok • restaurant & bar • gay & straight-owned/ run • $65-175

Alexis Hotel 1007 1st Ave (at Madison)
206/624-4844, 800/426-7033 • gay-friendly • luxury hotel w/ Aveda spa • kids/pets ok • wheelchair access • $215-595

Amaranth Inn 1451 S Main St (at 16th)
206/720-7161, 800/720-7161 • gay/ straight • 1890s mansion • full brkfst • nonsmoking • $75-165

Artist's Studio Loft B&B 16529 91st Ave SW, Vashon Island **206/463-2583** • gay-friendly • hot tub • nonsmoking • $95-175

Seattle

WHERE THE GIRLS ARE:
Living in the Capitol Hill District, south of Lake Union, and working in the Broadway Market, Pike Place Market, or somewhere in between.

LGBT PRIDE:
Last Sunday in June. 206/324-0405, web: www.seattlepride.org.

ANNUAL EVENTS:
September - AIDSwalk 206/329-6923.
October - Seattle Gay & Lesbian Film Festival 206/323-4274, web: www.seattlequeerfilm.com.

CITY INFO:
206/461-5800, web: www.seattle.com.

BEST VIEW:
Top of the Space Needle, or from Admiral Way Park in West Seattle.

WEATHER:
Winter's average temperature is 50° while summer temperatures can climb up into the 90°s. Be prepared for rain at any time during the year.

TRANSIT:
Farwest 206/622-1717.
Gray Top Cab 206/282-8222.
Airport Shuttle Express 206/622-1424.
Metropolitan Transit 206/553-3000, web: www.metrokc.gov/tran.htm.

ATTRACTIONS:
Experience Music Project, web: www.emplive.com.
International District.
Pike Place Market.
Pioneer Square.
Seattle Art Museum 206/654-3100, web: www.seattleartmuseum.org.
Seattle Center Monorail 206/441-6038, web: seattlemonorail.com
Space Needle 206/905-2100, web: www.spaceneedle.com.
Woodland Park Zoo 206/684-4800, web: www.zoo.org.

[Reply] [Forward]   [Delete]

Date: Dec 14, 2005 14:46:56
From: Girl-on-the-Go
To: Editor@Damron.com
Subject: Seattle

>Seattle's lush natural beauty—breathtaking views of Puget Sound and the Cascade Mountains—is actually more incredible than most let on.

>You can see for yourself from the deck of the Space Needle. This Seattle landmark is located in the Seattle Center, a complex that includes an opera house, the Arena Coliseum, the Experience Music Project, and the Pacific Science Center. If the line isn't too long, take the Monorail from downtown. (Be sure to sit on the right-hand side and keep your face pressed to the window. This scenic ride is over almost before it begins.) Another landmark is the quaint/touristy Pike Place Market (where all those commercials featuring mounds of fish are filmed).

>For the perfect day trip, ferry over to the Olympic Peninsula and enjoy the fresh wilderness, or cruise by "Dykiki," a water-front park on Lake Washington. If you enjoy island life, ferry over to the San Juan Islands for a relaxing stay at one of the lesbian-friendly guesthouses. Or head up north to Vancouver, British Columbia, Seattle's beautiful Canadian cousin.

>But Seattle is more than just another pretty place. It has a small-town friendliness that you won't always find in a big West Coast city, as well as an international reputation for sophisticated cafe culture and cyber-cool. Speaking of java, if you like yours strong, stop in at **Espresso Vivace** on Denny.

Bacon Mansion 959 Broadway E (at E Prospect) **206/329-1864, 800/240-1864** • gay/straight • Edwardian-style Tudor • nonsmoking • wheelchair access • $89-194

Bed & Breakfast on Broadway 722 Broadway Ave E (at Aloha) **206/329-8933** • gay-friendly • full brkfst • nonsmoking • $95-135

Chambered Nautilus B&B Inn 5005 22nd Ave NE (at N 50th St) **206/522-2536, 800/545-8459** • gay-friendly • colonial home • full brkfst • sundecks • $99-144

Chelsea Station on the Park 4915 Linden Ave N **206/547-6077, 800/400-6077** • gay/straight • award-winning B&B • full brkfst • $100-185

[Reply] [Forward]   [Delete]

>For lovely digs, stay at **Gaslight Inn.** Not only will you love their art-filled B&B in Capitol Hill, but you can also book their cottage in the San Juan Islands (Lopez Island) should you need a romantic island escape.

>For shopping, the Broadway Market in queer Capitol Hill is a multicultural shopping center. We're told the girl-watching is best from the Market's espresso bar. While you're in the neighborhood, stop by the dyke-owned **Toys in Babeland** for all your sex toy and erotica needs.

>Seattle's main women's bar is the **Wildrose Tavern.** Sassy local girls get down at the monthly **Girl 4 Girl** parties, and country gals can scoot their boots at **Timberline.** If you're looking for a mixed crowd, kick it up with the boys at **Neighbours** and **Re-bar.** To find out what else is going on, pick up a copy of the **Seattle Gay News.**

Gaslight Inn 1727 15th Ave (at E Howell St) 206/325-3654 • popular • gay/ straight • swimming • nonsmoking • gay-owned • $78-148

Gypsy Arms B&B 3628 Palatine Ave N 206/547-8194 • gay/ straight • Victorian inn w/ full dungeon • leather • hot tub • nonsmoking • gay-owned • $100-150

Hill House B&B 1113 E John St (at 12th Ave) 206/720-7161, 800/720-7161 • gay-friendly • full brkfst • nonsmoking • $75-165

Hotel Vintage Park 1100 5th Ave (at Spring) 206/624-8000, 800/624-4433 • gay/ straight • ultra-luxe sleep in Seattle • kids/ pets ok • also restaurant • wheelchair access • $159-269

MarQueen Hotel 600 Queen Anne Ave N (btwn Roy & Mercer) 206/282-7407, 888/445-3076 • gay/ straight • $125-325

Pioneer Square Hotel 77 Yesler Wy (btwn 1st Ave & Alaskan Wy) 206/340-1234, 800/800-5514 • gay-friendly • boutique hotel • gym • restaurant & saloon • wheelchair access • $89-289

Salisbury House B&B 750 16th Ave E (at Aloha) 206/328-8682 • gay-friendly • full brkfst • jacuzzi • nonsmoking • women-owned • $89-165

Seahurst Garden Studio 13713 16th Ave SW (at Ambaum Ave), Burien 206/551-7721 • women-only • self-sufficient garden studio for one or two women • wheelchair access • lesbian-owned • $36-60

Seattle Suites 1400 Hubbell Pl 206/232-2799 • gay/ straight • studio, 1 & 2-bdrm condos • nonsmoking • kids ok • woman-owned/ run • $128-165

Sweet Suite Seattle 1400 Hubbell Pl, Ste 812 (at Pike) 206/632-4210 • gay/ straight • condo • close to convention center • kids ok • gay-owned • $125-150 (2-night minimum)

W Seattle 1112 Fourth Ave 206/264-6000, 877/WHOTELS (RESERVATIONS ONLY) • gay-friendly • also restaurant • wheelchair access • $229-529

The Warwick Hotel 401 Lenora St (at 4th) 206/443-4300 • gay/ straight • full brkfst • swimming • jacuzzi • kids ok • wheelchair access • $119-245

Wild Lily Ranch B&B 360/793-2103 • popular • mostly gay men • cabins on Skykomish River • 1 hour from Seattle • riverside jacuzzi • swimming • camping available • nonsmoking • gay-owned • $95-110 (couple)

BARS

The Bad Juju Lounge 1518 11th Ave (at Pike) 206/709-9951 • 3pm-2am • gay/ straight • DJ • food served

The Baltic Room 1207 Pine St (at Melrose) 206/625-4444 • 5pm-2am • gay/ straight • live music

Beacon Pub 3057 Beacon Ave S 206/726-0238 • gay/ straight • neighborhood bar

CC Attle's 1501 E Madison (at 15th Ave) 206/726-0565 • 10am-2am, from 8am wknds • popular • mostly gay men • neighborhood bar • videos • also restaurant

Changes 2103 N 45th St (at Meridian) 206/545-8363 • noon-2am • mostly gay men • neighborhood bar • food served • karaoke • videos • wheelchair access

Chapel 1600 Melrose Ave (at E Pine) 206/447-4180 • 5pm-1am, till 2am wknds • gay/ straight • DJ • food served • upscale cocktails

The Crescent Lounge 1413 E Olive Wy (at Bellevue) 206/720-8188 • noon-2am • gay/ straight • neighborhood bar • karaoke nightly • wheelchair access

The Cuff 1533 13th Ave (at Pine) 206/323-1525 • 2pm-2am, after-hours wknds • popular • mostly gay men • dancing/DJ • levi crowd • 5 bar areas • wheelchair access

Double Header 407 2nd Ave S Extension (at Washington) 206/464-9918 • 10am-midnight, till 2am wknds • gay/ straight • neighborhood bar

Elite Tavern 622 Broadway East (at Roy) 206/324-4470 • 10am-2am • lesbians/ gay men • neighborhood bar • beer/ wine only • wheelchair access

Friends Martini Lounge 1509 Broadway (at Neighbours) 206/324-5358

Hana's Teriyaki & Lounge 1914 8th Ave (at Stewart) 206/340-1591 • noon-2am • mostly gay men • dancing/DJ • Korean food 10:30am-7:30pm • wheelchair access

Jade Pagoda 606 Broadway Ave E (at Mercer) 206/322-5900 • 5pm-2am • mostly gay men • neighborhood bar • food served • Chinese/ American • wheelchair access

Manray 514 E Pine (at Belmont) 206/568-0750 • 4pm-2am • mostly gay men • food served • videos

R Place 619 E Pine St (at Boylston) 206/322-8828 • 4pm-2am, from 2pm wknds • mostly gay men • neighborhood bar • dancing/ DJ • food served • karaoke • videos • 3 stories • wheelchair access

Rendezvous 2322 2nd Ave (at Battery) 206/441-5823 • 4pm-2am • gay/ straight • live bands • cabaret • theater • also restaurant

The Seattle Eagle 314 E Pike St (at Bellevue) 206/621-7591 • 2pm-2am • mostly gay men • Vibrator every 3rd Tue for "a club for dykes & their friends" • leather • rock 'n' roll • patio • wheelchair access

Thumpers 1500 E Madison St (at 15th) 206/328-3800 • 11am-2am • popular • mostly gay men • full restaurant • piano bar • videos • more women in dining room • wheelchair access • gay-owned

Timberline Spirits 1828 Yale Ave (at Howell) 206/883-0242 • 6pm-close, from 4pm Sun, clsd Mon • lesbians/ gay men • dancing/DJ • karaoke • country/ western Fri • disco T-dance Sun • cabaret lounge

Watertown 106 1st Ave N (at Denny) 206/284-5003 • 5pm-2am, till 3am Fri, 8pm-3am Sat, clsd Sun-Mon • gay-friendly • dancing/DJ Th-Sat

Wildrose Bar & Restaurant 1021 E Pike St (at 11th) 206/324-9210 • 3pm-2am, till 1am Sun & Mon • mostly women • neighborhood bar • dancing/DJ • karaoke • live shows • food served • wheelchair access

NIGHTCLUBS

Catwalk Club 172 S Washington St (at 2nd) 206/622-1863 • Fri-Sun • gay/ straight • call for events • also restaurant • cover

Century Ballroom 915 E Pine, 2nd flr 206/324-7263 • Outdancing 9:30pm 4th Fri, lessons at 8:30pm • lesbians/ gay men • dancing/DJ • also restaurant

Contour 807 1st Ave (at Columbia) 206/447-7704 • after-hours Fri-Sat w/ fire performances • gay-friendly • dancing/ DJ • also bar & restaurant

Girl4Girl Productions 1700 1st Ave S (at S Massachusetts St, at The Premier) • 3rd Sat only • mostly women • dancing/ DJ • live shows • go-go dancers

Jazz Alley 2033 6th Ave (at Lenora) 206/441-9729 • gay-friendly • call for events & reservations • live music • nonsmoking • cover charge • also restaurant

Neighbours Dance Club 1509 Broadway (at Pike & Pine) 206/324-5358 • 9pm-2am, till 4am Fri-Sat • popular • lesbians/gay men • dancing/DJ • 2 flrs • also 18+ room Th-Sat • young crowd • wheelchair access

Re-bar 1114 Howell (at Boren Ave) 206/233-9873 • 6pm-2am, clsd Mon • popular • gay/straight • more women Sat • dancing/DJ Thu-Sun • cabaret/theater

Showbox 1426 1st Ave (at Pike) 206/628-3151 • gay-friendly • live music venue • cover charge

The Vogue 1516 11th Ave (at Pine) 206/324-5778 • 6pm-2am • gay-friendly • fetish Sun • dancing/DJ • alternative • live shows • drag shows • theme nights

CAFES

Espresso Vivace 901 E Denny Wy #100 206/860-5869, 206/860-2722 • 6:30am-11pm • popular

Insomniax Coffee & Juice 102 15th Ave E 206/322-6477 • 6:30am-8pm, 9am-3pm wknds • wireless internet

RESTAURANTS

1200 Bistro & Lounge 1200 E Pike St (at 12th Ave) 206/320-1200 • dinner only • popular • full bar • gay-owned

Addis Cafe 1224 E Jefferson (at 12th) 206/325-7805 • lunch & dinner • popular • Ethiopian

Al Boccalino 1 Yesler Wy (at Alaskan) 206/622-7688 • lunch Tue-Fri, dinner nightly, clsd Mon • classy southern Italian

The Broadway Grill 314 Broadway E (at E Harrison) 206/328-7000 • 9am-2am, 8am-3am wknds • popular • full bar

Cafe Flora 2901 E Madison St 206/325-9100 • 11:30am-10pm, till 9pm Sun, 9am-2pm wknd brunch, clsd Mon • vegetarian • beer/wine • nonsmoking • wheelchair accessible

Cafe Septieme 214 Broadway Ave E (at Thomas & John) 206/860-8858 • 9am-midnight • popular • lesbians/gay men • also bar

Campagne 86 Pine St (at 1st) 206/728-2800 • dinner only • French • reservations advised • also bar • also Cafe Campagne, 206/728-2233

Dahlia Lounge 2001 4th Ave (at Virginia) 206/682-4142 • lunch Mon-Fri, dinner nightly • some veggie • full bar

Flying Fish 2234 1st Ave (at Bell) 206/728-8595 • lunch Mon-Fri, dinner nightly, bar till 2am • lesbian chef

Glo's 1621 E Olive Wy (at Summitt Ave E) 206/324-2577 • 7am-3pm, till 4pm wknds • brkfst only • popular

Mae's Phinney Ridge Cafe 6410 Phinney Ridge N (at 65th) 206/782-1222 • 7am-3pm • popular • brkfst menu • some veggie • wheelchair access

Mama's Mexican Kitchen 2234 2nd Ave (in Belltown) 206/728-6262 • lunch & dinner • cheap & funky

Queen City Grill 2201 1st Ave (at Blanchard) 206/443-0975 • dinner only • popular • fresh seafood • some veggie • wheelchair access

Rosebud Restaurant & Bar 719 E Pike St (at Harvard Ave) 206/323-6636 • dinner nightly, wknd brunch • nonsmoking

Sunlight Cafe 6403 Roosevelt Wy NE (at 64th) 206/522-9060 • 8am-9pm • vegetarian • beer/wine • wheelchair access

Szmania's 3321 W McGraw St (in Magnolia Bluff) 206/284-7305 • lunch Tue-Fri, dinner nightly, clsd Mon

Teapot Vegetarian House 125 5th Ave E 206/325-1010 • 11:30am-10pm • vegan

Wild Ginger Asian Restaurant & Triple Bar 1400 Western Ave (at Union) 206/623-4450 • lunch Mon-Sat, dinner nightly • popular • bar till 1am

ENTERTAINMENT & RECREATION

Alki Beach Park 1702 Alkai Ave SW, West Seattle • popular on warm days

Gay Bingo 860 Terry Ave N (at S Lake Union Naval Reserve Bldg) 206/323-0069, 206/328-8979 • monthly • run by the Chicken Soup Brigade

Harvard Exit 807 E Roy St 206/781-5755 • rep film theater

Northwest Lesbian & Gay History Museum Project 206/903-9517 • exhibits & publication

The Paramount Theatre 911 Pine St 206/467-5510 • historic Beaux Arts-style theater • tours 10am 1st Sat • live events regularly

Seattle Storm Key Arena 206/217-9622 • check out the Women's National Basketball Association while you're in Seattle

Tacky Tourist Clubs 800/807-5214 • fabulous social events

Bookstores

Bailey/ Coy Books 414 Broadway Ave E (at Harrison) 206/323-8842 • 10am-9pm, till 10pm Fri-Sat, till 7pm Sun • wheelchair access

Edge of the Circle 701 E Pike (at Boylston) 206/726-1999 • noon-9pm • alternative spirituality store

Fremont Place Book Company 621 N 35th (at Fremont Ave N) 206/547-5970 • 10am-8pm, noon-6pm Sun

Left Bank Books 92 Pike St (at 1st Ave) 206/622-0195 • 10am-7pm, 11am-6pm Sun • worker-owned collective • new & used books • LGBT section

Retail Shops

Archie McPhee 2428 NW Market St (in Ballard) 206/297-0240 • 9am-7pm, 10am-6pm Sun • weird & wonderful toys & trinkets • also mail order

Broadway Market 401 E Broadway (at Harrison & Republican) • popular mall full of funky, hip stores

Metropolis 7220 Greenwood Ave N (at 73rd) 206/782-7002 • 10am-7pm, till 6pm Sat, 11am-4pm Sun • cards & gifts

Sunshine Thrift Shops 1718 12th Ave (at Pike/ Broadway) 206/324-9774 • 10am-6pm, clsd Sun • nonprofit for AIDS organizations • call for details • wheelchair access

Publications

Magazine 99 360/312-8068 • arts, entertainment & lifestyle magazine for Pacific NW

Odyssey Magazine Northwest 206/621-8950 • dish on Pacific Northwest's club scene

Pink Pages 773/769-6328 • quarterly LGBT business directory & lifestyle magazine

SGN (Seattle Gay News) 206/324-4297 • weekly LGBT newspaper

The Stranger 206/323-7101 • queer-positive alternative weekly

Spiritual Groups

Dignity Seattle 5751 33rd Ave NE (at 60th St NE, at Methodist church) 206/325-7314 • 6pm Sun • Catholic

Grace Gospel Chapel 2052 64th St NW (at 22nd Ave N), Ballard 206/784-8495 • 11am Sun

MCC 16th Ave NE (at NE 45th St, University district) 206/325-2421 • 5:30pm Sun

Gyms & Health Clubs

Gold's Gym 825 Pike St (at 8th Ave) 206/583-0640 • gay-friendly

Hothouse Spa & Sauna 1019 E Pike St #HH (at 11th, 2 blocks E of Broadway) 206/568-3240 • noon-midnight, clsd Tue • women only • baths • hot tub • massage

Erotica

The Crypt Off Broadway 1113 10th Ave E (at Denny) 206/325-3882 • 9am-midnight, till 1am Fri-Sat, noon-10pm Sun

Fantasy Unlimited 2027 Westlake Ave (at 7th) 206/682-0167 • 24hrs

Hollywood Erotic Boutique 12706 Lake City Wy NE 206/363-0056 • toys • lingerie

Toys in Babeland 707 E Pike (btwn Harvard & Boylston) 206/328-2914 • 11am-10pm, noon-7pm Sun • wheelchair access • lesbian-owned • see ad in New York City, NY

Sequim

Accommodations

Bearheart Inn B&B 1290 Gardiner Beach Rd (at Hwy 101 & Diamond Pt Rd) 360/797-7500, 888/206-0899 • gay/ straight • full brkfst • kids ok • nonsmoking • lesbian-owned • $70-85

Sunset Marine Resort 40 Buzzard Ridge Rd 360/681-4166 • gay-friendly • waterfront cabins • nonsmoking • kids ok • lesbian-owned • $95-165

Spokane

Info Lines & Services

AA Gay/ Lesbian 301 S Freya (at 3rd, at Bethany Presbyterian church) 509/624-1442 • 7pm Wed

Rainbow Regional Community Center 508 W 2nd Ave 509/489-1914 • 10am-6pm, from 2pm Sat, clsd Sun • support groups • events • also art gallery

Accommodations

Montvale Hotel 1005 W First Ave (at Monroe) 509/747-1919, 866/668-8253 • gay-friendly • luxury, boutique hotel • transgender-friendly • also restaurant • gay-owned

Nightclubs

Dempseys Brass Rail 909 W 1st St (btwn Lincoln & Monroe) 509/747-5362 • 3pm-2am, till 4am Fri-Sat • popular • lesbians/gay men • dancing/DJ Th-Sat • drag shows Fri-Sat • also restaurant • wheelchair access

The Merq Cafe & Liquid Lounge 706 N Monroe (at Broadway) 509/325-3871 • 3pm-2am • gay-friendly • neighborhood bar • dancing/DJ • transgender-friendly • food served • live shows • karaoke • drag shows • wheelchair access • gay-owned

RESTAURANTS

Mizuna 214 N Howard 509/747-2004 • lunch Mon-Fri, dinner Tue-Sat • seasonal menu • plenty veggie • full bar

The Top Notch Cafe 825 N Monroe 509/327-7988 • 7am-2pm • homecookin'

BOOKSTORES

Auntie's Bookstore & Cafe 402 W Main St (at Washington) 509/838-0206 • 9am-9pm, till 10pm Fri, 11am-6pm Sun • wheelchair access

PUBLICATIONS

Stonewall News Northwest 509/456-8011 • monthly LGBT newspaper for Spokane & NW

SPIRITUAL GROUPS

Emmanuel MCC 301 S Freya 509/838-0085 • 5pm Sun

Suquamish

INFO LINES & SERVICES

Kitsap Lesbian/ Gay AA 18732 Division Ave NE (at Geneva St) 360/475-0775 • 7:30pm Sun

Tacoma

INFO LINES & SERVICES

AA Gay/ Lesbian 2150 Cushman (at the church) 253/474-8897 • 7:30pm Fri

Rainbow Center 917 Pacific Ave, Ste 304 253/383-2318 • open Mon-Sat • community center • call for meetings & events

Tacoma Lesbian Concern 253/272-3444 • social events • resource list • newsletter

ACCOMMODATIONS

Chinaberry Hill 302 Tacoma Ave N 253/272-1282 • gay-friendly • 1889 Victorian inn • also cottage • very romantic • full brkfst • jacuzzis • kids ok • nonsmoking • $125-195

Sheraton Tacoma Hotel 1320 Broadway Plaza (at S 15th) 253/572-3200, 800/325-3535 • gay-friendly • restaurants & bars • wheelchair access • $99-199

BARS

Airport Tavern 5406 S Tacoma Wy (at 54th) 253/475-9730 • 2pm-2am • lesbians/ gay men • neighborhood bar

On the Rocks 728 Pacific Ave (at 8th) 253/779-4700 • 6pm-2am, till 4am wknds • mostly gay men • neighborhood bar • dancing/DJ • drag shows

NIGHTCLUBS

Club Silverstone 739 1/2 St Helens Ave 253/404-0273 • 11am-2am • lesbians/ gay men • dancing/DJ • karaoke • drag shows • also restaurant

SPIRITUAL GROUPS

New Heart MCC 2150 S Cushman 253/272-2382 • 11am & 6pm Sun

EROTICA

Castle Superstore 6015 Tacoma Mall Blvd 253/471-0391

Vancouver

see also Portland, Oregon

BARS

North Bank 106 W 6th St (at Main) 360/695-3862 • 3pm-2am, from noon wknds • lesbians/ gay men • dancing/DJ • food served • karaoke Mon & Fri • drag shows • wheelchair access

SPIRITUAL GROUPS

MCC of the Gentle Shepherd 2200 Broadway, Stes E&F 360/695-1480 • 10:30am & 6:30pm Sun • wheelchair access

Wenatchee

CAFES

The Cellar Café 249 N Mission St (at 5th) 509/662-1722 • 9am-5pm, 10am-4pm Sat, clsd Sun • some veggie • beer/ wine • patio • lesbian-owned • $5-$9

Whidbey Island

ACCOMMODATIONS

Whidwood Inn 360/679-7472 • gay/ straight • near historic Coupeville • nonsmoking • gay-owned • $69-89

Winthrop

ACCOMMODATIONS

Chewuch Inn 223 White Ave **509/996-3107, 800/747-3107** • gay-friendly • inn & cabins • E of N Cascades Mtns • hot tub • kids ok • nonsmoking • $60-135

WEST VIRGINIA

Statewide

PUBLICATIONS

Graffiti **304/485-1891** • alternative entertainment guide • mostly straight

Beckley

EROTICA

Blue Moon Video 3427 Robert C Byrd Dr (at New River Dr) **304/255-1200**

Charleston

INFO LINES & SERVICES

West Virginia Lesbian/ Gay Coalition **304/344-3953**

BARS

The Tap Room/ Quarrier Diner 1022 Quarrier St **304/342-7453** • 6pm-close • mostly gay men • neighborhood bar • private club

NIGHTCLUBS

Broadway 210 Leon Sullivan Way (at Lee) **304/343-2162** • 4pm-3am, from 1pm wknds • mostly gay men • dancing/DJ • live shows

Trax 504 W Washington (at Maryland) **304/345-8931** • 4pm-3am, till 2:30am Sat • lesbians/ gay men • dancing/DJ Wed-Sun • live shows • drag shows

ENTERTAINMENT & RECREATION

Living AIDS Memorial Garden corner of Washington St E (at Sidney Ave) **304/346-0246**

SPIRITUAL GROUPS

Appalachian MCC 520 Kanawha Blvd W (in Unitarian Bldg) **304/727-7270** • 6pm Sun

Huntington

BARS

The Driftwood-Beehive Lounge 1121 7th Ave (at 11th St) **304/696-9858** • 5pm-3am • lesbians/ gay men • dancing/DJ • karaoke • live shows • videos • young crowd • wheelchair access

The Stonewall 820 7th Ave (enter rear) **304/523-2242** • 8pm-3am, clsd Mon • popular • lesbians/ gay men • dancing/DJ • karaoke • live shows • wheelchair access

RESTAURANTS

Fins Cafe/ Sharkey's 410 10th St **304/523-3200** • dinner Th-Sat, clsd Sun • bar till 3am

EROTICA

House of Video 1109 4th Ave (at 11th) **304/525-2194**

Lewisburg

ACCOMMODATIONS

Lee Street Inn B&B 200 N Lee St **304/647-5599, 888/228-7000** • gay-friendly • grand 1876 house • jacuzzi • garden • teens ok • gay-owned • $75-125

Lost River

ACCOMMODATIONS

The Guesthouse Settlers Valley Wy **304/897-5707** • lesbians/ gay men • full brkfst • also fine-dining restaurant • full bar • swimming • hot tub • gym • nonsmoking • $125-150

Martinsburg

EROTICA

Variety Books & Video 255 N Queen St (at Race) **304/263-4334** • 24hrs

Morgantown

INFO LINES & SERVICES

BGLM (Bisexual, Gay, Lesbian Mountaineers) **304/293-8200** • counseling, referrals & social group

NIGHTCLUBS

Vice Versa 335 High St (enter rear) **304/292-2010** • 8pm-3am Th-Sun • lesbians/ gay men • dancing/DJ • karaoke • live shows • private club • 18+ • wheelchair access

EROTICA

Oasis: The Other Book Store 275 Spruce St **304/291-6425** • noon-4am • books • videos • adult novelties

Parkersburg

BARS

True Colors 515 Market St **304/428-8783** • 7pm-3am • lesbians/ gay men • dancing/DJ • live shows • 18+ • private club

Princeton

EROTICA

Exotic Illusions Adult Bookstore 853 Frontage Rd/ Rte 460 (btwn Bluefield & Princeton) **304/487-2170** • 24hrs

Shepherdstown

ACCOMMODATIONS

Thomas Shepherd Inn 300 W German St (at Duke St) **304/876-3715, 888/889-8952** • gay-friendly • B&B • full brkfst • $100-150

BOOKSTORES

On the Wings of Dreams 129 W German St **304/876-0244** • 11am-6pm, wknd hours vary • metaphysical

Sissonville

RESTAURANTS

Topspot Country Cookin' 7139 Sissonville Rd **304/984-2816** • 7am-8pm, till 7pm Sun, clsd Mon

Upper Tract

ACCOMMODATIONS

Wildernest Inn **304/257-9076** • gay-friendly • full brkfst • hot tub • nonsmoking • $90-110

Waton

ACCOMMODATIONS

Long Fork Campgrounds 114 Longfork Camp Rd (at Charleston Rd), Walton **304/577-9347, 888/598-2267** • mostly men • 40 minutes from Charleston • pool • hot tub • wheelchair access • gay-owned

Wheeling

ACCOMMODATIONS

Best Western Wheeling Inn 949 Main St (at 10th St) **304/233-8500** • gay-friendly • also restaurant • $50-70

BARS

Twice as Nice 1056 Main St **304/232-3440** • 7pm-3am, clsd Mon • lesbians/ gay men • dancing/ DJ • gay-owned

EROTICA

Market St News 1437 Market St (at 14th St) **304/232-2414**

WISCONSIN

Statewide

PUBLICATIONS

Lavender Magazine **612/436-4660, 877/515-9969** • LGBT newsmagazine for MN, WI, IA, ND, SD

Algoma

RETAIL SHOPS

The Flying Pig N6975 Hwy 42 (at Tenth) **920/487-9902** • gay-friendly • 9am-6pm (May-Oct) & 10am-5pm, clsd Wed (Nov-April) • art gallery, beautiful garden & coffee bar • lesbian-owned

Appleton

BARS

Crossroads 1042 W Wisconsin Ave (at Summit) **920/830-1927** • 4pm-2am, till 2:30am Fri-Sat • lesbians/ gay men • dancing/ DJ • drag shows • food served • karaoke

Rascals Bar & Grill 702 E Wisconsin Ave (at Lawe) **920/954-9262** • 5pm-2am, from noon Sun • lesbians/ gay men • fish-fry Fri • patio

SPIRITUAL GROUPS

Angels of Hope MCC 815 N Richmond St **920/991-0128** • 6pm Sun

EROTICA

Eldorado's 2545 S Memorial Dr (at Hwys 47 & 441) **920/830-0042**

Baileys Harbor

ACCOMMODATIONS

Blacksmith Inn on the Shore 8152 Hwy 57 **920/839-9222, 800/769-8619** • gay-friendly • nonsmoking • wheelchair access • $115-235

Cumberland

ACCOMMODATIONS

Wild Iris Shores 2741 11th St **715/822-8594** • log cabins on 38 wooded acres • kids/ pets ok • nonsmoking • wheelchair access • woman-owned/ run • $95-120

Eagle River

ACCOMMODATIONS

The Edgewater Inn & Cottages 5054 Hwy 70 W **715/479–4011, 888/334–3987** • gay/ straight • also waterfront cottages • gay- owned • $39-70/ room & $80-175/ cottage

Eau Claire

INFO LINES & SERVICES

LGBT Community Center of the Chippewa Valley 510 S Farwell St **715/552–5428** • drop-in 7pm-10pm Fri, call for other hours • library & variety of events

BARS

Wolfe's Den 302 E Madison **715/832–9237** • 6pm-2am • mostly gay men • neighborhood bar • bears • karaoke Wed & Sun • drag shows • strippers

NIGHTCLUBS

Scooters 411 Galloway (at Farwell) **715/835–9959** • 3pm-2am • lesbians/ gay men • dancing/DJ • cabaret • drag shows • wheelchair access

Green Bay

INFO LINES & SERVICES

Gay AA 3607 Libal St (at Angels of Hope MCC) **920/494–9904** • 9.30am Sun, call for times & locations

BARS

Brandy's II 1126 Main St (near Webster Ave) **920/437–3917** • 5pm-2am • lesbians/ gay men • neighborhood bar • wheelchair access

Cricket's Fox River Lounge 715 S Broadway **920/884–2835** • 5pm-2am, from 3pm wknds • gay/ straight • live shows

Napalese Lounge 1351 Cedar St **920/432–9646** • 11am-2am, till 2:30am Fri-Sat • mostly gay men • neighborhood bar • DJ Fri- Sat • food served • drag shows • wheelchair access

Sass 840 S Broadway **920/437–7277** • 6pm- 2am, clsd Sun-Tue (summers) • lesbians/ gay men • dancing/DJ wknds

NIGHTCLUBS

The Shelter 730 N Quincy St (at 54302) **920/432–2662** • lesbians/ gay men • dancing/DJ • country/ western • bears • leather • transgender-friendly • food served • karaoke • drag shows • gay-owned

PUBLICATIONS

Quest **920/433–0611, 800/578–3785**

SPIRITUAL GROUPS

Angels of Hope MCC 3607 Libal St **920/983–7453** • 11am Sun

EROTICA

Adult Movieland/Books 'N' Things 836 S Broadway (at 5th) **920/433–9640**

Hayward

ACCOMMODATIONS

The Lake House 5793 Division, Stone Lake **715/865–6803** • lesbians/ gay men • full brkfst • swimming • nonsmoking • kids ok by arrangement • wheelchair access • lesbian- owned • $85-130

Hazelhurst

BARS

Willow Haven Resort/ Supper Club 4877 Haven Dr (at Willow Dam Rd) **715/453–3807** • noon-10pm, full bar open later • gay-friendly • lunch & dinner

Hurley

ACCOMMODATIONS

Anton-Walsh House 202 Copper St (at US Hwy 51) **715/561–2065** • gay-friendly • historic B&B • full brkfst • near skiing & Lake Superior • $75-110

Whitecap Mountains Ski Resort & Skye Golf County Hwy E (at Hwy 77), Montreal **715/561–2227, 800/933–7669** • gay-friendly • resort • full brkfst • kids/ pets ok • swimming • wheelchair access • $45-475

Kenosha

see also Racine

BARS

94 North 6305 120th Ave (on E frontage road of 94) **262/857–3240** • 7pm-2am, till 2:30am Fri-Sat, 3pm-2am Sun, clsd Mon • lesbians/ gay men • dancing/DJ • drag shows

La Crosse

ACCOMMODATIONS

Rainbow Ridge Farms B&B N 5732 Hauser Rd (at County S), Onalaska **608/783–8181** • gay-friendly • working hobby farm on 35 acres • hot tub • nonsmoking • $70-89

Trillium B&B **608/625–4492** • gay-friendly • cottage (sleeps 5) • 35 miles from La Crosse • full brkfst • kids ok • nonsmoking • $60-100

Bars

My Place 3201 South Ave (at East Ave)
608/788–9073 • noon-close • lesbians/ gay
men • friendly neighborhood bar • games •
gay-owned

Players 214 Main **608/784–2353** • 5pm-2am,
from 3pm Fri-Sun, till 2:30am Fri-Sat • popular
• lesbians/ gay men • dancing/DJ • live shows
• transgender-friendly • drag shows •
wheelchair access • gay-owned

Rainbow's End 417 Jay St (at 4th)
608/782–5105 • 2pm-11pm, till 2:30am Th-
Sat, from 3pm Sun • lesbians/ gay men •
neighborhood bar

Bookstores

Pearl Street Books 323 Pearl St
608/782–3424 • 9:30am-8pm, till 9pm Fri,
10am-5pm Sat, noon-5pm Sun • mostly used
• LGBT section

Lake Geneva

Accommodations

Allyn Mansion Inn 511 E Walworth Ave
(btwn 5th & 6th), Delavan **262/728–9090** •
gay/ straight • full brkfst • teens welcome •
nonsmoking • gay-owned • $100-150

Eleven Gables Inn on the Lake 493
Wrigley Dr **262/248–8393** • gay-friendly •
lakefront • full brkfst wknds • nonsmoking •
kids/ pets ok • wheelchair access • $109-330

Madison

Info Lines & Services

LesBiGay Campus Center 800 Langdon,
2nd flr Memorial Union, UW **608/265–3344** •
drop-in 9am-5pm, till 2:30pm Fri, clsd wknds •
social events • general info

OutReach, Inc. 600 Williamson St #P-1
608/255–8582 • 9am-9pm, noon-4pm Sat,
clsd Sun • drop-in center • library • newsletter
• referrals • call for listings & support group
times

Accommodations

Hawks Nest Log Home Rentals 2450,
2455 & 2459 Fairview (at Door Creek Rd),
Stoughton **608/445–7468** • lesbians/ gay men
• log homes on Lake Kegonsa • 20 minutes
from Madison • nonsmoking • lesbian-owned
• $150-190 (for 2)

Prairie Garden B&B W 13172 Hwy 188,
Lodi **608/592–5187, 800/380–8427** • mostly
gay men • 30 minutes N of Madison • full
brkfst • nonsmoking • pets by arrangement •
gay-owned • $90-220

Bars

Club 5 5 Applegate Ct (btwn Fish Hatchery
Rd & W Beltline Hwy) **608/277–9700,
877/648–9700** • 4pm-2am • popular •
lesbians/ gay men • dancing/DJ • karaoke • live
shows • restaurant • also The Foxhole
women's bar & Planet Q video bar • Tue 18+

Green Bush 914 Regent St (at Park)
608/257–2874 • 4pm-midnight, clsd Sun •
gay-friendly • also restaurant

Ray's Bar 2526 E Washington (at North)
608/241–9335 • 3pm-2am, from noon wknds
• lesbians/ gay men • neighborhood bar

Shamrock 117 W Main St (at Fairchild)
608/255–5029 • 11am-2am, from 2pm Sat,
Sun brunch • popular • lesbians/ gay men •
also grill

Nightclubs

Cardinal 418 E Wilson St (at S Franklin)
608/251–0080 • 8pm-2am, clsd Mon • gay-
friendly • more gay 2nd Tue & early Fri •
dancing/DJ • call for events

Club Majestic 115 King St **608/251–2582** •
9pm-2am, from 4pm Fri-Sun, clsd Mon-Tue •
lesbians/ gay men • dancing/DJ • live shows •
18+ Wed

Restaurants

Fyfe's 1344 E Washington (at Dickinson)
608/251–8700 • 11am-2pm & 5pm-close, clsd
Sun • full bar • live entertainment

La Hacienda 515 S Park St **608/255–8227** •
9am-3am • popular • Mexican

Monty's Blue Plate Diner 2089 Atwood Ave
(at Winnebago) **608/244–8505** • 7am-9pm, till
10pm Fri-Sat, from 7:30am wknds • some
veggie • beer/ wine • wheelchair access

Bookstores

**A Room of One's Own Feminist
Bookstore & Coffeehouse** 307 W Johnson
St **608/257–7888** • 8am-8pm, 9am-6pm Sat,
11am-5pm Sun • wheelchair access

Mimosa 260 W Gilman St **608/256–5432** •
11am-7pm, 10am-6pm Sat, noon-5pm Sun •
spiritual

Retail Shops

Look At That 917 Williamson St
608/663–2453 • 11am-8pm, clsd Sun & Mon
• biker leather, clothing & accessories • toys •
lesbian-owned

Piercing Lounge 461 W Gilman (at
University) **608/284–0870, 877/663–2349** •
noon-9pm

Tomboy girl 2334 Atwood Ave (at Ohio St) **608/242–1887** • 11am-6pm, 10am-5pm Sat, till 4pm Sun, clsd Mon • clothing designed w/ the tomboy girl in mind • lesbian-owned

SPIRITUAL GROUPS

Integrity/ Dignity 6205 University Ave (at St Dunstan Episcopal) **608/836–8886** • 6pm 2nd & 4th Sat (except July & Aug)

James Reeb Unitarian Universalist Church 2146 E Johnson St (at 4th St) **608/242–8887** • 10am Sun (summers) • 9am & 11am (winter)

Re-formed Congregation of the Goddess **608/226–9998** • call for gathering times & locations • visitors welcome

EROTICA

A Woman's Touch 600 Williamson (at Gateway Mall) **608/250–1928, 888/621–8880** • 11am-6pm, till 8pm Wed-Th, noon-5pm Sun • wheelchair access

Red Letter News 2528 E Washington (btwn North & Milwaukee) **608/241–9958** • 24hrs

Manitowoc

BARS

RiverBank Lounge 902 Jay St (at 9th St) **920/482–0032** • 5:30pm-close, 6pm-midnight Sun, clsd Mon-Wed • neighborhood bar • dancing/DJ • homemade hors d' oeuvres & desserts • in converted 1901 Victorian bank • gay-owned

Milwaukee

INFO LINES & SERVICES

AA Galano Club 315 W Court #201 (in LGBT Community Center) **414/276–6936** • call 6pm-10pm for meeting schedule

Gay People's Union Hotline 414/645–0585

Milwaukee LGBT Community Center 315 W Court #101 (btwn W Cherry & Galena) **414/271–2656** • 10am-10pm, from 6pm Sat, clsd Sun

ACCOMMODATIONS

Kilbourn Guesthouse 2825 W Kilbourn Ave (at N 28th St) **414/344–3167** • gay/ straight • nonsmoking • gay-owned • $79-159

The Milwaukee Hilton 509 W Wisconsin Ave (at 5th St) **414/271–7250, 800/445–8667** • gay-friendly • food service • swimming

Park East Hotel 916 E State St (at Marshall) **414/276–8800, 800/328–7275** • gay-friendly • also restaurant • wheelchair access • $90-200

BARS

Art Bar 722 E Burleigh St (at Fratney) **414/372–7880** • 4pm-1am, till 2:30am Fri-Sat • gay/ straight • live entertainment • also gallery • gay-owned

Boom/ The Room 625 S 2nd (at W Bruce) **414/277–5040** • 5pm-2am, from 11am Sun • lesbians/ gay men • neighborhood bar • food served • videos • patio • also martini bar

C'est La Vie 231 S 2nd St (at Pittsburgh) **414/291–9600** • 5pm-2:30am • lesbians/ gay men • drag shows

Fluid 819 S 2nd St (at W National) **414/643–5843** • 5pm-2am, till 2:30am Fri-Sat • mostly men • neighborhood bar

Henry's Pub & Grill 2523 E Belleview Pl (at Downer) **414/332–9690** • 3pm-2am • gay/ straight • full menu • wheelchair access

Kathy's Nut Hut 1500 W Scott (at 15th St) **414/647–2673** • 2pm-2am, from noon Fri-Sun • mostly women • neighborhood bar

M&M Club 124 N Water St (at Erie) **414/347–1962** • 11am-2am, from 10:30am Sun • lesbians/ gay men • cabaret • full restaurant • some veggie • Sun brunch • patio • wheelchair access

The Nomad 1403 E Brady St (at Warren) **414/224–8111** • 3pm-2am, from noon wknds • gay-friendly

Redroom Cocktail Lounge 1875 N Humboldt (at Kane) **414/224–7666** • 5pm-2:30am • gay/ straight • coffee bar • patio • wheelchair access

Switch 124 W National Ave (at 1st) **414/220–4340** • 5pm-2am, from 2pm wknds, lesbians/ gay men • neighborhood bar • karaoke • patio

Taylor's 795 N Jefferson St (at Wells) **414/271–2855** • 4pm-2am, 5pm-2:30am Fri-Sat • gay/ straight • neighborhood bar • patio • wheelchair access • gay-owned

The Tazzbah Bar & Grill 1712 W Pierce **414/672–8466** • 11am-2am, till 2:30am Fri-Sat, from noon Sun • mostly gay men • food served

Walker's Pint 818 S 2nd St **414/643–7468** • 4:30pm-2am, till 2:30am Fri-Sat, till midnight Sun, clsd Mon • lesbians/ gay men • neighborhood bar • live shows • karaoke • lesbian-owned

Woody's 1579 S 2nd St (at Lapham St) **414/672–0806** • 4pm-2am, from 2pm wknds • mostly men • neighborhood sports bar

NIGHTCLUBS

Cage/ Etcetera 801 S 2nd St (at National) **414/383-8330** • 5pm-2am, from 8pm wknds • popular • mostly gay men • more women wknds • dancing/DJ • live shows • videos • also martini bar • young crowd • wheelchair access

Club 219 219 S 2nd St (btwn Florida & Pittsburgh) **414/276-2711** • 7pm-2am, from 4pm wknds • lesbians/ gay men • dancing/DJ • multiracial • live shows • drag shows • strippers

Club Anything 807 S 5th St (at National) **414/383-5680** • 9pm-close, from 7pm wknds • gay/ straight • dancing/ DJ • live shows • gothic/ industrial

Mad Planet 533 E Center St **414/263-4555** • gay-friendly • retro dance Fri • dancing/DJ • live shows • live rock/ alternative shows

CAFES

Alterra Coffee Roasters 2211 N Prospect Ave (at North) **414/273-3753** • 6am-10pm, till 11pm Fri-Sat, from 7am Sat, from 8:30am Sun

Fuel Cafe 818 E Center St **414/374-3835** • 7am-11pm, from 9am wknds • infamous for their stong coffee

RESTAURANTS

Barossa 235 S 2nd St (at Oregon) **414/272-8466** • dinner, Sun brunch, clsd Mon • organic • plenty veggie

Cafe Vecchio Mondo 1137 N Old World Third St (at Juneau) **414/273-5700** • dinner, Sun brunch • full bar

Coquette Cafe 316 N Milwaukee St (btwn Buffalo & St Paul) **414/291-2655** • lunch Mon-Fri, dinner nightly, clsd Sun

Out N About 1407 S 1st St (at Greenfield) **414/643-0377** • 4pm-2am, till 2:30am Fri-Sat, from 11am Sun • lesbians/ gay men • also restaurant • Sun brunch • lesbian-owned

---

Milwaukee

WHERE THE GIRLS ARE:
In East Milwaukee south of downtown, spread out from Lake Michigan to S Layton Blvd.

LGBT PRIDE:
June. 414/272-3378, web: www.pridefest.com.

ANNUAL EVENTS:
June-July - Summerfest, web: www.summerfest.com.
August - Wisconsin State Fair 414/266-7000, web: wistatefair.com
September - AIDS Walk 800/348-WALK, web: www.aidswalkwis.org.

CITY INFO:
414/273-7222 or 800/231-0903, web: www.visitmilwaukee.org.

BEST VIEW:
Hyatt's revolving rooftop restaurant, Polaris 414/276-1234.

WEATHER:
Summer temperatures can get up into 90°s. Spring and fall are pleasantly moderate but too short. Winter brings snow, cold temperatures, and even colder wind chills.

TRANSIT:
Yellow Cab 414/271-1800.
Milwaukee Transit 414/344-6711, web: www.ridemcts.com.

ATTRACTIONS:
Annunciation Greek Orthodox Church 414/461-9400.
Breweries.
Grand Avenue.
Mitchell Park Horticultural Conservatory.
Pabst Theatre 414/286-3663, web: www.pabsttheater.org.

The Knick 1030 E Juneau Ave (at Waverly) **414/272-0011** • 11am-midnight, from 9am wknds • popular • some veggie • full bar • wheelchair access

La Perla 734 S 5th St (at National) **414/645-9888** • 11am-10pm, till 11pm Fri-Sat • Mexican • also bar

Range Line Inn 2635 W Mequon Rd, Mequon **262/242-0530** • 4:30pm-close, clsd Sun-Mon, American • reservations recommended

Sanford Restaurant 1547 N Jackson St **414/276-9608** • dinner only, clsd Sun • Milwaukee fine dining Euro-style

---

[**Reply**] [**Forward**]   [**Delete**]

```
Date: Dec 18, 2005 15:20:47
From: Girl-on-the-Go
To: Editor@Damron.com
Subject: Milwaukee
```

>Milwaukee holds a place of honor in the collective dyke cultural memory as the home of TV's *Laverne & Shirley*, a cute couple if we ever saw one. (You didn't really think that big *L* on Laverne's chest was a monogram, did you?)

>You'll find plenty of breweries in this historically German American city...and plenty of lesbians, too. On 2nd Street you will find a number of mixed lesbian/ gay bars including **Club 219** with dancing, shows, and a multiracial clientele and the lesbian-owned bar **Walker's Pint**. Hike over to Scott Street to check out the women's bar **Kathy's Nut Hut.**

>**OutWords** is the LGBT bookstore, and it's got an espresso bar to boot. Beer-drinking cinephiles will appreciate **Rosebud Cinema Drafthouse** in Wauwatosa, where they show mainstream and art house films, and offer nine beers on tap.

>Just an hour and a half west of Milwaukee is Madison—home of the University of Wisconsin, and, from what we hear, a hotbed of academic and cultural feminism. So if you live to make passes at girls who wear glasses—and who wouldn't?—then you'll love Madison. Call the **Campus Women's Center,** the **LesBiGay Campus Center,** or **OutReach** for current women's events. Better still, stop by the feminist bookstore **A Room of One's Own** for a cup of coffee and a good look around. Later, take your face out of that new book and get over to the **Foxhole** (at **Club 5**), the local women's bar.

ENTERTAINMENT & RECREATION

Boerner Botanical Gardens 9400 Boener Dr (in Whitnall Park), Hales Corners **414/525–5601** • 8am-dusk • 40-acre garden & arboretum, garden clsd in winter

Mitchell Park Domes 524 S Layton Blvd (27th St) (at Pierce) **414/649–9800** • 9am-5pm • botanical gardens

Rosebud Cinema & Drafthouse 6823 W North Ave, Wauwatosa **414/607–9672 (INFO)** • mainstream & art house films • food served • full bar

BOOKSTORES

Broad Vocabulary 2241 S Kinnickinnic Ave (at Lincoln) **414/744–8384** • 10am-8pm, 11am-5pm Sun • feminist • also gifts, magazines & more • also hosts readings, events, live music, workshops

OutWords Books, Gifts & Coffee 2710 N Murray Ave (at Park) **414/963–9089** • 11am-9pm, till 10pm Sat, till 6pm Sun • LGBT • pride items • wheelchair access

Peoples' Books 2122 E Locust St (at Maryland) **414/962–0575** • 11am-7pm, till 6pm Sat, clsd Sun

Schwartz Bookstore 2559 N Downer Ave **414/332–1181** • 9am-10pm, till 11pm Fri-Sat, till 9pm Sun

RETAIL SHOPS

Adambomb Gallery 524 S 2nd St (at Bruce) **414/276–2662** • 11am-9pm, clsd Mon • tattoo studio

Miss Groove 1225 E Brady (btwn Arlington & Franklin) **414/298–9185** • 11am-6pm, 10am-5pm Sat, noon-4pm Sun • accessories & gifts • gay-owned

Out of Solitude 918 E Brady (at Astor) **414/223–3101** • 11am-6pm, till 4pm Sat, clsd Sun • jewelry & gifts • gay-owned

Yellow Jacket 2225 N Humboldt Ave (at North Ave) **414/372–4744** • noon-7pm, till 5pm Sun • vintage clothes

PUBLICATIONS

Quest 920/433–0611, 800/578–3785 • good bar list

SPIRITUAL GROUPS

First Unitarian Society 1342 N Astor St (at Ogden) **414/273–5257** • 9:15am & 11:15am Sun, 10am (summers)

Milwaukee MCC 1239 W Mineral (btwn 12th & 13th) **414/383–1100** • 11am Sun

St James Episcopal Church 833 W Wisconsin Ave (at 8th) **414/271–1340** • 10:30am Sun

EROTICA

Booked Solid 7035 Greenfield Ave (at 70th), West Allis **414/774–7210** • 9am-6pm, till 8:30pm Fri, till 4:30pm Sat, till 3pm Sun

Water Front Video 225 N Water St (at Buffalo) **414/278–0636** • 8am-midnight, till 1am Th-Sat • toys • videos

Norwalk

ACCOMMODATIONS

Daughters of the Earth 18134 Index Ave **608/269–5301** • women only • women's land • camping • retreat space • lesbian-owned • $9/ night camping, $15/ night guest rooms

Oshkosh

see also Appleton

EROTICA

Pure Pleasure 1212 Oshkosh Ave (off Hwy 21) **920/235–9727**

Racine

ACCOMMODATIONS

Lochnaiar Inn 1121 Lake Ave (at 11th St) **262/633–3300** • gay-friendly • English Tudor on Lake Michigan • full brkfst • nonsmoking rooms available • wheelchair access • $90-225

BARS

What About Me? 600 6th St (at Villa) **262/632–0171** • 3pm-close, from 7pm Wed-Th & Sat, clsd Sun-Mon • lesbians/ gay men • neighborhood bar

NIGHTCLUBS

JoDee's International 2139 Racine St/ S Hwy 32 (at 22nd) **262/634–9804** • 7pm-close • lesbians/ gay men • dancing/DJ • live shows • karaoke • drag shows • courtyard • park in rear

EROTICA

Racine News & Video 316 Main St (at State) **262/634–9827**

Rhinelander

ACCOMMODATIONS

Musky Bay Resort 3724 N Limberlost Rd
(at County Hwy C) 715/365–7004,
866/855–9971 • gay-friendly • 3 cabins on the
Moens Chain of Lakes • kids/ pets ok •
lesbian-owned • $100-125/ night & $550-650/
week

Woodwind Health Spa & Resort
3033 Woodwind Wy (at S River Rd & Hwy 8)
715/362–8902 • gay/ straight • retreat & spa •
full gourmet brkfst • workshops • swimming •
nonsmoking • wheelchair access • lesbian-
owned • $85-110

Sheboygan

BARS

The Blue Lite 1029 N 8th St (off Rte 143)
920/457–1636 • 7pm-2am, from 3pm Sun •
lesbians/ gay men • neighborhood bar •
dancing/DJ Fri-Sat

CAFES

Wonderful World Coffeehouse 1022
Michigan Ave 920/694–0300 • 6am-10pm, till
1am Fri-Sat • live entertainment Sat • food
served

Stevens Point

BARS

Club Night Out 2533 County Rd M (4 miles
W of town) 715/342–5820 • 8pm-close, clsd
Mon-Tue • mostly men • neighborhood bar •
dancing/ DJ

Mortimer's Lounge 1501 Northpoint Dr (in
Country Springs Inn) 715/341–1340 • gay-
friendly • neighborhood bar • dancing/ DJ •
wheelchair accessible

EROTICA

Eldorado's 3219 Church St (at Business 51
S) 715/343–9877

Sturgeon Bay

ACCOMMODATIONS

The Chadwick Inn 25 N 8th Ave
920/743–2771 • gay-friendly • 1890 Queen
Anne • nonsmoking • lesbian-owned • $100-
135

The Chanticleer Guest House 4072 Cherry
Rd 920/746–0334, 866/682–0384 • popular •
gay-friendly • on 70 acres • swimming • hot
tub • nonsmoking • wheelchair access • gay-
owned • $120-320

Superior

BARS

JT's Bar & Grill 1506 N 3rd St (at Blaknik
Bridge) 715/394–2580 • 3pm-2am, from 1pm
wknds • popular • lesbians/ gay men •
neighborhood bar • dancing/DJ • food served
• karaoke • drag shows • strippers • patio •
wheelchair access

The Main Club 1217 Tower Ave (at 12th)
715/392–1756 • 3pm-2am, till 2:30am Fri-Sat
• popular • mostly gay men • dancing/DJ • live
shows • country/ western • leather • internet
access • wheelchair access

Two Rivers

RESTAURANTS

Cafe Alkamye 1033 22nd St (at Jackson)
920/553–2233 • 11am-9pm, till 10pm Fri-Sat •
European bistro • transgender-friendly • beer/
wine • wheelchair access • gay-owned

Wascott

ACCOMMODATIONS

Wilderness Way 715/466–2635 • women
only • resort property • cabins • camping • RV
sites • swimming • girls 12 years & up ok •
wheelchair access • lesbian-owned •
$14 (camping) & $60-94 (cabins)

Wausau

NIGHTCLUBS

Oz 320 Washington 715/842–3225 • 7pm-
2am, from 3pm Sun • mostly gay men •
dancing/DJ • karaoke • drag shows • videos

Wisconsin Dells

ACCOMMODATIONS

Rainbow Valley Resort 4125 River Rd (Hwy
13) 608/253–1818, 866/553–1818 • lesbians/
gay men • cottages, restaurant & nightclub
(Th-Sat) • 79-209

WYOMING

Cheyenne

INFO LINES & SERVICES

United Gays & Lesbians of Wyoming
307/778–7645 • 10am-3pm Mon-Fri • info •
referrals • also newsletter • support groups •
quarterly social activities

Etna

RETAIL SHOPS

Blue Fox Studio & Gallery 107452 N US
Hwy 89 307/883–3310 • open 7 days • hours
vary • pottery, jewelry & mask studio • local
travel info

Jackson

ACCOMMODATIONS

Bar H Ranch 208/354–2906 • mostly
women • seasonal • authentic working cattle
ranch • women-owned/ run • $125/night,
$750/week (3-night minimum)

Spring Creek Ranch 1800 Spirit Dance Rd
307/733–8833, 800/443–6139 • popular • gay-
friendly • food served • swimming •
nonsmoking rooms available • wheelchair
access • $150-310

ENTERTAINMENT & RECREATION

Fly Fishing Guide Service South Fork of
the Snake River 208/847–5262 • guided trips
on the Snake River • lesbian-owned

Laramie

INFO LINES & SERVICES

Rainbow Resource Center Knight Hall, Rm
112 (at University of Wyoming) 307/766–3478
• 8am-5pm, clsd wknds • safe & supportive
place for LGBT & questioning individuals &
allies • wheelchair access

Riverton

RESTAURANTS

Country Cove 301 E Main (at First)
307/856–9813 • 7am-3pm, till noon Sat, clsd
Sun • plenty veggie • wheelchair access •
women-owned/ run

Sheridan

RESTAURANTS

The Empire Grill 5 E Alger St (at Main)
307/674–4300 • clsd Sun & Mon • fresh
breads & desserts daily • full bar • mention
Damron for a 15% discount • gay-owned

ALBERTA

Calgary

INFO LINES & SERVICES

Front Runners AA 1227 Kensington Close NW (at Hillhurst United Church) **403/777-1212** • 8:30pm Tue, Th & Sat

Gay/ Lesbian Centre & Info Line 223 12th Ave SW #206 **403/234-8973** • 9am-9pm, till 5pm Fri, clsd wknds • many groups

Inside Out 1010, 1202 Centre St **403/234-8973** • 7pm Mon • support group for LGBTQ ages 15-25

ACCOMMODATIONS

11th Street Lodging 403/209-0111 • gay/ straight • kids 10+ ok • "no shoe" policy inside • nonsmoking • gay-owned • Can$47-149

Calgary Westways Guest House 216 25th Ave SW 403/229-1758, 866/846-7038 • gay/ straight • full brkfst • hot tub • nonsmoking • pets ok • gay-owned • Can$55-160

The Foxwood B&B 1725 12th St SW (17th Ave SW) **403/244-6693** • B&B • lesbians/ gay men • nonsmoking • indoor hot tub • some shared baths • gay-owned • Can$90-160

Home Plate Comforts B&B 403/263-2442 • women-only • B&B • full brkfst • jacuzzi • fragrance-free • Can$85-95 lesbian-owned

Westpoint Executive B&B 101 Westpoint Gardens SW (at Old Banff Coach Rd SW) **403/248-5668, 866/592-3974** • gay/ straight • on west side of Calgary • some shared baths • nonsmoking • gay-owned • Can$75-105

BARS

The Backlot 209 10th Ave SW (at 1st St SW) **403/265-5211** • 2pm-2am • mostly gay men • martini lounge • patio • wheelchair access

Detour/ Loading Dock 318 17th Ave SW **403/244-8537** • 3pm-3am • mostly gay men • Girls Night 1st Fri • neighborhood bar • dancing/DJ • also restaurant • drag show Sun

Ming 520 17th Ave SW **403/229-1986** • 4pm-2am • gay-friendly • martini lounge • food served

Money Pennies 1742 10th Ave SW (near 14th St) **403/263-7411** • 11am-close, 10am-10pm Sun • lesbians/ gay men • neighborhood bar • food served • karaoke • rooftop patio • wheelchair access

NIGHTCLUBS

The Warehouse 731 10th Ave SW (alley entrance) **403/264-0535** • 9pm-close Fri-Sat only, after-hours Sat • gay-friendly • dancing/DJ • young crowd • private club • guests welcome

CAFES

Cafe Beano 1613 9th St SW (at 17th Ave) **403/229-1232** • 6am-midnight, from 7am wknds • some veggie • wheelchair access

Timothy's World Coffee 1610 10th St SW (btwn 16th & 17th Ave) **403/244-7750** • 6am-11pm, till midnight Fri-Sat, from 7am Sat, 8am-10pm Sun • lesbians/ gay men • some veggie • patio • wheelchair access

RESTAURANTS

Melrose Cafe & Bar 730 17th Ave SW (at 7th St) **403/228-3566** • 11am-midnight, from 10am wknds • full bar till 2am • patio

Thai Sa-On 351 10th Ave SW (at 4th) **403/264-3526** • lunch & dinner, clsd wknds • Thai

Victoria's 306 17th Ave SW (at 3rd) **403/244-9991** • lunch, dinner, wknd brunch • homecooking • some veggie • full bar • wheelchair access

Wicked Wedge Pizza 618 17th Ave SW (at 6th St) **403/228-1024** • 11am-close, open late Fri-Sat

BOOKSTORES

A Woman's Place 2030 34th Ave SW (at 19th St SW) **403/263-5256** • 10am-6pm, from noon Wed, clsd Sun • women's bookstore • large LGBT section • wheelchair access

Daily Globe News Shop 1004 17th Ave SW (at 10th St) **403/244-2060** • 9am-11pm, till 10pm Sun • periodicals

Self Connection Books 4004 19th St NW **403/284-1486** • 10am-6pm, till 8pm Th, till 5pm Sat, clsd Sun • also 10816 Macleod Trail SE, 403/ 225-8887

With the Times 2203 4th St SW (at 22nd Ave) **403/244-8020** • 9am-11pm

RETAIL SHOPS

Priape 1322 17th Ave SW (enter on 16th) **403/215-1800, 800/461-6969 #25** • noon-9pm, till 6pm Sun • clubwear • leather • books • toys & more

PUBLICATIONS

Perceptions 306/244-1930 • covers the Canadian prairies

SPIRITUAL GROUPS

Integrity Calgary 1121 14th Ave SW (at St Stephen's Church) **403/701-5699** • worship 7pm 2nd Sun of the month • inter-denominational Christian fellowship

EROTICA

Adult Depot 524 6th Ave SE **403/264-7399** • clsd Sun • also 140 58th Ave SE, 403/258-2777

B&D Emporium 829 17th Ave SW **403/265-7789** • 11am-6pm, noon-5pm Sun • drag/ fetish items

Edmonton

INFO LINES & SERVICES

AA Gay/ Lesbian 12530 110th Ave (at Unitarian church, Green Room) **780/424-5900** • 8pm Fri, also 8pm Mon & Wed • call for location

Pride Centre of Edmonton 10010 - 109 St **780/488-3234** • 1:30pm-5:30pm & 7pm-10pm, clsd wknds • also youth group 7pm Sat

Womonspace 10010 - 109 Street (Pride Centre of Edmonton) **780/482-1794** • dances & other events

ACCOMMODATIONS

Labyrinth Lake Lodge **780/878-3301** • gay/ straight • lodge on private lake • hot tubs • kids/ pets ok • Can$200-250

Northern Lights B&B **780/483-1572** • lesbians/ gay men • full brkfst • swimming • gay-owned • Can$60-70

BARS

Boots/ Garage Burger Bar 10242 106th St (at 103rd Ave) **780/423-5014** • 3pm-1am • cafe 11am-8pm, till 10pm Fri • mostly gay men • dancing/DJ • drag shows • private club • wheelchair access

Prism 10524 101 St **780/990-0038** • 4pm-close, clsd Sun • mostly women • neighborhood bar • dancing/DJ • also restaurant • karaoke Tue • wheelchair access

The Roost 10345 104th St **780/426-3150** • 8pm-3am, clsd Mon • lesbians/ gay men • dancing/DJ • drag shows • strippers Wed • private club • patio

Woody's Pub & Cafe 11723 A Jasper (above Buddy's) **780/488-6557** • noon-12:30am, till 2am Fri-Sat • lesbians/ gay men • neighborhood bar • food served

NIGHTCLUBS

Buddy's Nite Club 11725 B Jasper **780/488-6636** • 9pm-3am, from 8pm Fri • lesbians/ gay men • dancing/DJ

RESTAURANTS

Cafe de Ville 10137 124th St (side entrance) **780/488-9188** • 11:30am-midnight Fri-Sat, 9:30am-2:30pm & 5pm-10pm Sun • nonsmoking • reservations recommended

ENTERTAINMENT & RECREATION

Gaywire CJSR FM 88.5 **780/492-5244** • 6pm-7pm Th • LGBT radio

BOOKSTORES

Audrey's Books 10702 Jasper Ave (at 107th) **780/423-3487** • 9am-9pm, 9:30am-5:30pm Sat, noon-5pm Sun • large LGBT section • wheelchair access

The Front Page 10356 Jasper Ave (btwn 103rd & 104th St) **780/426-1206** • 9am-8pm, 10am-6pm Sat, clsd Sun • periodicals

Greenwood's Bookshoppe 7925 104th St (at 80th) **780/439-2005, 800/661-2078** • 9am-9pm, till 5:30pm Sat, noon-5pm Sun

RETAIL SHOPS

Divine Decadence 10441 82nd Ave (at 105th) **780/439-2977** • hip fashions • accessories

PUBLICATIONS

Times .10 **780/415-5616**

SPIRITUAL GROUPS

Lambda Christian Community Church 11148 84th Ave (at Garneau United Church) **780/887-8611** • 7pm Sun

Lethbridge

INFO LINES & SERVICES

GALA/LA (Gay/ Lesbian Alliance of Lethbridge & Area) **403/308-2893** • peer support line 7pm-11pm Mon & Wed • coffee night Wed • dance last Sat • movie nights • youth group • also newsletter

BRITISH COLUMBIA

Birken

ACCOMMODATIONS

Birkenhead Resort Portage Rd 604/452-3255 • gay-friendly • cabins • campsites • hot tub • swimming • pets ok • also restaurant • lesbian-owned • Can$80-144

Chilliwack

RESTAURANTS

Bravo Restaurant & Lounge 46224 Yale Rd (at Nowell St) 604/792-7721 • 5pm-close, clsd Sun-Mon • also available for private functions • martinis • wheelchair access • gay-owned

Gibsons

ACCOMMODATIONS

Canoe Pass Seaside Cottage 604/687-7798, 866/587-7798 • gay/ straight • 2 self-contained suites • gay-owned • Can$100-350

Gulf Islands

INFO LINES & SERVICES

Gays & Lesbians of Salt Spring Island (GLOSSI) PO Box 644, Salt Spring Island V8K 2W2 250/537-7773, 250/537-0629 • social events • newsletter • support • info line

ACCOMMODATIONS

Anne's Oceanfront Hideaway B&B 168 Simson Rd, Salt Spring Island 250/537-0851, 888/474-2663 • gay-friendly • full brkfst • ocean views • nonsmoking • wheelchair access • Can$195-265

Bellhouse Inn 29 Farmhouse Rd, Galiano Island 250/539-5667, 800/970-7464 • gay/ straight • historic waterfront inn • full brkfst • nonsmoking • Can$85-195

Birdsong B&B 153 Rourke Rd, Salt Spring Island 250/537-4608 • gay/ straight • CAN$125-160

The Blue Ewe Private Cabin 1207 Beddis Rd, Salt Spring Island 250/537-9344 • lesbians/ gay men • hot tub w/ ocean view • nonsmoking • gay-owned • Can$150-175

Fulford Dunderry Guest House 2900 Fulford-Ganges Rd, Salt Spring Island 250/653-4860 • gay-friendly • oceanfront guesthouse close to pub, bakery, stores & kayak rental shop • gay-owned

Hawthorne House 6436 Porlier Pass Rd, Galiano Island 250/539-5815 • gay/ straight • guesthouse • sleeps 10 • nonsmoking • wheelchair access • lesbian-owned • Can$150-250

Hummingbird Lodge B&B 1597 Starbuck Ln (at Whalebone Dr), Gabriola 250/247-9300, 877/551-9383 • gay-friendly • private, luxurious atmosphere • close to beaches & kayaking • Can$89-139

Island Farmhouse B&B 185 Horel Rd W, Salt Spring Island 250/653-9898, 877/537-5912 • lesbians/ gay men • cottage • kids/ pets ok • nonsmoking • lesbian-owned • Can$120-160

The Owl Tree B&B 124 Webster, Salt Spring Island 250/653-2015 • gay/ straight • hot tub • Can$99-175

Sun Raven Lodge 1356 MacKinnon Rd (at Ferry Terminal), North Pender Island 250/629-6216 • mostly women • rental cottage • sauna • swimming • nonsmoking • lesbian-owned • Can$65-110

Tutu's B&B 3198 Jemima Rd, Denman Island 250/335-0546, 877/560-8888 • gay/ straight • lakefront • private dock • swimming • Can$50-90

Mission

EROTICA

XXXtreme Adult 115 B 32423 Lougheed Hwy 604/814-0488

Nanaimo

ACCOMMODATIONS

Dorchester Hotel 70 Church St 250/754-6835, 800/661-2449 • gay-friendly • $89-115

BARS

70 Below 70 Church St (under hotel) 250/716-0505 • 8pm-close, from 5pm Fri-Sun • lesbians/ gay men • neighborhood bar • dancing/DJ • alternative • live shows • karaoke • videos

Okanagan Lake

includes Kaleden, Kelowna, Oliver, Penticton & Vernon

INFO LINES & SERVICES

Okanagan Rainbow Coalition 991 Richter St, Kelowna 250/860-8555 • 24hr recorded info • support groups • social events • dances

Accommodations

Morningside B&B 1645 Carmi Ave (at Government St), Penticton **250/492–5874** • gay/ straight • full brkfst • shared baths • nonsmoking • Can$65-75

Rainbow's End 8282 Jackpine Rd, Vernon **250/542–4842** • lesbians/ gay men • full brkfst • hot tub • some shared baths • pets ok • wheelchair access • gay-owned • $35-45

Bars

Eagles Nest B&B 15620 Commonage Rd (at Carrs Landing Rd), Kelowna **250/766–9350, 866/766–9350** • mostly men • full brkfst • hot tub • gay-owned • $80-$150

Cafes

Bean Scene 274 Bernard Ave, Kelowna **250/763–1814** • 7am-10pm, till 11pm Fri-Sat • patio • wheelchair access

Restaurants

Greek House 3159 Woodsdale Rd, Kelowna **250/766–0090** • 4pm-9pm • cont'l

Powell River

Accommodations

Beacon B&B & Spa 3750 Marine Ave **604/485–5563, 877/485–5563** • gay-friendly • full brkfst • hot tub • massage • nonsmoking • wheelchair access • Can$85-155 + tax

Wilde Road Farm & Guesthouse 7420 Wilde Rd **604/483–4923** • gay/ straight • farmhouse & cabin close to ocean • full brkfst • kids/ pets ok • Can$30-50

Prince George

Info Lines & Services

GALA North **250/562–6253** • 24hr recorded info • social group • call for drop-in hours & location

Erotica

XXXtreme Adult 1412 Patricia Blvd **250/614–1411** • 24hrs • videos • magazines • toys • lingerie

Prince Rupert

Info Lines & Services

Prince Rupert Gay Info Line **250/627–8900**

Qualicum Beach

Accommodations

Bahari Oceanside Inn 5101 Island Hwy W **877/752–9278** • gay-friendly • full brkfst • hot tub • apt rental • nonsmoking • kids ok • Can$145-290

Tofino

Accommodations

Beachwood 1368 Chesterman Beach Rd **250/725–4250** • private house • steps to the beach • gay-friendly • gay-owned • $125-185

BriMar B&B 1375 Thornberg Crescent **250/725–3410, 800/714–9373** • gay/ straight • on the beach • full brkfst • teens ok • Can$110-200

Eagle Nook Wilderness Resort & Spa Barkley Sound **800/760–2777** • gay-friendly • private log cabins • gourmet meals • "all the comforts of a four-star resort" • adventure tours include kayaking, fishing & heli-venturing • health spa

Lone Cone Guest Suites 170 2nd St **250/725–3394** • gay/ straight • nonsmoking • pets ok • woman-owned/ run • Can$75-220

West Wind 1321 Pacific Rim **250/725–2777** • mostly gay men • cottage • 5 minutes from beach • hot tub • nudity ok • gym • sundecks • nonsmoking • lesbian & gay-owned • Can$125-195

Restaurants

Blue Heron 634 Campbell St **250/725–4266** • 7am-10pm • full bar • wheelchair access

Vancouver

Info Lines & Services

AA Gay/ Lesbian **604/434–3933**

The Greater Vancouver Pride Line **604/684–6869, 800/566–1170** • 7pm-10pm • info & support

Vancouver Gay/ Lesbian Centre 1170 Bute St (btwn Davie & Pendrell Sts) **604/684–5307, 800/566–1170** • also Out on the Shelves LGBT lending library • workshops • youth groups

Accommodations

A Place at Penny's 810 Commercial Dr (at Venables) **604/254–2229** • gay-friendly • antique-decorated B&B • kitchens • nonsmoking • kids/ pets ok • wheelchair access • $45-100

Aberdeen Mansion 1110 Victoria Dr **604/254–2229** • gay-friendly • B&B • $50-120

Absolutely Fabulous B&B at Johnson Heritage House 2278 W 34th Ave (at Vine) **604/266-4175** • gay-friendly • classic Craftsman home • full brkfst • nonsmoking • Can$96-154

Accommodations by Pillow Suites 2859 Manitoba St (btwn 12th & 13th Aves) **604/879-8977** • gay-friendly • apts w/ private entrances • kitchens • fireplaces • kids ok • wheelchair access • women-owned/ run • Can$85-255

Reply **Forward** **Delete**

Date: Dec 15, 2005 15:18:21
From: Girl-on-the-Go
To: Editor@Damron.com
Subject: Vancouver

>Just three hours north of Seattle is Vancouver, one of the most beautiful cities in the world. Much of its charm and attraction lie in natural scenery and outdoor activities. Great skiing is close by, and snow bunnies might want to schedule their trip to Vancouver around **Altitude,** Whistler's annual LGBT ski week (www.outontheslopes.com).

>Be sure to visit Stanley Park, the largest city park in North America. There you can see the Aquarium, the Zoo, and famous Native American totem poles. Also worth a visit is the historic Gastown district: a lively area of boutiques, antique shops, and a vast array of restaurants.

>Once you've seen these sites, it's time to appreciate the beauty of the women of Vancouver. Looking for a little flava? Check out **Lick,** Vancouver's only all-girl-operated queer nightclub. Or bust a move at one of the women's nights at a mixed bar such as **23 West.** If you are plugged in, log on to **www.flygirlproductions.com** to find out about the current line-up of girl parties in the city.

>For bookstores, try **Women in Print** or the famous LGBT bookstore, **Little Sister's.** At either one, you can pick up a copy of **Xtra! West,** British Columbia's splashy LGBT paper. Stop by **Melriches** for coffee and excellent girl-watching, and don't forget to check out **Womyn's Ware** for all your erotica needs.

>Vegetarians will fare well at **Naam** or **Dish,** the only vegetarian fast-food place we know of. Vancouver has tons of lesbian-friendly services, so inquire at the **Vancouver Gay/Lesbian Centre** to find the perfect activity.

Anthem House/ "O Canada" House
1114 Barclay St (at Thurlow) **604/688–0555, 877/688–1114** • gay/ straight • restored 1897 Victorian home • full brkfst • gay-owned • Can$135-265

Barclay House B&B 1351 Barclay St (at Jervis) **604/605–1351, 800/971–1351** • gay/ straight • restored Victorian • full brkfst • nonsmoking • gay-owned • $89-143

The Buchan Hotel 1906 Haro St (btwn Denman & Gilford) **604/685–5354, 800/668–6654** • gay-friendly • some shared baths • nonsmoking • kids ok • Can$45-135

Columbia Cottage B&B 205 W 14th Ave (at Manitoba) **604/874–7787** • gay-friendly • 1920s Tudor • full brkfst • nonsmoking • kids ok • Can$95-135 (winter rates lower)

Comfort Inn Downtown 654 Nelson St (at Granville St) **604/605–4333, 888/605–5333** • gay/ straight • hip boutique-style hotel in the heart of entertainment district • also Doolin's Irish Pub & Restaurant • gay-owned • Can$69-199 • ask for IGLTA Pride rate (10% off)

Downtown Suites Ltd/ Furnished Suites
604/694–8806, 877/454–8179 • gay-friendly • condos • swimming • kids ok • Can$1,110-3,500 (month)

Dufferin Hotel 900 Seymour St (at Smithe) **604/683–4251, 877/683–5522** • gay/ straight • restaurant • kids ok • $49-110 • also 3 bars • mostly men • karaoke • live shows

▲ **Hawks Ave B&B** 734 Hawks Ave **604/728–9441, 604/253–0989** • women only • town house • nonsmoking • near downtown • CAN$90

Hostelling International—Vancouver Central 1025 Granville St **604/685–5335, 888/203–8333** • gay/ straight • hostel right on Granville St • kids ok • also bar • wheelchair access • Can$20-26 (dorms)/ Can$59-68 (privates)

Hostelling International—Vancouver Downtown 1114 Burnaby St **604/684–4565, 888/203–4302** • gay/ straight • hostel in West End • kids ok • travel agent in lobby • wheelchair access • Can$20-28 (dorms)/ Can$59-77 (privates)

The Langtry 968 Nicola St **604/687–7892, 800/769–7892** • gay/ straight • B&B apts in West End • nonsmoking • gay-owned • Can$80-225

Les n' Bo's Escape for Womyn
604/886–4227 • women only • cabin rental • 40-min ferry ride from Vancouver • sauna • steps to beach • kids/ pets ok • $90

The Manor Guest House 345 W 13th Ave (at Cambie) **604/876-8494** • gay-friendly • full brkfst • hot tub • some shared baths • also apt available • nonsmoking • $57-111

Nelson House B&B 977 Broughton St (btwn Nelson & Barclay) **604/684-9793, 866/684-9793** • lesbians/ gay men • Edwardian mansion • full brkfst • jacuzzi in suite • sundeck • lesbian & gay-owned • Can$68-198

Vancouver

WHERE THE GIRLS ARE:
In the West End, between Stanley Park and Gastown, or exploring the beautiful scenery elsewhere.

LGBT PRIDE:
August. 604/687-0955, web: www.vanpride.bc.ca, www.rapturepridevancouver.com.

ANNUAL EVENTS:
January - New Year's Day Polar Bear Swim.
January-February - Gay & Lesbian Ski Week, web: www.outontheslopes.com.
May - Vancouver International Marathon 604/872-2928, web: www.adidasvanmarathon.ca
June - Dragon Boat Festival 604/688-2382, web: www.adbf.com
June-July - Vancouver Int'l Jazz Festival 604/872-5200, web: www.jazzvancouver.com
July - Folk Music Festival 604/602-9798, web: www.thefestival.com
August - Queer Film & Video Festival 604/844-1615, web: www.outonscreen.com
September/October - International Film Festival 604/685-0260, web: www.viff.org.

CITY INFO:
604/683-2000, web: www.tourismvancouver.com

BEST VIEW:
Biking in Stanley Park, or on a ferry between peninsulas and islands. Atop one of the surrounding mountains.

WEATHER:
It's cold and wet in the winter (32-45°F), but it's absolutely gorgeous in the summer (52-75°F)!

TRANSIT:
Yellow Cab 604/681-1111.
Vancouver Airporter 604/946-8866, web: www.yvrairporter.com.
TransLink 604/953-3333, web: www.translink.bc.ca
A Visitors' Map of all bus lines is available through the tourist office.

ATTRACTIONS:
Capilano Suspension Bridge, web: www.capbridge.com
Chinatown
Gastown
Science World 604/443-7443, web: www.scienceworld.bc.ca
Stanley Park, web: www.seestanley-park.com
Van Dusen Botanical Gardens 604/878-9274, web: www.vandusengarden.org.

Opus Hotel 322 Davie St (Yaletown) 604/642-6787, 866/642-6787 • gay-friendly • hip luxury boutique hotel • also bar & Elixer French brasserie • wheelchair access • Can$299-1,500

Penny Farthing Inn 2855 W 6th Ave (at MacDonald) 604/739-9002, 866/739-9002 • gay-friendly • 1910 heritage house in Kitsilano • full brkfst • nonsmoking • kids 12 years & up • Can$85-180

River Run Cottages 4551 River Rd W, Ladner 604/946-7778 • gay-friendly • on the Fraser River • full brkfst • wheelchair access • Can$130-210

Rural Roots B&B 604/856-2380 • lesbians/ gay men • 1 hour from Vancouver • full brkfst • nudity ok at hot tub • nonsmoking • wheelchair access • gay-owned • $50-75

Stay 'n Touch Guesthouse 1060 Alberni St, Apt 408 (at Burrard St) 604/681-2246 • women-only apt • jacuzzi • swimming • lesbian-owned • $75

Treehouse B&B 2490 W 49th Ave (btwn Larch & Balsam) 604/266-2962, 877/266-2960 • gay-friendly • full brkfst • jacuzzi • Can$115-175

The West End Guest House 1362 Haro St (at Broughton) 604/681-2889, 888/546-3327 • gay/ straight • 1906 historic Victorian • full brkfst • nonsmoking • gay-owned • Can$95-255

Bars

Dufferin Hotel 900 Seymour St (at Dufferin Hotel) 604/683-4251 • noon-2am, till midnight Sun • from noon • lesbians/gay men • 3 bars (tavern, pub & lounge) • karaoke • live shows • drag shows • strippers

The Fountainhead Pub 1025 Davie St 604/687-2222 • 11am-midnight, till 2am Fri-Sat • wknd brunch • lesbians/gay men • neighborhood bar • wknd brunch • transgender-friendly • patio

Gerard Lounge 845 Burrard St (in Sutton Place Hotel) 604/682-5511 • 11:30am-1am, 4:30pm-midnight Sun • gay-friendly • food served • great martinis

Lotus Lounge/ Honey 455 Abbott St (at Pender, in The Lotus Hotel) 604/685-7777 (HOTEL #) • clsd Sun • gay/ straight • dancing/DJ • food served • BodyPerveFetish Social last Sat

The Oasis 1240 Thurlow (at Davie) 604/685-1724 • 3:30pm-midnight, till 1am Fri-Sat • mostly gay men • martini bar • live shows • piano • tapas menu

Sugar Daddy's 1262 Davie St (at Jervis St) 604/632-1646 • 11am-11pm, till 1am Fri-Sat, from 10am wknds for brunch • lesbians/ gay men • video & sports bar • food served

Nightclubs

816 Granville/ The World 816 Granville • 1am-6am Fri, midnight-7am Sat • mostly gay men • dancing/DJ

Celebrities 1022 Davie St (at Burrard St) 604/681-6180 • lesbians/ gay men • more women Fri for Go • dancing/DJ

Club 23 West 23 W Cordova (at Carrall) 604/662-3277 • 10pm-4am Fri-Sat • lesbians/ gay men • Sin City 2nd Sat (fetish) • Z Girl 3rd Sat • mostly women • dancing/DJ • Drag King Vancouver 4th Sat

Drag King Vancouver 23 W Cordova (at Club 23 West) 604/662-3277 • from 9pm 4th Sat • mostly women • drag shows • cover charge

Flygirl Productions 604/839-9819 • mostly women • dance parties & events • check local listings for info

Go 1022 Davie St (at Celebrities) 604/681-6180 • Fri night only • mostly women • dancing/DJ

Lick 455 Abbott St (at Pender, in The Lotus Hotel) 604/685-7777 (HOTEL #) • mostly women • dancing/DJ

The Odyssey 1251 Howe St (at Davie) 604/689-5256 • 9pm-2am, till 3am Fri-Sat • popular • mostly gay men • dancing/DJ • drag shows • young crowd • theme nights • patio

Shine 364 Water St 604/408-4321 • 9pm-midnight Sun only for Nice • lesbians/ gay men • dancing/DJ

Skybar 670 Smithe St (Yaletown) 604/697-9199, 604/697-0990 • clsd Mon-Tue • gay/ straight • dancing/ DJ • food served • 3 flrs • rooftop patio

Z Girl 23 W Cordova (at Club 23 West) 604/837-7063 • 9pm-2am 3rd Sat • mostly women • dancing/DJ • hip-hop, funk, R&B

Cafes

Coffee A Go-Go 829 Davie St 604/687-2909 • 7am-9pm, 9am-6pm wknds • wireless internet • local art • food served

Delaney's 1105 Denman St 604/662-3344 • 6am-11pm, from 6:30am wknds • coffee shop

Melriches Coffeehouse 1244 Davie St 604/689-5282 • 6am-11pm, from 7am wknds

Sugar & Sugar 99 Powell St (in Gastown) 604/609-9939 • 10am-5pm, clsd wknds • art gallery & cocktail lounge

Sweet Revenge 4160 Main St (at 26th) **604/879-7933** • 7pm-midnight, till 1am Fri-Sat, from 2pm Sun • clsd Tue-Wed • patisserie • gay-owned

Restaurants

Accents Restaurant 1967 W Broadway (at Arbutus) **604/734-6660** • lunch noon-3pm Tue-Fri, dinner 5:30pm-close Tue-Sun • European/ int'l fine-dining • live shows Fri-Sat • gay-owned

Bin 941 941 Davie St **604/683-1246** • 5pm-2am, till midnight Sun • tiny tapas parlor • popular • also 1521 W Broadway, 604/734-9421

Café Deux Soleils 2094 Commercial Dr **604/254-1195** • 8am-midnight, till 5pm Sun • lesbians/ gay men • lots of veggie • live shows

Cafe Luxy 1235 Davie St (btwn Bute & Jervis) **604/669-5899** • 11am-10:30pm, wknd brunch 9am-3pm • some veggie • full bar • wheelchair access • live jazz

Chianti's 1850 W 4th Ave (at Burrard) **604/738-8411** • 11am-10pm, till 11pm Fri-Sat, from 3pm Sun

Cincin 1154 Robson St (off Bute) **604/688-7338** • lunch Mon-Fri, dinner nightly • Italian/ Mediterranean • full bar

Delilah's 1789 Comox St (at Denman) **604/687-3424** • 5:30pm-11pm • tapas menu • full bar • extensive martini menu • wheelchair access

The Dish 1068 Davie St **604/689-0208** • 7am-10pm, 9am-9am Sun • lowfat vegetarian fast food • gay-owned

Elbow Room Café 560 Davie St (at Seymour) **604/685-3628** • 8am-4pm, till 5pm wknds • great brkfast

Glowbal Grill & Satay Bar 1079 Mainland St (Yaletown) **604/602-0835** • lunch, dinner, brunch wknds • eclectic menu • martinis, extensive wine list • also check out Afterglow next door, nightly 6pm-late

Hamburger Mary's 1202 Davie St (at Bute) **604/687-1293** • 8am-3am, till 4am Fri-Sat, till 2am Sun • some veggie • full bar

Havana 1212 Commercial Dr **604/253-9119** • 11am-11pm, from 10am wknds • popular • Cuban fusion • full bar • patio • also gallery & theater

India Gate 616 Robson St (at Granville) **604/684-4617** • lunch Mon-Sat, dinner nightly

Jupiter Cafe 1216 Bute St (at Davie St) **604/609-6665** • live jazz Tue-Th, DJ's Fri-Sat

Lickerish 903 Davie St **604/696-0725** • 5:30pm-midnight, till 1am Th-Sun • global cuisine • cocktail lounge

Martini's Whole Wheat Pizza 151 W Broadway (btwn Cambie & Main) **604/873-0021** • 11am-2am, from 2pm Sat, till 1am Sun • great pizza • full bar

Naam 2724 W 4th St (at MacDonald) **604/738-7151** • 24hrs • vegetarian • wheelchair access

Shiraz 911 Denman St (at Barclay) **604/697-0501** • lunch Wed-Sun, dinner nightly • live jazz • full bar • gay/ straight

Zin Restaurant 1277 Robson St (in Pacific Palisades Hotel) **604/408-1700** • 7pm-midnight, till 1am Fri-Sat, from 8am wknds • contemporary int'l • trendy crowd

Entertainment & Recreation

Capilano Suspension Bridge 3735 Capilano Rd, N Vancouver **604/985-7474**

Cruisey T leaves from N foot of Denman St (at Harbor Cruises) **604/551-2628** • Sun (seasonal) • 4-hour party cruise around Vancouver Harbour • lesbians/ gay men • dancing/DJ • live shows • food served • Can$25 • tickets at Little Sisters, 1238 Davie, or online at www.cruiseyt.com

Laff Riot Girls **604/291-0291** • stand-up comedienne group • profits go to community groups

Lotus Land Tours 1251 Cardero St #2005 **604/684-4922, 800/528-3531** • day paddle trips, whale-watching trips • no experience necessary (price includes pickup & gourmet meal)

Queer FM CITR 101.9 FM **604/822-1242** • 6pm-8pm Sun • political & social issues in queer community

Rockwood Adventures 839 W 1st St #C, North Vancouver **604/980-7749, 888/236-6606** • rain forest walks for all levels w/ free hotel pick-up

Sunset Beach right in the West End • home of Vancouver AIDS memorial

Bookstores

Little Sister's 1238 Davie St (btwn Bute & Jervis) **604/669-1753, 800/567-1662 (IN CANADA ONLY)** • 10am-11pm • popular • LGBT • wheelchair access • please support this great store in their on-going legal battle against Canada Customs by buying a book today

RETAIL SHOPS

Mack's Leathers 1043 Granville (at Nelson) **604/688-6225** • 11am-7pm, noon-8pm Th-Fri • also body piercing

Next Body Piercing 1068 Granville St (at Nelson) **604/684-6398** • noon-6pm, 11am-7pm Fri-Sat • also tattooing

State of Mind 1100 Davie St (at Thurlow) **604/682-7116** • 10am-6pm • designer queer clothes

PUBLICATIONS

Magazine 99 360/312-8068 (WA #) • arts, entertainment & lifestyle magazine for Pacific NW

Odyssey Magazine Northwest 206/621-8950 • dish on Pacific Northwest's club scene

Xtra! West 604/684-9696 • LGBT newspaper

SPIRITUAL GROUPS

Christ Alive! MCC 1155 Thurlow **604/739-7959** • 7:15pm Sun

Dignity/ Integrity 604/432-1230 • call for info

GYMS & HEALTH CLUBS

Fitness World 1214 Howe St (at Davie) **604/681-3232** • gay-friendly • day passes $15

EROTICA

Love's Touch 1069 Davie St **604/681-7024**

Source Video 2838 E Hastings St **604/251-9191** • 24hrs • also 7994 Granville St, 604/264-4446

Tom's Video 2887 Granview Hwy (at Renfew) **604/433-1722** • 24hrs

Womyn's Ware 896 Commercial Dr (at Denables, in East End) **604/254-2543, 888/WYM-WARE (ORDERS ONLY)** • 11am-6pm, till 7pm Th-Fri, till 5:30pm Sun • toys • fetishwear • lesbian-owned

Victoria

INFO LINES & SERVICES

Front Runners AA 1112 Caledonia Ave (at St Nicholas Church) **250/383-7744 (AA#)** • 8pm Tue

Women's Creative Network 250/384-7701 • women's private social club • meetings • dances • events • visitors most welcome • check website for events: victoria.tc.ca/Community/WCN

ACCOMMODATIONS

Ambrosia Historic B&B 522 Quadra (at Humboldt) **250/380-7705, 877/262-7672** • gay/ straight • 5-star B&B 3 blocks from Victoria's inner harbor • full brkfst • jacuzzi • nonsmoking • $110-255

The Back Hills Guest House for Women 4470 Leefield Rd **250/478-9648** • women only • 30 minutes from Victoria in the Metchosin Hills • full brkfst • shared baths • nonsmoking • girls 10+ ok • lesbian-owned • Can$60-80

The Consulate, A Historic B&B 528 Goldstream (at Hwy 14) **250/474-9796** • gay-friendly • full brkfst • pagoda-shaped home • Can$80

The Fairmont Empress 721 Government St **250/384-8111, 800/441-1414** • gay-friendly • Victoria landmark • swimming • spa • afternoon tea • kids/ small pets ok • nonsmoking • wheelchair access • Can$159-479

Harris Green View Condo 505-930 Yates St (at Quadra) **250/380-6005** • gay/ straight • 2-bdrm condo • wheelchair access • $175-275 • gay-owned

Hostelling International—Victoria 516 Yates St **250/385-4511, 888/883-0099** • gay/ straight • hostel in heritage bldg dowtown • kids ok • wheelchair access • Can$17-24 (dorms)

Howard Johnson Hotel & Suites Victoria 4670 Elk Lake Dr **250/704-4656, 866/300-4656** • gay-friendly • swimming • hot tub • kids ok • restaurant & lounge • wheelchair access • Can$109-199

Ifanwen B&B 44 Simcoe St **250/384-3717** • lesbians/ gay men • full brkfst • gardens • sundeck • gay-owned • $60-99

Oak Bay Guest House 1052 Newport Ave **250/598-3812, 800/575-3812** • gay-friendly • 1912 Tudor-style house in quiet garden setting • full brkfst • near beaches • kids 10+ ok • nonsmoking • Can$80-205

BARS

Prism Lounge 642 Johnson (enter on Broad St) 250/388–0505 • 2pm-2am, from noon wknds • lesbians/ gay men • dancing/DJ • karaoke • drag shows • videos • wheelchair access

NIGHTCLUBS

Hush 1325 Government St (in basement) 250/385–0566 • 9pm-2am, till midnight Sun, clsd Mon-Tue • gay/ straight • dancing/DJ • drag shows Sun

RESTAURANTS

Green Cuisine 560 Johnson St #5 (in Market Square) 250/385–1809 • 10am-8pm • vegan • also juice bar & bakery

Rosie's Diner 235 Cook St 250/384–6090 • 8am-9pm • '50s & '60s music & videos • wheelchair access • gay-owned

Santiago's Cafe 660 Oswego St 250/388–7376 • 7:30am-9pm, from 7am summers • tapas bar • patio • gay-owned

BOOKSTORES

Bolen Books 1644 Hillside Ave #111 (in shopping center) 250/595–4232 • 8:30am-10pm • LGBT section

RETAIL SHOPS

Oceanside Gifts 812 Wharf St, Ste 102 (across from Empress Hotel on the lower causeway) 250/380–1777 • 9am-6pm, 7:30am-midnight summers • gifts from across Canada • wheelchair access

Side Show 559 Johnson St #43 (in Market Square) 250/920–7469 • 12:30pm-5:30pm • fetishwear

EROTICA

Kiss & Tell 531 Herald St 250/380–6995

Rubber Rainbow Condom Co 560 Johnson St #100 (in Market Square) 250/388–3532

Whistler

ACCOMMODATIONS

Coast Whistler Hotel 4005 Whistler Wy 604/932–2522, 800/663–5644 • gay-friendly • full-service resort hotel • full bar & restaurant • hot tub • swimming • nonsmoking • wheelchair access • Can$99-359

Hostelling International—Whistler 5678 Alta Lake Rd 604/932–5492 • gay/ straight • hostel in rustic lodge on Alta Lake • short drive from Whistler & Blackcomb Mtns • Can$20-28 (dorms)

Listel Whistler Hotel 4121 Village Green (at Whistler Way) 604/932–1133, 800/663–5472 • gay-friendly • hotel w/ swimming, sauna & outdoor hot tub • full brkfst • wheelchair access • $99-449

RESTAURANTS

Boston Pizza 2011 Innsbruck Dr 604/932–7070 • 11am-11pm, till midnight wknds • full bar

La Rua 4557 Blackcomb Blvd 604/932–5011 • 6pm-close, clsd Mon-Tue • Italian/ cont'l

Monks Grill 455 Blackcomb Wy 604/932–9677 • 11:30am-10pm • grill menu • full bar

White Rock

ACCOMMODATIONS

A Beach House B&B 15241 Marine Dr 604/536–5200 • gay-friendly • refurbished waterfront beachhouse w/ spectacular views • CAN$75-190

MANITOBA

St Pierre-Jolys

RESTAURANTS

La Table Des Bonnes Soeurs 432 Joubert St (at Hwy 59, in St Pierre Museum) 204/433–3878, 888/528–2253 • lunch & dinner, clsd Mon-Wed • eclectic, some veggie • wheelchair access • lesbian-owned

Winnipeg

INFO LINES & SERVICES

Rainbow Resource Centre 1-222 Osborne St S 204/474–0212, 204/284–5208 • 1pm-4:30pm Wed-Fri, 7:30pm-10pm Mon-Fri, clsd wknds • also info line • many social/ support groups

ACCOMMODATIONS

Winged Ox Guest House 82 Spence St 204/783–7408 • lesbians/ gay men • full brkfst • nonsmoking • shared baths • gay-owned • Can$40-55

BARS

Club 200 190 Garry St (at St Mary Ave) 204/943–6045 • 4pm-2am, 6pm-midnight Sun • lesbians/ gay men • dancing/DJ • karaoke • drag shows • go-go dancers • wheelchair access

NIGHTCLUBS

Club Desire 441 Main St 204/956–5544 •
lesbians/ gay men • dancing/ DJ • karaoke •
multi-level • theme nights

Gio's Club & Bar 155 Smith St
204/786–1236 • 4pm-3am, from 2pm wknds,
till midnight Sun, clsd Tue • lesbians/ gay men
• dancing/DJ • live shows • drag shows •
screened patio

CAFES

Theatro Café 126 Sherbrook St
204/775–3375 • 10am-11pm, from 11am
wknds • 2-story cafe w/ balcony • salads &
sandwiches

RESTAURANTS

Pizza Place E-3111 Portage Ave
204/940–6720

Right There! 472 Stradbrook Ave (at
Osborne) 204/775–5353 • noon-midnight,
4:30pm-10pm Sun • Korean

Step'N Out 157 Provencher Blvd
204/956–7837 • lunch & dinner, clsd Sun •
fresh dynamic entrees • wheelchair access

BOOKSTORES

Dominion News 262 Portage Ave (btwn
Garry & Smith) 204/942–6563 • 8am-9pm,
from 9am Sat, from noon Sun • some gay
periodicals

McNally Robinson 1120 Grant Ave #4000 (in
the mall) 204/453–2644 • 9am-10pm, till
11pm Fri-Sat, noon-6pm Sun • some gay titles
• wheelchair access

PUBLICATIONS

Perceptions 306/244–1930 • covers the
Canadian prairies

Swerve Media Inc. 204/942–4599 • LGBT
newspaper

SPIRITUAL GROUPS

**Unitarian Universalist Church of
Winnipeg** 603 Wellington Crescent
204/474–1261 • 10:30am Sun

EROTICA

Discreet Boutique 340 Donald (at Ellice)
204/947–1307, 800/247–0454 • also Discreet
Video next door

Love Nest 172 St Anne's Rd 204/254–0422 •
also 1341 Main St, 204/589–4141 • also
Portage & Westwood, 204/ 837–6475

NEW BRUNSWICK

Fredericton

RESTAURANTS

Molly's Cafe 554 Queen St 506/457–9305 •
full bar • garden patio • some veggie

BOOKSTORES

Beegie's Books 370 Prospect St (in
Fredericton Mall) 506/459–3636 • 9:30am-
9pm, till 6pm Sat, clsd Sun (summers) • some
LGBT titles

EROTICA

X-Citement 558 Queen St 506/458–2048 •
videos • magazines • adult novelties

Lower Sackville

EROTICA

X-Citement 295 Sackville Dr 902/864–4159 •
videos • magazines • adult novelties

Moncton

NIGHTCLUBS

Triangles 234 St George St (at Archibald)
506/857–8779 • 7pm-2am, from 8pm wknds •
lesbians/ gay men • neighborhood bar • more
women Tue • dancing/DJ • karaoke Th

CAFES

Cafe Joe Moka 837 Main St 506/852–3070 •
8am-6pm

RESTAURANTS

Calactus Cafe 125 Church (at St George)
506/388–4833 • lunch & dinner • vegetarian

EROTICA

X-Citement 203 St George St 506/855–2333
• videos • magazines • adult novelties

X-Citement 651 Mountain Rd 506/388–2226
• videos • magazines • adult novelties

Petit-Rocher

NIGHTCLUBS

Club GNG 702 rue Principle, Bloc C
506/783–7440 • some Sat, call for info •
lesbians/ gay men • dancing/DJ •19+

St John

ACCOMMODATIONS

Mahogany Manor 220 Germain St
506/636-8000, 800/796-7755 • gay/ straight •
full brkfst • nonsmoking • kids ok • wheelchair
access • gay-owned • Can$95-105

NIGHTCLUBS

Club Montréal 9 Sydney St (off King Square,
upstairs) **506/696-1900** • 9pm-2am, clsd
Mon-Tue • mostly gay men • dancing/DJ • live
shows

NEWFOUNDLAND

Dildo

ACCOMMODATIONS

Inn by the Bay 78-80 Front St **709/582-3170,
888/339-7829** • gay-friendly • B&B inn • full
brkfst • jacuzzi • nonsmoking • Can$79-149

St John's

ACCOMMODATIONS

A Gower House B&B 180 Gower St (at
Prescott St) **709/754-0058, 800/563-3959** •
gay/ straight • full brkfst • in downtown •
some shared baths • nonsmoking • $65-85

Abba Inn (Downtown) St John's 36
Queen's Rd (at Prescott St) **709/754-0058,
800/563-3959** • gay/ straight • B&B • full
brkfst • fireplaces • nonsmoking • pets ok •
CAN$69-189

Banberry House 116 Military Rd (at Rawlins
Cross) **709/579-8006, 877/579-8226** • gay/
straight • full brkfst • kids/ small pets ok •
nonsmoking • $99-169

Bluestone Inn 34 Queen's Rd (at Water St)
709/754-7544, 877/754-9876 • gay-friendly •
full brkfst • jacuzzi • gay-owned • Can$79-149

NaGeira House 7 Musgrave St (at Water St),
Carbonear **709/596-1888, 800/600-7757** •
gay-friendly • B&B • full brkfst • jacuzzi •
nonsmoking • kids ok • Can $99-149

Stonewall Inn B&B PO Box 1012,
Spaniard's Bay AOA 3XO **709/786-4386,
866/477-8404** • gay/straight • chalet-style
house overlooking the bay • full brkfst •
nonsmoking • Can$79-119 • gay-owned

BARS

Schroders 10 Bates Hill (off Queens Rd)
709/753-0807 • 4:30pm-1am, till 2am Fri-Sat,
till midnight Sun • gay-friendly • also Zapata's
restaurant downstairs • Mexican • some
veggie

NIGHTCLUBS

Zone 216 216 Water St **709/754-2492** •
9pm-close Th-Sat • lesbians/ gay men •
dancing/DJ

BOOKSTORES

Bennington Gate Bookstore 8-10 Rowan
St, Churchill Square (lower level, Terrace on
the Square) **709/576-6600** • 10am-6pm, till
9pm Th-Fri, 1pm-5pm Sun • LGBT section

NOVA SCOTIA

Annapolis Royal

ACCOMMODATIONS

Bailey House B&B 150 St George St (at
Drury Ln) **902/532-1285, 877/532-1285** •
gay/straight • full brkfst • nonsmoking •
Can$80-120

King George Inn 902/532-5286,
888/799-5464 • lesbians/ gay men • full brkfst
• jacuzzi • nonsmoking • seasonal • Can$89-
299

Baddeck

ACCOMMODATIONS

The Dunlop Inn 902/295-1100,
888/263-9840 • gay-friendly • waterfront B&B
inn • kids ok • Can$110-160

Chéticamp

ACCOMMODATIONS

Seashell Housekeeping Units 125
Chéticamp Island Rd **902/224-1563** • gay/
straight • housekeeping units on the ocean •
seasonal • kids/ small pets ok • nonsmoking •
lesbian-owned • Can$50-70

Digby

ACCOMMODATIONS

Harbourview Inn 25 Harbourview Rd (at
Hwy 1), Smith's Cove **902/245-5686,
877/449-0705** • gay-friendly • century-old
country inn • full brkfst • swimming • kids ok •
nonsmoking • wheelchair access • gay-owned
• $99-149

Guysborough

ACCOMMODATIONS

Barrens at Bay Coastal Cottages 6870 Hwy 16 (at Halfway Cove) **902/358-2157** • gay/straight • jacuzzi • kids/pets ok • nonsmoking • wheelchair access • gay-owned • Can$215-260

Halifax

ACCOMMODATIONS

Forevergreen House B&B 5560 Hwy 1, St Croix **902/792-1692** • gay-friendly • Victorian farmhouse • full brkfst • nonsmoking • women-owned • $65-85

Fresh Start B&B 2720 Gottingen St (at Black) **902/453-6616, 888/453-6616** • gay-friendly • Victorian mansion • some shared baths • kids/pets ok • women-owned • Can$70-110

BARS

Reflections Cabaret & Cigar Bar 5184 Sackville St (at Barrington) **902/422-2957** • 1pm-4am, from 4pm Sun • lesbians/gay men • dancing/DJ • live shows • cabaret • drag shows • wheelchair access

NIGHTCLUBS

Club NRG 2099 Gottingen St **902/422-4368** • 4pm-2am • lesbians/gay men • dancing/DJ • transgender-friendly • food served • karaoke Tue • drag shows • gay-owned

CAFES

The Daily Grind 5686 Spring Garden Rd (near South Park) **902/429-6397** • 7am-10pm, from 8am wknds • also newsstand

The Second Cup 5425 Spring Garden Rd **902/429-0883** • 7am-midnight, from 8pm wknds • internet access

RESTAURANTS

Satisfaction Feast 1581 Grafton St (off Blower St) **902/422-3540** • 11:30am-9pm, till 4pm Wed, till 10pm Fri, from 4pm Sun • vegetarian • patio

Soho 1667 Argyle **902/423-3049** • lunch & dinner • cont'l • live shows

Sweet Basil 1866 Upper Water St (near Duke) **902/425-2133** • 11:30am-9pm • full bar

Trinity Restaurant 1333 South Park (near Spring Garden Rd) **902/423-8428** • lunch & dinner, wknd brunch • full bar • wheelchair access

BOOKSTORES

Atlantic News 5560 Morris St (at Queen) **902/429-5468** • 8am-10pm daily • periodicals

Frog Hollow Books 5657 Spring Garden Rd (at Dresden Row) **902/429-3318** • 9:30am-6pm, till 9:30pm Th-Fri, clsd Sun

Schooner Used Books 5378 Inglis St (at Victoria Rd) **902/423-8419** • 9:30am-6pm, till 9pm Fri, till 5:30pm Sat, clsd Sun • rare & out-of-print books

Smithbooks 5201 Duke St (in Scotia Square) **902/423-6438** • 9:30am-6pm, till 9pm Fri-Sat

Trident Booksellers & Cafe 1256 Hollis St (at Morris St) **902/423-7100** • 8:30am-5pm, from 11am Sun • used • popular cafe

RETAIL SHOPS

Venus Envy 1598 Barrington St **902/422-0004** • 10am-6pm, till 8pm Th-Fri, noon-5pm Sun • "a store for women & the people who love them" • books • sex toys • alternative health products

SPIRITUAL GROUPS

Safe Harbour MCC 2786 Agricola St #108 (at Bloomfield Ctr) **902/453-9249** • 7pm Sun

EROTICA

Night Magic Fashions 5268 Sackville St **902/420-9309** • clsd Sun • lingerie, toys, videos

X-Citement 6260 Quinpool Rd **902/492-0026** • videos • magazines • adult novelties

Yarmouth

ACCOMMODATIONS

Charles C Richards House Historic B&B 17 Collins St **902/742-0042** • gay/straight • brick mansion • full brkfst • some shared baths • gay-owned • Can$95-210

Murray Manor B&B 225 Main St (at Forest St) **902/742-9625, 877/742-9629** • gay-friendly • heritage home w/ lovely gardens & greenhouse • full brkfst • shared baths • kids ok • one all-natural-fiber, environmentally friendly room available • $95

NW TERRITORIES

Yellowknife

ACCOMMODATIONS

Ptartan Ptarmigan 5120 51st St (at 52nd Ave) **867/669–7222** • gay/ straight • B&B • shared baths • smokfree • gay-owned • CAN$65-75

ONTARIO

Provincewide

PUBLICATIONS

fab 416/925–5221 • Ontario's gay scene magazine

Barrie

BARS

Club C'est La Vie 23 Collier St (at Clapperton) **705/720–9077** • lesbians/ gay men • neighborhood bar • dancing/ DJ • 19+

Brighton

ACCOMMODATIONS

Apple Manor 96 Main St, Box 11 613/475–0351 • gay-friendly • 150-year-old Victorian • full brkfst • shared baths • swimming • nonsmoking • $55-75

Butler Creek Country Inn 613/475–1248, 877/475–5827 • gay-friendly • Victorian home, circa 1905 • full brkfst • kids ok • nonsmoking • gay-owned • Can$85-115

BOOKSTORES

Lighthouse Books 65 Main St 613/475–1269 • 9:30am-5:30pm, clsd Sun-Mon

Brockville

ACCOMMODATIONS

The Calico Cat B&B 193 Brockmere Cliff (at Hwy 401) 613/342–0363 • gay-friendly • waterfront B&B located in the beautiful 1000 Islands • nonsmoking • C$75-100

Cobourg

ACCOMMODATIONS

Victoria View B&B Retreat 198 Bagot St (at Albert) 905/377–0620 • gay/ straight • 1874 heritage home • "an elegant & peaceful retreat destination" • gay-owned • $85-140

Elora

ACCOMMODATIONS

Log Cabin Heaven 7384 Middlebrook Rd (at Wellington Rd) 519/846–9439 • gay/ straight • pool • jacuzzi • nonsmoking • women-owned • Can$195

Gananoque

ACCOMMODATIONS

Boathouse Country Inn & Heritage Boat Tours 17–19 Front St, 1000 Islands, Rockport 613/659–2348, 877/434–1212 • gay/ straight • full brkfst • nonsmoking • also tavern • wheelchair access • $75-200

Rockport Village Cottage 11 Front St, 1000 Islands (at 1000 Islands Pkwy), Rockport 613/659–3845 • gay-friendly • riverside home • seasonal • nonsmoking • kids/ pets ok • women-owned/ run • Can$900/week

Trinity House Inn 90 Stone St S, 1000 Islands 613/382–8383, 800/265–4871 (ON ONLY) • gay-friendly • historic country inn • fine dining restaurant • nonsmoking • kids ok in suites • sailing charters • gay-owned • Can$90-243

Grand Valley

ACCOMMODATIONS

Rainbow Ridge Resort Country Rd 109 (at Hwy 25 S) 519/928–3262 • lesbians/ gay men • trailers & tents • located on 72 acres on Grand River • swimming • restaurant • dance hall • day visitors welcome • seasonal • pets ok • gay-owned • Can$15/ person

Guelph

INFO LINES & SERVICES

Out Line 519/836–4550 • volunteer hours vary

ACCOMMODATIONS

Dr WF Savage House B&B 45 Colborne St, Elora 519/846–5325 • lesbians/ gay men • full brkfst • nonsmoking • kids/ pets ok • wheelchair access • gay-owned • Can$75-100

BOOKSTORES

Bookshelf Cafe 41 Quebec St 519/821–3311 • 9am-10pm • also cinema, bar & restaurant • some veggie

Hamilton

ACCOMMODATIONS

Cedars Campground 1039 5th Concession W Rd, Millgrove **905/659-3655** • lesbians/ gay men • private campground • swimming • also bar • dancing/DJ • restaurant wknds • some veggie • Can$65-85 (cabins) & Can$15 (camping)

The Twisted Magnolia B&B 971 Lowers Lions Club Rd (at Wilson & Main W) **905/304-6130, 800/592-2303** • gay/ straight • Victorian farmhouse • full brkfst • swimming • fireplaces • kids ok • small legal gay weddings • Can$79-145

BARS

The Embassy Club 54 King St E (at Houston) **905/522-1100** • 8pm-2am, patio bar Fri-Sat • lesbians/ gay men • dancing/DJ • transgender-friendly • karaoke • drag shows • videos

The Werx 121 Hughson St N (at Canon) **905/972-9379, 866/796-0701** • 2pm-2am, from noon Sun • lesbians/ gay men • 3 levels • neighborhood bar • dancing/ DJ • karoke Fri • gay-owned

Kenora

INFO LINES & SERVICES

Kenora Lesbians Phone Line **807/468-5801** • phoneline staffed 7pm-9pm Tue • support & info

Kitchener

NIGHTCLUBS

Club Renaissance 24 Charles St W **519/570-2406, 877/635-2352** • 9pm-3am, clsd Mon-Tue • lesbians/ gay men • dancing/DJ • food served • drag shows • also billiards lounge

London

BARS

The Annex 347 Clarence St **519/640-6858** • 2pm-2am • lesbians/ gay men • dancing/DJ • karaoke • patio • wheelchair access

NIGHTCLUBS

Club 181 181 King St (at Richmond) **519/672-5182** • 8pm-3am Th-Sat • mostly gay men • dancing/DJ

RESTAURANTS

Blackfriars Cafe 46 Blackfriars (2 blocks S of Oxford) **519/667-4930** • lunch & dinner, Sun brunch • popular • plenty veggie • full bar

Magnolia Lane 460 King St (at Maitland) **519/858-8669** • dinner only, clsd Mon • French/ Cajun cuisine • gay-owned

Murano 394 Waterloo St (at Dundas) **519/434-7565** • dinner only, clsd Sun • northern Italian • terrace • gay-owned

Veranda 546 Dundas St (at William St) **519/434-6790** • dinner nightly, clsd Sun-Mon • gay-owned

ENTERTAINMENT & RECREATION

London Lesbian Film Festival c/o Reeling Spinsters, PO Box 46014, 956 Dundas St E, N6A 6B2 **519/434-0246** • women only • the only festival in North America of lesbian films

SPIRITUAL GROUPS

Holy Fellowship MCC 795 Dundas St E (in Aeolian Hall, corner of Dundas & Rectory) **519/645-0744** • 10:30am Sun • wheelchair access

Maynooth

ACCOMMODATIONS

Wildewood Guesthouse 613/338-3134 • lesbians/ gay men (mostly women) • brkfst & dinner included • hot tub • nonsmoking • wheelchair access • gay-owned • Can$175

Mississauga

EROTICA

Lovecraft 2200 Dundas St E (W of Hwy 427) **905/276-5772** • toys • lingerie • videos • women-owned/ run

Stag Shop 6020 Hurontario Rd **905/501-9855**

Morrisburg

ACCOMMODATIONS

The Village Antiques & Tea Room B&B 4326 County Rd 31, Williamsburg **613/535-2463, 877/264-3281** • gay-friendly • B&B inn • full brkfst • nonsmoking • dining room w/ excellent wine list • also antique shop & tea room • gay-owned • Can$65-105

Niagara Falls

see also **Niagara Falls & Buffalo, New York, USA**

ACCOMMODATIONS

Absolute Elegance B&B 6023 Culp St (at River Rd) **905/353-8522, 877/353-8522** • gay/ straight • restored Victorian near Niagara Falls • full brkfst • kids ok • nonsmoking • gay-owned • $100-170

Acute B&B 127 Mary St (at Hwy 55/ Mississauga St), Niagara-on-the-Lake **905/468-1328, 888/208-2340** • gay-friendly • 1843 home • full brkfst • garden • courtesy bikes • nonsmoking • Can$130-200

Amelia's 15526 Niagara River Pkwy, Niagara-on-the-Lake **905/468-5550** • gay/ straight • B&B-private home • full brkfst • swimming • small pets ok • gay-owned • Can$105-145

Angels Hideaway 4360 Simcoe St (at River Rd) **905/354-1119** • gay-friendly • B&B • full brkfst • jacuzzi • nonsmoking • Can$65-125

Avec Chateau Pebbles Stoney Creek **905/643-6627** • gay/ straight • B&B • Can$85-110

Bampfield Hall B&B 4761 Zimmerman Ave **905/353-8522, 877/353-8522** • gay/ straight • historic Gothic home near Niagara Falls • full brkfst • jacuzzi • kids ok • nonsmoking • gay-owned • $65-170

Britaly B&B 57 The Promenade (at Charlotte & John), Niagara-on-the-Lake **905/468-8778** • gay-friendly • B&B • full brkfst • gay-owned • Can$100-125

Fairbanks House/ Ellis House 4965 River Rd **905/371-3716, 866/246-6616** • gay/ straight • 1877 restored Victorian • full brkfst • fireplaces • also hosts same-sex weddings • kids ok • nonsmoking • lesbian & gay-owned • Can$75-160

Gretna Green B&B 5077 River Rd **905/357-2081, 888/504-3565** • gay/ straight • full brkfst • kids/ pets ok • nonsmoking • Can$85-125

Niagara Inn B&B 4300 Simcoe St (at River Rd) **905/353-8522, 877/353-8522** • gay-friendly • restored Victorian near Niagara Falls • full brkfst • kids ok • nonsmoking • gay-owned • $50-105

Niagara Falls

ACCOMMODATIONS

Sheraton Fallsview Hotel & Conference Centre 6755 Fallsview Blvd (at Stanley) **905/374-1077, 800/747-9045** • gay-friendly • 300 yds from Niagara Falls • swimming • full brkfst • pool & jacuzzi • kids/ pets ok • wheelchair access • $79-599

Niagara-on-the-Lake

ACCOMMODATIONS

The Pride of Niagara B&B 279 Nassau St, Box 485 (at Johnson) **905/468-8181, 877/586-1212** • gay/ straight • full brkfst • swimming • nonsmoking • gay-owned • from Can$135-150

Oshawa

NIGHTCLUBS

Club 717 717 Wilson Rd S #7 **905/434-4297** • 9pm-2am Th, till 3am Fri-Sat, till midnight Sun, clsd Mon-Wed • lesbians/ gay men • dancing • karaoke • drag shows • also referral service

EROTICA

Forbidden Pleasures 1268 Simcoe St N **905/728-0834**

Ottawa

see also Hull, Province of Québec

INFO LINES & SERVICES

237-XTRA 613/237-9872 • touch-tone LGBT info

Pink Triangle Services 177 Nepean St #508 (at Bank St) **613/563-4818** • many groups & services • library • call for times

ACCOMMODATIONS

Ambiance B&B 330 Nepean St **613/563-0421, 888/366-8772** • gay/ straight • full brkfst • some shared baths • kids ok • nonsmoking • lesbian-owned • Can$75-110

Home Sweetland Home B&B 62 Sweetland Ave (at Laurier Ave) **613/234-1871** • gay/ straight • full brkfst • kids ok • close to tourist attractions • nonsmoking • gay-owned • Can$72-120

Inn on Somerset 282 Somerset St W (at Elgin) **613/236-9309, 800/658-3564** • gay/ straight • 3-story Victorian • full brkfst • some shared baths • kids ok • nonsmoking • Can$75-140

Rideau Inn 177 Frank St **613/688-2753, 877/580-5015** • gay-friendly • Edwardian town house • some shared baths • nonsmoking • gay-owned • Can$ 70-110

BARS

Centretown Pub 340 Somerset St W (at Bank) **613/594-0233** • 2pm-2am • lesbians/ gay men • dancing/DJ • videos • leather bar upstairs • Silhouette Lounge piano bar Fri-Sat

Le Pub de Promenade 175 Promenade de Portage, Hull, QC 819/771-8810 • 11am-2am, from 2pm wknds • popular • lesbians/gay men • neighborhood bar • dancing/DJ • karaoke

The Lookout 41 York, 2nd flr (in Byward Market) 613/789-1624 • noon-2am • lesbians/gay men • food served • wheelchair access • lesbian-owned

Swizzles 246 Queen St 613/232-4200 • 11am-2am • lesbians/gay men • karaoke • drag shows

NIGHTCLUBS

Edge 212 Sparks St (at Bank) • clsd Mon & Wed • lesbians/gay men • dancing/DJ • drag shows • rooftop terrace

Pink 172 Rideau St (in Byward Market) 613/789-2658 • lesbians/gay men • dancing/DJ • drag shows

Surface 128 York St 613/562-9547 • gay-friendly • after-hours • dancing/DJ

Zaphod Beeblebrox 27 York 613/562-1010 • 4pm-2am • gay/straight • neighborhood bar • dancing/DJ • live music

CAFES

AE Micro Internet Cafe 288 Bank St (at Somerset) 613/230-9000 • 9am-1am • light menu

Bridgehead Coffee 366 Bank St (at Gilmour) 613/569-5600 • 7am-9pm • gay-owned

RESTAURANTS

Alfonsetti's 5830 Hazeldean Rd, Stittsville 613/831-3008 • lunch & dinner, clsd Sun • Italian • plenty veggie

The Buzz 374 Bank St 613/565-9595 • lunch & dinner, wknd brunch • beer/wine

Elgin Street Freehouse 296 Elgin St 613/233-5525 • full bar

Fairouz 343 Somerset St W (btwn Bank & O'Connor) 613/233-1536 • lunch & dinner, dinner only wknds • Lebanese

BOOKSTORES

After Stonewall 370 Bank St (near Gilmour) 613/567-2221 • 10am-6pm, till 8pm Fri, till 5:30pm Sat, noon-5pm Sun • LGBT

Mags & Fags 254 Elgin St (btwn Somerset & Cooper) 613/233-9651 • till 10pm • gay magazines

mother tongue books/femmes de parole 1067 Bank St (at Sunnyside Ave) 613/730-2346, 800/366-0514 (CANADA ONLY) • 10am-6pm, till 8pm Fri (clsd Sun summer)

Octopus Books 116 3rd Ave (at Bank) 613/233-2589 • 10am-6pm • progressive

RETAIL SHOPS

One in Ten 216 Bank St (at Nepean) 613/563-0110 • noon-10pm Mon-Fri, 1pm-8pm wknds • XXX video cinema • videos • toys

Venus Envy 110 Parent Ave 613/789-4646 • 11am-6pm, till 8pm Wed-Fri, till 7pm in winter, noon-5pm Sun • "a store for women & the people who love them" • books • sex toys • workshops

Wilde's 367 Bank St (at Gilmour) 613/234-5512 • 11am-9pm, noon-6pm Sun • pride items • videos • toys • magazines • leather • clothing • wheelchair access

PUBLICATIONS

Capital Xtra! 613/237-7133 • LGBT newspaper

To Be Publications 613/236-8888 • LGBT magazine covering Ottawa & Montreal

SPIRITUAL GROUPS

Dignity Ottawa Dignité PO Box 2102, Station D 613/746-7279 • call for hours & location

Perth

ACCOMMODATIONS

Perth Manor 23 Drummond St W (at D'Arcy & Boulton) 613/264-0050 • gay/straight • boutique hotel • kids/pets ok • English gardens • nonsmoking • gay-owned • Can$135

Peterborough

EROTICA

Forbidden Pleasures 91 George St N 705/742-3800

Picton

ACCOMMODATIONS

Henderson House B&B 116 Main St (at Hwy 33), Consecon 613/394-5093 • gay/straight • full brkfst • along Consecon River • nonsmoking • lesbian-owned • Can$80-95

Puslinch

ACCOMMODATIONS

Cedarbrook Farm B&B 812 8th Conc Rd W, RR 3 905/659-1566 • gay/straight • full brkfst • nonsmoking • lesbian-owned • $85-150

Sault Ste–Marie

ACCOMMODATIONS

St Christopher's Inn B&B 923 Queen St E (at Church St), Sault Ste-Marie **705/759–0870** • gay/ straight • kids/ pets ok • gay/ lesbian marriages can be performed on-site by owner • gay-owned • Can$65

St Catharines

BARS

The New Vouz 151 Queenston St **905/684–0451** • 8pm-2am, clsd Mon • lesbians/ gay men • neighborhood bar • gay owned/ run

Stratford

ACCOMMODATIONS

A Hundred Church Street 100 Church St **519/272–8845** • gay/ straight • full brkfst • hot tub • some shared baths • nonsmoking • kids 10+ ok • gay-owned • Can$85-120

The Maples of Stratford 220 Church St **519/273–0810** • gay-friendly • nonsmoking • some shared baths • woman-owned • Can$65-115

RESTAURANTS

Down the Street 30 Ontario St **519/273–5886** • 11am-midnight, dinner only Mon • popular • int'l • full bar till 2am

Sudbury

NIGHTCLUBS

Zig's 54 Elgin St (at Elm St) **705/673–3873** • 8pm-close • lesbians/ gay men • neighborhood bar • dancing/DJ • transgender-friendly • karaoke • drag shows

Thunder Bay

BOOKSTORES

Northern Women's Bookstore 65 Court St S (at Wilson) **807/344–7979** • 11am-6pm, clsd Sun-Mon • wheelchair access

EROTICA

Rainbow DVD & Video 264 Bay St (at Court St) **807/345–6272** • 11am-10pm, noon-6pm Sun • some books

Toronto

INFO LINES & SERVICES

519 Church St Community Centre 519 Church St (on Cawthra Park) **416/392–6874** • 9am-10pm, till 5pm wknds • numerous events • LGBT info center • cafe open 10am-3pm Mon-Fri • wheelchair access

925-XTRA 416/925–9872 • touch-tone LGBT visitors' info

AA Gay/ Lesbian 416/487–5591

Canadian Lesbian/ Gay Archives 56 Temperance St # 201 **416/777–2755** • 7:30pm-10pm Tue-Th & by appt

Pride Weddings 416/487–0211, 888/418–1188 • wedding planner for couples coming to Toronto to tie the knot

Toronto Area Gay/ Lesbian Phone Line 416/964–6600 • 7pm-10pm Tue & Th • counseling

ACCOMMODATIONS

213 Carlton Street—Toronto Townhouse 416/323–8898, 877/500–0466 • gay/ straight • upscale town house • full brkfst • some shared baths • nonsmoking • gay-owned • $61-199

A Seaton Dream 243 Seaton St (at Sherbourne & Gerrard) **416/929–3363, 866/878–8898** • gay/ straight • B&B • full brkfst • nonsmoking • garden patio • gay-owned • Can$85-130

Allenby B&B 223 Strathmore Blvd (near Danforth & Greenwood) **416/461–7095** • gay-friendly • nonsmoking • shared bath • Can$65+

Annex Townhouse B&B 384 Clinton St (at Bloor) **416/323–8898, 877/500–0466** • gay/ straight • B&B • jacuzzi • nonsmoking • gay-owned • $99-185

B "R" Guest B&B 367 Ontario St (at Gerrard & Parliament) **416/944–8579, 866/928–0187** • gay/ straight • B&B • full brkfst • kids ok • gay-owned • Can$85-200

Banting House Inn 73 Homewood Ave (at Wellesley) **416/924–1458, 800/823–8856** • lesbians/ gay men • Edwardian home • nonsmoking • gay-owned • Can$85-150

Bonnevue Manor B&B 33 Beaty Ave (at Queen St & Roncesvalles) **416/536–1455** • gay/ straight • B&B • full brkfst • kids ok • $75-130

Burwood Inn B&B 10 Monteith St (near Church & Wellesley) **416/351–1503, 877/580–5015** • gay/ straight • Victorian town house • some shared baths • garden • deck • gay-owned • Can$50-110

Cawthra Square Bed & Breakfast Inns
416/966-3074, 800/259-5474 • lesbians/gay
men • multiple Heritage homes • meeting
rooms • spa • nonsmoking • gay-owned •
$97-446

Dundonald House 35 Dundonald St (at
Church) 416/961-9888, 800/260-7227 •
mostly gay men • full brkfst • hot tub • sauna
• gym • bicycles • nonsmoking • gay-owned •
Can$85-195

Executive Apartments 416/918-8467 •
gay/ straight • full kitchens • wheelchair access
• Can$95-295

Toronto

WHERE THE GIRLS ARE:
In "The Ghetto"—south of Bloor St.,
between Yonge and Parliament.
The Cabbagetown area
(Parliament St.) is more laid-
back, while the intersection of
Church & Wellesley is queer
ground zero.

LGBT PRIDE:
June/July. 416/927-7433, web:
www.torontopride.com.

ANNUAL EVENTS:
May - International Gay & Lesbian
Comedy and Music Festival, web:
www.werefunnythatway.com
Inside Out: Lesbian & Gay Film and
Video Festival 416/977-6847,
web: insideout.on.ca
June - duMaurier Downtown Jazz
Festival, web: www.tojazz.com
International Dragon Boat Race
Festival 416/595-1739, web:
www.dragonboats.com
July - Caribana Caribbean festival,
web: www.caribana.com
September - International Film
Festival 416/968-3456, web:
www.e.bell.ca/filmfest.

BEST VIEW:
The top of one of the world's tallest
buildings, of course: the CN
Tower. Or try a sight-seeing air
tour or a three-masted sailing
ship tour.

WEATHER:
Summers are hot (upper 80°s-
90°s) and humid. Spring is
gorgeous. Fall brings cool, crisp
days. Winters are cold and snowy,
just as you'd imagined they
would be in Canada!

TRANSIT:
Co-op Taxi 416/504-2667.
Grey Coach 416/393-7911.
TTC 416/393-4636, web:
www.city.toronto.on.ca/ttc.

CITY INFO:
800/499-2514, web: www.toronto-
tourism.com.

ATTRACTIONS:
Art Gallery of Ontario 416/979-
6648, web: www.ago.net
Bata Shoe Museum, web:
www.batashoemuseum.ca
CN Tower 416/868-6937,
www.cntower.ca
Dr Flea's International Flea Market
416/745-3532, web:
www.drfleas.com
Gardiner Museum of Ceramic Art,
416/586-8080, web:
www.gardinermuseum.on.ca
Harbourfront Centre 416/973-4000,
www.harbourfront.on.ca
Hockey Hall of Fame 416/360-7735,
web: www.hhof.com
Kensington Market
Ontario Place 416/314-9900
Rogers Centre 416/341-3034, web:
www.rogerscentre.com
Royal Ontario Museum 416/586-
8000, www.rom.on.ca
Underground City.

| **Reply** | **Forward** | | **Delete** |

```
Date: Dec 14, 2005 14:51:53
From: Girl-on-the-Go
To: Editor@Damron.com
Subject: Toronto
```

>Toronto is more than just the capital city of Ontario, eh! It's the cultural and financial center of English-speaking Canada. And though it's not far from Buffalo, New York, and Niagara Falls, Toronto has a European ambiance, fostered by its eclectic architecture and peaceful diversity of cultures, that makes it a great vacation getaway.

>Restaurants and shops from Asia, India, Europe, and many other points on the globe attract natives and tourists alike to the exotic Kensington Market. And just around the corner from Kensington, you'll find a bargain hunter's bonanza: two blocks of vintage clothing stores.

>If your idea of high fashion doesn't include hand-me-downs, you can do some serious window-shopping in the upscale boutiques lining the quaint streets of the Bloor-Yorkville area. And, of course, there's something for everyone in the enormous Eaton Centre mall.

>For intrepid shoppers, Toronto has a lot to offer. **Out on the Street** carries LGBT accessories. **Good For Her** is a women's erotica shop. **Secrets from Your Sister** offers women's lingerie in "realistic sizes" (what a concept!). And the **Omega Centre** is the place for metaphysical literature and supplies.

>Toronto is home to Canada's largest LGBT community, and it shows. You'll see lesbians and gay men everywhere, but the heart of the community is the Church and Wellesley area. Stop in at the **519 Community Centre** to check the bulletin boards, then grab a cup of joe at **Second Cup** or **Timothy's.** Browse the magazines at **This Ain't the Rosedale Library,** then have some lunch—in the warmer months the patio at **Zelda's** is bustling.

>Over on Yonge Street, pay a visit to the LGBT **Glad Day Bookshop.** At the top of the stairs you'll find the latest issues of **Xtra!** (the LGBT weekly) and **fab** (Ontario's scene magazine), along with piles of flyers and ideas of things to do. In the evening, have a drink at **Tango,** the women's bar, or **Slack Alice,** a lesbian/ gay bar and restaurant popular with women.

Reply **Forward**   **Delete**

>You'll also find sisters in Old Cabbagetown, a funky neighborhood that's home to families, queers, and a mix of cultures. (West Coasters take note: It's also home to the strongest coffee in town— Jet Fuel.) While you're here, grab a pint and a bite to eat at the **House On Parliament Pub**.

>If it's more dancing you want, join the boys at **5ive** and, on Saturdays, at **Fly**. If you love salsa, don't miss Fridays and Saturdays at **El Convento Rico** in Little Italy. On Sundays, you'll find the girls getting down to great music at the small but hip **Ciao Edie**. For the latest queer hotspot or one-off party, check out the listings in *Klublife* magazine, found at bars and clubwear boutiques.

>If you're an outdoorsy type, you'll be glad to find that Toronto is rather green for such a large city. Don't miss Toronto Islands Park, the string of islands off the Waterfront area, dedicated to recreation. Take a ferry over and rent a bike. In addition to miles of bike paths, the islands feature an amusement park, picnic areas, sports field, boat rentals, and beaches (Hanlan's Beach is the gay beach).

>Toronto is also well-known for its repertory film scene, so try not to miss the Lesbian/Gay Film Fest in late May or early June, or the Film Festival of Festivals in September. In July, the city is host to Folsom Fair North, Toronto's answer to San Francisco's popular leather and kink fest of the same name. And Toronto Pride in June is said to be one of the largest gatherings of lesbians and gay men on the continent.

The Grange Hotel 165 Grange Ave (at Queen) **416/603–7700, 888/232–0002** • gay-friendly • kids ok • Can$100

House on McGill 110 McGill St (at Church & Carlton) **416/351–1503, 877/580–5015** • gay/straight • Victorian town house • shared baths • garden w/ deck • nonsmoking • gay-owned • Can$50-110

Huntley House 65 Huntley St (at Bloor) **416/923–6950** • gay-friendly • 1871 historic house • full brkfst • nonsmoking • Can$95-135

The Mansion 46 Dundonald St (at Church) **416/963–8385** • gay/straight • B&B • elegant Victorian • also 2 apts • Can$70-100

Pimblett's Rest B&B 242 Gerrard St E **416/929–9525, 416/921–6896** • Victorian • gay/ straight • full brkfst • hot tub • theme rooms • nonsmoking • gay-owned • Can$85-105

Toronto B&B Reservation Service **705/738–9449, 877/922–6522** • gay-friendly • reservation service • Can$80-170

Toronto Downtown Bed & Breakfast® 57 Chicora Ave **416/921–3533, 877/950–6200** • gay/ straight • luxurious • full brkfst • teens ok • nonsmoking • gay-owned • $199-259

Two Aberdeen B&B 2 Aberdeen Ave
416/944–1426 • lesbians/ gay men • 1883
Victorian in historic Cabbagetown • full brkfst
• rooftop garden • Can$101-170

Victoria's Mansion Guest House 68
Gloucester St **416/921–4625** • converted
mansion • kids/ small non-barking pets ok •
Can$75-145

Bars

Andy Poolhall 489 College St (at Markham)
416/923–5300 • 2pm-2am • gay/ straight •
Pop Art pool hall

Bar 501 501 Church St (at Wellesley)
416/944–3272 • 11am-2am • lesbians/ gay
men • neighborhood bar • drag shows •
infamous Window Show Sun

Ciao Edie 489 College St (at Markham)
416/927–7774 • 8pm-2am, clsd Mon-Tue •
gay/ straight • Here Kitty Kitty women's night
9pm Sun • cocktail lounge w/ DJ • food served

Crews/ Tango 508 Church St **416/972–1662** •
noon-2am • mostly gay men • neighborhood
bar • deck overlooking Church St • also Tango
from 8pm Mon-Sat • mostly women • popular
Sat • dancing/DJ • karaoke • drag shows

The Hair of the Dog 425 Church St (at
Wood) **416/964–2708** • 11:30am-2am •
lesbians/ gay men • neighborhood pub &
restaurant • patio

The House on Parliament Pub 456
Parliament St **416/925–4074** • 11am-2am •
gay/ straight • neighborhood bar • food served
• patio

Lo'la 7 Maitland (at Yonge) **416/920–0946** •
4pm-close • mostly gay men • lounge

Midtown 552 College St (W of Euclid)
416/920–4533 • 5pm-2am, from 3pm Fri-Sun
• gay-friendly • neighborhood pool bar • tapas
served

O'Grady's 518 Church St (at Maitland)
416/322–2822 • 11am-2am • gay/ straight •
casual dining • huge patio • also lounge
upstairs

Pegasus on Church 489-B Church St (at
Wellesley, upstairs) **416/927–8832** • 11am-
2am • lesbians/ gay men • neighborhood bar

Slack Alice 562 Church St (at Wellesley)
416/969–8742 • 4pm-2am, from 11am wknds
• popular • lesbians/ gay men • dancing/DJ Fri-
Sat • also restaurant • int'l fusion • brunch
wknds • comedy Th • videos

Statlers 471 Church St (at Maitland)
416/925–0341 • 2pm-2am • mostly gay men •
live shows nightly • piano • older crowd

Woody's/ Sailor 465–467 Church (at
Maitland) **416/972–0887** • 1pm-2am •
popular • mostly gay men • neighborhood bar
• live shows • drag shows Sun • videos • 18+
•wheelchair access

Zipperz 72 Carlton St (at Church)
416/921–0066 • noon-2am • mostly gay men
• dancing/DJ • drag shows • piano bar • patio

Nightclubs

5ive 5 St Josephs St (at Yonge) **416/964–8685**
• 10pm-3:30am, clsd Mon-Tue • popular •
mostly gay men • dancing/DJ • cover charge

Ambionce 26 Lombard St (at Club 26, use
back door) • 8pm-4am Fri only • women only
• dancing/ DJ

Chickitas • mostly women • dancing/DJ •
check website for upcoming parties:
www.chickitas.com

El Convento Rico 750 College St (at
Crawford) **416/588–7800** • 9pm-3:30am, clsd
Mon-Wed • popular • gay/ straight •
dancing/DJ • Latin/ salsa music • multiracial •
transgender-friendly • drag shows

Fly Nightclub 8 Gloucester St (2 streets N of
Yonge & Wellesley) **416/410–5426,
416/925–6222** • 10pm-7am, clsd Mon-Wed •
popular • mostly gay men • dancing/DJ • cover
charge

Lee's Palace/ Dance Cave 529 Bloor St
416/532–1598 • gay/ straight • live bands •
dance club upstairs

Lüb Lounge 487 Church St (S of Wellesley)
416/323–1489 • 4pm-midnight • gay/ straight
• women's night 9pm Wed (seasonal) •
dancing/ DJ • also restaurant • Sun brunch

Savour 489 College St (at Markham, at Andy
Poolhall) **416/923–5300 (club#)** • 10pm 4th
Sat only • mostly women • dancing/ DJ

Swallow 292 College St **647/439–5876** • gay/
straight • more gay Fri-Sat • dancing/ DJ

Tallulah's Cabaret 12 Alexander St (at
Buddies in Bad Times Theatre) **416/975–8555**
• 10:30pm Fri-Sat only • lesbians/ gay men •
eclectic performances • dancing/DJ • drag
shows last Fri

Cafes

Cafe Diplomatico 594 College St (at Clinton,
in Little Italy) **416/534–4637** • 8am-3am •
popular • patio

The Second Cup 548 Church St (at
Wellesley) **416/964–2457** • open late •
popular • coffee & desserts

Sweet City Bakery 24 Wellesley St W (at
Yonge) **416/962–0358** • 6am-5pm, clsd Sun

Timothy's 500 Church St (at Alexander) 416/925–8550 • lesbians/ gay men

RESTAURANTS

Allen's Restaurant 143 Danforth Ave (at Broadview) 416/463–3086 • lunch & dinner • great scotch selection • Irish music/ dancing • patio • CanS15

Avalon 270 Adelaide St W (at John) 416/979–9918 • dinner nightly, lunch Th only, clsd Sun-Mon • contemporary cont'l • intimate dining • nonsmoking • upscale

Bistro 422 422 College St 416/963–9416 • 4pm-2am • full bar

Byzantium 499 Church St (S of Wellesley) 416/922–3859 • 5:30pm-11pm • mostly gay men • chic • cont'l/ global • also martini bar till 2am • patio • gay-owned

Fire on the East Side 6 Gloucester St (at Yonge) 416/960–3473 • noon-1am, 10am-midnight wknds, clsd Mon-Tue • lesbians/ gay men • Southern comfort food • patio

Flo's Diner 70 Yorkville Ave (near Bay St) 416/961–4333 • 7:30am-10pm, till 7pm Mon, from 8am Sat, from 9am Sun • gay-owned

Golden Thai 105 Church St (at Richmond) 416/868–6668 • 11:30am-10:30pm, from 5pm wknds

The Gypsy Co-Op 817 Queen St W (W of Bathurst) 416/703–5069 • noon-3am, 6pm-2am Mon, clsd Sun • gay/ straight • also bar • eclectic & kitschy • resident spiritualists

Il Fornello 1560 Yonge St (1 block N of St Clair) 416/920–7347 • 11:30am-10pm, no lunch Sat • Italian • plenty veggie • also 214 King W (at Simcoe), 416/977-2855 • also 576 Danforth Ave (at Carlaw), 416/466-2931

Jamie Kennedy Wine Bar 9 Church St 416/362–1957 • tapas-style dishes

Joy Bistro 884 Queen St E 416/465–8855 • 8am-11pm, brunch wknds • nonsmoking • patio • also Over Joy lounge upstairs 6pm-2am

La Hacienda 640 Queen St W (near Bathurst) 416/703–3377 • lunch & dinner • Mexican • sleazy, loud & fun

Laurentian Room 51 Winchester St 416/925–8680 • dinner Tue-Sat • full bar • upscale

The Living Well Restaurant & Bar 692 Yonge St (at Isabella) 416/922–6770 • 11:30am-1am, till 1:30am Fri-Sat • lesbians/ gay men • plenty veggie • also upstairs bar • open 6pm-2am • live DJ • Dirty Bingo Mon • 2 patios

Mitzi's Sister 1554 Queen St W 416/532–2570 • 10am-2am, till midnight Sun, popular wknd brunch • upscale pub eats • full bar • gay-owned

Oasis 294 College St (at Spadina) 416/975–0845 • 5pm-2am • eclectic tapas • also bar • live shows

PJ Mellon's 489 Church St (at Wellesley) 416/966–3241 • 11:30am-10pm, from 11am Sun • some veggie • full bar • wheelchair access

Splendido 88 Harbord St (at Spadina) 416/929–7788 • 5pm-11pm, clsd Mon • great decor & gnocchi • full bar • wheelchair access

The Superior Restaurant 253 Yonge St (across from Eaton Centre) 416/214–0416 • 11:30am-midnight, clsd Sun • oysters • full bar • wheelchair access

Tantra 634 Church St (at Isabella) 416/926–0313 • lunch & dinner • also bar & lounge • patio

Trattoria Al Forno 459 Church St (at Carlton) 416/944–8852 • dinner nightly • full bar

The Village Rainbow 477 Church St (at Maitland) 416/961–0616 • 7am-midnight, till 1am Th-Sat, from 8am Sun • full bar • big patio

Zelda's 542 Church St 416/922–2526 • 11am-2am, from 10am wknds • Sun brunch popular • lesbians/gay men • drag shows • full bar • patio

ZiZi Trattoria 456 Bloor St W (E of Bathurst) 416/533–5117 • 5pm-close, from noon Fri-Sat, clsd Sun

ENTERTAINMENT & RECREATION

AIDS Memorial in Cawthra Park

The Bata Shoe Museum 327 Bloor St W 416/979–7799 • 10,000 shoes from over 4,500 years—including the platforms of Elton John and the pumps of Marilyn Monroe

Buddies in Bad Times Theatre 12 Alexander St 416/975–8555 • LGBT theater • also bar

Hanlan's Pt Beach Toronto Islands • nude beach • 10 minutes from downtown

BOOKSTORES

Glad Day Bookshop 598–A Yonge St (at Wellesley) 416/961–4161, 877/783–3725 • 10am-7pm, till 9pm Th-Fri, from noon Sun • popular • great selection of LGBT books, mags & videos

The Omega Centre 29 Yorkville Ave (btwn Yonge & Bay) 416/975–9086, 888/663–6377 (IN CANADA) • 10am-9pm, till 6pm Sat, 11am-5pm Sun • metaphysical

This Ain't The Rosedale Library 483 Church St (at Wellesley) 416/929–9912 • 10am-10pm, till 11pm Fri-Sat, 1pm-9pm Sun • popular • LGBT books & magazines

Toronto Women's Bookstore 73 Harbord St (at Spadina) 416/922–8744, 800/861–8233 • 10:30am-6pm, till 8pm Th-Fri, noon-5pm Sun

Wonderworks 79-A Harbord St (at Spadina) 416/323–3131 • 10:30am-6pm, till 8pm Th, noon-5pm Sun • books & gifts

RETAIL SHOPS

Out on the Street 551 Church St 416/967–2759, 800/263–5747 • 10am-8pm, from 11am Sun • LGBT accessories

Passage Body Piercing 473 Church St, 2nd flr 416/929–7330 • noon-7pm, clsd Mon • also tattoos & scarification

Secrets From Your Sister 476 Bloor St W 416/538–1234 • 11am-6pm, till 7pm Th-Fri, noon-6pm Sun • "beautiful lingerie in realistic sizes for the modern woman" • wheelchair access

Take A Walk On the Wild Side 161 Gerrard St E (at Jarvis) 416/921–6112 • "hotel, boutique & club for crossdressers, transvestites, transexuals & other persons of gender"

Vixon 620 Yonge St (at St Joseph) 416/960–6464 • 11am-8pm • clubwear

PUBLICATIONS

The Pink Pages 416/972–7418 • annual LGBT directory

Xtra! 416/925–6665 • LGBT newspaper

SPIRITUAL GROUPS

Christos MCC 427 Bloor St W (at Spadina in Trinity St Paul's Church) 416/925–7924 • 7pm Sun

Dignity Toronto Earl & Sherbourne Sts (at Our Lady of Lourdes Church library) 416/925–9872 x2011 • 7pm 4th Sat • upstairs in library

Integrity Toronto at Bloor & Avenue Rd (at Church of the Redeemer) 416/925–9872 x2050, 416/323–0389 • 7:30pm 3rd Mon

MCC Toronto 115 Simpson Ave (Broadview & Gerrard area) 416/406–6228 • 9am & 11am Sun • wheelchair access

GYMS & HEALTH CLUBS

Epic Fitness 9 St Josephs (at Yonge) 416/960–1705

SEX CLUBS

Pussy Palace Toronto 231 Mutual St (at Carlton) 416/925–9872x2115 • occasional women-only sex club • call for dates & info

EROTICA

ASLANLeather.com 135 Tecumseth St, Unit 6 (rear) 416/306–0462 • leather, rubber & vinyl dildo harnesses • fine bondage gear • toys

Come As You Are 701 Queen St W (at Bathurst) 416/504–7934 • 11am-7pm, till 9pm Th-Fri, till 6pm Sat, noon-5pm Sun • co-op-owned sex store

Good For Her 175 Harbord St (near Bathurst) 416/588–0900, 877/588–0900 • 11am-7pm, till 8pm Fri, till 6pm Sat, noon-5pm Sun (women- & trans-only Sun, also 11am-2pm Th) • women's sexuality products • wheelchair access

Lovecraft 27 Yorkville Ave (btwn Bay & Yonge) 416/923–7331 • toys • lingerie • videos • books

North Bound Leather 586 Yonge (W of Wellesley St) 416/972–1037 • toys & clothing • wheelchair access

Priape 465 Church St (at Wellesley, above Woody's) 416/586–9914, 800/461–6969 • popular • clubwear • leather • books • toys & more

Seduction 577 Yonge St 416/966–6969

Stag Shop 239 Yonge St 416/368–3507

Turkey Point

ACCOMMODATIONS

The Point Tent & Trailer Resort 918 Charlotteville Rd #2, RR 1, Vittoria 519/426–7275 • mostly gay men • nudity ok • swimming • leather • "tent & trailer resort" on 50 acres • gay-owned • Can$16-65

Waterloo

RESTAURANTS

Ethel's Lounge 114 King St N (at Spring) 519/725–2361 • 11:30am-2am • full bar • patio

Westport

ACCOMMODATIONS

Devil Lake B&B 8991 Perth Rd (at Hutchings Rd) 613/273–4001 • mostly women • swimming • lesbian owned/ run • Can$135

Windsor

see also Detroit, Michigan

ACCOMMODATIONS

The Windsor Inn on the River 3857 Riverside Dr E (at George Ave) 519/945–2110, 866/635–0055 • gay-friendly • jacuzzi • full brkfst • kids ok • nonsmoking • Can$79-149

BARS

The Honest Lawyer 300 Ouellete Ave 519/977–0599 • 11am-2am, from 4pm Sun • gay-friendly • food served

NIGHTCLUBS

The Complex 634 Chilver Rd (at Wyandotte East) 519/252–1774 • 2pm-2am • popular • lesbians/ gay men • dancing/DJ • food served • drag shows • video bar • karaoke Th & Sun • gay-owned

The Loop 156 Chatham St W (at Ferry St) 519/256–9844 • 9pm-2am • gay-friendly • dancing/DJ • alternative • live shows • theme nights • young crowd

The Wellington 800 Wellington 519/971–0428 • 8pm-close Wed-Sat • lesbians/ gay men • neighborhood bar • dancing/ DJ • karaoke

ENTERTAINMENT & RECREATION

Queer Radio CJAM 91.5 FM 519/253–4232 • 9pm Mon

SPIRITUAL GROUPS

MCC Windsor 1680 Dougall Ave (at Westminster United Church) 519/977–6897 • 1:30pm Sun

Woodstock

ACCOMMODATIONS

Nunn's Hollow Guest Suites 21 Delatre St (Dundas St) 519/539–9780 • mostly gay men • full brkfst • jacuzzi • also self-catering apt • gay-owned • Can$80-120

PRINCE EDWARD ISLAND

Albany

ACCOMMODATIONS

Evening Primrose 114 Lord's Pond Rd 902/437–3134 • 40 minutes from Charlottetown • B&B, cottage & studio • full brkfst • nonsmoking • kids/ pets ok • wheelchair access • gay-owned • Can$65/ night & $600/ week

Blooming Point

ENTERTAINMENT & RECREATION

Blooming Point • nude beach

Charlottetown

INFO LINES & SERVICES

Abegweit Rainbow Collective 902/894–5776, 877/380–5776 • 24hr info line, staffed 7pm-10pm Tue & Th • monthly dances & other social activities

ACCOMMODATIONS

Blooming Breezes Executive Cottage 108 Lowe Ln, Blooming Point 902/626–4475 • gay/ straight • cottage • close to beach • kids ok • gay-owned • Can$200-250/ night (weekly rates available)

Charlottetown Hotel 75 Kent St (at Pownall) 902/894–7371, 800/565–7633 • gay-friendly • swimming • also restaurant • cont'l/ seafood • lounge clsd Sun • wheelchair access • $109-192

Rainbow Lodge 902/651–2202, 800/268–7005 • lesbians/ gay men • full brkfst • 15 minutes outside of town • nonsmoking • gay-owned • Can$80

BARS

Baba's Lounge 81 University Ave 902/892–7377 • noon-2am, 5pm-midnight Sun • gay-friendly • live bands • also Cedars restaurant • Canadian/ Lebanese • some veggie

BOOKSTORES

Book Mark 172 Queen St (in mall) 902/566–4888 • 9am-5:30pm, till 9pm Th-Sat, clsd Sun • will order lesbian titles

EROTICA

Afternoon Delight 218 University Ave, Charlotte 902/892–3469, 877/424–5469 • woman-owned/ run

Cornwall

ACCOMMODATIONS

The Rainbow Inn PEI 4992 Rte 19 Nine Mile Creek **902/675–2393** • renovated farm house • full brkfst • kids/pets ok • lesbian-owned • Can$75

Souris

ACCOMMODATIONS

Johnson Shore Inn RR #3 Rte16 **902/687–1340, 877/510–9669** • gay/straight • country inn on 50 acres • full brkfst • kids 10+ ok • wheelchair access • lesbian-owned • Can$125-289

PROVINCE OF QUÉBEC

Provincewide

INFO LINES & SERVICES

Gay Line/Gai Ecoute **888/505–1010** • 7pm-11pm

Chicoutimi

see also Jonquière

BARS

Bistro des Anges 332 rue du Havre **418/698–4829** • 3pm-3am • lesbians/gay men • neighborhood bar • food served

NIGHTCLUBS

L'Arlequin 564 boul du Saguenay Ouest **418/696–2072** • 4pm-3am, from 9pm wknds, clsd Mon-Wed • lesbians/gay men • dancing/DJ

Drummondville

ACCOMMODATIONS

Motel Alouette 1975 boul Mercure **819/478–4166** • gay/straight • 3-star motel • sauna • hot tub • gay-owned • $80-120

BARS

Bar "G" Pob 901 Mercure Blvd **819/471–4252** • 8pm-3am, clsd Mon-Tue • lesbians/gay men • neighborhood bar • dancing/DJ • drag shows • 18+ • young crowd • terrace • wheelchair access

Granby

ACCOMMODATIONS

Le Campagnard B&B 146 Denison Ouest J2G 4C8 **450/770–1424** • gay-friendly • in a quiet village • bikes available • swimming • also camping • nonsmoking • Can$50-100

Hull

see also Ottawa, Ontario

Joliette

ACCOMMODATIONS

L'Oasis des Pins 381 boul Brassard, St-Paul-de-Joliette **450/754–3819** • lesbians/gay men • swimming • camping May-Sept • restaurant open year-round

Jonquière

see also Chicoutimi

Laurentides (Laurentian Mtns)

ACCOMMODATIONS

Auberge de la Gare 1694 chemin Pierre-Peladeau, Ste-Adèle **450/228–3140, 888/825–4273 (IN QUÉBEC ONLY)** • lesbians/gay men • B&B • superb ancestral home • near slopes • swimming • Can$65-80

Havre du Parc Auberge 2788 Rte 125 N, St-Donat **819/424–7686** • gay/straight • quiet lakeside inn for nature lovers • full brkfst • gay-owned • Can$130-150

Le Septentrion B&B 901 chemin St-Adolphe, Morin-Heights/St-Sauveur **450/226–2665** • lesbians/gay men • Victorian • full brkfst • swimming • hot tub • nonsmoking • gay-owned • Can$120-250

Magdalen Island

ACCOMMODATIONS

Les Réfugiés 955 chemin du Gros-Cap, L'Etang du Nord **418/986–4192** • gay-friendly • B&B • nonsmoking • gay-owned • Can$55-70

Magog

see also Sherbrooke

ACCOMMODATIONS

Au Gîte du Cerf Argenté 2984 chemin Georgeville Rd (off Hwy 10) **819/847–4264** • gay/straight • B&B in century-old farmhouse • 4 beaches nearby • kids ok • gay-owned • Can$140-195 (2 persons/2 nights)

Montréal

Note: M°=Metro station

INFO LINES & SERVICES

AA Gay/ Lesbian 514/376–9230 • call for info (in French or English)

Gay/ Lesbian Community Centre of Montréal 2075 rue Plessis, local 110 (at Ontario) 514/528-8424 • 10am-noon & 1pm-6pm, clsd wknds, library

Gay Line/ Gai Ecoute 514/866–5090 (ENGLISH), 888/505-1010 (IN CANADA ONLY) • 7pm-11pm

The Village Tourism Information Center/ Gay Chamber of Commerce 1260 rue St-Catherine Est #209 514/522–1885, 888/595-8110 • 11am-6pm, 10am-8pm Fri-Sun (May-Oct), 10am-6pm, clsd wknds (Oct-May)

ACCOMMODATIONS

Abri du Voyageur Hotel 9 Rue Ste-Catherine West 514/849–2922 • gay-friendly • charming, good-value hotel in downtown Montréal • 15-minute walk to the village • Can$42-99

Alexandre Logan 1631 rue Alexandre de Sève 514/598–0555, 866/895–0555 • gay-friendly • Can$75-175

Alexandrie-Montréal 1750 Amherst (at Robin) 514/525–9420 • gay-friendly • rooms & apts in the Village • kids/ pets ok • gay-owned • $40-200

Angelica Blue B&B 1213 Ste-Elisabeth (at Ste-Catherine) 514/844–5048, 800/878-5048 • gay/ straight • theme rooms • full brkfst • some shared baths • nonsmoking • Can$75-155

Montreal

WHERE THE GIRLS ARE:
In the popular Plateau Mont-Royal neighborhood or in the bohemian area on Ste-Catherine est.

LGBT PRIDE:
July/August. 514/285-4011, web: www.diverscite.org.

ANNUAL EVENTS:
June - Festival International de Jazz de Montréal 514/871-1881, www.montrealjazzfest.com
July - Just For Laughs Comedy Festival 888/244-3155, web: www.hahaha.com
August - Montréal World Film Festival 514/848-3883, web: www.ffm-montreal.org
September - International Gay/ Lesbian Film Festival, web: www.image-nation.org
October - Black & Blue Party 514/875-7026, web: www.bbcm.org. AIDS benefit dance & circuit party.

CITY INFO:
514/873–2015, web: www.tourism-montreal.org.

ATTRACTIONS:
Bonsecours Market 514/872-7730, web: www.marchebonsecours.qc.ca
Latin Quarter
Montréal Biodome 514/868–3000
Montréal Botanical Garden & Insectarium 514/872-1400
Montréal Museum of Fine Arts 514/285-2000, web: www.mmfa.qc.ca
Old Montréal & Old Port
Olympic Park
Underground City.

BEST VIEW:
From a caleche ride (horse-drawn carriage) or from the top of the Montréal Tower or from the patio of the old hunting lodge atop Mont Royal.

WEATHER:
It's north of New England so winters are for real. Beautiful spring and fall colors. Summers get hot and humid.

TRANSIT:
Diamond Cab 514/273-6331.
Montréal Urban Transit 514/786–4636, web: www.stcum.qc.ca.

Reply **Forward** **Delete**

Date: Nov 26, 2005 15:08:22
From: Girl-on-the-Go
To: Editor@Damron.com
Subject: Montréal

>Montréal is the world's second-largest French-speaking city. As you take in the architecture and arts, the fashion and the food, the style and sophistication of Canada's most cosmopolitan city, you will catch glimpses of the world's largest French-speaking city, Paris. But make no mistake; while it does have strong historical and cultural ties to Paris (it too has a Latin Quarter), Montréal is no "Paris-lite."

>Montréal is home to many museums, like the Musée d'art contemporain de Montréal and the Montréal Museum of Fine Arts. Theater, dance, and music companies as well as a celebrated symphony orchestra thrive in this historic city. There is also a wealth of Old World architecture in the streets of Old Montréal and around Mont Royal.

>Then there are the various symbols and events that mark Montréal as its own force in the contemporary world, like the World Film Festival (every August) and the Palais des Congrès and Montréal World Trade Center.

>But, clichéd as it may sound, what makes Montréal such a beautiful city to visit is its people. Just take a walk through the Plateau Mont-Royal neighborhood and stroll through St-Louis Square to the rue Prince-Arthur. You'll not only see an interesting mix of tourists and Quebeçois, but you'll also pass by **Lindsey's**, Montréal's premier women's guesthouse.

Au Stade B&B 514/899–4636 • mostly gay men • lesbians welcome

Auberge Belles Vues B&B 1407 Panet #2 **514/521–9998** • located in the Gay Village • Can$75-300

Auberge de la Fontaine 1301 rue Rachel Est (at Chambord) **514/597–0166, 800/597–0597** • gay/ straight • kids ok • wheelchair access • Can$129-253

Auberge La Raveaudiere B&B 11 Hatley Center, North Hatley **819/842–2554** • gay/ straight • 19th-c country inn • full brkfst • 1.5 hours from Montréal • gay-owned • Can$95-160

B&B Le Cartier 1219 rue Cartier (at Ste-Catherine Est) **514/917–1829, 877/524–0495** • gay/ straight • B&B • newly renovated 100-year-old stone house in Gay Village • Can$60-125 • gay-owned

Reply **Forward** **Delete**

>Or, better yet, head over to the Village, Montréal's gay community. For current hot spots, and the latest info, pop in at **The Village Tourism Info Center** where they can hook you up with area maps. Though at first glance the Village is a thriving Boys' Town, you'll see plenty of sisters in the bars and shops along Ste-Catherine. We hear there are plenty of cute girls to be found on the second floor of **Le Drugstore.** And **Club Parking** is said to be popular with the gals on Friday nights. Check the latest issue of **Fugues** for the latest in one-off parties.

>Just remember that the people of Montréal are proud of their French heritage and language. Most signs will be in French— sometimes with an English translation, sometimes not. So brush up on your French, or at least learn some of the polite basics: *s'il vous plaît* (please), *merci* (thank you), *pardon* (excuse me), and the all-important question, *Parlez-vous anglais?* (Do you speak English?).

Le Chasseur B&B 1567 rue St-André (at Maisonneuve) 514/521–2238, 800/451–2238 • mostly gay men • Victorian row house • summer terrace • gay-owned • Can$39-149

Chateau Cherrier 550 rue Cherrier (at St-Hubert) 514/844–0055, 800/816–0055 • lesbians/ gay men • full gourmet brkfst • gay-owned • $75-125

Chez Philippe 2457 rue Ste-Catherine Est (at Fullum) 514/890–1666, 877/890–1666 • B&B w/in walking distance of Gay Village • vegan brkfst • large terrace • gay/ straight • gay-owned • Can$65-135

Chez Roger Bontemps 1441 Wolfe (at Ste-Catherine) 514/598–9587, 888/634–9090 • gay/ straight • B&B in two 1873 homes • also furnished apts • Can$55-240

Crowne Plaza Metro Centre 505 rue Sherbrooke Est (at Berri) 514/842–8581, 800/561–4644 • gay-friendly • breathtaking views of Montréal • full brkfst • swimming • hot tub • also restaurant • full bar • wheelchair access • $139-450

Delta Montréal 475 President Kennedy (at City Councilor) 514/286–1986, 877/814–7706 • gay-friendly • hotel • hot tub • swimming • kids/ pets ok • restaurant • bar • garden terrace • Can$129-259

Gingerbread House B&B 1628 St-Christophe (at Maisonneuve) 514/597–2804 • lesbians/ gay men • full brkfst • shared bath • nonsmoking • gay-owned • Can$45-70

Hébergement Touristique du Plateau Mont–Royal 1131 rue Rachel Est 514/527–2394, 800/597–0597 • gay-friendly • reservation service

Hotel du Fort 1390 rue du Fort (at Ste-Catherine) 514/938–8333, 800/565–6333 • gay/ straight • wheelchair access • Can$135-475

Hotel Dynastie 1723 St-Hubert 514/529–5210, 877/529–5210 • gay/ straight • nonsmoking • gay-owned • Can$58-88

Hotel Kent 1216 rue St-Hubert (at Ste-Catherine) 514/845–9835 • gay-friendly • Can$40-90

Hotel le St-André 1285 rue St-André (at Ste-Catherine) **514/849–8167, 800/265–7071** • gay/ straight • B&B inn • on edge of Gay Village • kids ok • Can$68-148

Hotel Lord Berri 1199 rue Berri (at Ste-Catherine) **514/845–9236, 888/363–0363** • gay-friendly • nonsmoking rooms available • also Italian resto-bar • $99-159

Hotel Manoir des Alpes 1245 rue St-André (at Ste-Catherine) **514/845–9803, 800/465–2929** • gay-friendly • 3-star hotel • hot tub • kids ok • Can$60+

Hotel Pierre 169 Sherbrooke Est (btwn St-Denis & St-Laurent) **514/288–8519, 877/288–8577** • gay-friendly • kitchen • Can$95-125

Hotel XIXe Siecle 262 rue Saint-Jacques **877/553–0019, 514/985–0019** • gay-friendly • large, modern rooms • Can$140-335

The House of Angels B&B 1640 rue Alexandre de Sève (at Maisonneuve) **514/527–9890** • mostly gay men • rooms in cozy apt • shared baths • terrace access • gay-owned • Can$50-90

Jade Blue B&B 1225 de Bullion **514/878–9843, 800/878–5048** • gay/ straight • theme rooms • full brkfst • some shared baths • nonsmoking • Can$75-155

Lindsey's B&B 3974 av Laval (near Duluth) **514/843–4869, 888/655–8655** • popular • women only • charming town house near Square St-Louis & rue Prince Arthur • full brkfst • nonsmoking • lesbian-owned • Can$75-145

Loews Hotel Vogue 1425 rue de la Montagne (near Ste-Catherine) **514/285–5555, 800/465–6654** • gay-friendly • full-service 5-star hotel • wheelchair access • Can$175+

Montréal Boutique Suite Guesthouse 1269 rue de Champlain (at rue Sainte Catherine E) **514/521–9436** • gay-friendly • nonsmoking • gay-owned • Can$107-150

Le Roy d'Carreau Guest House 1637 rue Amherst (at Maisonneuve) **514/524–2493, 877/527–7975** • lesbians/ gay men • hot tub • sundeck • nonsmoking • in Gay Village • gay-owned • Can$100-250

Ruta Bagage 1345 rue Ste-Rose (at Panët) **514/598–1586** • gay/ straight • Victorian B&B • full brkfst • shared baths • Can$70-95

Le Traversin B&B/ Urban Spa 4124 rue St-Hubert (at Duluth) **514/597–1546** • gay & straight • B&B & urban spa • full brkfst • some shared baths • hot tub • massage • nonsmoking • gay-owned • Can$120-185

Turquoise B&B 1576 rue Alexandre de Sève (at Maisonneuve) **514/523–9943, 877/707–1576** • mostly gay men • Victorian B&B • shared baths • gay-owned • Can$50+

W Montréal 901 Square Victoria **514/395–3100, 877/WHOTELS (RESERVATIONS ONLY)** • gay-friendly • also spa, restaurant & 3 bars • wheelchair access • Can$249-5,000

Le Zebre B&B **514/528–6801** • elegant Victorian near Park Lafontaine & Gay Village • gay-owned

BARS

Bar Cajun 1574 rue Ste-Catherine Est (at Hotel Bourbon) **514/523–4679** • 3pm-3am • lesbians/ gay men

Cabaret Mado 1115 Ste-Catherine Est (at Amherst, below Le Campus) **514/525–7566** • 1pm-3am • popular • lesbians/ gay men • theme nights • dancing/DJ • karaoke • drag shows • owned by the fabulous Mado! • wheelchair access

Citibar 1603 Ontario Est (at Champlain) **514/525–4251** • 11am-3am • gay/ straight • neighborhood bar

Club Bolo 960 rue Amherst (at Viger) **514/849–4777** • 10pm-2am Fri • special events Sat • lesbians/ gay men • dancing/DJ • country/ western • T-dance from 4pm Sun • cover charge

Club Date 1218 rue Ste-Catherine Est (at Beaudry) **514/521–1242** • 1pm-2am • lesbians/ gay men • neighborhood bar • karaoke nightly • piano

Le Drugstore 1366 rue Ste-Catherine Est (at Panët) **514/524–1960** • 9am-3am • popular • lesbians/ gay men • 8-bar complex w/ boutiques, restaurants, even travel agency • 3 flrs • food served

Foufounes Electriques 87 Ste-Catherine Est (at St-Laurent) **514/844–5539** • 3pm-3am • gay-friendly • dancing/DJ • live bands • patio

Fun Spot 1151 rue Ontario Est (at Wolfe) **514/522–0416** • 11am-3am • lesbians/ gay men • neighborhood bar • dancing/DJ • transgender-friendly • food served • drag shows • karaoke

Lady Loft 990 rue St-Antoine Ouest (at Mansfield) **514/585–1393** • 9pm-close • lesbians/ gay men • dancing/ DJ

Météor 1661 rue Ste-Catherine Est (at Champlain) **514/523–1481** • 11am-3am • lesbians/ gay men • dancing/DJ • '60s-themed bar • ballroom dancing • square dancing • food served • karaoke • drag shows • 40+ crowd

Le Mystique 1424 rue Stanley (at Maisonneuve) 514/844–5711 • 4pm-3am • gay/ straight • English underground pub • poker machines

La Relaxe 1309 Ste-Catherine Est, 2nd flr 514/523–0578 • noon-3am • mostly gay men • neighborhood bar • open to the street • as the name implies, a good place to relax & people-watch

Taverne Rocky 1673 rue Ste-Catherine Est (at Papineau) 514/521–7865 • 10am-close • mostly gay men • videos • older crowd

West Side 1071 Beaver Hall (at Belmont) 514/866–4963 • 4pm-3am, from 7pm wknds • mostly gay men • nude dancers

NIGHTCLUBS

Cabaret Cleopatra 1230 boul St-Laurent (at Ste-Catherine) 514/871–8066, 514/871–8065 • 11pm-3am • mostly gay men • dancing/DJ • transgender-friendly • karaoke • live shows • theme nights

Club Parking 1296 rue Amherst 514/282–1199 • 3pm-3am • popular • mostly gay men • dancing/ DJ • leather • 2 flrs • women's night Fri

Femme Fridays 1296 rue Amherst (at Club Parking) 514/282–1199 (CLUB #) • Fri only • mostly women • dancing/ DJ

La Track 1584 Ste-Catherine Est 514/521–1419 • popular • mostly men • dancing/ DJ • older crowd • multi-level w/ outdoor terraces • cruisy

Meow Mix 4848 boul St-Laurent (at La Sala Rossa) 514/284–0122 • monthly party • mostly women • dancing/ DJ • check local listings for dates

Red Lite (After Hours) 1755 rue de Lierre, Laval 450/967–3057 • Fri-Sun only • popular • gay-friendly • after-hours club • cover

Sky Complex 1474 rue Ste-Catherine Est 514/529–6969 • 11am-3am • lesbians/ gay men • 3 levels • cabaret from 9pm Th-Sun • drag shows • dance club from 10pm Fri-Sun

Stéréo 858 rue Ste-Catherine Est 514/286–0325 • after-hours Fri-Sat only • gay/ straight • cover • popular

Unity II 1171 Ste-Catherine Est 514/523–2777 • 10pm-close, clsd Sun-Tue • lesbians/ gay men • dancing/DJ • 4 flrs & great rooftop terrace • live shows • young crowd

CAFES

Café Titanic 445 St-Pierre (in Old Montréal) 514/849–0894 • 8am-3pm, clsd wknds • popular • salad & soup

Presse Cafe 1263 rue Ste-Catherine Est 514/528–9530

The Second Cup 1351 Ste-Catherine Est 514/598–7727 • très gay coffee shop • nonsmoking

RESTAURANTS

L' Anecdote 801 rue Rachel Est (at St-Hubert) 514/526–7967 • 8am-10pm • lesbians/gay men • burgers • plenty veggie

Après le Jour 901 rue Rachel Est (at St-Andre) 514/527–4141 • 5pm-10pm, till 11pm Th-Sat • lesbians/ gay men • Italian/ French • seafood • bring your own wine • wheelchair access

Area 1429 rue Amherst 514/890–6691 • lunch Mon-Fri, dinner nightly • French/ Italian/ Asian fusion

L' Armoricain 1550 Fullum (at Maisonneuve) 514/523–2551 • lunch weekdays & dinner nightly, clsd Sun • gourmet French • beer/ wine • wheelchair access

Bato Thai 1310 rue Ste-Catherine Est 514/524–6705 • lunch weekdays & dinner nightly • lesbians/gay men • beer/ wine

Les Chevres 1201 Van Horne (M° Outremont) 514/270–1119 • lunch & dinner • mostly vegetarian • upscale

Chu Chai 4088 rue St-Denis (at Rachel) 514/843–4194 • lunch & dinner • vegetarian Thai • full bar • popular

Club Sandwich 1570 Ste-Catherine Est (in Bourbon Complex) 514/521–1419 • 24hr diner • wheelchair access

Commensal 1720 St-Denis (at Ontario) 514/845–2627 • 11am-11pm • vegetarian • other locations • beer/ wine • wheelchair access

L' Exception 1200 rue St-Hubert (at René-Lévèsque) 514/282–1282 • burgers & sandwiches • plenty veggie • terrace

L' Express 3927 rue St-Denis (at Duluth) 514/845–5333 • 8am-2am, 10am-close wknds • popular • French bistro • full bar • great pâté • reservations recommended • wheelchair access

La Paryse 302 rue Ontario Est (near Sanguinet) 514/842–2040 • 11am-11pm, from noon Sat, from 2pm Sun • lesbians/gay men • '50s-style diner • lesbian-owned • Can$8-10

Piccolo Diavolo 1336 rue Ste-Catherine Est (at Panêt) 514/526–1336 • 5pm-11pm, also lunch Th-Fri • popular • Italian • wheelchair access

Le Planète 1451 rue Ste-Catherine Est (at Plessis) 514/528-6953 • lunch weekdays & dinner nightly, brunch only Sun • global cuisine • young crowd • beer/ wine • Can$20 & under

Saloon Cafe 1333 rue Ste-Catherine Est (at Panêt) 514/522-1333 • 11:30am-midnight, from 10am wknds, till 2am Fri-Sat • popular • int'l • plenty veggie • big dishes & even bigger drinks • Can$20 & under •

Thai Grill 5101 boul St-Laurent (at Laurier) 514/270-5566 • lunch Sun-Th & dinner nightly • one of Montréal's best Thai eateries

ENTERTAINMENT & RECREATION

Ça Roule 27 rue de la Commune Est 514/866-0633 • join the beautiful people skating up & down Ste-Catherine

Cinéma du Parc 3575 Parc (btwn Milton & Prince Arthur) 514/281-1900 • repertory film theater

Prince Arthur Est at boul St-Laurent, not far from Sherbrooke Métro station • closed-off street w/ many outdoor restaurants & cafés • touristy but oh-so-European

RETAIL SHOPS

Cuir Mont-Royal 826-A Mont Royal Est (at St Hubert) 514/527-0238, 888/338-8283 • leather • fetish

Priape 1311 Ste-Catherine Est (at Visitation) 514 /521-8451, 800/461-6969 • 10am-9pm, noon-9pm Sun • clubwear • leather • books • toys & more

Screaming Eagle 1424 boul St-Laurent 514/849-2843 • leather shop • also 3915 Blvd Samson, Laval • 450/978-9237

PUBLICATIONS

Fugues 514/848-1854, 888/848-1854 • glossy LGBT bar/ entertainment guide

The Mirror 514/393-1010 • free queer-positive weekly • reviews, event listings & more in English

EROTICA

Il Bolero 6842-46 St-Hubert (btwn St-Zotique & Bélanger) 514/270-6065 • fetish & clubwear emporium • ask about monthly fetish party

North Hatley

see Sherbrooke

Québec City

ACCOMMODATIONS

L' Auberge du Quartier 170 Grande Allée Ouest (at av Cartier) 418/525-9726, 800/782-9441 • gay/ straight • cont'l brkfst • kids ok • nonsmoking • Can$79-120

Auberge Place D'Armes 24 rue Ste-Anne 418/694-9485, 866/333-9485 • gay-friendly • Can$90-190

Le Coureur des Bois Guest House 15 rue Ste-Ursule (at St-Jean, in Old Québec) 418/692-1117, 800/269-6414 • lesbians/ gay men • also apts • shared baths • nonsmoking • gay-owned • Can$65-135

Hoel-Motel Le Voyageur 2250 boul Sainte-Anne (at Estimauville) 418/661-7701, 800/463-5568 • gay/ straight • hotel • swimming • sauna • kids ok • restaurant • 2 bars • Can$65+

Hôtel Dominion 1912 126 rue St-Pierre 418/692-2224, 888/833-5253 • gay-friendly • boutique hotel in city's 1st skyscraper • wheelchair access • Can$205-305

Hôtel Germain Des Prés 1200 av Germain des Prés (at Laurier Blvd), Sainte-Foy 418/658-1224, 800/463-5253 • gay-friendly • hotel • modern & elegant • kids ok • restaurant • women-owned • Can$125+

Hotel Le Clos Saint-Louis 69 Saint-Louis (at Saint-Ursule) 418/694-1311, 800/461-1311 • gay/ straight • 1844 Victorian hotel located in historic district near shops & restaurants • Can$145-255

Loews Le Concorde 1225 cours du Général De Montcalm 418/647-2222, 800/463-5256 • gay-friendly • 4-star • located on Grand Allée • swimming • kids/ pets ok • revolving restaurant • wheelchair access • Can$109+

La Lucarne Enchantée 225 chemin Royal, St-Jean-De-L'Ile d'Orléans 418/829-3792 • gay/ straight • full brkfst • shared baths • animals on premises • near beach • swimming • lesbian-owned • Can$65-70

Maison du Cocher 31 rue Dauphine 418/261-6610 • gay-friendly • historic-style apts & coach house

Le Moulin de St-Laurent Chalets 754 Chemin Royal, St Laurent, Ile d' Orleans 418/829-3888, 888/629-3888 • gay/ straight • cottages • swimming • kids/ pets ok • also restaurant • Can$50-100/ person

BARS

L' Amour Sorcier 789 côte Ste-Geneviève (at St-Jean) **418/523-3395** • 2pm-3am • popular • lesbians/gay men • neighborhood bar • food served • videos • terrace

Bar 321 321 de la Couronne (at La Salle) **418/525-5107** • noon-3am • mostly gay men • neighborhood bar • transgender-friendly

Bar 889 889 côte Ste-Geneviève **418/524-5000** • 11am-3am • lesbians/gay men • neighborhood bar • patio

Bar Le Drague 815 rue St-Augustin (at St-Joachim) **418/649-7212** • 10am-3am • popular • 3 bars • mostly gay men • neighborhood bar • dancing/DJ Th-Sun • food served • drag shows • terrace • wheelchair access

Le Garage 670 rue Bouvier **418/628-0610** • 3pm-3am • mostly gay men • women's night Fri • dancing/DJ

Pub L'Echouerie 290 rue St-Joseph • mostly women • lounge • DJ wknds • live music

RESTAURANTS

Cafe Zorba 854 rue St-Jean (near Dufferin) **418/525-5509** • 24hrs • Canadian, Greek & Italian • BYOB • wheelchair access

Le Commensal 860 rue St-Jean **418/647-3733** • 11am-10pm • vegetarian/vegan • Can$5-12

Le Hobbit 700 rue St-Jean (at Ste-Geneviève) **418/647-2677** • 8am-close • some veggie

Le Poisson d'Avril 115 rue St-André (at St-Thomas) **418/692-1010, 877/692-1010** • lunch & dinner • name is French for "April Fools"

Restaurant Diana 849 rue St-Jean (at St-Augustine) **418/524-5794** • 8am-1am, till 2am Fri-Sat • popular • Italian & Greek

ENTERTAINMENT & RECREATION

Fairmont Le Château Frontenac 1 rue des Carrières **418/692-3861, 800/441-1414** • this hotel disguised as a castle remains the symbol of Québec—even if you can't afford the princess' ransom to stay the night, come & enjoy the view from outside

Quebec City

LGBT PRIDE:
September.

ANNUAL EVENTS:
January/February - Carnaval (Winter Celebration) 418/626-3716, web: www.carnaval.qc.ca
July - Summer Festival 888/992-5200, web: www.infofestival.com.

CITY INFO:
800/363-7777 and 514/873-2015, web: www.tourisme.gouv.qc.ca.

TRANSIT:
Taxi Québec 418/525-8123.
Autobus La Quebecoise 888/872-5525, web: www.autobus.qc.ca
STCUQ (bus service) 418/627-2511, web: www.stcuq.qc.ca.

ATTRACTIONS:
Change of Guards at the Citadel
Château Frontenac 418/692-3861, web: www.chateaufrontenac.com
Grand Allée
Hôtel du Parlement
Notre-Dame-de-Québec Basilica
Old Québec
Quartier du Petit-Champlain, web: www.quartierpetitchamplain.c

Ice Hotel Sainte-Catherine-de-la-Jacques-Cartier **418/875–4522, 877/505–0423** • sometimes getting put on ice isn't a bad thing—check this gay-friendly hotel out before it melts away, 9 km E of Québec City in Montmorency Falls Park (Jan-March only)

RETAIL SHOPS

FinFinaud 847 rue St–Jean **418/648–9526** • open 11am, club & fetish clothes

EROTICA

Importation André Dubois 46 côte de la Montagne (at Frontenac Castle) **418/692–0264** • transgender-friendly • wheelchair access

Rouyn-Noranda

BARS

Station D 82 Perreault Ouest **819/797–8696** • 4pm-close, clsd Mon-Tue • lesbians/ gay men • dancing/DJ • drag shows • karaoke • terrace

Saint-Ferréol-les-Neiges

ENTERTAINMENT & RECREATION

Les Sept Chutes 4520 Ave Royale, St Ferréol-les-Neiges **877/725–8837** • historical village w/ hiking trails

Saint-Joachim

ENTERTAINMENT & RECREATION

Cap Tourmente 570 chemin du Cap-Tourmente **418/827–4591** • Nat'l Wildlife area

Sherbrooke

BARS

L' Otre Zone 252 rue Dufferin **819/565–5333** • 4pm-3am, from 8pm Sat, clsd Mon-Wed • lesbians/ gay men • more women Fri • dancing/DJ • food served • terrace

NIGHTCLUBS

Complex 13–17 13–15–17 Bowen Sud (at rue King) **819/569–5580** • 11am-3am • lesbians/ gay men • dancing/DJ • pub & dance club • strippers Fri-Sun • lesbian bar downstairs • also sauna

St-Georges-de-Beauce

BARS

Bar L'envol 11270 1ère Ave, 5th floor, St-Georges **418/227–5550** • 4pm-close Th-Sat only • lesbians/ gay men • dancing/ DJ • drag shows

Ste-Catherine-de-Hatley

ACCOMMODATIONS

L' Auberge Ste-Catherine-de-Hatley 2 rue Grand **819/868–1212** • gay-friendly • also bar & restaurant • terrace • kids ok • Can$35-47/person

Trois Rivières

INFO LINES & SERVICES

Gay Ami 819/373–0771 • LGBT social contacts

ACCOMMODATIONS

Le Gîte du Huard 42 rue St-Louis **819/375–8771** • gay-friendly • B&B • Can$65-130

SASKATCHEWAN

Ravenscrag

ACCOMMODATIONS

Spring Valley Guest Ranch 306/295–4124 • popular • gay/ straight • 1913 character home • also cabin • full brkfst • kids/ pets ok • nonsmoking • also restaurant • country-style • gay-owned • Can$50-70

Regina

INFO LINES & SERVICES

The Gay & Lesbian Community of Regina 2070 Broad St (at Victoria) **306/569–1995, 306/522–7343** • 5pm-2am • also lounge & Homo-Depot gay store • deck

Pink Triangle Community Services 2070 Broad St **306/525–6046** • 7pm-10pm, clsd wknds • also store • library

NIGHTCLUBS

The Outside 2070 Broad St (at Victoria, at Gay Center) **306/569–1995, 306/522–7343** • 10:30pm-3am Fri-Sat only • lesbians/ gay men • dancing/DJ

RESTAURANTS

Abstractions Cafe 2161 Rose St **306/352–5374** • 7:30am-11pm, from 11am Sat, clsd Sun • some veggie

The Creek in Cathedral Bistro 3414 13th Ave **306/352–4448** • lunch & dinner, clsd Mon • contemporary

BOOKSTORES

Buzzword Books 2926 13th Ave **306/522–6562** • 11am-6pm, clsd Sun & holidays • some gay/ lesbian titles

PUBLICATIONS

Sensible Shoes News 306/775–0169 • "celebrating the diversity of Saskatchewan's lesbian, bisexual, & transgendered women's community"

SPIRITUAL GROUPS

Dignity Regina Dignité 1351 Elphinstone St **306/569–3666** • 6:30pm 3rd Sun

Saskatoon

INFO LINES & SERVICES

Circle of Choice Gay/ Lesbian AA 10th St & Broadway (at Grace Westminster United Church) **306/665–5626** • 8pm Wed

Gay/ Lesbian Line & Drop-In 203-220 3rd Ave S (at Gay/ Lesbian Health Services) **306/665–1224, 800/358–1833** • 10am-7:30pm, clsd wknds • library • many social/ support groups • queer gift store

NIGHTCLUBS

Diva's 220 3rd Ave S #110 (alley entrance) **306/665–0100** • 8pm-2am, clsd Tue • lesbians/ gay men • dancing/DJ • drag shows • private club (guests welcome)

RESTAURANTS

The Berry Barn 830 Valley Rd **306/978–9797** • open daily • seasonal • home-style eatery w/ views of river

Q Room Cafe 212 3rd Ave S **306/955–5775** • 9am-9pm Mon-Fri

Seasons Cafe & Eatery 102 Cardinal Crescent **306/665–8121** • 6:30am-10pm, till 11pm Fri-Sat, 7am-9pm Sun • fresh soups & salad bar

ENTERTAINMENT & RECREATION

Rainbow Radio 90.5 FM CFCR **306/664–6678** (STATION #) • 8pm Sun

RETAIL SHOPS

Out of the Closet 203-220 3rd Ave S, 3rd flr **306/665–1224** • boutique run by the Gay/ Lesbian Line • LGBT gifts, magazines, art, etc

The Trading Post 226 2nd Ave S **306/653–1769** • 10am-5:30pm, clsd Sun • clothing

PUBLICATIONS

Perceptions 306/244–1930 • covers the Canadian prairies

SPIRITUAL GROUPS

Unitarian Church of Saskatoon 912 Idylwyld Dr N **306/653–2402** • 10:30am Sun

YUKON

Whitehorse

INFO LINES & SERVICES

Gay/ Lesbian Alliance of the Yukon Territory PO Box 31678, Y1A 6L3 **867/333–5800** • events • newsletter • check web for current event listings: www.gaycanada.com/galayukon

Victoria Faulkner Women's Centre 503 Hanson St **867/667–2693** • drop in centre • 11am-3pm, clsd wknds • wheelchair access

ACCOMMODATIONS

Inn on the Lake Lot 76 McClintock Pl, Marsh Lake **867/660–5253** • gay-friendly • luxury lakefront log inn • Canada Select rated 4.5 stars • nonsmoking • Can$135-290

BAHAMAS

Nassau

BARS

Club Waterloo E Bay St (1/2 mile E of
Paradise Island Bridge) 242/393–7324 • 4pm-
close • gay-friendly • indoor/ outdoor complex
w/ 5 bars • dancing/DJ • live music • restaurant
• swimming

The Drop-Off Pub Bay St (at East St,
downstairs, across from Planet Hollywood)
242/322–3444 • 11am-6am • gay-friendly •
dancing/DJ from 10pm • also restaurant •
lunch & dinner • English/ Bahamian fare

CAFES

La Kasbah Bay (at Market) 242/325–2883 •
11am-midnight • also lounge

BARBADOS

Bridgetown

RESTAURANTS

The Waterfront Cafe The Careenage
246/427–0093 • 10am-midnight, clsd Sun •
trendy • also bar • live music • outdoor
seating (not surprisingly, on the waterfront)

BRITISH VIRGIN ISLANDS

see also US Virgin Islands

Tortola

ACCOMMODATIONS

▲ **Fort Recovery Villa Beach Resort**
284/495–4354, 800/367–8455 (WAIT FOR RING)
• gay-friendly • grand home on beach &
private beachfront villas • swimming • kids ok
• wheelchair access • women-owned/ run •
$160-797

ENTERTAINMENT & RECREATION

Yacht Ferdinand 284/499–4941 • gay-
friendly • charter yacht

DOMINICAN REPUBLIC

Puerto Plata

ACCOMMODATIONS

Tropix Hotel 809/571–2291 • gay-friendly •
full brkfst • garden setting near center of town
& beach • swimming • kids/ pets ok • lesbian
& gay-owned • $40-50

Santo Domingo

ACCOMMODATIONS

Caribe Colonial Hotel 159 Isabel Catolica
809/688–7799 • gay-friendly • boutique hotel

Hotel Venezia 45 Av Independencia
809/682–5108

Monaga Apartments Colonial Zone
809/686–1846 • apts w/in walking distance of
historical architecture, gay nightlife,
restaurants & the seaside boulevard

Renaissance Jaragua Hotel & Casino
367 George Washington Ave **809/221–2222,
800/331–3542** • 14-acre resort • tropical
gardens • lagoon • waterfalls • $140-900

Residencial El Candil Calle el Candil #2 (at
20 de Deciembre), Boca Chica **809/523–4252,
808/523–4253** • gay/ straight • apts •
5 minutes from beach • swimming • gay-
owned • $50-100

BARS

Bar Phoenix Calle Polvorin 10, Zona
Colonial **809/689–7572** • noon-2am • mostly
gay men • friendly neighborhood bar •
multiracial • 3 levels • also restaurant • gay-
owned

Llego/ Jay Dee's Jose Reyes 10, Zona
Colonial **809/335–5905** • 9pm-4am • mostly
gay men • neighborhood bar • strippers •
videos

CAFES

Mercure Hotel Cafe El Conde & Maria
Hostos **809/688–5500**

RESTAURANTS

La Bahia 19 de Marzo **809/682–4022** •
excellent seafood

Café Coco 53 Padre Billini (in Colonial Zone)
809/687–9624 • noon-10pm, till 3pm Sun,
clsd Mon • English • full bar • live shows

El Conuco 152 Casimiro de Moya (behind
Jaragua Hotel) **809/221–3231** • touristy local
landmark

Sosua

ACCOMMODATIONS

Club Escape Caribe Hotel Playa Laguna (at
Cabarete Rd), Escondido Bay **809/571–3560,
809/803–3588** • lesbians/ gay men • hotel •
swimming • full brkfst • private beach • $40-
125

DUTCH & FRENCH WEST INDIES

Aruba

BARS

Jimmy's Place Kruisstraat 15, Oranjestad
297/82–25–50 • 4pm-2am, till 4am Fri-Sat,
from 8pm Sun • more gay late • popular •
gay-friendly • neighborhood bar • dancing/ DJ
• food served

The Paddock LG Smith Blvd #13,
Oranjestad **297/83–23–34** • 10am-2am • gay/
straight • neighborhood bar • food served

NIGHTCLUBS

Club E Weststrraat 5 (in Bayside Mall)
297/93–67–84 • 9:30pm-late • gay/ straight •
dancing/DJ

RESTAURANTS

Cafe The Plaza Seaport Marketplace,
Oranjestad **297/583–8826** • 10am-2am •
lunch & dinner specials

ENTERTAINMENT & RECREATION

Shhh Don't Tell Mama La Cabana Resort &
Casino (in the Tropicana showroom),
Oranjestad **297/87-90-00, 800/835-7193** •
shows 9:30pm, from 11pm Wed, clsd Sun •
gay-friendly • drag shows • cover

Bonaire

ACCOMMODATIONS

Coco Palm Garden/ Casa Oleander Kaya
Statius van Eps 9 **599/717–2108,
599/790–2108** • gay/ straight • studios, apts &
houses • swimming • wheelchair access •
$66-95

Ocean View Villas Kaya Statius van Eps 6
599/717–6105 • gay/ straight • luxury apts w/
secluded patios & outdoor showers • gay-
owned • $80-140

Curaçao

INFO LINES & SERVICES

**Curaçao Hospitality & Tourism
Association** **5999/434–8200**

ACCOMMODATIONS

The Avila Beach Hotel 130 Penstraat,
Willemstad **800/747–8162** (FROM US &
CANADA), **5999/461–4377** • gay-friendly • $170-
275

Floris Suite Hotel Piscadera Bay
800/781–1011 (IN US & CANADA),
5999/462–6111 • gay-friendly • $160-285

Kura Hulanda Langestraat 8, Willemstad **5999/434–7700** • gay-friendly • also Jacob's Bar • $210-1,000

BARS

Limbo Bar on Keizerhof • 5pm-11pm daily • lesbians/ gay men

NIGHTCLUBS

Tu Tu Tango Plasa Mundo Merced, Punda • 11pm-4am • more gay Fri • also restaurant

Wet & Wild Beach Club Seaquarium Beach & Marina, Willemstad **5999/561–2477** • gay-friendly • more gay wknds

RESTAURANTS

Mambo Beach Bapor Kibra, Seaquarium Beach **5999/461–8999**

Saba

RESTAURANTS

My Kitchen The Road, Windwardside **599/416–2539** • 11am-8:30pm, clsd Sun • some veggie • patio

Rainforest Restaurant Windwardside **599/416–3888, 599/416–5507** • brkfst, lunch, dinner • fresh, home-made food • seafood, some veggie

St Barthélémy

ACCOMMODATIONS

Hotel le Village St-Jean St-Jean Hill **590–590/27–61–39, 800/651–83–66** • gay-friendly • hotel & cottages • swimming • €110-190 (rooms), €145-570 (cottages), €570-850 (villas)

Hotel Normandie **590–590/27-61-66** • gay-friendly

Hotel St-Barth Isle De France Plage des Flamands **508/528–7727, 800/421–3396** • gay-friendly • ultra-luxe hotel includes French cuisine • $500

St Barth's Beach Hotel Grand Cul de Sac **508/528–7727, 800/421–3396** • gay-friendly • swimming • $145-730

NIGHTCLUBS

Le Sélect Gustavia **590–590/ 27–86–87** • gay-friendly • more gay after 11pm

ENTERTAINMENT & RECREATION

Anse Gouverneur St-Jean Beach • nudity

Anse Grande Saline Beach • nudity • gay section on the right side of Saline

L'Orient Beach • gay beach

St Maarten

See also St Martin

ACCOMMODATIONS

Holland House 43 Front St, Philipsburg **599/542–2572** • gay-friendly • on the beach • restaurant • bar • $96+

RESTAURANTS

Cheri's Cafe Maho Reef **599/54–53–361** • 11am-1:30am, clsd Tue • popular • full bar • dancing • live music • touristy • wheelchair access

Wajang Doll 167 Front St, Philipsburg **599/54–22–687** • lunch weekdays & dinner nightly, clsd Sun • Indonesian • gay-owned

St Martin

see also St Maarten

ACCOMMODATIONS

Orient Beach Mont Vernon 1 **590–590/87–31–10, 800/818–5992** • gay-friendly • studios • 1 & 2-bdrm villas • steps from St-Martin's most beautiful clothing-optional beach • $115-340

BARS

Cohibar Nettle Bay **590–590/29–65–22** • 11pm-close Fri

Tantra Marigot (at the Royal Marina) **690/76–21–42** • 6pm-close • lesbians/ gay men

RESTAURANTS

L'Escapade 94 Blvd de Grand Case **590–590/87–75–04** • French • some veggie • reservations recommended

Le Pressoir 30 Blvd de Grand Case **590–590/87–76–62** • dinner nightly, clsd Sun • French

Rainbow 176 Blvd de Grand Case (at W end of beach) **590–590/87–55–80** • dinner nightly • French/ int'l

Splash Billy Folly Rd (in Simpson Bay) • dinner nightly

ENTERTAINMENT & RECREATION

Cupecoy Beach • gay beach

JAMAICA

Montego Bay

ACCOMMODATIONS

Half Moon Golf, Tennis & Beach Club
876/953–2211, 866/648–6951 • gay-friendly •
upscale resort • $200-600

Negril

ACCOMMODATIONS

Seagrape Villas West End Rd 831/625–1255
(US#) • gay/ straight • 3 seafront villas •
excellent sunsets • kids ok • $120-245

Ocho Rios

ACCOMMODATIONS

Golden Clouds Villa North Coast Rd,
Oracabessa 941/922–9191, 888/625–6007 •
gay-friendly • private estate • full brkfst • fully
staffed • jacuzzi • swimming • kids ok •
wheelchair access • gay-owned • $7,500-
15,100/ week

Port Antonio

ACCOMMODATIONS

Hotel Mocking Bird Hill 876/993–7267 •
gay-friendly • eco-friendly inn • fresh local
food served • swimming • massage • kids ok •
wheelchair access • lesbian-owned • $135-260

Westmoreland

ACCOMMODATIONS

Moun Tambrin Retreat set in the mtns 28
miles from Montego Bay 876/918–4486 •
gay/ straight • art deco estate furnished & built
from tropical woods • formerly owned by Alex
Haley • food served • swimming • $75 per
person (meals not included)

PUERTO RICO

Note: For those w/ rusty or no Spanish,
"carretera" means "highway." "Calle"
means "street."

Islandwide

PUBLICATIONS

Puerto Rico Breeze 787/722–5759 •
islandwide LGBT newspaper

Boqueron

ACCOMMODATIONS

A Boqueron Bay Guest House 10 Quintas
del Mar (at SR 307, Km 7.6, Interior)
787/847–4325 • lesbians/ gay men •
swimming • jacuzzi • pets ok • gay-owned •
$39-89

Fajardo

ACCOMMODATIONS

El Conquistador 1000 Conquistador Ave
787/863–1000 • gay-friendly • swimming •
panoramic views & luxurious rooms • "an
amazing Caribbean getaway" • wheelchair
access

Hormigueros

BARS

Station Bar Casablanca Shopping Center,
Rd #2 • from 7pm Wed-Sun • lesbians/ gay
men • dancing/DJ • entertainment • drag
shows • strippers

NIGHTCLUBS

Faces Hwy 2 (at km 164) 787/849–2005 •
9pm-late Th-Sun • mostly gay men •
dancing/DJ • drag shows • patio

Isabela

NIGHTCLUBS

Discoteca Ricomar Barrio Jobos, La Sierra
Carretera 459 (across from Brendy Pizza) •
10pm-close Fri-Sat only • lesbians/ gay men •
dancing/DJ • live shows • performance art •
terrace

Joyuda

BARS

Bayside Pub Carretera 102, km 14.9 • on
the water • open air • popular Sun

Luquillo

ACCOMMODATIONS

Coqui Villa 787/889-2098 • gay/ straight • tree house villa • private veranda • swimming • $600-850/wk

Moca

NIGHTCLUBS

Style Carr 111, Km 72 • 10pm-close Fri-Sat only • lesbians/ gay men • dancing/DJ • drag shows

Patillas

ACCOMMODATIONS

Caribe Playa Beach Resort Road #3, Km 112.1 Guardarraya 787/839-6339 • gay-friendly • inn • hot tub • swimming • kids/ pets ok • $79-104

Rincon

ACCOMMODATIONS

Horned Dorset Primavera Hotel Apartado 1132 800/633-1857 • gay/ straight • swimming pool

Villa Orleans Beachfront Vacation Home 787/433-6013 • gay-friendly • vacation rental • kids ok • $250-350

San German

BARS

Norman's Bar Ctra 318, Barrio Maresúa • 6pm-1am • lesbians/ gay men • neighborhood bar • dancing/DJ • salsa & merengue

San Juan

INFO LINES & SERVICES

LGBT Support Group 787/769-0077

ACCOMMODATIONS

Acacia Seaside Inn 8 Taft St 787/725-0668, 800/946-3244 • gay-friendly • hotel • kids ok • $125-150

At Home Vacation 1131 Ashford Ave, Apt 505 (at Calle Vendig) 787/633-8906, 787/635-1462 (CELL) • gay/ straight • furnished apts • kids/ pets ok • transgender-friendly • gay-owned • $75-125

At Wind Chimes Inn 1750 McLeary Ave, Condado 787/727-4153, 800/946-3244 • gay-friendly • restored Spanish villa • 1 block from Condado beach • swimming • kids/ pets ok • nonsmoking • wheelchair access • $75-140

Caribe Mountain Villas Carr 857, km 6.0, Carolina 787/769-0860 • gay-friendly • resort in Carolina rain forest (25 miles from San Juan) • tennis courts • swimming • gay-owned • $100-225

Casa Coqui 456 Calle Saldana, Santurce 787/268-0224 • apt rental in "Arts & Culture" district

Casa del Caribe Guest House Calle Caribe 57, Condado 787/722-7139, 877/722-7139 • gay-friendly • B&B in heart of Condado • kids ok • nonsmoking • $55-125

Condado Inn Av Condado 6 (at Av Ashford) 787/724-7145 • mostly men • near beach • also bar • gay-owned • $59-79

El San Juan Hotel & Casino 6063 Isla Verde Ave (at Baldorioty de Castro), Carolina 787/791-1000, 800/468-2818 (RESERVATIONS ONLY) • gay-friendly • resort on ocean • swimming • kids ok • great Asian restaurant & cigar bar • wheelchair access • $310-655

Hotel El Convento Calle Cristo 100, Old San Juan (btwn Caleta de las Monjas & Calle Sol) 787/723-9020, 800/468-2779 • popular • gay-friendly • 17th-c former Carmelite convent • swimming • "plunge" jacuzzi • $265+

Hotel Iberia Av Wilson 1464, Condado (btwn Avs de Diego & Washington) 787/722-5380, 787/723-0200 • gay/ straight • European-style hotel • nonsmoking • kids ok • also restaurant & bar La Fonda de Cervantes • lunch & dinner daily, Spanish/ int'l cuisine • wheelchair access • gay-owned • $75-132

L' Habitation Beach Guesthouse Calle Italia 1957, Ocean Park (near Santa Ana) 787/727-2499 • lesbians/ gay men • on the beach • also restaurant & bar • gay-owned • $70-111

Numero Uno on the Beach Calle Santa Ana 1, Ocean Park (near Calle Italia) 787/726-5010, 866/726-5010 • gay/ straight • swimming • also Pamela's, full bar & grill • Caribbean • brkfst, lunch & dinner • wheelchair access • $70-250

The Water Club Hotel 2 Tartak St (Isla Verde), Carolina 787/728-3666, 888/265-6699 • gay-friendly • boutique hotel on the beach • restaurant & lounge • kids ok • swimming • nonsmoking • wheelchair access $229-695

BARS

Bebo's Playa Piñones, Isla Verde 787/253-3143 • noon-close, clsd Mon-Tue • lesbians/ gay men • beachfront neighborhood bar • dancing/DJ • drag shows • strippers • fun crowd

Café Bohemio Calle Cristo 100, Old San Juan (in Gran Hotel El Convento) 787/723–9202, 787/723–9200 • 11am-2am • gay-friendly • professional crowd • more gay Tue • live music Th-Sat • also restaurant • Puerto Rican/ int'l • food served till 11pm

Cups Calle San Mateo 1708 (btwn Calles Barbe & San Jorge), Santurce 787/268–3570 • 7pm-close, from 8pm Sat, clsd Sun-Tue • popular • mostly women • dancing/ DJ • live music Wed & Sat

Excape Club 312 Avenida de Diego, Santurce • clsd Sun-Tue • gay/ straight • dancing/ DJ

Junior's Calle Condado 602 (btwn Calle Benito Alonso & Av Ponce de León), Santurce 787/723–9477 • 8pm-close • lesbians/ gay men • neighborhood bar • drag & strip shows • local crowd

Nuestro Ambiente Av Ponce de León 1412 (across from Central High School), Santurce 787/724–9093 • 8pm-close, clsd Mon-Tue • mostly women • dancing • live music wknds • comedy

Starz 365 Avenida de Diego (at Ponce de Leon Ave) • lesbians/ gay men

Steps 311 Roosevelt Ave, Hato Rey (above Condom World) • Th-Sat only • lesbians/ gay men • "upscale adult atmosphere"

Tia Maria's Av Jose de Diego, Stop 22 (at Ponce de León), Santurce 787/724–4011 • noon-2am • popular • lesbians/ gay men • neighborhood bar • professional crowd • also liquor shop

San Juan

LGBT Pride:
June.

Annual Events:
February - Ponce Carnival
February/ March - Festival Casals 787/721-7727, web: www.festcasalspr.gobierno.pr
June - Heineken Jazz Fest, web: www.heinekenpr.com/jazz
June - San Juan Bautista Day 787/721-2400. San Juan celebrates Puerto Rico's own saint w/ week-long music, dance, religious processions, parties. On midnight of the eve before June 24th (the official saint's day), revelers walk/jump backwards into the sea 3 to 7 times to ward off evil spirits & renew good luck for the coming year
November - Festival de Bomba y Plena (African-Caribbean music festival), Ponce 787/840-4141.

City Info:
Puerto Rico Tourism Company, 800/223-6530, web: www.gotopuertorico.com.

Best View:
From El Morro or alternatively, one of the harbor cruises that depart from Pier 2 in Old San Juan.

Weather:
Tropical sunshine year-round, with temperatures that average in the mid-80°s from November to May. Expect more rain on the northern coast.

Transit:
TaxiVan, 787/645-8294, web: taxivansanjuan.com.
Santana Taxi Service, 787/547-1926, www.taxituristico.com.
Metropolitan Bus Authority (AMA, its Spanish acronym) 787/250-6064. Metro Bus 787/763-4141.

Attractions:
Condado Beach
La Fortaleza 787/ 721–7000 x2323
Historic Old San Juan
El Morro Fortress & Fort San Cristobal (San Juan National Historic Site) 787/729-6777, web: www.nps.gov/saju
Pablo Casals Museum 787/723-9185
Quincentennial Plaza
San José Church
San Juan Museum of Art & History 787/724-1875.

NIGHTCLUBS

Club Lazer Calle Cruz 251, Old San Juan **787/725–7581** • 8pm-close • popular w/ gay cruises

Eros Av Ponce de León 1257 (btwn Calles Villamil & Labra), Santurce **787/722–1131** • 9pm-4am, clsd Mon • popular • lesbians/ gay men • dancing/DJ • drag shows • videos • theme nights • gay-owned

Kouros 1515 Ponce de Leon Ave, Santurce • 10pm-close • outdoor patio

The New Concept Av Chardón 9, Hato Rey (in Le Chateau), Hato Rey **787/751–2000** • 8pm-close, Sun only • lesbians/ gay men • dancing/DJ • popular drag shows

Prisma Calle Barranquitas 53, Condado (btwn Calle Mayagüez & Av Ashford) **787/602–5966** • 4pm-close, T-dance Sun • popular • mostly gay men • dancing/DJ • live shows

El Teatro Av Ponce de León 1420, Santurce **787/722–1130** • 9pm-late, clsd Mon-Tue • gay/ straight • dancing/DJ • drag shows • gay Sun & Wed

CAFES

Café Berlin Calle San Francisco 407, Plaza Colón, Old San Juan (btwn Calles Norzagary & O'Donnel) **787/722–5205** • 9am-11pm • popular • espresso bar • plenty veggie

RESTAURANTS

Aguaviva 364 Calle Fortaleza (in Old San Juan) **787/722–0665** • dinner nightly • fresh seafood & ceviche

Al Dente Calle Recinto S, Old San Juan **787/723–7303** • lunch & dinner, clsd Sun • Italian

La Bombonera Calle San Francisco 259, Old San Juan **787/722–0658** • 7:30am-8pm • popular • come for the strong coffee & pastries • since 1903!

Café Amadeus Calle San Sebastián 104, Old San Juan (btwn Calles San José & del Cristo) **787/722–8635** • lunch & dinner • popular • nouvelle Puerto Rican/ cont'l • also bar • gay-owned

Coloquios Cafe Local #11 Parking Covadonga (in Old San Juan) **787/723–5541** • dinner Wed-Sun & Sun brunch • gay/ straight

Dragonfly 364 S Fortaleza St (across from Parrot Club) **787/977–3886** • lunch & dinner • Latin/ Asian fusion

Fleria 1754 Calle Loiza, Santurce **787/268–0010** • lunch & dinner, clsd Sun-Mon • Greek • some veggie

La Querencia 320 Calle Fortaleza (in Old San Juan) **787/723–0357** • 6pm-11pm • gay-friendly • multiracial • excellent local food

Mona's 510 Ponce de Leon, Hato Rey **787/282–0207** • Mexican • live shows

The Parrot Club Calle Fortaleza 363, Old San Juan (btwn Plaza Colón & Callejón de la Capilla) **787/725–7370** • lunch & dinner • chic Nuevo Latino bistro & bar • live music

Transylvania Restaurant Recinto Sur 317, Old San Juan **787/977–2328** • 11am-2pm Tue-Sat & 5pm-11pm nightly • Romanian • also bar • art gallery • live music

ENTERTAINMENT & RECREATION

Saliendo del Closet WIAC 740AM **787/607–3939** • 9pm-11pm Wed

BOOKSTORES

Bookworm Av Ashford 1129, Condado (at Calle Vendig) **787/722–3344** • 10am-9pm, from 1pm Sun

RETAIL SHOPS

Matahari 202-B San Justo St (in Old San Juan) **787/724–5869** • ethnic art, clothing & gifts

The Rainbow Shop Av Ponce de León 1412 (inside Nuestro Ambiente), Santurce **787/721–0401, 787/721–2982** • 11am-6pm, 10am-3pm Sat-Tue • gay items, flags, stickers, etc

PUBLICATIONS

Puerto Rico Breeze **787/722–5759** • islandwide LGBT newspaper

SPIRITUAL GROUPS

Iglesia Comunitaria Metropolitana (MCC) 67 Calle Robles, Rio Piedras **787/281–6103**

GYMS & HEALTH CLUBS

International Fitness Av Ashford 1131, Condado (btwn Avs Cervantes & Caribe) **787/721–0717** • 5am-10pm, till 9pm Fri, call for wknd hours • gay/ straight

EROTICA

Condom World 311 Roosevelt Ave, Hato Rey **787/751–0997** • condoms, toys, videos & more • 21 locations in Puerto Rico

Pleasure Paradise Av Roosevelt 1367 (in Plazoleta Julio Garriga), Hato Rey **787/706–0855**

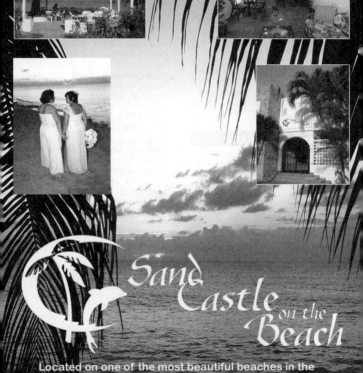

Vieques Island

ACCOMMODATIONS

Bravo! North Shore Rd (at Lighthouse) 787/741–1128 • gay/ straight • Vieques' "first true beachside designer hotel" w/ beautiful ocean views • gay-owned • $125-450

Casa de Amistad 27 Benitez Castano 787/741–3758 • gay-friendly • $60-90

Crow's Nest Inn PO Box 1521, 00765 787/741–0033, 877/276–9763 • gay-friendly • small inn • swimming • nonsmoking • restaurant • $94-199

Inn on the Blue Horizon 787/741–3318 • gay-friendly • country inn & cottages • beach access • restaurant • $175-370

Rainbow Realty 787/741–4312 • gay/ straight • 20 fully equipped properties available • most w/ views • some on the water • woman-owned/ run • $850-3,500

Villas of Vieques Island 787/741–0023 • gay/ straight • villa rentals • easy access to San Juan • woman-owned/ run • $900+/ week

TRINIDAD & TOBAGO

Tobago

ACCOMMODATIONS

Grafton Beach Resort 868/639-0191 • gay-friendly • food served • swimming • $168-450

Kariwak Village Hotel & Holistic Haven Store Bay Local Rd, Crown Point 868/639-8442, 868/639-8545 • gay-friendly • 1-room cabañas • kids ok • swimming • outdoor jacuzzi w/ waterfall • restaurant • $90-125

RESTAURANTS

Rouselles Bacolet St, Scarborough 868/639-4738 • West Indian/ int'l • nice sea view

Trinidad

BARS

Pier One on ocean, Chaguaramas 868/634-4472 • popular • gay-friendly • also party cruises

VIRGIN ISLANDS
see also British Virgin Islands

St Croix

ACCOMMODATIONS

Cormorant Beach Club & Hotel 4126 La Grande Princesse 340/778-8920, 800/548-4460 • popular • lesbians/ gay men • beachfront resort • food served • swimming • gay-owned • $110-265

King Christian Hotel 59 Kings Wharf, Christiansted 340/773-6330, 800/524-2012 • gay-friendly • swimming • also restaurant • $100-135

Pink Fancy Hotel 27 Prince St, Christiansted 340/773-8460, 800/524-2045 • gay-friendly • swimming • cont'l brkfst • kids ok • $85-150

▲ **Sand Castle on the Beach** 127 Smithfield, Frederiksted 340/772-1205, 800/524-2018 • lesbian, gay & straight-friendly • hotel • swimming • $79-339+tax • lesbian & gay-owned • see ad pg 515

RESTAURANTS

Le St-Tropez 67 King St (at Pier 69), Frederiksted 340/772-3000, 340/772-3335 • lunch weekdays & dinner nightly, clsd Sun • French cuisine • full bar

St John

ACCOMMODATIONS

Estate Concordia 20-27 Estate Concordia (at Rte 107) 340/693-5347 • gay-friendly • upscale eco-lodge • month-long volunteer program available • swimming • wheelchair access

Gallows Point Suite Resort Cruz Bay 340/776-6434, 800/323-7229 • gay-friendly • beachfront resort • all suites • swimming • kitchens • also restaurant • full bar • wheelchair access • $225-575

Island's End Hansen's Bay 888/205-2729 • gay/ straight • octagonal vacation villa w/ panoramic views • nonsmoking • lesbian-owned • $2,240-7,800/ week

Maho Bay Camps & Harmony Studios VI National Park 340/776-6226, 800/392-9004 • gay-friendly • tent cottages & studios • environmentally aware resort • kids ok • $75-200

Sago Palms Denis Bay 340/776-6876 • gay-friendly • private homes • $1,995-3,255 (weekly for two)

St John Inn 800/666-7688 • gay-friendly • kids ok • swimming • nonsmoking • $79-285

RESTAURANTS

Asolare Rte 20, Cruz Bay 340/779-4747 • 5:30pm-9:30pm • Asian/ French fusion • hip & elegant

Château Bordeaux Centerline Rd, Jct 10 340/776-6611 • 5:30pm-8:30pm • great view

ENTERTAINMENT & RECREATION

Solomon Bay • nude beach • 20-minute hike on Solomon Beach Trail

St Thomas

ACCOMMODATIONS

Club Villa Azul 6501 Red Hook Plaza, PMB #4, VI, 00802 340/513-1440, 800/898-9817 • gay-friendly • very private & intimate • each unit w/ own private plunge pool • walking-distance to Sapphire Beach

Danish Chalet Guest House 340/774-5292, 800/407-2567 • gay/ straight • overlooking harbor • spa • deck • limited wheelchair access • $98-160

Hotel 1829 Government Hill 340/776-1829, 800/524-2002 • gay-friendly • swimming • also full bar & restaurant • $105-220

The Inn at Blackbeard's Castle 340/776-1234, 800/344-5771 • gay/ straight • also a restaurant • $110-200

Pavilions & Pools Hotel 6400 Estate Smith Bay 340/775-6110, 800/524-2001 • gay-friendly • 1-bdrm villas each w/ own private swimming pool • $180-275

ENTERTAINMENT & RECREATION

Morning Star Beach • popular gay beach

MEXICO

Please Note: Mexican cities are often divided into districts or "Colonias" which we abbreviate as Col. Please use these when giving addresses for directions.

Acapulco

ACCOMMODATIONS

Calinda Beach Costera Miguel Alemán 1260 52-744/435-0600, 877/657-5799 • gay-friendly • overlooking ocean • swimming (2 pools)

Casa Condesa Bella Vista 125 52-744/484-1616, 800/816-4817 (US & CANADA) • mostly gay men • full brkfst • near beach • $75-150

Fiesta Americana Condesa Av Costera Miguel Alemán 1200 52-744/484-2828, 800/343-7821 • popular • gay-friendly • deluxe hotel above the gay beach • swimming • 4-star dining • $122+

Hotel Acapulco Tortuga Av Costera Miguel Alemán 132 52-744/484-8889, 800/832-7491 • gay-friendly • across from the gay beach

Las Brisas 52-744/469-6900, 888/559-4329 (US#) • popular • gay-friendly • luxury resort • private pools • kids ok • wheelchair access • $330+

Quinta Encanto Privada Roca Sola 108, Col. Club Deportivo (off Costera Blvd) 310/276-0752, 310/659-5384 (NIGHT) • gay-friendly • rental villa • sleeps up to 6 • swimming • full staff • $175-300

Sunscape Acapulco Calle Caracol 70 (Fracc. Amiento Farallón) 52-744/484-3707 • gay-friendly • swimming • food served • $59-125

Villa Estrella 169 Anahuac 52-744/460-1112 • gay-friendly • 6-bdrm villa (rent 4 rms or whole) • swimming • 180° view of bay • fully staffed • $400-1,000

BARS

Parranderías Av Cuauhtémoc (Col. Progresso, around corner from Hotel Palacio) • 11pm-close

NIGHTCLUBS

Prince Calle Juan de la Cosa 12 (across from the Hotel Continental) 52-744/484-7601 • after-hours • gay-friendly • popular • dancing/DJ

Relax Calle Lomas de Mar 4 (Zona Dorada) 52-744/484-0421 • 10pm-late, clsd Mon-Wed • popular • lesbians/ gay men • dancing/DJ • drag & strip shows wknds • videos • young crowd

RESTAURANTS

100% Natural Av Costera Miguel Alemán 200 (near Acapulco Plaza) 52-744/485-3982 • 24hr fast (healthy) food • plenty veggie

Beto's Beach Restaurant Av Costera Miguel Alemán 99 (at Condesa Beach) 52-744/484-0473 • 11am-midnight • lesbians/ gay men • full bar • palapas

El Cabrito Restaurante Av Costera M Alemán 1480 (near Convention Center) 52-744/484-7711 • local favorite, authentic

Carlos & Charlie's Av Costera Miguel Alemán #112 52-744/484-0039 • lunch & dinner • entertainment • int'l

Coyuca 22 Av Coyuca 22 52–744/482–3468, 52–7/483–5030 • open Nov-April • dress code • great views

Le Jardin des Artistes Vincente Yanez Pinzón 11 (in front of Hotel Continental Plaza) 52–744/484–8344 • 7pm-close • French • reservations required

Kookaburra Carretera Escénica (at Marina Las Brisas) 52–744/484–4418, 52–744/446–6039 • lunch & dinner • popular • int'l • expensive

La Cabaña de Caleta Playa Caleta Lado Oriente s/n (Fracc. las Playas) 52–744/482–5007 • seafood • right on Playa Caleta • great margaritas

La Tortuga Calle Lomas del Mar 5–A 52–744/484–6985 • 10am-2am • full bar • good Mexican, seafood • patio • gay-owned

Le Bistroquet Calle Andrea Doria 5 (Fracc. Costa Azul) 52–744/484–6860 • 6pm-midnight • popular • lesbians/ gay men • French • outdoor dining • reservations recommended • gay-owned

Madeiras Carretera Escénica 33-B (past La Vista shopping center) 52–744/446–5636 • 7pm-11pm • 4-course prix fixe • reservations recommended • incredible view

Su Casa/ La Margarita Av Anahuac 110 52–744/484–1261, 52–744/484–4350 • traditional cuisine • great views

Suntory de Acapulco Costera Miguel Alemán 52–744/484–8088 • Japanese • gardens

Zorrito's Av Costera Miguel Alemán 52–744/485–3735 • traditional Mexican • several locations along Costera • some all night

Aguascalientes

NIGHTCLUBS

Mandiles Av Lopez Mateos 730 W (btwn Agucate & Chabacano) 52–449/153–281 • 10pm-3am Fri-Sat only • lesbians/ gay men • dancing/DJ

Cabo San Lucas

ACCOMMODATIONS

Cabo Villas Resort Callejon del Pescador s/n (Col. El Medano) 52–624/143–9199, 877/382–2932 (RESERVATIONS US ONLY) • gay-friendly • resort on Medano Beach • 2 restaurants • swimming • $140-450

Hotel Hacienda Beach Resort Playa el Medano 52–624/143–0663, 800/733–2226 (US#) • gay-friendly • upscale • $175-440

Solmar Suites Av Solmar 1 52–624/143–3535, 800/344–3349 OR 310/459–9861 (US#) • gay-friendly • oceanfront suites at southernmost tip • 2 pools • hot tub • $145-330

The Todos Santos Inn Calle Legaspi #33 (Topete), Todos Santos 52–612/145–0040 • gay/ straight • colonial inn in Todos Santos' historic district • heated pool • courtyard • nonsmoking • also bar • gay-owned • $95-165

BARS

The Rainbow Bar Blvd de la Marina #39-E (Marina Cabo Plaza) 52–624/143–1455 • popular • lesbians/ gay men • dancing/DJ • patio

RESTAURANTS

Mi Casa Av Cabo San Lucas 52–624/143–1933 • lunch & dinner • great chicken mole • reservations recommended

Cancún

see also Cozumel & Playa del Carmen

ACCOMMODATIONS

Akul Hotel Blvd Kukulcán 5 52–998/838–330 OR 619/297–0897, 800/765–4370 • gay/ straight • 4-star beachfront hotel on 12 acres • swimming • tennis • volleyball • $99-119

Cancún Luxury Villas Palenque #17 #1-B, SM 29 281/914–4269 (RESERVATIONS, TX #), 52–998/892–4102 • gay-friendly • variety of private-owned, beachfront villas • swimming

Casa Cancún Puerto Morelos 212/598–0469 (US#) • gay/ straight • rental home on the beach • 20 minutes south of Cancún • nonsmoking • women-owned/ run • $120-140

Casa de los Amigos Isla Mujeres 52–998/44–01–877–1169 • gay-friendly • quiet cottage on Mexican Caribbean • gay-owned • $55-60 (4-day minimum)

Dreams Cancun Resort & Spa Paseo Kukulcán 52–998/848–7000, 877/722–6466 (US#) • gay-friendly • swimming • 2 beaches • several bars & restaurants including famous María Bonita

Rancho Sak Ol Puerto Morelos 52–998/871–0181 • gay-friendly • beachfront palapa-style B&B • 30 minutes from Cancún • $45-125

Villas Tacul Blvd Kukulcán km 5.5 (in Zona Hotelera) **52–998/883–0000, 800/842–0193** • gay-friendly • boutique hotel • swimming • gardens • restaurant • $145-1,275

Zona Hotelera (The Hotel Zone) Blvd Kukulcán • Cancún's answer to the Las Vegas Strip: resorts ranging from the Sheraton Cancún's Mayan pyramids to small boutique hotels

BARS

Picante Bar Av Tulúm 20, Centro (E of Av Uxmal, next to Plaza Galerías) **52–998/845–5587** • 9am-5am, clsd Mon • popular • mostly gay men • dancing/DJ • young crowd • drag shows & strippers Wed-Sat

NIGHTCLUBS

Glow Tulipanes 3 (SM 22, around the corner from Karamba) **52–998/898–4552** • 11pm-6:30am, clsd Sun-Mon • popular • lesbians/ gay men • women's night every other Fri • dancing/DJ (huge dance flr) • drag shows • strippers • rooftop terrace lounge

Karamba Av Tulúm 9 (Azucenas 2nd Flr, SM 22) **52–998/884–0032** • 10pm-6am, clsd Mon-Tue • popular • lesbians/ gay men • dancing/DJ • drag shows • go-go boys Fri

RESTAURANTS

100% Natural Sunyaxchen 6 **52–998/884–1617** • healthy fast food: sandwiches, salads & shakes • plenty veggie

Cafe D'Pa at corner of Las Palapas Park **52–998/883–0459** • opens afternoons • streetfront French restaurant • popular crepes • also bar • gay-owned

Casa Angelus Av Sayil 10 (Smza 4 Lote 72 y 73 Mza 12) **52–998/887–9444** • upscale Mediterranean • full bar

Modern Art Cafe Kukulcán Blvd km 12.5 (at La Isla Shopping Center) **52–998/883–4512** • full bar • gallery

Perico's Av Yachilan 71 **52–998/884–3152** • traditional Mexican served up w/ huge theatrical flare—run, don't walk if you love your waiters dressed as Mexican revolutionaries, want a sombrero put on your head when you enter, like to dance in conga lines & drink strong margaritas

ENTERTAINMENT & RECREATION

Chichén Itza • the must-see Mayan ruin 125 miles from Cancún

Playa Delfines in the Hotel Zone (next to Hilton's beach) • gay beach

Ciudad Juárez

see also El Paso, Texas, USA

BARS

Club La Escondida Calle Ignacio de la Peña 366 W • gay/ straight • neighborhood bar

Cordoba

BARS

Salon Bar El Metro Av 7 no. 117–C, 1 & 3 • lesbians/ gay men • dancing

Cozumel

see also Cancún & Playa del Carmen

ACCOMMODATIONS

El Cid La Ceiba Beach Hotel Carretera a Chankanaab km 4.5 **52–987/872–0844, 800/435–3240** • gay-friendly • 5-star beachfront resort • wheelchair access • $93-200

Sol Cabañas del Caribe Ctra Costera Norte km 5.1 **52–987/872–9870, 800/336–3542 (US#)** • gay-friendly • low-key resort • restaurant & bar • swimming • private beach • $86-195

Villa Las Anclas S 5th Ave #325 (btwn 3rd & 5th Sts) **52–987/872–5476, 52–987/872–6103** • gay-friendly • suites-hotel • 1 block from main plaza • $80-120

RESTAURANTS

Kiss My Cactus Av Melgar 100 (btwn 1 & Rosado Salas) **52–987/872–5793, 52–987/872–5798** • Mexican • also cafe & bar

Cuernavaca

INFO LINES & SERVICES

Centro Cultural Enkidu Juan Escutia 23 BIS, 03440 Mexico City **52–55/9180–1240 (MEXICO CITY #)** • provides a variety of services for LGBT travelers to Mexico City including a travel agency, tour guides & day trips • also publishes Enkidu LGBT magazine (www.enkidumagazine.com)

ACCOMMODATIONS

Casa del Angel Calle de Helechos #206 (Col. Jardin de Tetela) **52–777/364–6319** • gay-friendly • small guesthouse • spa • cooking school • tours available • gay-owned • $50-60 & $215-1,500 (whole house)

Hostería Las Quintas Resort Spa 9 Diaz Ordaz Blvd **52–777/362–3949, 800/990–1888** • gay-friendly • hotel & spa • restaurant & bar • botanical gardens • 3 pools • jacuzzi • $200-360

Las Mañanitas Ricardo Linares 107 **52–777/312–4646 & 314–1466, 888/413–9199 (US ONLY)** • gay-friendly • gardens • swimming • restaurant • peacocks! • $200-459

La Nuestra Calle Mesalina 18 (at Calle Neptuno) **52–777/315–2272, 404/806–9694** • gay/ straight • B&B • full brkfst • swimming • kids ok • lesbian-owned • $55-75

Quinta Las Flores Tlaquepaque 1 (Col. Las Palmas) **52–777/314–1244, 52–777/312–5769** • gay-friendly • small hotel • gardens • near downtown • swimming • $90-153

BARS

Barecito Comonfort 17 (at Morrow) **52–777/314–1325** • lesbians/ gay men • food served • lesbian-owned

NIGHTCLUBS

Club RA Madero 503 (at Col. Miraval) **52–777/318–2098** • lesbians/ gay men

Oxygen Dance Hall & Lounge Av Vincente Guerrero 1303 (near Sam's Club) **52–777/317–2714, 52–777/374–0649** • 10pm-close, Fri-Sat only • mostly gay men • dancing/DJ • food served • live shows • drag shows • videos • 18+ • young crowd

RESTAURANTS

Buba Cafe Morrow 9, Altos 3 **52–777/310–0432** • popular lunch buffet • plenty veggie • live music

La India Bonita Calle Dwight Morrow 106 **52–777/318–6967** • clsd Mon • in historic home of former US ambassador & father-in-law of Charles Lindbergh

Marco Polo Calle Hidalgo 30, Altos 9 (in front of cathedral, 2nd flr) **52–777/312–3484** • Italian (pasta & pizza) • overlooking cathedral

María Cristina Juárez 300 **52–777/318–5787, 52–777/318–6984** • very popular Sun brunch

ENTERTAINMENT & RECREATION

CETLALIC (Centro Tlahuica de Lenguas e Intercambio Cultural) Fl Madero 721 (Col. Miraval) **52–777/313–2637, 52–777/317–0850 & 313–5450** • offers intensive Spanish language & culture classes, including ones just for LGBTs w/ gay-friendly Mexican homestays • check out www.cetlalic.org.mx

Diego Rivera Murals Plaza de Museo (in Cuaunháhuac Regional Museum)

SPIRITUAL GROUPS

Iglesia de la Comunidad Metropolitana (ICM) Renovacion Leandro Valle 512 (Interior 1), Mexico City **52–777/7318–1517** • 9:30am Sat

Ensenada

ACCOMMODATIONS

Best Western El Cid Av Lopez Mateos 993 **52–646/178–2401** • gay-friendly • overlooking Ensenada Bay • free high-speed internet • secure parking • swimming • restaurant & bar w/ live music • $52-150

RESTAURANTS

Casamar Blvd Lázaro Cárdenas 987, Centro (at Blvd Costero) **52–646/174–0417** • 11am-11pm • popular • seafood • also bar • Ensenada landmark for 30 years

Guadalajara

INFO LINES & SERVICES

Centro Cultural Comunitario Gay de Guadalajara Av Alcalde 743

ACCOMMODATIONS

Casa de las Flores B&B Santos Degollado 175, Tlaquepaque **52–33/3659–3186** • gay-friendly • B&B 15 minutes from Guadalajara • great brkfsts & margaritas • $75-85

Hacienda Aldama Aldama 22 (off Main Crta), Ajijic **52–376/766–0944** • gay/ straight • 3 rooms in private home • full brkfst • nonsmoking • wheelchair access • gay-owned • $40-75

Hotel Calinda Roma Av Juárez 170 (Sector Juárez) **52–33/3614–8650** • gay-friendly • also rooftop restaurant

Hotel Casa Campos Francisco de Miranda 30 (Col. Centro), Tlaquepaque **52–33/3838–5296, 52–33/3838–5297** • gay-friendly • hotel 15 minutes SE of Guadalajara • also bar & restaurant • 850-1,250 pesos

Hotel El Aposento **52–33/3614–1612** • gay-straight • hotel in one of a kind 200-year-old mansion • full brkfst • wheelchair access • $65-95

Hotel Puerta del Sol Av López Mateos Sur 4205 (Col. Loma Bonita), Zapopan **52–33/3133–0808, 52–33/3133–0852 & 0862** • gay-friendly • hotel • swimming • bar & restaurant • 450-790 pesos

Hotel San Francisco Degollado 267 **52–33/3613–8954, 52–33/3613–8971** • popular • gay-friendly • hotel w/ Old World charm • courtyards & balconies • close to gay bars • also restaurant • $55+

Old Guadalajara B&B Belén 236 (Centro Histórico) **52–33/3613–9958** • gay/ straight • elegant private 16th-c home in downtown historic district • nonsmoking • gay-owned • $100

La Perla B&B Prado 128, Col. Americana (Vallarta y Lopez Cotilla) 52-33/3826-6961 • gay/straight • B&B in heart of Guadalajara • full brkfst • gay-owned

Bars

BE Café-Bar Lázaro Cárdenas 3750 52-33/3647-9160 • lesbians/gay men

Café Bar Butterfly Hidalgo 907 (casi esquina con cruz verde) • shows *The L Word* every Sun at 6:30pm

Cantina Ti@s Degollado 273 (Centro, across from Hotel Universo) • 8am-1am • lesbians/gay men

La Catrina Colón 389 (Las 9 Esquinas) 52-33/3658-3939 • lesbians/gay men • upscale lounge • live shows • patio

Chueca López Cotilla 1988 (Zona Centro Magno) 52-33/3615-5940 • from 6pm • mostly gay men • lounge • tapas menu

Julio Ranch Calle Degollado 187 (btwn Madero & López Cotilla) 52-33/3658-2838 • 1pm-3am • lesbians/gay men • dancing/DJ • drag shows

Luminare Hospital 882 (btwn Puebla & Federalismo) 52-33/3825-2085 • 6:30pm-12:30am, clsd Sun • lesbians/gay men • lounge • terrace

Máskara's Calle Maestranza 238 (at Prisciliano Sánchez) 52-33/3614-8103 • 8am-2am • lesbians/gay men • neighborhood bar • colorful atmosphere • live music • food served

Mundo Cool Café-Bar Prisciliano Sánchez 410 (Zona Centro) • lesbians/gay men • live shows • karaoke • strippers

La Prisciliana Prisciliano Sánchez 395 (Centro) 52-33/3562-0725

Sexos Bar Degollado 273 (Centro) • 6pm-3am • lesbians/gay men • dancing/DJ • shows

Nightclubs

Angels López Cotilla 1495-B, Col. Americana (btwn Av Chapultepec & Marsella, Zona Rosa) 52-33/3615-2525, 52-33/3630-5478 • 10pm-5am Fri-Sat, till 3am Wed, after-party Sun 6am-10am • mostly gay men • dancing/DJ • videos • cover charge • performance wknds • restaurant

Candilejas Calle Prisciliano Sánchez 407, Centro 52-33/3614-5512 • 8pm-4am • gay/straight • dancing/DJ • lavish drag shows • cover charge

Caudillo Platino Av Hidalgo 838 (Centro) 52-33/3563-4332 • 8pm-4am, clsd Mon • lesbians/gay men • dancing/DJ • transgender-friendly • drag shows • strippers

Circus Galeana 277 (at Prisciliano Sánchez, Centro Histórico) 52-33/3613-0299 • 9pm-5am • popular • lesbians/gay men • dancing • live shows

Enigma Galeana 378 (at 9 Las Esquinas) • 9pm-5am • gay-friendly • dancing/DJ • cabaret • drag shows • videos • 18+ • young crowd • gay-owned

Mónica's Disco Bar Av Álvaro Obregón 1713 (btwn Calles 68 & 70, Sector Libertad; no sign, look for canopy under a big palm tree) 52-33/3643-9544 • 10pm-5am, clsd Mon-Tue • popular after midnight • mostly gay men • dancing/DJ • drag/strip shows wknds • young crowd • cover charge • take a taxi to & from

SOS Club Av La Paz 1413 (Sector Hidalgo, Zona Centro) 52-33/3826-4179 • 9pm-3am, clsd Mon-Tue • lesbians/gay men • dancing/DJ • drag shows • strippers Fri-Sat (men only) & Sun (women only) • patio • cover charge

Restaurants

Mondo Caffe Av Chapultepec 48 (at Pedro Moreno) 52-33/3630-2232 • 8am-11pm • gay/straight • brkfast, lunch & dinner • coffee • smoothies • beer/wine • multiracial • free internet access

Sanborns Av Juárez 305 (at Av 16 de Septiembre) 52-33/3613-6264 • int'l • many locations

Sanborns Café Av Vallarta 2037 52-33/3615-7236 • int'l

La Séptima Vuelta Hidalgo 811 • lesbians/gay men • also bar

Entertainment & Recreation

Guadalajara Gay Radio 104.3 FM (Radio Universidad de Guadalajara) • gay radio station • check out www.gdlgayradio.com for shows

Spiritual Groups

Iglesia de la Comunidad Metropolitana (ICM) de Guadalajara Jose Cruz Bernabé Delgado 1293, Tonalá 52-33/3670-3073 • call for worship times

Iglesia de la Comunidad Metropolitana (ICM) de La Santa Cruz Medrano 1354 52-33/3617-1778 • 5pm Sun

Isla Mujeres

ACCOMMODATIONS

Casa de los Amigos 44.01/877-1169 • gay/straight • rental villa on Mayan Riviera • gay-owned • $330-390/ week

Jalapa

NIGHTCLUBS

La Mansión take a cab toward Banderillas (20 minutes NW of town, turn right at sign for El Paraíso Campestre & go past RR tracks) • 9pm-4am Fri-Sat only • lesbians/ gay men • dancing/DJ • live shows • cover charge

La Paz

ACCOMMODATIONS

La Casa Mexicana Inn Calle Nicolas Bravo 106 (btwn Madero & Mutualismo) 52-612/125-2748 • open Nov-June • gay/straight • Spanish/ Moorish retreat • 1 block from La Paz Bay • nonsmoking • wheelchair access • woman-owned • $65-125

Hotel Mediterrane Allende 36 (at Malecón) 52-612/125-1195 • gay/ straight • bar & restaurant • sun terrace • gay-owned • $55-85

BARS

Cafe La Pazta Allende 36 (at Hotel Mediterrane) 52-612/125-1195 • 7am-11pm • gay/ straight • neighborhood bar • young crowd • gay-owned

¡No Que No! Marcelo Rubio (btwn Cuauhtemoc & Sonora) • lesbians/ gay men • dancing/DJ

NIGHTCLUBS

Las Varitas Calle Independencia 111 (at Malecón) 52-612/125-2025 • 9pm-3am, clsd Mon • gay-friendly • dancing/DJ • live shows • rock 'n' roll bar

RESTAURANTS

La Pazta Allende 36 (at Hotel Mediterrane) 52-612/125-1195 • 3pm-11pm, clsd Tue • homemade Italian & Swiss

León

BARS

G*bar Madero at Gante (Centro Histórico) 52-477/716-3695 • 6pm-2am, from 5pm Sat-Sun • mostly gay men • café-bar w/ terrace • young crowd

NIGHTCLUBS

Biza Club 20 de Enero 204, Centro (off Calle Pedro Moreno) 52-477/716-3695, 52-477/713-7124 • 11am-3am, clsd Sun • mostly gay men • dancing/DJ • live shows • go-go boys Sat

La Madame Blvd A López Mateos 1709 Oriente (in front of Torre Banamex) 52-477/763-3086 • 10pm-3am, clsd Mon-Wed • mostly gay men • dancing/DJ • drag shows • go-go boys

Manzanillo

ACCOMMODATIONS

Las Hadas Av Vista Hermosa s/n (Fracc. Península de Santiago) 52-314/331-0101, 888/559-4329 • gay-friendly • great resort & location • $180+

Mexico's Villa Montaña Adventure Outpost 46 Los Angeles Locos, La Manzanilla 206/937-3882 • gay-friendly • 2-bdrm hilltop villa • ocean views • 1/2 hour N of Manzanillo • kids/ pets ok • nonsmoking • wheelchair access • $65-129

Los Sueños del Mar Calle Almendros 98 52-314/335-0482, 800/316-9032 (RESERVATIONS ONLY) • gay-friendly • casitas & guest rooms overlooking ocean • $125-185 (3-night minimum)

BARS

Evolution Blvd Miguel de la Madrid H 1550 (Zona Hotelera) • 7pm-3am • gay-friendly • drag shows Fri-Sat

OK Independencia 42 (Centro) • Th-Sun only • mostly gay men • dancing/DJ • drag shows • cover charge

Mazatlán

ACCOMMODATIONS

El Cid Resort 888/733-7308 & 800/525-1925 (US & CANADA), 52-669/913-3333 • gay-friendly • 4-hotel complex on 720 acres • $79-729

Hotel Los Sábalos Av Playa Gaviotas 100 (Zona Dorada) 52-669/983-5333, 800/528-8760 (US#) • gay-friendly • upscale resort • swimming • beach • health club • also popular Joe's Oyster Bar

The Pueblo Bonito Emerald Bay Ernesto Coppel Compañia 52-669/989-0525, 800/990-8250 • gay-friendly • resort on 20 acres • jacuzzi • swimming • restaurant • piano bar • gym • $145-370

BARS

La Alemana Calle Zaragoza 16 (at Benito Juarez & Serdan) • gay/ straight • sports bar

Pepe Toro Av de las Garzas 18, Zona Dorada (1 block W of Av Camarón Sábalo) 52–669/914–4176 • 9:30pm-4am, clsd Mon-Wed • popular • mostly gay men • dancing/DJ • drag/ strip shows

Vitrolas Bar Heribertos Frías 1608 (in El Centro) 52–669/985–2221 • lesbians/ gay men • lunch menu • karaoke • drag shows & strippers Sun

RESTAURANTS

Panamá Restaurant Pastelería at Avs de las Garzas & Camarón Sábalo 52–669/913–6977 • gay/ straight

Roca Mar Av del Mar (at Calle Isla de Lobos, Zona Costera) 52–669/981–6008 • till 2am • popular • seafood • full bar • lesbian-owned

Señor Frogs Av del Mar s/n, Zona Costera (Col. Palo Prietov) 52–669/982–1925, 52–669/985–1110 • upscale • seafood • full bar • dancing/DJ

Mérida

ACCOMMODATIONS

Angeles de Mérida Calle 74-A, #495-A x 57 y 59-A (at Calle 57 & Calle 59) 52–999/923–8163, 713/208–2482 (US#) • gay/ straight • B&B in 18th-c home on quietest streets of Mérida • nonsmoking • swimming • spa services available • gay-owned • $70-115

Los Arcos B&B Calle 66 52–999/928–0214 • gay-friendly • colonial home in the heart of Mérida's Centro • courtyard • gay-owned • $75-95

Casa Ana Calle 52 #469 (btwn 51 & 53) 52–999/924–0005 • gay-friendly • B&B in colonial home • swimming • nonsmoking • women-owned • $30-45

Casa San Juan B&B 545A Calle 62 (at Calle 69 & Calle 71) 52–999/986–2937 • gay/ straight • in historical center of Merida • courtyard • nonsmoking • kids ok • wheelchair access • gay-owned • $35-55

Gran Hotel Calle 60 #496 (at Calle 69, in Parque Hidalgo) 52–999/924–7730, 52–999/923–6963 • gay-friendly • historic turn-of-the-century hotel • courtyard w/ balconies • also restaurant

BARS

El Establo Calle 60 #482-A (btwn Calle 56 & 58) 52–999/924–2289 • gay-friendly • dancing/DJ • food served • popular w/ tourists & locals

Limbos Restaurant & Bar Paseo de Montejo x 37 y 39 52–999/901–1039 • gay-friendly • also restaurant

CAFES

El Edén Calle 55 (btwn Calle 56 & 58) • gay-friendly • café w/ large gay turnout • beer/ wine • also restaurant • gay-owned

RESTAURANTS

Café La Habana Calle 59 #511-A (at Calle 62) • 24hrs • also bar & café

La Bella Época Calle 60 #447 (upstairs in the Hotel del Parque) 52–999/928–1928 • 4pm-1am • Yucatécan cuisine • try to get one of the balcony tables • some veggie

Pop Calle 57 (btwn Calle 60 & 62) • cafetería w/ brkfst, lunch & "light dinner" • beer & wine

Mexicali

BARS

Cantine Tare at Calle Uxmal & Av Jalisco, Pueblo Nuevo (across the Rio Nuevo from downtown) • 6pm-2am, clsd Mon • mostly gay men • neighborhood bar • drag shows

Cinco Estrellas corner of Av Jalisco & Calle 3 (next door to Cantine Tare) • call for hours • popular • mostly women • neighborhood bar

Galerie 232 Av Zuazua 232 (in Zona Centro) 52–686/543–0161 • 1pm-midnight • dancing/DJ • videos • beer only

El Rey de Copas Av Baja California (at Av Tuxtla Gutierrez, Pueblo Nuevo) • open till 3am • lesbians/ gay men • neighborhood bar

El Taurino Av Juan de Zuazua 480 (near Morelos) • 1pm-2am, clsd Mon • popular • mostly gay men • dancing/DJ

NIGHTCLUBS

Mirage Disco Av Lerdo #430 (in Zona Centro) • 6pm-2am Wed-Sun • popular • dancing/DJ

Mexico City

Note: M°=Metro station

Note: Mexico City is divided into "Zonas" (ie, Zona Rosa) & "Colonias" (abbreviated here as Col.). Remember to use these when giving addresses to taxi drivers.

INFO LINES & SERVICES

Cálamo (LGBT AA) Av Chapultepec 265, desp. 202 (Col. Juárez) **52-55/5574-1210** • 8pm Mon-Fri, 7pm Sat, 6pm Sun • LGBT AA group

Centro Cultural de la Diversidad Sexual Colima 267 (Col. Roma) **52-55/5514-2565** • Mexico's city's LGBT center • also cafe

Centro Cultural Enkidu Juan Escutia 23 BIS (Ninos Heroes) **52-55/9180-1240** • variety of services for LGBT travelers to Mexico City including a travel agency, tour guides & day trips • also publishes Enkidu LGBT magazine (www.enkidumagazine.com)

Una Voz Interior (AA) Rosas Moreno 126 (Col. San Rafael) • 8pm Mon-Sat • AA group

ACCOMMODATIONS

Best Western Majestic Hotel Madero 73, Col. Centro **52-55/5521-8600, 800/528-1234** • gay-friendly • 4-star hotel on the Zócalo Plaza • rooftop restaurant • wheelchair access • $120+

Calinda Geneve Calle Londres 130 (Col. Juárez, Zona Rosa) **52-55/5080-0800, 800/714-6549 (IN MEXICO)** • gay-friendly • 3-story colonial-style hotel • Sanborns restaurant • also bar

Hostal San Sebastian Havre 41 (at Av Insurgentes, in Zona Rosa) **52-55/5208-6528** • gay-friendly • gay-owned • $23-34

Hotel Casa Blanca Lafragua 7 (Col. Tabacalera) **52-55/5096-4500, 800/905-2905 (US & CANADA #)** • gay-friendly • 5-star hotel • swimming • restaurant & bar • $116-445

Hotel Gillow Isabel la Católica 17 (Col. Centro) **52-55/5518-1440, 52-55/5510-2636** • gay-friendly • close to Zócalo • also restaurant & bar • $42-90

Hotel Polanco Edgar Allan Poe 8 (Col. Polanco) **52-55/5280-8082, 800/221-9044** • gay-friendly • posh location steps from Paseo de la Reforma • $115-140

Marco Polo Amberes 27, Col. Juárez (Zona Rosa) **52-55/5080-0063, 800/448-8355 (US#)** • gay-friendly • small boutique hotel • $88-248

NH Mexico City Liverpool 155 (Col. Juárez, Zona Rosa) **52-55/5648-0049** • gay-friendly • upscale • 2 restaurants • swimming • $125-3,000

W Mexico City Campos Eliseos 252 **52-55/9138-1800** • gay-friendly • ultracool hotel in trendy Polanco • 2 restaurants & bar • high-speed internet • $199+

BARS

Cafeína Nuevo Leon 73 (in Condesa) **52-55/5212-0090** • noon-2am • gay-friendly • dancing/ DJ • co-owned by Diego Luna of Y Tu Mama También fame

Enigma Calle Morelia 111, Col. Roma (4 blocks from M° Niños Héroes, Zona Rosa) **52-55/5207-7367** • 9pm-3:30am, 6pm-2am Sun • lesbians/ gay men • dancing/DJ • shows for women Th • live shows • cover charge

Lipstick Amberes 1 (at Paseo de la Reforma, Zona Rosa) **52-55/5514-4920** • clsd Sun-Tue • gay/ straight • more gay Fri-Sat • lounge • videos • live shows

NIGHTCLUBS

Anyway/ Exacto/ The Doors Calle Monterrey 47, Col. Roma (Zona Rosa) **52-55/5533-1691** • 9pm-4am • popular • lesbians/ gay men • 3 flrs • The Doors, 1st floor, is a mixed restaurant/ bar • Exacto, 2nd floor, is for women • Anyway, 3rd flr, is men's bar • food served • live shows • cover charge

Butterflies Calle Izazaga 9 (at Av Lazaro Cárdenas S, Centro Historico) **52-55/5761-1351, 52-55/5761-18.61** • 9pm-3am, till 4:30am Fri-Sat, clsd Mon • popular • lesbians/ gay men • dancing/DJ • 2 flrs • lavish drag shows Fri-Sat • cover charge

Cabaré-Tito Neón Calle Londres 136, Plaza del Angel (Zona Rosa) **52-55/5207-2543** • lesbians/ gay men • women's night Th • dancing/DJ • go-go dancers • drag shows Sun-Mon

Cabaré-Tito Safari Calle Londres 136 (Zona Rosa) **52-55/5207-2543** • lesbians/ gay men • theme nights • dancing/DJ • go-go dancers • drag shows

Cabaré-Tito VIP Calle Londres 104 (Zona Rosa) **52-55/5208-2305** • lesbians/ gay men • theme nights • dancing/DJ • go-go dancers • drag shows

Living Paseo de la Reforma 483 (Col. Cuauhtémoc) **55-55/5286-0671, 52-55/5286-0069** • clsd Mon, more gay Fri • popular • lesbians/ gay men • popular • theme nights

La Poule 39 Andromaco 39 (at Moliere, Col. Polanco) 52–55/5255–1747, 52–55/5255–1674 • lesbians/ gay men • huge club • dancing/DJ • check out www.box.com.mx for more info

Stereo Puebla 186 (Col. Roma) 52–55/5525–8681 • mostly gay men • monster club in converted theater w/ top DJs

CAFES

BGay BProud Amberes 12-B (in Zona Rosa) 52–55/5208–2547 • lively, pleasant cafe • mostly men • food served • younger crowd

La Chocolateria Juan de la Barrera 1-C (btwn Pachuga & Mazatlan) 52–55/5553–1362 • "unparalleled hot chocolate" • gay-owned

RESTAURANTS

La Antigua Cortesana Chiapas 173-A (Col. Roma) 52–55/5584–4678 • 1pm-11pm, till midnight Fri-Sat, till 7pm Sun • popular Mexican cuisine • also bar

Fonda San Ángel Plaza San Jacinto 3, Col. San Ángel (across from Bazar San Ángel) 52–55/550–1641, 52–55/550–1942 • popular after 7pm Fri-Sat • classic Mexican dishes

Ligaya Nuevo Leon 68 (in Condesa) 52–55/5286–6268 • nouvelle Mexican • dinner nightly • outdoor seating

Marrón Café Amberes 13 (Zona Rosa) 52–55/5514–5971 • popular before-clubbing hangout

La Nueva Opera Calle 5 de Mayo 10 (Centro Historico) 52–55/5512–8959 • 1pm-midnight, clsd Sun • legendary cantina since Pancho Villa fired a bullet into the ceiling

Punto y Aparte Amberes 62 (btwn Calles Londres & Liverpool, Zona Rosa) 52–55/5533–5442 • gay/ straight • int'l menu

Restaurante Lamm Alvaro Obregon 99, Roma 52–55/5514–8501 • hip Mexican-fusion restaurant on 3 level in old mansion • patio

Sanborns Madera 4 (in Casa de los Azulejos) 52–55/5518–6676 • brkfst, lunch & dinner • superstore

Virreinas Av México 54 (Col. Santa Cruz Atoyac) 52–55/5601–7460

ENTERTAINMENT & RECREATION

El Hábito Madrid 13 (Coyocán District) 52–55/5659–1139 • avante-garde theater & bar

Museo de Arte Carrillo Gil Av Revolución 1608 (San Angel) 52–55/5550–1254 • 10am-6pm, clsd Mon • contemporary art

Mexico City

LGBT PRIDE:
June/July, web: mexcity.8m.com.

CITY INFO:
InfoTur 52–55/525.93.80
Mexican Tourism 800-44-MEXICO (US #).

WEATHER:
Temperate and dry most of the year, with most of the annual rainfall coming in May-Oct. When the smog gets unbearable, head for a museum or other indoor activity.

TRANSIT:
52–55/516.60.20,
52–55/519.76.90.
Don't hail a taxi on the street. It costs more to call an official taxi, but it's worth it.
Metro & microbuses.

ATTRACTIONS:
Ballet Folklorico
Frida Kahlo House 52–55/545.999
Metropolitan Cathedral
Diego Rivera Web Museum, web: www.diegorivera.com
Museo Dolores Olmedo (largest collection of Kahlo's works) 52–55/555.10.16
Museum of Anthropology 52–55/553.62.66
Museum of the Palace of Fine Arts
Museum of Modern Art 52–55/553.62.33
Shrine to Our Lady of Guadalupe
Teotihuacan Pyramids.

Museo de Arte Moderno Paseo de la Reforma (at Gandhi, Chapultepec Forest) **52-55/5553-6233, 52-55/5211-8729** • 10am-6pm, clsd Mon

Museo de Frida Kahlo Calle Londres 247 (Coyoacán) **52-55/5554-5999** • 10am-5:45pm, clsd Mon • original paintings, furniture, letters & Frida's dresses • also garden & café

Museo Templo Mayor Calle Seminario 8 (at República de Guatemala, enter on plaza, near Cathedral) **52-55/5542-4784, 52-55/5542-4785 OR 4786** • 9am-5pm, clsd Mon • artifacts from the central Aztec temple at Tenochtitlán

National Museum of Anthropology Paseo de la Reforma (at Calle Gandhi) **52-55/5286-2923, 52-55/5553-6381** • 9am-7pm, clsd Mon

BOOKSTORES

El Armario Abierto Agustín Melgar 25 (Col. Condesa) **52-55/5286-0895** • Mexico's only bookstore specializing in sexuality • some LGBT titles

PUBLICATIONS

Homópolis **52-55/2616-0456, 52-55/2616-0457** • twice-weekly LGBT magazine & guide

LeS VOZ Magazine AP 33-091, 15900 **52-55/5535-0456** • "The magazine of Mexico's lesbian feminist culture, by and for women."

Rola Gay • national monthly LGBT newspaper w/ online verision at www.rolaclub.org.mx

Ser Gay **52-55/5511-0414** • quarterly magazine • covers all Mexico nightlife • limited resources

SPIRITUAL GROUPS

Iglesia de la Comunidad Metropolitana (ICM) Reconciliación Norte 77 #3218 (Col. Obrero Popular) **52-55/5396-7768** • 12:30pm & 7pm Sun

Shalom Amigos **52-55/5264-6888** • LGBT Jewish group • meets 6:30pm-8:30pm Sun

Mineral de Pozos

ACCOMMODATIONS

Casa Montana Plaza Principal, Jardin Juarez #4A (at Ocampo) **52-442/293-0032, 52-442/293-0033** • gay-friendly • boutique hotel in charming high desert town • full brkfst • garden restaurant & bar • woman-owned/run • $99-128

Monterrey

ACCOMMODATIONS

Hotel Rio Calle Padre Mier 194 N (at Garibaldi, Centro) **800/432-2520 (US#)** • gay-friendly • near Zona Rosa • swimming • also restaurant • $50-135

BARS

Divas Calle Zaragoza (at Issac Garza, Centro) • 10pm-close, clsd Sun-Tue • lesbians/ gay men • drag shows • strippers

Dorados de Villa Treviño 1813 (Col. Obrera) • 7pm-1am, clsd Sun-Tue • lesbians/ gay men • patio

Pink Boy Bar Alejandro de Humbolt 1119 (Col. Mirador) • lesbians/ gay men • videos

NIGHTCLUBS

Arcolris Calzado Madero 1707 (btwn Felix Gomez & JG Leal) **52-83/8372-8460** • 7pm-close • lesbians/ gay men • danncg/ DJ • strippers

Taboo Ocampo 433 Puente **52-81/8040-9458** • 9pm-close, clsd Mon-Tue • lesbians/ gay men • dancing/ DJ • strippers • videos

Venneno Club Av de los Héroes 47 (at Av Francisco I Madero) **52-81/8372-9019** • 9pm-close, clsd Mon-Tue • lesbians/ gay men • dancing/ DJ • drag shows • strippers

CAFES

Kaksan Aramberri 1217, Oriente (btwn Calle Carvajal y de la Cueva & Platón Sánchez) **52-81/8343-7325** • 6pm-midnight • lesbians/ gay men • also full bar

SPIRITUAL GROUPS

Iglesia de la Comunidad Metropolitana (ICM) Monterrey Diego de Montemayor 219 Sur (Col. Centro de la Ciudad) **52-81/8340-3789** • 8:15pm Fri & 6pm Sun

Morelia

ACCOMMODATIONS

Casa Camelinas B&B Jacarandas 172 (Col. Nueva Jacarandas) **52-443/324-5194, 707/942-4822 (US#)** • gay-friendly • mostly women • 3 1/2 hours from Mexico City • nonsmoking • also Spanish classes • $55-85

BARS

Amnesia Gertrudis Bocanegra 961 (at Lázaro Cárdenas) • 5pm-2am, clsd Sun • lesbians/ gay men • lounge w/ DJ

NIGHTCLUBS

Con la Rojas Aldama 343 (Centro) 52-443/312-1578 • 11pm-2am, clsd Sun-Wed • mostly gay men • upscale • dancing/DJ • cover charge

RESTAURANTS

La Capilla Ignacio Zaragoza 90 (at Posada de la Soledad Hotel) 52-443/312-1818 • in charming old hotel in converted convent

Fonda Las Mercedes Calle Leon Guzmán 47 52-443/312-6113, 52-443/313-3222 • popular • inside beautiful colonial home

Mulege

ACCOMMODATIONS

Las Casitas Madero 50 52-615/153-0019 • gay-friendly • restaurant & full bar

Oaxaca

ACCOMMODATIONS

El Camino Real Oaxaca Calle 5 de Mayo 300 52-951/516-0611, 800/722-6466 (US RESERVATIONS) • popular • gay-friendly • 5-star hotel in restored 16th-c convent • frescoes & courtyards abound • restaurant • swimming • $225-380

Casa Adobe B&B Independencia 11, Tlalixtac de Cabrera 52-951/517-7268 • gay/straight • full brkfst • 15 minutes from center of Oaxaca • gay-owned • $37-65

La Casa de Mis Recuerdos Pino Suárez 508 52-951/515-5645 • gay-friendly • full brkfst • $57-96 (3-night minimum)

Casa Sagrada Teotitlan del Valle 52-951/516-4275, 310/455-6085 • gay/straight • B&B located in weaving village 30 minutes from Oaxaca • full brkfst • kids ok • nonsmoking • cooking classes Fri • $85

Mision de los Angeles Hotel Calzada Porfirio Díaz 102 52-951/515-1500 OR 515-1000, 800/221-6509 (US#) OR 800/446-2922 • gay-friendly • resort w/ bungalows • restaurant & dance clubs • swimming • tennis courts • $128-182

NIGHTCLUBS

Club Privado 502 (aka El Número) Calle Porfirio Díaz 502 (Centro, ring to enter) • 10pm-close, clsd Sun-Tue • gay/ straight • dancing/DJ (wknds) • tourists welcome w/ proper ID • cover charge

Disco Snob Calzada Niños Héroes de Chupultepec (1 block W of bus station) • gay from 10pm Wed only • dancing/DJ

RESTAURANTS

El Asador Vasco Portal de Flores 10-A (Centro) 52-951/514-4755 • popular • great views • authentic Oaxacan cuisine (can you say ¡mole!)

Playa del Carmen

see also Cancún & Cozumel

ACCOMMODATIONS

Aventura Mexicana Resort Av 10 (at Calle 22) 52-984/873-1876 • gay-friendly • swimming • jacuzzi • nudity ok • 15 minutes to gay nude beach • also restaurant & bar • wheelchair access • $50-225

Pension San Juan 5a Av 165 (btwn Calles 6 & 8 Norte) 52-984/873-0647 • gay-friendly motel • nonsmoking • kids ok

RESTAURANTS

100% Natural Av 5 (btwn Calle 8 & Calle 10) • vegetarian

Jacobi's Restaurant 10th Ave & Calle 22 (at Aventura Mexicana Resort) 52-984/873-1876 • brkfst, lunch & dinner, poolside dining

Puebla

BARS

La Cigarra Calle 5 W 538 (at Calle 7, Centro) 52-22/246-6356 • 6pm-3am, clsd Sun • popular • mostly gay men • beer bar • videos

NIGHTCLUBS

Garrotos 22 Orient E 602 (close to Blvd 5 de Mayo, Xenenetla) 52-222/242-4232 • 9pm-3am Fri-Sat only • gay-friendly • dancing/DJ • cover charge

SPIRITUAL GROUPS

Afirmación México 52-222/200-1731 • lesbian/gay Mormons • monthly meetings

Puerto Vallarta

INFO LINES & SERVICES

Alano Insurgentes 181, #208 (at Cine Bahia Bldg) 52-322/223-0801 (BILL), 52-322/222-3906 (ANGELA) • English-speaking LGBT AA 11am Sat • women-only 11:30am Th

ACCOMMODATIONS

Amantes del Sol • gay-friendly • 2 condos w/ ocean views • near beach & nightlife • swimming • gay-owned • $35-75 • see www.amantesdelsol.com

Apartment Jacarandas Jacarandas 566, Jalisco (at Pulpito) **204/237–3840, 52–322/222–7126** • gay/ straight • main floor studio apt w/ fully equipped kitchen • discount for long-term rentals • $500/ week

Blue Chairs Beach Resort Malecon & Almendro 4 (on Playa Los Muertos) **229/336–9979 (US#), 866/514–7969 (US & CANADA)** • mostly gay men • popular • right on the beach • beach club bar & rooftop piano bar & cabaret • swimming • hot tub • wheelchair access • $49-219

Bugambilia Blanca Condos Carretera Barra de Navidad 602, Col. Emiliano Zapata (Off Hwy 200) **52–322/222–1152** • gay/ straight • 4 levels • suites • also 2 & 3-bdrm apts • 6-minute walk to gay beach • kids ok • gay-owned • $90-360

Casa Boana Torre Malibu Calle Amapas 325 **52–322/222–0099, 52–322/222–6695** • popular • gay/ straight • condo-hotel • bay views • food served • swimming • poolside bar • $40-190

Casa de los Arcos **52–322/222–5990, 212/561–5795 (US#)** • gay/ straight • private villa • sleeps 8 • swimming • terrace w/ amazing view of Bandera Bay • $100-240

Casa dos Comales Calle Aldama 274 **52–322/223–2042, 888/881–1822 (US#)** • gay-friendly • guesthouse & apts near Old Town • swimming • gay-owned • $50-125

Casa Fantasía Pino Suarez 203, Col. Emiliano Zapata (near the Rio Cuale) **52–322/223–2444** • gay/ straight • B&B made up of 3 traditional haciendas • full brkfst • terrace • swimming • nonsmoking • wheelchair access • gay-owned • $60-120

Casa Mariposa **401/849–8597, 866/849–8597** • mostly men • colorful condo w/ balcony 1 block from Los Muertos Beach • swimming pool • $65-100

Casa Tres Vidas **888/640–8100 (US#), 801/536–5850** • 3 luxury beachfront villas • swimming • hot tubs • kids ok • $450-750/ night + tax

Casa Ventana Calle Hortencias 135, Penthouse **649/376–6230** • gay-friendly • luxury condo • sleeps 6 • swimming • gay-owned • $300-625

Condominios Plazamar Lázaro Cárdenas 155 **702/496–4432 (NV#)** • gay-friendly • 1 & 2-bdrm beachfront condos • swimming • gay-owned • $90-180

Los Cuatro Vientos Matamoros 520 **52–322/222–0161** • gay-friendly • hotel that's home to popular El Nido rooftop bar & Chez Elena restaurant & sponsors annual week-long Women's Getaway • also commitment ceremonies

David's Beach Condo in PV 156 Amapas St #402 **415/487–0800** • gay-friendly • 4th-flr condo w/ ocean views • on gay beach • jacuzzi • swimming • $55-135

Discovery Vallarta **52–322/222–6918** • gay accommodations reservation service • also great website at www.discoveryvallarta.com

Doin It Right—in Puerto Vallarta **619/297–3642 (US#), 800/936–3646 (US#)** • Puerto Vallarta gay travel specialist since 1995 • villas & condos • 200+ page guide • coupons & more • also Costa Rica • www.DoinItRight.com

▲ **Hotel Mercurio** **52–322/222–4793** • popular • lesbians/ gay men • traditional & alternative families welcome • 1 1/2 blocks from beach • swimming • gay-owned • $50-90

Hotel Suites Descanso del Sol Pino Suárez 583, Zona Romantica **52–322/223–0277, 52–322/222–5229** • popular • mostly gay men • apts, casitas & tents • swimming • rooftop bar w/ sunset views • $45-110

Hotelito Desconocido Carretera a Mismaloya 479-102, 48380 Cruz de Loreto **52–322/222–2526, 800/851–1143** • gay/ straight • eco-resort on the beach • 60 miles S of Puerto Vallarta • swimming • sauna • $230-900

Paco's Hidden Paradise 30 minutes S of Puerto Vallarta **52–322/227–2189** • lesbians/ gay men • secluded beach resort accessible only by boat • condos & tents • bar • restaurant • gay-owned • $40-80

Quinta Maria Cortez Calle Sagitario 132, Playa Conchas Chinas **801/536–5850 (US#), 888/640–8100 (US#)** • gay/ straight • "Mexaterranian Villa" w/ sunny terraces & spectacular ocean views • swimming • $85-235 + tax

Villa Amapas **52–322/205–3907** • mostly gay men • luxury beachfront villa w/ heated pool & outdoor bar • 4 bdrms • 5 minutes from town • gay-owned • $850-1,200

Villa del Cielo Paseo de los Delfines 121 (at Residencial Conchas Chinas) **206/285–3503 (US#)** • gay/ straight • private villa on Conchas Chinas hillside • maid & houseman • swimming • kids ok • gay-owned • $395-750

Villa Safari Condo Francisca Rodriguez 203 269/469-0468 (US #) • gay/ straight • hillside 2-bdrm condo • 2 blocks from Los Muertos beach • swimming • nonsmoking • kids/ pets ok • gay-owned • $125-175

BARS

Los Amigos Bar Calle Venustiano Carranza 239 (upstairs, next to Paco's Ranch) 52-322/222-7802 • 5pm-2am • lesbians/ gay men • Mexican cantina • patio

Apaches Olas Altas 439 (at Rodriguez) 52-322/222-5235 • 5pm-2am, till 1am Sun-Mon • gay/ straight • classy martini bar • tapas • lesbian-owned

Blue Sunset Rooftop Bar Los Muertos Beach (at Blue Chairs Resort) • 2pm-10pm • mostly gay men • T-dance wknds • karaoke • drag shows • food served • also Blue Chairs Beach Bar & Blue Moon (cabaret & piano bar)

La Bola Calle Pilitas 174 (at Vallarta Cora hotel) 52-322/223-2815 • 3pm-11pm • popular poolside bar • mostly gay men • food served • meeting spot after Amadeus day cruises

Frida Lázaro Cárdenas 361 (at Insurgentes) • 1pm-2am, from 7pm Mon-Tue • gay/ straight • Mexican cantina • more gay later in evening • food served • gay-owned

Garbo Pulpito 142 (at Olas Altas) 52-322/223-5753 • 6pm-2am • gay/ straight • upscale martini lounge • live jazz Fri-Sat • piano Wed-Th • gay-owned • 18+

Kit Kat Bar Pulpito 120 (next door to Chiles restaurant) 52-322/223-0093 • 5pm-1:30am • popular • lesbians/ gay men • swanky New York–style cocktail lounge • drag shows 11:30pm some nights • also restaurant (pricey but fun) • gay-owned

La Noche Lázaro Cárdenas 257 (Zona Romantica) 52-322/222-3364 • 7pm-2am • lesbians/ gay men • cocktail lounge

The Palm Olas Altas 508 (at Rodolfo Gomez) 52-322/223-4818 • 7pm-2am • lesbians/ gay men • dancing/DJ • food served • live shows • cabaret • drag shows Sat • gay & lesbian-owned

Sama Olas Altas 510 52-322/223-3182 • 5pm-2am • lesbians/ gay men • small martini bar w/ sidewalk seating

NIGHTCLUBS

Anthropology Calle Morelos 101, Plaza Río (at Rodriguez) **52–322/222–6392** • noon-4am • lesbians/ gay men • 3 levels: intimate rooftop bar, cocktail lounge, basement disco • drag shows • strippers • young crowd • cover charge

Los Balcones Calle Juárez 182, 2nd flr (at Calle Libertad) **52–322/222–4671** • 9pm-3am, till 4am wknds • popular • mostly gay men • dancing/DJ • popular male strippers late night • T-dance 6pm-11pm Sun • cover charge

Club Paco Paco Calle Ignacio Vallarta 278 (at Carranza) **52–322/222–1899** • 1pm-6am • popular • lesbians/ gay men • cantina on 2nd flr • disco downstairs from 10pm • also rooftop terrace w/ live piano • cover charge • gay-owned

The Ranch Calle Venustiana Carranza 239 (walk thru Club Paco Paco to back of dance flr) **52–322/223–0537** • 8pm-6am • popular • mostly gay men • dancing/DJ • disco • packed for nightly strip shows • videos • cover charge • gay-owned

Sky Ignacio L Vallarta 399 **52–322/222–7261** • lesbians/ gay men • dancing/ DJ • wknds only • cover

CAFES

A Page in the Sun Olas Altas 299 **52–322/222–3608** • 8am-11pm • popular • coffee shop & English bookstore

Café San Angel Olas Altas 449 **52–322/223–2160** • 7am-1am • sidewalk café • also crepes, smoothies, salads & sandwiches

Choco Banana Calle Amapas 147 (at Calle Pulpito) • 8am-10pm, clsd Sun • coffee, smoothies, shakes—& chocolate-covered bananas!

The Coffee Cup Rodolfo Gómez 146-A (at Olas Altas) **52–322/222–8584** • 8am-10pm, clsd Sun in summer • gay-owned

CyberSmoothie Rodolfo Gómez 111 **52–322/223–4784** • internet cafe w/ smoothies, coffee, salads & sandwiches • owner is also certified massage therapist

Este Cafe Libertad 336, Centro (around corner from flea market) **52–322/222–4261** • 8am-10pm, clsd Sun • popular • espresso & juice bar • desserts • ice cream • gay-owned

The Net House Calle Ignacio Vallarta 232 **52–322/222–6953** • 8am-2am • popular • cybercafe • organic coffee & baked goods • also Buona Pizza • gay-owned

RESTAURANTS

Abadia Basilio Badillo & IL Vallarta, Old Town **52–322/222–6720** • 9am-midnight

Adobe Café Calle Basilio Badillo 252 (at Ignacio Vallarta) **52–322/222–6720** • 6pm-11pm, clsd Tue (clsd Aug-Sept) • popular • Southwestern flair • full bar • gay-owned

Bianco Insurgentes 190 (Col. Emiliano Zapata) **52–322/222–2177** • 6pm-11:30pm (bar till 2am), clsd Mon • popular • chic restaurant & lounge • live jazz certain nights

Bombo's Corona 327, Centro (at Matamoros) **52–322/222–5164** • 5pm-midnight • upscale French • great views of Bandera Bay • reservations required • gay-owned

Café Bohemio Rodolfo Gómez 127 (at Olas Altas) **52–322/223–4676** • 5pm-2am, clsd Sun • lesbians/ gay men • open-air café • grilled food • late-evening happy hour • gay-owned

Café des Artistes Calle Guadalupe Sánchez 740 (at Leona Vicario) **52–322/222–3228** • 6pm-11:30pm • popular • upscale French w/ a Mexican twist • reservations required • expensive

Chez Elena Matamoros 520, Centro (at Los Quatros Vientos) **52–322/222–0161** • 6pm-11pm • seasonal • garden restaurant • Mexican/ int'l • some veggie • also rooftop bar • woman-owned/ run

¡Chiles! Pulpito 122 (at Olas Altas) **52–322/223–0373** • 11am-6pm, clsd Sun, seasonal (clsd mid-May–late-Sept) • popular • roasted chicken • sandwiches • hamburgers • large patio • gay-owned

Daiquiri Dick's Olas Altas 314 (on Playa Los Muertos) **52–322/222–0566** • 9am-10:30pm, clsd Wed • popular • Cal-Mex

Le Bistro Jazz Café Isla Rio Cuale 16–A (on the island, at the East Bridge) **52–322/222–0283** • 9am-midnight, clsd Sun • popular • PV's classiest • gay-owned

Mama Dolores Olas Altas 534-B (Col. Emiliano Zapata) **52–322/228–4061** • 8am-10pm, clsd Mon • homestyle American & Mexican • daily happy hour

Memo's Casa de los Hotcakes Calle Basilio Badillo 289 **52–322/222–6272** • 8am-2pm • popular • long lines for cheap & good brkfst • indoor patio • cooking classes

Mezzaluna Ristorante Italiano Corona St at Hidalgo St **52–322/222–0393** • 6pm-11pm, clsd June 1st-Nov 1st

Planeta Vegetariano Iturbide 270 (Centro) **52–322/222–3073** • 8am-10pm, clsd Sun • buffet-style

Red Cabbage Calle Rivera del Rio 204-A (at Basilio Badillo) **52-322/223-0411** • 5pm-11pm • Mexican • on Rio Cuale w/ great kitschy decor • lesbian-owned

Trio Guerrero 264 **52-322/222-2196** • 6pm-midnight, clsd Sun • Mediterranean/ Mexican • patio • live music • reservations advised

ENTERTAINMENT & RECREATION

Boana Tours Calle Amapas 325 (at Casa Boana Torre Malibu) **52-322/222-0999** • horseback tours daily

Diana's Cruise the Bay Tour meet at Los Muertos pier **52-322/222-5040** • 10:30am-6pm Th (be at dock no later than 9:45am) • lesbians/ gay men • cruise on 33-ft trimaran • limited to 20 people • snorkeling equipment • food served • open bar • $65 • other tours available

Playa Los Muertos/ Playa del Sol S of Rio Cuale • popular • the gay beach • now spans "Blue Chairs" & "Green Chairs"

RETAIL SHOPS

La Rosa de Cristal Insurgentes 272 (at Cardenas) **52-322/222-5698** • 10am-8pm • local handicrafts & beautiful blown-glass items • gay-owned

Safari Accents Olas Altas 224 **52-322/223-2660** • 10am-11pm • pricey but beautiful home furnishings • gay-owned

GYMS & HEALTH CLUBS

Acqua Day Spa & Gym Calle Constitución 450 **52-322/223-5270** • 7am-9pm, till 6pm Sat, clsd Sun • spa w/ massage, pedicures & manicures, steam room & sauna • also small gym

Gold's Gym Calle Pablo Picasso s/n (Zona Hotelera Las Glorias) **52-322/293-3673, 52-322/226-3070** • 6am-10pm, 7am-7pm Sat, 9am-3pm Sun • full gym w/ classes, sauna, jacuzzi

Total Fitness Gym Calle Timon 1 (Marina) **52-322/221-0770** • women-only • offers wide variety of classes: yoga, aerobics, pilates, spinning & more

Querétaro

BARS

Villa Jardín/ Bar Oz Blvd Bernardo Quintana 556, Col. Arboledas (across from Cinemark) **52-442/24.13.96** • 10pm-3am Sat only • mostly gay men • dancing/DJ • cover charge

NIGHTCLUBS

La Creación Nuevo Milenio Monte Sinai 113, Col. Vista Hermosa (before Disco Qu) **52-442/13.51.90** • Fri-Sat • gay-friendly • dancing/DJ • cover charge

Rosarito Beach

ACCOMMODATIONS

Rosarito Beach Hotel Blvd Benito Juárez 31 **52-661/612-0144 OR 1111, 800/343-8582 (RESERVATIONS)** • gay-friendly • historic hotel that's hosted stars & royalty • swimming • also restaurant & full-service spa • $97-377

RosaritoRental.com La Paloma Beach & Tennis Club 760/318-9652 (US#) • gay-friendly • condo rentals • swimming • hot tub • private beach • gay-owned • $79-229

San Jose del Cabo

ACCOMMODATIONS

La Jolla Beachfront Resort beach 604/536-1948 • gay-friendly • private beachfront resort close to downtown • swimming • $500-700/ week

RESTAURANTS

Voila Cafe & Catering in Villa Valentina (at Carr Transp km 31.5) **52-624/130-7569** • 10am-6pm, clsd Sun • Mexican/ French fusion • full bar

San Luis Potosí

BARS

Sheik Prolongación Zacatecas 347 **52-444/812-7457** • 9pm-3am Fri-Sat • mostly gay men • dancing/DJ • drag shows Fri • strippers Sat • cover charge

NIGHTCLUBS

Disco Greko Av Venustino Carranza 763 (Centro) **52-444/812-3200** • lesbians/ gay men • dancing/DJ • drag shows Fri • strippers Fri-Sat • cover (Sat)

San Miguel de Allende

ACCOMMODATIONS

Casa de Sierra Nevada Calle Hospicio 35 (Centro) **52-415/152-7040** • gay-friendly • suites • horseback riding • also spa • swimming • fireplaces • patios

Casa Gayceta Quebrada 24 (btwn Umarán & Insurgentes, Centro) **52-415/152-0710** • lesbians/ gay men • charming B&B in historic house in downtown San Miguel de Allende • $60-150

Casa Schuck Boutique B&B Garita 3, Centro **52-415/152-0657, 937/684-4092 (US#)** • gay-friendly • boutique hotel w/ private garden & rooftop deck • full brkfst • swimming • $130-190

Dos Casas Calle Quebrada 101 (Guanajuato) **52-415/154-4073** • gay-friendly • luxury B&B 3 blocks from main square • full brkfst • $195-315

Las Terrazas San Miguel Santo Domingo 3 **52-415/152-5028, 707/534-1833 (US#)** • gay/ straight • 4 rental homes • nonsmoking • gay-owned • $390-960/ week & $1,380-3,330/ month

Tenancingo

ACCOMMODATIONS

Casa Mora B&B Malinalco Calle de la Cruz 18, Malinalco **52-714/147-0572** • gay-friendly • full brkfst • swimming • $125-260

Tijuana

BARS

Noa Noa Av D 150/ Miguel F Martínez (at Calle 1) **52-664/686-2207** • 5pm-3am, till 4am Fri, till 5am Sat • popular • lesbians/ gay men • dancing/DJ • drag shows • young crowd

NIGHTCLUBS

Los Equipales Calle 7/ Galeana #8236 (at Av Revolución, opposite Jai Alai Palace) **52-664/688-3006** • 9pm-3am, clsd Mon-Tue • popular • lesbians/ gay men • dancing/DJ • drag shows • young crowd

Extasis Larroque 213 (in Plaza Viva Tijuana, next to the border) **52-664/682-8339** • 8pm-late, clsd Mon-Wed • popular • mostly gay men • women's night Th • dancing/DJ • strippers • cover charge

Mike's Disco Av Revolución 1220 (at Calle 6A) **52-664/685-3534** • 8pm-5am, till 3am Th, clsd Wed • popular • lesbians/ gay men • dancing/DJ • drag shows • videos

Terraza 9 Calle 6/ Flores Magón #8150 (at Av Revolución) **52-664/685-3534** • 5pm-2am, till 5am Fri-Sat, clsd Mon • lesbians/ gay men • dancing/DJ • drag/ strip shows • cover charge

Veracruz

ACCOMMODATIONS

Casa de la Luz Bernardino Aguirre 15 (Tlacotalpan) **52-288/884-2331** • gay-friendly • charming studio apt • 3 blocks from town center • $25-35 (guesthouse) & $550 (apt)/ month

Hotel Villa del Mar Blvd Miguel Ávila Camacho 2707, Col. Zaragoza (across street from Playa del Mar beach) **52-229/989-6500 & 6501, 800/322-1212** • gay-friendly • hotel w/ separate motel & bungalows • near aquarium • moderate price

NIGHTCLUBS

Deeper Calle Icazo 1005 (btwn Avs Victoria & Revillagigedo N) **52-229/935-0265** • 9pm-4am Th-Sun • popular • mostly gay men • dancing/DJ • cover charge

Shotters Calle 3 #1221 (btwn Enriquez & Alcocer) • popular • lesbians/ gay men • dancing/DJ • drag/ strip shows • warehouse club in a residential neighborhood • 10-minute cab ride from downtown

ENTERTAINMENT & RECREATION

San Juan de Ulua Fortress • 9am-4:30pm, clsd Mon • impressive early colonial-era floating fortress

Veracruz Aquarium Blvd Avila (at Xicolencat) **52-229/932-7984** • 10am-7pm • one of the largest & best in the world • don't miss it!

Villahermosa

ACCOMMODATIONS

Hotel Don Carlos Av Madero 418, Centro **52-993/312-2499** • gay-friendly • food served

Hyatt Regency Villahermosa Av Juarez 106, Col. Lindavista (across from Tomas Garrido Park) **52-993/310-1234, 800/233-1234 (US#)** • gay-friendly

Yelapa

ACCOMMODATIONS

Casa Rosa Yelapa 415/897-5746 • mostly lesbian • rental homes (main house & casita) • lesbian-owned • $300-500/ week & $800-1,500/ month

Zacatecas

ACCOMMODATIONS

Quinta Real Zacatecas Av Ignacio Rayón 434 (Col. Centro) **52–492/922–9104 TO 07, 866/621–9288 (US#)** • gay-friendly • full-service, five-star hotel built into grandstand of bullfighting ring

NIGHTCLUBS

Escándalo Feria Zacatecan, Terraza 4 **52–492/922–0805** • 9pm-3am Fri-Sat • lesbians/ gay men • dancing/DJ • live shows

CAFES

Café Nevería Acrópolis Av Hidalgo • Greek/ Mexican, even ice cream (!)

Zihuatanejo

ACCOMMODATIONS

Hotel Las Palmas Calle de Aeropuerto (at lot 5) **52–755/557–0443, 52–755/557–0634 (CELL)** • gay-friendly • quiet B&B inn • full brkfst • swimming • $225

NIGHTCLUBS

Tequila Town Cuauhtehoc 3 (off Malecon) **52–755/48.587** • gay-friendly • more gay after 11pm • karaoke • videos

Wilde's Calle La Laja s/n (Col. Vicente Guerrero) **52–755/557–1042** • 8pm-4am • lesbians/ gay men • dancing/DJ • drag shows & strippers Fri-Sun

COSTA RICA

Nationwide

ACCOMMODATIONS

Doin It Right—in Costa Rica **619/297–3642 (US#), 800/936–3646 (US#)** • select gay properties, condos & villas • also Puerto Vallarta, Mexico • www.DoinItRight.com

Alajuela

see also San José

BARS

Marguiss (250 meters S of Almacénes Llobet, on 2nd flr) **506/443–5310** • 6pm-close, clsd Mon • popular • lesbians/ gay men • neighborhood bar • live shows last Sun

Arenal

ENTERTAINMENT & RECREATION

The Arenal Volcano • hourly eruptions

Dominical

ACCOMMODATIONS

Cabinas Alma Costarena Hwy, Hatillo de Aguirre, Puntarenas **506/850–9034** • gay-friendly • nestled between rain forest & ocean • swimming • full brkfst • kids/ pets ok • $45-60

Guanacasta

ACCOMMODATIONS

Key Lime Cottage Gaviota del Sol (Playa Hermosa) **612/362–0763** • lesbians/ gay men • nonsmoking • lesbians-owned • $1,400-2,500/ week

Guanacaste

ACCOMMODATIONS

Villa Decary Nuevo Arenal, 5717 Tilaran **506/383–3012** • former coffee farm on 7 acres overlooking Lake Arenal • gay-friendly • gay-owned • $75-129

Manuel Antonio, Quepos

ACCOMMODATIONS

Big Ruby's La Plantacion Pacific Coast **506/777–1332 OR 506/ 777–1115, 800/477–7829 (US#)** • mostly gay men • women welcome • infinity pool • clothing optional by pool & hot tub • shuttle service to gay beach • full brkfst • also Madres restaurant • gay-owned • $112-549

Casa Bumerango 213/330–0231 • gay/ straight • kids ok • wheelchair access • gay-owned • $95-125

Casa Romano 770/226–0054 • gay/ straight • swimming • near gay beach • kids over 8 years ok • wheelchair access • gay-owned • $150+ (weekly rates available)

Condominium Villas Mymosa Apdo 271-6350 **506/777–1254** • $55-140

Géminis del Pacífico 773/472–7127 • gay-friendly • luxurious vacation home • swimming • near beaches & bars • kids ok • nonsmoking • gay-owned • $2,500-3,500/ week

Hotel Casa Blanca 506/777–0253, 506/777–1790 • lesbians/ gay men • short hike to gay beach • swimming • kids ok • lesbian & gay-owned • $50-180 • ask about retreat

Hotel Del Mar 200 Meters Playa Espadilla, apdo 6350-31 **506/777–0543** • gay/ straight • nestled in jungle • near beach & Manuel Antonio Nat'l Park • kids/ pets ok • $35-100

Hotel Parador 506/777-1414 • gay-friendly • large luxury resort w/ mini golf course & health club • swimming • also gourmet restaurant • $130-800

Hotel Villa Roca 506/777-1349 • mostly gay men • great ocean views • near beaches • swimming • gay-owned • $49-155

Kekoldi Beach Hotel (El Dorado Mojado) 506/248-0804, 786/221-9011 (FROM US) • gay/ straight • rooms & villas in forest • swimming • gay-owned • $40-105

Makanda by the Sea 506/777-0442 • gay-friendly • private oasis • swimming • $175-460

La Mansion Inn 506/777-3489 • gay/ straight • luxury hotel • also restaurant • bar • ocean views

El Parque 506/777-0096, 506/777-5060 • gay-friendly • hillside condos w/ ocean views • waterfall swimming pool • restaurant • $66-229

Si Como No 506/777-0777, 800/282-0488 x300 • popular • gay-friendly • swimming • wheelchair access • $150-270

Villa Titi Manuel Antonio Rd 206/938-8603, 506/777-0408 • gay/ straight • rental home located above Manuel Antonio's gay beach • swimming • kids ok • gay-owned • $50-250

Villas las Estrellas 506/777-1286 • gay/ straight • 2-bdrm villas • $73-102

Villas Nicolas 506/777-0481 • gay-friendly • oceanview rental suites • swimming • $65-180

BARS

Cockatoo Bar across from Escuela d'Amore Spanish-language school (near Manuel Antonio Park) • 4pm-close • lesbians/ gay men • dancing/DJ

Hotel Vela Bar 1st Beach (at Vela Bar Hotel) 506/777-0413 • 7am-10:30pm • gay-friendly • also restaurant

Mar y Sombra on Playa Espadilla • 7pm-close • gay-friendly • local flavor • dancing/DJ (Nov-April) • oldest restaurant in town

RESTAURANTS

El Barba Roja Carretera al Parque Nacional 506/777-0331 • 7am-10pm, from 4pm Mon • American • popular • great sunset location

El Gran Escape & Fish Head Bar Quepos Centro 506/777-0395 • brkfst, lunch, dinner, clsd Tue • seafood • full bar

Karola's top of hill right in front of Cafe Milagro 506/777-1557 • 11am-11pm • popular • lunch & dinner w/ a view • some veggie • full bar • gay-owned

The Plinio at the Hotel Plinio 506/777-0055 • int'l • full bar • Asian • some veggie

Rico Tico paved road to national park (in Hotel Si Como No) • 6:30am-9:30pm • Tex/ Mex • includes use of pool bar • popular • live shows • also Claro Que Sí (seafood restaurant)

RETAIL SHOPS

Villas Selva Gifts (Jungle Village) Av 2 506/771-1192 • hand-crafted gifts, tourist items & more • gay-owned

Playa Jaco

ACCOMMODATIONS

Hotel Poseidon Calle del Bohio (30 meters W of Jaco Centro) 506/643-1642, 888/643-1242 • gay-friendly • 50 meters to beach • also bar & restaurant • $65-98

San José

INFO LINES & SERVICES

Uno @ Diez Calle 3 (at Av 7) 506/258-4561 • 10am-8pm, clsd Sun • LGBT tourist info center • internet access • cafeteria

ACCOMMODATIONS

Colours Oasis Resort El Triangulo Noroeste, Blvd Rohrmoser (200 meters before end of blvd) 506/232-3504 & 506/296-1880, 877/932-6652 OR 954/ 241-7472 • popular • mostly gay men • full-service accommodations w/ tours & reservation services throughout Costa Rica • swimming • also bar & restaurant • events • gay-owned • $59-189

Hotel Amon Plaza Av 11 & Calle 3 bis 800/575-1253 • gay-friendly • modern hotel • quiet location • food served • $80-120

Hotel Don Carlos 506/221-6707, 866/675-9259 • popular • gay-friendly • $60-80

Hotel Kekoldi Av 9 (btwn Calles 5 & 7, Barrio Amón) 506/248-0804, 786/221-9011 (FROM US) • gay/ straight • in art deco bldg in downtown • secluded garden • gay-owned • $60-105

Joluva Guesthouse Calle 3, Barrio Amón (btwn Avs 9 & 11) 506/223-7961 • lesbians/ gay men • gay-owned • $30-50

Melia Cariari 506/290-0798 • gay-friendly • luxury resort w/ great golfing • swimming

BARS

Poas Bar & Restaurant Av 7 Calle 3 & 5 (behind Holiday Inn) 506/223-8677

NIGHTCLUBS

La Avispa 834 Calle 1 (pink house btwn Avs 8 & 10) **506/223–5343** • 8pm-2am, popular T-dance from 5pm Sun, clsd Mon • lesbians/ gay men • mostly women last Wed • dancing/DJ

El Bochinche Calle 11 (btwn Avs 10 & 12, Paseo de los Estudiantes), San Pedro **506/221–0500** • 7pm-2am, till 5pm Fri-Sat, clsd Sun-Mon • also full restaurant • Mexican • dancing/DJ after 10pm • videos

Dejá Vú Calle 2 (btwn Avs 14 & 16) **506/223–3758** • 9pm-close, clsd Sun-Tue • popular • lesbians/ gay men • dancing/DJ • 2 dance flrs • take taxi to avoid bad area

Puchos Calle 11 & Av 8 (knock to enter) **506/256–1147** • 8pm-2:30am, clsd Sun • lesbians/ gay men • also restaurant • drag shows

CAFES

Café Britt in Teatro Nacional (on Av 2) **506/221-1329** • lunch

RESTAURANTS

Anochecer 2 km from Centro Aserri on Hwy to Tarbaca (near Colours) **506/230–5152** • 11am-midnight • full bar • authentic Tico dinners • scenic view

El Bochinche Calle 11 (btwn Avs 10 & 12, Paseo de los Estudiantes), San Pedro **506/221–0500** • lesbians/ gay men • 8pm-4am, clsd Sun-Tue • dancing/DJ after 10pm • 3 bars • also restaurant • videos • live shows

Cafe La Esquina NW corner of Rohrmoser Triangle (in Hotel Colours) **506/296–1880** • lunch & dinner • also full bar • theme parties • lesbians/ gay men

Café Mundo Av 9 & Calle 15 (200 meters E of parking lot for INS, Barrio Amón) **506/222–6190** • 11am-11pm, 5pm-midnight Sat, clsd Sun • Italian • garden seating • also cafe/ bar • gay-owned

La Cocina de Leña in El Pueblo complex **506/255–1360** • 11am-11pm • popular • 5 minutes from downtown • Costa Rican • reservations recommended

Olio Escalante **506/281–0541** • lunch & dinner, clsd Sun • Spanish • also full bar • popular

Restaurante Solera SE of Los Yoses **506/225–0034** • lunch weekdays, dinner nightly, clsd Sun

Vishnu Vegetarian Restaurant Av 1 (btwn Calles 3 & 1) **506/256–6063** • 8am-9:30pm • popular

PUBLICATIONS

Gente 10 Apdo Postal 1910-2100, Sector Guadalupe **506/280–8886** • bi-monthly LGBT magazine • also map w/ listings (en español w/ some English)

EROTICA

Tabú 50 meters N of Farmacia Fischel (in XXX World) **506/221–7165** • also locations in San Pedro, Alajuela, Escazú & Real Cariari

San Ramon

ACCOMMODATIONS

Angel Valley Farm B&B 200m N & 300m E of Iglesia de Los Angeles (at Autopista to Arenal Volcano) **506/447–4684, 506/308–7357** • gay/ straight • full brkfst • kids over 5 & small pets ok • nonsmoking • wheelchair access • $35-65

Inn at Coyote Mountain Calle San Francisco 3 **607/277–5279** • gay/ straight • eco-lodge • swimming • gay-owned • $99-230

Tamarindo

ACCOMMODATIONS

Cala Luna Hotel & Villas Playa Langosta (at Playa Tamarindo) **506/653–0214** • gay-friendly • hotel • swimming • kids ok • $139-405

Hotel Sueño del Mar Playa Langosta **506/653–0284** • gay-friendly • private hacienda on the beach • full brkfst • swimming • $120-240

Laz Divaz Casitas Apdo 05-5235, Playa Sámara, Guanacaste **506/656–0295** • B&B • full brkfst • lesbian-owned • $60-70

Uvita

ACCOMMODATIONS

Tucan Hotel Frente Ebais De Uvita (across from church) **506/743-8140** • gay-friendly • kids/ pets ok • near natural waterfalls • bisexual-owned/ run • $8-10 (dorm-style) & $18-30 (rooms)

ARGENTINA

Buenos Aires

INFO LINES & SERVICES

Comunidad Homosexual Argentina Tomas Liberti 1080 **54–11/4361–6382**

Grupo Nexo Av Callao 339, 5th flr **54–11/4375–0366, 54–11/4374–4484**

ACCOMMODATIONS

1555 Malabia House Malabia 1555, Palermo Viejo (at Honduras) **54–11/4832–3345** • gay-friendly • "Design B&B" • pets ok • $50-110

Bayres B&B Av Córdoba 5842 (in Palermo) **54–11/4772–3877** • gay-owned • $30-55

Crystal Suites Apart Uruguay 820, Capital Federal (at Av Cordoba) **54–11/5811–4169, 54–11/5811–4170** • lesbians/ gay men • kids ok • gay-owned • €72 & up

Don Sancho Youth Hostel Constitucion 4062 (at Boedo) **54–11/4923–1422** • gay/ straight • hostel • full brkfst • some shared baths • hot tub • kids ok • $7-15

Hotel Intercontinental Buenos Aires Moreno 809 **54–11/4340–7100, 888/303–1758** • gay-friendly • near commercial/ financial district • fitness center • bar • restaurants

Solar Soler B&B Soler 5676 (at Bonpland) **54–11/4476–3065** • gay-friendly • kids ok • nonsmoking • $45-75

BARS

Bach Bar Cabrera 4390 **54–11/4388–2875** • 11pm-close, clsd Mon • lesbians/ gay men • live shows Th-Fri • karaoke • videos

Bulnes Class Bulnes 1250 (Palermo) **54–11/4861–7492** • from 7pm Th & 11pm Fri-Sat • lesbians/ gay men • dancing/DJ

Cero Consecuencia Cabrera 3769 • 2pm-close, clsd Mon • lesbians/ gay men • "cultural pub"

Confusión Scalabrini Ortiz 1721 **54–11/4833–3543, 54–1/4166–6209** • lesbians/ gay men • dancing/DJ

Flux Bar Marcelo T de Alvear 980 • 6pm-close, from 8pm wknds • lesbians/ gay men • dancing/DJ

Goddess Av Córdoba 4185 (in Palermo) **54–11/4861–2961** • 8pm-close, clsd Sun-Mon • lesbians/ gay men

Inside Bartolomé Mitre 1571 **54–11/4372–5439** • 6pm-close • also restaurant • live shows • older crowd

Parada Obligada Charcas 4338 • 10pm-close, clsd Mon-Th • mostly gay men

Search Azcuénaga 1007 **54–11/4824–0932** • 11pm-close • drag shows • strippers

Shangay Av Córdoba **54–11/4866–3351** • 8pm-close, clsd Mon-Tue • lesbians/ gay men • cabaret & theater

Sitges Córdoba 4119 **54–11/4861–3763** • 11:30pm-close, from 7pm Sun, clsd Mon-Tue • table telephones

Tacla Av de Mayo 1114 **54–11/4381–8764** • gay/ straight • live shows • also restaurant

The Titanic Club Av Callao 1156 **54–11/4816–1333** • 7pm-close, clsd Sun • also restaurant • lesbians/ gay men • dancing/ DJ • strippers • videos

Water Club Uriburu 1018 • 6pm-4am, till midnight Fri-Sat • mostly men • bears Wed

NIGHTCLUBS

Amerika Gascón 1040 (at Cordoba) **54–11/4865–4416** • open late • mostly gay men • dancing/DJ • cruisy

Angel's Viamonte 2168 • midnight-close Th-Sun • mostly gay men • dancing/DJ

Glam Cabrera 3046 • midnight-close wknds, mostly men • popular • dancing/DJ

Palacio Buenos Aires Alsina 940 (near Plaza de Mayo) **54–11/4331–1277** • 1am Fri & 8pm Sun only • lesbians/ gay men

UNNA Suipacha 927 • 1am Sat • women only

CAFES

Pride Cafe Balcarce 869 (in San Telmo) **54–11/4300–6435**

RESTAURANTS

La Cabana Rodriguez Pena 1967 **54–11/4814–0001** • brkfst, lunch & dinner • upscale 2-flr steak house

Chueca Soler 3283 (Palermo) **54–11/4963–3420** • 9pm-close, clsd Sun-Tue

El Palacio de la Papa Frita Lavalle 735 **54–11/4393–5849** • popular • hearty traditional meals • also Av Corrientes 1612, 11/4374-8063

Empire Tres Sargentos 427 **54–11/4312–5706** • noon-midnight, 7pm-1am Sat • popular • Thai food, tapas • American bar

La Farmacia Bolivar 898 (in San Telmo) **54–11/4300–6151** • brkfst, lunch, dinner, clsd Mon • also bar & art gallery • gay-friendly

Filo San Martin 975 **54–11/4311–0312** • 8pm-close • Italian • trendy • also art gallery

Mark's Deli & Coffeehouse El Salvador 4107 (in Palermo) **54–11/4832–6244** • 11am-8pm, till 9pm Sun, clsd Mon • popular

Rave Gorriti 5092 **54–11/4833–7832** • lunch Tue-Sun & 9pm-nightly • popular

Scetta Restaurant French 2301 (Recoleta) **54–11/4508–9965**

ENTERTAINMENT & RECREATION

Museo Evita Lafinur 2988 (in Palermo) **54–11/4807–9433** • 2pm-7:30pm, clsd Mon

PUBLICATIONS

Imperio G Magazine **54–11/4304–6357** • monthly glossy w/ gay info

La Otra Guía Apartado 78 (Suc Olivos) • free gay monthly guide

The Ronda • gay pocket guide with local listings • www.theronda.com.ar

GYMS & HEALTH CLUBS

American Hot Gym Ayacucho 449 (M° Callao, Line B) **54–11/4951–7679** • clsd Sun

BRAZIL

Rio de Janeiro

Note: M°=Metro station

ACCOMMODATIONS

Copacabana Panorama 3806 Av Atlantica (at Souza Lima) **617/803–9164** • oceanfront condo w/ gorgeous view of Copacabana Beach, short walk to gay night life • $70-125

Ipanema Plaza Rua Farme Amoedo (at Rua Prudente de Morais) **55–21/3687–2000** • gay/straight • also restaurant • roof-top pool • $150-265

Nice Condos in Rio Rua Barata Ribeiro 669/604 **55–21/2256–2264, 55–21/9416–2665** • mostly gay men • condos • close to famous Copacabana & Ipanema beaches • swimming • kids/pets ok • wheelchair access • gay-owned • $20-100

O Veleiro B&B Rua Mundo Novo 1440 (at Rua Marquez de Olinda) **55–21/2554–8980** • rustic home in forested urban setting • minutes from Copacabana, Ipanema beaches, clubs & bars • pool • full brkfst • gay/straight • gay-owned • $39-89

Rio Penthouse **55–21/8181–9084** • gay-friendly • beachfront apts & penthouse suites

BARS

Blue Angel Rua Julio de Castilhos 15-B **55–21/2513–2501** • 6pm-close • lesbians/gay men • dancing/DJ • food served • live shows • videos

Dama de Ferro Rua Vinicius de Moraes 288 (Ipanema) **55–21/2247–2330** • lesbians/gay men • dancing/DJ

Galeria Cafe Rua Teixeira de Mello 31 (Ipanema) **55–21/2523–8250** • 10pm-close, clsd Mon • gay/straight • dancing/DJ • also gallery

Star's Club (Buraco da Lacraia) Rua André Cavalcante (Centro) **55–21/2242–0446** • popular • gay/straight • dancing/DJ

NIGHTCLUBS

Cabaré Casanova Av Mém de Sa 25 (Centro) • 11pm-close • mostly men • dancing/DJ • live shows • drag shows

The Copa Rua Aires Saldanha 13-A (Copacabana) **55–21/2256–7412** • clsd Mon • lesbians/gay men • dancing/DJ • also restaurant • funky atmosphere • LuLu Lounge (women) Tue

La Cueva Rua Miguel Lemos 51 (Copacabana) **55–21/2267–1364** • 11pm-close, clsd Mon • lesbians/gay men • dancing/DJ

Fosfobox Rua Siqueira Campos 143 (Copacabana) **55–21/2548–7498** • popular • gay/straight • dancing/DJ

La Girl Club Rua Raul Pompeia 102 (Copacabana) **55–21/2247–8342** • 9pm-3am, clsd Mon-Wed • popular • lesbians/gay men • dancing/DJ • strippers • young crowd • also Girl's Club from 9pm Th-Sun

Incontrus Praça Serzedelo Correa 15A (Copacabana) **55–21/2549–6498** • lesbians/gay men • dancing/DJ • transgender-friendly • drag shows

RESTAURANTS

Bofetada Rua Farme de Amoedo (Ipanema) **55–21/2227–1676** • 6pm-close • popular • post-beach meeting place • also bar

Tamino Rua Arnaldo Quintela 26 **55–21/2295–1849** • 7pm-4am, clsd Mon-Wed • club by night (lesbians/ gay men) • women's night Fri

ENTERTAINMENT & RECREATION

Copacabana Beach at Rua Rodolfo Dantas • gay across from Copacabana Palace Hotel

Ipanema Beach • gay E of Rua Farme Amoedo

CHILE

Santiago

Note: M°=Metro station

INFO LINES & SERVICES

Corporacion Chilena de Prevencion del SIDA General Jofré 179 **56–2/222–5255** • 10am-10pm Mon-Fri • AIDS info, testing & workshops

ACCOMMODATIONS

Hotel Castillo Pio Nono 420 (Bellavista) **56–2/735–0243** • lesbians/ gay men • 1920s building w/ ornate interior decor • includes brkfst • $25-40

Meintje Orsel Avda Diego de Almagro 2057 **56–2/204–0271** • gay-friendly • spacious colonial house w/ romantic garden • full brkfst • $25-60

BARS

Bar Willy Av 11 de Septiembre 2214 (Común Providencia) **56–2/381–1806** • 10pm-4am, till 5am wknds • lesbians/ gay men • live shows

Dionisio Bombero Nunez 111 (at Dardinac) **56–2/737–6065** • 9pm-close, clsd Sun-Mon • lesbians/ gay men • food served • live shows

Farinelli Bombero Nunez 159 (Recoleta) **56–2/732–8966** • 5pm-2am • internet access • food served • live shows • drag shows • strippers

Pub Friend's Bombero Nuñez 365 (at Dominica, barrio Bellavista) **56–2/777–3979** • 9:30pm-4am, till 5am Fri-Sat • lesbians/ gay men • women's night Th w/ female strippers, male strippers Fri

Vox Populi Ernesto Pinto Lagarrigue 364 (Bella Vista) **56–2/738–0532** • 9:30pm-3am, clsd Sun-Mon • mostly men • also restaurant • garden patio

NIGHTCLUBS

Bokhara Discoteque Pio Nono 430 (at Constitución, barrio Bellavista) **56–2/732–1050, 56–2/735–1271** • 10pm-6am, till 7am wknds • mostly gay men • dancing/DJ• food served • strippers • drag shows

Bunker Bombero Nuñez 159 (Bellavista) **56–2/737–1716** • 11pm-close Fri-Sat • lesbians/ gay men • dancing/DJ • food served • live shows

Femme Bombero Nuñez 169 (Bellavista, at Bunker) **56–2/738–2301, 56–2/738–2314** • 11pm-close Fri-Sat • mostly women • dancing/DJ • food served • live show Sat

Mascara Purísima 129 (Bellavista) • mostly women • dancing/DJ

Queen Coronel Santiago Bueras 128 **56–2/639–8703** • 11pm-close • lesbians/gay men • dancing/ DJ • drag shows

CAFES

Tavelli Andrés de Fuenzalida 34 (Providencia) **56–2/231–9862** • 8:30am-10pm, from 9:30am Sat • popular

RESTAURANTS

Amor del Bueno Ernesto Pinto Lagarrigue 106 **56–2/737–2790** • 5pm-1am, till 4am Fri-Sat • clsd Sun, mostly women • also bar • lesbian-owned

Capricho Español Purisima 65 (barrio Bellavista) **56–2/777–7674** • dinner only • Spanish • full bar

Conchas Negras Paseo El Manio 1665 (Zona Rosa Managua) **56–2/206–6030** • Chilean/ Italian

Holandesa Av Santa Rosa 31 • popular • soda fountain • late-night hangout

La Pizza Nostra Av Providencia 1975 & Pedro de Valdivia **56–2/231–9853** • Italian

El Toro Loreto 33 **56–2/737–5137** • noon-midnight

RETAIL SHOPS

Dimension House José Miguel de la Barra 572 (M° Bellas Artes) **56–2/683–7718** • casualwear • sportswear • DVDs

AUSTRIA

Vienna

INFO LINES & SERVICES

Gay & Lesbian AA 43-1/799-5599 • 7pm Sat • call for location

Hosi Zentrum Novarragasse 40 43-1/216-6604 • many groups & events • also publishes quarterly news magazine

Rosa-Lila-Villa Linke Wienzeile 102 (near Hofmühlgasse, U4-Pilgramgasse) 43-1/586-8150 (WOMEN), 43-1/585-4343 (MEN) • LGBT center • staffed 5pm-8pm Mon, Wed, Fri • info • gay city maps • also meeting place for various groups • also cafe-bar

ACCOMMODATIONS

Arcotel Wimberger Neubaugürtel 34–36 (at Goldschlagstr) 43-1/521-650 • gay-friendly • centrally located 4-star hotel • restaurant & bar on premises • also fitness club • €59+

Hotel Urania Obere Weißgerberstr 7 (U-Schwedenplatz) 43-1/713-1711 • gay-friendly • centrally located • pizzeria & bar on premises • wheelchair access

Pension Wild Lange Gasse 10 (off Lerchenfelder Str) 43-1/406-5174 • mostly gay men • rooms & apts • also restaurant • gay-owned • €37-102

Das Tyrol Mariahilfer Str 15 43-1/587-5415 • gay-friendly • small luxury hotel • €109-259

BARS

Brot & Rosen Ratschkygasse 48/ 2–4 43-1/996-2824 • 6pm-midnight • gay/ straight • cafe-bar • "intercultural feminist cafe" • special events include monthly Frauenfest

Café Savoy Linke Wienzeile 36 (at Köstlergasse) 43-1/586-7348 • 5pm-2am, from 9am Sat • popular • lesbians/ gay men • upscale cafe-bar

Frauencafé Lange Gasse 11 43-1/406-3754 • 7pm-midnight, till 2am Fri-Sat (sometimes clsd Sun-Mon) • mostly women • cafe-bar

Frauenzentrum Bar Währingerstr 59 (enter on Prechtlgasse) 43-1/402-8754 • 7pm-midnight Th-Fri, till 2am Sat • mostly women • dancing/DJ • food served

Operncafé Hartauer Riemergasse 9 (at Singer) 43-1/512-8981 • 6pm-2am, clsd Sun-Mon • gay/ straight • food served • terrace

Das Versteck Nikolaigasse 1 (at Grünangergasse, U1-Stephansplatz) 43-1/513-4053 • 6pm-midnight, from 7pm Sat, clsd Sun • gay/ straight • young crowd

NIGHTCLUBS

Heaven Gay Night at U4 Schönbrunner Str 222 (at Meidlinger, U4-Meidlinger Haupstr) 43-1/815-8307 • 10pm-5am Th only • popular • mostly gay men • dancing/DJ • transgender-friendly • live shows • wheelchair access

Why Not? Tiefer Graben 22 (at Wipplinger, U-Schottentor) 43-1/925-3024 • 10pm-close Fri-Sat & before public holidays • mostly gay men • dancing/DJ • live shows • videos

CAFES

Café Berg Berggasse 8 (at Wasagasse, U2-Schottentor) 43-1/319-5720 • 10am-1am • popular • lesbians/ gay men • cafe-bar • young crowd

Cafe Central Herrengasse 14 (at Strauchgasse) 43-1/533-376-424 • 7:30am-10pm, 10am-6pm Sun, 10am-10pm on public holidays, "world's most famous coffeehouse"

Cafe Savoy Linke Wienzeile 36 43-1/586-7348 • 5pm-2am, from 9pm Sat, clsd Sun • lesbians/ gay men

Das Mobel Burggasse 10 (Spittelberg) 43-1/524-9497 • 10am-1am • trendy • also art gallery • wireless internet

Smart Cafe Kostlergasse 9 43-1/585-7165 • 6pm-2am, Fri-Sat till 4am, clsd Sun-Mon • gay/ straight • S/M & fetish cafe

RESTAURANTS

Café-Restaurant Willendorf Linke Wienzeile 102 (near Hofmuhlgasse, U4-Pilgramgasse) 43-1/587-1789 • 6pm-2am, from 10am wknds, food served till midnight • lesbians/ gay men • plenty veggie • full bar • terrace

The Living Room Grosse Neugasse 31 43-1/589-1693 • 6pm-4am, bar open till 2am • lesbians/ gay men • Viennese

Motto Schönbrunner Str 30 (enter on Rüdigergasse) 43-1/587-0672 • 6pm-4am • popular • gay/ straight • trendy • also bar • patio • reservations recommended

ENTERTAINMENT & RECREATION

House of Music Seilerstätte 30 43-1/516-4810 • 10am-10pm • interactive museum

Kunsthistorisches Museum Maria-Theresien-Platz (enter Heldenplatz) **43–1/525–240** • 10am-6pm, till 9pm Th, clsd Mon • not to be missed • works from Ancient Egypt to the Renaissance to Klimt

Resis.Danse Novarragasse 40 (at Hosi Gay & Lesbian Center) **43–1/216–6604** • 7pm-midnight Fri • women only • ballroom dancing • dance classes • contact for dates and location

BOOKSTORES

American Discount Rechte Wienzeile 5 (at Paniglgasse) **43-1/587–5772** • 9:30am-6:30pm, till 5pm Sat, clsd Sun • int'l magazines & books • also Neubaugasse 39, 43-1/523.37.07 • also Donaustadt Str 1, 43-1/203.95.18

Frauenzimmer Zieglergasse 28 **43-1/522–4892** • 10am-6:30pm, till 5pm Sat, till 8pm Sun • women's

Vienna

LGBT PRIDE:
June

ANNUAL EVENTS:
February - Regenbogenball (Rainbow Ball), web: www.hosi-wien.at/ball.
May - Life Ball (AIDS benefit), web: www.lifeball.at
June - Queer Film Festival 43-1/524.62.74, web: www.identities.at
Summer - Vienna Festival 43-1/589.22.0web: www.festwochen.at
October - Vienna In Black

CITY INFO:
43–1/24.555, web: www.info.wien.at. In US, call 212/944-6880 or 310/477-3332.

BEST VIEW:
Overlooking the city from the top of the Giant Ferris Wheel.

WEATHER:
Mild, rainy summers and chilly winters. September is a good time to visit.

TRANSIT:
Vienna Airport Lines.
Vienna has an excellent public transit system. Consider purchasing a Vienna Card for 72 hours of unlimited travel by subway, bus, and tram, plus discounts on airport shuttle, at museums, and at many shops and restaurants. 43–1/798.44.00.128.

ATTRACTIONS:
Art Nouveau buildings
Belvedere Palace/Austrian Gallery 43–1/795.57.134
Sigmund Freud Museum 43–1/319.1596, web: www.freud-museum.at
House of Music 43-1/51.648, web: www.hdm.at
Imperial Palace
Jewish Museum 43–1/535.0431, web: www.jmw.at
Museum of Fine Arts 43–1/525.24.0, web: www.khm.at
Schönbrunn Palace 43–1/811.13, web: www.schoenbrunn.at
St Stephen's Cathedral 43-1/515.52.3526, web: www.st.stephan.at
State Opera House 43–1/514.44.2606, web: www.staatsoper.at
Vienna Boys' Choir 43–1/216.39.42, web; www.wsk.at.

Löwenherz Berggasse 8 (next to Cafe Berg, enter on Wasagasse, U2-Schottentor) **43–1/317–2982** • 10am-7pm, till 8pm Fri, till 6pm Sat, clsd Sun • LGBT • large selection of English titles

PUBLICATIONS

Vienna Gay Guide 43–1/789–1000 • city-map & guide

EROTICA

Art-X Percostr 3 43–1/258–0444, 43–2622/88.555 • 10am-8pm, till 5pm Sat, clsd Sun • leather, latex, rubber • toys • music • videos • magazines

Tiberius Lindengasse 2 (at Stiftgasse, U3-Neubaugasse) **43–1/522–0474** • clsd Sun • wheelchair access • leather, rubber & toys

CAFE

Café Stein Währinger Str 6–8 (near U-Schottentor) **43–1/319–7241** • 7am-1am, from 9am Sun • gay-friendly • cafe-bar • internet access • terrace

CZECH REPUBLIC

PRAGUE (PRAHA)

Note: M°=Metro station

Prague is divided into 10 city districts: Praha—1, Praha—2, etc.

Praha—1

ACCOMMODATIONS

Prague Center Guest Residence Stepanska Street (at Zitna) **36–309/323–334** • lesbians/ gay men • apt • near Wenceslas Square • kids ok • gay-owned • €70

BARS

Banana Cafe Stupartská 9 (Námestí Republiky, upstairs from La Provence restaurant) **420/222–324–801** • 8pm-2am • gay/ straight • drag shows • go-go dancers • gay-owned

Friends Bar Bartolomejská 11 **420/224–236–772** • 6pm-5am • popular • mostly men • dancing/ DJ • neighborhood bar • DJ Wed-Sat • videos • internet access

NIGHTCLUBS

Roxy Dlouhá 33 (M° Námestí Republiky) **420/224–826–296** • 9pm-6am• gay/ straight • dancing/ DJ • videos • young crowd • cool events • live bands

Tingl Tangl Karolíny Svetlé 12 **420/224–238–278** • 8pm-5am, clsd Sun • lesbians/ gay men • dancing/ DJ • cabaret • drag shows • also restaurant

CAFES

Cafe Cafe Rytirská 10 (at Perlová, near Oldtown Square) **420/224–210–597** • 10am-11pm, till midnight wknds

Café 'Erra Konviktská 11 **420/222–220–568** • 10am-midnight, from 11am wknds • gay/ straight • salads, sandwiches & entrées

Cafe Louvre Narodni Trida 20 (M° Narodni Trida) **420/224–930–912** • 8am-11:30pm, opens 9am wknds • gay/ straight • food served • billiard tables

RESTAURANTS

Country Life Melantrichova 15 (in Old Town) **420/2421–3366** • clsd Sat • vegetarian • nonsmoking

Lotos Platnerska 13 (M° Staromestska) **420/2232–2390** • 11am-10pm • veggie/ vegan fare

Petrinské Terasy Seminariská Zahrada 13, Petrin **420/290–000–457, 420/290–059–996** • 11am-1pm • in a former monastery • great view • gay-owned

La Provence Stupartska 9 (near Old Town Square) **420/257–535–050** • 11am-midnight, bar open till 1am • French • also Banana Cafe & Tapas Bar upstairs • gay-owned

Staromestska Restaurace Staromestske namesti 19 **420/224–213–015** • local Czech specialties

U Betlemske Kaple Betlemske nam 2 (M° Narodni Trida) **420/222–221–639** • 11am-10:30pm • local Czech specialities

Praha—2

ACCOMMODATIONS

Balbin Penzion Balbinova 26 (near Wenceslas Square) **420/222–250–660** • gay-friendly • located in city center • full brkfst • €40-100

Prague Saints Polska 32 (office location) (at Trebizkeho, at Saints Bar) **420/775–152–041, 420/775–152–042** • lesbians/ gay men • apts in gay Vinohrady district • gay-owned

BARS

Bar 21 Rimska 21 **420/724–254–048** • 4pm-4am • lesbians/ gay men • cellar bar • mostly Czechs

Fajn Bar Dittrichova 5 (near river)
420/224–917–409, 420/603–522–117 • 1pm-
1am, from 4pm wknds • lesbians/ gay men •
cafe-bar • occasional drag or strip shows

Saints Polska 32 (at Trebizkeho)
420/222–250–326 • 5pm-2am, till 4am Fri-Sat,
1pm-1am Sun • lesbians/ gay men

Stella Club Luzická 10 (in Vinohrady)
420/224–257–869 • 8pm-5am • lesbians/ gay
men • food served • cozy bar/ cafe • terrace

Street Cafe Blanická 28 **420/222–013–116** •
9am-11:30pm, till 4am Fri-Sat, 1pm-10pm Sun
• gay/ straight • dancing/DJ • food served

NIGHTCLUBS

Gejzeer Vinohradska 40 (in Vinohrady)
420/222–516–036 • 8pm-late, from 9pm Fri-
Sat, clsd Sun-Wed • popular • lesbians/ gay
men • dancing/ DJ • live shows • videos •
cover

Termix Trebizkeho 4 **420/222–710–462** •
8pm-5am • popular • lesbians/ gay men •
dancing/ DJ

RESTAURANTS

Celebrity Cafe Vinohradska 40 (in
Vinohrady) **420/222–511–343** • 8am-2am,
noon-3am Sat, till midnight Sun • gay/ straight
• also bar • right next door to Gejzeer
nightclub

Radost FX Belehradska 120, Vinohrady
420/224–254–776, 420/603.18.15.00 •
fabulous wknd brunch • vegetarian cafe • also
straight nightclub w/ popular monthly gay
party

Retro Francouzska 4 **420/603–176–111** •
8am-11pm • int'l • also bar

Prague (Praha)

LGBT PRIDE:
July.

ANNUAL EVENTS:
May/June - Prague Spring Music
Festival, web: www.festival.cz
October - International Jazz Festival
October - Mezipatra, Czech Gay &
Lesbian Film Festival, web:
www.mezipatra.cz

CITY INFO:
Tourist Info Center 420/12.44.
Staroměstské radnice, Old Town
Hall, 9am-7pm Mon-Fri, till 5pm
wknds, web: www.pis.cz.

ATTRACTIONS:
Charles Bridge
Jewish Museum 420/222.317.191,
web: www.jewishmuseum.cz
Museum of Fine Arts
420/222.220.218
Old Jewish Quarter
Prague Castle, web:
www.prague.cz/prague-
castle.asp
Wenceslas Square.

BEST VIEW:
For a great view of the whole of
Prague, head for the Observation
Tower (a mini version of the Eiffel
Tower) on Petrin Hill. The Old
Town Bridge Tower affords a
fabulous view of Old Town, the
Charles Bridge, and the Vltava
River.

WEATHER:
Continental climate. Late spring or
early fall are the best times to
visit, especially in June before the
tourist season is in full swing.
Winters can get very cold with
average daytime highs of 34° F.

TRANSIT:
Taxi AAA 420/222.333.222
Profi Taxi 420/261.314.151.
CSA shuttle.
There are 6 Transportation Info
Centers throughout city with info
on metro, trams, buses & funicu-
lar, Ruzyne Airport, web:
www.dp-praha.cz.

Praha—3

CAFES

Galerie Cafe Jagellonska 20, Vinohrady
420/222-730-056, 420/605-108-296 •
8:30am-10pm, from 5pm Sun, clsd Sat • gay/
straight • works by gay artists

ENTERTAINMENT & RECREATION

TV Tower Mahlerovy sady 1
420/267-005-778 • get a bird's-eye view of the
city from the top of this tower • also restaurant

GYMS & HEALTH CLUBS

Bravo Fitness Srobarova 9, Zizkov (at
Pisecká) 420/271-731-412 • 9am-10pm, 2pm-
9pm wknds • lesbians/ gay men • gay-owned

Praha—4

GYMS & HEALTH CLUBS

Plavecky Stadion Podoli Podolská 74
420/261-214-343 • gay/ straight • public
baths • restaurants • women's sauna Th-Fri &
Sun 10am-7:30pm

Praha—10

ACCOMMODATIONS

Ron's Rainbow Guest House Bulharska 4
(at Finská) 420/271-725-664 • gay/ straight •
jacuzzi • gay-owned • $50-75

DENMARK

Copenhagen

INFO LINES & SERVICES

**Wonderful Copenhagen Convention &
Visitors Bureau** Vesterbrogade 4A (Tourist
Office) 45-33/25.74.00 • check out
www.visitcopenhagen.com

ACCOMMODATIONS

Carstens Guesthouse Christians Brygge 28,
5th flr, 1559 45-33/14.91.07, 45-33/50.91.07 •
lesbians/ gay men • B&B in a private home •
also guesthouse • shared baths • kids/ pets
ok • 5 minutes from gay area • DKK420-1600

Copenhagen

WHERE THE GIRLS ARE:
Strolling Studiestraede with the
boys, or enjoying a beverage at
Cafe Ziraf.

LGBT PRIDE:
August.
www.copenhagenpride.dk/dk/.

ANNUAL EVENTS:
October - Gay & Lesbian Film
Festival, web: www.cglff.dk.

BEST VIEW:
From the dome of Marble Church,
or from the spiral tower of Our
Savior's Church.

TRANSIT:
Kobenhavns Taxa 3535-3535.
Metro 7015-1615, web: www.m.dk. Ask
about the Copenhagen Card,
which offers bargains on museums and public transportation.
Bycykler 3543-0110, web:
www.bycyklen.dk. 110 racks
around the city center offering
free bicycle rental!

ATTRACTIONS:
Botanisk Have (Botanical Garden)
3522-2240, web:
www.botanic-garden.ku.dk.
Dansk Design Center 3369-3369,
web: www.ddc.dk.
Latin Quarter.
The Little Mermaid.
Marmorkirken (Marble Church)
3315-0144, web:
www.marmorkirken.dk.
Museum Erotica, web:
www.museumerotica.dk.
Nationalmuseet (National Museum)
3313-4411, web:
www.natmus.dk.
Statens Museum for Kunst (Royal
Museum of Fine Arts)
3374-8494, web: www.smk.dk.
Strøget shopping district.
Tivoli 3515-1001, web:
www.tivoligardens.com.
Vor Frelsers Kirke (Our Savior's
Church) 3257-2798.

First Hotel Skt. Petri Krystalgade 22
45–33/45.91.00 • hotel embodying the ultra-coolest of Scandinavian design • great bar

Hotel Jørgensen Rømersgade 11
45–33/13.81.86 • gay-friendly • located downtown • dorm-style & private rooms • shared baths • kids ok • DKK130-700

Hotel Windsor Frederiksborggade 30, 1360
45–33/11.08.30 • mostly gay men • near gay scene • shared baths • gay-owned • €67-108

BARS

Amigo Bar Schønbergsgade 4, Frederiksberg
45–33/21.49.15 • 10pm-close • gay/ straight • karaoke

Cafe Ziraf Skt. Peder Straede 34
45–33/93.99.04 • 3pm-midnight, till 2am Fri-Sat, clsd Sun • mostly women • food served

Can-Can Mikkel Bryggers Gade 11
45–33/11.50.10 • 2pm-2am, till 5am Fri-Sat • mostly gay men • friendly neighborhood bar

Centralhjørnet Kattesundet 18
45–33/11.85.49 • 11am-1am, from noon wknds • mostly gay men

Cosy Bar Studiestræde 24 (in Latin Quarter)
45–33/12.74.27 • 10pm-6am • popular • mostly gay men

Masken Studiestræde 33 **45–33/91.67.80** • 4pm-midnight, 3pm-5am Fri-Sat • popular • lesbians/ gay men • cafe-bar • Girls' Night downstairs from 8pm Th

Men's Bar Teglgårdsstræde 3 **45–33/12.73.03** • 3pm-2am • mostly gay men • leather bar • popular brunch 1st Sun

Never Mind Nørre Voldgade 2
45–33/11.33.08 • 10pm-6am • gay/ straight

Oscar Bar Cafe Radhuspladsen 77
45–33/12.09.99 • noon-2am • mostly men • lesbians welcome • food served • great happy hour

Vela Viktoriagade 2-4 **45–33/31.34.19** • 8pm-midnight, till 5am Fri-Sat • mostly women • neighborhood bar

NIGHTCLUBS

Dunst • party/event maker in Copenhagen • check website for details at www.dunst.dk

Nasa Gothersgade 8F (2nd flr)
45–33/93.74.15 • popular • gay/ straight • dancing/DJ • gay night Th

Pan Disco Knabrostræde 3 **45–33/11.37.84** • 9pm-close, from 10pm Fri-Sat, clsd Sun-Tue • lesbians/ gay men • dancing/DJ • karaoke

XX Bar Gothersgade 37 (Kvindehuset)
45–33/14.28.04 • women-only party on third Fri of every month

CAFES

Cafe Intime Allegade 25, Frederiksberg
45–38/34.19.58 • 5pm-2am, from 8pm Sat • cafe-bar

Heaven Kompanistræde 18 **45–33/15.19.00** • noon-9pm, bar open till midnight • popular • mostly gay men

RESTAURANTS

Jailhouse Restaurant & Bar Stidiestraede 12 **45–33/15.22.55** • 1pm-midnight • popular

Riz Raz Kompagnistraede 20 (at Knabrostraede) **45–33/15.05.75** • 11:30am-midnight • popular • great vegetarian buffet

ENTERTAINMENT & RECREATION

Bellevue Beach • left end is nude & a mostly gay beach

BOOKSTORES

Pan Book Café Teglgardstræde 13
45–33/13.19.48 • 5pm-7pm Th • nonprofit bookshop & cafe run by LBL, nat'l lesbian/ gay organization

PUBLICATIONS

Pan Magazine 45–33/36.00.82, 45–33/36.00.83 • free monthly w/ news, personals, arts

ENGLAND

LONDON

London is divided into 6 regions:
London—Overview
London—Central
London—West
London—North
London—East
London—South

London—Overview

INFO LINES & SERVICES

Audre Lorde Clinic Royal London Hospital
44–(0)20/7377–7312, 44–(0)20/8846–1576/ 7 • 10am-5pm Fri • lesbian health clinic • call for appt & location

Black Lesbian/ Gay Centre 5/5A Westminster Bridge Rd, Rm 113
44–(0)20/7620–3885 • helpline staffed 2pm-5:30pm Sat

London Lesbian/ Gay Switchboard
44–(0)20/7837–7324 • 24hrs

Reply **Forward** **Delete**

```
Date: Dec 30, 2005 15:12:09
From: Girl-on-the-Go
To: Editor@Damron.com
Subject: London
```

>London is well known for its history, fine museums, and fog, but this world-class city offers much, much more. Over 7 million people, representing hundreds of cultures, languages, and religions, call London home. And the city has been going through yet another growth spurt in recent years: Haute cuisine and funky fusion restaurants abound. Cutting-edge buildings dot the skyline. And cellphones are omnipresent.

>Don't worry, though, you can still get bangers and mash. This sprawling city can easily accommodate change. As a matter of fact, when you start navigating around (recommendably via the Underground) you'll see that London is really a collection of smaller towns and neighborhoods, each with a distinct feel. Of these, you'll find more lesbians and gay men in Soho and Earl's Court.

>Like London itself, the women's scene is varied and vast. Take a break from sightseeing to visit **Silver Moon Women's Bookstore,** or **Gay's the Word,** and pick up a copy of **Diva**—London's slick lesbian magazine. To learn about the latest happenings, hop on **www.gingerbeer.co.uk,** a stylish online guide to the local lesbo scene. The free lesbian magazine **g3** will also give you all the latest 411.

In the evening, start out at one of London's trendy cafe-bars, like **Aquda, Freedom, Kudos,** or the **Box.**

>London has three (!) full-time women's bars—**Candy Bar, Glass Bar,** and the **Vespa Lounge**—and a vast array of women's nights at various mixed bars and clubs.

If you like dancing well into the morning hours, and mixing it up with the boys, check out one of London's popular clubs like **G.A.Y., Heaven, DTPM.** For a comprehensive listing of mixed clubs in and around London, pick up a copy of the **Pink Paper** or the scene guide **Time Out.**

>Now, when on earth are you going to find time to visit the Tate Gallery?

ACCOMMODATIONS

London First Choice Apartments
44–(0)20/8990–9033 • gay-friendly • short-term apt rentals • also hotel reservations • £75-300

ENTERTAINMENT & RECREATION

Wilde Tours: Gay & Lesbian Sightseeing London 1 Regent St (at London Visitor's Bureau) 44–(0)20/7209.4850 • seasonal • lesbians/gay men • Sat only • walking or bus tours • gay-owned

The Women's Library, London Metropolitan University Old Castle St 44–(0)20/7230–2222 • clsd Sun • also cafe • museum • cultural center • call for events • nonsmoking

PUBLICATIONS

Diva 44–207/424–7400 • glorious glossy lesbian magazine

g3 44–(0)20/7272–0093 • free monthly lesbian glossy

Gay Times 44–(0)20/7424–7400, 44–(0)20/8340–8644 • gay glossy

London

LGBT PRIDE:
June-July. www.pridelondon.org.

ANNUAL EVENTS:
April - Lesbian & Gay Film Festival 44–(0)20/7928-3232, web: www.llgff.org.uk
June-July - Pride Festival Fortnight, web: www.pridelondon.org
August - Mr Gay UK Contest, web: www.mrgayuk.co.uk.

CITY INFO:
44–(0)20/7292-2333, web: www.visitlondon.com, www.londoninformation.org.

BEST VIEW:
London Eye, 44–(0)87/0500-0600 web: www.londoneye.com

WEATHER:
London is warmer and less rainy than you may have heard. Summer temperatures reach the 70ºs and the average annual rainfall is about half of that of Atlanta, GA or Hartford, CT.

TRANSIT:
Freedom Cars 44–(0)20-7734-1313
Ladycabs 44–(0)20/7254-3501
Radio Taxi 44–(0)20/7272-0272.
London Travel Information (Tube & buses) 44–(0)20/7222-1234, 24hr info, web: www.tfl.gov.uk.

ATTRACTIONS:
British Museum 44–(0)20/7323-8299, www.thebritishmuseum.ac.uk
Buckingham Palace 44–(0)20/7766-7300
Globe Theatre 44–(0)20/7902–1400, web: www.shakespeares-globe.org
Kensington Palace 44–(0)87/0751-5170
Madame Tussaud's 44–(0)87/0400-3000, web: www.madame-tussauds.co.uk
National Gallery 44–(0)20/7747-2885, web: www.national-gallery.org.uk
Oscar Wilde's house (34 Tite Street)
St Paul's Cathedral 44–(0)20/7236-4128, www.stpauls.co.uk
Tate Gallery 44–(0)20/7887-8008, web: www.tate.org.uk
Tower of London 44–(0)87/0756–6060
Westminster Abbey 44–(0)20/7222–5152, www.westminster-abbey.org.

The Pink Paper 44–(0)20/7845–4300 • free LGBT newspaper

Time Out 44–(0)20/7813–3000 • weekly city scene guide w/ gay section

SPIRITUAL GROUPS

Jewish Gay/ Lesbian Group 44–(0)20/8952–0137

MCC London Camden Trinity URC (at Buck St and Kentish Town Rd) 44–(0)20/8802–0962 • 7pm Sun • also MCC Brixton, 44–020/8678–0200 • also MCC East London, 44–020/7538–8376

London—Central

London—Central includes Soho, Covent Garden, Bloomsbury, Mayfair, Westminster, Pimlico & Belgravia

ACCOMMODATIONS

Central London Guestrooms & Apts Tottenham Court Rd (at Charing Cross Rd) 44–(0)20/8743–5577 • lesbians/ gay men • guesthouse & apartment • nonsmoking • gay-owned • €75-185 (3-night minimum stay)

Checkin Accomodation London Tottenham Court Rd (at Shaftsbury Ave) 44–(0)78/0874–4847 • 3-bedroom flat in the heart of London's West End • rent a room or the whole apartment • nonsmoking • kids ok • gay-owned

Garth Hotel 69 Gower St (at Torrington Pl) 44–(0)20/7636–5761, 866/548–8653 • elegant Georgian town house • full brkfst • kids/ pets ok • £45-120

George Hotel 58–60 Cartwright Gardens (N of Russell Square) 44–(0)20/7387–8777 • gay-friendly • full brkfst • some shared baths • kids ok • £50-89

Lincoln House Hotel 33 Gloucester Pl, Marble Arch (at Baker St) 44–20/7486–7630 • gay/ straight • B&B • full brkfst • wheelchair access • £49-125

London Gay Accommodation 44–(0)20/7486–0855 • lesbians/ gay men • room in private apt • hot tub • shared bath • pets ok • gay-owned

Manors & Co 1 Baker St 44–(0)20/7486–5982, 800/454–4385 • gay-friendly • luxury apts • wheelchair access

Waverley House Hotel 130-134 Southampton Row (Bloomsbury) 44–(0)20/7833–3691, 44–(0)20/7833–2579 • gay-friendly • full brkfst • restaurant • bar • £120-220

BARS

• Note: "Pub hours" usually means 11am-11pm Mon-Sat and noon-3pm & 7pm-10:30pm Sun

The Admiral Duncan 54 Old Compton St (Soho) 44–(0)20/7437–5300 • pub hours • popular • lesbians/ gay men • neighborhood bar • transgender-friendly

Bar Aquda 13–14 Maiden Ln (btwn Bedford & Southampton, Covent Garden) 44–(0)20/7577–9891 • 4pm-11pm, from 3pm Sat, till 10:30pm Sun • popular • lesbians/ gay men • cafe-bar

The Candy Bar 4 Carlisle St, S (at Dean) 44–(0)20/7494–4041 • 5pm-11:30pm, till 2am Fri-Sat • women-only (men welcome as guests) • dancing/DJ • food served • karaoke • strippers • also a location in Brighton

Compton's of Soho 51-53 Old Compton St 44–(0)20/7479–7961 • noon-11pm, till 10:30pm Sun • popular • mostly gay men • leather • food served • wheelchair access

Duke of Wellington 77 Wardour (Soho) 44–(0)20/7439–1274 • noon-11pm, till 10:30pm Sun • lesbians/ gay men • food served • some veggie

The Edge 11 Soho Square 44–(0)20/7439–1313 • 11:30am-1am, till 10:30pm Sun • popular • 4 flrs • cafe-bar • dancing/DJ • live music • food served • outdoor seating • wheelchair access

The Escape 10a Brewer St (near Regent St) 44–(0)20/7734–2626 • 4pm-3am, till 10:30pm Sun • popular • mostly gay men • dancing/DJ • video

Friendly Society 79 Wardour St (the basement at Old Compton, enter Tisbury Ct) 44–(0)20/7439–1274 • noon-11:30pm • lesbians/ gay men • young crowd

The G.A.Y Bar 30 Old Compton St 44–(0)20/7494–2756 • noon-midnight, till 10:30pm Sun • lesbians/ gay men • basement women's bar (men as guests) • food seved • 3 flrs • soap operas & videos shown

Girls Go Down 30 Old Compton St (basement of G-A-Y bar) 44–(0)20/7494–2706 • 7pm-midnight, till 10:30pm Sun • video jukebox

Glass Bar West Lodge, 190 Euston Rd 44–(0)20/7387–6184, 44–(0)20/7387–4153 • 6pm-midnight, clsd Sun • women only • 2 flrs • food served • Tease comedy night 2nd Fri • theme nights • events • private club • £1 day membership

Glitterbug 11-12 Walkers Ct (at Too 2 Much, off Brewer St, Soho) 44–(0)77/8775–3623 • 9pm-3am monthly • check calendar or call for dates • burlesque shows

Ku Bar 75 Charing Cross Rd (at Shaftesbury, Soho) 44–(0)20/7437–4303 • pub hours • lesbians/ gay men • trendy cafe-bar • karaoke • young crowd

Kudos 10 Adelaide St (off the Strand) 44–(0)20/7379–4573 • pub hours • popular • lesbians/ gay men • professional crowd • trendy cafe-bar • multiracial • wheelchair access • gay-owned

The Retro Bar 2 George Ct (off the Strand) 44–(0)20/7321–2811 • pub hours • lesbians/ gay men • popular • neighborhood bar • more women Wed • dancing/DJ • alternative/ indie music • karaoke

Rupert Street 50 Rupert St (off Brewer) 44–(0)20/7292–7141, 44–(0)20/7734–5614 • pub hours • popular • lesbians/ gay men • upscale "fashiony-types" • food served • wheelchair access

Site 42 St Martin's Ln (off Charing Cross, near National Gallery, Covent Garden) 44–(0)20/7557–9851 • popular • mostly gay men • pre-club cocktail bar

Star at Night 22 Great Chapel St 44–(0)20/7434–3749 • Italian restaurant during day • 6pm-midnight, clsd Sun-Mon • mostly women • relaxed cafe/ bar • live shows

Too 2 Much 11-12 Walkers Ct (off Brewer St, Soho) 44–(0)20/7734–0377, 44–(0)20/7437–4400 • mostly men • dancing/DJ • cocktail bar

Vespa Lounge Centre Point House, St Giles High St (upstairs at The Conservatory) 44–(0)20/7836–8956 • 6pm-11pm, clsd Sun-Tue • mostly women (men welcome as guests) • theme nights • videos • comedy Sun [$] • private club

The Village Soho 81 Wardour St (at Old Compton) 44–(0)20/7434–2124 • 11:30pm-1am, noon-midnight Sun • popular • mostly gay men • trendy • videos • cafe menu till 5pm • young crowd • wheelchair access

The Yard 57 Rupert St (off Brewer) 44–(0)20/7437–2652 • pub hours • popular • lesbians/ gay men • 2 levels • young crowd • food served • wheelchair access

NIGHTCLUBS

Exilio Houghton St (at London School of Economics Underground) 44–(0)79/3137–4391, 44–(0)79/5698–3230 • 10pm-3am Sat, lesbians/ gay men • dancing/DJ • Latino/a clientele

G.A.Y. 157 Charing Cross Rd (at Oxford St, in London Astoria theatre complex) 44–(0)20/7734–6963 • 10:30pm-4am Mon & Th-Sat only • popular • mostly gay men • dancing/DJ • live shows • young crowd • Camp Attack Fri • cover charge

The Ghetto 5–6 Falconberg Court (off Charing Cross, behind G.A.Y.) 44–(0)20/7272–0093 • 10:30pm-3am, till 5am Fri-Sat • lesbians/ gay men • dancing/DJ • live shows • theme nights • more women for Pottymouth Mon, Miss-Shapes Th, Wig Out Sat

Heaven The Arches (off Villiers St) 44–(0)20/7930-2020 • Mon, Wed, Fri-Sat • popular • the mother of all London gay clubs • call for hours/ events • mostly gay men • dancing/DJ

Indulgence 29-35 Farringdon Rd (at Venus) 44–(0)20/7494–4041 • 7pm-midnight 1st Sun only • women-only lesbian strip night • £10

Long Yang Club Thai Square, 21-24 Cockspur St 44–(0)20/7311–5835 • mostly men • multiracial-Asian • dancing/DJ • karaoke

Lounge 93-107 Shaftsbury Ave (at Teatro) 44–(0)79/0620–5014 • 8pm-3am, Th monthly • call for schedule • men welcome as guests

Salvation 3 Coventry St (at Cafe de Paris, Leicester Square) 44–(0)87/1550–5544 • 1st Sun • gay/ straight • cover charge

Shadow Lounge 5 Brewer St (Soho) 44–(0)20/7287–7988 • 10pm-3am, from 9am Th-Sat • lesbians/ gay men • dancing/DJ • lounge • swanky late night club

Trash Palace 11 Wardour St (Soho) 44–(0)20/7734–0522 • 5pm-midnight, till 3am Wed & Fri-Sat • dancing/ DJ • alternative music • live shows

CAFES

Balans Cafe 34 Old Compton St 44–(0)20/7439–3309 • 24hrs • popular • lesbians/ gay men • sandwiches & salads • all-day brkfst • terrace

First Out 52 St Giles High St (btwn Charing Cross & Shaftesbury) 44–(0)20/7240–8042 • 10am-11pm, noon-10:30pm Sun • lesbians/ gay men • cont'l • some veggie • full bar • nonsmoking upstairs • women-only Fri for Girl Friday

Freedom Cafe-Bar 60–66 Wardour St (off Old Compton St) 44–(0)20/7734–0071 • 10am-3am, noon-midnight Sun • food served • trendy scene cafe • young crowd • live shows

RESTAURANTS

Asia de Cuba 45 St Martin's Ln (near Leicester Square) 44–(0)20/7300.5588 • noon-midnight, till 10:30pm Sun • reservations required • Cuban/Asian • chic scene

Balans 60 Old Compton St 44–(0)20/7439–2183 • 8am-5am, till 6am Fri-Sat, till 2am Sun • all-day/night brunch • popular • cafe-bar • transgender-friendly • live shows • wheelchair access

East@West 13-15 West St (at Shaftesbury Ave) 44–(0)20/7010–8600 • dinner Mon-Sat • full bar

Food for Thought 31 Neal St, downstairs (Covent Garden) 44–(0)20/7836–0239 • noon-8pm, till 4pm Sun • vegetarian • inexpensive hole-in-the-wall

The Gay Hussar 2 Greek St (on Soho Square) 44–(0)20/7437–0973 • lunch & dinner, clsd Sun • Hungarian • wheelchair access

Mildred's 45 Lexington 44–(0)20/7494–1634 • noon-11pm, clsd Sun • popular • vegetarian • plenty vegan

Nusa Dua 11–12 Dean St (Oxford Circus) 44–(0)20/7437–3559 • Indonesian

Steph's 39 Dean St (btwn Old Compton & Bateman) 44–(0)20/7734–5976 • noon-3pm Mon-Fri & 5:30pm-11:30pm Mon-Sat, clsd Sun • British

Wagamama Noodle Bar 10a Lexington St 44–(0)20/7292–0990, 44-020/7631–3140 • noon-11pm, 12:30pm-10pm Sun • Japanese • nonsmoking • chain w/ locations in Bloomsbury, Covent Garden, etc

ENTERTAINMENT & RECREATION

Comedy Camp 3–4 Archer St (at Barcode, btwn Windmill & Rupert, off Shaftesbury, Soho) 44–(0)20/7483–2960 • 8:30pm Tue • gay/straight • amateur & established comedy acts

Prince Charles Cinema 7 Leicester Pl (off Leicester Square) 44–(0)20/7494–3654 • sing-alongs • often show LGBT & alternative films

BOOKSTORES

Gay's the Word 66 Marchmont St (near Russell Square) 44–(0)20/7278–7654 • 10am-6:30pm, 2pm-6pm Sun • LGBT • new & used books • magazines

Silver Moon Women's Bookshop at Foyles 113-119 Charing Cross Rd, 3rd flr 44–(0)20/7440–1562 • lesbian/feminist • also videos & DVDs • wheelchair access

RETAIL SHOPS

American Retro 35 Old Compton St 44–(0)20/7734–3477 • 10:30am-7:30pm, till 7pm Sat, 1pm-6pm Sun • clothing & gifts

Metal Morphosis 10–11 Moor St (at Old Compton St) 44–(0)20/7434–4554 • tattooing • piercing studio • body jewelry • toys

Prowler Soho 5–7 Brewer St (behind Village Soho bar) 44–(0)20/7734–4031 • 11am-10pm, 1pm-9pm Sun • popular • large gay department store

EROTICA

Femme Boudoir 17b Riding House St 44–(0)20/7637–5794 • lingerie, corsets, leather, rubber, toys • woman-owned/run

RoB London 24 Wells St (near Berwick St) 44–(0)20/7735–7893 • leather/fetish shop • wheelchair access

London—West

London—West includes Earl's Court, Kensington, Chelsea & Bayswater

ACCOMMODATIONS

Comfort Inn Kensington 22–32 W Cromwell Rd (Earl's Court) 44–(0)20/7373–3300 • gay-friendly • kids ok • food served • also bar

Millennium Bailey's Hotel 140 Gloucester Rd (at Old Brompton Rd, Kensington) 44–(0)20/7373–6000, 866/866–8086 • gay-friendly 4-star hotel • located in the heart of Kensington • £120-210 • also Olives restaurant & bar • Mediterranean

BARS

The George Music Bar 114 Twickenham Rd (Isleworth) 44–(0)20/8560–1456 • 5pm-11pm, from noon wknds, till10:30pm Sun • transgender-friendly • George Cabaret every Fri-Sat & every other Sun • gay-owned

The Leinster 57 Ossington St (at Moscow Rd, Bayswater) 44–(0)20/7243–9541 • lesbians/ gay men • food served • sports bar • videos

Richmond Arms 20 The Square (at Princes, Richmond) 44–(0)20/8940–2118 • pub hours • lesbians/ gay men • dancing/DJ • professional crowd • karaoke • drag shows • cabaret

Ted's Place 305a North End Rd (at Lillie Rd, Earl's Ct) 44–(0)20/7385–9359 • 7pm-11pm, men-only Mon, Tue, Fri, clsd Sun • mostly gay men • dancing/DJ • transgender-friendly • karaoke Wed • drag shows • videos • private club

West Five (W5) 5 Popes Ln (South Ealing) 44–(0)20/8579–3266 • 7pm-11pm, till midnight Wed-Th, till late Fri-Sat, 1pm-midnight Sun, lunch served Sun • lesbians/ gay men • cabaret • lounge • piano bar • garden

Restaurants

Balans West 239 Old Brompton Rd 44–(0)20/7244–8838 • 8am-1am, till 2am Th-Sat • lesbians/ gay men • English

The Churchill Arms 119 Kensington Church St 44–(0)20/7727–4242 • inexpensive, fantastic Thai • also pub

Phoenicia 11–13 Abingdon Rd 44–(0)20/7937–0120 • Lebanese/ Mediterranean

Star of India 154 Old Brompton Rd 44–(0)20/737–2901 • lunch, dinner • upscale

Thai Princess 30-31 Philbeach Gardens (at the Philbeach Hotel) 44–(0)20/7835–1858, 44–(0)20/7373–1244

Entertainment & Recreation

Walking Tour of Gay SOHO 56 Old Compton St (at Admiral Duncan Pub) 44–(0)20/7437–6063 • 2pm Sun • world-famous historical walking tour covering over 600 years of gay history in London's "square mile of sin" • £5

Gyms & Health Clubs

Soho Athletic Club 254 Earls Ct Rd 44–(0)20/7370–1402 • gay-friendly • also at 193 Camden High St, 44–(0)20/7482–4524

London—North

London—North includes Paddington, Regents Park, Camden, St Pancras & Islington

Bars

Blush 8 Cazenove Rd (Stoke Newington) 44–(0)20/7923–9202 • 5pm-midnight, brunch from noon wknds, clsd Mon • lesbians/ gay men • friendly cafe-bar • beer garden • all-day brkfst • live music Sun • karaoke Fri • Bedroom 1st Sat, mostly women • lesbian-owned

Catch 22 679 Green Lanes (at Falkland Rd, Harringay) 44–(0)20/8881–1900 • till 2am Fri-Sat • lesbians/ gay men • neighborhood bar

Duke of Wellington 119 Balls Pond Rd (Islington) 44–(0)20/7254–4338 • pub hours • lesbians/ gay men • neighborhood bar

The Flag 29 Crouch Hill (Stroud Green) 44–(0)20/7272–4748 • lesbians/ gay men • friendly neighborhood pub

Kind William IV 77 Hamstead High St (Hampstead) 44–(0)20/7435–5747 • pub hours • gay/ straight • food served • beer garden

King Edward VI/ Sunroom Cafe 25 Bromfield St (at Parkfield St, Islington) 44–017/1704–0745 • noon-midnight, Sun lunch from 2pm-5pm • popular • mostly gay men • neighborhood cafe-bar • beer garden • wheelchair access

The Oak Bar 79 Green Lanes (Stoke Newington) 44–(0)20/7354–2791 • 5pm-midnight, till 2am Fri-Sat, from 1pm Sun • mostly women • Lower the Tone last Fri • dancing/DJ • food served • karaoke • dancers • theme nights • women-owned

Y-Bar 142 Essex Rd (Islington) 44–(0)20/7359–2661 • 4:30pm-midnight, till 1am Fri-Sat • popular • lesbians/ gay men • dancing/DJ • karaoke • women-only Tue

Nightclubs

Club Kali 1 Dartmouth Park Hill (at The Dome) 44–(0)20/7272–8153 (Dome #) • 10pm-3am 1st & 3rd Fri • popular • lesbians/ gay men • dancing/DJ • Asian-American clientele • transgender-friendly • South Asian music • cover charge

Egg 200 York Way (off Calendonian Rd) 44–(0)20/7609–8364 • 10pm-5am Fri-Sat, 5am-late afternoon Sun • gay/ straight • dancing/DJ • 3 flrs

Fiction Kings Cross Freight Depot (at The Cross, off York Way) 44–(0)20/7749–1199 • 11pm-late Fri • lesbians/ gay men • dancing/DJ • see-and-be-seen • cover charge

Liberté 18 Kentish Town Rd (at G Lounge, Camden) 44–(0)79/8997–8362 • 9pm-3am last Sat • women only • dancing/DJ • soul, rap, reggae • multiracial

Popstarz 213 Pentonville Rd (at The Scala, Kings Cross) 44–(0)20/7956–549246 • popular • 10pm-5am Fri • lesbians/ gay men • dancing/DJ • 4 rooms • Britpop, indie, alternative, disco, etc • cover charge

RESTAURANTS

Providores/ Tapa Room 109 Marylebone (at New Cavendish St) 44–(0)20/7935.6175 • lunch & dinner • Asian fusion • more casual Tapa room downstairs open for brkfst, lunch & dinner • tapas

Sauce 214 Camden High St 44–(0)20/7482–0777 • noon-10:30pm, till 4:30pm Sun • organic • lots of veggie

ENTERTAINMENT & RECREATION

Waltzing With Hilda 269a Archway Rd (Jackson Ln Art Centre, Highgate) 44–(0)79/3907–2958 • 7:45pm-midnight 2nd & last Sat • women only • Latin & ballroom dancing • also lessons • cover charge

RETAIL SHOPS

Fettered Pleasures 90 Holloway Rd 44–(0)20/7619–9333 • 11pm-7pm, clsd Sun • S/M & fetish gear

EROTICA

Prowler Camden 283 Camden High St (Camden Town) 44–(0)20/7284–0537, 44–(0)20/7267–0021 (MAIL ORDER) • 10:30am-6:30pm, clsd Sun • fetishwear • books • videos • sex toys • also King's Cross 020/7278-4335 • also mail order

London—East

London—East includes City, Tower, Clerkenwell & Shoreditch

BARS

Charlie's Bar 124 Globe Rd (Stepney) 44–(0)20/7790–1007 • pub hours • lesbians/ gay men •neighborhood pub

Essence 2-5 Carthusian St (Clerkenwell) • noon-11pm, till 2am wknds, from 7pm Sun • tapas bar & restaurant • also various queer nights

Royal Oak 73 Columbia Rd (Bethnal Green, in the flower market) 44–(0)20/7739–8204 • pub hours, from 8:30am Sun • popular • lesbians/gay men • neighborhood bar • transgender-friendly • food served

The Ship 17 Barnes St (Stepney) 44–(0)20/7790–4082 • 6pm-11pm, from 7:30pm Sat, 1pm-10:30pm Sun • lesbians/ gay men • neighborhood bar • cabaret • drag shows • wheelchair access

NIGHTCLUBS

The Angel Cabaret Bar 21 Church St (Stratford) 44–(0)20/8555–1148 • 7pm-midnight, till 2am Sat, from 2pm Sun • lesbians/ gay men • cabaret

Central Station–Walthamstow 80 Brunner Rd (Walthamstow) 44–(0)20/8520–4836 • 5:30pm-1am, till 2am Th-Sat, from 1pm Sun • lesbians/ gay men • dancing/DJ • cabaret

Club Wotever 2-5 Carthusian St (at Essence, Clerkenwell) 44–(0)79/3232–4374 • 9pm-2am, 2nd Sat, mostly women • dancing/DJ • gender queers & their admirers

Curves 3 Minster Ct Mincing Ln (at Agenda) 44–(0)79/4734–0967, 44–(0)79/6371–4603 • 8pm-2am 1st Sat only • dancing/DJ • upscale nightclub & lounge • cover charge

DTPM 77a Charterhouse St, Smithfield Mkt (at Fabric) 44–(0)20/7439–9009 (INFO LINE) • 10pm-5am Sun • popular • lesbians/ gay men • dancing/DJ • huge, stylish techno club • young crowd • cover charge

French Kiss 2-5 Carthusian St (at Essence) 44–078/1233–3257 • 9pm-2am 1st Sat only • very popular • women-only • dancing/DJ • cover charge

Pleasure Unit 359 Bethnal Green Rd (Bethnal Green) 44–(0)20/7729–0167 • lesbians/gay men • dancing/DJ • live music • more women for Unskinny Bop 3rd Sat

Rumours 64-73 Minories (at The Minories) 44–(0)20/7961–158375 • 8pm-2am 2nd, 3rd & last Sat • popular • women-only • dancing/DJ • 2 bars

Way Out Club 9 Crosswall (at Charlie's) 44–(0)20/8363–0948 • 9pm-4am Sat only • transsexuals & their friends • dancing/DJ • live shows • private club • cover charge

RESTAURANTS

Bonds Restaurant & Bar 5 Threadneedle St 44–(0)20/7657–8088 • hours vary Mon-Th, clsd wknds • formerly a bank lobby • tapas served

Café Spice Namaste 16 Prescott St 44–(0)20/7488–9242 • lunch Mon-Fri, dinner nightly, clsd Sun • Indian

Cantaloupe 35-42 Charlotte Rd (Shoreditch) 44–(0)20/7613–4411 • popular • 11pm-midnight, from noon wknds, till 11:30pm Sun • also bar

Les Trois Garçons 1 Club Row (at Bethnal, Shoreditch) 44–(0)20/7613–1924 • 7pm-midnight Mon-Sat • French • eclectic decor • reservations recommended

SoSho 2 Tabernacle St 44–(0)20/7920–0701 • 11am-close, till 3am Th-Sat, clsd Sun • also bar

EROTICA

Babes 57a Redchurch St 44–(0)20/7739–1910 • 11am-9pm, 10am-6pm Sun • toys for women

Expectations 75 Great Eastern St (Shoreditch) 44–(0)20/7739–0292 • 11am-7pm, till 8pm Sat, noon-5pm Sun • leather/rubber store • also mail order

Sh! 39 Coronet St (off Old St, Shoreditch) 44–(0)20/7613–5458 • 10am-8pm, till 5pm Sun • also mail order

London—South

> **London—South includes Southwark, Lambeth, Kennington, Vauxhall, Battersea, Lewisham & Greenwich**

BARS

Bar Lava 8 Westow St (Crystal Palace) 44–(0)87/1223–9243 • lesbians/gay men • café/ video wine bar • live music Fri

Bar Phoenix 25 Rennell St (Lewisham) 44–(0)20/8852–1705 • noon-2am, 1pm-12:30am Sun • lesbians/gay men • drag shows

Battersea Barge Riverside Walk Nine Elms Ln (Vauxhall) 44–(0)20/7498–0004 • 11:30am-late, clsd Mon • gay-friendly • cabaret • comedy • food served • some veggie • gay-owned

George & Dragon 2 Blackheath Hill (Greenwich) 44–(0)20/8691–3764 • 6pm-1am, till 3am Fri-Sat • mostly gay men • live shows • cabaret

Kazbar 50 Clapham High St (Clapham) 44–(0)20/7622–0070 • 4pm-midnight, from noon Sat, till 11:30pm Sun • lesbians/gay men • transgender-friendly • videos • cafe-bar

The Little Apple 98 Kennington Ln 44–(0)20/7735–2039 • noon-midnight, till 10:30pm Sun • lesbians/gay men • dancing/DJ • transgender-friendly • food served • terrace • wheelchair access

Southopia 146-148 Newington Butts (Kennington) 44–(0)20/7735–5306, 44–(0)20/7735–5178 • 5pm-11:30pm, till 2am Fri-Sat, noon-10:30pm Sun, clsd Mon • mostly women • women-only basement • dancing/DJ • live shows • private club, daily membership available

The Two Brewers 114 Clapham High St (Clapham) 44–(0)20/7498–4971 • 5pm-2am, till 3am Fri-Sat, 2pm-12:30am Sun • lesbians/gay men • dancing/DJ • karaoke • cabaret • videos

NIGHTCLUBS

A:M S Lambeth Rd (at Fire, Vauxhall) 44–(0)79/0503–5682 • after-hours, 3am-noon Sat • dancing/DJ • cover charge

Beyond 1 Nine Elms Ln (at Club Colosseum, Vauxhall) 44–(0)79/0503–5682 • 4:30am-late Sun • mostly gay men • dancing/DJ

Crash 66 Goding St, Albert Embankment (Vauxhall) 44–(0)20/7278–0995 • 10:30pm-late 2nd & last Sat • popular • lesbians/gay men • more women 2nd Fri for Bootylicious • dancing/DJ • cover charge

Diva Night Battersea Barge (at Nine Elms Ln) 44–(0)77/0916–6819 • 7pm-2am monthly, call for dates • lesbians/gay men • food served • live shows • cabaret • 18+

Duckie 372 Kennington Ln (at Royal Vauxhall Tavern) 44–(0)20/7737–4043 • 9pm-2am every Sat • popular • retro indie • short cabaret acts

Ego 82 Norwood High St 44–(0)20/8761–5200 • 7pm-close • lesbians/gay men • dancing/DJ • cabaret • Fatale Th (women only)

The Fridge 1 Town Hall Parade (Brixton Hill) 44–(0)20/7326–5100 • 9pm-3am Th, 10pm-6pm Fri-Sat • popular • gay/ straight • dancing/DJ • hosts Love Muscle Sat (mostly men • dancing/DJ) • Fusion 2nd & 4th Fri • call for current events

Gingerbeer's Lyrical Lounge Nine Elms Ln (at Battersea Barge) • quarterly party hosted by the fabulous lesbian website gingerbeer.com • mostly women • live music • cover charge

Hard On @ Club Wicked 2-4 Tooley St (under London Bridge) • lesbians/gay men • 3rd Sat • leather & SM party • private club

Royal Vauxhall Tavern 372 Kennington Ln (Vauxhall) 44–(0)20/7837–0596, 44–(0)20/7737–4043 • 9pm-2am, noon-midnight Sun • mostly gay men • neighborhood bar • dancing/DJ • transgender-friendly • drag shows • more women Sat for Duckie • wheelchair access

CAFES

Surf.Net Cafe 13 Deptford Church St (at Deptford Broadway) 44–(0)20/8488–1200 • 11am-8pm, till 6pm Sat, clsd Sun • cybercafe/wine bar

ENTERTAINMENT & RECREATION

Oval Theatre Cafe Bar 52-54 Kennington Oval 44–020/7582-7680 • call to inquire about current theatre & art • food served

RETAIL SHOPS

The Host 45 B S Lambeth Rd (Vauxhall) 44–(0)20/7793–1551 • 11am-7pm, clsd Sun • rubber & fetish gear

London Piercing Clinic 13 Portland Rd (S Norwood) 44–(0)20/8656–7180 • 11am-7pm, 2pm-6pm Sun • also tattoo • also branches in Croydon & Camden

FRANCE

PARIS

Note: M°=Métro station

Paris is divided by arrondissements (city districts); 01=1st arrondissement, 02=2nd arrondissement, etc

Paris—Overview

Note: When phoning Paris from the US, dial the country code + the city code + the local phone number

Paris

LGBT PRIDE:

June. web: www.gaypride.fr
Lesbian Pride (June). 33-1/40.37.79.87, web: www.multi-mania.com/fiertelesbienne.

ANNUAL EVENTS:

May-June - French Open tennis championship, web: www.rolandgarros.com
July - Tour de France, web: www.letour.fr
July 14 - Bastille Day
November-December - Paris Gay & Lesbian Film Festival, web: www.ffglp.net.

CITY INFO:

Carrousel de Louvre, 99 rue de Rivoli, web: www.parisinfo.com. Also www.paris.org.

BEST VIEW:

Eiffel Tower (but of course!) and Sacre Coeur.

WEATHER:

Paris really *is* beautiful in the springtime. Chilly in the winter, the temperatures reach the 70°s during the summer.

TRANSIT:

Alpha Taxi 33–1/45.85.85.85.
Taxi Bleu 33–1/49.36.10.10.
RATP (bus and Métro) web: www.ratp.fr.

ATTRACTIONS:

Arc de Triomphe 33-1/43.80.31.31
Notre Dame Cathedral 33–1/43.25.42.92
Eiffel Tower (up in lights for 10 minutes each hour from sunset till past midnight!) 33–1/44.11.23.45, web: www.tour-eiffel.fr
Louvre 33–1/40.20.51.51, web: www.louvre.fr
Musée d'Orsay 33–1/40.49.48.14, web: www.musee-orsay.fr
Picasso Museum 33–1/42.71.25.21, web: www.musee-picasso.fr
Rodin Musuem 33–1/44.18.61.10, web: www.musee-rodin.fr
Sacre-Coeur Basilica 33–1/42.51.17.02
Sainte-Chapelle 33–1/43.73.78.41.

Reply **Forward** **Delete**

```
Date: Dec 31, 2005 15:22:47
From: Girl-on-the-Go
To: Editor@Damron.com
Subject: Paris
```

>It's hard not to wax poetic about Paris. The most romantic city in the world, Paris has all the characteristics of a capricious lover. Beautiful and witty, dignified and grand, flirtatious and coy—Paris's admirers will tell you she's worthy of lifelong devotion. It's not surprising, then, that so many artists and thinkers have made Paris their home. Whether it's the museums, the couture, the cafes, the history, the churches, or the people...Paris seduces at every turn.*

>During the day, enjoy the incredible sights of Paris. After you've had your fill of famed landmarks, artworks, and boulevards, drop out of the tourist circuit and find out for yourself why they call it *"Gay Paree."* Of course, for Parisians, nowhere is as *très gai* as the Marais district (most of the Marais's listings can be found with those in the 4th arrondissement).

>To get the latest editions of Paris LGBT magazines and to scope out the latest in one-off parties and hot club nights of the moment, drop in at **Les Mots à la Bouche,** or pay a visit to the **Centre Gai et Lesbien** on rue Keller. To find out about lesbian-specific activities and events, drop in at the women's bookstore **La Librairie des Femmes.**

At night, Paris truly is "The City of Lights." Don't even dare turn in for bed until you've made the most of this city's incredible nightlife.

>There is a dizzying array of women's bars and clubs in Paris. For pre-dinner cocktails, stop by **L'Unity Bar** in Les Halles; **La Champmeslé** (a "lesbian landmark" located near the Palais Royal and the Bibliothéque Nationale); **Bliss Kfe** (in the heart of the Marais); **L'Utopia** (near the Centre Pompidou); or **3W Kafe,** located in the heart of the Marais. Or check out **Boobsbourg** for drinks and dinner. You'll also find plenty of hip urban dykes at one of the trendy, mixed cafe-bars like **L'Open Café.**

Reply Forward   Delete

>Then head for a lesbian-friendly restaurant; once again, there are choices! There are many lesbo-popular eateries in the Louvre/ Les Halles area, including **L'Amazonial, Aux Trois Petits Conchons,** and **Le Loup Blanc.** After dinner, groove till dawn at one of the (you guessed it!—there are several) women's nightclubs.... **Pulp** is popular and open late. **La Rive-Gauche** is open on Friday and Saturday nights only. Of course, there are also various one-nighters (see above) and plenty of mixed clubs (like the aptly named **Queen**).

*(Paris's streets, however, confuse if you don't understand there's a method to her madness. The city spirals out from the Louvre and Jardin des Tuileries in a string of districts called arrondissements. We've divided our listings according to arrondissements, using the following notation: 01=1st, 02=2nd, 03=3rd, etc. So, before you go, you might want to look over your maps and get a general idea of what falls in which district. Once you're there, you can get around using a combination of Métro stops and district names and numbers. *Bonne chance*—good luck!)

INFO LINES & SERVICES

Centre Gai et Lesbien 3 rue Keller (M° Bastille) **33-1/4357-2147** • drop-in 4pm-8pm, clsd Sun • call for other events/ groups • also wine bar

Ecoute Gaie 33-8/1081-1057 • helpline staffed 6pm-10pm Mon-Fri

Gay AA 7 rue August Vacquerie (at St George's Anglican) **33-1/4634-5965** • 7:30pm Tue

ACCOMMODATIONS

A Parisian Home 12 rue Mandar **33-1/4508-0337** • furnished apts in Paris, short-term rentals

Gay Accommodation Paris 271, rue du Faubourg Saint Antoine **33-1/4348-1382** • studios for rent in central Paris • gay-owned

Insightful Travelers 617/859-0720 (US#) • gay-friendly • short-term apt rentals • 3-day minimum stay • daily & monthly rates

Marais Flats/ Studios Rue Marie Stuart **33-6/1052-5935** • several spacious apts available for weekly or monthly rental in different Paris locations • close to gay districts • gay-owned • €720-1100/ week

Paris Marais Studios Marais District **33-1/4277-76240** • gay/ straight • apt rentals • private flats in historic homes • €90-250 (4-night minimum)

Paris Séjour Réservation 312/587-7707 (US#), 800/582-7274 (FAX #) • gay-friendly • short-term apt rentals • €75-450

RentParis.com LLC 33-1/6670-35471 • gay/ straight • fully furnished studios & apts • kids ok • nonsmoking • gay-owned • €50-300

ENTERTAINMENT & RECREATION

Cour et Jardin 33–1/3975–1908 • amateur LGBT theater group • call or see web for performance times & locations: www.france.qrd.org/assocs/cour-et-jardin/cj/index2.htm

O Chateau, Wine Tasting in Paris 39 Ave du Dr Netter 33–1/4473–9780 • gay-friendly • transgender-friendly • English-speaking French connoisseur

PUBLICATIONS

Lesbia 33–1/4348–8954 • monthly glossy magazine

Têtu 33–1/5680–2080 • stylish & intelligent LGBT monthly (en français)

SPIRITUAL GROUPS

Beit Haverim 33–1/4040–0071 • LGBT Jewish social group

David & Jonathan 92 bis, rue de Picpus (12) 33–1/4342–0949 • interdenominational LGBT Christian group

Paris — 01

ACCOMMODATIONS

Castille Sofitel Demeure Hotel 37 rue Cambon (near Place Concorde) 33–1/4458–4458, 800/448–8355 (US#) • gay-friendly • ultra-luxe hotel • wheelchair access • €288+

Hotel Louvre Richelieu 51 rue de Richelieu (M° Palais-Royal) 33–1/4297–4620 • gay/ straight • €78

Hotel Louvre Saint-Honoré 141 rue Saint-Honoré (at rue du Louvre) 33–1/4296–2323 • gay/ straight • modern 3-star hotel • full brkfst • kids ok • wheelchair access • €150-225

The Ritz 15 place Vendôme (M° Tuileries) 33–1/4316–3070, 800/223–6800 (US#) • gay-friendly • ultra-luxe hotel • €580-1,580

BARS

Le Banana Café 13–15 rue de la Ferronnerie (near rue St-Denis, M°Châtelet) 33–1/4233–3531 • 6pm-dawn • trendy • lesbians/ gay men • dancing/DJ • tropical decor • theme nights • piano bar • live shows • young crowd • wheelchair access • terrace

Le Cargo 37 rue des Lombards (M° Châtelet) 33–1/4028–0308 • noon-2am • lesbians/ gay men • cafe-bar • dancing/DJ • naval decor • T-dance Sun

Le Tropic Café 66 rue des Lombards (M° Châtelet) 33–1/4013–9262 • 4pm-5am • lesbians/ gay men • dancing/DJ Fri-Sat • transgender-friendly • kitschy, fun bar tapas served • terrace • young crowd • wheelchair access

Le Vagabon 14 rue Thérèse (at av de l'Opera, M° Pyramides) 33–1/4296–2723 • 6pm-close, clsd Mon • oldest gay bar & restaurant in Paris • older crowd

NIGHTCLUBS

Le Club 14 rue St-Denis (at rue des Lombards, M° Châtelet) 33–1/4508–9625 • midnight-close, till 7am Sat • lesbians/ gay men • dancing/DJ • multiracial clientele • food served • theme nights • strippers • private club • cover charge

RESTAURANTS

L' Amazonial 3 rue Ste-Opportune (at rue Ferronnerie, M°Châtelet) 33–1/4233–5313 • lunch & dinner, brunch wknds • lesbians/ gay men • Brazilian/ int'l • cabaret • drag shows • heated terrace • wheelchair access

Au Diable des Lombards 64 rue des Lombards (at rue St-Denis, M°Châtelet) 33–1/4233–8184 • 8am-1am • American • full bar • terrace

Au Rendez-Vous des Camionneurs 72 quai des Orfèvres (M°Pont Neuf) 33–1/4354–8874 • noon-2:30pm & 7pm-11:30pm, noon-11:30pm Sun • mostly gay men • traditional French bistro

Caribbean Coffee 15 rue du Roule 33–1/4233–2130 • clsd Sun-Mon • lesbians/ gay men • Creole bistro • also bar • women's T-dance Sun

La Mondetour 14 rue Mondetour 33–1/4236–0163 • lunch & dinner, also bar • popular • lesbians/ gay men

La Poule au Pot 9 rue Vauvilliers (M° Les Halles) 33–1/4236–3296 • 7pm-5am, clsd Mon • clsd Aug • bistro • traditional French •

ENTERTAINMENT & RECREATION

Forum des Halles 101 Porte Berger (M°Châtelet-Les Halles) • underground sports/ entertainment complex w/ museums, theater, shops, clubs, cafes & more

Paris—02

ACCOMMODATIONS

Frendy 7 rue des Fontaines du Temple 33–1/4508–9077 • lesbians/gay men • gay-owned • €65

BARS

La Champmeslé 4 rue Chabanais (at rue des Petits Champs, M° Pyramides) 33–1/4296–8520 • 5pm-late, clsd Sun • popular • mostly women • cabaret Th • theme nights • older crowd • wheelchair access • a lesbian landmark, in business for over 20 years

NIGHTCLUBS

Le Pulp 25 bd Poissonnière (M° Grands-Blvds) 33–1/4026–0193 • 11pm-close, clsd Sun-Tue • popular • mostly women • men welcome as guests • dancing/DJ • theme nights • cover charge Fri-Sat

Le Scorp 25 bd Poissonnière (M° Grands-Blvds) 33–1/4026–0130 • 11am-7am • popular • mostly gay men • dancing/DJ • shows Sun-Tue • young crowd • Oh La La on Th w/ old French hits

RESTAURANTS

Aux Trois Petits Cochons 31 rue Tiquetonne (at rue St-Denis, M°Etienne-Marcel) 33–1/4233–3969 • 8pm-1am • popular • lesbians/gay men • gourmet French made w/ fresh seasonal produce • menu changes daily • reservations recommended • gay-owned

Le Dénicheur 4 rue Tiquetonne (M° Etienne-Marcel) 33–1/4221–3101 • noon-midnight, clsd Mon • sandwiches, quiche, salads

Le Gut 64 rue Jean-Jacques Rousseau (M° Chatelet-Les-Halles) 33–1/4236–1490 • lesbians/gay men • 7:30am-7pm, noon-3pm Sat, clsd Sun • inexpensive bistro

L' Homosapiens 29 rue Tiquetonne (M°Etienne-Marcel) 33–1/4026–9485 • 7:30pm-11pm, clsd Sun-Mon (also clsd all Aug) • French • inexpensive

Le Loup Blanc 42 rue Tiquetonne (M° Etienne-Marcel) 33–1/4013–0835 • 7:30pm-midnight, till 1am Sat, also brunch 11am-4:30pm Sun • popular • lesbians/gay men • French/int'l

Mi Cayito 10 rue Marie-Stuart 33–1/4221–9886 • 7pm-midnight • Cuban

Paris—03

ACCOMMODATIONS

Absolu Living 3 Passage de l'Ancre 33–1/4454–9700 • lesbians/gay men • fully furnished apts in central Paris • short & long-term stays • gay-owned • €89-690

Adorable Apartment in Paris in the Marais, 3e arrondissement (M° Rambuteau) 415/397–6454 (US#) • gay-friendly • 2-bdrm flat in heart of Marais (sleeps 4-6) • nonsmoking • lesbian & gay-owned • $1,600/week & $4,000/month

Hôtel de Saintonge Le Marais 16 rue de Saintonge (off rue du Perche btwn rue Charlot & rue Vieille du Temple, M° Filles-du-Calvaire) 33–1/4277–9113 • gay-friendly • €105-170

BARS

Boobsbourg 26 rue Montmorency 33–1/4274–0482 • 5:30pm-2am, clsd Mon • mostly women • restaurant 6pm-11pm • lesbian-owned

Le Duplex 25 rue Michel-le-Comte (at rue Beaubourg, M° Rambuteau) 33–1/4272–8086 • 8pm-2am • lesbians/gay men • neighborhood bar • bohemian types • live shows • internet access

La Petite Vertu 15 rue des Vertus (M° Arts-et-Métiers) 33–1/4804–7709 • 5pm-2am, from noon wknds, clsd Sun-Mon • lesbians/gay men • food served

L' Unity Bar 176–178 rue St-Martin (near rue Réaumur, M° Rambuteau) 33–1/4272–7059 • 4pm-2am • mostly women • men welcome as guests • neighborhood bar • young crowd

L' Utopia 15 rue Michel-le-Comte (M° Rambuteau) 33–1/4271–6343 • 5pm-2am, clsd Sun (also clsd 8/1-8/15) • mostly women • men welcome as guests • neighborhood bar • live shows • theme nights • dancing/DJ Sat • internet access • wheelchair access

Villa Keops 58 blvd Sébastopol 33–1/4027–9992 • noon-3am, till 5am Fri-Sat, from 4pm Sat-Sun • lesbians/gay men • dancing/DJ Fri-Sat • also restaurant • clsd in August

NIGHTCLUBS

Les Bains 7 rue du Bourg-l'Abbé (at bd de Sébastopol, M°Etienne-Marcel) 33–1/4887–0180 • 11pm-close • gay-friendly • gay Sun-Mon • dancing/DJ • cover charge

Restaurants

Les Epicuriens du Marais 19 rue Commines (M° Filles-du-Calvaire) 33-1/4027-0083 • noon-3pm & 7pm-midnight, till 1:30am wknds • traditional French

La Fontaine Gourmande 11 rue Charlot 33-1/4278-7240 • noon-2pm Tue-Fri & 7:30pm-close Tue-Sun, clsd Mon • French •

Entertainment & Recreation

Musée Picasso 5 rue de Thorigny (in the Hôtel Salé, M° St-Paul) 33-1/4271-2521 • 9:30am-5:30pm, clsd Tue • wheelchair access

Erotica

Rexx 42 rue de Poitou (at rue Charlot, M° St-Sébastien-Froissard) 33-1/4277-5857 • clsd Sun • new, custom & secondhand leather & S/M accessories

Paris—04

Accommodations

Historic Rentals 100 W Kennedy Blvd #260, Tampa, FL 33602 800/537-5408 (US#) • gay-friendly • 1-bdrm apt • in the heart of the Marais • full kitchen • $600-900/week

Hôtel Beaubourg 11 rue Simon le Franc (btwn rue Beaubourg & rue du Temple, M° Hôtel-de-Ville) 33-1/4274-3424 • gay/straight • next to Centre Pompidou • €112-132

Hôtel de la Bretonnerie 22 rue Ste-Croix-de-la-Bretonnerie (M° Hôtel-de-Ville) 33-1/4887-7763 • gay-friendly • 17th-c hotel w/ Louis XIII decor • €80-120

Hôtel du Vieux Marais 8 rue du Plâtre (M° Hôtel-de-Ville) 33-1/4278-4722 • gay-friendly • centrally located • €92-106

Hotel Le Compostelle 31 rue du Roi de Sicile 33-1/4278-5999 • gay-friendly • in city center • €65+

Libertel Grand Turenne 6 rue de Turenne (at rue St-Antoine, M° St-Paul) 33-1/4278-4325, 800/949-7562(US#) • gay-friendly • €120+

Paris-Apart 14 rue Francois Miron • gay/straight • loft in old Le Marais • kids ok • gay-owned • €875/week • monthly rental available

Parisian Dream 6 cour Berard 33-6/7117-0169 • gay/straight • charming apt located in Marais district a short walk from gay Paris • gay-owned • €400 for 4 nights

Villa Malraux 6 rue des Archives 33-1/5301-9090 • gay/straight • in the heart of the Marais district • gay-owned

Bars

3W Kafe 8 rue des Ecouffes 33-1/4887-3926 • 5:30pm-2am • mostly women • dancing/DJ • live shows • videos

AccesSoir Café 41 rue des Blancs-Manteaux (M°Rambuteau) 33-1/4272-1289 • 6pm-2am • lesbians/gay men • drag shows • theme nights • food served

L' Amnésia Café 42 rue Vieille du Temple (at rue des Blancs-Manteaux, M°Hôtel-de-Ville) 33-1/4272-1694 • noon-2am • popular • lesbians/gay men • dancing • food served • brunch daily

Le Bar du Palmier 16 rue des Lombards (at bd de Sébastopol, M°Châtelet) 33-1/4278-5353 • 5pm-5am • lesbians/gay men • food served • terrace

Bliss Kfe 30 rue du Roi de Sicile (M°Hôtel-de-Ville) 33-1/4278-4936 • 5pm-2am • lesbians/gay men • stylish new bar • dancing/DJ • lesbian-owned

Le Carré 18 rue du Temple (M° Hôtel-de-Ville) 33-1/4459-3857 • 10am-4am, wknd brunch • lesbians/gay men • lounge & restaurant • terrace

Les Etages 35 rue Vieille du Temple 33-1/4278-7200 • 3:30pm-2am • mostly women • neighborhood bar

Le Masque Rouge 49 rue des Blancs-Manteaux (at rue du Temple, M° Hôtel-de-Ville) 33-1/4027-9742 • 5pm-2am • lesbians/gay men • T-dance Sun • nonsmoking

Le Mixer Bar 23 rue Ste-Croix-de-la-Bretonnerie (at rue des Archives, M° Hôtel-de-Ville) 33-1/4887-5544 • 4pm-2am • popular • lesbians/gay men • dancing/DJ • 3-flr techno/house bar • theme nights • young crowd

Morri's bar 27 rue Quincampoix 33-1/4272-8050 • 11pm-2am, from 5pm Mon-Tue • lesbians/gay men • neighborhood bar • food served

Oh! Fada 35 rue Ste-Croix-de-la-Bretonnerie (at rue du Temple, M°Hôtel-de-Ville) • 5pm-2am Th-Sun only • lesbians/gay men

Okawa 40 rue Vieille du Temple (at rue Ste-Croix-de-la-Bretonnerie, M° Hôtel-de-Ville) 33-1/4804-3069 • 11:30am-2am • gay/straight • trendy cafe-bar in 12th/13th-c caves • theme nights • cabaret • piano bar Tue-Wed • young crowd • also restaurant from 7pm

L' Open Café 17 rue des Archives (at rue Ste-Croix-de-la-Bretonnerie, M° Hôtel-de-Ville) **33-1/4272-2618** • 10am-2am, Sun brunch • popular • lesbians/gay men • sidewalk cafe-bar • also L'Open Coffee Shop • 23 rue du Temple, 33-1/4887-8025 • salads & sandwiches • young crowd

Le Polystar 94 rue St-Martin (M° Hôtel-de-Ville) **33-1/4454-9930** • 10pm-close, clsd Mon • dancing/DJ • karaoke • strippers

Le Raidd 23 rue du Temple (M° Hotel de ville) • 5:30pm-close • mostly men • danciing/ DJ • go-go boys

Le Troisieme Lieu 62 rue Quincampoix **33-1/4804-8564** • 6pm-2am, clsd Sun • lesbians/ gay men • also restaurant & nightclub

RESTAURANTS

Le Chant des Voyelles 4 rue des Lombards (M° Châtelet) **33-1/4277-7707** • 11:30am-3pm & 6:30pm-midnight (open all day in summer) • traditional French • terrace

Côté 9ème 29 rue du Bourg-Tibourg (M°Hôtel-de-Ville) **33-1/4274-4525** • dinner nightly

Le Crocman 6 rue Geoffroy l'Angevin (M° Rambuteau) **33-1/4277-6002** • 7pm-close, clsd Tue-Wed • mostly gay men

Le Dos de la Baleine 40 rue des Blancs-Manteaux (M° Rambuteau) **33-1/4272-3898** • lunch Tue-Fri, dinner Tue-Sat, clsd Sun-Mon (also clsd Aug) • gourmet seafood • reservations recommended

Equinox 33–35 rue des Rosiers (M° St-Paul) **33-1/4271-9241** • 7pm-midnight • Québecois/ French • full bar • piano bar • drag shows

Le Gai Moulin 4 rue St-Merri (at rue du Temple, M° Hôtel-de-Ville) **33-1/4887-4759** • dinner • lesbians/gay men • French/ int'l

Goldenbergs 7 rue des Rosiers (M° St-Paul) **33-1/4887-2016** • 8:30pm-midnight • Jewish

Le Passage 18 passage de la Bonne-Graine (M° Ledru-Rollin) **33-1/4700-7330** • lunch & dinner, clsd Sun • French

Le Petit Picard 42 rue Ste-Croix-de-la-Bretonnerie (M° Hôtel-de-Ville) **33-1/4278-5403** • lunch & dinner, clsd Mon • lesbians/gay men • reservations recommended

Les Piétons 8 rue des Lombards (M° Châtelet) **33-1/4887-8287** • 11am-2am, brunch noon-6pm Sun • gay/ straight • Spanish/ tapas • also bar • dancing/DJ from 8pm Wed

BOOKSTORES

Blue Book Paris 61 rue Quincampoix (at Rambuteau) **33-1/4887-0304** • 11am-11pm, from 1pm Sun-Mon • LGBT • also cafe & gallery

Les Mots à la Bouche 6 rue Ste-Croix-de-la-Bretonnerie (near rue du Vieille du Temple, M° Hôtel-de-Ville) **33-1/4278-8830** • 11am-11pm, 2pm-8pm Sun • LGBT • English titles

RETAIL SHOPS

Abraxas 9 rue St-Merri **33-1/4804-3355** • 11am-9pm, till 10pm Fri-Sat, from 3pm Sun • tattoos • piercing • large selection of body jewelry

Paris—05

ACCOMMODATIONS

Historic Rentals 100 W Kennedy Blvd #260, Tampa, FL 33602 **800/537-5408 (US#)** • gay-friendly • 1-bdrm apts • full kitchen • steps to Notre Dame & Luxembourg Gardens • $600-900/ week

Hôtel des Nations St Germain 54 rue Monge (near rue des Écoles, M° Pl-Monge) **33-1/4326-4524** • gay-friendly • small hotel in the Latin Quarter • pets ok

La Vie en Rose Quai de la Tournelle **888/866-4730 (US#)** • gay-friendly • luxury vessel on the Seine • full brkfst • nonsmoking • deck w/ garden • $650/ night • 3-night minimum stay

CAFES

Clickside 14 rue Domat (off rue Dante, M° Maubert-Mutualite) **33-1/5681-0300** • 10am-midnight, 1pm-11pm wknds & holidays • cybercafe • games & printing services • 11 English keyboards available

RESTAURANTS

Restaurant le Petit Prince de Paris 12 rue de Lanneau (M° Maubert-Mutualité) **33-1/4354-7726** • 2:30pm-midnight • popular • French

ENTERTAINMENT & RECREATION

Open-Air Sculpture Museum Quai Saint-Bernard **33-1/4326-9190** • along the Seine between the Jardin des Plantes & the Institut du Monde Arabe

Paris—06

ACCOMMODATIONS

L' Hôtel 13 rue des Beaux-Arts (btwn rue Bonaparte & rue de Seine, M° St-Germain-des-Près) **33–1/4441–9900** • gay-friendly • eccentric hotel where Oscar Wilde died • €260-600

NIGHTCLUBS

Le Rive-Gauche 1 rue du Sabot (M° St-Sulpice) **33–1/4020–4323** • 11pm-dawn Fri-Sat only • mostly women • dancing/DJ • cover charge

CAFES

Café de Flore 172 blvd St-Germain (M° St-Germain-des-Prés) **33–1/4548–5526** • 7am-2am • Dalí, Miró & Picasso's old hangout • great atmosphere

BOOKSTORES

Les Amazones 68 rue Bonaparte **33–1/4046–0837** • specializes in antique, lesbian & feminist books

La Librairie des Femmes Antoinette Fouque 6 **33–1/4222–6074** • 11am-7pm, clsd Sun • women's

The Village Voice 6 rue Princesse (M° Mabillon) **33–1/4633–3647** • 10am-8pm, from 2pm Sun-Mon, till 7pm Sun • English-language bookshop

Paris—07

ACCOMMODATIONS

Hôtel Muguet 11 rue Chevert (near av de Tourville, near the Eiffel Tower) **33–1/4705–0593** • gay-friendly • recently renovated • €85-130

Paris—08

ACCOMMODATIONS

Crillon 10 place de la Concorde **33–1/4471–1501, 800/888–4747 (US#)** • gay-friendly • ultra-luxe hotel • restaurant • €480-1550

BARS

Le Day-Off 10 rue de l'Isly (M° Gare-St-Lazare) **33–1/4522–8790** • 5pm-3am Mon-Fri only • mostly women • cocktail bar • food served • woman-owned

NIGHTCLUBS

Le Queen 102 av des Champs-Élysées (btwn rue Washington & rue de Berri, M° Georges-V) **33–8/9270–7330** • midnight-dawn • popular • mostly gay men • dancing/DJ • theme nights • drag shows • young crowd • selective door • cover charge

Paris—09

ACCOMMODATIONS

The Grand 2 rue Scribe **33–1/4007–3232, 800/327–0200 (US#)** • gay-friendly • ultra-luxe art deco hotel

NIGHTCLUBS

Folies Pigalle 11 place Pigalle (M° Pigalle) **33–1/48.78.55.25, 33–1/4280–1203 (BBB INFO LINE)** • midnight-dawn Tue-Sat • gay/ straight • dancing/DJ • more gay at popular Black, Blanc, Beur T-dance 6pm-midnight Sun • Escualita from midnight Sun • transgender-friendly • multiracial • cover charge

Paris—10

ACCOMMODATIONS

Hotel Louxor 4 rue Taylor (at bd St-Martin, M° République) **33–1/4208–2391** • gay-friendly • near Marais • free internet access • €51-82

Hôtel Moderne du Temple 3 rue d'Aix **33–1/4208–0904** • gay/ straight • economy-class hotel • some shared baths • kids ok • gay-owned • €24-44

RESTAURANTS

Le Châlet Maya 5 rue des Petits Hôtels (M° Gare de l'Est) **33–1/4770–5278** • 6:30pm-midnight • lesbians/ gay men • French

Paris—11

ACCOMMODATIONS

Hôtel Beaumarchais 3 rue Oberkampf (btwn bd Beaumarchais & bd Voltaire, M° Filles-du-Calvaire) **33–1/5336–8686** • gay/ straight • beautiful hotel • €85-140

Hôtel Mondia 22 rue du Grand-Prieuré (M° République) **33–1/4700–9344** • gay-friendly • hotel • quiet street • pets ok • woman-owned/run • €55-80

Libertel Croix-de-Malté 5 rue de Malté (M° Oberkampf) **33–1/4805–0936, 800/949–7562 (US#)** • gay-friendly • €100+

Studio in Paris 41 rue Saint Bernard 33–1/4930–0702 • gay/ straight • studio in Bastille area • gay-owned • €65-75

BARS

Interface 34 rue Keller (M° Bastille) 33–1/4700–6715 • 4pm-2am • mostly gay men • live shows

NIGHTCLUBS

Le Gibus Club 18 rue du Faubourg-du-Temple (M° République) 33–1/4700–7888 • midnight-close, clsd Mon-Tue • gay-friendly • gay Th & Sat • dancing/DJ • also piano bar • live music Sat • cover charge

RESTAURANTS

L' ArtiShow 3 cite Souzy 33–1/4348–5604 • lunch & dinner • French/ Thai • cabaret Sat

Le Temps Au Temps 13 rue Paul Bert (M° Faidherbe-Chaligny) 33–1/4379–6340 • 8pm-11pm, clsd Sun • lesbians/ gay men • French bistro • live shows • reservations recommended

Le Sofa 21 rue St-Sabin (M° Bastille) 33–1/4314–0746 • 6pm-midnight, till 2am Th-Sat • also bar

EROTICA

Démonia 10 Cité Joly (M° Pere-Lachaise) 33–1/4314–8270 • clsd Sun • BDSM shop • lingerie • videos • toys

Paris—12

GYMS & HEALTH CLUBS

Alantide 13 rue Parrot 33–1/4342–2243 • noon-close • gay-straight • Turkish bath • cabins • tanning • videos • women welcome

Paris—13

RESTAURANTS

Au Pet de Lapin 2 rue Dunois (M°Massena) 33–1/4586–5821 • noon-2pm & 8pm-10:30pm, clsd Sun-Mon (also clsd Aug) • foies gras & seafood

Paris—14

ENTERTAINMENT & RECREATION

Catacombes 1 place Denfert Rochereau 33–1/4322–4763 • a ghoulish yet intriguing tourist destination, these burial tunnels were the headquarters of the Résistance during World War II

Paris—15

RESTAURANTS

Le Boudoir 22 rue Frémicourt (M° La-Motte-Picquet) 33–1/4059–8228 • lunch & dinner, clsd Mon • French • also bar 5:30pm-1am

ENTERTAINMENT & RECREATION

Friday Night Fever Plaza Dautry (near Montparnasse Rail Station) 44–1/4336–8981 • 10pm-1am Fri (weather-permitting), meet 9:45pm • rollerblade through the city • gay/ straight

Paris—18

RESTAURANTS

Chez Catherine 66 rue de Provence (M° Chaussee d'Antin-La Fayette) 33–1/4526–7288 • lunch & dinner, clsd Sat-Mon • charming bistro • reservations required

Paris—19

ACCOMMODATIONS

A Week or More in Paris 33–1/4342–2156, 33–6/1362–9098 • gay/ straight • studio • pets ok • gay-owned • €500-600/ week

Paris—20

ACCOMMODATIONS

A Pink Froggy Gay/ Lesbian B&B Paris rue du Faubourg du Temple 33–6/2561–4944 • lesbians/ gay men • central & cozy • full brkfst • kids ok • info & free map to LGBT Paris • nonsmoking • lesbian-owned • €50

ENTERTAINMENT & RECREATION

Père Lachaise Cemetery bd de Ménilmontant (M°Père-Lachaise) • perhaps the world's most famous resting place, where lie such notables as Chopin, Gertrude Stein, Oscar Wilde, Sarah Bernhardt, Isadora Duncan, Edith Piaf & Jim Morrison

GERMANY

BERLIN

Berlin is divided into 5 regions:
Berlin—Overview
Berlin—Kreuzberg
Berlin—Prenzlauer Berg–Mitte
Berlin—Schöneberg-Tiergarten
Berlin—Outer

Berlin—Overview

INFO LINES & SERVICES

Compania FrauenKultureService Anklamer Str 38 (in Mitte) **49–30/4435–8704** • noon-7pm Mon-Fri • services & tours for lesbians • no sex

Gay AA for English Speakers at M-O-M **49–30/216–8008** • 5pm Tue, also Gay AA 8pm Th

Lesbenberatung (Lesbian Advice) Kulmer Str 20a (in Kreuzberg) **49–30/215–2000** • switchboard & center • staffed 4pm-7pm Mon, Tue & Th, 10am-1pm Wed & 2pm-5pm Fri • various meetings • youth line & young lesbians group

Mann-O-Meter Bülowstr 106 (at Nollendorfplatz) **49–30/216–3336, 49–23/638–142** • open 5pm-10pm, from 4pm wknds • gay switchboard & center • also cafe • also B&B referral service

Sonntags Club Greifenhagener Str 28 (S/U-Schönhauser Allee) **49–30/449–7590, 49–30/442–3702 (TRANSGENDER LINE)** • info line 10am-6pm daily • LGBT info • counseling • meetings • also cafe-bar • 5pm-midnight Mon-Sun • lesbians/gay men • transgender-friendly • live shows • videos • regular parties

Spinnboden Lesbian Archive & Library U-Bahn 8, Bernauerstr (in 2nd courtyard, 2nd flr) **49–30/448–5848** • call for hours • also by appt

SIEGESSÄULE
Europe's Biggest Queer City Mag
Presents OUT IN BERLIN

www.out-in-berlin.de

ACCOMMODATIONS

Enjoy B&B Bülowstr 106 (at M-O-M, gay center) **49-30/2362-3610** • lesbians/gay men • accommodations referral service • €18-30

NIGHTCLUBS

MegaDyke Productions Monumentenstr 1 **49-30/7870-3094** • popular parties & events for lesbians, including Subterra at SchwuZ & annual pride events for lesbians in other locations • check local publications for more details

Berlin

LGBT PRIDE:

Christopher Street Day, 3rd or 4th Saturday in June. 49-30/23.62.86.32 (M-O-M#), web: www.csd-berlin.de.

ANNUAL EVENTS:

February - Tuntenball. Drag ball, web: tuntenball.at

Berlinale: Berlin Int'l Film Festival w/ Queer Teddy Award, web: www.berlinale.de

June - Gay & Lesbian Street Fair 49-30/21.47.35.86, web: www.regenbogenfonds.de

July - Love Parade, web: www.loveparade.de

October - Jazz Fest Berlin, www.berlinerfestspiele.de

Lesbian Film Festival 49-30/787.181.08, web: www.lesbenfilmfestival.de

November - Verzaubert Int'l Queer Film Festival 49-30/861.45.32, web: www.verzaubertfilmfest.com.

CITY INFO:

Berlin-Tourism 49-30/25.00.25, web: www.btm.de

Europa Center 49-30/190.016.316, web: www.europa-center-berlin.de.

WEATHER:

Berlin is on the same parallel as Newfoundland, so if you're visiting in the winter, prepare for snow and bitter cold. Summer is balmy while spring and fall are beautiful, if sometimes rainy.

TRANSIT:

Taxifunk Berlin 49-30/44.33.222.

Jet Express-Bus X9 from Tegel Airport to central Berlin 49-30/11861.

U-Bahn (subway) and bus 49-30/194.49, web: www.bvg.de

S-Bahn (elevated train) 49-30/29.71.98.43

ATTRACTIONS:

Bauhaus Design Museum 49-30/254.00.20, web: www.bauhaus.de

Brandenburg Gate

Charlottenburg Palace 49-30/32.09.11

Egyptian Museum 49-30/20.90.55.77

Gay Museum 49-30/69.59.90.50, web: www.schwulesmuseum.de

Homo Memorial (at Nollendorfplatz station)

The Jewish Museum Berlin 49-30/25.99.33.00, web: www.jmberlin.de

Kaiser Wilhelm Memorial Church

Käthe-Kollwitz Museum 49-30/882.52.10, web: www.kaethe-kollwitz.de

Museuminsel (Museum Island) 49-30/20.90.55.55, web: www.smb.spk-berlin.de

New National Gallery 49-30/26.62.65

Reichstag 49-30/22.73.21.31.

Reply **Forward** **Delete**

```
Date: Dec 14, 2005 16:01:32
From: Girl-on-the-Go
To: Editor@Damron.com
Subject: Berlin
```

>In the past century, Berlin has seen just about everything: the outrageous art and cabaret of the Weimar era; the ravages of world war; ideological standoffs that physically divided families, lovers, and the city itself; and a largely peaceful revolution that brought Germany and the world together. Through it all, the Berliners have retained their own brand of cheeky humor—*Berliner Schnauze*, it's called—and a fierce loyalty to their city. While Berlin's museums and monuments are world-class, the city's real charm is in its cafes and countercultural milieu.

>You may find the women's scene in Berlin more political than in other places, but as a result you'll find a lot of support for women's culture and arts here, too. Although there are others, Berlin's main women's community/social center is **Schoko-Café** in Kreuzberg, a community center with a bar, cafe, and steam bath!

>After stopping in at one of the women's centers, grab a bite to eat and do some people-watching at **Café Berio.** If you're a girl who just wants to have fun, visit **Sexclusivitäten** for women's erotica.

>Later, check out the latest women's bar, **Neue Bar**. **Serene Bar** has popular girls' nights Thursday and Saturday. **SO 36, Die Busche,** and **SchwuZ** are popular mixed clubs; call for upcoming theme nights and women's nights. Pick up a copy of the local LGBT newsmagazine **Siegessäule** or the women's entertainment mag **L-Mag** (both in German) for the latest hot spots. Or give **MegaDyke Productions** a call—these women organize not-to-be-missed monthly parties and other events. After your night of dancing, wind down in Kreuzberg at **Roses,** a popular late-night spot.

>If the club scene is not your scene, you might enjoy spending some time at **Cafe Seidenfaden** (in Mitte)—a chem- and alcohol-free women's cafe. Check their info board for more ideas of things to do.

ENTERTAINMENT & RECREATION

The Jewish Museum Berlin Lindenstr 9-14 49–30/3087–85681 • 10am-8pm, till 10pm Mon • German-Jewish history & culture • €5

Schwules (Gay) Museum U6/U7 Mehringdamm 49–30/6959–9050 • 2pm-6pm, till 7pm Sat, clsd Tue • guided tours 5pm Sat (in German) • exhibits, archives & library

PUBLICATIONS

▲ **L-MAG** Jackwerth Verlag, L-MAG, Tempelhofer Ufer 11 49–30/235–5390, 49–30/2355–3932 • bimonthly nat'l lesbian magazine (in German)

▲ **Siegessäule** 49–30/235–5390, 49–30/2355–3932 • free monthly LGBT city magazine (in German) • awesome maps

SPIRITUAL GROUPS

Yachad—Lesbigay Jewish Association 49–30/624–8765 • brunch 1st Sun at Melitta Sundström • contact Mann-O-Meter for more info

Berlin—Kreuzberg

ACCOMMODATIONS

Hotel Transit Hagelberger Str 53–54 (U-Mehringdamm) 49–30/789–0470 • gay-friendly • loft-style hotel • some dormitory rooms • also bar • €52-60

BARS

Barbie Bar Mehringdamm 77 49–30/6956–8610 • 4pm-close • lesbians/gay men • lounge • terrace

Bargelb Mehringdamm 62 (U-Mehringdamm) 49–30/7889–9299 • 8pm-close • lesbians/gay men

Bierhimmel Oranienstr 183 (U-Kottbusser Tor) 49–30/615–3122 • 1pm-3am • gay/straight • young crowd

Kumpelnest 3000 Lützowstr 23 (at Potsdamer Str, U-Kurfürstenstr) 49–30/261–6918 • 5pm-5am, till 8am Fri-Sat • popular wknds • gay-friendly • cocktail bar • dancing/DJ • transgender-friendly • young crowd

Mobel Olfe Kottbusser Tor/ Dresden Str (U-Kottbusser Tor) • 6pm-close Wed-Sun • popular • lesbians/gay men

Germany's leading lesbian magazine www.L-mag.de

Roses Oranienstr 187 (at Kottbusser Tor) **49–30/615–6570** • 10pm-close • popular • lesbians/ gay men • transgender-friendly • young crowd

Sonnendeck Erkelenzdamm 47 **49–30/8179–7233** • lesbians/ gay men • more women Tue

NIGHTCLUBS

SchwuZ (SchwulenZentrum) Mehringdamm 61 (enter through Café Sundstroem) **49–30/693–7025** • from 11pm Fri-Sat • mostly gay men • more women 2nd Fri for Subterra • dancing/ DJ • live shows • younger crowd

Serene Bar Schwiebusser Str 2 **49–30/6904–1580** • lesbians/ gay men • popular Girls Bar Th • Girls Dance Sat

SO 36 Oranienstr 190 (at Kottbusser Tor) **49–30/6140–13067, 49–30/6140–1307** • popular • gay/ straight • dancing/DJ • transgender-friendly • live shows • videos • young crowd • wheelchair access • theme nights include Café Fatal (ballroom dancing) & Gayhane (Turkish night)

CAFES

Melitta Sundström Mehringdamm 61 (at Gneisenaustr, U-Mehringdamm) **49–30/692–4414** • 10am-8pm, till 4pm Sat, clsd Sun • lesbians/ gay men • terrace • wheelchair access • also LGBT bookstore

Muvuca Gneisenaustr 2a (at Mehringdamm) **49–30/6390–1756** • 4pm-close • radical/ political int'l cafe • food served

Schoko-Café Mariannenstr 6 (at Kottbusser Tor) **49–30/615–1561, 49–30/694–1077** • 5pm-close • women only • community center • also cafe & bar • Schokodisco 2nd Sat • dancing/DJ • live music • also Hamam steam bath

RESTAURANTS

Abendmahl Muskauer Str 9 (U-Görlitzer Bahnhof) **49–30/612–5170** • 6pm-11:30pm • vegetarian & seafood • also bar (open till 1am) • terrace • wheelchair access

Amrit Oranienstr 200 **49–30/612–5550** • Indian

Kaiserstein Mehringdamm 80 **49–30/7889–5887** • int'l

Locus Marheinekeplatz 4 **49–30/691–5637** • 10am-2am • popular • lesbians/ gay men • Mexican • full bar • lesbian-owned

SUMO Bergmanstr 89 **49–30/6900–4963** • trendy Japanese

EROTICA

Altelier Dos Santos Mehringdamm 119 (U Platz der Luftbrucke) **49–30/6823–7115** • lesbian-owned custom leather & fetish wear

Playstixx Waldemarstrasse 24 **49–30/6165–9500** • makers & sellers of silicone toys for women & lovers

Sexclusivitäten Fürbringer Str 2 **49–30/693–6666** • lesbian sex shop • toys • leather • videos • also escort service

Berlin—Prenzlauer Berg-Mitte

ACCOMMODATIONS

Hotel Transit Loft Greifswalder Str 219 (enter at Immanuelkirchstrasse 14) **49–30/4849–3773** • gay-friendly • loft-style hotel in 19th-c factory • some dormitory rooms • brkfst • also bar • € 19-59

Intermezzo Hotel for Women Gertrud-Kolmar Str 5 (at Brandenburger Tor) **49–30/2248–9096** • women-only • wheelchair access

Kunstlerheim Luise Luisenstr 19 (Mitte) **49–30/284–480** • gay-friendly • former palace w/ rooms re-imagined by local artists • near River Spree • $58 & up

Schall & Rauch Pension Gleimstr 23 (at Schönhauser Allee) **49–30/443–3970, 49–30/448–0770** • lesbians/ gay men • €24-110 • also bar & restaurant

BARS

Besenkammer Bar Rathausstr 1 (at Alexanderplatz, under the S-Bahn bridge) **49–30/242–4083** • 24hrs • lesbians/ gay men • tiny "beer bar"

Cafe Amsterdam Gleimstr 24 (at Schönhauser Allee) **49–30/448–0792, 49–30/231–6796** • 9am-3am, till 5am Fri-Sat • cafe-bar • gay/ straight • transgender-friendly • young crowd • terrace • wheelchair access • also pension • € 60-80

Flax Chodowieckistr 41 (off Greifswalder Str) **49–30/4404–6988, 49–30/441–9856** • 5pm-3am, 3pm-5am Sat, brunch from 10am Sun • lesbians/ gay men

Freizeitheim Schönhauser Allee 57 **49–30/17440–26444** • lesbians/ gay men • more women Th

Marietta Stargarder Str 13 **49–30/4372–0646** • lesbians/ gay men • popular gay night Wed

Offenbar Schreinerstr 5 (U-Samariterstr) **49–30/426–0930** • 10am-4am • lesbians/ gay men • brunch buffet wknds

Reingold Novalisstr 11 (U-Oranienburger Str) **49-30/2838-7676** • gay/ straight • lesbian-owned cocktail lounge

Sonderbar Käthe-Niederkirchner-Str 34 (near Märchenbrunnen) **49-30/4280-6425** • 8pm-8am • lesbians/ gay men • food served • terrace • young crowd • also art gallery

Stiller Don Erich-Weinert-Str 67 (at Schönhauser Allee) **49-17/2182-0168** • 8pm-close • popular • lesbians/ gay men • neighborhood bar • leather • food served

NIGHTCLUBS

Berghain Am Wrietzener (near Ostbahnhof station) • lesbians/ gay men • dancing/ DJ

Cafe Moskau (GMF) Karl-Marx-Allee 34 (U-Schillingstr) • mostly gay men • Sun T-dance

Klub International Karl-Marx-Allee 33 (at Kino International, U-Schillingstr) **49-30/2475-6011** • 11pm-close 1st Sat • lesbians/ gay men • dancing/ DJ • largest gay club in Berlin • cover charge

Sage Club Köpenicker Str 76 (at Brückenstr) **49-30/278-9830** • 11pm-7am Th-Sun • gay/ straight • more gay wknds • dancing/DJ • transgender-friendly

CAFES

Cafe Seidenfaden Dircksenstr 47 (U-Alexanderplatz) **49-30/283-2783** • noon-9pm, clsd Sun • women only • drug- & alcohol-free cafe • info board • nonsmoking

November Husemannstr 15 (at Sredzkistr) **49-30/442-8425** • 9am-2am • lesbians/ gay men • cafe-bar • terrace • brkfst buffet wknds

RESTAURANTS

Drei Lychener Str 30 (U-Eberswalder Str) **49-30/4473-8471** • pan-Asian

Rice Queen Danziger Str 13 (U-Eberswalder Str) **49-30/4404-5800** • Asian

Schall & Rauch Wirtshaus Gleimstr 23 (at Schönhauser Allee) **49-30/443-3970, 49-30/448-0770** • 10am-close • lesbians/ gay men • beer/ wine

Thüringer Stuben Stargarder Str 28 (at Dunckerstr, S/U-Schönhauser Allee) **49-30/4463-3391** • 4pm-1am, from noon wknds • full bar

BOOKSTORES

Ana Koluth Karl Liebknecht Str 13 (at Rosa Luxemburg Str, U-Alexanderplatz) **49-30/2472-6903** • 10am-8pm, till 4pm Sat, clsd Sun • lesbian-owned

EROTICA

Black Style Seelower Str 5 (S/U-Schönhauser Allee) **49-30/4468-8595** • clsd Sun • latex & rubber wear • also mail order

Lustwandel Raumerstr 20 (off Prenzlauer Allee & Danziger Str) **49-30/4404-0860** • lesbian-owned

Berlin—Schöneberg-Tiergarten

ACCOMMODATIONS

Arco Hotel Geisbergstr 30 (at Ansbacherstr, U-Wittenbergplatz) **49-30/235-1480** • gay/ straight • B&B inn • centrally located • kids/ pets ok • wheelchair access • gay-owned • €57-102

Hotel California Kurfürstendamm 35 (at Knesebeckstr, U-Uhlandstr) **49-30/880-120** • gay-friendly • full brkfst • nonsmoking flr • kids ok • €99-199

Hotel Hansablick Flotowstr 6 (at Bachstr, off Str des 17 Juni) **49-30/390-4800** • gay-friendly • full brkfst • kids/ pets ok • €82-120

Hotel Sachsenhof Motzstr 7 (at Nollendorfplatz) **49-30/216-2074** • gay/ straight • centrally located • €51-100

Pension Niebuhr Niebuhrstr 74 (at Savignyplatz) **49-30/324-9595, 49-30/324-9596** • gay/ straight • some shared baths • gay-owned • €40-75

BARS

Heile Welt Motzstr 5 **49-30/2191-7507** • 6pm-close • lesbians/ gay men • food served

Neue Bar Knesebeckstr 16 (at Goethestr) **49-30/3150-3062** • mostly women • dancing/DJ • food served

Neues Ufer Hauptstrasse 157 (U-Bahn Kleistpark) **49-30/784-1578** • 9am-2am, clsd wknds • lesbians/ gay men • older crowd

Together Hohenstauffenstr 53 (off Luther Str, U-Viktoria Luise Platz) **49-30/2191-6300** • lesbians/ gay men

NIGHTCLUBS

KitKat Club 2 Bessemerstr **49-30/2173-6841** • 8pm-close Th, 11pm-6am Fri-Sat • gay/ straight • theme nights • also S/M club

CAFES

Café Berio Maaßenstr 7 (at Winterfeldtstr, U-Nollendorfplatz) **49-30/216-1946** • 8am-1am • popular • int'l • brkfst all day • also bar • seasonal terrace • wheelchair access

Café Savigny Grolmanstr 53–54 (at Savignyplatz) **49-30/312-8195** • 9am-1am • artsy crowd • full bar • terrace

Windows Martin-Luther-Str 22 (at Motzstr, U-Wittenbergplatz) **49-30/214-2384** • 4pm-4am, from 3pm Sun • lesbians/ gay men • full bar • terrace

RESTAURANTS

Art Fasanenstr 81a (at Kantstr, in S-Bahn arches, Charlottenburg, S/U-Zoologischer Garten) **49-30/313-2625** • noon-2am, from 10:30am wknds • lesbians/ gay men • int'l cuisine • also bar • internet access • wheelchair access

Gnadenbrot Martin-Luther-Str 20a • cheap & good

ENTERTAINMENT & RECREATION

Xenon Kino Kolonnenstr 5-6 **49-30/792-8850** • gay & lesbian cinema

SEX CLUBS

Wildwechsel at Ajpnia eV Eisenacher Str 23 (U-Eisenacher Str) **49-30/425-5241** • last Fri only • women only • sex party

Berlin — Outer

ACCOMMODATIONS

Artemisia Women's Hotel Brandenburgischestr 18 (at Konstanzerstr) **49-30/873-8905, 49-30/869-9320** • the only hotel for women in Berlin • a real bargain • quiet rooms • bar • sundeck w/ an impressive view • some shared baths • nonsmoking rooms available • €49-104

Charlottenburger Hof Stuttgarter Platz 14 (at Wilmersdorfer Str) **49-30/329-070** • gay-friendly • centrally located • also Cafe Voltaire • open 24hrs • also bar • €75-160

Hotel Kronprinz Berlin Kronprinzendamm 1 (at Kurfürstendamm, in Halensee) **49-30/896-030** • gay-friendly • kids ok • wheelchair access • €115-250

BARS

Himmelreich Simon Dach Str 36 (off Warschauer Str, in Friedrichshain, U-Frankfurter Tor) **49-30/2936-9292** • from 6pm Mon-Fri, 2pm-close wknds • lesbians/ gay men • women's night Tue

HT Kopernikusstr 23 (in Friedrichshain) **49-30/2900-4965** • 5pm-2am • lesbians/ gay men • food served • terrace

NIGHTCLUBS

Die Busche Mühlenstr 11–12 (at Kurfürstenstr, in Friedrichshain, S/U-Warschauer Str) **49-30/296-0800** • 9:30pm-5am Wed & Sun, 10pm-6am Fri-Sat • popular • lesbians/ gay men • dancing/DJ • live shows • terrace • cover charge • also Kleine (Little) Busche • Warschauer Platz 18

CAFES

Schrader's Malplaquetstr 16b (at Utrechter Str, Wedding) **49-30/4508-2663** • also bar • gay-owned

RESTAURANTS

Cafe Rix Karl-Marx-Str 141 (in Neükolln) **49-30/686-9020** • 10am-5pm • Mediterranean • plenty veggie • also bar • open till 1am

ITALY

Rome

Note: M°=Metro station

INFO LINES & SERVICES

Circolo di Cultura Omosessual Mario Mieli Via Efeso 2a (M° San Paolo) **39-06/541-3985** • 10am-7pm Mon-Fri • switchboard, meetings & discussion groups • women-only club night

CLI (Collegamento Lesbiche Italiano) Via San Francesco di Sales 1/a (in basement of Casa Internazionale delle Donne) **39-06/686-4201** • call for hours • lesbian cultural center & archives • also publish newsletter

ACCOMMODATIONS

58 Le Real de Luxe Via Cavour 58, 4th flr (near Colosseum) **39-06/482-3566** • gay/ straight • B&B inn • hot tub • kids ok • wheelchair access • €75-115

Albergo Del Sole al Pantheon Piazza della Rotonda 63 **39-06/678-0441** • gay-friendly • 4-star hotel • jacuzzi • kids ok

Bologna B&B 6 Piazza Bologna (at Via Sambucuccio D'Alando) **39-06/4424-0244, 39/34781-04781 (CELL)** • gay/ straight • central location • some shared baths • kids/ pets ok • €40-123

Casariccia (near Piazza di Corte)Ariccia **39-06/933-2901** • gay-friendly • 15km outside Rome • 2-bdrm • kitchen • balcony • beautiful views • €600/ week

Domus International 39–06/6889–2918 •
gay/ straight • short-term apt rentals in the
heart of Rome • kids/pets ok • weekly rates

Gayopen B&B Via dello Statuto 44, Apt 18
(at Via Merulana, Piazza Vittorio)
39–06/482–0013 • gay/ straight • B&B • full
brkfst • kids/ pets ok • lesbian & gay-owned •
€45

Hotel Altavilla Via Principe Amedeo 9
39–06/474–1186 • gay-friendly • pets ok • also
bar • €65-220

Hotel Derby Via Vigna Pozzi 7 (Largo delle
Sette Chiese) 39–06/513–4955,
39–06/513–6978 • gay-friendly • small hotel in
heart of Rome • kids/pets ok • wheelchair
access • €91-124

Hotel Eden Via Ludovisi 49 39–06/478–121,
800/543–4300(US#) • gay-friendly • restaurant
& rooftop bar • kids/ pets ok • wheelchair
access • €460-3,600

Hotel Edera Via A Poliziano 75
39–06/7045–3888, 800/448–8355 • gay-
friendly • €103–196

Hotel Scott House Via Gioberti 30
39–06/446–5379 • gay-friendly • €35-88

Loft Colosseum Rione Monti-Colosseum
neighborhood (Piazza degli Zingari)
39–335/720–9383 • gay-friendly • large loft
only 5 minutes from Colosseum & Roman
Forum • kids/ pets ok • $90-190 (from 2-6
people)

Rome

WHERE THE GIRLS ARE:
Discussing politics at a cafe, or
dancing at one of the one-
nighters that make up lesbian
nightlife in Rome. Visit the
Coordinamento Lesbiche Italiano
center, the bulletin board at the
Libreria Babele, or the Circolo
Mario Mieli center for the latest
events.

LGBT PRIDE:
June/July.

ANNUAL EVENTS:
August-September - Gay Village,
web: www.gayvillage.it.
May - Maratona Gay/Lesbian
Festival.

CITY INFO:
Comune di Rome 39-06/90.63.00,
web: www.comune.roma.it
Enjoy Rome 39–6/445.18.43, web:
www.enjoyrome.com. Via
Marghera 8a.

WEATHER:
Late summer is hot and humid.
Winter is mild but rainy. The best
times to visit Rome are late
spring and early fall.

TRANSIT:
Taxi stands are located in several
popular piazzas. Only hire official
yellow or white taxis. You can
also call 3570 for pick-up service.
ATAC general info: 800/431.784 (in
Rome), tourist lines: 39-
06/46.95.22.52, web:
www.atac.roma.it.

ATTRACTIONS:
Baths of Caracalla 39–06/575.86.26
Campo dei Fiori
Capitoline Museums
39–06/399.678.00, web:
museicapitolini.org
Colosseum 39–06/399.677.00
Galleria Borghese 39–06/32.81.01,
web: galleriaborghese.it
Pantheon 39–06/6830.0230
Roman Forum 39–06/699.01.10
Spanish Steps
St. Peter's
Trevi Fountain
The Vatican and Vatican Museums
(includes National Etruscan
Museum, Sistine Chapel, and
Raphael Rooms)
39–06/698.833.33, web:
www.vatican.va.

Nicolas Inn Via Cavour 295 (at Via dei Serpenti) **39-06/9761-8483** • gay-friendly • elegant rooms located near the Colosseum & Roman Forum • owned/ operated by native English speaker • €90-150

Pensione Ottaviano Via Ottaviano 6 **39-06/3973-7253, 39-06/3973-8138** • gay-friendly • in quiet area near St Peter's Square • shared/ private rooms • €12-35

Rainbow B&B Via Accademia Ambrosiana 41 (at Via Leonri) **39-34/8710-8320** • gay-friendly • penthouse condo w/ great view • gay-owned • €64/ night, €390-600/ week

Roman Reference Via dei Capocci 94 **39-06/4890-3612** • gay-friendly • apts • kids ok

Sandy Hostel Via Cavour 136 **39-06/488-4585** • gay-friendly • great location near Colosseum, Roman Forum & Spanish Steps • €12-35

Scalinata di Spagna Piazza Trinità dei Monti 17 (M° Piazza di Spagna) **39-06/6994-0896, 39-06/679-3006 (BOOKING #)** • gay-friendly • roof garden • kids/ pets ok • €150-420

Valadier Via della Fontanella 15 **39-06/361-1998, 800/448-8355** • gay-friendly • 4-star hotel • kids ok • 2 restaurants & piano bar • €110-750

Villa Appennini 32 Via Appennini **39-06/855-1262** • gay/ straight • €52-83

BARS

Coming Out Via San Giovanni in Laterano 8 (near Colosseum) **39-06/700-9871** • 5pm-5am • popular • lesbians/ gay men • transgender-friendly • food served • live music Th • karaoke • movies Sun • lesbian-owned

Garbo Vicolo di Santa Margherita 1a (in Trastevere, Tram 8) **39-06/5832-0782, 39-06/581-6700** • 10pm-3am, clsd Mon • lesbians/ gay men • cocktail bar • food served • gay-owned

Matisse Via Montebello 68 **39-347/949-2601** • 9pm-2am, till 4am Fri-Sat, clsd Mon • lesbians/ gay men • dancing/DJ • food served • karaoke • young crowd • music videos & films shown

Shelter Via dei Vascellari 36 (in Trastevere, Tram 8) **39-06/588-0862** • 8pm-4am • lesbians/ gay men • transgender-friendly • cocktail bar • food served • live shows • private club

Side Meeting Point Via Pietro Verri 1 (near Colosseum) **39-348/692-9472** • 7pm-close • popular • lesbians/ gay men • dancing/DJ • food served • live shows • internet access • young crowd

Voice Via dei Conciatori 7/c (M° Piramide) **39-06/5728-8530** • 10pm-close Wed • women-only • dancing/ DJ

NIGHTCLUBS

L' Alibi Via di Monte Testaccio 40-44 (M° Piramide) **39-06/574-3448** • 11pm-4am, clsd Mon-Tue • popular • lesbians/ gay men • dancing/DJ • live shows • rooftop garden in summer • young crowd

Black Betty Via degli Aurunci 35, at Baltic (in San Lorenzo district) **39-06/347-244-5810** • 11pm-close Tue only • popular • lesbians/ gay men • dancing/DJ • "the gay side of R'n'B" • live entertainment

Coq Madame Via dei Lucani 22b (near the Atlantide Inn) • 10pm-close, last Fri • lesbians/ gay men • dancing/DJ • bears • live show

Frutta e Verdura Via Placido Zurla 68-70 (in Casilina) **39-347/879-7063, 39-348/450-0686** • from 5am Fri-Sat & public holiday eves • lesbians/ gay men • dancing/DJ

Muccassassina Via di Portonaccio 212 **39-06/541-3985** • 10:30pm-5am Fri only (Sept-June) • popular • lesbians/ gay men • dancing/DJ • karaoke • live shows • young crowd • cover charge • location changes so call ahead

CAFES

Oppio Café Via delle Terme di Titi 72 **39-06/474-5262, 39-347/510-8594 (CELL)** • brkfst, lunch & dinner • open 24hrs in Aug • popular • lesbians/ gay men • full bar • live shows • terrace w/ great view

RESTAURANTS

Asinocotto Ristorante Via dei Vascellari 48 (in Travestere, Tram 8) **39-06/589-8985, 212/858-5771 (US RESERVATIONS FAX LINE)** • lunch & dinner, clsd Mon • creative gourmet Mediterranean • reservations required • gay-owned

La Cicala e la Formica Via Leonina 17 **39-06/481-7490** • 7pm-midnight, clsd Sun

Ditirambo Piazza della Cancelleria 74-75 (near Campo dei Fiori) **39-06/687-1626**

Gelateria San Crispino Via Panetteria 42 (near Trevi Fountain) • gelato!

Jeliel Vicolo Montevecchio 8 (Plaza Navona) 39-06/6880-7025 • noon-1am • Italian • large pizza selection

Le Sorellastre 1 Via San Francesco de Sales 39-06/718-5288, 39-06/686-4201 • 7pm-2am, clsd Sun-Mon • women only

Taverna del Campo Campo dei Fiori 16 39-06/687-4402 • lunch & dinner • bruschetteria • plenty veggie

La Taverna di Edoardo II Vicolo Margana 14 39-06/6994-2419 • 7pm-12:30am, clsd Tue • lesbians/ gay men • full bar • wheelchair access

BOOKSTORES

Al Tempo Ritrovato Via dei Fienaroli 31d 39-06/581-7724 • 10am-8pm, from 3pm Mon, clsd Sun • women's • some lesbian & English titles • bulletin board

La Libreria Babele Via dei Banchi Vecchi 116 39-06/687-6628 • 10am-7:30pm, clsd Sun • LGBT • some English titles

Queer Via del Boschetto 25 (at Via Nazionale) 39-06/474-0691 • 9:30am-7:30pm, from 2:30pm Mon, clsd Sun • LGBT • also videos • pride items • T-shirts • cards & gadgets

Rinascita Via delle Botteghe Oscure 2 39-06/679-7460 • large LGBT section

PUBLICATIONS

Aut 39-06/541-3985 • monthly magazine w/ news & event listings • free around Rome

GYMS & HEALTH CLUBS

Balnea Club Via dei Pescatori 495a 39-06/335-800-9714 • Roman-style sauna • women-only 2nd Sat of month • private club

EROTICA

La Bancarella di Andy Capp Piazza Alessandria 2 (near Porta Pia, M° Repubblica) 39-06/853-0371 • erotic comics & LGBT magazines

Studio Know How Via di San Gallicano 13 39-06/5833-5692

NETHERLANDS

AMSTERDAM

Amsterdam is divided into 5 regions:

Amsterdam—Overview

INFO LINES & SERVICES

COC Amsterdam Rozenstraat 14 (in the Jordaan) 31-20/626-3087 • info line 10am-5pm, also cafe 8pm-11:30pm Wed-Fri • popular women-only disco every Sat 11pm-4am

Gay/ Lesbian Switchboard 31-20/623-6565 • noon-10pm, 4pm-8pm wknds • English spoken

Pink Point Westermarkt (in the Jordaan by Homomonument) • noon-6pm • info on Homomonument & general LGBT info • friendly volunteers • queer souvenirs & gifts

SAD-Schorerstichting PC Hoofstraat 5 31-20/573-9444 • resource center for queer health & well-being • info line (662-4206) 10am-4pm Mon-Fri

SOA 31-900/204-2040 (€.10 PER MINUTE) • 2pm-10pm Mon-Fri • 24hr automated info • HIV plus-line (31-20-685-0055)

Het Vrouwenhuis Nieuwe Herengracht 95 31-20/625-2066 • women's center & library • bulletin board • cultural events • internet access • bar at night

Wild Side 31-71/512-8632 • women's S/M support group • meetings, events & play parties • meets at COC

ACCOMMODATIONS

AmsterdamApartment Korte Lijnbaanssteeg 1 31-6/5024-7940 (CELL), 31-6/1656-2002 (CELL) • gay-friendly • short-term & long-term stay apts around Amsterdam • €80/ night – 3,500/ month

Country & Lake IJsselmeerdijk 26, Warder 31-299/372-190, 31-299/372-295 • gay/ straight • 2 beautiful apts in countryside 15 miles outside Amsterdam • one lakeview apt • €98-149 (3-night minimum)

Simply Amsterdam Apartments 31-20/620-6608 • gay-friendly • apts, studios, canal houses & houseboat • jacuzzi • kids/ pets ok • gay-owned • €120-280

ENTERTAINMENT & RECREATION

The Anne Frank House Prinsengracht 267 (in the Jordaan) 31-20/556-7100, 31-20/556-7105 (INFO TAPE) • the final hiding place of Amsterdam's most famous resident • €7.50

Boom Chicago Leidseplein 12 (Leidseplein Theater) 31–20/423–0101 (TICKET BOOKING) • English-language improvisational comedy • also dinner & drinks service • also distributes free *Boom!* magazine to Amsterdam for Americans • €18-20 (not including dinner or drinks)

Homomonument Westermarkt (in the Jordaan) • moving sculptural tribute to lesbians & gays killed by Nazis

Oxygen Bike Tours 31–6/1992–8556 • lesbians/ gay men • bike tours in & around Amsterdam • day trips

De Pijp near Albert Cuypmarkt • gay-friendly neighborhood teeming w/ lots of interesting shops & restaurants

The van Gogh Museum Paulus Potterstr 7 (on the Museumplein) 31–20/570–5200 • 10am-6pm, till 10pm Fri • a must-see museum dedicated to this Dutch master painter • €9

PUBLICATIONS

Boom! Leidseplein 12 31–20/530–7306 (OFFICE) • free magazine from the Boom Chicago comedy team • helpful & irreverent • geared toward the young American traveler • published 4 times per year

COC Update 31–20/623–4596 • news & events calendar for COC

Expreszo 31–20/623–4596 • for LGBT youth (in Dutch)

De GAY Krant 31–499/39–10–00 • nat'l LGBT newspaper in Dutch w/ English summaries

Gay News Amsterdam 31–20/679–1556 • bilingual paper • extensive listings

Gay & Night 31–20/625–5364 • free monthly bilingual entertainment paper w/ club listings

Squeeze 31–20/584–9020

SPIRITUAL GROUPS

Beit Ha Chidush Nieuwe Uilenburgerstraat 91 (at Uilenburgsynagoge) 31–20/422–8383, 31–20/776–5969 • queer Jewish group • monthly Friday services & Shabbat meals • weekly Torah study

CHJC Postbus 14722, 1001 LE 31–6/5323–4516 (CELL) • social group for lesbian & gay Christians

Stichting Dignity Nederland Spaarndammerstraat 460c 31–20/618–3164 • 2nd Sun 3pm worship

Amsterdam—Centrum

ACCOMMODATIONS

Amsterdam Central B&B Oudebrugsteeg 6-II (Warmoesstraat) 31–62/445–7593 • lesbians/ gay men • gay-owned • cozy B&B apts near main gay area & train station • full brkfst • €75-95

Amsterdam Escape Geldersekade 106 (at Centrum) 800/216–7295 (RESERVATIONS), 31–65/389–5642 (INFO) • gay/ straight • luxury apts & canal houses • €99-1,150

Bob's Youth Hostel Nieuwezijds Voorburgwal 92 31–20/623–0063 • women's, men's & mixed dorms • brkfst included • younger crowd • 3am curfew • €18

Bulldog Oudezijds Voorburgwal 220 31–20/620-3822 • gay-friendly • hostel in heart of Red Light District • no groups of over 5 men • dorms & private rms • brkfst included • coffeeshop & lounge/ bar • no lockout or curfew • €22-26 & €77-85 (private rms)

Cosmos Hostel Nieuwe nieuwstraat 17-1 31–20/625–2438 • gay-friendly • hostel in 17th-c bldg formerly a hotel • internet • no curfew • €27-35 (dorm) & €75 (rms)

Crowne Plaza Amsterdam City Centre NZ Voorburgwal 5 31–20/620–0500, 800/227–6936 (US#) • gay-friendly • swimming • wheelchair access • €305-335

NH City Centre Hotel Spuistraat 288–292 31–20/420–4545 • gay-friendly • kids/ pets ok • wheelchair access • €119-215

NH Grand Hotel Krasnapolsky Dam 9 31–20/554–9111 • gay-friendly • full-service hotel • in the city center opposite Royal Palace • business center • 5 restaurants • wheelchair access • €179-475

Stayokay Amsterdam Stadsdoelen Kloveniersburgwal 97 31–20/624–6832 • gay-friendly • hostel • in canal house in city center • dorm-style • €18.50-22.50

Victoria Hotel Amsterdam Damrak 1-5 (opposite Centraal Station) 31–20/623–4255, 800/814–70000 • gay-friendly • 4-star hotel • swimming • gym • restaurants • bar • wheelchair access • €265-505

Winston Hotel Warmoesstraat 129 31–20/623–1380 • gay-friendly • hipster hotel • rockers & artists • popular bar • live DJs • gallery • some shared baths • €60-90

BARS

De Barderij Zeedijk 14 31–20/420–5132 • 4pm-1am, till 3am Fri-Sat • mostly gay men • large neighborhood bar/ brown café

Getto Warmoesstraat 51 **31–20/421–5151** • 4pm-1am, from 7pm Tue, 1pm-midnight Sun • popular • lesbians/ gay men • women only 2nd Mon • live DJs • Tarot readings Sun • also restaurant till 11pm • Sun brunch • some veggie • €11-15

Vrankrijk Spuistraat 216 • gay/ straight • rowdy squat bar • alternative • more gay Mon

CAFES

Dampkring Handboogstr 29 (at Heiligeweg) **31–20/638–0705** • smoking coffeeshop • great fresh OJ

Gary's Late Night Reguliersdwarsstr 53 **31–20/420–2406** • noon-3am, til 4am Fri-Sat • popular • fresh muffins & bagels • organic fair-trade coffee

Puccini Staalstraat 17 **31–(0)20/626–5474** • If you love chocolate, do we have a cafe for you! (clsd Sun-Mon)

Rokerij Singel 8 **31–20/422–6643** • 1 of 4 smoking coffeeshops

RESTAURANTS

Cafe de Jaren Nieuwe Doelenstraat 20-22 **31–20/625–5771** • 10am-1am, till 2am Fri & Sat • int'l • some veggie • full bar • terrace • young crowd • cash only

Café de Schutter Voetboogstraat 13 (upstairs) **31–20/622–4608** • dinner (kitchen: 6pm-10:30pm) • popular local hangout • plenty veggie • full bar • terrace

Café Latei Zeedijk 143 (in Red Light District) **31–20/625–7485** • 8am-5pm, from 9am Sat, from 11am Sun • brkfst & lunch • great coffee hangout • everything you see you can buy, too

Amsterdam

LGBT PRIDE:
1st wknd in August, web: www.amsterdampride.nl.

ANNUAL EVENTS:
February - Carnaval. It's not Rio de Janeiro, but it's still fun
April 30 - Queen's Birthday
May 4-5 - Memorial Day & Liberation Day
June - Holland Festival
August - Heart's Day. Drag festival in the Red Light District
October - Leather Pride, web: www.leatherpride.nl.

CITY INFO:
VVV 0900/400-4040 (€.55 per minute). Visit their office directly opposite Centraal Station. Netherlands Board of Tourism, web: www.holland.com.

WEATHER:
Temperatures hover around freezing in the winter and rise to the mid-60°s in the summer. Rain is possible year-round.

TRANSIT:
31–20/677-7777.
Can also be found at taxi stands on the main squares.
KLM Bus.
GVB 0900-9292 (€.50 per minute), web: www.gvb.nl, or visit their office across from the Centraal Station (Stationsplein 10). Trams, buses & subway.

ATTRACTIONS:
Anne Frank House 31–20/556-7105, web: www.annefrank.org
Hermitage Amsterdam 31-20/530-8755, web: www.hermitage.nl
Homomonument
Jewish Historical Museum 31–20/626-9945, web: www.jhm.nl
Rembrandt House 31–20/520-0400
Rijksmuseum 31–20/674-7047, web: www.rijksmuseum.nl
Stedelijk Museum of Modern Art 31–20/573-2737, web: www.stedelijk.nl
Vincent van Gogh Museum 31–20/570-5252, web: www.vangoghmuseum.nl.

Reply Forward Delete

Date: Dec 12, 2005 16:58:12
From: Girl-on-the-Go
To: Editor@Damron.com
Subject: Amsterdam

>The day that Amsterdam is known as the *Lesbian* and Gay Capital of Europe, there will be a lot of "loud and proud" women-loving-women walking around. Until then, you're really going to have to search hard to find them.

>For the sad truth is that most Dutch dykes hold back more than just water. Still, we encourage you to keep the faith—not all Dutch girls are as straight-laced as they seem.

>In fact, just looking back over three centuries of dyke drama, there's reason to believe it's only a matter of time before the riot grrrls take Amsterdam. Way back in 1792, the jealous, murderous Bartha Schuurman was hung from the gallows for knifing her girl-friend's lover to death. In the 1970s, lesbian activists—in between scrawling pro-dyke graffiti—did manage to squat a few places and start some women's collectives. In fact, many of the women's establishments enjoyed today—ranging from bars to bookshops—emerged directly as a result of that era when Dutch dykes did indeed get mad and got rad.

>Until the spirit of those good ol' days returns, lesbian visitors can enjoy a pleasant time—if you can stand the ubiquitous cloud of smoke—at most of the gay establishments and the handful of lesbian and lesbian-welcoming bars and clubs like **Café Sappho** and **Saarein 2**. And one thing they definitely can share with those naughty Dutch boys is Amsterdam's largely tolerant atmosphere—just how tolerant is something that the people of Amsterdam are currently hashing out. (No pun intended.)

Cock & Feathers Zeedijk 23-25
31–20/624–3141 • 5pm-1am, till 3am Fri-Sat •
Dutch cuisine • also bar • mostly gay men

Dolores opposite NZ Voorburgwal 289
31–20/620–3302 • 11am-8pm, from noon Sun
(till 1am Th & 3am Fri-Sat in summers) •
organic burgers (veggie too) & other snacks;
small space w/ some outside tables

Green Planet Spuistraat 122
31–20/625–8280 • 11am-midnight (kitchen till
10:30pm), clsd Sun • vegetarian/ vegan • eat
w/ your cleanest conscience ever—everything
is organic, even the power (take-out packaging
is biodegradable))

Greenwoods Singel 103 (near Dam Square)
31–20/623–7071 • English-style brkfst & tea
snacks

Reply **Forward** **Delete**

>While you're out and about, experience a little of Amsterdam's touted counterculture for yourself...stop in at one of the famous "smoking coffeeshops."

>To find out what queer events are going on about town, or just to take a break from sight-seeing, stop by the **COC** center/cafe. Or head over to the women's bookstore **Xantippe Unlimited,** the LGBT bookstore **Vrolijk,** or the **American Book Center** to pick up some flyers, the local newspapers **Gay News Amsterdam** and **De GAY Krant,** the scene guide **Gay & Night**, and copies of the gay-friendly monthly calendar **Day By Day** and the quarterly entertainment guide **Boom!**

>Have a meal at one of the lesbian-friendly restaurants in town. Try **La Strada, Camp Café, Café De Jaren** or **'t Sluisje** (if you like your steak served by drag queens).

>At night, hang out with the lipstick femmes and cute baby dykes at **Vivelavie.** Later, hit the dance floor at the "trendy dancebar for gays and lesbos," **You II.** Don't miss the weekly women-only party at the **COC** nightclub on Saturdays.

>There are a number of popular mixed bars, including the hip **Getto** and **Mix Café.** The big gay clubs are **iT** and **Exit.**

>If you're looking for a different kind of "culture," don't miss the incredible masterworks this city's museums have to offer. (There is even an entire museum dedicated to van Gogh, and Russia's unparalleled Hermitage Museum has just opened an annex in Amsterdam.) One very Amsterdam-esque way to see them is to take the "Museum Boat" (www.lovers.nl) along the canal from museum to museum. The fare entitles you to discounted admissions.

Hemelse Modder Oude Waal 9-11 **31–20/624–3203** • 6pm-10pm, clsd Mon • popular w/ lesbians & gay men • French/ int'l • also full bar • wheelchair access • gay-owned

Krua Thai Staalstraat 22 **31–20/622–9533** • 6pm-10:30pm, clsd Sun-Mon • Thai • terrace • wheelchair access • also at Spuistraat 90a, 620-0623 • full bar

La Strada NZ Voorburgwal 93-95 **31–20/625–0276** • 4pm-1am, till 2am wknds • popular • food served till 10pm • Mediterranean • plenty veggie • full bar • terrace • lesbian-owned

Het Land van Walem Keizersgracht 449 **31–20/625–3544** • 10am-10:30pm • int'l • inexpensive • local crowd • canalside terrace • wheelchair access • lesbian-owned

Maoz Reguliersbreestraat 45 **31–20/624–9290**

Pygma-lion Nieuwe Spiegelstraat 5a (in Spiegelhof Arcade) **31–20/420–7022** • 11am-11pm, clsd Mon • South African cuisine • exotic meats & several veggie dishes • gay-owned/ run

't Sluisje Torensteeg 1 **31–20/624–0813** • 6pm-close, clsd Mon-Tue • popular steak house • transgender-friendly • full bar (open later) • drag shows nightly

Song Kwae Kloveniersburgwal 14a (near Nieuwmarkt & Chinatown) **31–20/624–2568** • 1pm-10:30pm • Thai • full bar • terrace

Bookstores

The American Book Center Kalverstraat 185 (at Heiligeweg) **31–20/625–5537** • 10am-8pm, till 9pm Th, 11am-6:30pm Sun • books & magazines in English imported from US & UK • large LGBT section • wheelchair access

Boekhandel Vrolijk Gay & Lesbian Bookshop Paleisstraat 135 (near Dam Square) **31–20/623–5142** • 10am-6pm, till 7pm Th, 11am-6pm Mon, 10am-5pm Sat, from 1pm Sun • LGBT books, videos & gadgets • also mail order

Retail Shops

Conscious Dreams Kokopelli Warmoesstr 12 **31–20/421–7000** • 11am-10pm • popular • "smart warehouse" • internet

Magic Mushroom Spuistraat 249 **31–20/427–5765** • 11am-7pm, till 8pm Fri-Sat • "smartshop": magic mushrooms & more • also Singel 524, 31-20/422-7845

Gyms & Health Clubs

The Garden Gym Jodenbreestraat 158 **31–20/626–8772** • health club • women very welcome

Splash Looiersgracht 26-30 **31–20/624–8404** • gym & wellness center • classes from pilates to yoga • massage

Erotica

Absolute Danny Oudezijds Achterburgwal 78 (in the Red Light District) **31–20/421–0915** • 11am-9pm, till 8pm wknds • upscale erotica • woman-owned

DeMask Zeedijk 64 **31–20/620–5603** • 10am-7pm, till 9pm Th, from 11am Sat, noon-5pm Sun • rubber & leather clothing

Female & Partners Spuistraat 100 **31–20/620–9152** • 11am-6pm, till 9pm Th, 1pm-6pm Sun • fashions & toys for women • also mail order

Amsterdam—Jordaan

Accommodations

Amsterdam B&B Barangay **31–6/2504–5432** • gay/ straight • 1777 town house • near tourist attractions • full brkfst • nonsmoking • gay-owned • €69-129

Amsterdam Lodge Eerste Boomdwarsstraat 10-I (at Westerstraat) **31–65/238–3920** • gay-friendly • B&B • kids ok • nonsmoking • €90-115

Blakes Keizersgracht 384 **31–20/530–2010** • gay-friendly • sleep in high style • 41 rms designed by London hotelier Anouska Hempe • also restaurant • high tea Sun • €250-400

The Brownstone B&B Rozengracht 158 **31–20/612–9320** • gay-friendly • turn-of-the-century bldg • nonsmoking • quiet hours 9pm-9am • gay-owned • €89+ (2-night minimum) • also apts from €135

Budget Hotel Clemens Amsterdam Raadhuisstraat 39 (at Herengracht) **31–20/624–6089** • gay-friendly • small hotel in Amsterdam's center • some shared baths • woman-owned/ run • €55-155

Canal Apartments Lijnbaansgracht 55 **31–20/626–4532, 877/283–7540 (US#)** • gay-friendly • studio, 1-bdrm & 2-bdrm apts • close to city center • €95 (night) – 599 (week)

En Suite Apartment Keizersgracht 320 **31–20/421–1887, 31–6/5234–3256 (CELL)** • gay-friendly • apt in historic 1675 canal house • fully equipped kitchen • €150-195 (2-night minimum)

Hotel Acacia Lindengracht 251 **31–20/622–1460** • gay-friendly • "homey hotel in heart of Jordaan" • also self-catering studios & houseboat • €65-130

Hotel Brian Singel 69 **31–20/624–4661** • gay-friendly • cheap & no frills but friendly • shared baths • €35-125 (5 beds)

Hotel New Amsterdam Herengracht 13-19 **31–20/522–2345** • gay-friendly • "the quiet hotel" • internet • €80-140

Hotel Pulitzer Prinsengracht 315–331 **31–20/523–5235** • gay-friendly • occupies 24 17th-c buildings on 2 of Amsterdam's most picturesque canals • €215-1,000

Maes B&B Herenstraat 26 hs **31–20/427–5165** • gay/ straight • nonsmoking • gay-owned • €95-285

Marnixkade Canalview Apartments
31-6/1012-1296 • popular • gay/ straight •
fully furnished apts in 19th-c canal house on a
quiet canal in heart of Jordaan • nonsmoking •
gay-owned • €110-150

Palace Rainbow Hotel Raadhuisstr 33
31-20/626-7086 • gay-friendly • centrally
located near the Homomonument • some
shared baths

Rembrandt Residence Hotel Herengracht
255 31-20/622-1727 • gay/ straight •
canalside hotel near Dam Square •
nonsmoking rooms available • €65-225

Sleep Happy Marnixstraat 198-II • gay-
friendly • renovated apt w/ kitchen • canal
views • can sleep up to 4 • €90-119 (cash
only)

Sunhead of 1617 Herengracht 152 (at
Leliegracht & Raadshuisstraat)
31-20/626-1809 • gay/ straight • B&B • full
brkfst • kids/ pets ok • nonsmoking • also 7
canal apts • gay-owned • €95-139

The Townhouse B&B Akoleienstraat 2
31-20/612-9320 • gay-friendly • in 19th-c
town house • nonsmoking • quiet hours 9pm-
9am • gay-owned • €99-125

Bars

Café de Gijs Lindengracht 249
31-20/638-0740 • 4pm-1am • 1st Wed of
month hosts T&T, social gathering for
transvestites & transsexuals, from 10pm •
trans-friendly rest of the time, too

Saarein 2 Elandsstraat 119 31-20/623-4901
• 5pm-1am, till 3am Fri-Sat, clsd Mon • mostly
women • food served • brown cafe

Nightclubs

COC Rozenstraat 14 31-20/626-3087 •
10pm-5am Fri • lesbians/ gay men •
dancing/DJ • women only 10pm-4am 2nd &
4th Sat (mostly women other Sats) •
multicultural disco 8pm-2am Sun • call for
many other parties/ events • cover charge

de Trut Bilderdijkstraat 165 31-20/612-3524
• 11pm-4am Sun only • lesbians/ gay men •
hip underground dance party in legalized
squat • alternative • young crowd

Cafes

Backstage Boutique & Coffee-Corner
Utrechtsedwarsstraat 67 31-20/622-3638 •
10am-6pm, clsd Sun • very kitschy lunchroom/
knitwear shop

Café Legendz Kinkerstraat 45
31-20/683-8513 • 8am-1am, till 3am Fri, from
11am Sat, clsd Sun • students by day, goths by
night

Café 't Smalle Egelantiersgracht 12
31-20/623-9617 • 10am-1pm • brown cafe •
full bar • outdoor seating

Reibach Brouwersgracht 139
31-20/626-7708 • 10am-6pm, from 11am Sun
• lunchroom • great brkfst • artsy crowd • gay-
owned

Rokerij Singel 8 31-20/422-6643 • 1 of 4
smoking coffeeshops

Tops Prinsengracht 480 31-20/627-3436 •
smoking coffeeshop & internet cafe

Restaurants

Bojo Lange Leidsedwarsstraat 49-51 (near
Leidseplein) 31-20/622-7434 • 4pm-2am, til
4am Fri-Sat, from noon wknds • popular •
Indonesian

De Bolhoed Prinsengracht 60 (at Tuinstr)
31-20/626-1803 • noon-10pm • vegetarian/
vegan

Burger's Patio 2e Tuindwarsstr 12
31-20/623-6854 • Italian • plenty veggie

Foodism Oude Leliestraat 8 31-20/427-5103
• 10:30am-10:30pm • brkst, lunch & dinner •
great soups & sandwiches • funky & fun

Granada Leidsekruisstraat 13
31-20/625-1073 • 5pm-close, clsd Tue •
Spanish • tapas • also bar • live music wknds

't Swarte Schaep Korte Leidsedwarsstraat
24 (near Leidseplein) 31-20/622-3021 •
noon-11pm • French

Vijf Prinsenstraat 10 31-20/428-2455 • 6pm-
10pm • lesbians/ gay men

De Vliegende Schotel Nieuwe Leliestraat
162 31-20/625-2041 • 4pm-11:30pm, kitchen
till 10:45pm, so come early • vegetarian & fish
• some vegan • nonsmoking section

Entertainment & Recreation

De Looier Art & Antiques Centre
Elandsgracht 109 31-20/624-9038 • 11am-
5pm, clsd Fri

Bookstores

Vrouwenindruk Westermarkt 5
31-20/624-5003 • 11am-6pm, till 5pm Sat,
clsd Sun-Mon • antiquarian & secondhand
books by & about women • also LGBT

Xantippe Unlimited Prinsengracht 290
31-20/623-5854 • 10am-7pm, till 6pm Sat,
noon-Sun, 1pm-7pm Mon • women's
bookstore • lesbian section • English titles •
lesbian-owned

RETAIL SHOPS

ClubWearHouse Spuistraat 250 (near Dam Square) 31–20/622-8766 • 11am-7pm, till 9pm Th, 1pm-6pm Sun-Mon • clothing • club tickets & flyers

Dare to Wear Buiten Oranjestraat 15 31–20/686-8679 • 11:30am-7:30pm, from 1pm Mon, clsd Sun • piercing, jewelry & accessories

House of Tattoos Haarlemmerdijk 130c 31–20/330-9046 • 11am-6pm, from noon Sun • great tattoos, great people

Lust for Leather Lindengracht 220 31–20/627-0778 • open Sat, appointment only • hip showroom • day & fetish wear

EROTICA

Black Body Lijnbaansgracht 292 (across from Rijksmuseum) 31–20/626-2553 • clsd Sun • rubber clothing specialists • leather • toys • wheelchair access

Amsterdam — Rembrandtplein

ACCOMMODATIONS

Amsterdam House 's Gravelandseveer 3-4 31–20/626-2577 & 624–6607 (HOTEL), 800/618-1008 (US#) • gay-friendly • 16-room hotel, 16 comfortably furnished apts & 10 lovely houseboats • €75 (hotel), €115+ (apt), €155+ (houseboat)

Best Western Eden Hotel Amstel 144 31–20/530-7878 • gay-friendly • 3-star hotel • nonsmoking rooms • brasserie overlooking River Amstel • wheelchair access • €125-195

Dikker & Thijs Fenice Hotel Prinsengracht 444 (at Leidsestraat) 31–20/620-1212 • gay-friendly • 4-star hotel on canal • nonsmoking rooms • bar & restaurant • €115-345

Hotel de l'Europe Nieuwe Doelenstraat 2-8 31–20/531-1777 • gay-friendly • grand hotel on the River Amstel • fitness center • swimming • €285-960

Hotel Monopole Amstel 60 31–20/624-6271 • gay-friendly • centrally located • nonsmoking rooms available • kids ok • €55-225 • also Cafe Rouge, 31-20/420–9881 • open 5pm-1am, till 3am Fri-Sat • mostly gay men

Hotel Orlando Prinsengracht 1099 (at Amstel River) 31–20/638-6915 • gay-friendly • beautifully restored 17th-c canal house • gay-owned • €70-130

Hotel Waterfront Singel 458 31–20/421-6621 • gay-friendly • rms & studios • brkfst • located in city's center • €95-150

ITC Hotel Prinsengracht 1051 (at Utrechtsestraat) 31–20/623-0230 • lesbians/ gay men • 18th-c canal house • great location • also bar & lounge • lesbian & gay-owned • €55-130

Jolly Hotel Carlton Vijzelstraat 4 31–20/622-2266 • gay-friendly • overlooking the famous flower market & Munt Tower • €115-310

Seven Bridges Reguliersgracht 31 31–20/623-1329 • gay-friendly • small & so elegant • canalside w/ view of 7 bridges (surprise!) • brkfst brought to you • €100-190

BARS

April Reguliersdwarsstraat 37 (at Rembrandtplein) 31–20/625-9572 • 2pm-1am, till 3am Fri-Sat • popular happy hour • mostly gay men • 3 bars • videos

ARC Reguliersdwarsstraat 44 31–20/689-7070 • 4pm-1am, till 3am Fri-Sat • gay/ straight • dancing/ DJ • hip 20-something crowd • also restaurant

The Back Door Cafe Amstelstraat 28-30 (beneath Back Door nightclub) 31–20/620-2333 • 6pm-1am, till 3am Fri-Sat, clsd Mon-Tue • gay/ straight • neighborhood bar • great cocktails • gay-owned

Café Sappho Vijzelstraat 103 31–20/423-1509 • 3pm-1am, till 3am Sat, clsd Mon • women's pub but men welcome • women-only Fri • DJs Fri-Sat

Entre-Nous Halvemaansteeg 14 (at Rembrandtplein) 31–20/623-1700 • 8pm-3am, till 4am Fri-Sat • lesbians/ gay men • neighborhood bar

Exit Café Reguliersdwarsstraat 42 31–20/625-8788 • 11am-4am, till 5am Fri-Sat • mostly gay men • upscale • part of 4-bar Exit complex

Habibi Ana Lange Leidsedwarsstraat 4-6 31–06/620-1788 • 7pm-1am, till 3am Fri-Sat • lesbians/ gay men • Arabian clientele • Arabian & int'l music • bellydancing shows wknds

Hot Spot Café Amstel 102 31–20/622-8335 • 8pm-3am, till 4am Fri-Sat

Mankind Weteringstraat 60 31–20/638-4755 • noon-midnight, clsd Sun • mostly gay men • canalside terrace • food served till 8pm • Dutch/ English

Mix Cafe Amstel 50 31–20/420-3388 • popular • 8pm-3am, till 4am Fri-Sat • lesbians/ gay men

Punto Latino Reguliersdwarsstraat 49 (gay entrance on right) • 8pm-3am, till 4am Fri-Sat • gay/ straight • dancing/DJ • Latino/a clientele

Soho Reguliersdwarsstraat 36 **31–20/330-4400** • 8pm-3am, till 4am Fri-Sat • popular • lesbians/ gay men • 2 flrs • young crowd • British pub 1st flr, American-style lounge upstairs • happy hour midnight-1am

Vivelavie Amstelstraat 7 (at Rembrandtplein) **31–20/624-0114** • 3pm-1am, till 3am Fri-Sat • mostly women

NIGHTCLUBS

The Back Door Amstelstraat 32 (near Rembrandtplein) **31–20/620-2333** • clsd Mon-Tue & Th • T-dance 10pm-4am Sun • mostly gay men • dancing/DJ • food served • gay-owned • cover charge

DJ Café Sol Rembrandtplein 18 **31–20/330-3279** • 10pm-4am, clsd Mon-Tue • "outside bar w/ the best music in town"

IT Amstelstraat 24 **31–20/618-6040** • 11pm-6am Fri-Sat • popular • gay/ straight • more gay Sat • dancing/DJ • private club • cover charge

Salvation at Escape Rembrandtplein 11 **31–20/622-1111 (ESCAPE #)** • 10pm-5am 1st Fri only • popular • mostly gay men• dancing/DJ • huge dance club • cover

Teadance • popular • mostly gay men• dancing/DJ • monthly party • www.teadance-amsterdam.nl

You II Amstel 178 (at Wagenstraat) **31–20/421-0900** • 10pm-4am, till 5am Fri-Sat, 4pm-1am Sun, clsd Mon-Wed • lesbians/ gay men• dancing/DJ • ladies night Sat

CAFES

Downtown Coffeeshop Reguliersdwarsstr 31 (at Koningsplein) **31–20/6-5087-2220** • 10am-8pm, till 10pm Fri-Sat • popular • mostly gay men • terrace open in summer

easyEverything Reguliersbreestraat 22 **31–20/320-6294** • 9am-10pm • hundreds of terminals (flat screens, net phone, webcams) • also at Damrak 33 near Centraal Station

Global Chillage Kerkstr 51 **31–20/777-9777** • 11am-midnight, till 1am Fri-Sat • smoking coffeeshop • publisher's choice

The Other Side Reguliersdwarsstr 6 (at Koningsplein) **31–20/421-1014** • 11am-1am • mostly gay men • smoking coffeeshop • gay-owned

RESTAURANTS

Barney's Breakfast Bar Haarlemmerstraat 102 **31–20/625-9761** • 7am-midnight • brkfst all day • lunch & dinner menu • plenty veggie

Camp Cafe Kerkstr 45 (at Leidsestr) **31–20/622-1506** • 8am-1am • popular • lesbians/ gay men • cont'l • kitchen open till 11:30pm • full bar • terrace • gay-owned

Garlic Queen Reguliersdwarsstr 27 **31–20/422-6426** • 6pm-close, clsd Mon-Tue • even the desserts are made with garlic!

Golden Temple Utrechtsestr 126 **31–20/626-8560** • 5pm-10pm • mix of Indian, Mexican & Mediterranean • oldest vegetarian & vegan restaurant in city • nonsmoking

Le Monde Rembrandtplein 6 **31–20/626-9922** • 8am-11pm, brkfst till 4pm (open 4pm-10pm Mon-Fri in winter) • lesbians/ gay men • Dutch/ Brazilian • plenty veggie • terrace dining • gay-owned

Rose's Cantina Reguliersdwarsstr 38–40 (near Rembrandtplein) **31–20/625-9797** • 5pm-11pm • popular • Tex-Mex • full bar

Saturnino Reguliersdwarsstr 5 **31–20/639-0102** • noon-midnight • lesbians/ gay men • Italian • full bar

RETAIL SHOPS

Conscious Dreams Dreamlounge Kerkstr 93 **31–20/626-6907** • 11am-7pm, till 8pm Th-Sat, noon-5pm Sun • "psychedelicatessen" • internet access • € 1.20 for 15 minutes

Amsterdam—Outer

ACCOMMODATIONS

Abba Budget Hotel Overtoom 122 (1st Constantyn Huygenstraat) **31–20/618-3058** • gay-friendly • brkfst buffet • free safety deposit boxes • "smoker"-friendly • € 40-80

AMS Hotel Holland PC Hooftstraat 162 **31–20/676-4253** • gay-friendly • ample parking • near museums• € 69-169

AMS Museum Hotel PC Hooftstraat 2 **31–20/662-1402** • gay-friendly • parking • also restaurant • € 130-260

AMS Toro Hotel Koningslaan 64 (next to Vondelpark) **31–20/673-7223** • gay-friendly • refurbished mansion • fax service • parking • € 89-210

Amsterdam B&B Roeterstraat 18 **31–20/624-0174** • gay-friendly • full brkfst • kids ok • nonsmoking • gay-owned • € 80-110

Amsterdam Room Service 2e van der Helststraat 26 III **31–20/679–4941** • gay/ straight • apt & B&B rooms in Amsterdam • cash only • gay-owned • €50-160

Between Art & Kitsch Ruysdaelkade 75-2 **31–20/679–0485** • gay-friendly • near museums • €80+up

The Collector B&B De Lairessestr 46 hs (in museum area) **31–6/1101–0105 (CELL)**, **31–20/673–6779** • gay-friendly • B&B • full brkfst • kids ok • gay-owned • €80-110

Downstairs B&B **31–20/676–2751** • gay-friendly • B&B • €75-110

The Flying Pig Vossiusstraat 46-47 (at Leidseplein) **31–20/400–4187** • gay-friendly • hostel • dorms • no curfew • kitchen facilities • also Centrum location • €20-90

Flynt B&B Amsterdam Eerste Helmersstraat 34 **31–20/618–4614, 31–0(6/5260–1160 (CELL)** • lesbians/ gay men • gay-owned • €70-120

Freeland Hotel Marnixstraat 386 **31–20/622–7511, 31–20/627–7578** • gay-friendly • 2-star hotel • full brkfst • gay-owned • €60-120

Hemp Hotel Frederiksplein 15 **31–20/625–4425** • only in Amsterdam: sleep on a hemp mattress, eat a hemp roll (THC-free) for brkfst or drink hemp beer in the downstairs Hemp Temple bar • €50-70

Hotel Aadam Wilhelmina Koninginneweg 169 **31–20/662–5467** • gay-friendly • charming • full brkfst buffet • some shared baths • €55-175

Hotel Arena Gravesandestraat 51 **31–20/850–2400** • gay-friendly • huge hotel in former orphanage • popular nightclub in former chapel • also restaurant & cafe/ bar • €100-175

Hotel Fita Jan Luykenstraat 37 **31–20/679–0976** • small family-owned hotel • nonsmoking • free telephone calls to US & w/in Europe • €90-140

Hotel Rembrandt Plantage Middenlaan 17 **31–20/627–2714** • gay-friendly • triples & quads available • beautiful brkfst room w/ 17th-c art • 10 minutes from Rembrandtplein • €70-170

Hotel Sander Jacob Obrechtstraat 69 **31–20/662–7574** • gay-friendly • also 24hr bar & coffee lounge • €100-205

International Budget Hostel Leidsegracht 76 (at Leidseplein) **31–20/624–2784** • gay-friendly • in 17th-c warehouse on canal • lounge w/ internet • clean 4-person dorms (€27-30) • some doubles (€65-75)

Johanna's B&B Van Hogendorpplein 62 **31–20/684–8596, 31–6/2413–3056 (CELL)** • mostly women but gay men welcome • full brkfst • nonsmoking • €90

Kerstin's B&B Kwakerstraat 2h **31–20/612–6969** • gay-friendly • B&B & self-catering apt • overlooking new canal • nonsmoking • kids ok • €80 (2-day minimum)

Liliane's Home Sarphatistraat 119 (at Weesperplein Station) **31–20/627–4006** • women only • brkfst • shared bath • nonsmoking • also apt • €100

Lloyd Hotel Oostelijke Handelskade 34 **31–20/561–3636** • gay-friendly • hip hotel for all budgets in cool Eastern Harbor area • €60-300

Prinsen Hotel Vondelstraat 36-38 (near Leidseplein) **31–20/616–2323** • gay-friendly • near the Centre • also bar • €110-210

Rubens B&B Rubensstraat 38 **31–20/662–9187** • gay/ straight • nonsmoking • €90-110 (3-night minimum)

Stayokay Amsterdam Vondelpark Zandpad 5 **31–20/589–8996** • gay-friendly • inside Vondelpark • brasserie & restaurant • €20-23 (dorms) & €65-77 (rooms)

NIGHTCLUBS

Melkweg Lijnbaansgracht 234 (at Leidseplein) **31–20/531–8181** • gay/ straight • popular live-music venue • restaurant • theater • cinema • gallery

ToNight @ Arena Gravesandestraat 51 (at Hotel Arena) **31–20/850–2400** • different events each night • come to see the club itself—a restored chapel from an orphanage

RESTAURANTS

An Weteringschans 76 (in Museum Quarter) **31–20/624–4672** • 6pm-11:30pm (kitchen till 10pm) • Japanese • patio • €14-21

Boom Chicago Leidseplein 12 (Leidseplein Theater) **31–20/530–7307 (BOOMBAR)** • noon-4pm lunch inside or on the square; dinner nightly from 6:30pm, then the famed comedy/improv show starts at 8:30pm (tickets not included in price)

Brasserie Van Gogh PC Hooftstraat 28 (at Hotel Smit) **31–20/673–8548**

De Waaghals Frans Halsstraat 29 **31–20/679–9609** • 5pm-11pm, kitchen open till 9:30pm, clsd Mon • int'l vegetarian

RETAIL SHOPS

Gallery Faubourg Overtoom 426 **31–20/676–1918** • clsd Mon • gay art & antique gallery

SPAIN

Barcelona

Note: M°=Metro station

INFO LINES & SERVICES

Casal Lambda Verdaguer y Callís 10 (M°Drassanes) 34/93-319-5550 • 5pm-9pm, till 11pm Sat, clsd Sun • community center • cafe • archives • library • also publish magazine

Colectivo Gay de Barcelona (CGB) 34/93-453-4125 • staffed 7pm-9pm Mon-Sat • also publishes Info Gai

Coordinadora Gai Lesbiana Finlàndia 45, E–08014 34/900-601-601, 34/902-120-140 • 6pm-10pm Mon-Fri • nat'l gay group

Stop SIDA Finlàndia 45 34–900/601–601 (IN SPAIN) • hotline 6pm-10pm Mon-Fri

ACCOMMODATIONS

Apartments Bonnois Via Augusta 37 34/651–060–338 • gay/ straight • gay-owned • €160

Aparts B&B Barcelona Gran Via de las Corts Catalanes 34/67–728–6263 • gay-friendly • hostel in city center • shared baths • €40-80

BarcelonaMarinaFlat.com Carrer Sant Miquel 52 (at Paseo Joan Borbo) 34/677–368–305 • gay-friendly • apt in Gothic Quarter near beach • full brkfst • gay-owned • €80+

Beauty & the Beach B&B 34/93–266–0562 • exclusively gay, lesbians welcome • B&B • full brkfst • right across from gay nude beach • nonsmoking • wheelchair access • gay-owned • €80-110

California Hotel Rauric 14 (at Fernando, M°Liceu) 34/93–317–7766 • gay/ straight • €49-115

Barcelona

LGBT PRIDE:
July.

ANNUAL EVENTS:
February - Carnival
July - Grec Summer Festival, web: www.barcelonafestival.com
August - Festa Major de Gràcia (huge street party), web: www.festamajordegracia.org
October/November - Gay/Lesbian Film Festival, 34/93.319.55.50, web: www.cinemalambda.com.

CITY INFO:
34/933.689.730 (outside Spain), 34/906.30.1282 (in Spain), web: www.barcelonaturisme.com.

WEATHER:
Barcelona boasts a mild Mediterranean climate, with summer temperatures in the 70°s-80°s, and 40°s-50°s in winter. Rain is possible year-round, with July being the driest month.

TRANSIT:
34/933.581.111
34/933.033.033, web: www.radiotaxio33.com.
Aerobus to Plaza de Cataluña 34/934.156.020.
Public transit: www.tmb.net.

ATTRACTIONS:
Barcelona Museum of Contemporary Art 34/93.412.08.10, web: www.macba.es
Barrì Gotic
Boqueria Market
Catedral de Barcelona 34/93.310.71.95
Fundació Joan Miró 34/93.443.94.70, web: www.bcn.fjmiro.es
Museu Picasso 34/93.319.63.10, web: www.museupicasso.bcn.es
National Museum of Catalan Art 34/93.622.03.76, web: www.mnac.es
Parc Güell
La Sagrada Familia 34/93.207.30.30, web: www.sagradafamilia.org.

[Reply] [Forward]   [Delete]

```
Date: Dec 9, 2005 15:26:01
From: Girl-on-the-Go
To: Editor@Damron.com
Subject: Barcelona
```

>An enormous open-air museum to its patron artist Gaudí, Barcelona is by turns handsome, quaint, sleek, wry, and hip. Gaudí's Dr. Seuss–like art nouveau apartment buildings are scattered throughout the city, and you can't miss his massive still-under-construction cathedral—La Sagrada Familia—or the amusing Park Güell overlooking the city.

>As all the guidebooks will tell you, the Barri Gotic is both the tourists' quarter and a crowded maze of ancient Gothic towers, narrow alleys, plazas, and cathedrals bisected by a wide pedestrian mall known as Las Ramblas.

>The Ramblas is the main artery of the quarter, and most days you can't walk more than a few feet without bumping into street hawkers, cartoonists, jugglers, clowns, live statues, and buskers of all sorts—in between the omnipresent bright red ¡Hola! bookstands, knots of tourists, and sidewalk cafes. Unlike many tourist areas, the Ramblas is also frequented by locals strolling for evening and weekend entertainment.

>A few blocks away, Raurich Street (carrer in Catalan, the local tongue of Barcelona; or calle in Spanish, pronounced "káh-yeh") meanders past most of the gay bars and bookstores in the Barri Gotic. But the heart of gay Barcelona is in L'Eixample, the most recently redeveloped part of town, with wide streets and sidewalks and plush middle-class businesses.

>Urban dykes may feel more at home in the less glossy Gracia neighborhood, home to a mix of queers, families of color, punks, and other misfits—most of whom still go to the Barri Gotic for excitement.

>During the day, visit the **Casal Lambda,** a community center and cafe that also publishes a local LGBT magazine. Or drop by one of the three LGBT bookstores in town: **Cómplices**, **Antinous,** and **Nosotras.**

Reply **Forward** **Delete**

>For casual hanging out, there's the popular **Bahía** or **La Illa**, a tiny, friendly dyke bar. The **Café de la Calle**, which is actually a bar-*cum*-community center, has a large lesbian clientele. It opens at 6pm but doesn't start filling up till 10pm. If you wander around its mazes, you'll find a narrow hallway in the back crammed with gay papers, flyers, free disco tickets, and all the current information you need.

>If you're in a dancing mood, many of the bars have music and small dance floors, earning them a classification as "*bares musicales.*" Get down with the girls at **D.Mer** or **La Rosa.** One of the larger dance clubs for women is **Aire,** a trendy cafe-bar and nightclub. It's is also within walking distance to bigger mixed clubs that stay open even later for the true night owls. For the hip, post-punk set, try **Pigalle** or the occasional **Bitch Club**.

>The most exciting women's nights are, of course, these and other monthly or periodic parties. Look for flyers advertising events for *dones* ("women" in Catalan), or ask the friendly bartenders, many of whom will answer you in English if your accent gives you away.

Catalonia Albéniz Aragó 591–593 **34/93-265-2626** • gay-friendly • food served • wheelchair access • €87-140

Catalonia Albinoni Avenida Portal de L'Angel 17 **34/93-318-4141** • gay-friendly • 3-star hotel • €121-172

Catalonia Barcelona Plaza Plaza d'Espanya 6–8 (across from Montjuïc Castle) **34/93-426-2600** • gay-friendly • swimming • jacuzzi • also restaurant & piano bar • €136-242

Catalonia Duques de Bergara Bergara 11 **34/93-301-5151** • gay-friendly • 4-star hotel in the heart of old Barcelona • food served • €143-242

Catalonia Roma Av de Roma 31 **34/93-410-6633** • gay-friendly • 4-star hotel next to the Sants train station • food served • €87-140

Gran Hotel Catalonia Balmes 142–146 **34/93-415-9090** • gay-friendly • 4-star hotel • kids ok • food served • wheelchair access • €129-242

Hotel Axel Aribau 33 (at Consell de Cent) **34/93-323-9393** • lesbians/ gay men • full brkfst • also restaurant • jacuzzi • swimming • wheelchair access • €90-300

Hotel Majestic Plaza de Gracia 68 (in city center) **34/93-487-3939, 866/376-7831 (FROM US)** • gay-friendly • swimming

Regencia Colon Hotel Sagristans 13–17 (in the Barri Gotic, Mºjaume I) **34/93-318-9858, 800/223-1356** • gay-friendly • some shared baths • swimming • €148 + 7% Tva-tax

The Seven Balconies (Natalia's) Cervantes 7 **34/654-238-161** • lesbians/ gay men • B&B • full brkfst • some shared baths • kids ok • €75-110

Suite Gaudi Barcelona B&B Rambla de Cataluña, 103, 1º-A (at Provença) **34/93-215-0658** • kids ok • lesbian-owned • €50-95

The Third Floor Av Diagonal 430 (at Paseo di Gracia) **34/93-217-3774** • lesbians/ gay men • B&B in stylish private apartment • gay-owned • €130-180

BARS

Aire/ Sala Diana Valencia 236 (btwn Enriq. Granados & c/ Balmes) **34/93-451-8462** • 11pm-3am, 6pm-10pm Sun, clsd Mon-Wed • mostly women • dancing/DJ • cafe-bar • women only Sun • young crowd

Bahía Carrer de Seneca 12 (in Gràcia) • till 2:30am • mostly women

Café de la Calle Vic 11 (M°Gracia) **34/93-218-3863** • 6pm-3am • lesbians/ gay men • food served • young crowd

Cafe Dietrich Consell de Cent 255 (btwn Muntaner & Aribau, M°Universitat) **34/93-451-7707** • 6pm-3am • popular • lesbians/ gay men • dancing/DJ • upscale • theater-cafe • drag shows • go-go dancers

Caligula Consejo de Ciento 257 (M°Universitat) **34/93-451-4892** • 8pm-3am • posh decor • lesbians/ gay men • live shows

D.Mer Plató 13 (ar Carrer Muntaner) **34/93-201-6207** • 11:30pm-4am, clsd Sun-Wed • mostly women • dancing/DJ

G Café Muntaner 24 (M°Universitat) • 4pm-2:30am & 6pm-3am, clsd Mon eve • funky decor • lesbians/ gay men

Gay T Dance Nou de la Rambla 113 (at Sala Apolo, M° Pariel) **34/93-511-5764** • lesbians/ gay men • dancing/DJ • go-go dancers • cover charge

La Illa Reig I Benet 3 (M°Joanic) • 7pm-11pm, till 3am Fri-Sat, closed Sun • women-only • food served

Machín Casanova 48 **34/93-530-4656** • 6pm-3am, clsd Mon • lesbians/ gay men • dancing/DJ • many events • also restaurant & internet cafe

Mandarina Diputación 157 **34/93-323-3393** • 6pm-3am • lesbians/ gay men • food served • terrace

Padam Padam Rauric 9 **34/93-302-5062** • 7pm-3am, clsd Sun • lesbians/ gay men • also cafe • classical music

Punto BCN Muntaner 63-65 (enter on Consejo de Ciento Yragón, M° Universitat) **34/93-453-6123** • 6pm-2:30am, till 3am wknds • popular • mostly gay men • upscale cafe-bar • wheelchair access

La Rosa Brusi 39 (btwn Augusta & San Elias, M°Plaza Molina) **34/93-414-6166** • 10pm-3am Th-Sun • mostly women • dancing/DJ • live shows • neighborhood bar

Sweet Café Casanova 75 (at Consell de Cent) **34/679-337-234** • 8pm-2:30am, till 3am Fri-Sat, clsd Mon • mostly gay men • dancing/DJ • cafeteria-style • food served • wheelchair access • gay-owned

Z:eltas Casanova 75 (M°Gran Vía/ Urgell) **34/93-454-1902** • 10:30pm-3am • mostly gay men • dancing/DJ • lounge • live shows • videos

NIGHTCLUBS

Arena Classic Diputación 233 (at Balmes, M° Universitat) **34/93-487-8342** • 12:30am-5am Fri-Sat only • popular • mostly gay men • dancing/DJ • Spanish music • live shows • videos • theme nights • young crowd • cover charge

Arena Sala Madre Balmes 32 (at Diputació, M°Universitat) **34/93-487-8342** • 12:30am-5am, from 7:30pm Sun, clsd Mon (except in Aug) • popular • mostly gay men • dancing/DJ • food served • live shows Wed • videos • young crowd • cover charge

The Bitch Club Calle Lincoln 19 • women-only • dancing/DJ • sign up for mailing list for current parties • www.bitch-club.com

Free Girls Maria Cubi 4 (M°Fontana or Diagonal) • 11pm-3am, 7pm-2am Sun & holidays • mostly women • ring bell for admittance • dancing/DJ

Free Women Casanova 43 (M°Urgell) • 6pm-dawn • mostly women • dancing/DJ

Metro Sepúlveda 185 (M° Universitat) **34/93-323-5227** • midnight-5am • popular • mostly gay men • dancing/DJ • leather • drag shows • videos • young crowd • T-dance 7pm-10:30pm Sun • also cafe • cover charge

Nextown Ladies Avda Manuel Azaña (at Ronda de Dalt, at Liquid) **34/67-682-8595** • contact for times & location

Pigalle Balmes 90 (btwn Mallorca & Valencia) • 11pm-3am, 7pm-1am Sun, clsd Mon-Wed • mostly women • dancing/DJ

Salvation Ronda San Pedro 19-21 (at Plaza Urquinaona) **34/93-318-0686** • midnight-close Fri-Sat only • mostly gay men • dancing/DJ • drag shows • strippers • videos • food served • young crowd • cover charge

Tatu Cayo Celio 7 (M°Plaza d'Espanya) **34/93-425-3350** • 10pm-4am, from 7pm Sun • mostly gay men • dancing/DJ • transgender-friendly • drag shows • videos • patio • cover charge • popular

CAFES

De Blanco Villarroel 71 (M° Urgell)
34/93-451-5986 • 7pm-3am • mostly gay men • full bar • young crowd

Quizás Diputación 161 (M° Urgell)
34/93-451-5258 • 9am-2:30am • lesbians/ gay men • breakfast & light lunch served • also bar

RESTAURANTS

7 Portes Passeig d'Isabel II, 14
34/93-319-3033 • 1pm-1am • Catalan • upscale • over 150 years old!

Botafumeiro El Gran de Gràcia 81
34/93-218-4230 • 1pm-1am • Galician seafood specialities • full bar • reservations recommended

Café Miranda Casanova 30 (btwn Gran Vía & Sepúlveda, M° Gran Vía) **34/93-453-5249** • 9pm-1am • popular • lesbians/ gay men • int'l/ Mediterranean • full bar • campy decor • live shows • drag shows • reservations recommended

Castro Casanova 85 (M°Urgell)
34/93-323-6784 • 1pm-4pm & 9pm-11:30pm, clsd Sun • mostly gay men • Catalan • full bar • leather • live shows

Comme-Bio Gran Via Corts Catalanes 603
34/93-301-0376 • from 2pm daily • vegetarian • also location at Via Laietana 28, 34/ 93-319-8968

dDivine Balmes 24 **34/93-317-2248** • 9:30-1am, clsd Mon • lesbians/ gay men • dinner show hosted by "Divine" • reservations reccomended

La Diva Diputació 172 (M°Universitat)
34/93-454-6398 • 1pm-3:30pm & 9pm-12:30am • popular • lesbians/ gay men • transgender-friendly • creative Mediterranean • fabulous drag cabaret • reservations recommended

La Flauta Magica c/ de Banys Vells 18
34/93-268-4694 • 1pm-4pm & 9pm-midnight • plenty veggie

Little Italy c/ del Rec 30 (near Plaza del Born)
34/93-319-7973 • 1:30pm-4pm & 9pm-midnight, clsd Sun • live shows

Madrid-Barcelona Carrer d'Arago 282 (M° Passeig de Gracia) **34/93-215-7027** • lunch & dinner, clsd Sun • located on old railway line • Catalan

La Veronica Avinyo 30 **34/93-412-1122** • noon-4pm & 8pm-12:30am, clsd Mon • pizza • terrace

BOOKSTORES

Antinous Josep Anselm Clavé 6 (btwn Las Ramblas & Ample, M°Drassanes)
34/93-301-9070 • clsd Sun • LGBT • books • gifts • also cafe • wheelchair access

Cómplices Cervantes 2 (at Avinyó, M°Liceu)
34/93-412-7283 • 10:30am-8:30pm, from noon Sat, clsd Sun • LGBT • Spanish & English titles

Nosotr@s Casanova 56 **34/93-451-5134** • LGBT books • magazines • gifts • videos • DVDs

PUBLICATIONS

Gay Barcelona Av Roma 152
34/93-454-9100 • monthy gay magazine

Info Gai **34/96-681-2303** • free bimonthly newspaper in Catalan

Nois **34/93-454-3805** • free gay monthly

Zero Pza Sta Ma Soledad Torres Acosta 2
34/93-917-01008

SPIRITUAL GROUPS

Associació Christiana de Gais I Lesbianes Finlandia 45 (at CGL)
34/93-486-3171 • activities 8:30pm Wed • service last Wed of month

EROTICA

Erotic Museum of Barcelona Ramblas 96
34/93-318-9865 • 10am-midnight (seasonal hours)

Madrid

Note: M°=Metro station

INFO LINES & SERVICES

COGAM (Colectivo de Lesbianas y Gays de Madrid) Fuencarral 37 (M°Tribunal)
34/91-522-4517 • LGBT center • groups • library • also cafe-bar

Gai Inform **34/91-523-0070** • 5pm-9pm Mon-Fri • helpline

ACCOMMODATIONS

Chueca Pension Gravina 4, 2nd flr (at Calle Hortaleza) **34/91-523-1473** • mostly gay men • hostel • kids ok • free Internet access • €37-47

Gay Hostal Puerta del Sol Plaza Puerta del Sol 14, 4° (at Calle de Alcalá, M°Sol)
34/91-522-5126 • mostly gay men • centrally located • wheelchair access • gay-owned • €60-100

Hostal Hispano Hortaleza 38, 2nd flr (at Perez Galdos, M°Chueca) **34/91-531-4871** • gay-friendly • €26-33

Hostal La Fontana Valverde 6, 1° (M°Gran Vía) 34/91–521–8449, 34/91–523–1561 • lesbians/ gay men • €36-45

Hostal Oporto Calle Zorilla 9, 1st flr (M°Sol) 34/91–429–7856 • gay-friendly • 10-minute walk to gay scene • some shared baths • €34-42

Hostal Sonsoles Fuencarral 18, 2nd flr (M°Chueca) 34/91–532–7523 • mostly gay men • €30-50

Hotel A Gaudí Gran Vía 9 (at Alcalá) 34/91–531–2222 • 4-star hotel • kids ok • wheelchair access • €122-192

Hotel Suecia Marqués de Casa Riera 4 34/91–531–6900, 800/448–8355 • gay-friendly • jacuzzis • €110-210

Hotel Urban Madrid Carrera de San Jerónimo 34 34/93–787–7770, 800/230–7330 • gay-friendly • upscale hotel w/ 3 restaurants & rooftop pool

The Westin Palace Plaza de Las Cortes, 7 34/91–360–8000, 800/325–3589 • gay-friendly • grand hotel w/ prices to match

BARS

La Bohemia Plaza de Chueca 10 (M°Chueca) • 8pm-close, from 9pm wknds • mostly women • neighborhood cafe-bar

Chueca's Friends Plaza de Chueca 9 • 5pm-4am • mostly women • seasonal terrace

Enfrente Infantas 12 (M°Gran Vía) • 8pm-3am • lesbians/ gay men • DJs Th & Sun

Lucas San Lucas 11 (M°Chueca) • 8:30pm-3:30am • lesbians/ gay men • dancing/DJ • drag shows • young crowd

La Lupe de Chueca Hortaleza 51 (in Chueca) 34/91–521–2564 • 2:30pm-2:30am, till 3:30am wknds • popular • lesbians/ gay men • neighborhood bar • bohemian crowd • live shows • also cafe

El Mojito Olmo 6 (M°Antón Martin) 34/91–539–4617 • 9pm-2:30am, till 3:30am Fri-Sat • lesbians/ gay men • cocktail bar

Museo Chicote Gran Vía 12 34/91–532–6737 • 10pm-3am • gay/ straight • hip, historic cocktail bar • also restaurant

Olivia 51 San Bartolomé 6 (btwn Figueroa & San Marcos) • 8pm-close Wed-Sat • mostly women • dance bar • live shows • food served

Madrid

LGBT PRIDE:
June, web: www.orgullogay.org.

ANNUAL EVENTS:
October/November - International Gay & Lesbian Film Festival, web: www.lesgaicinemad.com or www.fundaciontriangulo.es.

CITY INFO:
Oficina Municipale de Turismo 34/91.588.16.36, web: www.descubremadrid.com.

BEST VIEW:
From the funicular in the Parque des Atracciones.

WEATHER:
Winter temps average in the 40°s (and maybe even a little snow!). Summer days in Madrid are hot, with highs well into the 80°s.

TRANSIT:
Metro 34/91.522.59.09, web: www.metromadrid.es.

ATTRACTIONS:
Chueca
El Rastro (flea market)
Museo del Prado 34/91.330.28.00, web: http://museoprado.mcu.es
Museo Thyssen-Bornemisza 34/91.369.01.51, web: www.museothyssen.org
Museo de Reina Sofia (home of Picasso's 'Guernica') 34/91.467.50.62, web: http://museoreinasofia.mcu.es
El Retiro (park)
Royal Palace 34/91.542.00.59.

Reply **Forward** **Delete**

Date: Dec 10, 2005 11:27:21
From: Girl-on-the-Go
To: Editor@Damron.com
Subject: Madrid

───

>The sprawling capital of Spain, Madrid is both grandiose and intimate, more gifted in spirit and bustling street life than in tourist spots. Of course, even if museums aren't your thing, you shouldn't miss Picasso's *Guernica* in the Sophia Reina Museum, or Hieronymus Bosch's phantasmagoric paintings in the Prado museum. And definitely poke your head into one of the "Museo del Jamon" sandwich shops festooned with hanging hamhocks—it's a truly Madrileño experience.

>But the quintessential Madrileño activity—some would argue the quintessential Spanish activity—is *la marcha*, the full night of barhopping that most Spaniards apparently engage in many nights a week. What is not clear, is which—*la marcha* or the three-hour lunchtime siesta—came first, but now they are inextricably intertwined.

>After a modest dinner around 10pm—or perhaps just some *cañas* (half-bottles of beer) and *tapas* (hearty snackfood you're guaranteed with almost any alcohol purchase after 6pm)—it's off to another bar several blocks away for another single drink...then a 10- to 15-minute brisk walk to yet another bar for another single drink.

>The combination of friendly company, mild alcohol, plentiful snacks, and exercise is what keeps the evening going until at least 2 or 3am. Don't be surprised to find yourself in the middle of a crowded street or plaza at four or five in the morning!

>Generally the cafe-bars serving snacks close around midnight, and then it's on to a bar—which won't have wine, but may have *calamocho*, a *marcha*-fueling drink of wine mixed with cola. After 3am you'll have to find a night-club, which may charge a cover, at least on Fridays and Saturdays, but the cover usually includes a drink ticket.

>The lesbo stronghold of the city is Embajadores, southeast of the Center, bounded by the metro stations Lavapiés, Anton Martin, and Embajadores. Here you'll find the lesbian nightclub **Medea**.

>You'll also find plenty of sisters in the gay barrio of Chueca. After browsing the shelves at the LGBT **Berkana Bookstore**, visit the girls at **La Bohemia, Chueca's Friends,** or **Olivia 51**. Or get your groove on at **Truco**. For more nightlife ideas, pick up a copy of the free paper **Shangay Express**. Whatever you do, don't forget to take your siesta!

Priscilla San Bartolomé 6 (M°Gran Vía) • 7pm-3am, till 5am Fri-Sat • gay/ straight • trendy dance bar

Smoke San Bartolomé 11 (at Plaza de Chueca) • mostly women • neighborhood bar

Sunrise Barbieri 7 (btwn San Marcos & Infantas, M°Chueca) **34/91-523-2808** • midnight-close, clsd Mon-Tue • lesbians/ gay men • dancing/DJ • live shows

Truco Gravina 10 (at Plaza de Chueca) **34/91-532-8921** • 8pm-close, from 9pm Fri-Sat • popular • mostly women • dance bar • great parties • seasonal terrace

Why Not? San Bartolomé 7 (M°Gran Vía) **34/91-523-0581** • 10pm-close • popular • gay-friendly • fun dance bar • cover charge

NIGHTCLUBS

Cream Mesonero Romanos 13 (M°Callao) **34/91-531-4827** • 1am-6am Th only • lesbians/ gay men • dancing/DJ • cover charge

Escape Gravina 13 (at Plaza de Chueca) • open Th-Sun • lesbians/ gay men • dancing/DJ • drag shows

Joy Eslava arenal 11 (M°Sol) **34/91-366-3733** • 11:30pm-5:30am, till 6am Fri-Sat , clsd Sun• popular • fabulous crowd • converted theater

LL Pelayo 11 (M°Chueca) **34/91-523-3121** • 5pm-close • popular • gay/ straight • neighborhood bar • dancing • strippers • videos • darkroom • cruisy

Medea Cabeza 33 (M°Antón Martín) • 11pm-7am Th-Sat only • popular wknds • women only • men welcome as guests • dancing/DJ • cabaret • young crowd • cover charge

Mito Augusto Figueroa 3 **34/91-532-8851** • 11pm-6:30pm • lesbians/ gay men • neighborhood bar • dancing/ DJ • drag shows

Ohm Plaza de Callao 4 (at Sala Bash, M°Callao) • midnight-close Fri-Sat • popular • mostly gay men • dancing/DJ

Pasapoga Gran Vía 37 (M°Callao) **34/91-547-5711** • 12:30pm-6am Fri-Sat only • mostly gay men • dancing/DJ • drag shows • young crowd

Polana Barbieri 10 **34/91-532-3305** • 11pm-close • trendy • lesbians/ gay men • dancing/ DJ

Rick's Clavel 8 (at Infantas, M°Gran Vía, ring to enter) **34/91-531-9186** • 11pm-5am • popular • mostly gay men • dancing/DJ • young crowd • "see-and-be-scene"

Sachas Plaza de Chueca 1 (M°Chueca) • 8pm-5am Th-Sun, bar open 8pm-3am nightly • lesbians/ gay men • dancing/DJ • drag shows • terrace

Shangay Tea Dance Isabel la Catolica 6 **34/91-445-1741** • 10pm-3am Sun • popular • lesbians/ gay men • dancing/DJ • live shows • young crowd • cover charge

Tábata Vergara 12 (next to Teatro Real, M°Opera) **34/91-547-9735** • 11:30pm-late Wed-Sat • lesbians/ gay men • dancing/DJ • young crowd • cover charge

Week-end Plaza de Callao 4 (at Sala Bash, M°Callao) • midnight-6am Sun • popular • lesbians/ gay men • dancing/DJ • alternative • cover

CAFES

Baires Café Gravina 4 (M°Chueca) **34/91-532-9879** • 9am-2am, from 5pm Sun • lesbians/ gay men • also bar

Bonamara Hortaleza 51 (M°Gran Vía/ Chueca) **34/91-521-2564** • 3pm-3am • lesbians/ gay men • also bar

Cafe Acuarela Gravina 8-10 (M°Chueca) **34/91-532-8735, 34/91-570-6907** • 3pm-2am • lesbians/ gay men • bohemian cafe-bar • cocktails

Cafe Comercial Glorieta de Bilbao 7 **34/91-521-5655** • 8am-1am, from 9:30am Sun • spacious 19th-c cafe

Cafe Figueroa Augusto Figueroa 17 (at Hortaleza, M°Chueca) **34/91-521-1673** • noon-1:30am, till 2:30am Fri-Sat • lesbians/ gay men • also bar • theme parties

Café la Troje Pelayo 26 (at Figueroa, M°Chueca) **34/91-531-0535** • 2pm-2am, till 2:30am wknds • popular • lesbians/ gay men • full bar

Color Augusto Figueroa 11 (M°Chueca) **34/91-522-4820** • 3pm-midnight, from 5pm wknds • mostly gay men • tapas • desserts • full bar

D'Mystic Gravina 5 (M°Chueca) **34/91-308-2460** • 9:30am-close • gay/ straight • popular • hot food served • hip cafe-bar in Chueca area

El Jardin Infantas 9 **34/91-521-9045** • 10am-2am, till 3am wknds • lesbians/ gay men

Laan Cafe Pelayo 28 (M°Chueca) **34/91-522-6861** • 10am-close, from 4pm Sun • lesbians/ gay men • hip cafe-bar

Mama Inés Hortaleza 22 (M°Chueca) **34/91-523-2333** • gay/ straight • 10am-2am, till 3:30am Fri-Sat • sandwiches • pies

La Sastrería Hortaleza 74 (at Gravina, M°Chueca) **34/91-532-0771** • 10am-2am, till 3am Fri-Sat, from 11am wknds • lesbians/gay men • trendy cafe-bar • internet access

Star's Marqués de Valdeiglesias 5 (at Infantas, M°Banco) **34/91-522-2712** • 9am-6pm & 11pm-close, clsd Sun • mostly gay men • cafe-bar • dancing/DJ Th-Sat • €9-12

Urania's Cafe Fuencarral 37 (at COGAM center, M°Tribunal) **34/91-522-4517** • 5pm-midnight, till 1am Fri-Sat • lesbians/gay men • cafe-bar

RESTAURANTS

A Brasileira Pelayo 49 (M°Chueca) **34/91-308-3625** • lunch & dinner • Brazilian

Abaco Jovellanos 6 **34/91-420-1164** • dinner Mon-Sat, clsd Sun • int'l cuisine • elegant

Al Natural Zorrilla 11 (M°Sevilla) **34/91-369-4709** • lunch & dinner • vegetarian

El Armario San Bartolomé 7 (btwn Figueroa & San Marcos, M°Chueca) **34/91-532-8377** • lunch & dinner • lesbians/gay men • Mediterranean

Artemisa Ventura de la Vega 4 (at Zorrilla) **34/91-429-5092** • lesbians/gay men • vegetarian • also Tres Cruces 4 location, 34/91-521-8721

Café Miranda Barquillo 29 (downstairs) **34/91-521-2946** • 9pm-close • lesbians/gay men • kitschy decor • drag shows

Casa Vallejo San Lorenzo 9 **34/91-308-6158** • clsd Sun-Mon • creative homestyle

El Castro de San Francisco Hernán Cortés 19 (M°Chueca) **34/91-531-2740, 34/63-628-5232** • 11am-1:30am, clsd Sun • lesbians/gay men • upscale cafe-bar & restaurant

Chez Pomme Pelayo 4 (M°Chueca) **34/91-532-1646** • 1:30pm-4pm & 9pm-midnight • int'l/vegetarian

La Coqueta Libertad 3 **34/91-523-0647** • lunch & dinner • lesbians/gay men • Mediterranean

La Dame Noire Pérez Galdós 3 (M°Gran Vía) **34/91-531-0476** • 9pm-1am, till 2am Fri-Sat, clsd Mon • creative French

Divina La Cocina Colmenares 13 (at San Marcos, M°Chueca) **34/91-531-3765** • lunch & dinner, clsd Sun • lesbians/gay men • elegant & trendy

La Dolce Vita Cardenal Cisneros 58 (M°Quevedo) **34/91-445-0436** • 1:30pm-4pm & 9pm-midnight • Italian • full bar

Ecocentro Esquilache 4 (at Pablo Iglesias, M°Rios Rosas) **34/91-553-5502** • open till midnight • natural foods • also shop • herbalist school

Los Girasoles Hortaleza 106 **34/91-308-4494** • clsd Sun • creative Spanish • tapas

Gula Gula Infante 5 (M°Antón Martin) **34/91-420-2919** • lunch & dinner, clsd Mon • popular • lesbians/gay men • buffet/salad bar • full bar • drag shows • reservations required• also Gran Vía 1 location, 34/91-522-8764

Hudson Hortaleza 37 (M°Gran Vía) **34/91-532-3346** • 11:30am-3am, clsd Mon • mostly gay men • American food • pizza • also bar

El Kortijo de las Lokas Cuesta de Santo Domingo 3 **34/91-542-4208** • Wed & Fri nights are the best for live shows

Lemao Infantas 6 (M°Gran Vía/Chueca) **34/91-521-6792** • lunch & dinner, clsd Sun • popular lunch spot

Lombok Augusto Figueroa 32 **34/91-531-3566** • lunch & dinner, clsd Sun • int'l

Momo Augusto Figueroa 41 (M°Chueca) **34/91-532-7162** • lunch & dinner • nonsmoking • charming staff • gay-owned

Moskada Francisco Silvela 71 **34/91-563-0630**

Nina Manuel Malasana 10 **34/91-591-0046** • good food, service & atmosphere

Pink Pollo Infantas 18 (near Plaza Vazquez de Mella) **34/91-531-1675** • 12:30pm-12:30am, till 2:30am Fri-Sat • open daily for light meals/snacks • cute & casual

El Rincón de Pelayo Pelayo 19 (M°Chueca) **34/91-521-8407** • lunch & dinner • lesbians/gay men

BOOKSTORES

A Different Life Pelayo 30 (M°Chueca) **34/91-532-9652** • 11am-2pm & 5pm-10pm, till midnight Sat, clsd Sun • LGBT • books • magazines • music • videos • sex shop downstairs

Berkana Bookstore Hortaleza 64 **34/91-522-5599** • 10:30am-9pm, from 11:30am Sat, from noon Sun • Spanish & English titles • ask for free gay map of Madrid • wheelchair access

RETAIL SHOPS

La Catedral San Gregorio 3 (M°Chueca) 34/91–319–2874 • custom-made leather clothing • repairs • objects • fetish

PUBLICATIONS

Odisea Espiritu Santo 33 34/91–523–2154 • free monthly magazine (in Spanish)

Shangay Express 34/91–445–1741 • free biweekly gay paper • also publishes Shanguide

Zero 34/91–701–0089 • stylish & intelligent LGBT monthly (en español)

GYMS & HEALTH CLUBS

Energy Gym Hortaleza 19 (M°Gran Vía, Chueca) 34/91–531–1029

ExitFitness Espiritu Santo 2 (M°Tribunal) 34/91–523–2595

Gimnasio V35 Valverde 35 (M°Gran Via) 34/91–523–9352 • mostly gay men

Holiday Gym Princesa 40 34/91–547–4033 • gay-friendly • also locations at Plaza de Carlos Trias Bertran 4 & Plaza Republica Dominicana 8

EROTICA

California Valverde 20 (at Gran Vía)

SR Pelayo 7 34/91–523–1964 • fetish, military, leather • gay-owned

Sitges

ACCOMMODATIONS

Apartments Bonaventura San Buenaventura 7 34/93–894–9762 • gay-friendly • studio apts • €40-80

Los Globos 34/93–894–9374 • lesbians/ gay men • kids/ pets ok • also bar • terrace • gay-owned • €60-95

Hotel Liberty Isla de Cuba 45 (at A Carbonell) 34/93–811–0872 • lesbians/gay-men • seasonal • popular • wheelchair access • gay-owned • €65-150

Hotel Montserrat Espalter 27 34/93–894–0300 • popular • gay/ straight • €50-124

Hotel Renaixença Isla de Cuba 13 34/93–894–8375 • gay-friendly • some shared baths • €84-107

Hotel Romàntic Sant Isidre 33 34/93–894–8375 • popular • gay/ straight • 19th-c villa • full brkfst • some shared baths • seasonal • kids/ pets ok • also full bar • €47-107

Madison Bahía Hotel Parellades 31–33 34/93–894–0012 • popular • gay-friendly • also bar

Pensión Espalter Espalter 11 34/93–894–0300 • popular • gay-friendly • balconies • €48-76

San Sebastian Playa Port Alegre 53 34/93–894–8676, 866/376–7831 (IN US) • gay-friendly • swimming • €172-276

Sitges

ANNUAL EVENTS:
February - Carnival, web: www.sitges.com/carnaval
July - International Tango Festival, web: www.tangositges.com
August - Festa Major, web: www.sitgesmajor.com/festamajor
October - International Film Festival, web: www.cinemasitges.com.

CITY INFO:
34/93.894.42.51, web: www.sitgestur.com.

ATTRACTIONS:
Museu Cau Ferrat 34/93.894.03.64
Museu Maricel 34/93.894.03.64.

TRANSIT:
34/93.894.13.29.
34/93.893.70.60.

Sitges Holiday Apts Francisco Gum 25 34/93-894-1333 • gay-friendly • centrally located 1-brdrm apts • near beach • pets ok • €252-1,140/ week

Sitges, Spain Condo Pasco de la Ribera 32 954/563-1576 (US#) • lesbians/ gay men • beach condo • kids/ pets ok • gay-owned • €90-210

El Xalet Isla de Cuba 35 34/93-894-5579 • gay-friendly • food served

Bars

Bourbon's Sant Bonaventura 13 34/93-894-3347 • 10:30pm-3:30am (Sat only off-season) • popular • mostly gay men • dancing/DJ • videos • young crowd

Marypili Joan Tarrida Ferratges 14 • 4pm-3am • mostly women • dancing/DJ • terrace

Mediterraneo Sant Bonaventura 6 34/93-894-3347 • 10pm-3:30am • popular • mostly gay men • dance bar • patio • young crowd

Parrot's Pub Plaza Industria 2 & 3 (at Primero de Mayo) 34/93-894-7881 • seasonal, 5pm-3am, from 3pm wknds • popular • lesbians/ gay men • seasonal • leather • live shows • patio • also restaurant from 10am

Phillip's Port Alegre 10 (at San Sebastian Beach) 34/93-894-9743 • 10:30am-3am • gay/ straight • food served • terrace • seasonal

El Piano Bonaventura 37 • mostly gay men • piano bar • cabaret

Privilege Bonaire 24 • gay/ straight

Nightclubs

Organic Bonaire 15 34/93-894-2230 • midnight-6am (wknds only off-season) • mostly gay men • transgender-friendly • dancing/DJ

Trailer Angel Vidal 36 • midnight-6am • seasonal • popular • mostly gay men • dancing/DJ • young crowd

Restaurants

Al Fresco Pau Barrabeig 4 34/93-894-0600 • dinner only, clsd Mon • patio

Beach House Sant Pau 34 34/93-894-9029 • brkfst & dinner • full bar • patio • gay-owned

La Borda San Buenaventura 5 34/93-811-2002 • 1pm-4pm & 6pm-midnight

Can Pagès Sant Pere 24-26 34/93-894-1195 • 1pm-4pm & 8pm-midnight, clsd Mon • lesbians/ gay men

Casa Hidalgo Sant Pau 12 34/93-894-3895 • lunch & dinner, clsd Mon • Galician • seafood • wheelchair access

Flamboyant Pau Barrabeitg 16 34/93-894-5811 • 8pm-11pm, clsd Mon • mostly gay men • int'l • full bar • terrace dining • seasonal

Gabriel Sant Gaudenci 9 34/93-894-3046 • lunch & dinner, clsd Mon • patio

Ma Maison Bonaire 28 34/93-894-6054 • lunch & dinner • popular • lesbians/ gay men • French • full bar • terrace • clsd Nov

Mezzanine Espalter 8 34/93-894-9940 • dinner only

Monty's Passeig de la Ribera 19 34/93-811-0844 • lunch & dinner, clsd Tue • Italian • patio

Picnic Paseo de la Ribera 34/93-811-0040 • in front of gay beach • also internet cafe

Sucré-Salé Sant Pau 39 34/93-894-2302 • lunch & dinner, clsd Tue • lesbians/ gay men • crepes

El Trull Mossèn Felix Clará 3 (off Major) 34/93-894-4705 • dinner only, clsd Wed • popular • lesbians/ gay men • French/ int'l

El Velero Passeig de la Ribera 38 34/93-894-2051 • lunch & dinner • seafood • popular for dinner

Entertainment & Recreation

Gay Beach (Platja de la Bossa Rodona) • in front of Calipolis Hotel & Picnic cafe

Retail Shops

Oscar Marqués de Montroig 2 (at Plaza Industria) 34/93-894-1976 • designer clothing

FIND YOUR PLACE!

The outTraveler

Women of the world, unite!
The Out Traveler can help with tips, trends,
and advice for intrepid lesbian adventurers. Plus
our exclusive Out Traveler Ratings, which let you
know just where to go. Get it today
at your local newsstands or at outtraveler.com.

USA

ALABAMA

Geneva

Spring Creek Campground & Resort 163 Campground Rd (at Hwy 52 & Country Rd 4) **334/684–3891** • mostly gay men • cabins • also tent & RV sites • swimming • nudity ok • some theme wknds w/ DJ • gay-owned • $15-60

ALASKA

Fairbanks

Billie's Backpackers Hostel 2895 Mack Rd **907/479–2034** • gay-friendly • hostel & campsites • kids ok • food served • women-owned • $25

ARIZONA

Apache Junction

Susa's Serendipity Ranch 4375 E Superstition Blvd **480/288–9333** • women only • guesthouses on 15-acre ranch • 2 RV hookups • great views! • hot tub • nonsmoking • pets ok • lesbian-owned • $45-75/ night & $1500/ month

CALIFORNIA

Clear Lake

Edgewater Resort 6420 Soda Bay Rd (at Hohape Rd), Kelseyville **707/279–0208, 800/396–6224** • "gay-owned, straight-friendly" • cabin • camping & RV hookups • lake access & pool • theme wknds • boat facilities • smoking outside • kids/ pets ok • lesbian-owned • $28-400

Mendocino

Orr Hot Springs 13201 Orr Springs Rd, Ukiah **707/462–6277** • gay-friendly • mineral hot springs • swimming • hostel-style cabins, private cottages & campsites • clothing-optional • kids ok • guests must bring all own food • $40 (camping, 1 person) -$185 (cottage, 2 people)

Myers Flat

Giant Redwoods RV & Camp **707/943–3198** • gay-friendly • campsites • RV • located off the Avenue of the Giants on the Eel River • shared baths • kids/ pets ok • $23(tent)-35

Pescadero

Costanoa 2001 Rossi Rd **650/879–1100, 877/262–7848** • gay/ straight • also tent bungalows & cabins • 1 hour south of San Francisco • $40-350

Placerville

Rancho Cicada Retreat 209/245–4841, 877/553–9481 • mostly gay men • secluded riverside retreat in the Sierra foothills w/ 2-person tents & cabin • swimming • nudity • gay-owned • $100-200 (lower during week)

Russian River

Fifes Guest Ranch & Roadhouse Restaurant 16467 River Rd (at Brookside Ln), Guerneville **707/869–0656, 800/734–3371** • gay/ straight • 49 cabins • 60 campsites • swimming • also restaurant • 3 full bars • gym • day spa • wheelchair access • gay-owned • $65-305

Inn at the Willows 15905 River Rd (at Hwy 116), Guerneville **707/869–2824 (8AM-8PM PST), 800/953–2828** • lesbians/ gay men • old-fashioned country lodge & campground • nonsmoking • gay-owned • $79-159 ($25+ camping)

Sacramento

Verona Village River Resort 6985 Garden Hwy, Nicolaus **530/656–1321** • lesbians/ gay men • trailers for rent • full bar • restaurant • store • marina • RV space $18, tent space $12

Yosemite Nat'l Park

The Yosemite Bug Lodge & Hostel 6979 Hwy 140, Midpines **209/966–6666** • gay-friendly • hostel w/ dorms, cabins, private rooms & tents • some shared baths • kids ok • nonsmoking • wheelchair access • $18-120

COLORADO

Fort Collins

Never Summer Nordic 970/482-9411 • gay/ straight • camping in yurts (portable Mongolian round houses) in Colorado Rockies • sleep 5-9 • kids/ pets ok • mountain-biking & skiing • $60-110

Trinidad

Patmé Ranch PO Box 44, Aguilar 81020 719/846-5724 • mostly women • B&B • camping • on 400 acres • full brkfst • hot tub • kids/ pets ok • nonsmoking • lesbian-owned • $60

FLORIDA

Miami

Something Special, A Lesbian Venture 10178 Collins Ave #106 305/696-8826 • women only • 1-bdrm apt on beach • also camping & dining

Tampa

Sawmill Camping Resort 21710 US Hwy 98, Dade City 352/583-0664 • popular • gay/ straight • theme wknds w/ entertainment • RV hookups • cabins • tent spots • dancing • karaoke • swimming • nudity • gay-owned • $10.25-89

West Palm Beach

The Whimsy 561/686-1354 • referrals, resources & academic archives • political clearinghouse • also feminist/ women's land camping, RV spaces (4), picnicking & guesthouse (feminist-friendly men welcome) • wheelchair access • sliding scale

GEORGIA

Dahlonega

Swiftwaters Womanspace 706/864-3229, 888/808-5021 • women only • on scenic river • full brkfst • hot tub • seasonal • nonsmoking • deck • dogs ok • women-owned/ run • $69-95 (B&B)/ $40-50 (cabins)/ $10 (camping)

Dewy Rose

The River's Edge 2311 Pulliam Mill Rd 706/213-8081 • mostly gay men • cabins • camping • RV • live shows • swimming • nudity • nonsmoking • wheelchair access • $15-98

Macon

Lumberjack's Camping Resort 50 Hwy 230 (at Hwy 41), Unadilla 478/783-2267 • mostly gay men • 200 campsites & 85 RV hookups • on 150 acres • swimming • jacuzzi • pets ok • gay-owned

HAWAII

Hawaii (Big Island)

Margo's Corner Wakea/Kaikane Loop (Discovery Harbor) 808/929-9614 • cottage & 4 campsites • full brkfst & dinner • kids ok • sauna • lesbian-owned • $35-125

Kalani Oceanside Retreat 808/965-7828, 800/800-6886 • gay/ straight • coastal retreat & spa • on 113 acres • swimming • nudity • nonsmoking • food served • wheelchair access • straight & gay-owned • $20-30 camping • $60-240

Kulana: The Affordable Artists Sanctuary 808/985-9055 • mostly women • artist retreat • camping, cabins & guest rooms available • no smoking, drugs or alcohol • kids/ pets ok • women-owned/ run • $15 (campers) & $20-30 (cabin); $325/ month

Maui

Maluhia Kai Guesthouse 808/283-8966 • women only • ocean view • hot tub • swimming • 2 campsites ($35/ night) • lesbian-owned • $95

ILLINOIS

Du Quoin

The Pit 7403 Persimmon Rd 618/542-9470 • lesbians/ gay men • primitive camping • 18+ • nudity ok • swimming • gay-owned • free except $5 on holiday wknds

MAINE

Belfast

Greenhope Farm 124 Underpass Rd (at Rte 1), Brooks 207/722–3999 • mostly women • coastal retreat on 25 private acres • camping • horseback-riding • nonsmoking • kids ok • lesbian-owned • $75-175

Ogunquit

Beaver Dam Campground 551 School St, Rte 9, Berwick 207/698–2267 • gay-friendly • campground on beautiful 20-acre spring-fed pond • swimming • kids/pets ok • women-owned/ run • $25-38

Tenants Harbor

Blueberry Cove Camp Harts Neck Road 207/372–6353, 617/876–2897 (OFF-SEASON) • gay-friendly • cabins • private campsites • near Penobscot Bay

MICHIGAN

Cadillac

My Sister's Place 231/775–9730 • women's resort on lake • campsites, boats, bikes & other sports equipment available • kids welcome • women only • swimming • lesbian-owned • $20-135

Owendale

Windover Resort 3596 Blakely Rd 989/375–2586 • women only • seasonal private resort • campsites & RV hookups • swimming • $25/yr membership fee • $15-20 camping fee

Saugatuck

The Bunkhouse B&B 6635 118th Ave, Fennville 269/543–4335, 877/226–7481 • lesbians/ gay men • cabins • private baths • access to Campit Resort amenities (see listing below) • swimming • nonsmoking • lesbian & gay-owned • $60-125

Campit Outdoor Resort 6635 118th Ave, Fennville 269/543–4335, 877/226–7481 • lesbians/ gay men • campsites • RV hookups • separate women's area • swimming • seasonal • pets ok • membership required • lesbian & gay-owned • $17-45

MINNESOTA

Kenyon

Dancing Winds Farmstay Retreat 6863 County 12 Blvd 507/789–6606 • gay/ straight • B&B on working dairy farm • also tentsites • work exchange available • nonsmoking • lesbian-owned • $95-150

MISSISSIPPI

Ovett

Camp Sister Spirit 601/344–1411, 601/645–6479 • mostly women (some events women-only) • 120 acres of camping & RV sites • cabins • nonsmoking • clean & sober space • $15-30 (sliding scale includes kitchen use) • lesbian-owned

MISSOURI

Steelville

Country's Getaway 119 Big Bend Ln (near Hwy 8) 573/775–5534 • lesbians/ gay men • campground (open May 15-Oct 31) • 100 miles SW of St Louis • nudity ok • $10/ person (includes firewood)

NEW MEXICO

Ramah

Ancient Way Outpost 4018 Ice Caves Rd (at Hwy 53, mile marker 46), El Morro 506/783–4612 • cabins & RV park • also Ancient Ways Cafe • lesbian-owned

NEW YORK

Adirondack Mtns

Falls Brook Yurts in Adirondacks John Brannon Rd, Minerva 518/761–6187 • gay-friendly • stay in a comfortable yurt w/ a sky dome to view the stars • access to hiking, fishing & boating

Binghamton

Serenity Farms 607/656–4659 • gay/ straight • B&B • full brkfst • camping on 100 secluded acres • swimming • pets ok • gay-owned • $65-89

Catskill Mtns

Full Moon Resort Valley View Rd (at County Rt 47), Oliverea 845/254-5117 • gay/ straight • hotel, campsites, cabins available • located on 100 acres • swimming • kids ok • nonsmoking • wknd weddings • $75-165

NORTH CAROLINA

Asheville

Lofty Notions Campsite 411 Arrowood Rd (at Cove Rd), Rutherfordton 828/287-0069 • lesbians/ gay men • 1 campsite overlooking waterfall • SE of Asheville • swimming • kids ok • lesbian-owned • $200/ week

OHIO

Athens

SuBAMUH (Susan B Anthony Memorial UnRest Home) Women's Land Trust PO Box 5853, 45701 740/448-7242 • women only • cabins & camping • summer workshops • swimming • hot tub • nonsmoking • lesbian-owned • $7 (tent) – $12 (cabin) sliding scale

OKLAHOMA

Lexington

Blue Sky Ranch 14001 Banner 405/872-2583 • mostly women • cabin • camping • 2 RV hookups ($25) • swimming • pets ok • wheelchair access • lesbian-owned • $100-125

PENNSYLVANIA

Lehighton

The Woods Campground 845 Vaughn Acres Ln 610/377-9577 • lesbians/ gay men • tent/ RV spots • also cabins • swimming • 18+

New Milford

Oneida Camp & Lodge 570/465-7011 • mostly gay men • oldest gay-owned campground dedicated to the gay community • 12 RV hookups • 1 guest cottage • swimming • nudity • seasonal

Pittsburgh

Camp Davis 311 Red Brush Rd, Boyers 724/637-2402 • 2nd wknd April thru 2nd wknd in Oct • cabins, trailer, & campsites • lesbians/ gay men • adults 21+ only • dance 9pm-2am Sat • 1 hour from Pittsburgh • $17 (tent sites); $25 (cabins); $30 (trailer); rates per person

SOUTH DAKOTA

Rapid City

TW's 702 Box Elder Rd W (I-90 E, exit 63), Box Elder 605/923-2153 • 8pm-2am, clsd Sun-Mon • lesbians/ gay men • dancing/ DJ • karaoke • live shows • country/ western • leather • volleyball • bbq pit • also camping & RV • gay-owned

Salem

Camp America 25495 US 81 605/425-9085 • gay-friendly • 35 miles west of Sioux Falls • camping • RV hookups • kids/ pets ok • nonsmoking • lesbian-owned • $14-24

TENNESSEE

Gatlinburg

Big Creek Stables & Big Creek Outpost 5019 Rag Mtn Rd, Hartford 423/487-5742, 423/487-3490 • gay/ straight • cabins • camping • horseback-riding • kids ok • wheelchair access • gay-owned • $75-150

TEXAS

Groesbeck

Rainbow Ranch Campground 1662 LCR 800 254/729-5847, 888/875-7596 • lesbians/ gay men • open all year • on Lake Limestone • swimming • campsites & RV hookups • lesbian-owned • $10+/ person, $28/ RV site

Mission

Seldon Left Ranch 3000 Bentsen Palm Dr (I-83) 956/585-1215 • gay-friendly • RV hookups, furnished apts & park models • outdoor hot tub • located 10 miles outside Mexico & 1 hour from beach • wheelchair access • gay-owned • $10-30/ night & $165-500/ month

Shelbyville

English Bay Marina 186 D English Ln **936/368–2554** • gay/ straight • motel, cabins & RV hookups • in remote area overlooking Toledo Bend Lake • kids/ pets ok • wheelchair access • lesbian-owned • $35-50

Spring Branch

Mermaid's Cove 3660 Tanglewood Trail (at Eagle Rock Rd) **830/885–4297** • gay-straight • rustic campground w/ cabins • nonsmoking • lesbian-owned • $45-65 (cabins)/ $18-26 (RV)

VERMONT

Townshend

Townshend State Park 2755 State Forest Rd **802/365–7500** • gay-friendly • campground • great hiking • open Memorial Day wknd to Labor Day wknd

VIRGINIA

Charlottesville

CampOut 804/301–3553 • women only • 100-acre rustic campground w/ 50 campsites • nonsmoking • wheelchair access • women-owned/ run • $20 membership fee

Windsor

Blackwater Campground 7651 Whispering Pines Trail **757/357–7211** • gay-friendly • RV hook-ups & primitive camping • swimming • pagan, medieval & gay events on wknds • kids/ pets ok • $25 (full hookup) & $22 (water & electric) & $5 per night (primitive camping)

WASHINGTON

Hoquiam

Rivendell Ranch 100 Hensel Rd (at Hwy 101) **360/987–0088** • gay/ straight • campground & working ranch on Olympic Peninsula • kids ok • $10 • gay-owned

Long Beach Peninsula

Anthony's Home Court 1310 Pacific Hwy N, Long Beach **360/642–2802, 888/787–2754** • gay/ straight • cabins & RV hookups • gay-owned • $70-110

The Historic Sou'wester Lodge, Cabins & RV Park Beach Access Rd/ 38th Pl (PO Box 102), Seaview **360/642–2542** • gay-friendly • inexpensive suites • cabins w/ kitchens • vintage trailers • RV hookups • pets ok • nonsmoking • $49-149

San Juan Islands

Lopez Farm Cottages & Tent Camping 555 Fisherman Bay Rd, Lopez Island **360/468–3555, 800/440–3556** • gay/ straight • on 30-acre farm • hot tub • nonsmoking • also camping • $33 (camping) – 175 (cottages)

Seattle

Wild Lily Ranch B&B 360/793–2103 • popular • mostly gay men • cabins on Skykomish River • 1 hour from Seattle • riverside jacuzzi • swimming • camping available • nonsmoking • gay-owned • $95-110 (couple)

WISCONSIN

Norwalk

Daughters of the Earth 18134 Index Ave **608/269–5301** • women only • women's land • camping • retreat space • lesbian-owned • $9/ night camping & $15/ night guest rooms

Wascott

Wilderness Way 715/466–2635 • women only • resort property • cabins • camping • RV sites • swimming • girls 12 years & up ok • wheelchair access • lesbian-owned • $14 (camping) & $60-94 (cabins)

CANADA

BRITISH COLUMBIA

Birken

Birkenhead Resort Portage Rd
604/452–3255 • gay-friendly • cabins •
campsites • hot tub • swimming • pets
ok • also restaurant • lesbian-owned •
Can$80-144

ONTARIO

Grand Valley

Rainbow Ridge Resort Country Rd 109
(at Hwy 25 S) 519/928–3262 • lesbians/
gay men • trailers & tents • located on
72 acres on Grand River • swimming •
restaurant • dance hall • day visitors
welcome • seasonal • pets ok • gay-
owned • Can$15/ person

Hamilton

Cedars Campground
1039 5th Concession W Rd, Millgrove
905/659–3655 • lesbians/ gay men • private campground • swimming • also bar
• dancing/DJ • restaurant wknds • some
veggie • Can$65-85 (cabins) & Can$15
(camping)

Turkey Point

The Point Tent & Trailer Resort
918 Charlotteville Rd #2, RR 1, Vittoria
519/426–7275 • mostly gay men • nudity ok • swimming • leather • "tent &
trailer resort" on 50 acres • gay-owned •
Can$16-65

PROVINCE OF QUÉBEC

Granby

Le Campagnard B&B 146 Denison
Ouest J2G 4C8 450/770–1424 • gay-
friendly • in a quiet village • bikes available • swimming • also camping • nonsmoking • Can$50-100

Joliette

L'Oasis des Pins 381 boul Brassard, St-
Paul-de-Joliette 450/754–3819 • les-
bians/ gay men • swimming • camping
May-Sept • restaurant open year-round

CARIBBEAN

VIRGIN ISLANDS

St John

Maho Bay Camps & Harmony Studios
VI National Park 340/776–6226,
800/392–9004 • gay-friendly • tent cottages & studios • environmentally aware
resort • kids ok • $75-200

MEXICO

Puerto Vallarta

Hotel Suites Descanso del Sol Pino
Suárez 583, Zona Romantica
52–322/223–0277, 52–322/222–5229 •
popular • mostly gay men • apts, casitas
& tents • swimming • rooftop bar w/
sunset views • $45-110

Paco's Hidden Paradise 30 minutes S of
Puerto Vallarta 52–322/227–2189 • les-
bians/ gay men • secluded beach resort
accessible only by boat • condos & tents
• bar • restaurant • gay-owned • $40-80

GREAT OUTDOORS ADVENTURES

Women Only •

Adventure Associates 206/932–8352, 888/532–8352 PO Box 16304, Seattle, WA 98116 • stateside & int'l active & educational adventures • cruises, treks, safaris, hiking, kayaking, biking • cross-cultural connections • call for complete schedule • *www.adventureassociates.net*

Adventures for Women 973/644–3592 15 Victoria Ln, Morristown, NJ 07960 • hiking & kayaking in NJ, the Adirondacks & beyond • *www.adventuresforwomen.org*

Adventures in Good Company 410/435–1965, 877/439–4042 5913 Brackenridge Ave, Baltimore, MD 21212 • outdoor & adventure travel for women of all ages & abilities • call for complete catalog • *www.goodadventure.com*

Arctic Ladies 907/783-1954, 877/783–1954 PO Box 308, Girdwood, AK 99587 • small group adventure travel for women • *www.arcticladies.com*

Bar H Ranch 208/354–2906, 888/216–6025 PO Box 297, Driggs, ID 83422 • horseback riding adventures for women in Wyoming's Grand Teton Mtns • trips range from wilderness camping to luxury accommodations • near Jackson Hole, WY • *www.tetontrailrides.com*

Bushwise Women /61 266840178 PO Box 34, , Mullumbimby, NSW 2482, Australia • international escapes & adventures for women • wilderness & cultural trips in New Zealand, Australia, Egypt & Europe • also hosts The Women's Accomodation Network • *www.bushwise.co.nz*

Call of the Wild Adventure Travel 510/849–9292, 888/378–1978 (OUTSIDE CA) 2519 Cedar St, Berkeley, CA 94708 • hiking, kayaking, backpacking & wilderness trips for all levels in Western US, Alaska, Hawaii, Mexico, New Zealand & Peru • longest-running adventure travel company for women • *www.callwild.com*

Chicks with Picks 970/626–4424 PO Box 486, Ridgeway, CO 81432 • ice-climbing for women • all levels welcome • *www.chickswithpicks.net*

Cloud Canyon Expeditions 805/692–9615 4858 Ogram Rd, Santa Barbara, CA 93105 • seasonal wilderness backpacking in Utah • *www.cloudcanyon.com*

Coming About 52–322/222–4119 Marina Vallarta F-9, Puerto Vallarta, Mexico • 1-, 3- & 9-day sailing courses for women • *www.coming-about.com*

Earth Island Expeditions 802/425–4710 201 Ten Stones Cir, Charlotte, VT 05445 • wilderness trips for women with a spiritual focus • also co-ed trips • *www.earthislandexpeditions.org*

Equinox Wilderness Expeditions 604/222–1219 2440 E Tudor Rd, Anchorage, AK 99507 • wilderness trips in Alaska, British Columbia & the Southwest US by raft, canoe, sea kayak & backpack • also ski tours near Whistler, BC • *www.equinoxexpeditions.com*

Gaia Adventures 604/875–0066 2033 W 7th Ave #310, Vancouver, BC V6J 1T3, Canada • outdoor adventures for women • hiking & rock climbing • ecotourism • backpack the Grand Canyon & more • *www.gaiaadventures.com*

Grand Canyon Field Institute 866/471–4435 PO Box 399, Grand Canyon, AZ 86023 • women's educational backpacking classes in the Grand Canyon • also co-ed trips • *www.grandcanyon.org/fieldinstitute*

Herizen™ Sailing for Women Inc 250/753–4253 307-160 Vancouver Ave, Nanaimo, BC V9S 4E8, Canada • women-only sailing & self-awareness courses taught in a retreat format • *www.sailingforwomen.com*

Lottsa Women Walking 0034/6967–70742 (IN LONDON, ENGLAND) Andalucia, Spain • walking holidays for women in Andalucia, Spain • accommodations & meals included • *www.lottsawomen.com*

LunaTours 406/222–9631, 877/404–6476 200 Mountain Brook Rd, Livingston, MT 59047 • fully supported road bike tours in Greece, Vietnam, Costa Rica, Iceland & more • unique tours in CA, MT, UT & Canadian Rockies • all levels welcome • *www.lunatours.com*

Mangrove Mistress 305/745–8886 Murray Marine, 5710 US 1, Key West, FL 33040 • snorkeling • nature exploring • sunset cruises • land & sea ceremonies • *www.floridakeys.net/mangrovemistress*

Mariah Wilderness Expeditions 530/626–6049, 800/462–7424 PO Box 1160, Lotus, CA 95651 • unique vacations for women on roads less traveled • multi-sport adventures • unique cultural & eco-explorations • *www.mariahwe.com*

National Women's Sailing Association 401/682–2064, 866/631–6972 70A Pleasant St, Marblehead, MA 01945 • sailing seminars & workshops • *www.womensailing.org*

Nurture Through Nature 207/452–2929 77 Warren Rd, Denmark, ME 04022 • holistic canoe trips & adventure retreats for women • yoga, guided meditation, kayaking, hiking & camping • *www.ntnretreats.com*

Octopus Reef Dive Training & Tours 808/875–0183 Maui, HI • experienced instructors teaching & guiding SCUBA divers in Maui • *www.OctopusReef.com*

Pacific Yachting & Sailing 831/462–6835 OR 423–7245 790 Mariner Park Way, Santa Cruz, CA 95062 • international & local yachting vacations for lesbians & mixed groups • also sailing instruction • *www.pacificsail.com*

Sea Sense: The Women's Sailing & Powerboating School 727/865–1404, 800/332–1404 PO Box 1961, St Petersburg, FL 33731 • worldwide sailing & powerboating courses • custom courses • also private, co-ed "on your own boat" courses • *www.seasenseboating.com*

Sheri Griffith River Expeditions 435/259–8229, 800/332–2439 PO Box 1324, Moab, UT 84532 • women-only river journeys in Colorado, Utah & Oregon • rock climbing & canyoneering • yoga & massage • also co-ed trips • www.griffithexp.com

Silver Waters Sailing 315/594–1906 12025 Delling Rd , Wolcott, NY 14590 • sailing instruction on Lake Ontario • also day trips • www.silverwaters.com

South Sea Mermaid Tours Ltd 64 /4 973 0675 55A Townsend Rd, Miramar, Wellington, New Zealand • all-inclusive package tours & backpacker tours for the spirited woman! • NZ & abroad • www.southseamermaids.co.nz

Tethys Offshore Sailing for Women 877/379–3880 2442 NW Market St #498, Seattle, WA 98107 • join Capt Nancy Erley as learning crew for a week in the Pacific Northwest • www.tethysoffshore.com

Walking Women 44 0/1926 313321 22 Duke St, Leamington Spa, Warwicks CV32 4TR, United Kingdom • women's walking vacations of all shapes & sizes • from English Lake District to Nepal or Peru • some lesbian-only trips • all levels • www.walkingwomen.com/lesbians.htm

Wanderwomen 64 9/360 7330 PO Box 68-058, Newton, Auckland, New Zealand • sea kayaking, multi-activity wknds, adventure treks & more • all levels welcome • co-ed trips, too • www.wanderwomen.co.nz

Wild Women Expeditions 705/866–1260, 888/993–1222 PO Box 145, Stn B, Sudbury, ON P3E 4N5, Canada • Canada's outdoor adventure company for women • adventure trips in Ontario's near-North • backpacking on Canada's East & West coasts • x-country skiing & dogsledding • getaways at 200-acre waterfront property • www.wildwomenexp.com

Winter Moon Summer Sun 218/848–2442 3388 Petrell, Brimson, MN 55602 • dogsledding trips in winter • kayaking Lake Superior in summer • rustic accommodations with meals provided • wintermoonsummersun.com

Woman Tours 585/256–9807, 800/247–1444 2340 Elmwood Ave, Rochester, NY 14618 • bicycle tours for women • call for a free catalog • www.womantours.com

Womanship 410/267–6661, 800/342–9295 137 Conduit St, Annapolis, MD 21401 • daily or live-aboard learning cruises for women • sail & "see" adventures offered in 16 locations around the world • www.womanship.com

Women in the Wilderness 651/227–2284 566 Ottawa Ave, St Paul, MN 55107 • adventure travel for women of all ages, from the Arctic to the Amazon • currently Iceland, Canadian North, Yucatan, Peru • also writers' workshops • cancer survivors' retreats • www.judithniemi.com

▲ **Women On A Roll 310/578–8888** PO Box 5112, Santa Monica, CA 90409-5112 • travel, sporting, cultural & social club for women • wide range of events & trips • largest lesbian organization in Southern California • www.womenonaroll.com

Women Sail Alaska 907/463–3372, 888/272–4525 245 Irwin St, Juneau, AK 99801 • experience the pristine beauty of southeast AK with lesbian guides • groups of 4 or less on a private yacht • www.alaska.net/~sailak

Women's Flyfishing® 907/274–7113 PO Box 243963, Anchorage, AK 99524 • women-only fly-fishing schools & guided trips in different locations around Alaska • we provide all gear & equipment • beginners welcome! • www.womensflyfishing.net

Mostly Women

Journeyweavers 607/277–1416 313 Washington St, Ithaca, NY 14850 • hiking & birding trips in Costa Rica • www.journeyweavers.com

Mountain Trek Fitness Retreat & Health Spa 250/229–5636, 800/661–5161 Box 1352, Ainsworth Hot Springs, BC V0G 1A0, Canada • a vacation for the mind & body • comprehensive health programs • www.hiking.com

Venus Charters 305/292–9403, 305/304–1181 PO Box 4394, Key West, FL 33041 • snorkeling • light-tackle fishing • dolphin-watching • www.venuscharters.com

Gay/Lesbian

Alaska Fantastic Fishing Charters 800/478–7777 PO Box 2807, Homer, AK 99603 • deluxe cabin cruiser for big-game fishing (halibut) • *www.homeralaskafishing.com*

▲ **Alyson Adventures, Inc 305/296–9935, 800/825–9766** 923 White St, Key West, FL 33041-1638 • award-winning adventure travel & active vacations • hiking, biking & multi-sport activities • *www.AlysonAdventures.com*

OutWest Global Adventures 406/446–1533, 800/743–0458 PO Box 2050, Red Lodge, MT 59068 • specializing in gay/ lesbian active & adventure travel • worldwide • *www.outwestadventures.com*

Rainbow Adventures, Inc 808/965–9011 PO Box 983, Pahoa, HI 96778 • intimate hikes for 1 or more women • Volcano Nat'l Park • coastline lava tubes • ancient sacred sites • snorkeling • swimming with dolphins • also B&B • *alohafun.com*

South American Journeys, LLC 800/884–7474 Tujunga, CA 91042 • hiking, fishing, camping & more in Peru & South American • women-only & men-only trips available • *www.southamericanjourneys.com*

Undersea Expeditions 858/270–2900, 800/669–0310 PO Box 9455, Pacific Beach, CA 92169 • warm-water diving & scuba trips worldwide • *www.underseax.com*

Straight/Gay

10,000 Waves 406/549–6670, 800/537–8315 PO Box 7924, Missoula, MT 59807 • white-water & scenic rafting • kayaking • on Montana's premier rivers • *www.10000-waves.com*

Adventure Photo Tours 702/889–8687, 888/363–8687 3111 S Valley View Blvd #X-106, Las Vegas, NV 89102 • wonderful, romantic off-road adventures • private tours available • *www.adventurephototours.com*

Amphibious Horizons 410/267–8742, 888/458–8786 600 Quiet Waters Park Rd, Annapolis, MD 21403 • sea kayaking & adventure travel in the Chesapeake Bay Region • all levels • groups of any type welcome • 30 gorgeous paddle locations • *www.amphibioushorizons.com*

Atlantis Yacht Charters 415/332–0800, 800/65–YACHTS Schoonmaker Pt Marina, 85 Liberty Ship Way #110-A, Sausalito, CA 94965 • group charters • *www.yachtcharter.com*

Backroads 510/527–1555, 800/462–2848 801 Cedar St, Berkeley, CA 94710 • *www.backroads.com*

Barefoot Adventures Puerto Rico 787/245–1712 Luquillo, Puerto Rico • get to know Puerto Rico • local day trips • gay-owned • *www.geocities.com/bfapr*

Come 2 Africa 27 72/394–7625 75 Impala St, Hazyview 1242, South Africa • custom tours, including Kruger Nat'l Park • *www.comdzafrica.com*

GoNorth Alaska Adventure Travel Center 907/479–7272, 866/236–7272 3500 Davis Rd, Fairbanks, AK 99709 • guided tours throughout Alaska & the Arctic • air taxis & transportation • camper, canoe & bike rentals • hostel accommodations • RV & SUV rental • *www.gonorthalaska.com*

Great Canadian Ecoventures 867/920–7110, 800/667–9453 PO Box 2481, Yellowknife, NT X1A 2P8, Canada • Arctic Canada: wilderness & wildlife expeditions for the camera, paddle, heart & soul • *www.thelon.com*

Natural Habitat Adventures 303/449–3711, 800/543–8917 2945 Center Green Ct, Ste H, Boulder, CO 80301 • up-close encounters with the world's most amazing wildlife in its natural habitat • *www.nathab.com*

Open Eye Tours 808/280–5299 PO Box 324, Makawao, HI 96768 • customized private land tours of Maui & other islands • visit places seldom seen • refreshing, educational & fun, sharing Maui's best-kept secrets since 1983 • *www.openeyetours.com*

Outland Adventures 206/932–7012 PO Box 16343, Seattle, WA 98116 • ecologically sensitive cultural tours with snorkeling & biking in Central America, Canada, Alaska & Washington State • *www.outlandadventures.natureavenue.com*

Paddling South & Saddling South 707/942–4550, 800/398–6200 PO Box 827, Calistoga, CA 94515 • horseback, mountain biking & sea kayak trips in Baja • call for complete calendar • *www.tourbaja.com*

Passage to Utah 801/519–2400, 800/677–0553 1338 S Fooothill Dr, Salt Lake City, UT 84108 • custom trips in the West including hiking, horseback riding & river riding • *www.passagetoutah.com*

Puffin Family Charters 907/278–3346, 800/978–3346 PO Box 232813, Anchorage, AK 99523 • *www.puffincharters.com*

Rockwood Adventures 604/980–7749, 888/236–6606 839 W 1st St #C, North Vancouver, BC V7P 1A4, Canada • rain forest walks for all levels with free hotel pick-up • *www.rockwoodadventures.com*

Snow Lion Expeditions 801/355–6555, 800/525–8735 Oquirrh Pl, 350 South 400 East #G-2, Salt Lake City, UT 84111 • tours, treks & active vacations in the Himalayas, Tibet, SE Asia, China & more • gay & mixed tours available • *www.snowlion.com*

Voyager North Outfitters 218/365–3251, 800/848–5530 1829 E Sheridan, Ely, MN 55731 • canoe outfitting & trips • *www.vnorth.com*

Whitewater Connection 530/622–6446, 800/336–7238 PO Box 270, Coloma, CA 95613 • whitewater rafting adventures • *www.whitewaterconnection.com*

Wildlife Safari 925/376–5595, 800/221–8118 346 Rheem Blvd #107, Moraga, CA 94556 • photographic safaris • Eastern & Southern Africa, Egypt, Mauritius & Seychelles Islands • *www.wildlife-safari.com*

Sacred Journeys for Women

Sacred Journeys for Women is an internationally recognised women's travel company. We guide small groups on journeys to ancient sacred sites around the world.

We endeavor to travel lightly, eat organically, and rest in luxury whenever possible.

Sacred Journeys for Women
Toll-free: 1-888-779-6696
www.sacredjourneys.com
info@sacredjourneys.com

SPIRITUAL/HEALTH VACATIONS

Women Only

▲ **Sacred Journeys for Women 707/526–7888, 888/779–6696** PO Box 8007, Roseland Station, CA 95407 • pilgrimages focused on the Divine Feminine in England, Scotland, Ireland, Crete & Hawaii • *www.sacredjourneys.com*

Sounds & Furies 604/253–7189 PO Box 21510, 1424 Commercial Dr, Vancouver, BC V5L 5G2, Canada • economical goddess tours for women • *www.soundsandfuries.com*

Gay/Lesbian

Spirit Journeys 828/258–8880, 800/490–3684 PO Box 3046, Asheville, NC 28802 • spiritual retreats, workshops & adventure trips throughout the US & abroad • *www.spiritjouneys.com*

Tellardians 705/789–0058 GB 197, RR#4, Huntsville, ON P1H 2J6, Canada • guided spiritual wilderness retreats with rustic camping • also personal meditation cabins & hostels • canoe retreats into Algonquin Park & beyond • motor home retreats throughout Canada • *www.tellardians.com*

CRUISES

Women Only

▲ **Olivia Cruises 415/962–5700, 800/631–6277** 434 Brannan St, San Francisco, CA 94107 • exclusive cruise & resort vacations for lesbians • Bahamas, Caribbean, Alaska, Mexico, Tahiti, Barbados & more • see ad in front color section • *www.olivia.com*

Gay/Lesbian

Gayribbean Cruises 214/824–8765, 888/813–9947 PO Box 192506, Dallas, TX 75219 • gay & lesbian group cruises including annual Halloween Cruise from Galveston, TX • *www.gayribbeancruises.com*

Journeys By Sea 954/522–5865, 800/825–3632 PO Box 7438, Fort Lauderdale, FL 33338 • sailing in the Caribbean with gay captain & crew • *www.journeysbysea.com*

Ocean Voyager 321/783–6767, 800/435–2531 1980 North Atlantic Ave #916, Cocoa Beach, FL 32931 • hosted gay groups on mainstream upscale cruise ships • *www.oceanvoyager.com*

Port Yacht Charters 516/883–0998, 877/DO-A-BOAT 9 Belleview Ave, Port Washington, NY 11050 • custom charters worldwide, specializing in the Caribbean • commitment ceremonies • gourmet cuisine • *www.portyachtcharters.com*

▲ **R Family 866/732–6822** 5 Washington Ave, Nyack, NY 10960 • family-friendly vacations designed especially for the LGBT community • see ad in front color section • *www.rfamilyvacations.com*

Rainbow Charters 808/396–5995 939 Kawaiki Pl, Honolulu, HI 96825 • gay & lesbian weddings • custom sailing cruises • whale-watching • snorkeling

RSVP 612/729–1113, 800/328–7787 2800 University Ave SE, Minneapolis, MN 55414 • cruises & all-gay/ lesbian resorts in the Caribbean, Mexico & Alaska • *www.rsvp.net*

Sailing Affairs 917/453–6425 58 E 1st St #6-B, New York City, NY 10003 • gay sailboat charters, day trips, sunset sails & sailing vacations • East Coast & Caribbean • *www.sailingaffairs.com*

Straight/Gay

Amazon Tours & Cruises 305/227–2266, 800/423–2791 275 Fontainebleau Blvd #173, Miami, FL 33172 • weekly cruises in the upper Amazon • *www.amazontours.net*

Aquafest 800/592–9058 4801 Woodway #400-W, Houston, TX 77056 • lgbt groups mingle with mixed clientele on major cruise lines • *www.aquafest.net*

Whitney Yacht Charters 941/966–9767, 800/223–1426 3214 Casey Key Rd, Nokomis, FL 34275 • yacht charters in the Caribbean, Mediterranean & New England states • *www.whitneyyachtcharters.com*

THEMATIC TOURS

Women Only

▲ **12 Muses 603/323–9957, 800/926–6873** 11 Runnells Hall Rd, Chocorua, NH 03817 • cruises & tours led by women of distinction • see ad in front color section • *www.12Muses.com*

Canyon Calling 928/282–0916, 800/664–8922 200 Carol Canyon Dr, Sedona, AZ 86336 • multi-activity adventure trips for moderately fit women in the Southwest, Tetons, Canadian Rockies, Hawaii, Alaska, Costa Rica, The Alps, Greece & Fiji-New Zealand • *www.canyoncalling.com*

Club Skirts 888/44–DINAH 917 Folsom St, San Francisco, CA 94107 • Dinah Shore Women's Weekend parties • Dinah Shore hotline: 888-44-DINAH • *www.clubskirts.com*

Ela Brasil Tours 203/840–9010 14 Burlington Dr, Norwalk, CT 06851 • exclusive custom trips to Brazil • promoting responsible travel & cultural diversity • guided trips and custom itineraries year-round • EcoVolunteer programs • *www.elabrasil.com*

International Women's Studies Institute 650/654–6346 PO Box 1067, Palo Alto, CA 94302 • travel-study programs • cross-cultural • school credit available • *www.iwsi.org*

Purple Diamonds 718/623–9428 New York City, NY • stylish travel group for women of color • also special events • *www.purplediamonds.biz/homepage.htm*

Robin Tyler International Tours for Women 818/893–4075 15842 Chase St, North Hills, CA 91343 • lesbian travel • upscale international five-star operation • exotic locations include tours &private yacht cruises in Egypt, Galapagos, Amazon, Machu Picchu, Nepal, China, Asia & beyond • *www.robintylertours.com*

RVing Women 480/671–6226, 888/557–8464 PO Box 1940, Apache Jct, AZ 85217 • education & support organization for women who travel in RVs • *www.RVingWomen.com*

Shop Around Tours 212/684–3763 305 E 24th St #2-N, New York City, NY 10010 • for people who live to shop and love to travel • *www.shoparoundtours.com*

Tours of Exploration 604/886–7301, 800/690–7887 PO Box 1503, Gibsons, BC V0N 1V0, Canada • eco-cultural journeys to Ecuador for women • *www.toursexplore.com*

Towanda Women Motorcycle Tours 510/710–7748 (IN US), 64–3/313–9097 (IN NZ) PO Box 4437, Christchurch, New Zealand • women's motorcycle tours in the US, Europe, New Zealand & Australia • *www.towanda.org*

Women Travel Connection/ Ebony Travel 877/823–4373 1000 SW 86th Ave, Pembroke Pines, FL 33025 • travel group & agency designed exclusively by women for women travelers • *www.womentravelconnection.com*

Women's Motorcyclist Foundation 585/768–6054 7 Lent Ave, LeRoy, NY 14482 • works to improve the sport of motorcycling • also raises money for breast cancer • *www.womensmotorcyclistfoundation.org*

Gay/Lesbian

Adventure Tours, Inc 207/284–2804, 888/206–6523 PO Box 290, Saco, ME 04072 • custom individual & group packages to Costa Rica • www.gayadventuretours.com

Africa Outing 27–21/671–4028 5 Alcyone Rd, Claremont, Capetown 7708, South Africa • gay/lesbian safaris & more • tours customized to your needs • www.afouting.com

Arco Iris Gay Mexico Travel Experts 619/297–0897, 800/765–4370 1286 University Ave, #154, San Diego, CA 92103 • the original gay Mexico experts • group tours & individual trips to all of Mexico • www.arcoiristours.com

Brazil Fiesta Tours & Visa Service 415/986–1134, 800/200–0582 323 Geary St #615, San Francisco, CA 94102 • tours to Brazil • Brazilian visa service • www.brazilfiesta.com

Cruisin' the Castro 415/255–1821 584 Castro St #642, San Francisco, CA 94114 • award-winning, guided historical walking tour of the Castro • includes lunch • www.webcastro.com/castrotour/

DaSi Tours 877/276–6636 PO Box 2307, Seal Beach, CA 90740-1307 • independent & group tours in Spain & Portugal • www.da-sitours.com

Doin It Right – In Costa Rica 619/297–3642 (US#), 800/936–3646 Private Villa, Hotel & Gay Property Specialists • organized tours • FIT's • photography tours • www.DoinItRight.com

Doin It Right – In Puerto Vallarta 941/297–3642 (US#), 800/936–3646 1st ('95) Gay, Condo, Villa Puerto Vallarta Specialist • clients receive our 250+ page Vallarta Guide • $100 free coupons • honest descriptions • we've slept in most of our properties!! • www.DoinItRight.com

Gay Bali Tours 62–361/722 483 Griya Anyar 76A, Br. Kajeng-Suwung, 80361 Bali, Indonesia • exclusively gay & lesbian tours in Bali • special services in Bali & beyond • www.bali-rain-bows.com

Going Your Way Tours 860/861–2301 109 Dayton Rd #A, Waterford, CT 06385 • upscale customized group & individual itineraries worldwide • www.goingyourwaytours.com

MexGay Vacations 213/383–9491, 866/639–4299 611 S Catalina St #222, Los Angeles, CA 90005 • specializing in gay travel to Mexico • www.mexgay.com

National Gay Pilots Association 214/336–0873 PO Box 7271, Dallas, TX 75209 • several annual gatherings • call for more info • www.ngpa.org

Pacific Ocean Holidays 808/923–2400, 800/735–6600 Honolulu, HI • Hawaii vacation packages • gayhawaiivacations.com

Pink Travel 33-1/42-78-03-50 3 Passage de l'Ancre, Rue Saint Martin, 75003 Paris, France • inbound tour operator for gay & lesbian France • packages in Paris, Provence, Loire Valley, Nice & French Riviera • gay-owned/ run • www.gaytravelfrance.com

Pro Musica Tours 212/541–5122 458 W 52nd St #1-D, New York, NY 10019 • gay-only or mixed • performing arts/cultural tours • gay-owned/run • www.promusicatours.com

Venture Out 415/626–5678, 888/431–6789 575 Pierce St #604, San Francisco, CA 94117 • small-group escorted tours around the world • day trips & overnight excursions in Northern CA & San Francisco area • www.venture-out.com

Victorian Home Walks 415/252–9485 335 Powell, at Westin St Francis Hotel, San Francisco, CA • historical walking tour of San Francisco's Victorian homes • www.victorian-walk.com

Way To Go Costa Rica, Panama & Belize 919/782–1900, 800/835–1223 5171 Glenwood Ave # 111, Raleigh, NC 27612 • custom itineraries for individual travelers & groups • www.way-togocostarica.com

Winelovertours.com 860/861–2301 109 Dayton Rd #A, Waterford, CT 06385 • upscale group tours & individual itineraries for foodies & winelovers • www.winelovertours.com

Straight/Gay

Alaska Railroad Scenic Tours 907/265–2494, 800/544–0552 PO Box 107500, Anchorage, AK 99510-7500 • *www.akrr.com*

Asian Pacific Adventures 818/881–2745, 800/825–1680 6065 Calvin Ave, Tarzana, CA 91356 • custom tours to Asia, including India, Thailand, China, Tibet, Vietnam, Japan & more • festivals, tribes, safaris, art • hiking & biking • *www.asianpacificadventures.com*

Bophelo Tours & Safaris 27–0/12–654–7237 23 Kneen St, Valhalla, Pretoria, Gauteng 0185, South Africa • safaris & boat cruises in South Africa • gay-owned • *www.bophelo.com*

Earth Walks 505/988–4157 PO Box 8534, Santa Fe, NM 87504 • custom, guided tours of American Southwest & Mexico

Ecotour Expeditions, Inc 401/423–3377, 800/688–1822 PO Box 128, Jamestown, RI 02835-1822 • small group boat tours of the Amazon & more • call for color catalog • *www.naturetours.com*

Heritage Tours 212/206–8400, 800/378–4555 121 W 27th St #1201, New York, NY 10001 • custom trips to Turkey, Spain, Peru, Southern Africa & Morocco • *www.heritagetoursonline.com*

Holbrook Travel 800/451–7111 3540 NW 13th St, Gainesville, FL 32609 • natural history tours in Central America, South America & Africa • small groups • *www.holbrooktravel.com*

Kenny Tours, Ltd 410/548–2200, 800/648–1492 5530 Abbey Ln, Salisbury, MD 21801-2323 • trips to Ireland • *www.kenny-tours.com*

Lima Tours 51–1/619–6900 Belen 1040, Lima, Peru • customized, gay-friendly tours to Peru • *www.limatours.com.pe*

New England Vacation Tours 802/464–2076, 800/742–7669 PO Box 560, West Dover, VT 05356 • gay/lesbian tours (including fall foliage) conducted by a mainstream tour operator • *www.sover.net/~nevt*

Pacha Tours 800/722–4288 37 E 28th St #708, New York City, NY 10016 • trips to Turkey • *www.pachatours.com*

Stockler Expeditions 954/472–7163, 800/591–2955 10266 NW 4th Ct, Plantation, FL 33324 • trips to Brazil, Argentina, Peru, Ecuador, Chile & China

LUXURY TOURS

Gay/Lesbian

DavidTours 949/723–0699, 888/723–0699 310 Dahlia Pl, Ste A, Corona del Mar, CA 92625-2821 • luxury small-group tours to Europe, Africa, South America, Canada, Asia & the South Pacific • www.DavidTours.com

CUSTOM TOURS

Costa Rica Experts 773/935–1009, 800/827–9046 3166 N Lincoln Ave #424, Chicago, IL 60657 • www.costaricaexperts.com

Travel & Culture 922/152 18097 702 Panorama Center Office Plaza, 75530 Karachi, Pakistan • tours, safaris & hotel reservations in Pakistan • www.travel-culture.com

VARIOUS TOURS

Women Only

See Jayne Play 813/888–7965 7321 Canal Blvd, Tampa, FL 33615 • European tours for women • lesbian-owned • www.seejayneplay.com

Gay/Lesbian

Footprints 416/962–8111, 888/962–6211 506 Church St # 200, Toronto, ON M4Y 2C8, Canada • custom-designed, private tours arranged to worldwide destinations • www.footprintstravel.com

Friends of Dorothy Travel® 415/864–1600, 800/640–4918 1177 California St #B, San Francisco, CA 94108 • unique gay & lesbian adventures • individual & group arrangements • www.fodtravel.com

Out & About Travel 800/842–4753 161 Federal Street, Providence, RI 02903 • full-service gay-owned & operated travel agency specializing in gay & lesbian tours, cruises, adventure travel, ski trips & more! • gaytravelz.com

Postcard Destinations 814/539–4999, 800/484–3250 x2621 188 Crystal St, Johnstown, PA 15906 • for all your travel needs around the world • cruises, tours, hotels, flights • budget or deluxe • we find the best prices for you • www.postcarddestinations.com

Zoom Vacations 773/935–1728, 866/966–6822 716 W Buena #3C, Chicago, IL 60613 • group vacations taking gay travel to the next level • experience the best of a destination with surprises, insider events & a sense of magic • www.zoomvacations.com

EVENTS

January 2006

4-8: **Utah Gay/ Lesbian Ski Week**   *Park City, UT*
☎877/429–6368 EMAIL: wehojohn@aol.com WEB: www.gayskiing.org

15-22: **Aspen Gay Ski Week**   *Aspen, CO*
LGBT • 3000+ attendees ☎970/925–4123, 800/367–8290 (LODGING) ✉ c/o Aspen
Gay/Lesbian Community Fund, PO Box 3143, Aspen, CO 81612 EMAIL:
info@gayskiweek.com WEB: www.gayskiweek.com

February 2006

4-13: **Whistler Gay Ski Week: Altitude 2006**   *Whistler, BC, Canada*
annual gay/lesbian ski week • parties for boys & girls! • top-notch DJs & venues • popular destination 75 miles N of Vancouver • LGBT • 3000+ attendees ☎604/899–6209,
888/258–4883 ✉ c/o Out On The Slopes Productions, 2803-939 Homer St, Vancouver,
BC, Canada V6G 2W6 EMAIL: media@oosp.com WEB: www.outontheslopes.com

26-March 5: **Ascent**   *Lake Tahoe, CA*
sledding • snowshoeing • parties • major entertainment • and of course skiing during
this fabulous week in Tahoe • gay/lesbian ☎866/263–4167 EMAIL:
info@ascentlaketahoe.com WEB: www.ascentlaketahoe.com

28: **Mardi Gras**   *New Orleans, LA*
North America's rowdiest block party may be quieter in the wake of Hurricane Katrina •
check current conditions before making travel plans • mixed gay/straight
☎504/566–5011, 800/672–6124 ✉ c/o New Orleans Convention & Visitors Bureau,
1520 Sugarbowl Dr, New Orleans, LA 70112 WEB: www.neworleanscvb.com

TBA: **Hero**   *Auckland, New Zealand*
2-week LGBT celebration • movies, sports, readings & parties galore WEB:
www.hero.org.nz

March 2006

5-12: **Lake Tahoe WinterFest**   *Lake Tahoe, NV*
nightly entertainment • comedy show • Tahoe Cruise party boat • & of course skiing, at
6 world-class ski resorts • LGBT • 1000 attendees ☎877/777–4950 ✉ c/o Nevada Gay/
Lesbian Visitor & Convention Bureau, PO Box 2215, Carson City, NV 89702 EMAIL:
nglvcb@aol.com WEB: www.LakeTahoeWinterfest.com

27-April 2: **Kraft Nabisco Golf Championship**   *Palm Springs, CA*
previously known as the Dinah Shore Golf Championship • mostly women
☎760/324–4546 WEB: www.nabiscochampionship.com

29-April 2: **Club Skirts' Dinah Shore Weekend**   *Palm Springs, CA*
women only ☎888/44–DINAH ✉ c/o Club Skirts, 917 Folsom St, San Francisco, CA
94107 EMAIL: info@clubskirts.com WEB: www.clubskirts.com

29-April 2: **Girl Bar Dinah Shore Weekend**   *Palm Springs, CA*
huge gathering of lesbians for mega dance parties, huge pool parties, comedy, national
recording artists & yes, some golf watching • see ad in front color section • women only
WEB: www.dinahshoreweekend.com

April 2006

5-9: **OutBoard**   *Keystone, CO*
annual lesbian/ gay snowboarding festival • 300+ attendees EMAIL: ryan@outboard.org
WEB: www.outboard.org

27-30: **Philadelphia Black Gay Pride**   *Philadelphia, PA*
a weekend of social & cultural activities • films, BBQ, spoken word, parties & more •
lgbt ☎215/496-0330 ✉ c/o Philadelphia Black Pride, Inc, 1201 Chestnut St, 5th Fl,
Philadelphia, PA 19107 EMAIL: pride@coloursinc.org WEB: www.phillyblackpride.org

30: **Queensday**   *Amsterdam, Netherlands*
huge street festival to celebrate what was originally the birthday of the Queen Mother •
LGBT

TBA: **Boybutante Ball**   *Athens, GA*
LGBT • 1000+ attendees ☎706/227-3530 ✉ c/o Boybutante AIDS Foundation, Inc, PO
Box 6013, Athens, GA 30604-6013 EMAIL: missthing@boybutante.org WEB: www.boybu-
tante.org

TBA: **Splash: Houston Black Gay Pride**   *Houston, TX*
LGBT ☎832/443-1016 ✉ c/o Houston Splash, PO Box 667248, Houston, TX 77266
EMAIL: info@houstonsplash.com WEB: www.houstonsplash.com

May 2006

1-7: **Equality Forum**   *Philadelphia, PA*
largest national & int'l GLBT forum with 80+ programs, parties & special events
☎215/732-3378 ✉ 1420 Locust St #300, Philadelphia, PA 19102 EMAIL: info@equalityfo-
rum.com WEB: www.equalityforum.org

11-15: **Cancun Int'l Gay Festival**   *Cancun, Mexico*
LGBT ☎619/297-0897, 800/765-4370 EMAIL: gaymexicoexperts@aol.com WEB: www.can-
cungayfestival.com

24-29: **Annual Gay Bowling Tournament**   *Kansas City, MO*
also mid-year tournament in Michigan in November ☎414/482-1868 ✉ c/o IGBO, PO
Box 100339, Milwaukee, WI 53210 EMAIL: president@igbo.org WEB: www.igbo.org

25-29: **Pensacola Memorial Day Weekend**   *Pensacola, FL*
many parties on beaches & in bars • LGBT • 35,000+ attendees ☎850/438-0333

26-29: **Black Lesbian/ Gay Pride Weekend**   *Washington, DC*
LGBT ☎202/737-5767, 866/94-BLGPD ✉ c/o BLGPD, PO Box 77071, Washington, DC
20013 EMAIL: contactus@dcblackpride.org WEB: www.dcblackpride.org

26: **Gay/ Lesbian Night at Great America**   *Santa Clara, CA*
join 10,000 men & women for a special night at Northern California's favorite amusement park • live performances • dancing till 3am • LGBT

26-June 11: **Spoleto Festival USA**   *Charleston, SC*
one of the continent's premier avant-garde cultural arts festivals • mixed gay/straight
☎843/579-3100 ✉ c/o Spoleto Festival USA, PO Box 157, Charleston, SC 29402-0157
EMAIL: receptionist@spoletousa.org WEB: www.spoletousa.org

30-June 4: **Gay Days Orlando**   *Orlando, FL*
including Gay Day at Disney & Islands of Adventure • 4 days of parties & fun for boys &
girls alike! • LGBT ☎407/896-8431 ✉ c/o GayDays, Inc, 1011 Virginia Dr #101, Orlando,
FL 32803 EMAIL: chris@gaydays.com WEB: gaydays.com

TBA: **AIDS Walk New York**   *New York City, NY*
AIDS benefit • mixed gay/straight ☎212/807-9255 ✉ c/o Gay Men's Health Crisis, PO
Box 10, Old Chelsea Stn, New York, NY 10113-0010 EMAIL: awnyinfo@aidswalk.net WEB:
www.aidswalk.net

TBA: **Aqua Girl**   *Miami Beach, FL*
a weekend of hot women's parties in Miami • mostly women ☎305/532-1997 ✉ c/o
Women's Community Fund, 1521 Alton Rd #117, Miami Beach, FL 33139 EMAIL:
clara@aquagirl.org WEB: www.aquagirl.org

TBA: **Art for AIDS/ Art for Change**   *Pittsburgh, PA*
huge party benefitting AIDS charities • LGBT ☎412/441-9786 ✉ c/o Persad Center,
5150 Penn Ave, Pittsburgh, PA 15224 EMAIL: business@persadcenter.org WEB: persadcen-
ter.org

TBA: **Minnesota AIDS Walk**   *Minneapolis, MN*
enjoy a walk through Minnehaha Park & raise money for local AIDS organizations •
mixed gay/straight • 12,000 attendees ☎612/373–2411 ✉ c/o Minnesota AIDS Project,
1400 Park Ave S, Minneapolis, MN 55404 EMAIL: info@mnaidsproject.org WEB: www.mnaid-
sproject.org

TBA: **Russian River Women's Wknd**   *Guerneville, CA*
this tiny town is packed with dykes for a fun weekend of parties • 2 hours north of San
Francisco • mostly women ☎707/526–3416 WEB: www.russianriverwomensweekend.com

TBA: **We're Funny That Way**   *Toronto, ON, Canada*
comedians from around the world perform at Canada's International Gay/Lesbian
Comedy Festival • LGBT ☎416/975–8555, 416/907–9099 ✉ c/o WFTW Productions,
2060 Queen St E #45, Toronto, ON, Canada M4E 1C9 WEB: www.werefunnythatway.com

June 2006

1-5: **Girls in Wonderland**   *Orlando, FL*
official women's parties of Gay Days Orlando • 4 days of fun! • tickets available thru
www.girlsinwonderland.com • mostly women ☎305/495–6933 (TICKETS) ✉ c/o Pandora
Events, 800 West Ave #420, Miami Beach, FL 33139 EMAIL: info@girlsinwonderland.com
WEB: www.girlsinwonderland.com

on-going: **LGBT Pride**   *Everywhere, USA*
celebrate yourself & attend one – or many – of the hundreds of Gay Pride parades & fes-
tivities happening in cities around the world EMAIL: info@interpride.org WEB: www.inter-
pride.org

on-going: **Music in the Mountains**   *Nevada City, CA*
summer music festival • mixed gay/straight ☎530/265–6124, 800/218–2188 ✉ c/o
Music in the Mountains, PO Box 1451, Nevada City, CA 95959 EMAIL: mim@musicinthe-
mountains.org WEB: www.musicinthemountains.org

2-18: **Juneteenth Jamboree of New Plays**   *Louisville, KY*
annual theater festival • new works about the African American experience • many with
gay themes • Juneteenth@Apollo Talent Showcase & Juneteenth Bazaar • mixed
gay/straight ☎502/636–4200 ✉ c/o Juneteenth Legacy Theatre, PO Box 3463,
Louisville, KY 40201 EMAIL: juneteenthlegacy@aol.com WEB:
www.juneteenthlegacytheatre.com

3-30: **National Queer Arts Festival**   *San Francisco, CA*
performances & exhibitions in the San Francisco Bay Area highlighting artists from
around the country • LGBT ☎415/864–4124 ✉ c/o Queer Cultural Center, 934 Brannan
St, San Francisco, CA 94103 EMAIL: director@QueerCulturalCenter.org WEB:
www.QueerCulturalCenter.org

4-10: **AIDS LifeCycle**   *San Francisco to Los Angeles, CA*
bike from San Francisco to Los Angeles to raise money for HIV/AIDS services
☎866/BIKE–4AIDS ✉ c/o San Francisco AIDS Foundation, 995 Market St #200, San
Francisco, CA 94103 EMAIL: info@aidslifecycle.org WEB: www.aidslifecycle.org

5: **AIDS Walk & 5K Run Boston**   *Boston, MA*
mixed gay/straight • 12,000 attendees ☎617/437–6200 ✉ c/o AIDS Action Committee,
294 Washington Street, 5th floor, Boston, MA 02108 EMAIL: info@aac.org WEB:
www.aac.org

18: **Unofficial Gay Day at Cedar Point**   *Sandusky, OH*
wear red to show your support on the unofficial Gay Day at this popular amusement
park • mixed gay/straight EMAIL: info@lgcsc.org

19-25: **Black Pride NYC**   *New York City, NY*
multicultural LGBT festival with a wide array of entertainment, forums, workshops &
events • LGBT

21: **Pearl Day at Six Flags**   *Atlanta, GA*
unofficial gay celebration at Six Flags amusement park • show your support with a string
of Commemorative Pearls • proceeds go to local charities • LGBT ☎404/870–7821 WEB:
www.pearlday.com

commemorate.educate.liberate.celebrate.

SAN FRANCISCO LGBT PRIDE

June 24 & 25 2006

www.sfpride.org

22-26: **Mexico City Gay Pride Week**   *Mexico City, Mexico*
5 days of parties & more • LGBT ☎619/**297-0897**, 800/**765-4370** EMAIL: gaymexicoin-fo@aol.com WEB: www.mexcity.8m.com

24-25: **San Francisco LGBT Pride Parade/ Celebration**   *San Francisco, CA*
LGBT ☎415/**864-3733** ✉ c/o SFLGBTPCC, 1230 Market St PMB421, San Francisco, CA
94102 EMAIL: info@sfpride.org WEB: www.sfpride.org

25: **San Francisco Dyke March**   *San Francisco, CA*
join thousands of dykes of all shapes, colors & sizes for music, marching & more
through the streets of the Mission & the Castro • women only ☎415/**241-8882** EMAIL:
info@dykemarch.org WEB: www.dykemarch.org/SFO

26-28: **Int'l Assoc. of Country Western Dance Clubs Annual Convention**   *New York, NY*
also semi-annual conventions in March (Fort Lauderdale, FL) & October (San Francisco,
CA) • LGBT • 400-600 attendees ☎757/**456-5615**, 416/**923-8247** (**IN CANADA**) ✉ c/o
IAGLCWDC, 5534 Edmondson Pike, PMB 107, Nashville, TN 37211 EMAIL:
information@iaglcwdc.org WEB: www.outcountrydance.com

28-July 3: **At the Beach Weekend**   *Los Angeles, CA*
celebrate a weekend of Black gay pride in Malibu • LGBT ☎323/**293-4282** ✉ c/o At The
Beach Shorey, Inc, 4745 W Slauson Ave, Los Angeles, CA 90056 EMAIL: atbla@aol.com
WEB: www.atbla.com

30-July 3: **Int'l Gay Square Dance Clubs Convention**   *Santa Clara, CA*
☎800/**835-6462** ✉ c/o IAGSDC, PO BOX 87507, San Diego, CA 92138 EMAIL: informa-
tion@iagsdc.org WEB: www.iagsdc.org

TBA: **Black Gay Pride**   *Memphis, TN*
LGBT ☎901/**521-6922** WEB: www.memphisblackpride.com

TBA: **Black Lesbian/ Gay Pride**   *Oakland, CA*
celebrate with a weekend of conferences, awards ceremonies & parties • LGBT
☎510/**268-0646** EMAIL: tbhcafe@pacbell.net WEB: www.californiablackprides.info

TBA: **Boston Unity Pride**   *Boston, MA*
celebrate Black pride in Boston ☎617/**238-2404**

TBA: **EuroPride 2006**   *London, England*
parties, politics, performance & more • there is something for everyone at this massive
celebration of gay pride ☎49-177/**317 0943** ✉ c/o European Pride Organisers Assoc,
Buelowstrasse 106, Berlin, Germany D-10783 WEB: www.europride.no

TBA: **PrideFest**   *Milwaukee, WI*
celebrate LGBT pride at Henry W Maier Festival Park • LGBT ☎414/**272-3378** ✉ c/o
PrideFest, PO Box 511763, Milwaukee, WI 53203-0301 EMAIL: info@pridefest.com WEB:
www.pridefest.com

July 2006

6-9: **Chicago Black Pride**   *Chicago, IL*
a weekend of parties, seminars & more • LGBT

15-22: **Gay Games 2006**   *Chicago, IL*
8 days of sports, cultural events, arts & ceremonies in Chicago • LGBT ☎773/**907-2006**
EMAIL: info@gaygameschicago.org WEB: www.gaygameschicago.org

16: **AIDS Walk San Francisco**   *San Francisco, CA*
mixed gay/straight • 27,000+ attendees ☎415/**392-9255** ✉ c/o Miller Zeichik & Assoc,
PO Box 193920, San Francisco, CA 94119-3920 EMAIL: sfinfo@aidswalk.net WEB:
www.aidswalk.net

26-Aug 5: **1st World Outgames— Montreal 2006**   *Montréal, QC, Canada*
gay sport & cultural festival • LGBT ☎514/**252-5852** ✉ 4141 Ave Pierre de Coubertin,
Montreal, QC, Canada H1V 3N7 EMAIL: info@montreal2006.org WEB: www.montreal2006.org

26-29: **Hotter Than July Weekend**   *Detroit, MI*
celebrate more than a decade of black gay pride in the Motor City • LGBT
☎313/**289-8669** ✉ c/o The Black Pride Society, PO Box 3025, Detroit, MI 48231 EMAIL:
info@hotterthanjuly.com WEB: www.hotterthanjuly.com

TBA: **Crape Myrtle Festival**   *Raleigh-Durham, Chapel Hill, NC*
  weeklong festival to raise money for AIDS & LGBT concerns • gala Saturday • also sup-
  porting events throughout the year • mixed gay/straight • 1500+ attendees
  ☎919/832–2103 ⊠ c/o Crape Myrtle Festival, Inc, PO Box 10043, Raleigh, NC 27605
  EMAIL: info@crapemyrtlefest.org WEB: www.crapemyrtlefest.org

TBA: **Paradise Ride Hawaii**   *4 islands, HI*
  7-day cycling event to raise funds for HIV/AIDS service • 390 miles on the islands of
  Oahu, Kauai, Maui & Molokai ☎888/285–9866 ⊠ c/o Life Foundation, 233 Keawe St
  #226, Honolulu, HI 96813 EMAIL: info@paradiseridehawaii.org WEB: www.paradiseride-
  hawaii.org

August 2006

12-20: **National Gay Softball World Series**   *Fort Lauderdale, FL*
  LGBT ☎412/362–1247 ⊠ c/o NAGAAA, 1014 King Ave, Pittsburgh, PA 15206 EMAIL:
  board@nagaaa.org WEB: www.nagaaa.org

21: **AIDS Walk Colorado**   *Denver, CO*
  ☎303/861–9255 ⊠ c/o Colorado AIDS Project, PO Box 18529, Denver, CO 80218–0529
  EMAIL: info@aidswalkcolorado.org WEB: www.aidswalkcolorado.org

21-27: **"Camp" Camp**   *Kezar Falls, ME*
  summer camp for LGBT adults • sports, pottery, theater, yoga & more • LGBT • $924
  ☎888/924–8380 ⊠ c/o Camp Camp, 8 Perkins Ave, Hyde Park, MA 02136 EMAIL: camp-
  campinfo@msn.com WEB: www.campcamp.com

30-Sept 4: **Atlanta Black Pride Weekend**   *Atlanta, GA*
  celebrate Black Pride over Labor Day weekend in Atlanta • LGBT ☎404/872–6410 ⊠ c/o
  In The Life Atlanta, PO BOX 7206, Atlanta, GA 30357 EMAIL: info@inthelifeatl.com WEB:
  www.inthelifeatl.com

TBA: **Black Pride**   *Jacksonville, FL*
  celebrate African-American gay/lesbian culture • 2nd wknd in August • LGBT
  ☎904/858–3757 EMAIL: jaxbp@aol.com WEB: www.jaxxblackpride.com

TBA: **Black Unity Pride Celebration**   *Cleveland, OH*
  Ohio's oldest & largest event celebrating African American gay/lesbian culture • LGBT
  ☎216/937–2268 ⊠ c/o Black Out Unlimited, PO Box 6362, Cleveland, OH 44101 EMAIL:
  info@blackgayandproud-cleveland.com WEB: www.blackgayandproud-cleveland.com

TBA: **Northalsted Market Days**   *Chicago, IL*
  a good ol' summer block party on Main St of Boys' Town, USA • LGBT ☎773/303–0167
  ⊠ c/o Chicago Area Gay & Lesbian Chamber of Commerce, 210 W Rosedale, Chicago,
  IL 61660 EMAIL: info@glchamber.org WEB: www.glchamber.org

TBA: **Rendezvous 2006**   *Medicine Bow Nat'l Forest, WY*
  5-day camping festival to celebrate LGBT pride • 400+ attendees ☎307/778–7645 ⊠ c/o
  Wyoming Equality, PO Box 6837, Cheyenne, WY 82003 EMAIL: info@uglw.org WEB:
  www.uglw.org

TBA: **St Louis Black Gay & Lesbian Pride**   *St Louis, MO*
  ☎314/776–4966 ⊠ PO Box 4854, St Louis, MO 63108 EMAIL: president@stlouisblack-
  pride.org WEB: www.stlouisblackpride.org

TBA: **Wigstock**   *New York City, NY*
  outrageous & fierce wig/drag/performance festival • LGBT ☎212/243–3413 ⊠ c/o DBK
  Events, 20 W 20th St, 2nd flr, New York City, NY 10011 EMAIL: wigstock@wigstock.nu WEB:
  www.wigstock.nu

September 2006

1-4: **Festival of Babes** — *TBA, USA*
annual soccer tournament for women "in comfortable shoes" • women only EMAIL: fob-squadsf@yahoo.com WEB: www.festivalofthebabes.com

1-4: **Great Alberta Campout** — *Red Deer, AB, Canada*
3 days of friendly camping fun • meet & greet Friday • special meals all wknd • games, dances, more • presented by Gay & Lesbian Assoc of Central Alberta • always Labor Day wknd • LGBT ✉ c/o GALACA, Box 1078, Red Deer, AB, Canada T4N 6S5 EMAIL: gacampout@hotmail.com WEB: members.shaw.ca/GACampout/

2-9: **Gay Ski Week Queenstown** — *Queenstown, New Zealand*
WEB: www.gayskiweeknz.com

8: **Gay Day at Six Flags** — *Jackson, NJ*
unofficial Gay Day at this popular amusement park • LGBT WEB: www.hopinc.com

9-11: **Minnesota AIDS Trek** — *St Paul, MN*
annual 175-mile bike ride to fight AIDS • mixed gay/straight ☎651/**917-3504** ✉ 499 Lynhurst Ave W, St Paul, MN 55104 EMAIL: info@aids-trek.org WEB: www.aids-trek.org

17: **Out in the Park** — *Springfield, MA*
unofficial gay day at Six Flags New England • wear red to show your support • LGBT • 1000+ attendees EMAIL:

29: **Gay Night at Six Flags Magic Mountain** — *Valencia, CA*
LGBT ☎661/**251-1827** ✉ c/o Odyssey Adventures, PO Box 2566, Santa Clarita, CA 91386 EMAIL: odyssey@odysseyadventures.com WEB: www.odysseyadventures.com

TBA: **AIDS Walk for Life— Toronto** — *Toronto, ON, Canada*
walk in Toronto & cities across Canada to raise money to fight AIDS • LGBT ☎416/**340-8484** x249 ✉ c/o AIDS Committee of Toronto, 399 Church St 4th flr, Toronto, ON, Canada M5B 2J6 EMAIL: jkeystone@actoronto.org WEB: www.aidswalkforlife-toronto.ca

TBA: **AIDS Walk Seattle** — *Seattle, WA*
mixed gay/straight • 7000+ attendees ☎206/**323-9255** ✉ c/o Lifelong AIDS Alliance, 1002 E Seneca, Seattle, WA 98122 EMAIL: aidswalk@llaa.org WEB: www.llaa.org

TBA: **Houston Women's Festival** — *Houston, TX*
women from Texas & beyond gather to enjoy music, art, culture & community • produced by the Athena Art Project • mostly women ☎281/**338-7430** ✉ c/o Houston Women's Festival, PO Box 70102, Houston, TX 77270 EMAIL: info@hwfestival.org WEB: www.hwfestival.org

TBA: **Russian River Women's Wknd** — *Guerneville, CA*
this tiny town is packed with dykes for a fun weekend of parties • 2 hours north of San Francisco • mostly women ☎707/**526-3416**

TBA: **Wild Women's Weekend** — *Clearlake, CA*
dancing • BBQ • tournaments • breakfast • beer bust • fun & games • not for the mild mannered or politically correct! • women only ☎707/**279-0208**, 800/**396-6224** ✉ c/o Edgewater Resort, 6420 Soda Bay Rd, Kelseyville, CA 95451 EMAIL: business@edgewater-resort.net WEB: www.edgewaterresort.net

October 2006

on-going: **October is Breast Cancer Awareness Month** — *Cross-country, USA*
check local listings for fund-raising events in your area to fight breast cancer

1: **Castro Street Fair** — *San Francisco, CA*
arts & community groups street fair • co-founded by Harvey Milk ☎415/**841-1824** WEB: www.castrostreetfair.org

5-8: **Black Gay Pride** — *Dallas, TX*
LGBT ☎214/**540-4494** ✉ 3100 Main St #208, Dallas, TX 75226 EMAIL: info@dallassouthernpride.com WEB: www.dallasblackpride.com

6-9: **Baltimore Black Gay Pride**   *Baltimore, MD*
LGBT ☎443/691–9669 ✉ c/o BBGP Inc, 714 Park Ave
Lower Level, Baltimore, MD 21201 Email: info@bmoreblackpride.org Web: www.bmore-
blackpride.org

6-15: **Provincetown Women's Week**   *Provincetown, MA*
very popular – make your reservations early! • mostly women • 5000+ attendees ✉ c/o
Women Innkeepers of Provincetown, PO Box 573, Provincetown, MA 02657 Email:
info@womeninnkeepers.com Web: www.womeninnkeepers.com

11: **National Coming Out Day**   *Everytown, USA*
check local listings for events in your area or visit www.hrc.com/ncop ☎202/628–4160,
800/866–6263 ✉ c/o Human Rights Campaign, 1640 Rhode Island Ave, Washington, DC
20036 Email: ncop@hrc.org Web: www.hrc.org

14-16: **Sundance Stompede**   *San Francisco, CA*
San Francisco's annual country-western dance weekend • LGBT ☎415/820–1403 ✉ c/o
Sundance Assoc, 2261 Market St PMB 225, San Francisco, CA 94114 Web: www.stom-
pede.com

15: **AIDS Walk Philly**   *Philadelphia, PA*
LGBT ☎215/731–9255 ✉ c/o AIDSFUND, 1227 Locust St, Philadelphia, PA Email: aids-
fund@aidsfundphilly.org Web: www.aidsfundphilly.org

TBA: **AIDS Walk Atlanta**   *Atlanta, GA*
mixed gay/straight • 10,000+ attendees ☎404/876–9255 ✉ PO Box 78187, Atlanta, GA
30357 Web: walk.aidatlanta.org

TBA: **AIDS Walk LA**   *Los Angeles, CA*
annual AIDS fundraiser in West Hollywood • mixed gay/straight ☎213/201–9255 ✉ c/o
AIDS Walk LA, PO Box 933005, Los Angeles, CA 90093 Email: awlainfo@aidswalk.net
Web: www.aidswalk.net

TBA: **AIDS Walk St Louis**   *St Louis, MO*
☎314/367–7273 ✉ c/o AIDS Foundation of St Louis, 2340 Hampton Ave, St Louis, MO
63139 Email: aidstl@earthlink.net Web: www.aidstl.org

TBA: **Black Lesbian/ Gay Pride**   *San Francisco, CA*
celebrate with a weekend of conferences, awards ceremonies & parties • LGBT
☎510/268–0646 Email: tbhcafe@pacbell.net

TBA: **Black Pride**   *Nashville, TN*
gay/lesbian Email: brosunited@aol.com Web: www.brothersunited.com

TBA: **Desert AIDS Walk**   *Palm Springs, CA*
benefits Desert AIDS Project • LGBT ☎760/325–9255, 800/331–3344 ✉ c/o Desert AIDS
Project, PO Box 2890, Palm Springs, CA 92263 Web: www.desertaidsproject.org

November 2006

4-5: **Greater Palm Springs Pride**   *Palm Springs, CA*
come out for a weekend of gay films, dance parties, lots of people & a parade on Sunday
☎760/416–8711 ✉ 611 S Palm Canyon Dr PMB 7436, Palm Springs, CA 92264 Email:
administration@PSPride.org Web: www.PSPride.org

22-26: **Women's White Party**   *Miami Beach, FL*
join us for a wknd of special events, beautiful women & great DJs ☎954/288–8691
Email: yesi@pandoraevents.com Web: www.kissthegirlsproductions.com

TBA: **Glasgay**   *Glasgow, Scotland*
UK's largest lesbian & gay multi-arts festival ☎44-141/552–7575 ✉ c/o Gala Scotland,
Ltd, The Q Gallery
87-89 Saltmarket, Glasgow, Scotland G1 5LE Email: info@glasgay.co.uk Web: www.glas-
gay.co.uk

TBA: **IAGLBC Annual Bridge Tournament**   *Palm Springs, CA*
Int'l Association of Gay & Lesbian Bridge Clubs ☎877/429–6368 Email:
wehojohn@aol.com Web: www.GayBridge.org

December 2006

1-3: **Holly Folly**   *Provincetown, MA*
gay & lesbian holiday celebration • fabulous parties • holiday concert • open houses
WEB: ptown.org

31: **Mummer's Strut**   *Philadelphia, PA*
big New Year's Eve party • followed by New Year's Day Parade • mixed gay/straight •
$40-50 ☎215/336-3050 ✉ c/o Mummers Museum, 1100 S 2nd St, Philadelphia, PA
19147 EMAIL: parade@mummers.com WEB: mummers.com

WOMEN'S FESTIVALS & GATHERINGS

April 2006

13-16: **Gulf Coast Womyn's Sister Camp**   *Ovett, MS*
a celebration of womyn's land in the South! • 2 1/2 hours from New Orleans, LA • 1 1/2
hours from Mobile, AL • music, crafts, night stage, workshops & more • mostly women
• $50 ☎601/344-1411 ✉ c/o Camp SisterSpirit, PO Box 12, Ovett, MS 39464 EMAIL: sis-
terspir@aol.com WEB: www.campsisterspirit.com

20-24: **Southern Womyn's Festival**   *1 hour west of Atlanta, GA*
join womyn of the Southeast for music, camping, comedy, workshops & more! • women
only • 1000 attendees ☎904/725-8079 ✉ c/o SWF, PO Box 262, Macclenny, FL 32063
EMAIL: gaywomyn@aol.com WEB: www.gaywomyn.org/festival

May 2006

26-28: **Wiminfest**   *Albuquerque, NM*
music, comedy, drag king show • art, recreation & dances • open mic • kids
event • mostly women ☎800/499-5688, 505/899-3627 ✉ c/o Women in Movement in
New Mexico (WIMIN), PO Box 80204, Albuquerque, NM 87198 EMAIL:
wimin@wiminfest.org WEB: www.wiminfest.org

26-29: **Women Outdoors National Gathering**   *Hancock, NH*
camping • hiking • workshops • women only • 110+ attendees • $120-220 ✉ c/o
Women Outdoors, Inc, 55 Talbot Ave, Medford, MA 02155 EMAIL: info@women-
outdoors.org WEB: www.women-outdoors.org

TBA: **Herland Bi-Annual Retreats**   *Oklahoma City, OK*
music, workshops, campfire events & potluck • girls of all ages & boys under 10 welcome • also in September • women only ☎405/521-9696 ✉ c/o Herland Sister
Resources, 2312 NW 39th, Oklahoma City, OK 73112 WEB: www.herlandsisters.org

June 2006

8-11: **Womongathering**   *private camp, on NY/PA border*
women's spirituality fest • women only • 400+ attendees • $270 ☎856/694-2037,
301/598-9035 (TTY) ✉ c/o Womongathering, PO Box 559, Franklinville, NJ 08322 EMAIL:
womongathr@aol.com WEB: www.womongathering.com

22-25: **Golden Threads Celebration**   *Provincetown, MA*
annual gathering of older lesbians • all lesbians of all ages welcome • no age exclusion!
• women only ☎781/229-9028 ✉ c/o Golden Threads, 1 Nevada Rd, Burlington, MA
01803 EMAIL: joy@goldenthreadsptown.org WEB: www.goldenthreadsptown.org

TBA: **Southern Ontario Womyn's Drum Camp** *near Sarnia, ON and Port Huron, MI*
all levels welcome • on Lake Huron near Sarnia, ON and Port Huron, MI • Eastern
Ontario Women's Drum Camp in Ottawa, also in June • women only • 120 attendees •
$Can200-325 ☎519/435-0861 ✉ c/o JT Productions, 1090 Kipps Ln #116, London, ON,
Canada N5Y 4S7 EMAIL: info@drumcamps.ca WEB: www.drumcamps.ca

July 2006

14-16: Women's International Music Festival   *Akron, OH*
women from all over the US & Canada • food • and of course music! ☎330/219–0409
EMAIL: wimfest@hotmail.com WEB: www.wimfest.org

TBA: National Women's Music Festival   *TBA, USA*
check website for details • mostly women ☎317/713–1144 ✉ c/o Women in the Arts,
PO Box 1427, Indianapolis, IN 46206 EMAIL: wia@wiaonline.org WEB: www.wiaonline.org

TBA: Women's Voices Festival   *Plantagenet, ON, Canada*
camping, comedy & music in a lovely country setting • a one-of-a-kind outdoor festival
• volunteer-run • women only • 1200 attendees ☎613/850–0996 ✉ c/o Women's Voice
Festival, 207 Bank St #311, Ottawa, ON K2P 2N2 EMAIL: info@womensvoices.on.ca WEB:
www.womensvoices.on.ca

August 2006

8-13: Michigan Womyn's Music Festival   *near Hart, MI*
theater, music & dance performances • workshops, film festival & craft fair • ASL inter-
preting & differently-abled resources • child care • camping • women only • 5000-8000
attendees ☎231/757–4766x40 ✉ c/o WWTMC, PO Box 22, Walhalla, MI 49458 WEB:
www.michfest.com

24-27: Women in the Woods   *Portland, OR*
rustic cabins • natural hot springs • all meals included • women only • 100+ attendees
☎503/284–0722 ✉ c/o WIW, 7501 NE Glisan, Portland, OR 97213 EMAIL: swat@wom-
eninthewoods.com WEB: www.womeninthewoods.com

25-27: Carolina Lesbian: Women in the Woods   *Canon, GA*
grab your gear, your girl & some friends, & prepare to have a wild, fun weekend
☎704/246–9504 WEB: www.carolinalesbian.com

25-27: Women's Gathering   *Louisa, VA*
last wknd in Aug • camping, music & workshops • mixed gay/straight ☎540/894–5126
✉ c/o Twin Oaks Community, 138 Twin Oaks Rd, Luisa, VA 23093 EMAIL:
gathering@twinoaks.org WEB: www.twinoaks.org/community/women

26: Tri-State Womonfest   *Cincinnati, OH*
spend the day sharing music, food, crafts, workshops & fun • women only
☎513/545–3515 ✉ c/o Womonfest, PO Box 19223, Cincinnati, OH 45219 EMAIL:
info@tristatewomonfest.com WEB: www.tristatewomonfest.com

TBA: Northern California Women's Music Festival   *Laytonville, CA*
3 day festival of music, dance, workshops & more • 40 acres of upscale camping •
3 hours north of San Francisco • women only ☎530/265–6890 ✉ c/o Rose St
Productions, 23445 N Bloomfield Rd, Nevada City, CA 95959 EMAIL: info@norcalwom-
ensmusic.org WEB: www.norcalwomensmusic.org

September 2006

2-4: Camp Real Girls   *Southern CA*
weekend getaway camp for women in the mountains of Southern California • lesbian-
owned/ run • all-inclusive • activities • meals &
lodging ☎818/985–8885 ✉ 531-A N Hollywood Way #197, Burbank, CA 91505 EMAIL:
camprealgirls@adelphia.net WEB: www.camprealgirls.com

3: Midwest Womyn's Autumnfest   *Oregon, IL*
one-day outdoor festival on private land in the country • music, crafts, workshops &
more • celebration of women's culture & music • open to all supporters & allies •
women only ☎815/234–7557 ✉ c/o FEI, PO Box 74, Dekalb, IL 61061 EMAIL:
ranitiko@aol.com WEB: www.mwautumn.com

8-10: **Sisterspace Wknd**   *TBA, MD*
sliding scale • women only ☎215/546–4890 ✉ c/o Sisterspace of the Delaware Valley, 1315 Spruce St, Philadelphia, PA 19107 EMAIL: sweekend@sisterspace.org WEB: www.sisterspace.org

16: **Ohio Lesbian Festival**   *Kirkersville (near Columbus), OH*
women only • 3000 attendees ✉ c/o Ohio LBA, PO Box 82086, Colombus, OH 43202 EMAIL: webmistress@ohiolba.org WEB: www.ohiolba.org

TBA: **Iowa Women's Music Festival**   *Iowa City, IA*
mostly women ☎319/335–1486 ✉ c/o Prairie Voices Productions, PO Box 3411, Iowa City, IA 52244 EMAIL: festival@prairievoices.net WEB: www.prairievoices.net

TBA: **SISTAHfest**   *Los Angeles, CA*
a new world for the weekend w/ 500 Black lesbians! • comfortable lodging • provocative workshops • hot entertainment • film festival • dances • women only ☎323/960–5051 ✉ c/o ULOAH (United Lesbians of African Heritage), 1626 N Wilcox Ave #190, Los Angeles, CA 90028 EMAIL: sistahs@uloah.org WEB: www.uloah.org

October 2006

6-9: **Wyld Womyn's Weekend**   *Maui, HI*
concerts • games • workshops • craft fair • open talent night • women only ☎808/573–6868 ✉ c/o On Top Productions, PO Box 1185, Kula, HI 96790 EMAIL: CindiCatering@hotmail.com WEB: www.wyldwomyn.org

FILM FESTIVALS

January 2006

TBA: **Reel Out Queer Film & Video Festival**   *Kingston, ON, Canada*
celebrating the best of queer independent film & video ☎613/533–3189 ✉ 51 Bader Ln, Kingston, ON, Canada K7l 3N6 EMAIL: festival@reelout.com WEB: www.reelout.com

February 2006

17-19: **Out Far!**   *Phoenix, AZ*
Phoenix Int'l lesbian & gay film festival ☎602/410–1074 ✉ c/o Visions Events Productions, Inc, 619 E Vista Ave, Phoenix, AZ 85020 EMAIL: OutFarFilmFest@aol.com WEB: www.outfar.org

March 2006

23-April 9: **Out in Africa**   *Cape Town, South Africa*
the only film festival of its kind on the African continent • also in Johannesburg, Grahamstown, Pietermaritzburg, Ermelo, Mamelodi & Durban ☎27 21/461 40 27 63 ✉ PO Box 15707, 8000 Vlaeberg, South Africa EMAIL: info@oia.co.za WEB: www.oia.co.za

TBA: **Wingspan/ Tucson LGBT Film Festival**   *Tucson, AZ*
showcasing the best in new queer cinema ☎520/624–1779 ✉ c/o Wingspan LGBT Center, 425 E 7th St, Tucson, AZ 85705 EMAIL: wingspan@wingspan.org WEB: www.wingspan.org/filmfest

TBA: **Women in the Director's Chair Int'l Film & Video Festival**   *Chicago, IL*
largest & longest-running women's film festival • get your tickets early for "dyke night"! • also features work by transgendered directors • check website for updates • mostly women ☎773/235–4301 ✉ c/o WIDC, PO Box 11135, Chicago, IL 60611 EMAIL: widc@sbcglobal.net WEB: www.widc.org

April 2006

21-30: **Miami Gay & Lesbian Film Festival**   *Miami, FL*
☎305/534–9924 ✉ 1521 Alton Rd #147, Miami Beach, FL 33139 EMAIL: info@mglff.com
WEB: www.MGLFF.com

28-30: **London Lesbian Film Festival**   *London, ON, Canada*
women only Fri-Sat, open to all on Sunday ☎519/434–0246 ✉ c/o Reeling Spinsters,
PO Box 46014, London, ON, Canada N5W 6B2 EMAIL: llff@sympatico.ca WEB: www.llff.ca

TBA: **Mix: New York Lesbian/ Gay
Experimental Film/ Video Fest**   *New York City, NY*
film, videos, installations & media performances • write for info ☎212/742–8880 ✉ 29
John St PMB 132, New York, NY 10038 EMAIL: info@mixnyc.org WEB: www.mixnyc.org

May 2006

18-28: **Inside Out: Toronto LGBT Film & Video Festival**   *Toronto, ON, Canada*
☎416/977–6847, 416/925–XTRA EXT 2229 ✉ c/o Inside Out, 401 Richmond St W #219,
Toronto, ON, Canada M5V 3A8 EMAIL: inside@insideout.on.ca WEB: www.insideout.on.ca

18-21: **Q Cinema**   *Fort Worth, TX*
annual celebration of LGBT-themed movies ☎817/462–3368 ✉ c/o Q Cinema Inc, 9
Chase Ct, Fort Worth, TX 76110 EMAIL: tcamp@star-telegram.com WEB: www.qcinema.org

TBA: **Honolulu Rainbow Film Festival**   *Honolulu, HI*
☎808/381–1952 ✉ c/o Honolulu Gay & Lesbian Cultural Foundation, 1877 Kalakaua
Ave, Honolulu, HI 96815 EMAIL: info@hglcf.org WEB: www.hglcf.org

June 2006

1-11: **NewFest: New York LGBT Film Festival**   *New York City, NY*
☎212/571–2170 ✉ c/o The New Festival, 139 Fulton St #PH-3, New York, NY 10038
EMAIL: info@newfest.org WEB: www.newfest.org

2-10: **Connecticut Gay/ Lesbian Film Festival**   *Hartford, CT*
LGBT ☎860/586–1136, 860/232–3402 ✉ c/o Alternatives, Inc, PO Box 231192, Hartford,
CT 06123 EMAIL: glff@yahoo.com WEB: www.CTGLFF.org

14-18: **Provincetown Int'l Film Festival**   *Provincetown, MA*
mixed gay/straight ☎508/487–3456 ✉ PO Box 605, Provincetown, MA 02657 EMAIL:
info@ptownfilmfest.org WEB: www.ptownfilmfest.org

15-25: **San Francisco Int'l Lesbian/ Gay Film Festival**   *San Francisco, CA*
get your tickets early for a slew of films about us • LGBT • 65,000+ attendees • see ad in
front color section ☎415/703–8650 ✉ c/o Frameline, 145 9th St #300, San Francisco,
CA 94103 EMAIL: info@frameline.org WEB: www.frameline.org

July 2006

6-17: **Outfest**   *Los Angeles, CA*
Los Angeles' lesbian/gay film & video festival in mid-July ☎213/480–7088 ✉ c/o
Outfest, 3470 Wilshire Blvd #1022, Los Angeles, CA 90010 EMAIL: outfest@outfest.org
WEB: www.outfest.org

13-25: **Philadelphia Gay/ Lesbian Film Festival**   *Philadelphia, PA*
☎267/765–9700 ✉ c/o Philadelphia Film Society, 234 Market St, Philadelphia, PA
19106 EMAIL: info@phillyfests.com WEB: www.phillyfests.com/piglff

August 2006

8-13: **Rhode Island International Film Festival**   *Providence, RI*
don't miss the Gay & Lesbian Film Fest sidebar • mixed gay/straight ☎401/861–4445 ✉
c/o RIIFF, PO Box 162, Newport, RI 02840 EMAIL: info@film-festival.org WEB: www.film-festi-
val.org

TBA: **Austin Gay/ Lesbian International Film Festival**   *Austin, TX*
    ☎512/302–9889 ✉ c/o AGLIFF, 1216 E 51st St, Austin, TX 78723 EMAIL: info@agliff.org
    WEB: www.agliff.org

TBA: **North Carolina Gay/ Lesbian Film Festival**   *Durham, NC*
    ☎919/560–3040 ✉ c/o Carolina Theatre, 309 W Morgan St, Durham, NC 27701 WEB:
    www.carolinatheatre.org

TBA: **Vancouver Queer Film & Video Festival**   *Vancouver, BC, Canada*
    LGBT ☎604/844–1615 ✉ c/o Out on Screen, 405-207 West Hastings St, Vancouver, BC,
    Canada V6B 1H7 WEB: www.outonscreen.org

September 2006

on-going: **MadCat Women's Int'l Film Festival**   *San Francisco & Berkeley, CA*
    annual women's international film festival • also tours throughout the US each spring
    ☎415/436–9523 ✉ 639 Steiner St, San Francisco, CA 94117 EMAIL: info@madcatfilmfesti-
    val.org WEB: www.madcatfilmfestival.org

13-17: **Fresno Reel Pride**   *Fresno, CA*
    annual lesbian & gay film festival in central California ☎559/488–6562 ✉ PO Box 4647,
    Fresno, CA 93744 EMAIL: info@reelpride.com WEB: www.reelpride.com

TBA: **Pikes Peak Lavender Film Festival**   *Colorado Springs, CO*
    ☎719/386–6843, 719/475–0905 ✉ PO Box 1987, Colorado Springs, CO 80901 EMAIL:
    info@pplff.org WEB: www.pplff.org

October 2006

5-15: **Tampa Bay Int'l Gay/ Lesbian Film Festival**   *Tampa Bay, FL*
    ☎813/879–4220 ✉ c/o Friends of the Festival, PO Box 18445, Tampa, FL 33679 EMAIL:
    tickets@tiglff.com WEB: www.tiglff.com

17-22: **Hamburg Int'l Lesbian & Gay Film Festival**   *Hamburg, Germany*
    ☎49.40/3.48.06.70 ✉ Querbild e.V., Schanzenstr 45, Hamburg, Germany D-20357
    EMAIL: mail@lsf-hamburg.de WEB: www.lsf-hamburg.de

18-22: **St John's International Women's Film & Video Festival**   *St John's, NL, Canada*
    mixed gay/straight • 4500 attendees ☎709/754–3141 ✉ PO Box 984, St John's, NL,
    Canada A1C 5M3 EMAIL: womensfilmfest@nfld.net WEB: www.womensfilmfestival.com

TBA: **Barcelona Gay & Lesbian Film Festival**   *Barcelona, Spain*
    ☎34//93.319.55.50 EMAIL: cinema@lambdaweb.org WEB: www.cinemalambda.com

TBA: **Paris Gay & Lesbian Film Festival**   *Paris, France*
    ☎0143/56-53-66 ✉ 8 rue du Repos, Paris, France 75020 EMAIL: info@ffglp.net WEB:
    www.ffglp.net

TBA: **Pittsburgh International Lesbian & Gay Film Festival**   *Pittsburgh, PA*
    LGBT ☎412/422–6776 ✉ c/o PILGFF, PO Box 81237, Pittsburgh, PA 15217 EMAIL: pil-
    gff@aol.com WEB: www.pilgff.org

TBA: **Portland Lesbian & Gay Film Festival**   *Portland, OR*
    ☎866/206–2315 ✉ c/o Sensory Perceptions, PMB 282
    4110 SE Hawthorne Blvd, Portland, OR 97214 EMAIL: info@plgff.org WEB: www.sensoryper-
    ceptions.org

TBA: **Reel Affirmations Film Festival DC**   *Washington, DC*
    lesbian/gay films ☎202/986–1119 ✉ c/o One In Ten, PO Box 73587, Washington, DC
    20056 EMAIL: info@reelaffirmations.org WEB: www.reelaffirmations.org

TBA: **Seattle Lesbian/ Gay Film Festival**   *Seattle, WA*
    LGBT ☎206/323–4274 ✉ c/o Three Dollar Bill Cinema, 1122 E Pike St #1313, Seattle,
    WA 98122 EMAIL: filmfest@seattlequeerfilm.com WEB: www.seattlequeerfilm.com

November 2006

2-12: image+nation: Montréal Int'l LGBT Film Festival *Montréal, QC, Canada*
LGBT ☎514/285-4467 ✉ c/o Image + Nation, 4067 boul St Laurent #404, Montréal, QC
H2W 1Y7 EMAIL: info@image-nation.org WEB: www.image-nation.org

10-16: Long Island Gay & Lesbian Film Festival *Huntington, NY*
☎631/423-3456, 631/423-2696 ✉ PO Box 1477, Melville, NY 11747 EMAIL:
info@liglff.org WEB: www.liglff.org

TBA: Out on Film *Atlanta, GA*
LGBT ☎404/352-4225 ✉ c/o IMAGE Film & Video Center, 75 Bennett St NW, Ste N-1,
Atlanta, GA 30309 EMAIL: aff@imagefv.org WEB: www.outonfilm.com

TBA: Reeling 2005: Chicago Lesbian and Gay Int'l Film Fest *Chicago, IL*
☎773/293-1447 ✉ c/o Chicago Filmmakers, 5243 N Clark St, 2nd flr, Chicago, IL 60640
EMAIL: reeling@chicagofilmmakers.org WEB: www.reelingfilmfestival.org

LEATHER & FETISH

January 2006

13-15: Mid-Atlantic Leather Weekend *Washington, DC*
LGBT ☎202/388-1010 ✉ c/o Centaur MC, PO Box 34193, Washington, DC 20043 EMAIL:
registration@leatherweekend.com WEB: www.leatherweekend.com

20-22: Southwest Leather Conference *Phoenix, AZ*
workshops, vendors & fetish ball • MASTER/slave, Bootblack & Daddy/boy contests •
LGBT ✉ c/o SWLC, 4757 E Greenway Rd #107B
PMB 225, Phoenix, AZ 85032 EMAIL: swlcrobert@cox.net WEB: www.southwestleather.org

February 2006

17-20: Pantheon of Leather *Chicago, IL*
annual leather/SM/fetish community service awards • mixed gay/straight ✉ 5306
Romaine, Hollywood, CA 90029 EMAIL: tljandcuir@aol.com WEB:
www.TheLeatherJournal.com/pantheon.htm

April 2006

7-9: Leather Leadership Conference *TBA, USA*
join us to develop & strengthen problem-solving & camaraderie in the leather community • LGBT ✉ c/o LLC c/o John Weis, 265 W 19 St, New York, NY 10011 EMAIL: loli-
tassc@aol.com WEB: www.leatherleadership.org

7-9: Rubbout 14 *Vancouver, BC, Canada*
don't miss this annual gay rubber weekend • mostly men ☎604/683-8000 ✉ 901-1238
Seymour St, Vancouver, BC, Canada V6B 6J3 EMAIL: rubbout@shaw.ca WEB:
www.rubbout.ca

June 2006

9-11: Southeast Leatherfest *Atlanta, GA*
LGBT ☎718/662-6572 ✉ c/o Southeast Leatherfest, PO Box 487, Hiram, GA 30141
EMAIL: selfsecretary@yahoo.com WEB: www.seleatherfest.com

18: Folsom Street East *New York City, NY*
New York City's answer to the famous San Francisco fetish street fair • LGBT
☎212/727-9878 ✉ c/o GMSMA, 332 Bleecker St #D-23, New York City, NY 10014 EMAIL:
info@gmsma.org WEB: www.folsomstreeteast.org

July 2006

14-16: **International Ms Bootblack Contest** *Omaha, NE*
contest takes place the weekend of International Ms Leather weekend • mostly women ☎402/451–7987 ⊠ c/o Bare Images, 4332 Browne St, Omaha, NE 68111 EMAIL: bareimages@cox.net WEB: www.IMsL.org

14-16: **International Ms Leather Contest** *Omaha, NE*
contest • workshops • parties • vending • mixed gay/straight ☎402/451–7987 ⊠ c/o Bare Images, 4332 Browne St, Omaha, NE 68111 EMAIL: bareimages@cox.net WEB: www.IMsL.org

28-30: **Thunder in the Mountains** *Denver, CO*
weekend of pansexual leather events & seminars • kinky comedy revue • talent show • LGBT • 800+ attendees ☎303/698–1207 ⊠ c/o Thunder in the Mountains, LLC, 258 Acoma St, Denver 80223–1339 EMAIL: MrLthrCO@aol.com WEB: www.thunderinthemountains.com

TBA: **International Deaf Leather** *San Diego, CA*
weekend of events, including Mr and Ms Deaf Leather Contest ⊠ c/o Int'l Deaf Leather, PO Box 7355, Stockton, CA 95267 EMAIL: idlboard@earthlink.net WEB: internationaldeafleather.org

September 2006

2: **Folsom Europe** *Berlin, Germany*
⊠ c/o Folsom Europe e.v., Skalitzer Str 140, 10999 Berlin, Germany EMAIL: info@folsomeurope.com WEB: www.folsomeurope.com

24: **Folsom Street Fair** *San Francisco, CA*
huge SM/leather street fair, topping a week of kinky events • LGBT • thousands of local & visiting kinky men & women attendees ☎415/861–3247 ⊠ c/o Folsom Street Events, 584 Castro, PMB 553, San Francisco, CA 94114 EMAIL: info@folsomstreetevents.org WEB: folsomstreetevents.org

October 2006

6-9: **Portland Uniform Weekend** *Portland, OR*
LGBT ☎503/228–6935 ⊠ c/o In Uniform Magazine, PO Box 3226, Portland, OR 97208 EMAIL: uniformmag@aol.com WEB: www.inuniform.net

TBA: **Women at Amsterdam Leather Pride** *Amsterdam, Netherlands*
annual international women's SM conference • women only ☎31–71/512–8632 ⊠ c/o WALP, PO Box 842, 2300 AV Leiden, Netherlands EMAIL: walp@dds.nl WEB: www.walp.dds.nl

November 2006

4-6: **Santa Clara County Leather Weekend** *San Jose, CA*
3 days of leather celebration in the San Jose area • LGBT ⊠ c/o Santa Clara County Leather Assoc, c/o Billy deFrank LGBT Ctr 938 The Alameda, San Jose, CA 95126 EMAIL: info@sccleather.org WEB: www.SCCLeather.org

CONFERENCES & RETREATS

May 2006

12-14: **Saints & Sinners** *New Orleans, LA*
LGBT writers & readers from around the country gather for a hot weekend of readings, panels & performances • some past participants: Dorothy Allison, Michelle Tea & Christopher Rice • benefits NO/AIDS Task Force • 300 attendees • $100 ☎504/**821-2601** x217 ⌨ c/o NO/AIDS Task Force, 2601 Tulane Ave, Ste 500, New Orleans, LA 70119
EMAIL: saintandsinnola@aol.com WEB: www.sasfest.com

June 2006

8-11: **GCLS Literary Convention** *New Orleans, LA*
Golden Crown Literary Society's annual gathering to share & explore the many facets of lesbian literature ⌨ c/o GCLS, PO Box 357474, Gainesville, FL 32653 EMAIL: info@gclscon.com WEB: www.gclscon.com

TBA: **Lambda Literary Awards** *TBA, USA*
the Lammies are the Oscars of LGBT writing & publishing • LGBT ☎202/**682-0952** ⌨ c/o Lambda Literary Foundation, PO Box 73910, Washington, DC 20056 EMAIL: LLF@lambdalit.org WEB: www.lambdalit.org

September 2006

19-24: **Southern Comfort Conference** *Atlanta, GA*
entertainers & leaders from the entire spectrum of the transgender community offering 5 days of learning, networking & fun ☎702/**336-1202**, 850/**479-4137** ⌨ 3107 Alston Dr, Decatur, GA 30032 EMAIL: general_info@sccatl.org WEB: www.sccatl.org

TBA: **FTM 2006: A Gender Odyssey** *TBA, USA*
3 days of panels, workshops & caucuses • cabaret, spoken-word, art exhibit & vendors ⌨ PMB 796, 1122 E Pike St, Seattle, WA 98122 EMAIL: info@transconference.org WEB: www.transconference.org

TBA: **Healing Works: Nat'l Lesbian Health Conference** *Washington, DC*
sponsored by the Mautner Project for Lesbian Health ☎202/**332-5536** ⌨ c/o Mautner Project for Lesbian Health, 1707 L St NW, #230, Washington, DC 20036 EMAIL: mautner@mautnerproject.org WEB: www.mautnerproject.org

TBA: **Nat'l Lesbian & Gay Journalists Assoc. Convention** *Chicago, IL*
workshops • keynote speakers • entertainment • LGBT ☎202/**588-9888** ⌨ c/o NLGJA, 1420 K St NW #910, Washington, DC 20005 EMAIL: info@nlgja.org WEB: www.nlgja.org

October 2006

TBA: **National Lesbian & Gay MBA Conference** *TBA, USA*
discussions of sexual orientation in the workplace by MBA students & representatives from big-name companies • LGBT • 300+ attendees ⌨ c/o Reaching Out MBA, Inc, PO Box 691246, West Hollywood, CA 90069 EMAIL: info@reachingoutmba.org WEB: reachingoutmba.org

November 2006

8-12: **Creating Change Conference** *Kansas City, MO*
for lesbians, gays, bisexuals, transgendered people & queers into social activism • LGBT • 2500+ attendees ☎202/**639-6333** ⌨ c/o National Gay/Lesbian Task Force, 1325 Mass Ave NW #600, Washington, DC 20005 EMAIL: creatingchange@ngltf.org WEB: www.creatingchange.org

SPIRITUAL GATHERINGS

February 2006

17-20: **PantheaCon**   *San Jose, CA*
pagan convention • mixed gay/straight ☎510/653–3244 ✉ c/o Ancient Ways, 4075
Telegraph Ave, Oakland, CA 94609 EMAIL: store@ancientways.com WEB:
www.ancientways.com

May 2006

TBA: **A Gathering of Priestesses & Goddess Women**   *Wisconsin Dells, Southwestern WI*
women's spirituality conference • women only ☎608/226–9998 ✉ c/o Re-formed
Congregation of the Goddess, PO Box 6677, Madison, WI 53716 EMAIL: rcgi@rcgi.org
WEB: www.rcgi.org

June 2006

18-25: **Pagan Spirit Gathering**   *near Athens, OH*
summer solstice celebration in Ohio • primitive camping • workshops • rituals •
advance registration required • mixed gay/straight ☎608/924–2216 ✉ c/o Circle
Sanctuary, PO Box 9, Barneveld, WI 53507 EMAIL: circle@circlesanctuary.org WEB: www.cir-
clesanctuary.org/psg

TBA: **Ancient Ways Festival**   *Harbin Hot Springs, CA*
annual 4-day mixed gender/orientation spring festival • pan-pagan rituals, workshops &
music w/ lesbian/gay campsite • mixed gay/straight ☎510/653–3244 ✉ c/o Ancient
Ways, 4075 Telegraph Ave, Oakland, CA 94609 EMAIL: store@ancientways.com WEB:
www.ancientways.com

July 2006

29-Aug 5: **BC Witchcamp**   *near Vancouver, BC, Canada*
weeklong Wiccan intensive at Evans Lake • mixed gay/straight ☎604/253–7189,
604/253–7195 ✉ c/o BCWC, PO Box 21510, 1424 Commercial Dr, Vancouver, BC, Canada
V5L 5G2 EMAIL: infobcwc@yahoo.ca WEB: www.bcwitchcamp.org

August 2006

10-13: **Elderflower Womenspirit Festival**   *Mendocino, CA*
earth-based spirituality retreat • honoring the feminine through the Goddess • women
& girls only EMAIL: info@elderflower.org WEB: www.elderflower.org

October 2006

27-29: **Real Witches Ball**   *Columbus, OH*
weekend pagan celebration of Samhain • mixed gay/straight ☎614/421–7557 ✉ c/o
Salem West, 1209 N High St, Columbus, OH 43201 WEB: www.pagannation.com

BREAST CANCER BENEFITS

January 2006

on-going throughout the year: **Race for the Cure**   *Cross-country, USA*
5K & 1-mile run/fitness walks in cities around the country to fight breast cancer • call for local city dates • organized & funded by Susan G Komen Breast Cancer Foundation volunteers ☎888/603-7223 ✉ c/o Susan G Komen Breast Cancer Foundation: Race for the Cure, 5005 LBJ Fwy #370, Dallas, TX 75244 EMAIL: raceforthecure@komen.org WEB: www.raceforthecure.com

ongoing throughout the year: **Making Strides Against Breast Cancer**   *Cross-country, USA*
5-mile noncompetitive walks to raise awareness & money to fight breast cancer • donations go to American Cancer Society • check website or local listings for an event near you • mixed gay/straight WEB: www.cancer.org

August 2006

4-6: **Breast Cancer 3 Day**   *Boston, MA*
walk 60 miles in 3 days to raise money for the Susan G Komen Breast Cancer Foundation • mixed gay/straight ☎800/996-3329 WEB: www.the3day.org

11-13: **Breast Cancer 3 Day**   *TBA, MI*
walk 60 miles in 3 days to raise money for the Susan G Komen Breast Cancer Foundation • mixed gay/straight ☎800/996-3329 WEB: www.the3day.org

18-20: **Breast Cancer 3 Day**   *Minneapolis/St Paul, MN*
walk 60 miles in 3 days to raise money for the Susan G Komen Breast Cancer Foundation • mixed gay/straight ☎800/996-3329 WEB: www.the3day.org

25-27: **Breast Cancer 3 Day**   *Seattle, WA*
walk 60 miles in 3 days to raise money for the Susan G Komen Breast Cancer Foundation • mixed gay/straight ☎800/996-3329 WEB: www.the3day.org

September 2006

8-10: **Breast Cancer 3 Day**   *Chicago, IL*
walk 60 miles in 3 days to raise money for the Susan G Komen Breast Cancer Foundation • mixed gay/straight ☎800/996-3329 WEB: www.the3day.org

15-17: **Breast Cancer 3 Day**   *Kansas City, MO*
walk 60 miles in 3 days to raise money for the Susan G Komen Breast Cancer Foundation • mixed gay/straight ☎800/996-3329 WEB: www.the3day.org

October 2006

on-going: **October is Breast Cancer Awareness Month**   *Cross-country, USA*
check local listings for fund-raising events in your area to fight breast cancer

6-8: **Breast Cancer 3 Day**   *Philadelphia, PA*
walk 60 miles in 3 days to raise money for the Susan G Komen Breast Cancer Foundation • mixed gay/straight ☎800/996-3329 WEB: www.the3day.org

13-15: **Breast Cancer 3 Day**   *Tampa Bay, FL*
walk 60 miles in 3 days to raise money for the Susan G Komen Breast Cancer Foundation • mixed gay/straight ☎800/996-3329 WEB: www.the3day.org

20-22: **Breast Cancer 3 Day**   *Atlanta, GA*
walk 60 miles in 3 days to raise money for the Susan G Komen Breast Cancer Foundation • mixed gay/straight ☎800/996-3329 WEB: www.the3day.org

27-29: **Breast Cancer 3 Day**   *Dallas, TX*
walk 60 miles in 3 days to raise money for the Susan G Komen Breast Cancer Foundation • mixed gay/straight ☎800/996-3329 WEB: www.the3day.org

November 2006

3-5: **Breast Cancer 3 Day**   *TBA, AZ*
walk 60 miles in 3 days to raise money for the Susan G Komen Breast Cancer
Foundation • mixed gay/straight ☎800/**996–3329** WEB: www.the3day.org

10-12: **Breast Cancer 3 Day**   *San Diego, CA*
walk 60 miles in 3 days to raise money for the Susan G Komen Breast Cancer
Foundation • mixed gay/straight ☎800/**996–3329** WEB: www.the3day.org

KIDS' STUFF

July 2006

29-Aug 5: **Family Week**   *Provincetown, MA*
join hundreds of LGBT parents & their children for a week of clam bakes, BBQs, boat
rides, campfires, sandcastle competitions & more • LGBT ☎202/**331–5015** ✉ c/o
Family Pride Coalition, PO Box 65327, Washington, DC 20035 EMAIL: info@familypride.org
WEB: www.familypride.org

TBA: **Camp for Children of LGBT Parents**   *Halifax, NS, Canada*
fun-filled weekend where kids of LGBT parents are valued & respected ☎902/**455–0186**
✉ c/o **Family Pride Camping Association**, 121-3045 Robie St, Waverly, NS, Canada B3K
4P6 EMAIL: info@fpca.ca WEB: www.fpca.ca

TBA: **Camp Lavender Hill**   *Sierra Nevada, CA*
one-week summer camp for kids with LGBT parents • swimming • hiking • theater &
more • kids 7-17 ☎707/**544–8150** ✉ c/o **Camp Lavender Hill**, 16420 Cutten Dr,
Guerneville 95446 EMAIL: staff@camplavenderhill.org WEB: camplavenderhill.org

August 2006

TBA: **Camp It Up! Lesbian/ Gay Family Camp**   *Quincy, CA*
week-long program at Feather River Camp • swimming • horseback riding • arts & crafts
• music, dance & theater • family spa & salon! • 250+ attendees ☎510/**206–2727**
EMAIL: redros1214@aol.com WEB: www.campitup.org

TBA: **Camp Ten Trees**   *TBA, WA*
summer camp for LGBTQ youth, & for kids of LGBTQ family members (separate week-
long sessions for each) ☎206/**985–2864** ✉ c/o **Camp Ten Trees**, 1122 E Pike St, #1488,
Seattle, WA 98122 EMAIL: info@camptentrees.org WEB: www.camptentrees.org

TBA: **Mountain Meadow Summer Camp**   *Southern New Jersey*
camp for kids with LGBTQ parents & their allies • sliding scale fee • youth age 9-17
☎215/**772–1107** ✉ c/o **Mountain Meadow Country Experience**, 1315 Spruce St #407,
Philadelphia, PA 19107 EMAIL: inquiries@mountainmeadow.org WEB: www.mountainmead-
ow.org

September 2006

TBA: **Keshet Camp: Jewish Family Camp**   *Yosemite, CA*
a rainbow camp for LGBT families & their friends • sports, music, arts & crafts & more •
different sessions for different ages • LGBT ☎415/**543–2267** ✉ c/o **Camp Tawonga**, 131
Steuart St, San Francisco, CA 94105 EMAIL: info@tawonga.org WEB: www.tawonga.org

BOOKS & MAGAZINES

Amazon Bookstore Cooperative
☎612/821-9630 oldest independent feminist bookstore in North America • founded 1970 • no relation to Seattle's amazon.com • online orders available • women-owned & run ✉ 4755 Chicago Ave S, Minneapolis, MN 55407 WEB: www.amazonbookstorecoop.com

Bella Books ☎800/729-4992 lesbian press • many books, including all Naiad titles ✉ PO Box 10543, Tallahassee, FL 32302 EMAIL: info@bellabooks.com WEB: www.bellabooks.com

Bywater Books ☎866/390-7426 lesbian press founded by 3 women authors • many books • lesbian fiction contest ✉ PO Box 3671, Ann Arbor, MI 48106-3671 WEB: www.bywaterbooks.com

Curve ☎415/863-6538 the bestselling national lesbian magazine ✉ 1550 Bryant St #510, San Francisco, CA 94103 EMAIL: editor@curvemag.com WEB: www.curvemag.com

Kings Crossing Publishing
☎770/640-9963 black-women owned & operated • publishes & promotes authors & artists who are traditionally underrepresented ✉ PO Box 673121, Marietta, GA 30006 EMAIL: kingscrossing-pub@aol.com WEB: www.kingscrossingpub-lishing.com

Lesbian Connection ☎517/371-5257 free worldwide grassroots forum for, by, and about lesbians ✉ PO Box 811, East Lansing, MI 48826 EMAIL: elsiepub@aol.com WEB: www.lconline.org

Lesbian Health News, Inc ☎614/291-0038 ✉ PO Box 12121, Columbus, OH 43212 EMAIL: mason-middletown.1@osu.edu WEB: www.ohiowomeninc.org/orgs/lhn.html

Magus Books ☎612/379-7669, 800/99MAGUS 10am-9pm, til 6pm wknds, from noon Sun • alternative spirituality books • also mail order ✉ 1309 1/2 SE 4th St, Minneapolis, MN 55414 EMAIL: order@magusbooks.com WEB: www.magusbooks.com

RedBone Press ☎202/667-0392 "publishes work that celebrates the culture of black lesbians" ✉ PO Box 15571, Washington, DC 20003 EMAIL: redbone-press@yahoo.com WEB: www.redbone-press.com

Spinsters Ink ☎800/301-6860 (ORDERS ONLY) feminist fiction & non-fiction publishers • mail order ✉ Po Box 242, Midway, FL 32343 EMAIL: info@spinsters-ink.com WEB: www.spinsters-ink.com

▲ **Suspect Thoughts Press** ☎415/713-7159 voice-driven queer fiction, poetry, nonfiction • authors include Ali Liebegott, Patrick Califia, Jennifer Fink & Dodie Bellamy ✉ 2215-R Market St, PMB 544, San Francisco, CA 94114-1612 EMAIL: gregw@suspectthoughts.com WEB: www.suspectthoughtspress.com/press.htm

Wishing Well ☎858/270-2779 magazine designed for women-loving-women who want to locate their sisters ✉ PO Box 178440, San Diego, CA 92177-8440 WEB: www.wishingwellwomen.com/index.html

Women's Press ☎416/929-2774 lesbian/feminist book publisher • catalog available ✉ 180 Bloor St W #801, Toronto, ON M5S 2V6 EMAIL: info@womenspress.ca WEB: www.womenspress.ca

Damron City Guide

Our City Guide is the perfect companion to the **Men's Travel Guide** and the **Women's Traveller**! This attractive full-color guide features **more than 140 maps** with color-coded dots that pinpoint lesbian & gay bars, accommodations, and bookstores in **over 75 cities** and resorts worldwide.

Also included are restaurants, cafés, gyms, travel agencies, publications and more. "Info boxes" detail major annual gay events, local tourist attractions and food, transit, weather, best views of the city, and directions from the airport. It is also the only Damron guide that contains websites within its listings.

Damron Accommodations

Now you'll always have a home away from home! The first and only **full-color guide** to gay-friendly B&Bs, inns, hotels, and other accommodations in North America, Europe, Central America, South Africa, and Australia. Most listings include **color photographs** (not even straight B&B guides do this!) and a comprehensive description. Sophisticated travelers will appreciate the handy multiple cross-referenced index. Over 500 pages.

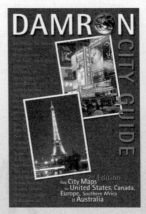

To order, call **(800) 462-6654**
Ask for our **FREE** Damron catalog of international lesbian & gay travel guides!

Visit **www.damron.com** for the latest and greatest gay travel updates!

CLOTHING

Family Evolutions ☎866/691–4476, 617/795–7370 clothing & accessories for lesbian & gay families ✉ 1784 Washington St #2, Auburndale, MA 02466 EMAIL: info@familyevolutions.com WEB: www.familyevolutions.com

Strip T's ☎603/755-2926 cat-lover T-shirts • jewelry • catalog ✉ PO Box 605, Farmington, NH 03835 EMAIL: piro@worldpath.net WEB: www.stephaniepiro.com

www.girlfiend.com ☎323/791–2207 hip dyke tees and accessories ✉ 264 S LaCienega Blvd #744, Beverly Hills, CA 90211 EMAIL: info@girlfiend.com WEB: www.girlfiend.com

JEWELRY

▲ **Jewelry by Poncé** ☎949/497–4154, 800/969-7464 specializing in commitment rings • free brochure ✉ 668 N Coast Hwy #331, Laguna Beach, CA 92651 EMAIL: jewelry@jewelrybyponce.com WEB: www.jewelrybyponce.com

Lizzie Brown/Pleiades ☎413/245-6552 woman-identified jewelry ✉ PO Box 389, Brimfield, MA 01010

Steel Toe Studios woman-owned blacksmith studio • unique belt buckles EMAIL: erica@steeltoestudios.com WEB: www.steeltoestudios.com

VARIETY

Avena Botanicals ☎207/594–0694, 866/282-8362 organically grown herbal products for women • catalog ✉ 219 Mill St, Rockport, ME 04856 EMAIL: avena@avenaherbs.com WEB: www.avena-herbs.com

Femail Creations ☎800/996–9223 catalog for, by & about womyn EMAIL: customerservice@femailcreations.com WEB: www.femailcreations.com

LadySlipper, Inc. ☎919/383–8773, 800/634-6044 women's music • videos ✉ PO Box 3124, Durham, NC 27715 EMAIL: info@ladyslipper.org WEB: www.ladyslipper.org

Snake & Snake Productions ☎919/401-9591 goddess • crone • astrology items ✉ 3037 Dixon Rd, Durham, NC 27707 EMAIL: susan@snake-andsnake.com WEB: www.snakeandsnake.com

No, it's not *The L Word* goes cowgirl. Harlequin romance, this ain't. These are hot tall tales about true lesbians who know how real roping and riding are done.

Leather, lust, riding a horse by day, a woman by night. While some of the tales have moments of easy ridin', most of them have a decided kink to their gallop, and even the occasional burr under the saddle.

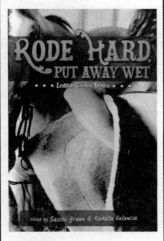

Rode Hard, Put Away Wet: Lesbian Cowboy Erotica

Sacchi Green & Rakelle Valencia, eds.

Lesbian Fiction/Erotica
Available at your local
bookstore or online.
$16.95

Suspect Thoughts Press
www.suspectthoughts.com

The Shenis ☎214/616-5454 the penis with a "she" • no more squatting to pee ✉ 5521 Greenville Ave #104-433, Dallas, TX 75206 EMAIL: kiki@shenis.com WEB: www.shenis.com

Women Fly Inc ☎800/304-9342 t-shirts • caps • coffee mugs • free catalog ✉ Po Box 246, Greensboro, MD 21639 EMAIL: womenfly@womenfly.com WEB: www.womenfly.com

EROTICA

Eve's Garden ☎212/757-8651, 800/848-3837 sex toys • books • videos • all from the first sexuality boutique created by women for women • send $3 for catalog ✉ 119 W 57th St # 1201, New York, NY 10019 EMAIL: customerservice@evesgarden.com WEB: www.evesgarden.com

▲ Good Vibrations ☎415/974-8990, 800/289-8423 lesbian-made erotica • sex toys • books • videos ✉ 938 Howard St #101, San Francisco, CA 94103 EMAIL: customerservice@goodvibes.com WEB: www.goodvibes.com

Greedy Dyke Productions ☎505/890-1376 women-crafted sex toys ✉ 301 Garcia Rd NW, Alameda, NM 87114 EMAIL: misskell@nmia.com WEB: www.nmia.com/~misskell/gdprod/

Pleasure Chest ☎800/316-9222 for all your erotic needs • catalog ✉ 7733 Santa Monica Blvd, West Hollywood, CA 90046 EMAIL: orders@thepleasurechest.com WEB: www.thepleasurechest.com

Pleasure Place ☎800/386-2386 erotic gifts • toys • catalog EMAIL: pleasure@pleasureplace.com WEB: www.pleasureplace.com

SIR Productions Sex, Indulgence, Rock & Roll • 100% dyke-owned/ run • award-winning movies in LGBT festivals worldwide EMAIL: info@sirvideo.com WEB: www.sirvideo.com

▲ Toys in Babeland ☎800/ 658-9119 women-owned & run sex toys store EMAIL: mailorder@babeland.com WEB: www.babeland.com

Wolfe Video ☎408/268-6782, 800/438-9653 LGBT feature films on video & DVD EMAIL: order@wolfevideo.com WEB: www.wolfevideo.com

▲ Xandria Collection ☎800/242-2823 sexual products from around the world • send $4 for catalog EMAIL: customerservice@xandria.com WEB: www.xandria.com